International Directory of
COMPANY
HISTORIES

International Directory of
COMPANY
HISTORIES

VOLUME 112

Editors

Derek Jacques and Paula Kepos

ST. JAMES PRESS
A part of Gale, Cengage Learning

Detroit • New York • San Francisco • New Haven, Conn • Waterville, Maine • London

GALE
CENGAGE Learning

International Directory of Company Histories, Volume 112

Derek Jacques and Paula Kepos, Editors

Project Editor: Miranda H. Ferrara

Editorial: Virgil Burton, Donna Craft, Louise Gagné, Peggy Geeseman, Julie Gough, Sonya Hill, Keith Jones, Matthew Miskelly, Lynn Pearce, Laura Peterson, Holly Selden, Justine Ventimiglia

Production Technology Specialist: Mike Weaver

Imaging and Multimedia: John Watkins

Composition and Electronic Prepress: Gary Leach, Evi Seoud

Manufacturing: Rhonda Dover

Product Manager: Jenai Drouillard

For product information and technology assistance, contact us at **Gale Customer Support, 1-800-877-4253.**
For permission to use material from this text or product, submit all requests online at **www.cengage.com/permissions.**
Further permissions questions can be emailed to **permissionrequest@cengage.com**

While every effort has been made to ensure the reliability of the information presented in this publication, Gale, a part of Cengage Learning, does not guarantee the accuracy of the data contained herein. Gale accepts no payment for listing; and inclusion in the publication of any organization, agency, institution, publication, service, or individual does not imply endorsement of the editors or publisher. Errors brought to the attention of the publisher and verified to the satisfaction of the publisher will be corrected in future editions.

EDITORIAL DATA PRIVACY POLICY: Does this product contain information about you as an individual? If so, for more information about our editorial data privacy policies, please see our Privacy Statement at www.gale.cengage.com.

Gale
27500 Drake Rd.
Farmington Hills, MI, 48331-3535

LIBRARY OF CONGRESS CATALOG NUMBER 89-190943
ISBN-13: 978-1-4144-4108-5
ISBN-10: 1-4144-4108-8

This title is also available as an e-book
ISBN-13: 978-1-55862-775-8 ISBN-10: 1-55862-775-8
Contact your Gale, a part of Cengage Learning sales representative for ordering information.

BRITISH LIBRARY CATALOGUING IN PUBLICATION DATA
International directory of company histories, Vol. 112
Derek Jacques and Paula Kepos
33.87409

Printed in the United States of America
1 2 3 4 5 6 7 14 13 12 11 10

Contents

Preface

The St. James Press series *The International Directory of Company Histories* (*IDCH*) is intended for reference use by students, business people, librarians, historians, economists, investors, job candidates, and others who seek to learn more about the historical development of the world's most important companies. To date, *IDCH* has profiled more than 10,785 companies in 112 volumes.

INCLUSION CRITERIA

Most companies chosen for inclusion in *IDCH* have achieved a minimum of US$25 million in annual sales and are leading influences in their industries or geographical locations. Companies may be publicly held, private, or nonprofit. State-owned companies that are important in their industries and that may operate much like public or private companies also are included. Wholly owned subsidiaries and divisions are profiled if they meet the requirements for inclusion. Entries on companies that have had major changes since they were last profiled may be selected for updating.

The *IDCH* series highlights 25% private and nonprofit companies, and features updated entries on approximately 35 companies per volume.

ENTRY FORMAT

Each entry begins with the company's legal name; the address of its headquarters; its telephone, toll-free, and fax numbers; and its web site. A statement of public, private, state, or parent ownership follows. A company with a legal name in both English and the language of its headquarters country is listed by the English name, with the native-language name in parentheses.

The company's founding or earliest incorporation date, the number of employees, and the most recent available sales figures follow. Sales figures are given in local currencies with equivalents in U.S. dollars. For some private companies, sales figures are estimates and indicated by the abbreviation *est.* The entry lists the exchanges on which the company's stock is traded and its ticker symbol, as well as the company's NAICS codes.

Entries generally contain a *Company Perspectives* box which provides a short summary of the company's mission, goals, and ideals; a *Key Dates* box highlighting milestones in the company's history; lists of *Principal Subsidiaries*, *Principal Divisions*, *Principal Operating Units*, *Principal Competitors*; and articles for *Further Reading*.

American spelling is used throughout *IDCH*, and the word "billion" is used in its U.S. sense of one thousand million.

SOURCES

Entries have been compiled from publicly accessible sources both in print and on the Internet such as general and academic periodicals, books, and annual reports, as well as material supplied by the companies themselves.

CUMULATIVE INDEXES

IDCH contains three indexes: the **Cumulative Index to Companies**, which provides an alphabetical index to companies profiled in the *IDCH* series, the **Index to Industries**, which allows researchers to locate companies by their principal industry, and the **Geographic Index**, which lists companies alphabetically by the country of their headquarters. The indexes are cumulative and specific instructions for using them are found immediately preceding each index.

SPECIAL TO THIS VOLUME

This volume of *IDCH* contains entries on five companies on the *Forbes* list of the 200 largest U.S. charities, including an update on United Way Worldwide, the number one charity in the United States in private donations.

SUGGESTIONS WELCOME

Comments and suggestions from users of *IDCH* on any aspect of the product as well as suggestions for companies to be included or updated are cordially invited. Please write:

> The Editor
> *International Directory of Company Histories*
> St. James Press
> Gale, Cengage Learning
> 27500 Drake Rd.
> Farmington Hills, Michigan 48331-3535

St. James Press does not endorse any of the companies or products mentioned in this series. Companies appearing in the *International Directory of Company Histories* were selected without reference to their wishes and have in no way endorsed their entries.

Notes on Contributors

Stephen V. Beitel
Writer and copyeditor based in East Amherst, New York.

Kecia Brown
Writer and editor in Washington, D.C.; contributor to the *African American National Biography*.

Joyce Helena Brusin
Writer and essayist; contributor to the *Encyclopedia of World Governments*.

Melanie Bush
Journalist and teacher in upstate New York.

Ed Dinger
Writer and editor based in Bronx, New York.

Melissa Doak
Writer and editor based in Ithaca, New York.

Doris L. Eder
Writer, editor, and president of Eder Editorial Enterprises in Norwalk, Connecticut.

Louise B. Ketz
Author, editor, book producer, and literary agent based in New York City; contributor to *Scribner Encyclopedia of American Lives*.

Eric Laursen
Writer and editor based in Buckland, Massachusetts.

Michael L. Levine
Writer and editor based in New York City.

Mary C. Lewis
Chicago–based editorial services professional specializing in reference books, educational publishing, copyediting, and developmental editing.

Maryellen Lo Bosco
Writer, editor and teacher based in Asheville, North Carolina.

Judson MacLaury
Retired historian of the U.S. Department of Labor; author of *To Advance Their Opportunities* (2008) and of numerous articles, reviews, and encyclopedia entries.

Doris Maxfield
Michigan-based editorial services professional specializing in reference works, textbooks, and nonprofit grants.

Stephen Meyer
Writer and editor based in Missoula, Montana.

Margaret L. Moser
Writer based in New York City; licensed attorney, former COO of boutique financial consulting firm, and onetime actor and director.

Grace Murphy
Writer based in upstate New York with specialties in health care, business, and reference.

Marie O'Sullivan
Researcher, writer, and editor based in Ireland; expertise includes international education, student mobility, and globalization; editor and writer for the IIEPassport Study Abroad Directories.

Roger Rouland
Writer and scholar specializing in company histories, literary criticism, literary essays, and poetry; freelance photographer specializing in nature photography.

Helga Schier
Writer, editor, and translator (German/English) based in Los Angeles.

Hanna Schonthal
Massachusetts-based writer and editor.

Roger K. Smith
Writer and writing instructor in Ithaca, New York; contributor to the *Gale Encyclopedia of World History: Governments*, CQ Press's *Political Handbook of the World*, and other reference titles.

Gillian Wolf
Writer and teacher living in Skokie, Illinois.

List of Abbreviations

€ European euro
¥ Japanese yen
£ United Kingdom pound
$ United States dollar

A

AB Aktiebolag (Finland, Sweden)
AB Oy Aktiebolag Osakeyhtiot (Finland)
A.E. Anonimos Eteria (Greece)
AED Emirati dirham
AG Aktiengesellschaft (Austria, Germany, Switzerland, Liechtenstein)
aG auf Gegenseitigkeit (Austria, Germany)
A.m.b.a. Andelsselskab med begraenset ansvar (Denmark)
A.O. Anonim Ortaklari/Ortakligi (Turkey)
ApS Amparteselskab (Denmark)
ARS Argentine peso
A.S. Anonim Sirketi (Turkey)
A/S Aksjeselskap (Norway)
A/S Aktieselskab (Denmark, Sweden)
Ay Avoinyhtio (Finland)
ATS Austrian shilling
AUD Australian dollar
Ay Avoinyhtio (Finland)

B

B.A. Buttengewone Aansprakeiijkheid (Netherlands)
BEF Belgian franc

BHD Bahraini dinar
Bhd. Berhad (Malaysia, Brunei)
BND Brunei dollar
BRL Brazilian real
B.V. Besloten Vennootschap (Belgium, Netherlands)

C

C. de R.L. Compania de Responsabilidad Limitada (Spain)
C. por A. Compania por Acciones (Dominican Republic)
C.A. Compania Anonima (Ecuador, Venezuela)
C.V. Commanditaire Vennootschap (Netherlands, Belgium)
CAD Canadian dollar
CEO Chief Executive Officer
CFO Chief Financial Officer
CHF Swiss franc
Cia. Compagnia (Italy)
Cia. Companhia (Brazil, Portugal)
Cia. Compania (Latin America [except Brazil], Spain)
Cie. Compagnie (Belgium, France, Luxembourg, Netherlands)
CIO Chief Information Officer
CLP Chilean peso
CNY Chinese yuan
Co. Company
COO Chief Operating Officer
Coop. Cooperative
COP Colombian peso

Corp. Corporation
CPT Cuideachta Phoibi Theoranta (Republic of Ireland)
CRL Companhia a Responsabilidao Limitida (Portugal, Spain)
CZK Czech koruna

D

D&B Dunn & Bradstreet
DEM German deutsche mark (W. Germany to 1990; unified Germany to 2002)
Div. Division (United States)
DKK Danish krone
DZD Algerian dinar

E

E.P.E. Etema Pemorismenis Evthynis (Greece)
EC Exempt Company (Arab countries)
Edms. Bpk. Eiendoms Beperk (South Africa)
EEK Estonian Kroon
eG eingetragene Genossenschaft (Germany)
EGMBH Eingetragene Genossenschaft mit beschraenkter Haftung (Austria, Germany)
EGP Egyptian pound
Ek For Ekonomisk Forening (Sweden)
EP Empresa Portuguesa (Portugal)

ESOP Employee Stock Options and Ownership
ESP Spanish peseta
Et(s). Etablissement(s) (Belgium, France, Luxembourg)
eV eingetragener Verein (Germany)
EUR European euro

F

FIM Finnish markka
FRF French franc

G

G.I.E. Groupement d'Interet Economique (France)
gGmbH gemeinnutzige Gesellschaft mit beschraenkter Haftung (Austria, Germany, Switzerland)
GmbH Gesellschaft mit beschraenkter Haftung (Austria, Germany, Switzerland)
GRD Greek drachma
GWA Gewerbte Amt (Austria, Germany)

H

HB Handelsbolag (Sweden)
HF Hlutafelag (Iceland)
HKD Hong Kong dollar
HUF Hungarian forint

I

IDR Indonesian rupiah
IEP Irish pound
ILS Israeli shekel (new)
Inc. Incorporated (United States, Canada)
INR Indian rupee
IPO Initial Public Offering
I/S Interesentselskap (Norway)
I/S Interessentselskab (Denmark)
ISK Icelandic krona
ITL Italian lira

J

JMD Jamaican dollar
JOD Jordanian dinar

K

KB Kommanditbolag (Sweden)
KES Kenyan schilling
Kft Korlatolt Felelossegu Tarsasag (Hungary)
KG Kommanditgesellschaft (Austria,

Germany, Switzerland)
KGaA Kommanditgesellschaft auf Aktien (Austria, Germany, Switzerland)
KK Kabushiki Kaisha (Japan)
KPW North Korean won
KRW South Korean won
K/S Kommanditselskab (Denmark)
K/S Kommandittselskap (Norway)
KWD Kuwaiti dinar
Ky Kommandiitiyhtio (Finland)

L

L.L.C. Limited Liability Company (Arab countries, Egypt, Greece, United States)
L.L.P. Limited Liability Partnership (United States)
L.P. Limited Partnership (Canada, South Africa, United Kingdom, United States)
LBO Leveraged Buyout
Lda. Limitada (Spain)
Ltd. Limited
Ltda. Limitada (Brazil, Portugal)
Ltee. Limitee (Canada, France)
LUF Luxembourg franc

M

mbH mit beschraenkter Haftung (Austria, Germany)
Mij. Maatschappij (Netherlands)
MUR Mauritian rupee
MXN Mexican peso
MYR Malaysian ringgit

N

N.A. National Association (United States)
N.V. Naamloze Vennootschap (Belgium, Netherlands)
NGN Nigerian naira
NLG Netherlands guilder
NOK Norwegian krone
NZD New Zealand dollar

O

OAO Otkrytoe Aktsionernoe Obshchestve (Russia)
OHG Offene Handelsgesellschaft (Austria, Germany, Switzerland)
OMR Omani rial
OOO Obschestvo s Ogranichennoi Otvetstvennostiu (Russia)

OOUR Osnova Organizacija Udruzenog Rada (Yugoslavia)
Oy Osakeyhtiö (Finland)

P

P.C. Private Corp. (United States)
P.L.L.C. Professional Limited Liability Corporation (United States)
P.T. Perusahaan/Perseroan Terbatas (Indonesia)
PEN Peruvian Nuevo Sol
PHP Philippine peso
PKR Pakistani rupee
P/L Part Lag (Norway)
PLC Public Limited Co. (United Kingdom, Ireland)
PLN Polish zloty
PTE Portuguese escudo
Pte. Private (Singapore)
Pty. Proprietary (Australia, South Africa, United Kingdom)
Pvt. Private (India, Zimbabwe)
PVBA Personen Vennootschap met Beperkte Aansprakelijkheid (Belgium)
PYG Paraguay guarani

Q

QAR Qatar riyal

R

REIT Real Estate Investment Trust
RMB Chinese renminbi
Rt Reszvenytarsasag (Hungary)
RUB Russian ruble

S

S.A. Sociedad Anónima (Latin America [except Brazil], Spain, Mexico)
S.A. Sociedades Anônimas (Brazil, Portugal)
S.A. Société Anonyme (Arab countries, Belgium, France, Jordan, Luxembourg, Switzerland)
S.A. de C.V. Sociedad Anonima de Capital Variable (Mexico)
S.A.B. de C.V. Sociedad Anónima Bursátil de Capital Variable (Mexico)
S.A.C. Sociedad Anonima Comercial (Latin America [except Brazil])
S.A.C.I. Sociedad Anonima Comercial e Industrial (Latin America [except Brazil])

S.A.C.I.y.F. Sociedad Anonima Comercial e Industrial y Financiera (Latin America [except Brazil])

S.A.R.L. Sociedade Anonima de Responsabilidade Limitada (Brazil, Portugal)

S.A.R.L. Société à Responsabilité Limitée (France, Belgium, Luxembourg)

S.A.S. Societe Anonyme Syrienne (Arab countries)

S.A.S. Societá in Accomandita Semplice (Italy)

S.C. Societe en Commandite (Belgium, France, Luxembourg)

S.C.A. Societe Cooperativa Agricole (France, Italy, Luxembourg)

S.C.I. Sociedad Cooperativa Ilimitada (Spain)

S.C.L. Sociedad Cooperativa Limitada (Spain)

S.C.R.L. Societe Cooperative a Responsabilite Limitee (Belgium)

S.E. Societas Europaea (European Union Member states

S.L. Sociedad Limitada (Latin America [except Brazil], Portugal, Spain)

S.N.C. Société en Nom Collectif (France)

S.p.A. Società per Azioni (Italy)

S.R.L. Sociedad de Responsabilidad Limitada (Spain, Mexico, Latin America [except Brazil])

S.R.L. Società a Responsabilità Limitata (Italy)

S.R.O. Spolecnost s Rucenim Omezenym (Czechoslovakia

S.S.K. Sherkate Sahami Khass (Iran)

S.V. Samemwerkende Vennootschap (Belgium)

S.Z.R.L. Societe Zairoise a Responsabilite Limitee (Zaire)

SAA Societe Anonyme Arabienne (Arab countries)

SAK Societe Anonyme Kuweitienne (Arab countries)

SAL Societe Anonyme Libanaise (Arab countries)

SAO Societe Anonyme Omanienne (Arab countries)

SAQ Societe Anonyme Qatarienne (Arab countries)

SAR Saudi riyal

Sdn. Bhd. Sendirian Berhad (Malaysia)

SEK Swedish krona

SGD Singapore dollar

S/L Salgslag (Norway)

Soc. Sociedad (Latin America [except Brazil], Spain)

Soc. Sociedade (Brazil, Portugal)

Soc. Societa (Italy)

Sp. z.o.o. Spólka z ograniczona odpowiedzialnoscia (Poland)

Ste. Societe (France, Belgium, Luxembourg, Switzerland)

Ste. Cve. Societe Cooperative (Belgium)

T

THB Thai baht

TND Tunisian dinar

TRL Turkish lira

TTD Trinidad and Tobago dollar

TWD Taiwan dollar (new)

U

U.A. Uitgesloten Aansporakeiijkheid (Netherlands)

u.p.a. utan personligt ansvar (Sweden)

V

V.O.f. Vennootschap onder firma (Netherlands)

VAG Verein der Arbeitgeber (Austria, Germany)

VEB Venezuelan bolivar

VERTR Vertriebs (Austria, Germany)

VND Vietnamese dong

VVAG Versicherungsverein auf Gegenseitigkeit (Austria, Germany)

W–Z

WA Wettelika Aansprakalikhaed (Netherlands)

WLL With Limited Liability (Bahrain, Kuwait, Qatar, Saudi Arabia)

YK Yugen Kaisha (Japan)

ZAO Zakrytoe Aktsionernoe Obshchestve (Russia)

ZAR South African rand

ZMK Zambian kwacha

ZWD Zimbabwean dollar

Akzo Nobel N.V. C

Strawinskylaan 2555
Post Office Box 75730
Amsterdam, 1070 AS
Netherlands
Telephone: (+31 20) 502 7555
Fax: (+31 20) 502 7666
Web site: http://www.akzonobel.com

Public Company
Incorporated: 1969 as Akzo N.V.
Employees: 57,060
Sales: EUR 13.89 billion ($19.37 billion) (2009)
Stock Exchanges: Euronext Amsterdam
Ticker Symbol: AKZA
NAICS: 325131 Inorganic Dye and Pigment Manufacturing; 325188 All Other Basic Inorganic Chemical Manufacturing; 325510 Paint and Coating Manufacturing; 325520 Adhesive Manufacturing; 325613 Surface Active Agent Manufacturing; 325998 All Other Miscellaneous Chemical Product and Preparation Manufacturing

∎ ∎ ∎

The Dutch company Akzo Nobel N.V. is the world's largest paint and coatings manufacturer and is also a top global manufacturer of specialty chemicals. Active in more than 80 countries around the world, Akzo Nobel organizes its operations into three major units: Specialty Chemicals (generating about 37 percent of sales), which produces industrial chemicals, functional chemicals, pulp and paper chemicals, and surfactants; Decorative Paints (34 percent), producer of paints for trade professionals and do-it-yourselfers under such brands as Sikkens, Dulux, and Hammerite; and Performance Coatings (29 percent), specializing in car refinishes, industrial coatings, marine and protective coatings, powder coatings, and wood finishes and adhesives. The company was formed through the 1994 merger of Akzo N.V. of the Netherlands and Nobel Industries AB of Sweden.

AKZO'S FORERUNNERS AND EARLY YEARS

The merger of Akzo and Nobel represented the culmination of more than a century of acquisitions and mergers that the two companies completed, in the process absorbing numerous firms with long histories. Some of the companies that Akzo acquired can be traced as far back as the 18th century. For example, one of the coating units that it acquired, Sikkens, was formed in 1792. Duyvis, a food company acquired by Akzo, was founded in 1806. Akzo's chemical interests in the United States were tied to Armour & Company, a leading meatpacking firm that began operating in the 1860s.

Akzo's foundation, however, was based on Vereinigte Glanzstoff-Fabriken, a German chemical company formed in 1899. In the early decades of the 20th century, Vereinigte established itself in the chemical industry as a leading producer of rayon and various paints and coatings. In 1929 Vereinigte merged with Nederlandsche Kunstzijdefabriek (known as Enka, for short), a competing Dutch manufacturer of rayon. The

COMPANY PERSPECTIVES

Often people achieve only incremental progress, because their view of tomorrow is determined by what they see today. At AkzoNobel, we believe the future belongs to those smart enough to challenge it. We believe that real progress belongs to those who not only think with courage, but also have the courage to deliver on the thought. Tomorrow's answers, delivered today.

What drives us is knowing that what is good for our customers today is not necessarily good enough for them tomorrow. What excites us is asking the unasked question. What inspires us is seeing the opportunity others cannot. What unites us is the intelligence to deliver where others have not. This benefits our customers because we sustain their future competitiveness and meet the consumers' unspoken needs.

This ambition defines us. This is the way we work. This is why we come to work. This is AkzoNobel.

resulting Dutch organization was named Algemene Kunstzijde Unie (AKU).

From the 1930s to the 1960s, AKU became a solid market leader in the development and manufacture of synthetic fibers. In addition to rayon, AKU began producing such breakthrough synthetics as nylon and polyester. Chief among the company's significant innovations was the invention of a material called aramid, a derivative of nylon. AKU experimented with this synthetic fiber in the late 1960s.

AKU had enjoyed generous profits from its core synthetic fiber products during the 1960s, and its corporate strategy looked sound for the 1970s. In 1969 AKU joined forces with Koninklijke Zout-Organon (KZO), a major Dutch producer of chemicals, drugs, detergents, and cosmetics, and the resultant organization became Akzo N.V. Further expansion plans on the part of Akzo were thwarted in the early 1970s, however, when actions by the Organization of Petroleum Exporting Countries (OPEC) oil cartel wreaked havoc with petrochemical markets. Akzo's businesses, particularly those related to synthetic fibers, suffered. In addition to these oil-related problems, the fibers market was affected by turbulence from other quarters. During this period,

many synthetic fibers became a commodity product, and low-cost Far Eastern manufacturers took control of many industry segments. Burdened by weak demand and manufacturing overcapacity, Akzo's profits plunged. By the late 1970s, some analysts speculated that Akzo was headed for bankruptcy.

Another setback came when in the 1980s, when the company was selling its new synthetic fiber under the name of Twaron. Unfortunately for Akzo, the fiber industry leader du Pont, headquartered in the United States, was simultaneously developing the fabric under the name of Kevlar, and du Pont began selling its product first. As a result, Akzo was both shut out of the lucrative U.S. market for the product and also faced stiff competition in its home market of Europe. Akzo's failure to carve out a market for Twaron proved to be the culmination of the setbacks that adversely affected its synthetic fibers operations throughout the 1970s.

REORGANIZATION STRATEGIES

Throughout this turbulent period, Akzo executives scrambled to overcome adversity. They reduced the percentage of revenues attributable to synthetic fibers from more than 50 percent in the early 1970s to less than 30 percent going into the 1980s. At the same time, they tried to supplant income from the struggling fiber division with higher-margin products such as paint coatings, noncommodity chemicals, and pharmaceuticals. Akzo executives made another significant move toward reorganizing the firm's operations in 1982, when they appointed Aarnout A. Loudon as chief executive of the company. Loudon, a 46-year-old attorney-turned-executive, had demonstrated impressive financial acumen in turning around Akzo subsidiaries in France and Brazil. Upon assuming leadership of the company, Loudon initiated an aggressive restructuring strategy designed to stabilize Akzo's unwieldy balance sheet and to ensure the company's long-term profitability.

Among other maneuvers, Loudon further reduced Akzo's emphasis on synthetic fibers to only 20 percent of corporate revenues and boosted its position in coatings and industries related to health care. He also decentralized decision making and eliminated management layers. At the same time, Loudon launched an ambitious acquisition drive in 1984 chiefly designed to increase Akzo's presence in the important U.S. market and to diversify into chemical businesses promising higher profit margins. Between 1984 and 1990, Akzo purchased more than 30 companies, mostly in the United States, at a cost of about $1.8 billion. The units were primarily involved in the production of salt, chemicals, and pharmaceuticals. To fund these purchases, Loudon simultaneously jettisoned poorly

KEY DATES

■

1646: Bofors is founded in Sweden.

1864: Alfred Nobel founds Nitroglycerin AB, forerunner of KemaNobel AB.

1929: Vereinigte Glanzstoff-Fabriken merges with Nederlandsche Kunstzijdefabriek to form Algemene Kunstzijde Unie (AKU).

1969: AKU merges with Koninklijke Zout-Organon to form Akzo N.V.

1984: Nobel Industries AB is created through the merger of KemaNobel and Bofors.

1994: Akzo merges with Nobel to form Akzo Nobel N.V. becoming one of the 10 largest chemical companies in the world.

1998: The firm acquires Courtaulds plc, a British coatings and fiber manufacturer.

1999: Akzo Nobel exits from the synthetic fiber industry by divesting its Acordis unit.

2007: Company sells its pharmaceutical unit, Organon BioSciences N.V., to Schering-Plough Corporation.

2008: Akzo Nobel buys the British coatings and specialty chemicals firm Imperial Chemical Industries PLC.

performing assets that were worth more than $1.5 billion. By the end of the acquisition campaign, Akzo had emerged as the leading global producer of salt and peroxides and one of the top 20 chemical companies in the world. Sales in 1990 approached $10 billion as profits surged.

STREAMLINING FOR GREATER EFFICIENCY

During the early 1990s, Akzo concentrated on improving efficiency. Compared to chemical companies in Japan and the United States, its operations were bloated, chiefly because of restrictive government and organized labor regulations in Europe. Gradual improvements in efficiency led to marked success in important divisions such as pharmaceuticals, which captured a key position in the reproductive medicine market. Its most notable product was Desogen, the top-selling birth-control formula in the world. Similarly, Akzo enjoyed consistent market-share gains in some of its paints and coatings divisions. The net result was that Akzo sustained steady sales and profits throughout the early 1990s, despite a global economic downturn.

Going into the mid-1990s, Akzo continued to reduce its emphasis on such low-profit commodities as salt and fibers and to boost its dependence on coatings and specialty chemicals. To that end, Akzo consummated a pivotal merger early in 1994 with Nobel Industries of Sweden. Nobel was a major contender in the global paint, coatings, and specialty chemicals industries. It operated subsidiaries worldwide and enjoyed a relatively strong position in the United States. The company that resulted, Akzo Nobel N.V., elevated Akzo's revenue figure by more than 25 percent, gave the new company a leadership role in the global paint and coatings industry, and bolstered the former Akzo's stance in the European and U.S. markets. The former Nobel Industries also was able to reduce costs because it could obtain needed materials more economically from Akzo, such as inexpensive access to such raw materials as salt and chlorates.

NOBEL INDUSTRIES AND ITS PREDECESSORS: 1864–1984

Akzo's merger partner was originally founded in 1864 by Alfred Nobel, the creator of the Nobel Prizes. Nobel was born in 1833 into a Swedish family that claimed heritage to the 17th-century Swedish scientist Olof Rudbeck. Alfred Nobel's father, Immanuel, was a self-educated inventor with an interest in explosives. An unsuccessful businessman, Immanuel was forced to file for bankruptcy in 1832 after the family's home burned down. In 1837 Immanuel moved to Russia, leaving his family behind, to start a new business. There, he invented an explosive device for which demand gradually increased. By 1842 Immanuel had achieved modest success with his invention, and he sent for his family. Alfred Nobel's exposure to that environment, combined with his natural interest in chemistry, prompted him to form his own company in 1864 called Nitroglycerin AB.

Nobel's key invention was a process of making nitroglycerin that did not explode during production and handling. The perfection of this technique, however, came at a great personal cost for Nobel in that an explosion killed his brother and four other workers during the testing process. This breakthrough led to Nobel's 1866 development of dynamite, which combined nitroglycerin and an absorbent earthy substance. Nobel went on to create blasting gelatin and smokeless powder, and he eventually claimed 350 patents. In an effort to overcome opposition from established gunpowder manufacturers and other competitors, Nobel and several associates formed the Nobel Dynamite Trust in 1886. This cartel eventually dominated five continents, and Nobel dynamite factories dotted the globe.

A surprising turn of events occurred for Nobel in 1888 when his brother Ludwig died and a local French newspaper accidentally reported the death of Alfred instead. To his dismay, Nobel read his own obituary, in which he was described as the inventor of dynamite and the "merchant of death," even though most of his explosives were used in nonmilitary applications. This experience motivated Nobel to demonstrate his true intent. Thus, when he died in 1896, his will directed that his entire fortune be entrusted to the Norwegian parliament and distributed annually as a reward to individuals who "shall have conferred the greatest benefit on mankind." Subsequently, the Nobel Foundation was established, and the first prize was awarded in 1901.

After his death, Nobel's conglomeration of businesses was divided into various corporations. Nobel's Swedish companies evolved into two separate organizations. His original company, Nitroglycerin AB, continued to make explosives. Its name was changed to Nitro Nobel AB in 1965 before it was bought out by a chemical group controlled by the prominent Wallenberg family in 1977. The resultant organization was named KemaNobel AB a year later. The other segment of the Swedish Nobel operations became Bofors, a manufacturer of munitions that traced its origins to 1646. In 1982 Erik Penser, a young Swedish stockbroker, engineered the purchase of Bofors. Two years later, he purchased KemaNobel, reuniting the two divisions in a company he called Nobel Industries AB.

In 1986 Penser's company won a five-year, $1.2 billion contract to supply field artillery to the Indian government. Business analysts lauded the deal as one of the largest orders ever secured by a Swedish company until it was discovered that Penser might have made illegal, covert payments of $4.5 million into a secret Swiss bank account to get the contract. To make matters worse, it was discovered in 1987 that Nobel Industries had illegally shipped arms to Iran, Iraq, and other countries not sanctioned for arms trade by the Swedish government. Meanwhile, Nobel's U.S. chemical subsidiary, Bofors Nobel, Inc., filed for bankruptcy in 1985, largely because the U.S. Department of Natural Resources had sued the division for $15 million in environmental cleanup costs. Initially, Bofors Nobel had agreed to pay the cleanup expenses, but once the higher-than-expected costs accrued, the subsidiary elected to file for bankruptcy instead.

THE MERGER: 1994

Despite the setbacks at Nobel Industries, Akzo executives viewed the company as a potential asset to their organization. In 1994 Akzo merged with Nobel and its six business groups, making the resultant Akzo Nobel

N.V. one of the 10 largest chemical companies in the world.

Shortly before the merger, Akzo had implemented a sweeping restructuring to dismantle the company's five major business divisions and reorganize them into four new groups: chemicals, fibers, coatings, and pharmaceuticals. Akzo had also continued to develop its U.S. operations aggressively, while working simultaneously to penetrate Asian and South American markets. By the time of the merger, Akzo had invested about 33 percent of its resources in the Netherlands, 20 percent in Germany, and 22 percent in the United States, with many of its remaining investments scattered throughout Europe. For 1994, its year of creation, Akzo Nobel posted sales of about $11.5 billion, roughly 5 percent of which was netted as income.

CHALLENGES, RESTRUCTURING, AND GROWTH

Akzo Nobel faced several challenges as it entered the mid-1990s. In 1995 its pharmaceutical unit, Organon, lost revenues following a scare linking its Marvelon and Mercilon oral contraceptive pills to increased risk of thrombosis (abnormal blood clotting). Falling fiber prices, stagnant markets, and declining sales in the coatings division also led to a mere 0.3 percent increase in profits in 1996. The firm did make some key partnerships, however, including a joint venture with Courtaulds plc to develop and market NewCell, a cellulosic filament yarn. The company also spent $240 million to expand its fluidized catalytic cracking (FCC) catalysts and hydroprocessing catalysts (HPC) capacity. The capital investment was made to attract partners to its FCC and HPC business. The firm also began restructuring its specialty surfactants business, which had been dealing with overcapacity as well as a stagnant market. As a result, the unit began cutting costs and consolidating production. Akzo Nobel also sold its North American salt business, Akzo Nobel Salt, Inc., in 1997 to Cargill, Incorporated, as part of its effort to focus on its core operations.

Akzo Nobel's restructuring of its pharmaceutical, coatings, and chemical businesses began to pay off and the balance sheet in 1997 reflected this. The company recorded a 7 percent increase in sales, and operating profits in its pharmaceutical interests climbed by 17 percent. Its coatings and chemicals divisions secured a 27 percent increase in operating profits.

In 1998 the firm focused on making key alliances and acquisitions as well as paring back less-profitable operations. An agreement with Bayer AG was reached in which the German-based firm would produce ethylene amines exclusively for Akzo Nobel. Three printing ink companies, Louis O. Werneke, Werneke & Mulheran, and Label Inks, were purchased to secure Akzo Nobel's position as a leading supplier of printing inks in the U.S. market. The company also acquired Courtaulds plc in July 1998 for NLG 6.1 billion ($3 billion) in a deal that created the world's largest coatings company. The firm subsequently merged its fiber business with that of Courtaulds into a newly created company, Acordis. At the same time, because of poor growth and overcapacity, Akzo Nobel continued to consolidate its surfactants operations. The company also sold its plastic packaging and laminate and aluminum tubes interests.

A disappointing 1 percent increase in net profits in 1998 led to a renewed focus on integrating its newly acquired firms into its current businesses. The firm's pharmaceutical operations, which were growing twice as fast as other companies in the industry, also became a major focus. The division had a strong position in the women's health-care market, and its Organon business operated as the world's fourth-largest producer of oral contraceptives. Akzo Nobel also strengthened its Intervet division with the EUR 546 million purchase of Hoechst Roussel Vet from Hoechst AG, a deal that doubled the size of its animal health-care business. Perhaps the most important move in 1999 was the sale of Acordis to CVC Capital Partners. The deal marked Akzo Nobel's exit from the synthetic fiber business and solidified the company's intent to focus on three core areas: pharmaceuticals, coatings, and chemicals.

As Akzo Nobel entered the 21st century, its pharmaceuticals business, the fastest-growing such concern in Europe, accounted for 47 percent of the company's total profits, with its core operations focusing on human and animal health care. The company's other divisions also fared well in 2000 despite weakening market conditions. The coatings division acquired the aerospace and specialty coatings business of Dexter Corporation, which strengthened its position in the global market and significantly increased the size of its aerospace coating operations. In January 2001 the chemicals division acquired Hopton Technologies, which was purchased to boost the paper chemicals business in the United States.

PHARMACEUTICAL DECLINE AND SALE

By 2002, however, the pharmaceuticals division was flagging, dragging down Akzo Nobel's overall profits. Earnings also took a hit from a strengthening of the euro against the U.S. dollar, which made U.S. products less expensively on the European market. The pharmaceuticals arm continued to struggle for a variety

of other reasons, including its thin "pipeline" of drugs nearing human trials, its weak record getting drugs approved by the U.S. Food and Drug Administration, and the expiration of the patent on its popular antidepressant drug Remeron, which allowed rivals to make generic versions of the drug.

Akzo Nobel continued to sell off some assets in order to focus on coatings, chemicals, and pharmaceuticals. In 2001 the company sold its medical diagnostics division as well as its printing inks business but bought the vehicle refinishes business of the U.S. firm MAC Specialty Coatings. When Hans Wijers succeeded Cees van Lede as CEO in 2003, he vowed to rejuvenate the pharmaceuticals segment. He immediately began downsizing, eliminating 3,300 jobs and selling off three of the company's chemical units. The divestments enabled Akzo Nobel to focus its chemicals business on a handful of key areas: pulp and paper chemicals, surfactants, functional chemicals, base chemicals, and polymer chemicals. By mid-decade, Akzo Nobel was buying coatings makers, including Swiss Lack, the leading paint company in Switzerland, in 2005, and Sico Inc., the leading coatings firm in Canada, in 2006.

In February 2006, having failed to breathe life into its pharmaceuticals arm, Akzo Nobel announced it would spin off the unit, Organon BioSciences N.V., the following year. In a surprise move, however, the U.S. firm Schering-Plough Corporation bought the unit for EUR 11 billion ($16.1 billion) in November 2007. The sale helped finance Akzo Nobel's purchase of the British coatings and specialty chemicals producer Imperial Chemical Industries PLC (ICI) for EUR 11.61 billion ($17.11 billion) the following January. ICI focused on specialty chemical products with higher profit margins than the commodity chemicals that had traditionally been the industry's base. In addition to expanding its specialty chemicals operations, the acquisition built up Akzo Nobel's retail decorative paints business and gave it a strong foothold in the North American coatings market.

POST-ICI RESTRUCTURING

Subsequent to the Organon sale and the acquisition of ICI, Akzo Nobel restructured its business operations into three segments: Decorative Paints, Performance Coatings, and Specialty Chemicals. Company revenues dropped in 2007, reflecting the divestment of Organon, before jumping back up to EUR 15.41 billion ($22.67 billion) the following year thanks to the takeover of ICI.

Akzo Nobel responded to the worldwide economic recession that began in late 2007 by cutting about 6 percent of its workforce and halting its share-buyback program. The difficult economic environment also led the company to lower the expected growth of the ICI operations it had acquired and to incur an after-tax impairment charge of EUR 1.2 billion in the fourth quarter of 2008. As a result, Akzo Nobel posted a net loss of EUR 1.09 billion ($1.6 billion) for the year.

In 2009 the company sold its nonstick coatings business as it continued to divest itself of noncore businesses. At the same time, Akzo Nobel pursued additional acquisitions to boost its paints, coatings, and specialty chemicals segments. It expanded further into Asian markets as well, building new manufacturing plants in China and India. In November 2009 the firm reached an agreement to buy Dow Chemical Company's powder coatings business. For the year, Akzo Nobel's revenues were down about 10 percent to EUR 13.89 billion ($19.37 billion), reflecting the poor economic climate, but the company returned to the black, posting net income of EUR 278 million ($386 million).

Akzo Nobel's actions during the early 21st century provided proof of its ability to adjust to adversity, be it the challenge of a struggling pharmaceutical arm, a weak dollar, or adverse economic circumstances. By divesting itself of unprofitable segments and acquiring businesses to help refocus on higher-margin coatings and specialty chemicals operations, the company showed itself to be highly nimble and responsive to economic conditions despite its huge, multinational presence. This responsiveness boded well for Akzo Nobel's future in a recovering global economy.

Dave Mote
Updated, Christina M. Stansell;
Melissa J. Doak

PRINCIPAL SUBSIDIARIES

Akzo Nobel Aerospace Coatings B.V.; Akzo Nobel Car Refinishes B.V.; Akzo Nobel Chemicals B.V.; Akzo Nobel Decorative Coatings B.V.; Akzo Nobel Functional Chemicals B.V.; Akzo Nobel Industrial Chemicals B.V.; Akzo Nobel Nederland B.V.; Akzo Nobel Salt B.V.; Alabastine Holland B.V.; SA Alba (Argentina); Akzo Nobel Pty Ltd. (Australia); Akzo Nobel Chemicals Ltd. (Canada); ICI Canada Inc.; Sico Inc. (Canada); Akzo Nobel (Asia) Co., Ltd. (China); Akzo Nobel (Shanghai) Co. Ltd. (China); Akzo Nobel S.A. (France); Akzo Nobel Chemicals GmbH (Germany); Akzo Nobel Coatings GmbH (Germany); Akzo Nobel GmbH (Germany);

Akzo Nobel Packaging Coatings GmbH (Germany); Schönox GmbH (Germany); ICI India Ltd.; PT ICI Paints Indonesia; Akzo Nobel K.K. (Japan); Akzo Nobel Industrial Coatings Mexico S.A. de C.V.; ICI Pakistan Limited; Akzo Nobel Paints (Asia Pacific) Pte. Ltd. (Singapore); Akzo Nobel AB (Sweden); Casco Adhesives AB (Sweden); Eka Chemicals AB (Sweden); Akzo Nobel Powder Coatings Ltd. (UK); Akzo Nobel UK Ltd.; ICI Paints (UK); International Paint Ltd. (UK); Akzo Nobel Chemicals, Inc. (USA); Akzo Nobel Coatings Inc. (USA); Akzo Nobel Inc. (USA); Akzo Nobel Paints LLC (USA); Akzo Nobel Polymer Chemicals LLC (USA); Akzo Nobel Surface Chemistry LLC (USA).

PRINCIPAL OPERATING UNITS

Decorative Paints; Performance Coatings; Specialty Chemicals.

PRINCIPAL COMPETITORS

BASF SE; E.I. du Pont de Nemours and Company; PPG Industries Inc.; RPM International Inc.; The Sherwin-Williams Company; The Valspar Corporation.

FURTHER READING

"Akzo Nobel Offers Premium for Courtaulds," *Chemical Market Reporter*, April 27, 1998, p. 8.

Cowan, Roberta B., "Akzo Halts Its Buyback, Plans Job Cuts," *Wall Street Journal*, September 30, 2008, p. B3.

Koster, Bart, and Maaike Noordhuis, "AkzoNobel CEO Plans Investment in China, Other Emerging Markets," *Wall Street Journal*, November 30, 2009, p. B4.

Milmo, Sean, "Akzo Nobel Focuses on Coatings," *Coatings World*, March 2006, pp. 18–19.

Short, Patricia, "A Slimmer Akzo," *Chemical and Engineering News*, March 5, 2007, pp. 37+.

Walen, Jeanne, Mike Esterl, and Tjeerd Wiersma, "Europe Drug Firms Join Slimming Trend: Akzo and Merck KGaA Look to Unload Units to Focus on Core Assets," *Wall Street Journal*, January 5, 2007, p. A4.

Walsh, Kerri, "Akzo Nobel to Acquire ICI for $16.1 Billion in Cash," *Chemical Week*, August 15, 2007, p. 6.

Young, Ian, "AkzoNobel: Portfolio Transformation Brings Added Focus," *Chemical Week*, December 22, 2008, pp. 16–19.

———, "AkzoNobel Writes Down Former ICI Assets, Posts a Big Fourth-Quarter Net Loss," *Chemical Week*, March 2, 2009, p. 6.

Allegheny Technologies Incorporated

—■—

1000 Six PPG Place
Pittsburgh, Pennsylvania 15222-5479
U.S.A.
Telephone: (412) 394-2800
Fax: (412) 394-3034
Web site: http://www.alleghenytechnologies.com

Public Company
Incorporated: 1938 as Allegheny Ludlum Steel Corporation
Employees: 8,500
Sales: $3.05 billion (2009)
Stock Exchanges: New York
Ticker Symbol: ATI
NAICS: 331210 Iron and Steel Pipe and Tube Manufacturing from Purchased Steel; 331491 Nonferrous Metal (except Copper and Aluminum) Rolling, Drawing, and Extruding; 331492 Secondary Smelting, Refining, and Alloying of Nonferrous Metal (except Copper and Aluminum)

■ ■ ■

Allegheny Technologies Incorporated (ATI) is one of the largest specialty metals firms in the United States. Although ATI traces its origins to the western Pennsylvania steel industry of the early 20th century, the company's present incarnation was formed in 1996, with the merger of Allegheny Ludlum Corporation with Teledyne Inc. In addition to being among the nation's leading producers of stainless steel, ATI is also a major manufacturer of titanium, nickel-based alloys, tungsten, and other metals. The company's operations are devoted to three principal product lines: high-performance metals, flat-rolled metal products, and engineered products such as tools and carbon forgings. Allegheny Technologies markets its products to a wide range of business sectors, including the defense, aerospace, and automotive industries.

CONSOLIDATION AND GROWTH: 1938–50

The genesis of Allegheny Technologies Incorporated can be traced to the 1938 merger of Allegheny Steel Company of Brackenridge, Pennsylvania, and Ludlum Steel Company of Watervliet, New York. Both companies were manufacturers of specialty steel, and each desired facilities the other possessed; for example, Allegheny wanted to enter the bar business, and Ludlum wished to get into the flat business. Consequently, the merger produced scarcely any duplication of facilities and enabled the newly formed corporation, named Allegheny Ludlum Steel Corporation (ALSC), to move to the forefront of the specialty steel market by virtue of the combined product lines of the two companies. W. F. Detwiler, a former night-shift apprentice for Allegheny Steel Company, became the corporation's first chairman of the board, and Hiland G. Batcheller, president of Ludlum Steel Company, was appointed its president.

At the completion of ALSC's first full year of operation in 1940, the demand for specialty steel had shown a steady increase for the past decade. ALSC reported more than $37 million in sales for the year, 58 percent of which were made in the final quarter. The

COMPANY PERSPECTIVES

Allegheny Technologies Incorporated is *Building the World's Best Specialty Metals Company*. The cornerstones of our value system are based on achieving the highest ethical standards, maintaining strong customer focus and providing challenging and rewarding opportunities for our employees.

Our objective is to provide an attractive investment to our stockholders by earning a premium return on our total invested capital over the long term.

We are driven by these strategies: Pursue high-margin global markets for specialty metals; leverage multi-materials capabilities; drive improved operating performance and customer service through the ATI Business System.

United States' entry into World War II took the steady increase of the market to unprecedented heights. As the demand for jet airplanes and armaments spiraled upward, research engineers at ALSC intensified their search for metal materials that would answer the growing demand. ALSC developed heat-resisting alloys for use in the construction of aircraft turbine engines. By 1944 the number of employees had ballooned to 17,000, almost three times the number at the outbreak of the war. Sales had climbed to more than $114 million, and ALSC parlayed this wartime-induced success toward an $80 million expansion and modernization program in 1946. The expansion program focused on increasing ALSC's production capacities of stainless steel (which had more than quadrupled in use since 1920) and the burgeoning demand for flat-rolled silicon electrical steel, used in the manufacture of electrical transformers and communication equipment.

INNOVATION AND DIVERSIFICATION: 1950–70

The 1950s, a decade of vast growth for the steel industry as a whole, occasioned only a marginal gain in sales for ALSC. At the conclusion of 1950, sales were just below $190 million and by the end of the decade had grown to only $230 million. However, during those 10 years, ALSC's sales figures fluctuated wildly, reaching a peak of $286 million in 1956 and a nadir of $170 million two years earlier. Although part of the blame for the vacillating sales was attributed to slackening demand, ALSC nevertheless remained steadfast to its long-term policy of expansion and modernization. By 1956 it had spent more than $100 million on such programs since the merger of Allegheny Steel and Ludlum Steel, and the company continued to fund further programs. ALSC's capacity for melting and refining special steel alloys was doubled in 1956, and in the same year, the company allotted $30 million to be spent over a two-year period for expanding its production of stainless, electrical, and other high-alloy specialty steels.

At this time, ALSC also made improvements in production efficiency and the quality of its products by installing the steel industry's first semiautomated system for hot working steel. Instead of having to set the measurements manually each time a slab of steel passed through a rolling mill (a process that could take up to 15 passes to achieve the desired thickness and shape), the semiautomated system required only one operator to insert a card containing the specifications for the slab into the system and then push a button. This procedure greatly diminished the chances of error, because the measurements were dictated by a computer. Consequently, the quality of the formed steel product was improved.

Having firmly established itself as one of the leading specialty steels manufacturers in the United States, ALSC began to turn to foreign markets as the backlog demand dating from World War II began to ebb. It was a direction that the steel industry as a whole followed by the mid-1960s, but in 1960 ALSC became one of the first U.S. steel companies to invest in overseas steel manufacturing. In a bid to capitalize on the rapid growth of specialty steel sales in the European Common Market area, ALSC formed a Belgian company in partnership with Evence Coppée & Cie. of Brussels and the Société Anonyme Metallurgique d'Esperance-Longdoz to produce and sell specialty steel.

ALSC also expanded once again on the home front. After posting sales of $292 million in 1964, its highest since 1956, the corporation invested $28 million in new plants and equipment, focusing its efforts on the conversion from open-hearth furnaces for silicon-steel production to basic-oxygen furnaces in 1966.

Two acquisitions in the late 1960s augured a change of market focus for ALSC. In 1967 the company acquired True Temper Corporation, a maker of sporting goods and garden tools. This acquisition, which represented a significant diversification of ALSC's product line, was followed in 1969 by the acquisition of Jacobsen Manufacturing Co., a maker of power lawn mowers, garden tractors, and snow blowers.

KEY DATES

1938: Allegheny Steel Company and Ludlum Steel Company merge to form the Allegheny Ludlum Steel Corporation.

1946: Allegheny Ludlum launches $80 million expansion and modernization program.

1967: Allegheny Ludlum acquires True Temper Corporation.

1969: Allegheny Ludlum purchases Jacobsen Manufacturing Company.

1980: George W. Tippins acquires Allegheny Ludlum in a leveraged buyout.

1996: Allegheny Ludlum merges with Teledyne Inc. to form Allegheny Teledyne Incorporated.

1999: Allegheny Teledyne Incorporated becomes Allegheny Technologies Incorporated.

2007: ATI expands titanium production capacity at plants in Pennsylvania, Oregon, and the Carolinas.

WEATHERING THE DOWNTURN: THE SEVENTIES

In early 1970 Allegheny Ludlum Steel Corporation changed its name to Allegheny Ludlum Industries Inc. (ALI). As a consequence of the name change, the specialty steel operation became a division of ALI but continued to bear the ALSC name. As quoted in the *Wall Street Journal*, a company spokesperson stated the name change "would reflect the changing nature of the business of Allegheny Ludlum." The 1970s, a horrendous decade for the steel industry, marked the decline of the specialty steel market as a major focus of ALI. By the end of 1970 a third of ALI's sales came from non-steel items.

In early 1972 ALI reached outside of the steel industry for a new president and chief operating officer (COO). Robert J. Buckley, who had held various positions in industrial management, was selected to lead ALI into a more diversified future. The announcement by ALI in the *Wall Street Journal* of Buckley's selection as president and COO reiterated the company's movement, articulated two years earlier, toward a more diversified product line. When questioned about the specific duties Buckley would assume as president, a spokesperson for the corporation stated Buckley would "run the day-to-day operations of Allegheny Ludlum Industries, which includes more than just a steel company." The qualifying statement clearly underscored

ALI's decision to branch out and aggressively pursue markets other than specialty steel.

By 1974 ALSC continued to be the major money earner for the parent company. Specialty steel accounted for 70 percent of the corporation's sales, producing over $500 million in revenue, but Buckley had already decided by 1973 to dispose of the specialty steel operation. He began to actively pursue buyers for a minority equity position in the subsidiary, but by 1976 he had found no satisfactory offers.

At this time, in the mid-1970s, the steel market was plummeting. If ever there was a time to exit the steel market, now was such a time. The steel industry was severely hampered by undercutting its own demand projections, slow worldwide economic growth, massive oil price increases, and increased foreign competition. By the end of the decade, ALSC had begun to feel the brunt of the harsh economic times. In 1978 Buckley engaged investment bankers to attempt to sell the specialty steel unit. The bar division had been spun off in 1976 as a leveraged buyout to existing management. When the bankers had no success in finding a buyer, ALI executive Richard P. Simmons received approval to try to put together his own buyout, while the bankers continued their efforts to find a buyer for the specialty steel operation.

Simmons, president of the steel division and executive vice president of ALI, had begun working for ALSC in 1953 as a metallurgist. Six years later he left ALSC and worked for two steel companies before returning to ALSC in 1968 to become vice president of manufacturing. After becoming president of ALSC in 1972, he merged manufacturing plants, reduced staff, established cost-control systems, and formulated the strategies that would carry the steel company into the next decade.

NEW OWNERSHIP AND A NEW DIRECTION: THE EIGHTIES

In 1980 Simmons and Clint W. Murchinson Jr., a Dallas financier who owned the Dallas Cowboys football team and held investments in petroleum and broadcasting properties, began negotiations for the sale of ALSC. By the end of the year an agreement had been reached. As part of the deal, Simmons agreed to leave ALI and become president of the spun-off specialty steel operation. In late December 1980 the sale of the corporation for approximately $195 million was approved by ALI shareholders. During final arrangements between Murchinson, Simmons, and the managers of the specialty steel subsidiary that held an invested interest in the sale, however, negotiations stalled due to last-minute disagreements, and Murchinson withdrew his offer.

As quickly as the deal fell through, however, it was revived when a wealthy Pittsburgh industrialist, George W. Tippins, entered the scene at the behest of Simmons. Tippins filled the void created by Murchinson's departure by offering the necessary financial backing to enable the sale of ALSC for the same amount offered by Murchinson (and exactly the same terms agreed to by both partners) to the private ownership of Tippins, Simmons, and 16 of his managers. The unexpected withdrawal of Murchinson's offer and the sale to the group headed by Tippins occurred virtually overnight. This 1980 leveraged buyout was the second largest at that point in time, and it was completed without investment bankers.

With Tippins as chairman of the board and Simmons as president and chief executive officer, ALSC braced itself for another downturn in the steel market. Large U.S. steel companies suffered disastrous losses, nearly $6 billion over a two-year period, during the early 1980s. Outdated facilities and inefficient production processes, as well as a decreasing demand for steel, were to blame for the losses. For years, steel manufacturers had looked toward raising prices rather than improving their productivity as a source for ameliorating their profits, and by 1983 their practices had begun to severely affect them. ALSC's largest competitor, Crucible Steel, went out of business during this difficult period, as did several other specialty steel producers. This was the most challenging time experienced by the steel industry, including specialty steel, going back to the Great Depression of the 1930s. Nevertheless, ALSC posted a profit for every quarter and every year.

The impact of foreign steel companies on U.S. steel manufacturers was one of the other major contributors to the ills of the steel industry during the 1980s. The increasing rate of foreign subsidized steel imports entering the U.S. market and the practice of foreign steel companies selling steel in the United States at prices below the cost of production in the U.S. market, referred to as "dumping," took its toll on the industry. Although the effect of foreign steel manufacturers had been felt years before, the U.S. steel industry began lobbying in earnest by the late 1970s for government intervention. In late 1984 their pleas were answered by the introduction of voluntary restraint agreement (VRA) curbs on illegally dumped and subsidized steel imports. The VRAs, in effect for five years and then subject to renewal, would restrict steel imports from 29 countries to just under a fifth of the U.S. market. The steel industry, ALSC included, used this grace period to finance capital-spending projects, totaling more than

$6.5 billion in a five-year period, to modernize their facilities and make them more efficient. The VRAs also aided ALSC by offering a respite from foreign competition at a time when imports were surging into the specialty steel market. Even during the period when VRAs were in effect, record input levels of specialty steel continued.

In 1985 Robert P. Bozzone, an employee of ALSC since 1955, succeeded Simmons as president of the company. Simmons remained as chief executive officer and a year later became the chairman of the board, replacing Tippins. The corporation remained financially healthy at this time, posting a profit every quarter since its buyout from ALI. Sales stood at $716 million by 1985, and ALSC's survival through the economic slide was attributed to its focus on product lines ignored by the big steel companies as well as its modern facilities that increased worker production. In 1986 ALSC changed its name to Allegheny Ludlum Corporation (ALC). A year later sales topped $1 billion, and in May the corporation went public.

By the end of the decade sales were hovering around $1.2 billion, and VRAs had been extended for another two and a half years, giving ALC additional incentive to boost its capital-spending projects by $25 million. Buoyed by a U.S. stainless steel market that had more than doubled over the past two decades, ALC entered the 1990s as another recession loomed on the horizon. Nonetheless, ALC was able to record profits, albeit at lower levels than previous years, throughout the downturn by adhering to the corporate strategies that had carried the company through decades of cyclical ups and downs since 1938. Since going private in 1980, Allegheny Ludlum had earned 15 percent on total capital employed, a record matched by few metals companies. By this time, ALC produced stainless steel and other specialty steel for a wide variety of uses beyond traditional markets. Its products were used in the production of stainless steel skis, home cookware, personal computer diskettes, and Gillette's Sensor razor, and in the creation of Biosphere 2, the scientific experiment that attempted to replicate a self-sustaining environment in a hermetically sealed complex. The search for new applications and markets for its products and the practice of eschewing overdependence on cyclical customers (both hallmarks of ALC's history) enabled the corporation to remain stable during an economic period that rocked many other steel companies.

MERGING WITH TELEDYNE: THE NINETIES

One of the linchpins of ALC's survival during the 20th century was its emphasis on innovative technology as a means of improving efficiency and lowering production costs. This focus continued into the 1990s. In 1992 ALC completed construction of the first prototype casting machine to produce stainless and carbon steel products from molten steel. The casting machine, called Coilcast and developed in cooperation with a company in Linz, Austria, eliminated the need for several stages of the production process, thereby improving the efficiency of production and lowering costs. When commercialized, it provided a continuing advantage for Allegheny Ludlum over its competition.

In the face of the cyclical, at times turbulent nature of the steel industry, ALC remained comparatively stable in the new decade, continuing to grow through the pursuit of its core objectives. Its strategies for seeking ways to remain cost competitive, identify new market niches, increase its exports, and remain sensitive to customer needs kept Allegheny Ludlum on an even keel during this period. At the same time, demand for Allegheny Ludlum's stainless steel grew at an annual rate of approximately 5 percent during the first years of the decade. By the early 1990s ALC had become the largest stainless steel manufacturer in the United States.

In spite of the company's continued dominance of its industry, larger economic forces began to take a toll on its bottom line. By 1993 the nation's steel business had slipped into a serious recession, causing a significant decline in Allegheny Ludlum's overall earnings. The company's profits slumped further in the first half of 1994, when a 70-day United Steelworkers strike resulted in a 40 percent decline in sales for the year's second quarter. As demand for steel continued to decline, ALC was compelled to explore new ways to increase revenues.

Allegheny Ludlum embarked on a new course in April 1996, when it announced a merger with Los Angeles-based Teledyne, Inc. At the time, the move surprised some analysts; a producer of specialty alloy products for the aviation, industrial, and consumer markets, Teledyne seemed an unlikely match for the steel manufacturer. In the eyes of ALC executives, however, the merger was a sound business move. In a statement quoted by Erle Norton and Andy Paszton in the *Globe and Mail*, ALC president and CEO Arthur Aronson cited Teledyne's "strong aviation and electronics, industrial and consumer-products businesses" as the primary impetus behind the deal, explaining that the merger would enable Allegheny Ludlum to balance "the cyclicality of the metals business" through product diversification. At the same time, Teledyne's surplus pension funds would help offset Allegheny Ludlum's underfunded pension plan.

The new company, Allegheny Teledyne Incorporated, was formed later that year, in a deal worth $3.2

billion. With the merger, the new company became the largest specialty steel firm in the world, with annual sales in the vicinity of $4 billion. Heading into the end of the decade, the company embarked on a series of strategic acquisitions, aimed at further expanding its share of the specialty metals market. In November 1997 Allegheny Teledyne purchased titanium producer Oregon Metallurgical Corporation for $560 million. A month later the company launched a hostile bid for Pennsylvania steel firm Lukens Incorporated. After a brief but intense bidding war between Allegheny Teledyne and rival Bethlehem Steel, in January 1998 the two companies reached an agreement to divide Lukens's key assets, with Allegheny Teledyne taking over the smaller company's stainless steel operations. To finance these mergers, the company was forced to undertake an aggressive restructuring project, shedding nine of its existing operating divisions. In 1999, as part of this streamlining process, the company adopted a new name, Allegheny Technologies Incorporated (ATI).

NEW PRODUCTS FOR A NEW MILLENNIUM

Allegheny Technologies struggled during the first years of the new century as slumping steel sales, combined with rising energy costs, led to an overall decrease in earnings. To confront this slump, the company launched an aggressive cost-cutting program. In December 2001 ATI closed its stainless steel plant in Houston, Pennsylvania, cutting more than 500 jobs, or roughly 5 percent of its total workforce. Even after returning to profitability, the company continued to streamline. In June 2004 ATI announced that it would cut an additional 650 jobs over a two-year span, with the aim of reducing operating costs by $200 million annually.

In the second half of the decade, ATI began to devote significant resources to expanding its titanium production. In March 2006 the company dedicated $25 million to increasing its titanium output, with the aim of raising production by 3.75 million pounds. In January 2007 the company earmarked an additional $215 million to expand titanium and nickel production at three of its facilities, and a month later it devoted $38 million to increasing titanium capacity at its plant in Albany, Oregon, to 4 million pounds. The new strategy came in response to increasing global demand for the specialty metal, particularly within the aerospace sector. Aerospace products accounted for roughly a third of ATI's business by March 2007. Between 2006 and 2007 the company's total value doubled, from $5 billion to $10 billion, driven largely by rapid growth in titanium sales.

In the face of the economic crisis of 2008, ATI saw its operating profits drop significantly as slumping demand for specialty metals forced companies to cut prices. By 2009 the company's revenues also began to slide as aviation giants like Boeing continued to reduce orders for titanium products. For the year's first quarter, ATI posted sales of only $831.6 million, compared with $1.34 billion for the same period the previous year. Third-quarter sales slipped even further, from $1.4 billion in 2008 to $697.6 million in 2009. As the decade drew to a close, it became apparent that ATI's future growth would depend a great deal on the global economic recovery.

Jeffrey L. Covell
Updated, Stephen Meyer

PRINCIPAL SUBSIDIARIES

ALC Funding Corporation; Allegheny Ludlum Corporation; ATI Funding Corporation; ATI Properties, Inc.; TDY Holdings LLC; TDY Industries, Inc.

PRINCIPAL COMPETITORS

Carpenter Technology Corporation; Nucor Corporation; RTI International Metals, Inc.; ThyssenKrupp Steel AG (Germany); Titanium Metals Corporation; United States Steel Corporation.

FURTHER READING

"Allegheny Ludlum Merger Details," *Steel*, May 23, 1938, p. 26.

Burger, John R., "ATI Expanding Titanium Sponge Production in Booming Market," *Metals Week*, March 27, 2006, p. 12.

Chakravraty, Subrata N., "A Farewell to Steel," *Forbes*, December 8, 1980, pp. 36–37.

Contavespi, Vicki, "It's a Good Thing the Steel Industry Worked So Hard in the 1980s to Prepare for the Next Recession," *Forbes*, January 6, 1992, p. 166.

Gilcrest, Laura, "Titanium Maker Allegheny Posts Loss amid Aircraft Slump," *Metals Week*, July 27, 2009, p. 2.

Norton, Erle, and Andy Pasztor, "Allegheny Ludlum, Teledyne to Merge," *Globe and Mail* (Toronto), April 2, 1996.

Petzinger, Thomas, Jr., "Allegheny Ludlum's Steel Operations Sold," *Wall Street Journal*, December 29, 1980, p. 4.

Russel, Mark, "Small Steelmakers Finding Profitable Market Niches," *Wall Street Journal*, January 8, 1987, p. 6.

"Sorting Out What's Left at Allegheny Ludlum," *BusinessWeek*, December 1, 1980, p. 49.

"Steel Mills Head into Push-button Era," *BusinessWeek*, January 12, 1957, pp. 80–82.

AMEC plc

— ■ —

76-78 Old Street
London, EC1V 9RU
United Kingdom
Telephone: (+44 20) 7539-5800
Fax: (+44 20) 7539-5900
Web site: http://www.amec.com

Public Company
Incorporated: 1982
Employees: 22,000
Sales: £2.61 billion ($3.77 billion) (2008)
Stock Exchanges: London
Ticker Symbol: AMEC
NAICS: 541330 Engineering Services

■ ■ ■

AMEC plc is a London-based global engineering, consultancy, and project management company serving the natural resources, power and process, and earth and environmental sectors. The Natural Resources Division is involved in the oil and gas services, oil sands, and mining sectors. Customers served by the Power & Process Division include both conventional and nuclear power suppliers, renewable and bio-process power providers, and transmission and distribution operators. The Earth & Environmental Division provides engineering and consulting help in such areas as air quality, asbestos and lead management, brownfields, groundwater supply, mine-water management, occupational health and safety, regulatory compliance, and waste management. A public company listed on the London Stock Exchange, AMEC maintains more than 250 offices in about 40 countries around the world.

NINETEENTH-CENTURY HERITAGE

AMEC is result of a merger between two major U.K. civil engineering groups, Fairclough Construction and William Press & Son. Fairclough was the older of the two, established in 1883 when a 30-year-old mason, Leonard Fairclough, launched a stone business in Adlington, England, focusing initially on monuments and artistic masonry. In time he became involved in the construction of schools, churches, and other structures as well as roads and bridges. At the start of the 20th century, his son Leonard Miller Fairclough joined him as an apprentice, and by 1927 when the founder died his son was ready to assume the helm as governing director of the company. Under the direction of Leonard M. Fairclough, the company completed a transition from regional masonry firm to major civil engineering contractor, taking on ever-larger projects, many of them in the late 1940s when England was recovering from the damage caused by World War II. The younger Fairclough ran the company until 1959, the same year it became a public entity.

Fairclough was still a midsize construction firm by 1970 when it began to grow through acquisitions, completing four major deals during the decade. As a result, revenues increased from £23 million in 1970 to more than £245 million 10 years later. Despite a worldwide recession, the company posted record profits in 1982. Although Fairclough enjoyed a robust business

---

---

in the United Kingdom, it sought to grow its international client base. To achieve that end, a merger was engineered in November 1982 with William Press, resulting in a holding company called AMEC plc. William Press had been established in London in 1913 and grew to become one of the country's leading gas and oil pipeline engineering firms. It was heavily involved in the country's conversion from coal to natural gas in the 1950s as well as the construction of pipelines and oil terminals.

CREATION OF MAJOR CONSTRUCTION FIRM

Not only did Press's international business account for 30 percent of its revenues, compared to 15 percent for Fairclough, Press also brought a strong industrial customer base that nicely complemented Fairclough's public and private clientele. In terms of capitalization, the merger created the fifth-largest construction firm in the United Kingdom. AMEC's performance during the first three years following the merger was not as strong as expected, however, largely because of problems at Press, some of which were unavoidable and some not. There was nothing Press could do about slumping gas prices, but mismanagement at a Press subsidiary led to significant losses created by missed deadlines or in some cases uncompleted projects. It was only Fairclough's strong performance that allowed AMEC to continue to increase profits during this period. In 1986 Press rebounded and ongoing growth at Fairclough led to pre-tax earnings surging to £30.5 million, up from the £5 million total for the previous year.

AMEC expanded further through external means in 1988 via a merger with the Matthew Hall Group of Companies, which possessed even deeper roots than Fairclough. It was founded in 1848 when a master plumber and lead worker named Matthew Hall moved from Newcastle, England, to London, where he set up his own lead works and plumbing business. Twenty years later he was joined by his nephew, Dr. Andrew Ainsley, and the company took on a number of projects

at such prominent sites as Buckingham Palace, Westminster Abbey, and Windsor Castle. In 1927 the business was reorganized as Matthew Hall Limited and began to grow into a global concern. By the time Matthew Hall merged with AMEC, it was generating revenues of £470 million a year from operations throughout Europe, the United States, the Middle East, Australia, and Asia.

ACQUISITION BID REJECTED: 1995

Fairclough, Press, and Matthew Hall continued to operate as independent entities into the 1990s, but the AMEC brand began to take root. Early in the decade the company's struggling process operation began doing business as AMEC, replacing the Press Offshore and Matthew Hall names in order to build the international business. Other reorganization efforts were also undertaken to offset the adverse impact of difficult economic conditions, and these initiatives helped AMEC's profits return to acceptable levels by 1994. The company's performance caught the attention of Norway's Kvaerner ASA, Europe's largest shipbuilder, which in November 1995 offered £360 million ($554 million) for AMEC as a way to expand its oil and gas offshore platform building business to the Pacific Rim, where AMEC controlled considerable offshore fabrication assets. AMEC quickly rejected the offer, insisting that it was "wholly inadequate."

At the same time it became an acquisition target, AMEC set its sights on Alfred McAlpine plc, a British home builder, offering £127 million in stock for the company. This effort also failed but AMEC was able to complete an important deal in 1995, adding New York-based Morse Diesel International, Inc., one of the world's top construction management firms, as a wholly owned subsidiary. The company, which had been formed as a 50-50 partnership between an AMEC unit and Morse/Diesel, Inc., maintained 13 offices across the United States and a branch in the United Kingdom. AMEC made another overseas acquisition in 1997 when it bought about 42 percent of Spie Batignolles S.A. (later SPIE S.A.), a French electrical contracting and construction firm that had been in business since the early 1880s when it was formed to build a machine for an abortive attempt to drill an English Channel tunnel.

As the 1990s came to a close, AMEC restructured its operations in an effort to be less dependent on competitively bid contracting work. Instead, under the leadership of its new chief, Peter Mason, AMEC sought to mitigate risk and add a measure of certainty by focusing on its core engineering, construction, development, and services capabilities and on long-term work in oil,

KEY DATES

1848: Matthew Hall starts plumbing and lead works business.
1883: Leonard Fairclough starts stone masonry business.
1913: William Press & Son is founded.
1982: Fairclough Construction and William Press merge to form AMEC plc.
1988: AMEC acquires Matthew Hall Group of Companies.

gas, utilities, rail, and facilities management. In keeping with this new direction, the Fairclough Homes subsidiary, builder of homes and apartments, became expendable and was sold for $170 million in 1999 to Centex Corporation, a major U.S. home builder that was eager to enter the U.K. market.

Completing the largest deal in its history, AMEC added significantly to its footprint in 2000 with the £221 million acquisition of AGRA Inc., a Canada-based provider of engineering, construction, environmental, and technology solutions with operations in about two-dozen countries, including the United States. The deal also added around £556 million in annual revenues. As a result of the investments in SPIE and AGRA, AMEC had clearly become an international concern. About 70 percent of the company's business had come from the United Kingdom in the mid-1990s, a percentage that had been cut in half by 2000.

NEW CENTURY, FRESH OPPORTUNITIES

AMEC was active on a number of fronts in the early years of the new decade. A few weeks after acquiring AGRA, AMEC launched a branding effort to bring all of its operations around the world under the AMEC identity, including AGRA and Morse Diesel in the United States. Later in 2000 AMEC bolstered its U.S. presence and doubled its environmental business by paying $17.5 million for Phoenix, Arizona-based Ogden Environmental and Energy Services Inc. This was also a year of achievement at home, where AMEC was able to take advantage of the United Kingdom's decision to sell off the country's public utilities, resulting in the company landing three major contracts. A year later, in the aftermath of the terrorist attacks on the World Trade Center in New York City and the Pentagon in

Washington, D.C., AMEC was awarded contracts to clear the rubble from both sites. New offices opened in Tokyo in 2001, followed a year later by an expansion of AMEC's business in China. The outstanding shares of SPIE were acquired in 2003, and that summer the AMEC SPIE brand was introduced across Europe.

AMEC also expanded its North American presence, especially in its Earth & Environmental business. Early in 2002 the division opened offices in Indiana and Minnesota, the first operations for the company in the midwestern United States. Later in the year an office was opened in New York City. In 2003 AMEC expanded its Denver-area Earth & Environmental office into a regional water resources hub with the acquisition of Water & Waste Engineering, Inc. An office was then opened in Washington, D.C., in 2004. Much of the work in the United States was contracted by the U.S. military, but with the war in Iraq, a large portion of those funds were reallocated to support that effort, reducing business for AMEC's environmental practice. The breadth of what the company had to offer paid off, however, as other arms of AMEC secured lucrative contracts to restore public works and water infrastructure in Iraq.

Despite the loss of U.S. military contracts related to the environment, AMEC continued to expand its operations in this area. Another acquisition completed in 2005 was that of Shapiro & Associates, Inc., a northwestern U.S. environmental consulting firm. Hydrosphere Resource Consultants, Inc., another Denver-area company, was acquired in 2007 to grow AMEC's water resources practice. Geomatrix Consultants, Inc., a California environmental specialist firm was brought into the fold in 2008, and a year later a Canadian environmental consultancy, Journeaux Bédard & Assoc. Inc., was added as well. In the meantime, AMEC expanded its environmental practice in the United Kingdom. In 2005 Environmental Advice Centre Limited was acquired, followed two years later by Applied Environmental Research Centre.

AMEC did not neglect other areas. In 2005 it acquired Houston-based Paragon Engineering Services, Inc., to bolster its oil and gas business. AMEC also expanded its European presence. In 2004 it acquired two French and one Spanish project management services companies. In 2005 AMEC completed an important acquisition in NNC Holdings Limited, the leading private-sector nuclear services firm in the United Kingdom. AMEC acquired a French nuclear services company, CIME SA, later in 2005 and majority control of a Romanian nuclear services firm the following year.

MASON RETIRES: 2006

Mason retired as chief executive in October 2006. His successor, Samir Brikho, undertook a strategic review and implemented a new strategy to focus on high-value consultancy, engineering, and project management services in the energy and industrial processes markets. AMEC SPIE was sold to a private-equity firm in 2006, and the following year the construction business and regeneration division was sold to Morgan Sindall plc. The Midwest Pipelines business was divested in 2007, followed in 2008 by the sale of AMEC's wind development business in the United Kingdom.

Acquisitions completed in the second half of the decade more than compensated for the divestitures, however. The largest independent engineering services company in Chile was purchased in 2007. Smith Williams Consultants, Inc., a mining consultancy, and Rider Hunt International Limited, a project services company, were acquired in 2008, while in Canada the oil sands specialist Bower Damberger Rolseth Engineering Limited was added. Acquisitions in 2009 included U.K.-based Performance Improvements Group Limited, a consultancy focusing on operations in the North Sea; Philips Engineering Ltd., a Canadian engineering consultancy; and GRD Limited, an Australian resources engineering company. Early in 2010, AMEC acquired another Australian company, Currie & Brown Pty Ltd., a leading cost and commercial management consultancy. There was every reason to believe that AMEC intended to remain a growth-oriented company for the long term.

Ed Dinger

PRINCIPAL SUBSIDIARIES

AGRA Foundations Limited (Canada); AMEC Americas Limited (Canada); AMEC Australia Pty Limited; AMEC BDR Limited (Canada); AMEC Cade Ingenieria y Desarrollo de Proyectos Limitada (Chile); AMEC Cade Servicios de Ingeniería Limitada (Chile); AMEC Earth & Environmental, Inc. (USA); AMEC Earth & Environmental (UK) Limited; AMEC E&C Services, Inc. (USA); AMEC Geomatrix, Inc. (USA); AMEC Group Limited; AMEC Holdings, Inc. (USA); AMEC Inc. (Canada); AMEC Infrastructure, Inc. (USA); AMEC Infrastructure Limited (Canada); AMEC International (Chile) S.A.; AMEC International Construction Limited; AMEC Kamtech, Inc. (USA); AMEC Nuclear UK Limited; AMEC NCL Limited (Canada); AMEC Nuclear Holdings Limited; AMEC Offshore Services Limited; AMEC Paragon, Inc. (USA); AMEC (Peru) S.A.; AMEC Utilities Limited; KL Ingenieurbau GmbH (Germany); Nuclear Safety Solutions Limited (Canada); Primat Recruitment Limited; Rider Hunt International Limited; Terra Nova Technologies, Inc. (USA).

PRINCIPAL DIVISIONS

Natural Resources; Power & Process; Earth & Environmental.

PRINCIPAL COMPETITORS

AECOM Technology Corporation; CH2M Hill Companies, Ltd.; Jacobs Engineering Group Inc.

FURTHER READING

Kavanagh, Michael, "Upbeat Amec Is Tapping the Benefits of Restructuring," *Financial Times*, August 29, 2008, p. 20.

Macalister, Terry, "Iraq War Puts Amec on the Defensive," *Guardian* (London), August 29, 2003, p. 23.

Morton, Ralph, and Andrew Ross, *Construction UK: Introduction to the Industry*. 2nd edition, Oxford: Blackwell, 2008.

Pretzlik, Charles, "Amec Discusses Disposal of Fairclough Arm," *Financial Times*, March 10, 1999, p. 44.

Stafford, Philip, "Amec Says Growth 'Assured,'" *Financial Times*, December 5, 2009, p. 14.

Taylor, Andrew, "Kvaerner Bid to Buy Amec Is Defeated," *Financial Times*, December 19, 1995, p. 17.

White, Garry, "AMEC Is Flush with Cash and Still Showing Growth," *Daily Telegraph* (London), March 13, 2009, p. 6.

American Red Cross

2025 E Street Northwest
Washington, D.C. 20006-5009
U.S.A.
Telephone: (202) 303-5000
Web site: http://www.redcross.org

Nonprofit Organization
Incorporated: 1881
Employees: 32,000
Sales: $3.3 billion (2009)
NAICS: 621991 Blood and Organ Banks; 624230
    Emergency and Other Relief Services

■ ■ ■

The American National Red Cross, more commonly known simply as the American Red Cross, is a nonprofit agency with a long history of providing relief to individuals affected by war and natural disaster. It was first formed in order to aid men wounded on the battlefield. The organization's network of more than 700 local chapters has volunteers who respond to flood, fire, earthquake, and drought. The American Red Cross has played an enormously important historical role in supporting U.S. troops in the two world wars and in ensuing conflicts. It has also been instrumental in organizing relief in countless natural disasters, from the Johnstown Flood to the Great San Francisco Earthquake to many more recent catastrophes, including the terrorist attacks against the United States of September 11, 2001. The organization's national presence and prestige allow it to spearhead fund-raising drives to benefit stricken communities, and it also often serves as the distribution network for funds and goods collected by other organizations or donated by the government.

Although the Red Cross was formed in response to war and disaster, it also developed a coherent peacetime mission, including teaching first aid and lifesaving, running blood banks, and providing assistance to fellow Red Cross and Red Crescent agencies worldwide. About half the organization's revenue comes from its Biomedical Services division, the division charged with collecting, processing, testing, and distributing blood products. Much of the remainder comes from charitable donations from individuals and corporations. It also receives money through the charitable fund-raising organization United Way.

INSPIRATION OF CLARA BARTON

The American Red Cross dates its formal beginning to 1881 but it was active before that. Its roots lie in Europe, where the International Red Cross was founded in Geneva, Switzerland, in 1864. The impetus for the founding of the international group was a book published in 1862 by a Swiss businessman, Jean-Henri Dunant. Dunant witnessed the horrific aftermath of a battle between Austrian and French forces near the Italian village of Solferino when he was traveling in the vicinity for business. Some 30,000 to 40,000 dead and wounded men lay on the battlefield, with no one to care for them. Dunant was so struck by the carnage that he wrote a book about what he had seen, and pleaded for the formation of volunteer civilian groups to aid wounded soldiers. Dunant spearheaded a group that soon formed the International Committee of the Red Cross. Although the United States sent an observer to the inaugural Red Cross conference, it did not at that time ratify what became known as the Geneva Convention.

The United States was in the midst of its own Civil War and paid little attention to this event in Switzerland. Nevertheless, battlefield relief for the wounded was vitally important. Clara Barton, a former schoolteacher and patent office clerk, became a one-woman force behind the Red Cross in the United States. Although she was not trained as a nurse and was a single woman of modest means, Barton had friends in high places in Washington through her patent office work. She began a crusade to bring supplies and aid to the Civil War wounded and went herself to the front lines, driving a mule wagon of supplies, serving hot soup, and nursing, all as needed.

After the war, she organized a search for missing prisoners of war. When ill health sent her to Europe for a rest, she became acquainted with the work of the Red Cross there. When she returned to the United States, she lobbied for a Red Cross in her home country, becoming a noted speaker all across the nation. With the war over in the United States, Barton had the idea of instituting the Red Cross as a disaster relief organization. Nothing like this existed at the time. Barton became the U.S. representative of the International Red Cross in 1881. In 1882 the U.S. Congress finally ratified the Geneva Convention.

In its earliest years, the American Red Cross existed almost solely through the energy of Barton. She shaped its mission and it was her political connections that made things work. She was an extraordinarily driven and hands-on person. The Red Cross did little without her direct involvement. One of the organization's first major disaster relief efforts was the Johnstown Flood of 1889, which drowned over 2,000 people and displaced most of Johnstown, Pennsylvania's 30,000 residents. Barton and her small staff went to Johnstown im-

mediately and stayed for five months. The Red Cross raised cash, disbursed goods, and oversaw the building of temporary housing with donated lumber.

The Red Cross became increasingly skilled at handling this kind of disaster and the organization won great praise for its domestic work. The limits of the organization's duties were not clearly spelled out, however, and the Red Cross extended itself to wherever Barton felt called. The Red Cross sent wheat to Russia to aid starving peasants in 1892 and Barton sailed to Turkey in 1896 to negotiate aid for the violently oppressed Armenians. During the Spanish-American War of 1898, the exact duties of the American Red Cross were not clear, leading to conflict with the Army Medical Corps. Although the Red Cross was usually seen as ultimately helpful, it was also criticized for overstepping bounds and sometimes for its accounting practices. Congress officially chartered the American Red Cross in 1900 but the group was nevertheless plagued with factionalism and lack of focus. Barton was elected president-for-life of the Red Cross in 1901 but resigned in 1904 after an aborted investigation into diversion of funds.

ROLE IN PEACE AND WAR

The group reincorporated under a new congressional charter in 1905, which made it a semigovernmental agency with some of its governors appointed by the president of the United States. The Red Cross developed a "peacetime" program around this time, defining a role for itself when neither war nor natural disaster threatened. It began training people in first aid and running courses in water safety. By 1917 the Red Cross had 267 chapters spread across the United States. It had working funds of about $200,000 and a paid staff nationwide of 167 people.

The group was exceedingly active in World War I, enrolling millions of volunteers to sew and knit clothing, roll bandages, and package food and supplies. The Red Cross sent thousands of nurses and ambulance drivers into the war and raised millions of dollars in donations. After the war, the group was criticized for allegedly mismanaging funds and for taking on duties that properly belonged to the government. The Red Cross restated its mission in 1922, dedicating itself first to military welfare and to disaster relief. Promotion of public health was its third area of concern. In addition, the group spelled out its intention not to duplicate the work of other agencies.

Membership grew and spread through the 1920s and 1930s, although the size of chapters and their level of funding varied considerably from place to place. By

KEY DATES

■

1864: International Red Cross is founded in Geneva.

1881: Clara Barton and others organize American Red Cross.

1900: Organization receives official charter from Congress.

1937: Red Cross begins blood bank activities.

1955–57: Three years of disasters drain organization's finances.

1980s: Red Cross begins screening donated blood for AIDS virus.

1993: Organization is under court order to improve blood services division.

2001: Donations pour into the Red Cross in response to September 11 terrorist attacks; criticism of the organization's handling of the donations follows.

2002: Red Cross launches its first for-profit venture, Pathogen Removal and Diagnostic Technologies, with ProMetic Life Sciences Inc.

2004: Red Cross updates its swimming and water safety program that reaches 2.2 million students annually.

2006: Food and Drug Administration fines organization $4.2 million for failing to correct record-keeping issues at blood banks.

2007: Johnson & Johnson unsuccessfully sues the Red Cross to stop it from using the red cross logo.

1941 total American Red Cross membership had grown to over nine million people. During World War II, membership swelled dramatically and the Red Cross raised more than $666.5 million. Anyone who donated a dollar or more to the organization was counted as a member. By 1945 over 25 percent of the U.S. population, 36.6 million people, were regarded as members. The group had close to 4,000 chapters.

RISE OF BLOOD BANKING

The Red Cross began operating blood banks in 1937. In 1940 it began a "Plasma for Britain" project to send blood to British soldiers. This was the first mass blood donation campaign and the first mass production of blood products. The plasma campaign was overseen by a pioneer of blood bank science, Dr. Charles R. Drew.

Drew, an African American, was a noted founder of blood storage technology. The U.S. military asked the Red Cross to provide blood for battlefield transfusion when the United States entered the war. Drew directed the Red Cross program for eight months but resigned in outrage because the Red Cross continued to comply with the military's request that the blood of black and white donors be segregated. The Red Cross continued to segregate blood by race until 1950.

During World War II the Red Cross collected blood from more than six million donors. Running blood banks became one of the most important missions of the Red Cross over the next 50 years. In 1948, with the war behind it, the Red Cross established the National Blood Donor Program to provide blood to hospitals. Blood was collected by local chapters and processed through 28 regional blood centers. Over the next decades, Red Cross researchers pioneered key aspects of blood bank technology. A Red Cross researcher discovered how to process blood for an antihemorrhaging agent; Red Cross scientists also crafted a method to process the clotting agent needed by hemophiliacs.

The Red Cross' donated blood was at first given without charge to hospitals but in the 1950s it began charging enough to recoup its costs. By the end of the 1970s, the Red Cross managed about half the nation's blood supply. By the first decade of the 21st century, this market share dropped to 40 percent. Nevertheless, in 2009 the Red Cross' Biomedical Services division turned some 6.5 million units of blood into 9.5 million blood products that were distributed at 3,000 hospitals and transfusion centers. It also continued to be a leader in the development and use of tests to detect infectious diseases transmissible in blood.

PERILS OF DISASTER RELIEF

The Red Cross continued its services to soldiers during the Korean War and after. Besides running blood banks, its peacetime mission consisted largely of disaster relief. Aid was provided to isolated victims, such as those whose homes burned, as well as to victims of devastating natural disasters. Each year the organization set aside a specific sum in its budget to pay for its disaster relief work. Extra money was put in a reserve fund. Then, in case of extreme need on the heels of a particularly devastating disaster, the group mounted fund-raising drives.

Chains of disasters often spelled financial peril for the organization. For example, hurricanes, floods, and tornadoes of unprecedented strength in 1955, 1956, and 1957 all but wiped out the Red Cross' reserves. The group relied on extra fund-raising campaigns to make up its losses. In 1985 the group budgeted $17 million annually for disaster relief. A succession of hurricanes that year forced the Red Cross to spend about $48 million, putting it severely over budget.

In the mid-1980s the Red Cross ran fund-raising campaigns by mailing out so-called disastergrams, which asked for money for victims of the latest catastrophe. Much of the charity's money came from the umbrella fund-raising organization United Way. Money brought in by disastergrams went to a general disaster fund. After the earthquake in San Francisco in 1989, the Red Cross allowed donors to specify that they wanted their money to go only to victims of a specific incident. This decision helped fend off allegations, which had been raised since Barton's time, that money raised for a specific cause might end up being spent elsewhere.

The Red Cross spent an increasing amount of money on disaster relief through the 1980s. It started the decade spending about $50 million per year, and by 1989 was spending over $100 million. Spending spiked to over $224 million in 1990. Although the organization provided relief on a massive scale, it was often criticized for the way it carried out its duties. By the early 1990s the group considered cutting back its services because so much of its budget was taken up with extraordinary disaster expenses. In 1991 Elizabeth Dole, who had held U.S. cabinet posts as secretary of labor and secretary of transportation, became president of the American Red Cross. Dole vowed to turn the organization around. The Red Cross was financially troubled because of its recent massive spending on disaster relief.

BLOOD SUPPLY SAFETY CONCERNS

Questions about the safety of the blood supply began dogging the Red Cross in the 1980s. At the time, the Red Cross used a test manufactured by Abbott Laboratories to screen donated blood for the acquired immunodeficiency syndrome (AIDS) virus. Despite known problems with the Abbott test, the Red Cross continued to use it into 1986. People who contracted AIDS through tainted blood transfusions later sued both Abbott and the Red Cross.

The Biomedical Services division was cited repeatedly in the 1980s and early 1990s for problems with its record keeping. A report by a U.S. Food and Drug Administration (FDA) investigator made public in 1990 recorded dozens of incidents of sloppy record keeping and computer errors. The FDA investigator told a congressional committee that ensuring the safety of the nation's blood supply was made difficult by the Red

Cross' problems. The investigator also found Red Cross officials were insufficiently concerned about mending its ways. When Dole took over the Red Cross, she announced a $120 million overhaul of the Biomedical Services division's record keeping and also scheduled improvements to staff training and blood testing. Eventually, the revamping of the Red Cross' blood banks cost around $287 million.

The changes, however, apparently did not go quickly enough. In 1993 the FDA filed suit against the Red Cross to force it to agree to make reforms. The Red Cross and the FDA settled the suit with a court-ordered consent decree outlining what the organization would do to improve. The Red Cross spent some $170 million to $180 million on computer systems and built eight regional blood testing laboratories in a move to centralize its operations. The cost of these changes put the Biomedical Services division in the red. By the late 1990s the division was in debt by about $300 million.

During this period, the Red Cross was nearing completion of its expensive overhaul of the Biomedical Services division. The division had evolved from a string of mainly autonomous regional blood centers to a much more centralized organization. Scott Hensley, in a June 22, 1998, article in *Modern Healthcare*, claimed the Red Cross "looks and feels more like a drug company." The Red Cross had remade its blood banks, significantly improving the safety of its products. The organization was said to have about 46 percent of the nation's blood supply market share, or almost half of the $2 billion industry. The Red Cross vowed to increase its market share, aiming for 65 percent over the next three years. This move was made specifically to enhance the blood division's finances.

COMPETITION IN THE MARKETPLACE

In 1995 the division brought in $937 million but was in the red by $113 million. Although the division brought in $1.1 billion in 1997, it still ran a deficit. The Red Cross began a campaign of tough competition, moving into markets that had traditionally been served by other companies. Its main competitor was a loose network of community blood banks that operated under the umbrella of America's Blood Centers (ABC). Blood banks had operated as virtual local monopolies since the 1970s, so that either the Red Cross, an ABC clinic, or a hospital blood bank would serve a particular community. In the mid-1990s the Red Cross began moving into markets from which it had been shut out of previously, such as Kansas City, Missouri; Dallas, Texas; and Phoenix, Arizona. It was often able to secure only a tiny market share, for example, 5 percent in Kansas City within two years of entering that market.

Nevertheless, the Red Cross had changed the way blood products were marketed by introducing direct competition. Some doctors and hospitals found that the new competitiveness brought prices down, while others worried that organizations vying for donors would ultimately scare the donors away. The new relationship between the Red Cross and its competitors became so acrimonious that the charity, ABC, and two other blood-banking societies engaged a professional mediator to allow them to discuss their differences. The industry leaders formed a working group called the Blood Forum and hoped to come up with rules that would allow them to compete gracefully. The level of hostility, however, was so high that an ABC official quoted in the *Modern Healthcare* article remarked the Blood Forum was "as bad as putting the Arabs and Israelis in the same room."

Aside from its problems with its Biomedical Services division, the Red Cross continued to strain to respond to unusual catastrophes in the 1990s. Flooding in the Midwest in 1993 led to the organization's largest relief effort ever, when over 20,000 workers assembled to combat the water damage. The Red Cross' most expensive disaster relief operation came just five years later, when Hurricane George in 1998 cost the charity more than $100 million.

Dole left the Red Cross in 1999 to pursue a run for president of the United States. Her successor was the first physician to head the agency in a hundred years, Bernadine Healy. Dr. Healy had been director of the National Institutes of Health, taught at Johns Hopkins University, and unsuccessfully run for the Senate. On taking over the Red Cross, Healy had to deal with the organization's ongoing fiscal and regulatory problems. She aimed to cut administrative positions to contain costs and streamline management. She also wanted the group to spend more money on research and development.

FDA CONCERNS AND FALLOUT FROM 9/11

At the end of 2000, the FDA again announced that the Red Cross was not doing enough to ensure the safety of its blood products. In response, Healy moved to borrow $100 million to fund improvements. The FDA, however, acted more aggressively than it had in the past and asked to be allowed to fine the Red Cross, which it said had been out of compliance with FDA regulations since 1985. Healy claimed to be amazed at the seriousness of the FDA's allegations of sloppiness, because the

Red Cross was supposed to have made drastic improvements in its blood operations after 1993. Healy was also faced with the ongoing problem of sour relationships with competitors of the Red Cross. In 2001 a California blood bank brought an antitrust suit against the Red Cross, alleging that the group artificially lowered prices in its region in order to drive other blood banks out of business.

In 2001 the American Red Cross responded to more than 67,000 disasters. The most memorable, however, were the September 11 terrorist jet hijackings that destroyed the World Trade Center in New York, damaged the Pentagon in Virginia, and resulted in a plane crash in Pennsylvania, sparking controversy and policy change. True to its mandate, the Red Cross responded immediately to the attacks with food, supplies, shelters, and counseling. As with any major disaster, the organization ran public service announcements asking people to assist in the response effort with money and blood donations. At one point, gifts were sent to the Red Cross' Liberty Relief Fund at the rate of three per second over the Internet.

The Liberty Relief Fund grew to a half-billion dollars. Soon the New York attorney general, who threatened to sue, and others were questioning what the Red Cross was doing with the money. Many people expected that cash would be distributed to victims, even though the Red Cross traditionally provided only vouchers and other types of assistance. Healy envisioned using what was left in the Liberty Relief Fund, after providing meals to first responders and investigators and mental health services to those affected by the attacks, to create contingency plans for future terrorist episodes. The outcry not only caused her to scuttle the plan but also forced her out of her job. Eventually more than 25,000 families and individuals did receive cash assistance; millions of dollars, however, went into the Disaster Relief Fund. In 2002 the organization began saying in its appeals that donations for a specific relief effort might be used for another, although under a new policy people could designate where they wanted their money to go. Another post-September 11 sore point concerned blood donations. Some were thrown away when their shelf life expired.

The Red Cross increased the cost of its blood products up to 31 percent in 2001 as it worked to improve safeguards. Faced with mounting pressure to ensure blood safety, the organization launched Pathogen Removal and Diagnostic Technologies Inc. with ProMetic Life Sciences Inc. in 2002 to seek out ways to detect disease agents. It was the Red Cross' first for-profit joint venture. Although the organization spent $1.7 billion yearly on biomedical services, it still was not in compliance with the 1993 FDA consent decree. A new FDA decree in 2003 was intended to finally correct labeling and record-keeping issues that made it difficult for the Red Cross to identify sources of contaminated blood products throughout its network of blood services operations. When the issues persisted, the FDA fined the organization $4.2 million in 2006. The Red Cross maintained five national testing laboratories, a biomedical research facility, and dozens of other support operations in 2009 to collect, test, and distribute safe blood. The same year its Biomedical Services division collected $2.2 billion in revenue.

HURRICANES WREAK HAVOC IN SOUTHERN UNITED STATES

With Hurricanes Katrina, Rita, and Wilma striking in consecutive months, 2005 was a disastrous year for southern states. More than 240,000 Red Cross workers responded to the affected areas. Katrina was the largest of the storms and it was the undoing of Marsha J. Evans, who had replaced Healy. Complaints about disorganization and not working with local organizations caused her to resign four months after Katrina.

Yahoo! Inc. and Amazon.com, Inc., helped the Red Cross raise funds online in 2005 for disaster relief. That effort not only drew donations for hurricane victims but also for victims of the December 2004 tsunami in more than 12 countries of Southeast Asia. The Tsunami Relief and Recovery Fund provided for immediate assistance and ongoing recovery services. The Red Cross received 72 percent of the monetary and in-kind donations and Federal Emergency Management Agency (FEMA) funds gathered for relief efforts, which totaled around $2.6 billion in fiscal year 2008. The organization was using the $21 million that remained to assist affected communities recover from the hurricanes.

After Katrina, the Red Cross organized a paid corps of skilled emergency responders who would be able to provide expert care most volunteers could not give. It also answered accusations of fraud by getting the Social Security numbers of volunteers and doing credit checks on money handlers. In addition, although the organization had an $80 million operating deficit, it stockpiled emergency supplies and made sure chapters had advanced communication technology.

REVAMP OF HEALTH AND SAFETY TRAINING

The Red Cross revamped its core swimming and water safety program in 2004. The upgrades aimed to make the instructors and lifeguards the program certified better swimmers and teachers of the 2.2 million students they oversaw in the water each year. Another Red Cross health and safety training area included cardiopulmonary resuscitation (CPR) and automated external defibrillators (AED). In 2007, 11 million people received instruction for CPR and AED use.

Also in 2007, Congress passed a new charter for Red Cross that would reduce the number of board members and give the CEO more authority by 2012. Previously the lead agency in disaster response, the federal government transferred that responsibility to FEMA.

When the American Red Cross started licensing use of the red cross symbol on products in 2004, Johnson & Johnson (J&J), which had been using the symbol as a trademark since 1887, decided it needed to protect its rights. Ironically, the Red Cross had also had rights to the symbol granted by a 1905 law. Furthermore, the $2 million made by the organization from branded products was a pittance compared to the $53.3 billion J&J generated from its products in 2006. The 2007 lawsuit filed by J&J was thrown out of court.

LEADERSHIP CHANGES CONTINUE

After a 16-month search for a replacement for Evans, the Red Cross hired former Internal Revenue Service Commissioner Mark W. Everson in 2007 as its new president and CEO. His tenure, however, lasted only four months after it was revealed he had had an affair with a chapter executive. The next year Gail J. McGovern was appointed president and CEO of the American Red Cross. The former corporate executive and marketing professor cut the Red Cross' $209 million operating deficit to $50 million by fiscal year-end, despite having to provide disaster relief during a banner year of hurricanes, tornadoes, wildfires, and flooding.

As the first decade of the 21st century came to a close, the American Red Cross, despite financial concerns, continued doing what it had been doing for nearly 130 years: providing relief to victims of disasters and helping people prevent, prepare for, and respond to emergencies. In January 2010 that included deploying supplies to Haiti in the aftermath of a 7.0-magnitude earthquake and helping people find out about their loved ones through its Family Links Web site. Some $3 million for the effort came in from people who made a $10 donation by simply texting "Haiti" to 90999 on their cell phones.

A. Woodward
Updated, Doris Maxfield

PRINCIPAL DIVISIONS

Biomedical Services; Blood Services; Disaster Services; Service to the Armed Forces; Health and Safety Services; International Services.

PRINCIPAL COMPETITORS

America's Blood Centers; Salvation Army.

FURTHER READING

"American Red Cross' New Swimming and Water Safety Program," *American Fitness*, July–August 2004, p. 38.

Babcock, Charles R., and Judith Havemann, "Managing an Agency and Image," *Washington Post*, February 16, 1999, p. A01.

Becker, Cinda, "Charity's New Business; Red Cross For-Profit Venture Targets Mad Cow Pathogens," *Modern Healthcare*, April 22, 2002, p. 22.

———, "FDA Accuses Red Cross of Unsafe Practices; Inspections at Embattled Blood Bank Turn Up 'Serious' Violations," *Modern Healthcare*, December 21, 2001, p. 10.

Burton, Thomas, "Panel Probes Early Abbott AIDS Test; Decision by Red Cross Is Questioned," *Wall Street Journal*, June 28, 1993, p. A11C.

"Bush Signs American Red Cross Governance Overhaul Bill," *Non-profit Times*, June 1, 2007, p. 22.

Carnes, Tony, "Too Much 9/11 Giving: Charities Overwhelmed by Task of Distributing $1.5 Billion Windfall," *Christianity Today*, January 7, 2002, p. 15.

Clolery, Paul, "Culling the Herd: Red Cross Responds Late to Its Own Disaster," *Non-profit Times*, February 1, 2008, p. 12.

———, "Exit Doors Rear and Aft: Red Cross Needs In-Aisle Path Lighting," *Non-profit Times*, January 1, 2008, p. 13.

"FDA, Red Cross Reach Agreement to Improve Blood Safety," *FDA Consumer*, July/August 2003, p. 35.

France, David, and David Noonan, "Blood and Money: Since September 11, Americans Have Given $1.4 Billion to Charity—Nearly Half to the Red Cross. Where Did All That Money Go? The Inside Story," *Newsweek*, December 17, 2001, p. 52.

Gose, Ben, "Marketing Expert Picked to Lead Red Cross," *Chronicle of Philanthropy*, April 17, 2008, p. 1.

———, "Ready or Not?" *Chronicle of Philanthropy*, July 26, 2007, p. 1.

Gregory, Sean, "Trying to Get It Right This Time," *Time*, September 26, 2005, p. 24.

Hensley, Scott, "Out for Blood," *Modern Healthcare*, June 22, 1998, p. 26.

———, "Rising to the Challenge," *Modern Healthcare*, May 1, 2000, p. 80.

Hrywna, Mark, "American Red Cross vs. J&J: Licensing and Image Key to Federal Lawsuit," *Non-profit Times*, September 1, 2007, p. 9.

Hurd, Charles, *The Compact History of the American Red Cross*, New York: Hawthorn Books, 1959.

Jones, Jeff, "9/11 Fall-out: Red Cross Changes to Generic Wording," *Non-profit Times*, July 1, 2002, p. 10.

Jones, Laurie, "FDA: Red Cross Record-Keeping May Hurt Blood Safety," *American Medical News*, July 27, 1990, p. 1.

Kaufman, Marc, "FDA Finds Problems with Red Cross Blood," *Washington Post*, December 2, 2000, p. A04.

Keizer, Gregg, "Red Cross Collects $209 Million Online; More Than Half of the $409 Million the American Red Cross Has Collected for Katrina Comes from the Web," *TechWeb News*, September 6, 2005.

Landers, Susan J., "Red Cross Faces Scrutiny, Possible Fines: While the Food and Drug Administration Says the Nation's Blood Supply Is Safe, It Believes Lax Management Has Led to Low Levels of Quality Assurance," *American Medical News*, January 14, 2002, p. 31.

Levine, Samantha, "Red Crossroads," *U.S. News & World Report*, November 19, 2001, p. 28.

McGuire, Stephen, "Judge Tosses J&J Logo Claim," *Medical Marketing & Media*, December 2007, p. 10.

Mulvihill, Kathleen, "Hectic Year Drains Red Cross's Fund for Disaster Relief," *Christian Science Monitor*, December 3, 1985, pp. 3, 4.

Neff, Jack, "J&J Targets Red Cross, Blunders into PR Firestorm," *Advertising Age*, August 13, 2007, p. 1.

"News Analysis: J&J Balances Its Legal and PR Objectives," *PR Week*, August 20, 2007, p. 8.

Nobles, Marla E., "Red Cross Turns Documents Over to Congress," *Non-profit Times*, April 1, 2006, p. 12.

O'Meara, Kelly Patricia, "Red Cross Feathers Its Own Nest First: After Receiving $546 Million to Aid Victims of the Sept. 11 Attacks, the Red Cross Admits Giving Only the Equivalent of Two Weeks' Financial Assistance to Families," *Insight on the News*, December 10, 2001, p. 15.

———, "The Red Cross in the Cross Hairs? Families of Oklahoma City Bombing Victims Say They Did Not Receive Funds Sent to Them by Mail and Handled by the Red Cross. And Questions Are Being Raised in New York City," *Insight on the News*, November 5, 2001, p. 18.

Perry, Suzanne, and Elizabeth Schwinn, "Pulling Back the Reins," *Chronicle of Philanthropy*, November 9, 2006, p. 1.

"Red Cross Urges Victims' Families to Accept Relief Funds," *Fund Raising Management*, November 2001, p. 8.

Reitman, Judith, *Bad Blood: Crisis in the American Red Cross*, New York: Kensington Publishing Corp., 1996.

Robledo, Rebecca, "Red Cross Updates Instructor Training," *Aquatics International*, April 2004, p. 12.

Sebastian, Pamela, "Red Cross Is Strained by Disasters Even as It Revamps Its Programs," *Wall Street Journal*, September 15, 1992, pp. A1, A10.

Tanner, Lisa, "Battling for Blood Business," *Dallas Business Journal*, March 21, 1997, p. 3.

Taylor, Mark, "Red Cross Faces Antitrust Lawsuit," *Modern*

Healthcare, January 1, 2001, p. 20.

"Trademark Travesty," *New Internationalist*, October 2007, p. 27.

Williamson, Richard, "Money Comes between Charities, Terror Victims: Red Cross Another Black Eye," *Non-profit Times*, December 1, 2001, p. 1.

Wolfe, Daniel, "Security Watch," *American Banker*, December 29, 2006, p. 5.

Aryzta AG

Talacker 41
Zurich, CH-8001
Switzerland
Telephone: (+41 44) 583 4200
Fax: (+41 44) 583 4249
Web site: http://www.aryzta.com

Public Company
Incorporated: 1897 as the Irish Co-Operative Agri-
    cultural Agency Society Ltd.; 2008 as Aryzta AG
Employees: 9,344
Sales: €3.21 billion ($4.38 billion) (2009)
Stock Exchanges: Switzerland Ireland
Ticker Symbol: ARYN YZA
NAICS: 311812 Commercial Bakeries; 311813 Frozen
    Bakery Product Manufacturing; 424420 Packaged
    Frozen Food Merchant Wholesalers; 424490 Other
    Grocery and Related Product Merchant Wholesalers

■ ■ ■

Aryzta AG is a global leader in the specialty baked
goods market, serving both the retail consumer and the
food-service industry. Based in Zurich, Switzerland,
Aryzta was formed in 2008 through a merger of IAWS
Group plc and Hiestand Holding AG, and has operations in Europe, North America, Southeast Asia, and
Australia. The company's four business segments are
Food Europe, Food North America, Food Developing
Markets, and Origin Enterprises plc. Food Europe is a
leading supplier of consumer and food industry baked
goods in Switzerland, Germany, Poland, the United

Kingdom, Ireland, and France. Its main brands include
Hiestand, Cuisine de France, Delice de France, and
Coup de Pates. With a product line that includes Otis
Spunkmeyer and La Brea Bakery, Food North America
is a market leader of freshly baked cookies and artisan
breads. Food Developing Markets has an eclectic
product line to suit the diverse tastes of the Japanese,
Malaysian, and Australian markets. Aryzta also holds a
71.4 percent interest in Origin Enterprises plc, one of
Ireland's main producers of cereal and other ambient
foods and a leader in the field of agri-nutrition in
Ireland, Poland, and the United Kingdom.

ORIGINS

According to the official centennial history of IAWS, the
cooperative movement in Ireland began in the late
1880s with dairy farms, whose products were being
displaced by new European methods of making butter.
At the same time, the short shelf life of dairy products
gave farmers little leverage with commercial creameries.
There soon evolved federations of individual cooperatives, which were concerned with both obtaining the
best prices for their members' wares and securing
adequate supplies.

Horace Plunkett, considered the founder of the
co-op movement, and others created an administrative
body in 1894 called the Irish Agricultural Organisation
Society (IAOC; renamed the Irish Co-Operative Or-
ganisational Society in 1979). The IAOC convinced the
Irish Co-Operative Agency Society Ltd. (IACSL),
founded in 1893, to focus on marketing butter and

dairy equipment. A new organization, the Irish Co-Operative Agricultural Agency Society Ltd. (ICAAS), was formed in Dublin on January 15, 1897, to address the problem of procuring quality supplies, particularly seeds and fertilizers. Plunkett was chairman for its first two years, and he was assisted, at first, by three employees. Lieutenant Colonel Loftus A. Bryan succeeded Plunkett in 1899.

ICAAS was renamed the Irish Agricultural Wholesale Society Ltd. (IAWS) in December 1897. Sales were £14,500 in the first year, and the agency showed a modest profit. Soon, IAWS had expanded its offerings to include hardware, flour, and insecticides, much to the ire of existing local traders. IAWS opened two additional stores, in Galway and Thurles, in 1899. An early venture into cattle trading proved disastrous, and by December 1900 IAWS was insolvent. Plunkett personally bailed out the agency with £2,000. An anonymous donor provided another £3,500 in 1903. By 1905 IAWS was again posting a profit.

In 1907 IAWS allowed its member societies to sell groceries. Irish Producers Ltd., an association of egg and honey producers, joined with IAWS in 1908. The group soon established facilities in Sligo and Enniskillen to package eggs under the brand name Karka. IAWS established a banking department in November 1910 to give the co-ops access to credit. The group also bought an interest in a ship to transport goods in late 1909, although the venture closed three years later.

A 1913 libel case against the head of the Department of Agriculture, T. W. Russell, who had claimed IAWS was insolvent, won the group no award for damages but garnered much positive press coverage. During World War I, IAWS worked to ensure a stable supply of food and kept bread prices in its stores at prewar levels. Otherwise, the group's business activities continued to grow, and IAWS set up a number of new departments. Harold Barbour, chairman between 1910 and 1922, helped guarantee the group's finances during this period of unrest and provided funds for a new warehouse. Sales exceeded £1 million in 1919.

The 1920 creation of Northern Ireland necessitated the formation of separate organizations in Ulster for both IAWS and its sister society, IAOS. In 1922 Barbour resigned IAWS to lead the newly created Ulster

Agricultural Organisation Society (UAOS); his place as chairman was taken by Dermod O'Brien, who was also designing the Irish Free State's new currency. By this time, IAWS was losing money as sales slipped to £700,000. Refinancing was obtained, pay cuts were instituted at all levels of the organization, and preference shareholders agreed to waive interest payments that were due to them in 1924 and 1925. Alongside these setbacks, IAWS benefited from two government initiatives in the late 1920s: new regulation of the creamery industry and the establishment of a factory to make sugar from beets, for which IAWS supplied the seed.

STRIVING FOR SELF-RELIANCE: 1930–70

In the 1930s the Great Depression and the Economic War with Britain curtailed the business of IAWS, its member co-ops, and their individual member farms. After coming to power in 1932, the Fianna Fáil party suspended annuity payments to the British throne. As a result, the Crown hammered Irish agricultural imports with huge duties. Fianna Fáil also placed a high priority on making Ireland self-sufficient, which tended to benefit IAWS. In 1934 IAWS was able to post a tiny profit for the first time in 14 years. In 1939 IAWS began importing Swedish wheat for growing and milling, replacing the wheat previously imported from Canada.

The need for self-reliance was increased by World War II, which cut off sources of many agricultural inputs, such as machinery, fertilizers, and twine. During the war, IAWS researched the domestic production of seeds for a variety of vegetables, and in 1941 the company formed Associated Seedgrowers Ltd. (ASG) with a consortium of seed companies. Dermott O'Brien died in 1945 and was succeeded as chairman by Thomas Westropp Bennett until his death in 1962. His successor, Owen Binchy, died only three years later and was replaced by Ned Wall. In 1971 Patrick I. Meagher assumed the position, where he remained until 1991.

IAWS achieved total sales of £2.25 million in 1950, although it represented just a quarter of the total business of its member co-ops. A number of interesting new ventures were launched during the decade. In 1956 IAWS began importing sugar into Northern Ireland for Comhlucht Siucre Eireann Teo (the Irish Sugar Company). This venture was broken up in the early 1970s after the latter company took a share in a competing distributor. After the introduction of a 50 percent import duty on stainless steel churns in 1959, IAWS began manufacturing its own. IAWS began operating a fishmeal factory in 1967. The group also started marketing a series of new high-nitrogen

KEY DATES

1897: Irish Co-Operative Agricultural Agency Society Ltd. is founded in Dublin.
1988: IAWS Group plc goes public.
1989: Shamrock Foods is acquired.
1990: IAWS acquires R&H Hall.
1998: Cuisine de France is acquired.
1999: Catering food company Delice de France is bought.
2001: U.S.-based La Brea Bakery is acquired; IAWS forms joint venture with Canada's Tim Hortons.
2005: Coup de Pates, the principal brand of Groupe Hubert, is acquired.
2006: U.S.-based Otis Spunkmeyer is acquired; Origin Enterprises plc is established as a separate operating company for the Group's agricultural and lifestyle food businesses.
2008: IAWS Group plc and Hiestand Holding AG merge to form Aryzta AG.

compound fertilizers for Richardson's of Belfast, which soon proved successful. Beginning in the late 1970s, IAWS produced its own blended fertilizers.

NEW CHALLENGES IN THE SEVENTIES AND EIGHTIES

Many changes, both positive and negative, occurred from 1970 to 1980. The political strife known as the Troubles made living and working dangerous at times. Ireland's entry into the European Economic Community (EEC) in 1973 opened up new markets for the country's agriculture and eventually resulted in IAWS receiving grants to develop, for example, grain-handling facilities.

A new competitor, Co-Operative Agricultural Purchases Ltd., had been set up in 1966. However, in 1974 it collapsed under the pressure of a global oil crisis and a bad year for cattle. IAWS sales were about £25 million at the time and, thanks largely to rampant inflation, reached £60 million in 1979. However, the organization was losing money again. To help rectify the situation, the board appointed Philip Lynch, formerly of R&H Hall, as managing director. Led by Lynch, who became CEO of IAWS in mid-1983, the management structure was also streamlined, and IAWS returned to profitability during the year.

Flour producer Boland Mills and the business of Townsend Flahavan, both in receivership, were acquired in 1984. IAWS also started a new venture to trade and export barley. The next year IAWS bolstered its fertilizer manufacturing base by acquiring a 30 percent holding in Gouldings. It acquired the remaining shares in 1986. Boland Mills was merged with three similar firms, Dock Milling Company, Davis Mosse, and Howard Brothers, in 1987. IAWS was divided into three divisions: Fertilisers, Food Products, and IAWS-Agri Ltd., which focused on producing and sourcing agricultural inputs.

GOING PUBLIC IN 1988

In the fall of 1988 a subsidiary company, IAWS Group plc, was created for listing on the Dublin Stock Exchange. The recapitalized entity continued to acquire companies. The group bought a 90 percent share in Sheriff & Sons Ltd., an English trader of grain, fertilizer, and chemicals. Shamrock Foods, a market leader in cooking and baking supplies in Ireland, was acquired in 1989. A subsequent investment in the First National Bakery Company (FNCB) involved IAWS in all phases of wheat production and consumption. FNBC launched its Irish Pride brand in 1990.

In that same year, IAWS took over the R&H Hall Group plc, a leading importer of ingredients for animal feed and a major producer of wheat. Acquiring Hall, which had been publicly traded since 1967, doubled IAWS's size. The purchase was worth IR£42 million. IAWS diversified by buying Suttons Ltd. and Suttons Oil Ltd., distributors of coal and oil. IAWS Group continued to grow. It acquired the Pertwee and Parson fertilizer business in 1992, and the Nordos fishmeal company in early 1994. The Malting Company of Ireland was added in July. Pretax profits rose from IR£10.1 million to IR£12.8 million (£12.6 million) in fiscal 1994. In 1995 IAWS acquired Scotland's United Fish Products for about IR£12 million. It also completed some important domestic acquisitions, including Unifood and Premier Proteins.

The Irish Agricultural Wholesale Society owned 64 percent of IAWS Group plc in the mid-1990s. Sales in 1995 exceeded IR£510 million; nearly a third of revenues were coming from the United Kingdom. In the spring of 1996, the Irish Agricultural Wholesale Society reduced its ownership in the IAWS Group to less than 51 percent, giving the Group better access to capital markets.

IAWS Group bought Master Foods, a distributor of Mars candy bars, in September 1996. The next January it acquired a stake in its first European producer by purchasing Groupe Ikem, a French fertilizer company with a 15 percent market share in France. At the time of its centenary in 1997, IAWS had 1,850 employees and continued to grow. Sales for the fiscal year ending July 31 were £581 million, producing a pretax profit of £21 million. In October 1997 the group made its largest purchase to date, acquiring the specialty bread maker Cuisine de France, which had 2,300 retail stores in the United Kingdom and Ireland, for IR£51 million. IAWS soon announced plans to increase its milling capacity to supply dough for its new acquisition, which was contracting out between 60 and 70 percent of its bread making.

BEYOND 2000

Catering food company Delice de France was bought for £35 million in 1999. The investments in convenience foods were paying off; IAWS Group's food division accounted for 40 percent of revenues (€982.2 million) and 50 percent of profits (£30.2 million, or €49.8 million) in 2000. The Cuisine de France line was developing a presence in North America, starting with 200 outlets in Chicago. To supply its Cuisine de France line, IAWS formed a bakery joint venture with Tim Hortons, a Canadian doughnut shop chain (and a subsidiary of Wendy's International) that also had a large par-baked bagels business. IAWS hoped the new bakery, built in Brantford, Ontario, would generate IR£108 million in sales in its first year. In July 2000 IAWS bought Pierre, the Irish specialty baking operations of its rival Northern Foods plc.

IAWS's expansion into the United States accelerated with the acquisition of 80 percent of La Brea Bakery, a $20 million Los Angeles specialty baker, in the last half of 2001. The $69 million purchase gave La Brea the means to expand to the U.S. East Coast. Construction soon began on a $50 million plant in New Jersey. Managing Director Philip Lynch described 2001 as "a superb year, our best." Sales rose 12 percent to €1.10 billion, while pretax profits (excluding exceptionals) of €59.8 million were 20 percent higher than in 2000.

In July 2003, IAWS acquired a 22 percent stake in Heistand AG, a Swiss company in the par-baked goods business, for $32 million,. On October 1, 2003, Owen Killian, who had been with IAWS since 1977 and who played a significant role in transforming the small co-op into a leading baked goods company, replaced Lynch, who had become IAWS's new chairman. Killian's plan was to turn IAWS into a global food company within the next decade. By now, the new East Coast La Brea plant was at full capacity, and its products were available in 3,000, or nearly 10 percent, of U.S. supermarkets. IAWS also had its Cuisine de France products in 1,000 retail shops in Chicago and the Baltimore/Washington, D.C., area, while in Britain and Ireland IAWS's reach

had extended to 7,000 stores. Since 1993, IAWS's shares had risen a staggering 900 percent.

In December 2004, in what would be Killian's first deal since taking over from Lynch and the company's largest acquisition to date, IAWS announced that it was acquiring Groupe Hubert for €130 million. Groupe Hubert was a leading developer and distributor of bakery products to France's food-service sector, and internationally recognized for its flagship brand, Coup de Pates. "The acquisition of Groupe Humbert is another key step in the internationalization of our business in the specialist artisan bakery subset of the food market," Killian said to Pat Boyle of the Irish *Independent* in December 2004.

ARYZTA IS FORMED

In July 2005 the IAWS Co-Operative officially ended when the members voted to float it on the stock exchange. They also renamed it One51plc in order to avoid confusion with the well-established food business segment, IAWS Group plc. In a departure from its usual food-related acquisitions, in August 2005 IAWS acquired TechRec Ireland, an electronic recycling firm. This was followed in October 2005 with the purchase of Querida Environmental Solutions (QES), a waste management company. By September 2006 IAWS's products were available in 60,000 convenience stores, supermarkets, and bakeries in Europe and North America, and the company boasted revenues of €1.56 billion. In November 2006 IAWS announced plans to create a new offshoot specialist company for its noncore milling, feed, and fertilizer businesses, which accounted for earnings before interest and taxation of €36.4 million. With Tom O'Mahony, IAWS's chief operating officer, assuming the position of CEO, Origin Enterprises plc determined to focus on the agribusiness and the non-lifestyle food products, such as Shamrock Foods Limited, and the Group's 50 percent interest in Odlum Group Milling.

IAWS's North American bakery business received a significant boost in 2007 when the company bought Otis Spunkmeyer for $463 million. Within three months of the purchase, Otis Spunkmeyer had generated revenues of $20 million. This new acquisition and the La Brea product line positioned IAWS as a "market leader in two complementary growth categories in the North American value-added bakery market," Killian said to Pat Boyle in the *Financial Times* in March 2007. By the close of the 2007 fiscal year, Otis Spunkmeyer had contributed €220.1 million to the Group's sales.

In June 2008 IAWS made the momentous announcement that it planned to merge with Hiestand, the Swiss company in which it already held a 32 percent stake. The merger would be an exchange of shares, with IAWS paying the U.K. equity firm Lion Capital €30 million for its 32 percent stake. The newly formed Aryzta AG would increase the geographic reach of both companies and create the world's leading developer and distributor of frozen, half-baked, and artisan bakery products. Aryzta was incorporated in Switzerland. Killian remained as CEO, and Denis Lucey, the nonexecutive chairman of IAWS, assumed the role of chairman of the board. The merger was completed by August 2008, with Aryzta trading on both the Swiss and Irish stock exchanges. Although the newly formed company reported a modest drop in Group revenues of 0.7 percent in June 2009, total revenues were still impressive at €2.4 billion ($3.4 billion). At a time when consumers were spending less as they weathered the global recession, Killian admitted that it was difficult to predict revenue growth under these economic conditions. By the end of November 2009, Aryzta recorded a 16 percent fall in quarterly revenues, with the agribusiness Origin Enterprises taking the hardest hit. As Killian looked toward 2010, he remained confident in the Group's business model, and according to industry analysts, intended to continue to invest in markets with large populations.

Frederick C. Ingram
Updated, Marie O'Sullivan

PRINCIPAL SUBSIDIARIES

BHH Limited (Northern Ireland, 35.7%); CillRyan's Bakery Limited (Canada, 50%); Continental Farmer's Group plc (Poland, 26.4%); Cuisine de France, Inc. (USA); Cuisine de France Limited (Ireland); Cuisine de France (UK) Limited; Delice de France plc (UK); Gallagher's Bakery Limited (Ireland); Goulding Chemicals Limited (Ireland, 71.4%); HiCoPain AG (60%); Hiestand Beteiligungsholding GmbH & Co; Hiestand International AG; Hiestand Schweiz AG; IAWS France SA; IAWS Management Services Limited Management (Ireland); IAWS Technology and Global Services Limited (Ireland); La Brea Bakery Holdings, Inc. (USA); Masstock Group Holdings Limited (UK, 71.4%); Odlum Group (Ireland, 71.4%); Origin Enterprises plc (Ireland, 71.4%); Origin Fertilisers (UK) Limited (71.4%); Otis Spunkmeyer, Inc. (USA); R&H Hall Limited (Ireland, 71.4%); Shamrock Foods (Ireland, 71.4%); Welcon Invest AS (Norway, 35.7%).

PRINCIPAL DIVISIONS

Food Developing Markets; Food Europe; Food North America; Origin Enterprises plc.

PRINCIPAL COMPETITORS

Associated British Foods plc; Brioche Pasquier S.A.; Interstate Bakeries Corporation.

FURTHER READING

Boyle, Pat, "French Deal Is Biggest-ever IAWS Takeover," *Independent* (Ireland), December 14, 2004.

———, "IAWS Nets Big Dough with US Bakery Unit," *Europe Intelligence Wire*, March 13, 2007.

Brown, John Murray, "IAWS Invests in Canadian Bakery Venture," *Financial Times* (London), March 7, 2001, p. 28.

———, "Ready-to-Bake Product Range Fattens IAWS," *Financial Times* (London), September 19, 2001, p. 28.

Fulmer, Melinda, "La Brea Bakery to Be Sold," *Los Angeles Times*, July 21, 2001, p. 1.

IAWS Group plc, *History of IAWS & the Co-Operative Movement*. Dublin: IAWS Group plc, 1997.

"Insight: Revenue 'Difficult' to Predict—Aryzta," Just-food. com, September 30, 2009, http://www.just-food.com/article. aspx?id=108186.

Masters, Brooke, "Ireland's IAWS Set for Merger with Swiss Baker," *Financial Times*, June 9, 2008, p. 19.

McGrath, Brendan, "IAWS Seeks £100 Million in Sales from Canadian Bakery," *Irish Times*, March 7, 2001, p. 20.

Morais, Richard C., "Rising Dough," *Forbes Global*, January 12, 2004, p. 40.

Shanahan, Ella, "IAWS Seeks US Supplier for Food Brands," *Irish Times*, January 6, 2001, p. 17.

Aspen Pharmacare Holdings Limited

———— ■ ————

Healthcare Park, Woodlands Drive, Woodmead
Sandton, Gauteng Province 2052
South Africa
Telephone: (+011 2711) 239-6100
Fax: (+011 2711) 239-6111
Web site: http://www.aspenpharma.com

Public Company
Founded: 1997 as Aspen Healthcare
Employees: 5,000
Sales: ZAR 8.5 billion ($1.12 billion) (2009)
Stock Exchanges: Johannesburg
Ticker Symbol: APN
NAICS: 325411 Medicinal and Medicine Manufacturing; 325412 Pharmaceutical Preparations Manufacturing; 424210 Pharmaceutical Merchant Wholesaling

■ ■ ■

Aspen Pharmacare Holdings Limited is South Africa's largest manufacturer of prescription drugs, personal care items, and infant formulas. The company operates through two principal divisions. Prescription drugs such as Aspen-Stavudene, a generic medication for the treatment of HIV/AIDS, are manufactured and marketed through the company's pharmaceutical division, while the consumer division handles products such as Woodward's Gripe Water, a tonic for babies, and Prep, a skin-soothing cream for shaving, sunburn, and minor insect bites. In addition to its two huge plants in East London and Port Elizabeth, both in South Africa's Cape Province, Aspen has manufacturing and marketing facilities in several countries, including India, Cyprus, Brazil, Tanzania, and the United Kingdom. All Aspen's products sell briskly, but the company owes its distinguished position in the pharmaceutical community to its line of generic antiretroviral drugs, or ARVs.

LAUNCH OF A YOUNG ENTREPENEUR

The seed of this huge company was planted in the late 1980s, when a young man named Stephen Saad completed his accountancy degree and took a sales job with a company called Quickmed. Rather than keeping finances straight, his job required him to sell medicines to doctors working in the provinces of KwaZulu and Gauteng. Soon the ambitious Saad was a co-owner of Quickmed, which he merged with a family-owned eye-drops manufacturer named Covan. He renamed the resulting business Zurich. In 1993 Saad sold Zurich to a company called Prempharm, a forerunner of pharmaceutical manufacturing company Adcock-Ingram. ZAR 75 million changed hands, leaving a 30-year-old Saad with ZAR 20 million, enough to allow him to retire.

Saad, however, was not about to retire. Instead, in 1997 he founded Aspen Healthcare, a small pharmaceutical company, which he headquartered in a little house in Greyville, Durban. This new venture was designed to greatly broaden the base of his pharmaceutical sales. As a first step, Saad, still at the head of this private company, initiated a reverse takeover of the public company Medhold in July 1998. This made

COMPANY PERSPECTIVES

Aspen is Africa's largest pharmaceutical manufacturer and a major supplier of branded and generic pharmaceutical, healthcare and nutritional products to southern Africa and selected international markets. Over the past decade Aspen has expanded its businesses substantially. The group now has a presence in South Africa, Australia, India, Brazil, the United Kingdom, Kenya, Tanzania, Venezuela, Mexico and Mauritius and also exports to many other territories across the globe.

Aspen a public company. It was listed on the Johannesburg Stock Exchange for the first time that year, after which the Medhold name was dropped.

Saad's next acquisition awed business analysts, describing the move as "a mouse swallowing an elephant." In March 1999 he bought the pharmaceutical interests of South African Druggists, the largest pharmaceutical manufacturing business in the country, for a highly leveraged ZAR 2.5 billion. This deal included manufacturing facilities as well as marketing and distribution channels, but the sellers advised him just to stick to marketing and not attempt manufacturing. As he later told Michael Bleby in *Business Day* that "the previous management told me 'Keep the brand; do not even think of manufacturing in South Africa given what China and India can do.'" However, as soon as he saw the South African Druggists' manufacturing plant in Port Elizabeth, Saad decided that the manufacturing operations had to stay. Also adopted was the second half of the Aspen name, Pharmacare, which had been used by South African Druggists to designate its pharmaceutical division.

BELIEFS ABOUT AIDS IN SOUTH AFRICA

While all this was going on, denial was widespread in South Africa about the link between the HIV virus and AIDS. Even President Thabo Mbeki denied this link. In addition, the thousands of AIDS victims in the country were often scorned and ostracized. As a result, many people who knew they had contracted the disease were afraid to seek medical help.

Additionally, patients encountered the fact that the available medications were frowned upon by the country's ultimate authorities, President Mbeki and his health minister, Manto Tshabalala-Msimanga. Both of them often warned of toxic effects from drugs used against AIDS, and the minister instead prescribed hearty helpings of lemon, garlic, beets, and African potatoes. As a result of this obfuscation, noted a Harvard School of Public Health calculation in 2008, there were 330,000 unnecessary deaths from AIDS in South Africa between 2000 and 2005.

ASPEN STEPS IN

The Aspen company saw things differently. From his experience in the townships of Gauteng and KwaZulu, Saad understood that there was an urgent need for both effective drugs and for education about hygiene and health care. Furthermore, he knew that these medications had to be affordable, because the poorest people anywhere typically afford only the poorest health care. For this reason, in 2001 he negotiated with Bristol-Myers Squibb, GlaxoSmithKline, and Boehringer Ingelheim, all international pharmaceutical companies, for permission to manufacture generic versions of their HIV/AIDS drugs under voluntary licenses. This was an unusual request, because Saad was asking these companies for permission to reproduce and sell their drugs for a far lower cost, even though their own exclusive patents had not run out. However, recognizing the desperate need of these patients for affordable medicines, all three companies agreed. According to Stavros Nicolau, a senior Aspen executive, this set of agreements brought the annual cost of treatment per patient down from an average ZAR 95,000 to about ZAR 1,200.

Careful research followed, along with organization of the manufacturing plant. All this took about 18 months, so Aspen announced its first generic AIDS drugs in 2003. One, called Aspen Stavudine, was a generic version of Bristol-Myers Squibb's Zerit. It was just as effective as Zerit at suppressing the HIV virus and preserving white cells, the patient's guards against infections. Its cost, however, was between 17 and 40 percent less than Zerit. Both advantages made doctors eager to prescribe it. By the end of the financial year, this drug had gone a long way toward making it possible for patients to control their disease while helping Aspen's earnings to reach ZAR 270.6 million, an increase of 24 percent over 2002.

ASPEN GOES INTERNATIONAL

Also in 2001 the company opened its first overseas facility. The new Australian subsidiary was concerned more with drugs for specialist areas than with generic drugs, and its stated objective was to create and market drugs for specific purposes

```
┌─────────────────────────────────────────────┐
│                                               │
│              KEY DATES                        │
│          ──────────■──────────                │
│                                               │
│  1997:  Aspen Healthcare is founded.          │
│  1998:  Aspen acquires the public company     │
│         Medhold; Aspen shares are offered     │
│         on the Johannesburg Stock Exchange.   │
│  1999:  Aspen buys Pharmacare Limited and     │
│         adopts the name Aspen Pharmacare.     │
│  2003:  Aspen produces the first locally      │
│         manufactured generic AIDS drug.       │
│  2005:  Aspen is chosen to provide generic    │
│         AIDS drugs for the Clinton Foundation │
│         and for the U.S. President's          │
│         Emergency Plan for AIDS Relief         │
│         (PEPFAR).                             │
│  2006:  Aspen reaches an agreement with Glaxo-│
│         SmithKline to market four new drugs to│
│         all territories except North America  │
│         and Japan; Aspen now has access to    │
│         markets in more than 100 countries.   │
│                                               │
└─────────────────────────────────────────────┘
```

Several huge strides were made by Aspen in 2005. The first event, occurring in January, was approval from the U.S. Food and Drug Administration to sell Aspen's generic AIDS drugs in the United States. This major coup, achieved only after a rigorous inspection of the Port Elizabeth plant, allowed Aspen to become an official supplier to the U.S. President's Emergency Plan for AIDS Relief (PEPFAR), an initiative founded by President George W. Bush in 2003 to treat and care for AIDS patients in developing countries.

In March another huge expansion was underway when a strategic partnership for AIDS generics was formed with Gilead Sciences, Inc., a California pharmaceutical company. In this nonexclusive partnership, Gilead would supply Aspen with the raw materials for manufacturing generic versions of certain AIDS drugs, which would then be supplied to about 90 countries under Gilead's Global Access Programme.

Also in 2005 the William J. Clinton Foundation chose Aspen as one of three ARV generics suppliers for its initiative to offer needy HIV/AIDS patients the necessary medications at an affordable price. Unsurprisingly, revenues for a banner 2005 year rose 30 percent to reach ZAR 2.9 billion.

In 2006, among other expansions, the company formed a collaboration with Matrix Laboratories in Hyderabad, where a Matrix subsidiary named Astrix Laboratories, jointly owned with Aspen, was opened to manufacture generic AIDS drugs to serve Australian and Asian markets. Revenue in that year rose a further 23 percent, reaching a total of ZAR 3.4 billion.

FURTHER DEVELOPMENTS

An agreement with GlaxoSmithKline in 2006 gave Aspen marketing rights for four new drugs: Eltroxin (for the treatment of hypothyroidism), Imuran (an immunosuppressant used for organ transplants), Lanoxin (used for certain heart ailments), and Zyloric (a gout remedy). These covered all territories except North America and Japan, which were already well covered. This deal, costing about ZAR 2.7 billion, gave Aspen access to markets in more than 100 countries. In return, GlaxoSmithKline announced that it was buying a 16 percent stake in Aspen, represented by 68.5 million shares.

Even more expansion occurred in 2007, when Aspen entered a joint venture with Strides Acrolab Ltd. of Bangalore, India. Through two Strides subsidiaries (Onco Therapies Ltd. based in India and Onco Laboratories Ltd. located in Cyprus), the company was able to develop a range of sterile products and generic drugs for cancer therapy.

Another expansion effort took the company to Tanzania, where Shelys Pharmaceuticals is headquartered, and also to neighboring Kenya, home of Beta Healthcare International. Both of these companies belong to the Shelys Africa Group, whose manufactured products include medications for fever and pain management, antimalarials, antibiotics, and contraceptives destined for consumers in Tanzania, Uganda, Rwanda, and Congo. Aspen began a partnership with these companies in 2008, and by 2009 sales resulting from this transaction had helped to bring Aspen Pharmacare's bottom line to ZAR 8.5 billion ($1.12 billion).

Gillian Wolf

PRINCIPAL SUBSIDIARIES

Aspen Pharmacare; Aspen Nutritionals; Shelys Africa; Shelys Pharmaceuticals; Beta Healthcare; Lakerose; Cellofarm; Solara and Mexicana; Sumifarma; Aspen Australia; Astrix; Onco Therapies; Aspen Global; Co-Pharma; Powercliff.

PRINCIPAL COMPETITORS

GlaxoSmithKline plc; Merck & Co., Inc.; Tiger Brands Limited.

FURTHER READING

"Aspen's Upward Slope: Can South Africa's Top Generics Manufacturer Become a Global Giant?" *Economist*, October 6, 2005.

Bleby, Michael, "Phamaceuticals Wizard Knows Potion for Success," *Business Day*, July 2, 2008.

"GSK Buys Into Aspen Pharmacare," SouthAfrica.info, May 13, 2009, http://www.southafrica.info/business/investing/gsk-130509.htm.

"SA Pharma Expands Global Presence." SouthAfrica.info, July 24, 2008, http://www.southafrica.info/business/success/aspen-240708.htm.

Zachariasen, Angela, "SA's Pharmaceutical Success Story," *Eastern Cape Madiba Action*, Winter 2008.

ASSA ABLOY

Assa Abloy AB

———————————■———————————

Klarabergsviadukten 90
PO Box 70340
Stockholm, SE-107 23
Sweden
Telephone: (+46 8) 506 485 00
Fax: (+46 8) 506 485 85
Web site: http://www.assaabloy.com

Public Company
Founded: 1994
Employees: 32,700
Sales: SEK 34.96 billion ($4.85 billion) (2009)
Stock Exchanges: Stockholm
Ticker Symbol: ASSAB
NAICS: 332510 Hardware Manufacturing; 332999 All
Other Miscellaneous Fabricated Metal Product
Manufacturing

■ ■ ■

Assa Abloy AB (the Group) is the global leader in the lock and door-opening solutions market. The company's product portfolio includes electromagnetic and electronic locks, mechanical locks and accessories, automatic doors, hotel locks, security doors, self-closing emergency doors, and identification technology. Formed in 1994 through the merger of Sweden's Assa and Finland's Abloy, the Group has experienced tremendous growth in its brief history through more than 150 strategic acquisitions, including such notable market leaders as Essex, Yale Intruder Security, HID, Besam, and Fargo Electronics. With companies in more than 50

countries and authorized distributors worldwide, the Group has a presence in every major region and is the market leader in Europe, North America, and Australia.

The Group operates through five divisions: Europe, the Middle East, and Africa (EMEA), the Americas, Asia Pacific, Global Technologies, and Entrance Systems. The EMEA, Americas, and Asia Pacific divisions manufacture and distribute locks, cylinders, electromechanical products, security doors, and fittings throughout each of their respective regions. Based in London, England, EMEA has 11,900 employees, and its product line includes such well-known brands as Yale and Vachette. With 8,600 employees, the Americas Division is located in New Haven, Connecticut, and its products include Medeco, Corbin Russwin, and Emtek. The Asia Pacific Division, with such brands as iRevo, Baodean, and Wangli, has 7,100 employees at its headquarters in Hong Kong.

HID Global and Assa Abloy Hospitality form the Global Technologies Division, based in Stockholm, Sweden. With a staff of 2,800, the division manufactures and sells identification technology and products for electronic access control and card issuance security, such as VingCard Elsafe, a leading hotel security technology. The Entrance Systems Division has 2,300 employees and manufactures and distributes automatic door systems worldwide under the Besam brand from the Group's Landkrona, Sweden, facility. In the rapidly growing and highly competitive security market, Assa Abloy aims to continue its expansion and retain its position as the global leader through acquisitions that are carefully chosen according to three distinct criteria:

COMPANY PERSPECTIVES

ASSA ABLOY's vision is: To be the true world leader, the most successful and innovative provider of total door opening solutions; To lead in innovation and offer well-designed, convenient, safe and secure solutions that create added value for our customers; To offer an attractive company to our employees.

geographic demand, focused product lines, and technological advances.

ASSA ABLOY'S BEGINNINGS

The Assa Abloy Group was formed in October 1994 through the merger of the Assa lock-making operation of the Swedish firm Securitas and the Finnish company Abloy. Abloy was a subsidiary of a company formerly known as Metra, which was renamed Wärtsilä in 2000. On November 8, 1994, with 4,700 employees and sales of SEK 3 billion, Assa Abloy AB was listed on the Stockholm Stock Exchange. The following month Wärtsilä (Metra) reduced its 55 percent stake in the Group to 48.3 percent, and Assa Abloy was no longer a subsidiary of Wärtsilä. By 2000 Wärtsilä had reduced its holding in the Group to 16.4 percent, and Assa Abloy ceased to be associated with the Finnish company.

The Group's expansion was rapid, both organically and through a series of acquisitions. The acquisition of Essex Holding in 1996 boosted Assa Abloy's annual sales to about SEK 5 billion. With the purchase of Essex Holding, the Group was able to enter the U.S. commercial security market. Other acquisitions in 1996 included the Dutch company Ambouw, Singapore's Secureware, and the Norwegian companies Grorud and NT Møller Undall and Låsgruppen.

In 1997 Assa Abloy acquired Abloy Security in Singapore, FAB a.s. Rychnov Nad Kreznou of the Czech Republic, and its French rival Vachette SA. The Vachette purchase brought with it Laperche SA, Bezault SA, JPM Chauvat (Europe's leading manufacturer of exit devices), and Litto SA (Belgium's leading lock company). In that same year, the Group's VingCard hotel security unit acquired the Norwegian company Elsafe, a leading supplier of hotel safes.

Assa Abloy opened its first office in China in 1998. That year the Group added Hong Kong's Precise Securities Supplies Ltd. to its Asia Pacific Division. Acquisitions in the Americas Division included Abloy in

Canada, Scovill in Mexico, and two U.S. companies, Securitron Magnalock and Medeco (a leading manufacturer of high-security cylinders used in pay phones, vending machines, and parking meters). The Group continued its European expansion with the purchase of Assa-Solid in Poland and Wilhelm Dorrenhaus in Germany. In a strategic move that significantly strengthened the Group's position in eastern Europe, Assa Abloy also acquired Urbis, Romania's leading lock manufacturer.

By 1999 Assa Abloy had 11,000 employees and reported year-end sales of SEK 8.5 billion. In April of that year, the Group purchased Stremler S.A., a leading French manufacturer of specialty locks for glass- and aluminum-framed doors. This acquisition opened up new markets for Assa Abloy, including glass- and aluminum-door manufacturers, installers, and shop front manufacturers. The Group expanded its electromechanical business with the purchase of Germany's effeff, which included operations in China, France, the United States, and Australia.

In December 1999 Assa Abloy acquired 89 percent of Mul-T-Lock, Israel's leading manufacturer of residential locks, padlocks, and high-security doors. The purchase included operations in the Netherlands, France, Canada, and the United States. The acquisition opened up sales channels in the do-it-yourself retail sector. Other acquisitions that year included Timelox and AKI Lasgrossisten in Sweden, Fichet in France, Sloth & Co. AIS in Denmark, AZBE in Spain, Bjorkboda Ias in Finland, and Arrow Lock in Canada.

MAJOR EXPANSION IN THE NEW MILLENNIUM

In 2000 Assa Abloy doubled its market share over its closest rival, Ingersoll-Rand, and became the world's largest lock manufacturer and distributor with the acquisition of Yale Intruder Security. The acquisition included operations in South Africa, China, Brazil, and Europe and brought with it some of the strongest brand names in locks, such as Yale, Chubb, Tesa, and Union. In November 2000 Assa Abloy entered the fast-growing electronic identification market with the acquisition of Hughes Identification Devices (HID) Corporation, a leading developer of electronic access control systems. Within six months Assa Abloy had launched its CLIQ technology, an intelligent lock that integrated electronics and mechanics for extra security. Other acquisitions that year included C.E.M. and Nuova Feb in Italy and TRI-MEC, an Australian manufacturer of electromechanical lock products.

In April 2001 Assa Abloy entered into a joint venture with UDP, a leading North American manufacturer of steel doors and frames for the nonresidential market. Assa Abloy held 80 percent ownership in the venture. With it came the CECO, Dominion Building Products, and Fleming brands. On September 23, 2001, with almost 100 companies and 25,000 employees worldwide, Assa Abloy participated in the launch of the Volvo Ocean Race.

Participation in this event was an effort to integrate the Group and develop Assa Abloy's corporate identity. "The challenge we are facing has much in common with the world's most exciting sailing race. It requires clear strategies, a well-functioning team and lots of hard work," President and Chief Executive Officer (CEO) Carl-Henric Svanberg said to Business Wire (August 11, 2000). Global acquisitions in 2001 included Viro in South Africa, Interlock in New Zealand, Indala in the United States, Phillips in Mexico, RIS in the Czech Republic, TESA in Spain, and MAB in Italy.

The acquisition frenzy continued into 2002, but Assa Abloy's most significant acquisition that year was Sweden's Besam, a leading manufacturer of automatic door operators for swinging, sliding, and revolving doors. Assa Abloy paid SEK 3 billion for the debt-free company, which had a presence in 60 countries and its own subsidiaries in one-third of those. The following year, Assa Abloy strengthened its position in Europe when it purchased from Black & Decker the cylinder and lock manufacturers Nemef BV in the Netherlands and Corbin Srl in Italy. In 2004 notable acquisitions included BEST Metaline in South Korea, Security Merchants Group in Australia and New Zealand, and a joint venture with Sweden's Brighthandle. In that same year, Assa Abloy launched its Hi-O Technology (highly

intelligent opening), a new system that simplified the installation and service of electronic doors.

The acquisitions of Doorman Services in the United Kingdom and Security World in South Africa followed in 2005. The Group also increased its presence in China through a joint venture with China's Wangli. In the deal Assa Abloy held a 70 percent stake for the manufacture and distribution of security doors and high-security locks throughout the country. The Group also streamlined its electronic door operations by merging Essex Industries and YSG Door Security Consultants to form Assa Abloy Door Security Solutions.

In 2006 Assa Abloy's subsidiary HID Global Corp. acquired Fargo Electronics Inc. for $326 million. HID manufactured and supplied security readers and card stock. In addition, the deal broadened the Assa Abloy's product line to include the systems used to issue secure ID cards. Other Assa Abloy acquisitions that year included Adams Rite, based in the United States, and Baron Metal Industries of Canada.

In 2007 the Group introduced a new branding strategy with most products cobranded with the Assa Abloy logo. Also in 2007 the Group made 17 acquisitions. These companies were carefully selected based on their product lines, technological achievements, or geographic location, such as iRevo, South Korea's leading provider of digital door locks to Korea and China. Another acquisition in the region was Baodean, a Chinese antitheft door lock manufacturer.

After the success of these two acquisitions, in 2008 Assa Abloy reinforced its position as the market leader in the Asia Pacific region with the purchases of Cheil in South Korea and Beijing Rianming's (BJTM) high-security door business. This was the same year in which Assa Abloy launched the Aperio wireless technology, a user-friendly protocol to convert locks from mechanical to electronic. Other acquisitions that year included Copiax in Sweden, Gardesa and Valli & Valli in Italy, and Rockwood in the United States. In 2009 Assa Abloy celebrated its 15th anniversary, having expanded tenfold, both organically and through the acquisition of more than 150 companies throughout the world. The year was marked by two major acquisitions: Ditec, Italy's leading supplier of entrance automation products, and Pan Pan, a Chinese company with 4,000 employees and the capacity to produce 2.4 million high-security doors per annum.

Between 1997 and 2009 the Group averaged organic growth of 5 percent a year, and Assa Abloy's new CEO, Johan Molin, expected this trend to continue. At the Group's capital markets day in London in November 2009, Molin noted that Assa Abloy also intended to grow an additional 5 percent annually through acquisitions in order to achieve the Group's target of 10 percent annual growth. In February 2010 Assa Abloy reported that its fourth-quarter net profits had doubled to SEK 192 million over the previous year because of increased cost controls. Although the company was experiencing a decline in its U.S. commercial segment, Assa Abloy projected that its long-term organic growth would continue at a positive rate through 2010.

Marie O'Sullivan

PRINCIPAL DIVISIONS

EMEA Division; Americas Division; Asia Pacific Division; Global Technologies Division; Entrance Systems Division.

PRINCIPAL OPERATING UNITS

HID Global; Assa Abloy Hospitality.

PRINCIPAL COMPETITORS

Eastern Company; Ingersoll Rand Security Technologies; Master Lock Company LLC.

FURTHER READING

"Assa Abloy Acquires Besam—World Leader in Door Automatics," PrimeZone Media Network, April 29, 2002.

"Assa Abloy Acquires Ditec, a Global Leader in Entrance Automation," Marketwire, July 29, 2009.

"Assa Abloy Acquires HID, World Leader in Identification Technology for Access Control," Business Wire, November 6, 2000.

"Assa Abloy Net Profit Jumps Due to Cost Control Q4 '09," *Nordic Business Report*, February 12, 2010.

Brown-Humes, Christopher, "UK: Yale Purchase Secures Assa as Leader in Locks," *Financial Times*, March 8, 2000, p. 25.

"Essex and YSG Merge to Form Assa Abloy Door Security Solutions," *Locksmith Ledger International Magazine*, May 2005, p. 78(1).

"HID Global's iClass Contactless SmartCard Technology Enables U.S. Bank's Award-Winning PayID Card," Business Wire, January 28, 2010.

McFadden, Maggie, "Assa Abloy Joins with Cisco to Offer Physical/Logical Access," *Security Distributing & Marketing*, December 2006, p. 28(1).

Shearer, Brent, "Fargo Buy Signals a Systems Approach to I.D. Smart Cards: HID Global's Acquisition of the I.D. Card Printing Company Boosts Its Ability to Offer Complete Security Packages," *Mergers & Acquisitions: The Dealmaker's Journal*, July 1, 2006.

"Skip a Trip to the Check-in Desk at Tech-Forward Aloft Hotels," Business Wire, February 16, 2010.

Barrick Gold Corporation

Brookfield Place
TD Canada Trust Tower
161 Bay Street, Suite 3700
Toronto, Ontario M5J 2S1
Canada
Telephone: (416) 861-9911
Toll Free: (800) 720-7415
Fax: (416) 861-2492
Web site: http://www.barrick.com

Public Company
Founded: 1980 as Barrick Petroleum Corporation
Employees: 20,000 (est.)
Sales: $7.91 billion (2008)
Stock Exchanges: Toronto New York
Ticker Symbol: ABX
NAICS: 212221 Gold Ore Mining; 212222 Silver Ore Mining; 212234 Copper Ore and Nickel Ore Mining

■ ■ ■

Barrick Gold Corporation is the largest gold producer in the world. The company oversees 26 mines on 5 continents, with major operations in South America, Australia, Papua New Guinea, Tanzania, and the United States. In 2008 the company produced 7.7 million ounces of gold and had total reserves of 138.5 million ounces, both first in the industry. Barrick has achieved much of its growth through acquisitions. Among the notable properties the company has purchased over the years are the Goldstrike Property in Nevada (1987), the

Homestake Mining Company (2001), and Placer Dome (2005). In addition to its gold mining operations, Barrick also controls more than a billion ounces of contained silver reserves, as well as 6.4 billion pounds of copper reserves.

INAUSPICIOUS BEGINNINGS

The story of gold is as old as time itself. Ancient civilizations appreciated the beauty and malleability of the precious metal, and many rulers had their likenesses fashioned onto coins. Gold's value was always an absolute. The possessor wielded both wealth and power. Barrick Gold Corporation's mission was never unique, yet how the company forged a name for itself and became the world's most profitable gold producer has been fodder for Canada's history books and led to studies at prestigious business schools. Few tales rival Barrick's meandering path to become a gold industry giant.

Although the gold standard was established in 1821, the story of Barrick Gold Corporation did not begin until more than 160 years later. Hungarian-born Peter Munk, whose family fled from the Nazis to Switzerland, came to Canada in 1948 with big dreams and even bigger ambition. After several ventures, some hits, others misses, Munk, his longtime partner David Gilmour, and several Arab investors founded Barrick Petroleum Corporation in 1980. The new company drew little notice until Munk and Gilmour bought Viking Petroleum and began working with the legendary D.O. "Swede" Nelson to find oil. Much to their dismay the partners never found any gushers, and the industry bottomed out.

COMPANY PERSPECTIVES

Barrick's vision is to be the world's best gold company by finding, acquiring, developing and producing quality reserves in a safe, profitable and socially responsible manner.

Munk then decided to go into precious metals, selecting gold as his venue, a field drastically in need of a boost. Targeting European pension funds with gold investments in South Africa, the new Barrick Resources Corporation (later renamed American Barrick Resources Corporation) hoped to get fund managers to invest their capital in North American gold stocks. With growing discord in South Africa's political and financial arenas, Munk and his partners believed Barrick could offer a more prudent investment. The new Barrick went public on the Toronto Stock Exchange in May 1983 with 1.3 million shares. The sale garnered only CAD 2.5 million, just enough to get the fledgling company on its way.

ACQUISITIONS

The company's mission was simple yet of grand scale: dominate the gold industry by becoming North America's largest producer, acquire established properties with sound futures, be fiscally conservative, and protect the bottom line through an aggressive hedging program. Hedging, used by precious metals producers, was the use of complicated financial contracts to arrange forward sales at fixed prices, regardless of (or rather in spite of) market fluctuations. The seemingly win-win formula (if prices went down producers were protected by their contracted prices, and if prices rose producers could sell additional reserves on the open market) was a boon for Barrick and such rivals as Vancouver's Placer Dome.

Barrick's second business tenet, to acquire working mines with potential, came into play just months after the company went public. The company bought a 23 percent stake in gold deposits in Alaska's Valdez Creek region and then joined up with Alaska Power & Light and the city of Juneau to explore more than two dozen sites. Barrick's next move was to buy a half-interest in Ontario's Renabie Mine. Although both the Valdez and Renabie mines produced gold, the former was eventually sold and the latter was closed.

In 1984 the tide turned with the acquisition of the debt-laden Camflo Mines Ltd. of Quebec. Camflo had a solid reputation for low-cost gold production and top-

notch people, including Robert Smith, Alan Hill, and Brian Meikle, who stayed on board to work with Barrick. In addition to the Camflo Mine came stakes in two other mines, one near Reno, Nevada, and another by Ontario's Kirkland Lake. The Ontario interest later became the Holt-McDermott Mine, Barrick's first major find from initial exploration to full production. The Nevada property led Munk and his team to staggering success and the coveted title of the world's most profitable gold producer. However, first there were trials and tribulations to wade through.

Barrick went public on the New York Stock Exchange in 1985, issuing shares at CAD 1.40 each. Although more successful than its IPO on the Toronto exchange, the company was still relatively unknown to Wall Street and its investors. With minor triumphs from mining operations at the Valdez and Camflo and on-going development of the Holt-McDermott Mine, Barrick was not only making money but hedging to stave off any market downswings. Bob Smith, who had come on board with the Camflo deal, was now Munk's leading developer and right-hand man. Smith helped spearhead Barrick's next acquisition, Utah's oft-closed Mercur Mine, a neglected property Texaco Inc. was looking to unload.

After arduously pulling together the $40 million asking price, Barrick excitedly took possession of Mercur Mine and its surrounding property in Utah. During the long negotiations Smith and former Camflo colleagues Hill and Meikle discovered that Mercur had much more to offer than expected. The acquisition turned out to be a major coup, not only because of additional gold deposits but also because Texaco had poured more than $100 million into updating the mine before deciding to sell. Barrick paid less than half of what Texaco had put into the mine, while gaining a property with considerably more assets than anticipated.

Mercur Mine brought Barrick into the big leagues of gold production. Barrick, in turn, brought increased production and state-of-the-art processing to Mercur. In the course of two years, Barrick's fortunes had multiplied: revenues jumped from $13 million with gold production of 34,000 ounces in 1984 to $42 million and 116,000 ounces in 1985.

ALL THAT GLITTERS IS GOLD

In 1986 Barrick had another year of hidden advantages after the company's prospectors traveled to the gold country of the Carlin Trend in north-central Nevada. On the surface buying the Goldstrike Property, along the United States' richest gold vein, was a good purchase. Beneath the layers of rock, Goldstrike more

KEY DATES

1980: Barrick Petroleum Corporation is founded.
1983: Company name changes to Barrick Resources Corporation; IPO on Toronto Stock Exchange is completed.
1985: Company name changes to American Barrick Resources Corporation.
1987: Barrick gains full ownership of Nevada's Goldstrike Property.
1995: Company is renamed Barrick Gold Corporation.
2001: Barrick acquires Homestake Mining Company.
2003: Gregory C. Wilkins becomes Barrick CEO.
2005: Barrick acquires Placer Dome.

than lived up to its name. The legendary Carlin Trend was home to several mines and mining companies, including one of Barrick's chief rivals, Newmont Mining Corporation. Newmont's Genesis Mine was a huge operation located adjacent to the Goldstrike Property. After negotiating two separate deals, each worth 50 percent, Barrick had complete control of Goldstrike. Despite some initial setbacks Goldstrike was confirmed as the richest gold deposit in North America and a wholly owned part of Barrick's growing empire.

By the late 1980s the Goldstrike Property was home to the exceptionally prolific Betze Mine (named for the two geologists who discovered it, Keith Bettles and Larry Kornze), with several developments under way. Barrick had increased productivity, sold some gold, and stored the rest for a rainy day. By now hedging was no longer a trend but the industry norm, with Barrick one of its leading proponents. Nonetheless, some analysts felt hedging was not in the best interests of shareholders if prices rose significantly, to which Munk said, "Isn't it more important to have no downside?" Then he needed only to point to the numbers. Stock valuation had gone up nearly 190 percent on the New York Stock Exchange for 1987 alone.

In 1989 Munk was the conquering hero to shareholders and the industry when gold prices took a dive to their lowest point in three years. Amazingly Barrick's earnings were robust, up over 20 percent, while stock prices rose an incredible 94 percent. Hedging, at least the Barrick way, had paid off tremendously. The same was true again in 1991 when lackluster prices brought devastating losses for many of Canada's

producers. However, Barrick surprised its shareholders and competitors with a 59 percent leap in earnings and a 68 percent jump in production. The next year Barrick reaped even greater rewards, with net income climbing 89 percent to $175 million on total revenues of $554 million, with production costs falling instead of rising and gold production reaching a new high of 1.3 million ounces.

The year 1992 was most significant for two other reasons. First, to continue its exploration of the Carlin Trend's Deep Post region, Barrick and rival Newmont agreed to a joint venture for the land adjacent to both their properties. This amicable agreement, the Newmont/Barrick HD Venture, came not long after Barrick considered a takeover of Newmont, which fell apart. In exchange for a 40 percent stake, Barrick performed the on-site drilling, while Newmont was responsible for the processing. Given the region's spectacular gold deposits, both companies had high hopes for the venture. Second, Barrick announced its intention to develop a massive underground reserve in what was called the Purple Vein. The new Meikle Mine, named after Brian Meikle, had more than 6.5 million ounces of particularly high-grade gold.

SALES PASS THE BILLION-DOLLAR MARK

In 1993 Munk received Canada's highest honor when he was named an Officer of the Order of Canada for his contributions to the country and beyond. The honor was both a personal and a professional triumph for Munk, who had come to Canada with high hopes, although it is unlikely that anyone had envisioned just how far he would take those aspirations.

Barrick, meanwhile, was full speed ahead. In 1994 came another banner year when the company won a bidding war for Lac Minerals Ltd., which turned out to be the largest gold company acquisition in North and South America at the time. Lac Minerals owned several properties, but the most exciting were in the El Indio gold belt in the Andes Mountains. Barrick's development team hoped El Indio's deposits might rival those found at Goldstrike.

By 1995 Barrick had 10 working mines and 4 in development. At the close of the year the company had produced 3.1 million ounces of gold and reported reserves of 37.6 million ounces, an all-time high. Sales surpassed the billion-dollar mark at $1.28 billion. Barrick was in fantastic form in 1996 with gold reserves of more than 51 million ounces, a 40 percent upswing from the previous year's reserves. The company had become the planet's most profitable gold company and its second-largest producer (behind Newmont).

Not only had Barrick mined 3 million ounces of gold during the year at an average cost of $193 per ounce (as opposed to the industry's standard of $269 per ounce), but the company had identified an additional 25 million ounces of new resources in the form of gold mineralization. On top of that the company had two years' worth of gold production in its hedging program and in nearly a decade of hedging had created $500 million in extra revenues.

"DO A BARRICK"

The company's name entered the vernacular, with investors and analysts searching for outfits that could "do a Barrick," or become as successful as Barrick had over the 13-plus years since it segued into gold mining. With the August 1996 takeover of Arequipa Resources, Ltd., of Vancouver came the Pierina Mine and an additional 47 properties in Peru with promising futures. Barrick put the Pierina deposits into development and continued its exploration of Chile's Pascua, which was now up to 10 million ounces in production.

The two properties were expected to generate up to 1 million additional ounces of gold to Barrick's annual output within a few years, while the company's joint venture with Newmont had brought in 1.2 million ounces in reserves since its creation the year before. The new Meikle Mine on the Goldstrike Property in Nevada also began production in 1996, on time and on budget. Sales for the year were $1.3 billion for 3.12 million ounces.

Just before the end of the year, Barrick seemingly had its industry by the tail: excellent cash flow, high gold reserves, and some of the richest gold properties in the world. Even so Peter Munk was determined not to take his company's fortunes for granted. As he had already stated in the corporate history by Peter C. Newman, which Barrick commissioned and published in 1995, "We tell each other not to get too euphoric. I remind them [his executive management team] not to be caught in the deadly sin of hubris. We must never start believing we're invincible; that would be fatal. I keep repeating to my people—and I make them repeat it back to me so I'm sure they get it—that we are still the same human beings we were 10 years ago when we were struggling. Balance sheets change but people don't. We'll never get too big for our britches."

Indeed a new gold find in Indonesia was about to rock the gold industry. Barrick would be right in the middle of the resulting maelstrom.

THE BUBBLE BURSTS

By the beginning of 1997, Barrick announced its pact with the Indonesian government to acquire a 75 percent

stake in the Bulsang gold deposit, believed to be the largest gold find since South Africa's Witwatersrand. Completion of the deal meant Barrick would shed its rank as second-largest gold producer in the world and rise to number one. Gold prices, however, bottomed out and no one was left unscathed. As Munk wrote in the company's 1997 annual report, "The past year brought a new and sobering reality to the gold business." This was putting it mildly as Barrick was assaulted on all fronts: financially, in the press, and by a lawsuit filed by Bre-X Minerals Ltd.

Although Barrick's size and reserves protected it from much financial fallout, the company announced the closure of its less efficient mines (numbering four) and took a major hit in the third quarter. According to *Maclean's*, the company had been valued on the stock market at $15.4 billion and by the end of 1997 had fallen to $8.6 billion with gold at a 12-year low of $295 per ounce.

Barrick also took heat for its hedging practices, with detractors accusing the company and the other major producers of manipulating the gold market, which Munk vehemently denied. In addition the Bulsang gold project in Borneo had become a vicious mess. Initially Barrick believed it had secured a 75 percent share of the mine, much to the dismay of the Calgary-based Bre-X, which had staked the claim and wound up with only a 25 percent interest.

It was a classic David and Goliath struggle. Bre-X accused Barrick of influence peddling, in the form of former Canadian prime minister Brian Mulroney (a Barrick board member since 1993) and former U.S. president George H. W. Bush (who had joined the board in 1995), to gain access to Indonesia's Suharto government. Before the dust settled accusations of graft and greed touched everyone involved, including Bre-X, which then leveled a lawsuit at Barrick for attempting to steal the golden egg. Barrick eventually withdrew from negotiations. Munk maintained that the company pulled out because the Indonesian government wanted too much control of the operation as well as 10 percent of the action.

For Barrick 1997 had been a rude awakening. The company was not above major market fluctuations regardless of its hedging program, which Munk still firmly believed in. Despite an earnings loss for the year, revenues were still a robust $1.28 billion, and gold production was 3 million ounces. The troubled year also brought a few executive changes: Bob Smith, president of Barrick since 1985, left his post to become vice-chairman, and John K. Carrington was named the new president and COO. Barrick, however, bounced back the following year.

MORE HARD TIMES

In 1998 operating cash flow was $539 million, after costs had declined 12 percent due to the program implemented the previous year. After Barrick slashed its operating mines to five, gold sales remained almost the same at $1.28 billion (up by $3 million) for the year, income topped $300 million for the first time, and gold production increased by 200,000 ounces. Barrick was still the most profitable gold company in the world, and for every ounce of gold sold, the company earned six times more profit than its competitors.

In October 1998 Barrick suffered a heavy blow when Vice-Chairman Bob Smith passed away. Generally referred to as "the soul of Barrick," Smith had helped steer the company to its preeminence in the 1990s. Smith's successor as vice-chairman was Carrington, and Randall Oliphant, formerly executive vice president and CFO, took over as president and CEO.

The company again came under fire in the late 1990s for its hedging practices, during another industry slump causing substantial losses. With prices reaching their lowest point in 20 years, and Barrick's sales soaring in 1999, the finger-pointing was inevitable. Barrick was accused of dumping too much gold on the market, triggering lower prices, when some of the blame lay with the banks and the International Monetary Fund's plans to unload substantial amounts of their gold reserves.

Because the gold market was in such disarray, Munk lobbied to get the banks and the IMF to reconsider. They complied. Gold prices soared, and everybody was content, until the next downswing. Several of the industry's top producers, including Barrick, Placer Dome, and Cambior, Inc., vowed to decrease their hedging programs.

While the Indonesian debacle was over but not forgotten, Barrick still went after promising properties. In 1999, following Placer Dome's lead, Barrick went to Africa. The company soon acquired Sutton Resources. Sutton had been exploring the Bulyanhulu property, situated in northwestern Tanzania, extolled as East Africa's largest gold deposit, with reserves of 8.8 million ounces of exceptionally high-grade gold. For every Bulsang, there was a Bulyanhulu, and Barrick had far more of the latter than the former. The company finished the year with gold sales of $1.42 billion, net income of $331 million (up 10 percent from the previous year), and production up another 500,000 ounces for a total of 3.7 million ounces of gold.

A NEW STRATEGY FOR GROWTH

Barrick headed into the new century with the same priorities that had helped shape the company for years:

acquisitions, steady production, and exceptional profit. In March 2000 the company reached an agreement with TNR Resources to buy many of its properties in Argentina, an area in which Barrick was already established through its El Indio gold belt explorations and mining. In July 2000 the company purchased Pangea Goldfields Inc. for $137.84 million. As part of the merger, Barrick took a 70 percent stake in the Tulawaka site in Tanzania. The site was located only 120 kilometers (74.6 miles) away from the company's existing mining operations at Bulyanhulu. The Pangea acquisition was part of a broader industry trend, as many of Barrick's principal competitors entered into successful mergers in 2000. One of the notable deals from that year was Newmont Mining's purchase of Battle Mountain Gold Corporation for $542 million.

Barrick concluded an even more impressive merger a year later, when it acquired the U.S. firm Homestake Mining Company for $2.3 billion. With the merger Barrick became the second-largest gold company in the world and the largest in North America. Overall the addition of the Homestake properties increased the company's production capacity by 40 percent.

At the time, many industry analysts applauded the ambition of Barrick's growth strategy. John Ing, head of Toronto-based brokerage firm Maison Placement Canada, spoke highly of the deal in the June 26, 2001, *Ottawa Citizen*, comparing the acquisition to a "huge new gold find for Barrick." In spite of the general enthusiasm for the merger, the integration of Homestake into its existing operations posed a unique set of challenges for Barrick. The company soon found itself contending with a range of unanticipated expenses and logistical issues.

SETTLING INTO THE NEW MILLENNIUM

Barrick faced other problems heading into 2002, as rising gold prices stoked investor concerns about the company's hedging strategy. The company's stock value fell 3 percent during the year, even as gold prices rose from $279 to $348 an ounce between January and December. Barrick was the only major gold producer to suffer a decrease in its market value in 2002. By comparison Newmont Gold saw its share price increase by more than 50 percent over the same span.

By February 2003, in the face of sluggish profits, Barrick had fired its CEO, Randall Oliphant, replacing him with Gregory C. Wilkins. Under Wilkins's stewardship Barrick embarked on a broad restructuring program, decentralizing its operations and creating regional divisions to oversee the company's principal geographical areas. More significantly the company began to rein in its hedging practices dramatically. In November 2003 Barrick founder Peter Munk even declared a 10-year moratorium on gold hedging.

Gold prices continued to rise in 2004, primarily as a result of the steadily declining value of the U.S. dollar. As prices showed no sign of declining in the near future, Barrick began to close many of its existing hedge agreements, selling 850,000 ounces of gold in the second quarter alone. By mid-2004 the company had reduced its reserves of hedged gold to 16 percent. Even as the company cut production in the early part of 2005, its profits increased dramatically. Net earnings rose to $51 million for the year's first quarter, nearly double the company's profits for the first quarter of 2004.

At the same time, Barrick remained focused on pursuing strategic acquisitions. In October 2005 the company launched a hostile takeover bid for Placer Dome, in a proposed deal worth $9.2 billion. According to reports Placer's initial reaction to the bid was lukewarm, forcing Barrick to increase its offer to $12 billion. After the two companies reached an agreement in December 2005, the merger became the largest acquisition in the history of the gold industry. The deal also made Barrick the leading gold producer in the world.

Barrick posted record profits in the second quarter of 2006, with net earnings of $459 million, compared to $47 million for the same period in 2005. Quarterly sales more than tripled over that span, from $463 million in 2005 to $1.5 billion a year later. Much of the company's rapid growth during this period was driven by a steady rise in gold prices. In mid-2006 gold was valued at $631 an ounce. In September 2007 the per-ounce price rose to $742. By March 2008 the price broke the $1,000 mark for the first time in history. In the midst of this booming market, Barrick produced roughly 8 million ounces of gold in 2007. In 2008 the company produced 7.7 million ounces, the most in the industry.

FAREWELL TO A FRIEND AND A LEADER

In 2008 Gregory Wilkins, after being diagnosed with cancer, resigned as CEO. Peter Munk filled the position for the remainder of the year before appointing a replacement, Aaron Regent, in January 2009. In the face of the prolonged financial crisis of 2009, Barrick continued to enjoy steady earnings, as global gold prices continued to rise.

As the decade drew to a close, however, the company suffered a serious and deeply personal blow.

On December 16, 2009, former CEO Gregory Wilkins died after his long battle with cancer. In addition to losing the principal architect of the company's turnaround during the middle of the decade, Barrick had lost a colleague and friend. Even with Barrick's financial prospects as strong as ever, Wilkins's death cast a somber light on the company as it headed into 2010.

Nelson Rhodes
Updated, Stephen Meyer

PRINCIPAL SUBSIDIARIES

ABX Financeco Inc. (USA); Arizona Star Resource Corp.; Atacama Copper Pty Limited (Australia, 50%); Barrick North America Holding Corporation (USA); Barrick PNG Limited (Papua New Guinea); BGC Holdings Ltd. (Cayman Islands); Dominicana Holdings Inc. (Barbados, 60%); PGI Acquisition Inc.; Placer Dome Africa Holdings (Cayman) Limited (Mauritius); Sutton Resources, Ltd.

PRINCIPAL OPERATING UNITS

Cortez Mine (USA); Goldstrike Property (USA); Lagunas Norte Mine (Peru); Porgera Mine (Papua New Guinea); Veladero Mine (Argentina); Zaldívar Mine (Chile).

PRINCIPAL COMPETITORS

AngloGold Ashanti Limited; Gold Fields Limited; Newmont Mining Corporation; Rio Tinto Limited.

FURTHER READING

Carr, Nancy, "Barrick Gold Profit Soars 43%," *Toronto Star*, February 14, 2004, p. D05.

Chadwick, John, "Barrick Goldstrike," *Mining Magazine*, November 1995, pp. 250+.

Davies, Charles, "So Big It's Brutal," *Globe and Mail* (Canada), May 26, 2006, p. 64.

"Good for Barrick, Bad for Gold?" *BusinessWeek*, October 25, 1999, p. 134.

Greenwood, John, "Bigger ... and Better: CEO Greg Wilkins Is More than Barrick Gold's Mr. Fix-it," *National Post's Financial Post & FP Investing* (Canada), February 1, 2006, p. 15.

"El Indio Rejuvenated Under Barrick Gold," *Mining Magazine*, January 1996, p. 6.

Ingram, Matthew, "Barrick Gold Is Winning a War It Helped to Start," *Globe and Mail* (Canada), June 26, 2001, p. B16.

Krantz, Matt, "Barrick Gold Bids $9.2B for Placer," *USA Today*, November 1, 2005, p. 1B.

Maurino, Romina, "Barrick Gold Profit Hits Record on Bullion Price, Placer Takeover," *Toronto Star*, August 3, 2006, p. C04.

Newman, Peter C., *Dreams & Rewards: The Barrick Story*. Toronto: Barrick Gold Corporation, 1995.

———, "Mining the Riches of Urban Real Estate," *Maclean's*, September 22, 1997, p. 60.

———, "Peter Munk: A Dreamer Who Became a King," *Maclean's*, December 9, 1996, p. 42.

"Newsroom Notes: The Making of a Mega-Deal," *Maclean's*, December 9, 1996, p. 4.

Perkins, Tara, "Barrick Gold Doubles Profits: Company Targets Production Growth of 40 Per Cent by the End of 2007," *Gazette* (Montreal), April 29, 2005, p. B5.

Petrou, Michael, "Barrick Gold to Grab Pangea: $204-Million Deal: Consolidation of Industry Is Accelerated," *National Post* (Canada), July 1, 2000, p. D01.

Rohmer, Richard, *Golden Phoenix: The Biography of Peter Munk*, Toronto: Key Porter Books, 1999.

Ross, Priscilla, "Barrick Buys into Top E African Mine," *African Business*, April 1999, p. 31.

"The Shine Is Off Barrick's Gold," *Maclean's*, December 8, 1997, p. 60.

Simon, Bernard, "Barrick Gold Fires Its Chief as Stock Price and Profits Lag," *New York Times*, February 13, 2003, p. 1.

Stueck, Wendy, "Revamped Barrick Keeps Eyes on the Hunt for the Golden Prize," *Globe and Mail* (Canada), September 17, 2005, p. B4.

Wells, Jennifer, "Greed, Graft, Gold: Canadians Find Treasure in One of the World's Most Corrupt Countries," *Maclean's*, March 3, 1997, p. 38.

———, "Gunning for Gold," *Maclean's*, February 17, 1997, p. 52.

———, "King of Gold: The Inside Story of Peter Munk's Indonesian Gold Coup," *Maclean's*, December 9, 1996, p. 32.

Wilkins, Greg, "Gold Provides a Haven from the Market Turmoil," *Daily Mail*, March 25, 2008, p. 67.

Wroughton, Lesley, "Tarnished Barrick Gold Misunderstood, Chief Says," *Toronto Star*, January 23, 2003, p. C06.

BayWa AG

Arabellastrasse 4
München, Bayern D-81925
Germany
Telephone: (+49 89) 9222 0
Fax: (+49 89) 9222 3448
Web site: http://www.baywa.com

Public Company
Founded: 1923
Incorporated: 1923
Employees: 16,500
Sales: €8.79 billion ($12.04 billion) (2008)
Stock Exchanges: Frankfurt
Ticker Symbol: BYW6
NAICS: 423820 Farm and Garden Machinery and Equipment Merchant Wholesalers; 424480 Fresh Fruit and Vegetable Merchant Wholesalers; 444220 Nursery, Garden Center, and Farm Supply Stores; 444130 Hardware Stores; 447110 Gasoline Stations with Convenience Stores; 441110 New Car Dealers

■ ■ ■

One of Europe's largest building materials and agricultural trade corporations, BayWa AG combines trading, logistics, and services in its three operating sectors: agriculture, building materials, and energy. Based in Munich, Germany, and rooted in the business of agricultural cooperatives, BayWa has been a strong force in rural regions for almost a century, offering proximity to customers and a tight sales network that guarantees a considerable competitive advantage for the members of the group.

The company's mainstay is traditional agribusiness, selling and distributing agricultural products (grain, oil, fertilizers, insecticides, feed, seed, fresh fruit) and equipment (farm buildings, machinery, tools). Its building materials sector reaches faraway regions with a widespread network of do-it-yourself stores and garden centers that feature products and services for new construction, modernization, and renovation. BayWa's energy segment offers light and heavy heating oil and fuel through an association of gas stations, 60 of which dispense biodiesel.

BayWa's customers include farmers as well as local authorities and retailers. In addition to its core region in southern Germany, the company is represented in Austria, Hungary, Bulgaria, Croatia, and Greece through joint ventures and franchise operations and employs more than 16,000 people. Its business caters to fundamental human needs such as food, shelter, energy, mobility, and warmth, while also looking forward to find renewable energy products and services.

COOPERATIVE ROOTS

The roots of the modern BayWa AG go back to the agricultural cooperatives established by Friedrich Wilhelm Raiffeisen starting in the late 19th century. Noticing that many farmers were at the mercy of usurers, Raiffeisen founded the first rural credit union in 1864. His idea was to combine trade and banking for a maximum advantage for both the cooperative and its members. The credit union, or savings and loan, would

BayWa is a high-performance company in the trading and logistics businesses and offers its customers a comprehensive product range and supplementary services in its operating segments of agriculture, building materials and energy. The extensive support and supply of a large number of customers, in particular outside large urban centers, requires a network which can provide full coverage through its efficient locations. Ensuring that the availability of products and services is within easy reach for customers in rural areas is BayWa's unique selling proposition in the competitive arena. And, ultimately, the offerings of the three segments of agriculture, building materials and energy, which mesh and complement one another, foster strong customer loyalty. The positive experience of customers of the one business segment is transferred to other business activities under the BayWa umbrella brand.

buy the products the farmers needed at bulk prices and then finance the purchasing needs of its mostly rural members. In other words, the trade arm of the cooperative would buy seed, feed, fertilizer, and tools at bulk prices, and the banking arm would offer farmers reasonable loans to buy the seed, feed, fertilizer, and tools.

The cooperative made a profit, while the farmers received better prices than they would have on their own. In addition, the trade arm of the cooperative would sell the harvest of its members to markets and retailers, making intermediaries unnecessary.

At the time, about 50 percent of the Bavarian population worked in agriculture, so the cooperative system benefited not only the cooperatives and their members but also all of Bavaria. During the agricultural crisis between 1870 and 1890, the cooperatives provided a safety net for many Bavarian farmers. In 1893 various cooperatives joined the Bayerische Landesverband landwirtschaftlicher Genossenschaftsverbände (the Bavarian Organization of Agricultural Cooperatives) to form one large cooperative. In 1900 the trade business of the cooperative was transferred to Bayerische Zentral-Darlehenskasse, a statewide credit union founded in 1893.

The continuous growth and expansion of cooperative trade sparked the idea for separating the trade business from the credit business. When runaway inflation

after World War I resulted in a dangerously lopsided relationship between the value of goods and the value of money, the two arms of the cooperative split. In a general meeting of the Bayerische Zentral-Darlehenskasse on January 17, 1923, the membership voted for the board's suggestion to focus only on the financial and credit business and to create a legally separate entity that would handle the trade business independently. Thus BayWa AG was born. Stockholders at the time included more than 1,000 Bavarian cooperatives and their central organization, the Bayerische Zentral-Darlehenskasse.

DIFFICULT BEGINNINGS UNDER THE NAZI REGIME

At its inception in 1923, the purpose of BayWa was to support its members in buying and selling agricultural products. First and foremost, the organization fulfilled two functions: it was the central trade union for the cooperatives and the primary market and distribution partner for Bavarian farmers. BayWa took over many storage facilities from individual trade cooperatives. In an attempt to make the company more profitable, BayWa had closed about half its storage facilities by 1925. To ensure that farmers in more remote areas could compete, the company began to provide transport and infrastructure logistics as well.

During the Nazi regime, BayWa was forced to join the Reichsnährstand, an NS organization that was established to fight *Erzeugungsschlacht*, or "the feeding war." The regime's aim was to have Germany's agricultural production and food supply completely self-sufficient and independent from other countries. In pursuit of this goal, in about 1933 the Reichsnährstand forced BayWa to join with its competitor, the Regensburger cooperative GeWa. BayWa's main task now was to seize and distribute agricultural products within Germany from the country's farmers in order to ensure the survival of its population during World War II. As the war wore on, this task became increasingly difficult, as many of the organization's warehouses were damaged or even destroyed, roads were blocked, and trucks were used for other aspects of the war effort.

INVESTMENT IN AGRICULTURAL EQUIPMENT IN POSTWAR GERMANY

After World War II BayWa resumed its work under the leadership of Josef Singer. From 1945 to 1962 Singer was chairman of the board at BayWa and at Bayerische Raiffeisen-Zentralkasse. Despite this shared leadership, the credit union and the trade company operated

KEY DATES

1923: Bavarian Trading Co. splits from the Bayerische Zentral-Darlehenskasse.

1933: Nazi regime forces the merger of BayWa and the Regensburg cooperative GeWa.

1948: BayWa shifts focus to mechanization of agriculture.

1991: First franchises open in the former East German states after German reunification.

1996: First franchises open in Austria.

1998: BayWa establishes franchise headquarters in Klagenfurt.

1999: BayWa and RWA Raiffeisen AG Vienna swap stock; BayWa now holds 48.3 percent of RWA stock.

2002: BayWa merges with WLZ Raiffeisen AG.

2009: BayWa Green Energy takes over Renerco Renewable Energy Concepts AG in Munich, MHH Solartechnik GmbH in Tübingen, and Aufwind Neue Energien GmbH in Regensburg.

independently. In 1947 Singer also became president of the Bavarian Senate, a post he held until 1967, illustrating a strong relationship between politics and agriculture in Bavaria.

After years of war and the resulting inflation, the German currency reform in 1948 signaled a new beginning for the entire country. The increasing mechanization of agriculture and the resulting unprecedented increase in production volume and quality made huge investments necessary. BayWa shifted its focus, becoming a company that would buy and sell not only agricultural products but also agricultural equipment such as seeders, tillage machinery, and harvesters. The trade with farming equipment naturally developed further, and soon the company's operations included servicing equipment as well. To fill this need, during the 1950s and 1960s BayWa established more than 300 repair stations and spare-parts centers for agricultural equipment, while also training hundreds of skilled mechanics to staff them.

The mechanization of agriculture resulted in increased production, which in turn required building more reception, drying, and storage units for fruit and other crops. Between 1948 and 1983 BayWa invested 1.5 billion DEM into these new sectors of the company, thus slowly changing its profile from being agricultural

merchant to both agricultural merchant and service provider. To this day BayWa offers a wide range of agricultural services aimed at increasing a farmer's efficiency and profitability, including soil and crop analysis, assistance in crop protection, new product research, and marketing strategies.

PRODUCT AND SERVICE EXPANSION

BayWa had become a driving force in rural areas, connecting farmers with each other, buying and reselling equipment, distributing product, and offering business and marketing support. Managing product supply and demand became as important to the company as quality control. During the 1970s the product line was further broadened to include energy products such as oil and gas. The BayWa subsidiary Tessol built gas stations all over Bavaria, and fuel trucks delivered to remote locations.

Around the same time the company's first do-it-yourself stores and garden centers were established. The BayWa-Märkte offered building materials and advice on energy-efficient construction to farmers in an attempt to improve the building quality in rural areas. With about 12,000 specialized employees in the early 1970s, BayWa was active even in areas with weak infrastructure, ensuring that rural areas remained sustainable despite the increasing urbanization of the country. A 1973 poll revealed that BayWa had become a household name: virtually everyone in Bavaria knew the company and its product and service lines.

As Germany's agricultural population decreased and urbanization increased, the company needed to make another shift in the 1980s. To ensure its future growth, the service and product lines were adjusted to suit the needs of urban areas and population sectors other than farmers. The DIY stores and garden centers were an easy fit even for urban areas, and the company began offering building materials and expertise to building professionals such as architects and construction companies. The company's pioneer use of renewable resources in the building sector offered an increasingly welcome alternative to traditional methods and materials. BayWa was growing from a regional merchant and service provider to a nationwide trading and building partner.

TURN OF THE 21ST CENTURY: FRANCHISE OPERATIONS MOVE BEYOND BAVARIA

The reunification of Germany in 1991 provided a new market for many German companies, and BayWa was no exception. Based on its experience rebuilding post-WWII Germany and faithful to the cooperatives that were at the root of the company's original success, BayWa became interested in assisting with the reintegration process of the former Eastern German states, as well as continuing to find new markets.

To the new BayWa CEO Wolfgang Deml, the franchise system was a natural extension of the agricultural cooperative business. Quickly establishing a tight network of independent entrepreneurs (home-improvement and garden centers) under the subsidiary BayWa Handels-Systeme-Service GmbH, BayWa offered West German products and expertise in the building sector through franchise operations in the former East German states.

In cooperation with RWA Raiffeisen Ware Austria AG, the franchise concept was expanded to Austria as early as 1996. In 1998 BayWa established the BayWa Franchise-Systemzentrale GmbH in Klagenfurt, Germany, to oversee the operations of national franchises in Bavaria and Hesse and international franchises in Austria. In 1999 RWA AG and BayWa AG consolidated their cooperation in Austria with a mutual stock swap, resulting in BayWa holding 48.3 percent of RWA stock.

The milestone merger between BayWa and WLZ Raiffeisen AG in 2002 allowed BayWa to expand its core operations in agriculture, building, and energy within Germany. Further acquisitions in Rheinland Pfalz and Nordrhein-Westphalia quickly followed. BayWa, already among Europe's largest agricultural corporations, became Germany's largest supplier of building materials. The merger with WLZ Raiffeisen also added car dealerships to the wide array of products and services under the BayWa umbrella. A total of 600 employees at 29 locations sold cars such as BMWs, Volkswagens, Audis, Fiats, Alfa Romeos, Peugeots, and Land Rovers. By 2009, in an effort to refocus on its core business, these car dealerships had been handed over to the BayWa subsidiary Deutsche Raiffeisen-Warenzentrale GmbH.

In 2004 the Bavarian state prosecutor's office launched an investigation of embezzlement allegations against BayWa and its former CEO Wolfgang Deml. According to allegations, BayWa had negotiated substantial discounts and bonus payments with producers and suppliers yet failed to pass on these benefits to its franchise operations. Over the years, more than 50 franchise operations had lost a total of more than €4.6 million, a loss that allegedly forced some franchises into bankruptcy.

By 2007 BayWa had voluntarily paid reparations of €6.9 million to more than 23 of its franchises and overhauled its data entry procedures to make the company's processes (purchases, storage, sales, distribution, prices, profits and losses, as well as the discounts and bonus payments in question) more transparent to every independent entrepreneur. The company's willingness to pay reparations and fix its data entry procedures led to a rather lenient sentence in 2009. BayWa had to pay a fine of only €950,000, and the case against Deml, by then retired, was dismissed.

NEW AND SUSTAINABLE HORIZONS

In 2008 Klaus Josef Lutz became CEO of the company. Under his leadership BayWa's focus turned to expanding the business in a sustainable fashion. While consolidating its core business in the agricultural and building sector, BayWa's goals may shift to renewable energies in the company's other main sector, energy. Aiming to become one of the leading trading houses for renewable energy sources in Europe, BayWa subsidiary Green Energy absorbed three pioneering companies. In 2009 it acquired 87.7 percent of shares of Renerco Renewable Energy Concepts AG stock and bought 100 percent of MHH Solartechnik GmbH, as well as Aufwind Neue Energien GmbH. BayWa Green Energy is primed to offer expertise in solar and wind energy as well as photovoltaic energy and bioenergy.

In more than 85 years of operation, BayWa has never reported losses. The company's diversified product and service line in agriculture, building materials, and energy, as well as its expanding customer base, has allowed the company to succeed and weather economic crises.

Helga Schier

PRINCIPAL SUBSIDIARIES

Tessol; BayWa Green Energy, RWA (Austria); Agrárház Kft (Hungary).

PRINCIPAL DIVISIONS

Agriculture; Construction; Energy.

PRINCIPAL COMPETITORS

AGRAVIS Raiffeisen AG; Bauhaus; Castorama; Migros; Obi; Raiffeisen-Warenzentrale Kurhessen-Thüringen GmbH; Raiffeisen-Waren-Zentrale Rhein-Main eG; ZG Raiffeisen eG.

FURTHER READING

"BayWa peilt Milliarden-Umsatz mit erneuerbaren Energien an," *Finanznachrichten.de*, December 6, 2009, http://www.

finanznachrichten.de/nachrichten-2009-12/15638030-baywa-peilt-milliarden-umsatz-mit-erneuerbaren-energien-an-016.htm.

Hüttl, Ludwig, "Bayerische Warenvermittlung landwirtschaftlicher Genossenschaften (BayWa)," *Historisches Lexikon Bayerns*, July 16, 2008, http://www.historisches-lexikon-bayerns.de/artikel/artikel_44429.

Liebrich, Silvia, "Pokern auf dem Acker," *Süddeutsche Zeitung*, August 22, 2008, http://www.sueddeutsche.de/wirtschaft/424/307378/text/.

Raiffeisen in Bayern 1893–1968, Jubiläumsschrift zu 75 Jahre Bayerischer Raiffeisenverband und Bayerische Raiffeisen- *Zentralkasse.* Neuwied: Raiffeisendruckerei GmbH, 1968.

Ritzer, Uwe, "Bayerische Rabattbetrüger," *Süddeutsche Zeitung*, March 15, 2009, http://www.sueddeutsche.de/wirtschaft/140/461762/text/.

———, "Ein geheimes System der Rückvergütung," *Süddeutsche Zeitung*, May 29, 2007, http://www.sueddeutsche.de/wirtschaft/937/343778/text/.

"Wachwechsel bei der BayWa: Einer für die nächsten Jahrzehnte," *Merkur-Online.de*, June 29, 2008, http://www.merkur-online.de/nachrichten/wirtschaft/wachwechsel-baywa-einer-naechsten-jahrzehnte-380240.html.

Billabong International
Limited

---

1 Billabong Place
Burleigh Heads, Queensland 4220
Australia
Telephone: (+61) 7-55-899-899
Fax: (+61) 7-55-899-800
Web site: http://www.billabong.com

Public Company
Founded: 1973
Incorporated: 1977 as Gordon & Rena Merchant Pty
    Ltd.
Employees: 4,500 (est.)
Sales: AUD 1.67 billion ($1.49 billion) (2009)
Stock Exchanges: Australian
Ticker Symbol: BBG
NAICS: 315223 Men's and Boys' Cut and Sew Shirt
    (except Work Shirt) Manufacturing; 315224 Men's
    and Boys' Cut and Sew Trouser, Slack, and Jean
    Manufacturing; 315228 Men's and Boys' Cut and
    Sew Other Outerwear Manufacturing; 315232
    Women's and Girls' Cut and Sew Blouse and Shirt
    Manufacturing; 315239 Women's and Girls' Cut
    and Sew Other Outerwear Manufacturing; 315999
    Other Apparel Accessories and Other Apparel
    Manufacturing; 316211 Rubber and Plastics
    Footwear Manufacturing; 339920 Sporting and
    Athletic Goods Manufacturing

■ ■ ■

Billabong International Limited manufactures and
markets apparel and accessories for surfing, skateboarding, and snowboarding enthusiasts. Billabong products
are sold both directly through the company and through
licensees, and they are available in sports shops in over
100 countries worldwide. Billabong's extensive product
line is aimed primarily at young men and women and
includes board shorts (for surfing), T-shirts, swimwear,
fleece tops, sweaters, jackets, backpacks, sports eyewear,
wetsuits, and surfboards. Billabong is the biggest name
in surfing apparel in Australia, and it is among the leading brands in the United States. In addition to the Billabong label, the company also markets its products under
a number of notable designer brands, including Nixon,
Element, Tigerlily, and Von Zipper.

FROM KITCHEN-TABLE
OPERATION TO INTERNATIONAL
BRAND: 1973–98

Billabong International started at the kitchen table in
Gordon and Rena Merchant's small, rented apartment
on the Gold Coast of Australia. In 1973 the husband-
and-wife team began to sew and sell knee-length board
shorts designed for the rigors of surfing. The Merchants
sold their board shorts to surfing shops on the Gold
Coast on consignment for AUD 4.50 per pair, and they
sold AUD 5,000 in merchandise their first year in
business.

The immediate success of the product and retailer
demand persuaded the Merchants to give a name to
their company and to add labels inside the board shorts
in 1974. They chose the name "Billabong" an aboriginal
word often used to mean "oasis," because of its uniqueness to Australia. They developed the wave logo to create a recognizable representation of the business.

Billabong International's values remain consistent with its foundation objectives, which include a commitment to brand protection and enhancement, the manufacture of design-relevant and functional products, marketing in the core boardsports channels, the professional development of staff and ongoing customer service and relationships.

The business continued to grow and Billabong opened its first factory, a 1,000-square-foot space in 1975. By 1977 annual sales reached AUD 100,000. That year the company failed to get a business loan, but the following year Billabong obtained its first bank loan of AUD 7,500, allowing the company to relocate to a larger, 7,500-square-foot production facility. With continued innovation and new products designed for the needs of surfers and beachcombers throughout Australia, Billabong reached the milestone of AUD 1 million in annual sales in 1981.

As surfing developed into a professional sport during the 1970s and 1980s, Billabong positioned its brand products as integral to the surfer lifestyle. Promotions centered on surfer magazines and sponsorship of surfing events and individual surfers. In 1984 Billabong began to sponsor the World Final Surfing Contest, held annually in Hawaii, its largest event to date. The event provided international exposure just as the company started to expand into international markets.

Billabong began to export products to Japan and the United States, particularly Hawaii, in 1979, and the company decided to license its name and product designs in the early 1980s. Licensees sold Billabong products in New Zealand, Japan, and the United States. In 1983 Billy International, cofounded by Bob Hurley, established Billabong in the United States at the center of the surf wear industry in Orange County, California, with a design and production facility located in Costa Mesa. After a decade in operation, Billy International built Billabong into a nationally recognized brand, with $25 million in annual sales. A 1988 license agreement established Billabong in the United Kingdom as a base for marketing and distribution throughout Europe. In 1992 Billabong took direct control of the European operations, relocating Billabong Europe's headquarters in Hossegor, France, with sales offices in Spain, France, and the United Kingdom, where most European sales originated. Billabong surf wear became available at

popular surfing areas in South Africa in 1989 through direct sales, and in Indonesia in 1991 through a licensee.

Billabong's growth as a popular brand and the expansion of its product line required new production facilities. The existing facility had been expanded several times to 40,000 square feet by 1989, when the company began operation of an in-house screen-printing shop. In 1992 the company opened a specially designed, 45,000-square-foot factory and sales showroom. New products at this time attracted crossover board sport enthusiasts in skateboarding and snowboarding. Billabong sold certain items to skateboarders using the "Bad Billy" logo in 1987 but did not target that group much until the mid-1990s. Thin Air, a subsidiary of Billabong formed in the early 1990s, produced jackets for use by surfers, for warming up after riding a few waves, or snowboarders. Thin Air produced snowboard carriers in the form of a backpack. International expansion at this time involved licensees in Brazil (1994), Peru (1995), South Africa (1995), Singapore (1996), and Chile (1997). By the end of fiscal year June 30, 1997, Billabong recorded revenues of AUD 47.4 million from direct product sales and licensing royalties, the latter at 5 percent to 7 percent of licensee sales. In 1998 Billabong built another, larger production facility and showroom at Burleigh Heads.

OVERSEAS EXPANSION IN THE LATE 1990S

In June 1998 Bob Hurley of Billy International decided not to renew his license to produce and sell Billabong apparel. Hurley did not want to follow the direction that the Merchants planned to take the company, selling accessories and junior women's clothing, and had decided to start his own line of surf wear. The news caused a wave of trepidation in the surf wear industry as Billabong rated among the top three brands in many surf shops, bringing approximately $70 million in sales to Billy International in 1998. Also, the pending debut of Hurley's line of surf wear raised speculation about new competition for Billabong. The brand was untested in the market, but Hurley had established a strong reputation as a businessman in the industry.

Billabong initially sought to find another licensee but decided to form its own subsidiary, Burleigh Point Ltd., doing business as Billabong USA. The formation of the subsidiary hinged on the infusion of new capital from a consortium of investors led by Gary Pemberton and Matthew Perrin. Pemberton, who became a nonexecutive chairman at Billabong, brought experience as chairman of Quantas Airways and leadership in other prominent Australian companies, particularly in the area

KEY DATES

1973: Gordon and Rena Merchant begin manufacturing and selling surfing shorts.
1975: Billabong opens its first factory.
1979: Billabong begins to export goods to Japan and the United States.
1981: Annual sales reach AUD 1 million.
1984: Billabong sponsors its first major surfing event, the World Final Surfing Contest in Hawaii.
1992: The company moves to a new production facility.
1998: Billabong USA is formed after a licensee decides not to renew.
2000: Initial offering of stock exceeds expectations, with the sale of stock closing early.
2002: CEO Matthew Perrin resigns amid share-dumping scandal.
2005: Billabong acquires Nixon Inc. for AUD 97 million.
2007: Billabong expands its women's clothing line through the purchase of the Tigerlily swimwear brand.

of international expansion. Perrin took the position of chief executive officer at Billabong while Gordon Merchant led Billabong USA. The consortium purchased Rena Merchant's 49 percent interest in Billabong for AUD 24.6 million ($14.3 million) in preparation for taking the company public. In support of the long-term well-being of the company, the investors provided capital to form Billabong USA.

Maintaining a presence in surf and extreme sports shops in the United States was essential for Billabong to expand its market share. Billy International's license expired in June 1999, and Billabong had to act quickly to maintain an uninterrupted flow of merchandise to surf shops. Hurley kept the manufacturing facility in Costa Mesa for his new company, so Billabong had to find a manufacturing facility and prepare it for operation in a matter of months. In November the company leased an 80,000 square-foot facility in Irvine, California.

Gordon Merchant selected Paul Naude, a former executive at surf wear manufacturer Gotcha International, for president of Billabong USA. While Hurley retained many key employees, many chose to remain with Billabong, including national sales manager

Richard Sanders and 10 of 14 sales representatives. For the sales staff, to stay with Hurley would mean a big cut in pay while selling an unknown brand under Hurley. Naude's reputation in the surf wear industry served to attract top designers and other high-profile staff members to Billabong. The hiring process generated controversy and change in the surf wear industry, with several positions being filled by people from competing companies.

When Billabong USA displayed samples of its summer 1999 line at the winter trade shows, it reassured surf wear retailers that the Billabong brand would endure the changes in operations. Billabong found itself in the rather odd position of having Hurley present Billabong surf wear as well, selling the line next to Hurley's debut line of surf apparel. Billabong was pleased with the Hurley's Billabong line and resulting sales. Billabong expected sales in the United States to account for approximately 50 percent of total revenues, as direct control of the market brought product revenues rather than royalties.

January 1999 Billabong debuted a line of clothing for girls and juniors. With Billabong Girls the company entered a largely untapped, niche market of young women, 16 to 22 years old, who often purchased young men's surf, skate, and snowboarding apparel. The line featured body-conscious knits, sheer knits, mesh, unusual floral prints, and bottoms that ranged from hot pants to Capri pants and loose, baggy-style pants. Wholesale prices ranged from $15 for a T-shirt to $120 for a jacket. Advertising targeted young women through general magazines, such as *Teen* and *Seventeen*, as well as specialty magazines, such as *Surfer*, *Surfing*, and *Wahine* (the Hawaiian word for "girl"). Billabong promoted the line through the sponsorship of girls surf and skate meets and through the endorsement of world-class surfers, such as Malia Jones and Layne Beachley, spokeswomen for Billabong and members of the Billabong Girls sports team. Merchant combined Billabong Girls with Billabong USA, operating the two subsidiaries as one division from the facility in Orange County.

GOING PUBLIC: 1999–2000

During 1999 and 2000 Billabong prepared to go public as a way of obtaining funds to diversify the company's product line and expand its reach internationally. With its products being sold in more than 60 countries through licensees, Billabong wanted to obtain direct control over production and distribution. Billabong signed licensing agreements with manufacturers in Israel in 1998 and in Venezuela in 1999. Billabong gained direct control of business in Canada and New Zealand in 1999 and 2000, respectively, where licensees had previously operated. The company also planned to convert Australian Accessories Business, maker of Billabong hats, backpacks, and other accessories, to direct company control in July 2000.

Through the direct operation of international operations, Billabong sought to improve the marketing and promotion of its products, gaining higher-margin income rather than royalty payments. Through management information systems, financial oversight, quality control, and economies of scale through central product sourcing, Billabong hoped to facilitate efficient market expansion as it diversified its product line. The company employed in-store merchandisers and account managers to oversee the in-store presentation of its branded merchandise, and the international network of commissioned salespeople became direct employees of Billabong, with regular pay and sales incentives. Billabong formed a central product sourcing subsidiary in Hong Kong in 1999. While external suppliers existed, 40 percent of licensee sourcing originated with Billabong, allowing the company to reduce costs, provide consistent quality, insure timely delivery, and become flexible with changing market conditions. Also, the company established direct distribution facilities in Victoria and New South Wales, Australia.

At the time of the initial public offering of stock, Billabong products were sold in more than 2,600 surf and extreme sports shops around the world. Revenues at Billabong nearly doubled from AUD 64.5 million during fiscal year ending June 30, 1998, to AUD 112.3 million during fiscal 1999 on the strength of the U.S. market. Billabong USA recorded revenues of AUD 25.6 million in 1999, resulting from three months in sales of men's products after taking over from Billy International, and six months of sales in young women's products after the debut of Billabong Girls. Billabong products were distributed through more than 900 surf, snow, and skate shops in the United States. In Australia sales to 600 accounts, for a total of 850 retail outlets, reached AUD 46.3 million in fiscal 1999. In Europe, where the product line included wet suits, accessories, and snowboarding equipment, Billabong products sold through 1,100 independent retail outlets in 25 countries and 2 company-owned stores in France. European sales generated AUD 40.4 million. Billabong planned to move into North Africa, the Middle East, and Asia, to expand its line of snowboard apparel and accessories in the United States, and to launch a line of swimwear for young women.

In July 2000 Billabong initiated the sale of 120.4 million shares of stock, including 11 million shares from oversubscription. Shares sold to institutions at AUD 2.60 per share and to retail investors at AUD 2.30 per share, each accounting for about half of stock purchases. The IPO raised AUD 295 million in capital, exceeding the goal of AUD 277 million. Strong demand for Billabong stock required the offering to close three days ahead of schedule, with the exchange price rising to more than AUD 3 per share on the Australian Stock Exchange. The stock offering included half of Gordon Merchant's 51 percent interest in the company, with 60 percent of total company shares sold.

One of the first actions that Billabong took in extending its international reach was to take over the licensee operation in Japan, the fourth-largest market for surf wear, after the United States, Europe, and Australia. While the licensee had sold $13 million in merchandise, compared with the leading surf wear brand, Quiksilver, at $43 million, Billabong planned to capture a greater share of the Japanese market. With headquarters in Osaka and a sales office in Tokyo, Billabong began official operation in Japan on January 1, 2001.

DIVERSIFICATION, CONTROVERSY, AND RECOVERY: 2001–05

In early 2001 Billabong sought to diversify its product line without diluting its brand name by purchasing two apparel and accessories companies, Von Zipper and Element, both based in the United States. Von Zipper specialized in sunglasses and eyewear for extreme sports, such as snow goggles. Von Zipper formed in 1999 and quickly established itself as an up-and-coming brand. Element, founded in the early 1990s, was considered one of the leading brands of skateboarding apparel and accessories worldwide. Billabong retained key staff at both companies and allowed them to retain their unique identities and independent operations, providing capital resources to expand product lines and distribution to select retailers. News of the acquisitions prompted an increase in Billabong's share price to over AUD 5.50.

By fiscal 2001, sales at Billabong increased to AUD 380.2 million, 15 percent higher than projected in the prospectus and 68 percent higher than the previous year. Net profit rose to AUD 42.1 million, 12.6 percent higher than forecast. Taking direct control of license distribution had a strong impact on revenues, as did the formation of Billabong USA. Sales in Australia and Asia increased 26 percent to AUD 118.8 million, sales in North America increased 50 percent to $179.3 million, and sales in Europe, where distributors in Italy and Belgium were converted to company-controlled operations, increased 50 percent to AUD 82.1 million. Billabong expected sales to grow approximately 15 percent in Australia/Asia and 25 percent in North America and

Europe in 2002. In the United States, Pacific Sunwear, a chain of beachwear clothing stores accounting for 20 percent of sales at Billabong USA, announced plans to double the number of outlets in the United States.

While Billabong has maintained its commitment to surfing throughout its history through sponsorship of events and athletes, in 2001 Billabong initiated a new extreme surfing event, the Billabong Odyssey. This event challenged surfers to a three-year search for the largest waves in the world, specifically, a search for the never-before-surfed 100-foot wave. The idea for the project came as an extension of Project Neptune, an expedition to a surf break 100 miles off the coast of San Diego. The legendary Cortes Bank seamount had never been surfed before, but Mike Parsons, a surfer on the Billabong Team, rode a 66-foot wave, winning the Swell XXL for the year's biggest wave. This adventure exhibited new possibilities for mid-ocean surfing by using motorized watercraft to tow surfers farther out to sea, an extreme form of surfing that began in the 1990s. Billabong invited internationally renowned surfers to participate in the event and planned eight expeditions of four to six surfers. Billabong offered a prize of AUD 1,000 per foot of face height to the surfer who rode the biggest wave each year and a prize of AUD 500,000 to any surfer to ride a 100-foot wave.

Even as the Billabong brand was becoming increasingly popular overseas, a scandal at home threatened to derail its long-term growth strategy. In August 2002 company CEO Matthew Perrin aroused suspicion when he suddenly sold AUD 66.4 million ($36.1 million) worth of Billabong stock. Of his 13 million shares, Perrin unloaded 8 million without informing the company's board of directors. Even as the company was declaring a 45 percent increase in profit for the year, Perrin's actions frightened nervous investors, and the company's stock value quickly dropped 20 percent. Although Perrin maintained the support of the company's chairman, Gary Pemberton, a number of prominent shareholders began to call for his ouster. Finally, in October, Perrin announced his resignation. In mid-November Billabong tapped Derek O'Neill, longtime head of the company's European operations, as Perrin's successor.

Entering 2003 Billabong's share value continued to decline steadily. In March the company's stock price dropped below AUD 5 per share, as earnings fell far short of the company's forecasts. Billabong's stock took another hit in August, when confidential internal documents were mysteriously leaked to several of the company's largest investors. The papers included an outline of weaker-than-expected sales projections and

hinted that founder Gordon Merchant was on the verge of selling his 22 percent ownership in the company. The company quickly denied the revelations, asserting that the information contained in the documents had been doctored. In spite of these refutations, the company's image among investors continued to suffer, and share values remained stagnant well into 2004.

By summer 2004 the company had found its bearing again as brisk orders and increased profits reassured shareholders. The bulk of the company's growth came in the United States, with sales in the region totaling AUD 229 million ($163.47 million) for 2003–04, an increase of 30 percent over the previous year. On the whole, the company enjoyed growth of 20 percent for the period and projected continued strong sales in the U.S. market. With the United States now accounting for 40 percent of Billabong's total revenues, maintaining growth in the region had become vital to the company's success.

GROWTH THROUGH ACQUISITION: 2005–10

Billabong continued to expand its global presence aggressively during the second half of the decade. In May 2005 the company announced that it would introduce a new line of footwear through its U.S. subsidiary, Element Skateboards. In December of that year Billabong acquired Nixon Inc., a U.S. watch and accessory maker, for AUD 97 million ($74.38 million). Billabong enjoyed record sales in 2005–06, surpassing the AUD 1 billion ($747.82 million) mark for the first time in the company's history. Of these revenues, more than half came from the United States, and another 20 percent came from Europe. Overall, sales in the United States rose nearly 33 percent for the year.

As its global business thrived, Billabong remained alert to new growth opportunities. In December 2007 the company acquired popular women's swimsuit brand Tigerlily, in the hope of increasing its share of the girl's and women's beachwear market. In July 2008 Billabong purchased Sector 9, a popular skateboard brand based in California; a month later the company expanded its winter clothing line when it acquired U.S. outerwear firm DaKine Hawaii. By late 2008, however, the company was hit by slumping global sales as the world economy slid into a recession. Even as sales grew to a record AUD 1.67 billion ($1.49 billion) for the year 2008–09, the company's profits fell more than 13 percent, to AUD 152.80 million ($137.06 million). Although strong Christmas sales helped the company rebound slightly at decade's end, its prospects remained uncertain in the face of what was proving to be a prolonged global downturn.

Mary Tradii
Updated, Stephen Meyer

PRINCIPAL SUBSIDIARIES

Amazon (New Zealand) Pty Ltd; Beach Culture International Pty Ltd; Billabong Retail, Inc. (USA); Burleigh Point Canada, Inc.; Burleigh Point, Ltd (USA); Element Skateboards, Inc. (USA); GSM (Central Sourcing) Pty Ltd; GSM (Duranbah) Pty Ltd; GSM (Europe) Pty Ltd; GSM (Japan) Limited; GSM (NZ Operations) Limited (New Zealand); GSM (Operations) Pty Ltd; GSM (Trademarks) Pty Ltd; GSM Trading (South Africa) Pty Ltd; GSM Brasil Ltda (Brazil); GSM England Retail Ltd; GSM Espana Operations Sociedad Limitada (Spain); GSM Investments Ltd (USA); GSM Rocket Australia Pty Ltd; GSM Trading (Singapore) Pty Ltd; Honolulu Surf International Ltd (USA); Nixon Europe SARL (France); Nixon Inc. (USA); Nixon Pacific Pty Ltd; Pineapple Trademarks Pty Ltd; Rocket Trademarks Pty Ltd; VeeZee, Inc. (USA).

PRINCIPAL COMPETITORS

The Burton Corporation; Hurley International LLC; Pacific Sunwear of California, Inc.; Quiksilver, Inc.; Rip Curl; Rusty International.

FURTHER READING

"Australia's Billabong Public Offer Closes after Strong Demand," *AsiaPulse News*, July 28, 2000.

"Billabong Founder on the Crest of a Wave as Firm Debuts on ASX," *AsiaPulse News*, August 11, 2000.

"Billabong's Rise Follows Pacific Sunwear," *Los Angeles Times*, March 8, 2001, p. 4.

Fraser, Andrew, "Billabong Chief Packs Swag and Walks the Plank," *Australian*, November 1, 2002, p. 21.

Lovett, Ian, "Leak Turns into a Tidal Wave of Trouble: Board Struggles to Contain 'Billabong-gate,'" *Daily Telegraph* (Sydney, Australia), August 7, 2003, p. 47.

Marlow, Michael, "Bob Hurley Giving Up Billabong's U.S. License," *Daily News Record*, June 10, 1998, p. 4.

Marriner, Cosima, "Billabong Catches Boomer," *Sydney Morning Herald*, August 12, 2000.

Ooi, Teresa, "Slump Leaves Billabong in the Doldrums," *Weekend Australian*, August 22, 2009, p. 29.

Rennie, Philip, "Meet the Chairman of the Surfboard," *Business Review Weekly*, December 1, 2000, p. 46.

Williamson, Rusty, "Billabong Catches U.S. Wave," *WWD*, June 3, 1999, p. 21.

Birks & Mayors Inc.

1240 Phillips Square
Montreal, Quebec H3B 3H4
Canada
Telephone: (+1 514) 397-2501
Fax: (+1 514) 397-2583
Web site: http://www.birksandmayors.com

Public Company
Founded: 1879
Incorporated: 2005 as Birks & Mayors Inc.
Employees: 935
Sales: $270.9 million (2009)
Stock Exchanges: NYSE Amex
Ticker Symbol: BMJ
NAICS: 334518 Watch, Clock, and Part Manufacturing;
    448310 Jewelry Stores; 339911 Jewelry, Precious
    Metal, Manufacturing; 332211 Cutlery and
    Flatware (Except Precious) Manufacturing; 454113
    Mail-Order Houses; 454111 Electronic Shopping

■ ■ ■

For more than a century, Birks & Mayors Inc. has made a premier name for itself in the luxury-goods market. Birks was founded in 1879. Mayors was established in 1983. A merger in 2005 enabled these firms to draw upon each company's strengths and develop brand-specific product lines and a uniform approach. Known for its distinctive aqua blue box, Birks has focused on selling fine jewelry, watches, sterling silver flatware and silver gifts, vintage jewelry, and designers' collections. Mayors' specialty has been luxury watches made by

Birks and other high-end designers, as well as custom-made jewelry. Both brands' stores have also offered appraisal, repair, and engraving services. In addition, a bridal registry has been a longtime component of the stores. During the 21st century, e-commerce became an adjunct to corporate sales and a mail-order business.

EARLY YEARS: 1879–1911

The origins of Birks go back to 1879, when Henry Birks opened his first jewelry shop in Montreal, Quebec. His father, too, had been a shopkeeper, working as a pharmacist. After graduating from high school, Henry Birks became an apprentice at Savage & Lyman, a well-known jewelry establishment in Montreal. Several years later, Birks's employer ran into financial difficulties. By that time, Birks was nearly 40 years old and had become a store manager. He used CAD $3,000 of his own money and began his own business.

Birks's parents were from Sheffield, an area of England known for its silversmiths. While part of his time at Savage & Lyman was spent learning the business of sales, merchandising, and customer service, he was also a silversmith's apprentice. In her profile of Birks in *American & European Jewelry, 1830–1914*, author Charlotte Gere noted, "[Birks'] trademark, a churchwarden's pipe, which is used on his best silver, was once that of a Birks ancestor, William, who made silver for Charles II." A trademark is a primary method by which appraisers and collectors can trace a piece's provenance and otherwise determine its value. In years to come, Birks' trademark would be joined by another mark used on all its packaging: a lion (calling to mind many of the

---

COMPANY PERSPECTIVES

The Birks & Mayors' mission is to deliver an unparalleled luxury brand experience through distinctively designed products crafted from quality materials and superior, personalized client service in a welcoming environment.

United Kingdom's symbols), shown above the company name, paired back-to-back with the letter *B*.

When his shop opened, Birks had a staff of three besides himself. According to Mark Kearney and Randy Ray in *I Know That Name!*, sales for the company's first year were CAD $30,000. A site for manufacturing jewelry was opened eight years later in Montreal. The facility brought Birks greater control over the quality of the rings, brooches, and watches he sold in his shop. In 1893 his sons, William M., John H., and Gerald W., became partners in the business. The company's new name reflected their involvement: Henry Birks & Sons Ltd.

In 1894 Birks & Sons moved to a newly built store with main offices. Designed by prominent architect Edward Maxwell, the headquarters and store were on St. Catherine Street's Phillips Square, an emerging core shopping district in Montreal. Seven years later, Birks opened its first store outside Montreal, in Ottawa, Ontario. Branching out to Ottawa was an indication of the influence of Birks's sons and their push for expansion. The company had more than 200 employees by 1904. Another headquarters and flagship store was built in 1911; the New Birks Building reoccupied the previous spot at Phillips Square.

THREE GENERATIONS OF OWNERSHIP

By 1923 Henry Birks and his family owned seven stores. According to Floyd Chalmers's article that year in a December issue of the *Financial Post*, "They operate stores under their own name in Halifax, Montreal, Ottawa, Winnipeg, Calgary, and Vancouver, and the Ryrie store in Toronto is owned almost outright." Chalmers added, "One of the grandsons, Henry G. Birks, is general manager of the business." The 83-year-old founder, all of his sons, and four of his nine grandchildren were focusing on jewelry and watch design, manufacturing, and sales.

In the 1920s Birks benefited from cross-border shopping. The Canadian government at the time did not assess a duty on unset diamonds and other precious stones entering Canada. As long as the stones were not placed into rings, pendants, or other settings, customers returning to the United States could avoid paying the 45 percent duty charged for set precious stones. Birks' mail-order business thrived at this time as well, due in part to customers in the United States who found Birks' price points more reasonable than those among comparable retailers elsewhere.

With seven stores (including locations in Montreal; Ottawa; Winnipeg, Manitoba; and Vancouver, British Columbia) in operation, increasing clientele from cross-border shoppers, and the mail-order business, Birks was experiencing a comfortable level of growth. In 1928, after a brief illness that forced him home from a trip to Florida, the founder Henry Birks died at the age of 87. Henry's son William became president of the company. William, his brothers, and many of their sons had already been responsible for day-to-day affairs of Birks, thus the staff at the main office and throughout the chain's stores included two more generations of Birks who already possessed extensive experience at running the jewelry business.

CHALLENGES AND STEADY GROWTH

One year after the company reached its 50th anniversary in 1929, worldwide depression put nearly all businesses in jeopardy. Sales of luxury goods tend to fall when consumers must watch their spending closely. Credit, a purchasing option for people with limited funds, became scarce during the 1930s. This, however, did not have much of an effect on Birks, as the firm's founder had set a tradition of always disdaining credit, preferring cash in all transactions. Despite the difficulties, William Birks and family managed to keep their company alive during this troublesome period.

Birks survived the Great Depression and the world war that followed, despite the shortage of raw materials that were being put to military use. The war's end in 1945 brought the return of servicemen and servicewomen and resulted in an uptick in marriages and births, and thus the need for engagement and wedding rings, wedding presents, and baby shower gifts.

More challenges ensued. Between 1949 and 1950, all three of the founder's sons died within months of each other. William's son Henry G. Birks became president of the company. His experience was quite broad; he had become the general manager in 1923. Even though the three deaths had a tremendous impact, the surviving family members' experiences in handling

```
┌─────────────────────────────────────────────────┐
│                                                   │
│                 KEY DATES                         │
│                                                   │
│                     ■                             │
│  ─────────────────────────────────────────────   │
│                                                   │
│  1879: Henry Birks opens his first jewelry shop in│
│        Montreal, Quebec.                          │
│  1893: The company's name becomes Henry Birks     │
│        & Sons Ltd.                                │
│  1901: Birks opens its first store outside Montreal.│
│  1928: Founder Henry Birks dies.                  │
│  1993: Italian firm Borgosesia acquires Birks.    │
│  2004: Birks opens a manufacturing plant in Rhode │
│        Island.                                    │
│  2005: Birks merges with Mayors Jewelers Inc.     │
│  2008: Canadian jewelry firm Brinkhaus is acquired.│
│                                                   │
└─────────────────────────────────────────────────┘
```

the tough Depression era gave the third generation of Birks the foundation for knowing how to proceed and prosper.

By 1972 the company had a total of 3,125 employees and three offices, in Montreal, Ottawa, and Vancouver. The Birks family was still at the helm. Henry G. Birks was the board chairman and remained in that role throughout the 1970s. Victor M. Birks was president and George D. Birks was vice president. As a century mark of doing business approached, the third and fourth generations of Birks directed their company's manufacture and retail of jewelry, silverware, and giftware.

GROWTH AND EXPANSION: THE EIGHTIES

The 1980s began with Birks having a total staff of 4,400 and main offices in Montreal and Ottawa. The Ottawa office held the holding company Henry Birks & Sons Ltd., while Henry Birks & Sons Montreal had become, at the same Phillips Square site as previously, a subsidiary. Five years later, Birks' staff had increased to 4,800. By the end of the decade, more than 5,700 employees worked for Birks, a 10-year rise of more than 30 percent. Sales for 1989 reached more than CAD $368 million.

By this time, the fourth and fifth generations of Birks were heading the company. In 1989 H. Jonathan Birks was president and T. M. and Barrie D. Birks were board members. The company's organization had changed. Henry Birks & Fils ("Sons" in English) Lim-itée of Montreal had become a subsidiary of Henry Birks Canada Inc. (Montreal). Henry Birks & Sons Ltd. (Ottawa) and Henry Birks Canada Inc. were holding companies. In the December 13, 1999, issue of the Tor-

onto magazine *Maclean's*, Brenda Branswell wrote that Birks "owned 220 stores at its peak in the 1980s, a period when it sold fashion jewelry and offered discount pricing." The Birks chain of the 1980s contrasted distinctly with the Birks chain of the founder's time. Just how much change had occurred would soon become evident.

SUBSIDIARIES AND RECESSION: 1990–93

A recession in the early 1990s made optimism difficult for the 220-store chain as consumers reined in their spending, profit margins went down, and the Canadian dollar weakened. Contrarily, the last development somewhat brightened the winter holidays retail season, always a time crucial for jewelers. In 1992 Canadian consumers took fewer cross-border shopping trips, exercising their limited buying power in Canada. Weddings and births also continued to offer retail opportunities, even in a recession.

Two developments challenged the company further. During the early 1990s Jonathan Birks conducted a buyout of his brothers' shares of stock. Although the company had considered a sale in 1990 of 40 of its stores in the United States to a Dallas-based firm, the deal did not go through. The 40 stores, in cities such as Washington, D.C.; Minneapolis, Minnesota; and Boston, were part of the Birks subsidiaries Shreve, Crump & Low of Boston and Henry Birks Jewelers Inc. of Minneapolis. Had the sale of stores been completed, it could have given Birks enough revenue to take care of a multimillion-dollar loan the company needed to repay to the Royal Bank of Canada. Instead, partly as a consequence of the family buyout and partly as a consequence of maintaining ownership of more than 200 stores, the company was experiencing significant indebtedness.

NEW OWNERSHIP, NEW LEADERSHIP: 1993–2004

In 1993 the Italian firm Borgosesia Acquisitions Corporation (which later became known as Regaluxe Investment S.a.r.l.) acquired Birks. The company was allowed to keep its original, family-based name because of its esteemed reputation. The positive name association had the potential for increased sales. After five generations, however, the Birks family's direct involvement with the company ended.

The acquisition was known as "rescue financing" which enabled Birks to avoid the bankruptcy protection it previously had applied for. Guiding the acquisition was Lorenzo Rossi di Montelera. A profile of Rossi by writer Jim Tobler appeared in the Autumn 2006 issue of *Nuvo*: "Dr. Rossi has been in the luxury business for a long time. He has been part of Regaluxe Investment … since he began his career." Some of his career was spent with Martini & Rossi, an Italian manufacturer perhaps best known for its brands of vermouth. After the acquisition, Rossi became board chairman and was instrumental in keeping the Birks name and hiring the company's next leader.

In 1996 Thomas Andruskevich, formerly of Tiffany's, became Birks' president and CEO. Andruskevich developed a strategic plan in 1999 that included a much-needed $30 million renovation of the interior and exterior of most of the 36 Canadian Birks stores. In 2000 the company sold its headquarters and flagship store in Montreal, deciding to lease the property.

In 2002 Birks bought more than 70 percent controlling interest in Mayors Jewelers Inc. This Florida-based firm, which also had stores in Georgia, had undergone some challenges of its own. A significant amount of its product lines was made for the wholesaler Sam's Clubs, as well as other similar sellers. These firms were considering handling their own manufacturing and marketing of jewelry, which would result in a loss of business for Mayors. Birks' controlling investment suggested interest in steering Mayors toward the higher-end of the jewelry business.

Two years later, Birks announced the opening of a manufacturing site in Woonsocket, Rhode Island, long known as a region where jewelry designers and silversmiths studied and created (it was also near to a plant owned by Tiffany's). The Rhode Island School of Design, located in Providence, had acquired a strong reputation for its metalworking, silversmith, and other jewelry courses. Also, the choice demonstrated Birks' commitment to increase its design and manufacture capabilities, which would, with Mayors' participation, upgrade the latter retailer's product development as well.

MERGER, IPO, AND REBIRTH: 2005–09

In 2005 Henry Birks & Sons Ltd. merged with Mayors Jewelers Inc., becoming Birks & Mayors Inc. The newly merged company underwent stock conversion of outstanding shares of Mayors stock and had an initial public offering (IPO), trading on the American Stock Exchange. At the time Birks & Mayors Inc. became a publicly held Canadian corporation, the company had 38 Birks stores in Canada, while 28 stores in Florida and Georgia carried the Mayors name. Net sales for 2005 were more than CAD $239 million, up 10.5 percent from the previous year.

In other noteworthy events, in 2008, not long after the company was named the official supplier of jewelry and commemorative items for the 2010 Winter Olympic Games in Vancouver, Birks acquired the Canadian jewelry firm Brinkhaus. Owned by Norbert Brinkhaus, a designer who specialized in diamonds, the acquisition might have seemed minor. The purchase added only two stores to the Birks' chain, one in Calgary, Alberta, and one in Vancouver. In 2000, however, Norbert Brinkhaus and fellow Calgarian Dieter Huebner had wowed crowds at an international diamonds show in Paris when a 2,000-diamond necklace they had designed was singled out for exhibition.

At the midpoint of 2009 Birks & Mayors had 69 retail locations, which were operating under the Birks and the Brinkhaus brand names in all major cities in Canada and the Mayors name in Florida and Georgia. Consolidation efforts for that year resulted in about 100 fewer employees than in 2008. Additionally, the plant in Rhode Island was closed in 2009. Steps were taken to focus more intensively on the computer-aided design and computer-aided manufacturing components of the company's facilities in Quebec.

In 2009, 95 percent of sales occurred through in-store retailing, with the rest obtained through the Internet, corporate sales, and other means, although online sales were growing in importance. In the stores, the well-trained, knowledgeable sales associates and the company's reputation for outstanding service and jewelry and watch design served Birks and its sister brands Mayors and Brinkhaus well.

Mary C. Lewis

PRINCIPAL SUBSIDIARIES

Mayor's Jewelers Inc.; Mayor's Jewelers of Florida Inc.; Mayor's Jewelers Intellectual Property Holding Co.; JBM Retail Company Inc.; Jan Bell Marketing/Puerto Rico Inc.; JBM Venture Company Inc.; Henry Birks & Sons U.S. Inc.

PRINCIPAL COMPETITORS

Cartier S.A.; LVMH Moët Hennessy Louis Vuitton S.A.; Tiffany & Co.

FURTHER READING

"Birks & Mayors Announces Acquisition of Brinkhaus," *Business Wire*, November 8, 2007.

"Birks & Mayors to Merge," *Jewelers Circular Keystone*, June 2005, p. 51.

"Birks and Mayor's to Open R.I. Facility," *South Florida Business Journal*, August 2, 2004.

"Birks Says It Will Keep U.S. Stores," *Financial Post Daily*, October 17, 1990, p. 24.

Branswell, Brenda, "Polishing Up Birks," *Maclean's*, December 13, 1999, pp. 43+.

Brown, Barry, "Diamonds Now Being Mined in Canada's Far North Territory," *Buffalo (NY) News*, December 29, 1998, p. A5.

Chalmers, Floyd B., "Sixty-six Years in Business Is the Record of Henry Birks," *Financial Post*, December 7, 1923, p. 10.

Dunn, Brian, and Melanie Kletter, "Birks Creates Blueprint for Mayor's," *WWD*, September 30, 2002, p. 18.

Gere, Charlotte, *American & European Jewelry, 1830–1914*, New York: Crown, 1975, pp. 151–52.

Giovis, Jaclyn, "Cartier, Tiffany's—and Mayors: Florida Chain's Owners Seek Niche at Top of Jewelry Business," *Knight-Ridder/Tribune Business News*, November 11, 2006, p. 1.

Gournay, Isabelle, and France Vanlaethem, eds., *Montreal Metropolis, 1880–1930*. Toronto: Canadian Centre for Architecture and Stoddart Publishing, 1998, pp. 83, 101, 159–60, 193.

Hood, Sarah B., "Reputation in a Blue Box," *Canadian Jeweller*, August 2008, pp. 74–79.

Kearney, Mark, and Randy Ray, *I Know That Name!: The People behind Canada's Best-Known Brand Names*, Toronto: Hounslow Book, 2002, pp. 42–44.

McMurdy, Deirdre, and Diane Brady, "Banking on Bliss," *Maclean's*, June 28, 1993, pp. 40–41.

"Milky Way of Diamonds (Calgarians Design Necklace Featured at the De Beer's Diamonds International Show 2000 in Paris)," *Report Newsmagazine*, February 7, 2000, p. 3.

Schupak, Hedda T., "Merge Right," *Jewelers Circular Keystone*, February 1, 2008, p. 84.

Tobler, Jim, "Brand (New) Loyalty, Count Lorenzo Rossi Brings Birks Back to the Top," *Nuvo*, Autumn 2006, pp. 56–65.

Wickens, Barbara, "Better Tidings," *Maclean's*, December 21, 1992, pp. 18–19.

Boston Apparel Group

35 United Drive
West Bridgewater, Massachusetts 02379
U.S.A.
Telephone: (508) 583-8110
Toll Free: (800) 525-6650
Fax: (508) 588-7994
Web site: www.chadwicks.com
Web site: www.metrostyle.com

Wholly Owned Subsidiary of Monomoy Capital Partners, L.P.
Founded: 1983 as Chadwick's of Boston
Incorporated: 1983
Employees: 445
Sales: $300 million (2008)
NAICS: 45411 Electronic Shopping & Mail-Order Houses

■ ■ ■

Chadwick's of Boston was launched in 1983 as the first "off-price" catalog company, offering women's fashion apparel of the same quality found in department and specialty stores but at much lower prices. A quarter of a century later, Chadwick's became the Boston Apparel Group, which operated the Chadwick's brand, catalog, and Internet retail operation, along with that of metrostyle, which targets women sizes 4–20 through misses, petite, and tall varieties. Since July 2008 Boston Apparel has been owned by New York private equity firm Monomoy Capital Partners, L.P., which acquired the Chadwick's and metrostyle operations from Redcats Group

Inc., a business unit of the French multinational PPR, S.A. In 2010 Monomoy acquired a third catalog and Internet retailer for Boston Apparel, Casual Living. Boston Apparel had 445 employees in Taunton and West Bridgewater, Massachusetts.

EMERGING IN THE EIGHTIES

Chadwick's of Boston made its debut in 1983 as an off-price mail-order company offering specialty women's apparel brand names and prices similar to those in the Zayre Corp.'s Hit or Miss chain of stores. Hit or Miss outlets were at the time selling brand name apparel at 20 to 50 percent off regular prices, and the close correspondence between Hit or Miss merchandise and that offered in Chadwick's catalogs allowed customers to handle and judge the products before trusting to catalog shopping from home. Originally considered an experimental project, Chadwick's had sales of $3 million in fiscal 1984 (the year ended in January 1984), $21 million in 1985, and $24 million in 1986, when Zayre's management decided that Chadwick's had achieved its goals and had proven a viable operation.

In 1987 Zayre spun off its off-price segment, consisting of its T. J. Maxx, Hit or Miss, and Chadwick's of Boston units, to a new subsidiary named The TJX Companies, Inc. As a division of TJX, Chadwick's function remained to feature off-price specialty items of women's apparel, much of which was also carried in the Hit or Miss stores, at prices significantly below conventional retailers and other mail-order catalogs. These items were said to consist of first quality, current fashion and classic merchandise, including sportswear,

---

COMPANY PERSPECTIVES

Great style doesn't have to be expensive. Chadwicks makes looking your best possible with the latest trends tailored to a flattering fit, then we keep the prices low so you can always look current while staying on a budget.

What is metrostyle? Fashion that will turn heads. Prices that won't bat an eye.

---

casual wear, dresses, suits, and accessories, in a mix of brand names and private labels. The clothing targeted 20- to 50-year-old women, including housewives as well as career women, who were interested in moderately to upper-moderately priced merchandise. Chadwick's delivered 23.7 million catalogs in 1987, an increase of 35 percent over the previous year. The division also developed an independent merchandising group during this time.

Chadwick's of Boston's sales grew from $33 million in 1987 to $43 million in 1988 and $47 million in 1989, when TJX's annual report declared that the division was selling "moderately-priced merchandise substantially below regular department store prices to a customer whose profile is similar to that of the Hit or Miss customer." This report said that the size of a typical Chadwick's catalog was about 56 pages and that nine mailings had been made during the fiscal year, including a focus book, or smaller book highlighting the best-selling items. About 35 percent of the goods sold were private label and 65 percent branded.

Chadwick's mailed 39 million catalogs during 1989. The TJX division also moved its base of operations from Stoughton, Massachusetts, to a new 175,000-square-foot fulfillment center in West Bridgewater. This state-of-the-art facility offered the long-term capacity of shipping four million orders per year. In addition, Chadwick's developed an independent buying staff for the organization.

Chadwick's fall 1989 catalog was redesigned to offer a more fashionable, visually appealing, and lifestyle-oriented presentation. Management considered the results encouraging and carried the new design into the winter and holiday catalogs, both of which were deemed successful. In response to what TJX's annual report called "the extremely promotional retail environment as well as specific promotions by other apparel catalogs," Chadwick's also successfully introduced an end-of-

season promotional sales catalog. In addition, during 1989 the division conducted market research in order to keep abreast of shifts in customer lifestyles. The number of Chadwick's catalogs reached 50 million in 1989. Sales in 1990 (the year ended January 27, 1990) reached $77 million.

DRAMATIC GROWTH: 1990–96

The calendar year 1990 was marked by dramatic expansion and other changes. Chadwick's mailed catalogs 20 times for a total distribution of about 67 million catalogs. TJX's annual report described it as "America's first company to offer the off-price concept in women's apparel nationally through the convenience of a mail-order catalog." The Chadwick's target customer was now described as the working woman between age 20 and 45, a group of women "who are interested in attractively priced merchandise and who enjoy the convenience of catalog shopping." A heavy focus was placed on career wear, including current fashions and classic styles in dresses and suits. Weekend apparel was also featured, and Chadwick's increased its assortment in petite sizes. Net sales reached $112.7 million in 1991.

During 1991 Chadwick's reported "resounding success" in shifting its focus quickly in response to an increase in demand for casual wear by mailing a casual wear focus book. The company also reported improvement in order fulfillment through better forecasting and more aggressive buying and further strengthened product quality-control programs, leading to reduced merchandise returns. Moreover, Chadwick's purchased its formerly leased West Bridgewater facility. Sales totaled $173.4 million in 1992, an increase of 56 percent over the previous year. Operating income rose by 44 percent, despite considerable increases in postal and United Parcel Service costs, as well as a national economic recession.

During this time Chadwick's took steps to improve its merchandise quality, an initiative it was hoped would attract more customers and reduce the volume of returned merchandise. The company also increased its telemarketing capacity and upgraded the existing system to improve the ordering process. This quality assurance program also focused on ensuring that merchandise orders were packed correctly. Finally, the company began test-marketing a line of menswear. Distribution capacity at Chadwick's more than doubled with the expansion of its fulfillment center from 175,000 square feet to more than 400,000 square feet. Chadwick's sales reached $291 million in 1993.

By the end of 1994 Chadwick's had added menswear to some of its catalog offerings and had

KEY DATES

1983: Zayre Company creates Chadwick's of Boston as a mail order company selling women's apparel.

1987: Zayre consolidates its off-price stores and catalogs, including Chadwick's, into a new subsidiary, The TJX Companies, Inc.

1996: TJX announces the sale of Chadwick's to Brylane LP for an estimated $328 million.

1999: Pinault-Printemps-Redoute S.A. completes the purchase of Brylane through its Redcats subsidiary.

2007: The company Chadwick's, renamed Boston Apparel Group, begins incorporating designs developed in house into its Chadwick's, metrostyle, and Jessica London brands and catalogs.

2008: Redcats sells Boston Apparel Group to Monomoy Capital Partners, L.P., a New York-based private equity firm.

2010: Monomoy acquires Casual Living U.S.A., Inc., a catalog and Internet retailer, and announces Casual Living's fulfillment, marketing, merchandising, and sourcing will be moved into Boston Apparel Group's existing operations.

expanded its offerings in large and petite sizes for women. Its target customers again included homemakers as well as career women. A further expansion of the fulfillment center completed that year brought the West Bridgewater facility to 676,000 square feet of space, while the company also leased 127,000 square feet nearby for offices and warehouse space. The Chadwick's customer database was proving valuable to its parent company, providing data for TJX's store siting, micro-marketing, and promotional strategies. Chadwick's also was planning a new catalog bearing the Cosmopolitan name, of magazine fame, geared toward young working women and offering the latest fashion trends at affordable prices.

A 1995 *Discount Store News* article declared that "Chadwick's appeals to the customer who needs to dress like she got it at Talbot's, but whose budget is more sensitive to discount values." Chadwick's sales volume grew so rapidly in 1994 (passing more than $420 million for 1995) that it experienced difficulty in filling orders. As a result, sales barely grew the next year, and

profits fell from 4 to 3 percent of revenues, and then to a nominal level.

Nevertheless, Chadwick's rebounded in 1996, registering sales of $472.4 million, operating profit of $26.6 million, and net income of $8.3 million. In fact, its operating profit made up about 84 percent of parent TJX's profit that year. The cataloger's fulfillment rate (the percentage of customers who actually received the apparel they wanted to order) improved significantly during this time. Because of rising paper costs, however, Chadwick's reduced its mailings by more than 16 percent, to 196 million catalogs.

TJX, in order to focus attention on its store-based retailing and pay down some of its debt, decided in 1996 to spin off Chadwick's of Boston as a separate company. Its plan was to sell 61 percent of the company in a $158-million initial public stock offering. The prospectus called Chadwick's "the nation's first and largest catalog retailer of off-price women's apparel," concentrating on careers, casual, and social wear at prices 25 to 50 percent below regular department stores. The company's six million active customers were said to be typically "middle- to upper-middle-income women between the age of 25 and 55." (The company had narrowed the upper limit of its target customer's age to 50 years in 1995.) Chadwick's also began publishing Bridgewater, a new catalog that included men's as well as women's off-price apparel.

A BRYLANE SUBSIDIARY: 1997

In July 1996 TJX postponed plans to spin off Chadwick's, citing a recent downturn in the stock market as exercising a dampening effect on new issues. Three months later, instead, it announced plans to sell the company to Brylane LP for an estimated $328 million in cash, notes, and receivables. Brylane, a rival catalog company, had an annual sales volume one-third larger than that of Chadwick's and specialized in plus-sized apparel for women as well as big-and-tall apparel for men. Interviewed for *Catalog Age* by Melissa Dowling, Brylane chairman and chief executive officer Peter Canzone observed that both enterprises had been "going after the same value-oriented apparel catalog customer" and added that "Chadwick's has some of the best merchandise negotiators in the catalog business."

Brylane made its initial public offering the following year, becoming Brylane Inc., while its new acquisition, Chadwick's of Boston, retained its identity as an independent subsidiary still based in West Bridgewater, Massachusetts. In March 1997 Chadwick's introduced the Jessica London catalog, a new catalog for larger-sized women. Two million copies were mailed to potential customers derived from a mailing list of those who had purchased larger-size clothing from Brylane in the past. A Chadwick's executive told Shannon Oberndorf in *Catalog Age*, "We've been building up our plus-size file for the past year after seeing the growth in orders of our regularly featured large sizes. We're not trying to go after the Brylane customer, but targeting a segment of our own buyers." The Jessica London catalog offered prices sharply below those of department and specialty stores and targeted younger, career-oriented women sizes 14W to 26W.

Under its new ownership, the Chadwick's catalog continued to target women between the ages of 25 and 55 who wore regular-sized apparel (sizes 4 to 20.) In addition, Chadwick's had expanded its merchandise offerings to target women who wore petite and special-size apparel (sizes 2 to 26). Private labels, including brand names such as Savannah, Fads, Stephanie Andrews, and JL Plum, accounted for 53 percent of Chadwick's net sales in 1997. Men's and children's apparel, women's special-size apparel, and accessories, gifts, and cosmetics (tested and offered on a limited basis) accounted for 22 percent of net sales. The company offered 73,000 stock keeping units (SKU) of merchandise at an average of about $27. The average order was $87. In its 1997 annual report, Brylane described Chadwick's market segment as about one-third, or 33 million, of all U.S. adult women. The medium age of the Chadwick's customer was said to be 42, with typical income equal to, or above, the national average.

Chadwick's announced plans in August 1997 to build a 330,000-square-foot distribution and customer-service center in an industrial park in Taunton, where the company had received property tax concessions. A portion of the company's ready-to-wear women's apparel catalog operations was moved to this location in the spring of the following year. The remainder of Chadwick's operations were still located in the Boston suburb of West Bridgewater. The company's overstock was marketed through retail outlet stores in Brockton, Massachusetts, and Nashua, New Hampshire.

PURCHASED BY REDCATS

By this time, Brylane was the largest specialty catalog retailer of value-priced apparel in the United States. It underwent a change of ownership the following year, when Pinault-Printemps-Redoute S.A., the Paris-based specialty retailer, purchased 49.9 percent of Brylane through Redcats, a subsidiary that was the world's third-largest mail order house. PPR completed the acquisition in March 1999, when it tendered for the balance of Brylane's shares.

Chadwick's cleared away a lingering legal dispute the same year when, as part of a group that included Polo Ralph Lauren Corp., Phillips-Van Heusen Corp., and Donna Karan International Inc., it agreed to accept independent monitoring of factories it used and contribute to a fund to compensate workers at factories in the Marianas Islands. The companies were due to be named as defendants in a class-action lawsuit filed by Sweatshop Watch, Global Exchange, UNITE (the Union of Needletrades, Industrial and Textile Employees), which also represented workers at Chadwick's West Bridgewater facility, and 70,000 garment workers in the Marianas. The lawsuit was one of three that accused American companies of "racketeering conspiracy" with contractors to use indentured labor on the Marianas island of Saipan.

PPR, meanwhile, had made its first move to build on the Chadwick's brand with the March launch of Real Comfort, a new casual wear catalog. "Chadwicks has been a careerwear catalog," Brylane CEO Peter Canzone told Robert Spiegel in *Catalog Age*. "But that customer has a need for casualwear appropriate for dress-down Fridays and off-work time." Real Comfort would mail four times a year starting in 2000.

A national recession and declining sales, however, were catching up with Chadwick's, and in April 2001 it announced that it would cut 20 percent of its workforce, or 300 jobs, at its order fulfillment centers in West Bridgewater and Taunton. Diane Caroselli, vice president of human resources, told Greg Gatlin in the *Boston Herald* that the layoffs stemmed from "concerns about slowing consumer sales" and "the uncertainty of future sales." Shortly thereafter, Brylane reorganized itself into three divisions: Special Size Group, Brylane Home Lifestyles Group, and Misses Apparel Group, the latter including Chadwick's, Jessica London, and Lerner, a casual wear catalog.

Chadwick's was also joining the pay-for-performance trend in its advertising strategy. Starting in 2000, it instituted a new model whereby it paid a commission to its advertiser only when a customer actually bought merchandise or requested a catalog. The new model went into effect when Chadwick's retained Chicago-based Performics to run its online advertising program. The pay-for-performance approach paid off quickly. As Chadwick's officials told Ann Meyer in *Catalog Age*, revenue from the Performics program rose 30 percent a month and overall online transactions rose 700 percent, while the average amount per order increased by 9 percent.

Despite this success, Brylane was working hard to redefine itself in the challenging post-recession market. In 2003 it closed its Indianapolis call center, which served many of the other catalogs in its portfolio, eliminating 415 jobs. Some of the savings would be used to improve productivity at Chadwick's call center in West Bridgewater, Brylane's new CEO, Russell Stravitz, told Paul Miller in *Catalog Age.* By this time, well over 20 percent of its total orders were coming from the Internet. Brylane also launched an initiative to reenergize its catalog books, adding, for example, a "Priority Report" to the Chadwick's fall 2003 book, which highlighted must-have items among its T-shirt, blazer, and ribbed sweater offerings.

Two years later Brylane, now renamed Redcats USA in an effort to strengthen PPR's global catalog brand, launched a new catalog through Chadwick's, titled Intimate Promise. The new, six-times-a-year book would sell plus-size lingerie, sleepwear, and swimsuits, including some items found in other Redcats titles. The expansion continued a month later, in February 2005, with the debuts of Brylane Catalog Outlet and Chadwick's Catalog Outlet, which sold discounted items from the company's other catalogs.

Another sign that the catalog business was reshaping itself came in April, when Redcats announced that it was closing its call center in West Bridgewater, eliminating 200 jobs, mostly year-round customer service representatives. Laura Chappell, senior vice president for customer relations at Redcats, told Jon Chesto in the *Patriot Ledger* that the cuts were due to concerns over high labor costs in Massachusetts and the difficulty of recruiting workers for call centers in the area. That left slightly more than 1,000 total employees in Chadwick's two sites in that town and in Taunton. The call center operations were consolidated with Redcats centers in El Paso and San Antonio, Texas. By then, nearly 35 percent of Redcats USA's sales took place over the Internet.

The importance of online sales was underscored in 2006, when Chadwick's revamped its Web site, part of an initiative by Redcats to improve its Web presence worldwide. "With the improved design of this website," Christophe Gaigneux, executive vice president of Chadwick's, said in a press release, "it will continue to transition the Chadwick's business and create a more comfortable and enjoyable online shopping experience for loyal customers, as well as capture a new share of the market."

As a company, Chadwick's morphed into a series of names (the Missy Group, then the Women's Apparel Group) before settling in as the Boston Apparel Group, retaining the Chadwick's name for the merchandise line. At this time the company was bringing design in-house, in an effort to identify its catalogs with fashion as well as discount prices. It set up a new design department in its West Bridgewater headquarters in late 2006 to create

all garment designs for the Chadwick's catalog as well as for the Lerner (renamed metrostyle) and Jessica London books. Boston Design Studio, a new line designed in-house and aimed at younger, contemporary-minded shoppers, was set to appear in the Chadwick's catalog starting in fall 2007, the *Boston Herald* reported.

BOUGHT BY PRIVATE EQUITY FIRM

Boston Apparel's parent company commenced its own change of direction. In January 2008 Redcats acquired United Retail Group Inc., a U.S. specialty retailer offering large-sized women's fashions. The purchase was part of a shift to focus more on special sizes and sports and leisure brands. Weeks later, reported Demitri Diakontonis in *The Deal,* Redcats began shopping around Boston Apparel Group, including Chadwick's, metrostyle, and the Brockton and Nashua outlet stores. In July Redcats announced the sale of the unit to Monomoy Capital Partners, L.P., a New York-based private equity firm with a broad portfolio of middle-market companies employing more than 5,000 people. The company was renamed Women's Apparel Group, LLC, but would do business as Boston Apparel Group.

Monomoy named Chas Hepler as CEO and David Myles as COO, both from SD Retail Consulting, Inc., a firm that advises on direct retail businesses. Acknowledging that Boston Apparel Group's customer base had been declining for some years, Hepler said he wanted to leverage Chadwick's well-known name to earn back its former customers. New management's plans included fixing inventory problems and streamlining catalog mailings. As of July 2008, Boston Apparel Group employed approximately 500 team members and generated more than $300 million in annual sales.

While no layoffs were planned initially, in May 2009 the company closed the Brockton overstock store and announced that the other, in Nashua, would close as well. The following February, Monomoy announced it had acquired Casual Living U.S.A., Inc., a catalog and Internet retailer based in Tampa, Florida, that sells casual wear for women between the ages of 45 and 60. Monomoy planned to move Casual Living's fulfillment, marketing, merchandising, and sourcing into Boston Apparel Group's existing operations.

"We are excited to add the Casual Living brand to the Boston Apparel family," Myles said in a 2010 press release. "In a difficult retail environment, the addition of Casual Living will substantially expand Boston Apparel's unique ability to provide customers with the right products at the right prices every day." A Monomoy official further stated in the press release, "Boston Apparel is now perfectly positioned to acquire additional brands and products that leverage its existing infrastructure and provide its customers with more choices and better value."

Robert Halasz
Updated, Eric Laursen

PRINCIPAL DIVISIONS

Chadwick's; metrostyle; Casual Living.

PRINCIPAL COMPETITORS

HSN, Inc.; J.C. Penney Company, Inc.; J. Crew Group, Inc.; Lands' End, Inc.; LL Bean, Inc.

FURTHER READING

Bailey, Steve, and Steven Syre, "Chadwick's Preparing Its IPO in Buyer's Market," *Boston Globe*, May 24, 1996, p. 52.

Bushnell, Davis, "Tax Incentives Draw Complaints," *Boston Globe*, January 11, 1998, p. 10.

Chesto, Jon, "200 Jobs Leaving W. Bridgewater; Catalog Retailer Redcats Blames High Labor Costs in Mass.," *Patriot Ledger*, April 28, 2005.

Cochrane, Thomas M., "Catalog Couture," *Barron's*, February 10, 1997, p. 53.

Del franco, Mark, "Brylane: How a Big Fish Is Getting Bigger," *Multichannel Merchant*, December 1, 2003.

Diakantonis, Demitri, "Monomoy Acquires Missy Group," *The Deal*, July 29, 2008.

Dowling, Melissa, "A Fitting Acquisition," *Catalog Age*, December 1996, p. 6.

Gatlin, Greg, "Chadwick's to Cut 300 Jobs Due to Slow Sales," *Boston Herald*, April 11, 2001.

"Mail Order Proves a Strategic Fit," *Discount Store News*, February 20, 1995, p. 20.

Meyer, Ann, "For Chadwicks', Pay-for-Performance Pays Off," *Catalog Age*, March 15, 2002.

Miller, Paul, "Brylane to Close Indianapolis Call Center," *Catalog Age*, May 1, 2003.

"Monomoy Is New Owner of Casual Living," *Tampa Bay Business Journal*, February 16, 2010.

Oberndorf, Shannon, "A Plus-Size Chadwick's," *Catalog Age*, June 1997, p. 12.

Radsken, Jill, "Chadwick's Chic: Frenchman Adds Soupcon of Style to Mass.-based Clothing Co.," *Boston Herald*, April 25, 2007.

Reidy, Chris, "TJX to Sell Chadwick's for $328m to Brylane," *Boston Globe*, October 22, 1996, p. C2.

Sloan, Allison, "The Unsavory World of Sweatshops," *Mothering*, January 1, 2000.

Spiegel, Robert, "Real Comfort," *Catalog Age*, January 1, 2000.

Wilson, Jeff, "Settlement to Mean Monitoring of Saipan Garment Shops," Associated Press, August 10, 1999.

Bridgelux, Inc.

1170 Sonora Court
Sunnyvale, California 94086
U.S.A.
Telephone: (408) 990-7500
Fax: (408) 990-7501
Web site: http://www.bridgelux.com

Private Company
Founded: 2002 as eLite Optoelectronics Inc.
Employees: 85 (est.)
NAICS: 423690 Other Electronic Parts and Equipment
    Merchant Wholesalers

■ ■ ■

Based in Sunnyvale, California, Bridgelux, Inc., is one of the world's leading developers and manufacturers of solid-state lighting (SSL), making use of light-emitting diode (LED) technology that will very likely transform the lighting industry, which has been dominated by energy-inefficient incandescent bulbs for more than a century. Bridgelux is one of only three vertically integrated LED manufacturers in the United States, controlling important intellectual property in core material technology, chip design, packaging technology, system technology, and manufacturing. The company offers LED Array products, an arrangement of LED lights for use in environments where lights are always on, including commercial, industrial, and hospitality settings. Bridgelux also sells LED chips to other companies for embedding into a variety of products,

such as cameras, signage, and cars. The company's corporate offices and manufacturing facilities are located in two separate Sunnyvale locations.

ELITE OPTOELECTRONICS INC.

Heng Liu founded the company in December 2002 in City of Industry, California, as eLite Optoelectronics Inc. During its first year of operation, eLite invested in Epitaxy technology, used to deposit a thin layer of crystals over a crystal substrate in semiconductors. By the end of 2003, the company had released its first Indium Tin Oxide (ITO) LED chip and received its initial funding.

In 2004 eLite made its first volume shipment of its high-power LED chip, many of which were used in camera-phone flashes as well as in signs and automobiles. The company pursued a "fab-less" business model, making use of Asia's existing high-volume indium gallium nitride (InGaN) LED production capacity to focus its efforts on design. ELite also applied for six U.S. patents related to InGaN LED chip design and device structure, and in March 2005 it received its first patent for a high-power, AllnGaN (aluminum indium gallium nitride)-based, multichip, light-emitting diode.

A NEW CEO

With eLite's operations successfully underway, the company brought in a new chief executive to serve as eLite's public face and to focus on growing the company, allowing Liu to serve as chief technology officer. In July 2005 Robert C. Walker took over as

COMPANY PERSPECTIVES

Bridgelux is the first, new US-based light-emitting diode (LED) manufacturer in the past 20 years. The Company's focus is bringing innovation to light by providing high power, energy-efficient and cost-effective LED solutions. Bridgelux actively supports its customers by delivering value-added, application-specific solutions that will open up new markets in solid-state lighting (SSL). Customers leverage Bridgelux's technology to replace traditional lamp and luminaire technologies (such as incandescent, halogen and fluorescent lighting solutions) with solid-state products that provide high performance and energy-efficient white light for the fast growing interior and exterior application areas such as street lights, track and downlights. Bridgelux's current and future-generation products support global clean energy initiatives by reducing energy consumption and offering environmentally friendly solutions for general lighting applications.

CEO, having served on the company's board of directors since August of the previous year. Soon after Walker took charge at eLite, the company moved its headquarters from City of Industry to Sunnyvale, California, where it also established a research and development center.

In April 2006 Walker oversaw a round of venture capital funding and raised $8.5 million from three California-based firms, Doll Capital Management, El Dorado Ventures, and Harris & Harris Group. Concurrently the company changed its name to Bridgelux, Inc. Later in 2006 Bridgelux released its BKO series LED chip, but soon found itself the subject of a patent infringement lawsuit filed by Cree Inc., a leader in LED technology. Cree charged that Bridgelux had violated a pair of its patents, one related to light extraction structures used in LEDs and the other to technology licensed from Boston University to Cree on an exclusive basis that involved semiconductor devices using a buffer technology based on gallium nitride (GaN).

MKO CHIP RELEASED

Despite the litigation, Bridgelux continued to grow, and in 2007 it released the MKO series LED chip. Also in 2007 Walker stepped aside, although he remained a

member of the senior management team and a board member, and Mark Swoboda took his place as CEO. A month later Bridgelux completed a third round of financing, raising $23 million from previous investors as well as newcomer Chrysalix Energy Venture Capital.

With ample cash in hand, Bridgelux now looked to build a manufacturing plant in the United States to not only bring production closer to its researchers but to also better protect its intellectual property. Bridgelux opened a state-of-the-art manufacturing site in Sunnyvale in 2008, which conducted volume production of its sixth-generation LED chip. Finding a larger-scale facility to ramp-up production when demand accelerated as expected proved more difficult, however. While California had plenty of former chip facilities, many were in a state of disrepair. Bridgelux desired to keep production in the United States, but its investors hesitated because of the high costs involved.

FOURTH FUNDING ROUND

Bridgelux also expanded its research and development center in 2008 and raised more money in a fourth round of funding. All told, the company received $30 million in private equity investment and another $10 million in bank lines of credit. The fourth round was led by a new investor, VentureTech Alliance, and joined by Doll Capital Management, El Dorado Ventures, Harris & Harris Group, and Chrysalix Energy Venture Capital. The money was earmarked for product development and market expansion.

Also in 2008 Bridgelux introduced a new LED array product line for use in SSL and other applications. The arrays were available in warm-, neutral-, and cool-white color temperatures and ranged from 400 to 2,000 lumens. Bridgelux continued to sell LED chips to third-party packaging houses, which in turn sold them to original equipment manufacturers and other customers. By offering the arrays, the company hoped to reduce design and system costs and open new markets for LED lighting applications. Essentially the arrays were plug-and-play devices that could be incorporated into a variety of lighting products. Bridgelux priced the arrays from one-to-two cents per lumen, depending on volume, far less than the two-to-six cents per lumen of the competitive LED-based emitter products.

At the end of 2008 Bridgelux settled the patent infringement suit with Cree and Boston University, eliminating all claims and counterclaims by agreeing to a license deal that included a fee and ongoing revenues. Moreover, the two companies forged a collaborative alli-

KEY DATES

2002: Heng Liu founds eLite Optoelectronics Inc.
2003: ELite offers the first LED chip for sale.
2005: Elite moves its headquarters to Sunnyvale, California.
2006: Elite changes its name to Bridgelux, Inc.
2009: Bridgelux introduces the LED array product line.

ance in which Cree became a supplier for Bridgelux. Other terms of the settlement were kept confidential.

A PROMISING FUTURE

In 2009 Bridgelux formed Lighting Services Group to help designers incorporate the arrays into lamp and luminaire designs. Also in 2009 Bridgelux received a U.S. patent for a surface-mountable LED chip. In early 2010 William D. Watkins succeeded Swoboda as CEO, and Bridgelux raised an additional $50 million in a round of funding led by VantagePoint Venture Partners in order to beef up its global manufacturing infrastructure. A Bridgelux IPO was likely to follow. There was also every reason to expect that LED technology would rapidly gain a significant share of the lighting market in the years to come, and Bridgelux would play an important role in that development.

Ed Dinger

PRINCIPAL SUBSIDIARIES

Lighting Services Group.

PRINCIPAL COMPETITORS

Cree, Inc.; Luminus Devices, Inc.; Lumiled Lighting US, Llc.

FURTHER READING

"Bridgelux Launches Lighting Services Group," *Wireless News*, May 9, 2009.

Duan, Mary, "Fan Propels Third Company Toward Public Arena," *San Jose Business Journal*, November 21, 2008.

Engardio, Pete, "Can the Future Be Built in America?" *Business Week*, September 10, 2009.

Henricks, Mark, "The Wave of Next-Generation Innovators," *Entrepreneur*, September 2006.

Johnston, Bob, "Lighten Up," *Forbes*, October 17, 2005, p. 56.

McDonald, JoAnn, "Robert Walker Becomes CEO of eLite," *LIGHTimes Online*, July 12, 2005.

Shieber, Jonathan, "Energy-Efficient Lighting Shines with Investors," *Wall Street Journal*, September 5, 2007.

BRITA GmbH

Heinrich-Hertz-Straße 4
Taunusstein, Hesse D-65232
Germany
Telephone: (+49 6128) 746-0
Fax: (+49 6128) 746-601
Web site: http://www.brita.net

Private Company
Incorporated: 1966
Employees: 950 (est.)
Sales: €283 million (2009)
NAICS: 333319 Water Purification Equipment
Manufacturing; 333415 Water Coolers Manu-
facturing

■ ■ ■

Headquartered in the small town of Taunusstein,
Germany, BRITA GmbH is the worldwide market
leader in household water filtration. The company,
founded in 1966, has grown from a one-man business
into an international enterprise with more than 900
employees worldwide. BRITA develops, produces, and
sells innovative drinking water filters for domestic and
professional use in more than 80 countries on all
continents, making it the only real global player in its
field. BRITA operates production facilities in Germany,
Great Britain, India, and Switzerland.

A ONE-MAN OPERATION

BRITA was established in Germany in 1966, when
Heinz Hankammer developed the AquaDeMat, a water

filter that demineralized tap water. The AquaDeMat offered consumers a cost-effective alternative to buying
distilled water for car batteries. All that was needed was
tap water and the water filter, which was soon sold at
garages and gas stations all over Germany. With pride
and affection Hankammer named his company after his
daughter Brita.

Realizing the need for healthier and better-tasting
drinking water, Hankammer moved on to developing a
water filter that optimized tap water using the simplest
means possible. At the time, most German households
bought bottled carbonated water for drinking, and
Hankammer set out to change that. His vision was to
put a water-filter pitcher on every German dinner table.
When Hankammer introduced his water-filter pitcher at
trade shows in 1970, he was met with disbelieving
smiles. Undeterred by naysayers, Hankammer patented
his table water filter, laying the foundation for the future
of his company.

A HIDDEN CHAMPION

In the 1980s Hankammer's vision expanded beyond the
German dinner table, and he began distributing water
pitchers internationally. Hankammer also realized that
improving the quality and taste of water could have a
strong commercial appeal. In 1980 BRITA began
manufacturing water filters for commercial use. BRITA
filters that reduced the lime and mineral content in tap
water not only produced better-tasting water, but also
increased the longevity of appliances, such as coffee and
espresso machines, vending machines, water coolers,
steamers, and dishwashers that were used by businesses,
such as restaurants.

COMPANY PERSPECTIVES

For more than 40 years BRITA has been involved in the filtration of water and has devoted itself to the future of this essential resource. As international market leader in the product category of water filter jugs we focus on our vision: Our vision is a world where drinking water of the highest quality is always available to everyone. Our contribution: We offer innovative products and solutions that enable people to experience the best possible drinking water according to their individual needs.

In 1984 BRITA began offering standard exchangeable filter cartridges for household and commercial use. By offering increased cost-efficiency through the use of its filters, BRITA quickly became the market leader. By 1987 BRITA had become synonymous with water filtration, clearly dominating the German market and making strong strides all over Europe and North America. In 1992 the company established the first recycling program for its exchangeable filter cartridges.

Four years later, in 1996, BRITA was one of the companies featured in Harvard professor Hermann Simon's study on small to midsize companies that, although relatively unknown, successfully dominated a market niche. Simon called these companies "hidden champions." Within only 30 years Heinz Hankammer had developed his one-man operation into a business that, well ahead of its time, had recognized a need for healthier and better-tasting drinking water and offered a cost-effective and sustainable solution that, literally, conquered the world.

A NEW GENERATION

In 1999 the second generation of Hankammers took over. Heinz Hankammer's son, Markus, who had been part of the company's leadership since 1996, became the new CEO of BRITA GmbH, while Heinz Hankammer became chairman of the newly founded supervisory board. Hankammer's daughter, Brita, also became a member of the supervisory board.

While continuing his father's vision of manufacturing and distributing a product that improves water quality, Markus Hankammer slightly shifted the company's focus. Instead of attempting to become the worldwide market leader with the already existing BRITA products, Markus Hankammer decided to focus the company's

resources on Europe instead. In 2000 he sold the North American distribution rights of all BRITA household products to the California-based CLOROX Company, pursuing product diversification rather than international expansion.

Markus Hankammer then launched several successful new product lines. In 2001 the first water heating kettle with an integrated BRITA filter first hit the British market, and in later years was introduced in other markets around the world. That same year the French market became the testing ground for the revolutionary BRITA On Tap system, offering a household water filtering system that attached directly to the faucet, thus circumventing the need for a table pitcher. By 2006 this system would also conquer other international markets.

A NEW CONCEPT AND MORE NEW PRODUCTS

In 2004 Markus Hankammer launched BRITA Integrated Solutions, a division that created partnerships with international manufacturers of domestic appliances, including BSH Bosch Siemens Haushaltsgeräte GmbH, Cloer, Breville and Pegler, to integrate BRITA's replaceable, water-filter cartridges into their appliances. This offered consumers BRITA-filtered water, while also increasing the life of their coffee and espresso machines, teakettles, chillers, dishwashers, refrigerators, and freezers.

Also in 2004 BRITA introduced AquaQuell PURITY and AquaQuell 1.5, two new commercial water-filter systems that utilized a unique four-step filtration system. In 2005 the company offered MAXTRA, a new, replaceable, household filter that used activated carbon and ion exchange resin to remove chlorine, heavy metals, and other impurities, while leaving behind the fluoride and minerals that promoted physical well-being. Also in 2005 BRITA introduced Elemaris, a jug water filter with a pour-through lid, enabling the jug to be filled with one hand, thus keeping alive consumer interest in the company's signature product, table pitchers.

OUTLOOK

In 2009 BRITA purchased the Enviva product line from Waterhouse ATT. Manufacturing, distributing, and servicing the line of water-dispensing furniture, such as water coolers for companies, drinking fountains for municipalities and water dispensers for hospitals, offered not only another established customer base for the BRITA water filtering systems, but also an additional product line with room for international growth. In

KEY DATES

1966: Heinz Hankammer founds BRITA GmbH.
1970: BRITA introduces its signature product, the household table water filter.
1999: Hankammer's son, Markus, becomes CEO; Heinz Hankammer becomes chairman of the newly founded supervisory board.
2004: BRITA launches Integrated Solutions.
2009: BRITA purchases Enviva product line from Waterhouse ATT and founds subsidiary Enviva GmbH.

January 2010 BRITA GmbH signaled its optimism for future growth with a move to new headquarters in Taunusstein, Germany.

Helga Schier

PRINCIPAL SUBSIDIARIES

BRITA GmbH, Germany (headquarters); BRITA Water Filter Systems PTY Ltd. (Australia); BRITA SARL (France); BRITA Manufacturing (UK); Limited BMC, (Great Britain); BRITA Water Filter Systems Ltd. (Great Britain); BRITA Italia S.r.l. Unipersonale (Italy); BRITA Japan KK (Japan); BRITA Korea (Korea); BRITA Benelux B.V. (Netherlands); BRITA Polska S.p.z.o.o. (Poland); BRITA AG (Switzerland); BRITA Spain S.L. (Spain); MAVEA LLC (USA); MAVEA Canada Inc. (Canada); ENVIVA GmbH; Usha Shriram BRITA Pvt. Ltd. (India, joint venture).

PRINCIPAL DIVISIONS

Household Water Filters; Professional Water Filters; Integrated Solutions; Enviva GmbH.

PRINCIPAL COMPETITORS

Alticor, Inc.; Culligan International Company; General Electric Company; The Procter & Gamble Company; Sun Water Systems, Inc.

FURTHER READING

Döbler, Yvonne, "Loslassen," Familienstrategie.de, April 2007, www.familienstrategie.de/media/public/pdf/artikel/hankammer_loslassen.pdf.

"Firmensitz BRITA GmbH," Business for Business Schwaben, January 25, 2010, www.b4bschwaben.de/Mittelstand/Artikel,-Firmensitz-BRITA-GmbH-_arid,44550_puid,1_pageid,246.html.

Kolb, Matthias, "Aerger um Sprudler aus Nahost," Sueddeutsche.de, September 3, 2009, www.sueddeutsche.de/politik/901/486318/text.

"German Standards." Cologne: Arcum Publishers, 1987.

Simon, Hermann, *Hidden Champions: Lessons from 500 of the World's Best Unknown Companies.* Boston: Harvard Business School Press, 1996.

Broadway Video Entertainment

1619 Broadway
New York, New York 10019-7412
U.S.A.
Telephone: (212) 265-7600
Fax: (212) 713-1535
Web site: http://www.broadwayvideo.com

Private Company
Founded: 1979
Employees: 235
Sales: $168 million (2008 est.)
NAICS: 512110 Motion Picture and Video Production;
    512120 Motion Picture and Video Distribution;
    512191 Teleproduction and Other Post-Production
    Services

■ ■ ■

Founded in 1979 by Lorne Michaels, the creator of *Saturday Night Live* (*SNL*), Broadway Video Entertainment began as a one-room post-production facility. Over its 30-year history the company has expanded to encompass development, production, and distribution of television programs, feature films, commercials, and other visual media. Broadway Video offers technical services including editing, graphic design, visual effects, sound design and original music, digital media, video duplication, and video encoding. Among the company's clients are the three major networks (ABC, CBS, and NBC), as well as numerous cable networks and corporations. In addition to *SNL* (1975–), the company is best known for production of the movies *The Blues Brothers* (1980) and *Wayne's World* (1992) and the primetime comedy *30 Rock* (2006–).

BEGINNINGS AND *SATURDAY NIGHT LIVE* SUCCESS: 1975–79

Lorne Michaels was born Lorne David Lipowitz in 1944 in Toronto, Canada. He worked as a standup comedian with partner Hart Pomerantz, whom he met while attending University College in Toronto. The two were invited to Hollywood in 1968 to write for the *Beautiful Phyllis Diller Show*, which ran for only nine weeks before being cancelled. The duo went on to write for other comedy shows produced in Los Angeles, including *Rowan and Martin's Laugh-In*, before returning to Canada when the CBC offered them a chance to write, produce, and star in their own shows. Michaels and Pomerantz created a series of comedy specials that showcased the format later made famous on *SNL*: an opening monologue, comic sketches performed by a repertory company, and musical guests.

Michaels returned to the United States alone in 1972. He was soon hired as a writer and producer by Lily Tomlin, one of the top comedians of the era. Michaels won two Emmys for his work on Tomlin's TV specials. In 1974 Johnny Carson informed NBC that he wanted the network to stop airing reruns of the *Tonight Show* on Saturday nights, which it had done for the prior 10 years, and NBC hired Michaels to produce an original show for that timeslot. *NBC's Saturday Night* aired for the first time on October 11, 1975 (it would be renamed *Saturday Night Live* two years later), and became an enormous hit, nominated for more than 80 Emmy awards, and entering its 35th season as of 2010.

COMPANY FOUNDED: 1979

Michaels and partner Ralph Kelsey started Broadway Video in 1979 to provide higher-quality post-production services for *Saturday Night Live*. Michaels believed there was no studio in New York that offered services comparable to what was available in Los Angeles at the time. The new company immediately began to handle all aspects of *SNL* that were pre-recorded, such as the show's trademark fake commercials and the show's graphics, including the famous opening credits.

Saturday Night Live served as the economic backbone of Broadway Video for 30 years, with Michaels heading both operations. In 1980 Broadway Video produced the first spinoffs of *SNL*. *The Blues Brothers* starred Dan Ackroyd and John Belushi as the improbable white bluesmen they had immortalized in the show. In 1983 the company produced an animated TV special based on extraterrestrial *SNL* family The Coneheads. Starring three former SNL cast members, Dan Ackroyd, Jane Curtin, and Laraine Newman, *The Coneheads* detailed the efforts of Beldar Conehead, his wife, Prymaat, and their daughter, Connie, recent arrivals from the planet Remulak, to adjust to life in suburban New Jersey. In 1986 Broadway Video produced the feature film *The Three Amigos* with show alumni Chevy Chase, Steve Martin, and Martin Short.

In 1989 Broadway Video began producing the comedy series *The Kids in the Hall* starring a five-member Canadian troupe of the same name. Airing concurrently in the United States and Canada, the show proved another success for Broadway and ran until 1995.

Also in 1989 the company acquired the rights to the pre-1974 television library of Rankin/Bass Productions. Included were such popular Christmas specials as *Rudolph the Red-Nosed Reindeer* (1964), *The*

Little Drummer Boy (1968), *Frosty the Snowman* (1969), and *Santa Claus Is Coming to Town* (1970). In addition to its Rankin/Bass holdings, Broadway Video developed an extensive library of programs for which it held broadcast rights, including more than 3,000 titles, such as the *Lassie* and *Lone Ranger* television series.

The company expanded its production services and equipment throughout the 1980s in its quest to become the top shop for post-production in New York. In 1989 Broadway Video opened a fully digital compositing suite. As one of the first companies to upgrade to digital facilities, Broadway Video believed it could provide "the most powerful environment possible for the compositing of video and graphic elements," company president Peter Rudoy told *Back Stage* in April 1989. The company now offered digital compositing in real time, rather than frame-by-frame, and had the ability to track each step in a session as it was completed. The digital upgrade offered customers access to all existing video formats: 1/2-inch, 3/4-inch, one-inch, and D-1 and D-2 formats; full edit-suite capabilities; and fast digital back-up.

FACILITIES AND SERVICES
GROW: 1990–99

Broadway staff had grown from seven when the company started to 90 in the early 1990s, when a design and graphics division was added, called Broadway Video Design. The Video Design operations were headed by vice president and executive producer Peter Ronick. In 1992 Broadway Video Digital Offline was inaugurated. BV Digital Offline produced HBO specials, projects for Oprah Winfrey and the National Football League, and promotional segments for numerous clients. This division also produced the popular and long-running *Unplugged* acoustic concert series for MTV. In 1993 Broadway Video also began producing *Late Night with Conan O'Brien* for NBC (later *Late Night with Jimmy Fallon*).

At this time the company was handling not only network television projects but also cable programming and commercial products. "We started with a bigger network segment," Rudoy told *SHOOT* magazine in June 1994, "and then as cable expanded it grew into our number-one segment, though network and cable have traded places a couple of times." Rudoy estimated that commercial projects accounted for approximately 25 percent of Broadway's work at that time. The company also expanded its graphics department into a separate division, Broadway Graphics, and opened Broadway Video Duplication later that year.

In 1995 Broadway Video opened a new sound design division, Broadway Video Sound, managed by

KEY DATES

1979: Broadway Video is founded by *Saturday Night Live* producer Lorne Michaels and Ralph Kelsey.

1988: Company purchases the pre-1974 catalog of Rankin/Bass animated television specials, including *Frosty the Snowman* and *Rudolph the Red-Nosed Reindeer*.

1994: Company expansion adds Broadway Graphics and Broadway Video Duplication divisions.

2003: Broadway Video Television begins operations in Los Angeles to develop original programming for television.

2006: The comedy series *30 Rock*, produced by Broadway Video and NBC Universal Television, debuts in October.

2007: Broadway Video Digital Media is established, providing broadcast support to networks, including standards conversion, closed captioning, custom formatting, and other services.

sound engineers Ralph Kelsey and Michael Ungar. Broadway Video Sound featured state-of-the-art equipment including mixing rooms with MIDI samplers, synthesizers, and Sonic Solutions digital audio workstations. Two of the three studios were mixing studios, with a third set up for voiceover recording and pre-lay. Routing switchers connected Broadway Sound to other resources available in the Broadway Video facility. At this point the company had 135 employees and had significantly expanded its marketing and client services departments.

The company also formed new companies in partnership with others in 1995. It joined forces with BAM! Software to form Broadway Interactive Group to produce interactive multimedia content that could boast broadcast quality production. That year also saw the inauguration of Broadway Comics, headed by the former editor-in-chief of Marvel Comics, Jim Shooter. In 1997 Broadway Video formed a partnership with TV Books to produce companion books for television series.

SUCCESSES IN TECHNOLOGY AND TELEVISION PRODUCTION: 2000–10

After the turn of the 21st century, *SNL* continued to act as the company's lifeblood and its main promotional

tool. In 2003 Broadway Video negotiated a deal with NBC to develop primetime comedy shows for the network and established Broadway Video Television in Los Angeles to begin development activities under the leadership of former NBC senior vice president JoAnn Alfano. Alfano's first project was the short-lived *Tracy Morgan Show*, which premiered in December 2003.

The effort paid off in 2006, however, when another *Saturday Night Live* spinoff show, *30 Rock*, hit the airwaves in October. Written by (and starring) *SNL* head writer and performer Tina Fey and jointly produced by Broadway Video and NBC Universal, *30 Rock* depicted the adventures of a head writer for a late-night comedy TV show. The show won critical acclaim and as of 2010 had received numerous honors, including Emmy awards for best comedy series three years in a row. Fey also had other hits produced by Broadway Video, including the popular films *Mean Girls* (2004) and *Baby Mama* (2008).

The company continued to upgrade its production technology and post production facilities in New York. In 2004 the company opened Broadway Video Encoding Services, an offshoot of Broadway Video Duplication, to offer customized digital encoding to broadcast and cable television networks. Specifically, this division enabled clients to use a data file format instead of videotape for production and distribution purposes. In 2007 the company combined the staff and resources of Broadway Video Duplication and Broadway Video Encoding to create Broadway Video Digital Media, which provided broadcast support, including duplication, standards conversion, closed captioning, custom formatting, and other services to television networks. By 2010 Broadway Video had grown to include state-of-the-art facilities, an industry-leading management team, experienced technicians, and operations on both coasts to develop, produce, and distribute television and film entertainment products.

Melanie Bush

PRINCIPAL DIVISIONS

Broadway Sound; Broadway Video Design; Broadway Video Digital Media; Broadway Video Editorial; Broadway Video Encoding Services; Broadway Video Enterprises; Broadway Video Film; Broadway Video Television.

PRINCIPAL COMPETITORS

Deluxe Entertainment; LaserPacific Media; Warner Bros.

FURTHER READING

"Broadway Video: Setting Its Sights on the Digital Future," *Shoot*, June 3, 1994, p. 69.

Clark, Andrew, *Stand & Deliver: Inside Canadian Comedy*. Toronto: Doubleday Canada, 1997.

Edgerton, Gary Richard, et al., eds., and *In the Eye of the Beholder: Critical Perspectives in Popular Film and Television*. Bowling Green, OH: Popular Press, 1997.

Schwartz, Tony, "Live (on Tape), from New York, It's Lorne Michaels ... Again," *New York*, January 9, 1984.

Winship, Michael P., *Television*. New York: Random House, 1988.

Cahill May Roberts Group Ltd.

---

1 Pharmapark
Chapelizod, Dublin 20,
Ireland
Telephone: (+353 1) 630 55 55
Fax: (+353 1) 630 55 99
Web site: http://www.cmrg.ie

Private Company
Founded: 1902
Incorporated: 1935 as May Roberts Ltd.
Employees: 225
Sales: €320.6 million ($464 million) (2008)
NAICS: 424210 Drugs and Druggists Sundries Merchant Wholesalers

■ ■ ■

Cahill May Roberts Group Ltd. (CMR) is one of Ireland's leading pharmaceutical distribution and wholesale companies. CMR's three trading divisions are Alchemy, Movianto Ireland (for pre-wholesale), and Wholesale. The Alchemy division provides specialized customer service, beginning with the initial product request and continuing to the supply of medication. Movianto, with branches in Dublin and Belfast, offers supply-chain solutions to more than 80 pharmaceutical manufacturers. CMR's Wholesale division has depots in Cork, Sligo, and Dublin and is responsible for distributing prescription and over-the-counter medications to pharmacies and hospitals throughout the country. It also acts as wholesaler, agent, and distributor of cosmetics, skincare products, veterinary products, and photo-

graphic goods. Its client base includes more than 1,200 retail customers and nearly 200 hospitals.

CMR's parent company is Celesio AG, a leading European service provider for the pharmaceutical industry. Celesio has three major service divisions (Solutions, Pharmacy, and Wholesale), and CMR is one of its 140 worldwide wholesalers serving more than 65,000 pharmacies.

MAY ROBERTS BEGINNINGS

Cahill May Roberts Group Ltd. began as two separate companies: May Roberts and Company and P. C. Cahill & Co. Ltd. Sam Roberts, a member of an Irish Quaker family that had immigrated to England, worked for May Roberts pharmaceutical wholesalers in London. In 1902 he returned to Ireland with his brothers, Frank and Calvert, and opened the Irish branch of the company.

May Roberts's first office was located on Price's Lane in Dublin, where the small staff would put together parcels of drugs and chemicals and distribute them throughout the country via handcarts, the railway system, and the postal service. By 1924 the company had implemented daily telesales calls, considerably increasing its outreach. As the business grew the brothers began to use delivery vans in the Dublin vicinity. By 1927 May Roberts had outgrown the Price's Lane office and relocated to Canal Quay, where Alex Davidson served as managing director.

In 1935 May Roberts was incorporated and established as an independent company. Around this time the Irish government enacted the Control of

COMPANY PERSPECTIVES

Our aim is to become the Healthcare Supplier of Choice in Ireland. We will achieve this through partnership between our customers and staff. We will continually work to improve the responsiveness, range and quality of our services whilst always recognizing the importance of our products and services to the customer. In this way, we will provide the greatest benefit for our customers, staff, shareholders and suppliers.

Manufacturing and Packaging Acts to encourage new industry, and May Roberts ventured into the manufacture and packaging of a wide variety of pharmaceuticals and cosmetics, such as Brylcreem, Milk of Magnesia, and Vaseline Hair Tonic.

POSTWAR GROWTH FOR MAY ROBERTS

By the 1940s there were about 15 pharmaceutical wholesalers in Ireland, including Ayrton Saunders, Dublin Drug, St. Dalmas, United Drug (which would become one of CMR's main competitors), and P. C. Cahill & Co. Ltd., the company with which May Roberts would one day merge. By 1954 May Roberts occupied a 50,000-square-foot space on Grand Canal Quay in Ringsend, Dublin, where it continued its wholesale operation. The company also served as an agent for a number of high-profile international pharmaceutical companies, including Pfizer, Parke-Davis, Glaxo, and Roche.

With the introduction of antibiotics and penicillin, there was a greater need to serve pharmacists outside Dublin, and May Roberts embarked on a decentralization plan. A new building was constructed in Limerick and, under the direction of Tom McAuliffe, served the major towns and cities in the counties of Limerick, Cork, Galway, Tipperary, and Mayo. In April 1966 the Carlow warehouse was opened with Declan Hickey, a successful Limerick pharmacist, installed as its general manager. Managed by Michael Ryan, the Cavan branch followed in November 1966 and served the northern expanse of Ireland.

By 1967 May Roberts had 97,000 square feet of warehouse space, was serving 1,300 customers with a fleet of 35 vans, and had sales of IEP 2.6 million. The following year the company acquired its first computer system at a cost of IEP 89,000. The new I.C.T. 1901 mainframe, installed by the Irish Computer Services Bureau, centralized the company's accounting function and streamlined the invoicing, stock control, and purchasing processes.

P. C. CAHILL BEGINNINGS

During Ireland's turbulent early 20th century, Arthur Cahill ran a pharmacy on the corner of Dorset Street and North Circular Road on Dublin's north side. Cahill was heavily involved in Irish politics and was a founding member of the Sinn Fein political party. He served as the operating chief of medical services during the 1916 Easter Rising and was interned at Knutsford and Frongoch prisons with his friend Sean T. O'Kelly, who would later become Ireland's president in 1945.

Cahill's son, Patrick, followed in his father's footsteps and fought in Ireland's war for independence. He too was put in an internment camp at Gormanston with O'Kelly. Patrick Cahill worked alongside his father in his Dublin pharmacy, receiving his pharmacist qualification in 1928. The younger Cahill was fluent in both English and Irish, and he soon opened his own pharmacy in Whitehall, an Irish-speaking neighborhood more commonly referred to in Ireland as "the Gaeltacht." During this time Patrick Cahill was also involved in a number of organizations related to the pharmaceutical industry and worked tirelessly to bring about change and improvements in business practices.

In 1936, along with a group of pharmacists and businesspeople, Patrick Cahill established P. C. Cahill & Co. Ltd., a manufacturing and wholesale company where he held the position of managing director until his death in 1951. Eamon McCarron, an Aer Lingus accountant, was the company's first chairman, and John P. Holland and J. J. Roche were on the board of directors. The business began with just one driver and three phones, serving the greater Dublin area. By 1947, under Eugene Davy as chairman, the company was covering the entire country and was launched on the Dublin Stock Exchange. Malachi Leonard was added to the board; Thomas Banks and James Hegarty were assistant managers; and Shane Gallagher, Bernie Duffy, and Charlie Roche were the regional representatives serving the outlying areas of the country.

P. C. CAHILL'S POSTWAR DIVERSIFICATION

In addition to its manufacturing and wholesale divisions, P. C. Cahill had become agents for international manufacturers such as Eli Lilly & Co. Ltd., Merck

KEY DATES

1902: Sam Roberts establishes May Roberts wholesalers in Dublin, Ireland.

1935: May Roberts is incorporated.

1936: Patrick C. Cahill establishes P. C. Cahill & Co. Ltd.

1950: P. C. Cahill enters the photography wholesale business.

1961: P. C. Cahill establishes Chem Labs Ltd. to market laboratory equipment and chemicals.

1970: May Roberts and P. C. Cahill merge, although the two companies continue to operate as separate entities.

1972: P. J. Carroll & Co. Ltd. acquires P. C. Cahill Ltd.

1976: The company is physically merged and renamed Cahill May Roberts Ltd.

1983: The company secures the rights for "Scripts," the country's first computerized retail pharmacy system.

1985: CMR launches "Colorcare," a photo-processing service.

1990: Cahill May Roberts Group PLC is floated on Unlisted Securities Market.

1992: AAH Holdings acquires CMR.

1995: AAH is taken over by Gehe, Germany's largest pharmaceutical wholesaler.

2001: Gehe acquires Crowley's Pharmacies chain.

2003: Gehe's name is changed to Celesio AG.

2007: CMR invests in a voice-enabled warehouse management system.

Sharp & Dohme Ltd., and British Drug Houses Ltd. Under Michael Phelan, P. C. Cahill began to diversify in 1950, becoming Ireland's largest photographic wholesaler. The company acted as the sole distributor for Zeiss-Ikon of Stuttgart, Germany, and other similar international companies. In 1960 P. C. Cahill opened a new factory on Bachelor's Walk in Dublin for the production of tablets and medications, including Nepecil, the first penicillin ointment to be produced in Ireland. In 1961 the company established a wholly owned subsidiary, Chem Labs Ltd., to market laboratory equipment and chemicals.

The following year P. C. Cahill embarked on an extensive decentralization plan, beginning with the acquisition of the St. Dalmas wholesale company in Cork. The new facility on Anglesea Street in Cork

covered the entire southern province of Munster. This was followed in 1966 with the establishment of a wholesale branch in Finisklin, Sligo, which covered the northwestern provinces. By 1969 the city of Dublin was becoming too congested, and the company searched for a more strategic location. New wholesale, office, and agency space was built five miles outside of the city in California Heights, Chapelizod, where the country's main roads all converged.

MERGER OF MAY ROBERTS AND P. C. CAHILL

Throughout its development, P. C. Cahill's main competitor was May Roberts. By 1970 each company's worth was approximately IEP 500,000, and both agreed that sales and profits would be maximized through a merger. On December 4, 1970, the deal was completed, and Tom McAuliffe was appointed managing director. McAuliffe and Tom Ruddock joined Cahill's board, and Cahill's J. P. Holland and Jim Hegarty joined the board of May Roberts. Although merged on paper, the two companies continued to operate as separate entities until 1976.

In 1972 the Irish tobacco company P. J. Carroll & Co. Ltd. acquired 100 percent of P. C. Cahill Ltd. May Roberts also closed its facilities in Sligo, Mayo, and Donegal but acquired a new site in Togher, Cork County, to replace the Anglesea premises in the city of Cork. The portfolio of the combined companies boasted an impressive list of brands, such as Upjohn, Roche Products, and Ciba Labs, and was Ireland's leading pharmaceutical agency and wholesale business.

On March 3, 1976, with Hegarty as the new chairman of the board, the group was renamed Cahill May Roberts Ltd. (CMR). All activities were moved to the new purpose-built facility in Chapelizod, and the company streamlined its operations and reduced the wholesale business to six branches operating in the counties of Dublin, Cork, Limerick, Sligo, Carlow, and Cavan. In 1983 it secured the rights for "Scripts," the first computerized retail pharmacy system, greatly increasing the efficiency of its prescription pricing and labeling functions. In 1985, in conjunction with Spectra Laboratories, the group launched "Colorcare," a photo-processing service.

Paul Higgins, the managing director in 1988, successfully led a group of managers, a director, and Allied Irish Bank's venture capital company, ACT, in a management buyout. Under the scheme, Niall Crowley was appointed chairman, ACT's Niall Carroll and Aidan Byrnes joined the board, and profit sharing was offered to employees and customers. The newly named Cahill

May Roberts Group PLC was floated on the Unlisted Securities Market at 55 pence per share on May 14, 1990. CMR also established a consultative body of retail and hospital pharmacists in order to improve its customer service. In 1991 the company expanded with the acquisition of Natureline and AG & S Cope, a Manchester-based cash-and-carry. The company continued to grow during the 1990s, adding Elizabeth Arden, Wellcome, and other well-known names to its portfolio.

TAKEOVERS AND BUYOUTS

In September 1992 AAH Holdings, who also owned AAH Pharmaceuticals and Castlereagh Pharmaceuticals in Northern Ireland, acquired the total share capital of CMR. As part of the deal, CMR took over Castlereagh's pre-wholesale business, marking the company's entrance into Northern Ireland. In April 1995 AAH was taken over by the Germany company Gehe, Europe's largest pharmaceutical wholesaler. CMR became a subsidiary of the prestigious Gehe, which was renamed Celesio AG in 2003. The first steps Gehe took were to expand the agency warehouse in Chapelizod and close three of its wholesale warehouses. The remaining wholesale warehouses in the counties of Sligo, Cork, and Dublin were also expanded and modernized.

In 2001 Gehe acquired Crowley's Pharmacies, an Irish retail chain, which negatively impacted CMR's business. Pharmacists feared the increasing dominance of the German company and preferred to purchase their drugs and cosmetics from CMR's two main competitors, UniPhar and United Drug. In 2003 CMR, which was now Ireland's second-leading pharmaceutical wholesaler, saw a 3 percent fall in sales in the first nine months of the year. Further adding to the fall in profits was the recent opening of several discount retail pharmacy chains throughout the country and UniPhar's acquisition of Walsh Pharmacy Group.

A year later CMR reported a 19 percent increase in sales for the first nine months of 2004. Analysts speculated that the turnaround was due to the fact that CMR had won a tender to supply vaccines to all of Ireland's doctors, while Celesio attributed the positive results to cost cutting and improved logistical equipment. In 2005 CMR continued to lose market share to United Drug and UniPhar, slipping to third place in the rankings of Ireland's pharmaceutical distributors. Although its revenues rose by approximately 10 percent, this was still lower than its competitors. Analysts maintained that it was Celesio's decision to purchase retail pharmacies that caused the

decrease. CMR managed to turn things around again in 2006, and sales were up 20 percent for the first nine months of the year.

In March 2007 CMR reported a 17 percent increase in revenues to €299 million. In that same month the company announced that it had made a substantial investment in a voice-enabled warehouse management system. The new system, which managed every warehouse function, was expected to increase productivity by 25 percent and ensure 99.99 percent accuracy. Cahill May Roberts decided to share its success with the community that had supported the company for more than a century. Its social initiatives included the endowment of the Cahill May Roberts Lecture Theatre in the School of Pharmacy at Trinity College and the annual conferring of the CMR Prize and Paul Higgins Memorial Prize.

In 2008 CMR reported revenues in excess of €320 million. With Celesio's commitment to develop its core businesses throughout Europe, the company was positioned to continue to grow organically well into the future.

Marie O'Sullivan

PRINCIPAL DIVISIONS

Alchemy; Movianto Ireland; Wholesale.

PRINCIPAL COMPETITORS

UniPhar Group; United Drug Plc.

FURTHER READING

"Acquisition Boosts AAH Holdings," *Cosmetics International*, September 10, 1993, p. 13.

O'Hora, Ailish, "Sales Up 20pc at Cahill May Roberts," *Irish Independent*, November 14, 2006.

———, "Strong Irish Growth for Chemist Group Celesio," *Irish Independent*, March 16, 2007.

Sweeney, David. *The History of Cahill May Roberts*. Dublin: Cahill May Roberts Group Ltd., 2002.

Thesing, Gabi, "The Business & Finance Company of the Year," *Business & Finance*, November 21, 2002.

Weston, Charlie, "Cahill May Drugs Sales Dip by 3pc," *Irish Independent*, November 14, 2003.

———, "Cahill May Loses Market Share to Rivals," *Irish Independent*, March 19, 2005.

———, "Cahill May Roberts Sales Rise by 19pc," *Irish Independent*, November 16, 2004.

Callaway Golf Company

2180 Rutherford Road
Carlsbad, California 92008-7328
U.S.A.
Telephone: (760) 931-1771
Toll Free: (800) 588-9836
Fax: (760) 930-5015
Web site: http://www.callawaygolf.com

Public Company
Incorporated: 1982
Employees: 2,700
Sales: $1.18 billion
Stock Exchanges: New York
Ticker Symbol: ELY
NAICS: 339920 Sporting and Athletic Goods Manu-
    facturing

■ ■ ■

Callaway Golf Company is a leading U.S. manufacturer
of golf clubs and golf balls. In addition to a line of drivers, Callaway also makes irons, putters, and golf balls. It
licenses Callaway golf wear through apparel makers Ash-
worth Inc. and Perry Ellis, and it partners with other
firms to sell golf electronics and other gear. Its various
clubs and golf balls rank first or second in market share.
The company began a meteoric rise to fame and fortune
with the introduction of the powerful Big Bertha driver
in 1991. The success of Callaway Golf is attributed to
Ely Callaway, who over two decades transformed a modest company into a worldwide powerhouse.

EARLY CAREER IN TEXTILES AND WINE

Ely Reeves Callaway Jr. was born in La Grange, Georgia,
a small town about 60 miles southwest of Atlanta. Ely's
grandfather, a Baptist preacher, owned and operated a
plantation with approximately 20 slaves. When the
Union forces defeated the Confederacy in the American
Civil War during the 1860s, the Callaways lost their
entire fortune. Ely's uncle, Fuller Callaway, was the
primary force behind the family's resurgence. He first
went into farming, then into dry goods, later into banking, and finally into the cotton mill trade. Ely's father
worked for his uncle, but when Ely Jr. graduated from
Emory University, his father advised him not to work
for the family.

In June 1940 Ely Jr. was working as a runner in the
factoring department of the Trust Company of Georgia
and decided to take an army reserve correspondence
course. Commissioned six weeks later, Callaway went to
Philadelphia and began working in the apparel procurement division of the quartermaster's depot. Callaway
was soon promoted to major, a significant achievement
for a young man of 24, and was in charge of 70 civilians
and 2 lawyers. During this time, he was buying approximately 70 percent of the total wartime production
of the U.S. cotton apparel industry and was dealing
with such companies as Levi Strauss; Hart, Schaffner &
Marx; and Arrow Shirt on a daily basis. When the war
ended, Callaway decided to go to work for Deering,
Milliken & Company in order to continue a career in
the textile and apparel industry.

Callaway rose quickly in his chosen profession. In 1954, however, after he became involved in a disagreement with Roger Milliken's brother-in-law, Milliken fired him unceremoniously. Undismayed, Callaway found a job at Textron Industries and, under the supervision of Royal Little, oversaw the merger of Robbins Mills and American Woolen, two large textile mills. When Textron sold the division Callaway worked in to Burlington Industries, Callaway was part of the package deal. By 1968 Callaway was appointed president of Burlington Industries.

Callaway's new post as president of the largest and most influential textile company in the world merely fueled his ambition. When he was passed over for the position of chairman in 1973, Callaway quit abruptly. Picking up his family, he moved from the East Coast to California in order to start a wine-making company in the tiny town of Temecula. Although the land that Callaway had purchased was not prime grape-growing country, nonetheless he persevered until his venture began to pay off. Callaway Vineyard & Winery was soon supplying its products to well-known restaurants such as the Four Seasons in New York City. He sold the operation to Hiram Walker Resources, Ltd., in 1981 at a price of $14 million. In just a few short years, Callaway had garnered a profit of more than $9 million.

STARTING OVER WITH GOLF

At the age of 60, Callaway thought it was time to relax and, hearkening back to his youth and the years when he was a tournament champion, he began in earnest to resume his game of golf. One day on the golf course, he became acquainted with a hickory-shaft club that had a steel core. The club was made by Hickory Stick, a tiny California company run by two entrepreneurs, Richard Parente and Dick De La Cruz. Callaway liked the golf club so much that he called up its manufacturers to tell

them so. Parente and De La Cruz, short of money and looking for someone to invest in their company, asked Callaway for help. In 1984 Callaway purchased the small enterprise at the bargain basement price of $400,000, and pinned his own name to the company.

Callaway Golf Company, under the direction of Callaway himself, immediately began to conceive of strategies to increase both its profile and its revenues in the highly competitive sports equipment market. Callaway decided the best way to achieve these goals was to introduce new products. Within four years of acquiring the company, he had his design staff come up with a new premium-priced item that did away with a large amount of the neck of the club, while extending the shaft through the clubhead. This club was called the S2H2, short for Short Straight Hollow Hosel.

Callaway funded development of the new club by signing up investors, including the General Electric Pension Fund. The pension fund invested $10 million in Callaway Golf in 1988. The response to Callaway's new design was nothing less than phenomenal. Golfers responded to the heavier-weighted clubheads that included a lower center of gravity, and sales shot up dramatically, as did the profile and reputation of Callaway's company. By the end of 1988, company sales amounted to approximately $5 million. One year later, sales had doubled to $10.5 million. In 1990 sales doubled again; by 1991 revenues skyrocketed to $54.7 million, an increase of nearly 150 percent.

BIG BERTHA MAKES AN IMPACT

In 1991 Callaway created the Big Bertha driver, an oversized driver named for the huge gun used by the Germans during World War I to drop shells on Paris from six miles away. The principle behind Callaway's creation of the metal wood driver was that it put more weight around the perimeter of the head of the club, resulting in a thinner face. According to Callaway, this gave the golfer a greater "feel" at the time of impact with the ball. Moreover, the golfer did not have to hit the ball precisely on the button to obtain directional control and good distance. Soon golfers were swearing by them and sales surpassed all the other brands of golf clubs made in America.

With the company growing rapidly, Callaway decided to take it public in February 1992. With 2.6 million shares of stock offered on the New York Stock Exchange at $20 per share, the stock had jumped to $36 per share by the end of the day. The capital provided by the stock offering enabled Callaway to expand his manufacturing capacity. The demand for the company's golf club was rising at unexpected rates, and manage-

KEY DATES

1984: Ely Callaway buys Hickory Stick, which becomes Callaway Golf.
1991: Company launches Big Bertha driver.
1992: Company goes public.
1998: Company claims approximately 70 percent of pro golfers worldwide use Callaway clubs.
2000: Callaway golf balls debut.
2001: Ely Callaway dies.
2002: U.S. Golf Association bans high-performance driver from competition.
2003: Company acquires Top-Flite and Ben Hogan ball brands.
2009: Callaway raises $140 million with stock sale.

ment at the firm needed more cash to take advantage of what has always been regarded as a notoriously faddish market in the golf equipment industry. By the end of 1992, sales had reached $132 million. At the end of April 1993, the price per share of Callaway Golf Company stock had increased to an impressive $54. In 1993, when sales were reported at $255 million, the company had surpassed the better-known names in the sporting goods industry, such as Wilson Sporting Goods Company, Spalding, and MacGregor Golf Company, to become the revenue leader in the field. As sales and the stock price continued to climb, Ely Callaway's personal share rose to a hefty $86 million.

In 1994 Callaway Golf Company introduced an innovative design for irons that would accompany the highly successful Big Bertha metal wood drivers. The new irons, created with the same principles in mind as Callaway's Big Berthas, were an immediate hit on the golf course. Priced at $125, the steel-shafted irons were approximately 20 percent more costly than conventional premium clubs. For $175, a golfer could purchase the new design with a graphite shaft. Because nearly all the company's clubs relied on a new development in casting technology, supplies of the new clubs were limited and helped keep the price per iron high. A total set of nine irons and three woods purchased from Callaway Golf Company at the suggested retail price amounted to the small fortune of $2,325. Nevertheless, golfing enthusiasts, both amateur and professional, happily bought the company's wares. By the end of fiscal 1994, sales had risen to $449 million.

At the beginning of 1995 there were only three major companies in the golf equipment industry, includ-

ing Callaway Golf, Cobra Golf Inc., and TaylorMade, a division of Salomon, which was a prominent manufacturer of skis in France. These three firms were clobbering the remaining competition. Revenues at Callaway Golf in 1994 had increased substantially over the previous year, while revenues at Cobra Golf shot up an astounding 121 percent during the same period. There seemed to be no end to the prospects for these three companies. Nearly 400 golf courses were opened in the United States in 1994, with approximately 800 more under construction. The baby boomer generation was approaching its golfing years and the sport was gaining in popularity all over the world, especially in the countries of the Pacific Rim.

COMPETITION INCREASES

Trouble, however, loomed on the horizon as increased competition among the three major companies and a growing group of both new and old golf equipment firms threatened to cut into profit margins. Wilson, Spalding, and other companies saw an opportunity to secure a share of the market with new products made from aerospace-grade materials and composites. When a golfer swings a club, the wrists rotate, and the head and shaft of the club twist, creating a centrifugal force that tends to pull the club from the golfer's hands. When the golfer then hits the ball, for every millimeter the ball is hit off the center of the club's head, there is a corresponding penalty in distance.

When Callaway's designers created Big Bertha, they revolutionized the industry by taking advantage of a major technological innovation, namely, investment casting. This process was an improved technique for making metal clubheads and enabled designers to shift the weight of the club around with greater precision than ever before. Along with other innovations, Callaway's people designed a club that allowed a golfer to actually control more of the centrifugal force of a swing directly onto the ball.

One company, Goldwin Golf, began to use 7075-T6 aluminum, an aerospace-grade material, in its manufacture of golf clubs. Management at Goldwin guarded their production process as carefully as a national secret. Another development by the same company resulted in the design of a clubhead that weighed a mere 140 grams, approximately 30 percent less than the average weight. GolfGear International, Inc., another firm on the cutting edge of golfing technology, began using an aluminum-vanadium alloy. Only three firms in the industry could forge the new metal. Some companies also began using titanium, which is lighter and denser than steel, resulting in a longer driving range. Titanium drivers were particularly popular in Japan, where they made up over 60 percent of all drivers used. In that market, the seemingly prohibitive cost of approximately $700 for a club was not an insurmountable deterrent.

In spite of the competition, however, Callaway Golf Company continued as the leader in the golf equipment industry. In the mid-1990s the company built a $9 million research, development, and test facility for the purpose of staying ahead of the game. The facility was a state-of-the-art complex, including a 260-yard driving range, which was peppered with hundreds of testing sensors, four kinds of bunkers, and three types of grass in order to simulate the golfing conditions at any course around the world. Callaway expected the highly sophisticated setup to yield even more innovative golf club designs. Because the development of new technologies for designing and new material for manufacturing golf clubs had become so essential to keeping abreast of the industry, the inability to introduce a new product for even two or three years could spell disaster for any golf equipment company.

KEEPING AFLOAT IN THE LATE NINETIES

By the late 1990s Callaway's sales had risen to over $800 million, up from only $5 million a decade earlier. The company's production facility churned out expensive clubs, running three shifts six days a week. Every golfer knew the Big Bertha, and a score of famous amateurs accepted Callaway stock as recompense for appearing in advertisements for the club. Entertainers including rock star Alice Cooper and Canadian singer Céline Dion endorsed the Big Bertha. Even computer mogul Bill Gates took time off from running Microsoft Corporation to appear in a Big Bertha commercial. By 1998 Callaway claimed that almost 70 percent of all professional golfers worldwide used a Callaway driver. The company held about a third of the U.S. driver market, and a company spokesperson told *Golf Magazine* (May 1998) that Callaway wanted 100 percent. Callaway's annual sales were double that of its nearest competitor and the company hoped to break the billion-dollar mark soon.

Conditions, however, were not absolutely favorable to Callaway's continued advance. Wet weather brought on by El Niño in 1998 kept sales flat and the crash in the Asian financial market also dampened matters. Over 16 percent of Callaway's total sales came from Asia, and the weakened economy there had a direct effect on the company. In response, the firm began to diversify. Callaway acquired a putter manufacturer, Odyssey Golf, in 1997, and revamped a small publishing company run by Ely Callaway's son into Callaway Golf Media, which

put out coffee-table books on golf. Callaway also launched Callaway Golf Experience in the late 1990s, a computer- and video-aided fitting center designed to align customers with the right clubs.

Callaway also introduced new clubs, bringing out the Big Bertha Steelhead metal wood line in mid-1998, and followed with the Great Big Bertha Hawk Eye woods the next year. Nevertheless, Callaway's most dramatic move was into the golf ball market. By 1998 Callaway let it be known that it had invested at least $100 million in developing a new golf ball. The ball market ran a high-profit margin, and sales industry-wide were growing at a steady pace. With its excellent brand-name recognition, the move into balls seemed appropriate for Callaway.

These new strategies may have meant long-term gains, but in the short term, the company was not doing well. Imitators with lower priced drivers had snatched market share from Callaway. Two upstart companies, Orlimar Golf Equipment Co. and Adams Golf Inc., together took over 20 percent of the U.S. driver market by the fall of 1998, sending Callaway's share down. By the end of 1998, Callaway stock had crashed, sales were down 17 percent, and profits had dropped 80 percent. Ely Callaway, who had stepped away from the day-to-day running of the company in 1996, agreed to come back full time as chief executive and try to turn things around. Callaway promptly axed 700 employees, divested unprofitable lines, and trimmed costs all around.

ENTERING THE NEW MILLENNIUM AT A TURNING POINT

As the company entered the new century, it also went in new directions and faced new difficulties. Ely Callaway continued to fight for the firm's reputation and market share, but his leadership of the company he had brought to prominence was soon superseded by time and mortality. Additionally, new ventures he helped bring about faced challenges.

The first challenge came when the company brought out its pricey, high-tech Rule 35 golf ball in 2000. The long-anticipated product launch did not prove as immediately beneficial to the company as had been hoped. Nike Golf, a division of the well-known shoe company, also brought out a golf ball that year and persuaded golf superstar Tiger Woods to use it. Woods won three championships in 2000 using the Nike balls. Ely Callaway had expected ball sales of about $70 million for 2000, but because of this competition, sales were less than half that. Subsequently he restructured the company, folding the previously separate ball unit operations into the parent company.

The firm surpassed the size of even the biggest Big Bertha with release of the ERC II in 2000, a new driver with the largest "sweet spot" yet. Unfortunately, the U.S. Golf Association (USGA) ruled that the carefully engineered club did not conform to its technical specifications and allowed too much "whip-saw" action. When the USGA banned the ERC II from its competitions, Callaway appealed the decision and also filed suit against the Royal Canadian Golf Association over the same issue, beginning a wrangle over nonconforming drivers that endured through the decade.

Ely Callaway was diagnosed with pancreatic cancer in the spring of 2001 and died in July of that year. He had never instituted a succession plan, so succeeding CEOs had difficulty establishing their leadership. The company initially carried on under the direction of Ron Drapeau, the first in a series of successor CEOs. With the whole economy slowing in the wake of the September 11, 2001, terrorist attacks on the United States, the company did not predict a return to its former growth rate. Nevertheless, it appeared to be in sound shape on some fronts. It had no debt and had a sizable cash reserve, and it was positioned to continue much as Ely Callaway had done, concentrating on innovative product introductions aimed at the average golfer.

PRODUCTS AND MARKETING: 2001–09

Throughout the first decade of 21st century, Callaway Golf continued to introduce new products and to market them in innovative ways. In what it hailed as its most dramatic product introduction to that time, in 2001 it rolled out seven new offerings, ranging from an oversized driver with a composite head to high-performance premium golf balls. It topped this in 2004 with 11 new products, including a new ERC Fusion Driver and an HX Tour Golf Ball. In 2008, taking advantage of relaxed USGA rules on club adjustability, it unveiled I-MIX Technology, an advance in do-it-yourself club customization that allowed golfers to match a wide range of Callaway clubheads with a range of shaft brands.

Callaway actively promoted the contested ERC II nonconforming driver, despite the continued ban by the USGA. In 2001 golf legend Gary Player endorsed Callaway clubs and balls and used the ERC II driver in the British Open that year. The company was whiplashed by the USGA in 2002. The body first issued a compromise on its standards allowing limited competitive use of the

ERC II in the United States until 2008. Then a few months later Callaway was sent reeling when the USGA rescinded the change, arguing that it might confuse golfers. The company had no backup product for the driver and, despite being lured into a price war with competitor TaylorMade, lost market share to its archrival. This, combined with the low profitability of the golf ball division, led to a precipitous slide in Callaway's stock prices and the resignation of CEO Drapeau in 2004. Critics said the company had failed to emphasize or maximize the more profitable golf hardware business.

Good marketing was always key in the highly competitive golf products industry. During the decade Callaway launched a number of creative marketing ploys. In 2002 it introduced Trade In! Trade Up!, the first manufacturer-sponsored program of its kind allowing golfers to trade in various brands of old clubs for new Callaways. In 2005 the company sought to boost sales by shifting its ad focus from specific products to brand image, emphasizing the company's computer modeling and technological prowess. In 2007 it initiated a $30 million-plus yearlong campaign incorporating television and print, program entitlement, in-house publications, and an inaugural Web television venture. In its first 30 days, the latter, dubbed Callaway TV, drew more than 150,000 video viewers, lured by exclusive videos with Phil Mickelson, Annika Sorenstam, and Gary Player.

Callaway also entered into product partnerships involving a wide range of nongolf products, including Swiss Army Brands, Timberland travel gear, Fossil timepieces, and Perry Ellis apparel. In 2005 Callaway Golf and Verizon Wireless announced the Callaway Golf Mobile Caddie that allowed customers to manage their game, research golf information, and shop from the Callaway catalog. In a real coup, in 2008 it forged a groundbreaking partnership with the world-famous St. Andrews Links to have their logo appear on a range of Callaway Golf products as part of a fund-raising effort to preserve ancient Scottish golf links.

STRENGTHENING FINANCES AND LOOKING ABROAD

Away from the product marketplace, Callaway adjusted its financial position as needed in response to changing internal and external conditions. When share prices fell sharply in 2001, an investor group, seeing a bargain price for the company's shares, approached a major Callaway stakeholder seeking to buy him out, presumably with an eye to taking control of the company. To fight this off, the company was authorized to repurchase $100 million in common stock. That fended off this takeover attempt but in 2005 the company reversed its position and engaged the investment banking firm Lazard Group, LLC, to help it find a buyer in 2005. Bids of as much as $1.24 billion were received for the company. Apparently the price was not right, and there was no takeover. In 2007, for purely internal reasons, the company repurchased another $100 million of its common stock. Then in 2009, to reduce indebtedness and improve its cash position, it sold $140 million worth of convertible preferred stock and, in an unusual move, reduced its quarterly stock dividend to one penny.

Despite the volatile financial and economic conditions of the decade, Callaway forged ahead with several acquisitions designed to improve its market share. In 2003 the company acquired all of the golf-related assets of bankrupt TFGC Estate Inc., which manufactured and sold the popular Top-Flite and Ben Hogan ball brands. The deal eventually cost Callaway a hefty $169 million. In 2006 it acquired the assets of Tour Golf Company, and in 2009 it acquired uPlay, a consumer electronics company that had developed uPro, a Global Positioning System-based device that provided golfers with aerial and satellite golf-course imagery.

As the decade came to an end, Callaway and its competitors were facing pressure from the shrinking domestic golf market as baby boomers aged and the younger generations were less interested in golf. The bright side was an expected 25 percent growth rate for golf products in China and other foreign markets. With its innovative tradition, essential in a market in which consumers continually seek newer and better products, and an already significant commitment to foreign sales (50 percent of total sales in 2008), Callaway was well-positioned to take advantage of a worldwide recovery after the economic crash that began in 2008.

Thomas Derdak
Updated, A. Woodward; Judson MacLaury

PRINCIPAL SUBSIDIARIES

Callaway Golf Ball Company.

PRINCIPAL COMPETITORS

Cleveland Golf; Fortune Brands Inc.; Nike Golf; Ping Golf; TaylorMade-adidas Golf.

FURTHER READING

Barker, Robert, "Why Is Callaway Chasing Golf Balls?" *Business Week*, September 1, 2003, p. 100.

Barkow, Al, "A Controversy Going Longer Than the Drives," *New York Times*, July 15, 2001, p. SP11.

"Ely Callaway: He Did It His Way," *Business Week*, July 23, 2001, p. 44.

Impoco, Jim, "Ely Callaway Hits the Green," *U.S. News & World Report*, April 11, 1994, p. 47.

Jaffe, Thomas, "Big Bertha's Big Bucks," *Forbes*, December 21, 1992, p. 344.

Leavens, Sydney, "Callaway's New CEO Plans to Keep Grip on Old Strategy," *Wall Street Journal*, August 8, 2001, p. B4.

Perry, Nancy J., "How Golf's Big Bertha Grew," *Fortune*, May 18, 1992, p. 113.

Purkey, Mike, Tara Gravel, and Scott Kramer, "Great Big Empire," *Golf Magazine*, May 1998, p. 102.

Strege, John, "Callaway Combines Club, Ball Divisions to Bolster Efficiency," *Golf World*, August 18, 2000, p. S1.

Thomaselli, Rich, "Club Ban Stuns Makers," *Advertising Age*, August 12, 2002, pp. 4.

Canada Council
for the Arts

Canada Council for the Arts

———— ■ ————

350 Albert Street, P.O. Box 1047
Ottawa, Ontario K1P 5V8
Canada
Telephone: (613) 566-4414
Toll Free: (800) 263-5588
Fax: (613) 566-4390
Web site: http://www.canadacouncil.ca

Nonprofit
Founded: 1957
Employees: 208
Total Assets: CAD 264.05 million ($255.5) (2009)
NAICS: 831211 Grantmaking Foundations

■ ■ ■

The Canada Council for the Arts (Canada Council, or Council) is Canada's foremost supporter of the arts. Classified as a charity under the country's income tax laws, the Council is a hybrid creation of parliament that operates as a national entity while holding itself as an independent body outside actual government control. That is, it is accountable to parliament, but not run by it. Since its founding in 1957, the Council's impact on Canadian society has been immense, lifting the country out of a cultural backwater status into a position of artistic prominence. It fulfills its mandate "to foster and promote the study, enjoyment and production of works in the arts" via a variety of grants, endowments, and awards, as well as by administering the Art Bank, Killam Program, Public Lending Right Commission (PLRC), and Canadian Commission for the United Nations

Educational Scientific and Cultural Organization (UNESCO). The Council went through some difficult times in the mid-1990s, forcing budget cuts and staff reduction, but it had rallied by the end of the decade. By the time of its 50th anniversary in 2007, it had broadened its scope considerably and launched a new strategic plan to guide it through the next three to five years. Perhaps even more important, Canada's once nearly nonexistent artistic community had become a vital and mature one that was respected all over the world.

THE MASSEY COMMISSION

As the second half of the 20th century approached, Canada was at a unique crossroad. It had been part of the British Commonwealth since 1867, and the requisite nation building that resulted had been a long and arduous process. Part of the difficulty was simply inherent to any new nation's struggles, but Canada's efforts to eradicate its colonial mentality were further hampered by the vastness of the country itself, the presence of a thriving French Canadian culture within its borders, and its proximity to the United States. The latter became particularly important for two reasons. First, the lack of cultural opportunity in a nation still seeking its own identity was causing Canadian artists to emigrate in droves. Second, the existing void was increasingly being filled by imports from the United States. Thus, the artists, intellectuals, and general citizenry began to put pressure on the Canadian government to help create an artistic infrastructure that would both assist the creative community and promote a genuine Canadian culture.

The government's response was to initiate the Royal Commission on National Development in the Arts, Letters and Sciences on April 8, 1949. The commission was made up of an august group of citizens, including Montreal civil engineer Arthur Surveyer, President Norman A. M. MacKenzie of the University of British Columbia, Dean Georges-Henri Levesque of Laval University's Faculty of Social Sciences, and history professor Hilda Neatby of the University of Saskatchewan. The group's chairman, Vincent Massey, perhaps lent the most cachet and visibility, and the assembly became known as the Massey Commission.

Massey was born in Toronto on February 20, 1887. His great grandfather had founded the extremely successful farm implement company Massey-Harris in 1847, and the family enjoyed great wealth as a result. An advantageous birthright did not prevent Massey from forging an impressive path on his own, however. His many professional pursuits included service as president of the family business (1921–25), cabinet minister for Prime Minister Mackenzie King (1925), diplomatic representative to the United States (Canada's first, 1926–30), high commissioner for Canada in the United Kingdom (1935–46), chancellor of the University of Toronto (1947–53), and Canada's inaugural native-born governor general (1952–59). He was also quite active in the arts, beginning as an actor and director at the University of Toronto, moving on to hold such posts as chairman of London's National and Tate Galleries and chair of the National Gallery of Canada, and writing several books. (Artistic endeavors were something of a family tradition, it appears, as Massey's brother was noted Hollywood actor Raymond Massey.) Distinguished and accomplished, Massey was named to head the commission that would change the face of Canadian culture.

The Massey Commission held 114 public hearings between August 1949 and July 1950. More than 450 formal submissions were considered, and various experts submitted special reports. The culmination of that investigation was the "Massey Report," which was issued in 1951. Extensive and thoughtful, the report explored the past, examined the present, and made recommendations for the future. Its proposals included the creation of a national library, federal funding for universities, and a revamping of the radio and television industry. Not incidentally, it also recommended the establishment of a Canada Council for the Encouragement of the Arts, Letters, Humanities and Social Sciences in order to develop the country's native cultural and intellectual talents. It would take time to bear fruit, but the seeds of the Council had been planted.

CREATION OF THE COUNCIL

The Massey Commission's ideas were both groundbreaking and a product of their time. State patronage of the arts was then a suspect proposition in North America, unlike in Europe. Additionally, there was much reluctance in Canada's provinces, especially Quebec, to cede power to the federal government. The former objection particularly resonated in the aftermath of World War II, and the commission took great pains to articulate that a Canada Council would be supported, but not controlled, by the government. The latter reluctance led to years of territorial squabbling. Nonetheless, the Canada Council came to fruition through an act of parliament on March 28, 1957. Most of the other major recommendations of the commission were also implemented that year.

Fundamental to the Council's mandate was its independence from government. This was done by fashioning the organization to operate at arm's length from the state while still being accountable to parliament through the minister of Canadian heritage. Its broader instruction, however, as quoted on the Council's Web site, was to "foster and promote the study and enjoyment of, and production of works in, the arts, humanities and social sciences" through a variety of grants, endowments, and services to the artistic community. At the time of its founding, the Council was also tasked with responsibility for the Canadian Commission for UNESCO. Initial funding for the newly minted organization was obtained from the estate taxes of two important, but very different, Canadian industrialists: Izaak Walton Killam and Sir James Hamet Dunn.

Killam was born in Nova Scotia in 1885 and worked his way up from humble beginnings to catch the eye of Max Aitken (later Lord Beaverbrook) at the

KEY DATES

1949: Royal Commission on National Development in the Arts, Letters, and Sciences, chaired by Vincent Massey, is formed.

1951: Massey Commission Report is published.

1957: Canada Council for the Arts is created by parliamentary act and initially funded through the estate taxes of Sir James Dunn and Izaak Walton Killam.

1995: Budget and staff cuts are instituted.

2007: Council celebrates 50th anniversary and launches new strategic plan.

Union Bank of Halifax. He joined Aitken's new investment firm, the Royal Securities Corporation, in 1904, and he replaced his mentor as president 10 years later. Killam remained head of Royal Securities for 40 years, establishing a vast empire that included interests in publishing, pulp and paper, utilities, construction, and even chocolate, and becoming one of the richest Canadians of the time in the process. Despite such fantastic success, however, he was reticent and little known to the general public, preferring the comparatively modest pleasures of salmon fishing, baseball, and the company of his wife, Dorothy.

Dunn, on the other hand, was somewhat more ostentatious. He shared a modest background with Killam, as well as the friendship of Aitken and an unerring sense of business, but the similarities stopped there. Dunn began his career as a salesman, went on to become a lawyer, spent a number of years in international finance, and wound down his professional life with the coup of covertly orchestrating the resurrection of the once-bankrupt Algoma Steel Corporation. While such occupational triumphs would not have been unknown to Killam, the three wives, personal brand of whiskey, and Salvador Dali painting of Dunn as Caesar might have given the more reticent mogul pause. The same might be said of the fits of pique or entitlement that caused Dunn to, for instance, send one of his personal airplanes to fetch fresh blueberries for dinner out of season or heave table settings to the floor when a hapless waiter displeased him.

For all their disparity of temperament, however, Killam and Dunn were major contributors to the arts during their lifetimes. (Killam characteristically operated anonymously, while Dunn, just as true to type, was suspicious of large bequests because of their perceived potential to create dependency.) It was therefore fitting that upon their respective deaths in 1955 and 1956, the ensuing combined revenues of approximately $100 million went to funding the Canada Council in its infancy.

MOVING INTO THE 21 CENTURY

As the years passed, the Council was inarguably successful in fulfilling its mandate. In its first year of operation, for example, it granted assistance to nine orchestras, three theater companies, three dance companies, and two periodicals. By 1992 those numbers had grown to 33 orchestras, 197 theater groups, 35 dance companies, approximately 100 periodicals, and more than 700 arts organizations overall. In 2007 the Council awarded grants to nearly 1,600 arts organizations that had expanded to include opera companies, art galleries, media arts concerns, and interdisciplinary arts, as well as to more than 2,300 individuals. Furthermore, its responsibilities had increased to include the administration of many prominent awards, the Art Bank, the Killam Program, and the Public Lending Right Commission (PLRC).

The Council had encountered challenges along the way. The Canadian government underwent some major belt-tightening in the mid-1990s, and the Council was not immune to the effects. Cost-reducing measures, such as cutting its staff by one-third, reorganizing the arts sections to seven rather than ten, and paring its board members from 21 down to 11, were invoked in a bid to shrink administrative costs by close to 50 percent over three years. Happily, the restructuring was successful, and the Council was entering a period of renaissance by the close of the decade.

The Council marked its 50th anniversary in 2007 with a broadened scope and new strategic plan, the action phase of which was released in 2008. The five key elements of the plan were to reinforce the Council's commitment to individual artists, strengthen its efforts in all areas of the country, enhance its role in promoting equity in the arts, nurture partnerships with other organizations to effectively further its mandate, and shore up its internal structure and services to maximize its support of the arts. It was a sweeping proposal, but no less so than the Council's original reason for being Canada's artistic community no longer required support simply to discover itself and become viable. Under the auspices of the Council, it had matured and developed into a diverse, well-established, and highly respected community both within the country's borders and abroad. It was still in need of financial support, as is the nature of the arts the world over, but the "genuine

Canadian culture" envisioned by the Massey Commission had long since become a reality.

Margaret L. Moser

FURTHER READING

Barnes, Michael, *Great Northern Characters*. Burnstown, Ontario: General Store Publishing House, 1995, pp. 163–70.

Bélanger, Claude, "Readings in Quebec History: Massey Report," Marianopolis College, 1998, revised August 23, 2000, http://faculty.marianopolis.edu/c.belanger/quebechistory/readings/massey.htm.

"Board Profile—Canada Council for the Arts," Government of Canada, June 4, 2009, http://www.appointments-nominations.gc.ca/boardProfileOrg.asp?OrgID=CCL&type-typ=2&lang=eng.

"Canada Council," National Center for Charitable Statistics, http://nccsdataweb.urban.org/PubApps/showVals.php?ft=bmf&ein=986000843.

Carter, Don, "His Excellency, The Right Honourable Vincent Massey," Library and Archives Canada, January 27, 2001, http://www.collectionscanada.gc.ca/massey/h5-200-e.html.

"Izaak Walton Killam," Killam Trusts, http://www.killamtrusts.ca/izaak.asp.

Maingot, Jen, "The Elusive Grant: An Interview with the Canada Council for the Arts," Writer's Block, Fall 2002, http://www.writersblock.ca/fall2002/interv.htm.

"Milestones, Jan. 16, 1956," *Time*, http://www.time.com/time/magazine/article/0,9171,861861,00.html.

The Cleveland Clinic
Foundation

9500 Euclid Avenue
Cleveland, Ohio 44195
U.S.A.
Telephone: (216) 444-2200
Toll Free: (800) 223-2273
Web site: http://www.clevelandclinic.org

Nonprofit
Founded: 1921
Employees: 27,273
Gross Receipts: $3.5 billion (2008)
NAICS: 622110 General Medical and Surgical Hospital

■ ■ ■

The Cleveland Clinic Foundation is among the largest and most respected hospital systems in the United States, with 4.2 million patient visits and more than 50,000 inpatient hospital admissions in 2008. Developed from a group practice following World War I, by 2010 the Cleveland Clinic employed nearly 2,000 physicians and scientists and comprised 10 regional hospitals in northeast Ohio, hospitals in Florida and Ontario, Canada, the Sheikh Khalifa Medical City in Abu Dhabi, and the Lou Ruvo Center for Brain Health in Las Vegas. The Clinic's heart program is among the best in the world and was ranked number one in the United States by *U.S. News & World Report* for 15 years in a row beginning in 1995. The Clinic's programs in urology, rheumatology, and gastrointestinal disorders are also ranked among the best in the nation.

FOUNDED AS A GROUP PRACTICE IN 1921

The Cleveland Clinic was founded in 1921 by three medical doctors, George Crile, Frank E. Bunts, and William Lower, who had returned to the United States following their service as surgeons in World War I. Each had been impressed by the efficiency he observed in military hospitals, where members of medical and surgical specialties worked as a single team to save lives. This type of health care collaboration was new at the time and had not been implemented in the country's civilian hospitals. Making teamwork the basis for their new clinic, the physicians took as their motto: "Better care of the sick, investigation into their problems, and further education of those who serve."

To round out their capabilities the founders included Dr. John Phillips, a respected clinician and expert in internal medicine. The Cleveland Clinic opened for business in February 1921 in a building now known as the T building, with 13 doctors and four nurses. Its success was immediate, and the popularity of the clinic allowed the founders to construct a new 184-bed hospital to expand the Clinic's campus in 1924.

From the outset, the Clinic developed specialized divisions, with individual physicians overseeing clinical laboratories and departments of dermatology, endocrinology, urology, and otolaryngology. As the practice grew, specialists in plastic surgery, gynecology, thoracic surgery, vascular surgery, and colorectal surgery came on board. One of these early doctors, Russell L. Haden, who served as chief of medicine from 1930 to

1949, was a laboratory-oriented scientist who made important contributions to the field of blood disease.

TRAGIC FIRE KILLS 123 IN 1929

On May 15, 1929, tragedy struck: 80 patients and 43 staff members, including founder Dr. John Phillips, were killed at the Clinic when a fire exploded in a basement storage room and released clouds of toxic yellow gas that spread throughout the building. The gas was generated by the ignition of nitro-cellulose x-ray film that had been placed too close to a bare 100-watt light bulb. Most of the deaths in the incident were caused by inhalation of the gases as people were overcome before they could escape from the burning building. The disaster resulted in many improvements to safety regulations for the storage of x-ray film, the mandatory use of safety film that would not explode, and for better protection from smoke inhalation for police and firefighters. The Cleveland Clinic was eventually absolved of legal responsibility for the fire, including $3 million in lawsuits, because the film had been stored properly according to laws of the time, and they settled the case out of court for $45,000.

Following the tragedy the remaining founders renewed their commitment to the Clinic. However, their medical building was unusable, with extensive damage to the interior including brown stains from the smoke

and clouds of gas. Rumors circulated that the building continued to emit fumes, making patients reluctant to enter. The headmistress of a girls' school directly across the street from the damaged building came to the rescue, offering all three floors of the school's dormitory. The Clinic reopened there on May 20, only five days after the disaster.

FACING CHALLENGES DURING THE GREAT DEPRESSION

In October 1929 the stock market crashed, and the country was plunged into the Great Depression. As the Depression deepened and dragged on, all staff members took a series of significant pay cuts. The Clinic, however, was simultaneously growing rapidly both in prestige and in practice. Although they were worried about the economic climate in the country, as well as about lingering court cases from the disaster that might still go against them, the founders decided to build an addition to the Clinic. Financial growth of the Clinic during the early 1930s was steady, although this was mainly due to donations made by the doctors. The men borrowed $850,000 to construct the new building, a loan for which Crile and Lower put up their own life insurance policies as collateral.

Building commenced by the end of 1929, and by 1931 there existed what Crile called a "beautiful cathedral for service." Dr. Crile, who was 70 years old in 1934, developed glaucoma and then cataracts, and began to direct his efforts toward research. The area of Crile's research (analyzing the adrenal system as a means of possible treatment for conditions including hypertension, peptic ulcer, and epilepsy) was considered controversial, and his work attracted little attention or funding. Fortunately for the Clinic, however, other staff physicians were initiating a series of astonishing medical breakthroughs that would continue to occur at Cleveland Clinic at a steady pace for the next 70 years.

GROWTH AND SUCCESS FOLLOWING WORLD WAR II

By the end of the Great Depression the Clinic was on stable ground and growing steadily. The number of employees had increased from 216 to 739, and the Clinic had been able to repay all debts incurred in constructing the new building. Henry S. Sherman succeeded Crile as president in 1940 and then became chairman in 1943, at which time Edward C. Daoust assumed the role of president. The transition of power among the doctors was rocky at times, and hot-tempered personalities among them led to contentious meetings. Fortunately these same men, chief of medicine

KEY DATES

■

1921: Cleveland Clinic opens in February with 13 doctors and four nurses.
1929: The main building of the Clinic catches fire, killing 123 people including founder Dr. John Phillips.
1967: Heart surgeon Dr. René Favaloro pioneers coronary bypass surgery.
1985: The Crile Building, an outpatient facility designed by Cesar Pelli, opens.
1988: The Clinic's 120 heart transplants set a national record for a single hospital.
2002: The Cleveland Clinic Lerner College of Medicine opens.
2008: The Sydell and Arnold Miller Family Heart & Vascular Institute and the Glickman Urological and Kidney Institute open.
2009: The Cleveland Clinic Lou Ruvo Center for Brain Health opens in Las Vegas.

Dr. Russell Haden, chief of surgery Dr. Thomas E. Jones, Dr. A. D. Ruedemann, and many other Clinic physicians, were achieving breakthroughs in medical science that overshadowed their disagreements.

During World War II the Clinic further enhanced its reputation for excellence in patient care. Medical specialties became more clearly defined, and patient registration for 1947 reached 31,504, three times what it had been a decade before. Medical milestones of the 1940s included the discovery of the connection between high blood pressure and heart disease by Dr. Irvine H. Page, director of the Research Division. In 1948 Dr. Page isolated the brain chemical serotonin, which gained enormous importance for the understanding of emotional health over the following decades.

George Lower, the last of the founders, died in 1948, and that same year Clarence M. Taylor, former executive vice president of Lincoln Electric Company, became the Clinic's executive director. Taylor implemented a business model to organize the physicians' responsibilities more clearly, but over the next few years Ruedemann and Haden left the Clinic and Jones died. Medical breakthroughs during the 1950s included the identification of carpal tunnel syndrome, another discovery that would achieve increased importance in decades to come. In 1958 cardiologist F. Mason Sones Jr. developed coronary arteriography, the viewing of the heart and its vessels through moving X-rays. One day

Sones had accidentally injected a large amount of dye into a coronary artery, and when no ill effects occurred, he deliberately injected smaller doses that provided a clear X-ray picture. Sones used his technique to locate blockages in the arteries, and it later enabled doctors to evaluate the success of coronary bypass operations.

In 1955 the Clinic initiated a new form of self-governance by creating a Board of Governors, of which physician Fay A. LeFevre became president. The Board dealt democratically with pressing issues at hand, such as voting to acquire property on which to build new facilities and to create more subspecialties of clinical practice. During LeFevre's tenure, a west wing was added to the hospital building. To add further space, the Board voted to shut down its obstetrical service to make more space for cardiac surgery. As the obstetrics ward was by law completely separated from the rest of the hospital, this move would have tremendous import for the Clinic as the consolidation of operating rooms, recovery rooms, intensive care units, and convalescent wards helped the Clinic build what would soon be its most famous department. In 1967 Dr. René Favaloro performed the world's first coronary bypass surgery in the new cardiovascular ward, an operation that by the 21st century saved tens of thousands of lives every year.

EXPANSION INTO THE MODERN ERA AFTER 1970

The Cleveland Clinic's modern era is considered to begin with the appointment of George E. Wasmuth as chairman of the Board of Governors in 1969. He was the Clinic's first physician administrator, having been formerly the head of the Department of Anesthesiology. The most urgent task facing the new administration was the creation of more space, and Wasmuth immediately began raising money to add a south hospital wing, a new research building, a hotel, and two parking garages. The Clinic borrowed money from local banks for the first time to finance these expansions, as the federal government imposed price and wage controls on physicians during the early 1970s, and funding the project from within the institution became impossible.

Wasmuth presciently persuaded the governors and trustees that all available land around the Clinic should be purchased. He is credited with foreseeing the Clinic's role as a national and international health powerhouse in the years to come. There was some resistance from the surrounding community to the unfettered expansion of the Clinic, and the organization had to go to court several times to resolve issues such as zoning changes, neighborhood use variances, the building of viaducts over city streets, and street closures. In most cases the Clinic prevailed.

Many members of the Clinic staff and the larger community found Wasmuth's management style to be autocratic, however, and he was replaced as chairman of the Board of Governors in 1977 by William S. Kiser. Under Kiser's leadership, management was reorganized under a more traditionally corporate model. Unlike Wasmuth, Kiser preferred delegating responsibility among a group of physician managers and other administrators. Kiser addressed the Clinic's continued need for expansion by authorizing a sale of long-term bonds to raise $228 million in June 1982. The bonds, which all sold promptly, represented the largest use of private financing in the history of U.S. health care to date.

PREPARING FOR THE FUTURE
1980–99

Kiser also set up offices that had not previously been established, including departments devoted to public affairs, development, archives, and long-range planning. This last became the forum for the Century Project, which involved adding several new buildings to the Clinic's footprint, plus a pedestrian walkway, and another garage. One of these new buildings, the Crile building, was designed by noted architect Cesar Pelli. Opened in 1985, the new building boasted 520,000 square feet of space and was used to house some 70 percent of the staff and 17 medical departments. During Kiser's tenure, the Cleveland Clinic had its peak number of staffed beds: 1,018. Kiser also presided over the opening of the Clinic's first satellite hospital, Cleveland Clinic Florida in February 1988, in Fort Lauderdale with 28 staff physicians.

Medical advances multiplied along with the Clinic's floor space. In 1988 the Clinic performed 120 heart transplants, a national record for a single hospital, with survival rates that were also higher than the national average. This scale of expansion led to financial difficulties for the Clinic, however, especially when it was revealed that the land in Florida was worth less than half of the $55,000 per acre that the Clinic had paid for it. A project to transfer billing and medical records to an electronic format also failed, costing the Clinic millions. The trustees asked Kiser and the Board of Governors to bring in McKinsey & Company, an outside consulting firm with expertise in rescuing floundering companies to implement what became known as the Economic Improvement Program. McKinsey's analysis of the Clinic's finances was that if decisive action were not taken, the Clinic would have a negative cash flow of $75

million within 18 months and would enter a terminal freefall.

Kiser stepped down in the summer of 1989 to be replaced by Dr. Floyd D. Loop, chairman of the Clinic's Department of Thoracic and Cardiovascular Surgery. Loop had joined the staff in 1970 and was appointed department chairman in 1975. He is credited with overseeing the Clinic's financial recovery and ensuring its future stability. In his first Health of the Clinic Address, Loop said, "[f]or the first time we need to think strategically. We must adapt or we will go the way of the dinosaurs ourselves.... In other words, if we want to stay the same, things will have to change." Loop appointed a team of management professionals from both inside and outside the Clinic to help with the financial recovery, including Dr. Melinda Estes, the first woman member of the Board of Governors, who was appointed head of a newly created Office of Clinical Effectiveness. By the end of 1990 Loop's efforts had created the turnaround: Cash flow exceeded $30 million.

Loop also steered the Clinic smoothly into the era of managed care, brokering a contract with Kaiser Permanente in 1992 under which the Cleveland Clinic Hospital became the primary inpatient destination for Kaiser subscribers in northern Ohio. This in turn led to the development of five satellite Family Health Centers, each located 30 to 45 minutes' driving time from the main campus. A new Emergency Medicine and Access Center was also opened in 1994. Chief among Loop's achievements during the 1990s was the formation of the Cleveland Health Network, an affiliation among 10 area hospitals that would better enable all of them to provide services under the managed care system. Loop also reinstated the Clinic's obstetrical program, which had been shut down in 1966 to add space for the cardiac surgery program. It was also during Loop's tenure that the cardiology department became one of the world's most respected centers for heart care.

Beginning in the mid-1990s, Loop began sowing the seeds for what would become known as the Cleveland Clinic Health System. This was an enormous expansion comprising the acquisition of nine hospitals in the northeast Ohio region, the assembly of the Cleveland Clinic Health System, and the formation of the Physician Organization; the construction of integrated clinics and hospitals in Naples and Fort Lauderdale, Florida; the creation of 14 family health centers; construction of a research and education institute, an eye institute, and a cancer center on the Cleveland campus; expanded emergency services including 24 new operating rooms; and the founding of the Cleveland Clinic Lerner College of Medicine.

ADVANCES IN RESEARCH, EDUCATION, PATIENT CARE: 2000–10

The Cleveland Clinic Lerner College of Medicine came into existence in May 2002 through an agreement with Case Western Reserve University and a gift of $100 million from Alfred Lerner, president of the Cleveland Clinic Foundation. The Lerner College sought to promote research careers among medical graduates, stating that the new medical school was to train "physician investigators through innovative approaches to the integration of basic science, research and clinical medicine." The first class of 32 students enrolled in July 2004.

Medical breakthroughs at the Cleveland Clinic during the first decade of the 21st century included the discovery of the first gene linked to juvenile macular degeneration (2000); the discovery of first gene linked to coronary artery disease (2003); the first kidney surgery performed through a port in the patient's navel (2007); and the nation's first near-total face transplant (2008). This last highly publicized operation involved a multidisciplinary team of doctors and surgeons led by Dr. Maria Siemionow, who performed a 22-hour operation to transplant 80 percent of the face of a woman who had suffered severe facial trauma.

On June 2004 Floyd Loop retired after nearly 15 years as chief executive officer. The Board of Trustees announced the election of Delos M. "Toby" Cosgrove as the Clinic's next CEO. Cosgrove inherited a very different organization from the one Loop had joined. Research had moved from the sidelines of the Clinic's work to a sophisticated and central position. Fundraising had become highly organized, and the Clinic's endowment had increased during the Loop years from $150 million to $800 million. The organization had grown enormously to become a world-class medical center and teaching institute.

In 2008 the Cleveland Clinic established the Sydell and Arnold Miller Family Heart & Vascular Institute and the Glickman Urological and Kidney Institute. That year the Clinic employed about 2,000 full-time salaried physicians and researchers and 7,600 nurses in more than 100 medical specialties. It opened the Cleveland Clinic Lou Ruvo Center for Brain Health in Las Vegas and operated internationally in Toronto, Canada, and in Abu Dhabi, United Arab Emirates. In addition to managing the Sheikh Khalifa Medical City in Abu Dhabi, the Clinic was building a hospital nearby on Sowwah Island that was scheduled for completion in 2012.

The Cleveland Clinic, which began modestly with a group of doctors returning from war to civilian practice, had by 2010 grown into a world-renowned research and care organization that treated patients each year from every state and more than 80 foreign countries. With its well-endowed facilities and academic programs, it prepared for continued expansion in delivering state-of-the-art care.

Melanie Bush

PRINCIPAL DIVISIONS

Education; Patient Care; Research.

FURTHER READING

Altman, Lawrence, "First Face Transplant Performed in the U.S.," *New York Times*, December 16, 2008.

Choate, Alan, "Clinic's CEO Wants to Help: Cosgrove Hints at What Institution Might Bring to Las Vegas," *Las Vegas Review-Journal*, September 24, 2009.

Clough, John D., M.D., ed. *To Act as A Unit: The Story of the Cleveland Clinic*, Cleveland: Cleveland Clinic Foundation, 2004.

Jesitus, John, "Facing Forward: Cleveland Clinic Performs First U.S. Transplant; Ethical Concerns Remain," *Dermatology Times*, February 2009.

Krugman, Paul, "Drugs, Devices and Doctors," *New York Times*, December 16, 2005.

"World's 1st Total Artificial Heart to Dual Heart & Liver Transplant Performed at Cleveland Clinic," *Blood Weekly*, November 19, 2009.

Zawacki, Michael, "Prescription: Innovation: Cleveland Clinic CEO Toby Cosgrove Says a Region Needs Smart People and Good Ideas to Compete in the Knowledge Economy," *Inside Business*, March 2005.

Comcast Corporation

―――――――■――――――――

1 Comcast Center
Philadelphia, Pennsylvania 19103
U.S.A.
Telephone: (215) 286-1700
Toll Free: (800) 266-2278
Fax: (215) 981-7790
Web site: http://www.comcast.com

Public Company
Founded: 1963 as American Cable Systems, Inc.
Incorporated: 1969
Employees: 100,000
Sales: $35.76 billion (2009)
Stock Exchanges: NASDAQ
Ticker Symbol: CMCSA, CMCSK
NAICS: 515210 Cable and Other Subscription Programming; 517210 Wireless Telecommunications Carriers (except Satellite)

■ ■ ■

Comcast Corporation is a leading cable, telecommunications, and entertainment firm. Comcast is among the largest cable television companies in the United States, with 23.8 million customers in 39 states. The company is also a major provider of wireless telecommunications products and services, serving nearly 16 million Internet subscribers and an additional 7.4 million telephone customers. Since the emergence of broadband technologies in the 1990s, Comcast has been one of the fastest-growing cable and communications companies in the country, acquiring rival AT&T broadband in 2002 and swallowing up a host of smaller regional cable and Internet firms. In late 2009 Comcast made an aggressive push to become a major producer of video content when it offered $30 billion to acquire NBC Universal.

BIRTH OF A CABLE TELEVISION COMPANY: THE SIXTIES

Comcast has its origin in the early 1960s with American Cable Systems, Inc., a small cable operation serving Tupelo, Mississippi. At the time, American Cable was one of only a few community antenna television (CATV) services in the nation. The CATV business was predicated on the fact that rural areas were underserved by commercial television stations, which catered to large metropolitan areas. Without CATVs huge antennas that pulled in distant signals, consumers in these areas had little use for television. Although they were required to pay for CATV, customers considered the benefits worth the cost.

In 1963 Ralph J. Roberts and his brother Joe sold their interest in Pioneer Industries, a men's accessories business in Philadelphia, and were looking to invest the proceeds in a new industry. After some research, they learned that the Jerrold Electronics Company, the owner of American Cable Systems, wished to sell the CATV concern. The Roberts brothers enlisted a young accountant named Julian Brodsky, who had helped them liquidate Pioneer Industries, and Daniel Aaron, a former system director at Jerrold Electronics, to help them evaluate the opportunity. The four agreed that while the system carried only five channels and served only 1,500 customers, the investment had great potential. Ralph

COMPANY PERSPECTIVES

When Comcast was founded, Ralph J. Roberts's dream was to bring more choice in content and a better quality television picture to our customers. Today, in an age of constantly changing technology, we are still committed to big dreams—and to making those dreams a reality for our customers, our employees, and the communities we serve.

Our promise is made real through: The Customer's Experience. We want our customers to be amazed with the choice Comcast offers, excited by the innovation Comcast provides and satisfied with the service and reliability of every interaction with Comcast. The Reliability of Our Products. High quality products and services are what our customers expect and what we will deliver. Superior Products. Superior products offer more choice and value. Innovation is a constant at Comcast. We will continue to find new ways to give our customers more than ever before.

Roberts bought American Cable Systems and later asked Brodsky and Aaron to join him in managing the company.

Growth within Tupelo was difficult, however. At times, the three were forced to serve as door-to-door salesmen. By 1964 they decided to buy additional franchises in Meridian, Laurel, and West Point, in eastern Mississippi. The following year, American Cable acquired more franchises in Okolona and Baldwyn, Mississippi. While these acquisitions succeeded in increasing subscribership, they failed to have much effect on penetration; there remained an insufficient number of subscribers to deliver a high return given the cost of setting up a local system.

Roberts turned his attention to the larger potential market of Philadelphia. In 1966 he bid successfully for cable franchises in Abington, Cheltenham, and Upper Darby, all northern suburbs of Philadelphia. He then purchased the Westmoreland cable system that served four other communities in western Pennsylvania. To achieve better economies of scale, Roberts dovetailed Westmoreland's operations with those of his other franchises. After establishing a strong foothold in suburban Philadelphia, Roberts extended his company's presence into six additional local communities.

Highly leveraged from this acquisition binge, but eager for more opportunities, Roberts enlisted the *Philadelphia Bulletin* newspaper for a joint venture to build additional cable systems serving Sarasota and Venice, Florida. As part of a limited diversification in 1968, Ralph Roberts joined his brother Joe (by then a minor partner in American Cable but also an executive vice president of Muzak Corporation) in purchasing a large franchise to provide the subscription "elevator music" service in Orlando, Florida.

Having decided that the name American Cable Systems sounded too generic for his growing company, Roberts decided in 1969 to change its name. In an effort to build a more technological identity, he took portions of the words "communication" and "broadcast," creating Comcast Corporation and reincorporating the company in Pennsylvania.

EXPANSION INTO NEW MARKETS: THE SEVENTIES AND EIGHTIES

Comcast reorganized its operations somewhat in 1970, selling off its Florida operations to Storer Communications and forming a limited partnership to purchase Multiview Cable, a local franchise serving Hartford County in Maryland. Limited partnerships enabled Comcast to finance growth with a minimal use of operating funds and were used to finance subsequent acquisitions. Predicting growth in the Muzak business, Comcast also acquired a franchise in 1970 for the service in Denver. The company later purchased Muzak franchises in Dallas, Texas; San Diego, California; Detroit, Michigan; and Hartford, Connecticut.

Boasting 40,000 customers but hampered by a continued stagnation in subscriber penetration rates, Comcast still needed funds to finance further expansion. In 1972 Roberts decided to take the company public, offering shares on the over-the-counter market. In 1974 Comcast purchased a cable franchise for Paducah, Kentucky, and in 1976 it acquired systems in Flint, Hillsdale, and Jonesville, Michigan. The following year, Comcast bought out its partners' interest in Multiview.

Cable by this time had become much more than an antenna service. For several years, cable operators had included local access and special programming channels, as well as programming from large independent stations such as WGN in Chicago and WTBS in Atlanta. The government restricted what programming a cable operator could offer, often blocking access to programs that customers clearly wanted. Dan Aaron, a manager with Comcast, was active in the National Cable Television Association (NCTA), lobbying effectively for the relaxation of programming and other restrictions. In 1977, as chairman of the NCTA, Aaron brought many of the industry's efforts to fruition. As the cable industry was allowed to mature, additional cable-only stations were added, making the service viable within metropolitan areas that were already well served by broadcasters.

With this added strength in the company's product offerings, Comcast was able to win franchises to serve parts of northern New Jersey in 1978, as well as Lower Merion, Pennsylvania, and Warren and Clinton, Michigan, in 1979. Through limited partnerships, the company later won franchises for Sterling Heights and St. Clair Shores, Michigan, and Corinth, Mississippi. By 1983 Comcast had purchased Muzak franchises in Indianapolis, Indiana; Buffalo, New York; Scranton, Pennsylvania; and Peoria, Illinois.

The company made an important move in 1983 when, in partnership with a British gambling and entertainment enterprise, Ladbroke, it won a license to establish a cable television system in the residential suburbs of London, England. Most cable licenses in the United States had been taken, and those that remained were expensive or only marginally profitable. The industry was still in its infancy in the United Kingdom, however. In addition, British viewers would appreciate cable's selection; Britain had only about five stations, offering mostly government-supported programming.

In 1984, as Comcast added a cable partnership in Baltimore County and a Muzak franchise in Tyler, Texas, an important change took place in another industry. After a half century of antitrust litigation, the U.S. government broke up the Bell System. As a result, AT&T and its long-distance operations were separated from 22 local Bell companies. Each of these Bell companies was organized into one of seven companies that saw cable television as the next logical course of progression for their telephone networks. The U.S. Congress, however, had already enacted legislation that would prevent telephone companies from taking over the still-fragile cable industry. The Cable Act, which was written primarily to guarantee fair pole attachment rates to cable companies, had the effect of locking telephone companies out of the cable business.

Free for the moment from the ominous threat of competition from any of these multibillion-dollar companies, Comcast proceeded with growth through acquisitions. In 1985, after purchasing cable operations in Pontiac/Waterford, Michigan, Fort Wayne, Indiana, and Jones County, Mississippi, Comcast won a plum: the right to serve the densely populated northeastern Philadelphia area. In 1986 Comcast took over a cable system serving Indianapolis and purchased a 26 percent share in Group W, one of the country's largest cable companies. This brought the company's subscribership to more than one million customers. The following year Comcast acquired a cable system in northwestern Philadelphia from Heritage Communications, thereby cementing its position in suburban Philadelphia.

Turning more toward investments in other cable companies than in actual franchises, Comcast purchased a 20 percent share of Heritage Communications and a 50 percent share of Storer Communications in 1988. The Storer acquisition brought subscribership to more than two million customers and elevated Comcast to the fifth-largest cable company in the United States. Consolidating its partnerships, the company took full control of its Maryland Limited Partnership, Comcast Cablevision of Indiana, and Comcast Cable Investors, a venture capital subsidiary.

ENTERING THE CELLULAR PHONE BUSINESS: THE LATE EIGHTIES AND EARLY NINETIES

Also in 1988 Comcast turned an important strategic corner regarding telephone companies when it purchased American Cellular Network, or Amcell, a cellular telephone business serving New Jersey. For the first time, cable and telephone companies, prevented from competition in landline services, were facing each other in the cellular telephone business. Also for the first time, a cable company was able to offer telephone customers an alternative to the telephone company.

In 1990, a year after relocating the corporate offices from Bala Cynwyd, Pennsylvania, to Philadelphia, Ralph Roberts shocked the company and the industry by naming his 30-year-old son, Brian, to succeed him as president of the company, while Ralph Roberts remained as chairman. Brian Roberts, who had impeccable academic credentials, silenced critics by proving to be a highly effective manager. In addition, having begun work in the company at the age of 7, he had 23 years' seniority, more than virtually anyone but his father.

That same year, after having purchased an interest in an additional franchise serving suburban London, the company's newly formed international unit won more British franchises, allowing the company to serve Cambridge and Birmingham. Comcast now counted more than one million customers in Britain alone. Increasingly, however, Comcast's smaller companies, such as Amcell, were beginning to experience slower growth. Rather than allow Amcell to be swallowed up later by a larger suitor, Comcast struck a deal in 1991 with the Metromedia Company, in which it purchased that company's Metrophone cellular unit for $1.1 billion. The new joint company, established in 1992, quadrupled Comcast's potential market to more than 7.3 million customers.

Later that year, the company's offices at One Meridian Plaza in Philadelphia were destroyed by a fire that took 19 hours to put out. Only 8 days later, the company set up shop 4 blocks away at 1234 Market Street. It was a temporary location, but the company's 250 employees were once again in business.

In September 1992 Comcast staged a five-way international telephone call using the Comcast network and a long-distance carrier. The purpose was to demonstrate that the company could handle telephone calls and completely bypass the local telephone network. While the demonstration was intended to raise investor interest in such bypass operations, it also succeeded in scaring telephone companies sufficiently to argue for permission to offer cable television services. The company continued to bolster its position in the bypass business in 1992, when it gained a 20 percent interest (later reduced to 15 percent) in Teleport Communications Corporation, operator of a fiberoptic-based bypass telecommunications network that was serving more than 50 major markets nationwide by the mid-1990s.

Late in 1992 Comcast took over 50 percent of Storer Communications, dividing the assets of that company with Denver-based Tele-Communications, another leading cable firm. Storer was forced into dissolution by heavy debt carried at high interest. The proceeds from the sale enabled Storer's parent company, SCI Holdings, to retire much of that debt.

SEARCHING FOR NEW GROWTH OPPORTUNITIES: 1992–99

The mid-1990s saw a frenzy of activity throughout the cable and telecommunications industries as deregulation increasingly brought cable and telephone companies sometimes into competition with each other, other times into partnerships. The period also saw a flurry of acquisitions, mergers, and system swaps in the cable industry as companies sought to build networks of contiguous systems to improve efficiencies. Comcast was at the center of all of this activity, and it also made aggressive moves into the area of programming content.

As early as 1992 Comcast had begun testing a forerunner of what eventually became known as the Sprint PCS (personal communications services) digital cellular technology, which delivered crisper sound and more security than analog cellular phone technology. In 1994 Comcast entered into an alliance that formed the Sprint Telecommunications Venture, renamed Sprint Spectrum LP in 1995. The alliance partners were Sprint Corp. (owning 40 percent of the venture), Tele-Communications Inc. (30 percent), and Comcast and Cox Communications Inc. (15 percent each). In the early 1995 Federal Communications Commission (FCC) auction of PCS licenses, Sprint Spectrum was the biggest winner, gaining the rights to wireless licenses in 31 major U.S. markets, covering a population of 156 million. The venture was soon renamed Sprint PCS, and the four partners spent millions of dollars building a wireless network. In 1997 Comcast's cellular operations in Pennsylvania, New Jersey, and Delaware were converted to the digital technology, but by then the company considered Sprint PCS, which faced tough competition from cellular veterans such as AT&T Corp., a drag on earnings. In May 1998 the Sprint PCS partners announced that they planned to sell 10 percent of the venture to the public through a public offering, with Sprint PCS set up as a tracking stock under Sprint's corporate domain. (Shareholders of tracking stocks have very limited voting rights.) This move was considered the first step toward the possible exit of Comcast, Cox, and TCI from the joint venture. Meanwhile, in January 1998 Comcast acquired Global-Com Telecommunications, a regional long-distance service provider. Along with the company's other operations, the addition of GlobalCom (renamed Comcast Telecommunications) enabled Comcast to offer a full range of telecommunications services.

In cable, Comcast in 1994 acquired Maclean Hunter's U.S. cable operations for $1.27 billion, gaining an additional 550,000 customers. In November 1996 Comcast acquired the cable properties of E. W. Scripps Co. in a $1.575 billion stock swap. Scripps's 800,000 customers brought Comcast's cable holdings to more than 4.3 million customers in 21 states, the fourth-largest cable system in the United States. In February 1998 the company agreed to sell its underperforming U.K. cable operations to NTL Inc. for $600 million in stock plus the assumption of $397 million in debt. Three months later Comcast announced that it would spend $500 million over the next several years to take over the 30 percent interest in Jones Intercable Inc., held by the Canada-based BCI Telecom Holding Inc. Jones had a technologically advanced, one-million-customer cable system, much of which was in the suburbs of Washington, D.C., strategically contiguous to some of Comcast's main markets.

Comcast's aggressive moves to become a major provider of entertainment content were perhaps the company's most dramatic actions of this period. Already holding a 13 percent stake in QVC, Inc., the number-one cable shopping channel, Comcast in July 1994 scuttled a planned merger between QVC and CBS Inc. by offering to pay $2.2 billion for a controlling interest in QVC. CBS, refusing to engage in a bidding war, immediately retreated, leaving Comcast to increase its QVC interest to 57 percent. In early 1996 Comcast paid $250 million to acquire a 66 percent stake in a new venture, Comcast-Spectacor, L.P. Most of the remaining ownership interest was held by Spectacor, which owned the Philadelphia Flyers NHL hockey team and two sports arenas in Philadelphia. Comcast-Spectacor was set up to own and operate the Flyers, the Philadelphia 76ers NBA basketball team, and their two arenas. Comcast then leveraged these ownership interests into establishing Comcast SportsNet, a 24-hour regional cable sports channel, which debuted in the fall of 1997 and featured telecasts of Flyers, 76ers, and Philadelphia Phillies (Major League Baseball) games, in addition to other sports programming. In March 1997 Comcast partnered with the Walt Disney Company to acquire a majority interest in E! Entertainment Television, a 24-hour cable network devoted exclusively to entertainment and celebrity programming. E! was available in more than 45 million homes in more than 120 countries around the world.

In June 1997 Microsoft Corp. announced that it would invest $1 billion in Comcast in return for an 11.5 percent nonvoting interest. Microsoft wanted a cable partner for testing interactive television and high-speed computer services, and the company chose Comcast because its cable system was one of the most technologically advanced in the country. By the end of 1997 Comcast had converted about 70 percent of its customers to a new hybrid fiber-coaxial technology, which was more reliable, offered improved signal quality, and had the capacity to deliver more services. The company was also a partner (with a 12 percent interest) in At Home Corporation. ComcastHome was launched in December 1996, offering high-speed interactive services, including 24-hour unlimited Internet access, through a cable modem to customers in Baltimore County, Maryland, and Sarasota, Florida. Additional markets were soon added.

In 1987 Comcast Corporation was almost exclusively a cable television company. Just 10 years later, cable was no longer even the company's largest unit. Out of 1997 revenues of $4.91 billion, $2.08 billion (42.4 percent) came from the company's content operations, $2.07 billion (42.2 percent) came from cable, and $444.9 million (9.1 percent) came from cellular services. Clearly, Comcast was not a firm that rested on its laurels. Furthermore, the partnership with Microsoft promised involvement in additional innovative technologies and services, and Comcast seemed certain to be a central player in the high-tech world of the 21st century.

As the decade drew to a close, Comcast began to focus more intently on expanding its cable and high-speed communications business. In January 1999 the company decided to shed its cellular phone operations, selling the unit to Texas-based SBC Communications for roughly $1.7 billion. Two months later the company began acquisition talks with MediaOne, a Colorado-based broadband company, with a bid valued at roughly $48 billion. If successful, the merger would more than double Comcast's subscriber base while expanding its geographical reach significantly. The proposed deal divided industry analysts. Some thought the merger had the potential to accelerate innovation in the broadband industry, while others considered the price of the bid to be overvalued. By May, however, Comcast had been outbid by rival AT&T. With the failure of the Media-One merger, Comcast's ambitious growth strategy was put on hold.

BECOMING A NATIONWIDE CABLE GIANT: 2000–10

Entering the new century, Comcast did not hesitate to pursue new opportunities. In mid-2001 the company launched an aggressive bid to acquire AT&T's broadband business. Although AT&T rejected the company's initial offer of $44.5 billion, Comcast eventually raised its bid to $72 billion, and by December of that year the two firms had reached a tentative agreement. In spite of widespread protests from other cable firms and consumer groups, the deal achieved final regulatory approval in November 2002. The merger made Comcast the largest cable company in the United States, with 21.8 million subscribers. By comparison, the nation's second-largest cable provider, AOL Time Warner, had only 12.8 million customers.

As it emerged as the dominant player in the pay-TV sector, Comcast was also quietly becoming an industry leader in the area of high-speed Internet access. By 2003 the company had built its broadband customer base to 3.6 million, surpassing such rivals as MSN and AOL. In October 2003 Comcast strengthened its market share even more when it announced that it would double its Internet connection speeds to 3 megabytes per second before the end of the year. Even more attractive to Comcast customers, monthly rates would remain unchanged.

Comcast attempted another bold move in February 2004 when it launched a $49.1 billion hostile bid to acquire the Walt Disney Company. In April, however, Comcast withdrew its offer after it became clear that Disney executives had no interest in negotiating a merger. In the wake of the failed Disney bid, Comcast began to seek other avenues of expansion. In April 2005 the company entered a joint partnership with AOL Time Warner to acquire Adelphia Communications. As part of the deal, Comcast would receive 1.8 million of Adelphia's existing subscribers, raising its total number of customers to 23.3 million.

By 2006 the company's profits were soaring. In the year's first quarter, net earnings ballooned to $466 million, compared with $143 million for the same period in 2005, an increase of more than 300 percent. Meanwhile, the company's total first-quarter sales grew 10 percent to $5.9 billion. As the decade drew to a close and the country sank into a deep recession, Comcast managed to remain highly profitable. Even after Microsoft sold its 7.26 percent stake in the company in January 2009, Comcast continued to see steady earnings growth. Second-quarter profits for 2009 rose to $967 million, an increase of 53 percent over the same period in 2008. Revenues, meanwhile, rose 4.5 percent to $8.94 billion. Much of this growth was driven by an increase in the company's subscriber base, as well as by price increases.

With this competitive advantage over its struggling rivals, Comcast remained aggressive in its pursuit of new growth opportunities. In late 2009 the company reached a tentative agreement with General Electric to acquire a controlling stake in NBC Universal in a deal worth a projected $30 billion. As part of the merger, Comcast would fold its own television channels, including E! Entertainment and Versus, into the joint venture. The agreement, however, soon ran into opposition from consumer groups and federal agencies, which feared that the merger would give Comcast unparalleled control over both distribution and content creation in the cable industry. By January 2010 it was clear that the company would need to clear numerous hurdles before the deal could gain regulatory approval.

John Simley
Updated, David E. Salamie; Stephen Meyer

PRINCIPAL SUBSIDIARIES

More than 1,000 subsidiaries throughout the world, including principal U.S. subsidiaries Comcast Cable Communications, LLC; Comcast Cable Communications Holdings, Inc.; Comcast Cable Holdings, LLC; Comcast MO Group, Inc.; Comcast MO of Delaware, LLC.

PRINCIPAL COMPETITORS

The DIRECTV Group, Inc.; Dish Network Corporation; Time Warner Cable Inc.

FURTHER READING

Brown, Rich, "Brian Roberts: Stretching Comcast's Reach through New Technology," *Broadcasting & Cable*, August 2, 1993, p. 29.

Cohen, Warren, "Scrambled Signals in the TV World: Comcast Scuttles the Vaunted CBS-QVC Deal," *U.S. News & World Report*, July 25, 1994, p. 43.

Fabrikant, Geraldine, "The Heir Is Clearly Apparent at Comcast," *New York Times*, June 22, 1997, pp. 1, 12.

Fernandez, Bob, "Comcast CEO: On the Sidelines for 'Tonight Show' Flap," *Philadelphia Inquirer*, January 28, 2010, p. C2.

Hazelton, Lynette, "Comcast Online Makes Its Debut," *Philadelphia Business Journal*, July 18, 1997, p. 10.

Higgins, John M., and Richard Tedesco, "PC/TV à la Bill Gates: Comcast Deal Is the Latest Evidence of Microsoft's Quest to Grab a Large Piece of TV Action," *Broadcasting & Cable*, June 16, 1997, p. 6.

Landro, Laura, "Comcast Names Brian Roberts President, Extending Family's Hold on Cable Firm," *Wall Street Journal*, February 8, 1990, p. B6.

Lieberman, David, "AT&T Broadband, Comcast Get Merger OK," *USA Today*, November 14, 2002, p. 1B.

McGraw, Dan, "No Ordinary Cable Guys," *U.S. News & World Report*, July 8, 1996, p. 44.

Stern, Christopher, "Comcast Makes Its Play: Advancing with a Flurry of Acquisitions, the Cable Firm Prepares to Reap the Benefits of a Customer 'Super-Cluster,'" *Washington Post*, August 28, 2000, p. F16.

Weber, Joseph, "Comcast Plays Hard to Get," *Business Week*, November 29, 1993, pp. 82–83.

CONSECO®
Conseco, Inc.

11825 North Pennsylvania Street
Carmel, Indiana 46032-4555
U.S.A.
Telephone: (317) 817-6100
Fax: (317) 817-2847
Web site: http://www.conseco.com

Public Company
Incorporated: 1979 as Security National of Indiana Corp.
Employees: 3,700
Sales: $4.19 billion (2008)
Stock Exchanges: New York
Ticker Symbol: CNO
NAICS: 524113 Direct Life Insurance Carriers; 524114 Direct Health and Medical Insurance Carriers; 524126 Direct Property and Casualty Insurance Carriers

■ ■ ■

Conseco, Inc., is a diversified insurance company based in Carmel, Indiana. Conseco underwrites a range of policies in the areas of life, health, and property and casualty insurance. At the same time, the company also offers its customers a range of annuity and retirement fund products. In the 1990s Conseco grew to become one of the largest and most successful insurance firms in the United States. By the early 21st century, however, the company was forced to declare bankruptcy after a disastrous attempt to expand into the consumer lending and financial planning industries. Upon exiting bankruptcy protection in 2003, Conseco once again

became committed to building its core insurance businesses.

INNOVATIVE BEGINNINGS

Stephen C. Hilbert founded the company and guided its meteoric rise. Hilbert had an unusual background for a chairman of a major financial institution. He was raised in a small rural community near Terre Haute, Indiana, and attended nearby Indiana State University. After only two years of college, however, Hilbert became restless. "I dropped out to sell encyclopedias," Hilbert explained to *Barron's* in 1991. "After I made $19,000 my first year as a 19-year-old, I knew I didn't need a college education to make a good living."

Hilbert drifted into the insurance business in the 1970s. After working for a small company for a few years, he got a taste of the corporate world at Aetna. Although Hilbert admired the muscle of Aetna and its corporate counterparts, he was frustrated by their lack of innovation. During this experience he conceived the idea for a new kind of enterprise, a life insurance company that would combine the flexibility and innovation of a small firm with the marketing savvy, financial strength, and computer systems of a big financial institution.

Just as he had done to sell encyclopedias in the mid-1960s, Hilbert started knocking on doors in the late 1970s. This time, however, he was looking for seed capital to fund his business start-up, Security National of Indiana Corp. Although several regional securities firms laughed Hilbert and his five-page business plan out the door, by the early 1980s he had raised $3 mil-

COMPANY PERSPECTIVES

Conseco's mission is to be a leading provider of financial security for life, health and retirement needs of middle market Americans. Headquartered in suburban Indianapolis, Indiana, our companies provide supplemental health insurance, life insurance and annuities. Through our subsidiaries and a nationwide network of distributors, Conseco helps more than 4 million customers step up to a better, more secure future.

lion in capital. In 1982 Hilbert acquired his first life insurance company, Executive Income Life Insurance Co., for $1.3 million. By slashing the fat and inefficiency out of his new purchase, Hilbert was able to return the ailing insurer to profitability after only one year.

True to his original concept of combining size with innovation, Hilbert established his enterprise in 1982 under two separate companies. Security National Corp. was formed to acquire and manage existing life insurance companies. To complement that holding company's subsidiaries, Security National of Indiana was established to develop and market new life insurance products and services. Although the two companies merged to form one holding company late in 1983, internal operations still reflected Hilbert's original concept.

Hilbert's company acquired Consolidated National Life Insurance Co. in August 1983. In December of that year Hilbert's two holding companies were merged under the name Conseco, Inc. With about 25 employees and assets worth $3 million, Conseco substantially improved the performance of its two acquisitions during 1983 and 1984. The company then purchased Lincoln American Life Insurance Co. early in 1985 for $25 million. Lincoln's headquarters in Memphis, Tennessee, were quickly moved to Conseco's burgeoning offices in Carmel. Hilbert, with a few successful acquisitions under his belt, took Conseco public in 1985 in an effort to boost its investment capital. By the end of the year the company's asset base had increased to $102 million.

FOCUS ON EXPANSION: THE LATE EIGHTIES

Galvanized by its proven ability to acquire and improve insurance companies, Conseco stepped up its acquisition

efforts during the second half of the decade. In 1986 it purchased Lincoln Income Life Insurance Co. for $32 million and Bankers National Life Insurance Co. for $118 million. In 1987 it added Western National Life Insurance to its portfolio at a cost of $262 million. By the end of 1987, Conseco's assets had grown to an impressive $3.4 billion, and its workforce had grown almost 20-fold since 1984, to nearly 500.

Conseco reorganized and caught its breath in 1988. It moved the balance of the operations from its largest purchase, Bankers National, to its ballooning Carmel headquarters. It also moved much of its Lincoln Income Life subsidiary from Kentucky. Although it increased the value of its holdings to more than $4 billion in 1988, Conseco was able to reduce its workforce by almost 10 percent.

After nearly two years since its last acquisition, Hilbert raised $68 million in June 1989 to purchase National Fidelity Life Insurance Co. It moved that concern's headquarters from Dallas, Texas, to Carmel. To house its expanding staff and operations in Carmel, Conseco built a 40,000-square-foot data-processing center in 1990.

Throughout the 1980s Wall Street perceived Conseco as young and inexperienced. Nevertheless, the company's rapid growth finally began to pique the interest of industry analysts and mainstream investors. Hilbert's strategy seemed relatively simple to most observers: purchase troubled insurance companies with potential and increase their value by turning them around. When Conseco went hunting for acquisition candidates, it looked for organizations with sound asset portfolios. For example, it avoided the many companies that in the 1980s had invested heavily in risky real estate and junk bonds. In addition, Hilbert sought firms that had developed unique insurance and annuity products or had devised innovative distribution systems for their offerings.

Importantly, Hilbert also searched for insurers that were inefficient and bloated with excess personnel. He slashed the aggregate workforce of the five companies he had purchased between 1985 and 1989, for example, from 850 to 450 by 1993. Conseco's 1989 annual report boasted that it had eliminated 83 percent of the employees from one of its acquisitions. Many of the cutbacks were accomplished by integrating Conseco's consolidated marketing, investment, and product development operations into the companies that it purchased. In addition, Conseco typically achieved significant efficiency gains by implementing advanced information and data-processing systems.

KEY DATES

KEY DATES

1979: Stephen C. Hilbert forms Security National of Indiana Corp.

1982: Security National begins operations.

1983: Company changes name to Conseco, Inc.

1985: Conseco goes public.

1992: Company establishes Conseco Capital Management, Inc.

1998: Conseco acquires Green Tree Financial and expands into the financial services sector.

2000: CEO Hilbert resigns in the face of the company's severe financial woes.

2002: Conseco files for bankruptcy protection.

2003: Conseco divests its financial services subsidiary, Conseco Finance.

2008: Conseco suffers net losses of $1.12 billion for the year.

BECOMING A MAJOR INSURER

By 1989 Conseco's assets were valued at $5.2 billion. Although Conseco's rise was impressive, rampant acquisition and expansion had a downside for the holding company. By the late 1980s Conseco had accumulated about twice as much debt as equity. In order to continue acquiring new companies, Hilbert knew that he would have to find a new source of funding that was not linked to debt-burdened Conseco. Therefore, in 1990 Hilbert organized Conseco Capital Partners (CCP), a limited partnership that included several well-financed companies. The company was intended to serve as the primary vehicle for new life insurance acquisitions. CCP's first acquisition was Great American Reserve Insurance Co. for $135 million. It also purchased Jefferson National Life Group in 1990 ($171 million) and Beneficial Standard Life in 1991 ($141 million).

Continued gains in the value of Conseco holdings combined with the success of CCP investments resulted in dynamic growth during 1990 and 1991. Although many insurers suffered severe setbacks during the U.S. recession in that period and experienced staggering declines in the value of their portfolios, Conseco swelled its asset base to $11.8 billion and doubled its workforce to almost 1,100. As the insurance industry weathered record insolvencies, Conseco expanded its headquarters and opened an entirely new hub, the Conseco Annuity Center, in Dallas. Entering 1992 the company was valued at more than $800 million.

Because Conseco's performance contrasted so sharply with that of most of its competitors in the early 1990s, many analysts were skeptical. Critics charged that Conseco's amazing asset growth was largely the result of questionable accounting techniques. They pointed to the company's relatively low net worth, which was equal to only 2 percent of its total assets in 1991. Some analysts believed that it was just a matter of time before Conseco would fall prey to the asset devaluation that had plagued other fast-growing insurers of the 1980s.

Despite Hilbert's insistence that Conseco's success reflected a commitment to sound business practices, skepticism continued. Conseco endured a string of disparaging articles in major business journals in the early 1990s that questioned its integrity. Short sellers (investors who had bet on Conseco's downfall) were enraged when its earnings continued to multiply. "This [criticism] goes back to instinct and gut feeling, and no hard facts," said money manager Martin Lizt in a January 1993 issue of *Financial World*. "You [have to] ask the question, 'Have they found a new way to make white bread?'"

As detractors waited for Conseco's money machine to disintegrate in the early 1990s, Hilbert clung to his original guiding principles. As stated in the company's 1993 annual report, "Our operating strategy is to consolidate and streamline the administrative functions of the acquired companies, to improve their investment yield through active asset management ... and to eliminate unprofitable products and distribution channels."

Analysts familiar with Conseco's portfolios attested that the company's investments were much more liquid, of higher quality, and more conservative than those of most insurers. In addition to avoiding real estate and junk bonds, Conseco's portfolio managers steered away from other risky and trendy investment vehicles of the 1980s, particularly guaranteed income contracts. A study of the top U.S. insurers in 1991 showed that only 48 percent of their investments were fixed maturities, whereas over 50 percent were tied up in real estate and other less dependable assets. In contrast, fixed maturities constituted more than 80 percent of Conseco's portfolio, and only 2 percent consisted of real estate holdings.

ADDING VALUE: 1992–94

In 1992 Conseco founded Conseco Capital Management, Inc., (CCM) to capitalize on its investment expertise. CCM provided a variety of financial and investment advisory services on a fee basis to both affiliated and nonaffiliated insurers. CCM was managing about $19 billion worth of assets going into 1994. Also in 1992, CCP shelled out $600 million to acquire Bankers Life and Casualty Co., one of the nation's largest writers of individual health insurance policies. In early 1993 Conseco acquired a controlling interest in MDS/Bankmark, a major marketer of annuity and mutual fund products.

The Conseco organization continued to add value to its holdings in the early 1990s and to achieve success with both CCM and CCP, experiencing stellar growth during 1992 and 1993. The company's net income increased 46 percent in 1992 to $170 million and 75 percent in 1993 to $297 million. During the same period, the value of Conseco's assets ballooned from $11.8 billion to $16.6 billion, a gain of about 30 percent. As Conseco increased its value and expanded its asset base, suspicions about its performance began to wane in 1993 and 1994. Importantly, the company had eliminated much of its debt burden by 1994.

From an encyclopedia salesman in eastern Indiana, Hilbert had successfully boosted his status to that of corporate multimillionaire. In 1992, just 10 years after starting his business, Hilbert was one of the highest-paid executives in the United States. He received $8.8 million in pay and exercised stock options worth almost $30 million. Although some critics derided his benefits package and called it exorbitant, Hilbert was quick to point out that his compensation was tied to the company's performance. After all, a $100 investment in Conseco in 1988 would have returned $2,062 in 1993.

CONTINUED EXPANSION: 1994

Entering the mid-1990s, Conseco was poised for continued growth. Its goals for 1994 included increasing its assets under management by 30 percent. To help achieve this objective, Conseco formed a new limited partnership in early 1994, Conseco Capital Partners II, L.P. (CCP II). CCP II included 36 limited partners who had a combined investment potential of $5 billion to $7 billion. In contrast to CCP, the new partnership was designed to focus on the acquisition and improvement of larger companies valued at $350 million to $1.5 billion. The original CCP partnership was renamed CCP Insurance, Inc., in 1993, and began acting as a holding company for its three subsidiaries.

In addition to its insurance and financial management divisions, which accounted for more than 85 percent of Conseco's operations in 1993, the company was broadening its scope to include some nontraditional ventures. Conseco was investing tens of millions of dollars into new entertainment-related projects late in 1993 and 1994, including some riverboat gambling proposals.

In October 1993 Hilbert formed Conseco Entertainment Inc., a holding company for Conseco's future entertainment investments. Other ventures included outdoor and indoor theaters in Indiana and Ohio. In addition, in 1992 the company paid $15 million for a 31 percent share of Chicago-based Eagle Credit Corp., an organization formed to provide financing to Harley-Davidson dealers and their customers. Conseco also agreed to commit $5 million in 1993 to Rick Galles Racing, an Indy-car racing team in which Conseco owned a 33 percent share.

To its investors' chagrin, however, several of Conseco's past forays into nontraditional investments had not performed as well as its core insurance and financial holdings. In 1989, for instance, Conseco invested in a powdered drink mix developed by an Indiana doctor. The venture failed. Similarly, an investment in a restaurant chain that featured buckets of spaghetti fizzled. "You have to know where your strengths are," acknowledged Ngaire E. Cuneo, executive vice-president of corporate development, in the October 25, 1993, issue of *Indianapolis Business Journal*. "We are going to stay away from food and beverage." Despite a few unwise choices, Conseco was recognized for its highly conservative approach to investing.

In May 1994 CCP II made the first in a series of expected acquisitions when it agreed to purchase Statesman Group, Inc., for $350 million. In September the company entered into a $344 million partnership with American Life Holdings, Inc., which included subsidiaries American Life and Casualty and Vulcan Life. Conseco acquired the remaining 63 percent interest in American Life in September 1996. Conseco planned to retain its proven strategy of using innovative management techniques to increase the value of acquired holdings. Hilbert moved his main personal office to New York, where he planned to direct Conseco's CCP II. Nevertheless, Conseco's headquarters remained in Carmel, and Hilbert planned to sustain his active management role there. "This is what I love to do," Hilbert proclaimed in the June 7, 1993, issue of *Indianapolis Business Journal*. "I think you'd hear the same thing if you were talking to ... Bill Gates or anyone [else] who has achieved success ... it's their baby."

Continuing on its acquisition spree, Conseco entered into agreements to merge with Kemper Corporation, a much larger insurance company, for about $2.6 billion. Conseco withdrew from the deal after deciding that the asking price would cause too much accumulation of debt. Termination of the agreement, however, created bank and accounting fees of about $36 million and spurred a Merrill Lynch analyst to downgrade the company's stock. Conseco subsequently severed its relationship with Merrill Lynch, which had handled Conseco's initial public offering.

GROWTH THROUGH ACQUISITIONS

In 1995 Conseco formed a new division, Conseco Global Investments, and purchased the remaining shares of CCP. CCP was then merged into Conseco, and Beneficial Standard Life Insurance and Great American Reserve Insurance, both subsidiaries of CCP, became subsidiaries of Conseco. The company also acquired additional shares of Bankers Life Holding Corp., a holding company for Bankers Life and Casualty, upping its stake to 81 percent in 1995. The following year Conseco increased its share to 90 percent.

Over the next two years Conseco continued to gobble up insurance companies, acquiring eight in 1996 and 1997. Conseco Risk Management acquired Wells & Company, which offered casualty and property insurance products. The purchase created the largest independent casualty/property agency in the state of Indiana. In July 1996 Conseco bought Life Partners Group, Inc., for about $840 million. The purchase included Massachusetts General Life, Philadelphia Life, Lamar Life, and Wabash Life. At the end of 1996 Conseco made two more acquisitions, American Travellers Corp. for $880 million and Transport Holdings, Inc., for $228 million. American Travellers offered long-term care insurance and Transport provided cancer insurance. Another cancer insurance provider, Capitol American Financial Corp., was purchased by Conseco for $696 million in March 1997. Then, in May, Conseco paid $505 million to acquire Pioneer Financial Services, Inc., a provider of life and health insurance products. Conseco rounded out the year with two additional purchases: Colonial Penn Group, which sold life insurance to older U.S. citizens, and Washington National Corp., a provider of life and health insurance and annuities.

As Conseco headed into 1998, the company had a number of accomplishments under its belt. In 1996 the company was named to the *Fortune* 500 and in 1997 Conseco was added to the Standard & Poor's 500 Index. The company's stock had returned an average of 39 percent a year since becoming a public company in 1985. Total revenues, after dropping from $3 billion in 1993 to $2.36 billion in 1994, climbed steadily, rising to $3.56 billion in 1995 and $3.79 billion in 1996. In 1997 total revenues reached $6.85 billion, a significant increase over the previous year.

GREEN TREE ACQUISITION CAUSES CONCERN: 1998

In 1998 Conseco hoped to continue its growth and strong financial performance. To meet these goals, Conseco in March agreed to acquire Green Tree Financial Corporation, a diversified financial services company that offered home equity and home improvement loans, financing packages for the purchases of recreational vehicles and equipment, and credit cards. Green Tree was best known, however, as the leading U.S. lender for mobile home purchases. Green Tree was Conseco's first acquisition not related to insurance; it was also the largest of Conseco's acquisitions. Conseco reportedly paid about $6 billion in stock for Green Tree. Conseco claimed the acquisition was a perfect fit, as both companies served the same target market; many industry observers, however, were skeptical and Conseco's stock took a plunge. Not only did the company's stock fall about 15 percent upon announcement of the acquisition agreement but it also continued to drop; from a high of $58.12 a share in April 1998, Conseco stock dropped to about $20 a share in late 1999.

The Green Tree acquisition stirred up numerous questions, including whether Conseco had too much debt and whether Green Tree, which had a past of dubious accounting practices, was growing too rapidly, 25 to 30 percent a year, and providing loans to high-risk borrowers. The company's stock decline also led to a deficit of collateral on company-guaranteed loans used by Conseco executives to purchase Conseco stock. Questions persisted and in late 1999 Conseco announced plans to pare debt and slow growth. The company said it would divest its noncore assets and it sold 7 percent of its stock to the private investment firm Thomas H. Lee Company for $478 million.

Falling stock prices did not completely hinder Conseco. With plans to form a new subsidiary dedicated to supplemental health insurance distribution, in 1999 Conseco acquired three health insurance marketing companies: Consolidated Marketing Group; Inter-State Service, Inc.; and TLC National Marketing Company, which sold products door-to-door. In 1998 Conseco had begun placing additional emphasis on building brand awareness. Not only did Conseco launch a major advertising campaign pushing the company as the "Wal-Mart of financial services," but it also sponsored the Indiana Pacers basketball team and the Conseco Fieldhouse, an 18,500-seat facility that opened in late 1999.

PARTNERSHIP WITH NASCAR: 1999

In 1999 Conseco secured a marketing partnership with the National Association for Stock Car Auto Racing

(NASCAR) to become the "Official Financial Services Provider of NASCAR" and entered the second phase of its marketing campaign. In 1998 Hilbert received about $69.7 million in compensation. Although this was significantly lower than his 1997 pay of $119 million, it was enough for Hilbert to retain his reputation as one of the highest-paid CEOs in the nation.

Conseco renamed Green Tree as Conseco Finance Corp. in 1999 and moved toward the next century intent on strengthening operations. The company, after 20 years in business, had grown tremendously. Conseco's total managed financial assets had expanded from $8.2 billion in 1988 to $87.2 billion a decade later. Moreover, despite the company's stock price troubles, total revenues continued to grow; for the nine months ended September 30, 1999, revenues reached $5.92 billion, up from $5.75 billion for the comparable period in 1998.

Hilbert demonstrated his confidence in the company by acquiring more than 638,000 shares in October 1999, pushing his total stake in Conseco to 10.4 million shares. Hilbert could not understand why industry insiders continued to hold reservations about Conseco. Hilbert told the *Indianapolis Star and News* in November 1999, "Everything at Conseco is hitting on all cylinders except the stock price. ... I hate where our stock price is, but I cannot control the market. What's somewhat baffling is we haven't missed a [earnings] number. But my net worth's in Conseco. All I can say is, I'm buying more." As the company approached its 21st year of operations, Conseco remained confident that it could successfully attain its goals: to provide middle America with a wide array of financial and insurance products and services.

ON THE BRINK OF DISASTER: 2000

Nevertheless, Conseco's move into the consumer lending business proved to be short-lived; by early 2000 it found itself overextended financially. The company's efforts to diversify had also proved unpopular with investors. On the eve of its purchase of Green Tree Financial, Conseco's stock value exceeded $58 per share. By the spring of 2000 Conseco stock had dropped to roughly $11 a share, a decline of 80 percent.

Intent on shifting its focus back to its core business, the company decided it had no choice but to sell its financial services unit. CEO Hilbert was straightforward in his assessment of the company's struggles. In an article appearing in the April 1, 2000, edition of the *New York Times*, Hilbert declared that the company was "through giving guidance on earnings," describing the

"pain threshold" for the company's investors as "just too great." The company's earnings also took a hit during this period, as profits for fiscal year 1999 fell to $595.1 million, a decline of 38 percent from the previous year's total of $962.6 million. By late April 2000, in the face of mounting shareholder unrest, Hilbert was forced to step down as company chairman and CEO.

In June of that year, Conseco hired Gary C. Wendt, former head of GE Capital, to help reverse the company's fortune. For the second quarter of 2000, Conseco lost $404.7 million, compared to profits of $213.3 million for the same period in 1999. Facing more than $2 billion in debt, the company soon announced a series of dramatic cost-cutting measures, including the elimination of more than 2,000 jobs, while also divesting a number of its holdings. In the third quarter, the company posted further losses of $489.5 million; meanwhile, the company's shares were trading at between $5 and $7. By April 2001 Conseco was forced to cut another 3,000 jobs, roughly 20 percent of its domestic workforce. At the same time, the company announced its intention to outsource approximately 2,000 new jobs to India.

FILING FOR BANKRUPTCY: 2002

By August 2002 Conseco's debts had swollen to $6.5 billion. To make matters worse, the company had become the target of a Securities and Exchange Commission investigation over alleged accounting violations. In December of that year, Conseco filed for bankruptcy. With total assets of $52 billion, the company had become the third-largest corporation in history to that date to fail. In March 2003, after nearly three years, the company finally sold its financial services unit, Conseco Finance, for just over $1 billion. By September of that year, the company was able to exit bankruptcy protection, having trimmed its debt from $7 billion to $1.4 billion. A year later, Conseco filed a lawsuit against several of the company's former executives, including founder Hilbert, in an effort to recover more than $650 million in stock loans the company had guaranteed the executives during their tenures with the company. According to the company's court filings, Hilbert alone owed more than $220 million.

Although Conseco briefly regained some stability after it emerged from bankruptcy, as the decade drew to a close, the company once again began to suffer substantial losses. In 2006 the company posted net earnings of $106 million for the year. In 2007 it suffered a loss of $179.9 million and in 2008 losses topped $1.12 billion. By 2009 industry observers had begun to speculate that Conseco might have to declare bankruptcy again.

In order to stave off financial ruin, Conseco began to explore ways to aggressively pare down its debt. In October of that year, the company's life insurance subsidiary, Bankers Life and Casualty Company, entered into an agreement with Wilton Reassurance Company to coinsure roughly 234,000 of its existing policies. That same month, Conseco sold a 9.9 percent stake in the company to hedge fund manager John Paulson. In December Conseco initiated a public stock offering, selling nearly 50 million shares of common stock at a rate of $4.75 per share. Although these measures were clearly positive steps, Conseco continued to face grave uncertainty, and the question of the company's solvency remained a major concern entering the next decade.

Dave Mote
Updated, Mariko Fujinaka; Stephen Meyer

PRINCIPAL SUBSIDIARIES

Administrators Service Corporation; American Life and Casualty Marketing Division Co.; Association Management Corporation; Bankers Conseco Life Insurance Company; Bankers Life and Casualty Company; BLC Financial Services, Inc.; Carmel Fifth, LLC; CDOC, Inc.; Codelinks, LLC; Colonial Penn Life Insurance Company; Conseco Data Services (India) Private Limited; Conseco Health Insurance Company; Conseco Health Services, Inc.; Conseco Insurance Company; Conseco Life Insurance Company; Conseco Life Insurance Company of Texas; Conseco Management Services Company; Conseco Marketing, L.L.C.; Conseco Securities, Inc.; Conseco Services, LLC; C.P. Real Estate Services Corp.; Design Benefit Plans, Inc.; Erie International Insurance Company, Inc. (Turks and Caicos); 40|86 Advisors, Inc.; 40|86 Mortgage Capital, Inc.; General Acceptance Corporation Reinsurance Limited (Turks and Caicos); Geneva International Insurance Company, Inc. (Turks and Caicos); Hawthorne Advertising Agency, Incorporated; K. F. Agency, Inc.; K. F. Insurance Agency of Massachusetts, Inc.; NAL Financial Group, Inc.; Performance Matters Associates, Inc.; Performance Matters Associates of Texas, Inc.; ResortPort Holding of Delaware, Inc.; 3037953 Nova Scotia Company (Canada); Washington National Insurance Company.

PRINCIPAL COMPETITORS

Aflac Incorporated; Hartford Life, Inc.; Metlife, Inc.; New York Life Insurance Company; Protective Life Corporation; Pruco Life Insurance Company; Unum Group.

FURTHER READING

Ambrose, Eileen, "Green Tree Is Deal of Different Color for Conseco," *Indianapolis Star*, April 12, 1998, p. E1.

Andrews, Greg, "Conseco Move Marks Evolution," *Indianapolis Business Journal*, September 20, 1993.

———, "Conseco Pouring Millions into Entertainment Venture," *Indianapolis Business Journal*, October 25, 1993, pp. 1A+.

"Buoyed by Their Biggest Year Ever, Hilbert and Conseco Aim Higher," *Indianapolis Business Journal*, June 7, 1993, pp. 10A+.

Francis, Mary, "Carmel, Ind.-Based Financial Firm's CEO Tries to Prove Wall Street Wrong," *Indianapolis Star and News*, November 14, 1999.

Gogoi, Pallavi, "Back to Square One at Conseco," *Business Week*, April 15, 2002, p. 104.

Laing, Jonathan R., "Deferred Risk? A Hard Look at Conseco, a Fast-Growing Life Insurer," *Barron's*, February 11, 1991, p. 10.

Mercado, Darla, "Beleaguered Conseco May Face Bankruptcy—Again; Much Hinges on Report from Its Auditors, According to Analysts," *Investment News*, March 9, 2009, p. 3.

Miller, James, "Conseco Partnership Agreement to Acquire Statesman for $350 Million," *Wall Street Journal*, May 3, 1994.

Norris, Floyd, "Conseco to Sell Loan Unit, Giving Up Brief Effort to Diversify," *New York Times*, April 1, 2000, p. 1C.

———, "Its Price Share Sagging, Conseco Refocuses on Its Balance Sheet and Gets an Immediate Response," *New York Times*, December 1, 1999, p. 18.

Panchapakesan, Meenakshi, and Michael K. Ozanian, "Loaded for Bear: Why High-Flying Conseco Is Proving Its Numerous Detractors Wrong," *Financial World*, January 19, 1993.

Sparks, Debra, "Conseco's Morning After," *Business Week*, June 5, 2000, p. 108.

Consolidated Edison, Inc.

4 Irving Place
New York, New York 10003
U.S.A.
Telephone: (212) 460-4600
Fax: (212) 982-7816
Web site: http://www.conedison.com

Public Company
Founded: 1823 as New York Gas Light Company
Incorporated: 1936 as Consolidated Edison Company of New York
Employees: 15,628
Sales: $13.58 billion (2008)
Stock Exchanges: New York
Ticker Symbol: ED
NAICS: 551112 Public Utility Holding Companies

■ ■ ■

Consolidated Edison, Inc., (Con Ed) is one of the largest publicly owned utility holding companies in the United States. The company's core business is the transmission and distribution of electricity, gas, and steam, which is managed by two regulated subsidiaries. Consolidated Edison Company of New York, Inc., serves New York City and Westchester County, New York. Orange and Rockland Utilities, Inc., serves parts of New York, New Jersey, and Pennsylvania. Con Ed's unregulated subsidiaries include Consolidated Edison Solutions, Inc. (a retail energy services company), Consolidated Edison Energy, Inc. (a supplier of wholesale energy), and Consolidated Edison Development, Inc. (an energy infrastructure developer).

LIGHTING NEW YORK

Con Ed began as New York Gas Light Company, which was founded in 1823 to provide gas for New York's street lamps and homes. Gas illumination had been introduced only recently in the United States and, at first, met widespread resistance due to concerns about safety, but its economy and efficiency soon made gas the standard light source for much of the 19th century. By the last quarter of the century, New York Gas Light and five rival companies were supplying gas to the majority of New York's already vast population.

By the 1870s electricity had come under intense scrutiny as an alternative source of illumination. In that decade, after years of experimentation, the first electric arc lights began appearing in U.S. cities, and it was soon obvious that electricity would one day become the standard illuminant. The arc light was, nevertheless, a crude and dangerous innovation, suitable only for outdoor lighting of public space. A host of inventors around the world continued searching for an acceptable alternative.

Among the men who became interested in the future of electric light was Thomas Alva Edison, already famous for his invention of the phonograph and a series of improvements in telegraphy. It was clear to Edison that electricity was destined to light the world, and in 1878 he focused his energies on solving the problems remaining in its development. To make electric light truly universal, two things were needed: a sturdy and

COMPANY PERSPECTIVES

Con Edison is one of the largest companies in New York State and plays a major role in the sustainable economic development of New York metropolitan area. We employ more than 15,000 people, we purchase goods and services from community-based organizations, and we are one of the largest taxpayers in both the city and the state. We embrace our economic responsibility to our stakeholders in several ways.

By adding to shareholder value, we attract new investors and improve our capability to support the growth of our community.

economical form of incandescent illumination and a power grid able to distribute safe, reliable electric current from its source of generation into distant homes, something that had not been attempted on a large scale. Incandescence was a well-known method of illumination, but no one had found a material able to withstand long hours of operation without burning up.

Edison proposed designing and building a system of electric power distribution. Literally everything had to be created, such as generators, transmission lines, switching equipment, and protective devices, and, within the home or office, internal wiring, outlets, lamps, meters, and even the lightbulb itself. Such an immense project required capital, and in October 1878 Edison joined forces with Wall Street financiers and formed the Edison Electric Light Company. Edison's backers, including J. P. Morgan and the Vanderbilts, saw the potential of the new system. With his financing in place, Edison redoubled his experiments, and by the end of 1879 he had devised a workable incandescent light using a filament of high-heat- and electric-resistant "thread" in an evacuated glass globe.

THE FIRST ELECTRIC POWER STATION

Edison simultaneously had solved most of the generation and transmission problems and by 1880 was ready to apply to the city of New York for permission to build the nation's first commercial electric power station. At that point a legal technicality forced the creation of a subsidiary corporation, Edison Electric Illuminating Company, to act as an operating company on behalf of Edison Electric Light, which would remain only a hold-

ing company and in control of all patents. The newly formed Edison Electric Illuminating applied for and received a license.

At 3 p.m. on September 4, 1881, current began to flow from the generators at 255–57 Pearl Street in lower Manhattan. The Pearl Street Station could supply power only a mile or two in any direction from the plant before its direct-current electricity began to lose voltage, but for several years its design was unchallenged. Edison and his associates incorporated many subsidiary manufacturing companies in order to build power stations wherever they were wanted, and by the spring of 1883 there were some 334 plants in operation, most of them considerably smaller than the one on Pearl Street. By 1884 Edison had gained control of Edison Light as well as Edison Illuminating, and by the late 1880s he was no longer actively participating in his electrical holdings.

GAS AND ELECTRIC CONSOLIDATE

In 1890 a group of German financiers led by Henry Villard proposed the formation of a new electrical combination to include all of Edison's manufacturing companies and the valuable stock of Edison Electric Light, the holding company. Although the latter had come under the managing direction of Edison's group in an 1884 proxy fight, its largest block was controlled by the interests of J. P. Morgan. In the complex negotiations leading to the creation of Villard's new company, later known as General Electric, Morgan used his stock position and financial muscle to demand and win 40 percent of General Electric's stock, while Edison settled for 10 percent and enough cash to make his fortune. Meanwhile, the creation of General Electric led to Edison Illuminating being spun off on its own.

New York's gas companies were hardly pleased by the success of electric lighting. Edison's earliest announcements on the subject had sent gas stocks reeling, and in 1884 the city's six largest gas concerns (including New York Gas Light Company) joined forces in a new utility giant called Consolidated Gas Company of New York. This merger initiated a long process whereby the scores of small electricity, gas, and steam companies in the greater New York area would be melded into a single and far more efficient entity (known since 1936 as Consolidated Edison Company of New York).

At first the electric and gas concerns faced each other as rivals, each side augmenting its forces by annexing or combining with neighboring firms. In 1898 the bulk of Manhattan's electricity supply was collected under the umbrella of the New York Gas & Electric Light, Heat & Power Company (NYG&ELH&P).

KEY DATES

1823: New York Gas Light Company is founded.

1884: New York Gas Light Company merges with five other gas companies to form the Consolidated Gas Company of New York.

1899: The company buys the New York Gas & Electric Light, Heat & Power Company.

1901: The company merges with Edison's Illuminating Company to create the New York Edison Company.

1936: Consolidated Edison Company of New York is created from the combined holdings of New York Edison.

1967: Charles F. Luce is appointed chairman.

1974: New York State buys two of Con Ed's generating plants for $612 million.

2001: Terrorist attacks on the World Trade Center destroy two Con Ed substations and interrupt power to 12,000 customers.

2004: Con Ed pays $7.2 million to settle a lawsuit filed by the family of a woman who was killed by an exposed wire in one of the company's service boxes.

2006: A massive blackout in Queens leaves 175,000 Con Edison customers without power for more than a week.

NYG&ELH&P also gained a controlling share of Edison Electric Illuminating.

In 1899 Consolidated Gas bought NYG&ELH&P. The purchase was part of an effort by the gas company to overcome a growing technological gap by buying up as many electricity companies as it could. In 1901 Consolidated Gas merged the electric companies it controlled into a single subsidiary known as the New York Edison Company. Thus the gas companies themselves became providers of electricity and by 1910 controlled most of the electricity generated in Manhattan and the western portion of the Bronx.

By that time, electricity had become the standard source of power not only for illumination but also for a widening variety of household appliances and industrial tools. Very large central generators capable of serving vast numbers of customers at long distances were built. New York Edison gradually replaced its last few small stations, and the city's power network began to assume its modern structure.

REGULATORY CONTROL

As it became apparent that large-scale power distribution would be a monopoly, utility companies came under the regulatory control of the state legislature in Albany, New York. The power of the legislature to fix rates of return for utilities was tested in a landmark court case arising out of its 1906 attempt to limit Consolidated Gas's price for its gas to 80 cents per 1,000 cubic feet. The U.S. Supreme Court eventually ruled that while governmental bodies had a clear right to oversee the operation of utilities, they could not set rates so low as to prevent the utilities from earning a reasonable rate of return on investment. In the case of Consolidated Gas, however, the rate of 80 cents was not found to be excessively low. In the course of its analysis, the Court estimated Consolidated Gas's asset value at $56 million.

For many years Consolidated Gas and its subsidiary New York Edison grew quietly. The long process of unifying New York's various power companies continued, and by 1932 Consolidated Gas was the world's largest company providing electrical service. The final step occurred in 1936, when Consolidated Gas became Consolidated Edison Company of New York. Under the direction of President Hudson R. Searing, the previously cool relations between Edison's gas and electric divisions quietly improved, and the gigantic company took on its present configuration as New York City's sole power company.

DAMAGED REPUTATION

As the single purveyor of light and electricity to New York's millions of inhabitants and workers, Con Ed attracted suspicion and criticism. When Mayor Fiorello La Guardia threatened to create a municipal power utility to compete with Con Ed during the Great Depression, company executives worked to develop closer relationships with other members of the city's government. Con Ed was also the city's largest employer of construction workers and paid more taxes than any other single organization in the city, so it was able to stave off La Guardia's threat. The interests of New York City and Con Ed meshed from the mid-1930s on.

In 1955 Con Ed was among the first utilities to apply for permission from the Atomic Energy Commission to build and operate a private atomic power plant. Once permission was granted, Con Ed built its reactor at Indian Point, New York, some miles up the Hudson River from New York City, inaugurating what it hoped would be an era of clean, inexpensive power for New York. The project took far longer and much more money to build than anyone expected. When it was completed in the early 1960s, Indian Point's cost per kilowatt of capacity was two and a half times that of a conventional generator, adding to a general growing perception among New Yorkers that Con Ed was an inefficient utility.

Supplying power in the complex environment of New York City was fraught with difficulties. Since the 19th century, most utility lines and pipes were required by law to be laid underground, vastly increasing Con Ed's expense for upkeep and expansion of its system. New York's extremely dense population created additional problems, and the high percentage of residential users necessitated the metering, billing, and servicing of thousands of relatively small accounts, in contrast to a utility with a higher proportion of industrial customers. Because of the preponderance of office workers in Manhattan, Con Ed had to be prepared to supply a midday peak of electricity far greater than its 24-hour average, forcing the construction and maintenance of a generating capacity larger than would otherwise be needed. Such underutilized capacity is highly inefficient for power companies, whose single greatest burden is the cost of construction and upkeep.

POOR PERFORMANCE

Con Ed paid extremely high taxes, which it passed on to customers through its rates. Thus Con Ed, in effect, collected taxes on behalf of the various city, state, and federal agencies, that helped make Con Ed the nation's most expensive utility for many years. Finally, space restrictions in New York made it much easier for Con Ed to repair old power stations than to build new ones, which meant that by the 1950s much of its physical plant was antiquated and inefficient. Despite that handicap, Con Ed was the subject of some of the earliest restrictions on air pollution adopted in the United States, further increasing its already excessive costs.

By the 1960s, Con Ed had become an expensive and erratic provider of gas, electricity, and steam, and some of its problems lay with its management. Chairman Charles Eble and his team of top advisers had all been with the company for a number of years, and many felt that they had developed an aloof, isolated mentality that angered New Yorkers, who were irate over poor service, high bills, and a series of famous blackouts beginning in 1959. Typical of the company's poor handling of public relations was its 1962 effort to build a second atomic power plant in the middle of the borough of Queens.

Equally damaging was Con Ed's poor financial performance. While 1965 revenues of $840 million made Con Ed the nation's largest utility, its revenue growth was very slow, net earnings were low, and earn-

ings per share were moving up at only 4 percent per year, or half the pace of a typical competitor, such as Commonwealth Edison in Chicago.

CRISIS AND RENEWAL

The man chosen to lead Con Ed out of its troubles was Charles F. Luce. Appointed chairman in mid-1967, Luce was formerly an undersecretary with the U.S. Department of the Interior. He was chosen for his abilities and because he was an outsider to New York power politics. The new chief executive took a number of decisive steps toward the renewal of Con Ed, including a virtual makeover of top management; division of the company into six operating divisions (one for each city borough plus one for suburban Westchester County); the addition of several new plants; plans to replace aging equipment; and a new emphasis on customer service.

Con Ed's stock price continued to drop, however, and the company soon found itself in the worst crisis of its history. After agreeing in 1972 to halt the use of coal for environmental reasons, Con Ed was dependent on oil for 85 percent of its generating capacity. The following year the OPEC oil embargo doubled the price of crude oil. As fuel price increases could not be passed along to customers for about four months, and because Con Ed was in the midst of more construction projects to increase capacity, the company was suddenly faced with a critical shortage of cash. Luce took the unprecedented step of withholding dividends in the first quarter of 1974, unleashing an avalanche of criticism from stockholders, Wall Street, and other utilities, who watched their own stocks follow Con Ed on a sharp decline.

Luce had a second, far more important strategy. Knowing that the state government had no interest in seeing New York's power supply disrupted by financial collapse, Luce persuaded it to buy two of Con Ed's generating plants that were still under construction. Con Ed received $612 million in cash and was relieved of the heavy cost burden associated with new plant construction. What additional power Con Ed required was bought back from the state, but 1973 and 1974 also marked the beginning of a long decline in the expansion rate of New York's energy usage. This decline was partially in response to the high price of oil and partially a result of vigorous conservation campaigns promoted by Con Ed, which realized that nothing could be better from a financial perspective than an end to the cycle of borrowing required for generating new equipment and plants.

STABLE OPERATIONS

By 1978 Con Ed was regarded as one of the most efficient and profitable utilities in the country, and Chairman Luce was credited with the remarkable turnaround. Customer complaints dropped off dramatically, and earnings per share and the stock price rose. Con Ed gradually eased itself back into a more balanced pattern of fuel usage, much of it natural gas and nuclear. In the 1980s Con Ed operated smoothly and quietly. The generally conservative pattern of energy usage in New York allowed Con Ed to avoid the costly construction projects that once threatened to sink it, keeping earnings high. During the late 1980s, Con Ed began posting the lowest rates of customer interruption for any utility in the country, which, in light of its long tradition of subpar performance, may be its most impressive achievement.

Luce retired in September 1982 and was succeeded by Arthur Hauspurg. By this time Con Ed had begun an era of stability in its electric rates. A rate increase requested in April 1982 and granted the following year was its last for a decade. Hauspurg retired in September 1990 without requesting a single electric rate increase. During his tenure, electric sales rose, fuel prices generally declined, and dividends were increased annually. Con Ed had ample capacity to meet the demand generated by the healthy local economy.

Eugene R. McGrath became chairman, president, and chief executive officer upon Hauspurg's retirement, and he faced a somewhat different situation than his predecessor. Con Ed remained financially strong, but the New York City area's economy had weakened. Con Ed launched a major energy conservation program in 1990, with the goal of reducing customers' electric energy usage by 15 percent by 2008. Con Ed planned to spend about $4.2 billion on the program. To maintain its power supply, Con Ed continued modernizing its existing plants and signed contracts with several prospective independent power producers.

COST CUTTING AND LAYOFFS

In 1992 Con Ed requested and received a rate hike, the first in almost 10 years. Despite long-term rate stability, Con Ed still had extremely high rates, and its 12 cents a kilowatt hour was double the national average. With its aging plants and the city's stringent environmental controls, Con Ed could only generate power at 7 cents a kilowatt hour, compared to independent power producers, who could manage at 5 cents a kilowatt hour. In addition, taxes accounted for 25 percent of Con Ed's revenues in 1993, by far the highest in the country.

Cost cutting and more efficient operations were high priorities for Chairman McGrath in the 1990s, as the company prepared for the deregulation of the electric generating market. Between 1990 and 1993 the

company laid off 3,000 workers, and by 2000 it had reduced its workforce by another 3,000.

McGrath's plans called for Con Ed to minimize its power generation and maximize its power distribution after deregulation. The company's greatest assets in the mid-1990s were its transmission and distribution systems, whereas the generating plants accounted for only 20 percent of company assets. McGrath refused to upgrade or build new plants in anticipation of selling them off and buying power from independent producers after deregulation.

DEREGULATION

In 1997 the first phase of a five-year process of deregulation began, allowing some commercial and residential customers to choose their power supplier. Although only 10,000 commercial customers and 50,000 residential customers in New York could purchase electricity on the open market by 1998, by 2002 all of Con Ed's three million customers would have that freedom. Con Ed, however, continued to distribute the power, regardless of who generated it.

Deregulation required Con Ed to develop a plan with government agencies and consumer groups for its organization and operation. As part of that plan, Con Ed reorganized under a new holding company, Consolidated Edison, Inc., in 1998, with different subsidiaries handling its regulated and nonregulated businesses, including a new power marketing group. The same year, Con Ed announced plans to buy Orange and Rockland Utilities, Inc., which operated in New York State, New Jersey, and Pennsylvania. The $790 million deal was completed in 1999 and helped protect Con Ed from acquisition by a large national power company.

McGrath's long-held plan to sell off the company's generating plants came to fruition in 1999, when Northern States Power, KeySpan, and Orion Power paid a total of $1.65 billion for the facilities. Con Ed used the money to finance its Orange and Rockland acquisition, to buy back some of its stock, and to entice other possible merger partners.

The company found such a partner quickly, arranging to purchase Northeast Utilities for $3.5 billion in cash and stock and the assumption of $3.9 billion of Northeast's debt. After numerous talks with regulators and consumer groups on how to divide the savings generated by the merger, the deal fell through in 2001.

9/11 TERRORIST ATTACKS

Enthusiasm for deregulation waned in 2000 when a summer power shortage caused blackouts in New York

City. Although Con Ed received the brunt of consumers' criticism, it had little actual power to control the situation, having in large part exited the power generation business. In addition, Con Ed had been required by deregulation to reduce its long-term contracts with energy suppliers, forcing the company to pay high spot prices during peak demand.

The September 11, 2001, terrorist attacks on the World Trade Center severely damaged Con Ed's infrastructure in lower Manhattan. Two substations adjacent to the Twin Towers were destroyed and major transmission cables were significantly damaged, leaving 12,000 customers without electricity. The company moved quickly to bring generators, new cables, and about 2,000 repair workers into the area to restore service.

Even as Con Ed scrambled to restore its power-generating capacity in the months following the terrorist attacks, the company soon found itself confronting a host of other problems. In August 2003 a severe blackout cut off electricity to 3.1 million Con Ed customers. The incident raised questions about the company's obligation to compensate customers for any food products that were spoiled during the outage. A month after the blackout, Con Ed insisted that it was not liable for any damages resulting from lost power, since the incident was caused by events that occurred outside of New York City.

LAWSUITS, SANCTIONS, AND PENALTIES

Con Ed found itself dealing with a more serious public relations disaster in January 2004, when Jodie S. Lane was killed after stepping onto an electrified metal plate while walking her dog. A subsequent investigation revealed that there was an exposed wire in one of the company's service boxes beneath the street. Con Ed immediately began to inspect an additional 250,000 service boxes throughout the city for potential problems. The incident sparked angry protests among neighborhood residents, who blamed the company for failing to adhere to basic safety standards. Con Ed later paid $7.2 million to settle a lawsuit filed by Lane's family.

In August 2004 the Public Service Commission imposed tighter safety restrictions on the utility, requiring the company to conduct tests of all of its electrical equipment. Between December 2004 and November 2005, Con Ed detected more than 1,200 stray voltage sites throughout the city. Meanwhile, the company's decaying infrastructure continued to pose a significant hazard to city residents. During this period the company named Kenneth Burke as its new CEO.

In February 2006 several people were shocked by an exposed cable near the Port Authority Bus Station, and less than a week later, a dog was electrocuted in Brooklyn. In July 2006 the company found itself confronting one of the worst blackouts in its history, as an outage in several neighborhoods in Queens left nearly 175,000 residents without power for almost 10 days. An official report released in January 2007 found Con Ed made virtually no effort to support customers during the crisis. In November 2007 Con Ed was fined $18 million for a range of service violations, including its handling of the power outage in Queens.

SKYROCKETING COSTS

In May 2007 in order to confront the rising costs involved with infrastructure improvements, Con Edison requested permission for a 17 percent rate hike. Critics of Con Ed decried the request, complaining that the company's own incompetence was primarily responsible for its troubles. To many consumer advocates, the steep increase in the company's profits in recent years made the request for a rate increase particularly offensive.

Many industry observers blamed deregulation for the decline in safety and quality standards, arguing that the company's efforts to transport energy across greater distances in pursuit of new markets were weakening its power infrastructure. Although state regulators initially denied the company's request, in March 2008 the Public Service Commission approved a smaller rate hike of $425 million. Although the increase fell far short of the company's original appeal for an increase of $1.2 billion, it still represented the largest single increase in energy costs in the history of New York City.

As global fuel prices continued to skyrocket toward the end of the decade, Con Ed remained focused on covering its increasing operational costs. In May 2008 the company filed for permission to increase rates by 7.3 percent per year. The following January state regulators approved a rate hike of 5.6 percent. In November 2009 the company received approval for another rate hike, which would increase its revenues by $1.1 billion over a three-year span. While the city's residents and editorial writers fumed, Con Ed had reason to be optimistic, having positioned itself to enjoy steady earnings growth well into the new decade.

Jonathan Martin
Updated, Susan Windisch Brown; Stephen Meyer

PRINCIPAL SUBSIDIARIES

Consolidated Edison Company of New York, Inc.; Consolidated Edison Development, Inc.; Consolidated

Edison Energy, Inc.; Consolidated Edison Solutions, Inc.; Orange and Rockland Utilities, Inc.

PRINCIPAL COMPETITORS

American Electric Power Company, Inc.; Energy East Corporation; National Grid USA; Northeast Utilities.

FURTHER READING

"Government Alert: Con Ed Won't Charge More," *Crain's New York Business*, October 15, 2001, p. 12.

Keenan, Charles, "Businesses Jolted; Deregulation Spurs Megabills for Megawatts," *Crain's New York Business*, August 7, 2000, p. 1.

Lentz, Philip, "Con Ed Fighting to Keep Savings in Big Merger," *Crain's New York Business*, October 18, 1999, p. 1.

Lisberg, Adam, "Shocker! Con Ed Reveals It Will Hike Rates over Next Three Years," *New York Daily News*, November 25, 2009, p. 2.

Norman, James R., "A Beleaguered Tax Collector," *Forbes*, December 20, 1993, pp. 47–48.

O'Hanlon, Thomas, "Con Edison: The Company You Love to Hate," *Fortune*, March 1966.

Perrow, Charles, "The Government's Con Ed Bill," *New York Times*, July 8, 2007, p. 13.

"The Real Story on Power Woes," *Crain's New York Business*, July 3, 2000, p. 8.

Silverberg, Robert, *Light for the World: Edison and the Power Industry*. Princeton, NJ: Van Nostrand, 1967.

Urbina, Ian, "Con Ed Blames Faulty Work in Electrocution," *New York Times*, January 30, 2004.

Cordis Corporation

430 Route 22 East
Bridgewater, New Jersey 08807
U.S.A.
Telephone: (908) 541-4100
Toll Free: (800) 447-7585
Fax: (800) 997-1122
Web site: http://www.cordis.com

Wholly Owned Subsidiary of Johnson & Johnson
Incorporated: 1957 as Medical Development Corp.
Employees: 5,000
Sales: $3.1 billion (2008 est.)
NAICS: 339112 Surgical and Medical Instrument
    Manufacturing; 334510 Electromedical and Electro-
    therapeutic Apparatus Manufacturing

■ ■ ■

Cordis Corporation, a Johnson & Johnson (J&J) company, operates as a leading developer and manufacturer in the circulatory disease management industry. Cordis's products include guidewires, balloons, catheters, and stents that are used to treat circulatory system problems, including coronary artery disease and cerebral aneurysms. In 2002 Cordis revolutionized the treatment of cardiovascular diseases with the launch of the Cypher Sirolimus-eluting coronary stent, the first stent to employ a drug treatment as a means of reducing recurrences of artery blockage. By the end of the decade, Cordis had emerged as the industry leader in the manufacture of stent devices, achieving total sales of $3.1 billion in 2008.

POSTWAR ORIGINS

The medical device company was founded in Miami, Florida, by William Murphy. The son of the Nobel laureate William Parry Murphy, Murphy was immersed in medicine from his youngest days. The younger Murphy also realized early on that he had a particular aptitude for mechanical engineering. The self-described "tinkerer" even designed his own medical devices as a teen.

After pursuing a dual education in medicine and engineering, Murphy was involved in the creation of the first artificial kidney. He also served briefly at Dade Reagents Inc. in Miami. When that company was bought out by American Hospital Supply Corp., it became clear to the ambitious Murphy that his career at this large, relatively anonymous company was limited. Murphy formed Medical Development Corp. in 1957.

One of the first products Murphy developed was a "lumbar puncture tray," a disposable set of needles and tools used for spinal taps. Noticing that doctors performing this procedure often used dull and sometimes burred needles, making the test difficult and often painful, Murphy developed the concept of using a disposable kit, meaning that each patient would get a sterile, sharp needle. Murphy developed several elaborations on this basic concept, patented them, and licensed the core concept to Mead John & Co. He used the $300,000 in royalties that accrued over the next couple of years to finance research and development at his own company.

In 1959, realizing that his strengths lay more in research and development than operational management, Murphy recruited John Sterner to serve as president of his small but growing company, which had moved from its original garage headquarters to a house. Sterner, a physicist, introduced Murphy to the venture capitalist Georges F. Doriot. Doriot's American Research and Development Corp. would invest nearly a quarter of a million dollars in the start-up business.

By 1960 Murphy had changed the business's name to the more distinctive Cordis ("of the heart"), a name that indicated the primary focus of the company's efforts. During the decade Cordis became involved in the relatively new field of cardiac pacemaking, which utilizes a small, usually battery-operated electronic device called a pacer to stimulate the heartbeat with electrical charges. By the early 1970s, Cordis ranked second only to Medtronic among America's pacemaker manufacturers. Cordis introduced its first remotely programmable pacemaker in 1973 and launched improved electrodes (which make the actual connection to the heart muscle) by the mid-1970s.

Despite infusions of more than $500,000 in cash in its first few years, Cordis had a rocky start. Under Murphy the company was so devoted to research and development that it did not achieve a positive net operating cash flow until 1980. Murphy and Sterner

were forced to sell their stock to keep the firm afloat. By 1984 they held less than 5 percent between them.

QUALITY CONTROL CRISIS

In the mid-1970s Cordis faced poor quality control within its own manufacturing operations and in components from an important supplier. Flawed circuits from its supplier CTS Corp. and an internal rejection rate that soared to 30 percent contributed to the U.S. Food and Drug Administration's (FDA) issue of a product advisory against Cordis in 1974. Cordis's share of the pacemaker market declined from 20 percent in 1975 to 13 percent in 1978. With sales and net worth plummeting, corporate executives were compelled to cut salaries by 20 percent across the board.

CTS Corp. agreed to keep Cordis afloat, injecting $5 million of capital in exchange for control of nearly one-fourth of the pacemaker manufacturer's stock. For its part, Cordis promised to buy back the shares at a premium, doing so in 1977. Hoping to reinvigorate the company, Murphy and Sterner brought in a new president, Norman Weldon, in 1979. Characterized by *Forbes* as "a husky Indiana farm boy turned biochemist, economist, and businessman," Weldon had served as CTS's president before moving to Cordis.

For two years Sterner, Murphy, and Weldon formed a management troika that focused on a costly restructuring of Cordis's manufacturing and marketing operations. Among other moves, Weldon organized the company's first independent marketing department and boosted the sales force by 30 percent. The restructuring cost dearly. Cordis lost $8.3 million in 1981 and by that time had racked up $89 million in debt.

A SECOND DILEMMA

Cordis's luck appeared to be changing in the early 1980s. Four years after a competitor launched the first lithium-powered implantable pacemaker, Cordis introduced its first lithium model in 1979. The Miami company's version featured an encapsulated battery that purported to be smaller and more efficient than its predecessor's. Just three years later, Cordis won FDA approval for an innovative "physiological" or "synchronous" pacemaker, which issued electric pulses only when needed by regulating two chambers of the heart instead of one. At the same time, several competitors (including Intermedics, which had supplanted Cordis as number two in pacemakers in 1979) were reeling from a kickback scandal.

Cordis took good advantage of the situation, increasing sales by more than 75 percent, from $117.7 million in 1984 to $207 million. It also recovered from

KEY DATES

1957: William Murphy establishes the Medical Development Corp.

1960: The firm's name is changed to Cordis.

1973: Cordis introduces its first remotely programmable pacemaker.

1978: The firm's share of the pacemaker market falls to 13 percent.

1983: Cordis's pacemakers are recalled.

1987: The pacemaker division is sold.

1990: Cordis's angiography operations account for 85 percent of company revenues.

1996: Cordis becomes a Johnson & Johnson subsidiary in a $1.8 billion stock swap.

2001: Cordis receives FDA approval to begin its SIRIUS study of the Sirolimus pharmaceutical-coated Bx Velocity coronary stent.

2002: Cordis begins marketing its Cypher Sirolimus-eluting coronary stent in Europe.

2003: Cordis receives FDA approval to begin selling the Cypher stent in the United States.

2004: Cordis introduces its second-generation restenosis-reducing stent, the Cypher Select.

2006: Cordis launches the Cypher Select Plus.

2009: Cordis celebrates its 50th anniversary.

a net loss of $8.2 million to more than $10 million in profits during the period. Furthermore, it regained the number two rank among pacemaker manufacturers. In the meantime, however, engineers at the company had discovered two potentially devastating problems with the lithium-powered pacer.

First, they learned that their method of encapsulating the battery had a high potential for corrosion and possibly leakage. Although the company was not legally obligated to do so at the time, Cordis modified the battery and notified both doctors and the FDA about the possibility that the device could become corrupted. The close monitoring of the 8,500 patients who had already received the pacers revealed a second, more serious problem. A totally unforeseen chemical reaction was sapping the power of the batteries. The FDA ordered recalls of Cordis's pacemakers in 1983 and 1985 and prohibited the company from testing and selling new products for 18 months.

Cordis's sales were more than halved from 1984's $207 million down to just $80 million in 1986. In 1987 the company sold the pacemaker division, which had at one time contributed more than half its annual revenues. Cordis also reached a $5.7 million settlement with claimants two years later. Chief Financial Officer Robert Strauss succeeded Weldon as president and CEO upon the latter's resignation in 1987.

RAPID GROWTH

Under Strauss, Cordis fell back on a secondary business interest, diagnostic cardiac catheters, in the late 1980s. These fine-gauge tubes are used in angiography, the injection of special dyes into blood vessels and the heart chambers to conduct tests for impairment of this vital muscle. By 1990 Cordis had captured 40 percent of the global angiography market, and this business segment constituted 85 percent of the company's total revenues.

During the first half of the 1990s, Strauss guided what investment bankers Hambrecht & Quist characterized as a "metamorphosis" from a "troubled, unfocused, regulatory-hindered Cordis [to] a streamlined one." Moreover, Strauss planned to transform Cordis from a firm focused almost exclusively on development of new technology to one emphasizing customers' needs. Having eradicated the company's pacemaker obligations, Strauss focused on maintaining Cordis's leading share in angiography catheters and diversifying into the larger and more profitable therapeutic heart catheter market. Commonly known as angioplasty, this therapy uses specialized catheters to ream out blockages in the arteries around the heart or, in the case of balloon angioplasty, to expand the artery to allow increased blood flow.

Strauss hoped to increase Cordis's share of the therapeutic catheter market from 2 percent in 1991 to 15 percent by mid-decade, but he faced daunting competition from well-established giants in the medical business, including the market-leading Eli Lilly & Co. and Pfizer Inc. He reorganized Cordis's staff into product-oriented teams, focusing on balloon catheters, interventional catheters, steerable guidewires, and diagnostics, thereby encouraging the development of a comprehensive line. Using competitive pricing and dynamic marketing, Strauss made Cordis the industry's fastest-growing competitor in the early 1990s. By 1994 the company had captured 10 percent of total U.S. angioplasty sales, short of Strauss's ambitious goal but an impressive expansion nonetheless.

Perhaps more important, the company made dramatic inroads into the global heart catheter business, achieving a third-ranking 17 percent of the worldwide angioplasty market by the middle of 1994. By that time, overseas sales constituted more than 50 percent of Cordis's total annual revenues. Strauss also reduced the company's debt from $31.6 million in 1990 to a mere $1.1 million by the end of 1993. Sales increased from $202.6 million in 1990 to more than $443 million in 1994, while net income multiplied from $20.1 million to $50.2 million.

PRODUCT DEVELOPMENT
UNDER JOHNSON & JOHNSON

Cordis's speedy growth attracted the attention of the health-care giant Johnson & Johnson, which initiated a highly unusual (for this industry) hostile takeover of Cordis in October 1995. Eager to create a total cardiac package of products, J&J offered $100.00 per share in cash for a company that was then trading at $81.00. Cordis initially resisted the assault, but in November it agreed to a stock swap valued at $1.8 billion. Cordis became a J&J company in February 1996. The merger combined J&J's cardiac stents (minuscule steel tubes that repair damaged arteries) with Cordis's balloon catheters, which were used to deliver the stents, forming a globally significant manufacturer of cardiac devices.

Under the leadership of its new parent, Cordis spent the remainder of the 1990s developing new products. In 1997 the company formed its Endovascular Division to focus on vascular disease treatments. In an attempt to bolster J&J's share of the stent market, Cordis also began to manufacture several different stents, including the Palmaz-Schatz Crown stent, the CrossFlex hybrid stent, and the S.M.A.R.T. stent.

Cordis also made several key acquisitions and formed strategic partnerships during this time period. In 1997 the firm teamed up with Cardiometrics Inc. in a codistribution agreement involving Cardiometrics' testing products. Cordis also settled a patent dispute with Medtronic Inc. by forming a patent cross-license agreement for certain stents and stent delivery systems. In 1998 Cordis acquired various assets of IsoStent Inc., including the BX stent. The following year, AngioGuard Inc. was purchased, giving Cordis access to the firm's technology that was developed to protect the heart and brain during medical procedures.

The deals continued into the new millennium. In 2000 Cordis resolved another patent dispute with Guidant Corp. Under the terms of the agreement, Cordis was able to provide its U.S. customers with rapid exchange catheters, which were used in interventional cardiology procedures, including angioplasty and stent placement. Cordis also acquired Atrionix Inc., a developer of catheter-based systems used in the treatment of atrial fibrillation, a disruption in the heart's normal sinus rhythm. In 2001 TERAMed Inc., a developer of catheter-based systems utilized to treat abdominal aortic aneurysms, was purchased.

RECLAIMING THE STENT
MARKET

The most significant moves for the company during the late 1990s and into the new millennium, however, were its attempts to reinvent itself in the stent market. In 1994 J&J had introduced the coronary stent and saw sales of the product increase rapidly to $500 million by 1996. By 1997, however, its 95 percent market share had fallen to just 5 percent, and revenues had dropped to $200 million. *Forbes* commented on J&J's falter in a 2001 article, claiming that the company had "angered doctors with high prices, ignored demands for better technology, and wrongly assumed its patents would stall rivals. When competitors invaded in 1997, doctors were only too happy to switch."

Headed by Robert Croce, Cordis began to develop new stents and increased its sales force by 40 percent. Along with the less profitable Crown and CrossFlex stents released in the late 1990s, in 2000 Cordis launched the Bx Velocity stent, which proved to be the success J&J needed to regain market share. In 2001 the Velocity Hepacoat stent was introduced. This stent was coated with a blood thinner that prevented blood clots from forming and quickly became responsible for nearly 20 percent of the company's stent sales.

Cordis then put plans in motion to launch a drug-coated stent that would prevent restenosis, a reclogging of the artery that occurred in 25 percent of patients who received stents. By this time stents were used in 80 percent of angioplasties performed in the United States. Stents accounted for $1.4 billion in annual sales. J. P. Morgan Chase predicted that the release of the new stent could potentially increase U.S. market sales to $3 billion.

Cordis, which received FDA approval for its SIRIUS study of the Sirolimus pharmaceutical-coated Bx Velocity coronary stent, hoped to launch the breakthrough product in 2003. The move would position it ahead of competitors by one year. Cordis chose the name SIRIUS (in reference to the brightest star in the heavens) to symbolize the advantages of the new restenosis-preventing stent. The release of this new product had the potential to position both Cordis and J&J at the forefront of the stent market.

A PRODUCT BREAKTHROUGH:
2003–09

In early 2002 Cordis received European approval for its new restenosis-reducing stent. Dubbed the Cypher

Sirolimus-eluting coronary stent, Cordis's drug-enhanced stent was proven to reduce or eliminate many of the complications involved with traditional procedures. According to trial studies in the United States, the restenosis rate with the Cypher stent was only 9 percent. Traditional stents had a rate of 36 percent.

Cordis officially launched the Cypher stent in the United Kingdom in May 2002. In an article published in the *Northern Echo* (May 2, 2002), the British cardiologist Jim Hall hailed the trial results of the Cypher stent as "spectacular," while reporting a high level of patient interest in the new device. Nevertheless, the high cost of the stent was prohibitive, and preliminary sales of the Cypher were slow. By the end of 2002, Cordis's new stent accounted for only 10 percent of the total European market.

After launching the Cypher in Europe, Cordis turned its attention to marketing the stent in the United States. Even before receiving final FDA approval, the new stent was being hailed as a milestone in the treatment of heart disease. Speaking to the *New York Times* (January 3, 2003), Kurt Kruger of Banc of America Securities speculated that Cordis's Cypher would single-handedly double U.S. stent sales. Calling the device "an absolute gold mine" for the Johnson & Johnson subsidiary, Kruger expected the domestic market for stents to swell to $3.2 billion in 2003. At the time, Kruger predicted that Cordis's stent sales would increase to $2.8 billion for the year, compared to $415 million in 2002.

Cordis received final FDA approval for the new stent in April 2003. From the beginning, the Cypher cost $3,000, roughly three times the cost of stents currently on the market. In spite of the device's hefty price tag, sales of the Cypher stent had an immediate impact on the company's bottom line. For the second quarter of 2003, Cordis posted revenues of $599 million, an increase of 47 percent over the same period for 2002. Sales in the United States rose even more sharply, with earnings topping $360 million, 56 percent higher than the previous year's figures. The American Heart Association ranked the Cypher stent as one of the 10 most significant medical developments of 2003.

GROWTH IN THE NEW MILLENNIUM

Throughout the middle of the decade, Cordis continued to pursue an aggressive growth strategy. In 2004 a second-generation version of the company's ground-breaking restenosis-reducing stent, the Cypher Select, became available in overseas markets. By early 2006 the company had sold more than two million Cypher stents worldwide. In May of that year, Cordis launched the S.M.A.R.T. stent, for use in unclogging iliac arteries. That same month, the company founded the Cordis Global Cardiac & Vascular Institute, an educational outreach program aimed at promoting technological advances in the treatment of cardiovascular diseases.

In July 2006 Cordis acquired the California-based Ensure Medical, a device manufacturer specializing in the treatment of femoral artery blockages. Three months later the company unveiled its third-generation Cypher stent, the Cypher Select Plus. By 2008 Cypher stents had been used to treat more than three million patients across the globe. For the year, the company recorded revenues of $3.1 billion, with more than half of its total sales coming from overseas markets. As the company celebrated its 50th anniversary in April 2009, its financial outlook remained as promising as ever.

April Dougal Gasbarre
Updated, Christina M. Stansell; Stephen Meyer

PRINCIPAL OPERATING UNITS

Cordis Cardiology; Cordis Endovascular; Conor Medsystems LLC; Biosense Webster, Inc.; Cordis Biologics Delivery Systems Group.

PRINCIPAL COMPETITORS

Abbot Laboratories; Boston Scientific Corporation; C. R. Bard Inc.; Medtronic CardioVascular.

FURTHER READING

Abelson, Reed, "Cordis Corp.," *Fortune*, June 5, 1989, p. 176.

———, "A Rare Chance to Take Back a Market; Johnson & Johnson's New Stent May Dominate Angioplasties," *New York Times*, January 3, 2003, p. C1.

Breen, Julia, "New Heart Treatment Could Cut Waiting," *Northern Echo*, May 2, 2002, p. 15.

"Cardiometrics Inc.," *Health Industry Today*, July 1997, p. 14.

"Catheters Unclog Cordis' Growth," *Florida Trend*, January 1994, p. 8.

"Cordis," *BBI Newsletter*, August 1999, p. 186.

"Cordis," *BBI Newsletter*, March 2001, p. 80.

"Cordis: Building Marketing Muscle to Pump Up Strength in Biomedicine," *Business Week*, December 20, 1982, p. 63.

"Cordis Celebrates 50 Years of Transforming Cardiovascular Care," *Biotech Business Week*, April 6, 2009, p. 1525.

"Cordis Completes Enrollment in Landmark U.S. Trial," *PR Newswire*, August 30, 2001.

"Cordis Corporation to Develop Global Cardiac and Vascular Institute," *Drug Week*, May 5, 2006, p. 994.

"Cordis Faces Import Sanctions, Begins Heart-Valve Recall," *South Florida Business Journal*, May 18, 1992, p. 7.

"Cordis Quality Starts with Suppliers," *Florida Trend,* May 1988, pp. 50–52.

"Cordis Receives Approval for New Catheter," *South Florida Business Journal*, March 19, 1990, p. 6.

Davis, Philip M., "Beware of Corporate Criminal Conduct," *Design News*, November 7, 1988, p. 214.

Dooley, Kerry, "Cypher Stent Sales Buoy Johnson & Johnson Earnings: Profit Meets Street Target," *National Post's Financial Post & FP Investing* (Canada), July 16, 2003, p. 16.

Engardio, Pete, "Why Cordis' Heart Wasn't in Pacemakers," *Business Week*, March 16, 1987, p. 80.

Farley, Dixie, "Firm Pleads Guilty to Selling Faulty Pacemakers," *FDA Consumer*, September 1989, pp. 38–39.

"Johnson & Johnson Launches Hostile Bid for Miami Firm," *Atlanta Constitution*, October 20, 1995, p. F6.

Keller, Katrina, "Cardiac Comeback," *Forbes*, April 30, 2001, p. 164.

Linden, Eugene, "The Role of the Founder: Murphy's Law," *Inc.*, July 1984, pp. 90–96.

McGough, Robert, "Choppy Waters," *Forbes*, September 12, 1983, p. 183.

———, "Mr. Clean," *Forbes*, April 23, 1984, pp. 141–142.

Miller, Susan R., "Snag Slows Down Cordis Deal with Johnson & Johnson," *South Florida Business Journal*, December 29, 1995, pp. 3–4.

Nesse, Leslie Kraft, "Change in Cordis' Structure Leads to Increased Sales, Profits," *South Florida Business Journal*, June 10, 1994, pp. 8–9B.

———, "Cordis in Licensing Agreement," *South Florida Business Journal*, June 17, 1994, pp. 3–4.

Paltrow, Scot J., "Cordis Stock Plunges on J&J Delay," *Los Angeles Times*, December 28, 1995, p. D2.

Petruno, Tom, "Johnson & Johnson Makes Bid for Cordis," *Los Angeles Times*, October 20, 1995, p. D2.

Price, Joyce Howard, "New Artery Device Gets FDA Approval; Cypher Stent Reduces Reclogging Risks," *Washington Times*, April 25, 2003, p. A06.

Raloff, J., "Keeping Pace," *Datamation*, January 1984, p. 38.

Resnick, Rosalind, "Cordis Recovers; Can It Catch Up?" *Florida Trend*, June 1991, pp. 41–43.

Waresh, Julie, "Back to the Drawing Board," *South Florida Business Journal*, August 14, 1989, pp. 1–2.

———, "Spin-offs Lift Burden from Cordis Corp.," *South Florida Business Journal*, December 12, 1988, pp. 5–6.

Westlund, Richard, "Cordis Corporation: A Wellness Program with 'Heart,'" *South Florida Business Journal*, June 9, 1995, p. 12B.

Cornell Companies, Inc.

1700 West Loop South, Suite 1500
Houston, Texas 77027
U.S.A.
Telephone: (713) 623-0790
Toll Free: (888) 624-0816
Fax: (713) 623-2853
Web site: http://cornellcompanies.com

Public Company
Founded: 1990 as Cornell Cox Group
Employees: 4,300
Sales: $412.38 million (2009)
Stock Exchanges: NYSE
Ticker Symbol: CRN
NAICS: 922140 Correctional Institutions

■ ■ ■

Cornell Companies, Inc., is the fourth-largest publicly traded provider of correctional and treatment services in the United States. Its customers include the Federal Bureau of Prisons (BOP), the U.S. Marshals Service, and state and local departments of correction and human services. Cornell provides services for adults and juveniles, including incarceration and detention, transition from incarceration, drug and alcohol treatment programs, behavioral rehabilitation and treatment, and alternative education for grades 3 to 12. In 2010 Cornell operated 68 facilities in 15 states and the District of Columbia with a total service capacity of 21,392 individuals.

COMPANY FOUNDED: 1990

Cornell was founded in 1990 as Cornell Cox Group, a firm that provided consulting services to the developing private prison industry in the United States. Company founder David M. Cornell had served as a special projects operations manager for the engineering and construction giant Bechtel and as chief financial officer of one of Bechtel's subsidiaries, Becom, from 1983 to 1990. He served as CEO of Cornell from 1990 to 2000. Cornell received initial financing to build and operate prisons primarily from the investment firm Dillon, Read & Co., which had accumulated 44 percent of Cornell's common stock by the time the company made its IPO in 1996 and was thus the controlling shareholder.

Cornell built its first correctional facilities in 1991, including the Donald W. Wyatt Detention Facility in Central Falls, Rhode Island. The federal government had agreed to pay Cornell $83 per day to house its detainees, but by 1993 the prison was largely empty, according to Jeff Gerth and Stephen Labaton in the *New York Times*. Threatened by insolvency and angry shareholders, Cornell sought prisoners outside the federal system and, through a deal brokered by the lawyer Richard Crane, 232 prisoners from North Carolina were housed at Wyatt. In addition to building facilities, during this time the company bought Eclectic Communications, which operated 11 pre-release facilities in California. In 1995 the company lost $7.4 million on total revenues of $20.7 million.

By 1996 Cornell Corrections had become the fourth-largest operator of detention and pre-release

COMPANY PERSPECTIVES

By providing safe and secure environments, teaching values, and offering quality programs and opportunities for change in an environment of dignity and respect for the individual, people can change. They can be successful, productive citizens who are no longer a threat to society and can have a second chance at life. This is the fundamental belief that is interwoven throughout our company and binds our employees, programs, departments, and facilities together.

services in the United States. It held contracts with the U.S. Marshals Service, the Immigration and Naturalization Service (later Immigration and Customs Enforcement), and the states of California and Texas. The company operated 20 private detention facilities totaling 3,349 beds, and five of the facilities had been designed, built, and financed by Cornell. That year the company acquired two Texas companies: MidTex in Big Spring, which operated three secure facilities with a capacity of 1,305 beds for prisoners supplied by the BOP, and the Ben A. Reid Community Residential Facility in Houston, the state's largest pre-release facility.

Cornell Corrections went public in 1996 with an initial public offering of about three million shares of common stock on the American Exchange for a total of $56 million. In the *Houston Business Journal*, Cornell's chief financial officer, Steve W. Logan, noted that "Most of the cost savings from privatization—as much as 30 percent—comes from our early design and construction of the facilities. We don't have to take over somebody else's problem."

GROWTH THROUGH ACQUISITIONS: 1997–99

In 1997 Cornell Corrections acquired Abraxas Youth Family Services, a Pennsylvania-based company that provided programs supporting the juvenile justice system. Abraxas offered residential and detention care with various levels of security, as well as shelter care, counseling, treatment, educational services, and recreation programs for youths aged 10 to 18. In December 1998 Cornell Corrections debuted on the New York Stock Exchange under a new name, Cornell Companies, retaining the ticker symbol CRN. That year the company had contracts to operate 52 facilities with a total offender capacity of 10,525.

In 1999 Cornell Corrections acquired Interventions, a nonprofit Chicago corporation that had existed since 1974 providing adult and juvenile treatment in Illinois. The assets included seven residential facilities and more than 30 programs within 13 facilities throughout Illinois. Cornell also bought Archway Programs, Inc., and Archway Programs Delaware, Inc., two New Jersey-based not-for-profit corporations. That year the company was selected by the State of Utah to design, build, and operate a 209,000-square-foot facility that would be Utah's first medium-security private prison.

In July 1999 David Cornell suffered a mild heart attack, and Steve Logan replaced him as acting chief executive officer. Logan became the company's second CEO a year later when Cornell officially stepped down. In August 1999 Cornell Companies reported second-quarter net income growth of 39 percent and revenue growth of 50 percent, attributable largely to more than 2,400 new offenders under contract during the second half of 1998 and the first six months of 1999.

FACING CRITICS: 2000–01

The new millennium started off on a high note for Cornell Companies when American Capital Strategies, Ltd., invested $30 million to finance the company's further growth. The Teachers Insurance and Annuity Association-College Retirement Equities Fund (TIAA-CREF), the world's largest retirement system, also invested $10 million.

Cornell received unwelcome publicity, however, in April 2001 following a disturbance at one of its operations, New Mexico's Santa Fe County jail. The prison had already been on lockdown because three federal inmates had escaped by breaking a window and sawing through metal bars, using tools given to them by jail guards employed by Cornell. Inmates complained about conditions at the jail during Cornell's administration, including lack of medical care and basic sanitation such as toilet paper. Such problems supported the claims of critics of prison privatization, who noted that jail administrators were under the authority of their corporate management, not the local sheriff's department, which removed accountability for the prison from the local community and made profit a motive in operation the facility. Another firm, Management & Training Corp. of Utah, took over the jail in October 2001.

The year 2001 saw a heightened interest in the prison industry, especially on detaining illegal aliens, after the terrorist attacks against the United States on September 11. "What we are seeing is an increased scrutiny, a tightening up of the borders," CEO Logan

KEY DATES

1990: Cornell Corrections founded to take advantage of a national trend toward prison privatization.

1998: Cornell Companies, Inc., (CRN) begins trading on the New York Stock Exchange.

2001: Cornell sells 11 of its facilities to Municipal Corrections Finance L.P. in a $173 million sale-leaseback deal brokered by Lehman Brothers.

2002: Company investigated by the Securities and Exchange Commission (SEC) for possible conflict of interest with Lehman Brothers.

2004: SEC investigation concludes with no enforcement action against the company.

2010: Company enters a 10-year, $205-million agreement to house more than 2,500 low-security federal inmates at the D. Ray James Correctional Facility in Georgia.

reported during a conference call reported in *Colorlines.* "Some of that means that people don't get through. But the other side of that is more people are gonna get caught.... So that's a positive for our business." Opponents of privatized prisons, such as the activist group Not With Our Money, disputed Logan's claim, saying there had actually been no demand for additional detention facilities as a result of the 2001 terrorist attacks, but that if additional bed spaces were created, harsher incarceration policies would be enacted to fill them.

LEASE DEAL LEADS TO INVESTIGATION, LAWSUITS: 2001–02

In August 2001 Cornell sold 11 of its facilities to Municipal Corrections Finance L.P. (MCF) in a $173 million sale-leaseback deal intended to allow Cornell to expand its operations while leasing the facilities and continuing to operate them. MCF was an entity created specifically to acquire these properties. The transaction was brokered by Lehman Brothers, and it reduced Lehman Brothers' own substantial equity share in Cornell. Also in 2001 the company made a public offering of over three million newly issued shares of its common stock in an offering led by Lehman Brothers.

In March 2002 four class action lawsuits were filed against Cornell by its shareholders, accusing the

company of violating federal securities laws. The lawsuits alleged that the company had made misleading statements that sent the stock as high as $18.40 per share in its November 2001 offering of 3.4 million shares, which had raised $48 million for the company. Later that month Cornell was investigated by the SEC for its payment of $3.65 million to Lehman Brothers. Although the company claimed it had been a retainer to Lehman Brothers for future services, it could have also been a payment for Lehman Brothers' role in setting up MCF, the creation of which reduced Lehman Brothers' equity share in Cornell below the level required by SEC law. (Lack of sufficient outside ownership was the same thing that had revealed Enron's illegal accounting practices.) News of the SEC investigation set off a rapid downturn in Cornell's shares on the New York Stock Exchange, where they lost more than half their value. The company restated its financial statements for the fiscal year ended December 31, 2000, and its financial statements for three of the four quarters of 2001.

Toward the end of 2004, the SEC announced that it had terminated its investigation into Cornell's revised financial statements and that no enforcement action had been recommended. The class action suit brought against Cornell by its shareholders was ultimately settled in 2006 for $7 million. Under the terms of the settlement the company admitted to no wrongdoing.

A CHANGE IN LEADERSHIP: 2002–04

In September 2002 Steve Logan resigned. He was succeeded as CEO by Thomas R. Jenkins, who had previously been the company's senior vice president and chief operating officer. That year Cornell closed one of its youth facilities, New Morgan Academy, after six inmates had escaped and reports of sexual assaults on juvenile inmates by employees had been filed.

Despite such problems, in 2003 Cornell was contracted to operate two new juvenile programs in South Dakota, which had previously sent youths out of state for correctional detention. The detention center was expected to generate annual revenue of approximately $2 million. In August 2003 Harry J. Phillips Jr. succeeded Thomas R. Jenkins as CEO. Jenkins retained the roles of president and chief operating officer.

In 2004 the company began building Moshannon Valley Correctional Center, a $68 million federal prison for 1,000 adult male prisoners and 300 adult females in Clearfield County, Pennsylvania. Also that year Cornell signed a five-year agreement to provide alternative education services to 3rd and 4th grade students in the

School District of Philadelphia. This agreement would generate $2 million in annualized revenue. In 2004 Cornell opened the Regional Correctional Center (RCC) in Albuquerque, New Mexico, a 528-bed facility in what had been formerly the Bernalillo County Detention Center. A second section of the prison opened later that year, bringing the total inmate capacity to 970. The RCC was expected to generate annualized revenue of $24 million.

In August 2004 a group of shareholders angry about the company's disappointing financial performance (Cornell's market value had sunk to $166 million from $228 million in 2001) lobbied for its sale. Management was rumored to have held meetings with several potential buyers, including Geo Group, Corrections Corp. of America, and Management & Training Corp. Another shareholder faction merely wanted management replaced. Shareholders expressed frustration that the company held many lucrative corrections contracts, yet rarely managed to profit from them. "Our capital is being wasted here, and our company is being undermanaged," said Zachary George of Pirate Capital, a Connecticut hedge fund. Speaking directly to CEO Harry Phillips, he predicted: "In the next year, we're going to be here, and you won't."

THE HYMAN ERA: 2005–10

George was right. In January 2005 James E. Hyman, a Harvard graduate with a background in finance, succeeded Phillips as Cornell's chief executive officer. That same month Cornell acquired one of its competitors, Correctional Systems, Inc., a San Diego-based provider of privatized jail and alternative sentencing services, for $10 million. This purchase added eight jails, six community corrections facilities, and five alternative sentencing programs to Cornell's inventory. Cornell reopened the New Morgan juvenile center as Abraxas Academy with a new staff and revised procedures in 2006.

In 2007 the Immigration and Customs Enforcement (ICE) agency pulled more than 600 detainees from the Cornell-managed RCC in Albuquerque, New Mexico, after months of "allegations of filthy conditions, subpar medical attention and bad food," as reported by Kate Nash in the *Albuquerque Tribune*. "We took our people out of the RCC facility because we are skeptical about Cornell's ability to run the facility in a way that maintains the safety, health and well-being of our detainees," Gary Mead, ICE's assistant director for detention and removal operations, told Sue Major Holmes in the *Santa Fe New Mexican*. In response, Cornell undertook several improvements in the facility and its management, including improved security monitor-

ing and recreation programs, cleaning and painting the center, and revising the operations manual.

In August 2009 Cornell announced that it had received a contract from the State of Alaska Department of Corrections to house 1,250 state prisoners in Hudson, Colorado. Approximately 800 Alaskan inmates jailed in Arizona were to be transferred by plane to the Colorado prison, thus saving Alaska $6 per day per prisoner.

In February 2010, reporting its earnings for the year ending December 31, 2009, Cornell noted that revenue grew 6.6 percent from $386.72 million in 2008 to $412.38 million in 2009. The growth resulted from expansions at the Great Plains Correctional Facility in Oklahoma and the Walnut Gove Youth Correctional Facility in Mississippi, the opening of the new facility in Hudson, Colorado, and an increase in populations at the RCC in New Mexico and the Reid Community Facility in Texas.

Also in early 2010 Cornell announced a 10-year, $205-million agreement with the BOP to house 2,507 low-security federal inmates at the D. Ray James Correctional Facility in Folkston, Georgia. With this contract, Cornell management expressed confidence in its future, stating, "We believe this sets a trajectory for Cornell of solid long-term growth despite the challenging budget environment that we face with our customers in 2010."

Melanie Bush

PRINCIPAL DIVISIONS

Abraxas Youth and Family Services; Adult Community-Based Services; Adult Secure Services.

PRINCIPAL COMPETITORS

Corrections Corporation of America; The Geo Group, Inc.; Management and Training Corporation; The Wackenhut Corporation.

FURTHER READING

Bernstein, Nina, "New Scrutiny as Immigrants Die in Custody," *New York Times*, June 26, 2007.

Carrillo, Karen Juanita, "Locking away Profits: Capitalizing on Immigrant Detentions Has Turned into a Booming Business for Lehman Brothers," *Color Lines*, Fall 2002.

Gerth, Jeff, and Stephen Labaton, "Prisons for Profit: A Special Report; Jail Business Shows Its Weaknesses," *New York Times*, November 24, 1995.

Holland, Megan, "Alaska Prisoners to Move from Arizona to Colorado: $1.75 million Saved: Current Arizona Facility Is

$6 a Day More for Each of Its 800 Alaska Inmates," *Anchorage Daily News*, August 10, 2009.

Wahlgren, Eric, "Investing in Crime and Punishment," *BusinessWeek Online*, October 21, 2003, http://www. businessweek.com/bwdaily/dnflash/oct2003/nf20031021_0464_db014.htm.

Xiong, Nzong, "Private Prisons: A Question of Savings," *New York Times*, July 13, 1997.

CSL Limited

---

45 Poplar Road
Parkville, VIC 3052
Australia
Telephone: (+61 613) 9389-1911
Fax: (+61 613) 9389-1434
Web site: http://www.csl.com.au

Public Company
Founded: 1916
Incorporated: 1991
Employees: 10,000
Sales: AUD 4.62 billion ($4.22 billion) (2009)
Stock Exchanges: Australia
Ticker Symbol: CSL
NAICS: 325412 Pharmaceutical Preparation Manufacturing; 325411 Medicinal and Botanical Manufacturing; 325414 Biological Product (except Diagnostic) Manufacturing; 424210 Drugs and Druggists' Sundries Merchant Wholesalers; 541710 Research and Development in the Physical Sciences and Engineering Sciences; 551112 Offices of Other Holding Companies

■ ■ ■

CSL Limited is a leading global biopharmaceutical company in the plasma industry and is a worldwide provider of influenza vaccines. Based in Melbourne, Australia, the CSL Group (CSL) operates major facilities in Germany, Switzerland, and the United States and has 10,000 employees working in 27 countries. The company's three main operating divisions are Plasma Products, Vaccines and Pharmaceuticals, and Research and Development. The core businesses in the Plasma Products division include CSL Behring (for the manufacture of plasma-derived and recombinant products), CSL Plasma (a plasma collection network), CSL Bioplasma (a plasma fractionator), and Immunohaematology (for the manufacture and marketing of in vitro diagnostic products).

CSL Biotherapies manufactures and distributes a broad range of vaccines and antivenoms throughout Australia, New Zealand, the United States, and many other countries. In partnership with academic institutions and corporations throughout Asia, North America, Europe, and Australia, CSL R&D is committed to developing new products and improving existing products to help treat and prevent serious human medical conditions. In 2007 the Biopharmaceutical Formulation Centre in Melbourne was established to develop liquid pharmaceuticals. The CSL Group's contributions to medicine and human health span more than 100 years, and the company remains committed to investing heavily in its R&D efforts in the areas of plasma replacement therapies, vaccines, immunomodulators, and recombinant therapeutic proteins.

CSL'S ORIGINS

For the duration of World War I, Australia was largely cut off from the rest of the world, on which it depended for its vaccines, serums, and other bacteriological products. In 1916 the Commonwealth Serum Laboratories (CSL), a federal serum institute, was established in Australia to meet these needs. Under the

COMPANY PERSPECTIVES

CSL Limited is a global, specialty biopharmaceutical company that researches, develops, manufactures and markets products to treat and prevent serious human medical conditions. The CSL Group has a combined heritage of outstanding contributions to medicine and human health with more than 90 years experience in the development and manufacture of vaccines and plasma protein biotherapies. Our strong commitment to funding research and development of protein based biological medicines for unmet medical needs underpins our continuing growth.

direction of William Penfold, a bacteriologist from the Lister Institute of Preventive Medicine in the United Kingdom, CSL developed and manufactured lifesaving medications and treatments.

In 1917 the prestigious Walter and Eliza Hall Institute of Medical Research (WEHI) of Melbourne offered CSL temporary accommodation in its facility. In what would become an enduring professional relationship, CSL would collaborate over the next century with WEHI's world-class researchers on several medical breakthroughs. As recently as September 2009 CSL and WEHI signed a $2.2 million agreement to develop the next generation of treatments for inflammatory diseases.

COMBATING EPIDEMICS: POST–WORLD WAR I

By 1918 the Spanish influenza had the world in its grips, and the ports of Melbourne and Sydney were placed under quarantine. CSL set up permanent quarters at its site in Parkville, Melbourne, where the company's first course of action was to prepare advance doses of the vaccine in preparation for an influenza outbreak in Australia. The flu hit Australia with a vengeance in January 1919. To deal with the outbreak, authorities closed public venues, such as schools, theaters, and cinemas, turning many into makeshift hospitals. CSL temporarily tripled its staff to meet the needs of Australia's population, producing three million doses of the bacterial vaccine.

Diphtheria, which is easily spread by a cough or a sneeze, had reached epidemic proportions by the 1920s. In late 1920 a toxin-antitoxin was introduced to combat the highly infectious and potentially fatal disease. The immunization treatment, which essentially eradicated

diphtheria, was based on the work of Emil von Behring, who won the first Nobel Prize in Medicine in 1901 for his work on serum therapies. In 1904 in Marburg, Germany, Behring also established the Behringwerke to produce vaccines and other serums. By 1946 the company had become the first in Europe to separate human plasma proteins on an industrial scale.

DEVELOPING NEW PRODUCTS

By the 1920s CSL's product range included various diagnostic agents, 5 therapeutic serums, 24 vaccines, and 4 tuberculins. In 1922 CSL entered into the veterinary market and began to produce vaccines and a broad range of other veterinary products. Also in 1922 Frederick Banting and Charles Best of Canada isolated insulin, a groundbreaking achievement that would save the lives of millions of diabetes sufferers throughout the world. CSL became one of the first laboratories to produce an experimental batch of the insulin and by 1923 was one of only four labs in the world licensed to manufacture the treatment. By August 1923 CSL was producing enough insulin to serve Australia's population.

Throughout the decade CSL continued to expand its product lines. A number of medical breakthroughs were made using blood products to develop serums that would prevent and treat such diseases as poliomyelitis, measles, and scarlet fever. Through these achievements, CSL and other medical laboratories began to produce large quantities of human serum that would prove useful during World War II, when blood transfusions were greatly needed. In 1930, in collaboration with WEHI, CSL released its tiger snake antivenom, the first of many antivenom treatments that CSL would manufacture to fight snake and spider bites. As CSL's operations grew, the company required its own independent research facility, and under the direction of E. V. Keogh, CSL established an in-house research section.

With the onset of World War II, the need for tetanus prevention was greater than ever, and CSL produced enough of the vaccine to immunize all of Australia's military personnel. As a result, not a single Australian serviceperson contracted the dreaded disease. Forces in Asia and the Middle East also required biological products, and CSL answered the call, manufacturing millions of doses to fight smallpox, typhoid fever, plague, and cholera. By 1940 CSL had begun to produce pooled human serum.

Along with a team of scientists at Oxford University in England, Australia's Howard Florey discovered the therapeutic properties of penicillin, for which he and his colleague Ernst B. Chain earned the 1945 Nobel Prize in Physiology or Medicine. In response to this discovery, CSL recalled its staff member Val Bazeley (later CSL's

KEY DATES

1904: Emil von Behring founds Behringwerke in Marburg, Germany, for the manufacture of vaccines.

1916: Commonwealth Serum Laboratories (CSL) is founded.

1918: CSL establishes permanent headquarters in Parkville, Melbourne, Australia.

1922: CSL enters the veterinary market.

1952: CSL Bioplasma business is established.

1991: CSL Limited is incorporated; Brian McNamee is named managing director and chief executive officer.

1994: CSL Limited is listed on the Australian Stock Exchange.

2000: CSL acquires Rotkreuzstiftung Zentrallaboratorium Blutspendedientst SRK (ZLB).

2010: CSL begins restructuring its top management team.

director) from the army to supervise the production of penicillin. Bazeley was immediately dispatched to the United States to study penicillin manufacturing techniques. Upon his return to Australia, he recruited soldiers who were awaiting discharge to work as his night production staff.

Within 10 weeks the crew was producing more than 750 bottles of penicillin per day. By February 1944 penicillin supplies had reached the front, supplying not only the Australian forces but also many of the Allied forces serving in the Pacific. Two months later production levels were so high that penicillin could be freely dispensed to Australia's civilians. By 1948 CSL was producing 44,000 bottles of penicillin per day.

CSL POST–WORLD WAR II

In 1949 the Zentrallaboratorium Blutspendedienst (ZLB) was established as a department of the Swiss Red Cross in Bern, Switzerland, where ZLB held its first blood donor sessions. ZLB would grow to become one of the world's largest blood plasma groups and would be acquired by CSL 50 years later. In 1952 CSL established its CSL Bioplasma business for blood fractionation, which was based on the Cohn process developed by Edwin Cohn of Harvard University during World War II. The following year, CSL developed immune serum globulin derived from pooled human blood, a product that would be used in the prevention of certain viruses,

such as measles and rubella. Also in 1953 the company introduced the Triple Antigen vaccine, for the immunization of infants and young children against tetanus, diphtheria, and pertussis. This was followed in 1954 with CSL's first issue of albumin, an essential blood protein.

In 1954 Bazeley returned to the United States to serve as Jonas Salk's assistant in the development of the poliomyelitis vaccine at the University of Pittsburgh in Pennsylvania. The following year, after successful clinical trials in the United States, Bazeley returned to Australia to begin CSL's production of the Salk vaccine. By June 1956 CSL's production of the vaccine had risen to 390,000 doses per year. Within two years this number had increased to five million doses per year, and under an agreement with the Commonwealth Government, the vaccine was administered free of charge to Australian residents and Australian nationals living abroad.

In 1961 CSL issued an antihemophiliac globulin product produced from plasma. This was followed in 1962 with the release of the first polyvalent snake antivenom for the treatment of bites by venomous snake originating in Australia and Papua New Guinea. In 1966 CSL became the world's first company to issue on a national basis the Rh(D) Immunoglobulin plasma derivative, used in the treatment of hemolytic disease in newborns.

Bluetongue, a viral disease that affects livestock, was identified in Australia in 1977. Having recently completed construction of a maximum-security laboratory, CSL moved swiftly to use this facility for the development of a vaccine to combat the disease. In 1981 the first pasteurized factor VIII product reached the European market. The von Willebrand factor complex, Haemate Human Plasma Factor VIII was developed for the prevention and treatment of bleeding in hemophilia A.

Also in 1981 Struan Sutherland, CSL's head of immunology from 1966 to 1994, developed the pressure-immobilization first aid technique and snake venom detection kit, revolutionizing the treatment of snakebites. Sutherland also developed a lifesaving funnel-web spider antivenom. In 1983 CSL began manufacturing the GLANVAC vaccine for the prevention of clostridial diseases and "cheesy gland" (*Caseous lymphadenitis*) in sheep.

INCORPORATION AND ACQUISITIONS

In 1991, with the Commonwealth Government holding all shares, CSL Limited was incorporated as a public company. Brian McNamee was appointed managing director and chief executive officer (CEO). McNamee's vision was to grow CSL to become one of Australia's leading independent companies through mergers and acquisitions. In 1992 CSL entered into an agreement with Merck Sharp & Dohme (Australia) Pty Ltd and Merck & Co to develop a combination vaccine for children in Australia, New Zealand, and the Asia-Pacific region.

At this same time, CSL Bioplasma began toll manufacturing for Malaysia, while its new plasma products facility, which opened in Broadmeadows, Australia, in 1994, boasted the world's largest chromatographic albumin plant. During 1993 CSL signed a 10-year agreement with the Commonwealth to manufacture and supply a range of plasma-derived products to the Australian market. CSL also participated in two Cooperative Research Centre programs that focused on the development and commercialization of Australian innovative technology.

On May 30, 1994, after a public float, CSL was listed on the Australian Stock Exchange. In this same year, CSL acquired a majority interest in Sweden's Iscotec AB and 100 percent of JRH Biosciences, Inc., a U.S. cell culture company. After many years of positive performance, CSL sold JRH Biosciences in 2005 to Sigma-Aldrich Corporation for a record AUD 492 million, more than three times the value that CSL placed on the business. By 1995 CSL had become Australia's second-largest pharmaceutical company and the only one in the country that manufactured products from human plasma. CSL was now a fully listed public company, with 50 percent of the shares held by retail investors and the remaining 50 percent split among domestic and foreign institutions.

CSL expanded its veterinary business with the opening of a new viral vaccine facility in New Zealand. This was followed in 1998 with the acquisition of Biocor, a U.S. veterinary vaccine manufacturing plant. On November 18, 1998, CSL opened a new Pharmaceutical Packaging dispensing center. By February 1999 CSL's half-year pretax profits were up 17.6 percent. That year CSL Bioplasma signed a lucrative product development and manufacturing agreement with the American Red Cross.

In 2000 the company signed a 10-year agreement with GroPep Pty Ltd. for the exclusive worldwide marketing of a range of its recombinant growth factor products. One of CSL's most significant acquisitions was the purchase of Rotkreuzstiftung Zentrallaboratorium Blutspendedienst SRK (ZLB), a nonprofit organization affiliated with the Swiss Red Cross and the world's fifth-largest manufacturer of plasma products. CSL's shares soared on the heels of this announcement but fell again in January 2001 over fears that the company's human plasma products could be affected by mad cow disease, although analysts maintained that the risk of transference was minimal.

CONTINUED GLOBAL GROWTH

CSL was confident in its product line, and shares rose 23 percent in June 2001 after the announcement that the company was purchasing 47 U.S.-based plasma collection centers and associated lab facilities from Nabi. By September 2001, with the plasma supply secured, ZLB Plasma Services was ready to begin operations, and McNamee was eyeing other acquisition opportunities. In December 2001, in a deal that the two companies hoped would increase their presence in the U.S. animal health market, CSL began distribution of BresaGen Ltd.'s horse drug EquiGen. The following month, in a strategic move, CSL began a $10 million expansion of its Biocor site in Omaha, Nebraska. In 2002 CSL doubled production of the influenza vaccine to meet the needs of the Southern and Northern hemispheres. That year CSL also opened its first regional office in Hong Kong and introduced Menjugate, a meningococcal C vaccine licensed from Chiron Corporation, to the Australian market.

CSL began construction of CSL Bioplasma's new purpose-built nucleic acid testing laboratory in 2003. In that same year, CSL launched the Fluvax influenza vaccine and, in partnership with the University of Queensland, obtained the U.S. patent for the human papillomavirus 16 serotype developed by Merck & Co. By 2006 the collaboration had proved a success when the cervical cancer vaccine GARDASIL received FDA approval. Also in 2006 CSL's Vivaglobin, a treatment for people with primary immunodeficiency, was approved for distribution in the U.S. and U.K. markets.

In 2004 CSL completed the acquisition of Aventis Behring SA and merged it with ZLB Bioplasma to create ZLB Behring. Later renamed CSL Behring, the newly formed business created a world leader in plasma therapeutics and catapulted the CSL Group to second place in the global blood products industry. In a move that was welcomed by investors, CSL also decided to sell its animal health business to Pfizer, Inc. By 2005 CSL had doubled its net profit, helped in part by its divestiture of JRH Biosciences.

ADAPTING FOR THE 21ST CENTURY

In June 2006 CSL Biotherapies entered the U.S. influenza market when it partnered with the National Institute of Allergy and Infectious Diseases, a division of the National Institutes of Health, to begin clinical trials of its vaccine. In July 2006 the company acquired Zenyth Therapeutics Ltd., which McNamee projected would "double the company's activity in biotechnology," according to *AAP News* (July 17, 2006). Following the acquisition, CSL moved 50 of its scientists to the University of Melbourne's Bio21 Molecular Science and Biotechnology Institute, significantly increasing the company's research capacity. In 2007 the CSL Behring global plasma therapeutics business was showing strong growth, and the company announced that it would be investing $15 million to expand its manufacturing facility in Kankakee, Illinois. The high-speed, single-dose syringe filling operation, which was licensed by the U.S. Food and Drug Administration (FDA) in August 2009, would provide filling and packaging services for the seasonal influenza vaccine manufactured by CSL Biotherapies.

In January 2008 CSL entered into an agreement with Celltrion, Inc., a Korean biopharmaceutical company for the development and supply of CSL 360, an experimental therapy for the treatment of acute myeloid leukemia. CSL Biotherapies became the first vaccine manufacturer to conduct clinical trials of the H1N1 (swine flu) influenza vaccine. In August 2009 it was announced that the company had signed an initial contract valued at $180 million to supply the U.S. Department of Health and Human Services with the H1N1 antigen. On September 15, 2009, the FDA approved the H1N1 flu vaccine.

In November 2009 CSL Biotherapies succeeded in securing accelerated FDA approval for its pediatric Afluria influenza vaccine. After more than 10 years, CSL announced in December 2009 that its gum disease vaccine was in the advanced stages of development. The vaccine would combat periodontitis, a common oral health problem that scientists had linked to an increased risk of developing heart disease, dementia, and cancer.

At the start of 2010, CSL Ltd. implemented a restructuring of its top management team, with McNamee expected to continue as CEO for at least three years. The company also merged its two manufacturing facilities in Parkville and Broadmeadows, Australia. McNamee said to the *Australian* (December 9, 2009), "These changes signal increased alignment of our international operations which have grown through a number of successful acquisitions. We are strengthening the future of the Australian businesses."

Marie O'Sullivan

PRINCIPAL SUBSIDIARIES

CSL Employee Share Trust; CSL Biotherapies Pty Ltd; Cervax Pty Ltd (74%); CSL Biotherapies (NZ) Limited;

Isotec AB (Sweden); Zenyth Therapeutics Pty Ltd; CSL International Pty Ltd; CSLB Holdings Inc (USA); CSL Behring Verwaltungs GmbH (Germany); CSL Biotherapies Asia Pacific Limited (Hong Kong); CSL Behring S.A. (Argentina); CSL Behring Holdings Ltd (England).

PRINCIPAL DIVISIONS

Plasma Products; Vaccines & Pharmaceuticals; Research & Development.

PRINCIPAL OPERATING UNITS

CSL Bioplasma incorporating Immunohaematology; CSL Biotherapies; CSL Behring incorporating CSL Plasma.

PRINCIPAL COMPETITORS

Baxter International Inc.; Grifols, S.A.; Novartis AG.

FURTHER READING

Ambler, Emma, "CSL Makes $108 Million Takeover Bid for Zenyth," *AAP News*, July 17, 2006.

"Australia's Biopharmaceutical Co CSL Signs Deal with GroPep," *AsiaPulse News*, April 6, 2000, p. 0214.

"Australia's CSL Caught in Regulatory Crossfire in U.S.," *AsiaPulse News*, May 25, 2009.

"Australia's CSL H1 Net Profit Jumps 46 Pct on Behring Plasma Ops," *AFX Asia (Focus)*, February 20, 2007.

"Australia's CSL Reports 76 Pct Fall in Annual Net Profit," *AsiaPulse News*, August 23, 2006.

"Australia's CSL Says Full Year Net Profit May Reach US$226.3 Mln," *AsiaPulse News*, June 28, 2005.

"Australia's CSL Says FY Net Profit May Touch US$154 Mln," *AsiaPulse News*, August 3, 2004.

"Australia's CSL to Acquire Switzerland's ZLB Plasma Business," *AsiaPulse News*, June 8, 2000, p. 0430.

"Australia's CSL to Sell Animal Health Business to Pfizer," *AsiaPulse News*, December 16, 2003.

"Australian Pharmaceutical Group CSL Says Interim Profit Up," *AsiaPulse News*, February 10, 1999.

Brogan, A. H., *A History of the Commonwealth Serum Laboratories*. Melbourne: Hyland House, 1990.

"Celltrion and CSL Announce Collaboration to Develop and Manufacture Monoclonal Antibody," *PR Newswire*, January 10, 2008.

Chappell, Trevor, "CSL Announces New Share Buyback," *Asia Africa Intelligence*, June 28, 2005.

———, "CSL Shares Tumble Almost 10pc after Merrill Lynch Downgrade," *Asia Africa Intelligence Wire*, June 12, 2002.

———, "WRAP-CSL Shares Plunge as FX Movements Expected to Cut Earnings," *Asia Africa Intelligence Wire*, October 17, 2002.

"CSL and Australian University Obtain Patent for HPV 16 Serotype," *AsiaPulse News*, September 3, 2003.

"CSL Behring to Build High-Speed Syringe Fill Line at Its Kankakee (IL) Facility," *Business Wire*, August 1, 2007.

"CSL Biotherapies, a New Entrant into U.S. Flu Market, Starts Influenza Vaccine Biological Licensure Trial," *PR Newswire*, June 5, 2006.

"CSL Biotherapies Secures FDA Accelerated Approval for Its Seasonal Flu Vaccine," *Wireless News*, November 16, 2009.

"CSL Biotherapies Starts Shipment of Seasonal Influenza Vaccine for the 2009–2010 Flu Season," *Chemical Business Newsbase*, July 27, 2009.

"CSL Completes Acquisition of Aventis Behring to Create ZLB Behring," *PR Newswire*, April 1, 2004.

"CSL Decision to Cut Q Fever Vaccine Angers Vets," *AAP News*, November 21, 2005.

"CSL Limited to Apply for License to Market Influenza Vaccine in the U.S.; Major Vaccine Manufacturer to Double Capacity," *Business Wire*, February 7, 2006.

"CSL Makes Transition to Growth and Geographic Expansion," *Pharmaceutical Business News*, July 31, 1995, p. 26(4).

"CSL Shares Plunge on Concerns over Blood Plasma Market," *Asia Africa Intelligence Wire*, August 6, 2002.

"Dose of Swine Flu Vaccine Works in 10 Days," *Business Recorder*, September 12, 2009.

Epstein, Victor, "Australian Company Bets on Nebraska Animal Pharmaceuticals Market," *Knight-Ridder/Tribune Business News*, January 28, 2002.

"EvoGenix Announces Antibody Collaboration with CSL," *PR Newswire*, June 1, 2006.

"FDA OKs CSL Biotherapies' Influenza Vaccine Filling and Packaging Facility in Illinois," *Wireless News*, August 21, 2009.

Greenblat, Eli, "Cancer Drug Gives CSL Mammoth Earnings Boost," *Australasian Business Intelligence*, August 22, 2007.

"Hepatitis Vaccine Collaboration Signed," *Pharma Business Week*, February 9, 2004, p. 242.

McIntyre, David, and Trevor Chappell, "CSL to Buy Back 9% of Shares after Dropping Talecris Deal," *AAP News*, June 9, 2009.

Neergaard, Lauran, "US Government Approves New Swine Flu Vaccine," *America's Intelligence Wire*, September 15, 2009.

Neufeld, Sonya, "CSL Reaffirms 2005/06 Guidance Ahead of Aventis Charge," *AAP News*, June 21, 2006.

Noonan, Richard, "Australia's CSL Doubles Pft, Pays Special Div," *FWN Select*, August 24, 2005.

———, "DJ Update: Australia's CSL Signals Cap Return after Sale," *FWN Select*, January 19, 2005.

Ooi, Theresa, "Some New Blood in Management Shake-up, but CSL Chief Stays," *Australian*, December 9, 2009.

Puliyenthuruthel, Josey, "Aventis' Plasma Unit Fetches $925M," *Daily Deal*, December 10, 2003.

Rose, Danny, "FED: Vaccine to Prevent Common Gum Disease Nears," *AAP News*, December 10, 2009.

Samandar, Lema, "CSL Says More Solid Growth Expected," *Bulletin Wire*, February 18, 2009.

"Shares in Australia's CSL Hit Three Year Lows on U.S. Concerns," *AsiaPulse News*, February 10, 2003, p. 4478.

"Shares in Australia's CSL Surge over 23 Pct on US Acquisition News," *AsiaPulse News*, June 27, 2001, p. 0729.

"Shares in Australian Drug Co CSL Fall Further on Mad Cow Panic," *AsiaPulse News*, January 12, 2001, p. 0611.

"Shares in Australian CSL Surge after Positive Vaccine Results," *AsiaPulse News*, November 21, 2002.

Singer, Glenn, "Australian Firm Buys Most of Boca Raton, Fla.-based Nabi Plasma Centers," *South Florida Sun Sentinel*, June 26, 2001.

"WEHI Spin-out Murigen Restructures G-CSF Antagonist Program with CSL," *AsiaPulse News*, October 29, 2008.

Wolf, Alan M., "CSL Will Fight for Talecris: Feds Will Sue to Block Deal," *News & Observer* (Raleigh, N.C.), May 28, 2009.

"World's First Cervical Cancer Vaccine Available to Australian Women," *Xinhua News Agency*, August 27, 2006.

Young, Donna, "CSL, Talecris Drop Merger Plans under FTC Pressure," *BioWorld Today*, June 9, 2009.

———, "Talecris Opts for $3.1B Merger Instead of IPO," *BioWorld Today*, August 14, 2008.

D. Swarovski & Co.

Swarovskistrasse 30
Wattens, A-6112
Austria
Telephone: (+43) 5224-5000
Fax: (+43) 5224-5010
Web site: http://www.swarovski.com

Private Company
Incorporated: 1895 as Daniel Swarovski & Co.
Employees: 25,995
Sales: EUR 2.25 billion (2009)
NAICS: 333314 Optical Instrument and Lens Manufacturing; 333515 Cutting Tool and Machine Tool Accessory Manufacturing; 335121 Residential Electric Lighting Fixture Manufacturing; 339911 Jewelry (Except Costume) Manufacturing; 541490 Other Specialized Design Services

■ ■ ■

Founded in 1895, the Austrian manufacturer D. Swarovski & Co. has become nearly synonymous with crystal production. Through its many subsidiaries, the company produces crystal jewelry stones, crystal gifts and objects, including its famed collection of miniature animals, as well as accessories, crystal-based materials for the fashion industry, and components for crystal chandeliers. Swarovski's Crystal Palace collections include lighting, furniture, and architectural designs created in collaboration with prominent international designers. The company's Schonbek subsidiary, long known for its chandeliers, also designs and manufactures

lighting systems for both residential and industrial use. Swarovski is also well-known for its Swarovski Optik subsidiary's line of high-performance telescopes, gun sights, and binoculars for hunting and bird-watching enthusiasts. Another company subsidiary, Swareflex, manufactures roadside reflectors and related highway safety products. The company's Tyrolit subsidiary produces a catalog of more than 80,000 grinding, cutting, and drilling tools and systems. Enlightened–Swarovski Elements, known as Signity until 2008, is the company's brand of genuine and manmade gemstones. Finally, Amazar Holding AG is the subsidiary dedicated to exploring and developing opportunities and concepts that extend beyond the company's core business models. With worldwide operations including factories in Argentina, Brazil, Italy, Mexico, the United States, and elsewhere, Swarovski employed nearly 26,000 people in 2009. More than 100 years after its founding it remained owned and led by the Swarovski family.

FOUNDED BY CRYSTAL CUTTER IN 1895

Swarovski and Co. was founded by Daniel Swarovski, a glass cutter who moved from the Bohemia region of the former Austro-Hungarian empire to Wattens, Austria. Originally trained to cut crystal by hand, Swarovski invented and patented an automatic grinding machine to industrialize the process, and the mountain rivers near Wattens provided an inexpensive source of energy to run the machine. Swarovski's invention, and a process that remained a jealously guarded family secret, was to revolutionize the crystal industry and provide the basis

COMPANY PERSPECTIVES

Over the course of its history, Swarovski has produced innovations and inspired creative trends in fields as varied as jewelry, fashion, accessories, lighting and interior design, culture and industrial research and development. The company draws its richness of expression from the cultural heritage of Central Europe and its talent for forging links between the arts, science and economics. Today, the name of Swarovski stands for exacting workmanship, quality and creativity all over the world.

for the family company's long-lasting success. Swarovski established his firm, Daniel Swarovski & Co., in 1895.

Swarovski's invention produced crystal gemstones of outstanding quality, and the patented process enabled the company to become the world's leading producer of crystal gemstones. The company's earliest products were especially valued by the jewelry and fashion industries. By the end of World War I, the company began to target the industrial community as well. In 1917 Swarovski began developing grinding and polishing equipment for its own production uses. By 1919, however, the company saw the opportunity to market these tools as a new product line. In that year, Swarovski launched its first subsidiary and brand name, Tyrolit, taking its name from the Tyrolean region of Austria in which the company was located. Originally designed for cutting and polishing crystal gemstones, the Tyrolit line of products later expanded to include a wide variety of applications.

The 1930s saw several significant developments in Swarovski's history. The first of these was a line of crystal "trimmings," which debuted in 1931. The Swarovski trimmings featured the company's crystal gemstones prepared in a variety of ready-to-use formats for edging, hems, and borders. Also known as rhinestones, Swarovski's gemstones were of such high quality that they were often mistaken for real diamonds.

Also in the 1930s Wilhelm Swarovski, the son of Daniel Swarovski, began work on a prototype for a pair of field binoculars. The younger Swarovski, who had inherited his father's inventiveness, had joined the family company at the age of 17 and had long been conducting experiments in glass smelting techniques. Wilhelm Swarovski finished his prototype field glasses in 1935, developing new techniques for the field glasses'

hand-ground and polished optical components. The company began production of optical lenses in 1939 on the eve of World War II. The company's field glasses were to remain in the prototype stage, however, until after the war ended.

Swarovski moved into a third area of operations toward the end of the decade when it launched a line of reflective glass that quickly found a number of applications, such as road and rail reflectors, reflector strips for guardrails, and other safety uses. Launched in 1937, these products resulted in the creation of the Swareflex brand in 1950.

EXPANDED PRODUCT LINES AFTER WORLD WAR II

Emerging from World War II, the company built on Wilhelm Swarovski's optical experiments to begin the production of eyeglass lenses in 1945. This was to become an important part of the company's operations and remained a key component of its catalog until the early 1980s. Swarovski not only ground lenses, it also launched an initiative to train opticians for the Austrian market, founding the Industrial and Vocational School for Optics, Glass, Iron, and Metal, which later became the Trade School for Opticians, producing a large share of the country's opticians.

The company's optical glass activities grew quickly. By 1948, production of optical glass had outgrown the company's Wattens glass-cutting headquarters. The company opened a new facility in nearby Absam, forming the operation as the subsidiary Swarovski Optik KG in 1949. While eyeglass lenses represented the largest share of the new subsidiary's production (up to 300,000 lenses ground per month), Swarovski Optik launched production of its first pair of binoculars, the 7 x 24, which was quickly embraced by Europe's hunting enthusiasts.

During the 1950s Swarovski's reflective glass operations had also begun to grow as the postwar European economic boom and the rapidly growing numbers of automobiles on the continent's highways helped to stimulate demand for the Swareflex line. Meanwhile, Swarovski's Tyrolit operations were also outpacing its Wattens production capacity, and those operations were moved to a new production plant, in Schwaz, Austria, in 1950.

A new generation of Swarovskis had taken a place in the company's leadership, as Daniel Swarovski's grandson Manfred took over the company's direction in the 1950s. Manfred Swarovski set the company in a new direction and won acclaim when, working with designer Christian Dior, the company created its famed

KEY DATES

1895: Daniel Swarovski establishes crystal cutting company.
1919: Company launches Tyrolit tool subsidiary.
1939: Daniel Swarovski & Co. begins production of optical lenses.
1949: Swarovski Optik is formed.
1956: Company creates Aurora Borealis crystal in collaboration with Christian Dior.
1976: Swarovski & Co. launches line of crystal animals.
1977: Company launches Swarovski jewelry line.
1999: Company forms Signity joint venture.
2002: Company introduces Crystal Palace collection.
2008: Company debuts Enlightened–Swarovski Elements brand of gemstones and synthetic stones.

multicolored Aurora Borealis crystal stones in 1956. The collaboration with Dior marked the beginning of an era of close cooperation between the crystal company and the world's fashion industry.

The company's other divisions were also producing their share of technical innovations in the 1950s. Through the decade, Swarovski Optik rolled out a number of binocular designs, including the wide-angle Habicht binoculars. The company also began developing a range of opera glasses, which debuted in 1957. Two years later, Swarovski Optik debuted its first rifle scope, a line that was to become one of its most important. Meanwhile, Tyrolit was enjoying increasing international success, leading the subsidiary to open its first foreign sales office, in Milan, Italy, in 1953. The company's international reputation was equally helped by a new range of fiberglass-reinforced grinding wheels, launched in 1952.

COLLECTIBLE ANIMAL FIGURINES INTRODUCED: 1976

Tyrolit was also leading Swarovski's international development. In 1960 the company opened its first manufacturing plant outside of Austria, founding the grinding tool production facility Abrasivos Austromex in Mexico City, Mexico. The company opened a new foreign plant in Buenos Aires, Argentina, in 1968. This expansion coincided with the launch of a line of res-inoid bonded diamond grinding tools the year earlier.

Swarovski's crystal operations were also growing. In 1965 the company began producing crystal chandelier components, dressing up such famed chandeliers as those in the Metropolitan Opera House in New York City and France's Palace of Versailles. Two years later, Swarovski began producing a new range of natural and artificial gemstones, including cubic zirconia. The company developed the first mechanical process for cutting cubic zirconia by the end of the decade.

The 1970s marked the beginning of an important era for Swarovski. Until then, the company had never ventured into the consumer retail market. The worldwide recession of the decade, the result of the Arab Oil Embargo of 1973, had caused a dramatic drop in demand for the company's crystal gemstones. Manfred Swarovski was searching for a way to prop up the company's sales. As his granddaughter, and future company vice president Nadja Swarovski told the *Financial Times:* "My grandfather was fiddling around in his office with a few little crystals when it occurred to him that the pieces, arranged in a certain fashion, resembled a tiny mouse. That was his light bulb moment."

That moment led the company to launch the first in what was to become one of the world's most sought-after collector's series, a tiny crystal mouse, in 1976. The mouse and the many other animals in the series, the production of which was placed under a new Tabletop Division, brought the Swarovski name into the consumer world for the first time. The company's consumer products, which at first represented a means to guarantee cash flow during industry down-cycles, nonetheless quickly became an integral part of the company's operations. In 1977 Swarovski followed up the worldwide success of its crystal animals by launching its own line of jewelry. This move led to the creation of a new subsidiary and brand, the Daniel Swarovski line of jewelry and accessories in 1989. By then, the growing international demand for the company's crystal animals also led the company to establish the Swarovski Collectors Society, which quickly boasted a membership of more than 300,000. The company also changed its logo, formerly featuring the Tyrolean edelweiss, to a more elegant swan symbol.

OPTICS, FASHION PRODUCTS INTRODUCED: 1990–99

Swarovski continued to build its several businesses through the 1990s. Tyrolit, which had introduced such new products as laser-welded diamond tools targeted to the stone industry, also continued its international development. After opening a production plant in San Luis, Argentina, the company moved into North

America, buying a share of Diamond Products, in the United States. In 1997 Tyrolit cemented its North American position with the acquisition of Bay State/Sterling Company, based in Massachusetts, then the second largest manufacturer of bonded grinding tools in the U.S. market. Tyrolit also strengthened its European position through the decade, opening a plant in Stans, Austria, for high-precision grinding tools in 1992; acquiring the Italian diamond tools producer Vincent in 1993; and capping the decade with the acquisition of US Veglio S.p.A, a metal bonded diamond tools manufacturer based in Italy.

Swarovski Optik meanwhile had built an international reputation for its high-quality binoculars, telescopes, and gun sights. After discontinuing production of eyeglass lenses in 1983, the company began expanding its range, adding hand-held night-vision binoculars and pocket binoculars during the decade. In 1991 the subsidiary moved into the U.S. market, founding Swarovski Optik North America. Swarovski continued to introduce new products, such as laser range finders, leading to the company's patented LRS product and a rifle scope with integrated range finder, a market first. In the late 1990s the company began designing and producing specialty binoculars for bird-watching enthusiasts.

By then, Swarovski itself was enjoying renewed enthusiasm from the fashion industry. Helping to inspire this trend, which saw Swarovski's crystals glitter from creations by the world's top fashion designers, was Nadja Swarovski, who joined the company's New York branch in 1995. Swarovski actively sought partnerships with such noted designers as Anand Jon, Alexander McQueen, Philip Treacy, and others, helping to raise Swarovski's name from the kitsch of its crystal animals to the ranks of global haute couture. In 1999 the company introduced Signity, a joint-venture with Geneva, Switzerland-based Golay Buchel, to produce precision-cut genuine gemstones and synthetic and imitation stones.

With a new century fast approaching, the company also cast an eye to creating a lasting bridge between the old and new millennia. Kristallwelten (Crystal Worlds), designed by the multimedia artist André Heller to celebrate Swarovski's first 100 years, was built in Wattens in 1995 to provide visitors with a multisensory museum experience showcasing the full range of Swarovski products. Attracting millions of visitors per year, the site became a major Austrian tourist attraction and was expanded in 2003 and 2007. Kristallwelten had attracted more than nine million visitors from around the world by 2010.

EMPHASIS ON ART AND DESIGN: 2000–10

Swarovski's association with haute couture advanced rapidly in the first decade of the 21st century as the company sponsored young designers like Jason Wu, Kate and Laura Mulleavy (Rodarte), and Alexander Wang. The launch in 2007 of Atelier Swarovski, the company's own line of luxury fashion accessories, promoted collaborations between Swarovski and top designers, including Christopher Kane, Jack McCollough and Lazaro Hernandez (Proenza Schouler), and the architect Zaha Hadid. Incorporating Swarovski's precision-cut crystal brands, Crystallized–Swarovski Elements and Enlightened–Swarovski Elements, creations ranging from pendants to fabrics pushed the limits of crystal-based design. The company further extended its international fashion brand by sponsoring design competitions, including a watch design contest in 2008 and a jewelry design competition in 2009.

Building on its 2003 Runway Rocks gem collection, which was designed for display on the runway, in 2005 the company hosted Fashion Rocks, a charity event blending rock music and high fashion, to benefit Monaco's Prince's Trust. During this period, Swarovski continued to develop its line of cut crystals, including the star-shaped Xilion crystal (2004). In 2006 it assumed full ownership of Signity, which would become a subsidiary. Renamed Enlightened–Swarovski Elements in 2008, the brand defined the market for premium quality precision-cut gemstones and synthetic stones, including cubic zirconium, synthetic corundum, synthetic spinel, and Alpinite. In 2009, in New York, Swarovski opened the first Swarovski Crystallized jewelry store, providing customers with the opportunity to customize their jewelry designs. Looking ahead, the company expanded its exploration of new, alternative market applications for its products. Crystal-based designs for eyeglass frames, tableware, portable electronic devices, and writing implements gained both popularity and market share.

Beyond wearable fashion, the company also made an imprint in the area of décor. With the 2002 launch of the Crystal Palace collection, the brainchild of Nadja Swarovski, the company's artistic vision expanded to include sculptural lighting design, with a focus on chandeliers. Each year, the company commissioned a lighting collection designed by a prominent designer. Past collections had included works by Tord Boontje and Yves Béhar. In 2007 Swarovski purchased Schonbek, a European chandelier design and manufacturing firm, further expanding into the world of residential and industrial lighting. To promote and showcase innovative uses of crystal and light, Crystal Palace sponsored yearly design installations created in collaboration with such designers as Greg Lynn and Arik Levy. By 2010 the scope of the Crystal Palace collection had expanded to include furniture and architectural designs, and the company had its own line of architectural and lighting design products and services.

The success of Swarovski's varied product lines resulted in financial growth throughout the first decade of the new millennium, and sales increased from EUR 1.63 billion in 2001 to EUR 2.53 billion in 2008. Led by members of the fourth and fifth generations of the Swarovski family, the company's quest for new avenues for its glittering designs continued to enhance the firm's international brand recognition, reputation for quality, and financial strength.

M. L. Cohen
Updated, H. Schonthal

PRINCIPAL SUBSIDIARIES

Amazar Holding AG (Switzerland); Atelier Swarovski; Daniel Swarovski; Daniel Swarovski Paris; Schonbek Worldwide Lighting Inc.; Strass Swarovski Crystal; Swareflex; Swarovski AG; Swarovski Crystallized; Swarovski Crystal Palace; Swarovski Enlightened; Swarovski Kristallwelten; Swarovski Optik; Swarovski SCS; Tyrolit Schleifmittelwerke Swarovski KG (Austria).

PRINCIPAL COMPETITORS

ARC International; Avimo Group Limited; Konica Corporation; Leica Camera AG; Nikon Corporation; Société du Louvre; Steuben Glass LLC; Tiffany & Co.; Carl-Zeiss-Stiftung; Waterford Wedgwood PLC.

FURTHER READING

Adams, Susan, "Hawk Eyes," *Forbes*, November 13, 2000, p. 402.

Becker, Vivienne, *Daniel Swarovski: A World of Beauty*, New York: Thames & Hudson, Inc., 2005.

Carpenter, Lea, "A Many Spangled Thing," *Financial Times*, February 10, 2001.

Rickey, Melanie, "The Glitter Band," *Independent*, December 19, 1998, p. 27.

Slowey, Anne, "Fashion Spotlight: Swarovski," *Elle*, December 23, 2009.

White, Lesley, "Nadja Swarovski: Chip off the Old Rock," *Sunday Times*, April 29, 2009.

DeBruce Grain, Inc.

4100 North Mulberry Drive
Kansas City, Missouri 64116-1787
U.S.A.
Telephone: (816) 421-8182
Toll Free: (800) 821-5210
Fax: (816) 584-2350
Web site: http://www.debruce.com

Private Company
Incorporated: 1978
Employees: 550
Sales: $5.76 billion (2008)
NAICS: 311119 Other Animal Food Manufacturing; 311222 Soybean Processing; 424510 Grain and Field Bean Merchant Wholesalers; 424910 Farm Supplies Merchant Wholesalers; 444220 Nursery, Garden Center, and Farm Supply Stores

■ ■ ■

DeBruce Grain, Inc., is a leading midwestern and North American agribusiness firm that stores, processes, manages, and sells grain and fertilizer. With grain businesses in eight states and Mexico, the company owns and operates grain elevators, grain-handling facilities, fertilizer distribution terminals, wholesale and retail fertilizer businesses, grain-flaking facilities, and a soybean-processing plant. Additionally, DeBruce operates a grain transportation business, runs a freight brokerage, and trades grain and other feed ingredients. As of 2009, the company was the seventh-largest grain-storage firm in North America, with a capacity of 115 million bushels,

and was ranked by *Forbes* as the 56th-largest private company in the United States based on annual revenues.

ORIGINS AND EARLY YEARS

Paul DeBruce grew up in an area filled with farms and grain elevators in southwestern Kansas. As an adult, believing there was a market for a regional grain trading company, he founded DeBruce Grain, Inc., in 1978. Based in northwestern Missouri, in Kansas City, De-Bruce started his company with limited finances and with limited personnel. During the company's first two years of existence, Paul DeBruce served as company president and treasurer and his wife, Wanda, as vice president and secretary. The two were the only members of the company's board of directors. According to the company's articles of incorporation, DeBruce Grain was formed to "buy, sell, store, and otherwise handle and deal in grain, feeds, soybeans and all manufactured products" related to these commodities. In 1979 Paul DeBruce established the company's first subsidiary, the Kansas City-based DeBruce Fertilizer, Inc., as a merchandiser and wholesale operator of fertilizer distribution terminals.

In 1981 DeBruce Grain purchased its first grain-storage operation, in Abilene, Kansas. Located in the central area of the state, the facility served a range of clients, including poultry users, flour mills, and processors, and transported commodities and products to the Gulf of Mexico, the Pacific Northwest, and Mexico for export. The operation became part of DeBruce's cross-country merchandising business through which non-grain products such as salt and rock were trucked out of

COMPANY PERSPECTIVES

DeBruce has been proud to serve agricultural communities throughout the Midwest for more than two decades. The DeBruce philosophy encourages a spirit of cooperation, trust, courtesy and integrity towards our customers and a stimulating, entrepreneurial environment for our people. An innovative spirit along with a sound fundamental business practice has earned DeBruce recognition as being a viable competitor as well as a good business partner.

the area, and a return haul of grain was delivered to Abilene. DeBruce also formed its first version of the subsidiary DeBruce Feed Ingredients, Inc., in 1981. DeBruce acquired its second grain operation in 1984 in Nebraska City, Nebraska, along the Missouri River. The facility shipped to feedlots and to poultry markets in the southern states and also exported grain to Mexico.

DeBruce expanded its trading company operations and established DeBruce Futures, Inc., to serve as a broker for commodities futures and options in 1986. That same year, the company formed a related subsidiary, DeBruce Finance, Inc., to invest in stock and other financial ventures. The company also dissolved its DeBruce Feed Ingredients subsidiary.

During the late 1980s the company expanded its Nebraska activities with the acquisition of two grain elevator operations, located in Fremont and Lexington. The Fremont operation handled grain and beans coming from the Dakotas, Minnesota, Iowa, and Nebraska; was situated on both the Union Pacific and Burlington Northern Santa Fe railroads; and became part of the company's cross-country program. The Lexington facility was located on the Union Pacific mainline railroad and served Pacific Northwest locations, West Coast feed mills, and domestic flour millers. It also handled shipments to the Gulf and exports to Mexico.

NEW BUSINESS LINES AND NEW SUBSIDIARIES

DeBruce expanded its business lines during the 1990s through the establishment of new subsidiaries. In 1990 the subsidiary DeBruce Ag Service Inc. was formed as a retail arm of DeBruce Fertilizer. Established as a farm supply business, DeBruce Ag Service offered fertilizers and crop-protection products and sold directly to farmers. Over time, the subsidiary established six retail

facilities, three in Iowa and three in Texas: Benton, Creston, and Shenandoah, Iowa, and Farwell, Hale Center, and Lockney, Texas. The subsidiary DeBruce Transportation, Inc., was established in 1995 to offer merchandising and bulk transportation services.

During the second half of the 1990s, DeBruce further developed its footprint in Nebraska and Kansas and established a presence in the Texas Panhandle. In 1996 DeBruce acquired the Garvey Grain terminal in Haysville, Kansas, from the Chicago-based company Garvey Grain. Half a mile long with a storage capacity of 24 million bushels, the elevator was the world's largest under one head house, according to the *Guinness Book of World Records*. Originally built in the 1950s, the Haysville facility was served by three area railroads and provided both elevator- and farmer-owned grain throughout Kansas and parts of Colorado and Oklahoma and shipped grain to Mexican end users. In 1996 and 1997 DeBruce also acquired two grain elevators in Amarillo, Texas, with a combined storage capacity of 5.9 million bushels. Both were served by the Burlington Northern Santa Fe and the Union Pacific railroads. The Amarillo properties gave DeBruce the ability to originate corn for area feedlots and milo and wheat for export and delivery to the West Coast. In 1998 DeBruce acquired its fourth Nebraska grain operation, a facility located in Thumel with a storage capacity of 5.6 million bushels. Activities at this site included shipments via train to the Pacific Northwest, the Gulf, and Mexico.

Soon after the inception of DeBruce Grain, it began exporting grain to Mexico. Following the implementation of the North American Free Trade Agreement in 1994, DeBruce's exports to Mexico substantially increased. To better take advantage of improving merchandising and trading opportunities, the company in January 1998 formed a Mexico-based grain and feed firm called DeBruce Grain de Mexico S.A. de C.V., which was based in a Querétaro trading office near Mexico City. With a 1.6-million-bushel storage facility in Guadalajara to serve Mexican clients, DeBruce Grain de Mexico sold grain and feed products from the United States as well as grain grown in Mexico.

EXPLOSION AT KANSAS ELEVATOR

On June 8, 1998, a massive explosion at the DeBruce grain elevator facilities in Haysville, Kansas, killed seven workers. The blast was heard for miles around, shot metal into the air, and ripped the elevator's underbelly completely into two pieces. Two weeks after the explosion, with six workers confirmed dead and one man still

```
┌─────────────────────────────────────────────┐
│                                               │
│              KEY DATES                        │
│                   ■                           │
│  ┌─────────────────────────────────────────┐ │
│                                               │
│  1978:  Company is founded by Paul DeBruce.   │
│  1981:  Company buys its first grain-storage  │
│         operation.                            │
│  1990:  DeBruce Ag Service Inc. is formed.    │
│  1998:  DeBruce Grain de Mexico S.A. de C.V. is│
│         established; an explosion at the company's│
│         Haysville, Kansas, grain elevator kills seven│
│         employees.                            │
│  2000:  DeBruce Feed Ingredients, Inc., is formed.│
│  2002:  Company opens a grain-shipping facility in│
│         Daviess County, Kentucky, its first facility│
│         east of the Mississippi River.        │
│  2005:  DeBruce surpasses 100-million-bushel storage│
│         capacity with acquisitions in Iowa and Texas.│
│  2008:  DeBruce constructs an 800,000-bushel grain-│
│         storage facility in Rosedale, Mississippi.│
│                                               │
└─────────────────────────────────────────────┘
```

reported missing, DeBruce announced plans to reopen part of the grain elevator. Nearly three weeks after the incident, the missing worker was found dead in the conveyor-belt tunnel, beneath the elevator, where the explosion was initially set off.

DeBruce was notified it could face both criminal charges related to the explosion and resulting deaths and civil charges from the Occupational Safety and Health Administration (OSHA) that carried hefty fines. A war of words in the media between OSHA and DeBruce Grain ensued, set off by a series of OSHA press releases, one of which quoted Secretary of Labor Alexis Herman saying that it was "unforgivable that DeBruce officials would so callously disregard federal safety standards and risk the lives of their workers." The company responded by claiming that OSHA was "scapegoating and getting publicity out of it," and the company's president, Paul DeBruce, told the *Wichita Eagle* that "Sometimes an accident is just that, an accident," even though federal investigators by that point had claimed a faulty conveyor-belt bearing was the cause of the explosion.

By February 1999, with a criminal investigation still being conducted, OSHA formally charged DeBruce Grain with 36 counts of seriously and willfully violating federal safety regulations. These charges carried a total of $1.7 million in possible fines. Among its charges, OSHA alleged that the company failed to fix dust collection systems, failed to add belt-alignment and motion-detector systems, and failed to hold employee safety meetings. Most serious, OSHA claimed that De-

Bruce should have been aware of and addressed the conditions that caused the fatal explosion. The company denied all of OSHA's charges. By November 1999, however, DeBruce was negotiating with OSHA over a fine settlement.

LAUNCH OF NEW SUBSIDIARY

By the end of the decade, DeBruce ranked 299th on the *Forbes* list of the 500 largest private companies in the United States, based on the previous year's annual revenues of $772 million (in 1999 the company logged $890 million in sales). In two decades, the company had grown from a one-man operation to a leading regional grain operation with 250 employees. The company entered the new century with a continued focus on expanding its territory west of the Mississippi through acquisitions and the establishment of complementary business activities. In 2000, a year in which revenues for the first time surpassed $1 billion, DeBruce launched a new business, DeBruce Feed Ingredients, Inc. Based in Kansas City, Missouri, the subsidiary was designed as a merchandiser of feed ingredients and grain-processing by-products with warehouses to handle a variety of commodities, including canola meal, cottonseed meal and hulls, whole cottonseed, distillers' grain, gluten feed pellets, and soybean meal.

After the 1998 fatal explosion, DeBruce did rebuild the largest grain elevator in the world, which came to be known in company literature as the Wichita—not Haysville—Elevator. In February 2001, with criminal charges against DeBruce related to the explosion already dismissed, the company and OSHA reached a settlement whereby OSHA agreed to reduce the number of charges to 14, with none of the remaining charges to include the word *willful*. In return, DeBruce agreed to a fine settlement of $685,000.

EXPANSION INTO IOWA, KENTUCKY, AND OKLAHOMA

DeBruce expanded into Iowa in March 2002 with the acquisition of several properties at a liquidation auction, including fertilizer and grain operations and a bean-processing plant from the bankrupt Crestland Cooperative. DeBruce paid $6.5 million for assets that included the company's first fertilizer business in Iowa and several facilities in Creston, Iowa, including the Crestland headquarters, a 7.5-million-bushel grain-storage facility and feed mill, and a four-year-old bean-processing plant. The Creston facility was built to extract soybean oil for the food-processing industry and to process soybeans into high-protein animal and human food products. The plant was located on the Burlington Northern railway and had the capacity to produce 600 tons of soybean meal or white flakes daily. Separately, DeBruce acquired a feed mill and grain elevator in Shenandoah, Iowa; a chemical building and dry fertilizer facility in Corning, Iowa; and other properties in towns in southern Iowa.

In September 2002 DeBruce opened its first facility east of the Mississippi River, a new grain-shipping facility in Daviess County, Kentucky. The shipping operation included two pits for receiving and a barge loader with the capacity to handle 50,000 bushels per hour. The company also planned to build grain-storage facilities in Daviess County. DeBruce's entry into the county provided the area with competition where once there had been none, with Owensboro Grain previously having a virtual monopoly. DeBruce planned to ship 8 million to 10 million bushels from Daviess County in 2002 but a drought made securing contracts difficult in the company's first year in the county.

In 2002 DeBruce also established its first joint venture, with Saginaw Flakes, in Dimmitt, Texas. The venture represented the company's initial foray into the grain-flaking business. In addition, it further expanded DeBruce's growing operations in the Texas Panhandle.

DeBruce expanded into Oklahoma in 2004 with the construction of a grain and fertilizer facility at the Tulsa Port of Catoosa, located near Tulsa at the head of the McClellan-Kerr Arkansas River Navigation System, a 445-mile riverway connecting Oklahoma to ports in five adjacent states as well as other ports via New Orleans and the Gulf Intracoastal Waterway. The $6 million facility was constructed on the Arkansas River where it was expected to produce a 20 percent increase in barge traffic. The facility also was connected to two area railways. It was equipped with three pits, two for trucks and one for rail unloading. DeBruce leased 10.5 acres near the head of the Arkansas River for the facility, designed to transport fertilizer and gather grain from the Midwest. In addition, the Tulsa Port facility was built with storage capacity for 500,000 bushels of grain and 30,000 tons of fertilizer. By the end of 2004, DeBruce was one of the 10 largest North American grain companies with a grain-storage capacity of 89 million bushels. It controlled 30 terminals for handling grain, grain by-products, and fertilizer in six states and Mexico.

ACQUISITIONS IN IOWA AND TEXAS

Via acquisitions completed in August 2005, DeBruce added 15.5 million bushels of storage space in Iowa and Texas. The purchases included a Joice, Iowa, facility that the company quickly began expanding, adding 260

percent more storage capacity and a truck unloading pit and enhancing the facility's ability to dry grain. DeBruce also acquired a Lake Mills, Iowa, operation with a per-day processing capacity of 800 tons. The Lake Mills facility was considered a potential boon for the Creston bean-processing plant, as it had the capability to originate particular specialty soybeans. In addition, four separate facilities were acquired in Dimmitt, Texas, that were expected to complement the company's nearby flaking operations. The acquisitions together brought the company's total storage capacity to more than 100 million bushels.

After improving its grain-flaking business, by doubling the size of operations in Dimmitt in 2004 and then acquiring additional nearby storage space in 2005, DeBruce formed a second 50-50 joint venture with Saginaw Flakes in 2006 in order to create a grain-flaking facility able to annually generate 350,000 tons of flaked grain using DeBruce's existing Etter, Texas, facility. The targeted clientele for the flaked grain was the burgeoning Etter dairy industry.

DeBruce upgraded and expanded existing facilities in 2006 and 2007 not only by adding storage space but also by improving grain-handling speed. At the Port of Catoosa, storage space was enhanced by 1.5 million bushels, allowing product to more easily come into Catoosa via truck or train and then go out by barge. The additional space brought company-wide capacity to more than 101 million bushels. During the same two years, significant improvements and additions were made at Etter, Texas, resulting in two separate facilities with a combined storage capacity of 3.1 billion bushels. Following this upgrade, the Etter operation was able to handle both 100-car feed-ingredient trains and 110-car grain trains. High-speed grain-handling equipment was added, and the total handling capacity of feed ingredients was increased, a move expected to complement the facility's existing flaking operations.

The Etter expansion project allowed the company to purchase and sell more bulk products to dairy and cattle farms and feed yards as well as acquire more trainloads of distillers' grains to service new ethanol plants. In 2006 the company also improved its four-year-old Owensboro, Kentucky, facility, which was increasingly doing more business with nontraditional farmers. Total storage capacity was raised to 935,000 bushels, providing the facility with the flexibility to handle five types of grains at one time. In addition, the facility's barge-loading speed was increased and a dryer was added to provide the capability of dealing with moisture-laden grain.

RISING REVENUES AND FURTHER EXPANSION

During the second half of the decade, the company's revenues and status as a leading handler of grain grew substantially. Escalating grain prices in 2007 prompted farmers to hold onto their products and not to sell that year, a fact that was a boon to DeBruce's grain-storage business. Between 2005 and 2007, DeBruce's revenues nearly doubled, to $4.62 billion. Meanwhile, the company in 2007 moved up to number 76 on the *Forbes* list of the largest U.S. private companies.

In 2008 DeBruce began construction on an 800,000-bushel grain-storage facility in Rosedale, Mississippi. The new facility included a high-speed truck-unload area and was designed to move product to both barge and storage simultaneously at 70,000 bushels an hour. DeBruce planned to later add more storage space with the possibility of including an ingredient barn.

DeBruce moved into the state of Wisconsin in 2009 by leasing a barge loading and transfer facility on the Mississippi River in Prairie du Chien. The facility, with a 55,000-bushel storage tank, was able to transfer grain directly from truck or rail to barge. DeBruce planned to use the Wisconsin operation to store and transfer corn, wheat, and soybeans.

In December 2009 DeBruce acquired property in Phelps City, Missouri, in order to build a 2.4-million-bushel greenfield grain-handling operation in an area served by the Burlington Northern railroad. The shuttle facility, which featured a loop-track design, was configured to accommodate up to a 130-car train, with the capacity to unload cars at 80,000 bushels per hour. The Phelps City operation was expected to include four receiving pits for unloading trucks at a rate of 75,000 bushels per hour. Geared for Growth with Product and Geographic Diversification

As it entered the second decade of the 21st century, DeBruce's business strategy was focused on a number of different fronts it had developed in the previous five years. It had a growing presence in west Texas and the Texas Panhandle. It had increased its ability to ship long-distance by barge, having recently added or expanded barge-loading facilities in Owensboro, Kentucky; Catoosa, Oklahoma; Rosedale, Mississippi; and Prairie du Chien, Wisconsin. It also had added grain flaking to its business lines, and it had updated some of its more active facilities to increase loading and unloading speed and to add storage capacity.

For the company, growth by acquisition was its strategy for producing consistently rising revenues, which topped $5.75 billion in fiscal 2008. As Paul De-

Bruce, company founder and president, told Chris Grenz of the *Kansas City Business Journal* in 2006, "We are always looking for additional acquisitions." The company seemed to have a knack for making strategic acquisitions and also was not afraid to invest in facility expansions and improvements and product diversification. DeBruce Grain apparently had sustained itself on its diversification and geographical spread even when farmers had less than excellent years. Paul De-Bruce viewed the bottom line on the company's future in more basic terms. "The good news is that people keep eating. Cows, hogs and chickens all keep eating," he told Grenz. "So there's always demand for grains. There'll be a continuing opportunity for what we do."

Roger Rouland

PRINCIPAL SUBSIDIARIES

DeBruce Fertilizer, Inc.; DeBruce Ag Service Inc.; Creston Bean Processing, LLC; DeBruce Feed Ingredients, Inc.; DeBruce Transportation, Inc.; DeBruce Grain de Mexico S.A. de C.V.

PRINCIPAL OPERATING UNITS

Grain; Fertilizer; Bean Crushing; Feed Ingredients; Transportation; Specialty Contracts; Risk Services.

PRINCIPAL COMPETITORS

Archer-Daniels-Midland Company; Bunge Limited; Cargill, Incorporated.

FURTHER READING

Cookson, Brian, "DeBruce Will Expand in Iowa with Purchases from Cooperative," *Kansas City Business Journal*, March 8, 2002.

"DeBruce, OSHA Reach Settlement with No Admission of Wrongdoing," *Milling and Baking News*, February 13, 2001, p. 9.

"DeBruce Says Explosion Caused by Industrial Maintenance Lapses," *Milling and Baking News*, January 18, 2000, p. 9.

"DeBruce to Operate Barge Facility," *Feedstuffs*, April 6, 2009, p. 23.

Droege, Tom, "Grain Firm to Build Port Facility in Tulsa, Okla.," *Tulsa World*, June 18, 2004.

Grenz, Chris, "DeBruce Known in Its Field but Unsung in Its Hometown," *Kansas City Business Journal*, June 23, 2006.

House, Charles, "DeBruce Grain, OSHA at Odds over Allegations, Investigation," *Feedstuffs*, April 19, 1999, p. 37.

——, "Elevator Explosion among the Worst in 20 Years," *Feedstuffs* June 15, 1998, pp. 1+.

Howie, Michael, "DeBruce Expands in Etter," *Feedstuffs*, June 5, 2006, p. 32.

——, "DeBruce Grain Buys Iowa, Texas Operations," *Feedstuffs*, August 29, 2005, p. 20.

"Owner of DeBruce Grain Elevator Claims Safety Meetings Were Held," *Topeka (KS) Capital-Journal*, June 4, 1999.

Sosland, L. Joshua, "DeBruce Fighting for Reputation in Face of Proposed Citations," *Milling and Baking News*, January 19, 1999, pp. 1+.

Delta Dental of California

---■---

100 First Street
San Francisco, California 94105
U.S.A.
Telephone: (415) 972-8300
Fax: (415) 972-8466
Web site: http://www.deltadentalins.com

Nonprofit Company
Founded: 1955 as California Dental Association Service
Employees: 2,471
Sales: $5.9 billion (2008)
NAICS: 524114 Direct Health and Medical Insurance
    Carriers

■ ■ ■

Delta Dental of California, a private, nonprofit company, is California's largest dental health plan and covers 17.5 million people in its commercial and government programs throughout the state. It is part of a national holding company that covers 24 million people in 15 states, the District of Columbia, and Puerto Rico. By 2009 it had total revenues of $5.9 billion (with general reserves of $348 million) and was processing nearly 27 million claims per year, with 18,111 dentist locations statewide and access to 103,000 locations nationwide. Delta Dental of California is headquartered in San Francisco and has offices in San Diego, Sacramento, Fresno, and Cerritos.

BEGINNINGS

In 1954 the International Longshoreman's and Warehousemen's Union and the Pacific Maritime As-

sociation (ILWU-PMA) decided to create a dental care program for their members' children. With a $750,000 fund, the ILWU-PMA approached the dental associations in California, Oregon, and Washington, all of which welcomed the request to create new programs that would promote prevention of tooth problems and retention of natural teeth. The Washington Dental Service was created in that year, and the Oregon Dental Service followed in February 1955. The California Dental Association, which then represented only northern California dentists, formed the California Dental Association Service (CDAS) in May. Later in the decade, the Western Conference of Dental Service Plans was established, and in 1960 the Southern California Dental Association lent its support to the CDAS, which changed its name to California Dental Services (CDS) in 1963.

In response to a recommendation from the American Dental Association for a national coordinating agency, CDS and other service plans helped create the National Association of Dental Service Plans in 1965, which was renamed Delta Dental Plans Association (DDPA) in 1969. In 1957 CDAS had covered only 1,800 children in one dental benefits program, paying out $60,000 in about a thousand claims. When it changed its name to CDS in 1963, however, there were more than a quarter million enrollees, 6,370 participating dentists, and 83,000 claims processed. The growth in its first ten years, more than half a million enrollees from 79 clients by 1965, was accomplished by two sales staff and through word of mouth. CDAS's plans featured patient's freedom to choose a dentist, reimbursement to dentists on a fee-for-service basis, and an emphasis on high standards quality, all very important features for clients and participating dentists.

This early growth is attributable to Dr. F. Gene Dixon, who as managing director of CDAS implemented many of the company's early innovations, policies, and procedures that continue to serve as industry standards. These included guaranteed copayments and review of claims by trained dental auditors and dental consultants to make sure that treatment met contract specifications. The Delta Difference, a trademarked set of promises pleased purchasers, and by 1974 CDS's payments to dentists climbed to $150 million per year. Aerospace industry giants, such as Lockheed Martin, McDonnell Douglas, Northrop, and Rockwell International, brought in nearly 200,000 enrollees. Kaiser Industries had started in 1971 with 20,000 new enrollees, later having 47,000 enrollees from 11 companies in the United States and seven foreign countries.

WORKING WITH THE STATE OF CALIFORNIA

In 1974, during the administration of then-Governor Ronald Reagan, California entered into a risk-sharing agreement with CDS to oversee the dental portion of the state's Medicaid program. Denti-Cal, as the program was called, began with 2.2 million beneficiaries receiving treatment at 8,000 dental offices. By 1978 the number of eligible enrollees was 2.85 million, with 12,500 dental offices participating and receiving $109 million. Outside California, CDS in 1969 helped establish

Dental Service Plans Insurance Company (DSPIC), a for profit insurer to underwrite and administer dental plans in states without a Delta Dental service company. DSPIC was headquartered in Chicago.

Dr. Dixon retired in 1977, and Dr. Erik D. Olsen became the chief executive officer, leading the phenomenal growth of CDS for fifteen years, including going after dental benefits contracts with government agencies and other public organizations. CDS also established a new company in 1977, Datamedic of California, to market minicomputers to dental offices for claims processing. By 1980 there were 200 Datamedic minicomputers in California dental offices, handling billing and treatment forms for all dental carriers. New government regulations and growing competition in the minicomputer field, however, led CDS to sell its ownership interest to Datamedic Corporation of New York.

In 1979 CDS had 2,091 clients with 5 million enrollees and paid nearly $250 million to 14,000 participating dentists. That same year, CDS introduced Supertooth, a voluntary and free fluoride mouth rinse program for California elementary schoolchildren in both public and private schools. In its first year more than a quarter million children benefited from the program, which continued through the 1980–81 school year and helped a half million children.

MULTIMEDIA AND THE 1980S

"We have a plan to keep you smiling" became the CDS slogan when it began multimedia advertising with a strong dental health message in 1980. During the early part of the decade, CDS also added some new prestigious clients, including the California state university system, state of California employees, and the Motion Picture Industry Pension & Health Plans.

DSPIC's actuarial and accounting functions were transferred from Chicago to San Francisco in 1980, and that city became DSPIC's central office. Most of DSPIC's employees, however, stayed in regional claims offices in Atlanta, Dallas, Gadsden in Alabama, and Lincoln, Nebraska. In 1992 DSPIC became Delta Dental Insurance Company and the following year consolidated its operations in Atlanta. Delta Dental Insurance Company moved its main office to Alpharetta, Georgia, in 1996.

CDS continued administrating California's Denti-Cal program on six-month extensions until 1981, when the state's director of the Department of Health was authorized by the state assembly to enter into a three-year contract with CDS. They continued to be awarded administration of the program contract into the 21st

KEY DATES

1955: California Dental Association Service (CDAS) is formed.

1963: CDAS changes its name to California Dental Services (CDS).

1969: National Association of Dental Service Plans, formed in 1965, changes its name to Delta Dental Plans Association; CDS helps establish Dental Services Plans Insurance Company (DSPIC).

1974: CDS enters into an agreement with the state of California to oversee the dental portion of the state's Medicaid program (Denti-Cal).

1986: CDS changes its name to Delta Dental Plan of California; the U.S. Department of Defense awards a three-year contract to the company for a dental program covering eligible dependents of active duty uniformed service personnel.

1990: DeltaUSA, a commercial extension of the program covering uniformed service personnel, is established; company revenues reach $1 billion.

1999: Company is providing dental plan coverage for one-third of all Californians.

2000: Holding company Dentegra is formed.

2002: Delta Dental starts pilot program for AARP members in Maryland, Texas, and the District of Columbia.

2003: Delta Dental Plan of California changes name to Delta Dental of California.

century. In 1982 CDS also covered nearly 65 percent of California's public school districts, and it moved its Government Programs division to a computer center in Sacramento to handle the Denti-Cal program and to back up its San Francisco computer. In 1983 the company added 180 new clients.

Changing trends in the dental benefits market led CDS in 1984 to create Pacesetter, a program that combined elements of fee-for-service and HMO programs, which was marketed exclusively in San Diego and covered 15,000 people in its first year. That same year, CDS acquired Private Medical-Care, Inc., later known as PMI Dental Health Plan, Inc., and a few years later Pacesetter was managed by PMI. The acquisition of PMI increased CDS's ability to offer a good

dental HMO program and retain clients that might be lost to competing HMOs. The acquisition also gave CDS the dual feature of being able to offer fee-for-service programs in conjunction with HMO programs.

In 1986 CDS changed its name to Delta Dental Plan of California, which gave it national name recognition by association with the Chicago-based Delta Dental Plans Association (DDPA), of which it had been a member since the 1960s. Construction also began in 1986 on a new San Francisco headquarters office. That same year, Delta Dental Plan of California obtained a controlling interest in Deltanet, Inc., an information technology company that provided claims processing for 26 DDPA member companies. Deltanet would become the information technology division of Delta Dental of California in 2005.

The Delta Dental system's ability to take on large accounts through its network of dentists was a deciding point in the U.S. Department of Defense's 1987 awarding Delta Dental Plan of California and its partner, Delta Dental Plan of Michigan, a contract for a dental program for more than 2 millions eligible dependents of active duty uniformed personnel. DDP Delta was a first-time, three-year contract valued at $363 million. Another program was introduced in 1987, the DeltaPreferred Option (DPO), a mid-priced preferred provider program, later called Delta Dental PPO, that included the provider access of the traditional Delta Dental Premier program.

NEW TECHNOLOGY

At the beginning of the 20th century's last decade, Delta Dental Plan of California's revenue reached $1 billion. DeltaUSA, the commercial extension of the government's DDP Delta program, was established by implementing new technology and software that also helped with electronic claims and benefits processing. DIAL (Delta Information Access Line) provided automated eligibility and benefits over the telephone. DeltaUSA's first two clients were World Savings and Armored Transport, starting in 1992, the year William T. Ward became Delta Dental of California's new president and chief executive officer. There were also 4.7 million Denti-Cal beneficiaries, and a joint marketing venture with Kaiser Health Plan had 11,000 covered Californians.

In 1995 Delta Dental was unsuccessful in its bid for renewal of the DDP Delta (later called TRICARE-FMDP) contract. Despite this loss, annual revenues were more than $2 billion in 1996, and Delta Dental Insurance Company added 80,000 new enrollees in its 10-state operating area. In 1997 Delta Dental was awarded a five-year TRICARE Retiree Dental Program contract, which offered a voluntary PPO plan to more than 4 million uniformed services retirees and family members throughout the United States, its territories, and Canada. Delta Dental's Health, Education, and Research Fund, set up in 1995 to sponsor community health programs and advance dental health and access, awarded its first grant in 1997, to the University of California, San Francisco School of Dentistry, for a study focused on curing tooth decay and preservation of tooth structure. Also in that year, Delta Dental Plan of California launched its Web site, making a wealth of information available to its clients, brokers, dentists, enrollees, the media, and the general public.

The company successfully renewed its bid for the Denti-Cal contract and in 1998 was one of four carriers chosen to administer Healthy Families, California's new dental program for uninsured children of working families. Delta Dental was the only program offered in all California counties, and 26,000 Healthy Families enrollees, half the total number of eligible enrollees, chose Delta Dental. In 1999 the California Managed Risk Medical Insurance Board awarded Delta Dental $5.8 million in new funding to serve the state's rural areas and the children of seasonal and migrant workers. With all of its commercial and government programs, in 1999 Delta Dental covered one in three Californians.

DENTEGRA AND THE 21ST CENTURY

In 2000, the revenues of Delta Dental of California were $2.9 billion, almost triple those of 1990. At the end of 2000, Ward retired as president and CEO, and Delta Dental of California, Delta Dental of Pennsylvania, and affiliate companies joined together in a new holding company system. Gary D. Radine, president and CEO of Delta Dental of Pennsylvania and the mid-Atlantic Delta Dental affiliated companies, took on those positions at Delta Dental of California, as well as the holding company. Radine's vision for the new enterprise, as he was later quoted in a company document prepared for the company's 50th anniversary, was to share "the best practices of all the companies, advancing our technology, more fully understanding our competitors, developing new markets, and providing world-class customer service."

Delta Dental Insurance Company experienced great growth in 2000, and by 2002 its enrollment surpassed a million enrollees. That same year, the TRICARE Retiree Dental Program was renewed for five more years. Delta Dental also began a two-year pilot voluntary dental program for the 1.6 million members of AARP in Maryland, Texas, and the District of Columbia, expand-ing in 2003 to Pennsylvania and Alabama. In 2003 Delta Dental's large client list grew, and the company dropped "Plan" from its name to become Delta Dental of California. The company was able to contribute more than $1 million in cash and services to oral health causes and education. Such efforts included scholarships and donations to dental clinics primarily serving the disabled, elderly, and low-income populations. In mid-2003 Delta Dental of California relocated most of its commercial operations division from San Francisco to Pennsylvania and Rancho Cordova, California, where the Sacramento office had moved in 1999 into the first of what became a four-building campus.

Early in 2004 Delta Dental of California was again chosen to administer the Denti-Cal program for four years and three one-year extensions. This $3 billion contract was most likely the largest dental benefits contract in the United States. By the end of 2004 the company had launched Passport, a dual choice program that allowed enrollees to change their dental plan at any time of the year, and the company expanded its Small Business Advantage program in other states. That year, it posted $3.8 billion in annual revenue. In 2007 the Department of Defense renewed Delta Dental's TRI-CARE contract, and by 2010 AARP members were covered in all 50 states, the District of Columbia, Puerto Rico, and the U.S. Virgin Islands by Delta Dental Insurance Company and affiliate Dentegra Insurance Company.

During its 50th anniversary celebrations in May 2005, Delta Dental of California asked Radine and the three former CEOs to share their thoughts about their years at Delta Dental and their outlook for its future. As quoted in a company document prepared for the occasion, Dr. Dixon (who served from 1959 to 1977) said: "While there are many factors that have contributed to Delta of California's success, in my view, the most important one is the program of dental professional supervision that was established during the formative years. This has given our product a uniqueness without which Delta would have become 'just another insurance company.'" On the key to Delta Dental's future success, Dr. Olsen (CEO from 1977 to 1992) said, "Sticking to our knitting—Delta should always be aware of its history with the dental profession and maintain ... continued close involvement with the profession in setting dental policies. ... And, always remember to 'have a plan to keep them smiling.'" William Ward (serving from 1992 to 2000) attributed past and future success to the same idea: "Delta has always been very customer-oriented. That, along with having the support of the dental profession, has allowed us to offer quality dental care programs at affordable prices." Gary Radine (who began in 2001) offered the following for future success: "We have to keep nimble and stay responsive. The world, our environment, health care in the U.S., are going to continue to change on us. We need to be ready to leverage our strengths to meet the challenges of tomorrow."

Louise B. Ketz

PRINCIPAL SUBSIDIARIES

Delta Dental Insurance Company.

PRINCIPAL DIVISIONS

Delta Dental Premier; Delta Dental PPO; DeltaCare USA.

PRINCIPAL COMPETITORS

Aetna Inc.; Cigna Corporation; Guardian Life Insurance Company of America; Metropolitan Life Insurance Company; United Health Group Incorporated.

FURTHER READING

"About Us," Delta Dental of California, http://www. deltadentalins.com/about/index.html.

"Delta Dental Brings Out New HMO Options for California Residents," *Health & Beauty Close-Up* September 11, 2009.

"Delta Dental Cost Management Measures Produce Substantial Customer Savings," *Managed Care Outlook,* May 1, 2006, p. 11.

"Delta Dental Offers New HMO Dental Plan Options for California Individuals and Families," *Pediatrics Week,* September 26, 2009, p. 83.

"Delta Dental Wins Bid for Military Retiree Dental Plan; Five-Year, $1.5 Billion Contract to Cover Up to 4 Million Eligibles," *Business Wire,* October 23, 1997.

"Interactive Technology from Syntellect Helps Delta Dental Brush Up On Customer Service," *PR Newswire,* April 7, 1997.

Publication commemorating company's 50th anniversary, San Francisco, CA: Delta Dental of California, 2005.

Risber, Elizabeth. Intervies with Louise B. Ketz. January, 2010.

Robinson, Cynthia, "Dental Plans Unite to Take Bigger Bite of Market," *San Francisco Business Times*, March 24, 2000, p. 3.

DISH Network Corporation

9601 South Meridian Road
Englewood, Colorado 80112
U.S.A.
Telephone: (303) 723-1000
Toll Free: (866) 443-5162
Fax: (303) 723-1999
Web site: http://www.dishnetwork.com

Public Company
Founded: 1980 as Echosphere
Incorporated: 1995 as EchoStar Communications
Employees: 26,000
Sales: $11.62 billion (2008)
Stock Exchanges: NASDAQ
Ticker Symbol: DISH
NAICS: 517110 Satellite Television Distribution
    Systems

■ ■ ■

Formerly EchoStar Communications Corporation, DISH Network Corporation provides satellite-delivered digital television. It is the second-largest satellite TV provider and third-largest of all pay-TV providers. It offers hundreds of audio and video channels. Among pay-TV providers, it offered the most HD channels and the greatest number of international channels in 2010. DISH has frequently finished first among all satellite and cable TV companies in consumer satisfaction. It rapidly increased its customer base starting in the late 1990s, with a slowdown in 2007 and 2008 due partly to external conditions and partly as a result of internal problems. By 2010, however, the company was hopeful that changes in management and improved market conditions would lead to continued growth.

ORIGINS: 1980–93

The company that became EchoStar Communications and then DISH Network was founded by Charles Ergen in 1980 as a small retail store that sold direct-to-home satellite television products and services. During the 1980s it was primarily a manufacturer and distributor of C-band hardware. C-band satellites were used for the most part to broadcast shows to cable system operators, not to individuals, because reception equipment cost about $2,500 and included a 10-foot dish antenna. By the mid-1980s the company, then known as Echosphere Corp., was a leading supplier of direct-to-home hardware and services worldwide.

Foreseeing changes in the satellite industry, Ergen applied to the Federal Communications Commission (FCC) in 1987 for a direct broadcast satellite (DBS) license. In 1992 EchoStar Communications won a license to broadcast from one of three slots within the broadcasting range of the entire continental United States. The slot, among eight set aside by the FCC, was located above the city of Los Angeles. EchoStar Satellite Corp. was established to build, launch, and operate the company's satellites.

In December 1993 EchoStar Communications was incorporated in Nevada, with headquarters in Englewood, Colorado, as a holding company for 13 direct and indirect subsidiaries. EchoStar claimed to lead the U.S. market for home satellite reception products, with a 30 percent domestic market share. The company had an existing distribution network of 5,000 dealers. For 1993 revenues from subsidiaries were $220.9 million, 33.8 percent more than in 1992, with net income of $20.4 million, nearly double 1992's net income of $10.8 million.

ESTABLISHING THE NETWORK: 1994

In January 1994, EchoStar made arrangements with DirectSat Corporation, a subsidiary of SSE Telecom that had also won a license to put a satellite above Los Angeles, to pool their licenses and resources to offer 110 channels of television, 250 audio channels, and data feeds of financial and weather information.

In 1994 EchoStar Communications offered $624 million in senior secured notes along with 3.7 million common stock purchase warrants. Proceeds to the company were about $335 million. These so-called "junk bonds" had an interest rate of nearly 13 percent, with payment deferred until 1999. The proceeds would be used primarily to construct, launch, insure, and operate two direct broadcast satellites to be built by Martin Marietta Corp. (later Lockheed Martin Corp.) for $159 million. The launches were planned to take place in China in 1995 and 1996, with insurance costing $206.3 million.

If successful, the two satellites would be worth $881 million once service was initiated. They would enable EchoStar to begin broadcasting more than 100 channels of television programming to 18-inch receiver dishes that cost an estimated $500 each. The company's target audience would be the 11.5 million U.S. households not wired for cable and 20.4 million households wired for cable but with limited channel capacity.

AT&T would operate EchoStar I and provide tracking, telemetry, control, and maintenance services for the satellite. AT&T would also provide consulting services to Martin Marietta, the satellite's builder. It was unclear at first who would supply the receiving equipment for consumers. At this point, access to the 18-inch satellite receiver was controlled by DirecTV, owned by the Hughes Electronics Corp., a subsidiary of General Motors.

LAUNCHING ECHOSTAR I: 1995

In 1995 EchoStar Communications was building a $50 million uplink facility in Cheyenne, Wyoming, that would be operational by August 1995, and EchoStar I was scheduled to launch October 1, 1995. The company was busy lining up programming. Its initial hardware would consist of an 18-inch dish, set-top box, and remote. It intended to compete directly with the Digital Satellite System offered by Thomson Consumer Electronics and DirecTV.

EchoStar issued a prospectus for a four-million share initial public offering (IPO) in July 1995. By August 1995 EchoStar had signed programming deals with Viacom to carry its basic and premium channels, including Showtime, The Movie Channel, MTV, VH1, and Nickelodeon. It also had signed deals with HBO, CNN, The Disney Channel, Turner Classic Movies, ESPN, C-SPAN, and The Learning Channel.

EchoStar's initial satellite launch was delayed because of problems with its Chinese partner, China Great Wall Industry Corp., which had experienced two launch failures in 1995. Meanwhile, DBS competitors DirecTV and Primestar were mounting extensive marketing campaigns to gain market share.

The company's first satellite was launched from China on December 28, 1995. EchoStar also acquired more channels by purchasing the 22 channel assignments of Direct Broadcast Satellite Corporation (DBSC) for $8 million. EchoStar had acquired a 40 percent interest in DBSC in 1994 and in 1996 acquired the remaining 60 percent for an estimated $23 million.

EchoStar's DBS service would be called the DISH TV Network, with DISH standing for Digital Sky Highway. The service was scheduled to launch in February 1996 with 100 channels. It would compete directly with DirecTV and less directly with Primestar, which required a larger dish and had fewer channels.

DIRECT BROADCAST SATELLITE SERVICE BEGINS: 1996

At the beginning of 1996 the FCC auctioned two blocks of DBS channels, one of which went to MCI

1987: EchoStar founder Charles Ergen files for a direct broadcast satellite license with the FCC.

1995: The company's first satellite, EchoStar I, is launched from China.

1996: The company's DBS service, DISH TV Network, is launched.

1998: EchoStar acquires the assets of American Sky Broadcasting.

1999: Company introduces the first integrated satellite TV receiver and Internet browser; Congress passes the Satellite Home Viewers Act, allowing DBS providers to broadcast local programming in local markets.

2004: DISH becomes the first satellite provider to carry local channels to local markets in all 50 states plus the District of Columbia.

2008: EchoStar Communications Corp. divides into DISH Network Corp. and EchoStar Corp.

2009: DISH broadcasts to 14 million subscribers by year's end.

1,500 subscribers per day and forecast up to 400,000 subscribers by the end of 1996. DISH Network reached 100,000 subscribers by August 1996. EchoStar was offering its satellite dish and programming for low prices, and the competitors were soon forced to lower their prices as well.

EchoStar II launched on September 10, 1996, from French Guiana, doubling EchoStar's channel capacity from 80 to 160. The company added two new basic packages: America's Top 40, which consisted of 40 basic networks for $19.95 per month, and America's Top 50, which included a 30-channel audio feed plus 10 more channels, for $24.99.

In November 1996 EchoStar Communications introduced a new promotion with computer manufacturer Gateway Inc. Customers who purchased certain Gateway computers would receive a coupon for a free satellite receiver system with the purchase of one year of DISH Network programming. The company would continue to use free dish promotions as an integral part of its marketing programs to attract new subscribers to DISH Network TV. The company added 65,000 subscribers in December 1996, its strongest month, giving the DISH Network 350,000 subscribers by year's end. Meanwhile, DirecTV added 165,000 subscribers in December, giving it 2.3 million subscribers at year's end.

MERGER PLANS WITH MURDOCH FAIL: SPRING 1997

Seeking to expand its services beyond DBS, the company began entering into agreements for more satellites and fixed satellites. The fixed satellite business required a higher degree of capitalization than EchoStar could command, and the company was admittedly seeking financial partners, among them TCI Satellite Entertainment. By February 1997 the company had $800 million of debt on its balance sheet. Its stock hit a 52-week high of $37 in February 1996, but a year later was worth about 60 percent less. It reached a 52-week low of $15 on January 29, 1997.

By the end of February 1997 it appeared that EchoStar had found its financial partner in Rupert Murdoch and News Corporation Limited. Murdoch was in the process of building an uplink center in Arizona for ASkyB, his proposed joint venture with MCI Worldcom. Murdoch's News Corp. planned to buy a 40 percent stake in EchoStar Communications for about $1 billion. The deal would give EchoStar seven satellites able to deliver 500 channels, including the capacity to carry local stations. As part of the deal, MCI would own 10 percent of EchoStar. The remaining 50 percent of

and the other to EchoStar Communications. EchoStar's slot was too far to the west to be able to serve the East Coast, while MCI purchased the last DBS slot with full coverage of the continental United States. MCI and News Corp. were planning a joint satellite venture to be called American Sky Broadcasting Co. (ASkyB).

When EchoStar began offering DBS service in spring 1996, there were three competitors already offering similar services: DirecTV, United States Satellite Broadcasting, and Primestar. EchoStar was the only DBS service to have the capacity for two national DBS systems. Its receivers would be made by the French manufacturer Groupe Sagem and the U.S. company SCI Systems. Philips would market EchoStar DBS dishes under its Philips and Magnavox brands.

EchoStar Communications previewed its DISH TV Network at a trade show in March 1996, and by May the service was rolled out to consumers, who could chose from five programming packages with monthly fees ranging from $19.99 to $59.99. At the same time the company launched a $40 million advertising campaign to promote the DISH Network. By June 1996 EchoStar claimed to have 50,000 subscribers. The company would continue to offer various price promotions to gain subscribers. EchoStar was adding about

EchoStar would be retained by the company's shareholders. Under the terms of the agreement, Ergen would continue as CEO of EchoStar, and Murdoch would become chairman.

EchoStar quickly announced it would invest $500 million to build eight regional uplink centers with the capability of delivering local broadcast channels. Analysts agreed that a DBS service that offered local programming would be the first really serious threat to cable television, but the proposed merger with News Corp.'s satellite business was soon running into opposition.

News Corp. had failed to obtain permission from broadcasters to retransmit their signals, and the FCC was being asked to deny the ASkyB-EchoStar merger. When Murdoch insisted on management control over the merged company, the deal came undone. With News Corp. and EchoStar disagreeing on several technical issues, EchoStar went to court to force News Corp. to make good on a $200 million interest-free loan that was part of the merger agreement. Murdoch countered by insisting that Ergen resign as CEO and give up management of the venture.

On May 9, EchoStar sued News Corp. for breach of contract, claiming $5 billion in damages, with News Corp. filing a countersuit the next month. Meanwhile, News Corp. and Primestar reached an agreement in principle to merge their DBS operations, but that proposed merger was also subsequently called off by federal regulators.

EXPANDED SERVICES AND SUBSCRIPTION GAINS: 1997

EchoStar Communications continued to seek financial partners and filed with the SEC for a $378 million debt offering, in part to raise an additional $305 million to cover the costs of four planned satellites. As it negotiated with Lockheed Martin to reschedule its payments, the company's debt reached $1.2 billion.

The company began a new promotion on June 1, 1997, whereby consumers could purchase EchoStar hardware for $199 without buying an annual subscription, subscribing on a monthly basis instead. By mid-1997 EchoStar had 590,000 subscribers and was adding nearly 50,000 new subscribers per month. EchoStar III launched in October 1997 from Cape Canaveral, Florida, and would serve primarily the East Coast of the United States. The company also purchased for $7.5 million a 190,000-square-foot building and 32.2 acres in Littleton, Colorado, for its new campus-style corporate headquarters.

A $99 installation promotion resulted in 105,000 new subscribers in September. By the end of October,

EchoStar had 895,000 subscribers and was warning that a shortage of receivers would temporarily limit the number of new subscribers. However, the company had met its financing needs by raising more than $650 million through debt and equity offerings following its proposed merger with News Corp. fell through. The company reached an agreement with Sears, Roebuck & Co. to offer its $199 package in 800 Sears outlets.

For 1997 net losses rose 210 percent to $321.3 million on revenues of $477.4 million, up 140 percent. The company ended the year about $1.4 billion in debt after raising $750 million in debt during the year. The company also ended the year with 1.2 million subscribers.

MORE CHANNEL CAPACITY: 1998

In January 1998 EchoStar Communications began beaming the local signals of the top four networks' broadcast affiliates into their respective markets in Atlanta, Boston, Chicago, Dallas, New York, and Washington, D.C., with additional cities scheduled to follow. Ten more western cities would be added after the launch of EchoStar IV in the spring, according to EchoStar's plan to reach more than 40 percent of U.S. television households. The company introduced a new Top 60 programming package in May for $28.99 per month to replace the Top 50 package, adding such channels as American Movie Classics, Bravo, and the SportsChannel, among others. New subscribers were offered a $60 credit if they submitted a copy of their latest cable bill.

EchoStar IV launched on May 8, 1998, from Kazakhstan. Following the launch, the company encountered problems deploying the solar panels on the satellite. It subsequently found that one primary and one backup transponder on EchoStar IV failed. Additional capacity was gained through an alliance with Loral Skynet to deliver niche programming through one of Loral's satellites. EchoStar was also preparing to deliver data to consumers. It was already supplying data to niche markets through AgCast, an agricultural report, and Signal, a stock report. It began competing more directly with DirecTV by offering a $100 bounty to any DirecTV subscribers who switched to EchoStar. DirecTV responded by doubling the bounty for DISH TV subscribers who switched to DirecTV.

EchoStar Communications received permission from the FCC to broadcast local network signals to "unserved" homes in Denver, Phoenix, San Francisco, and Salt Lake City from its EchoStar IV satellite. Industry periodical *Broadcasting & Cable* noted that the political climate was good for moving "local-to-local" service ahead, because it was seen as providing competition to cable television and possibly reducing cable subscriber rates. By September it was clear that Congress was working to pass legislation that would permit satellite TV companies to deliver local broadcast signals.

In October, EchoStar announced a three-month promotion to new subscribers, giving them a $249 rebate on the cost of receiving hardware in exchange for a one-year subscription to the DISH Network's America's Top 100 CD programming package. DirecTV and Primestar had their own promotions underway and declined to match the offer. At the beginning of the month DISH TV had about 1.6 million subscribers, compared with 4 million for DirecTV and 2.6 million for Primestar. EchoStar also announced that in 1999 it planned to offer interactive television nationally, including e-mail and home banking, using software from OpenTV Inc. of Mountain View, California.

ACQUIRES AMERICAN SKY BROADCASTING

In December 1998 the News Corp. agreed to sell its satellite television assets to EchoStar Communications, which would increase EchoStar's channels from 200 to 500. Under terms of the agreement, EchoStar would pay $1.25 billion to buy the DBS assets of the MCI Worldcom-News Corp. venture ASkyB. The stock deal would give MCI and News Corp. a 37 percent interest in EchoStar and end the litigation over the failed merger attempt in 1997. EchoStar would receive ASkyB's uplink center in Gilbert, Arizona, as well as a license to operate at another orbital location, and two satellites then under construction. EchoStar also got a three-year retransmission deal to carry FOX Network's local signals and agreed to carry the FOX News Channel. Following the merger, EchoStar would control more than half the satellite slots over the United States. With FCC approval of ASkyB's license transfer to EchoStar, the deal closed in June 1999, with EchoStar issuing 8.6 million shares of Class A stock.

Competitor DirecTV responded by acquiring its longtime partner, U.S. Satellite Broadcasting Co., for $1.3 billion in December 1998. The acquisition gave DirecTV an improved programming package and 200,000 new subscribers. In January DirecTV announced it would acquire rival Primestar for $1.82 billion, leaving DirecTV and EchoStar as the number one and two DBS providers. EchoStar saw an opportunity to pick up Primestar's old subscribers and offered a $200 bounty to its dealers for every Primestar customer they could switch to DISH TV. Analysts estimated that as many as 1,000 Primestar customers per day were switching to DISH TV.

THE TOP TWO SATELLITE TV SERVICES IN 1999

In an effort to provide interactive television services, EchoStar Communications announced a partnership with Microsoft's WebTV to include the WebTV Network Plus Internet TV service in a new generation of EchoStar integrated receiver/decoders that would be available in spring 1999. The service would deliver Web page content to viewers and allow them to pause a program for up to 30 minutes before resuming it. In June, EchoStar rolled out its DISHPlayer, a satellite receiver with an integrated WebTV service that allowed users to surf the Internet, send e-mail, and play video games. The DISHPlayer was priced at $199, plus a subscription fee for programming service and another fee for Internet access.

In March, EchoStar surpassed the two million subscriber mark for DISH TV. With federal cable rate regulations expiring in March 1999, lawmakers were seeking to find ways to increase competition for cable, rather than extend the rate regulations. In May, a House bill on satellite reform passed that would allow DBS companies to provide a programming package that included local programming. For the rest of the year the Satellite Home Viewer Act (SHVA) would be the subject of intense lobbying on the part of satellite providers, cable operators, television station owners, and cable and broadcast networks. Hurdles to offering local-into-local service included passage of appropriate legislation, FCC approval of orbital license transfers, and retransmission deals with every local broadcaster. The company's stock reached a 52-week high of $142.63 and later rose to more than $176 before settling around $151.

By the end of August 1999 EchoStar had 2.84 million DISH TV subscribers. EchoStar V was launched on September 23, 1999, from Cape Canaveral. Following a stock split EchoStar's stock was trading at a 52-week adjusted high of $88.25.

In November SHVA passed Congress and was signed into law by President Bill Clinton. It gave DBS providers like EchoStar and DirecTV permission to offer local broadcast channels to their subscribers in those local markets, making them more competitive with cable television operators. EchoStar was immediately able to provide full market coverage in 13 cities covering 31 million homes, with other cities to follow, while DirecTV offered local broadcast affiliate programming to nearly 12 million households in New York and Los Angeles with other markets to follow.

GROWTH AND COMPETITION: 1999–2006

The passage of SHVA sparked a sharp growth in DISH Network subscriptions. During the first quarter of 2000, 455,000 new subscribers joined DISH Network, 40 percent more than in the first quarter of 1999 and the most that DISH had ever gained in a single quarter. At the time of SHVA's passage, DISH had three million customers. Just five months later, in April 2000, it reached four million, and by June 2001, six million. The number of subscribers continued to grow, reaching 9 million in September 2003 and 11 million in January 2005. At the end of 2006, DISH had 13 million subscribers, compared with 16 million for DirecTV.

Although DirecTV remained the top DBS provider through the first decade of the 21st century, for most of those years DISH Network remained highly competitive as the second largest. In various areas of competition, DISH led the industry. In 2004 it became the first to carry local channels to local markets in all 50 states plus the District of Columbia. In 2006 it offered the largest HD lineup, utilizing MPEG-4 technology to expand its HD offerings. It was the first to market a satellite receiver with a built-in digital video recorder. According to surveys by J. D. Powers and Associates, DISH Network led all satellite and cable television companies in consumer satisfaction in 1999, 2000, and 2004. DISH was also rated highest by satellite and cable television consumers in 2004, 2005, and 2007, according to the American Customer Satisfaction (ACSI) Index.

Competing with DirecTV, EchoStar's DISH Network continued offering special pricing and free equipment to attract new customers. These deals, added to the high initial costs involved in acquiring subscribers, meant that DISH Network, despite surging subscriptions, continued losing money. In a bold move, CEO Ergen tried to tackle this problem by ending EchoStar's competition with DirecTV through a merger of the two in 2001. Another motive was to block an attempt by Murdoch's News Corp. from acquiring DirecTV. The bid was dropped the following year after antimonopoly objections from the Justice Department and the FCC. This failure opened the door for Murdoch to turn the table on Ergen, which he did in 2003 when News Corp. bought DirecTV. Ownership by the wealthy News Corp. gave DirecTV a competitive boost.

TROUBLED TIMES AND TURNAROUND: 2007–09

In January 2008, EchoStar Communications Corp. divided into two publicly traded companies, DISH Network Corp. and EchoStar Corp., the latter partner-ing with DISH to provide it with technical products and services. The split was accompanied by bad news for DISH. Court rulings against DISH and EchoStar were upheld in a patent infringement suit brought by TiVo. Meanwhile, with DISH Network's customer numbers having leveled off in 2007, the company lost 25,000 subscribers in the second quarter of 2008, its first quarterly loss ever. From mid-2008 to mid-2009, subscriber numbers went down from 13.8 million to 13.6 million. Meanwhile, DirecTV continued to gain customers.

One reason for declining subscriptions was the overall economic decline experienced in the United States that began in 2007 and led to a worldwide financial crisis in late 2008. Another was the semi-saturation of the market for pay TV in the United States. DISH Network faced more trouble when, in mid-2008, AT&T announced that as of the end of the year it would conclude its distribution deal with the satellite TV firm. DISH relied on telecoms like AT&T to market its services to customers. Also, cable and telecommunications companies were providing stiffer competition.

However, as DISH Network itself acknowledged, not all of its troubles were external. Some came from within. In a March 2009 assessment, Ergen said that the corporation's product was too complex, making it hard for other companies to work with DISH. He also stated that in the past few years the firm had let its operations deteriorate. This included customer service, which, he admitted, was deficient in everything from taking customer calls, to installation, and dealing with customer problems. Ineffective marketing was another issue, the CEO commented. He also said that increasing piracy and fraud had kept customer growth down and that DISH had been slow in dealing with it.

Ergen believed, however, that changes in management personnel and a focused commitment to improve would serve DISH Network well in the future. Subscription numbers rebounded to reach 14 million customers by the end of 2009, and the company got another boost in January 2010. A federal court ruling made it easier for DISH Network to fight piracy when it handed down a $51 million judgment against a Florida man who posted software to the Internet that unlocked encrypted satellite broadcasts.

David P. Bianco
Updated, Michael Levine

PRINCIPAL SUBSIDIARIES

DISH DBS; DISH Network LLC.

PRINCIPAL COMPETITORS

Comcast Corporation; DirecTV Group Inc.; Time Warner Cable Inc.

FURTHER READING

Albiniak, Paige, "At Long Last, Local," *Broadcasting & Cable*, November 29, 1999, p. 4.

Brull, Steven V., "Now, Beam up Some Customers," *Business Week*, December 28, 1998, p. 52.

Dickson, Glen, "Sat TV Goes Interactive," *Broadcasting & Cable*, January 11, 1999, p. 15.

"EchoStar and Dish STB with Integrated Slingbox," *Screen Digest*, February 2009, p. 58.

Griffin, Greg, "Littleton, Colo.-Based Satellite-TV Firm Ranks First in Customer Satisfaction," *Denver Post*, September 7, 2000.

Grover, Ronald, "DISH Starts Falling to Earth: The Satellite TV Network Is Struggling to Keep Subscribers from Fleeing," *Business Week*, August 4, 2008, p. 65.

Littleton, Cynthia, and Harry A. Jessel, "Murdoch, Ergen Take to Sky," *Broadcasting & Cable*, March 3, 1997, p. 41.

Mundy, Alicia, "EchoStar Woos Rival's Subs," *Mediaweek*, February 1, 1999, p. 5.

Perman, Stacy, "EchoStar's New Orbit," *Time*, March 10, 1997, p. 56.

Watts, Thomas, "EchoStar Dishes It Out Once Again," *Interspace*, August 27, 2003.

EchoStar Corporation

90 Inverness Circle East
Englewood, Colorado 80112
U.S.A.
Telephone: (303) 723-1000
Fax: (303) 723-1499
Web site: http://www.echostar.com

Public Company
Incorporated: 2008
Employees: 2,400
Sales: $2.15 billion (2008)
Stock Exchanges: NASDAQ
Ticker Symbol: SATS
NAICS: 334220 Radio and Television Broadcast and Wireless Communications Equipment Manufacturing

■ ■ ■

EchoStar Corporation provides hardware, software, and services for digital pay-TV broadcasting through its three wholly owned subsidiaries: EchoStar International Corporation, EchoStar Satellite Services LLC, and Echo-Star Technologies LLC. Spun off from DISH Network in 2008, that satellite TV firm remains EchoStar's primary customer. However, EchoStar also develops products for cable, telecommunications, Internet protocol television (IPTV), and other market segments. Sling Media, Inc., a wholly owned subsidiary of Echo-Star Technologies, has been a pioneer in TV signal placeshifting through its Slingbox products, which enable consumers to watch their home TV programming anywhere in the world. The success of Slingbox is considered a key to EchoStar Corp.'s future profitability.

SATELLITE TV COMPANY FOUNDED: 1980

In 1980 Charles Ergen, his wife, Cantey Ergen, and his friend James DeFranco joined to form Echosphere, a satellite TV business later named EchoStar Communications Corporation. The firm was headed by Ergen, who had been a financial analyst for Frito-Lay. At first, Ergen and his partners worked mostly in rural Colorado, manufacturing and selling C-band satellite television products and services. These included direct broadcast satellite (DBS) television dishes, set-top boxes (STBs), programming, installation, and third-party consumer financing. By the mid-1980s it had become one of the world's major sources of these goods and services.

In 1987 Ergen took the next step: requesting a DBS license from the Federal Communications Commission (FCC). During March 1992 the FCC granted it, assigning EchoStar Communications 11 high-power DBS frequencies at longitude 119° west. Seven months later EchoStar began constructing its first satellite, which was launched from Xichang, China, as EchoStar I on December 29, 1995. At the same time EchoStar created DISH Network as its broadcasting subsidiary. In 1995 it built an uplink in Cheyenne, Colorado, and by the end of the year it had made programming arrangements with Viacom to broadcast its basic channels and premium channels such as HBO, Showtime, CNN, and others. Making its first broadcast in March 1996, Echo-Star had 100,000 subscribers at mid-year and more than one million by the end of 1997. It ranked second in the satellite TV field, which was led by DirecTV, owned by the Hughes Electronics Corp., a subsidiary of General Motors.

Ergen helped organize lobbying support for the Satellite Home Viewer Improvement Act of 1999, which allowed satellite broadcasters to carry local TV channels in their own local markets. This legislation sparked a significant increase in subscribers for both DISH Network and DirecTV as local affiliates of the four broadcast networks signed up to have their local stations carried by satellite. It also intensified the competition between DISH and DirecTV over the years, with DISH luring customers through cut-rate prices and rebates. At times it offered free satellite dishes and receivers in exchange for long-term contracts.

A LEADER IN SATELLITE TV INNOVATIONS: 2000–07

DirecTV, strengthened when it was purchased by the wealthy News Corporation of Rupert Murdoch, led the satellite broadcasting industry through the first decade of the 21st century. DISH, however, remained a competitive number two for most of those years. In May 2000 it had four million customers. Subscriptions leaped to 10 million in June 2004 and 13 million by the end of 2006, compared with DirecTV's nearly 16 million. In 1999 DISH Network became the first satellite system to provide 500 channels. In 2004 it became the first such system to beam local channels to local markets in all 50 states and the District of Columbia. By the end of 2007, EchoStar Communications had launched 10 satellites in all.

EchoStar Communications kept pace with and often led the industry in technological innovation. At the beginning of 2000, EchoStar began selling its new DISH HD receiver, enabling the firm to broadcast high-definition television. During the same year it introduced DISH DVD, the world's first combination satellite television receiver and embedded DVD player. Extensive DVD features included multiple language and subtitle tracks, multiple angles, and four fast-forward and rewind speeds. During 2001 EchoStar launched the DISH Network Pro 501, which recorded 30 hours of

video programming, compared with the 12 hours of the DISH Player, which had been initiated two years earlier.

In 2003 EchoStar's state-of-the art satellite receiver DISHPVR 921 (personal video recorder) arrived on the market. It was described as the first satellite TV receiver with complete capability to pick up both satellite and terrestrially launched HD video broadcasts. The new product gave consumers added flexibility in recording, watching, or pausing a program, watching instant replays, and using functions such as fast forward and fast reverse on multiple HD programs. The year 2005 brought the HD-DVR 942. Providing high definition support, it also could drive a standard definition display in another room using a second, RF (radio frequency) remote control.

Also in 2005, EchoStar Communications presented the PocketDISH, a portable media player with capability for carrying TV programs and movies, playing music, and storing digital photos. In 2006 the company introduced the country's largest HD programming lineup, available to DISH Network customers with the Network's new MPEG4 satellite receivers. In 2007 EchoStar brought forward MobileDISH, which made it possible for automobiles to receive satellite programming via a dish on the roof of the vehicle. At the same time, the corporation also made public the ViP622 HD DVR, which increased DVR storage capacity to 500 gigabytes.

SLING MEDIA FOUNDED: 2004

In 2004 Blake Krikorian cofounded and became the CEO of the privately held U.S. firm Sling Media, Inc., whose aim was to introduce innovative digital media products. In its first year of operation the company obtained $10.5 million in venture funding from Mobius Venture Capital, DCM-Doll Capital Management, and an undisclosed investor. At the International Consumer Electronics Show (CES) in Las Vegas in January 2005, the firm introduced its signature product: the Slingbox. As Krikorian explained to *Online Reporter*, the Slingbox, installed at home, "picks up the TV signal from a cable box, satellite receiver, or PVR to wherever the viewer requests, be it in the next room, across the country or around the world, as long as there's a high-speed Internet connection." The initial Slingbox shifted TV signals only to a single Windows XP-based PC. Initially sold for $250 and carrying no subscription fees, the silver-colored Slingbox was about the size and shape of a large chocolate bar.

Just as the introduction of the VCR in the 1970s made "timeshifting" possible for television viewing, the Slingbox introduced "placeshifting." It enabled viewers to watch programs from anywhere on the globe

KEY DATES

1980: Charles Ergen founds a satellite television business later known as EchoStar Communications Corporation.

2005: Sling Media, Inc., introduces the Slingbox, which placeshifts television signals to PCs at any location.

2007: EchoStar Communications purchases Sling Media.

2008: EchoStar Corporation, including Sling Media, is formed when EchoStar Communications is divided in two.

2009: Ergen resigns as EchoStar Corporation's CEO; EchoStar T2200S is the first HD DVR set-top box with Slingbox capability.

on their home television screen, including local programming. Sling Media did not report sales figures, but in Amazon.com's electronics category, the Slingbox consistently ranked among the 100 most popular products among the 60,000 listed. The question for the future, however, was whether the Slingbox could sufficiently extend its appeal beyond frequently traveling businesspersons to maintain good initial sales.

In the meantime, however, the Slingbox's early success drew further interest from investors. In February 2006 Sling Media obtained $46.6 million in additional financing from a cluster of firms headed by Goldman Sachs, Liberty Media, and EchoStar Communications. EchoStar's interest was likely linked to the fact that during the preceding year it had adopted the concept of mobility with the introduction of its PocketDISH product.

IMPROVING THE SLINGBOX: 2006–07

Sling Media software innovations in March 2006 made the Slingbox more versatile. The company announced the SlingPlayer Mac, which made it possible for Apple's Macintosh computers to receive home TV programming. Sling Media also presented a new software package called SlingPlayer Mobile. This made it possible for Slingbox owners to watch their home television from any network-enabled mobile phone or handheld computer (PDA) powered by Windows Mobile.

In September 2006 three new Slingbox models emerged: the Slingbox TUNER, designed for users who

did not have a cable box or a DVR; the Slingbox AV, which connected to a digital cable box, a satellite receiver, or a DVR; and the Slingbox Pro HD, which supported high definition TV. Along with this launch, Sling Media initiated a higher level of customer support for installation: subscribers could talk to technical support representatives as they set up the Slingbox, and the representative, with the customer's permission, could remotely control the customer's computer to help in the installation.

In an interview at the end of 2006, Krikorian estimated that Sling Media had about a 95 percent market share. He attributed this to his company's constant innovation and adjustments. Yet despite the initial buzz surrounding the Slingbox, he stated the following year that Slingbox sales were in the hundreds of thousands, not an overwhelming figure. At the January 2007 CES, the company introduced the SlingCatcher, which carried Web matter of any format to a TV, reversing the flow originally generated by the Slingbox. Six months later Sling Media presented two HomePlug power line products to make it easier to connect a Slingbox or other device to a home network.

CREATING A NEW CORPORATION: 2007–08

In September 2007 these two companies came together when EchoStar Communications Corp. announced it was purchasing Sling Media, Inc., for an estimated $380 million. EchoStar Communications, already an investor in Sling Media, believed that the latter's placeshifting software would give its set-top boxes (STBs) for DISH Network a significant edge over the set-top boxes used by DirecTV and by other pay-TV providers. At a time when DISH's subscriber numbers were flat while DirecTV continued adding customers, this seemed like a well-calculated enhancement. For its part, Sling Media believed that combining the two companies' resources and technologies would quickly enlarge its open multi-platform product offerings. Sling Media needed a boost, losing $32.8 million on revenues of $23.2 million in 2007.

Shortly afterward, in January 2008, EchoStar Communications split into separately traded public corporations. EchoStar Communications continued under a new name, DISH Network, consisting of the satellite pay-TV operation. A new company, EchoStar Corporation, was formed by spinning off parts of EchoStar Communications. One part was technology and services for satellite and other forms of pay TV. They were to be provided by EchoStar Technologies LLC and EchoStar Satellite Services LLC, subsidiaries of the new corporation. Another part was Sling Media, now to be a subsidiary of EchoStar Technologies. An additional subsidiary, EchoStar International Corporation, was established to handle non-European foreign business. EchoStar Europe, an operating unit of EchoStar Technologies, dealt with the particular needs of European customers.

The new firm was partnered with DISH Network to provide technology products and services for it. Almost all of EchoStar Corporation's business was with DISH at first, and the firm expected business with DISH to be the major source of its revenue in the foreseeable future. In addition, EchoStar was free to expand its customer base beyond DISH to cable operators, telecommunications firms, other pay TV providers, and even to DirecTV.

Charles Ergen was the CEO of both EchoStar Corp. and DISH Network Corp., and Blake Krikorian continued as head of Sling Media until January 2009. Early in 2008 EchoStar took the industry lead in offering digital converter boxes for consumers in anticipation of the FCC's 2009 deadline for an end to broadcaster transmission of analog signals. The converters were priced so that with the federal government's $40 subsidy, they would cost the consumer almost nothing. Writing in the *Denver Post*, Kimberly S. Johnson stated that "it's a bold move that positions the Douglas County-based satellite-TV company at the forefront of the coming digital transition."

At the same time, Sling Media quickly tried to demonstrate that its new status as an EchoStar subsidiary did not mean that it would be restricted to serving DISH subscribers. Krikorian declared that Sling Media intended to sell the modem through original equipment manufacturers (OEMs), namely TV, cable, and telecommunications companies. The idea was to make Slingbox technology a built-in feature of STBs that would be sold wholesale, thus improving on the flattening retail sales of Slingboxes as a stand-alone retail product. This was the idea behind the EchoStar T2200S, introduced in March 2009. It was the first HD DVR set-top box with Slingbox capability designed for the cable TV industry. The question was whether the cable industry would purchase Slingbox software.

SEEKING BREAKTHROUGHS: 2008 ON

Three international developments contributed to EchoStar's income in 2008 and 2009. In November 2008, EchoStar Corp. joined with MVS Comunicaciones, a Mexican media and telecommunications conglomerate, to announce a joint venture, a direct-to-home (DTH)

satellite TV service available to consumers across Mexico. In December 2008, EchoStar Europe stated that its HD STB had been introduced by Cyfrowy Polsat, a Polish satellite television platform with 2.4 million subscribers in Poland. In June 2009 EchoStar and Asia Satellite Telecommunications Company (AsiaSat), Asia's leading satellite operator, announced a joint venture to bring DTH satellite television to Taiwan and other targeted regions in Asia.

In December 2008 EchoStar Corp. and EchoStar Satellite Services were cited by World Teleport Services as among its Global Top 20 satellite communications firms. The following month EchoStar Corp. and EchoStar Satellite Services announced an agreement with Vredes, Inc., to provide satellite services for emergency management and other remote location broadcast demands. The oil and gas industries would be among those utilizing these services.

In 2008 and 2009 Sling Media continued offering new versions of the Slingbox, including models that streamed HD television content and mobile models for iPhones and BlackBerry smartphones. Beyond these incremental developments, Sling Media sought to make itself a household name by establishing in December 2008 a free entertainment destination called Sling.com. Once Sling Media and its Slingbox became commonly known, it was hoped, TV manufacturers, cable companies, and others would license Slingbox technology. Ultimately, the goal was to make Slingbox software as common as DVRs.

Toward the end of 2009, however, EchoStar Corp. management acknowledged that the company was having difficulty achieving the breakthroughs it sought. In November, CEO Ergen stated that EchoStar's efforts to sell its technology to cable companies had not progressed far and that Sling Media had not succeeded in converting its technology product into a built-in feature. This was confirmed by the fact that in 2009, 90 percent of EchoStar's STB shipments still went to DISH Network. To make things worse, stagnation in DISH subscriber numbers reduced EchoStar's business with its largest customer.

In mid-November, the 56-year-old Ergen resigned as EchoStar CEO but remained as chairman of the board. He was replaced by Michael Dugan, a key technological innovator for EchoStar and DISH. Ergen did not place major blame on the economic recession or financial crisis of the years 2008 and 2009. Rather, according to *Fair Disclosure Wire*, he commented that "we're still kind of a breakeven company that's still kind of finding its way out there that has a lot of building blocks in place, and it's up to our management to take those and find a way to make money at them."

Michael Levine

PRINCIPAL SUBSIDIARIES

EchoStar International Corporation; EchoStar Satellite Services LLC; EchoStar Technologies LLC.

PRINCIPAL COMPETITORS

Cisco Systems Inc.; Intelstat Ltd.; Motorola Inc.

FURTHER READING

Baumgartner, Jeff, "Take Your TV with You; Can 'Place-shifting' Drive the Upstream and Premium Broadband Services?" *CED*, May 2005, p. 46.

"DBS Systems Drive Set-top Box Demand," *Electronic News*, September 11, 1995, p. 28.

Donohue, Steve, "Charlie Ergen: 'From a 98-Pound Weakling to a 400-Pound Gorilla,'" *Electronic Media*, January 25, 1999, p. 58.

Downey, Kevin, "Blake Krikorian," *Broadcasting & Cable*, April 14, 2008, p. 40.

Johnson, Kimberly S., "EchoStar Leads in Digital Switch," *Denver Post*, January 8, 2008.

Kharif, Olga, "Will Sling Media Shift Places?" *BusinessWeek Online*, March 3, 2006, http://www.businessweek.com/technology/content/mar2006/tc20060303_485877.htm.

"Q3 2009 EchoStar Corporation Earnings Conference Call," *Fair Disclosure Wire*, November 9, 2009.

"Sling Media's Slingbox Turns a PC into a Personal TV," *Online Reporter*, January 15, 2005, p. 1.

"Television's Next Big Shift," *The Economist* (U.S.), March 11, 2006, p. 16.

Edwards Lifesciences LLC

One Edwards Way
Irvine, California 92614
U.S.A.
Telephone: (949) 250-2500
Toll Free: (800) 424-3278
Fax: (949) 250-2525
Web site: http://www.edwards.com

Public Company
Founded: 1961 as Edwards Laboratories
Incorporated: 2000 as Edwards Lifesciences
Employees: 6,300
Sales: $1.32 billion (2009)
Stock Exchanges: New York
Ticker Symbol: EW
NAICS: 339112 Surgical and Medical Instrument Manufacturing; 339113 Surgical Appliance and Supplies Manufacturing

∎ ∎ ∎

Edwards Lifesciences LLC, an Irvine, California-based medical device company, is the world leader in heart valve technology. Its line of tissue heart valves and valve repair products dominate the market. A global leader in critical care products, Edwards is recognized for its pioneering hemodynamic monitoring technologies (including the Swan-Ganz catheter), which are devices inserted directly into the heart or blood vessels to precisely measure cardiac function in acutely ill and surgical patients. The company is also a world leader in vascular therapy products, used to repair diseased blood vessels. As the premier innovator of devices for minimally invasive heart repair, Edwards consistently puts significant resources into the development of new therapies for advanced cardiovascular disease, in 2009 investing up to 13 percent of sales in research and development. Home to the world's most prominent heart valve museum, Edwards makes its headquarters in Irvine, California. The company manufactures products around the globe for distribution in nearly 100 countries.

FIRST COMMERCIAL HEART VALVES

In 1958 retired mechanical engineer Miles "Lowell" Edwards developed an idea for an artificial heart based on his work in hydraulic engineering, the branch of civil engineering concerned with the flow of fluid in a system. A two-time survivor of rheumatic fever as a teenager, Lowell Edwards had always been fascinated by the mechanics of the heart. Armed with a design concept, Edwards consulted Dr. Albert Starr, a surgeon at the University of Oregon, who suggested that Edwards redirect his efforts toward the development of an artificial heart valve instead. Heart valves, which control the flow of blood in the heart, are vital to the heart's ability to pump blood to the body. A successful valve implant had the potential to benefit many thousands of patients with severely reduced cardiac function due to diseased heart valves.

Within two years Edwards and Starr had pioneered a design to replace the mitral valve, which controls the flow of blood from the left upper chamber, or atrium, of the heart to the left lower chamber, or ventricle, of the heart. The artificial valve, consisting of a Silastic ball enclosed by a stainless steel cage attached to a Teflon ring and called the Starr-Edwards mitral ball valve, was considered a design breakthrough. On September 21, 1960, after several animal trials, Starr successfully implanted the first valve into a 52-year-old man with mitral valve disease, an event that was reported worldwide. The patient, the first to survive longer than three months with an implanted mitral valve, lived for 10 years before dying from unrelated causes.

The design of the Starr-Edwards valve would go on to become an industry standard. Within a year of introducing their implantable mitral valve, Edwards and Starr would introduce a mechanical replacement for the aortic valve, the structure that controls the flow of blood from the left ventricle of the heart to the aorta, the largest artery in the body. For the first time, people with severe heart valve disease could look forward to longer, healthier lives. Spurred by these early successes, and in need of a way to manufacture the valves, Edwards went on to found Edwards Laboratories in April 1961, with Starr on board as a consultant. Over the next few years Edwards and Starr redesigned their ball valve several times to improve its safety and function. A version of their original valve design is still in use in the 21st century.

By the late 1960s the competition for new valve designs had heated up. Valve replacement with a mechanical device had saved the lives of hundreds of people. However, recipients of the device were required to take blood thinning medication for the rest of their lives to reduce the risk of blood clots, a requirement that carried serious risks of its own. As a result, new designs aimed at reducing the risk of blood clot formation were developed. These included a mechanical valve with a tilting disk mechanism and the first porcine valve, a biologic tissue valve made from the heart valve of a pig. In 1969, after several years of experimentation, a team led by French surgeon and biochemist Alain Car-

pentier published early clinical results of their work with a chemically treated porcine valve mounted on a Teflon-coated stent, or small metal frame, for smooth insertion. In 1975 Edwards's company would become the first to manufacture this device, called a bioprosthesis, initiating a line of tissue heart valves, manufactured under the Carpentier-Edwards brand, that would come to dominate the global market.

THE SEARCH FOR INNOVATION AND GROWTH

Edwards Laboratories' early forays into the critical care market included the production and marketing of the Fogarty embolectomy catheter, the first balloon catheter, in 1963. The device, developed by cardiovascular surgeon Thomas Fogarty, consisted of a thin tube, inserted into a blood vessel through a small incision, that could be inflated after insertion. Blood clots could then be removed from blood vessels in the arms and legs without the need for major surgery. Use of the Fogarty catheter would transform what was once a high-risk surgical procedure into a minimally invasive procedure with a much better safety profile.

In 1966 American Hospital Supply Corporation acquired Edwards Laboratories, and the company was renamed American Edwards Laboratories. In 1970 American Edwards continued its expansion into critical care with the first Swan-Ganz pulmonary artery catheter, developed in collaboration with two cardiologists, Jeffrey Swan and William Ganz, of Cedars-Sinai Medical Center in Los Angeles. This revolutionary hemodynamic monitoring device gave physicians a quick and relatively simple way to monitor the heart function of critically ill and surgical patients. Over time, the information provided by Swan-Ganz catheters would serve to greatly expand cardiologists' understanding of how the heart works.

On the cardiovascular front, the decision by American Edwards to manufacture the heart valve bioprosthesis introduced by Carpentier was in many ways a bold one, because the new technology presented a direct challenge to the existing Starr-Edwards valve. Carpentier worked closely with American Edwards to develop their line of bioprosthetic heart valves as well as products used in valve repair. In 1974 American Edwards introduced the Carpentier-Edwards Classic annuloplasty ring, a valve repair device, launching a product line that would eventually become the global market leader. A year later the company introduced its first tissue heart valve, the Carpentier-Edwards porcine bioprosthesis. Biologic tissue valves were fast becoming the valve of choice because of their durability, a global trend that would continue into the 21st century.

KEY DATES

1961: Edwards Laboratories is established.
1966: Edwards Laboratories is acquired by American Hospital Supply Corporation to become American Edwards Laboratories.
1985: Baxter International Inc. acquires American Edwards.
2000: Edwards Lifesciences is incorporated.
2004: Percutaneous Valve Technologies Inc. is purchased.

In 1980 American Edwards, now 1,600 employees strong, reorganized into three commercial divisions: cardiovascular, critical care, and noninvasive. In 1981 the first Carpentier-Edwards PERIMOUNT pericardial heart valve was introduced. The PERIMOUNT line of mitral and aortic valve replacements would become the leading tissue valve products worldwide. In 1985, American Edwards was purchased by Baxter International Inc., becoming the cardiovascular arm of that company. The 1990s brought continued growth, with the introduction of the Cosgrove-Edwards valve repair products and the first Vigilance monitor, which provided health care providers with a clear, detailed record of a patient's hemodynamic status. Motivated by a desire for faster growth, in 2000 Edwards would spin off from Baxter and incorporate under a new name, Edwards Lifesciences.

THE 21ST CENTURY: TRANSCATHETER HEART VALVE TECHNOLOGY AND BEYOND

The beginning of the 21st century saw continued growth for the company in the heart valve sector. Working with Alain Cribier, a French interventional cardiologist specializing in transcatheter heart valve surgery, a minimally invasive surgical procedure, Edwards began development of its own transcatheter heart valve technology. Committed to the rapid development of this new technology, which made valve replacement an option for many patients too frail to undergo open-heart surgery, Edwards purchased the start-up Percutaneous Valve Technologies in 2004 for more than $125 million. Clinical trials in patients with heart valve disease began almost immediately. Despite some early setbacks, clinical results proved encouraging, and in 2007 the company launched the Edwards-SAPIEN aortic transcatheter valve in Europe and other international markets. In 2009 annual sales for this heart valve technology topped $110

million, and development of the next generation of products was under way. In the United States, a large-scale clinical trial (PARTNER) of the Edwards-SAPIEN aortic valve technology was ongoing in 2010.

Edwards continued to develop its FloTrac minimally invasive monitoring system, first launched in 2005, for use in monitoring critically ill and surgical patients. In 2010, in a major advance that would expand access to the critical care market, the company made its advanced monitoring technologies compatible with display monitors manufactured by Phillips Healthcare, the industry leader in acute-care patient monitors. Other early 21st century developments included the Odyssey program, an innovative, minimally invasive valve technology that built on the Carpentier-Edwards PERIMOUNT system, and new valve repair products. The TRITON study, a feasibility study for the Odyssey line of minimally invasive aortic valve replacement products, was launched in Europe in 2010.

Driven by strong heart valve sales, Edwards reported annual sales of $1.32 billion for 2009, representing an 11 percent underlying sales growth from the previous year. International sales topped domestic sales at $765.3 million and $556.1 million, respectively, in 2009, as reported in a February 2010 press release.

The near-term and future outlook for Edwards appeared promising, based on the company's continued investment in research and development in its core areas of valve technology and critical care. With its expanding pipeline of new products, continued strong sales of existing products, and divestment of noncore product lines, Edwards Lifesciences expected to benefit from continued growth both in the United States and internationally.

Hanna Schonthal

PRINCIPAL SUBSIDIARIES

Edwards Lifesciences (Asia) Pte. Ltd. (Singapore); Edwards Lifesciences Canada, Inc.; Edwards Lifesciences Comércio de Produtos Médico-Cirúrgicos Ltda. (Brazil); Edwards Lifesciences DR (Dominican Republic); Edwards Lifesciences Ltd. (Japan); Edwards Lifesciences Puerto Rico; Edwards Lifesciences, S.A. (Switzerland).

PRINCIPAL DIVISIONS

Cardiac Surgery Systems and Vascular; Critical Care; Heart Valve Therapy; Transcatheter Valve Replacement.

PRINCIPAL COMPETITORS

Becton, Dickinson and Company; Hospira, Inc.; LeMaitre Vascular, Inc.; Medtronic, Inc.; St. Jude Medical,

Inc.; Terumo Cardiovascular Systems Corporation; W. L. Gore and Associates, Inc.

FURTHER READING

Carpentier, Alain, "The Surprising Rise of Nonthrombogenic Valvular Surgery," *Nature Medicine*, October 2007, p. xvii.

Chaikoff, Elliot L., "The Development of Prosthetic Heart Valves—Lessons in Form and Function," *New England Journal of Medicine*, October 4, 2007, p. 1368.

Chatterjee, Kanu, "The Swan-Ganz Catheters: Past, Present, and Future," *Circulation*, 2009, p. 147.

Conroy, Sherrie, "Edwards Lifesciences: A Passion for Patients," Medical Device and Diagnostic Industry, November 2009, http://www.devicelink.com/mddi/archive/09/11/002.html.

"Edwards Lifesciences' Critical Care Technologies to Be Available via Philips Monitors," Marketwire, January 11, 2010, http://www.marketwire.com/press-release/Edwards-Lifesciences-Critical-Care-Technologies-to-Be-Available-via-Philips-Monitors-NYSE-EW-1099750.htm.

"Edwards Lifesciences Initiates Clinical Study of Minimally Invasive Aortic Valve Surgery System," Marketwire, January 25, 2010, http://www.marketwire.com/press-release/Edwards-Lifesciences-Initiates-Clinical-Study-Minimally-Invasive-Aortic-Valve-Surgery-NYSE-EW-1106385.htm.

"Edwards Lifesciences Reports Strong Fourth Quarter Results," Marketwire, February 4, 2010, http://www.marketwire.com/press-release/Edwards-Lifesciences-Reports-Strong-Fourth-Quarter-Results-NYSE-EW-1112693.htm.

Starr, Albert, "The Artificial Heart Valve," *Nature Medicine*, October 2007, p. xii.

Stewart, Colin, "Heart Repair Overhaul," *Orange County Register*, March 15, 2007.

Strauss, Evelyn, "2007 Winners: Albert Lasker Clinical Medicine Research Award; Award Description—Alain Carpentier and Albert Starr," Lasker Foundation, http://www.laskerfoundation.org/awards/2007_c_description.htm.

Entegris, Inc.

3500 Lyman Boulevard
Chaska, Minnesota 55318
U.S.A.
Telephone: (952) 556-4181
Toll Free: (800) 394-4083
Fax: (952) 556-8022
Web site: http://www.entegris.com

Public Company
Incorporated: 1966 as Fluoroware, Inc.
Employees: 2,200
Sales: $398.6 million (2009)
Stock Exchanges: NASDAQ
Ticker Symbol: ENTG
NAICS: 326122 Plastics Pipe and Pipe Fitting Manufacturing

■ ■ ■

A NASDAQ-listed company, Entegris, Inc., provides the semiconductor and other high technology industries with a broad range of products, materials, and systems that purify, protect from contamination, and transport critical materials used in the manufacturing process. The production of semiconductors is highly complex, requiring multiple steps to build raw silicon wafers into complex integrated circuits. Not only do the raw silicon wafers have to be shipped intact and uncontaminated to semiconductor manufacturers, they are repeatedly combined with silicon, chemicals, gases, and metals as layers of materials are deposited to create the circuit elements of a semiconductor. Entegris products help in the purification and handling of these critical materials through all the steps in the production of a semiconductor device. The company provides similar products and services for high-technology items that employ many of the same manufacturing processes, such as flat panel displays, solar cells, gas lasers, optical and magnetic storage devices, fiber optic cables, aerospace components, biomedical devices, and fuel cells.

Entegris products include wafer carriers and shippers that prevent the contamination and breakage of semiconductor wafers and solar cells during and after manufacturing. Other products include shippers and trays for the manufacture and transport of disk drive components, specialty coatings that purify and protect manufacturing materials, graphite materials for high-end performance applications, and fluid handling and filtration products that purify process gases and fluids and aid in their transport and dispensing. Entegris customers include wafer growers, original equipment manufacturers, and semiconductor manufacturers, including the likes of IBM, Seagate Technology, Samsung, Taiwan Semiconductor Manufacturing, and Freescale Semiconductor. Although based in Chaska, Minnesota, Entegris has global reach, operating manufacturing plants in the United States as well as Yonezawa, Japan, and Kulim, Malaysia. Service centers and other operations are also conducted in China, France, Germany, Israel, Singapore, and Taiwan. About one-third of the company's sale are drawn from Asia, 29 percent from the United States, 21 percent from Japan, and the balance from Europe.

COMPANY PERSPECTIVES

■

Entegris is the global leader in materials integrity management. Its mission is to purify, protect and transport critical materials used in high technology products, processes and services. The Entegris brand will reflect the value Entegris provides to its key stakeholders, including customers, shareholders, employees and communities in which we live.

EARLY YEARS

The origins of Entegris date to 1966 when Fluoroware, Inc., was spun off by Thermotech Industries, founded by Bob Booker and Victor Wallestad. The former established Booker Company in Minnesota in 1947, and Wallestad, a North Dakota farmer who had become involved in the tool and die industry, joined him later. In 1949 they incorporated Thermotech, a plastic injection molding company. Three years later Thermotech formed the Booker & Wallestad division, which would begin serving the needs of semiconductor manufacturers through a referral from DuPont. Delco Radio, a General Motors subsidiary, had crafted some rough semiconductor wafer carriers out of Teflon blocks for making solid state radio circuits and asked DuPont if there was a molding company that could do a better job. DuPont recommended Booker & Wallestad. Delco representative Earl Fowler spent a day at Booker & Wallestad, explaining the microelectronics marketplace to a group of personnel that included the man who would become the longtime chief executive and chairman of Fluoroware and the first chairman of Entegris, Dan Quernemoen. He spearheaded the investigation of this emerging marketplace.

Soon Booker & Wallestad worked up some wafer carrier designs, and Quernemoen began making cold calls to potential customers, asking to speak with the person working with processing wafers. "The receptionist looks at you like, what are you from Mars or something," he recalled in an interview with Craig Addison in 2004 for the trade association Semiconductor and Equipment and Materials International (SEMI). Instead, Quernemoen found a novel way to identify potential customers. Before the lunch hour, he set up a display table of wafer carriers in a company's lobby. "I just cleaned the magazines off the table and set up the products like a Tupperware show and it wasn't long before engineers gathered around and wanted to know what those products were for. ... They [soon] had me in a conference room with six or eight engineers gathered around and really wanted to talk seriously about this stuff and so I did that at more than one place."

FLUOROWARE SPUN OFF: 1966

In addition to making wafer carriers Booker & Wallestad used its expertise in molding Teflon to develop tanks, beakers, and other handling devices used by semiconductor manufacturers. As sales of these products increased in the early 1960s, it became apparent that the operation, which was engaged in a different kind of molding than the rest of Thermotech, needed to be a standalone business. In 1966, with Wallestad providing the money and becoming the sole owner, the niche unit was spun off as Fluoroware, the name drawn from the fluorocarbon materials used in the company's products, which at the time fell under the category of lab ware.

During Fluoroware's first year in business, Quernemoen was not involved, having left to start a plastic molding company in Phoenix, Q&W Plastics, involved in the making of hearing aid parts. He also did some subcontract molding for Fluoroware, which enjoyed immediate success, becoming profitable in its first year. Wallestad soon proposed buying Q&W and having Quernemoen establish a sales and marketing operating in San Francisco, the heart of the semiconductor industry. Quernemoen agreed and relocated to the Bay Area. He ran the California division until 1970, when a slump in semiconductors, which would become a common occurrence in the highly cyclical business, led Fluoroware to shut it down. Quernemoen returned to Minnesota and eventually became Fluoroware's general manager.

One of the Thermotech employees Wallestad took with him to Fluoroware was mold maker Joel Elftman, who also held a job as a die maker for another company. He became Fluoroware's supervisor of design and tool making. Later, when the company was hired by Collins Radio to build a silicon wafer drying mechanism, Elftman headed the team that invented the semiconductor industry's first centrifugal spin dryer. The success of this product led to the development of a wafer rinsing and drying system. Because it strayed from the core business of Fluoroware, this nascent equipment business was spun off in 1973 as Fluoroware Systems, Inc. By contract, Fluoroware Systems was required to change its name within two years to avoid marketplace confusion, and it became FSI International, Inc. Holding a 25 percent interest, Elftman ran the company, and Wallestad owned the remaining stake.

Spinning off FSI made sense, because Fluoroware was having trouble keeping pace with demand for its

KEY DATES

1966: Fluoroware, Inc., is founded.
1973: Fluoroware Systems, Inc., is spun off.
1980: Empak, Inc., is spun off.
1997: Koroean joint venture is formed.
1999: Empak merger results in name change to Entegris, Inc.
2005: Entegris merges with Mykrolis Corporation.
2008: Poco Graphite, Inc., is acquired.

core products. Quernemoen was continually frustrated by shortages of Teflon from DuPont, which failed to recognize the potential of the semiconductor processing market. After years of paying regular visits to DuPont's Delaware headquarters, and taking DuPont personnel to trade shows to witness the worldwide clamor for Fluoroware's Teflon products, Quernemoen was able to finally secure a meeting with DuPont's chief executive and arrange a reliable supply of Teflon to meet the Fluoroware's growing needs.

QUERNEMOEN NAMED PRESIDENT: 1979

Wallestad developed Parkinson's disease and by 1979 was unable to run the company, naming Quernemoen to take over as president. At the time, Fluoroware employed 125 people and posted annual revenues of $10 million. It was also around this time that another spin-off took shape. Fluoroware had been producing shipping containers for wafer growers as a natural extension of their business, but as orders increased, the company's molding equipment could not handle the volume. In 1980 Empak, Inc., was spun off to concentrate on this market, with employee Wayne Bongard buying the business at an amount just above book value. It was one of the last deals Wallestad was involved in before his death.

Quernemoen established a goal of becoming a $100 million company. Fluoroware increased market share steadily in the first half of the 1980s, but sales began to tail off at the end of 1985 when the semiconductor industry underwent another downturn. As a result, the company placed greater emphasis on exporting as well as increasing revenues through the development of new products and marketplaces. One Fluoroware subsidiary, Galtek Corp., established early in Quernemoen's tenure as chief executive, enjoyed especially good success overseas. The company, whose name was shorthand for

"gas and liquid handling technology," produced fittings, tubes, and valves for the chemical processing industry. In 1981 exports accounted for 8.5 percent of sales, but that amount increased to 20 percent just three years later. By 1987 the unit was contributing about 25 percent of Fluoroware's $30 million in annual revenues. At this point, duplication was developing between Galtek and its parent company, and in March 1987 much of Galtek's manufacturing operation was folded into Fluoroware to money. Galtek would eventually become merely a brand in Entegris' fluid and handling product lines.

NEW CHIEF EXECUTIVE: 1996

After the semiconductor industry rebounded, Fluoroware resumed its pattern of strong growth. In early 1992 the company bought 30 more acres of land in Chaska to expand its facilities. In the first half of the 1990s sales increased more than 200 percent, totaling $190 million in fiscal 1996, well above Quernemoen's $100 million goal. By this time Fluoroware was manufacturing its products in Germany and Japan as well as the United States, and it maintained sales and marketing offices in more than 40 countries. The company looked to bolster its international footprint through joint ventures. In 1996 it teamed with First Engineering Plastic of Singapore, forming Fluoroware Asia South to manufacture Fluoroware products in Woodlands, Singapore. A year later a similar joint venture was established in Korea. Called F.J.V. Korea Ltd., it was co-owned with Jell Chemical Co., Ltd., and Nippon Valqua Industries. With Korea emerging as that region's most important market in the semiconductor industry, the country was clearly an important market for Fluoroware. The Singapore and Korea ventures were struck during the tenure of a new CEO. Upon reaching the age of 65 in 1996, Quernemoen turned over day-to-day control of Fluoroware to 47-year-old Stan Geyer, who had been with the company since 1978 and had played an important role in its growth. Quernemoen remained chairman of the board.

Revenues increased to $277.3 million and net income to $19.2 million in fiscal 1997. During the rest of the 1990s the numbers fell off, however, slipping to sales of $242 million and earnings of $6 million in 1999. A major reason for this diminished performance was competition from the company Fluoroware had spun off some 20 years earlier, Empak. Because of its shared heritage with Fluoroware, Empak knew how to mold Teflon and eventually decided to become a competitor. Empak had manufacturing operations in Minnesota, Colorado, Korea, and Malaysia, as well as an Advanced Polymers group in Houston that recycled and purified polymers. The presence of Empak in the critical materials management market allowed customers to play Empak and Fluoroware off one another, leading to serious price erosion. Fluoroware approached Empak about a possible merger that would not only increase their mutual market share in overlapping products but also return the packaging business to Fluoroware to create a broader-based company, one that could service the entire supply chain for semiconductor manufacturing.

ENTEGRIS NAME ADOPTED: 1999

Bongard, who remained Empak's owner, showed little initial interest in a merger, but the attraction of the idea grew. Unfortunately, Bongard suffered a heart attack and died in 1998. Before his passing, however, he indicated to his CEO a desire to make the deal, albeit with certain conditions. The merger was negotiated with these stipulations in mind and finally completed in the summer of 1999. The combined enterprise now began doing business under a new name, Entegris, Inc., chosen for its similarity to the word "integrity."

Following the merger, Entegris made plans to go public, conducting an initial offering of stock in July 2000. Although it raised $143 million, the company was disappointed in the price it fetched, hoping for $18 a share but settling for $11. The stock then began trading on the NASDAQ. For fiscal year 2000, Entegris reported revenues of $343.5 million and net income of nearly $48 million.

Early in 2001 the next steps in a succession plan were implemented. Geyer stepped down as CEO and became chairman, while Quernemoen retired and became chairman emeritus. Taking over as president and CEO was chief operating officer, Jim Dauwalter, who had been with the company since his college days in the early 1970s. It was not, however, the best of times to take the helm. With the crash of the high technology sector, the semiconductor industry experienced the worst slump in its history. Entegris was forced to close a Minnesota plant, resulting in a loss of 130 jobs. Revenues dipped to $343.4 million and net income to $38.6 million in fiscal 2001. The impact of the downturn became more evident in fiscal 2002 when sales plummeted to $219.8 million and earnings dropped to $2.8 million. Between 2002 and 2003 the company closed six plants.

Entegris sought diversification to limit its exposure to the cyclical nature of the semiconductor industry, and fortunately its advantageous cash position, as well as stock that was now available, allowed it to buy into other businesses. In January 2003 the company pursued the life sciences market by acquiring Electrol Specialties

Company, a maker of "Clean-in-Place" technology products used by biotechnology firms. The idea was to marry the expertise of Entegris in fluoropolymer materials and fluid handling with Electrol's stainless steel fabrication skills to develop innovative products for the life science field. Another new area for Entegris was the fuel cell market, which the company entered in October 2002. As part of its development in this market, the company installed a 5-kilowatt fuel cell in its Chaska factory in August 2003 to meet some of its power needs. Entegris made other acquisitions as well to support its core business. In February 2003 it bought the wafer and reticle carrier product lines of Asyst Technologies, Inc., and in May 2004 Entegris expanded its presence in Europe by acquiring a precision parts cleaning business in Montpellier, France. The company was able to rebuild revenues to $329 million in fiscal 2004 and $347.3 million in fiscal 2005.

COMPANY MERGES WITH MYKROLIS CORPORATION: 2005

A more important transaction was completed in 2005 when Entegris merged with Mykrolis Corporation, a Boston-area company that provided purification systems for liquid and gases used in the semiconductor industry. Entegris and Mykrolis were an excellent fit because they manufactured different products but sold to many of the same customers. Mykrolis had been spun off from MicroElectronics, Inc., in 2001 and later in the year went public. In the Entegris and Mykrolis merger, Entegris became the surviving entity after the $1.3 billion stock exchange was completed. The deal also brought a new CEO, Gideon Argov, the chief executive of Mykrolis.

Shortly after Argov took charge, Entegris elected to divest its life science, fuel cell, and other interests in order to grow its core business and pursue other, more promising opportunities. In 2006 it expanded its manufacturing facility in Kulim, Malaysia, and a year later acquired the semiconductor coating business of Surmet Corporation. In 2008 it also acquired Poco Graphite, a leading provider of high performance graphite and silicon carbide, the addition of which opened doors to such markets as medical, aerospace, and specialty industrial. The enlarged Entegris recorded revenues of $672.9 million in 2006 (the fiscal and calendar years now coinciding), but difficult business conditions once again visited the industry, and revenues fell to $626.2 million in 2007 and $544.7 million in 2008. By 2009 revenues had dropped to $398.6 million. Forced to cut costs, the company closed a plant and warehouse in Chaska in 2009 and moved manufacturing to other sites in the United States and Asia. While painful in the short run, these and other cost control measures, as well as putting new growth initiatives in place, promised to lay the foundation for future growth.

Ed Dinger

PRINCIPAL SUBSIDIARIES

Entegris Asia LLC; Entegris Pacific Lts.; Entegris International Holdings B.V.; Entegris Malaysia Sdn. Bhd.; Entegris Precision Technology Corp.; Entegris logistics, Inc.; Entegris Materials, Inc.; Poco Graphite Holdings, Inc.

PRINCIPAL COMPETITORS

3M Company; Pall Corporation; SAES Pure Gas Inc.

FURTHER READING

Addison, Craig, "SEMI Oral History Interview: Dan Quernemoen," SEMI, Feburary 24, 2004, http://www.semi. org/en/P038687.

Beal, Dave, "Squaring Off a Cyclical Industry," *Saint Paul Pioneer Press*, February 6, 2005.

Bocklage, Judy, "Entegris Agrees to Buy Mykrolis for $578 Million," *Wall Street Journal*, March 22, 2005, p. D6.

Davis, Riccardo A., "Fluoroware Shuffles Top Management," *Saint Paul Pioneer Press*, October 17, 1996, p. 3E.

"Fluoroware, Empak Agree to Merge," *Electronic News*, March 22, 1999, p. 24.

Jones, Jim, "Small Chaska Firm Takes Big Role in Export Market," *Star Tribune* (Minneapolis, MN), May 29, 1987, p. 7B.

Kennedy, Patrick, "Entegris Inc. IPO Raised $143 Million on First Day," *Star Tribune* (Minneapolis, MN), July 12, 2000, p. 1D.

Lipchitz, Rebecca, "Mykrolis in $1.3 Billion Merger," *Sun* (Lowell, MA), March 22, 2005.

Olson, Mark W., "Entegris—A Changing, Growing Industry," *Chaska Herald* (Chaska, MN), March 22, 2001.

St. Anthony, Neal, "Entegris to Acquire Boston Firm," *Star Tribune* (Minneapolis, MN), March 22, 2005, p. 1D.

FirstEnergy Corp.

76 South Main Street
Akron, Ohio 44308
U.S.A.
Toll Free: (800) 633-4766
Fax: (330) 384-3866
Web site: http://www.firstenergycorp.com

Public Company
Incorporated: 1930 as Ohio Edison Company
Employees: 14,698
Sales: $12.97 billion (2009)
Stock Exchanges: New York
Ticker Symbol: FE
NAICS: 221112 Fossil Fuel Electric Power Generation; 221113 Nuclear Electric Power Generation; 221121 Electric Bulk Power Transmission and Control; 221122 Electric Power Distribution

■ ■ ■

Based in Akron, Ohio, FirstEnergy Corp. is the fifth-largest investor-owned power company in the United States, with 4.5 million customers. Through its regional subsidiaries, FirstEnergy has a total power generating capacity of 14,000 watts, serving consumers in Ohio, New Jersey, and Pennsylvania. Its unregulated subsidiary, First Energy Solutions, sells electricity to customers outside FirstEnergy's core region. While the bulk of FirstEnergy's electricity is derived from coal-burning power plants, the company also operates a number of nuclear power facilities.

EMERGENCE OF A MAJOR UTILITY

FirstEnergy began as the Ohio Edison Company, founded in June 1930 by the Commonwealth and Southern Corporation when it consolidated five Ohio public utility companies: Northern Ohio Power & Light Company of Akron, Pennsylvania-Ohio Power & Light Company of Youngstown, Ohio Edison Company of Springfield, London Light & Power Company, and Akron Steam Heating Company. Ohio Edison established headquarters in Akron, Ohio. A. C. Blinn became vice president and general manager. The company began operations without a president.

During its first full year of operation, Ohio Edison grew despite the Great Depression. It constructed a new office building in Youngstown, Ohio, and acquired electric distribution systems through a trade, which brought it properties in Ravenna, Medina, Doylestown, and Seville, Ohio, in exchange for less-profitable assets north of Springfield, Ohio. In 1931 Ohio Edison began construction of an East Akron power transmission line, which replaced power purchased from a Cleveland utility company. Ohio Edison's finances were strained during the Depression, however, and both lower-level and senior-management workers took pay cuts to keep their jobs, and stockholder dividends were suspended. The company often had to wait for customers to pay their bills, but it met its payroll.

As a means of boosting electric sales, from its outset Ohio Edison promoted and marketed electric appliances, an aspect of operations that endured for more than four decades. During the early 1930s, division offices established small-appliance service departments and sales departments, which expanded their inventory as new products entered the marketplace. Blinn became Ohio Edison's first president in 1938 and continued to guide the company through most of World War II. After the United States entered the war in 1941, Ohio Edison and other utilities were placed under the supervision of the War Production Board and were temporarily restricted from selling appliances and constructing new power lines.

Industrial electricity sales skyrocketed with wartime production. In response to the increased need for power generation during the war, Ohio Edison constructed the new R.E. Burger plant in Belmont County, Ohio, and expanded plants in Akron, Marion, and Warren, Ohio. In 1944 Blinn was replaced as president by the expansion-minded Walter Sammis, who had been instrumental in forming the company 14 years earlier. In 1944 in one of his first moves as president, Sammis orchestrated the acquisition of Pennsylvania Power Company (Penn Power) from Commonwealth & Southern. Penn Power had been incorporated through a consolidation move the same year Ohio Edison was formed, and as a new wholly owned subsidiary, it gave the Ohio Edison system more than 1,500 square miles of service area in western Pennsylvania.

GROWTH IN THE POSTWAR ERA

Following the war, restrictions on utilities were lifted. Postwar prosperity made it easier to obtain credit, and Ohio Edison sales of new appliances boomed. At the same time, industrial expansion gave rise to increased residential and nonresidential electric sales and left the company in need of increased power generation. Ohio Edison responded to that need in the first few years following the war with additions to the Burger plant and to facilities in Springfield and Akron.

In 1949 in its first postwar acquisition, Ohio Edison acquired an electric distribution system serving Mc-

Donald, Ohio. Also in 1949 Ohio Edison became an independent company after the Securities and Exchange Commission (SEC) forced Commonwealth & Southern to divest its interests in Ohio Edison. As a result of another SEC divestiture order, Ohio Edison's competitor, Ohio Public Service Company (OPS), also became an independent company in 1949, and in 1950 Ohio Edison acquired OPS. The OPS merger added the Ohio communities of Sandusky, Marion, Mansfield, Massillon, Lorain, and Warren to the Ohio Edison system, pushing the company's customer base to more than 500,000 and making Ohio Edison the tenth-largest electric utility in the United States in operating revenues.

During the mid-1950s, Ohio Edison continued to add to its system and acquired distribution systems in the Ohio communities of Leroy, Huron, and Plain City. To keep pace with those acquisitions and increased electrical use, postwar power plant expansion followed, and in 1954 the company added a new plant in Niles, Ohio. Ohio Edison also made additions to the Burger and Edgewater plants in Lorain, Ohio, and in 1959 it opened the W. H. Sammis plant in Stratton.

CONSOLIDATION AND TRANSITION

By the early 1960s, Ohio Edison's service area had grown to within five miles of Cleveland's city limits, and its subsidiary Penn Power was within three miles of Pittsburgh. In 1962 Penn Power expanded its service area northward from Pittsburgh and acquired a 121-square-mile distribution system in Crawford County, Pennsylvania, abutting its parent company's Ohio network. After 20 years at the helm, Sammis retired in 1964 and was replaced by D. Bruce Mansfield, who quickly moved Ohio Edison into an era of electric utility power pools formed through joint plant ownership. In 1965 Ohio Edison acquired the municipally owned distribution system of Lowellville, Ohio, just southeast of Youngstown. That same year Ohio Edison made its first move toward forming a power pool and joined with Cleveland Electric Illuminating Company (CEIC) to construct and operate a power plant addition for their common areas of service.

In 1967 Ohio Edison joined with CEIC, Duquesne Light Company, and Toledo Edison Company to form a power pool known as Central Area Power Coordination Group (CAPCO), designed to share the burden of constructing and operating power plants. CAPCO members initially committed to the installation of six large generating units. In 1970 Ohio Edison began construction in Shippingport, Pennsylvania, on a CAPCO project, the firm's first nuclear-powered facility,

KEY DATES

1930: The Ohio Edison Company is founded.
1938: A. C. Blinn becomes first president of Ohio Edison.
1944: Walter Sammis succeeds A. C. Blinn as company president.
1967: Ohio Edison joins Cleveland Electric Illuminating Company, Duquesne Light Company, and Toledo Edison Company to form the Central Area Power Coordination Group.
1997: Ohio Edison and Centerior Energy Corporation merge to form FirstEnergy Corp.
2001: FirstEnergy acquires GPU Inc.
2003: The North American Electric Reliability Council finds FirstEnergy guilty of violations relating to a major blackout in the northeast United States.
2010: FirstEnergy reaches a preliminary agreement to purchase Allegheny Energy Inc.

Beaver Valley power station. Three years later the company discontinued its appliance sales operations, which had been declining since the 1950s.

In 1972 Ohio Edison acquired the 5700-customer municipal electric system of Norwalk, Ohio. In 1975 it added the Hiram, Ohio, municipal system serving 271 customers and the former East Palatine, Ohio, municipal system with 2,653 customers. Also in 1975 John R. White, a former executive vice president and 22-year veteran of the company, succeeded Mansfield as president, and CAPCO's first new facility, the Bruce Mansfield plant in Shippingport, Pennsylvania, began operation under control of Ohio Edison's subsidiary Penn Power. In 1976 the first unit of the Beaver Valley nuclear plant began operation under the control of Duquesne Light Company. Ohio Edison owned a 35 percent share.

WEATHER, LABOR, AND ENVIRONMENTAL PROBLEMS

Despite the company's increased power capacity, White's five-year tenure as president was marred by weather, labor, and environmental complications. A long period of sub-zero days in January 1977 resulted in record electricity demand and made the Ohio River impassible for barges bringing coal to company plants. One year later, the worst blizzard in Ohio's history, on January 26

and 27, resulted in major power outages, with high winds and frigid temperatures stalling repairs for a time.

In 1978 a 109-day coal miners' strike depleted Ohio Edison's fuel reserves at its coal-fired generating plants, forcing the company to turn to backup generating sources and to purchase power from other utilities. That same year, 2,000 members of the Utility Workers Union of America went on strike for two months at five of Ohio Edison's nine plants and at its two largest power-line operations. Foremen, supervisory personnel, and technicians ran the operations. The strike was resolved only after the company threatened to hire permanent replacement workers.

During the miners' strike, the U.S. Environmental Protection Agency (EPA) filed suit against Ohio Edison to push the company into compliance with the Clean Air Act standards and install pollution-control devices. In a settlement reached three years later, Ohio Edison agreed to pay the government more than $1.5 million for past emission violations and install more than $500 million in antipollution devices, with the bulk earmarked for the company's Sammis plant.

NEW FOCUS ON PROFITABILITY

Mansfield retired in 1980 and was replaced by Justin T. Rogers Jr., an executive vice president and 22-year veteran of the company. Rogers took over a company that officials conceded was suffering from inflation, a bulging construction budget, high fuel prices, and a low bond rating. In one of his first moves as president, Rogers took Ohio Edison out of what had become its unprofitable steam power operations. He also sold steam systems in Akron and Youngstown and abandoned a similar operation in Springfield. Citing the political and regulatory problems facing nuclear plants following a 1979 accident at Three Mile Island power plant, in 1980 CAPCO agreed to cancel four nuclear power plants scheduled for construction.

During his first two years in office, Rogers led the company over four major legal hurdles, including the 1981 settlement with the EPA over emission controls at the Sammis plant. In February 1980 Ohio Edison was one of four utilities that agreed to settle an antitrust suit filed by the city of Cleveland five years earlier. Ohio Edison denied charges of conspiring to force the city's municipal electric light plant out of business, but agreed to pay $500,000 to the city to avoid future litigation. It also was to provide technical assistance to the city's plant.

In March 1980 Ohio Edison dropped a one-year-old suit against Exxon Corporation over delivery of nuclear fuel, after Exxon agreed to renegotiate its contract. One year later North American Coal Co. consented to dropping a breach-of-contract suit it had filed against Ohio Edison, after the fuel supplier agreed to a contract giving the utility more favorable options for the purchase and delivery of coal.

With the help of new contracts, Ohio Edison's average fuel costs were the lowest in the state for an investor-owned electric company by 1982. That same year Rogers began streamlining operations and cutting staff. The company also began marketing its increased electric generating capacity in 1982, and during the next two years landed long-term, bulk-sales contracts with utilities in New Jersey, Ohio, and Washington, D.C. In 1984 the company initiated a price incentive program for new or expanding industries to increase industrial sales in its own service area.

ADAPTING TO SHIFTING MARKET CONDITIONS

In 1985 Ohio Edison suspended construction of the second unit of a nuclear power plant in North Perry, Ohio, but continued work on its Perry 1 and Beaver Valley 2 nuclear units, which became operational in November 1987. To reduce the revenue required to provide a profit on the two nuclear units, Ohio Edison agreed to sell and then lease back portions of the units upon their completion, while retaining a 35 percent interest in Perry 1 and a 41 percent interest in Beaver Valley 2. With the opening of the two nuclear units, Ohio Edison's credit rating received a boost in 1987. That same year, the company negotiated a 13-year coal contract with North American Coal. Ohio Edison also renegotiated a power sale agreement with Potomac Electric Power Company of Washington, D.C., with an 18-year agreement expected to give Ohio Edison $150 million in annual sales.

With bulk sales on the rise and Ohio Edison's service area seeing an influx of diverse business and industry, Ohio Edison's total sales surpassed the $2 billion mark for the first time in 1988. That same year the company formed two wholly owned finance-related subsidiaries, OES Capital, Incorporated, and OES Fuel, Incorporated. Both subsidiaries began doing business in 1989, with OES Capital financing customer accounts receivable and OES Fuel financing the purchase of nuclear fuel.

During the late 1980s, Ohio Edison began to actively change its image on environmental matters. In 1989 a coal technology project that reduced emissions at its Lorain, Ohio, plant received the Ohio Governor's Award for Outstanding Achievement in Waste Management and Pollution Control. In 1990 Ohio Edison began studying the feasibility of burning treated municipal waste at coal-fired generating plants and became the first Ohio utility to test-burn waste tires. The following year Ohio Edison was one of a group of utilities that won a $33 million government contract to build a system at the company's Niles plant to reduce pollutants associated with acid rain.

In line with its ongoing plans to trim payroll costs, Ohio Edison initiated an employee stock ownership program in 1990 to help the company reduce costs of matching contributions to employee savings plans, and it suspended its bonus program for senior management. Ohio Edison began 1991 with 1,100 fewer employees than it had a decade earlier and was committed to further workforce reductions. In the early part of the decade, the company's new strategy called for delaying costly plant construction by encouraging off-peak hour use through rate incentives, maintaining its customer base with reasonable rates, and broadening sales through further incentives to new and expanding businesses. At the time the company appeared to be in a strong position, with enough generating capacity to carry it through the end of the 20th century and to accommodate anticipated sales growth both in its service area and through power sale agreements. Ohio Edison also seemed poised to meet the 1996 compliance deadline established by the 1990 Clean Air Act amendments, with almost half of the company's generating capacity coming from nuclear or other units that would not need major additions of sulfur-dioxide control equipment.

AGE OF DEREGULATION

The 1990s was an era of unprecedented consolidation in the power industry, as deregulation enabled utilities to begin vying for customers outside of their core geographical regions. In order to remain viable in this increasingly competitive marketplace, Ohio Edison was forced to seek ways to reduce expenses, while also exploring new areas for expansion. In September 1996 the company announced a plan to acquire Centerior Energy Corporation for $1.61 billion. Based in Independence, Ohio, Centerior was created in 1985 by the merger of Toledo Edison and Cleveland Electric Illuminating. Centerior had struggled in recent years, as high operating costs and significant investments in nuclear power had left the company unable to offer competitive rates. In the eyes of many analysts, the merger of Ohio Edison and Centerior made sound fiscal sense.

Upon completion of the deal, a new energy holding company, FirstEnergy Corp., was formed. Ohio Edison continued to exist as a subsidiary of the new entity. The combined company immediately became the 11th largest investor-owned power company in the United States, with 2.1 million customers throughout Ohio and western Pennsylvania and combined annual revenues of $5 billion. The merger also promised to enable FirstEnergy to implement significant cost savings over the coming decade, primarily through reductions in its workforce and the elimination of redundancies at its various facilities. According to company estimates, the cost-cutting measures had the potential to lower operating expenses by $1 billion over a ten-year period.

Entering the new decade, FirstEnergy remained intent on increasing its market strength through expansion into new territories. In mid-2000 the company announced its purchase of GPU Inc., a utility with operations in New Jersey and Pennsylvania, in a deal worth roughly $12 billion. The acquisition gave FirstEnergy the sixth-largest customer base among investor-owned energy companies in the United States. After clearing a series of regulatory hurdles in several states, the merger was completed in November 2001. That same month, FirstEnergy sold four of its power plants to Minnesota-based NRG Energy Inc. for $1.36 billion, a move designed to help finance the GPU acquisition.

FirstEnergy's ambitious growth strategy soon began to take a toll on its financial health, however, and by mid-2003 the company was $12.5 billion in debt. In August, a U.S. district court found the company in violation of the Clean Air Act, dating back to its renovation of a power plant in Stratton, Ohio, during the 1980s and 1990s. That same month, FirstEnergy was implicated in a power outage that left approximately 50 million people in the United States and Canada without electricity. The outage was deemed by many observers to be the worst blackout in North American history, and its source was eventually traced to four of the company's power lines outside of Cleveland. In a report filed in November 2003, the North American Electric Reliability Council (NERC) determined that the blackout could have been prevented if FirstEnergy had been in compliance with NERC standards.

FOCUSED ON EXPANSION

In 2005 the U.S. Congress passed the Energy Policy Act, a law designed to promote further consolidation in the power industry. The law prompted a great deal of speculation regarding FirstEnergy's future, as many observers wondered whether the company would continue to grow through acquisitions or become the target of a takeover by a larger company. As the decade came to a close, the company found itself fighting to retain control over its existing customer base, as more and more competitors began to seek ways to enter the Ohio energy market. One new rival, the nonprofit

Northeast Ohio Public Energy Council (NOPEC), had already attracted more than 535,000 of FirstEnergy's customers by July 2009.

In the face of this competition, FirstEnergy remained determined to increase efficiency through acquisition. In February 2010 the company reached a preliminary agreement to purchase rival Allegheny Energy Inc., a utility based in Pennsylvania, for $8.5 billion. With the acquisition, FirstEnergy expected to become one of the largest utilities in the nation, with 6.1 million customers and projected revenues of $16 billion a year. In an increasingly cutthroat energy market, FirstEnergy's focus on expansion seemed like a sound business strategy going forward.

Roger W. Rouland
Updated, Stephen Meyer

PRINCIPAL SUBSIDIARIES

American Transmission Systems, Inc.; Cleveland Electric Illuminating Company; FirstEnergy Generation Corp.; FirstEnergy Nuclear Operating Company; FirstEnergy Service Company; FirstEnergy Solutions Corp.; Jersey Central Power & Light Company; Metropolitan Edison Company; Ohio Edison Company; Pennsylvania Electric Company; Pennsylvania Power Company; Toledo Edison Company.

PRINCIPAL COMPETITORS

American Electric Power Company, Inc.; Dominion Resources, Inc.; Public Service Enterprise Group Incorporated.

FURTHER READING

Block, Donna, and Claire Poole, "FirstEnergy to Acquire Allegheny Energy in $8.5B Deal," *Daily Deal*, February 11, 2010.

Fabrikant, Geraldine, "FirstEnergy Said to Be in Talks to Acquire GPU for $4.4 Billion," *New York Times*, August 7, 2000.

The Fiftieth Anniversary Issue: Ohio Edisonian. Akron: Ohio Edison Company, 1980.

Finer, Jonathan, "FirstEnergy Faced String of Difficulties," *Washington Post*, August 19, 2003.

Maugans, Edward H., "The Cleveland Electric-Toledo Edison Affiliation: Stars in the Right Places," *Public Utilities Fortnightly*, July 24, 1986.

Miller, Jay, "FirstEnergy, Competitor in Power Struggle; Nonprofit NOPEC Vies for Market Share," *Crain's Cleveland Business*, July 20, 2009.

————, "New Act Sparks Merger Talk in Electric Industry; Will FirstEnergy Be Hunter or Hunted?" *Crain's Cleveland Business*, January 16, 2006.

Salpukas, Agis, "Ohio Edison Plans to Buy Another Utility for $1.6 Billion," *New York Times*, September 17, 1996.

Teather, David, "FirstEnergy Loses Power," *Guardian* (London), August 19, 2003.

Truini, Joe, "Power Industry Suffers Setback; FirstEnergy Loses Landmark Case," *Waste News*, August 18, 2003, p. 1.

Fluor Corporation

———— ■ ————

6700 Las Colinas Boulevard
Irving, Texas 75039
U.S.A.
Telephone: (469) 398-7000
Fax: (469) 398-7255
Web site: http://www.fluor.com

Public Company
Incorporated: 1924 as Fluor Construction Company
Employees: 46,000
Sales: $22.32 billion (2008)
Stock Exchanges: New York
Ticker Symbol: FLR
NAICS: 541330 Engineering Services; 236220 Commercial and Institutional Building Construction; 237310 Highway Construction; 238190 Other Foundation, Structure, and Building Exterior Contractors; 541310 Architectural Services; 811310 Commercial and Industrial Machinery Repair and Maintenance Services

■ ■ ■

Fluor Corporation is one of the world's largest engineering, procurement, construction, and maintenance companies. Its five main segments, Energy and Chemicals, Industrial and Infrastructure, Government, Power, and Global Services, provide a full range of services to public and private clients in the United States and more than 15 other countries. For several years Fluor has been ranked within the Fortune 500 and has also been rated among the top companies of its kind in

terms of size, quality of management, innovative strategies, and safety measures. *Fortune* magazine, the National Safety Council, and other independent observers recognize that Fluor demonstrates an exceptional ability to complete the terms of its contracts, even when faced with extreme challenges in far-flung locations.

EARLY DECADES: 1912–29

In 1912 Fluor Construction Company was founded by John Simon Fluor Sr., who had immigrated from Switzerland to the United States in the late 1880s. A carpenter, Fluor helped two brothers start a saw and paper mill in Wisconsin in 1890. He served as manager at the mill. Twelve years later Fluor headed to California, where he started his own general construction business.

As J. Robert Fluor remarked in a speech he gave in 1977, J. Simon Fluor Sr. was known as a highly ethical perfectionist. During the company's early years, the founder and his venture's reputation spread quickly. The Southern California Gas Company hired him to build an office and meter shops in 1915. That year Industrial Fuel Supply Company offered Fluor a construction contract for a compressor station (where gas is reduced in volume).

Discoveries of oil during that time were adding momentum to California's petroleum industry. Fluor began to pursue ways to meet the industry's demands. For example, in 1921 a client hired him to design and erect a cooling tower to reduce inefficiency and waste. Called the "Buddha tower" because of its appearance, his structure was a landmark product and held such

COMPANY PERSPECTIVES

Fluor is a FORTUNE 500 company that delivers engineering, procurement, construction, maintenance (EPCM), and project management to governments and clients in diverse industries around the world. For nearly a century, clients have selected Fluor as their company of choice to complete challenging projects in remote parts of the world.

Founded as a construction company in 1912, Fluor quickly built a reputation for applying innovative methods and performing precise engineering and construction work within the emerging petroleum industry. Today, Fluor continues to develop and implement innovative solutions for complex project issues in diverse industries, including chemicals and petrochemicals, commercial and institutional (C&I), government services, life sciences, manufacturing, mining, oil and gas, power, renewable energy, telecommunications, and transportation infrastructure.

merit that other companies in California, such as Julian Petroleum, hired Fluor to construct similar towers at their sites.

In 1924 Fluor incorporated his business with a capital investment of $100,000. Clients and projects continued. In 1925, recognizing a need to have specially trained staff, Fluor hired his first engineer, Donald Darnell. Others joining the company were the founder's sons, two of whom (J. Simon Fluor Jr. and Peter Fluor) became particularly notable.

Peter Fluor had a degree of salesmanship that earned him the nickname "the company engine." Between 1924 and 1929 annual sales grew from $100,000 to $1.5 million. In need of additional capital, in 1929 the company reincorporated and changed its name to Fluor Corporation Ltd. Peter Fluor and J. Simon Fluor Jr. encouraged company employees to take advantage of the company's success by offering them a stock purchasing opportunity.

A DOMESTIC AND INTERNATIONAL OUTLOOK: 1930–49

In 1930 Peter Fluor convinced his father and brothers to adopt a more expansive approach. Until that year the company had operated within California. Peter Fluor

persuaded his family members to let him propose a project with the Panhandle Eastern Pipeline Company. Panhandle hired Fluor to build compressor stations along an extensive pipeline being built to deliver oil from Texas to Indianapolis, Indiana, and then to Chicago, Illinois. The project with Panhandle resulted in enough approval from J. Simon Fluor Sr. that he also agreed in the early 1930s to open a Midwestern office, in Kansas City, Missouri.

Despite the Great Depression, Fluor's progress continued. Shell Oil Company hired the firm to build a $100,000 refining unit in Wood River, Illinois. The company founder registered patents on two important products of this period. The Fluor aerator tower was patented in 1932, and the Fluor air-cooler muffler was patented in 1938.

World War II brought specific energy needs. Early in the war years, Fluor was hired to establish facilities and train personnel in high-octane gasoline and synthetic rubber production (required for military fleets and operations). Sinclair Oil Company selected Fluor to design and build such a plant using a sulfuric acid alkylation process at Sinclair's Watson, California, refinery. Because of Fluor's success with these activities, more jobs emerged, and the company was involved with more than one-third of the high-octane gasoline produced in the United States during this era.

J. Simon Fluor Sr. died in 1944. Peter Fluor succeeded him as president, and J. Simon Fluor Jr. became executive vice president. From 1945 to 1947 Fluor received contracts for facility construction or expansion of refineries and natural gas plants in Canada, Venezuela, and Saudi Arabia. On the domestic scene, in 1946 Carter Oil Company commissioned Fluor to take responsibility for building a refinery in Billings, Montana, and making it operational. With these design and construction projects completed or under way, Fluor's reputation as a refinery engineering firm was growing significantly.

In 1947 Peter Fluor died unexpectedly at age 52. After an interim replacement, in 1949 Darnell, the company's first professional engineer, became head of Fluor. Meanwhile, despite these shifts in leadership, the company's substantial international expansion in North and South America and in the Middle East was such that Fluor formed its Gas-Gasoline Division, centered in Houston, Texas, in 1948.

GOVERNMENT CONTRACTS AND PROJECTS ABROAD

At the start of the 1950s the company's stock began trading over the counter. Leadership changed, too. Darnell became chairman of the company. J. Simon Fluor

KEY DATES

1912: J. Simon Fluor Sr. moves to California and founds Fluor Construction Company.

1915: Fluor Construction is awarded its first contract in the oil and gas industry.

1925: Flour Construction hires its first engineer, Donald W. Darnell.

1929: The company is reincorporated as Fluor Corporation Ltd. and reports its first $1 million year.

1930: Operations expand beyond California.

1946: Fluor lands its first major refinery building project, in Billings, Montana.

1950: Fluor's stock begins trading over the counter.

1957: The company's stock begins trading on the New York and Pacific Stock Exchanges; its first office abroad opens.

1967: Fluor diversifies into offshore oil drilling.

1969: The company's name is changed to Fluor Corporation, purchases Utah Construction and Mining Company.

1977: Fluor's acquisition of Daniel International Inc. is one of the year's largest transactions of its kind.

1986: Fluor divests itself of its businesses in South Africa.

1998: Philip Carroll becomes the first outsider in company history to be named chief executive officer.

2000: After reincorporating, Fluor has a reverse spin-off from Massey Energy Company, its coal mining entity.

2006: Fluor moves its corporate headquarters to Irving, Texas.

Jr. became president and chief executive officer (CEO), and J. Robert Fluor, the founder's grandson, became executive vice president. Together they steered the company's next series of moves.

When the Korean War created massive petroleum product needs, Fluor's experience with meeting wartime-related demands and its expertise with oil and gas facilities design and construction led to significant business opportunities. Once again government contracts ensued. For the U.S. Air Force, Fluor designed and constructed Dhahran Air Base in Saudi Arabia. The three-year project was completed in 1955.

Nuclear energy became a new direction for the company to pursue. Fluor participated in construction of a large materials testing reactor for the Atomic Energy Commission in Arco, Idaho. In the next decade other assignments in the nuclear field followed.

EXPANSION AND INNOVATION

In the early 1950s, recognizing a need to improve its design methods, Fluor introduced the use of scale models for the design of its process facilities. The technique became an industry standard. The company also actively engaged in diversification. These efforts included designing and building petrochemical and helium plants in Canada, Scotland, Australia, South Africa, and Britain. In 1957 the company opened an office in London, and Fluor's stock began trading on the New York and Pacific exchanges.

During this period the need for staff recruitment and training became evident. Fluor began an in-house program in conjunction with a Los Angeles–area community college, eventually offering specialized drafting courses, office worker and engineering secretarial skills development classes, and college tuition reimbursement programs.

GLOBAL EFFORTS WITH OIL, ENERGY, AND MINING: 1960–70

In 1962 J. Robert Fluor, an engineer and a former U.S. Air Force pilot, became the company's president and CEO. Internationalization, computerization, and acquisitions emerged as activities. In 1963 and 1965 two more nations were added to Fluor's construction roster with refinery projects in Korea and Iran. The company also began using computers to handle its engineering projects and management needs.

In 1967 five oil drilling companies were acquired by Fluor and were renamed Coral Drilling Inc. By establishing a subsidiary, Deep Oil Technology (the result of a joint venture with Ocean Science and Engineering), Fluor focused efforts on deep-ocean recovery of oil. Continuing in this vein, in 1968 the company created Fluor Ocean Services Inc. Fluor's largest offshore drilling acquisition of that period occurred in 1969, with the purchase of Pike Corporation. That year shareholders agreed to change the company's name from Fluor Corporation Ltd. to Fluor Corporation.

Involvement with the mining and metals industry also began in 1969, when the company purchased Utah Construction and Mining Company and formed the subsidiary Fluor Mining and Metals Inc. Another mining interest, Fluor Australia, was set up soon afterward.

For the next 30 years mining would become a significant interest for Fluor. In 1971 Fluor consolidated its engineering and construction activities into Fluor Engineers and Constructors Inc. The 1960s ended with a worldwide concentration on offshore and oceanic oil facility projects and increased engagement with the mining and metals fields. According to an article in *Financial World* (August 15, 1973), the company's operating revenues went from $144.2 million in 1963 to $374.9 million in 1967 to $513.4 million in 1970.

INTERNATIONAL EXPANSION: 1970–77

During the 1970s the company's activities continued heavily overseas. To maximize its effectiveness and efficiency, Fluor set up or expanded subsidiaries or management organizations in England, Holland, Greece, West Germany, Indonesia, South Africa, and Saudi Arabia, the last in response to a $5 billion contract. In 1973 Fluor consolidated its oil and gas activities into Fluor Oil and Gas Corporation. In 1976 it completed an offshore facility for natural gas production in Java, at that time the largest such facility in the world. Even though Fluor's projects of this period included participation in the start-up of the Alaska pipeline, its overseas commissions were the company's overriding focus.

The company's increasing revenues reflected its expansion. In 1973 Fluor took in $1.3 billion. Revenues increased to $4.4 billion in 1974 and $9 billion in 1975. New corporate offices opened in Houston and Irvine, California, to accommodate the rapidly growing staff. Along with international involvement, one of the company's most significant domestic moves was its acquisition in 1977 of the industrial contracting firm Daniel International Corporation for $221.5 million. According to *Mergers & Acquisitions* (Fall 1977), the purchase of Daniel was the third-largest transaction in dollar value of the year's second quarter.

A DIVERSE CLIENTELE: 1980–90

The decade began for Fluor with its purchase of St. Joe Minerals Corporation in 1981. Fluor had a healthy cash flow from its growing engineering and construction sectors. Management knew about the mining business from having entered the industry in 1969 and forming the subsidiary Fluor Mining and Metals Inc. shortly thereafter. Because metals prices ran countercyclically to the market variations in the construction industry, mining seemed a suitable complement to building. The company successfully bid $2.2 billion for St. Joe Minerals, which included A. T. Massey Coal Company Inc.

Events followed that caused concern, however. Not long after the acquisition of St. Joe, metals prices crashed. A deep recession ensued, as did a collapse in petrochemical plant building and an oversupply of oil, decreasing Fluor's strategy of complementing mining with petrochemicals jobs. J. Robert Fluor's death in 1984 spurred another change at the top. David S. Tappan Jr. became CEO at a time when Fluor had accumulated substantial debt, amounting to $724 million by 1985.

Tappan sought to ease the company's dependence on oil contracts while also pursuing ways to regain profitability. Fluor sold all of the oil properties and some of the gold affiliated with its St. Joe Minerals operation, all of its offshore drilling facilities, and some of the corporate offices it had opened during the previous decade. The company also decided to undergo some divestiture, focusing this strategy on its South African operations in 1986 and retaining a repurchase option on these assets.

Fluor also underwent extensive restructuring and embraced a more diversified clientele. In 1986 Fluor merged Daniel International with Fluor Engineers and Constructors to create Fluor Daniel Inc. Operating as Fluor Corporation's major subsidiary, Fluor Daniel took advantage of its principal strength as an industrial contractor, pursuing plant modernizations, chemical plant constructions, factory retrofits, and high-tech plant construction. To further reinforce this move, Fluor was reorganized into the process, power, industrial, hydrocarbon, and government market sectors. The transformation proved successful.

After losing $60 million in 1986, Fluor posted a profit in 1987 of $26 million. By the end of the decade Fluor's earnings were $147 million, on more than $7 billion in sales. Although Fluor continued to construct petroleum refineries for $1 billion and up (most notably in Saudi Arabia), recovery was due largely to its diversified clientele. Fluor entered the 1990s with a roster of design, construction, and maintenance projects of buildings and equipment in more than 30 industries.

BROAD EXPANSION: 1990–96

This diverse customer base served Fluor well in the early 1990s. A recession crippled many construction companies, but Fluor increased its operating profit, benefiting from a $5 billion contract signed with Saudi Arabia's Aramco in 1990 as well as reconstruction work in the Middle East after Kuwait's petroleum facilities were destroyed during the 1991 Persian Gulf War. Fluor's decisions of the previous decade had involved a great deal of reorganization, with the overall purpose of greatly reducing reliance on oil and gas contracts. David Jefferson pointed out in the *Wall Street Journal* (April 18, 1991) that "the company [was] again tempted by the siren song of oil."

In 1992, under the stewardship of CEO Leslie G. McCraw, Fluor moved into a period of aggressive expansion and increasing profits. Fluor Daniel alone recorded a 15 percent rise in operating profit from 1991 to $191 million. Revenues for the year were buoyed by a $4 billion federal government contract to manage the cleanup and dismantling of a plutonium plant in Fernald, Ohio. Meanwhile the company continued its investment in the coal industry. A. T. Massey increased its reserves to nearly one billion tons and generated an operating profit of $80 million, ranking it among the five largest U.S. coal companies.

By early 1995 Fluor Daniel had operations in more than 80 countries and in 25 industry areas. The corporation created a new unit, the Diversified Services Group, to provide engineering- and construction-related services that included procurement, temporary staffing, and equipment rental and sales. Revenues soared, from $7.85 billion in 1993 to $11.02 billion in 1996, while net income climbed from $166.8 million to $268.1 million over the same period. Among Fluor Daniel's major projects during this period, either alone or through a consortium, were a $1 billion petrochemical complex (Kuwait), a $5 billion cleanup effort at a former plutonium production facility (Hanford, Washington), a $1.6 million Batu Hijau copper and gold mining project (Indonesia), and a $4.8 billion high-speed rail system (Florida).

CHALLENGES: 1996–99

The expansion hit a snag. In early 1997 the company accepted some contracts that had low margins. The difference between payment and actual cost was a great deal more than had been estimated, and the company lost money on the contracts. Increasing competition for projects also resulted in reduced profits. Fluor had overhead expenses of nearly $700 million in 1997. A number of new overseas offices were shuttered, staff was cut, and then, in response to economic conditions in Asia, the company announced further restructuring decisions. Fluor Daniel was reorganized into the energy and chemicals segment, the industrial segment, the mining and minerals segment, and the government, environment, and telecommunications segment.

After McCraw retired in early 1998, Philip J. Carroll became the first outsider in company history to be named chairman and CEO. Carroll's start at Fluor was followed by two key events. That year Fluor abandoned

an attempt to sell American Equipment Company, its equipment rental and sales arm. Carroll then initiated a restructuring, which was announced in 1999. Fluor's reorganization featured three principal, semiautonomous business units: Fluor Daniel, A. T. Massey Coal, and Fluor Global Services. The last was a successor to the company's Diversified Services Group and included American Equipment, staffing services, operations and maintenance services, consulting services, and services for Fluor's governmental and telecommunications sectors.

The restructuring also involved a large-scale overhaul of Fluor Daniel. While not abandoning any existing contracts, Fluor Daniel was to concentrate on five core areas: chemicals and process (including pharmaceuticals and biotechnology), infrastructure (transportation), mining, manufacturing (particularly consumer products, food and beverage, microelectronics, and light metals), and oil, gas, and power. The goal was to have Fluor Daniel focus on its 200 largest customers and those industries in which its projects achieved the largest profit margins. Initial results were encouraging. Unlike in 1997 and 1998, in 1999 Fluor could present its shareholders with a positive consolidated backlog of projects that totaled $9.1 billion. For this industry, which measures success in part based on payments a firm anticipates from contracts obtained and jobs under way, this consolidated figure was good news.

AHEAD FOR FLUOR

Fluor began the 21st century ready to make definitive choices and equally definitive progress. It was decided that a reverse spin-off was needed for Massey Energy alongside a subsequent recapitalization of Fluor. This occurred with shareholders' approval late in 2000, with Fluor becoming reincorporated under its same name as before and Massey becoming a separate entity whose coal operations were discontinued. Although the 2000 annual report showed a 12 percent loss from the previous year, in terms of new projects it also posted a 42 percent increase from 1999. Among these were several projects implemented by the company's Oil & Gas, Industrial & Infrastructure, Power, and Government divisions.

The bookings continued. In 2000 Fluor Daniel, as part of a consortium, obtained a $1 billion, three-year contract to build the Hamaca crude oil refinery in northeastern Venezuela. In 2002 the pharmaceutical giant Pfizer commissioned a Fluor subsidiary, Fluor Ltd., for a three-year, $113 million construction project in Sandwich, U.K., that would become Pfizer's European research and development headquarters. In 2003 the company began an $80 million engineering and procurement services job for Exxon Neftegas Ltd.'s offshore oil and gas project at Sakhalin Island in Russia. A joint venture was awarded with Airtricity in 2007 to develop a 140-turbine wind farm off the coast of Suffolk, U.K.

Figures presented in Fluor's 2008 annual report showed that its Oil & Gas Division was the company's top performer, with a 55 percent increase from 2007. Some reorganization occurred in 2009, when the Oil & Gas segment became the Energy & Chemicals segment, as jobs featuring the growing industry of polysilicon production were added to Fluor's roster and the Power segment similarly pursued projects involving renewable energy. That year Fluor's Offshore Solutions unit announced a partnership with Global Industries, a U.K.-based firm with which Fluor would pursue oil and gas projects in the Middle East and North Africa. Contracts obtained in 2009 with the U.S. Army Corps of Engineers focused on military vehicle maintenance and site management in Iraq. A completion goal of 2010 was set to align with the U.S. military's schedule for activity in that country. In late 2009 Fluor won a project involving a $1.1 billion expansion of an important interstate highway in Utah.

After a period of leasing its main offices in Irvine, Fluor moved to its own corporate headquarters in Irving, Texas, in 2006. Despite a global recession, its industries' traditionally cyclical nature, and the somewhat risky aspects of these businesses, Fluor was thriving. With its four-pronged focus of engineering, procurement, construction, and maintenance (EPCM) services, this Fortune 200 corporation has earned its global reputation. The company is known for accurately assessing project value, meeting job schedules on time, tackling such challenges as remote settings, occupational hazards, and geopolitical issues, and applying innovative approaches to standards and design elements. Clients in the public and private sectors have commissioned Fluor as a suitable fit for their EPCM plans.

Jeffrey L. Covell
Updated, David E. Salamie; Mary C. Lewis

PRINCIPAL SUBSIDIARIES

American Equipment Company Inc.; Del-Jen Inc.; Fluor Arabia Ltd.; Fluor Australia Ltd.; Fluor Canada Ltd.; Fluor Constructors International Inc.; Fluor Daniel Inc.; Fluor Daniel International Inc.; Fluor Enterprises Inc.; Fluor Europe BV; Fluor Federal Services Inc.; Fluor Fernald Inc.; Fluor Hanford Inc.; Fluor Ltd. (UK); Fluor SA; Plant Performance Services LLC; Tecnoconsult SA (Venezuela); TRS Staffing Solutions Inc.

PRINCIPAL DIVISIONS

Energy and Chemicals; Industrial and Infrastructure; Government; Power; Global Services.

PRINCIPAL OPERATING UNITS

Fluor Daniel; Fluor Offshore Solutions.

PRINCIPAL COMPETITORS

AMEC plc; Bechtel Group Inc; Chicago Bridge and Iron Company NV; CH2M Hill Companies Ltd.; Foster Wheeler AG; Jacobs Engineering Group Inc.; KBR Inc.; Shaw Group; Skanska AB; URS Corporation; Technip; WorleyParsons Ltd.

FURTHER READING

"After McCraw, Fluor Changes Tack," *Engineering News Record*, December 22, 1997, p. 12.

"Annual Meeting Briefs: Fluor," *Wall Street Journal*, May 20, 1969, p. 2.

Aron, Ravi, and Jitendra V. Singh, "Getting Offshoring Right," *Harvard Business Review*, December 2005, pp. 135–143.

Berry, Mary Clay, *The Alaska Pipeline, the Politics of Oil and Native Land Claims.* Bloomington: Indiana University Press, 1975.

"Bigger Inch," *Time*, March 3, 1947, p. 85.

Boschee, Pam, "Sakhalin-1 Technology Conquers Unique Challenges," *Offshore*, December 2005, p. 38.

Byrne, Harlan S., "Fluor Corp.," *Barron's*, October 21, 1991, pp. 51–52.

"Capital Conscious," *Economist*, April 27, 1968, p. 76.

Cunningham, Storm, *The Restoration Economy: The Greatest New Growth Frontier.* San Francisco: Berrett-Koehler, 2002.

"Digest of Earnings Reports," *Wall Street Journal*, March 13, 1962, p. 20.

"Duke/Fluor Wins CMS, DTE Deal," *Independent Energy*, January/February 1999.

Emshwiller, John R., "Fluor Plans New Round of Cutbacks," *Wall Street Journal*, March 10, 1999, p. B16.

"Fluor," *Texas Contractor*, July 17, 2006, p. 18.

"Fluor Awarded $16 Million Order for Korean Oil Refinery," *Wall Street Journal*, November 2, 1962, p. 5.

"Fluor Awarded U.K. Pfizer Project," *Pharmaceutical Technology Europe*, October 2002, p. 6.

"Fluor Completes Acquisition of Pike, Names Two to Board," *Wall Street Journal*, January 3, 1969, p. 9.

"Fluor Corporation," *Petroleum Economist*, September 2000, p. 53.

"Fluor Flourisheth," *Forbes*, November 1, 1973, pp. 26–27.

Fluor, J. Robert, *Fluor Corporation: A 65-Year History.* New York: Newcomen Society, 1978.

"Fluor Offshore Solutions Partners with Global Industries," *International Resource News*, August 4, 2009.

"Fluor Provides Construction Management for Coming Facility in Taiwan," *M2 Presswire*, February 22, 2005.

"Fluor: Ready to Capitalize on the Hidden Assets in St. Joe," *Business Week*, April 27, 1981, pp. 104, 108.

"Fluor to Provide Engineering and Procurement Services for Major Russian Oil & Gas Project; Adds to Construction Management Work Already Under Way," *PR Newswire*, February 25, 2004.

"Fluor's Feast," *Forbes*, August 1, 1967, p. 41.

"Fluor Wins New Iraq Contracts from U.S. Army Corps of Engineers," *Defense & Aerospace Week*, November 18, 2009, p. 67.

"The Forbes Yardsticks: 1976, Construction," *Forbes*, January 1, 1977.

"Forty Million Dollar Pipe Line Is Finished to Mississippi," *Chicago Tribune*, July 16, 1931, p. 23.

Galluccio, Nick, "The Growth Engineer," *Forbes*, March 30, 1981, p. 62.

Geraghty, Barbara, *Visionary Selling: How to Get to Top Executives—And How to Sell Them When You're There*. New York: Simon and Schuster, 1998.

"Green Light for Windfarms, On and Off Shore," *Utility Week*, February 23, 2007, p. 6.

Guarnieri, Timothy J., "The Real Cost of Sustainable Development," *AACE International Transactions*, June 1, 2008, pp. HP31–HP37.

"Investors Bet on Fluor," *Financial World*, August 15, 1973, p. 10.

Jefferson, David J., "Global Reach: Biggest Builder, Fluor, Sees Kuwaiti Contracts as a Mixed Blessing," *Wall Street Journal*, April 18, 1991, p. A1.

"Mapping Fluor's Strategy: Builder Drives to Broaden," *Chemical Week*, April 26, 1958, pp. 82–84, 86.

McCraw, Leslie G., "Developing Global Strategies at Fluor Corp.," *Site Selection and Industrial Development*, April 1990, pp. 391–392.

McQuade, Walter, "Bob Fluor, Global Superbuilder," *Fortune*, February 26, 1979, pp. 54–60+.

"Mitchell Explains What Texas Gas Means to City," *Chicago Tribune*, July 16, 1931, p. 23.

Nulty, Peter, "How to Clean Up on the Cheap," *Fortune*, December 16, 1991, p. 102.

O'Dell, John, "Fluor Taps Shell Oil President as CEO," *Los Angeles Times*, April 16, 1998, p. D1.

Perry, Nancy J., "Flush Times for Fluor," *Fortune*, November 6, 1989, p. 113.

Poole, Claire, "Construction," *Forbes*, January 7, 1991, pp. 126–128.

Ramirez, Anthony, "The Big Chill at Fluor," *Fortune*, May 13, 1985, pp. 42–46.

Reingold, Jennifer, "No Respect," *Financial World*, March 14, 1995, pp. 36–38.

Rose, Frederick, "Fluor, after Touting Big Expansion, Tightens Its Belt," *Wall Street Journal*, May 5, 1997, p. B4.

———, "Fluor Plans Restructuring and Retains Search Firm to Find a Chief Executive," *Wall Street Journal*, December 12, 1997, p. B1.

Schine, Eric, "Cleaning Up at Fluor," *Business Week*, October 5, 1992, p. 112+.

"United States: Utah DOT Selects Fluor-Led Team for $1.1 Billion Major Expansion of I-15 Corridor," *Tenders Info*, December 12, 2009.

"Washington at Work: Reactor," *Wall Street Journal*, February 27, 1962, p. 6.

"Where the Constructors Strike It Rich," *Business Week*, August 23, 1976, pp. 46–49, 51–53.

Wrubel, Robert, "Transforming Fluor," *Financial World*, May 30, 1989, pp. 28-29.

Forest City Enterprises, Inc.

———— ■ ————

1100 Terminal Tower
50 Public Square
Cleveland, Ohio 44113-2203
U.S.A.
Telephone: (216) 621-6060
Fax: (216) 263-6208
Web site: http://www.forestcity.net

Public Company
Founded: 1920 as Forest City Material
Incorporated: 1960
Employees: 3,237
Sales: $1.29 billion (2009)
Stock Exchanges: New York
Ticker Symbol: FCEB
NAICS: 531110 Lessors of Residential Buildings and
Dwellings; 531120 Lessors of Nonresidential Build-
ings (except Miniwarehouses); 531311 Residential
Property Managers; 531312 Nonresidential
Property Managers

■ ■ ■

With total assets of $11.9 billion in 2009, Forest City
Enterprises, Inc., is a leading developer and manager of
commercial and residential real estate. Headquartered in
Cleveland, Ohio, the company oversees an extensive
portfolio of hotels, apartment communities, and retail
and office space. Over the years, Forest City has
established a reputation for its development of mixed-
use properties, its emphasis on innovative architectural
designs, and its focus on utilizing sustainable building

strategies. The company's activities are concentrated
primarily in large, urban markets. Indeed Forest City
has carved out a sizable niche in a number of key
metropolitan areas throughout the United States,
notably Boston, Chicago, New York City, Denver, Los
Angeles, San Francisco, and Washington, D.C.

FOUNDATION AND DEVELOPMENT IN THE EARLY 20TH CENTURY

The family affair began in 1905, when members of the
Ratner clan began to immigrate to the United States
from their native Poland. Charles Ratner, the eldest and
first to arrive in Cleveland, Ohio, founded Forest City
Material in 1920. Upon their arrival, Leonard Ratner
and his younger siblings Max, Fannye, and Dora Ratner
borrowed money to start a small creamery offering milk,
butter, and eggs. Trained as a weaver, Leonard Ratner
joined his older brother in the lumber business, opening
Buckeye Lumber in 1924. Two years later the Ratners
sold their creameries to focus on the lumber and building materials market.

In the late 1920s Leonard and Charles Ratner
turned over the lumberyard to their brother Max Ratner, who had just earned a law degree from Case
Western Reserve's John Marshall Law School. Fannye
Ratner's husband, Nathan Shafran, came into the
lumber business around this same time. Leonard and
Charles Ratner then founded B & F Building Co.,
which constructed single-family homes on Cleveland's
east side. Leonard Ratner rejoined the family lumber
firm in 1934, bringing with him his expertise in
residential construction.

COMPANY PERSPECTIVES

Forest City is a national owner and developer of real estate, committed to building superior, long-term value for its shareholders and customers. We accomplish this through the operation, acquisition and development of commercial, rental housing and land development projects. We operate by developing meaningful relationships and leveraging our entrepreneurial capabilities with creative talent in a fully integrated real estate organization.

Although the company sold construction materials primarily to contractors in the 1920s, 1930s, and 1940s, it had also reached out to the general public during the Great Depression. At this time Forest City Lumber started a lending program that enabled homeless people to borrow $549 toward the purchase of building materials. By investing their own "sweat equity," these struggling individuals could build inexpensive homes.

EXPANSION INTO REAL ESTATE

Forest City made its first forays into the real estate business during the 1930s and 1940s by acquiring inexpensive land repossessed by banks and other institutions. Some lots were purchased for as little as $10 each. During the interwar period, the company provided land and building materials to local builders with the understanding that they would pay for both when the homes were sold. In 1941 Forest City became a pioneer in the construction of prefabricated homes, but this activity was interrupted by World War II. To help in the war effort, Forest City made wooden munitions boxes for the government.

Sam Miller, who joined the company in 1947, was credited with launching Sunrise Land Co., the land development arm of the business. Miller became a full-fledged member of the family when he married Leonard Ratner's daughter Ruth. Envisioning an opportunity for growth in the postwar housing shortage, the Ratners entered residential construction. The company was a key developer of some of Cleveland's largest suburbs.

The group also began to develop its extensive land holdings into apartments and shopping centers. This new focus on consumers may have led the company to begin converting its lumberyards into do-it-yourself home stores in 1955. Forest City's early entry into this

important market helped make the firm Ohio's largest building materials company by the end of the decade.

INCORPORATION SIGNALS
TRANSITION: 1960–79

Forest City Enterprises was incorporated in 1960, with Leonard Ratner as chairman and Max Ratner as president. In an initial public stock offering that same year, the Ratners sold a 19.5 percent stake of the company at a face value of $4.5 million. Forest City's stock was listed on the American Stock Exchange by 1965. Although the company continued to develop its retail and wholesale lumber businesses during the 1960s and 1970s, this corporate reorganization represented a turning point for Forest City, when real estate came to the fore.

Beginning in 1966, under the direction of Max Ratner's son Charles, Forest City's building materials chain grew from $12 million in annual sales to nearly $200 million over the next two decades. In 1969 the division added to its portfolio one of the nation's largest lumber distributors, an Oregon company. Over the course of the 1960s and 1970s, Forest City opened stores in Detroit, Chicago, and Akron, Ohio. By the late 1970s the chain boasted 20 do-it-yourself centers.

Forest City's real estate developments took several forms. The company built, owned, and operated shopping centers, malls, office buildings, industrial parks, and hotels. It also acquired the Akron-based construction firm Thomas J. Dillon & Co., Inc., in 1968. Under the guidance of Shafran, Forest City applied its patented method of modular high-rise housing construction to this new subsidiary. Through its "Operation Breakthrough" program, over the next 30 years the firm erected nearly 60,000 units of low-cost housing for the elderly.

By the end of the 1970s, Forest City owned 17 shopping centers and 39 apartment buildings with a combined total of 10,800 housing units. The company had also diversified into mortgage banking, property leasing, and property management, as well as petroleum and natural gas development. Albert B. Ratner advanced to the presidency in 1973, when Max Ratner assumed the chairmanship and Leonard Ratner took the title of founder-chairman. Corporate revenues increased from $32 million in 1963 to $235.3 million by 1979, but net income grew only from $1 million to $1.4 million.

1980–92: MAJOR URBAN
PROJECTS

At the dawn of the 1980s, Forest City began to phase out its smaller ventures and concentrate its resources on

KEY DATES

1920: Charles Ratner founds Forest City Material in Cleveland, Ohio.

1941: Forest City begins building prefabricated homes.

1955: The Ratners begin converting their lumberyards into do-it-yourself home stores.

1960: Forest City Enterprises is incorporated and makes an initial public offering.

1980: The company acquires the historic Terminal Tower in Cleveland and launches an extensive renovation project.

1990: The Terminal Tower redevelopment is completed and renamed Tower City.

1993: Forest City partners with a Mexican company to develop commercial properties in Mexico.

2001: Forest City breaks ground on the redevelopment of the former Stapleton Airport in Denver, Colorado.

2005: Forest City earns approval to build a multiuse development in the Atlantic Yards neighborhood of Brooklyn, New York.

2007: Forest City establishes a branch office in London, England.

million-square-foot, multiuse urban renewal redevelopment featured hotels, a mall, and offices. Renamed Tower City, the project helped push Forest City's real estate portfolio over $2 billion in 1991.

Major retail and commercial projects in Boston, Pittsburgh, Brooklyn, Los Angeles, Tucson, San Francisco, Chicago, and elsewhere echoed the scale and impact of Tower City in Cleveland. Throughout this period Forest City also continued to pursue residential developments, creating everything from single-family inner-city projects to luxury apartments and condominiums. Forest City sailed through the credit crunch of the late 1980s and early 1990s better than many of its competitors. Nevertheless, it was compelled to eliminate its quarterly dividend in 1991 and put the brakes on 17 projects in 1992.

INTERNATIONAL INVESTMENTS AND CASINO DEVELOPMENT

Having specialized in large, urban redevelopments for about a decade, a confident Forest City wagered future prosperity on international projects and gambling houses. The company made its first international foray in 1993 via a joint venture with Mexico's Grupo Protexa. Ian Bacon, the executive in charge of this endeavor, compared Mexico to the United States of the 1950s and 1960s. Mexico was a market ripe for the development of regional malls and shopping centers.

In the mid-1990s Forest City became increasingly involved in the construction and management of casinos, euphemistically dubbed "urban entertainment" in the industry. Projects in Pittsburgh, Las Vegas, and Atlantic City either planned for or proposed gambling. Although gambling and its social and economic effects were hotly debated topics in the early 1990s, Forest City executives recognized the gambling industry's business potential. The analyst Sheldon Grodsky told the *Cleveland Plain Dealer*'s Bill Lubinger, "This is what they do, whether they do it with gambling-related property or retail or mixed use or apartments—that's real estate development."

Charles A. Ratner, son of Max Ratner, became president and chief operating officer and then assumed the role of chief executive officer (CEO) after his father's death in 1995. The year also marked the company's 75th anniversary, and Forest City's new CEO revealed a strategic plan outlining financial goals and the strategies necessary to reach them, a mission statement, and a set of core values. Two years later, in 1997, the company moved its stock listing from the American Stock Exchange to the New York Stock Exchange. Also in 1997 Forest City relocated its

larger urban developments. The most significant divestment of this transition came in 1987, when the company sold its Forest City Materials chain to Handy Andy Home Improvement Centers, Inc. Forest City had dominated the local home improvement market until the early 1980s, when DIY Home Warehouse and Kmart Corp.'s Builders Square infiltrated Cleveland. Forest City tried to match the competition with deep discounts and a switch to a warehouse format but soon realized that it needed more volume and more buying power to compete with these large, well-financed national chains. This dramatic break with the company's traditional business freed Forest City to focus on the megaprojects for which it would become nationally known in the 1980s and 1990s.

Forest City played a key role in the revitalization of downtown Cleveland and then applied the skills it had gained to urban projects throughout the United States. In 1980 the company bought Cleveland's Terminal Tower, a passenger rail terminal built before the Great Depression. Although the $250 million project endured several fits and starts, it would become a cornerstone of the city's rebirth. When completed in 1990, the three corporate headquarters to Tower City, its recently developed high-profile Cleveland property.

NEW PROJECTS FOR THE NEW MILLENNIUM: 1998–2002

Forest City closed out the 20th century with a burst of urban development activity. Among the projects the company completed in 1998 and 1999 were a large office building in the Massachusetts Institute of Technology's University Park and a luxury apartment high-rise in Bethesda, Maryland. The company also built a mall near San Diego, California, and a shopping center in New Jersey. As these new properties were opening, Forest City had plenty in the pipeline to replace them.

In 1998 alone Forest City launched more than a dozen projects. Two high-profile jobs were on opposite coasts. In New York City the company began construction of a 300,000-square-foot hotel and entertainment complex in Times Square. In San Francisco it kicked off redevelopment of the city's historic Emporium building near Union Square.

One of Forest City's largest and most unusual projects came in 1999, when the company was awarded the $4 billion job of redeveloping Denver's obsolete Stapleton Airport. The project was delayed by numerous obstacles before finally commencing in early 2001. The redevelopment involved converting some 3,000 acres of former airport land into a community complete with housing, retail space, and office space. By the time the company broke ground on the Stapleton project, it was in the midst of planning for a number of other developments, including a Times Square headquarters for the venerable New York Times Company, a one-million-square-foot mall (Richmond, Virginia), an upscale shopping area (Pasadena, California), and a state-of-the-art facility designed to house telecommunications and IT companies (Cleveland).

In 2001, as businesses across the United States struggled with a difficult economy, Forest City weathered the storm well. For the year, the company achieved record results in both revenues and earnings and took steps to strengthen its financial liquidity. It also made a secondary public offering of 3.9 million shares (which generated $118 million) and sold seven properties, including a $108 million mall in Tucson. The influx of capital allowed the company to reduce its nonrecourse mortgage debt by almost $96 million.

Forest City stormed into 2002, completing nine property acquisitions and opening five new developments, all in the first half of the fiscal year. It also continued to make significant progress in ongoing developments at Denver's Stapleton Airport and MIT's University Park. For the second quarter, the company posted an increase of about 8 percent in both revenues and earnings over the same period in 2001.

ENTERING NEW MARKETS: 2003–08

Heading into the middle of the decade, Forest City Enterprises remained intent on pursuing new real estate opportunities in key geographical areas. In December 2003 Hawaii Military Communities, LCC, a partnership between Forest City and C. F. Jordan, LP, won a $358 million contract from the U.S. Navy to construct and manage close to 2,000 naval residences on the island of Oahu. The following March, the company concluded a deal to develop the Southeast Federal Center, a 44-acre area along the Anacostia River in Washington, D.C. As part of the project, the company would build 1.8 million square feet of commercial space, as well as 2,800 residential dwellings.

The company launched one of its most ambitious projects in May 2005, when its New York subsidiary Forest City Ratner Companies received preliminary approval to redevelop a 21-acre area in Brooklyn's Atlantic Yards neighborhood. In a project that would cost an estimated $2.5 billion, the company planned to build a multiuse commercial and residential complex on an area formerly used as a storage yard for the Long Island Rail Road. The centerpiece of the development would be a new arena for the New Jersey Nets basketball franchise, of which Forest City Ratner had purchased a share the previous year. As part of the proposal, the arena would be designed by the acclaimed architect Frank Gehry.

By mid-2007 Forest City owned nearly 36 million square feet of commercial real estate, in addition to roughly 44,000 residential properties. Around this time the company began to explore real estate opportunities in foreign markets. In June 2007 the company established a branch office in London, England. The following April, Forest City executives traveled to India to discuss a multiuse development project with an Indian real estate group. By the end of 2008, however, as the global financial crisis steadily worsened, the company found itself forced to rein in its growth ambitions.

FACING THE GLOBAL FINANCIAL CRISIS

In December 2008 Forest City placed a freeze on new building projects so that it could focus on the management of its existing properties. Speaking in the *Crain's Cleveland Business* (December 15, 2008), CEO Charles

Ratner announced that the company would "put virtually all new development on hold" until economic conditions improved. Ratner also offered a concise summation of the company's guiding philosophy: "When you can't make money, you don't do it."

In spite of this general slowdown, the company remained committed to completing its existing projects. These included the Atlantic Yards complex, which had become stalled by lawsuits and other legal issues. However, as the worldwide credit market continued to stagnate and real estate prices stumbled, Forest City found itself struggling to maintain steady earnings. In early 2009 the company began to sell a number of its assets in an effort to pay down its debt and raise capital.

Among the properties listed during this period were four retail sites in New York City, as well as a share of a new development project in Boston. With these sales, the company hoped to generate up to $1.15 billion. At the same time, Forest City also began to offer consulting services to other real estate developers struggling to complete projects in the midst of the recession. As the decade drew to a close, Forest City's ability to adapt to market conditions would play a crucial role in determining its long-term financial health.

April Dougal Gasbarre
Updated, Shawna Brynildssen; Stephen Meyer

PRINCIPAL SUBSIDIARIES

FC Basketball, Inc.; Forest City Ratner Companies; Forest City Rental Properties Corporation; Ironwood Insurance Company.

PRINCIPAL COMPETITORS

Boston Properties, Inc.; Equity Office Properties Trust; Inland Real Estate Group of Companies, Inc.; Jones Lang LaSalle Corporation; Tishman Speyer Properties, L.P.; Trammell Crow Company; Trump Organization; Vornado Realty Trust.

FURTHER READING

Bullard, Stan, "Forest City Puts Desirable Assets in Play; Market Conditions Lead Developer to List Properties in D.C., NYC—but None Here," *Crain's Cleveland Business*, March 16, 2009, p. 1.

Gerdel, Thomas, "Forest City Goes Full Speed on Its Development Course," *Cleveland Plain Dealer*, July 31, 1990, pp. 1D, 8D.

Gleisser, Marcus, "Business Leader Max Ratner Dies," *Cleveland Plain Dealer*, June 2, 1995, pp. 1A, 12A.

Koshar, John Leo, "Ambitious Projects Fill Forest City's Drawing Boards," *Cleveland Plain Dealer*, July 1, 1984, p. 1G.

Lubinger, Bill, "Forest City Forges Gambling Ties," *Cleveland Plain Dealer*, July 10, 1996, pp. 1C, 3C.

Moore, Paula, "Stapleton's Ambitious Developer: Founded as a Lumber Company, Forest City Tackles Monstrous Airport Project," *Denver Business Journal*, January 29, 1999, p. 3B.

Perez, Christine, "From Lumberer to Developer, Forest City's Roots Run Deep," *National Real Estate Investor*, June 1, 2007, p. 8.

Phillips, Stephen, "Forest City Betting on Projects," *Cleveland Plain Dealer*, July 1, 1994, pp. 1C, 2C.

Sartin, V. David, "Save Tower City, Kucinich Demands," *Cleveland Plain Dealer*, September 1, 1984, pp. 1A, 11A.

Sullivan, Elizabeth, "Hilton, Forest City Sign Deal on Downtown Hotel," *Cleveland Plain Dealer*, July 27, 1983, pp. 1A, 8A.

Fossil, Inc.

2280 North Greenville Avenue
Richardson, Texas 75082
U.S.A.
Telephone: (972) 234-2525
Toll Free: (800) 969-0900
Fax: (972) 234-4669
Web site: http://www.fossil.com

Public Company
Founded: 1984 as Overseas Products International
Incorporated: 1987 as Fossil, Inc.
Employees: 7,355
Sales: $1.58 billion (2008)
Stock Exchanges: NASDAQ (Global Select Market)
Ticker Symbol: FOSL
NAICS: 334518 Watch, Clock, and Part Manufacturing;
448310 Jewelry and New Watches Stores; 448150
Clothing Accessories Stores; 448320 Leather Goods
Stores; 448140 Unisex Clothing Stores; 454111
Web Retailers

■ ■ ■

Owner of an extremely popular brand name, Fossil, Inc., designs, markets, and distributes watches, leather goods, sunglasses, jeans, and other merchandise for retail sale worldwide. The company's five divisions (Fossil United States, Fossil Direct to Consumer, Fossil Europe, Fossil Other International, and Fossil Corporate) reflect a geographically based business approach that combines e-commerce and direct to consumer marketing in its overall strategic plan. Fossil's in-house design team and their 1930s-, 1940s- and 1950s-inspired watch and packaging designs have resulted in phenomenal success in the United States and more than 50 countries. In addition to marketing merchandise under the Fossil brand name, the company contracts with well-known fashion designers and film studios to produce watches and other merchandise that promote newly released films, commemorate special events, or drive holiday sales. Whether Fossil has worked on products for other companies or focused on its own lines, the company has become a leader in its specialty. As of 2008, Fossil was ranked in the S&P 400 stock index.

FOSSIL'S BEGINNING

Founded in 1984, Fossil represented Tom Kartsotis's second entrepreneurial effort. A former Texas A&M student in his early twenties, Kartsotis was living in Dallas and operating a moderately successful ticket brokerage business, selling tickets for such events as Dallas Cowboy football games. The inspiration that led Kartsotis into his second business venture came from a suggestion by his older brother, Kosta, a merchandising executive at Sanger Harris, a Dallas-based department store chain. Kosta's experience as a buyer had caused him to notice opportunities for importing moderately priced fashion watches made in the Far East. Made by a Swiss-based firm, Swatch watches were the rage of the day, enjoying international popularity. Tom Kartsotis withdrew his savings and sold his half of the ticket brokerage business, which gave the young entrepreneur $200,000 to start his new business.

Tom Kartsotis flew to Hong Kong to investigate the possibilities of starting an import/export enterprise.

COMPANY PERSPECTIVES

The heart and soul of the FOSSIL brand—its people, products and culture—is about a unique kind of inspired creativity. Representing the concept of accessible cool, Fossil's identity is anchored in vintage authentic style mixed with a creative spirit and a sense of humor that extends into all its product offerings, graphics and one-of-a-kind, trademark collectible tins. Fossil creates modern yet vintage products for everyone, a simple yet compelling idea reflected in the Company's tagline, What Vintage Are You?

Founded in 1984, Fossil was the first American brand to bring value and style to the watch category transforming the concept of timekeeping from the merely functional to chic and stylish must-haves for the wrist. Since then, Fossil has always been in the avant-garde, whether in terms of technology, the choice of materials or design.

During his travels around Hong Kong, Kartsotis explored various import/export options and finally settled on his brother's suggestion. Kartsotis hired a Hong Kong manufacturer and brought 1,500 watches back to the United States where he sold the products to Dallas department stores and specialty shops. These sales marked the fledgling moments of his new company, Overseas Products International.

Shortly afterward, the 24-year-old Kartsotis hired a friend, Lynne Stafford, as Overseas Products' first designer. Stafford was instrumental in creating the "retro" design style that became the signature of the company's brand and would fuel its growth. Of the three watch product lines the company was selling in 1985, the most popular was a design that Stafford based on a retro look from the 1950s. Although Kartsotis was not a designer, the retro look became part of his product offering early on, due partly to his father, whom he and Kosta had nicknamed "Fossil" and who had a preference for items from the 1950s. Overseas Products came out with its first officially branded Fossil wristwatch in 1986.

EXPLOSIVE GROWTH: 1987–89

With Tom Kartsotis at the helm, the company grew exponentially during the 1980s by attracting young consumers with designs reminiscent of their parents' or grandparents' eras. As William P. Barrett pointed out in his profile in a November 1993 issue of *Forbes*, "Inspiration for new ... designs and marketing gimmicks, then as now, came largely from ads in the pages of old magazines, like *Life, Look* and *Time*." By taking careful note of the fashion styles illustrated in these advertisements, Kartsotis and Stafford devised a design concept that went beyond one watch, was more than mere whimsy, and was embraced increasingly by a new generation of consumers.

However, the company needed more than nostalgic watch designs to progress beyond its start-up venture status. Kartsotis's company stood on the brink of explosive growth. In 1987, the same year that Kartsotis renamed his company Fossil, Inc., the firm had $2 million in sales. With this revenue generated, the company was able to undertake two more steps. The first was to increase its in-house design staff, which would enable the company to avoid the expense of royalty payments and to own and control the design concept, and the second step was to control the quality of its products. The first step was handled significantly in 1987, when Tim Hale became the full-time design director, and the company's leading design force. The other step of that period came about as noted by Matthew Porter in his article in the March/April 2003 issue of *Communication Arts*: "Success enabled the company to focus next on manufacturing. Better product, better sales, led to a world-class distribution network."

In 1988 Kosta Kartsotis joined the company. Kosta's expertise as a buyer and his years of working at department stores made him an important element in his brother's company. By the end of the decade, there was ample evidence of success. In 1989 the company generated $20 million in sales, having increased its revenue volume tenfold in two years, and made a substantive change in its marketing approach. In 1989 Hale's creative guidance led the company to begin packaging its watches in elaborately decorated tin containers and wooden boxes, which strengthened the nostalgic appeal of Fossil merchandise. To further excite consumer demand, a marketing campaign was launched featuring Fossil watches on the wrists of models engaged in adventurous activities, evoking comparisons to the *Indiana Jones* films that were popular at that time.

The leap from $2 million to $20 million in sales between 1987 and 1989 bred optimism for the 1990s. The company was becoming a fast-rising firm. Tom and Kosta Kartsotis, Hale, and the rest of the company had tapped into a mystique and an audience of consumers whose interest in affordable, retro products seemed unlimited. As with any company that underwent robust financial growth, strategies for the future were likely to

KEY DATES

1984: Tom Kartsotis founds Overseas Products International.

1986: The company's first wristwatch with the Fossil brand name debuts.

1987: Overseas Products International becomes Fossil, Inc.

1990: The company begins selling leather goods; first international subsidiary is established.

1993: Fossil completes an IPO.

1994: The company celebrates its 10th anniversary.

2001: The company adds apparel to its product lines.

2003: The company debuts wristwatches with personal digital assistant (PDA) technology.

2009: Fossil's 25th anniversary year includes the launch of a footwear line.

include, for example, international markets, domestic expansion, and the introduction of other product lines.

NEW PRODUCTS: 1990–92

At the start of the 1990s, roughly 3 percent of Fossil's sales came from international markets. This would soon change, as would its reliance on the sale of watches as the sole source of revenue. In 1990 the company introduced a line of leather goods and a new brand of watches. In years to come the new product line expanded to include handbags, wallets, belts, and other items. A new watch brand, Relic, was marketed as a lower-priced alternative to Fossil watches and sold to retail chains such as Sears and JCPenney. Concurrently, Fossil began to develop its international business more diligently, moving first into Europe, where it established a subsidiary in Traunstein, Germany. Although the push overseas had begun, it would be several years before the company possessed adequate financial resources to expand internationally with vigor.

Enviable sales growth continued, with sales climbing from $20 million in 1989 to $32.5 million in 1990. A greater increase was recorded the following year, when sales leaped to $57.1 million. During this period, heightened awareness of the Fossil name was achieved by allying with one of the best-known retailers in the country. In 1991 Macy's opened a 300-square-foot Fossil "super shop" on the main floor accessories department of its flagship store in New York City. An ideal location for a small, fast-growing company, the Fossil

shop at Macy's represented a marketing boon for the Texas-based company and was a precursor to the retail outlets Fossil would open on its own during the mid-1990s. Fossil's "door" (the company's means of accessing customers) had opened in a noteworthy way.

Sales in 1992 jumped to $73.8 million, more than 90 percent of which was generated by the sale of Fossil and Relic watches. The company's foray into the design and marketing of leather goods accounted for less than five percent of total sales by this point, but this complementary side business would grow in importance to Fossil's bottom line in the near future. Although tremendous financial growth had been achieved, overseas expansion in earnest and other strategic pursuits were yet to come. Before the objectives of international expansion, building brand name recognition, and strategic diversification were fully embraced, the company made a move that provided the financial resources to execute its plans for the future.

IPO: 1993

In 1993 Fossil completed its initial public offering (IPO) of stock, selling 20 percent of the company to investors. Tom Kartsotis retained 40.5 percent control over the company, and Kosta retained 18.8 percent ownership. The conversion to public ownership yielded Fossil $19 million. The stock offering's proceeds went in part to pay off debts and also to fund plans to undergo expansion. By this point, Fossil was producing more than 4 million watches per year. Although the company's in-house team designed the timepieces in Texas, manufacturing took place overseas, in Hong Kong, Uruguay, China, and Brazil.

The year of Fossil's initial public offering of stock proved to be a busy one for the nine-year-old company. Fossil's 500-watch product line was being revamped five times a year. Fossil watches were sold at more than 2,000 locations, including Carter Hawley Hales stores, Dayton Hudson stores, Dillard's, Federated department stores, May department stores, and Macy's, as well as numerous specialty shops. Relic watches, targeted for a different market, appeared in Ames department stores, JCPenney, Service Merchandise stores, and Target stores. The company's office in Dallas employed 240 people who focused on design, marketing, and distribution in the United States and South America. Domestic sales rose from $32 million in 1990 to more than $90 million in 1993.

It was this strong domestic business that the company sought to extend overseas. In 1993 Fossil operated several subsidiaries in Europe, led by Fossil Europe GmbH, the company's primary European operation located in Germany. Other subsidiaries included Fossil France S.A.R.L. and Fossil Italia S.R.L., which served as Fossil's marketing and distribution entities in these countries. Fossil B.V. was formed in 1993 as a holding company for these three European subsidiaries, with Texas-based Fossil, Inc., controlling 70 percent of its newly formed European holding company.

Even though Fossil's staff embraced the idea of international distribution and used fax machines to ease their communications and reporting procedures, only when the company adapted to the realities of international communication did certain issues get resolved. For instance, operations and sales in South America experienced some lag until a fluent Spanish-speaking manager was hired. In an article in the October 8, 1993, issue of *Dallas Business Journal*, Bill Bowen reported on this situation: "By communicating directly with distributors, the company solved problems that it didn't even know existed." Bowen added, "And the company is filling 98% of its orders from South American distributors. ... The lesson hasn't been lost on Fossil officials, who believe the company's philosophy is central to its success overseas." In years to come, an appreciation of language-specific components would reemerge.

INTERNATIONAL MARKETS AND CONCEPT SHOPS: 1994–97

In 1994 the company celebrated its 10th anniversary. That year, foreign sales, increased brand name recognition, and diversified product lines were accomplished via three developments. Fossil launched a line of men's leather goods, in time for Father's Day. The company signed a five-year agreement with Seiko Corporation, gaining entrance into the Japanese market and giving its rival Japanese distribution rights through Seiko's subsidiary Fostim. In addition, Fossil announced it would open 150 concept shops within department stores and planned to increase the number of its shops at outlet malls to 500 by 1996.

By the end of 1994, sales had reached $161.1 million, a one-year increase of $56 million. Despite the continued surge in sales, domestic sales of Fossil watches were flagging, prompting efforts to increase the company's market presence worldwide and to continue diversifying. One achievement of this type occurred in 1994, for instance, when DKNY, an apparel company, undertook a licensing agreement with Fossil. DKNY hired Fossil to design and distribute a line of watches for the winter holiday season, called "DKNY Time." In 1995 Fossil introduced a line of sunglasses, including specially made cases, lessening its reliance on watch sales and increasing its commitment to accessories as product

lines that might fuel growth. That year also brought an increase to 88 percent of the company's stake in Fossil B.V., the holding company for the Fossil subsidiaries in Europe.

As Fossil headed for the mid-1990s, two main strategies were under way. One strategy involved international expansion. In 1995 Fossil watches and accessories were sold in department stores and upscale retail settings in more than 50 countries, a broad geographic foundation to support its business. International sales, particularly those derived from European markets, were accounting for much of the company's sales growth. Other markets experiencing sales growth for Fossil included those in South America. Another strategy involved the operation of Fossil's own freestanding retail locations. By early 1996 the company was operating 20 such shops, compared with 4 units the year before.

An acquisition in 1996 enabled Fossil to build on its Asian market and take advantage of a previous arrangement. The company acquired 81 percent of Fostim, a $700,000 cash purchase that gave Fossil substantial control over the distribution of its products in Japan. Fostim was renamed Fossil Japan and, along with the company's longstanding dealings in Hong Kong, became a primary focus for Fossil in Asia. Although prolific sales growth had characterized the company's existence during its first decade of business, the next decade brought the challenges of how a retailer with a distinctive brand name and image would continue to attract consumers around the globe.

INNOVATION, DESIGN, AND TECHNOLOGY: 1998–2009

Fossil continued its progress. In 1998 Harley-Davidson commissioned Fossil's designers to create products to commemorate the motorcycle manufacturer's 95th anniversary. Fossil's design team also launched a print media campaign that year inspired by the 1940s and featuring the address of the company's Web site. Three magazines received ads specific to their readers: *Details* ran a sports watch ad, *Seventeen* ran an ad for "Big Tic," a blinking watch, and the ad in *Jane* featured a bangle-like fashion watch. These publications shared Fossil's target audience, middle- and upper-income men and women ages 14 to 44. According to Becky Ebenkamp's article in the November 2, 1998, issue of *Brandweek*, "Last holiday season, the company ran inserts in the more mainstream *Glamour* and *GQ* featuring collages of its retro Americana imagery, but opted this time for edgier books."

The media campaign was accompanied by Fossil's relaunch of a Web site whose improvements, thanks to the in-house Web content designers, made direct consumer sales efficient and speedy, gave Fossil greater control, and laid the groundwork for interactive engagement with customers. Because the company had already initiated foreign distribution and sales, global e-commerce was a natural outgrowth. The international online presence, http://global.fossil.com, grew to include translations in languages specific to Fossil's customer base, such as the Netherlands, France, Italy, Spain, and Germany.

As the 21st century began, more gains occurred. The consumer-oriented Web site Bizrate.com gave Fossil.com the 2001 Circle of Excellence award because more than one million consumers had rated Fossil's e-commerce as superior. A 2001 cover story in *Graphis*, an international journal of industrial and graphic arts, highlighted Fossil's design team. Fossil launched an apparel line in 2001 of jeans, T-shirts, and jackets, opening 18 stores in one month, including one in New York City's premier art gallery district, and using its Web site to extend the launch worldwide. Internationally, Fossil bought three Swiss watch and watch-parts companies that year. The acquisitions led to Fossil relocating its European headquarters to Switzerland. The year ended with the purchase of a 500,000-square-foot distribution center in Dallas, whose maximum capacity could reach 800,000 square feet.

Advances in technology remained at the forefront. In 2003, 2004, and 2006, through licensing agreements or collaborations with Microsoft, Pelikon, and Sony Ericsson, Fossil launched wristwatches with personal digital assistant (PDA) features, watches with an animated and illuminated display, and watches with "caller ID" that operated in tandem with the wearer's mobile phone. Affordability was equally vital. A partnership with Wal-Mart in 2005 resulted in private label watches sold at more than 500 Wal-Mart locations. In 2009, Fossil's 25th anniversary, another product line, footwear, got under way, along with "Fossil Finds," special items for collectors to purchase online. With longevity on its side, Fossil has experienced success with design, innovation, and technology that could be measured along an extensive timeline.

Jeffrey L. Covell
Updated, Mary C. Lewis

PRINCIPAL SUBSIDIARIES

Fossil Intermediate Inc.; Fossil Stores I Inc.; Arrow Merchandising Inc.; Fossil Canada Inc.; Fossil Europe B.V. (Netherlands); Fossil Japan K.K.; Fossil Holdings LLC; Fossil Holdings (Gibraltar) Ltd.; Fossil International Holdings Inc.; Swiss Technology Holding GmbH (Switzerland); Fossil Holding LLC Luxembourg S.C.S.

PRINCIPAL DIVISIONS

Fossil United States; Fossil Direct to Consumer; Fossil Europe; Fossil Other International; Fossil Corporate.

PRINCIPAL OPERATING UNITS

Fossil Austria GmbH; Fossil Mexico S.A. de C.V. (52%); Fossil (East) Limited (Hong Kong); Fossil Luxembourg S.A.R.L.; Pulse Time Center Company Ltd. (Hong King, 96%); Fossil (Asia) Ltd. (Hong Kong); Fossil Singapore Ptd. Ltd.; FDT Ltd. (Design Time Ltd.) (Hong Kong, 51%); Fossil (New Zealand) Ltd.; Fossil Time Malaysia Sdn. Bhd.; Fossil Industries Ltd. (Hong Kong); Fossil Trading (Shanghai) Company Ltd. (China); Fossil Europe GmbH (Germany); Fossil Italia S.r.l. (Italy); Gum S.A. (France); Fossil S.L. (Spain, 50%); FESCO GmbH (Germany); Fossil Swiss No Time GmbH (Switzerland); Fossil Swiss X Time GmbH (Switzerland); In Time—Portugal (50%); Fossil U.K. Ltd.; Fossil Stores U.K. Ltd.; Montres Antima S.A. (Switzerland); Fossil Group Europe GmbH (Switzerland); Fossil France S.A.; Logisav S.A.R.L. (France); Trotime Espana S.L. (Spain, 51%); Fossil Retail Stores (Australia) Pty. Ltd.; Fossil Management Services Pty. Ltd. (Australia); Fossil Scandinavia A.B. (Sweden); Fossil Norway A.S.; Fossil Denmark A.S.; Fossil Stores France S.A.S.; Fossil Stores S.r.l. (Italy); Fossil Korea Ltd.; Fossil Macau Limited; Fossil India Private Co. Ltd.; Trylink International Ltd. (Hong Kong, 85%); Fossil Newtime Ltd. (Hong Kong); Fossil Stores Belgium B.V.B.A. (Belgium); Fossil Stores Denmark A.S.; Fossil Stores Spain S.L.; Fossil Stores Sweden A.B.; MW Asia Ltd. (Hong Kong).

PRINCIPAL COMPETITORS

Guess Inc.; LVMH Moöt Hennessy Louis Vuitton S.A.; Swatch Group Ltd.

FURTHER READING

Barrett, William P., "Selling Nostalgia and Whimsy," *Forbes*, November 8, 1993, p. 224.

Bowen, Bill, "Fossil Digs Up Big Sales in Foreign Markets," *Dallas Business Journal*, October 8, 1993, p. B5.

Chabbott, Sophia, "A Matter of Time; Main-Floor Women's Watchmakers Add Swiss Functionality to New Spring Styles," *WWD*, October 24, 2005, p. 54S.

Chen, I-Chun, and David Wethe, "Fossil Buys Swiss Companies (Dallas Wins)," *Dallas Business Journal*, November 16, 2001, p. 21.

Dodge, Fred, *Antique Tins: Identification & Values, Book II*. Paducah, KY: Collector Books, p. 5.

Ebenkamp, Becky, "Fossil Test Could Spur Regular Media Sked," *Brandweek*, November 2, 1998, p. 6.

Fishel, Catharine, and Stacey King Gordon, *The Little Book of Big Packaging Ideas*. Gloucester, MA: Rockport Publishers, 2007, p. 200–07.

"Fossil Acquires Controlling Stake in Fossil Japan from Seiko," *Daily News Record*, April 19, 1996, p. 5.

"Fossil and Pelikon Team Up to Change the Face of Watches," PR Newswire, August 24, 2004.

"Fossil Announces Partnership with Wal-Mart to Produce Fashion Watch Line," PR Newswire, November 18, 2005.

"Fossil.com Recognized with 'Circle of Excellence' Award by Bizrate.com; Over 1 Million Consumers Select Fossil.com for Superior Online Shopping Experience," Business Wire, February 7, 2001, p. 1.

"Fossil Earnings Soar 64.3%," *WWD*, November 16, 1998.

"Fossil Jeans Store Opens in the Heart of New York City's SoHo," Business Wire, July 31, 2001, p. 2021.

Hallett, Vicky, "It's Time for Wristy Business," *U.S. News and World Report*, July 21, 2003, p. 62.

Harrison, Crayton, "Who's Calling? It's at Your Wrist: Fossil Stresses Style over Technology," *Knight Ridder Tribune Business News*, September 28, 2006, p. 1.

Hart, Elena, "Macy's N.Y. Flagship Unfurls Fossil Shop," *Daily News Record*, November 15, 1991, p. 3.

Hicks, Mike, "Fossil, Inc.: The Brand as the Product (How to Sell a $65 Tin with a Free Watch Inside)," *Graphis*, July/August 2001, p. 146–59.

"In Brief: Surfing the Wrist," *WWD*, January 10, 2003, p. 2.

Meadus, Amanda, "Fossil Falters but Watches Tick On," *WWD*, December 11, 1995, p. 8.

Panchuk, Kerri, "Best Real Estate Deals of 2001," *Dallas Business Journal*, February 22, 2002, p. B28.

Pate, Carter, and Harlan Platt, *The Phoenix Effect: 9 Revitalizing Strategies No Business Can Do Without*. New York: John Wiley and Sons, 2002, p. 87–89.

Porter, Matthew, "Lovely Bones: Fossil's (Very) Clever (In-House) Design," *Communication Arts*, March/April 2003, p. 84–91.

Russolillo, Steven, "Fossil Digs Out of Sales Slump by Wooing Young Adults," *Chicago Tribune*, December 23, 2007, p. 8.

Schutze, Jim, "To a Watchmaker, It's Fashion First," *New York Times*, January 19, 2003.

Tell, Caroline, "Fossil Launches Growth Initiatives in Step with 25th Anniversary," *WWD*, July 20, 2009, p. 21.

Vargo, Julie, "Fossil's New Fuel," *Daily News Record*, February 11, 1994, p. S12.

Welch, David, "Despite Stock Slide, Fossil Still Has Some True Believers," *Dallas Business Journal*, December 1, 1995, p. 7.

Wood, Sean, "Watchmaker Plans IPO to Fund Acquisitions, Expansion," *Dallas Business Journal*, February 7, 1992, p. 3.

GENERAL ATOMICS

General Atomics

3550 General Atomics Court
San Diego, California 92121-1122
U.S.A.
Telephone: (858) 455-3000
Fax: (858) 455-3621
Web site: http://www.ga.com

Private Company
Incorporated: 1955 as General Atomic Division
Employees: 5,000 (est.)
NAICS: 212291 Uranium-Radium-Vanadium Ore Mining; 331419 Primary Smelting and Refining of Nonferrous Metal (except Copper and Aluminum); 332410 Power Boiler and Heat Exchanger Manufacturing; 332999 All Other Miscellaneous Fabricated Metal Product Manufacturing; 334111 Electronic Computer Manufacturing; 334416 Electronic Coil, Transformer, and Other Inductor Manufacturing; 334511 Search, Detection, Navigation, Guidance, Aeronautical, and Nautical System and Instrument Manufacturing; 335314 Relay and Industrial Control Manufacturing; 335999 All Other Miscellaneous Electrical Equipment and Component Manufacturing; 336411 Aircraft Manufacturing; 541690 Other Scientific and Technical Consulting Services; 541712 Research and Development in the Physical, Engineering, and Life Sciences (except Biotechnology).

■ ■ ■

General Atomics is a leading manufacturer of high-technology systems for a wide range of business sectors, among them energy, defense, transportation, and construction. The company's diverse products and services include aircraft launch and recovery equipment, superconducting magnets, computer systems, radar systems, logistical support solutions, particle accelerators, and hazardous material destruction systems. Over the years, General Atomics has played a pioneering role in the development of nuclear technology, constructing innovative fusion and fission reactors for both the domestic and global markets. Through its wholly owned subsidiary, General Atomics Aeronautical Systems, Inc., (GA-ASI) the company has also emerged as a major supplier of aircraft to the U.S. military, becoming most famous in recent years for its Predator unmanned aerial vehicle (UAV).

ORIGINS AND GROWTH: 1950–67

General Atomics (GA) was established as a division of General Dynamics Corporation in mid-1955. Originally known as General Atomic, the division was the creation of General Dynamics chairman John Jay Hopkins and Frederic de Hoffmann, GA's first general manager and president. De Hoffmann was a veteran of the Manhattan Project at the Los Alamos National Laboratory in New Mexico. GA's first offices were in the General Dynamics facility on Hancock Street in San Diego, California.

The next summer some of the most eminent nuclear scientists and engineers of the day gathered at GA's next temporary headquarters, a schoolhouse on San Diego's Barnard Street. (GA would later "adopt" the school in 1994 as part of its Education Outreach program.) Their order of business was to find suitable peacetime uses for nuclear energy and to come up with a commercial product for GA to produce.

San Diego voters approved the transfer of land to GA for permanent facilities at Torrey Pines. The John Jay Hopkins Laboratory for Pure and Applied Science was formally dedicated there on June 25, 1959, with these words from its namesake: "We are establishing here a timeless institution, a thing of the mind and spirit, devoted to man's progress." GA's staff already numbered 700, and the firm was involved with several research projects.

A prototype for a small, safe research reactor, the TRIGA, had debuted on May 3, 1958. GA developed special uranium-zirconium hydride fuel elements for the reactor, which gave it a level of what was called "inherent safety," rather than the engineered safety of most reactors. Marketable within four years, the TRIGA would be one of GA's most enduring and successful projects. In the next 40 years, more than 65 TRIGA reactors would be built in two dozen countries around the world.

The company spent the next 20 years trying to make high-temperature gas-cooled reactor (HTGR) technology competitive with the light-water technology that was preferred in the 1950s. The latter used water to cool the reactor. GA's process used helium, reducing pollution and overheating concerns and lessening the amount of fuel needed. Helium also did not become radioactive, unlike water. GA's reactor design used a graphite core, which could tolerate an increase of several thousand degrees above its 850 degrees Celsius operating temperature without damage.

GA began to develop a Maritime Gas Cooled Reactor for the Atomic Energy Commission and studied controlled fusion for a group of Texas utilities. A prototype gas-cooled reactor built on the system of the Philadelphia Electric Co. went on line in the 1960s.

Project Orion was an attempt to design a 4,000-ton, long-range spacecraft powered by controlled nuclear pulses, or explosions, to the point that a small test vehicle (dubbed "Hot Rod") powered by conventional explosives was built. However, Orion was canceled in 1965 due to political and technical challenges.

OWNED BY GULF, ROYAL DUTCH/SHELL IN THE SEVENTIES

Gulf Oil acquired GA in 1967, and Royal Dutch/Shell became a partner in GA in 1973 with a $200 million investment. It added another $200 million to $300 million in another two years. GA, which had been known under the name Gulf General Atomic, then Gulf Energy & Environmental Systems, became the General Atomic Company in January 1974.

Construction of GA's first commercial power plant, built for the Public Service Co. of Colorado (PSCO), was completed in 1973. However, the reactor did not go on line for another three years, and then it experienced several equipment failures until it was shut down in 1989. Other utilities committed to buy 10 more reactors in the mid-1970s, but these commitments were canceled. GA then focused on reactor technology research. In 1977, joined by 28 utilities, it formed Gas Cooled Reactor Associates (GCRA).

Founding President Frederic de Hoffmann had left GA in 1969 and went on to head the Salk Institute. GA was led during the mid-1970s by Bill Finley. Finley's 1977 Business Plan set forth new goals of profitability and diversification. Dr. Harold Agnew, formerly director of the Los Alamos Scientific Laboratory, became president of GA in March 1979. The next month, the Three Mile Island accident dramatically affected the entire nuclear power industry. GA claimed its gas-cooled reactors were the safest in the world and would have been capable of averting the Three Mile Island disaster. Nonetheless, the new regulatory environment raised the cost of operating any type of nuclear plant.

Agnew set GA on a course of diversification. It used its concrete structure expertise to build offshore oil tanks. The company also looked abroad, participating in a joint U.S.-Japanese fusion power development project called Doublet III.

From December 1975 to June 1984, GA was embroiled in litigation by Westinghouse Electric Corp.

<table>
<tr><td colspan="2">

KEY DATES

■

</td></tr>
<tr><td>1955:</td><td>General Atomic Division (GA) is formed as a unit of General Dynamics.</td></tr>
<tr><td>1958:</td><td>TRIGA research reactor prototype is produced.</td></tr>
<tr><td>1959:</td><td>John Jay Hopkins Laboratory is dedicated at Torrey Pines.</td></tr>
<tr><td>1967:</td><td>Gulf Oil acquires GA.</td></tr>
<tr><td>1974:</td><td>Royal Dutch/Shell becomes equal partner in GA with Gulf Oil.</td></tr>
<tr><td>1986:</td><td>Denver investors Neal and Linden Blue acquire GA.</td></tr>
<tr><td>1992:</td><td>General Atomics Aeronautical Systems (GA-ASI) is formed.</td></tr>
<tr><td>1994:</td><td>Predator UAV makes its first flight.</td></tr>
<tr><td>2004:</td><td>GA enters into agreement with U.S. Navy to design and build electromagnetic aircraft launch system (EMALS).</td></tr>
<tr><td>2006:</td><td>GA receives grant from U.S. Department of Energy to explore development of a next-generation nuclear power plant.</td></tr>
</table>

and United Nuclear Corp. (UNC), alleging an international price-fixing conspiracy. Twenty-eight other companies were also charged in lawsuits in Illinois and New Mexico. GA ended up settling claims against it for $200 million.

CHANGING HANDS: 1982–88

GA had revenues of $115 million in 1980, most of it ($85 million) from government nuclear-energy research contracts. The company employed about 2,200 people, down 600 from its mid-1970s peak.

Gulf Oil bought out its 50/50 partner, Royal Dutch/Shell Group's Scallop Nuclear Inc., effective January 1, 1982. Gulf became full owner of General Atomic, while Scallop received a large piece of land next to GA's San Diego headquarters. General Atomic then became known as GA Technologies Inc. Chevron became GA's owner after its merger with Gulf Oil in mid-1984.

A systems and services group was started in 1982 as GA sought to become less dependent on government funding, specifically the Department of Energy. Among the group's offerings was toxic waste disposal. GA was also involved in the research of particle-beam weapons and a space-based nuclear reactor for the Department of Defense. Revenues reached $154.5 million in 1985.

GA joined with the University of California–San Diego (UCSD) to launch the San Diego Supercomputer Center in 1985. The center received most of its funding from the National Science Foundation and performed research on earthquakes, the global climate, and other analytical and mathematical problems.

Two Denver-area investors, Neal and Linden Blue, acquired GA from Chevron Corporation for more than $50 million in 1986. The company was then known as GA Technologies. After the purchase, Dr. Kerry Dance, who had submitted an employee buyout bid, left the company as president, a position he had held since January 1985 following the retirement of Dr. Harold Agnew. Neal Blue became CEO and board chairman, while Linden Blue became vice chairman overseeing reactor programs. In 1988 the company changed its name to General Atomics.

TAKING WING: 1990–2000

GA formed a 50/50 radioactive cleanup joint venture with Indiana-based hazardous waste firm Canonie Environmental Services Corp. in 1990. Nuclear Remediation Technologies Corp. was founded with about six employees and $3 million in start-up capital. In the fall of 1989 the Department of Energy had identified 10 military nuclear-weapon sites for remediation over the next three decades.

In 1991 GA acquired Chevron Corp.'s North American uranium assets. These holdings included the largest known uranium deposit in the United States, at Mount Taylor, New Mexico.

The breakup of the Soviet Union allowed for closer cooperation between GA and Russian nuclear researchers. In 1993 the Russian Ministry for Atomic Energy teamed with GA in designing a new prototype of a gas-cooled reactor. The aim was to generate commercial sales of the reactors around the world.

Former Admiral Thomas P. Cassidy and six engineers formed General Atomics Aeronautical Systems Inc. (GA-ASI) as an affiliated company of GA in 1992. The unit's mission was to develop unmanned aerial vehicles (UAVs). Drones in the past had been limited by range restrictions and the need to process film from their cameras. GA-ASI set out to develop an unmanned craft that could be controlled from greater distances while transmitting battlefield pictures in real time.

The company's first craft was called the Gnat. It could remain airborne for more than 40 hours. The Gnat was used in combat, but another UAV would become better known to military planners. First flown in 1994, the Predator was used over the skies of Bosnia during the NATO intervention there in the late 1990s. After the conflict, GA-ASI signed deals with several European companies to meet local requirements for UAVs. GA-ASI was spun off as an independent company in 1994. The Predator's real-time battlefield coverage capabilities made headlines over the skies of Afghanistan and Iraq after September 11, 2001.

In the mid-1990s GA had about 1,300 employees in San Diego. GA was involved in nuclear space power systems, weapons destruction, and superconducting magnets in addition to nuclear reactors and fusion.

PROMISING RESEARCH: THE NEW MILLENNIUM

GA was involved in a number of unique research projects in the late 1990s and beyond. One of them was a ship using a superconducting magnet to detonate mines at sea. It was also helping to market a Russian design for high-temperature batteries used to power sensors on oil rigs. In December 1999 a GA-led team was one of two to win a contract to design an electromagnetic aircraft launcher for U.S. Navy carriers. GA began selling its new high-resolution LYNX radar system to the U.S. Army in 2000.

Some of GA's research involved using fusion processes to generate energy. In one process, a D-shaped magnetic field keeps plasma in place inside a chamber 15 feet in diameter, called a tokamak. The plasma is spun from 10 to 100 miles per second, creating pressure, while the temperature reaches millions of degrees. The reactions, which last only a few seconds, combine light elements such as deuterium and tritium to produce heavy elements and energy. However, scientists had been unable to produce a fusion reaction that yielded more energy than the large amount needed to sustain them in a lab.

Another GA team developed the equivalent of "lightning in a bottle." Its Rotating Tube Discharge kept a long column of plasma in place inside a spinning tube. A number of industrial applications were envisioned. In other developments in the year 2000, Chong Yuan, an expert in enzyme technology, joined GA as director of Diazyme Laboratories, a new biotechnology division.

GA was also leading several Pennsylvania-based agencies in the Urban Maglev consortium to develop a rail system based on magnetic levitation. The research was sponsored by the Federal Transit Administration. In one test in early 2002, GA engineers levitated a ton of weight using a single magnet module, which could be combined with others to suspend an entire 40,000-pound train.

In 2003 GA and its affiliates were involved in a wide range of other projects at the leading edge of technology, including flexible flat panel displays (called organic light emitting diodes). The Energy Products Division had won a contract to produce 2,500 capacitors for Sandia National Laboratories. GA entered a joint venture with Royal Philips Electronics to develop chipsets using GA's ultra-wideband (UWB) wireless networking technology. The Energy Products Division had been formed in 2000 from business lines acquired from San Diego's Maxwell Technologies. The division was subsequently merged with GA's Sorrento Electronics unit, a supplier of products for the petroleum and nuclear power industries.

EXPANSION DURING WARTIME: 2004 ON

During the second half of the decade, General Atomics continued to increase its presence in the defense sector, both at home and abroad. In April 2004 GA won a $145 million bid to build electromagnetic aircraft catapults for the U.S. Navy. According to reports, the new electromagnetic aircraft launch system (EMALS) would reduce the personnel needed to operate the equipment by 30 percent, making it far more efficient than traditional steam-powered catapults. EMALS would also have a capacity to launch a wider variety of aircraft. Later that year, the company's principal subsidiary, GA-ASI, entered an agreement with two of Germany's leading defense contractors, Rheinmetall Defense Electronics and Diehl BGT Defense, to begin marketing the Predator UAV in Germany. As part of the deal, the companies eventually hoped to expand the market for the Predator into other European nations.

In February 2005 General Atomics sealed a $46 million contract to develop a new warship motor for the Navy. Under the terms of the deal, GA would design, build, and test an innovative propulsion system using superconductor technology. That June, General Atomics announced that it would fold its Reconnaissance Systems unit into GA-ASI. According to a statement quoted in the June 9, 2005, issue of *Aerospace Daily & Defense Report*, the merging of the two units reflected the company's "commitment to delivering comprehensive solutions on a cost effective basis." Two months later GA-ASI outbid rival Northrup Grumman for a lucrative new contract to manufacture extended-range/multi-purpose (ERMP) UAVs for the U.S. Army. In a deal worth $214.4 million, GA-ASI would build a total of 132 UAVs, more than double the original order of 60.

While its defense business thrived, General Atomics continued to explore new opportunities in other business sectors. In February 2006 GA entered an agreement to help develop a nuclear test reactor in West Texas. The new reactor, the HT3R, would be based on the company's helium-cooled reactor technology, and it would have an output capacity of 25 thermal megawatts. That October, GA was one of three companies tapped by the U.S. Department of Energy to begin exploring the possibility of constructing a next-generation nuclear power plant within the next decade and a half. In February 2008 GA joined with Texas AgriLife Research to begin researching potential ways to extract biofuels from microalgae.

While General Atomics remained active in a wide range of technological fields, by the end of the decade it was clear that defense had become one of the company's principal revenue sources. In 2009 the U.S. Navy awarded GA a $573 million contract for the production of the electromagnetic aircraft launch system for the CVN-78 aircraft carrier, as well as a $107 million contract for production of the advanced arresting gear ship set for the same vessel.

At the same time, the company's subsidiary GA-ASI was also thriving. By 2010 General Atomics had grown to more than 5,000 employees, well more than double its workforce at the beginning of the decade. Of this total, roughly 3,000 worked for GA-ASI. Much of the subsidiary's rapid growth over this period had been driven by widespread demand for its unmanned aerial vehicles, in particular its Predator UAVs. In light of this trend, it became clear that defense contracts would be a principal engine of growth at General Atomics for many years to come.

Frederick C. Ingram
Updated, Stephen Meyer

PRINCIPAL SUBSIDIARIES

General Atomics Aeronautical Systems, Inc. (GA-ASI); General Atomics Electronics Systems, Inc.

PRINCIPAL DIVISIONS

Electromagnetic Systems.

PRINCIPAL OPERATING UNITS

Advanced Technologies Group; Energy Group; Nuclear Fuels Group.

PRINCIPAL COMPETITORS

Boeing Integrated Defense Systems; Computer Sciences Corporation; General Electric Company; Lockheed Martin Corporation; Northrop Grumman Corporation.

FURTHER READING

Dant, Jennifer, "It's No More Wait and See for GA," *San Diego Business Journal*, July 8, 1996, p. 5.

Emshwiller, John R., "General Atomics Ready for Nuclear Power Resurgence," *Wall Street Journal*, June 7, 1993, p. B2.

Graves, Brad, "GA Makes Fusion Breakthrough," *San Diego Business Journal*, July 9, 2001, p. 8.

Kuzela, Lad, "A Nuclear Pioneer Tries the Power of Persuasion," *Industry Week*, April 20, 1981, p. 73.

Loveless, Bill, "New Contracts Mark Opening Steps for Next Generation Nuclear Plant," *Inside Energy with Federal Lands*, October 2, 2006, p. 12.

Morrocco, John D., "Predator Builder Teams with Europeans," *Aviation Week & Space Technology*, June 28, 1999, p. 49.

Pae, Peter, "Future Is Now for Creator of Predator; Unmanned Vehicle Made by San Diego's General Atomics Is Helping Revolutionize Warfare in Skies over Afghanistan," *Los Angeles Times*, January 3, 2002, p. C1.

"Reactors Fuel GA's New Approach," *San Diego Union-Tribune*, February 22, 1988.

Squeo, Anne Marie, "Small Maker of Unmanned Jets Fights Big; Goliath Competitors Scramble to Move in on General Atomic's Specialty," *Wall Street Journal*, January 29, 2003, p. B8.

Warwick, Graham, "GA Catapults to US Navy Aircraft Carrier Contract; Manufacturer to Develop Electromagnetic Launcher in a Five-year Deal Worth over $145m," *Flight International*, April 20, 2004, p. 18.

Hasbro, Inc.

———————■———————

1027 Newport Avenue
Pawtucket, Rhode Island 02862-1059
U.S.A.
Telephone: (401) 431-8697
Toll Free: (800) 255-5516
Fax: (401) 431-8535
Web site: http://www.hasbro.com

Public Company
Founded: 1923
Incorporated: 1926 as Hassenfeld Brothers Inc.
Employees: 5,800
Sales: $4.07 billion (2009)
Stock Exchanges: New York London
Ticker Symbol: HAS
NAICS: 339931 Doll and Stuffed Toy Manufacturing;
    339932 Game, Toy, and Children's Vehicle
    Manufacturing; 511210 Software Publishers

■ ■ ■

Truly successful toy companies do not just make toys. They manufacture popular culture. Hasbro, Inc., which is the second largest toy maker in the world, behind number one Mattel, Inc., certainly fits that description. From an iconic military action hero to a plastic anthropomorphized potato to vehicles that transform into robots to the largest bird in the world, Hasbro toys are instantly recognized by millions of Americans. Hasbro makes G.I. Joe, Mr. Potato Head, and Transformers, and owns licenses for Sesame Street characters. Through numerous acquisitions beginning in the 1980s, it also

became the maker of Playskool and Romper Room preschool toys, Tonka trucks, Nerf toys, Cabbage Patch Kids, and Pokemon game cards. Hasbro has become dominant in the area of board games and puzzles through its ownership of Milton Bradley (maker of Scrabble and Parcheesi) and Parker Brothers (maker of Monopoly). It is also licensed to develop toys based on Disney Studios movie releases. In 2010 Hasbro entered television production, introducing the children's television channel The Hub in conjunction with TV giant Discovery Communications.

EARLY HISTORY: 1923–35

Hasbro traces its origin to an enterprise founded in Providence, Rhode Island, in 1923 by Henry, Hilal, and Herman Hassenfeld, brothers who had immigrated to the United States from Poland. The Hassenfeld brothers engaged in the textile remnant business, selling cloth leftovers. By the mid-1920s they were using the remnants to make hat liners and pencil-box covers. After realizing the popularity of the covers, they soon began making the boxes themselves with eight employees, all of whom were family members. In 1926 the company incorporated under the name Hassenfeld Brothers Inc.

Hilal Hassenfeld became involved in other textile ventures, and Henry took control of the new company. Although a paternalistic employer, Henry Hassenfeld was also a tough and shrewd businessman. During the Great Depression, with 150 employees in 1929 and 200 employees in 1930, Hassenfeld Brothers commanded annual sales of $500,000 from sales of pencil boxes and cloth zipper pouches filled with school supplies. At that point, however, the company's pencil supplier decided to raise its prices and sell its own boxes at prices lower than Hassenfeld's. Henry Hassenfeld responded with a vow to enter the pencil business himself, and in 1935 Hassenfeld Brothers began manufacturing pencils. This product line would provide the company with a steady source of revenue for the next 45 years.

TRANSFORMATION TO TOY MANUFACTURING: 1935 TO 1960

During the late 1930s the Hassenfeld Brothers began to manufacture toys, an extension of the company's line of school supplies. Initial offerings included medical sets for junior nurses and doctors and modeling clay. During World War II Henry's younger son, Merrill Hassenfeld, acted on a customer's suggestion to make and market a junior air raid warden kit, which came complete with flashlights and toy gas masks.

By 1942, as demand for school supplies tapered off, the company had become primarily a toy company, although it continued its large, profitable pencil business. Hilal Hassenfeld died in 1943, at which point Henry Hassenfeld became CEO and his son Merrill Hassenfeld became president. Also during World War II, the company ventured into plastics but was forced, due to labor shortages, to reduce employment to 75.

After the war Merrill Hassenfeld began marketing a girls' makeup kit after seeing his four-year-old daughter play with candy as though it were lipstick and rouge. In 1952 the company introduced its still-classic Mr. Potato Head, the first toy to be advertised on television. In 1954 Hassenfeld became a major licensee for Disney characters. By 1960 revenues reached $12 million, and Hassenfeld Brothers had become one of the largest private toy companies in the United States.

TURBULENT TIMES: 1960–69

Henry Hassenfeld died in 1960. Merrill Hassenfeld then assumed full control of the parent company, while his older brother Harold Hassenfeld, continued to run the pencil-making operations. Merrill Hassenfeld's succession was logical given his interest and expertise in the toy business, but it also marked the beginning of an intramural rivalry between the two sides of the company. Harold Hassenfeld would come to resent the fact that the pencil business received a lower percentage of capital investment even though it was a steadier performer and accounted for a higher percentage of profits than toys.

Hassenfeld Brothers seemed to defy the vagaries of the toy business in the early 1960s when it introduced what would become one of its most famous and successful product lines. According to author Marvin Kaye in *A Toy Is Born*, the company conceived G.I. Joe in 1963 when a licensing agent suggested a merchandise tie-in with a television program about the U.S. Marine Corps called *The Lieutenant*. The company liked the idea of a military doll, but did not want to pin its fate on a TV show that might prove short-lived. Instead, Hassenfeld Brothers created its own concept, and in 1964 the company introduced G.I. Joe, a 12-inch "action figure" with articulated joints. In its first two years, G.I. Joe brought in between $35 and $40 million and accounted for nearly two-thirds of the company's total sales.

The company changed its name to Hasbro Industries, Inc., in 1968. It had sold its toys under the Hasbro trade name for some time. It also went public but issued only a small portion of Hasbro stock on the open market. The majority stake remained in the hands of the Hassenfeld family. At the same time, Hasbro decided that it could no longer ignore the public's growing disapproval of war toys, which was fueled by disillusionment with the Vietnam War. In 1969 G.I. Joe, still the company's leading moneymaker, was repackaged in a less militaristic "adventure" motif, with a different range of accessories. Also in 1969, the company acquired Burt Claster Enterprises, the Baltimore, Maryland-based television production company responsible for the popular *Romper Room* show for preschoolers. Burt Claster Enterprises had also begun to manufacture a line of Romper Room toys. Nevertheless, a month-long Teamsters strike and troubles with suppliers in Asia hurt Hasbro in 1969, and the company posted a $1 million loss for the year.

TURBULENCE CONTINUES: 1970–79

The 1960s ended on a turbulent note for Hasbro, providing a foretaste of the decade to come. In 1970

KEY DATES

◼

1923: Polish immigrant brothers Henry and Hilal Hassenfeld found a textile remnant business in Providence, Rhode Island.

1935: Hassenfeld Brothers begins manufacturing pencils, one of its stalwart revenue sources until 1980.

1942: By the end of World War II, the company had expanded its product line to include toys, such as paint sets, wax crayons, and doctor and nurse kits.

1952: Mr. Potato Head, the first toy to be advertised on television, is introduced.

1968: Company name changed to Hasbro Industries, Inc.; the company goes public with a small portion of stock; the rest remains with the Hassenfeld family.

1984: Alan Hassenfeld becomes president of Hasbro; the company acquires the Milton Bradley Co. and its subsidiary Playskool; company is renamed Hasbro Bradley Inc.

1985: Hasbro unites its four subsidiaries (Hasbro Toys, Milton Bradley, Playskool, and Playskool Baby) under the name Hasbro, Inc.

1995: Company acquires Larami Corp., makers of SuperSoaker brand water guns; Hasbro begins releasing CD-ROM versions of board games such as Monopoly and Scrabble, and other popular toys, including Tonka and Mr. Potato Head.

1997: Company acquires licensing rights to three new Star Wars prequels for almost $600 million and over 7 percent of Hasbro stock.

2003: Alfred Verrecchia becomes CEO.

Hasbro began to diversify, and it opened a chain of nursery schools franchised under the Romper Room name. The company hoped to take advantage of President Richard M. Nixon's Family Assistance Plan, which subsidized day care for working mothers. Running the preschools proved problematic for the company. Merrill Hassenfeld's son, Alan Hassenfeld, told the *Wall Street Journal*, "We'd get phone calls saying, 'We can't find one of the kids.' The whole company would stop." Within five years Hasbro had left the day care business. Another ill-fated diversification move was Hasbro's line of Galloping Gourmet cookware, which

sought to capitalize on a contemporary television cooking show of the same name. That venture literally fell apart when termites ate salad bowls stacked in a warehouse.

In addition, two products from Hasbro's 1970 line turned into public relations disasters: Javelin Lawn Darts were declared unsafe by the government, and Hypo-Squirt, a water gun shaped like a hypodermic needle, was dubbed by the press a "junior junkie" kit. Both products were promptly removed from the market. The continuing success of *Romper Room* and its related toy line proved to be a bright spot for Hasbro, although the company came under fire from the citizens group Action for Children's Television, which accused the program of becoming an advertising vehicle for toys.

In 1974 Merrill Hassenfeld became CEO of Hasbro, and his son, Stephen D. Hassenfeld, became president. Hasbro regained its profitability but floundered once again later in the decade. Poor cash flow accounted for some of the problems, but the company's underlying mistake was casting its net too far and too wide in an effort to compensate for G.I. Joe's declining popularity. Hasbro discontinued G.I. Joe in 1975 because of the rising price of plastic. By 1977, the year Hasbro acquired the licensing rights to Peanuts cartoon characters, the company suffered $2.5 million in losses and carried a heavy debt.

The financial situation became serious enough that Hasbro's bankers forced it to suspend dividend payments in early 1979. The toy division's poor performance fueled Harold Hassenfeld's resentment that the Empire Pencil subsidiary continued to receive a smaller proportion of capital spending to profits than did the toy division. The dam threatened to burst in 1979 when Merrill Hassenfeld died at age 61. Stephen Hassenfeld was chairman Merrill Hassenfeld's heir apparent, but Harold Hassenfeld refused to recognize Stephen Hassenfeld's authority.

CORE PRODUCTS REFUEL
SUCCESS: 1980–83

The feud was resolved in 1980, when Hasbro spun off Empire Pencil, which had become the nation's largest pencil maker, and Harold exchanged his Hasbro shares for shares of the new company. At the same time, Stephen Hassenfeld became CEO and chairman of the board of the toy company and dedicated himself to turning Hasbro around. Where it had once been overextended, the company slashed its product line by one-third between 1978 and 1981, and its annual number of new products was cut in half. Hasbro also refocused on simpler toys, such as Mr. Potato Head:

products that were inexpensive to make, could be sold at lower prices, and had longer life cycles. This conservative philosophy precluded Hasbro from entering the hot new field of electronic games, as did the fact that it could not spare the cash to develop such toys. The decision to stay out of the market was vindicated in the early 1980s when the electronics boom turned bust and shook out many competitors.

Perhaps the most important event in Hasbro's revival was the 1982 return of G.I. Joe. The U.S. political climate at the time made military toys popular again, and G.I. Joe was reintroduced as an antiterrorist commando, complete with a cast of comrades and exotic villains, whose personalities were sculpted with the help of Marvel Comics. Two years later, Hasbro introduced its highly successful Transformers line featuring toy vehicles and guns that could be reconfigured into toy robots. Transformers were tied into a children's animated TV series and proved so popular that *People* magazine asked Stephen Hassenfeld to pose with them for a cover photo.

In 1983 Hasbro acquired GLENCO Infant Items, a manufacturer of infant products and the world's largest bib producer. Hasbro also sold about 37 percent of its own stock to Warner Communications in exchange for cash and Warner's struggling Knickerbocker Toy Company subsidiary, which made Raggedy Ann and Raggedy Andy dolls. The new Warner holdings did not threaten the company's autonomy, however. The shares were put into a voting trust controlled by the Hassenfeld brothers and other Hasbro executives. In 1984 Stephen Hassenfeld turned over the position of president to his brother, Alan, while remaining CEO and chairman.

MERGING WITH MILTON BRADLEY: 1984

In the early 1980s Hasbro was the nation's sixth best-selling toy maker, with revenues of $225.4 million and $15.2 million in profits. Flush with newfound strength, in 1984 it acquired Milton Bradley, the nation's fifth best-selling toy maker, and second only to Parker Brothers in production of board games and puzzles. Milton Bradley had been founded by a Springfield, Massachusetts, lithographer who set up shop in 1860 and immediately turned out a popular reproduction of a portrait of presidential candidate Abraham Lincoln. Bradley's portrait, however, showed Lincoln clean-shaven, so when Lincoln grew his beard, sales fell off. Looking for a way to stay in business, Bradley invented and produced a board game called the Checkered Game of Life, a distant precursor of a popular Milton Bradley game, the Game of Life, which was introduced in 1960.

The game's success convinced Bradley to stay in the game business. During the Civil War he produced a lightweight packet of board games for the amusement of Union troops. The company incorporated in 1882.

During the late 19th century, Milton Bradley (MB) relied mostly on such favorites as chess and checkers and traditional European games. During the 20th century, however, the company designed and marketed more original games, sometimes with great success. During the Depression, a Milton Bradley financial game called Easy Money became popular. In the 1950s Milton Bradley pioneered games with tie-ins to television shows, including the early favorite Concentration. In 1968 MB acquired Chicago-based Playskool Manufacturing, which was noted for its preschool toys. Among Milton Bradley's later successes was the "body action" classic Twister, which was published in 1971 and became a popular prop with talk show hosts for a while after Johnny Carson challenged Eva Gabor to a go-around on the *Tonight Show*.

In 1984, however, Milton Bradley had found itself in an uncertain financial position after fending off a hostile takeover from British conglomerate Hanson Trust. In the wake of that failed bid, several unidentified parties bought up large blocks of MB stock, fueling speculation that another takeover attempt was imminent. Finally, in May 1984, MB agreed to be acquired by Hasbro for $360 million. MB's strength in board games and puzzles complemented Hasbro's plastic toys and stuffed animals. Milton Bradley's Playskool subsidiary provided a solid preschool line including such classics as Lincoln Logs and ABC blocks. The new Hasbro Bradley Inc. immediately challenged Mattel's position as the nation's leading toy maker. In 1985 Hasbro Bradley became Hasbro, Inc.

If the Hasbro and Milton Bradley product lines merged well, their chief executives did not. Stephen Hassenfeld became president and CEO of Hasbro Bradley, with Milton Bradley chief James Shea Jr. becoming chairman. After only a few months, however, Shea resigned. Stephen Hassenfeld became chairman, with his brother Alan Hassenfeld replacing him as president.

REACHING THE TOP: 1985–89

Hasbro surpassed Mattel to become the largest toy company in the world in the mid-1980s. Having done so, it then attempted to dethrone Mattel's Barbie, queen of the fashion doll market. In 1986 Hasbro introduced Jem, a fashion doll given the dual identity of business woman/record producer and purple-haired rock musician. While Jem posted strong initial sales, her popularity quickly faded and she was retired the following year. In 1988 the company brought out Maxie, a blonde doll scaled to match Barbie in size so that she could wear Barbie clothing and accessories. Maxie was discontinued in 1990.

In 1989 Hasbro acquired bankrupt rival Coleco Industries, owners of the Cabbage Patch Dolls, for $85 million. The Coleco acquisition proved to be Stephen Hassenfeld's final business achievement. In 1989 he died at age 47, having converted the relatively modest toy company that his grandfather had founded into a juggernaut at the top of its industry with 1989 sales of $1.41 billion, a huge increase over the $104 million figure of the year he took over.

ACQUISITIONS CONTINUE:
1990–95

A new and more challenging era began when 41-year-old Alan Hassenfeld became chairman and CEO of Hasbro. The younger Hassenfeld continued the acquisition trend of the 1980s, as Hasbro acquired Tonka Corporation in 1991 for $486 million. With the deal, Hasbro added not only the Tonka line of toy trucks but also Tonka's Parker Brothers unit, the maker of Monopoly, and Kenner Products, which featured Batman figures and the Strawberry Shortcake doll. The Parker Brothers unit was merged into Hasbro's already strong Milton Bradley division. Hasbro took a $59 million charge in 1991 to cover costs of consolidating the Tonka acquisition and restructuring overall operations.

In the late 1980s Alan Hassenfeld had spearheaded an effort to increase Hasbro's international sales, primarily by taking toys that failed in the U.S. market and remarketing them overseas at prices as high as four times their original prices. He had helped increase international sales from $268 million in 1985 to $433 million in 1988. It was not surprising, then, that as chairman he pushed to increase Hasbro's international presence. He did just that in 1991, establishing operations in Greece, Hungary, and Mexico.

It was the Far East, however, that Hassenfeld saw as a critical market for Hasbro to develop. The company gained two more distribution channels there in 1992 by purchasing Nomura Toys Ltd., based in Japan, and buying a majority stake in Palmyra, a Southeast Asian toy distributor. Thanks to these efforts, by 1995, Hasbro's international sales had reached $1.28 billion, which represented almost 45 percent of total sales, a significant increase over the 22 percent figure of 1985. More than 46 percent of the company's operating profit was attributable to operations outside the United States in 1995. One international setback came in 1993 when

Hasbro lost out to arch-rival Mattel in a bid for J.W. Spear, a U.K.-based maker of games.

While international results were improving, Hasbro began to show some weaknesses on the domestic front. Much of the growth since 1980 had come from the company's various acquisitions, along with Hasbro's largely successful efforts to leverage the new assets it gained through the deals. Many new product development activities, on the other hand, were not as successful, with the exception of product lines developed to tie in with the movie *Jurassic Park* and the popular children's television show *Barney & Friends*. As a result, domestic sales stagnated in the early 1990s, and actually fell from $1.67 billion in 1993 to $1.58 billion in 1995.

Worldwide sales showed much slower growth as well. From 1991, the year of the Tonka acquisition, to 1995, sales increased only 33.5 percent, with half of the increase occurring in 1992 alone. To help improve the company's domestic performance, a reorganization was completed in 1994 that merged the Hasbro Toy, Playskool, Playskool Baby, Kenner, and Kid Dimension units into a new Hasbro Toy Group. Meanwhile, in 1993 rival Mattel acquired Fisher-Price and soon thereafter regained the number one spot in the toy industry.

ENTERING THE ELECTRONIC
GAME MARKET: 1995

Also contributing to Hasbro's challenges in the 1990s was its belated struggle to enter the market for electronic games. Eventually, in 1992, the company began development of a mass-market virtual reality game system. Although such a system was successfully developed, it was judged too expensive for the mass market and the project was abandoned in 1995, resulting in a charge of $31.1 million. In 1993 Hasbro bought a 15 percent stake in Virgin Interactive Entertainment, a producer of game software for Sega and Nintendo systems, with the intention of developing software based on Hasbro toys and games. Two years later, however, Hasbro dissolved the partnership and sold its stake.

A more promising venture began in 1995 with the establishment of Hasbro Interactive and the release of its first product that same year, a CD-ROM version of Monopoly. More than 180,000 units were sold in the first eight weeks following its release. Additional titles released in 1996 included Risk, Battleship, and Playskool-brand games.

MERGER WITH MATTEL
AVERTED: 1996

In 1995 Mattel approached Hasbro about a possible merger of the two largest toy companies in the world.

Negotiations took place in secret over the course of several months until the Hasbro board early in 1996 unanimously turned down a $5.2 billion merger proposal that would have given Hasbro stockholders a 73 percent premium over the then-current selling price. Hasbro officials expressed doubts that the merger could pass antitrust challenges and wanted a large up-front payment to help the company's performance during what would have likely been a lengthy antitrust review and to protect itself against the possibility that the merger would collapse. Mattel officials, on the other hand, maintained that the merger would have had little difficulty gaining approval, but backed away, and did not initiate a hostile takeover, when Hasbro waged a vigorous media campaign emphasizing the possible negative ramifications of such a mega-merger. Also clouding the deal was an ongoing Federal Trade Commission investigation into alleged exclusionary policies between toy manufacturers and toy retailers, involving most notably the Toys "R" Us chain.

Having maintained its independence, Hasbro took several steps in an attempt to reinvigorate its performance. These included leveraging its well-known brands in new ways; stepping up efforts to market electronic versions of established games, particularly through the Hasbro Interactive initiative; continuing to grow internationally; and bolstering new product development primarily through media tie-ins. Already planned for 1997 were several promising film tie-in prospects, including the movies *Jurassic Park 2*, *Batman and Robin*, and *Barney's Great Adventure*, as well as the theatrical re-release of *Star Wars*.

Hasbro also sought to regain the top spot in children's toys and entertainment, a market that was becoming increasingly international and driven by new media. In 1995 the company acquired Larami Corp., creators of the SuperSoaker line of water guns. Within three years it had added Tiger Electronics, makers of Furby and Poo-Chi interactive toys. In the April 16, 1999, issue of the *Wall Street Journal*, Joseph Pereira stated that Furby generated about 10 percent of Hasbro's total revenue for the quarter as the "must-have" toy of the 1998 Christmas season. That same year also marked the procurement of Galoob Toys, Inc., makers of MicroMachines. The following year Hasbro not only acquired Wizards of the Coast, makers of Pokemon game cards, but they also reaped huge dividends from merchandise associated with the first of three *Star Wars* prequels, *The Phantom Menace*. The movie broke the single-day record for box office receipts in its first 24 hours of release and helped influence high sales of the Phantom Menace line of action figures. With two more prequels to be released in the following decade, Star Wars looked to be a continuous source of revenue for

Hasbro, justifying the steep price paid for the license in 1997: almost $600 million and a 7.4 percent stake in Hasbro, Inc.

As the 20th century came to a close, Hasbro seemed prepared to challenge incumbent children's toy leader Mattel. However, precipitous drop-offs in Pokemon and Star Wars merchandise sales and a weak interactive games market led to Hasbro's first negative financial quarter since 1995. Hasbro's software games division, Hasbro Interactive, and their interactive gaming Web site, Games.com, had lost over $100 million in 1999 and in 2000. For the final quarter of 2000, Hasbro posted an overall net loss of $180 million.

Determined to return to profitability in 2001, Hasbro took decisive action. It sold Hasbro Interactive and Games.com to French video game company Infogrames Entertainment and consolidated its U.S. toy group in Pawtucket, Rhode Island, shutting down plants in Cincinnati, San Francisco, and Napa, reducing its workforce by 850 jobs. The company refocused attention on its core group of brands and more traditional toy lines, including Mr. Potato Head, Monopoly, and G.I. Joe. Hasbro dedicated itself to expanding these brands and toys beyond their traditional markets, and announced movie licenses with Pixar and Disney, as well as Harry Potter movie tie-in trading cards by Wizards of the Coast.

CONTINUING STRUGGLES: 2000–03

Despite Hasbro's best efforts, as the new century dawned the losses continued, amounting to $463 million in the last quarter of 2001. Hasbro, like its competitors, faced both old and new difficulties and needed to operate in innovative ways to deal with them. Hasbro's traditional child market was being shrunk as kids began to grow out of dolls and toys at younger ages. The costs associated with licensing deals with major studios had been underestimated, resulting in reduced or zero profits for movie tie-in products. Under the continuing leadership of CEO Alan Hassenfeld, Hasbro started emphasizing educational toys, seizing on the needs of time-starved parents for entertaining products that also contributed to their children's growth and development. It also focused more on adults, launching a major promotion of board and parlor games for that demographic before the holiday season in 2001 that resulted in a significant gain in the adult category. Foreign markets were another source of income, and Hasbro reported a 22 percent jump in international sales in the third quarter of 2003.

At this crucial time in its history, an important changing of the guard at Hasbro began a new era filled with high hopes and the potential for turning the company's direction and fortunes around. In August 2003 the Hassenfeld family ended its unbroken era of control of the top position when Alan Hassenfeld stepped down as CEO after what some considered a chaotic reign. His replacement was Alfred Verrecchia, who had worked at Hasbro for 38 years, starting as a junior accountant. Industry analysts praised Verrecchia's elevation, seeing him as someone who would be more hands-on and decisive than consensus-building Hassenfeld.

NEW BLOOD, NEW DIRECTIONS: 2005–08

The Verrecchia era emphasized acquisitions and initiated major ventures into publications, digitization, and entertainment media. The acquisitions of Wrebbit, a manufacturer of three-dimensional puzzles, in 2005, and Cranium, Inc., with its wide range of branded games, in 2008, added to Hasbro's toy arsenal. In March 2008 Hasbro acquired all rights to Trivial Pursuit, which it had been marketing under license to Horn Abbot, Ltd., since 1983.

During this same period Habro's license for the rich library of more than 5,000 Marvel Comics characters entered into effect. The first Marvel characters to be marketed sprang from the highly successful movie *Spider-Man 3*. Hasbro also emphasized comic books and other publications involving its own characters, such as Transformers and the venerable G.I. Joe, and built on long-standing deals with children's publishers. In 2007 Hasbro announced a strategic licensing agreement with Electronic Arts that brought together two of the most powerful entertainment companies in an attempt to transform the landscape of interactive family entertainment by giving EA worldwide rights to create digital games based on Monopoly, Yahtzee, Nerf, and other Hasbro properties. Reversing the past pattern of licensing characters from movies, Hasbro partnered with Universal Pictures in an agreement for them to produce motion pictures based on such Hasbro properties as Monopoly, Clue, and Candy Land.

Al Verrecchia's tenure was one of the most productive in company history. While revenue growth only recovered moderately from the lows of 2000 and 2001, the company's diversification and willingness to enter into new ventures enhanced its standing in the industry. In 2007 Hasbro was cited by *World Trade* magazine as one of its leading manufacturers of the year. Describing the company's strengths, the magazine particularly noted Hasbro's ability to efficiently manage dual supply chains in the United States and abroad in a responsible and ethical manner.

Verrecchia, who was 59 years old when appointed CEO, announced his retirement in 2008. He was succeeded by Brian Goldner, 44, who was serving as the company's chief operating officer. Goldner quickly added major ventures with Discovery Communications and Sesame Workshop to the Hasbro portfolio.

MULTIMEDIA VENTURES: 2009 ON

In April 2009 Hasbro and Discovery entered into a joint venture to develop quality family entertainment and educational programming for television and the Internet built around some of the most popular brands from both companies. In January 2010 the partner companies announced the planned rollout of the venture in the fall of that year. Known as The Hub, it was a children's television network reaching 60 million families on the existing Discovery Kids network. The goal was to offer young viewers and their parents creative television and Web content ranging from new comedies and animated adventures to live-action franchises and game shows emphasizing childhood concepts of fun and play.

Just before announcing The Hub, in December 2009 Hasbro scored a major coup when it won a 10-year partnership with Sesame Workshop, the nonprofit organization behind the *Sesame Street* television program. Hasbro was given the rights to manufacture and market a wide range of toys and games based on Elmo, Cookie Monster, Abby Cadabby, and other characters from the beloved show.

By 2009 Hasbro had returned to solid profitability, registering its fifth consecutive year of revenue growth. The strategy of innovative ventures in a context of corporate responsibility was meeting significant success, despite the deep U.S. recession of 2008 and 2009. Hasbro seemed well-positioned for further success over the long term as it executed its global strategy of marketing branded play.

Douglas Sun
Updated, David E. Salamie;
Jerod L. Allen; Judson MacLaury

PRINCIPAL SUBSIDIARIES

Cranium, Inc.; Milton Bradley Co.; Parker Brothers & Co.; Playskool, Inc.; Tonka Corp.; Tiger Electronics Inc.; Wizards of the Coast, Inc.

PRINCIPAL COMPETITORS

The LEGO Group; Mattel Inc.

FURTHER READING

Arner, Faith, "Pass Go and Collect the Job of CEO: After 38 Years at Hasbro, the Toy-and-Game giant, Al Verrecchia Wins the Prize," *BusinessWeek*, August 4, 2003, p. 84.

Jereski, Laura, "It's Kid Brother's Turn to Keep Hasbro Hot," *BusinessWeek*, June 26, 1989, pp. 152, 155.

Kaye, Marvin, *A Toy Is Born*, New York: Stein and Day, 1973.

Kimelman, John, "No Babe in Toyland," *Financial World*, January 4, 1994, pp. 34–36.

Michlig, John, *G.I. Joe: The Complete Story of America's Favorite Man of Action*, San Francisco: Chronicle Books, 1998.

Miller, G. Wayne, *Toy Wars: The Epic Struggle between G.I. Joe, Barbie, and the Companies That Make Them*, New York: Times Books-Random House, 1998.

"Not Toying Around," *Forbes*, January 3, 1994, p. 131.

Pesek, William, Jr., "Toy Wars," *Barron's*, May 24, 1999, pp. 17–19.

Petrecca, Laura, "Hasbro Hopes Star Wars Toys Prosper without Sequel," *Advertising Age*, March 6, 2000, p. 58.

Sansweet, Stephen J., "Toy Story: Mattel Offers $5 Billion in Unsolicited Bid for Rival Hasbro," *Wall Street Journal*, January 25, 1996, pp. A3, A10.

Heifer Project International

■

1 World Avenue
Little Rock, Arkansas 72202
U.S.A.
Toll Free: (800) 422-0474
Fax: (501) 907-2902
Web site: http://www.heifer.org

Nonprofit Organization
Founded: 1944 as Heifers for Relief
Incorporated: 1953 as Heifer Project
Employees: 889
Revenues: $98 million (year ending June 30, 2009)
NAICS: 813319 Antipoverty Advocacy Organizations;
    813312 Environmental Advocacy Organizations

■ ■ ■

Heifer Project International is a nonprofit organization dedicated to eradicating hunger and poverty throughout the world. It pursues this goal via a unique program that distributes animals to needy families as a means of providing eventual self-sufficiency. Key to this concept is the agreement that recipients "pass on the gift" by sharing the livestock's offspring, as well as their newly acquired knowledge and skills, with others, thereby creating a broader network of independence. Based in Little Rock, Arkansas, Heifer has made enormous strides since its first shipment of 17 heifers was sent to Puerto Rico in 1944. By 2009 it had distributed 30 kinds of animals, including goats, bees, chicks, and water buffalo,

to assist 8.5 million people in more than 125 countries (including the United States).

FOUNDED IN 1944

Heifer was the brainchild of an ardent pacifist, unapologetic idealist, and effective pragmatist named Dan West. Born in 1893 in Preble County, Ohio, West was reared in the Church of the Brethren, whose precepts included community responsibility and the sanctity of human life. In 1937, during the Spanish Civil War, West traveled to Spain with a relief effort organized by three pacifist churches: the Society of Friends (Quakers), the Mennonites, and the Brethren. Distributing food and clothing to both sides of the conflict, West witnessed the deprivations of war and poverty. In January 1938, after he had spent another day giving cups of powdered milk to hungry children, West realized that the refugees needed "a cow, not a cup," giving a family a chance at long-term survival as opposed to the stop-gap measure of daily donations from outside entities.

West brought his ideas before his church and his neighbors upon his return to Indiana. The positive response led to the formation of the Heifers for Relief Committee in 1939. After further consultation with other farmers, academics, and the U.S. Department of Agriculture, West received approval for his initiative as a national project in 1942. World War II delayed progress, but Heifers for Relief officially became a nonprofit organization in 1944. That same year it made its first shipment of 17 heifers (young, female cows that have not yet calved) from Pennsylvania to Puerto Rico.

1945–89: GLOBAL EXPANSION AND RECOGNITION

Heifer's first paid employee and long-time executive director was Thurl Metzger, another member of the Brethren with tremendous drive and energy, which he capably channeled into making West's ideas tangible and broadening Heifer's impact. He began his association with the program in 1946 as a "seagoing cowboy," a volunteer who accompanied livestock shipments to their destinations abroad. As Europe, Asia, and North Africa struggled to rebuild after World War II, countries desperately needed to replenish their supplies of livestock lost during the war. Heifer partnered with the United Nations Relief and Rehabilitation Administration to bring aid to these war-torn areas. Each animal gift from Heifer carried the condition that the recipient family "pass on the gift," giving their heifer's first female offspring to another family in the community, which would in turn have the obligation to "pass on the gift" when that heifer calved. In this way, it was estimated that each gift would be passed on 40 times over the course of a decade, propagating the benefits throughout the community.

Before long, Metzger was hired as Heifer's European representative, and in 1951 West asked him to sign on as Heifer's first executive director, a position he went on to hold for 30 years. In 1953 he spearheaded the organization's incorporation as a nonprofit under the name "Heifer Project" in 1953.

Metzger expanded Heifer's geographic range and diversified the program's offerings. The project's experiences around the globe taught Metzger that a flexible approach was necessary. For example, gifts of heifers were complicated in India, where cattle are considered sacred; meanwhile, the ready availability of chickenfeed in North Korea made gifts of chicks and hatchlings extremely successful. Heifer added chickens, pigs, rabbits, goats, and other animals to its offerings, collecting the donations on farms in the United States for later shipment overseas.

During the Cold War, Heifer's willingness to provide aid in countries around the world, regardless of politics or ideology, was not always popular in the United States. For example, Metzger's travels to Poland and the Soviet Union brought the scrutiny of the FBI. However, the project endured, and its mission shifted from providing aid in war-torn areas to helping the developing world, in partnership with the Peace Corps. In the early 1970s, Heifer consolidated its U.S. distribution network by buying several large farms, including a 1,200-acre ranch in Perryville, Arkansas, as livestock holding facilities. The organization moved its headquarters to Little Rock, near the Perryville ranch, in 1971. In 1973 the organization was renamed Heifer Project International.

By the time of Metzger's retirement in 1981, Heifer had grown from having one paid employee to more than 200 and to providing services in 115 countries. In 1986 President Ronald Reagan recognized Heifer with the Volunteer Action Award, and in 1990 President George H. W. Bush granted the organization the Presidential End Hunger Award.

A NEW FOCUS IN THE 1990S

Although Heifer was an established and respected charity, it was also small and not very well known to the public. The organization was determined to modernize itself for the new millennium. A first step, in 1990, was the establishment of the Heifer Foundation, a separate entity dedicated to building an endowment for Heifer's mission.

In 1992 Jo Luck became Heifer's president and CEO. Luck, a former member of Arkansas Governor Bill Clinton's cabinet, had joined Heifer in 1989 as Director of International Programs, focusing on sustainable development. Even before Luck took over as CEO, Heifer began phasing out the practice of raising livestock in the United States for distribution abroad, recognizing that purchasing local or regional breeds saved transportation costs and had less impact on the environment.

Over time Heifer's ranches in the U.S. were converted into education centers where people could learn more about sustainable farming, both in the United States and around the world. Education formed the centerpiece of Heifer's activities in the United States, through partnerships with such organizations as the New American Sustainable Agriculture Project to teach immigrants sustainable farming techniques and familiarize them with American plants and farming tools, and Growing Power, which taught urban farming in Wisconsin.

Under Luck's leadership, Heifer expanded upon the "pass on the gift" philosophy to introduce a set of core principles known as the "12 Cornerstones," which were based on the acronym "PASSING GIFTS." These are:

KEY DATES

1937: Church of the Brethren member Dan West participates in relief effort during Spanish Civil War.
1944: Heifers for Relief is founded by West.
1953: Heifers for Relief is incorporated as the Heifer Project.
1973: Name is changed to Heifer Project International.
2008: Heifer receives $42.8 million grant from the Bill & Melinda Gates Foundation.

passing on the gift, accountability, sharing and caring, sustainability and self-reliance, improved animal management, nutrition and income, gender and family focus, genuine need and justice, improving the environment, full participation, training and education, and spirituality. The cornerstones represented an expansion of Heifer's mission, particularly in areas such as sustainability and gender parity. "For forty years [Heifer] had been training the men [to care for gift animals], but the women were the ones caring for the animals and never got the training," Luck told Jacqueline Hornor Plumez in an interview for the book *Mother Power*. Under Luck, Heifer emphasized empowering women through training and by encouraging education and leadership.

Another way in which Heifer modernized was by embracing the Internet. The organization established its online presence in 1997 and a year later was ahead of many other charities by offering an online catalog complete with credit card payment system. By 2000 Heifer was the top U.S. nonprofit in online donations, according to *Arkansas Business*, with more than $3 million in donations collected.

PUT IN THE SPOTLIGHT BY
BEATRICE'S GOAT

Heifer would soon make even more extensive use of its new fundraising infrastructure. In 2001 Simon & Schuster published *Beatrice's Goat*, the story of a Ugandan girl whose family was lifted from poverty by the gift of a goat from Heifer. The girl, Beatrice Biira, was able to pursue an education with the money her mother made from selling the goat's milk and one of its kids. The book was a sensation, a *New York Times* best seller that promoted Heifer's mission of defeating poverty through the gift of livestock.

It was the type of publicity money could not buy. Biira, by then an articulate 16-year-old, traveled to the United States to promote the book. She did interviews, including one on the *Oprah Winfrey Show*, and appeared in later profiles by *60 Minutes* and the *New York Times*. Celebrity supporters of Heifer, including Susan Sarandon, Ted Danson, Goldie Hawn, and Bradley Whitford, helped to spread the word, and Whitford even arranged to incorporate Heifer into a storyline on the television drama *The West Wing*.

The media attention was reflected in Heifer's fundraising. According to *Arkansas Business*, between 1998 and 2003 the charity's revenues rose from $15.6 million to $56 million. In 2002 *Worth* magazine selected Heifer as one of its top 100 charities, and a year later *Forbes* declared it one of the top ten nonprofits. The greatest accolade arrived in the form of the $1 million Conrad N. Hilton Humanitarian Award, which the project received in 2004. "The million dollar Hilton prize will be a powerful tool in Heifer's fight against hunger and poverty, and will help to accelerate the vision of a world living in peace, equitably sharing the resources of a healthy planet," Luck said, accepting the prize.

In 2006 the organization dedicated a new headquarters, a state-of-the art eco-friendly facility that earned a Leadership in Energy and Environmental Design (LEED) designation from the U.S. Green Building Council and a National Institute Honor Award from the American Institute of Architects, one of architecture's most prestigious accolades. Heifer Village, a dedicated educational center, was added in 2009 on the campus of the Little Rock headquarters.

Heifer continued to experience robust growth. Between 2004 and 2008 revenues increased by more than 75 percent. In 2008 alone, largely owing to a four-year $42.8 million grant from the Bill & Melinda Gates Foundation, the largest single donation in Heifer's history, the organization's numbers rose by more than 25 percent. Heifer employed 1,119 people, 340 of whom worked in the United States, with 240 of those in Arkansas. By 2009, Heifer was engaged in some 870 active projects incorporating approximately 29 species of plants and animals in 53 countries or provinces and 27 states. Since its inception in 1944, Heifer had provided assistance to 8.5 million people in more than 125 countries.

EFFECTS OF ECONOMIC
DOWNTURN, 2009

Beginning in 2009, however, Heifer felt the effects of a global economic downturn as donations fell and revenues decreased accordingly. Management instituted a hiring freeze, a 3 percent salary reduction for top executives, and layoffs of 18 percent of the workface. While the layoffs were painful, many believed they were necessary to make Heifer a leaner, more efficient operation. During the years of plenty, Heifer COO Steve Denne told Gwen Moritz of *Arkansas Business*, "capacity was lagging the revenue, so the focus was always on 'How can we get more staff? How can we keep up?'" However, because of the decentralized nature of Heifer's projects, the operation had become laden with redundancy. In some ways, the project's restructuring was very much in keeping with two of Heifer's cornerstones: accountability and sustainability.

In January 2010 Heifer announced that Luck was relinquishing the title of CEO to concentrate on writing a book about her experiences with the charity. During her 17 years as CEO, Heifer went from $7 million in assets to well over $100 million and brought the organization's unique message of eradicating poverty through sustainable development to a new and much larger generation of supporters.

Margaret L. Moser

FURTHER READING

Blake, Harriet, "Heifer International Takes Sustainability to Heart," Green Right Now, KABC-TV Los Angeles, December 4, 2009, http://www.greenrightnow.com/wabc/2009/12/04/heifer-international-takes-sustainability-to-heart/.

Cummins, Roz, "'A Cow, Not a Cup,'" Culinate, December 5, 2007, http://www.culinate.com/articles/our_table/heifer_international (January 12, 2010).

"Dan West," Hagerstown Church of the Brethren, http://www.hagerstoncob.org/UnsungBrethren_Dan_West.html (January 12, 2010).

Eaton, Joe, and Ron Sullivan, "Getting Poverty's Goat," *Earth Island Journal*, Summer, 2005, p. 31.

"Global Updates from World View," World View at UNC-Chapel Hill, June 2009, http://www.unc.edu/world/Global_Updates_2009/May_June/June_09.htm.

"Hard Times at Heifer," *Arkansas Business*, April 6, 2009, p. 3(2).

"Heifer International Has Been Named the Winner of the 2004 Award for Outstanding Achievement in Internet Fundraising by the Association of Fundraising Professionals," *Arkansas Business*, March 22, 2004, p. 10.

McBrier, Page, and Lori Lohstoeter, *Beatrice's Goat*,; New York, NY: Athenium Books for Young Readers, 2001.

Moritz, Gwen, "Heifer COO Sees Chance for Change: Decline in Revenue Creates Opportunity," *Arkansas Business*, August 3, 2009, p. 1(2).

"Now, for the Good News," *Arkansas Business*, September 28, 2009, p. 5(2).

Plumez, Jacqueline Hornor, *Mother Power: Discover the Difference That Women Have Made All over the World*,; Naperville, IL: Sourcebooks, Inc., 2002.

Shireman, Pamela, "Thurl Metzger," Keepsakes Project, http://www.thispublicaddress.com/keepsakes/metzger.html.

Waldon, George, "As Heifer Grows, So Do Questions of Accountability," *Arkansas Business*, July 2, 2007, p. 1(3).

Host Hotels & Resorts, Inc.

———■———

6903 Rockledge Drive, Suite 1500
Bethesda, Maryland 20817
U.S.A.
Telephone: (240) 744-1000
Fax: (301) 380-8957
Web site: http://www.hosthotels.com

Public Company
Incorporated: 1993
Employees: 215
Sales: $4.16 billion (2009)
Stock Exchanges: NYSE
Ticker Symbol: HST
NAICS: 721110 Hotels (except Casino Hotels) and
   Motels

■ ■ ■

Host Hotels & Resorts, Inc., is a real estate investment trust (REIT) that owns or has a controlling interest in more than 100 lodging properties in prime urban, airport, resort, and convention locations primarily in North America and Europe. In accordance with regulations defining real estate investment trusts, it must pay 90 percent of its taxable income back to its shareholders every year and is then entitled to deduct those dividends from its corporate tax obligation. Host Hotels, which is both a Standard & Poor's 500 and Fortune 500 company, began life as a corporation after it was spun off from its parent, Marriott Corp. Host Hotels partners with such premium brands as Marriott, Ritz-Carlton, Sheraton, and Hyatt, among others.

CREATED AS SPIN-OFF OF MARRIOTT CORP.: 1993

The Marriott Corp., founded by J. Willard Marriott as an A&W Root Beer stand in 1927, soon morphed into a chain of Hot Shoppes and food service businesses. Marriott continued to successfully expand his operations, opening his first hotel in 1957 in Arlington, Virginia. By 1989, the Marriott Corp., now under the leadership of J. W. (Bill) Marriott Jr., opened its 500th hotel.

The company first ran into difficulty after a buying spree in the 1980s. According to *Forbes Magazine*, the "build-sell-manage" strategy worked well until 1986, when Congress reduced real estate tax shelters. Marriott had a lot of debt, and two Japanese banks backed out of their commitments to buy hotels from Marriott in 1990, which would have amounted to a $700 million sale. Saddled with distressed real estate and $3.4 billion in debt, the company could no longer expand quickly.

Bill Marriott and CEO Stephen Bollenbach conceived a plan to reorganize the company. By creating two companies from one in 1993, the Marriott organization was able to establish separate entities to own and to operate its properties, thus freeing the hotel company to continue expanding through both selling and acquiring properties. The new companies were Marriott International, which continued as a lodging operator and contract-services provider, and Host Marriott, which now owned the real-estate portfolio and operated the former company's concessions at airports, travel plazas, and similar venues. The reorganization was not well received by bond holders, who feared that the Host

COMPANY PERSPECTIVES

Our vision is to be the premier lodging real estate company. We create value through aggressive asset management and disciplined capital allocation. Our success over the years is the result of the careful execution of a focused and disciplined long-term strategic plan to acquire high quality lodging assets in prime urban and resort locations which have the potential for significant capital appreciation. We seek to maximize stockholders' returns through a combination of dividends, growth in funds from operations and increases to net asset value per share.

Marriott would not be able to service the lion's share of debt it had taken on from the parent company. Marriott was sued by the bond holders, although their suits were eventually dismissed, and their fears proved unfounded, as both companies continued on successfully.

TRANSFORMED INTO REAL ESTATE INVESTMENT TRUST: 1999

At first the two companies, Marriott International and Host Marriott, worked closely together and had more flexibility. Bollenbach was the first CEO of Host Marriott. Host Marriott had ownership of 24 full-service hotels, 102 limited-service hotels, 14 senior-living communities, and the Host Marriott Operating Group, which ran the concessions. In 1994 Host Hotels embarked on a strategy to specialize in the ownership of full-service hotels and thus sold its senior-living communities and some of its limited-services properties while acquiring 15 full-service hotels.

Over the next few years, Host Marriott continued this strategy and finally spun off the Host Marriott Operating Group as a separate company (called Host Marriott Services) in 1995. By 1998 diversification had come to mean acquiring luxury and upscale hotels, often carrying brand names associated with opulence. That year Host Marriott Corp. bought the New York-based Blackstone Group portfolio of 12 luxury hotels operating under several brands, including Ritz-Carlton and Four Seasons.

In order to take advantage of the tax benefits of REIT laws, the company became a real estate investment trust in 1999. Strict laws limited non-real estate activities by REITs, and Host Marriott was required to

lease its properties to a third party. It accomplished this by spinning off still another corporation, Crestline Capital Corporation. Host Marriott now leased its properties from Crestline and returned most of its taxable income to its shareholders every year in accordance with the law. After the REIT Modernization Act of 1999 took effect in 2001, Host Marriott was allowed to lease its hotels to wholly owned subsidiaries. The company now returned to Crestline to buy the subsidiaries that owned the leasing rights to Host's properties. With this arrangement, Host could better manage and control its assets.

In 2001 the company suffered a severe setback, like all other hospitality businesses, when the United States endured terrorist attacks on New York City and Washington, D.C., on September 11. The New York Marriott World Trade Center Hotel was all but destroyed at 3 World Trade Center, and the company's stock value plummeted. The following year, however, the company bounced back, and stock prices returned to their previous levels.

DEVELOPED LUXURY BUSINESS BEYOND MARRIOTT: 2002 AND BEYOND

In the following years Host Marriott continued to sell off limited-service hotels and buy full-service properties. By 2002 Host Marriott's portfolio included 123 hotels of which 99 percent were full-service, upscale and luxury properties. In that year the company owned 40 percent of the Ritz-Carlton hotels in the United States. In November 2005 the company bought hotels from Starwood Hotels & Resorts Worldwide, Inc., under the brand names Luxury Collection, Sheraton, St. Regis, W, and Westin. According to *Buildings* magazine, "The difficult-to-duplicate location of Host Marriott properties is part of what defines them as 'premier' assets." For example, the Marriott Marquis on 44th and Broadway in New York City cost $500 million to build, and the location of the hotel means that it will hold its value longer than if it were in a less choice location.

Host Marriott officially changed its name to Host Hotels & Resorts, Inc., in 2006. The reason for the name change was to further separate itself from the Marriott franchise, especially because its portfolio now reflected a diversity of name brands well beyond the Marriott name. As part of its aggressive asset management plan, the company worked closely with the managers of each hotel to reduce operating costs and increase revenues. Host Hotels also initiated selective capital improvements and expansions to improve operations. The company planned to continue buying revenue for 2009 ($4.16 billion in revenue) compared with 2008 ($5.29 billion), which had also shown a decline over the previous year ($5.41 billion). Despite the negative economic conditions, Host Hotels remained positioned for success. In 2009 the company was ranked first in the Real Estate category by *Fortune* magazine in its list of most admired companies, with Host receiving high marks for its global competitiveness, long-term investment strategy, people management practices, and business innovation.

Maryellen Lo Bosco

PRINCIPAL COMPETITORS

Hilton Worldwide; Hyatt Corporation; LaSalle Hotel Properties.

FURTHER READING

Evans, Judith, "The REIT Place at the Right Time; Host Marriott Spin-off Seeks to Hammer Out Its Own Identity by Managing Trusts' Hotel Assets," *Washington Post*, March 1, 1999, p. F15.

Freeman, Tyson, "Better REIT or Wrong?" *National Real Estate Investor*, December 1999, p. 44.

Koselka, Rita, "Marriott, Meet Marriott," *Forbes*, March 13 1995, p. 48.

Madsen, Jana J., "The Ultimate Host: Host Marriott Corp. Strives for Best-in-Class Status," *Buildings*, November 2002, p. 25.

McDowell, Edwin, "The Marriott Prospers as Three Separate Companies," *New York Times*, November 29, 1996, p. D9.

Tarquinio, J. Alex, "5 Years and Counting for Real Estate Surge," *New York Times*, October 8, 2006.

Webb, Steve, "Ready to Pounce," *National Real Estate Investor*, July 1, 2002.

KEY DATES

1993: Host Marriott Corp. is split off from Marriott Corp. as the owner of Marriott's real estate portfolio and the operator of its concessions at airports and toll roads.

1995: Host Marriott Corp. spins off Host Marriott Services Corp. to operate the food and gift shops at airports, travel plazas, and stadiums.

1998: Host Marriott Corp. buys the New York-based Blackstone Group portfolio of 12 luxury hotels, including Ritz-Carlton and Four Seasons.

1999: Host Marriott Corp. changes its corporate status to a publicly traded real estate investment trust and spins off Crestline Capital Corp. as an independent company listed on the New York Stock Exchange.

2006: Host Marriott Corp. changes its name to Host Hotels & Resorts, Inc., to reflect that the company now operates hotels with brands owned by companies other than Marriott.

---

and selling assets worldwide to enhance its existing luxury and "upper upscale" portfolio.

The problems wrought by the economic downturn in 2008 and 2009 hurt the entire travel and leisure industry. Host Hotels, like all other businesses, faced a challenging financial environment. The company's operating results were affected, and a preliminary annual report to shareholders noted a 19.1 percent decrease in

HOLDING

Hypo Real Estate Holding AG

———————— ■ ————————

Freisinger Straße 5
Unterschleißheim, Bavaria 85716
Germany
Telephone: (+49 89) 2880-0
Fax: (+49 89) 2880-10319
Web site: http://www.hyporealestate.com

Public Company
Founded: 2003
Employees: 1,480 (est.)
Total Assets: €373.8 billion ($547.5 billion) (2009)
Stock Exchanges: Frankfurt
Ticker Symbol: HRX
NAICS: 522292 Real Estate Credit; 522110 Commercial Banking

■ ■ ■

The Hypo Real Estate Holding AG (HRE), headquartered in Munich, Germany, is a public umbrella company housing the Deutsche Pfandbriefbank AG, also headquartered in Munich, and the DEPFA Bank, headquartered in Dublin, Ireland. The Group's name hints at its core business: *Hypo* is short for *Hypothek*, the German word for "mortgage." In 2003 HRE began as a spin-off of the commercial real estate financing business from the HypoVereinsbank. At its inception the Group included the Hypo Real Estate Bank AG, the Hypo Real Estate Bank International, and the Württembergische Hypothekenbank AG. At the time, the Group was a leading international real estate financing company combining commercial real estate with modern investment banking. The first few years were characterized by continuous growth and profits, leading to an invitation to the Frankfurt stock exchange (DAX) in 2005, after only two years of operation.

In 2009 HRE faced bankruptcy. To ensure solvency HRE stockholders agreed to the nationalization of the company through SoFFin, the Financial Market Stabilization Fund of the Federal Republic of Germany. The Group's core bank now operates under a new name, the Deutsche Pfandbriefbank AG, while the original brand name Hypo Real Estate has been relegated to the umbrella, Hypo Real Estate Holding AG. The Group's turbulent history, from successful inception through stellar rise to DAX trading to takeover by the German government, ran its course against the backdrop of a worldwide real estate and finance market crisis.

PREDECESSORS

The history of the Hypo Real Estate Holding AG goes back to the Bayerische Hypo- und Vereinsbank AG, the second-largest German bank, which in 1998 was created as a merger of the Bayerische Vereinsbank AG and the Bayerische Hypotheken- und Wechselbank AG, ending a rivalry that had endured for more than a century. The Bayerische Hypotheken- und Wechselbank, established by King Ludwig I of Bavaria in 1835 as a mortgage bank, issued real estate loans at first and, since 1864, mortgage bonds. The Bayerische Vereinsbank was created a generation later (in 1869) by King Ludwig II of

COMPANY PERSPECTIVES

Hypo Real Estate Group is in the process of realigning its business as a specialist bank for real estate and public finance. The Group will also concentrate its activities in regional terms, and will in future focus on Germany and Europe. Depending on the particular area of activity, it will also be active in other international markets. The focus will always be on the eligibility of business for Pfandbrief funding.

The Hypo Real Estate Group has mission-critical know-how for this business model. It has access to the relevant markets, for the acquisition of customers and also as a result of its expertise in the Pfandbrief market. The Pfandbrief itself is a superior security. The German Pfandbrief, which is a positive USP of the German capital market, has also held up relatively well in the financial crisis.

Bavaria, initially offering commercial loans to encourage Bavarian business expansion. In 1871 the Bayerische Vereinsbank was granted permission to also issue real estate mortgages and mortgage bonds. Thus the rivalry was born.

Throughout most of their early history, the Bayerische Vereinsbank and the Bayerische Hypotheken- und Wechselbank (Hypo-Bank) remained regional banks. When at the end of the 19th century Germany became a nation under Bismarck, several large national banks formed (Deutsche Bank, Dresdner Bank, and Commerzbank, all headquartered in Berlin), often by swallowing smaller regional banks in the former independent states. Loyal to their original customer base, the Bayerische Vereinsbank and Hypo-Bank remained in Bavaria.

To fend off early 20th-century takeover bids by the Prussian national banks, regional banks signed community-of-interest agreements with other regional banks. The Hypo-Bank joined the Barmer Bankverein and the Allgemeine Deutsche Creditanstalt of Leipzig. The Bayerische Vereinsbank joined Mendelssohn & Company, a prestigious banking house based in Berlin and Amsterdam. Not only did these measures guarantee the survival of both banks, but they also helped them prosper. By 1916 Hypo-Bank had become Germany's largest mortgage bank. Thus secured, both banks weathered the storm of the depression in the 1920s–30s.

POST–WORLD WAR II

Both the Bayerische Vereinsbank and Hypo-Bank prospered in the years of the German Wirtschaftswunder after World War II. In 1958 the Hypo-Bank and Bayerische Vereinsbank established the Internationale Immobilien-Institut GmbH (iii-investments), which was the first investment company for open real estate funds in Germany. In 1969 the Bayerische Vereinsbank and the Hypo-Bank began merger talks, which failed due to the state's insistence that a third bank, the Bayerische Staatsbank, would be included in the merger. While the Hypo-Bank wanted out, the Bayerische Vereinsbank bought the Bayerische Staatsbank and grew.

Throughout the 1970s and 1980s, the two banks competed for the number-four spot in the German banking industry (behind the Deutsche Bank, Dresdner Bank, and Commerzbank). In 1985 the Bayerische Vereinsbank invested in the West German defense industry by acquiring a 5 percent stake in Messerschmidt-Boelkov-Bloehm and by acquiring, together with the Dresdner Bank, Krauss-Maffai, maker of the leopard tanker. By increasing its stakes in other regional banks, the Bayerische Vereinsbank became a superregional bank in the 1990s. Hypo-Bank, on the other hand, did not stray from its core business, the mortgage and securities industry.

German reunification in 1991 opened a new market and seemingly new opportunities in the former Eastern states. The Bayerische Vereinsbank rapidly expanded into the East, opening 80 branches by 1994, while the Hypo-Bank funded a record number of real estate projects in East Germany. In addition the Bayerische Vereinsbank invested in technology, offering telephone banking and online banking throughout reunited Germany. By the mid-1990s both banks were outperforming the three larger German banks.

Such positive balance sheets did not go unnoticed. In 1996 the Deutsche Bank bought a 5 percent stake in the Bayerische Vereinsbank. Allianz, the German insurance giant with interests in the Dresdner Bank, held a 10 percent stake in the Hypo-Bank. Anticipating a possible takeover bid by a larger national bank, Hypo-Bank CEO Martini and Bayerische Vereinsbank CEO Schmidt struck a merger deal in July 1997.

HYPOVEREINSBANK

The merger took effect on September 1, 1998, creating the Bayerische Hypo- und Vereinsbank AG (also called HypoVereinsbank), the second-largest bank in Germany after only the Deutsche Bank. The new bank immediately had to deal with a negative legacy from the

KEY DATES

1835: The Bayerische Hypotheken- und Wechselbank AG is established.

1864: The Bayerische Hypotheken- und Wechselbank AG introduces mortgage bonds.

1869: The Bayerische Vereinsbank AG is established.

1998: The Bayerische Hypotheken- und Wechselbank AG and Bayerische Vereinsbank AG merge to become the Bayerische Hypo- und Vereinsbank AG, or HypoVereinsbank.

2003: A spin-off of the real estate portfolio from HypoVereinsbank establishes Hypo Real Estate Holding AG.

2008: Hypo Real Estate stock plummets; SoFFin begins operations as an agency of the Deutsche Bundesbank in a federal program to stabilize the German financial market and buys 8.7 percent of Hypo Real Estate Group stock.

2009: SoFFin completes the nationalization of Hypo Real Estate.

past. The reunification process in Germany had not developed as well or as rapidly as anticipated. Many former East German states suffered from depopulation and high unemployment rates, and thus many of the mortgage deals underwritten by the former Hypo-Bank went bust. The bank incurred high losses, and as a result all former Hypo-Bank executives had to resign in 1999. What had originally been marketed as a merger of equals was really a takeover by the Bayerische Vereinsbank.

Hypo-Bank's bad mortgage deals would come back to haunt the newly established bank. The recession in the beginning of the new millennium hit hard. During a massive restructuring process in 2001, HypoVereinsbank closed numerous branches and eliminated 10,000 jobs, almost 14 percent of its payroll. It had to take €3.8 billion ($5.5 billion) in bad loan provisions, partly due to a stagnating economy, but mainly due to the repercussions of the bad loans in the former East German states. In 2002 the bank reported a record loss of €858 million.

In early 2003 HypoVereinsbank initiated another restructuring process, creating three main operating units: (1) Germany, (2) Austria and Central and Eastern Europe, and (3) Corporates and Markets. A fourth unit,

housing the bank's commercial real estate finance business, including the bad loans in the Eastern German states, was prepared for a spin-off. The new company, with assets of almost $170 billion, housing the mortgage portfolio of the HypoVereinsbank, was to operate independently as the Hypo Real Estate Holding AG.

STELLAR RISE

The spin-off took effect in October 2003. The newly established Hypo Real Estate Holding AG (HRE) was first listed on the Frankfurt stock exchange (SDAX) on October 6, 2003. On March 22, 2004, the company was admitted to the MDAX. Initially focusing on a massive restructuring process, then CEO Markus Fell divided the Hypo Real Estate Bank AG into three operating units: Hypo Real Estate International (which was to consolidate all international business), the Württembergische Hypothekenbank (which was focused on bonds and debentures, or Pfandbrief), and Hypo Real Estate Germany. Hypo Real Estate Germany had inherited the ailing mortgage loans from the Hypo-Bank.

In September 2004 Hypo Real Estate Germany sold its nonperforming loan portfolio to the U.S. investment company Lone Star to improve profitability. The single transaction with a volume of €3.6 billion was the largest transaction of this kind ever carried out in the world, reducing Hypo Real Estate Germany by 75 percent. In October 2004 the bank sold an additional package of subperforming loans, with a volume of €394 million, to Morgan Stanley Real Estate Funds and Citigroup. Now rid of its ailing loan package, Hypo Real Estate Germany was set to once again become a major player in the German mortgage business.

Free for new business, HRE Group aggressively pursued expansion. Initially the Group's business focused on state finance (54 percent), commercial real estate (27 percent), and residential (19 percent) real estate. The HRE Group was active mostly in Germany (62 percent) but also conducted business in France, the United States, and the Netherlands, as well as Scandinavia, Italy, and Spain. In 2004 the HRE Group recorded a pretax net income of €221 million, which represented a 44 percent growth in just one year of operation. The first dividend to stockholders was paid at €0.35 per share.

DIVERSIFICATION AND FURTHER RESTRUCTURING

Still in the midst of the initial restructuring process in 2005, the Group portfolio increased its commercial real estate business to 48 percent, reducing the residential real estate business to only 5 percent. In addition HRE pursued further geographical diversification. Only 50 percent of business stayed at home in Germany, while the other 50 percent was generated abroad: 13 percent in the United Kingdom, 11 percent in the United States, and the remainder in France, the Netherlands, Scandinavia, Spain, Japan, and Italy. At the end of 2005, within only two years of its inception, the company recorded an 84.6 percent growth with a €443 million pretax profit. Dividends were paid out at €1 per share. Crowning the company's stellar success, the shares of HRE were first listed on the German stock exchange index (DAX) on December 19, 2005.

Further restructuring in 2006 dissolved the Württembergische Hypothekenbank AG and consolidated all international credit business in the Hypo Real Estate International Bank, Stuttgart, while the Hypo Real Estate Bank AG, Munich, took over all domestic financing arrangements from the Württembergische Hypothekenbank AG. Hypo Public Finance in Dublin consolidated all asset-based and infrastructure finance. HRE still experienced growth and profitability in 2006: it recorded €558 million pretax earnings, which amounted to a 29 percent growth. Dividends were paid out at €1.50 per share.

DEPFA JOINS THE GROUP

In October 2007 HRE acquired the DEPFA Bank, Dublin, Ireland, one of the world's leading providers of public finance. DEPFA had been established in 1922 by the German government to provide financing for residential construction and had grown to be the largest German underwriter of public covered bonds (Pfandbrief). When its tax-free status expired in the 1970s, the company moved to Dublin, Ireland. The DEPFA portfolio with its focus on the public sector and infrastructure finance complemented rather than doubled the business of HRE, which was first and foremost a commercial real estate lender. For HRE, now comprising four subsidiaries (Hypo Real Estate Bank International AG, Hypo Real Estate Bank AG, DEPFA Bank plc, and DEPFA Deutsche Pfandbrief AG) and handling commercial real estate, public sector and infrastructure finance, capital markets, and asset management, the milestone acquisition seemed to provide natural risk diversification. CEO Georg Funke predicted that HRE would provide a 15 percent increase of equity return by 2010.

The turbulent real estate and finance market since mid-2007, however, had already had a negative impact by the time DEPFA joined the Group. In 2007 HRE recorded a pretax profit of only €587 million, which represented a virtual 0 percent growth compared to 2006. Dividends were paid out at only €0.50 per share. The downward spiral had begun. Only one year later, by the end of 2008, the very existence of the Hypo Real Estate Group was in danger.

DEPFA had joined the HRE Group with a seemingly attractive portfolio of long-term loans. DEPFA financed these loans with short-term credit from other banks. While this was not an unusual practice, it certainly was risky business, because to finance long-term loans with short-term credit requires that credit is readily available. During the worldwide credit crunch beginning in mid-2007, this was not the case.

THE CREDIT CRUNCH

About 80 percent of U.S. mortgages issued since the late 1990s were adjustable-rate mortgages. When the U.S. housing market began its steep decline in mid-2006, refinancing became more difficult, adjustable-rate mortgages reset at higher rates, and mortgage delinquencies soared. Securities backed with subprime mortgages lost most of their value. Banks heavily invested in the subprime mortgage market were in danger. Lehman Brothers, the fourth-largest investment bank in the United States, was forced to adjust the value of its investments in residential mortgages and commercial property and, in the summer of 2007, made write-downs first of $700 million.

Within just one year this figure rose to $7.8 billion. As a result Lehman stock tumbled more than 95 percent within a single year, eventually forcing the company into bankruptcy. Lehman's steady decline and eventual collapse on September 15, 2008, led to a virtual collapse of the interbank market, which severely tightened credit around the world. DEPFA's interbank credit source had slowly dried up since mid-2007, and, stuck with long-term loans, found itself in a serious liquidity impasse by early 2008.

HRE announced write-downs of €390 million in January 2008. As a result the stock plummeted. In early 2008 shares still traded at about €30 a share. In June 2008 the American investment firm J. C. Flowers & Co. LLC became a majority shareholder after buying 24.7 percent of HRE stock at €22.50 per share. The decline continued nonetheless. By September 2008 HRE stock was worth only €16 a share. Despite the issuance of new shares to raise capital, the DEPFA credit crisis threatened the entire HRE Group.

BAILOUT ATTEMPTS

To save the company from insolvency, HRE requested a €35 billion bailout package from the German federal government and a consortium of banks. When the rescue package was announced on September 29, 2008, the stock plummeted further to a mere €3.52.

When it quickly became apparent that even further rescue packages were necessary to keep the company afloat, CEO Georg Funke was heavily attacked for allegedly misrepresenting the severity of the company's situation. As a result, Funke resigned on October 7, 2008. Axel Wieandt became CEO, joining HRE from the board of the Deutsche Bank. On December 19, 2008, the supervisory board began to turn over the entire management and fired CFO Marjus Fell and other managers.

At the same time, former CEO Funke and other members of the board were investigated for misconduct. Funke, according to the allegations, should have changed DEPFA's credit policies as early as 2007, when the potentially damaging results of the worldwide credit crisis became readily apparent. Instead, so the charge claimed, Funke misrepresented the company's situation in late 2007 (the HRE annual report) and 2008 (HRE interim reports), thus misleading stockholders and manipulating the stock price. As a result HRE stock continued to fall, reaching €3.05 by December 2008. Within a single year the stock had plummeted by 90 percent.

In early 2009 it became apparent that even additional bailout packages would not suffice. The federal government initiated a takeover plan through SoFFin, a government program to stabilize and restore confidence in the German financial system. SoFFin began operations on October 27, 2008, as an agency of the Deutsche Bundesbank, at the time buying 8.7 percent of HRE stock. In May 2009 SoFFin increased its share to 47.31 percent. In June 2009 a capital increase program issuing new stock solely underwritten by SoFFin increased the government's stake in HRE to 90 percent.

In its interim report of September 30, 2009, HRE reported pretax losses of €1,779 million for the first three quarters of the year and estimated that the company would not be able to pay off its debt until 2015. At the general meeting on October 5, 2009, HRE shareholders had little choice but to accept a squeeze-out at €1.30 per share. Investors such as J. C. Flowers & Co. LLC, which less than a year earlier had paid €22.50 per share, incurred tremendous losses.

On October 13, 2009, SoFFin became the sole owner of HRE. This takeover by the Federal Republic of Germany was the first nationalization of a bank since the country's inception in 1949.

OUTLOOK

In preparation of and since the SoFFin takeover, the Hypo Real Estate Group began to implement a strategy meant to heal the company. Over a period of three years, the Group planned to simplify its corporate structure. The ongoing strategic realignment aimed to reposition Hypo Real Estate Group as a leading specialist for real estate and public-sector finance in Germany and Europe, with a funding strategy focused on issuing bonds and debentures (Pfandbrief). Deutsche Pfandbriefbank AG became the core bank of the Hypo Real Estate Group. The bank was established in a merger of the Hypo Real Estate Bank AG and DEPFA Deutsche Pfandbrief AG.

As a first important step in this process, the Deutsche Pfandbriefbank AG auctioned off its claims in the Lehman Brothers bankruptcy case (€332.5 million) on October 19, 2009. A few days later Deutsche Pfandbriefbank AG sold its U.S. collateralized debt obligations (€759 million). In a further positive development HRE Holding announced on November 4, 2009, that SoFFin intended to grant further support. SoFFin agreed to issue a further capital contribution of €3 billion and to extend the €52 billion liquidity guarantee (originally in place only until November 18, 2009) until June 30, 2010.

On November 27, 2009, the Deutsche Pfandbriefbank AG and Westdeutsche Immobilien AG announced an investment of €48.5 million for Arka's Alfa Shopping Center in Poland. On December 10, 2009, the Deutsche Pfandbriefbank and ADIF, the Spanish railway infrastructure company, extended a €200 million public finance loan for the development of Spain's high-speed railway network.

Helga Schier

PRINCIPAL SUBSIDIARIES

Deutsche Pfandbriefbank AG, Munich; DEPFA Bank plc, Dublin, Ireland.

PRINCIPAL OPERATING UNITS

Commercial Real Estate; Public Sector and Infrastructure Finance; Capital Market and Asset Management.

PRINCIPAL COMPETITORS

Bayerische Hypo-und Vereinsbank AG; Deutsche Bank AG; Commerzbank AG; Landesbank Baden-Württemberg.

FURTHER READING

Balzli, Beat, Dinah Deckstein, and Jorg Schmitt, "Germany Probes Hypo Real Estate," *BusinessWeek*, December 29, 2008, http://www.businessweek.com/globalbiz/content/dec2008/gb20081229_172397.htm?link_position=link11.

Dougherty, Carter, "U.S. Investor Has No Allies in Battle over German Bank," *New York Times*, April 27, 2009, http://query.nytimes.com/gst/fullpage.html?res=9906E1DC1339F934A15757C0A96F9C8B63.

Fairlamb, David, "Down for the Count at HVB: Will Bad Debt Crush the German Banking Giant?" *BusinessWeek*, January 20, 2003, http://www.businessweek.com/magazine/content/03_03/b3816139.htm.

"Hypo Real Estate verstaatlicht," Süddeutsche, October 5, 2009, http://www.sueddeutsche.de/finanzen/653/490034/text/.

Ott, Klaus, "Hypo Real Estate: Vorwürfe gegen Funke," Süddeutsche, December 1, 2009, http://www.sueddeutsche.de/finanzen/843/496162/text/.

———, "Der Niedergang der Hypo Real Estate," Süddeutsche, January 15, 2009, http://www.sueddeutsche.de/finanzen/897/454579/text/.

Weller, Ludwig, "Bailout of Germany's Hypo Real Estate: A Bottomless Pit," World Socialist Web Site, February 23, 2009, http://www.wsws.org/articles/2009/feb2009/germ-f23.shtml.

IASIS Healthcare
Corporation

117 Seaboard Lane, Building E
Franklin, Tennessee 37067
U.S.A
Telephone: (615) 844-2747
Fax: (615) 846-3006
Web site: http://www.iasishealthcare.com

Private Company
Founded: 1998
Employees: 10,959
Sales: $2.36 billion (2009)
NAICS: 622110 General Medical and Surgical
    Hospitals; 621111 Offices of Physicians (except
    Mental Health Specialists); 621610 Home Health
    Care Services

∎∎∎

Founded in 1998 and headquartered in Franklin, Tennessee, IASIS Healthcare Corporation takes its name from the Greek word for "process of healing." The founders of IASIS, including the company's first chief executive officer, Wayne Gower, sought to create a company that could run strong community hospitals. IASIS owns and operates 15 community hospitals in high-growth urban and suburban markets in six states: Arizona, Utah, Nevada, Louisiana, Texas, and Florida. These acute-care hospitals offer a variety of medical services, including emergency care, orthopedics, general surgery, internal medicine, cardiology, obstetrics, psychiatry, and physical rehabilitation. IASIS also oper-

ates several outpatient facilities that offer auxiliary medical services such as medical imaging, radiation therapy, and outpatient surgery. IASIS emphasizes its commitment to high-quality, cost-effective healthcare and strives to build strong relationships as it interacts with physicians, employees, patients, and payers.

In 1999, shortly after its founding the previous year, IASIS received equity backing from the New York investment firm Joseph Littlejohn & Levy (JLL) to purchase 15 hospitals in Utah, Arizona, and Florida. Valued at $800 million, the deal covered 5 hospitals previously owned by Paracelsus Healthcare Corporation and 10 previously owned by Tenet Healthcare Corporation. Each of the hospitals needed updating and renovation and they had been for sale for some time, but IASIS executives saw the potential for tremendous growth. Instead of dictating changes to be made, the company asked the physicians working at each of the 15 hospitals to name needed improvements. Physicians usually suggested upgrades to the medical imaging, emergency, and obstetric departments. Using the input received, IASIS put together a five-year plan to upgrade its new hospitals.

Only one of the 15 hospitals acquired, Paracelsus Regional in South Salt Lake, was renamed. Gower explained in an interview with Norma Wagner for Knight Ridder/Tribune newspapers in August 1999 that the company was not interested in trying to "brand these hospitals with our corporate name. Our focus is emphasizing and trying to add value to the community presence they already have."

COMPANY PERSPECTIVES

At IASIS Healthcare we are highly motivated and compassionate people, using advanced systems and technology to become the healthcare provider of choice and to improve the quality of life for the individuals and communities we serve. IASIS employees, physicians, and volunteers share and are guided by enduring values. We care about people and treat our patients and one another with dignity, compassion, and respect. We act with honesty and integrity. We are accountable, one to another and as an organization, to build and maintain trust. We encourage innovative thinking and leadership excellence, which promotes the advancement of quality and healthcare delivery. We persevere and constantly strive to be better.

HOSPITAL AGAINST HOSPITAL

In April 2000 IASIS reopened Rocky Mountain Healthcare Center in Salt Lake City, Utah. Having purchased the facility from Paracelsus Healthcare Corporation the previous autumn for $40 million, IASIS invested approximately $20 million in the center. When the anticipated amount of patients and revenue did not materialize, the hospital experienced losses of $1 million per month, and Rocky Mountain sued nearby St. Mark's hospital in August 2000. Rocky Mountain alleged that St. Mark's contracts with some of Utah's major health insurance providers penalized the insurers with costs up to 20 percent higher if those companies also did business with Rocky Mountain Healthcare Center. Rocky Mountain petitioned the court to award appropriate damages and prohibit what it called an illegal group boycott that violated Utah's Antitrust Act. A St. Mark's Hospital spokesperson disputed the allegations, according to Barbara Kirchheimer in *Modern Healthcare*, asserting that the hospital remained "confident that our managed-care contracting and all of our business practices are in line and legal." Kirchheimer characterized the allegations as the most recent "example of a growing trend of hospital turning against hospital to address financial losses and competitive issues."

While the lawsuit remained pending in Utah's Third District Court, IASIS announced plans in June 2001 to close the Rocky Mountain Healthcare Center. Rocky Mountain CEO Jim Rogers explained the closure in an interview published June 1 on Business Wire: "We

have a beautiful facility in a prime location and an excellent staff. We were equipped with the latest in technology to deliver exceptional services to patients. Despite these advantages, our prolonged inability to serve physicians and patients who are providers or members of some of the largest payers in our market ultimately proved too costly for us." In February 2004 IASIS completed sale of the former Rocky Mountain Healthcare Center property to the Board of Education of the Granite School District of Salt Lake City for approximately $15.2 million.

In January 2001 IASIS announced plans for an initial public offering of 13.4 million shares of stock. According to articles in the *St. Petersburg Times*, the company hoped to raise as much as $201 million to pay down debt. At the end of 2000 the market had been providing for-profit hospital companies with a favorable investment climate. In April 2001, however, the company reversed course and postponed the offering indefinitely. The first quarter of 2001 had revealed a turbulent market that seemed to be rewarding only those for-profit companies with a strong track record of steady price increases and investor earnings. In addition to being an untested player on the open market, IASIS had suffered recent unexpected revenue losses at its Rocky Mountain Healthcare Center. IASIS joined 78 other companies that also withdrew planned initial public offerings during the first quarter of 2001.

NEW MAJORITY STAKEHOLDER CONTINUES BEST PRACTICES

In 2004 Texas Pacific Group acquired majority shareholder status in IASIS for $1.4 billion. Based in Fort Worth, Texas, Pacific was a private investment partnership managing over $13 billion in assets.

In 2005 IASIS instituted an innovative new program to recruit physicians and nurses to work in its hospitals. To ensure a sufficient number of nurses at each of its hospitals, the company sent its chief nursing officer to India to recruit well-trained nurses with 10 or more years of experience who spoke English fluently. The initial recruitment brought more than 40 nurses from India to work at IASIS-owned hospitals and ensure adequate staffing in the face of potential nursing shortages.

By 2006 IASIS was expanding its tradition of actively involving the physicians who practiced in its hospitals in the company's management and business decisions. Physician syndication, or the opportunity for physicians to own a part of the hospital in which they practice, offered opportunities for income growth for physicians and provided IASIS with capital for renova-

KEY DATES

1998: IASIS is founded in Franklin, Tennessee.
1999: With financial backing from private equity firm Joseph Littlejohn & Levy, IASIS purchases 15 hospitals.
2001: IASIS postpones its planned initial public offering.
2004: Texas Pacific Group becomes the majority shareholder in IASIS.
2008: False-claims allegations against IASIS are dismissed.

tion and expansion projects. In 2006 physician syndication was in place at four out of 15 IASIS-owned hospitals. In addition to the financial opportunities provided, the company executives determined that syndication opportunities increased the level of commitment physicians and others employed at the hospital felt toward the hospital's mission.

ALLEGATIONS OF FALSE CLAIMS

In September 2005 IASIS revealed that it had received a subpoena from the federal Department of Health and Human Services for all documents pertaining to contractual relationships between physicians and IASIS-owned hospitals dating back to 1999. Documents subpoenaed included leases for offices and buildings, medical directorship appointments, and physician recruitment agreements. Former employees of the Department of Health and Human Services speculated that a whistleblower complaint had probably initiated the subpoena.

In 2007 a federal whistleblower lawsuit against IASIS that had been kept under wraps for two years was unsealed in an Arizona court. Jerre Frazier, a former IASIS vice president for ethics and compliance, alleged in the suit (filed on behalf of the federal government) that IASIS had engaged in illegal acts to boost profits, paid kickbacks to doctors for patient referrals, and performed unnecessary medical procedures. IASIS disputed the allegations, saying through a spokesperson in an interview on August 30 with Carol Gentry in the *Tampa Tribune* that "we intend to vigorously defend ourselves."

In April 2008 an Arizona judge dismissed the lawsuit, but Frazier' attorneys, Phillips & Cohen LLC, announced plans to appeal the decision to the Ninth Circuit Court of Appeals. Interviewed for an article in the Mesa, Arizona, *Tribune*, attorney Mary Louise Co-

hen told Edward Gately that "we feel strongly it's an important case. We think the complaint outlines significant violations and should continue." In the same article, IASIS spokesperson Tomi Galin said, "We are confident the court's decision is correct, and we continue to maintain that the allegations made by Jerre Frazier are baseless and without merit."

SIGNS OF GROWTH

In September 2009 *Inc.* magazine named IASIS to its Top 10 list of the 5,000 privately held companies that had achieved the highest percentage of growth over the previous three years. Of the companies considered for the award, IASIS ranked 10th largest by total revenue. David R. White, chairman and chief executive officer of IASIS, commented in a September 4, 2009, interview with *Economics Week* that the *Inc. 5000* list "is largely composed of private companies that have been able to make a substantial impact on the U.S. economy in a relatively short period of time. We are proud to be included in such an innovative and successful group of businesses."

At the beginning of 2010 IASIS maintained 2,644 hospital beds in six states: Arizona, Texas, Florida, Utah, Nevada, and Louisiana. It owned and operated 15 acute-care facilities and one behavioral health facility. The health plan Health Choice Arizona, Inc., managed by Medicare and Medicaid was its primary subsidiary and served approximately 145,000 people in Phoenix, Arizona. Investment in the privately held IASIS was led by three private-equity firms: Texas Pacific Group, JLL Partners, and Trimaran Fund Management.

Joyce Helena Brusin

PRINCIPAL SUBSIDIARIES

Health Choice Arizona, Inc.

PRINCIPAL COMPETITORS

HCA, Inc.; Vanguard Health Systems, Inc.; Bay Care Health System; Methodist Healthcare System of San Antonio, Ltd., LLP; CHRISTUS Health; University of Utah Hospitals and Clinics.

FURTHER READING

Gately, Edward, "Lawsuit against Mesa General Owner Dismissed," *Tribune* (Mesa, AZ), April 2, 2008.

Gentry, Carol, "Lawsuit Accuses IASIS of Fraud," *Tampa Tribune*, August 30, 2007.

"Hospital Makeover: COO Sandra McRee Says That Instead of Assuming Absolute Power This Healthcare Corporation Looked to Its Physicians for Guidance," *Health Executive*, September 2005.

"IASIS Healthcare Announces Closing of Rocky Mountain Medical Center," Business Wire, June 1, 2001.

"IASIS Healthcare Included in Inc. 5000's Top 10-by-Revenue List," *Economics Week*, September 4, 2009, p. 10.

"Joseph Littlejohn and IASIS to Acquire 15 Hospitals," *New York Times*, August 18, 1999.

Kirchheimer, Barbara. "Change in Plans: Rapidly Deteriorating Conditions Force IASIS to Cancel Trip to IPO Market," *Modern Healthcare*, April 9, 2001.

———, "IASIS Healthcare Emerges: Nashville Firm to Own 15 Tenet and Paracelsus Hospitals," *Modern Healthcare*, August 23, 1999, p. 2.

———, "Salt Lake Face-off: Hospital in Legal Duel over Charges of Anticompetitive Tactics," *Modern Healthcare*, August 28, 2000, p. 6.

Oberbeck, Steven. "Salt Lake City Medical Center Sues Nearby Hospital," *Salt Lake City Tribune*, August 23, 2000.

"Private Equity Group to Buy IASIS Healthcare," *New York Times*, May 6, 2004, p. C4.

Rai, Saritha, "Indian Nurses Sought to Staff U.S. Hospitals," *New York Times*, February 10, 2003.

Rivlin, Richard, "Group Formed to Buy Hospitals," *Financial Times*, August 18, 1999, p. 24.

Wagner, Norma, "Nashville, Tenn., Firm Announces Purchase of Utah Hospitals," Knight Ridder/Tribune Business News, August 18, 1999.

John Paul Mitchell Systems

—■—

9701 Wilshire Boulevard, Suite 1205
Beverly Hills, California 90212-2019
U.S.A.
Telephone: (310) 248-3888
Toll Free: (800) 793-8790
Fax: (310) 248-2780
Web site: http://www.paulmitchell.com

Private Company
Incorporated: 1980
Employees: 175
Sales: $900 million (2009 est.)
NAICS: 325620 Toilet Preparation Manufacturing

■ ■ ■

A recognized leader in the beauty industry, John Paul Mitchell Systems markets more than 90 different hair-care products in 81 countries, selling its products exclusively at authorized hair salons. John Paul Mitchell, a celebrated hairstylist, and John Paul DeJoria, a struggling salesman, founded John Paul Mitchell Systems in 1980. Together, until Mitchell's death in 1989, the two men shaped their entrepreneurial creation into a market winner, succeeding through Mitchell's haircutting demonstrations, DeJoria's renowned marketing skills, and the company's signature Awapuhi shampoo, made from Hawaiian gingerroot. John Paul Mitchell Systems uses a three-stage marketing system to drive its sales. The company ships its hair-care products to distributors who deliver the merchandise to hair salons where consumers purchase the company's products, all pack-aged in white bottles with black lettering. John Paul Mitchell Systems' distributor-to-salon-to-consumer approach has been credited for much of the company's success.

The simple black-and-white packaging of John Paul Mitchell Systems' products reflected the company's modest beginnings, and the starkness belied the colorful personalities behind the company. From its outset, John Paul Mitchell Systems was a unique enterprise started and stewarded by unconventional corporate leaders, a characterization from which John Paul Mitchell and John Paul Jones DeJoria did not shirk and even embraced. DeJoria and, in particular, Mitchell, had enjoyed success in their careers before starting John Paul Mitchell Systems, but both were, for different reasons, at turning points in their lives, and John Paul Mitchell Systems represented a way forward, a vehicle to disengage them from the past.

BACKGROUND ON MITCHELL

Born in Scotland, Mitchell grew up during the 1940s in London, where his father was employed as chief engineer at Buckingham Palace. In London, Mitchell pursued a career decidedly unlike his father's, becoming one of the city's flamboyant hairstylists. Studying under the tutelage of the famed Vidal Sassoon, Mitchell became one of the most sought-after hairstylists in London during the early 1960s, earning the esteem of the city's "swinging" high society. His rise to the ephemeral top of the salon scene was fueled in large part by the dozens of traveling clinics he conducted. He transformed haircutting presentations into artistic performances, which entertained and attracted clientele and cast Mitchell in the spotlight as an indefatigable showman.

By the mid-1970s, Mitchell was, in his own words as related to Joseph Kahn of *Inc.* magazine in 1987, "one of the most recognized hair artists in the world" and profoundly disenchanted by his own success. Life in the limelight had disagreed with him, and he was "totally burned out on the whole success trip." To distance himself from the flash and frenetic pace of working as a "hair artist," Mitchell went into seclusion. He decided to live his life according to a new philosophy. The new lifestyle he eagerly embraced later served to underpin the philosophy of John Paul Mitchell Systems itself.

To lose himself from the hairstyling crowd, Mitchell moved to Hawaii in 1975. There, he struggled to find a new perspective on life, a new course for his future. "For nearly a year," Mitchell related to *Inc.*, "I lived in a one-room beach shack, doing nothing but yoga, meditation, and vegetarianism. Hawaii healed me." On those few occasions when the hairdresser accepted visitors, Swami Muktananda, an Eastern mystic, was his company of choice.

As Mitchell was experiencing life as a tropical-bound, soul-searching recluse, his future business partner was on an entirely different path. His experiences, too, would have considerable influence on the personality of John Paul Mitchell Systems.

BACKGROUND ON DEJORIA

Unlike Mitchell's prolific rise to stardom and success during his years before the formation of John Paul Mitchell Systems, John Paul Jones DeJoria spent his years before the company's creation desperately trying to climb the rungs of success, quite frequently losing his

purchase. Ten years Mitchell's junior, DeJoria was a Los Angeles native who left the U.S. Navy in 1964 to enroll in dental school. His plans for dental school were scotched, however, when he was unable to raise the tuition money, forcing him in a different career direction altogether. DeJoria began selling encyclopedias, then he switched to selling copying machines. Insurance became his next focal point as a salesman, a door-to-door job that lasted three months. Next, he sold medical linens, but nothing seemed to work for the young DeJoria. By age 26, he was ready to have a go at the publishing business and landed a job at Time, Inc., as a sales manager. DeJoria's stay at Time came to an abrupt end when he remarked to his bosses that his office would be more productive if he was permitted to increase commissions and thereby devote less time to supervising his sales force.

Forced to find another job, DeJoria was at a crossroads in his selling career. "I suppose the reason the jobs lasted such a short time," he later mused, in a 1991 profile by Christopher Palmeri in *Forbes*, "was that I didn't like what I was selling." DeJoria's next job, however, introduced him to products he did enjoy selling. The one constant thread—sales—that ran through an otherwise erratic career life intersected with the world in which Mitchell excelled. DeJoria joined the ranks of the hair-care industry.

With the help of a friend who worked at an employment agency, DeJoria secured an interview at Redken Laboratories Inc. in 1971. Redken, a pioneer in the distribution of shampoo through hair salons, was a member of a business society tailored to the tastes of DeJoria. "I saw all these salesman in beautiful Italian suits," a friend of DeJoria's related to *Forbes*, "and I knew it was the place for John." DeJoria quickly affirmed his friend's appraisal, rising in a short time to rank as one of Redken's top salespeople. Generating $1,000 in sales a day, DeJoria leaped up the corporate ladder at Redken, becoming a sales manager within six months and, after 18 months, being appointed national manager of the company's schools and training salons.

DeJoria then hit a brick wall. "They said I wasn't a businessman," DeJoria later explained to *Forbes*, "that I had gone as far as I could." Remaining in the beauty business after his departure from Redken, DeJoria served two more stints as a salesman for beauty products companies, with one job ending when he found himself in the untenable position of "making more money than the guy that owned the company." By 1980 DeJoria was ready for a new challenge and yet in need of constancy, searching for a career opportunity that would enable him to use his talent as a salesman to its full advantage.

KEY DATES

1980: Company is founded by John Paul DeJoria and Paul Mitchell.
1986: Company's products are introduced in China.
1989: Mitchell dies of pancreatic cancer; DeJoria assumes full control.
2004: Company devotes advertising dollars on a consumer education campaign regarding counterfeit products.

FOUNDING AND RAPID GROWTH

In 1980 DeJoria was in Hawaii and there became reacquainted with Mitchell. The two had met for the first time nine years earlier. "It's a show-business industry," DeJoria explained to *Inc.* in 1987, "and Paul [Mitchell] and I crossed paths often." Each looking to move in a new direction, DeJoria and Mitchell decided to start a business together, with Mitchell cast as the hair-products expert and DeJoria as the marketing expert. The partners pooled their resources and came up with $700, which represented a paltry sum to launch a new enterprise, but neither was disheartened by the modest start. Mitchell and DeJoria were invigorated by the prospects of a new beginning and hoped to create a business fundamentally different from any other in existence. With the formation of John Paul Mitchell Systems, Mitchell and DeJoria created a business vehicle to express their unique perspectives, a corporate megaphone that each used to articulate his personal philosophy.

Considering the precarious financial foundation Mitchell and DeJoria stood on when they embarked on their business plan, any means of saving money was searched for and embraced. The need to get the business up and running for under $1,000 led to two money-saving alternatives in particular that distinguished the company in the years to come. First, the partners decided to use generic white bottles with black lettering as their packaging, a move that saved them a considerable amount of money and, as it turned out, served as an effective marketing tool years later when the company was collecting more than $100 million in sales a year.

The second money-saving decision was more ingenious, a move that enabled Mitchell and DeJoria to realize their entrepreneurial dream shortly after they hatched their business plan. Instead of underwriting the cost of a production facility, they persuaded a small Los

Angeles-based hair- and skin-care maker named Star Laboratories Inc. to produce their products for them. By subcontracting production, Mitchell and DeJoria were able to begin producing and marketing John Paul Mitchell Systems products before the end of 1980, saving much-needed cash for the development of their shampoo and other hair-care products.

PRODUCT DEVELOPMENT AND MARKETING

Every dollar saved by cutting corners wherever possible was invested in developing new products, including shampoo that featured the ginger plant Awapuhi. The investment paid large dividends quickly, as John Paul Mitchell Systems shampoo became a best seller. To market the company's products, DeJoria drew on the approach he had witnessed at Redken, selling John Paul Mitchell Systems products through professional salons only. At first, Mitchell performed haircutting presentations in individual salons, then DeJoria remained behind after the show was finished, vowing not to leave until the last bottle of John Paul Mitchell Systems product was sold. Moving from salon to salon in this way, Mitchell and DeJoria traveled throughout Hawaii, scoring considerable success and creating a stable foundation for their fledgling enterprise. Once the pair had firmly established themselves in Hawaii, they were ready to make the leap to the mainland, where sales of the company's hair-care products soon flourished.

The overwhelming initial success of the company stood conventional wisdom on its head. Traditional corporate leaders and industry observers may have smirked at the small and lean upstart coming out of Hawaii but by the early 1980s no one could ignore the explosive growth of the company. This was even more true by the mid-1980s, after expansion had taken the company as far away as China, where John Paul Mitchell Systems products were introduced in late 1986. John Paul Mitchell Systems was a corporate phenomenon, operating with a small staff, little overhead, and capable of generating $5 million in sales a month. In 1986, with sales hovering around the $100 million mark, the company ranked 71st on *Inc.* magazine's list of the 500 fastest-growing companies in the United States.

Despite this, there were only 27 employees on the company's corporate payroll. The true personnel strength of the company was elsewhere, vested in the 34 distributors scattered throughout the United States, in the 7 distributors operating overseas, and primarily in the 350 John Paul Mitchell Systems Associates: the hairstylists who promoted the company's products by giving demonstrations at beauty schools and hair shows. Mitchell, by this point, had settled into semiretirement on the Hawaiian island of Oahu, conducting the majority of his business from the porch above his hot tub. Although the company bore his name, Mitchell was beginning to recede from the day-to-day affairs of the company, leaving DeJoria in full command. A personal tragedy two years later left no doubt as to who was in control of John Paul Mitchell Systems.

DIVIDENDS OF A UNIQUE BUSINESS MODEL

Mitchell was diagnosed with pancreatic cancer and died in 1989, stripping the company of one of its integral spiritual leaders. Despite the loss of Mitchell, the performance recorded by John Paul Mitchell Systems hardly missed a beat, as the company entered the 1990s with DeJoria firmly in control. In the *Forbes* profile published in 1991, DeJoria declared, "I'm the American dream," a living testament to the quintessential "rags-to-riches" story. Before entering into a partnership with Mitchell, DeJoria had relegated himself to living in a car, but a decade later he stood atop an exceptionally successful company that was collecting more than $100 million in sales a year. Much of his success during the 1980s was attributable to his partnership with Mitchell, whose marquee name enabled the company to make strides quickly, but considerable credit went to DeJoria as well. His tireless marketing work created a consistent, long-term money earner, providing the framework that truly supported John Paul Mitchell Systems.

As the 1990s progressed, the strength of this framework was reflected in the continued success of the company. John Paul Mitchell Systems continued to distinguish itself as a success story. With sales topping $150 million by mid-decade, the company reigned as a market leader, its ever-expanding product line winning consumers over in the United States and overseas. The company's three-stage distributor-to-salon-to-consumer marketing system was heralded as the key to its success, convincing DeJoria, who presided as chairman and CEO, that he should never market the company's products through traditional retail methods.

The business model relied on a team of independent distributors with whom DeJoria kept in close touch, across the geographical breadth of the company's markets. The company also maintained a network of hundreds of hairstylists known as Paul Mitchell Associates, who not only used and marketed the products in their salons but also, in many cases, ran satellites of "Paul Mitchell—The School" to train the next generation of hairdressers. In a reciprocally rewarding relationship, the company offered these stylists instruction in the optimal use of Paul Mitchell products and other business development resources, while the

professionals provided input to keep the company ahead of contemporary fashion trends. Overseeing this relationship between the company and its base in the industry were a small design team, a style team, and a creative team known as the Paul Mitchell Artistic Core Group.

While John Paul Mitchell Systems' unique business structure provided a remarkably stable platform for growth, it did have some disadvantages. The proliferation of bootlegging and counterfeiting was a serious liability. In 1999 a California man pleaded guilty to delivering 10 tractor-trailer loads of phony products with Paul Mitchell labels to a New York distributor.

The laws were more ambiguous in the case of "gray-market" products diverted from their normal distribution chain and found on the shelves of retail stores or sold over the Internet. Because of the brand's popularity, chain drugstores found it profitable to stock Paul Mitchell products despite the illegitimate distribution and the possibility that the product itself could be tainted, and laws generally permitted them to do so unless the products could be proven counterfeit. In 2004 the company was forced to devote advertising dollars to a consumer education campaign, reminding the public that Paul Mitchell products were guaranteed only when sold through authorized salons and individual stylists. That year, DeJoria told *Business Week Online*, "This is robbing us of millions of dollars in sales."

DEJORIA IN THE EARLY 21ST CENTURY

Nevertheless, DeJoria refused to countenance a change in the company's operating methods and declined numerous acquisition offers. Prospective buyers, he told Brenna Fisher of *Success* magazine in 2009, were eager to "immediately go mass retail with it and double the sales. I never wanted that to happen because I promised hair stylists we would always stay with the professional beauty industry."

DeJoria himself went on to become one of the 100 wealthiest Americans, according to *Forbes*. He had cofounded the Patrón Spirits Company in 1989 to market high-end, "ultrapremium" tequila. Patrón rose to the top of its niche and was second only to José Cuervo in global tequila sales, becoming even more profitable than DeJoria's beauty company. His wife, Eloise, an actress, became the company's "spokesmodel" and the familiar face of its advertising. The billionaire couple also became deeply involved in philanthropic efforts. Along with Nelson Mandela, actor Brad Pitt, and British entrepreneur Richard Branson, DeJoria served as a patron of Mineseeker, a leading land-mine detection and de-mining agency. He also partnered with Mandela to support the organization Food for Africa and the "46664" AIDS charity concert series.

Jeffrey L. Covell
Updated, Roger K. Smith

PRINCIPAL COMPETITORS

Aubrey Organics, Inc.; Aveda Corporation; Jean Louis David; Redken Laboratories Inc.; Vidal Sassoon Co.

FURTHER READING

Arguelles, Alannah, "Good Hair, Good Deeds," *Vanity Fair*, December 1, 2008, http://www.vanityfair.com/online/daily/2008/12/john-paul-mitchell.html.

Fisher, Brenna, "Down but Never Out: John Paul DeJoria's Perseverance Took Him from Homeless to a $900 Million Hair Products Empire," *Success*, January 2009, pp. 38+.

"John Paul Mitchell Systems: Teamwork Pays Off," *Drug and Cosmetic Industry*, August 1997, pp. 22–25.

Kahn, Joseph P., "Are We Having Fun Yet? John Paul Mitchell Systems Is a New-Wave Profit Machine with Few Moving Parts and a Direct Connection to Paradise," *Inc.*, October 1987, pp. 106+.

Palmeri, Christopher, "Often Down but Never Out," *Forbes*, March 4, 1991, p. 138.

Romero, Dennis, "Homelessness, Hair Care, and 12,000 Bottles of Tequila: How John Paul DeJoria Became a Billionaire," *Entrepreneur*, July 2009, pp. 58+.

"This Is Robbing Us of Millions" (interview with John Paul DeJoria), *Business Week Online*, December 17, 2004, http://www.businessweek.com/bwdaily/dnflash/dec2004/nf20041217_2945_db049.htm.

Jujamcyn Theaters Corporation

———■———

246 West 44th Street
New York, New York 10036
U.S.A.
Telephone: (212) 840-8181
Fax: (212) 944-0708
Web site: http://www.jujamcyn.com

Private Company
Founded: 1956
Employees: 450
Sales: $24.1 million (2007)
NAICS: 531120 Lessors of Nonresidential Buildings
  (except Miniwarehouses)

■ ■ ■

Jujamcyn Theaters Corporation owns and operates five Broadway theaters (the St. James, Al Hirschfield, August Wilson, Eugene O'Neill, and Walter Kerr), rendering it the third-largest player on the Great White Way. The largest Broadway theater company is the Shubert Organization, with 17 houses, followed by the Nederlander Organization's group of 9 theaters. However, being comparatively small has not stopped Jujamcyn. The company often acts as a producing entity, presenting major hits such as *Angels in America*, *The Producers*, *Smoky Joe's Cafe*, and *Spring Awakening*.

Innovation has been a hallmark of Jujamcyn as well. Its establishment of a residential theater model of operation and its controversial introduction of premium ticket pricing made a tremendous impact on how Broadway plies its trade. Much of the company's success

can be attributed to former Jujamcyn president and co-owner Rocco Landesman, but the influence of late chairman James H. Binger and his wife, Virginia McKnight Binger, should not be understated.

As the first decade of the 21st century came to a close, the company appeared poised to make new inroads into the business with the September 2009 appointment of Jordan Roth as president and co-owner. Just 33 years old at the time, Roth was expected to inject a much-needed shot of youth into the industry.

JUJAMCYN'S BEGINNINGS

Jujamcyn began as a business venture of William L. McKnight, chairman and president of Minnesota manufacturing behemoth 3M. After buying the St. James Theater at 246 West 44th Street in New York City in 1956, McKnight purchased Broadway's Martin Beck Theater (later renamed the Al Hirschfield) and the Colonial Theater in Boston. The name of his theatrical enterprise was an amalgamation of the names of his daughter Virginia's children, Judith, James, and Cynthia.

Virginia's husband, James H. Binger, would eventually initiate the transformation of Jujamcyn into a major force on Broadway. A Yale University and University of Minnesota Law School graduate, Binger had swapped a legal career for one in the burgeoning electronics industry by signing on with Honeywell Inc. in 1943. The move proved both wise and lucrative, as he was elevated to vice president in 1952, president in 1961, and chairman in 1965. Binger and his father-in-law had a number of things in common, not the least of which were a canny business sense, a love of horse racing, and a devotion to Virginia. All three were to play pivotal roles in Binger's life.

The Bingers took over Jujamcyn in 1976 and sold the Colonial Theater shortly thereafter. Binger retired from Honeywell two years later, allowing the couple time to devote more attention to the new enterprise. Although they had shared an appreciation for the stage since they were teenagers, sentiment now took a back seat to value in Binger's practical eyes. In a 1982 profile by the *New York Times*, Binger said, "(Jujamcyn is) an investment matter, but one that I find fascinating. If there were no return on the investment I would lose my enthusiasm fast."

Fortunately for Binger, there was an adequate success ratio to prompt him to increase the company's portfolio. He acquired the Ritz (later renamed the Walter Kerr) and the ANTA (first rechristened the Virginia in honor of his wife and later becoming the August Wilson) theaters in 1981. A year later Binger completed his New York holdings with the purchase of the Eugene O'Neill Theater, bringing the total to five and positioning Jujamcyn as the third-largest theater company on Broadway.

Being a prominent theatrical landlord was good, but it was not sufficient in itself to attract the cachet (and profits) necessary to place a comparatively small fish such as Jujamcyn in the Broadway big leagues. Fortuitously, however, Binger's love of horse racing (he was a major horse breeder with the McKnight-established Tartan Farms in Florida) produced a friendship with up-and-coming producer Rocco Landesman. The two met when Landesman produced the Tony Award–winning *Big River* in 1985 and cemented their mutual admiration at the racetrack. In 1987 Landesman

signed on as Jujamcyn's president, creating a partnership that would, in some ways, alter the course of Broadway itself.

ENTER LANDESMAN

Landesman was born in St. Louis, Missouri, where his father and uncle owned a cabaret theater that featured entertainers such as Barbra Streisand, Mike Nichols, Elaine May, the Smothers Brothers, and Lenny Bruce. Despite dabbling in acting for a time, Landesman did not initially aspire to a life in the theater. Rather, he received an undergraduate education at Colby College in Maine and at the University of Wisconsin before earning a doctorate in criticism and dramatic literature from the Yale School of Drama.

After teaching at Yale for four years, Landesman left his post in 1977 to start a private investment venture, the Cardinal Fund. He also became involved in the racing business, eventually owning a dozen horses. In 1985 the theater came into his life once again when Landesman and his then-wife, Heidi, decided to produce *Big River*, the hit Broadway musical based on *Adventures of Huckleberry Finn*.

When Landesman accepted Binger's offer to run Jujamcyn, the company was lagging significantly behind the top two games in town, Shubert and Nederlander. Jujamcyn had been operating solely as a landlord and not an especially profitable one. Binger recognized that change was required in order to turn the business around and believed that Landesman was the person to do it.

Realizing that Jujamcyn had neither the venues nor the bank account to compete directly with Shubert and Nederlander, Landesman decided to take a different approach to grow the business. First, he altered the internal structure of Jujamcyn to mimic that of a repertory theater by hiring a creative director and a resident director. The idea was to get involved with projects in the early stages, sometimes even developing them in-house, to avoid the futile attempts to outbid rivals with deeper pockets. This effort was further enhanced by cultivating relationships with out-of-town resident companies such as the American Repertory Theater in Cambridge, Massachusetts, and La Jolla Playhouse in California, both of which had helped bring *Big River* to New York. Even more important was the fact that Landesman was an active producer himself.

The new formula proved to be a winning one. By 1990 the Jujamcyn theaters were making money and had nabbed 44 of that year's 75 Tony nominations, outstripping Shubert and Nederlander by a wide margin. Four of those productions (*The Piano Lesson*,

The Grapes of Wrath, *City of Angels*, and *Grand Hotel*) were produced or coproduced by Jujamcyn. (*The Grapes of Wrath* and *City of Angels* won top accolades as best play and best musical, respectively.) Jujamcyn and Landesman had garnered awards before, but this level of success was unprecedented for the company.

ONGOING SUCCESS

Binger, mainly from his Minnesota base, and Landesman, at the center of the action in New York, continued to maintain Jujamcyn's edge as the years passed. Staying ahead of the curve was an ongoing purpose, and the partners suited one another well toward that end. As the 21st century dawned, they scored their biggest hit ever with *The Producers*, a musical rendition of the Mel Brooks movie. It opened on March 21, 2001, at the St. James and was an instant popular and critical success, earning a record 12 Tony Awards. The play also launched one of Jujamcyn's most influential, and controversial, innovations: the premium ticket.

The Producers had already broken the Broadway record for expensive seating with $100 tickets when it was announced in October of 2001 that the show would also offer a set number of seats at $480 apiece. Ostensibly aimed at corporate and high-end individuals in a bid to bypass scalpers and unaffiliated ticket brokers, the concept caused an uproar and was widely predicted to fail. However, as with other Jujamcyn ideas, the competition soon followed suit. All Broadway houses eventually sold premium seating of some kind.

Following the passing of Binger in 2004 (his wife had predeceased him in 2002), Landesman purchased Jujamcyn in February 2005. He had already produced nearly 50 plays during his tenure as president, and his new role placed him in the unusual position of being both owner and active producer. Jujamcyn experienced continued success during Landesman's time as proprietor. He coproduced *Jersey Boys*, which opened at the August Wilson in 2005 and won a Tony for best musical in 2006. *Spring Awakening*, the 2007 Tony winner for best musical, opened at the Eugene O'Neill in 2006.

The landscape shifted in 2009, however, when Landesman was tapped to become chief of the U.S. National Endowment for the Arts (NEA). It was a challenge he could not resist, but it marked another harbinger of change for Jujamcyn. When Landesman departed for the NEA, he retained co-ownership of Jujamcyn and named Princeton-educated Jordan Roth as president and co-owner. Roth had joined Jujamcyn in 2005 as vice president and had cut his Broadway-producing teeth with the 2000 production of *The Rocky Horror Picture Show*. As Landesman had been when he came onboard Jujamcyn, Roth, who was 33 when he assumed his new duties, promised to bring an infusion of youthful perspective to a business long in the hands of an older sensibility.

Margaret L. Moser

PRINCIPAL COMPETITORS

Nederlander Producing Company of America; Shubert Organization.

FURTHER READING

Cohen, Patricia, "A New Force on Broadway," *New York Times*, September 8, 2009.

Franklin, Robert, and Rohan Preston, "James Binger/1916–2004; A Star Player in the Theater Business Exits the Stage," *Minneapolis Star Tribune*, November 5, 2004, p. 01A.

Jones, Kenneth, "Producer Rocco Landesman Will Buy Jujamcyn Theatres, Representing Five Jewels in Broadway's Crown," *Playbill*, November 5, 2004.

McKinley, Jesse, "For the Asking, a $480 Seat," *New York Times*, October 26, 2001, p. A1.

———, "James H. Binger, 88, Leader of Broadway Theater Chain," *New York Times*, November 5, 2004, p. A29.

Rothstein, Mervyn, "A Life in the Theatre: Jujamcyn Theatres' President Rocco Landesman," *Playbill*, August 17, 2006.

———, "Theater; How a High Roller Bets on Broadway," *New York Times*, June 3, 1990.

Kelly-Moore Paint Company, Inc.

---■---

987 Commercial Street
San Carlos, California 94070
U.S.A.
Telephone: (650) 592-8337
Toll Free: (800) 874-4436
Fax: (650) 508-8563
Web site: http://www.kellymoore.com

Private Company
Founded: 1946
Incorporated: 1946
Employees: 1,800
Sales: $281 million (2008)
NAICS: 325510 Paint and Coating Manufacturing

■ ■ ■

Kelly-Moore Paint Company, Inc., is an employee-owned regional paint manufacturer and retailer, with headquarters in San Carlos, California. The company concentrates its efforts on the West and Southwest, operating more than 160 stores in 8 U.S. states and the unincorporated territory of Guam. Its 3 manufacturing facilities, capable of producing 20 million gallons of more than 100 types of paints and finishes each year, are located in Seattle, Washington; Hurst, Texas; and San Carlos, California.

As has been the case for more than 60 years, Kelly-Moore caters primarily to professional contractors and the do-it-yourself market and has built a well-earned reputation for selling high-quality products while providing strong service. Retail sales account for less than 15 percent of the business; the company describes itself as "The Painter's Paint Store." In the first decade of the 21st century, Kelly-Moore focused on moving past asbestos lawsuits regarding its pre-1978 joint compound by offering new, environmentally friendly product lines and waste-reduction programs. These "green" practices won the company numerous awards.

WILLIAM E. MOORE'S PATH TO THE PAINT BUSINESS

The driving force behind Kelly-Moore was the company's cofounder, William E. Moore, who was born in the small town of Hartford, Arkansas, the son of a barber. According to a video tribute produced by his alma mater, Georgia Tech, Moore was ambitious from an early age. He started shining shoes at nine in order to fund his college education, and he learned how to play tennis on a makeshift court in front of his home. When he began his studies at Georgia Tech in 1934, he was accomplished enough at tennis to win a scholarship as a walk-on.

Nevertheless, Moore needed to support himself through his college years. He held eight odd jobs simultaneously while maintaining high grades and achieving an impressive athletic record. In the process Moore became something of a local legend. When he graduated in 1938 with a dual degree in industrial management and chemical engineering, America was still very much in the grips of the Great Depression. Moore was happy to find any job, accepting a position as a salesman for National Theatre Supply at a salary of $110 per month, a considerable falloff considering he

COMPANY PERSPECTIVES
■

Our Mission: To be a service-oriented paint company that provides a broad selection of high quality paint and paint related products at fair prices to Painting Contractors, Commercial and Maintenance Accounts and Do-It-Yourself Consumers through strategically located neighborhood paint stores.

had been able to cobble together $150 per month from his part-time college jobs.

Moore soon found work at Glidden Paint as a salesman and lab technician. Starting with a $160 per month draw, he set a goal of earning $1,000 each month and launched a systematic approach to achieving that amount. By analyzing sales information he determined that just 20 percent of his customers accounted for 80 percent of his sales. Rather than continue to spend the same amount of time on all of his customers, he decided to return his smaller accounts to the company in order to focus his efforts on the top 20 percent. As a result, he reached his target goal of $1,000 per month within the first year and ultimately became Glidden's top West Coast producer.

Moore's business career was interrupted by a stint in the navy during World War II, when he served on a destroyer in the Pacific. However, his time at Glidden had convinced him that his future lay in the paint business, and he devoted much of his spare time in the service studying two books on paint making. Like many in his generation, the war had a profound effect on Moore. Having lost several years of his life to the service, he felt that he had fallen behind schedule, which fueled his already ambitious nature. In 1946, at the age of 29, Moore got married and decided to strike out on his own in the paint business.

FOUNDING KELLY-MOORE

Moore studied the Southern California market and concluded that the ideal location for his enterprise was San Carlos, located some 30 minutes north of San Jose, in the heart of what would one day become the Silicon Valley. At the time, the city was home to a large number of orchards, some of which were being converted to tract-home communities. Seed money to establish a single store and manufacturing facility came from the funds Moore had saved during his stint at Glidden, which he had invested during the war in Tulsa, Oklahoma, real estate.

All Moore needed now was someone experienced in mixing paint. He found the ideal partner in William H. Kelly, a retired superintendent at Glidden who had the time and was interested in starting a small factory. The plan was to mix paint in the mornings, and Moore would make deliveries in the afternoons, with the hope that the start-up business would show a $500 profit each month. Moore and Kelly did not anticipate the pent-up demand for housing caused by the privations of war that resulted in a dramatic building boom. In the first six months of existence, instead of a $3,000 profit Kelly-Moore made $30,000.

The company's success was more than fortuitous timing, however. Moore's decisions and innovations were smart ones and would impact the future growth of the business. From the start, he had decided to focus on the tract-home paint contractors, a market segment that was being overlooked by the national brands that were eagerly pursuing consumer sales. To win over contractors, Kelly-Moore developed the kind of high-quality paint required by them, one that could do the job with a single coat. The store also maintained the high inventory levels that contractors required and could rely on.

As the business grew the company opened stores larger than was the norm in the industry, in effect serving as a warehouse for paint contractors, who mostly worked out of their homes and were unable to store large quantities of paint. In addition, Kelly-Moore was in the vanguard of making credit a function of sales, treating its customers like partners. The company further separated itself from the competition by offering innovative customer service. It opened early in the day and served free coffee, a small gesture but one that meant a great deal to paint contractors who regularly put in long, tiring days of work. Kelly-Moore was also the first to own a fleet of its own delivery trucks. In the end, the company's success was built on the character and ideas of Moore, whose dedication to honest business dealings and to producing a high-quality product supported by superior customer service resulted in repeat business.

BUYING OUT KELLY

Moore bought out Kelly in 1952, but he continued to carry his partner's name as the business grew beyond northern California. There was no doubt, however, that the success of Kelly-Moore was dependent on the integrity, skills, and hands-on leadership of Moore. He was instrumental in every area of the business, including the development of manufacturing techniques and the design of company-owned stores.

Of key importance was Moore's savvy choice of real estate. He established stores at locations with reason-

```
┌─────────────────────────────────────────────┐
│                                               │
│              KEY DATES                        │
│                    ■                          │
│  ─────────────────────────────────────────    │
│                                               │
│  1946:  Kelly-Moore Paint Company, Inc., is founded │
│         by William E. Moore and William H. Kelly.   │
│  1952:  Moore buys out Kelly.                 │
│  1985:  Joseph P. Cristiano succeeds Moore as │
│         president and CEO.                    │
│  1994:  Kelly-Moore acquires Preservative Paint Co.; │
│         company begins paint-recycling effort. │
│  1998:  Employee stock ownership program is   │
│         instituted.                           │
│  2002:  Herb R. Giffins replaces Cristiano as │
│         president and CEO.                     │
│  2006:  Steve DeVoe is appointed president.   │
│  2010:  Company wins Green Large Business of the │
│         Year Award from California Green Business │
│         Committee.                            │
│                                               │
└─────────────────────────────────────────────┘
```

able rental rates, which helped to produce high margins for the business. By operating larger stores and thereby acting as a warehouse for customers, Kelly-Moore could better plan its inventories, which also resulted in strong net margins.

It was also at Moore's insistence that the company never succumbed to the temptation of saving money by cutting back on product quality, instead relying on high-quality raw materials such as titanium in the formulation of all of its paints. In addition to tough, company-wide quality-control measures, Kelly-Moore's sales department maintained its own quality-control testing.

Over the years Kelly-Moore picked up some consumer sales, largely due to contractors leaving behind touch-up cans, which served as both a product sample and a professional endorsement for the company. By 1974 consumer sales accounted for about one-quarter of total revenues. That amount would grow over the next decade to 37 percent, the result of a changing marketplace in which an increasing number of home-owners were opting to do their own painting.

Despite the rise of the do-it-yourself customer and an ever-changing housing market, Kelly-Moore was able to maintain a decade of growth. By the time Moore began the process of retiring and turning over day-to-day responsibilities to a new chief executive in 1984, Kelly-Moore generated sales of 136 million and a profit of more than $11 million, with more than 80 stores located in California, Arizona, Colorado, Texas, Oklahoma, and the Pacific Northwest.

NEW LEADERSHIP AND STEADY GROWTH

After building a successful business, Moore, approaching 70 years old, set about the task of making sure the company was in a position to carry on without him. His 33-year-old daughter was in charge of advertising, but to find his replacement at the top of the organization, Moore recruited outside the company. He hired Joseph P. Cristiano, who had actually been dispatched by a competing paint company, Sherwin-Williams, in an effort to acquire Kelly-Moore. Instead, Moore sold Cristiano on coming to work for him. For the first six months Cristiano was on the road with sales representatives, learning firsthand how Kelly-Moore operated. In January 1985 Moore officially turned over the reins to Cristiano, although Moore continued to serve as the company's chairman of the board and retained about 97 percent of the stock.

Cristiano adhered to the formula established by Moore, and the company continued its steady growth over the next 10 years. Although Kelly-Moore primarily relied on internal growth, it used external means as well. In 1994 it acquired Seattle-based Preservative Paint Co., which became a wholly owned subsidiary, adding 2 stores in Alaska and 15 in Washington, as well as a pump and compressor center. A year later Kelly-Moore bought K-M Universal, gaining a factory in Tempe, Arizona, as well as additional stores in Arizona and California. Kelly-Moore added to this new subsidiary in 1996 when it folded in another purchase, the Guam-based paint division of Island Equipment Co.

BRANCHING OUT INTO RECYCLING

Kelly-Moore experienced some internal growth during this period by becoming involved in paint recycling. The effort started out on a small scale as a pet program that allowed paint contractors to return unused paint at no cost. This was a useful service because professionals were not permitted to use free public paint collection facilities. The company stockpiled a large amount of recycled paint and began to seek a market for it.

In the summer of 1994, Kelly-Moore landed a contract for 50,000 gallons of recycled latex paint with the federal General Services Administration (GSA). The contract called for a product that contained at least a 50 percent postconsumer recycled content, which was packaged under the company's "e coat" brand name, to be used by military installations, U.S. forestry facilities, and other federal outlets. As a result, the "e coat" line became listed in the GSA catalog, which gave Kelly-Moore a leg up on future contracts for recycled paint. In addition, the company moved aggressively to sell its recycled paint product at the state and local levels to schools and other facilities.

As Kelly-Moore reached its 50th year in business in 1996, it was generating some $240 million in annual sales; boasting 140 stores in Guam and 10 states (Alaska, Arizona, Arkansas, California, Colorado, Nevada, Oklahoma, Oregon, Texas, and Washington); and employing more than 2,300 people. Its continued success remained based on a longtime formula of producing quality paints and offering superior service to the contract painter. Moreover, the company was able to adjust to changing circumstances in the marketplace. The state of California instituted tough volatile organic compounds (VOC) standards, forcing Kelly-Moore and other paint companies doing business in the state to reformulate their products. Kelly-Moore's efforts in new product development were now devoted to waterborne products, as opposed to oil-based paints, with the challenge of maintaining the high quality of its architectural coatings and high-gloss exteriors.

ESTABLISHING ESOP

Aside from keeping pace with regulatory changes, Kelly-Moore took other measures to remain competitive. In 1998 Moore and his wife established a combined retirement and employee stock ownership program (ESOP), which allowed qualifying employees to gain an ownership stake in the business. The plan was instrumental in helping the company retain personnel and instill an even greater degree of loyalty in its employees. It subsequently became the largest employee-owned U.S. paint company.

Kelly-Moore also developed marketing partnerships to help it compete with national brands. In 1999 it formed a marketing alliance with Pennsylvania-based M. A. Bruder & Sons, a company of similar size and philosophy that operated primarily in the eastern states. Because their territories did not overlap, the two companies were able to share national accounts, with M. A. Bruder responsible for East Coast projects and Kelly-Moore for West Coast projects. As a result of the venture, the companies were jointly listed in the American Institute of Architects' MASTERSPEC finishes directory, which is used by about 5,500 architectural and construction firms and includes only a handful of other paint companies.

The company's marketing alliance grew in 2000 with the addition of Diamond Vogel Paints, based in Orange City, Iowa. The resulting venture was named Paint America, a key component in the regional partners' efforts to resist industry consolidation and

maintain independence while still serving national retail chains and property management customers. West Coast paint company Dunn-Edwards soon joined Paint America as well. To a small degree Kelly-Moore took part in the consolidation of the paint industry in 2000, when it acquired Ponderosa Paint Manufacturing Inc., adding 15 stores in Oregon, Utah, and Idaho.

After almost 20 years at the helm, Cristiano stepped down as president and CEO of Kelly-Moore. Although his retirement was not official until January 2003, in November 2002 he was replaced by Herb R. Giffins, an executive with 24 years of experience in the paint industry. He in turn was replaced by long-time Kelly-Moore employee Steve DeVoe in 2006, who reemphasized the company's focus on customer service by personally having dinner with store customers around the nation to hear about their concerns.

ASBESTOS LAWSUITS AND "GREEN" PRACTICES

In the first decade of the 21st century, Kelly-Moore began to receive recognition for its technological innovation in developing environmentally friendly paints. It received the 2007 Northern California, Large Facility, Certificate of Merit from the California Water Environment Association because of its meeting of environmental pollution standards. The following year the company launched two new zero-VOC paint lines, Enviro Coat and Green Coat, and was certified as a "green business" by the California State Assembly. In January 2010 Kelly-Moore won the Green Large Business of the Year Award from the California Green Business Committee.

The company had not always been considered so "green," however. In 2001 a contractor living in Texas was awarded $55.5 million by a jury that found his cancer was caused by asbestos in a Kelly-Moore joint compound he worked with during the 1970s. The plaintiff's attorneys successfully argued that Kelly-Moore continued to use asbestos in its products even after their health dangers were known. Kelly-Moore, for its part, denied that its joint compounds had ever contained unsafe levels of asbestos.

Kelly-Moore then did an about-face. After asserting in lawsuits for years that its product was not harmful, the company acknowledged its toxicity and sued Union Carbide Corporation, one of its suppliers, claiming that it had concealed the dangers of asbestos. Kelly-Moore's lawyer, Mark Lanier, told Nathan Koppel of *American Lawyer* that the company took the risk because it had already paid $240 million in damages, including the huge award in Texas, and faced over a billion dollars more in the future. "This," he said, "was their best chance to stay alive."

During a six-week trial in 2004, the jury heard evidence that Carbide was what Koppel termed "callous and manipulative." However, Lanier had a difficult time convincing the jury that Kelly-Moore was an innocent victim. When the jury found in favor of Carbide, Kelly-Moore was opened up to seemingly endless lawsuits.

Despite predictions otherwise, Kelly-Moore survived the lawsuits; most of the damages for asbestos exposure were paid by the company's insurance policies. However, by 2008 its sales numbers and employment figures had declined, in large part because of the global economic recession that began in late 2007. Industry magazine *Coatings World* reported in its 2009 Top Companies Report that Kelly-Moore's sales figures had slipped to $281 million in 2008 and its employees numbered 1,500, down from 2,300 at the beginning of the decade. The company had also dropped in the magazine's annual ranking, from No. 32 in 2002 to No. 44 in 2008. Although still a small player compared to the industry giants, Kelly-Moore remained a very successful business, well entrenched in its niche in the market and positioned to thrive for the foreseeable future.

Ed Dinger
Updated, Melissa Doak

PRINCIPAL SUBSIDIARIES

Preservative Paint Co.; K-M Universal.

PRINCIPAL COMPETITORS

Benjamin Moore and Co.; E.I. du Pont de Nemours & Company; The Sherwin-Williams Company.

FURTHER READING

Burrows, Kate, "Paint for the Pros: For More than 60 Years, Kelly-Moore Paint Says It Has Ensured All Customers Receive Personalized Service from Its Skilled Employees," *U.S. Business Review*, January 2008, p. 63.

Dill, Larry, "Paint Recycling: Kelly-Moore Is Supplying the Federal Government and Looking for Other Markets," *Modern Paint and Coatings*, January 1, 1995, p. 19.

Dorich, Alan, "Painting Perfection: As It Celebrates Its 60th Anniversary, Kelly-Moore Paint Co. Says It Will Continue Providing Contractors High-Quality Paint and Personalized Service," *U.S. Business Review*, August 2006, p. 22.

"Kelly-Moore Receives 'Green Large Business of the Year' Award," *Marketwire*, January 27, 2010.

Koppel, Nathan, "Showdown in a Small Town," *American Lawyer*, February 2005.

"Man Wins $55 Million Verdict against Kelly-Moore Paint," *New York Times*, August 31, 2001, p. 3.

Neal, Roger, "Color It Profitable," *Forbes*, January 28, 1985, p. 76.

Sharkey, Mike, "Kelly-Moore Paints: True Colors," *American Executive*, September 30, 2007.

Simmers, Tim, "Paint Makers Heat Up Competition," *Oakland Tribune*, August 3, 2005.

Valero, Greg, and Bill Schmitt, "Regional Paint Makers Link to Serve National Accounts," *Chemical Week*, May 17, 2000, p. 39.

Kingston Technology
Company, Inc.

17600 Newhope Street
Fountain Valley, California 92708
U.S.A.
Telephone: (714) 435-2600
Toll Free: (877) 546-4786
Fax: (714) 435-2699
Web site: http://www.kingston.com

Private Company
Founded: 1987
Employees: 4,000 (est.)
Sales: $4 billion (2008 est.)
NAICS: 334112 Computer Storage Device Manufacturing; 334413 Semiconductor and Related Device Manufacturing

■ ■ ■

Kingston Technology Company, Inc., is among the world's leading producers of memory storage devices for computers and other digital media products. Kingston's core business involves the design and manufacture of portable memory drives, processor upgrades, storage subsystems, and networking products for personal computers, workstations, and laser printers. At the same time, the company is one of the world's largest providers of enhancement products for PCs, laptops, notebooks, servers, workstations and printers. Kingston maintains regional headquarters in three strategic locations worldwide: the United States, which manages the company's operations in North and South America, Eastern Europe, and Russia; the United Kingdom,

which oversees the company's European and African branches; and Taiwan, which is responsible for the company's activities in Asia and the Pacific Rim.

CAPITALIZING ON THE DEMAND
FOR MORE MEMORY: 1980–89

Kingston Technology Company was founded in 1987 by John Tu (originally from Shanghai) and David Sun (originally from Taiwan). Tu and Sun had met in 1982 and started Camintonn Corporation, a manufacturer of enhancement products for DEC systems. This fly-by-night company began in Tu's garage, with the two businessmen carrying computer memory chips in the back seats of their cars. By 1986 business took off with sales of $9 million. That year they sold the company to AST Research for $6 million, investing their gains in the stock market.

When the stock market crashed in 1987, Tu and Sun lost almost everything. Then they saw an opportunity to recoup their losses. At that time the computer industry was suffering from a shortage of memory modules for personal computers. Tu and Sun seized a simple solution to the problem, designing an industry standard Single In-Line Memory Module (SIMM) with an alternative chip that was readily available. This product and a mere $4,000 launched Kingston's operations, and the company soon began developing memory products for PCs.

A skeptical businessman, Tu found it difficult to believe that the simple solution the two had found to the memory crisis would result in a lasting company. He bet Sun a Jaguar that Kingston would not live past its

COMPANY PERSPECTIVES

∎

At Kingston Technology Company Inc., we have a long standing commitment to performing our business in a socially responsible and ethical manner. We recognize our responsibility to contribute positively to our employees' success and to provide a work environment that is respectful, safe and healthy for all.

Kingston's Core Values are: respect for one another in our culturally diverse environment; loyalty to our long-term partnerships; integrity and fairness in all aspects of our business; flexibility and adaptability in responding to our customers' needs; investing in our employees to continually improve our most valuable resource; having fun working in the company of friends.

first year. The PC market was beginning to produce computers that ran on separate proprietary systems, leaving the door open for Kingston to design and produce several unique memory upgrade devices for each individual market. In its first year the company achieved $12.8 million in sales. Tu lost his bet, and Sun later bestowed the Jaguar upon an employee who had long dreamed of owning one.

By 1989, just two years after Kingston's emergence, the marketplace had changed. Chips were in ready supply once again, and as a result so were memory enhancement products. However, Kingston remained the clear leader in the memory market, and in 1989 the company earned $36.5 million in sales.

THE EMERGENCE OF AN INDUSTRY LEADER: 1990–95

One of the ways in which Kingston quickly differentiated itself from its competition was the high level of customer service, including 100 percent testing of its products, comprehensive 5-year warranties, domestic 24-hour shipping, and free technical support. The company promised to immediately replace defective parts with no questions asked.

Beyond customer service, Kingston established a holistic way of operating a family-style company. The company's philosophy places the customer third, after employees and suppliers. According to Kingston, if the company takes care of its employees and suppliers, the customers will be taken care of as well. Kingston

employees are among the highest paid in the industry (as much as 30 percent above average), and an egalitarian work environment is demonstrated by the fact that Tu and Sun's working suites are cubicles among their staff. Showing a generosity that is rare in corporate America, Kingston distributed 5 percent of pretax quarterly profits to employees as a bonus and matched employee contributions to 401(k) plans dollar for dollar. Furthermore, managing the company conservatively, Tu and Sun ensured employees that should the company go out of business at any time, employees would be granted a full year's salary in order to find a suitable position elsewhere. Appreciative of such unusual treatment, Kingston employees tended to stay, with less than 2 percent annual attrition as of 1994.

Given such perquisites, one would imagine that job seekers clamor to work at Kingston. However, securing a position with the company is no easy task. Tu and Sun value experience over credentials and seek employees who would be good members of the family. About 80 percent of new hires are the result of internal referrals. By hiring slowly, the company succeeds in gradually implanting its family culture in each employee. One of the most multicultural companies in the industry, Kingston employs a mix of whites, blacks, Chinese, Vietnamese, and Hispanic workers, with two-thirds of its workers in 1995 representing ethnic minorities.

RELATIONSHIPS WITH SUPPLIERS

Suppliers, the company's number two priority, are also treated well. The company never turns away shipments from chip vendors, nor does it renegotiate when market chip prices fall below contractual agreement levels. Kingston seeks to establish long-term relationships with vendors, working with them as partners over many years. Long-term relationships are also key to managing currency risk, and Kingston has cultivated strong relationships with its foreign distributors based on mutual favors and support. When sterling fell against the dollar, for example, Kingston's U.K. vendor could not meet the cost of a more expensive dollar. At the expense of its profit margins, Kingston lowered its prices. The company in such a situation, however, expects the vendor to return the favor when sterling's value again increases.

Kingston's early success was also due to the cutthroat computer market, where manufacturers customarily produced low-quality hardware products and made money on upgrades. With Kingston's upgrade products, these machines could handle the demands of word-processing and Internet software. Kingston soon became known for the speed with which it designed and delivered upgrades, sometimes producing the upgrade

KEY DATES

■

1987: John Tu and David Sun found the Kingston Technology Company.

1994: Kingston names Henry Tchen the company's first chief financial officer.

1996: The Japanese firm Softbank Corporation acquires an 80 percent stake in Kingston Technology.

1997: Kingston opens European headquarters in England.

1999: Kingston founders Tu and Sun buy back Softbank's shares in the company; Kingston Technology once again becomes a private company.

2006: Kingston launches the DataTraveler Elite Privacy Edition, a security-enhanced memory storage device.

2009: Kingston subsidiary Kingston Technology Europe Limited enters into a retail pact with Staples.

for a product before that product was even released to the consumer. Whereas most PC producers allow orders to pile up while they shop for the best bargains, shipping bulk orders every month or so, Kingston fills all purchase orders daily. The company places the quality of its relationship with suppliers and customers above any savings associated with waiting to fill orders. The result is that Kingston is the fastest company to meet its customers' orders. Its reputation for speedy response is so strong that original equipment manufacturers (OEMs) have been known to refer their own customers to Kingston when they cannot meet customer needs in a timely way. Filling orders quickly has another advantage: Kingston carries no inventory.

GROWTH: 1989–94

All of these qualities set Kingston apart from the competition during its first few years in business. In 1989 Kingston extended beyond memory products, entering the storage upgrade market. The next year, the company began offering processor upgrades, the company's first nonmemory product line. The introduction of Windows 3.0 in 1990 gave sales a boost, as computers required more memory than what was contained within PCs. Revenues almost tripled in 1990, reaching $87.8 million, and in 1991 sales again surged, to $140.7 million. The demand for memory was

spurred in 1991 by the rise of the memory-intensive workstation market. Kingston created a special department to serve this market in 1991. By this time the company employed 110 people.

In 1992 Kingston was ranked the fastest-growing private company in America by *Inc.* magazine. With no debt and no venture capital, revenues surged to $251 million (with about one-third coming from international markets), and the company grew to employ 175 people. Competing with about 15 companies, Kingston held a 45 percent share of the computer memory market in 1992. That year the company continued to diversify its offerings, adding a line of Ethernet and Token Ring networking products. In 1993 new networking and storage product lines were introduced. That year it became apparent that the company's innovative vendor relationships were working. Demand for semiconductors exceeded supply, with suppliers shipping to Kingston when orders from other buyers were delayed. Sales for 1993 were $433 million, and the number of employees grew to 255.

By 1994 Kingston had developed nine separate processor upgrade products and a full line of portable products. The company entered the portable market with its introduction of DataTraveler, a portable hard disk drive, and DataPak, a portable PCMCIA hard disk drive. The billion-dollar mark began to feel reachable, as 1994 revenues climbed to $800 million.

Kingston's competition had increased, with 70 companies in the $7.2 billion dynamic random-access memory (DRAM) module market, but Kingston was still number one. The company's growth was physically evident. The workstation memory group was moved to a different building, and Kingston purchased bicycles to shuttle employees between the two worksites.

However, growth began to present questions for the company. In 1994 Kingston hired its first chief financial officer, former Wall Street investment banker Henry Tchen, and issued security badges to employees. Outsiders wondered if the company's family environment would be tossed aside when revenues reached the billion dollar mark.

EXPANSION AT HOME AND ABROAD: 1995–96

When Microsoft introduced the Windows 95 operating system, in 1995, demand for Kingston's memory upgrades skyrocketed. Windows required more memory than most consumers had in their existing hardware. The company surpassed a billion dollars in sales that year, earning $1.3 billion with 450 employees.

International development became a major focus about this time. Expanding its worldwide distribution network, Kingston opened a branch office in Munich, Germany, in 1995. The next year a branch office was opened in Paris. Kingston worked with Legend Technology Limited to develop computers for the Chinese market in 1996. Also in 1996 the company introduced the TurboChip 133 processor upgrade, which gave a 486 computer the power of a 75 megahertz Pentium chip, and three new plug-and-play Ethernet adapters.

By this time Tu and Sun had become two of America's wealthiest entrepreneurs, occupying places on the *Forbes* list of America's 400 richest people. Leading the company, Tu focused on sales and marketing while Sun oversaw engineering. As a team, Tu and Sun were noted for their quick decision-making. The pair often decided to launch new products while walking from their cars to the Kingston headquarters, and the success rate for new products was an unheard-of 90 percent in 1992. Kingston's founders did not wish to take the company public, desiring to maintain the family environment they had built.

In 1996 the price of DRAM had dropped dramatically, forcing upgrade vendors to boost sales volume and enter new markets. Kingston responded by pursuing the OEM market, courting companies such as Compaq Computer Corp., IBM Corp., and Sun Microsystems, Inc.

ACQUISITION BY SOFTBANK

Taking analysts by surprise, Kingston was acquired in 1996 by Softbank Corporation, the world's largest publisher of computer-related magazines and books and the world's largest producer of technology-related trade shows and expositions. Softbank was also the largest distributor of computer software, peripherals, and systems in Japan. Softbank purchased 80 percent of the company for $1.5 billion, and Kingston characteristically shared $100 million with its employees as a holiday bonus (doling out approximately $75,000 to each employee).

Softbank's revenues for fiscal year 1996 were $1.6 billion, and the company had 6,000 employees across the world. Under the terms of the acquisition, Tu and Sun remain in charge of the company's operations. What was surprising about the acquisition was that Tu and Sun, who had been extremely financially conservative from the outset (never even agreeing to take out a bank loan), had agreed to be purchased by a company that was in the process of a takeover spending spree with high financing. Why would Kingston agree to such an alliance?

The answer was that Softbank's strong distribution channels in Japan, where Kingston had virtually no pres-

ence, would be an asset to Kingston's expansion plans. The company's dominance of the distribution channels selling to America's *Fortune* 1000 had made it the largest memory module manufacturer, but outside markets remained unconquered.

With Softbank's acquisition the company began targeting international growth. In 1997 Kingston announced a $40 million expansion plan, involving the construction of production facilities in Europe and Asia and the expansion of its U.S. facility to include a new manufacturing center. The goal of the expansion was to achieve faster turnaround times and lower prices amid the plummeting price of memory, which had dropped 80 percent during 1996–97. Kingston opened a European headquarters in the United Kingdom and announced plans to open a manufacturing site there as well.

In its first decade Kingston grew from a company that manufactured a single memory module to an international corporation with more than a billion dollars in revenues. The company achieved its astounding growth by eschewing the cutthroat bargain-oriented mentality of its competitors, instead valuing long-term relationships and employee satisfaction. With its acquisition by Softbank and its expansion in Europe and Asia, Kingston entered a new phase of development in its second decade of existence. These developments raised an intriguing question about the company's future: Could the family-style management that had secured Kingston's leadership place in the market continue to coexist with the demands of a billion dollar business?

A SHIFT IN DIRECTION: 1999–2003

The union of Kingston and Softbank proved to be short-lived. By the late 1990s Softbank had begun to devote more of its resources to the emerging Internet commerce segment, purchasing substantial shares of such companies as Yahoo! and E*Trade. With this shift in Softbank's business model, Kingston's memory products suddenly became superfluous to the Japanese firm's long-term strategy. At the same time, Kingston was struggling toward the end of the decade, as market prices for DRAM products continued to slide. For the fiscal year ending March 31, 1999, Kingston suffered an annual loss of more than $50 million.

In July 1999 Softbank agreed to sell its 80 percent ownership in Kingston back to the company's founders, Sun and Tu, for $450 million, roughly a third of what Softbank had paid for its stake only three years before. While many observers believed that Softbank could have received far more money in the transaction, a prior agreement with Sun and Tu had prohibited it from selling the company to outside parties. In the wake of the stock repurchase, the newly privatized Kingston once again became fully committed to developing its core product line. The company rebounded quickly from its losses, with total earnings for 1999 reaching the $1.5 billion mark. In the year 2000 Kingston was ranked 141 on *Forbes* magazine's list of the nation's leading private companies.

Kingston continued to grow steadily during the early years of the 21st century. By 2003 it had become the largest independent manufacturer of memory products worldwide, with an international workforce of 1,800 employees. In 2003 the company achieved total sales of $1.8 billion. In an interview appearing in the *Daily Telegraph* on July 19, 2003, Kingston cofounder John Tu attributed the company's success to luck and trust. "It is important to trust people," Tu told reporter Rosie Murray-West. "People have to come first." This philosophy applied equally to the company's internal operations, as Kingston routinely paid large annual bonuses to its employees. Kingston's business practices frequently earned the company recognition as one of the best employers in the industry.

BRISK EARNINGS GROWTH

The middle of the decade saw the emergence of several new products at Kingston. In 2004 Kingston unveiled its HyperX DDR2 memory module, which featured higher speed and bandwidth capacities, while also operating at higher energy efficiency. Two years later the firm launched the Kingston DataTraveler Elite Privacy Edition, a secure USB memory device featuring encryption software and other password safeguarding utilities. Other notable new products from these years included the MMCmobile flash card (a memory storage device for cell phones) and DataTraveler Secure (a waterproof flash drive with enhanced security features).

With this focus on constant innovation, Kingston enjoyed brisk earnings growth heading into the end of the decade. The company's earnings rose from $2.4 billion in 2004 to $4.5 billion in 2007; near the end of that period, *Inc.* magazine ranked Kingston the nation's fastest growing private company on the basis of earnings.

In the face of the global economic downturn, Kingston's sales suffered a slight dip in 2008, with total revenues falling to $4 billion for the year. Nevertheless,

the company remained focused on new opportunities for expansion, both at home and abroad. In 2009 the company's European subsidiary, Kingston Technology Europe Ltd., entered into a joint partnership with office supply chain Staples to begin selling memory products in four countries. With the company widely regarded to be the industry leader in the manufacture of memory storage devices, Kingston had reason to remain confident about its prospects heading into the new decade.

Heidi Feldman
Updated, Stephen Meyer

PRINCIPAL SUBSIDIARIES

Kingston Technology Europe Limited (United Kingdom); Kingston Technology Far East Co. (Taiwan).

PRINCIPAL COMPETITORS

Elpida Memory, Inc.; Hynix Semiconductor Inc. ; Lexar Media, Inc.; Micron Technology, Inc.; PNY Technologies, Inc.; Samsung Electronics Co., Ltd.; SanDisk Corporation; SMART Modular Technologies, Inc.; STEC, Inc.

FURTHER READING

Burck, Charles, "The Real World of the Entrepreneur," *Fortune*, April 5, 1993, pp. 62–81.

Davidson, John, "Softbank to Kingston: Thanks for the Memory," *Australian Financial Review*, July 16, 1999, p. 58.

Doebele, Justin, "Kingston: King of Retrofit," *Forbes*, December 19, 1994, pp. 312–13.

———, "Memory Gain," *Fortune*, September 9, 1996, p. 16.

"Kingston Technology Announces Retail Deal with Staples," *Telecomworldwire*, March 12, 2009.

Laabe, Jennifer J., "Kingston Employees Get Huge Bonuses," *Workforce*, February 1997, p. 11.

McKeefry, Hailey Lynne, "Kingston Plans Major Expansion: Memory Maker Will Add Two Overseas Facilities," *Electronic Buyers' News*, May 5, 1997, p. 74.

Murray-West, Rosie, "The Yin and Yang of Selling Memory Chips," *Daily Telegraph*, July 19, 2003, p. 32.

The Ultimate Memory Guide. Fountain Valley, CA: Kingston Technology Corporation, 1995.

Welles, Edward G., "The 1992 Inc. 500: Built on Speed," *Inc.*, October, 1992, pp. 82–88.

Wachstum erleben.

K+S Aktiengesellschaft

Bertha-von-Suttner Street 7
Kassel, Hesse 34131
Germany
Telephone: (+49 561) 9301 0
Fax: (+49 561) 9301 1753
Web site: http://www.k-plus-s.com

Public Company
Founded: 1889 as Aktiengesellschaft für Bergbau und
    Tiefbohrung
Employees: 15,000 (est.)
Sales: €4.79 billion ($6.53 billion) (2008)
Stock Exchanges: Frankfurt
Ticker Symbol: SDF
NAICS: 212391 Potash, Soda, and Borate Mineral Min-
    ing; 212393 Other Chemical and Fertilizer Mineral
    Mining; 325311 Nitrogenous Fertilizer Manufactur-
    ing; 325998 All Other Miscellaneous Chemical
    Product and Preparation Manufacturing; 424690
    Other Chemical and Allied Products Merchant
    Wholesalers; 424910 Farm Supplies Merchant
    Wholesalers

■ ■ ■

The K+S Aktiengesellschaft, headquartered in Kassel, Germany, is Europe's leading potash and salt mining company and one of the world's leading suppliers of specialty and standard fertilizers and plant-care and salt products. Its subsidiary K+S Nitrogen is the world's leading supplier of ammonia sulfate and the second-largest supplier of fertilizer, potting soils, and plant nutrients. With the acquisition of the U.S.-based giant Morton Salt, K+S also became the world's leading salt producer. This enormous international success has been prepared by a 120-year history of predecessors aiming to integrate the entire German potash industry through mergers and acquisitions. Today K+S is active in Europe, South America, and the United States. About 15,000 employees work for K+S worldwide. K+S subsidiaries are primarily engaged in marketing and distributing their own product, as well as in related services such as logistics, waste disposal, and recycling. K+S stock trades on the German stock market (MDAX).

THE GERMAN POTASH MONOPOLY

In the mid-1900s the German chemist Justus von Liebig discovered the significance of mineral fertilizers for agriculture, which were based on three basic ingredients: phosphate, nitrogen, and potash. Potash is the common name of potassium carbonate and various mined and manufactured salts that contain the element potassium in water-soluble form. In the decades following Liebig's discovery, potash became a sought-after commodity.

The economic boom following the founding years of the German Reich in 1870–71 further increased the demand for potash, and accelerated mining began in several new, mostly state-run mines in northern Germany around Hannover, Braunschweig, and Hildesheim. In 1883 the German salt industry was privatized, and in 1889 Guido Henkel von Donnersmarck founded the Aktiengesellschaft für Bergbau und Tiefbohrung in Goslar, Germany. Here begins the his-

COMPANY PERSPECTIVES

Growth lies at the heart of our vision. K+S is one of the world's leading suppliers of specialty and standard fertilizers, plant care as well as salt products. We offer our customers a range of goods that meet needs and serve as the basis for growth in almost all areas of day-to-day life in the form of tailor-made and branded products. In doing so, we assume active responsibility for the sustained growth of our world. Our approximately 15,000 employees display their commitment towards this goal day in day out by applying their knowledge and experience.

tory of K+S Aktiengesellschaft, a name echoing the founding ingredients of its success, *Kali* (potash) and *Salz* (salt).

The new company mined in northern Germany searching for potash and in 1892 found the potash salt Sylvinit in Salzdetfurth near Hildesheim. Construction of shafts and tunnels 700 meters below ground began immediately. Upon completion in 1899 the company moved its headquarters to Salzdetfurth and changed its name to Kaliwerke Salzdetfurth AG.

The fast growth of the potash industry at the turn of the century produced other mining companies, among them the Bohrgesellschaft Wintershall (1894, renamed the Wintershall AG in 1929) and the Kaliwerke Kruegershall AG (1905, renamed the Burbach Kaliwerke AG in 1928), both predecessors that would eventually blend within the K+S AG. At the end of the 19th century, the German Reich was the only country in the world mining for potash and producing related products, mainly agricultural fertilizers and industrial salts. In an effort to protect this monopoly, the companies formed cartels. Price arrangements and supply caps allowed the companies to take hold of a volatile market and increase their share. In 1901 the Salzdetfurth AG joined the Kali-Kartell, an association of the 12 leading potash mining companies in Germany.

An increased need for German agricultural production that would make up for the loss of agricultural imports during World War I made it necessary to find a replacement for nitrate from South America, so agricultural fertilizers could be produced with only German resources. A mixture of nitrogen and hydrogen, produced by the chemical company BASF, did the trick. Hence BASF, now a player in the fertilizer business, was

well positioned to become a future majority shareholder of the Salzdetfurth AG.

NAVIGATING THE INTERNATIONAL COMPETITION

Alsace-Lorraine, a geographical area at the border between France and Germany, became part of France in 1919, following World War I. Up to this time the area had been mined exclusively by the German potash industry. While only an insignificant amount of potash was mined there, this territorial change signaled the end of the German potash monopoly. Soon German potash producers had to compete with international companies, mainly from the United States, Canada, the Soviet Union, southern Europe, and South America, particularly Chile and Brazil. In the 1920s about 70 percent of the world's potash still came from German mines, but by 1935 the percentage had dropped to 62 percent.

To counteract this development and to remain competitive, German potash mining companies sought to strengthen their market position by forming associations. During the economic crisis caused by inflation in the 1920s, Deutsche Bank, Commerzbank, and Dresdner Bank, as well as the Solvay-Werke, invested in the Salzdetfurth AG, becoming major shareholders. The same banks also held shares in other German potash companies, which provided an easy gateway to market negotiations that would allow price fixing and supply regulations.

In 1922 several of these companies, the Consolidirten Alkaliwerke Westeregeln AG, the Kaliwerke Aschersleben AG, and the Salzdetfurth AG, went a step further and associated in an organization, the Werksgruppe Salzdetfurth-Aschersleben-Westeregeln. The companies bought each other's shares, with the Salzdetfurth AG holding 40 percent of the total stock, thus emerging as the leader of the group. Together the group held about 20 percent of the potash market, slowly catching up with the market leader at the time, the Wintershall AG, which dominated about 40 percent of the market. In 1926, in an effort to further consolidate their market share, virtually all potash companies other than Wintershall (the Salzdetfurth AG, the Burbach Kaliwerke AG, the Kali-Chemie AG, and the Deutsche Solvay-Werke) united in a potash syndicate, the so-called Kali-Block. The Kali-Block supported its participating companies mainly with regard to distribution, together holding about 50 percent of the market.

In 1927 a transport company was established on the island of Wilhelmsburg on the Elbe River near Hamburg, where modern warehouse and handling facilities satisfied the growing demand for transport services.

KEY DATES

1889: The Aktiengesellschaft für Bergbau und Tiefbohrung is founded in Goslar, Germany; Joe Morton acquires a major interest in Richmond & Company, Agents for Onondaga Salt, and renames the company Jay Morton & Company.

1894: The Bohrgesellschaft Wintershall (renamed the Wintershall AG in 1929) is founded in Bochum.

1899: The Aktiengesellschaft für Bergbau und Tiefbohrung moves to Salzdetfurth, Germany, and is renamed Kaliwerke Salzdetfurth AG.

1901: The Kaliwerke Salzdetfurth AG joins the Kali-Kartell.

1934: The Wintershall AG purchases 45.5 percent of the Burbach Kaliwerke AG.

1937: The Wintershall AG buys stock of the Salzdetfurth AG, becoming a shareholder in the competition.

1945: Some 60 percent of the German potash mining capacity is locked behind the Iron Curtain in East Germany.

1955: The Wintershall AG becomes majority shareholder at the Burbach Kaliwerke.

1960: The Salzdetfurth AG becomes sole owner of the Kölner Chemische Fabrik Kalk.

1968: BASF becomes majority owner of the Wintershall AG.

1971: Merger between the Salzdetfurth AG and the Wintershall/Burbach Group forms the Kali und Salz AG.

1983: The K+S Consulting GmbH opens its doors.

1990: The Kali und Salz Entsorgung GmbH is established in Kassel.

1993: The Kali und Salz AG and the Deutsche Treuhandanstalt merge with the East German Mitteldeutsche Kali AG and the West German Kali und Salz AG to form the all-German Kali und Salz GmbH.

1994: The Kali und Salz GmbH changes its name to Kali und Salz Beteiligungs AG.

1998: The Kali und Salz Beteiligungs AG purchases the remaining 49 percent of the Kali und Salz GmbH share capital completing the privatization of the former East German potash companies; the Kali und Salz Beteiligungs AG is first listed on the German stock exchange (MDAX).

1999: Company changes name to K+S Aktiengesellschaft.

2000: K+S acquires the UBT- See- und Hafenspedition GmbH Rostock.

2004: K+S buys out Sovay and takes over esco; also takes over the French potash company SPCA.

2006: K+S acquires Sociedad Punta de Lobos S.A. (SPL) in Chile.

2009: K+S acquires Morton Salt Inc., USA.

Commissioned by the state of Prussia, a port was built within a very short time and placed at the disposal of the Kali-Block. In 1928 another port facility was built in Bremen. Together the two ports offered sufficient storage space for 190,000 tons of potash salt, which allowed the Kali-Block to compete in the growing international potash trade.

WORLD WAR II AND ITS RAMIFICATIONS

The rise of the Nazis in Germany during the 1930s signaled another period of national economic self-reliance. The government drastically controlled all areas of the German economy and pressured producers to avoid imports, aiming for an economic boost the country badly needed after the economic crisis in the 1920s. Traditional trade associations that would negotiate price levels and control supply and demand were a thing of the past. The government practically forced the Werksgruppe Salzdetfurth-Aschersleben-Westeregeln to fuse into the Salzdetfurth AG and to move headquarters to Berlin. The Nazi policy of Aryanization, which aimed at Aryan control of all sectors of the economy, encouraged any company to force out Jewish stockholders. In 1937 Wintershall bought all Salzdetfurth AG shares owned by the Jewish family Petschek and thus became a shareholder in its largest competitor. This created the foundation for an eventual "super merger" decades later.

During World War II much of the potash mining was done by forced laborers who were gathered from

German concentration camps. Toward the end of the war, when Allied forces had begun air raids on Germany, some of the potash mining shafts became hiding places for military supplies as well as valuables from museums, libraries, galleries and banks in an effort to store and preserve them in allegedly safe locations, far below the surface and out of sight of Allied forces. Today the Merkers Mine Adventure Museum marks this dark portion of the company's history.

In 1945 Germany was divided into four occupation zones and later into two separate countries, East Germany and West Germany. As a result only about 40 percent of the previous potash production capacity remained on West German territory. The remaining 60 percent were in Communist East Germany. Under Soviet rule the East German potash mines were nationalized, and the former owners, among them the Salzdetfurth AG and the Wintershall AG, were expropriated. The Salzdetfurth AG left West Berlin and moved back to Salzdetfurth in West Germany. Encouraged by the hope for an era of postwar economic boom promised by the Marshall Plan, the Salzdetfurth AG managed to overcome its loss. Alongside the Wintershall AG, the Burbach-Kaliwerke AG, the Kali-Chemie AG, and Preussag, the Salzdetfurth AG by 1948 once again belonged to the leaders of the German potash industry.

POSTWAR CONSOLIDATION

The postwar economic boom in Germany had positive effects on the German potash industry. Technological advances quickly increased the mining output to prewar capacity, an enormous accomplishment given the fact that the Salzdetfurth AG was left with less than half of its mines. To increase capacity and compete on the tight market, the Salzdetfurth AG purchased 25 percent of stock in the Kölner Chemische Fabrik Kalk in Cologne, Germany, in 1952, increased its shares to 75 percent in 1957, and finally took over 100 percent in 1960. This was a natural step considering that the Kölner Chemische Fabrik Kalk had been one of Salzdetfurth's main potash customers since the 1940s and offered a more diverse line of fertilizers, which in later years would become a portion of the company's signature COMPO products.

In the 1960s the international competition grew. In an effort to consolidate its market position, the Salzdetfurth AG sought cooperation with its major competitor, the Wintershall AG. Wintershall, which already owned 15 percent of Salzdetfurth stock, had also become a majority shareholder at the Burbach Kaliwerke AG in 1955. The German potash industry was well on its way toward consolidation.

In 1968 the chemical giant BASF took over Wintershall. BASF was less interested in Wintershall's potash mining and more in its crude oil business. Wintershall had found crude oil by accident, when in 1930 oil had accidentally leaked into one of its potash mines. Since that time the company also mined for oil, which, due to the increased motorization of Germany and the world, soon became its major source of revenue. On a campaign to secure natural resources to regain the chemical-production monopoly held by IG Farben before World War II as an oligopoly of three companies (BASF, Bayer, and Hoechst), BASF was not opposed to splitting off Wintershall's potash division.

Consequently, just a few years later, in 1971, a merger between the Salzdetfurth AG and the potash segment of the Wintershall/Burbach Group created the Kali und Salz GmbH, headquartered in Kassel, Germany. Through its subsidiary Wintershall, BASF became the majority shareholder of the new corporation.

As a result of the merger, BASF also became a 50 percent shareholder of COMPO, a producer of consumer fertilizers, which the Salzdetfurth AG had founded with the Sprenger and Todenhagen KG in 1967. COMPO had made its mark with the potting soil COMPO SANA, one of the first potting soils available in consumer-friendly bags. Now as a member of the newly founded Kali und Salz GmbH, COMPO entered the market as a provider of specialized fertilizers for professional use. As such, COMPO also took over distribution of the specialized fertilizers produced at the Kölner Chemische Fabrik Kalk.

The 1970s and 1980s were further characterized by an expansion into new business segments and services. In 1983 the K+S Consulting GmbH was founded to offer mining-related technical and research services. In 1990 the Kali und Salz Entsorgung GmbH was established to coordinate the waste management activities of the corporation.

RESTRUCTURING AFTER GERMAN REUNIFICATION

In July 1990, after the breakdown of the Soviet Empire, East and West Germany signed a treaty that sealed economic, social, and monetary union. Part of this treaty defined and prescribed the process of privatization of the thus far nationalized East German economy. The Deutsche Treuhandanstalt became the privatization agency in charge and as such was the sole owner of the Mitteldeutsche Kali AG, which had quickly been established as a holding company for the former state-run East German potash mining companies. In 1993 the Kali und Salz GmbH and the Deutsche Treuhandanstalt drew up a merger concept aimed at creating a competitive all-German potash industry. The Kali und Salz GmbH was to hold 51 percent, and the Deutsche Treuhandanstalt 49 percent. In the wake of this merger, several unprofitable mines in the former Eastern states were closed, for which the Kali und Salz GmbH drew heavy criticism.

In 1994 the Kali und Salz GmbH changed its name to Kali und Salz Beteiligungs AG. The sole focus of its business activities was investment management, with the Kali und Salz GmbH being the corporation's largest investment. In 1997 BASF sold 25 percent of its stock in the Kali und Salz Beteiligungs GmbH to a number of financial investors, thus reducing its share to 49.5 percent.

In 1998 the Kali und Salz Beteiligungs AG was first listed on the German stock exchange (MDAX). That same year marked the final privatization of the former East German potash industry, when the Kali und Salz Beteiligungs AG purchased the 49 percent holding in the Kali und Salz GmbH still owned by the Deutsche Treuhandanstalt successor, the Bundesanstalt für vereingungsbedingte Sonderaufgaben (Federal Office for Reunification-Related Special Tasks). At the same time, the Kali und Salz Beteiligungs AG began its stock repurchasing program, further reducing the BASF holdings in the company to 25 percent, thus encouraging a much broader range of investors. BASF reduced its shares one year later to 15 percent and by 2003 to a mere 10 percent. In 1999 Kali und Salz Beteiligungs AG was renamed K+S Aktiengesellschaft.

INTERNATIONAL EXPANSION IN THE NEW MILLENNIUM

In 1999 K+S repurchased the COMPO shares held by BASF since the 1971 merger between the Salzdetfurth AG and the Wintershall AG. This move made K+S Europe's second-largest supplier of fertilizers. The distribution and marketing of these fertilizers was managed by the newly established K+S subsidiary called fertiva GmbH. COMPO, a pioneer in environmentally friendly fertilizers, made K+S a leader in the European "green" market, with its many products for the leisure or hobby area, as well as specialized agricultural fertilizers. In 2009 fertiva and portions of the COMPO professional services were merged in the company's new subsidiary, K+S Nitrogen GmbH.

Preparing for continued international expansion required a reorganization of infrastructure and logistics, which since 1999 were in the hands of the transport corporation Kali-Transport Gesellschaft (KTG). KTG had grown out of the Prussian transport company established in 1927. In 2000 K+S acquired the UBT-See- und Hafenspedition GmbH Rostock, also grown from the Prussian transport company, to handle increased shipment demands.

In 2002 K+S and Solvay founded esco in Hannover, Germany, set up as a joint venture in the salt sector, serving the European market with a complete salt-related product range for consumer, agricultural, and industrial use. Only two years later, in 2004, K+S bought Solvay's 38 percent participation in the venture, becoming esco's sole owner. With esco, K+S moved its salt products into the Netherlands and Scandinavia. The acquisition of the French potash and salt company SPCA that same year guaranteed K+S presence in France. Two years later K+S acquired SPL in Chile, increasing its stature in South America.

The year 2009 was marked by the company's purchase of the U.S.-based salt producer Morton Salt Inc. With this bold move K+S became the world's largest supplier of salt. The acquisition doubled the company's revenues from its salt sector, making salt the source of almost a quarter of its income.

While the acquisition thus cushioned the more volatile potash market, the half-year K+S 2009 financial report warned of a significant decline in overall revenues due to a weakening of the fertilizer business. The fertilizer market suffered greatly from the crash of all commodity prices and the shortage of farm credit in the wake of the worldwide credit crunch in 2007 and 2008, forcing most potash producers, including K+S, to curtail production dramatically.

Despite these problems K+S looked toward the future, pursuing potash trade agreements in China, the world's largest potash market, and presenting a groundwater-protection program, aiming to reduce and reverse the adverse effects of potash mining on drinking water in affected rivers in Hesse and Thuringia by 2015. In January 2010 Merrill Lynch removed K+S from its list of underperforming companies, upgrading it to be a preferred company.

Helga Schier

PRINCIPAL SUBSIDIARIES

K+S Kali GmbH; COMPO GmbH & Co. KG; K+S Nitrogen GmbH; esco–European Salt Company GmbH & Co. KG; Sociedad Punta de Lobos S.A. (SPL); Morton Salt Inc.; Kali-Transport Gesellschaft mbH (KTG); UBT See- und Hafenspedition GmbH; K+S Consulting GmbH; K+S Entsorgung GmbH; Chemische Fabrik Kalk GmbH (CFK).

PRINCIPAL DIVISIONS

Potash and magnesium products; nitrogen-based fertilizers; salt; related businesses.

PRINCIPAL COMPETITORS

Cargill, Incorporated; McCormick & Company, Incorporated; Potash Corporation of Saskatchewan, Inc.

FURTHER READING

Erman, Michael, "K+S to Focus on Potash after Morton Salt Buy," Reuters UK, October 5, 2009, http://uk.reuters.com/article/idUKN0528841520091005.

Hanneman, Dick, "German Based K+S Buys Morton Salt," Salt Institute, BizCentral.org, April 1, 2009, http://www.bizcentral.org/salt-institute/2009/04/germanbased-ks-buys-morton-sal.php.

Helmer, John, "German Potash Finds Growth in China," *Asia Times Online*, April 30, 2009, http://www.atimes.com/atimes/China_Business/KD30Cb01.html.

Montague-Jones, Guy, "Morton Salt Buy Makes K+S Biggest Global Salt Producer," FoodNavigator-USA.com, September 29, 2009, http://www.foodnavigator-usa.com/Product-Categories/Preservatives-and-acidulants/Morton-Salt-buy-makes-K-S-biggest-global-salt-producer.

Reder, Dirk, Severin Roeseling, and Thomas Prüfer, *Wachstum erleben: Die Geschichte der K+S Gruppe*. Kassel: K+S Aktiengesellschaft, 2006.

Stroux, Sigrid, *US and EC Oligopoly Control*. The Hague: Kluwer Law International, 2004, pp. 206–08.

Weaver, Courtney, "Brokers Review Banks' Prospects," *Financial Times* (FT.com), January 5, 2010, http://www.ft.com/cms/s/0/287d7892-f9e8-11de-adb4-00144feab49a.html?nclick_check=1.

Kum & Go, L.C.

6400 Westown Parkway
West Des Moines, Iowa 50266
U.S.A.
Telephone: (515) 226-0128
Fax: (515) 226-1595
Web site: http://www.kumandgo.com

Subsidiary of Krause Gentle Corporation
Founded: 1959 as Hampton Oil Company
Incorporated: 1973 as Krause Gentle Oil Corporation
Employees: 3,663
Sales: $1.43 billion (2008)
NAICS: 447190 Other Gasoline Stations; 445120
    Convenience Stores; 447110 Gasoline Stations with
    Convenience Stores; 445110 Supermarkets and
    Other Grocery (except Convenience); 452910
    Warehouse Clubs and Supercenters

∎∎∎

Kum & Go, L.C., is a leading force in the convenience store and gas station retail industry. From 1959, its founding year, to 2009, its 50th anniversary, Kum & Go has continued to demonstrate how the company defines excellence in customer service and easy access to general merchandise. The company's achievements have been such that *Convenience Store People* named William Krause, a Kum & Go cofounder, Retail Leader of the Year in 2006. In 2005 the industry publication ranked him among the Top Ten Most Influential CEOs. By 2008 Kum & Go's sales of more than $1.4 billion brought the company to within the top 25 of the largest U.S. chain store firms. Known for entrepreneurship, building relationships with managers, employees, and customers, and proactive engagement with circumstances, Kum & Go has made a lasting impression in its field.

FULL SERVICE: GAS STATION AND STATION STORE: 1959–69

Kum & Go began in 1959, two years after one of its founders, William A. Krause, graduated from the University of Iowa with a degree in public relations. A job in sales for Continental Oil Company (Conoco Philips) was about to force him to relocate to Wyoming, quite a distance from his future wife and her family. His future father-in-law, drugstore owner Tony S. Gentle, offered seed money to buy a gas station in Hampton, Iowa, and asked Krause to manage the two-pump establishment. With Gentle acting as silent partner providing merchandising and retail experience and Krause showing his interest in the gas business, the native Iowans opened their first station in 1959.

Hampton Oil Company began at a time when three factors were among those influencing the business. The federal Interstate Highway Act funded the expansion and paving of roads throughout the country, including some in Iowa. In addition Krause and Gentle's ownership positioned them as small independents, overshadowed correspondingly by major corporations such as Shell Corporation, Texaco Inc., Standard Company of Ohio (Sohio), and Pure Oil Company and by major, semi-independents such as Continental Oil Company and Murphy Oil Company.

COMPANY PERSPECTIVES

We are dedicated to going all out in providing fast, friendly, convenient service and products to our customers. Through the growth of our company, we will provide opportunities for people to succeed personally, professionally and financially.

However, with more and more drivers traveling newly paved highways and more families shifting from cities to suburbs, opportunities for growth were available. Plus there was an additional factor of location: in north-central Iowa, Hampton was in the path of highways and railroads that linked the town in several directions. Access to merchandise, supplies, and consumers would prove instrumental to the company's growth.

Less than five years after they began their company, Krause and Gentle added a "station store" to their gas station. A predecessor of the convenience store, this gave customers a quick, simple way to purchase such items as snacks, beverages, and road maps. Other gas stations were implementing similar efforts. The full-service treatment featured a range of offerings, from the one-stop approach with food, motel and gas, automotive expertise that gave vehicles top-notch maintenance and repair services, and even marriage ceremonies. Krause and Gentle kept things simple, preferring cautious strategizing to fancy appeals or somewhat outrageous gimmickry. Most important to the pair, it seemed, was the long-term goal. Krause and Gentle's customers returned to their cars and their trips with a clear sense of getting the kind of friendly, exceptional service and convenience that would induce them to return.

The company's next important step came not long after the addition of the store. Krause and Gentle became fuel transporters in 1964 when Solar Transport Trucking was born. This, too, proved timely. The early to mid-1960s were still part of the era when fuel got shipped to gas stations primarily via tank trucks. Even though this delivery method got supplanted over time by pipelines, railroads, and barges, involvement in fuel transportation gave Krause and Gentle more of a proactive stance as gas retailers.

EXPANSION AND INGENUITY: 1970–79

Hampton Oil Company's growth ran headlong into major challenges from the industry. At a customary height of long trips by car, a nationwide gas shortage the summer of 1973 resulted in gasoline rationing among oil companies, dealers, and station owners. Then the Organization of Petroleum Exporting Countries (OPEC) imposed an embargo and worsened the shortage for another year. Even though the United States instituted a different federal energy policy, for Krause and Gentle, who also had a fuel transport trucking business (they were known as jobbers), these events threatened their survival. As Fred C. Allvine and James M. Patterson remarked in their book *Highway Robbery*, "In normal times such market withdrawals would have meant little, but in time of shortage, it meant these small businesses—many of which had expanded at the insistence of their former suppliers—would be unable to find new suppliers and, hence, would be forced out of business." Krause and Gentle needed to pursue additional avenues.

One such avenue involved the purchase of a snowmobiling distributorship, indicating Krause and Gentle's willingness to apply the "turn lemons into lemonade" principle to their operations. Snowmobiles had evolved into an attractive venture. In a state known for its wintry seasons, a distributorship like this seemed a worthwhile opportunity to seize.

In 1973 Krause and Gentle changed the company name to Kum & Go, a variation of the phrase "come and go" using the first initials of their last names. A structural change also took place. Kum & Go became a subsidiary of Krause Gentle Oil Corporation. In 1977 there were 65 Kum & Go locations, more than 325 people worked for the company, and sales reached $2 million.

INNOVATIONS IN OWNERSHIP AND CONVENIENCE: 1980–89

In 1984 the company gave employees an unusual opportunity that went beyond typical incentives in retailing (which were offered by Kum & Go as well), such as contests, mystery shoppers, and bonuses. Krause and Gentle formed Chieftain Corporation to give long-standing associates the chance to invest $5,000 and become owner-operators of Kum & Go sites. Initially 11 such employees made the investment. By 1998 owner-operator-investor participation in Chieftain had grown to 26 employees. Chieftain's profits exceeded $1.5 million in 1997. As Barbara Grondin Francella noted in her profile on Kum & Go in *Convenience Store News* (August 3, 1998), "One employee, for instance, last year earned $70,000 in income from her original $5,000 investment."

The early to mid-1980s was also a time when Krause and Gentle began introducing in-store food

KEY DATES

1959: Tony S. Gentle and William A. Krause buy their first gasoline station, in Hampton, Iowa.

1973: The company's name changes to Kum & Go, a subsidiary of Krause Gentle Oil Corporation.

1984: Krause and Gentle start Chieftain Corporation, an investment opportunity for longtime associates to become owner-operators of Kum & Go sites.

1998: Kum & Go's acquisition of more than 100 convenience stores brings its geographic reach to 12 states.

2003: The company forms a partnership with Cenex Energy to manage 36 Cenex stores as dual-branded units.

2006: Kyle Krause becomes president and CEO of Kum & Go; cofounder Tony Gentle dies.

service. At this time customers rarely had a chance to buy prepared food as they purchased gas and shopped. In 1983 Kum & Go had 47 convenience stores, each with a delicatessen, an in-store bakery at 2 of the stores, and 20 c-stores with hot food service. The company's first items of this type were pizza and Mexican food. By the following year the number of Kum & Go c-stores had increased to 65.

About the same time, Krause and Gentle began acquiring small banks. Not long afterward, full-service banks became an additional feature of Kum & Go stores. The company was adopting a broader, more meaningful, and more profitable style of retailing. By 1988 Krause Gentle Oil Corporation had become Krause Gentle Corporation. The parent company and its subsidiary Kum & Go relocated from their hometown of Hampton to West Des Moines in the central part of Iowa. Later that year Krause acquired a semipro basketball team and relocated the team from Cincinnati, Ohio, to Cedar Rapids, Iowa. In an article appearing in the October 1988 issue of *National Petroleum News*, Peggy Smedley stated, "The owner of the Krause Gentle [Corporation] expects the purchase of the basketball team will increase traffic and gallonage at the Kum & Go outlets."

A STRATEGIC PLAN: 1990–99

Over the next decade Kum & Go's progress maintained an upward trajectory. The company began the 1990s

with 134 units in Iowa, Colorado, Missouri, Montana, New Mexico, and North Dakota. Recognition followed. In 1992 *Inc.* and *Chain Store Age Executive* named Krause entrepreneur of the year in the retail category. That same year Krause won the Entrepreneurial Spirit Award from the *Des Moines Business Record*.

Other food-service offerings emerged for sale at Kum & Go. Unlike the previous debuts, these often involved well-known brands. Blimpie Subs & Salads, Cinnamon Street Bakery, and Burger King were among the fast-food outlets customers could find at Kum & Go locations, depending on franchise or owner-operator arrangements. As the list of branded outlets indicated, customers could expect to find a selection of prepared food that would keep them inside Kum & Go rather than outside, on their way elsewhere to eat. This period also saw the reemergence of the regionally known brand Hiland potato chips, acquired by Kum & Go and sold in its units. By the end of the decade, a line of other Hiland products, including a special sandwich, bottled water, and candy, was being sold, too. Near future plans featured other private-label products such as ground coffee.

Acquisitions of units became a dedicated strategy for more sites getting the Kum & Go logo. Near the end of the decade Kum & Go undertook a major, distinctly different purchase. In 1998 the company acquired 113 stores from Contemporary Industries Corporation, which had gone bankrupt. Fourteen of the stores, better known as 7-Eleven units, were closed. By becoming part of Kum & Go's existing 158 units, the other 99 c-stores enabled Kum & Go to extend its brand of service and convenience across a 12-state expanse: Arkansas, Colorado, Iowa, Kansas, Minnesota, Missouri, Montana, Nebraska, North Dakota, Oklahoma, South Dakota, and Wyoming. The 99 new Kum & Go units were up to speed with their remerchandising within six weeks of the acquisition.

A strategic plan was set forth in 1995. Known as Vision 2000, the plan laid the groundwork for the company's targeted achievements from 1995 to 2000. Goals included $200 million in sales by 2000 and an average of one new c-store per month. Results were outstanding. In 1997 Kum & Go's sales reached the $200 million goal and one new store per month was opened for the second straight year. At the end of 1999 the company reported $251 million in sales. Between 1996 and 1999, due in part to the 7-Eleven acquisition, Kum & Go had 203 additional stores. This was a decade of exceptional growth and progress for Kum & Go.

LEADERSHIP IN SERVICE AND CONVENIENCE: 2000–07

Kum & Go ended the 1990s with an advertising campaign whose budget concentrated mainly on TV and radio. Two years later the company's total number of units was 306 and remained in 12 states. Having outperformed its own projections for the last part of the 1990s, entrepreneurial spirit kicked in as Kum & Go entered the 21st century.

Thoughtful innovation seemed the catchphrase for Kum & Go. For example, in 2003 the company underwent a partnership with Cenex Energy. As part of the initial terms of the agreement, 36 Cenex c-stores in Iowa, Minnesota, Montana, South Dakota, and Wyoming would carry the Kum & Go name and its private-label brands of coffee, potato chips, and other products, and Cenex would still own these stores. Responsibility for matters such as licensing and taxes would fall on Cenex. Future aspects of the deal included the possibility that Cenex's gasoline brand might get improvements in systems of inventory and methods of distribution that Kum & Go would have available throughout its network. The Kum & Go–Cenex deal resulted in a total of 349 units that Kum & Go operated in 2003 in 14 states.

Three years later two more landmarks became part of Kum & Go's history. William Krause's son Kyle Krause took a leadership position as president and CEO. Tony Gentle, having stepped down from those roles for health-related reasons, died in 2006. Far from being a name-only participant, Kyle Krause had worked for his father and grandfather early on, earned an MBA, and consequently became known for his devotion to structure and his close relationship with his father. Kyle Krause's skill at running other family-owned ventures was recognized as well. In 2005 he started Amici Espresso, a small local chain of coffeehouses whose products became part of Kum & Go's private-label offerings after 2006. He also ran the fuel trucking firm Solar Transport and a professional soccer team in Des Moines.

THE NEXT ROUTES FOR KUM & GO

As a family-run, multigenerational business, Kum & Go continued to show interest in new ideas. One of these ideas was actually a mixture of old and new. Global warming and dependence on oil imports were among the most attention-grabbing issues of the 21st century's first decade. Increasingly biofuel appealed to customers as retailers did what was needed to make these choices more convenient and cost effective. One such move

came in 2007 at a Kum & Go site near Iowa City, Iowa.

The Iowa City unit began selling E-85, comprising 85 percent ethanol (a well-known alternative fuel) and 15 percent gasoline. This was not a new practice, however. Kum & Go had been featuring E-85 among its gas offerings since the late 1990s. The debut at this site was fortuitous. Iowa City, home to a university, was a natural location; college students and others for reasons of thrift and ecological perspective would likely want to purchase an alternative fuel. E-85 had a lower cost per gallon in 2007 than regular gasoline. With tax breaks the state began offering in 2005 to ease installation expenses, and the University of Iowa's motor pool of cars using E-85, the attraction for Kum & Go was also apparent. In 2008 the company's first certified store for Leadership in Energy and Environmental Design (LEED) began construction.

In 2008 and 2009 the company implemented other, possibly near-term strategies. Twenty-one smaller units were sold in 2008 in Iowa, Missouri, Montana, Nebraska, North Dakota, South Dakota, and Wyoming. While maintaining a presence in these states, the decision was made to build large stores, such as a new unit that opened in Colorado late in 2009 with 3,400 square feet, eight pumps, and the branded in-store food service that customers expected from Kum & Go. If the company were to continue the strategy the size would put at least some of its c-stores in the category of supercenters and warehouse clubs for which other retailers, such as Sam's Clubs and Wal-mart, have held dominant positions for several years.

More familiar decisions have been made as well. While continuing to acquire other, declining c-store chains, such as Cody's, whose units in Missouri were purchased by Kum & Go in 2009, a distinguishing aspect should be noted. Cody's was named after William Frederick "Buffalo Bill" Cody, a pioneer of the 19th century who was said to have camped on occasion around Rogersville, Missouri, where the first Cody's unit existed. Before completing its rebranding, Kum & Go honored that history, erecting a plaque that described what made the former c-store chain special in its surrounding communities. Respect for tradition, energetic commitment to customer service, and high standards of professionalism have been among the company's stated values. With the Krause family's leadership the future for Kum & Go had progress on the horizon.

Mary C. Lewis

PRINCIPAL COMPETITORS

Casey's General Stores Inc.; Chevron Corporation; Exxon Mobile Corporation.

FURTHER READING

Allvine, Fred C., and James M. Patterson, *Highway Robbery: An Analysis of the Gas Crisis.* Bloomington: Indiana University Press, 1974, pp. 3–15, 21.

"Celsius Launches in 438 Kum & Go Locations in the Midwest," *Business Wire,* December 1, 2008.

Chase, Brett, "More Kum & Go Banks in Krause's Plans," *Des Moines Business Record,* April 3, 1995, p. 1-1.

Day, Bill, "Friendly Rivals," *Des Moines Business Record,* December 1, 1997, p. 10.

Dietrich, Robert F., "Consumers in Crisis: They've Changed Their Ways of Shopping," *Progressive Grocer,* April 1974, pp. 45–47, 50, 52, 54.

"Dirt Poor to Entrepreneur, William Krause Builds on Empire in Iowa," *Chain Store Age Executive with Shopping Center Age,* February 1993, pp. 36+.

Francella, Barbara Grondin, "A Kinder, Gentler Retailer," *Convenience Store News,* August 3, 1998, p. 30.

———, "Moooving in on Bill Krause," *Convenience Store News,* January 8, 2001, p. 82.

"General Merchandise," *Progressive Grocer,* January 1978, pp. 48–52, 54, 56, 59–60.

"Industry Springs at Merger, Acquisition Opportunities," *Convenience Store News,* April 20, 2009.

Jakle, John A., "The American Gasoline Station, 1920 to 1970," *Journal of American Culture,* Fall 1978, pp. 520–42.

"Kum & Go Continues to Grow," *Convenience Store News,* October 21, 2008.

"Kum & Go Honors Acquired Chain's History," *Convenience Store News,* November 11, 2009.

"Kum & Go Opens New Store in Colorado," *Convenience Store News,* December 4, 2009.

Margolies, John, *Pump and Circumstance: Glory Days of the Gas Station.* Boston: Little, Brown, 1993, pp. 86–88, 96–99, 110, 112–113.

Margonelli, Lisa, *Oil on the Brain: Adventures from the Pump to the Pipeline.* New York: Nan A. Talese/Doubleday, 2007, pp. 13–19.

"Now, the No-Service Station," *Time,* August 22, 1977, p. 43.

"One Thousand New-Style Convenience Stores Target of Open Pantry Food Marts," *Progressive Grocer,* April 1964, pp. 100–104.

"A Red-Hot Winter for Snowmobiles," *Business Week,* January 10, 1970, pp. 34–35.

Von Koschembahr, John C., "The Convenience Stores, Twisting the Behemoths' Tails for Cheers and Profits," *Financial World,* November 1, 1977, pp. 33–35, 47.

Walzer, Ed, "Forty-first Annual Report of Grocery Industry: Sales Top $113 Billion as Inflation Changes Everything," *Progressive Grocer,* April 1974, pp. 67–75.

Lagardère

Lagardère SCA

---

4 rue de Presbourg
Paris, 75116
France
Telephone: (+33 1) 4069 1600
Fax: (+33 1) 4069 2272
Web site: http://www.lagardere.com

Public Company
Founded: 1945 as Matra; 1993 as Lagardère Group S.A.
Employees: 29,393
Sales: €8.21 billion ($11.52 billion) (2008)
Stock Exchanges: Paris
Ticker Symbol: MMB
NAICS: 336411 Aircraft Manufacturing; 336414
Guided Missile and Space Vehicle Manufacturing;
511110 Newspaper Publishers; 511120 Periodical
Publishers; 511130 Book Publishers; 515111 Radio
Networks; 515112 Radio Stations; 515120 Televi-
sion Broadcasting; 541611 Administrative Manage-
ment and General Management Consulting
Services; 541820 Public Relations Services; 711410
Agents and Managers for Artists, Athletes,
Entertainers, and Other Public Figures

■ ■ ■

Lagardère SCA, an expansive, wide-ranging media
group, operates in 40 countries on five continents. The
group's four distinct business lines are Lagardère
Publishing, Lagardère Active, Lagardère Services, and
Lagardère Sports. The Publishing division is the world's
second-largest trade-book publisher serving the general

public and educational markets. Its prestigious brands
include the Hachette Book Group in the United States,
the Grasset, Larousse and Hatier imprint in France, and
Anaya in Spain. The Active division specializes in the
production of multimedia content across six business
lines: magazine publishing, radio broadcasting, television
broadcasting, audiovisual production, digital activities,
and advertising sales. The Services division is a global
leader in travel retail and press distribution. It operates a
network of duty-free shops, convenience stores, and
concept stores in 21 countries throughout North
America, Asia, and the Pacific region. The Sports division organizes and launches major sporting events, and
it is a leading player in the sports economy market,
which includes the Sportfive Group, IEC in Sports, Up-
solut Sports AG, PrEvent, and the World Sport Group
Pte Ltd. Created in April 2009, Lagardère Unlimited
manages international athletes and celebrities, such as
Andy Roddick and Fernando Gonzalez, and develops
sports and cultural events. With offices in Paris,
London, and Miami, the subsidiary also manages sports
academies throughout the world. The European
Aeronautic Defence and Space Company (EADS), of
which Lagardère has joint control and holds a 7.5
percent stake, is the leading European manufacturer of
aircraft, nonmilitary helicopters, commercial launches,
and missile systems. Its five business divisions are Airbus, Military Transport Aircraft, Eurocopter, Defence
and Security Systems, and Astrium.

LAGARDÈRE'S ORIGINS

Louis Hachette was a third-year student at l'École Nor-
male Supérieure when Monsignor Denis Frayssinous

COMPANY PERSPECTIVES

Lagardère develops, promotes and disseminates information and culture across five continents. It has distinguished itself as a market leader in the sectors of book publishing, distribution of cultural products, print and audiovisual media, and management and marketing of sporting rights. Lagardère holds a 7.5% stake in the European Aeronautic Defence and Space Company (EADS), over which it exercises joint control. Lagardère's values, together with the quality of its corporate culture, rest on two pillars—its rich and varied history and the qualities of the people who embody it, both now and in the past. The Lagardère Group has always sought to boldly expand its horizons by investing in new business sectors in which it has acquired both legitimacy and competence. As a highly entrepreneurial pure media company, the Lagardère Group has always been managed from a long-term perspective and has never indulged in fleeting trends.

decided to close the prestigious institution. A gifted student, Hachette embarked on a new path. In 1826 he bought a bookstore and publishing house in Paris called Librairie de Jacques-Francois Brédif. Renamed Librairie Louis Hachette, the venture set in motion what would become one of the world's most successful trade publishers 150 years later, and Lagardère SCA's main business line. Hachette published his first periodical, a journal for teachers, in 1827. Four years later Hachette was publishing a range of textbooks for primary schools. In 1832 he began to diversify, introducing a classical publishing division, and he published his first catalog. In 1833 Hachette's business turned the corner after the French government enacted a law requiring free public schooling, and the Ministry of Public Education placed an order for 500,000 reading primers and 40,000 math books. The following year Hachette's sales had tripled since the founding of the company seven years earlier.

Hachette, who had now added dictionaries to his product line and had two ambitious projects in progress, needed a partner. In 1840 Louis Breton came on board, and the two began publishing the works of such English luminaries as William Makepeace Thackeray, Henry Wadsworth Longfellow, and Charles Dickens. While in England, Hachette was impressed by the news agent business of W. H. Smith. Upon his return to France in 1852, he established his own book and newspaper

stands in railway stations, and he added newspaper and magazine publishing to the company's portfolio. In 1855 Hachette published *Le Journal pour Tous*, one of France's first entertainment magazines aimed at the general public. In that same year, after acquiring Librairie Victor Lecou, the company gained the rights to publish the works of numerous notable writers, including George Sand, Victor Hugo, Gerard de Nerval, and Gustave Doré. Hachette's first overseas expansion was in 1859 when it established a foreign-language bookstore in London.

Hachette was in the process of publishing Émile Littré's *Dictionary of the French Language* in 1863, but he died the following year. He left Breton and a small group of investors to manage the company while his son, Georges, inherited the Hachette bookselling license. The Librairie Louis Hachette now employed 165 people, with sales reaching FRF 18 million by 1878. Breton died in 1883, but the company continued to thrive, with tourism guides being one of Hachette's biggest sellers. In 1891 the company published its first women's magazine, *La Mode Practique*, and opened its first newsstand in France's Metro subway system in 1900. The formation of Messageries d'Hachette in 1897, a book and press distribution organization, was a turning point for the company. By 1914 the organization was serving the entire country and employed more than 700 people.

With the onset of World War I, many of Hachette's skilled workers were called into action, and they were replaced by an inexperienced, predominantly female workforce. This proved to be no obstacle to the company as it continued to expand through this difficult period. In 1914 Hachette purchased Hetzel, the publisher of the Jules Verne books. This was followed in 1916 with the acquisition of Pierre Lafitte, which included several newspapers, bestsellers, a bookshop, and a photographic studio. After the war the company underwent a restructuring. Prompted by a need to increase its capital and to issue redeemable stock, Hachette became a public company. Keeping it in the family, the new public limited company now had 29 partners, all of whom were related to Hachette and Breton in some way.

POSTWAR EXPANSION

With its increased capital base, the company began to invest in leading French printing and binding companies, and a new subsidiary, Librairie Generale Française, was formed in 1922. A decade later the company began to secure exclusive distribution rights for other publishers, such as N. R. F. Gallimard, which later became a subsidiary. In 1939, with its capital hav-

KEY DATES

1826: Louis Hachette buys a bookstore and publishing house in Paris, France.

1945: The first issue of *Elle* is launched; Matra (Mécanique Aviation TRAction) is formed.

1953: In partnership with Henri Filipacchi, Hachette launches Livre de Poche.

1961: Matra is selected as the first prime contractor for satellites for the newly established European space program.

1963: Jean-Luc Lagardère is appointed CEO of Matra.

1983: The Espace, Matra's "one-box" vehicle, is launched under the Renault brand.

1984: Hachette acquires U.K. Seymour Press and merges it with Cordon & Gotch to form Seymour International Distributor Ltd.

1993: Matra and Hachette merge and Lagardère Group S.A. is formed.

1996: Matra BAe Dynamics is formed through the merger of British Aerospace Dynamics Group and Matra.

1997: Hachette Filipacchi Presse and Filipacchi Médias merge to form Hachette Filipacchi Médias (HFM).

2000: Lagardère sells Grolier Inc.; the European Aeronautic Defence and Space Company (EADS) is created from the merger of Aerospatiale Matra, Aeronauticas SA, and DaimlerChrysler Aerospace AG.

2003: Jean-Luc Lagardère dies, and his son, Arnaud, becomes chairman.

2009: Lagardère Unlimited is formed.

ing increased ninefold since going public, the company gained control of AGLP, a book and newspaper wholesaler and the owner of several bookshops throughout South America and Europe. Between World War I and World War II, Hachette's business volume tripled, but this growth halted with the start of World War II.

During the four years of German occupation, Hachette successfully resisted takeover attempts made by the Nazis. Through organized passive resistance, as early as 1944 the directors were returning to the Librairie. Messageries Françaises de la Presse was created to compensate for the badly affected Messageries

d'Hachette. In 1945 Hachette launched the first issue of the hugely successful *Elle* magazine. This was also the same year that Matra (Mécanique Aviation TRAction) was created and began development of the world's fastest twin-engine propeller plane. In 1951 Matra would be the first to break the sound barrier in horizontal flight in Europe with its Mach 1.4 engine. Hachette and Matra would merge decades later in a deal engineered by Jean-Luc Lagardère.

When Messageries Françaises de la Presse failed, along with other postwar recovery attempts, Hachette established Nouvelles Messageries de la Presse Parisienne (NMPP) in 1947. By 1963 NMPP had achieved sales of FRF 1.5 billion, half the sales of Hachette. By 1991 Hachette owned 49 percent of NMPP, with the remaining 51 percent held by nine other magazine and newspaper publishers. After World War II Hachette expanded its book division through acquisitions and organically. In 1953, in partnership with Henri Filipacchi, the company launched the Livre de Poche, an inexpensive paperback series of modern and classic literature. Within one year 15 million books in the Livre de Poche series were sold, and by 1955 this number climbed to 24 million. Also in 1954, Hachette gained a controlling interest in Editions Bernard Grasset, the publisher of Marcel Proust, Paul Morand, and Henry de Montherlant. Grasset soon merged with Fasquelle, another subsidiary in which Hachette held a majority stake since 1931. Hachette also added to its stake in Librairie Fayard to become a majority shareholder. By 1963, with 36 subsidiaries and branch offices throughout the world, Hachette was a complex and expansive organization of public limited companies and limited liability companies, and it had sales of FRF 1.5 billion, not including NMPP.

HACHETTE, MATRA, AND LAGARDÈRE

In 1961 the European space program began, and Matra was selected as the first prime contractor for satellites. Two years later, when Matra had a workforce of 1,450, Jean-Luc Lagardère was appointed chief executive officer. Lagardère was pushing Matra toward automotive design, and the company unveiled the Matra 530 sports car at the Geneva Motor Show in 1967. In a 1984 *Forbes* article, Rosemary Brady quoted Lagardère as saying that "race cars gave an image of a new group not just devoted to military activities." His strategy paid off. In 1972 Matra was appointed the lead contractor on France's first urban transport system, the VAL. By 1974 Matra had achieved three consecutive victories at the Le Mans 24-hour rally, and it had won its second World Championship title for the Matra-Simca. The first VAL automated Metro line opened in Lille in 1983, while the Espace, Matra's "one-box" vehicle, was launched under the Renault brand.

Between 1964 and 1976 Hachette continued to grow under the leadership of Robert Meunier de Houssoy before passing the reins to Jacques Marchandise. The company experienced a setback in 1970 when Hachette lost the rights to distribute Gallimard's books after the two companies separated. In 1975 the company reentered the dictionary business with the highly successful 12-volume, 100,000-word set of Encyclopédie Générale d'Hachette. Celebrating its 150th anniversary in 1976, Hachette acquired the company Jean Prouvost, owner of *Paris Match* and the French television guide, *Tele 7 Jours*. In 1977 Marchandise officially changed the company's name from Librairie Hachette to the more modern Hachette. The following year, Hachette drew worldwide attention when it opened the Centre de National de Distribution du Livre (CDL), a 50,000-square-meter storage and distribution facility run almost entirely by robots.

Under the weight of stodgy family-business management, these achievements were not enough to keep Hachette ahead of its competition. By 1980 the company's share price had fallen low enough to attract a takeover attempt, and Lagardère, who was named France's Manager of the Year in 1979, became the controlling owner of Hachette stock. Lagardère immediately implemented a restructuring of Hachette, which resulted in 400 job cuts by June 1981. While many companies fell under French government control, Lagardère managed to retain the private status of most of his holdings. In October 1981 Lagardère acquired the publisher Jean-Claude Lattès, and he appointed Lattès the managing director of the book division. Lagardère's vision was to make the book division the largest multimedia group in the world, and he gave Lattès free rein to pursue acquisitions in France and abroad.

In 1984 U.K. Seymour Press was acquired and merged with Cordon & Gotch to form Seymour International Press Distributor Ltd. For the first time, Hachette recorded annual sales in excess of FRF 10 billion. The following year, Hachette bought 50 percent of Harlequin's romance novel business, and the publisher launched a new series for young readers in its Hachette Jeunesse division. In that same year, the first American version of *Elle* magazine was produced in a joint venture with Rupert Murdoch. By 1988 *Elle* was being distributed in 17 countries, including China and Japan, and boasted a global circulation of 2.5 million copies. Hachette acquired Curtis Circulation Co. in 1986, the second-largest magazine distributor in the United States, and reestablished Dupuis, the Belgium-based publisher of Europe's first comic strip. The company also bought a controlling interest in Europe 1, one of France's leading radio stations, and shortly thereafter helped to establish Europe 2.

The company suffered a setback in 1986 when Lattès launched the Succès du Livre, a series of reprinted bestsellers that were to be sold at a 30 percent discount. After spending FRF 15 million on marketing, the product line was poorly received, and it was eventually sold to a clearance dealer. This was just a minor inconvenience to Lagardère, whose holding company, MMB S.A., had grown to become France's third largest, and who now had his sights set on substantially increasing Hachette's presence in the U.S. market. For starters, Hachette paid $448.6 million in 1988 to purchase Grolier, the publisher of *Encyclopedia Americana*, and instantly became the world's third-largest book publisher. This was followed with the acquisition of Diamandis Corporation, publisher of *Woman's Day, Car and Driver*, and *Stereo Review*, for $712 million. In 1989 Lagardère turned his attention to Spain, where Hachette bought Salvat, the country's fifth-largest publisher of encyclopedias and dictionaries. In that same year, the Spanish government awarded the contract for its Hispasat communications satellites to Matra. As the new decade approached, Lagardère was confident that his mission was on the correct path.

THE BIRTH OF LAGARDÈRE SCA

Lagardère still needed to add television to his multimedia empire after an unsuccessful takeover attempt in 1988 of TFI, France's leading television network. In 1990 he acquired 25 percent of the ailing La Cinq, France's fifth television station, which was best known for airing late-night soft porn. In the deal, Hachette agreed to become the station's operator, so confident was Lagardère that he could return the station to profitability. His gamble was a failure, and by the end of 1991 La Cinq had filed for bankruptcy as Hachette recorded a loss of FRF 1.9 billion ($350 million). By April 1992 La Cinq was off the air at a cost to Hachette of $630 million, and the company was facing collapse. The following month, Lagardère announced a recapitalization plan of FRF 2.8 billion ($510 million), in which Hachette would merge fully with debt-free Matra. Hachette's largest financiers, the state-owned Credit Lyonnais, Banque Nationale de Paris, and Groupe des Assurances Nationales, agreed to the bailout rather than allow the media group to fall into foreign hands.

By the end of 1993 the merger was complete, creating a media and defense company operating under the name Lagardère Group S.A. The new company's annual revenues remained flat between 1992 and 1994, but its net income rebounded to FRF 615 million ($152 million) during that same period. International sales surpassed domestic sales for the first time in 1994, and Hachette, which was now operating in 40 countries, was ranked as one of the top magazine publishers in the world. The subsidiary Hachette Filipacchi NBC launched *Tell*, a quarterly teen-oriented magazine, while the Chinese version of *Elle* was now published bimonthly instead of twice a year. In the multimedia sector, Matra Hachette Multimédia launched the Epsis imaging technology for the satellite industries, a process commonly used for advertising at sports events.

In 1995 Hachette Distribution Services acquired UCS, Canada's leading newsstand chain, becoming the country's third-largest retail press company. Hachette Filipacchi Magazines acquired *Family Life* from Warner Media and *Mirabella* from News Corp., and it entered a joint venture with the New World Communications Group to acquire the movie magazine *Premiere*, which was launched in South Korea, Spain, and Taiwan by year's end. In May 1996 the $1.5 billion merger between British Aerospace Dynamics Group and Matra was finalized after three years of negotiations, and Matra BAe Dynamics became the world's third-largest space group and one of Europe's leading missile-design houses. In publishing, the Hachette Livre subsidiary acquired the Hatier Group, France's third-largest educational publisher.

The acquisitions and merger frenzy continued for the rest of the decade. In 1997 Hachette Filipacchi Presse and Filipacchi Médias were merged to form France's largest media company, Hachette Filipacchi Médias (HFM). The following year Matra Hautes Technologies merged with Aerospatiale to form Aerospatiale Matra. The merge created one of Europe's largest defense firms, with total sales of FRF 80 billion and 56,000 employees. The Lagardère Group, now known as Lagardère SCA, also acquired the French newspaper *Nice Matin* and the Japanese women's magazine *Fujin Gaho*. In June 1998 HFM announced that it had entered into an agreement with the Paxnet TV network to produce a magazine-style program based on its range of women's magazines, which now had a combined monthly readership in excess of 9 million.

In 1999 Lagardère acquired the French multimedia bookshop Extrapole and 80 percent of the Italian publisher Rusconi Editore. In that same year Lagardère's son and co-CEO of the Group, Arnaud, was named president of Europe 1 Communication, and Aerospatiale Matra was quoted on the stock market for the first time. Hachette Livre, which had grown significantly through international acquisitions, was merged with Grolier Interactive to form Hachette Multimedia.

The final year of the decade brought with it some of Lagardère's most momentous changes, and developing its digital business became the company's priority. In May 2000 Lagardère sold Grolier Inc. to Scholastic Corp. for $400 million as "part of the wider policy of hiving off non-core assets," Lagardère stated in a press release, according to *European Report*. The sale did not include Grolier Interactive, now part of Hachette Multimedia, which was responsible for handling all multimedia production and the company's growing on-line business, including Club Internet. The European Aeronautic Defence and Space Company (EADS) was created from the merger of Aerospatiale Matra, Aeronauticas SA, and DaimlerChrysler Aerospace AG, and the A380 Airbus program was launched. In 1999 Lagardère had acquired a 34 percent stake in CanalSatellite (Canal+) for FRF 5.8 billion ($805 million). In September 2000 the two companies formed an alliance to develop interactive applications and launch a series of new information-driven channels. While Hachette Filipacchi Magazines ceased publishing *Audio* and *Mirabella*, Lagardère paid $1 billion in stock for the remaining one-third interest in HFM.

LAGARDÈRE IN THE NEW MILLENIUM

Although Hachette Filipacchi Magazines made the decision in 2001 to also cease publication of *George*, the late John F. Kennedy Jr.'s political magazine, it still remained the world's largest magazine publisher with approximately 200 titles distributed to more than 30 countries. Meanwhile, Hachette Livre acquired the Spanish educational publisher Grupo Editorial Bruño and Britain's Octopus Publishing, strengthening its position in the international publishing sector. In October 2002 Lagardère announced that it would be acquiring Vivendi Universal's publishing businesses in Europe and Latin America, Editis, for €1.25 billion. Through the Hachette Distribution Services (HDS) subsidiary, Lagardère acquired the Virgin Stores brand and Virgin Megastores in France. The following year Lagardère opened its Barbès (Paris) store, making it France's 31st Virgin outlet.

In a global strategic move to strengthen its Internet and digital businesses, Lagardère SCA created the Lagardère Active division to focus on developing electronic media and next-generation media platforms. With separate operating units in North America, Europe, and Asia, the new division aimed to maximize the synergies between HFM, Hachette Filipacchi Magazines, and RTM Productions, HFM's new media division and a supplier of original television programming. In August

2001 Lagardère Active North America and Hachette Filipacchi Magazines launched ELLEgirl.com, an online magazine geared for the teen market. In that same month, Lagardère Active announced the inclusion of 360-degree videos on flyingmag.com, the official Web site of *Flying* magazine. In October 2001 the new division entered into an agreement with Healthology, Inc., a leading media health company, to provide an online women's health video resource on WomansDay.com.

Arnaud Lagardère assumed complete control as CEO of the Lagardère Group in 2001. Two years later, in March 2003, his father Jean-Luc died of a rare neurological disease at the age of 75, leaving the 42-year-old Arnaud sole chairman. The group's annual results were to be announced within days of the founder's death: The company had fallen to a net loss of €291 million, compared with a net profit in 2001 of €616 million. Lagardère had taken a big hit the previous year when Renault took over construction of the fourth generation of the Espace minivan, leaving the slow-selling Renault Avantime to Matra's assembly business. Earlier in 2003 Lagardère had sold his 1.3 percent stake in Renault and resigned from the board. The bottom line was grim, but Arnaud forged ahead with the presentation of the annual results, knowing that it was essential that he convey to the group's investors a seamless transfer of executive control. "I will follow the same path he set without hesitation and in the same spirit," Arnaud Lagardère said at the presentation. He announced that the group would be closing Matra's Romorantin plant in Central France and selling off its automobile engineering activities, which were eventually acquired by Italy's Pininfarina Group.

One year after the patriarch's death, Lagardère SCA announced that strong performance by its media business had put the group back into the black, posting net profits of €334 million. A key contributor to the positive bottom line was Hachette Livre's global sales of more than five million copies of author Dan Brown's novel *The Da Vinci Code*. The upward trend continued the following year, with Lagardère reporting a 50 percent increase in revenues from the book publishing business. The Editis and Hodder Headline acquisitions were cited as two of the main reasons for this success. Hodder Headline, a British publisher acquired by Lagardère in 2004 for $400 million, contributed €61.1 million in its first three months when Andrea Levy's novel *Small Island* won the Whitbread Book of the Year award.

With the strong performance of the book publishing business, Lagardère was anxious to increase its activities in the United States, where it had little presence. Time Warner's decision to sell its book group, which

was the fifth-largest book publisher in the United States, came at the perfect time. In February 2006 Lagardère purchased the Time Warner Book Group for $537.5 million, making it the world's third-largest book publisher. Lagardère then increased its stake in Vivendi Universal's pay-television arm, Canal+, to 20 percent with an option to increase its holding to 34 percent in three years. When shares of EADS soared on April 4, 2006, Lagardère seized the opportunity to sell 7.5 percent of the stake for €2 billion, preferring to place its focus on the media business.

In August 2006 Lagardère announced that it had received the licenses to launch two new television stations in Romania, where it already operated two radio stations. The two channels, Europa 1 TV and Europa 2 TV, would also include the construction of two new studios in Bucharest. In November 2006 Lagardère agreed to purchase Sportfive for €865 million ($1.1 billion), marking the company's entrance into the market for soccer television broadcasting rights.

CHALLENGING TIMES FOR LAGARDÈRE

Despite reporting a 19.5 percent drop in operating profits in its press division in September 2006, Lagardère said it planned to continue to acquire and develop new periodicals. Lower sales in print advertising in American automobile magazines, men's magazines in general, and regional newspapers, particularly in France, were cited as the reasons for the decline. "We are a magazine company and we will remain one," Arnaud Lagardère told an interviewer for the newspaper *Journal du Dimanche*, as quoted by Europe Intelligence Wire. Lagardère was forced to renege on this commitment when, in January 2007, it was announced that his company planned to discontinue or publish through third parties about 20 magazines, resulting in approximately 700 to 1,000 job cuts. It was estimated that the restructuring would cost between €80 and €100 million, with an aim of achieving a total annual savings of €78 million by the end of 2009.

The first step of the restructuring plan was the announcement in April 2007 that Hachette Filipacchi Norway had been sold to Hjemmet Mortensen AS for an undisclosed sum. Lagardère Media, however, was planning to hire 200 new staff members for its Internet activities and digital publishing business. In April 2007 Lagardère had to reassure shareholders that his company would remain diversified and rejected claims that it was taking a "digital only" approach.

In August 2007 Lagardère Active acquired the online advertising company ID Regie. This was followed in that same month with the acquisition of the French interactive media agency Nextedia. In February 2008, in a joint venture with Kagiso Media, Lagardère Active Radio International (LARI) acquired Acceleration Media, a South African online media agency. As advertising markets continued to weaken in the United States, Spain, France, the United Kingdom, and Japan, Lagardère began to look toward Russia and China for growth opportunities. In May 2009 Lagardère received a boost when Blue Entertainment Sports Television (BEST) announced that the former BEST Tennis Division president, Kenneth Meyerson, and a number of high-profile players, such as Andy Roddick, would immediately be joining Lagardère Unlimited LLC, the new athlete and celebrity management division that was created in April 2009. Also in May 2009, the group entered the mobile advertising business when its French media agency, Lagardère Publicité, began selling advertising space on iPhone applications from the Lagardère product range. Initially, seven applications from Lagardère Active were available, with plans to release more in the near future.

In September 2009 Lagardère Publishing was the only publisher among the five largest trade houses in the United States that posted increases in both sales and profits for the first six months of the year. Total revenue for the period was 58 percent higher than for the same time the previous year, while operating profits had increased by 62 percent. Later that month Lagardère Services announced that it had entered an agreement with the Australian fashion stationery chain, Smiggle, to open and operate its stores in airports throughout the Asia Pacific region. In December 2009 Lagardère Unlimited acquired Sporteam, a French company that represents professional rugby players. With its entrepreneurial spirit and capacity to develop alternative strategies to retain its competitive edge, Lagardère is well positioned to meet the challenges of the ever-changing and complex world of media.

Marie O'Sullivan

PRINCIPAL SUBSIDIARIES

European Aeronautic Defence and Space Company (EADS) (7.5%); Hachette SA; Hachette Livre SA; Lagardère Active SAS; Lagardère Services SA; Lagardère Sports SAS; Lagardère Unlimited.

PRINCIPAL DIVISIONS

Lagardère Publishing; Lagardère Active; Lagardère Services; Lagardère Sports.

PRINCIPAL COMPETITORS

The Bauer Publishing Group; Bertelsmann AG; Hearst Corporation.

FURTHER READING

"After the Musketeer; Face Value," *Economist*, March 22, 2003.

"Arnaud Lagardère Announces Hachette Productions Television Deal with Paxnet TV," PR Newswire, June 3, 1998.

"Arnaud Lagardère Takes Over Group," Europe Intelligence Wire, March 17, 2003.

"Aust Stationery Chain Smiggle Inks Store Deal with Lagardère," *AsiaPulse News*, September 16, 2009.

"BAe and Lagardère Form Missile Venture," *Navy News & Undersea Technology*, August 26, 1996.

Barrie, Douglas, and Kevin O'Toole, "Dynamic Duo," *Flight International*, May 22, 1996, p. 27.

Benjamin, Daniel, "Publishing with a French Accent: Hachette Spends $2 Billion to Become a Major Player in the U.S.," *Time*, April 25, 1988, p. 60.

Betts, Paul, "Lagardère Strikes a Light at Paris Match," *Financial Times*, June 30, 2006, p. 18.

Brady, Rosemary, "My Way," *Forbes*, June 18, 1984, p. 34.

"CanalSatellite Relies on Lagardère for Interactive Traction," *Broadcasting & Cable's TV International*, September 4, 2000, p. 2.

Chang, Alicia, "Lagardère Full-year Profit Falls to A291 Million," America's Intelligence Wire, March 12, 2007.

de Saint-Seine, Sylviane, "Founder Dies as Mantra Closes," *Automotive News Europe*, March 24, 2003, p. 20.

Done, Kevin, and James Mackintosh, "Daimler and Lagardère Cut EADS Stakes Aerospace," *Financial Times*, April 5, 2006, p. 25.

"France-Lagardère Active to Acquire Internet Media Agency Nextedia," Europe Intelligence Wire, August 30, 2007.

"France-Lagardère Buys Online Ad Agency ID Regie," Europe Intelligence Wire, August 29, 2007.

"French Industrialist Jean-Luc Lagardère," *WWD*, March 17, 2003, p. 23.

"French Media Group Lagardère Purchases Romanian Radio, TV Stations," *BBC Monitoring International Reports*, August 2, 2006.

"French Racing Loses Its Godfather as Lagardère Dies," Europe Intelligence Wire, March 14, 2003.

Gurubacharya, Binaj, "Lagardère Wins European Championship, African Cup Soccer Rights in Sportfive Deal," America's Intelligence Wire, November 20, 2006.

"Hachette Filipacchi Magazines and Lagardère Active North America Announce the Launch of ELLEgirl.com," Business Wire, June 25, 2001, p. 2231.

"Hachette Job for Elle: French Parent Lagardère Said to Be Talking to Hearst," *New York Post*, July 29, 2009, p. 34.

Hall, Ben, "Lagardère Seeks to Expand to Counter Ad Decline," *Financial Times*, August 11, 2008, p. 16.

Hollinger, Peggy, "Lagardère Resists Pressure on EADS Aerospace," *Financial Times*, June 22, 2006, p. 26.

———, "Lagardère's Easy Ride," *Financial Times*, October 26, 2007, p. 16.

———, and Adam Jones, "Lagardère Focus Comes Back Down to Earth as It Cuts Its EADS Stake," *Financial Times*, April 6, 2006, p. 26.

Hopewell, John, and Emiliano De Pablos, "Growing Gallic Giant Targets Production," *Daily Variety*, April 10, 2008, p. 6.

"Jean-Luc Lagardère, Chairman of EADS, Wins Prestigious Aviation Week Laureate Award," Business Wire, April 26, 2001, p. 0483.

Jones, Adam, "Lagardère Cuts up to 1,000 Jobs," *Financial Times*, January 26, 2007, p. 28.

———, "Lagardère Head Supports Curbs on 'Golden Parachute' Payments," *Financial Times*, April 28, 2007, p. 10.

———, "Lagardère Unveils Euros 4bn Media War Chest," *Financial Times*, May 3, 2006, p. 23.

"Kagiso, Lagardère Acquire Acceleration Media," Africa News Service, February 26, 2008.

"Lagardère Acquires Editorial Aique," *South American Business Information*, October 24, 2002.

"Lagardère Active iTV and OpenTV to Provide Interactive TV Services to DIRECTV Latin America," Business Wire, October 22, 2001, p. 2005.

"Lagardère Active Media Targets 10 Pct Reduction in Headcount in France," Europe Intelligence Wire, March 26, 2007.

"Lagardère Active North America Expands Multi-platform Efforts Supporting Flying Magazine," Business Wire, August 9, 2001, p. 2419.

"Lagardère Active North American to Provide Content for Lucent Technologies' MiRingBack," Telecomworldwire, October 26, 2004.

"Lagardère Active Teams with Healthology to Provide a Video Women's Health Resource on WomansDay.com," PR Newswire, October 23, 2001.

"Lagardère Affirms Commitment to Magazine Business, to Aim for Synergies," Europe Intelligence Wire, September 17, 2006.

"Lagardère Defends Diversified Model as Providing 'Secure' Long-term Growth," Europe Intelligence Wire, April 27, 2007.

"Lagardère Enters TV Soccer-Rights Arena with $1.1 Billion Buy," America's Intelligence Wire, November 20, 2006.

"Lagardère Media Boosted by Books," Europe Intelligence Wire, September 15, 2005.

"Lagardère on Media Business Shopping Spree," *Screen Digest*, August 2001, p. 233.

"Lagardère Says It Will Continue Acquiring, Developing Magazines," Europe Intelligence Wire, September 13, 2006.

"Lagardère Seeks Continuity after Death of Founder," Europe Intelligence Wire, March 17, 2003.

"Lagardère SCA and Its Subsidiary Hachette Filipacchi Medias Form Lagardère Active," Business Wire, February 15, 2001, p. 2454.

"Lagardère SCA Sells Grolier Inc. to Scholastic Corp.," *European Report*, May 3, 2000.

"Lagardère Sells Hachette Filipacchi Norway to Local Player, Terms Undisclosed," Europe Intelligence Wire, April 10, 2007.

"Lagardère Starts Selling Ad Space on Its iPhone Apps," Europe Intelligence Wire, May 20, 2009.

"Lagardère to Axe Magazines in Favour of Digital Services," Europe Intelligence Wire, January 26, 2007.

"Lagardère Unlimited Boosts Growth in the USA," PR Newswire, May 7, 2009.

"Lagardère Unlimited Creates a Rugby Division," PR Newswire, December 2, 2009.

Lewis, Jakema, "Lagardère Debuts in U.S. Private Market, Buy-side Interest Strong," *Private Placement Letter*, November 27, 2000.

Lottman, Herbert R., "French Plan to Sell Grolier," *Publishers Weekly*, November 29, 1999, p. 21.

———, "New Look for France's Big Publishing Groups," *Publishers Weekly*, January 4, 1993, p. 20.

Macrae, Duncan, "Lagardère's Comeback," *Interavia Business & Technology*, September 1998, p. 5.

McCarthy, Ellen, "Lagardère Swings Back to Profit Thanks to Media, EADS Stake," America's Intelligence Wire, March 15, 2004.

McGuirk, Rod, "Lagardère Reaches Deal with Vivendi for Stake in Canal Plus Pay TV," American's Intelligence Wire, February 17, 2006.

Milliot, Jim, "It's Good to Be Hachette: Publisher Outdistances Rivals in First Half of 2009," *Publishers Weekly*, September 14, 2009, p. 3.

———, "Lagardère Makes Its Move: TW Deal Plants French Giant in the U.S.," *Publishers Weekly*, February 13, 2006, p. 4.

Sage, Adam, "Bid for Le Monde Triggers Power Struggle," *Times* (London), January 14, 2008, p. 47.

"Sales up at Lagardère," *Publishers Weekly*, November 9, 2009, p. 6.

Sasseen, Jane, "Family Dynasty," *International Management*, February 1990, p. 24.

Silbert, Nathalie, and Bruno Trevidic, "No Immediate Lagardère Bail-out of EADS," *Financial Times*, September 13, 2007, p. 19.

Sutel, Seth, "Time Warner Sells Book Group to France's Lagardère," America's Intelligence Wire, February 6, 2006.

Tagliabue, John, "Jean-Luc, 75, Executive Dies: Founded an Aerospace and Media Empire," *New York Times*, March 16, 2003, p. 31.

"The Odd Couple: Matra and Hachette," *Economist*, May 9, 1992, p. 89.

"The World: Prague-Lagardère Buys into Slovakian Radio Station Okey," *Campaign*, April 6, 2007, p. 12.

Tiernan, Ross, "Lagardère Extends Reach," *Sunday Business* (London), February 13, 2005.

Tran, Pierre, "French Publishing Baron Lagardère Closes Book on Vivendi Unit's Buyout," *Sunday Business* (London), December 14, 2003.

———, "Lagardère Aims to Make His Name at Le Monde,"

Sunday Business (London), March 6, 2005.

"Vivendi Universal Plans to Sell Its Publishing Businesses, Except for Houghton Mifflin, to the Lagardère Group," *Canadian Corporate News*, October 23, 2002.

Whitney, Craig, "France Sells a Third of Aerospatiale to Groupe Lagardère," *New York Times*, February 16, 1999.

Lorillard, Inc.

714 Green Valley Road
Greensboro, North Carolina 27408
U.S.A.
Telephone: (336) 335-7000
Fax: (336) 335-7550
Web site: http://www.lorillard.com

Public Company
Incorporated: 2007
Employees: 2,800
Sales: $5.23 billion (2009)
Stock Exchanges: New York
Ticker Symbol: LO
NAICS: 312221 Cigarette Manufacturing

■ ■ ■

Lorillard, Inc., is the third-largest cigarette manufacturer in the United States. Founded in New York City in 1760, Lorillard has since moved its headquarters to Greensboro, North Carolina. The company is the oldest manufacturer of tobacco products in the United States and one of the country's oldest operating businesses in any field. Its leading brand, Newport, is the highest-selling menthol brand and the second-highest-selling U.S. brand overall. Lorillard's other cigarette brands include Kent, Kent III, Kent Golden Lights, Old Gold, Newport Stripes, True, Max, and Triumph. After 40 years as a subsidiary of Loews Corporation, Lorillard became an independent corporation again in 2008, operating in a shrinking market facing tightening regulations and higher taxes.

1760: PIERRE LORILLARD'S TOBACCO SHOP

Pierre Lorillard, a French immigrant to the United States, set up a tobacco shop in the bustling coastal city of New York in 1760. P. Lorillard Company specialized in manufacturing and selling snuff, the then-fashionable powdered form of tobacco customarily consumed by sniffing. The shop also sold pipe tobacco and plug tobacco for chewing. After Lorillard was killed during the Revolutionary War, his sons, Pierre II (known as Peter) and George, continued the enterprise. In 1792 the brothers constructed a water-powered factory for grinding snuff along the Bronx River, more than 10 miles northeast of New York City.

The company issued the earliest known U.S. tobacco advertisements in the late 1780s. In 1830 it solicited U.S. postmasters to stock its products in their offices, which often served as general stores and community gathering places. This gave P. Lorillard the first effective national distribution network for tobacco products.

After Peter died in 1843, company leadership passed to Pierre Lorillard III and Pierre Lorillard IV and stayed in the family's hands through the early 1900s. During this time the Lorillards also became prominent members of New York's high society. To stay in line with popular consumption trends in the early 19th century, P. Lorillard shifted its focus to plug tobacco for chewing. The company also offered fine-cut tobacco suited for hand-rolled cigarettes.

In 1870 Lorillard opened a new factory in Jersey City, New Jersey, and by 1900 as many as 4,000

COMPANY PERSPECTIVES

As clearly set forth in the Tobacco Industry's Cigarette Advertising and Promotion Code (the "Code"), to which Lorillard has adhered for many years, Lorillard believes that cigarette smoking is an adult custom and that children should not smoke. Accordingly, Lorillard advertises and promotes its cigarettes only to adult smokers. Moreover, Lorillard believes that laws prohibiting the sale of cigarettes to minors should be strictly enforced. By entering into the Master Settlement Agreement (the "MSA") with state attorneys general in November 1998, Lorillard agreed to various other restrictions and prohibitions relating to the marketing and promotion of our cigarettes. These are consistent with our long-standing commitment to preventing youth smoking. We intend to strictly comply with both the letter and spirit of these restrictions and prohibitions, and all other obligations we have undertaken pursuant to the MSA.

employees (many of them young women) worked there. Around this time, the company patented and introduced tin tags stamped with distinctive logos to mark its tobacco as genuine. P. Lorillard also marketed cigars, some labeled with the names of famous actors or literary characters.

P. LORILLARD AND THE RISE OF THE CIGARETTE

In 1898 P. Lorillard joined American Tobacco Company, a trust devised to control the tobacco industry, but was allowed to remain autonomous under its existing management. After 1900 the Roosevelt and Taft administrations filed lawsuits to break up many industrial trusts, seeking enforcement of the Sherman Antitrust Act against monopolies. A U.S. Supreme Court 1911 ruling ordered the dissolution of the American Tobacco Company trust, which resulted in four main firms producing cigarettes and pipe and chewing tobacco: American Tobacco, P. Lorillard & Co., R. J. Reynolds, and Liggett & Myers. All of these companies would remain among the industry's leaders for the next several decades.

P. Lorillard enjoyed strong shares in cigarettes, smoking tobacco, and little cigars shortly after the trust breakup. Around this time, the company featured a

series of "Turkish" cigarette brands such as Helmar, Mogul, Murad, and Zubelda. These cigarettes were made from imported aromatic tobacco and were typically packaged in colorful labels depicting exotic (sometimes erotic) scenes. P. Lorillard drove sales by inserting trade cards and giving out premiums in exchange for product labels.

Beginning in 1913 with R. J. Reynolds's Camel brand, manufacturers introduced "standard-blend" cigarettes that combined domestic and imported tobaccos to create tastes that seemed to appeal to more consumers. Aggressive promotion of standard-blend brands helped push cigarettes to become the predominant tobacco product in the United States. From 1911 to 1945 annual per capita cigarette consumption soared from 108 to 2,027.

P. Lorillard lagged in adapting to this decisive shift. In 1926 the company finally introduced a successful standard-blend brand, Old Gold. It supported the launch with extensive (and expensive) advertising, some of which openly appealed to the rising numbers of female smokers. Old Gold soon became the fourth-leading cigarette brand after Camel, Lucky Strike, and Chesterfields. Despite this, P. Lorillard's share of aggregate income among the "Big Four" tobacco companies plunged from 15.96 percent in 1912 to 5.14 percent in 1930.

During the late 1920s and early 1930s, the company used the slogan "Not a Cough in a Carload" to hint that its cigarettes were healthier to smoke than rival products. P. Lorillard and fellow cigarette manufacturers also sought to allay health fears by featuring testimonials from physicians and athletes in print ads. Another effective promotional technique was a series of contests that required contestants to submit answers to a long list of questions (accompanied by plenty of Old Gold wrappers). The publicity culminated in 1937 when a $100,000 first prize prompted about two million entries.

Boosted by all the attention, Old Gold, along with other leading brands, enjoyed steady sales growth throughout the 1930s and 1940s, despite the Depression and World War II. In 1947 Lorillard launched Embassy, a king-sized brand that became a mainstay of the manufacturer's export trade. It sponsored numerous radio and television programs and presented the Old Gold Dancing Packs during the 1950s.

FILTERS COME TO THE RESCUE

By the early 1950s medical research studies had convincingly linked cigarette smoking to higher rates of lung cancer. The appearance of articles discussing these

```
┌─────────────────────────────────────────────────────┐
│                                                       │
│                    KEY DATES                          │
│                       ■                               │
│  1760:  Pierre Lorillard founds P. Lorillard Company, │
│         a tobacco shop in New York City.              │
│  1792:  Lorillard's sons, Peter and George, establish │
│         water-powered snuff mill on the Bronx River,  │
│         north of New York City.                       │
│  1830:  Company begins national distribution of       │
│         products through U.S. post offices.           │
│  1870:  P. Lorillard opens new factory in Jersey City,│
│         New Jersey.                                   │
│  1898:  P. Lorillard is incorporated as the American  │
│         Tobacco Company.                              │
│  1911:  P. Lorillard & Co. reemerges after court-     │
│         ordered breakup of American Tobacco.          │
│  1926:  Company introduces Old Gold, which            │
│         becomes its most popular cigarette brand.     │
│  1952:  P. Lorillard introduces Kent, one of the first│
│         popular filter cigarette brands in the United │
│         States.                                       │
│  1968:  Loews Theatres acquires P. Lorillard.         │
│  1998:  P. Lorillard accedes to landmark settlement of│
│         suits filed by state attorneys general for    │
│         reimbursement of health care costs linked to  │
│         smoking.                                      │
│  2002:  Loews issues Carolina Group tracking stock    │
│         for P. Lorillard.                             │
│  2008:  Lorillard, Inc., once again becomes an        │
│         independent corporation.                      │
│                                                       │
└─────────────────────────────────────────────────────┘
```

findings in popular magazines such as *Reader's Digest* and *Time* in 1952 and 1953 marked a watershed in public awareness of cigarettes' dangers. The industry responded by collaborating with organizations such as the Tobacco Industry Research Council and the Tobacco Institute to defend its products' reputation, refusing to admit that cigarette smoking could actually harm people's health.

Reacting to the medical findings, tobacco companies promoted cigarettes with filters that supposedly removed much of the potentially harmful chemicals before smokers could inhale them. In 1952 P. Lorillard had already introduced Kent, one of the first major brands of filtered cigarettes on the U.S. market. The company's success with Kent was short-lived, however. Its sales declined in 1954 and 1955, attributed in part to the onslaught of lower-priced filter brands and the difficulty of puffing through the thick filter.

Around this time, P. Lorillard replaced many of its executives, starting at the top with new chairman Lewis Gruber. The company relaunched Kent with an "improved" filter in 1957, billing it as lower in tar and nicotine than other filter brands. Sales of the brand soared the following year, leaping from tenth to fifth among brands, as the company rode Kent's revival to rise from the sixth- to the third-leading tobacco firm in the United States. Filter brands in general accounted for around 25 percent of total U.S. cigarette sales by 1956 and more than 50 percent by 1960. P. Lorillard also introduced several brand extensions of Old Gold during the 1950s and launched Newport, a mildly mentholated brand.

As if to confirm the triumph of cigarettes, the manufacturer withdrew its cigars from the market in 1958, although it continued to be a leading producer of little cigars (sometimes offered in packaging resembling cigarette packs). In 1956 P. Lorillard closed its Jersey City plant and opened a new plant in Greensboro, North Carolina, closer to the core tobacco-growing region. It also moved its headquarters into a newly constructed 29-floor office building in New York City in 1958.

DIVERSIFICATION AND ACQUISITION BY LOEWS

In the early 1960s tobacco companies started investing in other industries, hedging against tightened regulation and declining cigarette sales as evidence of smoking's health risks mounted. In 1962 P. Lorillard stockholders voted to allow the company to expand into nontobacco businesses, which had been banned in the company's 1911 charter. In 1964 it acquired Usen Canning Company, the second-largest canned cat food manufacturer in the United States, for around $7 million of stock. Two years later it purchased Reed Candy Co.

P. Lorillard was also expanding abroad, where cigarette sales were increasing faster than in the United States. The company established joint-venture manufacturing subsidiaries in Hong Kong and Luxembourg. Chairman Manuel Yellen, who had succeeded Gruber the year before, boasted to the *New York Times* in 1965 that the company had licensing agreements in 12 countries and that its products were marketed in 125 countries.

Despite its acquisitions and several brand introductions, P. Lorillard's overall sales and earnings stagnated during the 1960s. An agreement announced in March 1967 to purchase liquor producer Schenley Industries fell through. The following year Laurence Tisch, coowner of Loews Theatres, learned that P. Lorillard was seeking a merger with a suitable partner. Tisch and his brother Bob decided to add P. Lorillard to their rapidly growing conglomerate, Loews Theatres (later renamed Loews Corporation). P. Lorillard's undervalued stock and its steady sales of consumer staples particularly attracted the Tisches, who swiftly purchased it for more than $400 million in stock. The new owners quickly replaced Yellen and many other P. Lorillard executives, convinced that their management of the company had been inept. By the early 1970s Loews Corporation had sold off P. Lorillard's pet food and candy divisions.

STEADY PROGRESS AS SHADOW LOOMS

Concentrating on tobacco appeared to be a financially smart move for P. Lorillard. Throughout the late 20th century it remained a profitable mainstay of Loews's business. However, the company stayed well behind industry giants Philip Morris and R. J. Reynolds, with a market share hovering between 8 and 10 percent throughout most of this period.

The unit continued to roll out new brands and brand variants to adapt to a market increasingly segmented by taste, length, and tar content. The company's True brand, a filtered cigarette launched in 1966, overtly stressed its purported healthiness. It was marketed specifically to smokers who were thinking of quitting the habit. P. Lorillard had another modestly successful launch with Satin, a cigarette brand introduced nationally in 1983 and aimed at women.

However, its most dramatic brand success was the once faltering Newport. P. Lorillard revitalized the brand by reformulating the menthol concentration and through advertising campaigns featuring young, attractive couples cavorting outdoors. Much of its marketing targeted urban African Americans, for whom mentholated brands seemed to have particular appeal. Newport's share surged from 0.74 percent in 1972 to 2.79 percent by 1983 and would continue to rise.

Employing adept public relations and protected by its many political friends, the cigarette industry skillfully defended its power and profits, even after the U.S. Surgeon General officially declared in January 1964 that cigarette smoking caused lung cancer. Mandatory warning labels on cigarette packs and a ban on television advertising effective January 1, 1971, made little immediate dent in cigarette sales. However, the industry's horizons would slowly constrict, at least in the United States. The percentage of smokers among U.S. adults declined from more than 40 percent in 1964 to about 25 percent by 1994. During this time federal and state excise tax rates on cigarettes also rose. In 1977 P. Lorillard sold all its international trademark rights to the British tobacco giant BAT Industries PLC, a fateful decision in an industry where international markets were becoming major drivers of profits.

A New Jersey court case that came to trial in 1987 dramatized the increasing legal risks that P. Lorillard and other tobacco companies faced. The lawsuit was filed on behalf of Rose Cippolone, a lifelong smoker who had died of lung cancer. P. Lorillard was not found liable for damages, and verdicts against all defendants were reversed on appeal. However, the plaintiff's attorneys had forced the disclosure of a trove of internal company documents as evidence during the trial. The attorneys pointed to a report from a P. Lorillard researcher in 1946 discussing the possible health hazards of smoking as proof that the tobacco companies had been well aware for decades that they were selling dangerous products but had chosen to deny publicly that cigarettes could do any permanent harm. While P. Lorillard and its peers preserved legal impunity, their public reputation could never fully recover.

LOEWS HANGS ON TO P. LORILLARD IN AN EMBATTLED INDUSTRY

Relying on full-priced brands, P. Lorillard was vulnerable to the popularity of discount brands in the early 1990s. It responded first by launching a new discount brand, Style, in 1992. Over the next three years, the company chopped retail prices for Newport (which had become its mainstay brand), relaunched the venerable Old Gold as a discount brand, and introduced a low-priced extension of Kent, whose high-class reputation handicapped the brand as smoking became more socially stigmatized and concentrated among working-class people.

Meanwhile in 1986 famed motorcycle manufacturer Harley-Davidson had agreed to license its trademark to P. Lorillard, which hoped to develop themed cigarettes to attract younger men. However, after the company had spent several years researching and test marketing the product, it cancelled a planned launch in 1993. By then Harley-Davidson decided it no longer wanted to associate its name with tobacco. It tried to revoke the licensing agreement, but P. Lorillard won a court ruling to keep the right to use the name. Early in 1997 a proposed FDA regulation that would forbid licensed tobacco products prompted the manufacturer to pull Harley-Davidson cigarettes from the market and replace them with the Maverick brand.

By the early 1990s the Tisches, who had become prominent in the media and philanthropy, were feeling pressure to distance Loews from the tobacco industry. Speaking to biographer Christopher Winans, Laurence Tisch and other members of the nonsmoking Tisch family acknowledged qualms about their company earning so much profit from cigarettes but insisted that selling off P. Lorillard would make no moral difference. Defenders of Loews pointed out that if the company sold P. Lorillard, it could still be found liable for harm caused by tobacco products marketed during its ownership, so it might as well keep the unit and enjoy the profits as long as it could. In 1996, for example, Lorillard's $2.24 billion in revenue contributed around 11 percent of Loews's overall revenue of $20.47 billion, and its $444.4 million in net income accounted for a disproportionate 32 percent of Loews's $1.34 billion net income.

By the late 1990s Lorillard began paying settlement costs from successful lawsuits; these amounts rose from $122.0 million in 1997 to $637.3 million in 1999. In December 1998, to settle lawsuits brought by the attorneys general of various U.S. states, the tobacco industry agreed to pay $246 billion through the 2020s to compensate the states for Medicaid expenses related to smoking. The tobacco manufacturers also agreed to cease outdoor advertising and to fund youth smoking-prevention programs. P. Lorillard would be obliged to charge off many billions of dollars a year from these settlements, however, it could recoup much of the losses by hiking retail prices.

LOEWS STEERS P. LORILLARD TOWARD INDEPENDENCE

As a new century began, the Tisch family was preparing to ease its company out of the tobacco trade. Thousands of tobacco product liability suits, many of which named P. Lorillard as a defendant, were winding their way through U.S. courts. The most prominent case, *Engle v. R. J. Reynolds Tobacco Co., et al*, resulted in an award of $144.9 billion in punitive damages in 2000; P. Lorillard was held responsible for $16.25 billion. Ultimately, P. Lorillard and its codefendants escaped financial liability, as the judgment was reversed in 2001 and the Florida Supreme Court confirmed the reversal in 2006.

In 2002 Loews gained $1.1 billion by issuing shares in Carolina Group, a tracking stock for P. Lorillard. This move was intended mainly to support Loews's other divisions and help the parent company pay off debt. Carolina Group shareholders received only dividends; Loews still owned 100 percent of P. Lorillard. Loews disposed of much of its Carolina Group stock, reducing its holdings to 38 percent by 2005. It declared in December 2007 that P. Lorillard would become an independent corporation the following year.

Lorillard, Inc., offered its stock on the New York Stock Exchange on June 10, 2008. Many analysts recommended buying the stock, citing the company's high profit margins and rising market share as sales of mentholated cigarettes were shrinking more slowly than those of standard cigarettes. Newport, the leading menthol brand in the United States, now supplied more than 90 percent of the company's sales and revenue. In addition, cigarette sales were not closely linked with wider economic trends, which comforted investors as the economic crisis intensified. However, share prices fell from the offering price of $74.00 to as low as $52.24 in December 2008.

In response to a proposed bill in Congress in 2008 to outlaw flavored tobacco products, African-American health activists and politicians urged that the bill include menthol, as many menthol brands such as Newport were aimed chiefly at urban blacks. The enacted bill did not cover menthol, so for the time being Lorillard had dodged another threatened blow to its business. The company's share price rebounded to more than $80 by October 2009. Industry rumors pegged Lorillard as an attractive takeover target for a larger competitor, but no offers had been announced as of early 2010.

Stephen V. Beitel

PRINCIPAL COMPETITORS

Commonwealth Brands, Inc.; Philip Morris USA Inc.; Reynolds American Inc.

FURTHER READING

Brandt, Allan M., *The Cigarette Century: The Rise, Fall, and Deadly Persistence of the Product That Defined America*. New York: Basic Books, 2007.

Cox, Reavis, *Competition in the American Tobacco Industry, 1911–1930*. New York: Columbia University Press, 1933.

Elliott, Stuart, "Lorillard Attempts a Tricky Balance by Selling Kent Cigarettes as Both a Premium and Discount Brand," *New York Times*, January 6, 1995.

Fabrikant, Geraldine, "Loews to Spin Off Lorillard Tobacco," *New York Times*, December 18, 2007.

"Filters' Friend: Lewis Gruber," *Time*, February 2, 1959.

Gardner, James, "Newport Smokes Out a Surprising Comeback," *Marketing & Media Decisions*, Spring 1984, p. 89.

Hammer, Alexander R., "Cigarette Exports Rise Sharply," *New York Times*, September 8, 1965, pp. 63, 71.

Huhn, Mary, "Lorillard Cancels Plans for Harley-Davidson Launch," *Mediaweek*, August 9, 1993, p. 5.

Lorillard and Tobacco: 200th Anniversary, P. Lorillard Company, 1760–1960. New York: P. Lorillard Company, 1960.

"Lorillard Now Free to Diversify: Ban on Non-Tobacco Ventures Ended by Holders," *New York Times*, April 4, 1962.

"P. Lorillard to Close Its Factory in Jersey City and Move South," *New York Times*, January 14, 1956, pp. 23, 26.

Reckert, Clare M., "Lorillard Company Diversifies; Purchases Maker of Pet Foods," *New York Times*, December 22, 1964, p. 39.

Robert, Joseph C., *The Story of Tobacco in America*. New York: Alfred A. Knopf, 1949.

Rothenberg, Randall, "Verdict Expected to Focus Attention on Early Tobacco Ads," *New York Times*, June 15, 1988.

Saul, Stephanie, "Black Caucus Seeks Limits on Menthol Cigarettes," *New York Times*, July 1, 2008.

———, "Profits in Hand, Wealthy Family Uses Spinoff to Cut Tobacco Tie," *New York Times*, June 11, 2008, p. A18.

Teinovitz, Ira, "Harley Cig First Casualty of FDA Rule?" *Advertising Age*, February 7, 1997, p. 3.

"This Stock May Harm Your Portfolio's Health," *BusinessWeek*, February 4, 2002, p. 80.

"U.S. Business: To the Package Store," *Time*, March 24, 1967.

Winans, Christopher, *The King of Cash: The Inside Story of Laurence Tisch*. New York: Wiley, 1995.

Marvell Technology Group Ltd.

Canon's Court
22 Victoria Street
Hamilton, HM 12
Bermuda
Telephone: (441) 296-6395
Web site: http://www.marvell.com

Public Company
Incorporated: 1995
Employees: 5,552
Sales: $2.95 billion (2009)
Stock Exchanges: NASDAQ
Ticker Symbol: MRVL
NAICS: 334413 Semiconductor and Related Device
Manufacturing

■■■

A NASDAQ-listed company headquartered in Hamilton, Bermuda, Marvell Technology Group Ltd. is a fabless (contracting out its manufacturing) semiconductor company that has dominated virtually every field it has entered with innovative designs and a ruthless work ethic exemplified by its founders, talented engineers in their own right who also serve as the company's chief executives. Marvell products are application-specific System-on-a-Chip (SoC) storage and communication devices that serve such platforms as smartphones, smartbooks, mobile Internet devices, and e-readers. At the heart of the SoC devices is Marvell's Sheeva Central Processing unit. The company also offers storage, wireless, switching, power management, enterprise transceiver, broadband, PC connectivity, system controllers, and digital entertainment solutions. In addition to its principal executive offices in Bermuda, Marvell maintains offices in the United States, Singapore, Tokyo, Israel, and India.

BEGINNING WITH A CIRCUIT

Husband and wife Sehat Sutardja and Weili Dai and Sutardja's younger brother, Pantas Sutardja, founded Marvell in 1995. They assembled seed money from friends and family and used their electrical engineering knowledge and talents to design a circuit that fetched $200,000 in licensing. For the name of their company, they chose the word *marvel*. "We wanted to build a marvelous company," Dai explained in a 2001 *San Jose Business Journal* article. To differentiate themselves from Marvel, the comic book publisher, they added an "l," resulting in Marvell Technology Group, which they incorporated in Bermuda. Marvell Semiconductor, Inc., then became its operating unit in the United States.

Marvell originally set up shop in Cupertino, California. Knowing they wanted to design a fast chip that could translate analog data into digital data, the brothers looked for a suitable market, finally targeting disk drives, which not only sold in the hundreds of millions each year but also comprised a niche with no standard bodies controlled by the major companies, allowing an easy entry into the market. Moreover, they felt confident they could design processing chips that were faster, smaller, and cooler running than anything available.

COMPANY PERSPECTIVES

■

A leading fabless semiconductor company, Marvell ships over one billion chips a year. Marvell's expertise in microprocessor architecture and digital signal processing, drives multiple platforms including high volume storage solutions, mobile and wireless, networking, consumer and green products. World class engineering and mixed-signal design expertise helps Marvell deliver critical building blocks to its customers, giving them the competitive edge to succeed in today's dynamic market.

A FAST BEGINNING

Dai's job was to cold-call potential customers. She eventually called Seagate Technology, which was not pleased with the speed of the chips that they were using for transmitting data in and out of drives. Dai promised to send her two best engineers to investigate the matter, and in short order her husband and brother-in-law were on a flight to Seagate's Minnesota office. A year later the brothers completed the design of a chip 20 percent faster than what Seagate's supplier, T1, had to offer, and Marvell seized Seagate's business.

In 1999, its first year of shipping, Marvell sold $21 million in chips, an amount that grew larger as other storage companies followed Seagate's lead and contracted with Marvell. These companies included Fujitsu Ltd., Hitachi Ltd. Samsung Semiconductor, Toshiba Corporation, and Western Digital Corporation.

Marvell's success with disk drives attracted the attention of Diosdado Banatao, a famed Silicon Valley serial entrepreneur who had been involved in several successful chip start-up companies. He became Marvell's first investor, contributing $1 million. In the meantime, Marvell turned its attention to the broadband communications market, using its technology to develop a chip that could provide a tenfold increase in speed in the amount of data that could be transmitted through an Ethernet port. This breakthrough led to a development deal with Intel, and a first-generation product introduced in late 1999 spearheaded an effort to take Marvell public in 2000.

Not everyone was convinced, however, that Marvell would succeed as a public company. According to David Whelan, writing in *Forbes Global* in 2006, "Morgan Stanley rejected the group, as did late-stage venture capitalists, because of concerns over how the family-run company would handle corporate governance." The cofounders did not alleviate these concerns when, two months before the scheduled initial public offering (IPO), they abruptly fired the chief financial officer.

IPO COMPLETED

Also complicating the IPO was a high-technology sector that was suddenly collapsing in the stock market, led by Internet ventures. Marvell stayed the course and found a receptive market for the IPO. Instead of the asking price of $9 to $11 per share, Marvell commanded $15 when the offering was held in June 2000, netting $103.5 million. Moreover, the share price soared on its first day of trading on the NASDQ to nearly $56 per share and continued to climb, peaking at almost $110 per share in mid-September before leveling off. As a result, the cofounders each possessed a net worth in excess of $600 million.

The IPO also provided Marvell with stock to use in making acquisitions. In early 2001 the company used $2.7 billion in stock to acquire an Israeli company, Galileo Technology Ltd., which maintained its operating headquarters in San Jose, California. Galileo produced chips used in networking switching, local routing, and system management. With the deal Marvell acquired technology, more than 250 engineers, and a presence in new markets.

Also in 2001 Marvell was sued for misappropriating trade secrets. It had been negotiating to buy patents from Jasmine Networks when Marvell executives neglected to disconnect a phone after leaving a message for Jasmine officials. An ensuing conversation was recorded, during which, according to Whelan writing in *Forbes Global* in 2006, "Marvell's patent attorney Eric Janofsky wondered aloud if Sehat would go to jail and moments later remarked: 'If we took the [intellectual property] on the pretense of just evaluating it.'" As of early 2010 the matter was still wending through the court system.

MORE ACQUISITIONS

Marvell continued its expansion into new markets. In February 2006 it paid $240 million to acquire the printer semiconductor division of Avago Technologies Limited. Marvell then arranged to add the mobile phone chip business of Intel Corporation in 2006, paying $600 million a little more than three weeks after Intel put it on the block. Intel had lost money on the business, but Marvell, which did not buy Intel's factories, was confident that its fabless business model would allow it to greatly cut costs by moving produc-

```
                KEY DATES
                     ■
1995:  Sehat Sutardja, Weili Dai, and Pantas Sutardja
       found Marvell.
1999:  Marvell sells $21 million in chips.
2000:  Marvell files its initial public offering.
2006:  Marvell acquires the printer semiconductor
       division of Avago Technologies Limited and
       the mobile phone chip business of Intel
       Corporation.
2008:  The Securities and Exchange Commission
       fines Marvell $10 million for backdating
       stock options.
```

tion to less-expensive Taiwanese plants.

The acquisitions cut into profit margins, as Marvell posted a $12 million loss on revenues of $2.24 billion for the fiscal year ending January 27, 2007. Losses grew to $114.4 million on sales of $2.89 billion in fiscal 2008. A year later revenues improved to $2.95 billion and the company recorded net income of $147.2 million as expenses leveled off after the company successfully digested its acquisitions.

SEC INQUIRY

While admired for its success in many quarters, Marvell was despised by rival firms it had shoved aside in markets they had once dominated. The company, in the words of Whelan writing in *Forbes Global* in 2006, was "a tough place to work, with its up-all-night work habits and short-fuse product development." On the other hand, hundreds of Marvell engineers had become millionaires from company stock. The way the company handled stock options, however, eventually caught the attention of authorities.

In 2006 Marvell received a subpoena from the Securities and Exchange Commission (SEC) and a grand jury requesting information on its practices. The Marvell board of directors launched an internal investigation, but waited 10 months before interviewing the only members of the stock option committee: Sehat Sutardja and Weili Dai. The investigation eventually concluded that Dai had participated in backdating. As a result, she relinquished her role as chief operating officer and director for a lesser position in May 2007.

The chief financial officer resigned, and the board urged Sehat Sutardja to give up the chairmanship, but he refused. In 2008 the SEC weighed in, fining Marvell

$10 million for backdating options from 2001 to 2004, an especially large amount because of the delay in interviewing Sutardja and Dai. Dai also agreed to a settlement in which she paid $500,000 and was barred for five years from serving as an officer or director.

MOMENTUM CONTINUES

In 2009, as consumers began to accumulate large amounts of digital entertainment and other data, Marvell anticipated the emergence of a new data-storage model and unveiled its plan for so-called plug computers, compact storage devices powered by Marvell chips that could be plugged into an electrical outlet connected by an Ethernet cable to a home router or storage device via a USB cord. The data these units stored could then be accessed via the Internet by multiple users. This concept was just one of many possibilities Marvell pursued to drive further growth, impressing investors who over most of 2009 bid up the price of the company's stock to new 52-week highs.

Momentum continued to mount in early 2010 when Marvell unveiled a host of new products at the annual International Consumer Electronics Show in Las Vegas. The company's new chips were positioned to power a vast range of "always-on" devices that included storage, information appliances, intelligent displays, mobile computing, telephony, gaming, data, and entertainment. The underlying vision was a next-wave lifestyle that provided consumers with live digital content "where ever they want it, whenever they want it and in the format they want it in," as Dai explained in a January 2010 press statement. Whether or not consumers would embrace such a lifestyle remained to be seen, but in whichever direction consumers turned, Marvell was poised to have a chip ready to make the fulfillment of their desires a little bit faster.

Ed Dinger

PRINCIPAL SUBSIDIARIES

Marvell International Ltd.; Marvell Semiconductor, Inc.

PRINCIPAL COMPETITORS

LSI Corporation; STMicroelectronics N.V.; Texas Instruments Incorporated.

FURTHER READING

Alpert, Bill, "Simply Marvell-ous," *Barron's*, February 25, 2008, p. 31.

Charles, John, "Basketball Semipro-Turned-Exec Keeps Her Eyes on the Goal," *San Jose Business Journal*, May 18, 2001, p. 36.

Deogun, Nikhil, and Molly Williams, "Marvell Technology Purchases Israel's Galileo in $2.7 Billion Deal," *Wall Street Journal*, October 17, 2000.

Dunn, Darrell, "Marvell Expands Ethernet Lineup," *Electronic Buyers' News*, August 21, 2000, p. 40.

Elinson, Zusha, "Marvell Technology to Pay $10 Million Fine over Backdating," *Legal Intelligencer*, May 12, 2008.

Hall, Thomas C., "Multimillionaire Startup Exec Brushes Off Her Good Fortune," *Business Journal*, September 22, 2000, p. 3.

Shwiff, Kathy, "Marvell Set to Cut Staff After Loss," *Wall Street Journal*, March 6, 2009.

Whelan, David, "Meet Marvell," *Forbes Global*, September 4, 2006, p. 142.

White, Bill, "Marvell Is Branching Out Beyond Read-Channel Roots," *Electronic Buyers' News*, November 27, 2000, p. 20.

Meyer Natural Angus L.L.C.

4850 Hahns Peak Drive, Suite 250
Loveland, Colorado 80538
U.S.A.
Telephone: (970) 292-5006
Toll Free: (800) 856-6765
Fax: (970) 272-5567
Web site: http://www.meyernaturalangus.com

Privately Owned Subsidiary of Meyer Foods
Founded: 1996
Employees: 38
Sales: $150 million (2008)
NAICS: 311611 Animal (except Poultry) Slaughtering;
    311612 Meat Processed from Carcasses

■ ■ ■

Meyer Natural Angus L.L.C. (MNA) is the largest U.S. producer of natural beef, or beef derived from cattle raised without the use of antibiotics or hormones. MNA slaughters some 120,000 cattle per year. The cattle come from the MNA-owned, 43,000-acre ranch in western Montana and more than 250 ranches around the country whose owners contract with MNA to follow its protocols. These protocols not only forbid the use of antibiotics and hormones but are also designed to promote environmentally sound use of land and humane treatment of cattle. The protocols are consistent with growing consumer concerns about health, the environment, and animal welfare. As a result of these concerns and MNA's purchase of leading competitors,

MNA beef sales grew dramatically during the first decade of the 21st century.

GETTING STARTED

A successful entrepreneur in the fields of pharmaceuticals, investment banking, and commercial real estate, Robert Meyer began in the 1980s to seek land acquisitions with the goal of establishing a cattle ranch. On this ranch Red Angus cattle would be raised the "old-fashioned way" to produce "natural beef," concepts that would be further developed in the 1990s. The purpose was to achieve the best possible beef flavor, better than the taste of the nonbranded, commercial beef that dominated the market. Meyer wanted to achieve this in a way that was respectful of the land, of the needs of the animals, and of the health of his customers.

Meyer decided to locate his ranch in the Blackfoot Valley of western Montana, around Helmville. His first purchase, made in 1990, was the 6,000-acre Wales Ranch, where purebred Percherons (French draft workhorses) had been raised. Next Meyer bought the Company Ranch, which in its prime had been a sheep operation. After buying many additional land parcels in the vicinity, Meyer emerged with a large, contiguous spread known as the Meyer Company Ranch.

In 1996 Meyer founded Meyer Natural Angus L.L.C. Over the next 15 years, MNA contracted with more than 250 Angus cattle ranchers around the country who agreed to follow the protocols of the Meyer Company Ranch. To ensure that standards were maintained, MNA regularly audited these ranches and the Meyer Company Ranch as well, even though MNA and the Meyer Company Ranch were both owned by Meyer. In 2000 MNA became a subsidiary of Meyer Foods, also owned by Meyer.

MEYER NATURAL ANGUS PROTOCOLS: QUALITY AND SAFETY

By 2000 MNA protocols had been shaped and formalized. They were based on several principles. Producing superior-tasting beef was the fundamental goal, for without that there would be no market for MNA beef. To that end MNA selected Angus cattle, known for beef with substantial marbling (all cuts were choice and above), juiciness, tenderness, flavor, and consistent portion sizing. The Red Angus was selected over the Black Angus because of its greater adaptability to cold and heat and because it does not have a white udder, which can sunburn, or white eyes, which can become cancerous.

To protect the quality, healthfulness, and safety of MNA beef, the company took measures to ensure that all cattle were fully traceable. Affidavits tracked the movement of cattle from their original seller to other owners, shippers, feeders, and truckers. In addition, all MNA producers had to certify that their cattle were born, raised, and fed in the United States. The genetic integrity of MNA herds was perpetuated through a breeding program using embryo transplants and artificial insemination.

"Natural beef" was defined as beef from cattle raised without antibiotics and growth hormones. Some experts believed that beef with high antibiotic content could create a resistance to antibiotics in the humans who ate the beef (although others asserted that evidence for this problem was lacking). Cattle that required antibiotics for their health were removed from the herd and sold in the commercial beef market. MNA beef was not organic, however, as some sprays were used to

forestall invasion of weeds. All MNA beef was tested for E. coli before it was shipped out for distribution.

ENVIRONMENTAL CONCERNS AND HUMANE TREATMENT

Participating ranchers were required to operate in an environmentally sound way. Riparian areas were restored with bank stabilization and fencing. Cattle were grazed at a level below the land's carrying capacity. Also helping to preserve the land was an elaborate and rapid system of pasture rotation.

Humane treatment of the cattle was another element of the protocols. Contrasting with the great majority of ranches, cattle on ranches following MNA procedures were worked and moved by ranch hands on horses rather than on four wheelers or motorcycles. This practice was easier on both the animals and the land. (It also reflected Meyer's nostalgia for doing things the old way.)

Electric cattle prods were never used. The cattle were provided with shade and sprinklers in the summer. They were also given sufficient space to accommodate their natural movements as well as clean and ample water. The animals received a healthful, strictly vegetarian grass-and-grain diet.

DEVELOPING THE MEYER BRAND

The Meyer protocols reflected the concerns of a growing number of consumers who were very demanding with the healthfulness and taste of their food and who cared about the well-being of the environment and the welfare of animals. This segment of the population accounted for the double-digit annual increase in natural beef sales during the 1990s. These consumers were from the middle class and up and could afford to pay the 25 percent extra that the natural beef cost. MNA saw the branding of its beef products (that is, the establishment of points of difference between its beef and the beef of its competitors) as the key to sales growth. The protocols branded MNA beef in ways that would appeal to these consumers.

That branding was enhanced by the certifications and awards MNA won in the first years of the 21st century. In 2000 the American Humane Association (AHA) introduced a new food label called Free Farmed to certify the compassionate treatment of animals. The requirements for certification would be enforced by inspection performed by the AHA's Farm Animal Services division, with the U.S. Department of Agriculture auditing the results. MNA was among the first three food companies to win this certification.

```
┌─────────────────────────────────────────┐
│                                           │
│              KEY DATES                    │
│                 ■                         │
│                                           │
│  1990:  Robert Meyer begins purchasing    │
│         land around Helmville, Colorado,  │
│         to establish the Meyer Company    │
│         Ranch.                            │
│  1996:  Meyer Natural Angus (MNA) is      │
│         founded.                          │
│  2001:  The T.G.I. Friday's restaurant    │
│         chain announces that it will      │
│         serve hamburgers made from MNA    │
│         beef.                             │
│  2007:  Sales of MNA beef double.         │
│  2008:  MNA purchases Laura's Lean Beef   │
│         Company and the natural and       │
│         organic beef division of          │
│         Coleman's Natural Foods.          │
│                                           │
└─────────────────────────────────────────┘
```

In 2003 Humane Farm Animal Care, a nonprofit organization financed by the American Society for the Prevention of Cruelty to Animals, introduced a certification program that awarded a Certified Humane Raised and Handled label to qualifying companies. MNA was among the first to earn this label. MNA also won a gold medal from the American Tasting Institute (2001) and a GridMaster award from the Red Angus Association of America (2003). The GridMaster is awarded to cattle producers and feeders who reach the organization's strict carcass quality specifications.

MARKETING IN THE NEW MILLENNIUM

In addition to branding, MNA employed various marketing devices, from the retail level upward, to appeal to customers. MNA worked with supermarkets and groceries to draw attention to its beef, offering marketing materials to retailers and helping them in advancing MNA's promotional objectives. MNA encouraged product demonstrations, the use of coupons, and giveaways. Store employees were given buttons that read "Ask me about Meyer Natural Angus Beef." During summer weekends, representatives of national retailers, restaurants, and food service organizations were invited to stay at the Meyer Company Ranch's two-story guesthouse to see how the cattle were raised.

At the other end of the marketing spectrum, MNA worked with the U.S. Meat Export Federation (USMEF) to promote sales around the world, in such countries as China, Thailand, and the Caribbean. In the spring of 2007, for example, at a Hong Kong fair, USMEF set up a booth that included MNA beef. In June 2009 USMEF brought eight Caribbean retailers to MNA's headquarters in Loveland, Colorado. The retail-

ers were taught how muscle seaming and cutting methods could help maximize yield and quality.

MNA also added customers by introducing convenience items, such as frozen hamburgers in 2003 and frozen steaks in 2005. The firm did not rule out the possibility of producing prepared food in the future. To widen customer choice, MNA offered dry-aged premium steaks. Dry aging is a process that takes several months, during which the meat's natural enzymes dissolve tough connective tissues. The result was more tender beef with a richer, earthier flavor that some steak lovers preferred.

EXPANSION

With MNA's reputation as a natural beef producer growing in the new century and the demand for natural beef increasing, the company's sales of ground beef, bulk and preformed patties, frozen steaks and cuts, and dry-aged steaks rose rapidly after 2000. Originally found in specialty stores, the products began to appear in mainstream restaurants, supermarkets, and groceries. In 2001 T.G.I. Friday's, a nationwide casual restaurant chain that serves standard American cuisine, announced that it would begin selling hamburgers made from MNA beef. Growing during the decade to more than 1,000 restaurants in 50 countries, T.G.I. Friday's was the largest chain to that time to feature MNA beef. In 2002 it was selling almost one million of the hamburgers per month.

The next year the Chipotle Mexican Grill chain, a string of hundreds of restaurants in the United States and Canada, specializing in burritos and tacos and owned by McDonald's, began using MNA beef. By the end of 2003 some of MNA's other customers included Whole Food Markets in the Northeast, Florida, Texas, and Chicago. Andronico Markets, Dreager's Markets, Mollie Stone's, and PW Markets introduced MNA beef in northern California. Shaw, Wegman's, and Roche Brothers in the Northeast also began selling MNA beef.

One of the fastest-growing suppliers of natural beef, in 2003 MNA realized a sales growth of 40 percent over the preceding year. A case of bovine spongiform encephalopathy (BSE), commonly called mad cow disease, in Washington State in December 2003 and another case in 2005 boosted the sales of MNA's natural beef by more than 25 percent. BSE, for example, convinced Heinen Fine Foods (an Ohio-based owner of 15 stores) to change to MNA, first because its cattle were fully traceable and second because MNA's beef was certified under the Humane Farm Animal Care program. In 2007 MNA's sales doubled.

In 2008 MNA made acquisitions that more than doubled its size. First it purchased Laura's Lean Beef

Company, a major natural beef producer. Later in the year it bought out the natural and organic beef division of Coleman's Natural Foods, one of the largest natural beef producers in the United States. With these purchases MNA now controlled more than half the U.S. natural beef market.

In all of 2001 MNA had slaughtered approximately 18,000 head of cattle. By 2010 it was slaughtering 10,000 cattle per month. Nonetheless, this figure was dwarfed by the 40,000 cattle killed each day by large commercial beef producers. In 2009 MNA doubled its office space at the company's Loveland headquarters in preparation for the introduction of online ordering by retail customers.

Michael Levine

PRINCIPAL COMPETITORS

Dakota Beef L.L.C.; Maverick Ranch Association, Inc.; Niman Ranch, Inc.

FURTHER READING

Briggeman, Kim, "Cows, Naturally," *Missoulian*, April 13, 2008, p. A1.

Fabricant, Florence, "Judging Beef by Its Grade, Cut, and Eating Habits," *New York Times*, May 21, 1997, p. C1.

Fulmer, Melinda, "New Food Label to Certify Humane Treatment of Animals," *Los Angeles Times*, September 20, 2000, p. 1.

"Natural Foods: More Consumers Are Demanding Natural Beef and Other Meat Products," *Grocery Headquarters*, September 1, 2004, p. S74.

Peck, Clint, "Natural Strategy," *BEEF*, April 1, 2004, p. 36.

Raabe, Steve, "Natural Beef Firms Soon to Reveal Deal; Loveland-Based Meyer Natural Angus Is Expected to Acquire the Coleman Beef Brand, out of Golden," *Denver Post*, April 4, 2008, p. B-09.

"Skip the Tube Socks, Give the Gift of Prime Natural Beef," *PR Newswire*, October 26, 2009.

"Winn Meat Company Debuts Meyer Natural Angus Beef on Premier Product Line-up," *PR Newswire*, June 9, 2008.

Minnesota Twins

—————■—————

34 Kirby Puckett Place
Minneapolis, Minnesota 55415
U.S.A.
Telephone: (615) 375-1366
Fax: (612) 375-7473
Web site: http://minnesota.twins.mlb.com

Private Company
Founded: 1901
Employees: 900
NAICS: 711211 Sports Teams and Clubs

■ ■ ■

The Minnesota Twins is an American League franchise of Major League Baseball playing in the Minneapolis–St. Paul, Minnesota, market. Formerly the Washington Senators, the Twins have played in the Twin Cities since the 1961 season, winning two World Series, the last in 1991. Since then, the economics of baseball have made it increasingly difficult for small-market teams like the Twins, which lack lucrative local television contracts and other ancillary income, to compete against the New York Yankees, Boston Red Sox, and other large market clubs. Nevertheless, the Twins have developed a formula for success, relying mostly on an excellent player development program. The Twins take advantage of baseball's free agency system that allows clubs to keep player salaries at relatively modest levels for several years. As players near free agency, when their salaries can escalate dramatically, the Twins trade their star players for young prospects, feeding on the minor league "farm system" that replenishes the ranks of the major league team. After a quarter-century playing in the Hubert H. Humphrey Metrocenter, a dank indoor stadium, the Twins moved in 2010 into a new outdoor stadium, providing the team with new revenue sources and allowing the franchise to become even more competitive in the Central Division of the American League. The Twins have been owned by the Pohlad family since 1984.

BIRTH OF THE FRANCHISE AND AMERICAN LEAGUE: 1901

The origins of the Minnesota Twins date to 1901, when the upstart American League of professional baseball established a team in Washington, D.C. In business since 1876, the well-established National League had already outlived rivals, most notably the American Association, which went out of business in 1891. The National League, because of its strength in New York and other major cities, had the ability to dictate the outlines of "Organized Baseball," essentially declaring itself the "major" league and all others to be subservient "minor" leagues, whose players could be taken ("drafted") at the pleasure of a major league team, which also determined the proper price of the transaction. To not abide by the rules of organized baseball, called the National Agreement, meant a league and all of its players would be branded as outlaws and forbidden from playing in organized baseball. Virtually all of the professional leagues gave in to the demands of the National League.

The significant exception was a former newspaperman named Byron Bancroft "Ban" Johnson who ran the

Professional baseball in Minnesota dates back to 1884 with various teams and leagues. However since 1961, the baseball spotlight in Minnesota has focused mainly on the major league game. ... Minnesota Twins.

Western League, which had teams throughout the Midwest, including Minneapolis. In 1900 the National League contracted from 12 teams to 8, eliminating franchises in Baltimore, Cleveland, Louisville, and Washington. Sensing an opportunity, Johnson rechristened the Western League as the American League and began to move some of his franchises to eastern cities. A year later Johnson declared the American League to be a major league on an equal footing with the National League, resulting in an intense bidding war for players and eventually a truce that led to the champions of the two leagues playing in the World Series and the present-day configuration of Major League Baseball.

As part of Johnson's bid to challenge the National League, he established a team in Washington, D.C., in 1901. Originally called the Nationals (although informally called the Senators, as the National League had previously named the team), the club was essentially the Kansas City team of the Western League, whose players and owner-manager, Jimmy Manning, relocated to Washington. It was supposedly owned by the club's president, Detroit hotelier Fred Postal, but while Manning and Postal may have held interests, in reality Johnson was the owner of the Senators. In 1904 he sold the team to a syndicate of local investors, led by newspaperman Thomas C. Noyes, owner of the *Washington Evening Star*.

CLARK GRIFFITH GAINS CONTROL: 1919

The Senators enjoyed little success on the field during its early years, although at the start of the 1910 season they established a long-standing baseball tradition of having a sitting president throw the first pitch, persuading President William Howard Taft to launch the first ball of the season. Catching the president's toss that day was a young pitcher named Walter Johnson, who would play a key role in the team's improved performance and one day, eventually considered one of the game's greatest pitchers, would become a member of baseball's Hall of

Fame. A year later a new manager, himself a former pitching star, Clark Calvin Griffith, took the reins and transformed the lowly Senators into a winning club for the next 20 years. He rarely challenged for the league championship, primarily due to the team's lack of money to acquire top-notch players. Griffith had mortgaged his Montana ranch to buy a 10 percent stake in the team and gain a seat on the board of directors. In 1919 he urged the board to spend more money on players, and when he was turned down, he decided to buy out his fellow owners with the backing of Philadelphia grain merchant William Richardson. Griffith took out a bank loan and mortgaged personal property to raise $100,000 of the $290,000 needed to acquire an 80 percent stake in the club. Richardson gave an equal share to Griffith, who as club president, now had control of the franchise. His financial situation, however, was no less precarious.

Griffith resigned as manager in 1921 and had difficulty in finding the right man to lead the Senators on the field. Finally in 1924 he made a surprise choice for a manager, 27-year-old second baseman Bucky Harris, a decision that proved to be inspired. In 1924 Harris led the Senators to their only World Series championship, defeating the New York Giants in the 12th inning of the 7th game. A year later the Senators again won the American League pennant, although this time the team lost in seven games to the Pittsburgh Pirates. With Walter Johnson as manager, the Senators won another pennant in 1933, before mediocrity became the norm for the team, leading to the well-worn adage about the Washington Senators: "First in War, First in Peace, and Last in the American League."

In 1949 Richardson's estate sold its stake in the Senators. Although Griffith no longer held a controlling interest, the minority shareholders elected him president in 1950, a post he held until his death in 1955. Now assuming control was his adoptive son, Calvin Griffith (actually his nephew, whom Clark Griffith had raised since the death of his wife's brother). By the time Calvin Griffith took charge, baseball was undergoing some sea changes. What had once been limited to markets east of the Mississippi River due to travel constrictions, baseball was taking advantage of air travel to expand the game geographically, as clubs began eying prosperous new markets. The Boston Braves, long overshadowed by the Red Sox, was the first team to make the jump, relocating in 1953 to Milwaukee, where they enjoyed record attendance and excellent results on the field. The Braves were followed by the St. Louis Browns, which moved to Baltimore, and the Philadelphia A's, which made a stop in Kansas City before eventually relocating a second time to Oakland, California. The Brooklyn Dodgers and New York Giants

```
┌─────────────────────────────────────────────────┐
│                                                   │
│               KEY DATES                           │
│                     ▪                             │
│  ─────────────────────────────────────────────   │
│                                                   │
│  1901:  The American League baseball franchise is │
│         established in Washington, D.C.           │
│  1919:  Clark Griffith gains control of the       │
│         Washington Senators.                      │
│  1924:  The Senators win the World Series.        │
│  1955:  Calvin Griffith succeeds his father as club│
│         president.                                │
│  1961:  The Senators move to Minnesota and are    │
│         renamed the Twins.                        │
│  1982:  The Twins begin play in the Metrodome.    │
│  1984:  Carl Pohlad acquires the Twins.           │
│  1987:  The Twins win the World Series.           │
│  1991:  The Twins win the World Series.           │
│  2007:  Ground is broken on a new baseball park.  │
│  2009:  Carl Pohlad dies.                         │
│  2010:  The Twins begin play in their new stadium,│
│         Target Field.                             │
│                                                   │
└─────────────────────────────────────────────────┘
```

would also find new homes in California, in Los Angeles and San Francisco, respectively. By 1958 Calvin Griffith was making plans to move the Senators to Minneapolis.

SENATORS AGREE TO MOVE TO MINNESOTA: 1960

Because the Senators were located in Washington, D.C., Griffith encountered more resistance than other club owners. Not only did Congress oppose the move, so did President Dwight D. Eisenhower. Major League Baseball was reluctant to upset the federal government, especially in light of the special status bestowed upon it by Congress that made it exempt from antitrust legislation. Team owners, however, were well aware that even during good seasons, the Senators did not draw well, and eventually an accommodation was reached in October 1960: Griffith would be allowed to move the Senators to Minneapolis, and Washington would receive one of the new franchises as Major League Baseball began to expand beyond the eight teams that had been the norm in each of the two leagues for the past 60 years.

Minneapolis and St. Paul had been home to popular minor league teams—the Millers in the former and the Saints in the latter. In 1956 the Millers moved into a new ballpark in suburban Minneapolis called Metropolitan Stadium. It became the home for the transplanted Senators, which now supplanted the Millers and the Saints and adopted the name of the Minnesota Twins. The community embraced the team, which pos-

sessed some emerging talent, including home-run hitter Harmon Killebrew. More stars were to follow, and in 1965 the Twins found themselves in the World Series, where they ultimately lost to the Los Angeles Dodgers in seven games. The Twins did not play in another World Series in the 1960s or 1970s. Although the team won a pair of division championships, its failure to win consistently began to take a toll on attendance.

CARL POHLAD BUYS TWINS: 1984

In 1982 the Twins moved into a new downtown home (along with the National Football League's Vikings), the Hubert H. Humphrey Metrodome, which became baseball's third domed stadium. Attendance did not show much improvement, however, and Calvin Griffith decided the time had come to sell his majority interest in the franchise and take advantage of an escape clause in the stadium lease that allowed him to cancel it if the Twins failed to attract 4.2 million fans over a three-year period. In 1984 the team would have to draw 2.4 million to reach the threshold number binding Griffith to another three-year term. Griffith lined up an interested buyer who wanted to move the franchise to Tampa, Florida, and who had already bought out a minority partner to gain a sizable stake in the club. A group of Minnesota investors were interested in retaining the team but did not wish to enter into a bidding war with the Tampa group. In order to outmaneuver Griffith, the local group raised money to purchase large quantities of tickets to boost attendance. Fearful that he would be trapped for another three money-losing years in the Metrodome, Griffith agreed to sell the twins to Minnesota financier Carl Pohlad, who then had little trouble buying out the minority shareholders in Tampa. Pohlad paid $44 million for the Twins in 1984.

Pohlad inherited a team with an emerging core of talented players that would soon be augmented by a future hall-of-fame center fielder, Kirby Puckett. Attendance matched the team's rising fortunes, and in 1987 the franchise was rewarded with the second World Series championship in franchise history when the Twins defeated the St. Louis Cardinals. A year later the team became the first American League club to draw 3 million fans in a season, but as quickly as the Twins reached the top, they fell off, finishing last in 1990. Just one year later, however, they vaulted back to first place, and again gained a World Series berth facing the Atlanta Braves team that had itself finished at the bottom of its division the previous year. Trailing in the Series three games to two, the Twins rallied to win their second World Series title in five years.

After a second place finish in the American League's West Division in 1992, the Twins again suffered through lean times. The economic realties of baseball were changing, making it increasingly difficult for teams operating in smaller markets like Minneapolis–St. Paul to compete against well-heeled clubs in New York, Los Angeles, Chicago, and Boston. The Twins' situation was exacerbated by a stadium agreement that offered no share of parking, concessions, or stadium advertising revenues. Pohlad claimed the team lost $10 million to $12 million each year, and he began urging the state to help finance a new outdoor stadium that could provide the Twins with the extra income necessary to compete with the larger clubs. Although he said he had no desire to sell the Twins, Pohlad used an offer from a North Carolina investor group eager to move the Twins to Charlotte to help spur action from lawmakers. In 1997 he even offered to give the state 49 percent of the Twins and contribute $82.5 million in cash if Minnesota would finance a new ballpark.

BID FOR ST. PAUL STADIUM FAILS: 1997

In 1997 the Minnesota General Assembly failed to pass a bill to sell revenue bonds to finance a new ballpark. While other efforts continued, Pohlad made a pact with Glen Taylor, owner of the Minnesota Timberwolves of the National Basketball Association, and Robert Naegle Jr., owner of the Minnesota Wild of the National Hockey League, to sell them the Twins for $120 million. The deal was contingent on St. Paul and the state providing two-thirds of the funds necessary to build a new ballpark in St. Paul. A referendum was put to St. Paul residents for a half-cent sales tax increase to fund the city's share of the project in November 1999, but the measure was defeated and the deal to sell the Twins to Taylor and Naegle never came to fruition.

In 2001 Major League Baseball considered shrinking the leagues, eliminating two teams. Word leaked through labor negotiations between baseball players and team owners that the Montreal Expos and the Twins were the teams slated to be bought out and dissolved. The possibility caused an uproar in Minnesota, and the contraction plan was stymied by a Minnesota judge who issued an injunction that forced the Twins to fulfill its lease at the Metrodome in 2002. To Twins' fans, Pohlad had committed the unforgivable sin. Even though the deal had never come close to being consummated, his mere consideration of dissolving the Twins was deemed the ultimate act of betrayal. Pohlad, in his own defense, claimed that no one in the community had supported the Twins as he had, covering losses of $150 million in the previous decade.

Momentum for a new stadium increased as Pohlad also looked for ways to increase revenues. Following in the footsteps of the New York Yankees, which had successfully established its own cable TV sports channel, the Twins launched Victory Sports One in 2004. The Twins lacked the market influence of the Yankees, however, and were unable to persuade the four major cable operators in their market as well as satellite companies DirecTV and Echostar to pay the $2.12 per subscriber Victory demanded. Even a drop in price failed to win over carriers, and after six weeks the Twins admitted defeat, sold the local cable rights to the games to Fox Sports Net North, and folded Victory.

While the Twins struggled off the field to engineer a stadium deal or improve its finances, it was finding a good deal of success on the field. The Twins became the model small market franchise in the way it developed talent and eschewed bidding wars over free agents. The team won the American League Central Division three consecutive years, from 2001 to 2003, and won it again in 2005. They were not, however, able to win their way into the World Series. In the meantime, progress was being made in the political arena. In 2006 the Hennepin County Broad voted for a $500 million ballpark to be funded through an increase in the state's sales tax within the county.

CARL POHLAD DIES: 2009

Ground was broken on the new ballpark in 2007, but Carl Pohlad would not live to see the finished structure. He died in early 2009 at the age of 93. Succeeding him as "control executive" as stipulated by Major League Baseball was his son. Jim Pohlad had been preparing for the position since the late 1990s, when he began participating in Twins' management sessions as well as baseball ownership meetings. He took over a team that once again overachieved, mounting a comeback late in the 2009 season to secure another Central Division championship before being eliminated in the first round of the playoffs by the New York Yankees. Late in 2009 the Twins' new ballpark, christened Target Field, was completed ahead of schedule and ready for the next season. The terms of the stadium lease made it difficult for the Pohlad family to sell the team, but Jim Pohlad indicated that he, his sons, and his nephews planned to run the team well into the future. With the prospect of increased attendance at the new park and additional revenue streams, the Twins appeared poised to enjoy an extended run of success.

Ed Dinger

PRINCIPAL SUBSIDIARIES

Rochester Community Baseball, Inc.; New Britain Baseball Club, Inc.

PRINCIPAL COMPETITORS

Chicago White Sox Ltd.; Cleveland Indians Baseball Company, Inc.; Detroit Tigers, Inc.

FURTHER READING

Baar, Aaron, "Minnesota Twins Propose Novel Deal for New Stadium," *Bond Buyer*, January 10, 1997, p. 1.

Catanoso, Justin, "Bottom of the Ninth; The Twins Could Be the First MLB Team to Move in 25 Years," *Business Week*, November 3, 1997, p. 48.

Deveaux, Tom, *The Washington Senators, 1901–1971.* Jefferson, NC: McFarland & Company, 2001.

Fatsis, Stefan, "Minnesota Twins Offer 49% Interest to State in Return for a New Stadium," *Wall Street Journal*, January 9, 1997, p. B5.

Kahn, Aron, "Future of Ballpark Plan Weighs on Minds of Potential Minnesota-Twins Owners," *Saint Paul Pioneer Press*, November 5, 2001.

———, "Minnesota Twins Are Safe for a Season," *Saint Paul Pioneer Press*, February 5, 2002.

Mackay, Harvey, "'I'd Like 15,000 Tickets for Tonight's Game, Please,'" *Sales & Marketing Management*, May 1988, p. 24.

Miller, Phil, "Twins' Leader Already in Place," *Saint Paul Pioneer Press*, January 7, 2009, p. D1.

Pietrusza, David, Matthew Silverman, and Michael Gershman, *Baseball: The Biographical Encyclopedia.* New York, NY: Total Sports Illustrated, 2000.

Riess, Steven A., *Encyclopedia of Major League Baseball Clubs.* Westport, CN: Greenwood Press, 2006.

St. Anthony, Neal, "Carl Pohlad 1915–2009," *Star Tribune*, January 6, 2009, p. 1A.

Thorn, John, and Pete Palmer, *Total Baseball.* New York, NY: Warner Books, 1989.

Mount Sinai Medical Center

5 East 98th Street
New York, New York 10029
U.S.A.
Telephone: (212) 241-6500
Toll Free: (866) 674-3721
Web site: http://www.mountsinai.org

Private Company
Founded: 1852 (Hospital); 1949 (Medical Center)
Employees: 3,500
Sales: $5.62 billion (2008 est.)
NAICS: 622110 General Medical and Surgical Hospitals; 611310 Colleges, Universities, and Professional Schools

■ ■ ■

Mount Sinai Medical Center, founded in 1949, is based in New York and oversees Mount Sinai Hospital and Mount Sinai School of Medicine. Mount Sinai Hospital is one of the oldest and largest voluntary teaching hospitals in the United States, internationally acclaimed for excellence in patient care, physician education, and medical research. The hospital is a regional center for rehabilitation of spinal cord and brain injury. Its programs in geriatrics, hemophilia, and HIV/AIDS are recognized regionally and nationally. The hospital is also home to the world's only center dedicated to the diagnosis and treatment of genetically acquired diseases that predominantly affect individuals in the Jewish population.

FOUNDING OF MOUNT SINAI

Mount Sinai was founded by nine men from the Jewish community on January 15, 1852, to establish a hospital to care for indigent Jews in New York. In the mid-19th century religious communities were expected to provide care for their members. Construction of the hospital, originally known as Jews' Hospital, began in the fall of 1853, and the doors opened to patients on June 5, 1855. The hospital served a variety of people and prided itself on never turning away an emergency case regardless of a patient's religious background.

Jews' Hospital could accommodate 45 patients and was located on West 28th Street between 7th Avenue and 8th Avenue. During the Civil War the building was enlarged to accommodate Union Army soldiers, and in 1864 one of the hospital's surgeons, Willard Parker, performed the first appendectomy in the United States. In 1866, in recognition of the hospital's increasing number of non-Jewish patients, its name was changed to Mount Sinai Hospital.

A SECOND HOME

Mount Sinai left its original building in 1872 and moved to a new, larger location on Lexington Avenue between 66th and 67th streets, where its capacity increased to 120 beds. The hospital complex consisted of a four-story brick building with two wings. An outpatient clinic and nurses' dormitory were added in 1875, and a training school for nurses was established in 1881. Its graduates became the hospital's first professional nurses, replacing the male and female attendants who had previously provided nursing care.

Mount Sinai Hospital was supported by individual dues that ranged from $5 to $100 per year, which in the 1890s raised approximately $65,000 a year. Families could also donate $2,500 toward a "perpetual bed" that would memorialize a loved one. The hospital also raised funds through the Mount Sinai Alliance, the Ladies' Auxiliary Society, and local organizations such as the Purim Association and the Saturday and Sunday Association.

The hospital cared for approximately 3,000 patients annually at an estimated cost of $1.25 each per day. Its outpatient dispensary treated approximately 33,700 people a year and an Outdoor Relief and District Service department delivered free care to an additional 170 people a year. Mount Sinai was founded as a charitable institution and provided care to those least able to pay. At the turn of the 20th century, 86 percent of patients received services for free. The rest paid according to their ability, usually less than the cost of their care.

A MEDICAL RESEARCH CENTER

During the late 19th century Mount Sinai became a center of medical research. It established its first laboratory in 1893 in response to the changing nature of patient care and the need for bacteriology to support physicians' bedside observations. Care also changed in other ways. Specialty wards, including surgery, pediatrics, neurology, and dermatology, began serving patients.

Well-known researchers at Mount Sinai included neurologist Bernard Sachs, who described the first American case of Tay-Sachs disease in 1887. In 1888

Arpad Gerster, a Hungarian-born Mount Sinai surgeon, published *Rules of Aseptic and Antiseptic Surgery*, the first American textbook on the importance of avoiding contamination and germs during surgery. According to an 1897 article in the *New York Times*, "After nearly a half century's existence, the hospital has attained among the hospitals of this city a position of the highest respect, and its fame as a broad-minded and well-managed institution is not confined to its country's boundaries."

A THIRD HOME AND INCREASED SPECIALIZATION

In March of 1904 Mount Sinai relocated to its present location between Fifth Avenue and Madison Avenue and 100th and 101th streets. Major buildings included the Children's Pavilion, the Private Pavilion, and the Pathological Building. The emerging concerns of medicine were evident in the hospital's design, which stressed light, ventilation, disinfection, and isolation.

In addition to the hospital's 456 beds, new specialty departments and clinics emerged to reflect a growing perspective on health and patient care. A nutrition and dietetics department was added in 1905, a social-work department in 1906, physical therapy in 1911, and gastroenterology in 1913. Burrill B. Crohn, a physician in the gastroenterology department, identified the disease that bears his name in 1932. In 1933 the hospital's social-service department began an occupational therapy program to rehabilitate and support the efforts of people unemployed during the Depression.

MOUNT SINAI MEDICAL CENTER AND SCHOOL OF MEDICINE ESTABLISHED

Mount Sinai Medical Center, a for-profit private company, was established in 1949, in part to oversee the operation of Mount Sinai Hospital. The Mount Sinai School of Medicine was established in 1963, providing the hospital with well-qualified doctors for its training programs and house staff. The medical school also gave a new home to Mount Sinai's medical research department, which continued to gain recognition. The medical school went on to establish an academic affiliation with the City University of New York and became known as the Mount Sinai School of Medicine of the City University of New York.

Mount Sinai was reorganized during the 1980s. The 1990s saw the creation of the Mount Sinai Health System, an affiliated network of hospitals, nursing homes, and medical practices serving the New York,

KEY DATES

1852:	Jews' Hospital is founded in New York.
1866:	Hospital name is changed to Mount Sinai Hospital.
1881:	Mount Sinai Training School for Nurses is established.
1949:	Mount Sinai Medical Center is founded.
1963:	Mount Sinai School of Medicine is founded.

Connecticut, and New Jersey tristate area that offered patients increased access to specialty services and referrals to member institutions.

Mount Sinai began an extended fund-raising drive in the late 1980s to replace outdated buildings and facilities, and in 1992 the hospital dedicated the Guggenheim Pavilion, which replaced 11 outdated buildings. The pavilion featured a new emergency room, 625 patient beds, and areas dedicated specifically to organ transplants, orthopedic surgery, and neurosurgery. Designed by famed architect I. M. Pei and partially financed by a donation from the Guggenheim family of New York, the pavilion's design echoed the original building's emphasis on the importance of light and air in a healing environment.

MERGERS AND FINANCIAL CRISIS

In 1998 the structure of Mount Sinai underwent a fundamental change with the creation of the Mount Sinai–New York University (NYU) Medical Center and Health System. The merger linked four New York City hospitals: Mount Sinai, the NYU Medical Center, the Hospital for Joint Diseases' Orthopaedic Institute, and the NYU Downtown Hospital. In the aftermath of the merger, the Mount Sinai School of Medicine changed its academic affiliation from the City University of New York to NYU. It did not, however, merge its medical school with the NYU School of Medicine.

In 1999 Mount Sinai purchased the Western Queens Community Hospital, formerly known as Astoria General, renaming it Mount Sinai Hospital of Queens. The newly acquired hospital helped Mount Sinai continue to fulfill its mission of serving the community at large.

Mount Sinai began to dismantle its merger with NYU in 2001. As the merger dissolved, Mount Sinai experienced a serious financial crisis. The hospital board brought in the Hunter Group, an outside consulting firm, which provided a road map for change under newly appointed hospital president and Mount Sinai surgeon Larry Hollier. The financial crisis receded, and Mount Sinai, which previously had prided itself on its sound financial structure, managed to right itself.

In July 2009 *U.S. News & World Report* named Mount Sinai Medical Center to its list of the best hospitals in the United States. The report ranked it 19th overall and 3rd in the nation in geriatrics. By the beginning of 2010, Mount Sinai Hospital offered 1,171 beds and utilized the services of 2,181 attending physicians, 689 residents and fellows, and 1,800 nurses to treat more than 47,000 inpatients and 427, 000 outpatients annually. Its services expanded to encompass more than 300 specialty clinics, programs, and departments, including occupational health, palliative care, and surgical weight loss.

In 2010 the Mount Sinai Health System included 17 affiliated hospitals, 7 affiliated nursing homes and long-term care facilities, and 3 affiliated physician practices in the tristate area. The Mount Sinai School of Medicine offered postgraduate and other training programs as well as master's and doctoral degree programs in a variety of scientific and medical disciplines. The National Institutes of Health ranked the Mount Sinai School of Medicine among the top 20 medical schools in the United States.

Joyce Helena Brusin

PRINCIPAL DIVISIONS

Mount Sinai Hospital; Mount Sinai School of Medicine.

PRINCIPAL COMPETITORS

New York-Presbyterian Hospital; University Hospitals of Columbia and Cornell; New York University Medical Center; Memorial Sloan-Kettering Cancer Center; Rockefeller University Hospital; St. Luke's-Roosevelt Hospital Center.

FURTHER READING

Aufses, Arthur H., Jr., and Barbara Niss, *This House of Noble Deeds: The Mount Sinai Hospital, 1852–2002.* New York: NYU Press, 2002.

Finkelstein, Katherine E., "Layoffs Feared as Consultant Examines Mount Sinai's Budget," *New York Times,* November 29, 2001.

Hirsh, Joseph, and Beka Doherty. *The First Hundred Years of the Mount Sinai Hospital of New York, 1852–1952.* New York: Random House, 1952.

"Hospital a Model of Sanitary Science," *New York Times*, March 12, 1904.

Lewis, Marjorie Gulla, and Sylvia M. Barker, *The Sinai Nurse: A History of Nursing at the Mount Sinai Hospital, 1852–2000.* New York: Mount Sinai Hospital, 2001.

Morse, Edward B., "Mount Sinai Hospital," *New York Times*, November 28, 1897.

"Mount Sinai Opens a Medical Pavilion," *New York Times*, September 24, 1992.

Page, Leigh, "It's Academic: A Physician Takes the Reins as President of Mount Sinai Hospital," *Modern Physician*, June 10, 2002.

"Practical Benevolence: Mount Sinai Training School for Nurses and Its Work," *New York Times*, June 9, 1895.

The National Rifle Association of America

11250 Waples Mill Road
Fairfax, Virginia 22030
U.S.A.
Telephone: (703) 267-1200
Toll Free: (800) 672-3888
Fax: (703) 267-3989
Web site: http://www.nra.org

Nonprofit Organization
Incorporated: 1871
Employees: 500
NAICS: 813940 Political Organizations; 813319 Firearms Advocacy Organizations

■ ■ ■

The National Rifle Association of America (NRA), is a nonprofit organization that works to promote and protect the right to bear arms as outlined in the Second Amendment of the U.S. Constitution. Long respected by some and feared by others on Capitol Hill, the association has grown to become one of the most powerful political lobbying groups in the country, committing enormous financial resources to electoral campaigns and other legislative efforts. With more than four million members, the NRA reaches young men and women through a range of educational programs, including a program for young hunters. At the same time, thousands of marksmen compete nationally in the association's annual shooting competitions.

ORIGINS: 1871

The NRA traces its origins to the 1870s, when two former Union army officers, Colonel William Conant Church and General George Wood Wingate, formed the NRA to foster marksmanship. The association was chartered in the state of New York on November 17, 1871. Another well-known Civil War veteran, General Ambrose Burnside, served as the group's first president. Burnside had been a U.S. senator and governor of Rhode Island. Although he lobbied very effectively for funding, he was not otherwise actively involved in the fledgling group and resigned within a year.

Through the founders' efforts, the state of New York granted the NRA $25,000 to create a practice ground on a 100-acre lot on Long Island. The Creedmoor range opened there in 1873 and hosted the Irish Rifle Association in a two-entrant international shooting competition held the next year. The event drew 8,000 spectators. Even in those early days, however, the NRA faced antigun sentiment in the cities, and in 1892 the land grant was rescinded and the range was moved to Sea Girt, New Jersey.

New York Governor Alonzo Cornell, predicting a long age of peace, had cut the NRA's funding in 1880. Nevertheless, technological innovations and events overseas soon made weapons training relevant again. Dutch South African farmers demonstrated the effectiveness of new, highly accurate rifles in the Boer War, which led to a renewed interest in marksmanship and military preparedness in the British Empire and in the United States.

A revitalized NRA began setting up programs at colleges and military schools in 1903. Within three years there were more than 200 young men competing at the shooting contest in New Jersey.

NRA headquarters moved to Washington, D.C., in 1907. According to Osha Gray Davidson's book, *Under Fire*, the NRA persuaded Congress and the War Department to first sell, then give away, surplus rifles and ammunition to NRA-sponsored shooting clubs. Between World War I and World War II, 200,000 rifles were reportedly distributed at cost to NRA members, whose ranks were ballooning. The NRA also received federal money and army assistance for its shooting competitions during this time.

FORMATION OF LEGISLATIVE AFFAIRS DIVISION: 1934

The association's Legislative Affairs Division was created in 1934 to disseminate information to its members regarding pending gun control legislation. Among the vehicles of communication was the group's flagship publication, the *American Rifleman*, published sporadically at first and later gaining a large and regular readership. A huge NRA letter-writing campaign helped temper one wave of gun control sentiment so that the National Firearms Act of 1934 would extend only to regulating machine guns and sawed-off shotguns. In 1938 the NRA supported provisions to limit the sale of guns across state lines and prevent the sale of guns to fugitives and convicted felons.

At the start of World War II in 1939, the NRA collected 7,000 guns to aid Great Britain's defense. When the United States was drawn into the war in 1941, the NRA offered its facilities and encouraged its members to guard factories.

In the postwar years, the NRA focused on hunting issues, developing a pioneering hunter education program with the state of New York. The association also began a program for instructing police officers in marksmanship; it would introduce the country's only national law enforcement certification program in 1960. Membership in the NRA reached nearly 300,000 and employment 140 in the 1950s.

CONTROVERSY IN THE SIXTIES AND SEVENTIES

The assassination of President John F. Kennedy in November 1963 prompted the nation to rethink the availability of guns in the United States, which ultimately led to the Gun Control Act of 1968. This act banned the sale of guns through the mail. Kennedy's accused assassin, Lee Harvey Oswald, had ordered his rifle from the pages of *American Rifleman* for just $19.95.

A new NRA shooting range, Camp Perry, had been constructed in Ohio on the Lake Erie shore, and during this time it became home to the NRA's National Matches. The U.S. government supplied $3 million per year and the use of 5,000 troops each year for these tournaments. Opposition to such government aid to the NRA was challenged; Senator Edward Kennedy attempted to cut off the financial aid in the late 1960s and routinely fought NRA-backed bills in Congress throughout his career.

The NRA launched a new magazine, the *American Hunter*, in 1973, addressing hunting issues only. Two years later, the NRA formed the Institute for Legislative Action (ILA), designed specifically as a lobby for Second Amendment rights. The ILA was headed by Harlon B. Carter, a Texan who became controversial when his conviction in the shooting death of a Hispanic youth, which had occurred when Carter was a teenager and of which he was later cleared, came to the attention of the media in 1981. The goals of the NRA during the 1970s had become twofold. Sportsmanship and safety, embodied in the *American Hunter*, competed for attention with the role of the ILA as a gun lobby.

During this time, the NRA acquired 37,000 acres of land in the New Mexico wilderness. Controversy in the organization arose, according to Davidson's *Under Fire*, when some proposed that the New Mexico lands be designated as a shooting center, while others favored an outdoor center, dedicated to camping, wilderness survival, environmentalism, and other wide-ranging concerns, in addition to marksmanship and safety. The

KEY DATES

1871: The National Rifle Association (NRA) is chartered in New York.
1903: Shooting programs for students are set up.
1907: National headquarters moves to Washington, D.C.
1934: The Legislative Affairs Division is created to organize political action.
1968: First significant gun control legislation in 30 years is passed.
1975: Institute for Legislative Action, the NRA's lobbying unit, is created.
1994: The Brady Bill, calling for waiting periods and background checks, is passed.
1998: NRA hosts its largest convention ever and names actor Charlton Heston president.
2004: With the help of NRA lobbying, 1994 ban on assault weapons is allowed to expire.
2008: Former NRA President Charlton Heston dies.

rift in the NRA between those supporting the single issue of Second Amendment rights and those hoping to broaden the scope of the NRA culminated, according to Davidson, at the NRA national convention of 1977 in Cincinnati. Led by Carter, the so-called hard-liners took over the convention in what became known as the Cincinnati Revolt. In short, Carter and his supporters, fervently opposed to any form of gun control, wrested control of the NRA from the existing leaders (whose concerns included sportsmanship and environmentalism), turning the NRA into a single-issue gun lobby, according to Davidson. Carter was named executive vice president, the most powerful position in the organization.

REGAINING STRENGTH IN THE REAGAN YEARS: THE EIGHTIES

With newly reorganized management and purpose, the NRA entered the 1980s on more cohesive footing. Energies were focused on opposing gun control. When a few local communities, such as Morton Grove, Illinois, enacted city ordinances to ban handguns all together in 1981, the NRA fought the ban unsuccessfully in court. The group then battled similar legislation on the state level, helping defeat Proposition 15 in California, which called for a ban on the sale of new handguns. The NRA, however, was unable to overturn a new ban on handguns in Maryland in 1988.

A national print advertising campaign launched by the NRA in January 1982 gained wide attention. With the tagline "I am the NRA," a variety of individuals (including an eight-year-old boy, former astronaut Wally Schirra, former Dallas Cowboys cheerleader Jo Anne Hall, and actor/singer Roy Rogers) highlighted the group's diverse member base. While several magazines refused to run the ads, particularly the ads depicting handguns, some 45 magazines did run them, and they were credited with raising the NRA's profile considerably. The NRA had more than one million members in 1977; its ranks would reach 2.6 million by 1983, when Ronald Reagan became the first U.S. president to address the group. Reagan's speech at the annual meeting of the NRA was regarded as an important affirmation of NRA principles; the president averred that "we will never disarm any American who seeks to protect his or her family from fear or harm."

G. Ray Arnett was picked to succeed Carter in 1985. Surrounded by scandal, however, Arnett lasted only until May 1986, when ILA leader J. Warren Cassidy became the next executive vice president.

In 1986 the NRA had three million members and income of about $66 million a year. During this time, the group was sponsoring the McClure-Volkmer Act, which amended restrictions in the Gun Control Act of 1968 and was eventually passed. The group also fought to temper legislation banning Teflon-coated "cop killer" bullets. By this time, the issue of gun control in the United States had become highly fragmented and charged with emotion. The association was beginning to find itself on different sides of gun control issues with many of the country's police officials. In the late 1980s the NRA ran political ads and direct-mail campaigns against several police chiefs who favored regulating handguns.

Although many of its members were Democrats, the NRA spent an estimated $7 million to defeat Democratic candidate Michael Dukakis, a staunch supporter of gun control, in the 1988 presidential campaign. Republican George H. W. Bush broke ranks with some in the NRA while campaigning for the presidential nomination, calling for a ban on "plastic" handguns. Still, as an avid hunter, veteran, and NRA member, he appealed to the group and won its approval.

NEW CHALLENGES IN THE EARLY NINETIES

As the U.S. public became ever more aware of increases in violence involving firearms, the NRA again sought to address issues beyond gun ownership. The NRA Foundation was created in 1990 to raise tax-exempt funds for gun education. The Eddie Eagle Gun Safety Program, started two years earlier, taught elementary and middle school children to avoid guns and report them to adults. Moreover, Refuse to Be a Victim seminars, introduced in 1993, lectured women on personal safety issues. According to the NRA, three out of four women would suffer a violent crime in their lifetime.

The early 1990s were difficult years financially for the organization. According to NRA figures cited by *Fortune* magazine, the NRA lost $10 million in 1991, $38 million in 1992, and $22 million in 1993. In 1991 the board replaced Cassidy (whose reputation was tainted by a sex scandal, less-than-stellar financial results, and diminishing popularity due to what some perceived as a willingness to compromise the association's mission) with longtime politico Wayne LaPierre, another former leader of the group's lobbying arm, the ILA.

The NRA then faced several challenges to its mission. Efforts to overturn New Jersey's ban on semiautomatic weapons and Virginia's gun-rationing program in 1993 both failed. In the late 1980s the NRA had lobbied unsuccessfully against a national ban of certain semiautomatic assault rifles. Moreover, after several years of struggle, in 1994 the Brady Bill passed. Named for White House Press Secretary Jim Brady, who had been shot and partially paralyzed during an assassination attempt on Reagan (who also was wounded), the bill mandated a five-day waiting period and a background check for gun purchasers. (This process was replaced by a computerized verification system run by the Federal Bureau of Investigation in 1998.) The Brady Bill, however, did not apply to flea markets and gun shows, and gun sales at these venues boomed.

Annual revenues for the NRA approached $150 million in 1994 as the group attracted a more active and high-profile membership. The group spent $15 million on a new headquarters in Fairfax, Virginia, in the mid-1990s and also invested in a new computer system.

To address issues of increasing violent crime in the country, the NRA called for more prisons, tougher sentences, and more law enforcement officers. The association, however, continued to struggle with public relations issues and alienated certain law enforcement groups. Michigan Congressman John Dingell, an NRA board member, had called the U.S. Department of Alcohol, Tobacco, and Firearms a "jack-booted group of fascists" in one of the group's promotional films in 1981. The NRA repeated the rhetoric in a 1995 fundraising letter, prompting former President Bush to rescind his life membership.

A LITIGIOUS CLIMATE IN THE LATE NINETIES

In October 1997, nine firearms manufacturers, including Smith & Wesson Corp., announced they were voluntarily adding child-safety locks to their products. The unprecedented break from NRA policy was prompted by a litigious climate that had cities such as Chicago and New Orleans filing lawsuits similar to the ones that had been launched against the cigarette industry. The gunmakers risked a boycott by NRA members who opposed compromise of any kind. According to *Newsweek*, the publicly traded Sturm, Ruger & Company, Inc., had faced such a boycott earlier in the decade after it came out in favor of limiting high-capacity ammunition clips for assault weapons.

In 1997, in the face of such challenges, the NRA began publishing the *American Guardian*, designed to appeal to a more general audience, with less emphasis on technical subjects and more on self-defense and sporting uses for firearms. Membership in the NRA, after reaching 3.5 million, had fallen by about one million in the mid-1990s. Nonetheless, the group held the largest convention in its history in 1998, attracting 41,000 attendees. In the same year, the NRA elected as its president the actor Charlton Heston, perhaps best known for his performance as Moses in the epic film *The Ten Commandments*. Another famous actor, Tom Selleck, appeared in a new round of magazine advertising for the NRA.

In the late 1990s, following several highly publicized incidents of violence involving guns among U.S. teenagers, some polls indicated that 70 to 80 percent of Americans favored stricter gun control laws. *Newsweek*, however, reported that the fear of political retaliation from the NRA killed a new round of gun control bills in June 1999. NRA membership climbed again late in the decade. By May 2000 the association reported 3.7 million members.

EMERGING AS A FORMIDABLE POLITICAL FORCE IN THE TWENTY-FIRST CENTURY

At the dawn of the 21st century, the NRA had emerged as one of the most powerful and influential political organizations in the United States. As the NRA grew in popularity, its financial contributions increased, swelling the group's annual budget to $168 million. The organization also grew more confrontational during this period, accusing major Democratic politicians such as Bill Clinton and Al Gore of wanting to repeal the Second Amendment. In one television spot, the group dubbed Clinton and Gore the "face of gun hatred in America." During the group's annual convention in the summer of 2000, spokesman Heston famously told supporters that if Gore were to try to take away his right to bear arms, he would have to pry it out of his "cold, dead hands!"

With the presidential election of 2000 approaching, the NRA became increasingly active in its efforts to create broad, nationwide support for gun rights. In the eyes of many of the group's leaders, the Second Amendment was gaining in popularity among the U.S. public at large, in spite of continued efforts by lawmakers to impose restrictions on firearms. In an article published in the August 6, 2000, edition of the *Washington Post*, NRA Executive Vice President LaPierre was quoted by reporter Michael Powell as saying that the organization's main goal was to put "the NRA and the Second Amendment right where it belongs: in the American mainstream." That same month, the group launched a campaign accusing Democrats of not defending the right to bear arms, placing full-page ads in major newspapers and running television spots during the Democratic National Convention.

In spite of its strong support for George W. Bush, however, the NRA refused to formally endorse the Republican candidate, out of fear that the Democrats would exploit the publicity to their advantage. However, the organization played an active role in campaigning for the Republican nominee. In the month of September alone, the NRA's Political Victory Fund spent nearly $1 million on pro-Bush advertising. By November 2000 the group had received roughly $11.4 million in outside donations, more than double the amount raised in 1996. According to some estimates, the NRA's total political spending for the year was between $15 million and $20 million. In May 2001 the NRA was named the top lobbying group in the United States by *Fortune* magazine.

As the Republicans took control over the executive and the legislative branches of government, the NRA began to seek ways to use this political advantage to expand gun rights across the country. A major battle emerged in 2004, when Democratic gun-control advocates in Congress attempted to renew the ban on assault weapons, originally signed in 1994 and set to expire in September 2004. Even President Bush, along with a number of the nation's most prominent police chiefs, supported the ban's renewal. The law was ultimately allowed to expire, however, due in large part to NRA pressure on the Republican-controlled House and Senate.

LEGAL BATTLES CONTINUE

Sensing that public sentiment had shifted even further in its favor, the NRA soon became involved in other efforts to relax firearm restrictions, both on the federal and state levels. In April 2005 the group announced its support for a new Florida law granting citizens "the right to stand his or her ground and meet force with force, including deadly force if he or she reasonably believes it is necessary to do so to prevent death or great bodily harm." After the law passed easily in the Florida legislature, the NRA launched a major campaign endorsing similar legislation in other states. In an interview with Manuel Roig-Franzia that appeared in the *Washington Post* on April 26, 2005, LaPierre asserted: "There's a big tailwind we have, moving from state legislature to state legislature." The state of Florida gave the organization another political victory a year later, when it passed a law requiring hunting, fishing, and trapping licensors to provide customers with voter registration cards.

By April 2007, however, in the wake of a mass shooting at Virginia Tech University that left 32 people dead, proponents of gun control suddenly had new ammunition in their battle against the NRA. In June of that year, the Democratic-controlled Congress reached an agreement with the organization requiring stricter background checks for gun purchasers. In a testament to the NRA's power, the Democrats were forced to offer the group a number of key concessions, including a prohibition on the collection of fees. In March 2008 the NRA was once again at the center of the Florida legislative process, when it threw its lobbying power behind a new law allowing gun owners to carry firearms to their place of work.

In April 2008 former NRA President Heston died after suffering from Alzheimer's disease. That same month, the NRA called for the arrest of Philadelphia Mayor Michael Nutter on grounds of "official oppression," after Nutter and the city council attempted to pass a package of comprehensive gun control laws. In May a judge ruled in favor of the organization's efforts to block the legislation, forcing the issue to the state court. A month later, the NRA scored another major political victory, when the U.S. Supreme Court decided that a gun ban in Washington, D.C., was unconstitutional. Buoyed by the ruling, the group immediately set out to challenge similar laws in Chicago and San Francisco. Throughout this period, the NRA was again devoting major resources to electoral politics, spending $40 million over the course of the year; of that sum, $15 million was specifically aimed at preventing the election of Democratic presidential candidate Barack Obama.

As the decade drew to a close, the NRA became involved in several controversial legal battles, as it continued to fight against the rights of cities and states to regulate gun ownership. In June 2009, an appeals court in Chicago ruled that the Second Amendment did not apply to local law. The NRA immediately appealed the ruling to the Supreme Court, setting up another major showdown on the issue of gun rights. After narrowly winning the Washington, D.C., gun ban ruling a year earlier, the organization had reason for confidence as it headed into its next legal battle.

Frederick C. Ingram
Updated, Stephen Meyer

PRINCIPAL DIVISIONS

Institute for Legislative Action; NRA Foundation.

FURTHER READING

Bai, Matt, "Caught in the Cross-Fire," *Newsweek*, June 28, 1999, pp. 31–32.

Birnbaum, Jeffrey H., "Under the Gun," *Fortune*, December 6, 1999, pp. 211–18.

Davidson, Osha Gray, *Under Fire: The NRA and the Battle for Gun Control*. New York: Henry Holt, 1993.

Dionne, E. J., Jr, "Beyond the NRA's Absolutism," *Washington Post*, December 10, 2009, p. A29.

Feldman, Richard, *Ricochet: Confessions of a Gun Lobbyist*. Hoboken, NJ: John Wiley & Sons, 2008, 296 p.

Fineman, Howard, "The Gun War Comes Home," *Newsweek*, August 23, 1999, pp. 26–32.

Hornblower, Margot, "Have Gun, Will Travel," *Time*, July 6, 1998, pp. 44–46.

Leddy, Edward, *Magnum Force Lobby*. Lanham, MD: University Press of America, 1987.

Melzer, Scott, *Gun Crusaders: The NRA's Culture War*. New York: New York University Press, 2009, 323 p.

Novak, Viveca, "Picking a Fight with the NRA," *Time*, May 31, 1999, p. 54.

Powell, Michael, "Call to Arms," *Washington Post*, August 6, 2000, p. W8.

Roig-Franzia, Manuel, "Fla. Gun Law to Expand Leeway for Self-Defense; NRA to Promote Idea in Other States," *Washington Post*, April 26, 2005, p. A1.

Smolowe, Jill, and Andrea Sachs, "The NRA: Go Ahead, Make Our Day," *Time*, May 29, 1995, p. 18.

Trefethen, James, and James Serven, *Americans and Their Guns: The National Rifle Association's Story through Nearly a Century of Service to the Nation*. Harrisburg, PA: Stackpole Books, 1967.

NextWave Wireless Inc.

10350 Science Center Drive, Suite 210
San Diego, California 92121
U.S.A.
Telephone: (858) 480-3100
Fax: (858) 480-3105
Web site: http://www.nextwave.com

Public Company
Incorporated: 1995 as NextWave Telecom, Inc.
Employees: 442
Sales: $63.01 million (2008)
Stock Exchanges: NASDAQ
Ticker Symbol: WAVE
NAICS: 517210 Wireless Telecommunications Carriers

■ ■ ■

NextWave Wireless Inc. is a mobile multimedia and wireless broadband company active in multimedia endeavors and the management of wireless spectrum assets. Multimedia operations are conducted through its subsidiary, PacketVideo Corporation (PV), which develops and markets software to deliver media services over wireless networks to mobile phones, handheld computers, and laptops. Incorporated into more than 300 devices, PV software supports all audio and video formats. NextWave's U.S. wireless spectrum holdings total about 220 million MHz POPs (the license divided by the population of the area covered by the license). The company also holds about 145 million international POPs, with a large presence in Canada and nationwide licenses in Austria, Croatia, Germany, Norway, Slovakia, and Switzerland. NextWave has used sales of its wireless spectrum assets to pay down debt. James Brailean, a cofounder of PV, serves as NextWave's chief executive officer, and NextWave founder Allen Salmasi is the company's chairman.

FOUNDED IN 1995

Allen Salmasi was born into a wealthy family in Iran in 1954. His family fled the country following the Islamic revolution that toppled the secular government in 1979, but Salmasi was already in the United States, having emigrated in 1971 to pursue his education. He earned degrees in electrical engineering and management economics from Purdue University in 1977. Two years later he received master's degrees in electrical engineering from Purdue and in applied mathematics from the University of Southern California, where he also completed the course work for a Ph.D. in electrical engineering. In 1979 Salmasi went to work for the National Aeronautics and Space Administration Jet Propulsion Laboratory, holding several technical and management posts during his five-year tenure. With $14 million in backing from his family, now relocated to Los Angeles, Salmasi founded Omninet Corporation in 1984, applying lessons learned at NASA to develop a truck fleet satellite-tracking system. He then merged Omninet with Qualcomm Inc. in 1988 and established the tracking service in the trucking industry. By 1995 it accounted for more than half of the $387 million in revenues Qualcomm recorded.

Salmasi left Qualcomm in 1995 to take advantage of the decision by the Federal Communications Commission (FCC) to auction personal communication services (PCS) licenses to entrepreneurs and small businesses. In July 1995 Salmasi formed NextWave Telecom, Inc., investing $7 million of his own money for a 14 percent stake. He was soon joined by a pair of senior Qualcomm executives, and Qualcomm itself invested $20 million in the new venture. Other backers were the Sony Corporation and a South Korean steel company. In 1996 the company formed subsidiary NextWave Wireless Inc. Salmasi's plan was to develop a nationwide PCS network that served carriers, who in turn would serve consumers and pay NextWave a fee for using the network.

NEXTWAVE WINS SPECTRUM AUCTION: 1996

The PCS auction, which was expected to bring in about $5 billion for the federal government, was fraught with delays. When the bidding finally began in 1996, firms with large backers forced prices upward, and small companies fell out of contention. In all, more than $10.2 billion was raised by FCC through the auction. NextWave stunned observers when it agreed to pay $4.74 billion for PCS licenses in 95 urban markets in the United States. Other bidders cried foul, accusing NextWave of being little more than a front for Qualcomm.

It was NextWave's foreign investors, however, that led to legal challenges. FCC rules limited foreign ownership to no more than 25 percent of a participating company, and at one point NextWave had allowed foreign owners to hold debt that had the potential of resulting in an equity stake as high as 36 percent. Although other domestic investors were added to bring those percentages in line, NextWave's rivals challenged the auction results in June 1996, forcing NextWave to postpone an initial public offering (IPO) of stock in which the company hoped to raise the money needed to pay the FCC for the licenses and begin building the network.

Before the IPO was shelved, NextWave was able to make a 10 percent down payment on the licenses, $500 million, and agreed to pay the rest in installments spread over 10 years. When it was unable to meet the payments, NextWave filed for Chapter 11 bankruptcy protection in December 1998. The company then argued in bankruptcy court that it had been unfairly forced to overpay for the licenses because after the auction the FCC flooded the market with spectrum. NextWave claimed that prices were depressed, making it impossible to secure financing to pay for the licenses. In truth, holders of 337 licenses went bankrupt during this period. The court then ruled that the licenses were now only worth $1.02 billion, news that helped NextWave attract $1.6 billion to build its network from the likes of Liberty Media Corp. and Global Crossings Ltd. in December 1999.

NextWave also became the object of an $8.3 billion hostile takeover bid by Nextel Communications, Inc. The offer was soon withdrawn by Nextel when it became apparent that the FCC would seize the PCS licenses and again put them up for sale after the U.S. Second Court of appeals overturned the bankruptcy court ruling on the value of the licenses. The court also maintained that the FCC had exclusive jurisdiction over the licenses, thus opening the way for the FCC to take back the licenses. The FCC re-auctioned them in January 2001. Because no new spectrum had been sold for a period of time, the value of NextWave's licenses skyrocketed to $16 billion.

SUPREME COURT RULES IN NEXTWAVE'S FAVOR: 2003

Salmasi did not give up the licenses easily. He pursued the matter in the U.S. Court of Appeals, hiring prominent attorney Theodore Olson to represent NextWave. Olson, who later became the U.S. Solicitor General, successfully argued that the FCC had violated federal bankruptcy laws by taking back the licenses while NextWave was under Chapter 11 protection, and the agency was no different from any other creditor. In June 2001 the appeals court ruled in favor of NextWave, and the licenses were returned to the company, which was then able to secure $2.5 billion in financing from UBS Warburg to build a 3G wireless network. In the meantime, the court case made its way to the final arbitrator, the U.S. Supreme Court, which in March 2002 agreed to rule on the FCC's contention that spectrum auctions should be exempt from bankruptcy protection because wireless spectrums were public assets that should not be allowed to go unused because a company defaulted on its payments and tied them up in bankruptcy proceedings. Early in 2003 the Supreme

KEY DATES

1995: NextWave Telecom Inc. is formed.
1996: NextWave Wireless is formed; company wins $4.74 billion wireless spectrum auction.
1998: NextWave declares bankruptcy.
2001: FCC re-auctions NextWave's licenses.
2003: U.S. Supreme Court ruling returns spectrum licenses to NextWave.
2005: NextWave emerges from bankruptcy, acquires PacketVideo Corporation.
2009: NextWave sells 35 percent stake in PacketVideo.

Court upheld the appeals court decision that the FCC could not seize the licenses.

While the matter was pending before the Supreme Court, however, a settlement was cobbled together that would allow the FCC to complete the second auction and fetch more money for the licenses. The agency met with NextWave and the group of telecommunications firms that won the re-auction. The parties reached an agreement in which the telecoms paid $15.9 billion for the NextWave Licenses, $10 billion of which was earmarked for the government and the balance to NextWave. In the end, NextWave's investors were handsomely repaid for their patience, sharing $3 billion, or about $7 per share.

The plan was approved by the bankruptcy court in March 2005, and NextWave Telecom was in effect liquidated. A new NextWave Wireless Inc. was formed, with about 1,300 shareholders of the old NextWave reinvesting in the company. The new NextWave began business with $550 million in the bank. NextWave Wireless was reincorporated in Delaware in 2006 and became a public company listed on the NASDAQ in 2007.

PACKETVIDEO ACQUIRED: 2005

Looking to find a niche in the wireless market, Next-Wave spent $46.7 million of its funds in July 2005 to acquire PacketVideo (PV) Corporation. PV was founded in 1998 by Motorola executives James Carol and James Brailean, the latter an engineer who supplied the company's vision of bringing streaming video to cell phones. The company demonstrated its technology at a 1999 trade show and attracted several investors. Even after the collapse of the technology sector, which prevented the company from going public, PV was able

to raise more than $100 million. The capabilities of wireless networks failed to keep pace with the technology, however, and carriers grew less willing to invest in network upgrades after the wireless industry and the economy slumped. As a result, NextWave, with a war chest at its disposal, was able to take advantage of PV's plight to acquire the company at a reasonable price.

PV was now able to dip into NextWave's pockets to expand its business through acquisitions. It paid $2.6 million in April 2006 for Tusonic Corporation, a developer of database applications for downloadable music. A month later it spent $2.2 million for the multimedia business of Openbit Ltd., and in September it acquired TwonkyVision GmbH for $3.5 million. Based in Berlin, Germany, TwonkyVision developed universal plug-and-play audio-video middleware for media servers as well as embedded devices. Another deal, completed in early 2007, was the $17.8 million acquisition of SDC AG, a Switzerland-based company that offered a JAVA music client for downloading music with digital rights management (DRM) protection in order to fend off piracy. Later in 2007, PV added another Swiss company, paying $5.8 million for Digital World Services AG, which also developed secure digital content delivery software.

In addition to the multimedia endeavors of PV, NextWave invested in wireless network infrastructure companies. In 2006 it acquired CYGNUS Communications, maker of WiMAX products. In February 2007, it added GO Networks Inc., a developer of municipal Wi-Fi networks, purchased for $13.3 million. The Next-Wave Broadband unit also beefed up its engineering team to develop Wi-Fi and WiMAX technologies. The company spent about $50 million on research and development in 2006 and increased the budget to $150 million in 2007.

NextWave also built up a portfolio of wireless spectrum licenses. In 2006 the company paid $115.5 million for 16 wireless communication services (WCS) licenses and 154 advanced wireless services (AWS) licenses, resulting in a portfolio of more than 248 million POPs. Through a joint venture in 2006, NextWave acquired its first international spectrum, located in Germany. A year later, another 142 million POPs were added in the United States, Argentina, Austria, Canada, Croatia, Germany, Norway, Slovakia, and Switzerland.

To support its growth, NextWave grossed nearly $300 million by issuing senior secured notes in 2006. NextWave raised more funds in 2007 to pursue its plan of becoming a player in the wireless broadband field. Salmasi and board member Douglas Manchester each invested $50 million, and a further $255 million was added through a private placement of stock. Some of that money, $25 million, and $75 million in stock, was then used in May 2007 to acquire IPWireless, developer of the TD-CDMA (time division code division multiple access) technology and a leader in UMTS (universal mobile telecommunications system) broadband technology.

COMPANY RESTRUCTURES BUSINESS: 2008

In 2008 NextWave restructured its operation. Rather than use its spectrum licenses to build a national wireless network, which could be used to support customers who bought the company's products and services, NextWave elected to focus on its multimedia business, primarily PV. The decision was also made to begin selling off the company's wireless spectrum interests to pay down debt and support NextWave's multimedia efforts. In July 2008 the company sold 63 percent of its AWS spectrum for $145.5 million. Also in the second half of 2008, NextWave sold its controlling interest in IPWireless and discontinued the operations of its network infrastructure businesses, including the Go Networks and CYGNUS subsidiaries. The company also initiated bankruptcy proceedings for infrastructure subsidiaries in Canada, Denmark, and Israel as a way to exit those countries.

Because of PV's increasing importance, the subsidiary's CEO, James Brailean, took over as the CEO of NextWave in 2009, replacing Salmasi, who remained chairman. In July of that year, NextWave sold a 35 percent interest in PV to Japanese wireless carrier DoCoMo for $45.5 million in order to pay off senior secured notes due in July 2010. Clearly struggling, NextWave found little support from Wall Street as its stock traded in the vicinity of 50 cents. In January, 2010, the company received a delisting notice from the NASDAQ. PacketVideo, on the other hand, held some

promise as consumers increased their consumption of media on mobile phones, handheld computers, and laptops. NextWave also continued to own valuable spectrum licenses. Nevertheless, the company's future prospects were far from certain.

Ed Dinger

PRINCIPAL SUBSIDIARIES

PacketVideo Corporation.

PRINCIPAL COMPETITORS

Alcatel-Lucent; Flextronics International Ltd.; Nokia Siemens Networks.

FURTHER READING

Glasner, Joanna, and Elisa Batista, "NextWave Telecom's Twisted Tale," *Wired*, March 12, 2002.

Harris, Nicole, "Nextel Withdraws Its Hostile Bid for NextWave," *Wall Street Journal*, December 27, 1999, p. 1.

———, "NextWave Telecom Raises $1.6 Billion to Build Network," *Wall Street Journal*, December 17, 1999, p. 1.

Karr, Albert R., "NextWave, Winner in Wireless Auction, Considers How to Pay for FCC Licenses," *Wall Street Journal*, May 20, 1996, p. A13.

Naik, Gautam, and Bryan Gruley, "NextWave's Tactics at Wireless Auction Are under Fire," *Wall Street Journal*, May 6, 1996, p. B4.

"NextWave Sells off Part of S.D.-based PacketVideo," *San Diego Union-Tribune*, July 7, 2009.

"NextWave Wireless Makes Management Changes as Part of Reorganization," *Wireless News*, May 11, 2009.

Schine, Eric, "Entrepreneurs Right Party, Wrong Number?" *BusinessWeek*, December 23, 1996, p. 86.

Silva, Jeffrey, "Allen Salmasi's Next Wave," *RCR Wireless News*, June 18, 2007, p. 6.

Veverka, Mark, "Son of NextWave," *Barron's*, May 5, 2008, p. 28.

19 Entertainment Limited

32/33 Ransomes Dock
35-37 Parkgate Road
London, SW11 4NP
United Kingdom
Telephone: (+44 20) 7801-1919
Fax: (+44 20) 7801-1920
Web site: http://www.19.co.uk

Wholly Owned Subsidiary of CKX, Inc.
Founded: 1985
Employees: 100
Sales: £17.9 million ($28.5 million) (2009 est.)
NAICS: 711410 Agents and Managers for Artists, Athletes, Entertainers, and Other Public Figures; 711320 Promoters of Performing Arts, Sports, and Similar Events; 512110 Motion Picture and Video Production

■ ■ ■

19 Entertainment Limited is a global media and entertainment business whose parent company is CKX Inc. Created by trend-spotter Simon Fuller in 1985 with one client, 19 Entertainment has grown to be a highly successful representative of music and television entertainers and sports and fashion celebrities, including former Spice Girl Victoria ("Posh") Beckham and her husband, soccer star David Beckham, as well as singer Annie Lennox. It also owns the trademark for the worldwide *Pop Idol* series, including the hugely popular television series *American Idol*, all created by Fuller. In 2008 *Billboard* magazine declared Fuller to be the most

successful British music manager of all time. In February 2010 Fuller was succeeded by Robert Dodds as the CEO of 19 Entertainment.

MUSIC, MUSIC, MUSIC

Fuller was 25 and working at Chrysalis Music Limited and Chrysalis Records, managing the singer Paul Hardcastle in 1985, when he created 19 Entertainment, naming it after Hardcastle's first number-one hit, "19," a Vietnam war song. The company also began managing the solo career of Lennox after her popular duo the Eurythmics split in 1990, including the release of her platinum-selling album *Diva* in 1991. Under 19's management, she won an Academy Award, four Grammy Awards, eight BRIT Awards, and a Golden Globe.

The company has also managed hit songwriters and producers, notably Cathy Dennis. She first met Fuller in the 1980s as a singer for D Mob, and he guided her to being Britain's number-one female songwriter, with hits for Britney Spears, Pink, and many others. Amy Winehouse was discovered by 19 Entertainment in 2002. They produced her first award-winning album but she left 19 Entertainment in 2006.

Fuller managed the Spice Girls, masterminding such hits as "Wannabe" and garnering lucrative commercial sponsorships in deals with Pepsi and Polaroid, among others. Under 19 Entertainment's management, the Spice Girls sold over 37 million records in three years. They left 19 in November 1997 to manage their own career. The group later disbanded but two members, Emma Bunton and Victoria Adams, approached Fuller to manage their careers. In 2007, 19 Entertainment organized the Spice Girls reunion tour, which began in December and earned each of the group's members $10 million. Since January 2000 Fuller has been an investor in and director of Popworld Limited, a multimedia music company.

IDOL SERIES

Fuller and 19 Entertainment ventured into television with the *Pop Idol* format in 1998. The series broke television records in the United Kingdom during its first two seasons. In 2000 the show was sold to Fox Entertainment in the United States and *American Idol* became the number-one rated show. Following the U.K. format, a panel of judges rated the on-air auditions of thousands of singers who were reduced to a much smaller pool of performers who were then voted for by viewers. The singer who received the most votes, sent in by phone or text messages, was selected as the winner, and then signed for representation with 19 Entertainment. (For example, 90 million votes were cast in May 2008, making David Cook the seventh idol.) The show made stars of the host, Ryan Seacrest, and the three judges: bassist, singer, and record producer Randy Jackson; singer-dancer Paula Abdul; and music producer Simon Cowell. Seacrest's career grew to include producing reality television shows such as *Keeping Up with the Kardashians*.

In 2004, after Cowell launched the television show *The X Factor*, a similar singer-audition competition with no age limits, Fuller sued and gained a share of that show and Cowell received a multimillion-dollar salary for his participation on *American Idol*. Other controversy erupted the same year, over the standard *American Idol* contract, which bound all winners and some finalists to 19 Entertainment for recording, management, and marketing. Clay Aiken, the runner-up during *American Idol*'s second season, with the aid of a lawyer, was able to extricate himself from the management and marketing parts of the contract. In the fourth season, finalist Mario Vazquez left the show for undisclosed reasons, but it appeared to be his unwillingness to sign the contract.

Nevertheless, *American Idol* continued to rank high in the U.S. television ratings, so any back-end loss of revenue was offset by higher front-end earnings. By 2009 *Pop Idol* was one of the world's highest-earning television formats, valued at more than $2.5 billion, with income from sponsors, merchandising, music sales, and advertising revenues. *Advertising Age* in 2009 reported that *American Idol* was a very close second only to the spy-thriller drama *24* in television advertising revenues.

Network Ten of Australia purchased the rights for *Australian Idol*; a similar sale was made in Canada for a show that aired on CTV. With local adaptations of the *Idol* television format, *Idol* programs in 2010 aired in more than 100 countries. In 2010 Ellen DeGeneres, popular comedian and daytime talk-show host took over Abdul's chair on the *American Idol* judges panel. Abdul left the show after failing to reach a new agreement with 19 Entertainment and FremantleMedia North America.

IDOL TOURS AND RECORDING STARS

The American Idol Live! tour took off at the end of each season of *American Idol*, with the top 10 finalists performing from July through September in more than 50 North American cities in 2010. A division of 19 Entertainment, 19 Recordings, held exclusive recording rights for such winners of *American Idol* as Kelly Clarkson, Carrie Underwood, Chris Daughtry, and David Cook, and selected finalists, selling more than 50 million copies of *American Idol* music in North America since the show was first broadcast.

Underwood, the winner in 2005, became a 4-time Grammy Award winner, had 10 number-one hits, and in 2009 was named the Academy of Country Music's Entertainer of the Year. Adam Lambert, the openly gay runner-up in season eight (2009) was marketed widely by 19 Entertainment, and his popularity grew in the few months before the end-of-the year release of his debut album, *For Your Entertainment*, which opened at the number-three spot on the *Billboard* 200 chart.

OTHER TELEVISION

In 1999, 19 Entertainment auditioned 10,000 people to create S Club 7, which became a successful pop group and was featured in a BBC TV show that was seen in more than 100 British territories. Group members Rachel Stevens, Jon Lee, and Hannah Spearritt went on with successful solo careers in music and movies.

In 2004 Fuller launched *So You Think You Can Dance* with creator Nigel Lythgoe on the Fox network. The Emmy Award-winning show became a summer hit

KEY DATES

1985: 19 Entertainment is formed by Simon Fuller.
1998: *Pop Idol* is television show launched in the United Kingdom.
2000: *American Idol* television show begins in the United States.
2003: Agreement is signed with Spice Girl Victoria Beckham and soccer superstar David Beckham.
2005: 19 Entertainment is sold to CKX.
2006: 19 Entertainment enters fashion industry with joint-venture agreement with designer Roland Mouret.
2009: 19 Entertainment moves into motion picture industry with production of the film *Bel Ami*.
2010: Robert Dodds becomes company CEO.

for Fox, with 60 million viewer votes being cast in the fourth season. Sam Nixon and Mark Rhodes, finalists two and three, respectively, in *Pop Idol*'s second season, were also represented by 19 Entertainment; the pair became two of the most popular British television presenters, hosting the hit children's Saturday morning show *TMi* starting in 2006 and the number-one rated *Who Wants to Be a Superhero?* beginning in 2009.

In 2007 Victoria and David Beckham moved to Los Angeles and Fuller produced the documentary *Victoria Beckham: Coming to America*. In the same year, 19 Entertainment signed a deal with comedians Matt Lucas and David Williams to develop their award-winning BBC TV show *Little Britain* for the United States (as *Little Britain USA*). In 2009 a new production deal was made with television host Seacrest. The live-streaming reality show *If I Can Dream*, in which participants were filmed around-the-clock living in a Hollywood house while they pursue their dreams in their chosen creative fields, was launched in 2010. Fuller received the 2008 Visionary Award from the Producers Guild of America for his creativity, entrepreneurialism, and charity work.

COMPANY SOLD TO CKX 2005

Fuller sold 19 Entertainment in March 2005 to CKX, Inc., for more than $210 million in cash and stock, but remained as president of 19 Enterprises. He also became a director of CKX, taking on responsibility for Elvis Presley Enterprises, which owned and controlled the commercial use of Presley's name, image, and likeness; the operation of the Graceland museum; and the

revenue derived from Presley's television specials, films, and some of his music.

In addition, Fuller took responsibility for the business interests of former boxer Muhammad Ali and his wife, Lonnie, and the rights to his name, image, and likeness. In 2007 Fuller was included on *Time* magazine's annual list of the top 100 most influential people in the world.

FASHION

In a joint venture with noted fashion designer Roland Mouret, creator of the Galaxy dress made famous by Hollywood celebrities, 19 Entertainment entered the fashion world in August 2006 with its 19 RM division. Later that year *GQ* magazine named Fuller Entrepreneur of the Year. In 2010 a menswear collection was added to the division.

Victoria Adams and David Beckham had been introduced at a football charity event by Fuller, and the two 19 Entertainment clients married in 1997. After 19 signed Victoria with Telstar Records in 2002, 19 Entertainment signed a new deal with Victoria and David Beckham to manage all of Victoria's career and business interests and to market the Beckhams as a brand. Their fashion brand, dVb, included denim styles, sunglasses, and a billion-dollar his-and-her fragrances line introduced in 2006.

In 2008 Victoria launched her first collection of dresses to critical acclaim. The dVb label became one of the world's most successful celebrity lines, with a retail value over $200 million. By 2009 the Beckhams total wealth was around $225 million. That same year Fuller purchased a 51 percent share in the renowned British modeling agency Storm Model Management, with models Kate Moss and Cindy Crawford.

In September 2009, 19 Entertainment partnered with Sojin Lee to launch the London-based fashion-entertainment online site Fashionair.com. In a September 4, 2009, interview with Forbes.com reporter Lauren Sherman, Lee said: "Having someone like Simon backing us is definitely a benefit. ... The level of exposure we've already received is definitely a result."

BRANCHING OUT INTO SPORTS AND MOTION PICTURES

Fuller and 19 Entertainment began sports management in the mid-1990s. He formed a joint-venture partnership with David Beckham, who played for many seasons with Manchester United and Real Madrid, and negotiated Beckham's $250 million move to the Los Angeles Galaxy in 2007. Fuller formed the sports company named 1966 to help improve the public image of the

England football (soccer) team members, starting with the players' charity, which in two years raised £1 million for charitable causes.

Sports Illustrated declared Ali "Sportsman of the Century" in 1999, and BBC TV declared him "Sports Personality of the Century." CKX and 19 Entertainment took on management of the Ali name, image, and likeness in the 21st century to maintain a lasting legacy for the popular and iconic athlete.

In 2007, 19 Entertainment became the first company to successfully promote the environment in car racing. Their Earth Car was driven in the Formula One season by Brazilian racer Rubens Barrichello, who joined with Fuller and David Beckham in a World of Sport concept with a resort and land preserve in Brazil. In tennis, 19 Entertainment began representation in 2009 of world-ranked Scottish player Andy Murray and his doubles-winning brother Jamie Murray.

In 2009, 19 Entertainment moved into the Hollywood film industry with plans to do film treatments of the lives of Presley and Ali as part of their contracts with Ali and the Presley estate. The first project was a film adaptation of the erotic novel *Bel Ami*, written by Guy de Maupassant in 1885, starring British singer and heartthrob Robert Pattinson. Fuller served as executive producer. Filming began in 2010 amid speculation about Fuller's music management experience and Pattinson's future career. *Bel Ami* was scheduled for completion in April 2010 and release in 2011.

FULLER AND THE FUTURE

As chief executive officer of 19 Entertainment, Fuller's total compensation in 2008 was over $4 million. As Robert F. X. Sillerman, chairman and CEO of CKX, said in a March 18, 2005, *Business Wire* article, after the purchase of 19 Entertainment: "Simon Fuller and his associates at 19 Entertainment have a long history of developing and building some of the most impactful entertainment properties in the world. ... The content that 19 owns, controls, is developing, or develops in the future will become important elements in our effort to refocus the relationship between the creators of content and the distributors of that content." On January 14,

2010, Fuller and CKX announced an agreement to a long-term contract to keep Fuller involved in the firm's key shows, while freeing him to launch a new entertainment company. Fuller was to stay in place as executive producer behind *American Idol*, *So You Think You Can Dance*, and *If I Can Dream*, and provide general consulting services to CKX, and CKX had the option to invest in Fuller's new company, XIX Entertainment Limited.

Louise B. Ketz

PRINCIPAL DIVISIONS

19 Management; 19 Recordings; 19 RM; 1966.

PRINCIPAL COMPETITORS

All3Media; Endemol B.V.; Live Nation, Inc.; RDF Media Group PLC; Shed Media PLC; Shine Ltd.

FURTHER READING

"American Idol Joins Elvis at CKX, Inc.; Robert F.X. Sillerman's CKX Acquires 19 Entertainment, Creator of American Idol, and Partners with Founder, Simon Fuller," *Business Wire* March 18, 2005.

Beckham, David, "The Time 100: Simon Fuller," *Time*, May 3, 2007.

Garrahan, Matthew, "The Unlikely Impresario," *Financial Times*, May 24, 2008.

"The Independent: First Music, Then Modelling—Now Fuller Trains Sights on Hollywood," *Financial Times*, November 4, 2009.

McNicholas, Kym, "A Dancing Machine," Forbes.com, August 28, 2009, http://video.forbes.com/fvn/personalbest/nigel-lythgoe-a-dancing-machine.

Sherman, Lauren, "Fashion's New Visionary?" Forbes.com, September 4, 2009, http://www.forbes.com/2009/09/04/fashionair-designer-fashion-lifestyle-style-shopping-online.html.

Smith, Caspar Llewellyn, "The Starmaker," *Daily Telegraph* (London), September 28, 2002.

Sweney, Mark, "19 Entertainment Profits Soar," *Guardian* (London), March 3, 2009.

Timms, Dominic, "Fuller Scores Beckham Brand Deal," *Guardian* (London), July 24, 2003.

Orica Ltd.

1 Nicholson Street
East Melbourne, Victoria 3002
Australia
Telephone: (+61 3) 9665-7111
Fax: (+61 3) 9665-7937
Web site: http://www.orica.com

Public Company
Founded: 1874 as Jones, Scott and Company
Incorporated: 1928 as Imperial Chemical Industries of Australia and New Zealand Ltd.
Employees: 15,000
Sales: $7.41 billion (2009)
Stock Exchanges: Australian
Ticker Symbol: ORI
NAICS: 325920 Explosives Manufacturing; 333131 Drilling Equipment, Underground Mining-Type Manufacturing; 325199 Basic Organic Chemicals Manufacturing; 325132 Synthetic Organic Dye and Pigment Manufacturing; 325211 Plastics Manufacturing; 325510 Paints Manufacturing

∎ ∎ ∎

Orica Ltd. has remained at the forefront of its industries for several decades. Previously owned by Imperial Chemical Industries, a pioneer in chemical engineering, dye compositions, and other advances, Orica became a stand-alone company in the late 1990s. Since then, Orica's four main business segments have focused on manufacturing and distributing commercial explosives; drilling equipment and other products for tunnels, mines, and infrastructure projects; industrial and specialty chemicals for construction, pulp and paper, water treatment, beverage, agriculture and other uses; and paint and product treatments for homes, vehicles, and business exteriors and interiors. As of 2009, Orica had a workforce of 15,000 and sales of more than $7 billion, and it was ranked within the top 50 companies listed on the Australian Stock Exchange.

THE EARLY YEARS

Orica Ltd. began in 1874 as Jones, Scott and Company in Victoria, Australia. At that time, discoveries of gold were attracting a great deal of attention from miners, their investors, and those who supplied the mines with necessities, such as dynamite. Two men who provided dynamite were Robert Steel Scott and Thomas Tolley Jones. Scott was an agent for Krebs & Company, a German manufacturer of dynamite, and Jones was his partner, located in London. Krebs wanted to establish a factory in Victoria so its product would be closer to the growing demand of the gold mines and it could avoid the time-consuming, costly, and risky transportation from Germany and the expensive duty that Victoria charged on dynamite imports.

Thomas Jones secured the necessary licensing agreement for a factory in Victoria and obtained an initial £30,000 in investments so Jones, Scott and Company could begin operations. The company faced several challenges at first, including high production costs and limited production. William J. Reader, author of *Imperial Chemical Industries: A History* wrote, "Worse still, the company was prevented from making gelatinous

COMPANY PERSPECTIVES

Orica's proud traditions of leadership, innovation, quality and safety are shared by our 15,000 people located in around 50 countries across six continents. Orica turns science into the solutions that satisfy basic human needs. Our products, brands and services can be trusted for their reliability, range and quality. Each of our businesses—Orica Mining Services, Minova, Orica Chemicals and Dulux-Group—is the leader in its chosen market and enjoys a world class reputation.

explosives until [inventor of dynamite Alfred] Nobel's patents ran out in 1890, and even after that was not very good at them. Nevertheless it was profitable enough to survive, and in the mid-nineties it had about one-fifth of the total Australian market for explosives."

In 1888 Nobel acquired Jones and Scott's company, enabling him to pursue production of blasting gelatin outside of England. By the late 1800s Nobel had controlling stakes and licensing deals with several chemical manufacturers. These firms comprised Nobel-Dynamite Trust, which later, as Nobel Industries Ltd. was one of four chemical companies that merged in 1926 in response to competition in Germany. The merged company was Imperial Chemical Industries Plc (ICI), with subsidiaries that included the company that Jones and Scott had founded. In 1928 Jones and Scott's company became Imperial Chemical Industries of Australia and New Zealand Ltd.

THE SUBSIDIARY YEARS

As a subsidiary, Imperial Chemical Industries of Australia and New Zealand was subject to its parent company's policies, practices, and commitment to its shareholders. In addition, since ICI of Australia and New Zealand was an international component of a corporation that supplied materials to commodity-based industries, the state of the mining industry in Australia and New Zealand, currency rates, and the cyclical nature of commodities were among the impacts on the subsidiary's progress. As ICI and its subsidiaries experienced their first two decades of consolidation, they held on during the Great Depression and then undertook leading efforts to join other companies, including Du Pont of the United States, in keeping their factories operating on behalf of the Allied forces during World War II.

By the 1960s ICI had definitive progress to report to its shareholders. Four decades after its merger, ICI was listed by *Fortune* magazine as the fourth largest industrial corporation outside the United States. In 1967 the company's sales were $2.7 billion and more than 175,000 employees worked there. Also in 1967 Sir Peter Allen became board chairman. According to *Fortune*, "he took over from Sir Paul Chambers, who switched ICI from its drowsy Commonwealth-oriented policy to a highly competitive drive for European markets."

INDEPENDENCE AND EXPANSION

In 1971 ICI reorganized and Imperial Chemical Industries of Australia and New Zealand became ICI Australia Ltd. The parent company later decided to shift its core activities more toward the manufacturing of pharmaceutical products, and in 1997 ICI divested its 62.4 percent stake in ICI Australia. The newly divested company was now free to concentrate on how to best use its knowledge of the Pacific Rim to remain a leading manufacturer. Less than one year after the sale, ICI Australia Ltd. signified the change with a new name, Orica Ltd.

In 1998, just before the name change became official, ICI Australia bought its former parent's explosives businesses. In an article in the January 7, 1998, issue of *Chemical Week*, Ian Young reported, "The sale to ICI Australia comprises manufacturing operations in Canada, Mexico, Brazil, and the U.K., as well as a distribution business in the U.S.... With the deal, ICI Australia emerges as the global leader in explosives, with a market share of about 20%. It will also gain its first manufacturing operation outside Australia."

The purchase of ICI's explosives businesses indicated Orica's position and financial standing. The 1998 edition of *Jobson's Year Book of Public Companies* listed more than 15 subsidiaries for Orica. Prominent among these was Incitec Ltd., which manufactured fertilizer. It merged with ICI in 1995 to become Australia's leading agricultural chemicals producer and was part of the split-off deal from ICI. The Australian-based paints, chemicals, and plastics businesses that were former ICI subsidiaries and also became arms of Orica included such well-known brands as Dulux and Berger paints, Cabot's wood-care products, and Armor All protective coating for cars. Orica's revenue for 1994–95 was $3.5 billion, and even though the company experienced downturns in 2001 that included a weakened construction industry, a poorly performing Australian dollar, and cutbacks in employees, Orica bounced back.

KEY DATES

1874: Thomas Tolley Jones and Robert Steel Scott found Jones, Scott and Company.

1926: Four major chemical companies, including Nobel Industries Ltd., merge and form Imperial Chemical Industries Plc.

1971: Imperial Chemical Industries of Australia and New Zealand Ltd. is renamed ICI Australia Ltd.

1998: ICI Australia is renamed Orica Ltd.; the company buys ICI Plc's explosives businesses in Europe and North and South America.

2006: Orica acquires Minova.

PERFORMANCE AND PROSPECTS

In 2006 Orica sold its resins and adhesives plants in Australia and New Zealand to Hexion Specialty Chemicals, a company based in the United States. The sale signaled Orica's strategy for the coming years to concentrate on primary successes and let go of secondary functions. This was also the year that Orica acquired Minova for more than $646 million. As Soh Cheok Hui observed in the October 2006 issue of *ICIS Chemical Business*, "Orica is looking to tap into Minova's business in China, Russia and Kazakhstan, which is seeing robust demand for mining chemicals."

Expansion continued in 2007 as Orica completed a takeover of Excel Mining Systems, a company specializing in roof support products for tunnels and mines. This enabled Orica to extend its operations geographically and within the mining services industry. Around the same period, Orica bought parts of Dyno Nobel Ltd.'s explosives business and sold its 70 percent stake in Incitec, the fertilizer manufacturer. Around the time that Orica acquired Excel, Incitec purchased a 13 percent interest in Dyno Nobel, a stake that culminated in 2008 when Incitec acquired Dyno Nobel. Orica was not immune, and a consortium's takeover bid for Orica in 2007 was rejected for undervaluation reasons.

Focused growth was in evidence at Orica. A joint venture in Indonesia, planned since 2006, was resulting in construction in 2009 of Southeast Asia's largest ammonium nitrate factory to date. This vital chemical for the mining industry had another connection, to Orica's acquisition of Minova, which had been doing business in China. The factory in Indonesia showed how Orica was targeting its decisions in complementary ways. Another piece of the strategic plan emerged in 2009 when Orica announced upcoming construction on a detonator plant in China, with expansions ahead for Africa and Eastern Europe.

In a letter to shareholders in 2009, Orica's board chairman Don Mercer wrote: "In a year of extreme volatility in global markets, Orica's strategy of pursuing leadership positions in markets offering long term, sustainable growth with limited exposure to the vagaries of commodity price cycles has been tested and reaffirmed." The company had encountered challenges, including the difficult, upcoming choice of splitting off its paints and product care businesses. Orica planned to center its commitment on manufacturing commercial explosives, mining and tunneling equipment, and industrial chemicals. The industries in which it had made its start would serve as the foundation for its prospects and performance.

Mary C. Lewis

PRINCIPAL SUBSIDIARIES

Orica USA Inc.; Orica Canada Inc.; Minova International Ltd.; Selleys; Dulux; Orica Europe Ltd.; Cabot's; Orica Australia Pty Ltd.; Orica New Zealand Ltd.; Orica Mining Services Latin America.

PRINCIPAL DIVISIONS

Orica Mining Services; Minova; Orica Chemicals; DuluxGroup.

PRINCIPAL OPERATING UNITS

Mining Chemicals; Chemicals Australia; Chemnet New Zealand; Orica Chemicals Latin America (Chile); Marplex; Orica Watercare; Orica Powder Coatings (New Zealand); Altona Properties Pty Ltd. (37.4%); Bamble Mekaniske Industri AS (Norway, 40%); Beijing Ruichy Minova Synthetic Material Company Ltd. (China, 45%); Bronson & Jacobs International Company Ltd. (Thailand, 51%); Dyno NitroMed AD (Bulgaria, 40%); Dyno Nobel VH Company LLC (Canada, 49%); Emirates Explosives LLC (United Arab Emirates, 35%); GeoNitro Ltd. (Georgia, 40%); Hunan Orica Nanling Civil Explosives Company Ltd. (China, 49%); Nitro Asia Company Inc. (Philippines, 41.6%); Northwest Energetic Services LLC (U.S., 48.7%); Orica-CCM Energy Systems Sdn Bhd (Malaysia, 45%); Orica-GM Holdings Ltd. (U.K., 49%); Orica Eesti OÜ (Estonia, 35%); Orica Nitro Patlayici Maddeler Sanayi ve Ticaret Anonim Sirketi (Turkey, 49%); Sprengmittelvertrieb in Bayem GmbH (Germany, 49%); Teradoran Pty. Ltd. (33%); TOO "Minova Kasachstan" (Kazakhstan, 40%).

PRINCIPAL COMPETITORS

Dyno Nobel Ltd.; GEA Group Aktiengesellschaft; Sasol Ltd.

FURTHER READING

"Australia's Orica Aims to Expand in China, E. Europe, Africa," *Asia Pulse News*, October 16, 2009.

"Changes at the Top of the Top, the Fortune Directory: The 200 Largest Industrials Outside the U.S.," *Fortune*, September 15, 1968, pp. 129–31.

Hui, Cheok Soh, "Orica Digs Deep to Fund Expansion," *ICIS Chemical Business (Weekly)*, October 23, 2006, p. 13.

Jobson's Year Book of Public Companies 1998–99. Chatswood, NSW: Dun & Bradstreet Marketing Pty Ltd., 1998, pp. 248, 336–37.

Moldofsky, Leora, "Orica Sets Off Mines Expansion with Excel Takeover," *Financial Times (London)*, September 25, 2007, p. 17.

Reader, William Joseph, *Imperial Chemical Industries: A History.* Vol. 1, *The Forerunners: 1870–1926*. London: Oxford University Press, 1970, pp. 59–63, 66–71, appendix 5.

"RI to Have Largest Explosives Plant in SE Asia," *Jakarta Post*, June 4, 2009, p. 13.

Robinson, Simon, "Orica Signs Off Adhesives Arm: Hexion Specialty Chemicals Acquires the Adhesives Business," *ICIS Chemical Business (Weekly)*, September 4, 2006, p. 15.

Warner, Frederick, "Engineers and International Cooperation," *Engineering*, August 1971, pp. 537–40.

Young, Ian, "ICI Sells Explosives Businesses to Orica," *Chemical Week*, January 7, 1998, p. 21.

PacketVideo Corporation

10350 Science Center Drive, Suite 210
San Diego, California 92121
U.S.A.
Telephone: (858) 731-5300
Fax: (858) 731-5301
Web site: http://www.packetvideo.com

Wholly Owned Subsidiary of NextWave Wireless Inc.
Incorporated: 1998
Employees: 400
Sales: $63 million (2008)
NAICS: 511210 Software Publishers

■ ■ ■

A subsidiary of NextWave Wireless Inc., PacketVideo Corporation (PV) is a San Diego-based company that develops and sells software that delivers media services over wireless and wireline networks to mobile phones, handheld computers, laptops, and connected devices. PV products include CORE, a rich abstraction layer that allows customers to easily change media applications, and OpenCORE, a subset of CORE that allows for the development of multimedia services on the open-source Android platform. MediaFusion is a client-server media platform that aggregates and delivers content to multiple screens and is applicable to various business models including merchandising and previewing. Another product, TwonkyMedia comprises a set of software solutions that allow users to play content of connected devices throughout the digital home. Introduced in 2009, TwonkyBeam is a Web browser ap-

plication that provides a way for Web-based media to be wirelessly delivered to a television or audio receiver via network devices. PV software supports all audio and video formats, is incorporated into hundreds of millions of devices, and boasts more than 400 design awards. The company maintains offices in Boston, Charlotte, and Chicago, as well as Europe and Asia.

BACKGROUND AND ORIGINS: 1996

PacketVideo was cofounded in 1998 by James Z. Carol, the company's first chief executive officer, and James C. Brailean, the chief technology officer who provided the vision for the company and later became CEO as well. The son of a Ford Motor Company engineer, Brailean shared his father's mechanical gifts but preferred technology over automobiles. After receiving an undergraduate degree in electrical engineering from the University of Michigan, he earned a master of science in electrical engineering from the University of Southern California, followed by a doctorate in the subject from Northwestern University.

It was at Northwestern in the early 1990s that Brailean became familiar with digital video. He went to work as a staff engineer at the Motorola Corporate Research and Development Laboratories in Chicago and managed the Advanced Video Algorithm Group that developed advanced video compression and imaging algorithms. Brailean also served on an international committee of scientists, the Motion Picture Experts Group (MPEG), to approve a compression standard that would enable high quality video to be transmitted over narrow bandwidth channels. The group had already adopted a video compression standard for direct-broadcast satellite and digital TV transmission called MPEG2. The new work brought a compression standard to error-prone networks, generally IP-based and wireless networks, eventually taking the name MPEG4. During his time at Motorola Brailean also began working with Jim Carol.

Carol grew up in Pittsburgh, Pennsylvania, and attended West Virginia Wesleyan College on a baseball scholarship, graduating in 1979 with a degree in government and business. He attended Marine Corps officer candidate school but declined the commission. He moved to California to pursue law school, deferred admission, and instead began selling word processors for Digital Equipment Corporation. He spent more than eight years with the computer manufacturer, selling mainframe computers and becoming senior account manager. He then joined Motorola as a vice president of sales and marketing, his new unit charged with selling communications components to original equipment manufacturers.

Working out of Orange County, California, Carol also created a side venture in Motorola that pursued the idea of transmitting voice and video via Internet protocol over wired networks. In 1996 he met Brailean, who began working with him on the voice and video project. While it became clear that the project had little hope of succeeding within Motorola, Carol and Brailean developed a strong rapport. "I told Jim if he ever had a great idea," Carol told *San Diego Business Journal* in 2001, "to put it in a little treasure chest, lock it up and bring it to me, and I'd go find the money to start it."

COMPANY FOUNDED: 1998

An idea had already been taking shape for Brailean as he worked with MPEG: delivering multimedia to cell phones. An MPEG colleague who had worked on video-phone technology for AT&T dampened his enthusiasm, however, insisting that video on small devices, something they had tried at AT&T, would never work.

Brailean regained interest in the idea in 1997 while visiting a research park in Japan built by wireless carrier DoCoMo Inc. Here in a country that was on the cutting edge of cell phone technology he found people who shared his vision for video on cell phones.

Brailean returned to the United States and met Carol at Steamboat, Colorado, and on a ski lift he shared his idea of developing wireless video software for the new generation of processors coming on line and a market that he was convinced would eventually demand media delivered on cell phones and other wireless devices. According to company lore, by the time the lift reached the top of the hill, the two men were ready to tell their wives they were quitting their jobs and going into business together.

In July 1998 Carol and Brailean cobbled together $1 million in seed money. To raise his share of $300,000, Brailean sold his house and cashed out his retirement savings. Also investing in the start-up and serving as an adviser was William D. Cvengros, CEO of the Newport, California investment firm, Pimco Advisors LP. In August 1998 they incorporated PacketVideo Corporation in Delaware. The company name referred to the method in which data was compressed into formatted units (or "packets"), transmitted piecemeal, and then reassembled for play on a wireless device.

The company set up shop in San Diego because Brailean wanted to work with two engineering friends from Northwestern, Cheuk Chan and Mark Banham. Chan lived in San Diego, as did Banham's sister. While launching the company Brailean stayed in Chan's guest room. Brailean's wife, an engineer herself, kept her job at Motorola and temporarily moved in with her parents.

INSPIRING INVESTMENT: 1999

Also playing an important role at this juncture in PV's development was attorney Joel Espelien, whose law firm, Cooley Godward, advised start-up companies. Another contributor was Osama Alshayhk, a talented engineer whom Brailean had met during his years working with the MPEG committee. Together, this team helped to flesh out what was a skeletal business plan, in essence selling video software to computer chip manufacturers because there was no market among cell phone manufacturers. Rather than wait for a market to develop for mobile video, PV helped to foster one. At a trade show in 1999 PV unveiled its technology by connecting a handheld computer to a cell phone to stream real time video at five frames per second over a cell phone network that was not designed to carry video. At a speed one-sixth that of television, the video stuttered, but it still offered a vivid demonstration of the technology's potential.

KEY DATES

1998: Company is founded.
2003: Network division is sold.
2005: Company is sold to NextWave Wireless Inc.
2006: TwonkyVision GmbH is acquired.
2009: Japanese firm DoCoMo acquires 35 percent interest in company.

In June 1999 the company was able to complete another round of financing, raising $4 million from Intel Corporation and Siemens Mustang Ventures GmbH, the investment arm of a German telecom company. A third round followed in December 1999, when PV raised $21 million from Intel and Siemens Mustang Ventures, along with Credit Suisse First Boston, Nexus Group LLC, Qualcomm, Reuters Group PLC, and Rockefeller. PV also hired a president of programming, recruiting Robert Tercek from Columbia TriStar Television, where he had been senior vice president of digital media. His task was to create programming to entice wireless carriers to employ PV's technology.

Cvengros now took over as CEO, and Carol became chairman, as PV prepared to make an initial public offering of stock, hoping to raise $64 million. Papers were filed in March 2000, but soon the NASDAQ began to falter because of a collapse of the technology sector. Five weeks later PV shelved the offering and again turned to private sources of capital, raising $16.5 million from Royal Philips Electronics, Sonera, Texas Instruments, and Time Warner. Another $100 million was then raised in February 2001 from a host of investors, most of whom already held interests in the company.

STRUCTURE AND OWNERSHIP CHANGES: 2003

Carol resumed his post as chief executive, but Brailean soon succeeded him as PV continued to test its software and wait for the market to catch up to its vision. While PV and Sprint PCS launched the first wireless video service in 2000, and in that same year Warner Bros. agreed to produce an original animated series for cell phone delivery, PV had to wait for wireless providers to upgrade their networks in order to have the capability of transmitting digital video before the service became commercially viable. Those providers, however, were reluctant to invest in upgrades as the wireless industry slumped, as did the economy in general. Brailean was

forced to lay off about one-third of PV's employees. In November 2003 he took a more drastic step, selling the network division to Alcatel, a wireless infrastructure company. Carol left the company in the fall of 2003 to pursue other interests.

No longer providing multimedia technology to wireless networks, PV focused its efforts on producing multimedia software for mobile phones and other devices. The company already had deals in place with eight carriers, including DoCoMo. In 2003 PV provided a media player for DoCoMo's 3G FOMA services in Japan and also launched a media player with Orange World service in France and Europe. The U.S. market lagged behind. It was not until 2005 that PV and Verizon Wireless launched VCAST Video on Demand.

PV did not become a public company. Instead, its investors cashed out in July 2005 when PV was sold to NextWave Wireless Inc., formed by NextWave Telecom in that same year. NextWave Telecom had been founded in the mid-1990s by former Qualcomm board member Allen Salmasi and made a mark by successfully bidding $4.7 billion for federal wireless spectrum licenses. Because the company was unable to pay for them, the government seized the licenses and re-auctioned them. NextWave sued and eventually won a decision in the U.S. Supreme Court in 2003. NextWave was then able to sell its spectrum to Verizon Wireless for $3 billion, pay off its creditors, and emerge from bankruptcy with $550 million in its coffers to launch NextWave Wireless and make acquisitions, such as PV; GO Networks Inc., a developer of municipal Wi-Fi networks; and IP Wireless, developer of the TD-CDMA (time division code division multiple access) technology.

TWONKYVISION ACQUIRED: 2006

With NextWave's backing, PV continued to develop its technology while pursuing external growth. In 2006 PV acquired SDC AG, a Swiss company that offered a JAVA music client for downloading music with digital rights management (DRM) protection to fend off piracy. The deal allowed PV to add JAVA clients to the multimedia client software it had to offer. SDC's Basel, Switzerland, office also became the PacketVideo development center for SDC (secure digital container) technology. PV acquired another European company in 2006, adding TwonkyVision GmbH, based in Berlin, Germany. A 2000 spin-off of Fraunhofer FOKUS Institute for Open Communications Systems, TwonkyVision developed universal plug-and-play audio-video middleware for media servers as well as embedded devices. By acquiring TwonkyVision's technology, PV hoped to speed up the convergence of mobile phones and consumer electronics. Moreover, TwonkyVision, which became PacketVideo Germany, enhanced PV's European presence.

The market was now catching up to PV, as consumers increasingly demanded more media content on their mobile phones and other handheld devices. In 2006 PV software was shipped in more than 60 million handsets. In that same year, DoCoMo used PV software to add Internet content within its media player, and PV won an Innovations Award at the highly influential Consumer Electronics Show. The following year PV software was included in more than 200 different devices and shipped in more than 200 million handsets. To keep pace, PV stepped up hiring, adding about 120 people in the course of a year. In later 2007 PV introduced an on-device portal for media services that in 2008 emerged as the MediaFusion content management and delivery platform, a single interface that allowed users access music, video, and interactive live TV.

PV found a way to tap into the success of Apple's iPhone in 2009, by developing a DVB-T broadcast receiver called "Telly" to deliver broadcast TV to iPhones as well as other Wi-Fi–enabled phones, portable media players, and computers. TwonkyVision, in the meantime, sought to take advantage of a growing demand for playing Internet video on flat screen televisions and home stereo systems. A number of set top boxes to play Internet content had emerged, and TwonkyVision in the fall of 2009 unveiled a media-sharing software solution, TwonkyBeam, that allowed consumers to send or "beam" Web-based media through wireless network-enabled devices for play on home audio-video equipment.

While PV was enjoying a strong market for its product offerings, its parent company was struggling, and the price of NextWave stock dipped below 10 cents. In late 2008 NextWave sold off its majority stake in IP Wireless for a fraction of the $100 million it paid just one year earlier. PV was now NextWave's main subsidiary. In July 2009, NextWave sold a 35 percent interest in it to DoCoMo for $45.5 million, using the money to pay down senior secured notes due in July 2010. Although NextWave's stock was trading at close to 50 cents in early 2010 and the future of the company was uncertain, PacketVideo remained a viable concern that was likely to enjoy strong growth as consumers increased their consumption of media on mobile phones, handheld computers, laptops, and other connected devices.

Ed Dinger

PRINCIPAL DIVISIONS

TwonkyMedia.

PRINCIPAL COMPETITORS

Motorola Inc.; Nokia Corporation; Samsung Group.

FURTHER READING

Allen, Mike, "Japanese Phone Company Takes Stake in Packet-Video," *San Diego Business Journal*, July 13, 2009, p. 6.

———, "PacketVideo Cuts Its Staff, Moves Back to Old Digs," *San Diego Business Journal*, April 15, 2002, p. 8.

Balint, Kathryn, "Events Finally Prove the Skeptics Wrong," *San Diego Union-Tribune*, May 17, 2005, p. C1.

———, "'Insatiable Appetite' NextWave See WiMax Feeding Popularity of Mobile Broadband," *San Diego Union-Tribune*, February 16, 2007, p. C1.

Brull, Steven V., "Coming to a Cell Phone Near You …; PacketVideo gives Hollywood an Entrée to the Mobile Net," *BusinessWeek*, July 3, 2000, p. 105.

Dano, Mike, "Alcatel Purchases PacketVideo Network Division," *RCR Wireless News*, p. 13.

Davies, Jennifer, "PacketVideo Forgoes IPO in Favor of Private Funding," *San Diego Union-Tribune*, March 13, 2001, p. C1.

"PacketVideo Lands Funding Windfall," *Wireless Week*, March 19, 2001, p. 18.

Schuk, Carolyn, "Bridging the Gap between 'Smart' Content, 'Dumb' Smartphones," *Broadcast Engineering*, March 3, 2009.

"Streaming with a Vision; Jim Carol," *Electronic Media*, March 5, 2001, p. 21.

RAND Corporation

—■—

1776 Main Street
P.O. Box 2138
Santa Monica, California 90407-2138
U.S.A.
Telephone: (310) 393-0411
Fax: (310) 393-4818
Web site: http://www.rand.org

Private Company
Founded: 1945 as Project RAND
Incorporated: 1948 as the RAND Corporation
Employees: 1,600 (est.)
Sales: $232.6 million (2009)
NAICS: 541910 Marketing Research and Public Opinion Polling; 541712 Research and Development in the Physical, Engineering, and Life Sciences (except Biotechnology); 541720 Research and Development in the Social Sciences and Humanities

■ ■ ■

A nonprofit public policy research institution based in Santa Monica, California, the RAND Corporation is the original think tank, providing research and analysis to decision makers in both the public and private sectors. For many years RAND focused primarily on U.S. military matters. The organization has expanded its purview to include a wide range of research areas, including the arts, civil justice, education, energy and environment, health care, population and aging, public safety, science and technology, terrorism and Homeland Security, transportation and infrastructure, and work-force and workplace concerns. More than 30 Nobel Prize winners have been associated with RAND over the course of its history. In addition to its Santa Monica campus, RAND maintains major offices in Arlington, Virginia, and Pittsburgh, Pennsylvania. International offices are located in the United Kingdom, Belgium, and Qatar. The organization also operates the Frederick S. Pardee RAND Graduate School, which offers advanced degrees in public policy analysis, and publishes the *RAND Journal of Economics*.

POST–WORLD WAR II ORIGINS

The seeds for the RAND Corporation were planted during World War II, which more than in previous wars was impacted by the contributions of scientists and engineers, whether it be efforts in cracking military codes, the development of radar, or the crash program to build the atom bomb. The British coined the term *think tank* during the war, but it was the general of the U.S. Army Air Forces, H. H. "Hap" Arnold, who vehemently argued that a private organization was needed to retain the scientists the war had brought together. This would enable them to continue their research and development efforts after the war's end in order to maintain national security, rather than wait for the next conflict and start from scratch. The advent of nuclear weapons, of course, made such an improvised approach obsolete and inadequate.

In October 1945, two months after the war ended, Arnold and several other men met at Hamilton Field in California to lay the groundwork for a new organization. They included Edward Bowles, a consultant to the secretary of war, from M.I.T.; Donald Douglas, president of Douglas Aircraft Company; Arthur Raymond, Douglas's chief engineer; and Franklin Collbohm, Raymond's assistant. It was Raymond who suggested the name Project RAND, which stood for research and development, and Collbohm who volunteered to run the operation while he recruited a permanent director. This temporary post lasted more than 20 years.

Project RAND was launched in December 1945 with an Army Air Force contract as a unit of Douglas Aircraft Company, operating out of a Douglas facility at Santa Monica's municipal airport. About six months later the organization issued its first report, a feasibility study that explored the concept of man-made satellites and set the standard for all RAND reports to follow. It combined solid engineering, compelling recommendations, and clear and concise prose to influence the way the Air Force, and the United States, viewed space initiatives for years to come. The report discussed possible propellants, optimum acceleration rates, the effectiveness of multiple-stage rockets, and the potential for someday using satellites to guide missiles to their targets.

INCORPORATION: 1947

RAND moved to offices in downtown Santa Monica in 1947 and ramped up the hiring of engineers, physicists, and aerodynamicists, as well as chemists, mathematicians, economists, and even psychologists. Another office was soon opened in Washington, D.C. Already the idea of severing ties with Douglas was being considered. These discussions led to the formation of the RAND Corporation as a nonprofit company under the laws of the State of California in May 1948. In November of that year Douglas transferred the Project RAND contract to the nonprofit.

In the meantime RAND had also arranged for financing from the Ford Foundation in the form of an interest-free loan. This would help RAND pursue nonmilitary research projects. The company soon made plans to construct a purpose-built facility. In 1953 it

moved into its new headquarters, where offices were arranged around a group of outdoor courtyards in such a way as to force chance encounters between researchers of different disciplines, thus helping to foster the collaborative spirit on which RAND was envisioned.

In many respects RAND enjoyed a golden era during the 1950s and 1960s, when its studies and recommendations had the greatest influence on the U.S. military and government. A RAND study shaped the Air Force's ballistic-missile program, which in turn laid the foundation for jump-starting the U.S. space program.

RAND analysts also played a key role in the United States' decision to base its nuclear deterrent bomber force in the United States rather than in Europe, where the planes were more vulnerable to sabotage or attack by the Soviet Union. As a result bombers carrying nuclear bombs were in the air at all times and were refueled in midair. Other recommendations eventually became accepted U.S military doctrine, including "fail-safe" procedures to recall bombers in the event of a mistake that could lead to war.

FOREIGN AND PUBLIC POLICY INFLUENCE: 1960–80

The cold calculation exhibited by the nuclear war strategists gave RAND a negative image in some quarters. While RAND maintained an air of detachment and objectivity, as well as being nonpolitical, it worked within a Cold War frame of reference in which, critics charged, the supremacy of American values was taken for granted and the need to counter Marxists at all costs was a given. Hence RAND researchers helped foster a foreign policy in which the United States supported military dictatorships rather than democracies (such as the case of South Vietnam), with less than desired outcomes. On the other hand, it was also a RAND researcher, Daniel Ellsberg, who in an effort to end the war in Vietnam made public a study of U.S. government decision making on Vietnam, the so-called Pentagon Papers, that created a political firestorm in 1971.

While some aspects of RAND's work may have been controversial, there was no doubt that the organization made a host of valuable contributions. In addition to laying the foundation for the space program, RAND contributed to the development of computers, linear programming, and digital communications. It also helped in the development of video recording technology, pioneered the concept of packet switching (which laid the foundation for the Internet), and championed systems analysis and game theory.

RAND's abilities were widely recognized, leading to more nonmilitary work in the 1970s, although the organization had had a considerable impact on social policy in the previous decade. Many of its more prominent members either joined or consulted for the Kennedy administration. Secretary of Defense Robert McNamara's "Whiz Kids" (many of them former RAND employees) championed the RAND-developed planning, programming, and budgeting system (PPBS) that would become a mandated federal standard by President Lyndon Johnson's subsequent administration. During this period RAND also pursued some less than ordinary topics. It studied the effects of LSD in the early 1960s. Later in the decade a RAND aeronautical engineer wrote a seminal study on the concept of windsurfing.

In the 1970s RAND devoted much of its time to a number of domestic projects, including studies related to urban governance, insurance, and health care issues. It also worked internationally, for example studying storm barriers on the northern coast of the Netherlands. With the election of Ronald Reagan as president in 1980, military spending was increased, leading to more Pentagon funding for RAND. At the same time, federal funding for research on social policy issues was cut, leading to RAND taking on work from business consortiums, international organizations such as the World Bank, and foreign governments.

COLD WAR END CHANGES FOCUS

By the end of the 1980s the Soviet Union was beginning to collapse. Upon the Soviet Union's dissolution in the early 1990s, the United States became interested in enjoying the benefits of a "peace dividend," leading to sharp cuts in military spending. At the height of the Reagan administration, about 97 percent of RAND's funds came from federal, state, or local government coffers. With three-quarters of its revenues still derived from the military, RAND shed some jobs and began to revise its mission, hoping to achieve a 50-50 mix of military and civilian funding.

In its search for new revenue streams, RAND opened an office in the Netherlands and looked to other locales as well. At home it solicited more projects related to education and health care. In Santa Monica it learned some of the obstacles inherent in making the transition to civilian projects. Hired to study Santa Monica High School's condom-distribution program, RAND provoked the ire of parents upset over some of the questions its researchers asked.

In 1995 RAND decided the time had come to study itself. In the process of forging a new long-term strategic business plan, RAND reorganized its operation and replaced three of the vice presidents heading its five primary research divisions. In addition, for the first time in its history, RAND launched a major fund-raising drive to attract private-sector contributions to its endowment. It was not an easy transition. In the mid-1990s only 13.5 percent of the organization's work came from nongovernment clients. The wider RAND cast its net, the more it risked losing its luster and becoming just another one of the research organizations that had opened over the years.

RAND's reorganization continued in the new century. The company sold its 11.3-acre headquarters to the city of Santa Monica for $53 million in April 2000. RAND then leased the facility from the city while planning a new headquarters on property not owned by the city. The new headquarters eventually opened in 2004. RAND also moved its fast-growing Washington, D.C., office to larger accommodations in nearby Arlington, Virginia, and a second East Coast office was opened in Pittsburgh, Pennsylvania, in 2000. In addition RAND began the 2000s with its first public fund-raising effort, part of a $100 million campaign. In 2001 RAND established an office in Cambridge, England, to perform public policy research in the United Kingdom.

FIRST NON-AMERICAN TRUSTEE

The international flavor of RAND increased as the new century unfolded. In 2002 it elected its first trustee from outside the United States: Carl Bildt, a former prime minister of Sweden. RAND reached an agreement the following year to open an operation in Qatar, the RAND-Qatar Policy Institute. In 2008 RAND opened an office in Brussels, Belgium, to expand its opportunities in Europe. At the same time, RAND expanded the breadth of its work in the United States, adding research areas as well as new offices, including Jackson, Mississippi, in 2006, and Boston in 2009. RAND was expected to continue to have a major voice in public policy, whether it involved national security or social issues, both in the United States and abroad.

Ed Dinger

PRINCIPAL SUBSIDIARIES

Frederick S. Pardee RAND Graduate School; RAND Journal of Economics.

PRINCIPAL COMPETITORS

Aerospace Corporation; Institute for Defense Analyses; MITRE Corporation.

FURTHER READING

Abella, Alex, *Soldiers of Reason*. New York: Harcourt, 2008.

Campbell, Virginia, "How RAND Invented the Postwar World," *Invention & Technology*, Summer 2004.

Daniels, Wade, and Daniel Taub, "Think Tank Targets New Client Base," *Los Angeles Business Journal*, September 29, 1997, p. 1.

Deady, Tim, "Rand Scopes Out New Raison d'etre in Post-Cold War Social Structure," *Los Angeles Business Journal*, June 14, 1993, p. 23.

———, "Southland Think Tanks Are Rethinking Their Future," *Los Angeles Business Journal*, September 21, 1992, p. 6.

Harris, Roy J., Jr., "Peace Games: After the Cold War, Rand Remakes Itself as a Civilian Expert," *Wall Street Journal*, June 18, 1993, p. A1.

King, Danny, "Rand Corp. Expected to Stay at Its Home by the Sea," *Los Angeles Business Journal*, May 20, 2002, p. 12.

Stern, Sol, "Who Thinks in a Think Tank?" *New York Times*, April 16, 1967.

Realogy Corporation

1 Campus Drive
Parsippany, New Jersey 07054-4407
U.S.A.
Telephone: (973) 407-2000
Fax: (973) 407-7004
Web site: http://www.realogy.com

Private Company
Incorporated: 2006
Employees: 11,400
Sales: $3.9 million (2009)
NAICS: 531210 Offices of Real Estate Agents and Brokers; 531390 Other Activities Related to Real Estate; 541191 Title Abstract and Settlement Offices

∎ ∎ ∎

Based in Parsippany, New Jersey, Realogy Corporation is one of the largest global providers of real estate and relocation services. It has both franchised and company-owned brokerages, operating as Better Homes and Gardens Real Estate, Century 21, Coldwell Banker, Coldwell Banker Commercial, Corcoran Group, ERA, ONCOR International, and Sotheby's International Realty. It also provides worldwide relocation management through Cartus Corporation, as well as title and settlement services.

HFS ROOTS

Although Realogy Corporation did not become known by that name until 2006, the roots of the organization were formed over a decade earlier. In 1995 Hospitality Franchise Systems (HFS), a fast-growing corporation that was involved in hotel franchising, decided to venture into real estate and acquired Century 21 Real Estate Corporation, the world's largest brokerage franchisor, for $200 million. The following year, HFS increased its real estate interests and, for $36.8 million, purchased ERA Franchise Systems Inc. It followed this by buying Coldwell Banker Real Estate Corporation, for which it paid $640 million in cash and repaid an additional $105 million in debt.

In 1997, extending its real estate interests beyond brokerage firms, HFS acquired PHH Group, an automobile fleet management company that had a real estate and relocation division. That same year, HFS merged with CUC International Inc., a global marketing company, and HFS and CUC became jointly known as Cendant Corporation. In a joint venture with Apollo Management, a New York-based private-equity real estate firm, Cendant formed the National Realty Trust LLC (NRT) in order to manage and acquire company-owned brokerage firms and separate them from the franchised brokerages. In keeping with Cendant's cross-marketing strategy, PHH became the sole mortgage provider for all NRT acquisitions.

Shortly after the HFS and CUC merger, however, fraudulent accounting practices at CUC were uncovered. The value of Cendant Corporation stock was halved in a single day and then continued to dive. While the former chairman and the former president of CUC were indicted on criminal charges, Henry Silverman, founder of HFS, became the CEO of Cendant. Silverman worked to repair the damage from the massive account-

COMPANY PERSPECTIVES

Realogy's business model is structured around our unique "Value Circle" approach. The integration of our company's service offerings provides our business units with excellent cross-selling opportunities while enabling customers to enjoy the convenience of a single-source solution for all their real estate needs.

ing scandal. Within two years the company was recovering and back to making acquisitions.

GROWTH OF NRT

During this time, NRT had been growing at a remarkable rate. Less than three years after it had been founded, NRT had acquired more than 157 companies. In 2000 the company had the industry's top closed sales volume of $105 billion. In 2002 Cendant further expanded its real estate investments and purchased complete interest in NRT, paying $230 million in stock and assuming a $300 million debt.

In 2004 Cendant bought Sotheby's International Realty, a high-end brokerage firm, for $100 million. Cendant, already the nation's largest real estate company had become even larger. Sotheby's competed in New York with Corcoran Realty, which Cendant had previously acquired. In the February 18, 2004, issue of *Newsday* writer Murray Christian quoted Richard A. Smith, chief executive of Cendant's Real Estate Services Division, as he reflected on the Cendant acquisition policy, "There is room for competition. Until we have 100 percent market share we all have room."

Despite Cendant's solid growth, the stock price did not, in the judgment of Cendant management, reflect the organization's worth. CEO Silverman, who had been criticized for being one of the highest-paid corporate executives while the Cendant shares lost value, announced that, by 2006, the company would spin off its various components, including the real estate interests, into separate companies. Cendant had already made PHH, its mortgage unit, independent.

BIRTH OF REALOGY

In July 2006 the Cendant Corporation holdings were divided into four separate companies and the real estate business became the publicly traded Realogy. The name (pronounced REEL-uh-gee) was created from a fusion of the term *real estate* and the Greek root *-logy*, meaning "study of." Realogy began trading on the New York Stock Exchange under the ticker symbol H, chosen to represent homes, and Cendant shareholders received one share of Realogy for every four shares of Cendant common stock. They would also receive compensation for the other units of Cendant that were part of the spin-off.

Realogy now consisted of the Cendant companies that focused on residential and commercial real estate, relocation services, and title and settlement units. Silverman became the Realogy CEO.

The new organization maintained the structure that existed when it was part of Cendant and consisted of four units: Realogy Franchise Group, NRT, Cartus (formerly Cendant Mobility), and Title Resource Group. The franchise group included several companies whose brands competed with one another but collectively had a major share of the real estate market. Century 21, formed in Southern California in 1971, had become the world's largest residential real estate sales organization. ERA Real Estate (originally called Electronic Realty Associates) capitalized on its tradition of innovation and technological savvy. Coldwell Banker, founded in the aftermath of the 1906 San Francisco earthquake, had become a leading residential and commercial brokerage brand. Sotheby's International Realty, benefiting from its affiliation with the well-known auction house, specialized in luxury real estate. ONCOR International, acquired soon after the spin-off, was a worldwide commercial real estate referral network. All these companies had a global reach and an extensive franchise network.

NRT, as the nation's largest real estate brokerage firm, operated the brokerage offices that were directly owned by Realogy. Its operations were usually affiliated with Realogy's franchise brands, although some were associated with more local brands, such as the Corcoran Group and Citi Habitats. Cartus Corporation provided worldwide employee relocation services and had more than half of the *Fortune* 500 companies as clients. The Title Resource Group, operating under a multitude of distinct brand names, provided closing, title, and settlement services for real estate transactions. In 2006 the *Wall Street Journal*'s inaugural listing of the "Real Estate Top 200" gave all four top awards to Realogy brokerages. The scope and reach of the newly minted real estate empire were enormous.

GOING PRIVATE

On April 10, 2007, Realogy was sold to an affiliate of Apollo Management L.P., the same organization that had helped form NRT in 1997, for $8.5 billion. Real-

KEY DATES

1995: Hospitality Franchise Systems (HFS) acquires Century 21.

1997: Company merges with CUC International and becomes Cendant Corporation.

2004: Cendant buys Sotheby's International Realty.

2006: Realogy is listed on the New York Stock Exchange.

2007: Company is sold to Apollo Management.

2010: Primacy Relocation is acquired.

ogy ceased trading on the New York Stock Exchange and stockholders were paid $30 per share. Although the purchase of Realogy took place as the real estate market was faltering, Realogy management believed that the private-equity firm could take a longer-term view of the company's value than stockholders had. According to Silverman, quoted in the December 19, 2006, *Wall Street Journal*, "The view of the board is that companies with declining earnings and no visible growth should be private. ... The people who own our stock have a five-second view. ... They don't have that kind of patience."

In 2008 Smith, CEO of the Cendant Real Estate Services Division, became the Realogy CEO. The housing market continued to be weak but Realogy remained bullish on real estate's long-term prospects. In July 2008 it unveiled a licensing deal with *Better Homes and Gardens* magazine (owned by Meredith Corporation) to promote a branded real estate operation based on the magazine's iconic name. The licensing agreement between Realogy and Better Homes and Gardens Real Estate specified a 50-year term, with a renewal option for another 50 years. Realogy also continued to expand its innovative Internet marketing techniques, using partnerships with Google, Openhouse and Homescape to extend its Internet presence.

By June 2009 Realogy had approximately 14,400 franchised and company-owned offices and 270,000 sales associates in the United States and 92 other countries and territories around the world. This included over 790 company-owned-and-operated brokerage offices. Nevertheless, the shaky economy, the fragile real estate market, and the debt Realogy assumed when it was bought by Apollo Management had a serious effect on Realogy's bottom line. Although Realogy initiated many new policies to cut costs and function more efficiently, including reducing its lobbying budget, it continued to struggle. In early 2009 Realogy looked close to bankruptcy.

ICAHN FILES LAWSUIT

In 2008 the company had attempted to reduce the impact of its indebtedness through restructuring its obligations. The company's toggle note holders (a debt whose interest payments can be deferred until the note's maturity), led by financier Carl Icahn and the Bank of New York Mellon, filed a lawsuit in Delaware to prevent the move. The court ruled against Realogy.

In September 2009, however, Realogy was rescued from default through $515 million raised in new loans, more than half of which were slated to reduce the company's older debts. Around 30 percent of the loan was provided by Icahn. Apollo increased its investment in Realogy by purchasing approximately $970 million in bonds.

Although the company remained $6.3 billion in debt, Realogy viewed these investments as a sign of investor confidence in the long-term value of the organization and a way to ensure its flexibility. By the third quarter of 2009, Realogy, as well as the rest of the real estate industry, was experiencing some positive results as a result of the first-time homebuyer tax credit that had been passed by the U.S. Congress as part of an economic stimulus package. Realogy reported net revenue of $1.2 billion, a profit of $58 million, and a slight improvement in home sales.

Soon afterward, Sotheby's International Realty, a Realogy subsidiary, expanded its presence in Germany and the Caribbean. Coldwell Banker launched a new online property search Web site. In early 2010 Realogy was back in the acquisition business. Cartus, a Realogy relocation business unit, bought Primacy Relocation, a Tennessee firm with 25 global offices. The terms of the transaction were not disclosed. Despite the economy, the company's debt, and the weak real estate market, with this acquisition, Realogy was repositioning itself for strategic growth.

Grace Murphy

PRINCIPAL SUBSIDIARIES

Better Homes and Gardens Real Estate LLC; Century 21 Real Estate LLC; Coldwell Banker Real Estate LLC; Coldwell Banker Commercial; ERA Franchise Systems LLC; NRT LLC; ONCOR International LLC; Sotheby's International Realty Affiliates LLC.

PRINCIPAL DIVISIONS

Realogy Franchise Group; Cartus Corporation; Title Resource Group.

PRINCIPAL COMPETITORS

HomeServices of America, Inc.; LandAmerica Financial Group, Inc.; Cushman & Wakefield, Inc.; CB Richard Ellis Group, Inc.; RE/MAX International, Inc.; Weichert Realtors.

FURTHER READING

Berman, Dennis K., and James R. Hagerty, "Apollo Management Is Poised to Acquire Realogy," *Wall Street Journal*, December 18, 2006, p. A3.

Evans, Blanche, "Realogy Goes Private," *RealtyTimes*, December 19, 2006, http://realtytimes.com/rtpages/20061219_realogyprivate.htm.

Farzad, Roben, "Heads They Win, Tails You Lose; Expect to Hear More Tales Like Cendant's: A Dealmaking Disaster for Investors," *Business Week*, December 8, 2008.

"Franchisor Puts Scandal Behind It; Cendant Turns Corner, Shows Sharp Gains in Revenues, Switches Approach,"

Crain's New York Business, January 19, 2004.

Ives, Nat, "Licensing Deal: Home Run—Or House of Cards?" *Advertising Age*, October 8, 2007.

Juliano, Michael C., "Cartus Buys Rival Primacy," *Connecticut Post*, January 21, 2010.

Murray, Christian, "New York-Based Real Estate Firm Cendant Buys Sotheby's International Realty," *Newsday*, February 18, 2004.

Perrotta, Adam, "Realogy Expands Commercial Activity with ONCOR Acquisition," *Commercial Property News*, October 5, 2006.

"Realogy Closes on $515 Million of Expected $650 Million of Second Lien Incremental Term Loans," *Internet Wire*, September 28, 2009.

"Realogy Subsidiary, Cartus, Acquires Primacy Relocation Acquisition Positions Realogy for Strategic Growth across Its International and Domestic Businesses," PRinside.com, January 21, 2010.

Red Spot Paint & Varnish Company, Inc.

1107 East Louisiana Street
Evansville, Indiana 47711-4747
U.S.A.
Telephone: (812) 428-9100
Toll Free: (800) 457-3544
Fax: (812) 428-9167
Web site: http://www.redspot.com

Wholly Owned Subsidiary of Fujikura Kasei Co., Ltd.
Founded: 1903 as Evansville Paint & Varnish Company
Employees: 262
Sales: $50 million (2009 est.)
NAICS: 325510 Paint and Coating Manufacturing

■ ■ ■

Red Spot Paint & Varnish Company, Inc., a subsidiary of the Japanese company Fujikura Kasei Co., Ltd., is a leading supplier of coatings for plastics. Founded as a hardware retailer in 1903, Red Spot has concentrated on plastics since the 1930s. The company formulates and manufactures paints and primers for sporting equipment, personal electronics, aerospace components, cosmetics packaging, and business machines. The bulk of its business, however, is in the automotive sector, where it supplies an array of coatings that are used on cars—from bumper to bumper, both inside and out. General Motors Corporation, Ford Motor Company, Chrysler Group LLC, and Toyota Motor Corporation are among Red Spot's major automotive customers.

The company's technologically innovative coatings developed in the 1990s and early 21st century, including

its environmentally friendly ultraviolet-curable coatings, helped it top $100 million in sales by 2002. Nevertheless, the shrinking automotive market, the global economic recession that began in late 2007, and an environmental contamination lawsuit led to a reversal in the company's fortunes. Fujikura Kasei bought Red Spot in 2008 for $63.2 million, ending four generations of family ownership. By the next year Red Spot faced a costly cleanup of toxic chemicals around its Evansville plant, its workforce had shrunk to around half of what it had been at its peak early in the decade, and its sales had been slashed to only $50 million.

PAINTING PLASTIC IN THE EARLY 20TH CENTURY

In 1903 Harry D. Bourland founded Evansville Paint & Varnish Co. in Evansville, Indiana. Bourland initially sold hardware and turpentine wholesale to dealers, but the company flourished as he expanded the product offerings and opened his own retail hardware stores in the tristate area where Indiana, Kentucky, and Illinois meet. Seeking to broaden his company's appeal in the region, Bourland changed its name to Red Spot Paint & Varnish in 1921. The company's bull's-eye logo became a familiar sight in the area.

In 1927 Rozaline Bourland, the daughter of Red Spot's founder, married Milton Z. Thorson. This marriage proved auspicious for the family business as Thorson ultimately transformed the company from an Indiana-based paint seller to an international force in paints and plastics. Thorson gradually rose through the company ranks, moving up from brush cleaner to traveling salesman. In 1937 he was approached by a representative of Hoosier Cardinal, Inc., a plastics manufacturer that was experimenting with a paint which could be applied to the back side of clear plastic. Hoosier called the end result a "see deep finish." The plastics industry was young, and Hoosier needed someone to manufacture this novel paint. Hoosier's request seemed an odd one, as no one had previously considered mixing plastics and paints. When Thorson ran the idea by Red Spot's only researcher, he laughed and told Thorson to focus on furniture coatings.

Disregarding this advice, however, Thorson followed his gut and made Red Spot the exclusive paint supplier to Hoosier. Red Spot opened a coating development laboratory and a production facility to accommodate Hoosier's needs. The partnership flourished, and by the late 1930s the Evansville area was referred to as "Plastics Valley."

WORLD WAR II AND THE MATURATION OF THE PLASTICS INDUSTRY

Red Spot's rise was closely linked to that of the plastics industry as a whole. The outbreak of World War II in 1939 created great demand for all sorts of plastic products, particularly those that could substitute for materials, such as rubber, that were in short supply because of the war effort. During the war years, Thorson landed Red Spot contracts for defense supplies. For example, Red Spot provided salt-resistant paints, in the obligatory olive drab combat colors, to Chrysler Corporation's ammunition plant.

Even beyond the short-term economic opportunities, the war had a profound effect on the plastics industry as a whole. With the tremendous national push for the large-scale production of synthetic rubbers, researchers undertook an extensive examination of the chemistry of polymer formations to figure out how best to achieve this goal. Their findings markedly broadened the industry's understanding of the ways plastics could be created and the range of feasible uses for them. In the decade following the war, plastics producers developed such industry workhorses as polypropylene

and high-density polyethylene, which had a broad spectrum of important applications.

Red Spot was determined to be a part of the expansion of the postwar plastics industry. Using its wartime relationship with Chrysler as a jumping-off point, Red Spot spent the immediate postwar years looking for new markets. It courted both appliance and automotive manufacturers, who were incorporating new plastics into their products and needed coatings for these materials. While these efforts bore some fruit during the 1950s, the company's field of vision still did not extend far beyond the tristate area. Red Spot ended the decade still regarded primarily as a house paint manufacturer and hardware retailer for the Indiana-Illinois-Kentucky region.

Thorson had a different vision for Red Spot. Recognizing that the plastics business was likely to go global as Europe and Asia continued to rebound from the devastation of the war years, Thorson took his first overseas trip to Paris in 1959 to drum up business for his paints. The company was so shocked by what it perceived to be another of Thorson's quirky ideas that he was forced to pay for his trip himself. Undeterred, Thorson followed up his European tour with trips to the Far East, and by the early 1960s Red Spot was doing business with Japanese electronics companies. At the same time, Red Spot obtained manufacturing licenses in England and Australia and found sales agents in Japan and Hong Kong. An interesting dichotomy developed, as Red Spot's domestic sales were driven by its house paints and other maintenance coatings, while it built its reputation overseas on industrial coatings. The industrial side of the business grew rapidly in the succeeding years.

DRAMATIC CHANGES 1970–90

The plastics industry continued to evolve rapidly. The 1970s saw the introduction of extremely dense plastics, particularly linear low-density polyethylene, released in 1978, which were sufficiently strong and reliable to compete with more "traditional" materials, such as metal, wood, paper, glass, and leather. As large-scale production of this new generation of plastics began, the costs of these materials fell dramatically. Consequently, manufacturers in a variety of industries turned to these high-performance and inexpensive new plastics to replace the more expensive natural materials on which they had previously relied. Seizing this opportunity, plastics producers began to tinker with alloys and blends of polymers, which made it possible to create individualized plastics capable of satisfying specific performance requirements. This customization further broadened the uses to which these plastics could be put. Automobile

KEY DATES

1903: Harry D. Bourland founds Evansville Paint & Varnish in Evansville, Indiana.

1921: The company is renamed Red Spot Paint & Varnish.

1937: Company develops the first decorative coating for plastic in the world.

1959: Red Spot begins to market its products outside the United States.

2000: Red Spot forms a global alliance with Sonneborn & Rieck Ltd. and Fujikura Kasei Co., Ltd.

2005: Ecology Coatings, Inc., grants Red Spot a license to manufacture and sell its ultraviolet-curable coatings.

2008: Fujikura Kasei buys Red Spot through its U.S. subsidiary, Fujichem, Inc.

2009: Red Spot settles pollution lawsuit with real estate developer 1100 West.

manufacturers were particularly interested in these strong, resilient, and comparatively inexpensive new plastics. As they were significantly lighter than traditional materials, they increased fuel efficiency, a notable concern during the decade's energy crisis.

Car companies had some very particular requirements, however. They needed specialized coatings for the new materials. They were also extremely concerned that the plastics used in cars did not look or feel like traditional industrial plastics, as consumers were adamant about avoiding coldly "institutional" vehicles. Automakers turned to coatings manufacturers such as Red Spot for color-keyed interior auto parts and specialized lacquer coatings. Red Spot in turn developed vacuum metallizing coatings that allowed mirror-bright finishes on plastics, which the auto industry cherished.

Red Spot grew significantly in the 1980s. One key factor in its success was its development of a urethane coating flexible enough to withstand impact on newly developed plastic. In other words, Red Spot produced the first paint that could be used on a plastic car bumper. To boost production, Red Spot expanded its facilities with an eye toward accommodating the needs of the Detroit automotive sector. The company purchased a manufacturing plant in Westland, Michigan, in 1987 and a sales office in Plymouth, Michigan, two years later. Despite its increased attention to production and sales, the company remained focused

on product development. Nearly one-quarter of Red Spot's employees were involved in research and development.

By the early 1990s, Red Spot was at a crossroads. Its hardware stores, once the core of its business, were struggling to remain profitable, and it was clear that the company's future centered on automotive coatings, not consumer paints. In 1991, therefore, the company eliminated its retail division, severing that link with its roots.

NEW ENVIRONMENTAL REGULATIONS

The 1990s brought a multitude of changes to the coatings industry in the form of more vigilant environmental regulations. The Clean Air Act Amendments of 1990 empowered the Environmental Protection Agency to regulate and limit the devastating environmental impact of volatile organic compounds (VOCs), which were a common component of many coatings. Many states, most notably California, adopted even tougher standards. These new restrictions required the coatings industry not only to limit VOCs in the coatings produced but also to change the process by which the coatings were applied. Many of the high-tech coatings developed for the automotive industry in the 1970s and 1980s used solvent solutions to apply the coatings, which were out of compliance with the new environmental laws.

Car manufacturers did not want to have to choose between innovative, high-quality coatings and environmental compliance. The onus thus fell on coatings manufacturers to develop cost-effective, high-tech coatings that met the new regulations. Moving away from the lacquers, enamels, and solvent-borne (or solvent-applied) paints that had been the primary coatings used for carmakers in the 1960s and 1970s, coatings manufacturers in the 1990s perfected high-solid enamels (which contained fewer VOCs than the earlier enamels), waterborne coatings (instead of solvent-borne ones), and powder coatings. This change was a dramatic one. "These new products represent a 95 percent turnover in chemistries from just ten years ago," an industry insider told *Industrial Paint and Powder* in October 1994. This burst of innovation belied the chorus of complaints that had been raised by both the automotive and coatings industries about the apocalyptic impact the stricter regulations would have on their businesses. Red Spot was particularly well positioned to benefit from the changes necessitated by the new laws. The company had always placed a premium on innovation and new technology rather than on the mass production of basic coatings.

ADJUSTING TO GLOBALIZING CUSTOMERS

New environmental regulations were not the only dramatic change for the automotive coatings industry in the early 1990s. The globalization of the automotive sector raised the bar for coatings producers still further during this period. Thorson had indeed seen the future in 1959 when he had boarded a plane to Paris to drum up overseas business. As they moved away from their national roots to become multinational conglomerates, car companies wanted relationships with fewer suppliers. They wanted coatings producers who could make all the coatings needed for a given car, and they wanted to build partnerships with coatings companies that had a global base. Once again, Red Spot was in an ideal position to benefit from this change. By 1993 Red Spot was ringing up $70 million in sales annually, with about 18 percent of the revenues generated in international markets.

In 1994 Red Spot opened a new facility that promised to meet its dual needs, increasing both manufacturing capacity and its research and development base. This $8.3 million, 53,500-square-foot plant was the world's largest facility for the development of automotive plastics. The company planned to use its new facility to create environmentally friendly coatings for plastics used in cars.

Red Spot, however, was not the only company seeking to make bold technological leaps. In the mid-1990s Red Spot found itself in a race against rival Morton Automotive Coatings to develop a waterborne "soft-touch" coating. Auto designers were interested in cutting manufacturing costs by limiting the amount of foam and upholstery used on the interior of a car. Rather than layering a soft material on top of plastic, they wanted a coating that would be soft to the touch. In other words, they wanted a paint for car interiors that felt like velvet. The real challenge was to develop this coating without a solvent-borne application. By 1995 Red Spot had produced the first waterborne soft-touch coating, which it named Soft Feel. Two years later, General Motors selected the coating for the interior of the Pontiac Grand Am.

Buoyed by this success, Red Spot opened a 28,000-square-foot Coatings Application Center in Plymouth, Michigan, in 1998. The facility was intended for the development of application systems as well as pioneering new decorative coatings. That same year, however, Red Spot reported the first losing year in its history, when Ford, its longtime mainstay customer, chose a different supplier. Red Spot subsequently diversified its automotive clients to lessen its reliance on Ford.

A REVERSAL OF FORTUNES IN THE NEW MILLENNIUM

The red ink of 1998 was the first sign of a reversal in Red Spot's fortunes. At the dawn of the 21st century, Red Spot attempted to grow its international sales, which by 2000 had risen to account for over 20 percent of total revenue, by establishing additional licenses and sales agents. It also formed several alliances with key international partners. Most importantly, Red Spot in 2000 entered into a global alliance with the English coatings manufacturer Sonneborn & Rieck Ltd. and the Japanese firm Fujikura Kasei. This partnership was well devised because the products manufactured by these companies complemented Red Spot's. For example, Fujikura specialized in the production of the raw acrylics that Red Spot used in its coatings.

Red Spot expanded its reach even further in December 2000 when it acquired Michigan-based Seibert-Oxidermo, Inc., which specialized in primers for plastics and other coatings used in the transportation industry. Red Spot's president declared that the move provided "further penetration into other areas of the transportation sector and complements our core businesses." In 2001, however, when sales topped $95 million, the company barely survived the economic downturn and at one point hovered close to bankruptcy.

During the decade, Red Spot invested heavily in research into improved ultraviolet-curable coatings. These coatings contained no water or solvents that would need to evaporate in order for the coating to set. This reduced the space needed to coat a product, lowered energy consumption by 75 percent, and made the coating more environmentally sound. In 2005 Ecology Coatings, Inc., granted Red Spot a license to manufacture and sell its ultraviolet-curable coatings, and by 2006 the company had partnered in a venture to develop an ultraviolet-curable powder coating that would produce a chrome finish. The process had been improved enough by 2009 that it was being used for taillight surrounds and some interior door parts in some car models. Another research partnership developed a powder-priming technique for sheet molding compound.

END OF FAMILY OWNERSHIP

In 2008 Fujikura Kasei acquired Red Spot for $63.2 million, ending four generations of family ownership. Red Spot became a wholly owned subsidiary of Fujichem, Inc., itself a subsidiary of Fujikura Kasei. CEO Charles Storms, a grandson of Milton Thorson, became a senior adviser to Red Spot, while Hiro Araki became Red Spot's president and CEO. The headquarters remained in Evansville, and none of its 345 workers was laid off at that time.

Part of the motivation for selling Red Spot may have been a pending environmental-contamination lawsuit, filed in 2003 by 1100 West LLC, a real estate development firm in Evansville. Soon after the sale was complete, the federal judge in the case declared that Red Spot had failed to be truthful about its use of toxic chlorinated solvents, hiding damning evidence and making "a mockery of the discovery process," reported Dan Shaw in the July 4, 2009, *Evansville Courier and Press.* The judge ordered Red Spot to clean up the site, giving the two companies six months to settle on an amount to pay for the cleanup. In November 2009 Shaw reported that the two companies had settled for an undisclosed amount.

In addition, the global economic recession that began in late 2007 and hit U.S. automakers hard also had a devastating impact on Red Spot. The U.S. auto industry had focused much of its attention on sport-utility vehicles, which, as the decade wore on and fuel prices continued to increase, became less popular with U.S. consumers. Additionally, as credit tightened and unemployment rose, sales of new vehicles plunged. U.S. carmakers, who had pinned their profitability on gas-guzzling large vehicles, were particularly hard hit. In late 2008 and 2009 the U.S. government gave millions in emergency assistance to General Motors and Chrysler, both of which ultimately filed for bankruptcy, and provided a line of credit to Ford. The big three U.S. automakers closed factories, shut down brands altogether, and produced fewer cars, leading to a huge drop-off in demand for Red Spot's automotive coatings.

The decade that had started with such promise for the company ended with much uncertainty. Nearly 100 employees were laid off in late 2008 and 2009, and company sales dropped to only $50 million in 2009. The environmental-contamination lawsuit had damaged the company's credibility. The shaky nature of the U.S. auto industry was an even greater threat to Red Spot's continued profitability. It remained unclear whether Red Spot would be able to recover as the nation began on a path to an economic rebound.

Rebecca Stanfel
Updated, Melissa J. Doak

PRINCIPAL SUBSIDIARIES

Red Spot Paint Canada Ltd.; Red Spot Westland, Inc.

PRINCIPAL COMPETITORS

Akzo Nobel N.V.; E.I. du Pont de Nemours and Company; The Valspar Corporation.

FURTHER READING

Bailey, Jane M., "Top Coatings Manufacturers Speak Out," *Industrial Paint and Powder,* June 1994, pp. 14–19.

———, "Where Paint Meets the Environment," *Industrial Paint and Powder,* October 1994, pp. 14–17.

"Milton Thorson: Paints, Plastics Executive," *Evansville (IN) Courier and Press,* December 3, 1999.

Schuch, Linda K., "New Wave Waterborne Offers Soft Feel Finish," *Industrial Paint and Powder,* March 1997, pp. 14+.

"Seibert-Oxidermo Acquired by Red Spot," *Journal of Coatings Technology,* December 2000, p. 20.

Shaw, Dan, "Jobs Lost at Red Spot; Falling Demand Blamed for Reduction," *Evansville (IN) Courier and Press,* May 15, 2009, p. B10.

———, "Red Spot Has Month to Plan Cleanup," *Evansville (IN) Courier and Press,* July 4, 2009, p. A1.

———, "Red Spot May Settle Pollution Suit," *Evansville (IN) Courier and Press,* November 10, 2009, p. B10.

Success When You Least Expect It: The Story of the Red Spot Paint & Varnish Company, 1903–2003 and Beyond, Evansville, IN: Red Spot Paint & Varnish Company, 2008, 264 p.

Wersich, Carol, "Local Paint Company Grows to Global Proportions," *Evansville (IN) Courier and Press,* November 1, 2005, p. E26.

———, "Red Spot Sold to Japanese Firm; None of Company's 345 Workers Will Be Cut," *Evansville (IN) Courier and Press,* April 22, 2008, p. B6.

Reichhold, Inc.

———————————◼———————————

2400 Ellis Road
Durham, North Carolina 27703-5543
U.S.A.
Telephone: (919) 990-7500
Toll Free: (800) 448-3482
Fax: (919) 990-7711
Web site: http://www.reichhold.com

Private Company
Founded: 1927
Incorporated: 1930
Employees: 1,400
Sales: $876 million (2009)
NAICS: 324121 Asphalt Paving Mixture and Block Manufacturing; 324122 Asphalt Shingle and Coating Materials Manufacturing; 325211 Plastics Material and Resin Manufacturing; 325510 Paint and Coating Manufacturing; 325520 Adhesive Manufacturing; 325613 Surface Active Agent Manufacturing

◼ ◼ ◼

One of the original developers of alkyd resins for the paint industry, Reichhold, Inc., is a leading manufacturer of coating resins and unsaturated polyester resins for use in composites. The company was founded in the 1920s by a German immigrant who provided new, fast-drying paints to the automotive industry. Since that time Reichhold's products have been used in bath and shower manufacturing, marine construction, the transportation industry, and wind energy applications,

among others. In the coatings business, Reichhold resins are used in urethanes, epoxies, paints, varnishes, and other products. Reichhold resins are also used in graphic arts applications, in both traditional and digital printing. Under Japanese ownership beginning in the late 1980s, Reichhold was purchased by its U.S. management team in 2005, and the new owners outlined a business plan that emphasized controlling costs, improving productivity, and providing customer value. In addition, Reichhold began an expansion into Asian markets, specifically China and India.

EARLY YEARS: 1924–38

Helmuth (Henry) Reichhold emigrated from Germany to the United States in 1924 to study surface-finishing methods in the U.S. automobile industry. He began his career as a lab assistant at the Ford Motor Company in Detroit, Michigan, but soon was promoted to head of the paint laboratory. At the time, Ford was using finishes on its cars that took days to dry, which was an obstacle to mass production.

In 1925 Henry Reichhold learned that Beck, Koller & Company in Vienna, where Reichhold's father was a principal, had developed a heat-hardening and oil-soluble resin that dried in hours rather than days. Reichhold began importing these resins to create a quick-drying paint for the Model-T. He opened his own paint and varnish factory in 1927 as a subsidiary of his father's business. In 1929 Reichhold bought Synthe-Copal Company of Buffalo, New York, which manufactured ester gums, the raw material used to cre-

COMPANY PERSPECTIVES

COMPANY PERSPECTIVES

Reichhold achieves success only when our customers succeed. We strive to create value for customers through innovative products, unmatched customer service and value-added services which all combine to give our customers the tools they need for success in the markets they serve.

ate synthetic resins. By 1930 Reichhold and his business partner, Charles J. O'Connor, had incorporated the company.

During the Great Depression, Henry Reichhold developed his corporate strategy, which was to become a complete supplier to his customers and to build factories in areas where he intended to grow market share. To this end, he moved the Synthe-Copal plant from Buffalo to Michigan, where it became the largest individual ester gum/resin plant in the world. In the 1930s the company also began manufacturing the chemicals needed to make its resins. By 1938, Reichhold changed the name of the company to Reichhold Chemicals, Inc. (RCI).

REICHHOLD BECOMES AN INTERNATIONAL COMPANY: 1938–87

RCI continued to expand its manufacturing facilities on the East Coast by buying a Brooklyn company that produced chemical pigments. During World War II, the Brooklyn plant became a primary source for the U.S. military's coatings for vehicles of war, as well as for such consumer goods as radios and furniture. Reichhold was also developing substitute chemicals for its coatings and opened a plant in Alabama that made synthetic phenol. By 1942, company sales were $10 million, and in the next 10 years they increased to $100 million.

As plants multiplied the company established Reichhold Chemicals (Canada) Ltd. Reichhold moved its corporate headquarters from Michigan to New York City to make it easier to forge international alliances. In 1951 Reichhold entered into an agreement with a Swiss company to manufacture resins and embarked on a joint venture with the Japanese firm Dainippon Printing Ink Manufacturing Company. By 1953, Reichhold ran 10 plants in the United States and 19 plants around the world, with facilities and licenses in 13 countries and subsidiaries in Australia, Canada, England, and France. Reichhold also began producing bonding resins (used in

plywood, plastics, and foundry cores) during the 1950s. In 1955 the company raised money for expansion by making 200,000 shares available on the New York Stock Exchange. Reichhold had become a public company.

Between 1957 and 1960, Reichhold bought more plants and established a Mexican subsidiary. The company diversified its product line by adding plastics and fiberglass to its core offering of resins and polymers. Structoglas was acquired in the 1960s, and RCI added reinforced plastics to its portfolio. In the late 1960s RCI entered the rubber latex field through an acquisition.

In the 1970s, through additional acquisitions, Reichhold began producing plywood, as well as emulsion polymers for textile products, adhesives, leather finishing products, paper chemicals, and rubber products. By 1981, sales reached $1 billion, and RCI was named a Fortune 500 company. In the mid-1980s Reichhold acquired Swift Adhesives and gained prominence in the adhesive market. In 1987 Dainippon Ink and Chemicals, Inc., (DIC) bought RCI, which became a wholly owned subsidiary of Tokyo-based Dainippon and reverted to private status.

REICHHOLD AS A DAINIPPON SUBSIDIARY: 1987–2005

Through DIC, Reichhold gained new markets and expanded its presence in existing ones. It relocated its corporate headquarters and research operations to North Carolina in 1992. Dainippon continued to acquire companies to expand the composites and coatings business, including Resana Resins & Polymer in Brazil (1996), Jotun Polymer in Norway (1997), and NCS Resins in South Africa (2000). In 2000 Reichhold restructured into strategic business units producing composites, coatings, emulsions, and adhesives as the company moved from an organization that operated regionally to one that served customers globally.

Discussing the years immediately before and after the turn of the 21st century with Amanda Jacob in *Reinforced Plastics*, chairman and CEO John Gaither recalled that it was a period of high staff turnover and reorganization. He noted that DIC brought in new managers, sometimes with no knowledge of the composite business and that, while the company spent a lot of money on plants, productivity did not improve.

Gaither had retired from Reichhold in 1998 as a senior executive, after 32 years of service, when sales were $1.3 billion. He returned to lead the company in 2004 in an effort to revive sagging profits. In 2002 the company sold its adhesives unit to the Swiss firm Forbo

KEY DATES

1927: Helmuth (Henry) Reichhold founds a subsidiary of his father's European company, Beck, Koller & Company, in Detroit.

1938: Renamed Reichhold Chemicals Inc. (RCI), the company has three production plants and $3 million in annual sales.

1951: RCI corporate headquarters moves from Ferndale, Michigan, to New York City, with the company focus shifting to overseas markets.

1955: Reichhold becomes a public company and offers 200,000 shares on the New York Stock Exchange.

1981: Sales reach $1 billion; Reichhold is named a Fortune 500 Company.

1987: RCI is acquired by the Japanese firm Dainippon Ink and Chemicals (DIC) and is no longer a public corporation.

1992: Reichhold moves its headquarters to Research Triangle Park in North Carolina.

2005: DIC agrees to a management buyout; Reichhold's executive team, led by John Gaither, re-establishes Reichhold as a privately held U.S. company.

Holding AG and combined its emulsions business with a business unit of Dow Chemical. The joint venture focused on the specialty latex market, an industry that produced a variety of products, from running tracks to latex gloves. Nonetheless, by 2003, Reichhold sales had fallen to $800 million, with net losses of $112 million. Net losses were $214 million by 2004, which is when Gaither approached DIC about a buyout. Dainippon refused but asked him to return as the CEO, and Gaither agreed.

Reichhold continued its poor performance, the reason Dainippon cited for ultimately agreeing to sell the company to Gaither and the Reichhold management team. In the autumn of 2005 the Reichhold unit was sold for a dollar, with DIC forgiving $229 million of its subsidiary's $431 million debt. Reichhold agreed to pay the remaining $202 million in increments of $30 million on the day of the sale and the rest over a three-year period. Under the agreement DIC retained the Austrian coatings operations, but both DIC and Reichhold would be free to continue supplying the worldwide coatings market.

RETURNING TO BASICS: 2005 ON

Gaither and Doug Frey, executive vice president of global composites, believed that Reichhold's core strength was in the experience and knowledge of its managers. Strategic development issues were put on hold as the company refocused on costs, customer service, and quality. Reichhold undertook a company-wide effort to increase efficiency throughout its plants by eliminating unnecessary manufacturing bottlenecks. Gaither told Jacob, "It's about trying to create more value for our customers—producing quality products, in spec, on time, at competitive costs—and then getting the value for the products that they deserve."

Reichhold was committed to its core values of operating ethically and legally, creating value for its customers, and keeping the company intact. It continued to invest in new technologies and created new products to meet increasingly stringent environmental regulations for VOCs (volatile organic chemicals). Some of the new products included solvent-cut alkyds for industrial finishes, environmentally friendly polyurethanes for floor finishes, waterborne epoxy curing agents for industrial maintenance applications, and a water-based epoxy coating for metal surfaces.

In December 2008 Reichhold's joint venture with Dow Chemical Company, Dow Reichhold Specialty Latex LLC, closed the doors of its headquarters in Durham, a production plant in Delaware, offices in Malaysia, and a laboratory and offices in Shanghai, China. Pieces of the business were sold to three separate companies. Meanwhile, Reichhold began assessing new markets in Asia. In October 2009 the company opened a manufacturing facility in India at Ranjangaon, a village not far from Pune. The plant made unsaturated polyester resins for wind turbines, glass-reinforced pipe, engineering stone, chemical equipment, and automobiles, among other purposes. Reichhold was also building a plant in Tianjin, China, for the manufacture of resins, under the auspices of Reichhold (Tianjin) Company Limited. The plant would produce vinyl esters, gel coats, and structural adhesives. Reichhold simultaneously opened a business office and applications lab in Beijing to provide sales and technical support for the new plant.

As of 2010 Reichhold operated manufacturing plants in 13 countries throughout the Americas, the Middle East, Europe, and Asia, as well as administrative centers in North Carolina, Germany, and the Netherlands. Research product and development testing facilities are located at its North Carolina headquarters as well as in Brazil, England, Mexico, and Norway. Sales in 2009 were $876 million, up from an estimated $865 million the previous year.

Maryellen Lo Bosco

PRINCIPAL COMPETITORS

Dainippon Ink and Chemicals; Dow Chemical Company; E. I. du Pont De Nemours and Company; PPG Industries, Inc.

FURTHER READING

"80 Years and Going Strong: Reichhold Makes a Comeback," *PCI Magazine*, April 9, 2007, pp. 102–05.

Baysden, Chris, "John Gaither, Returning to Right the Listing Ship," *Triangle Business Journal*, June 11, 2004, p. 5.

Blocker, Edward, Betty Wong, and Christopher T. McKittrick, "Making Bottom-Up ABC Work at Reichhold, Inc.," *Strategic Finance*, April 2002.

"Chemicals: The Little Giant," *Time*, September 7, 1953.

Jacob, Amanda, "Getting Back to Basics," *Reinforced Plastics*, December 2006, pp. 1–3.

Narvaez, Alfonso A., "Henry H. Reichhold Dies at 88; Founder of a Chemical Company," *New York Times*, December 13, 1989.

Related Companies, L.P.

—■—

60 Columbus Circle
New York, New York 10023
U.S.A.
Telephone: (212) 421-5333
Fax: (212) 751-3550
Web site: http://www.related.com

Private Company
Founded: 1972
Employees: 2,000 (est.)
Total Assets: $15 billion (real estate)
NAICS: 531110 Lessors of Residential Buildings and
 Dwellings; 531120 Lessors of Nonresidential Build-
 ings (except Miniwarehouses); 531190 Lessors of
 Other Real Estate Property; 531311 Residential
 Property Managers; 531312 Nonresidential
 Property Managers; 531390 Other Activities
 Related to Real Estate

■ ■ ■

Related Companies, L.P., is a privately owned company
that develops, finances, and manages retail, commercial,
residential, and mixed-use properties in the United
States. It has been involved in diverse projects that range
from affordable housing to the high-profile Time
Warner Center, a 2.8-million-square-foot retail/office/
hotel/condominium/cultural complex located in
Manhattan's Columbus Circle. Headquartered in New
York City, Related also has offices and major projects in
Boston, Los Angeles, San Francisco, Chicago, Las Vegas,
and other cities worldwide.

BEGINNINGS

Stephen Ross, founder of Related, began his career as a
tax attorney in Detroit, Michigan, and later worked for
two New York investment banks, specializing in real
estate and corporate finance. In 1972 Ross saw the opportunities in a newly enacted New York State law
providing tax incentives for affordable housing. He created the Related Housing Company to finance and
develop government-subsidized multifamily apartments.

Related's reputation for innovative financing began
with its early projects. Initially Ross syndicated interests
in government-assisted housing that was built by other
developers. Soon, however, Related began developing its
own projects. By 1980 the company had over $40 mil-
lion in equity invested in more than 50 development
ventures.

Related then began diversifying its holdings and
expanding its locations. The company opened offices in
Los Angeles, Miami, and Chicago. During the 1980s
Related developed large-scale office and commercial
properties and solidified its preeminent position in
creating mixed-use properties, such as the Copley Place
shopping mall in Boston. Although the Tax Reform Act
of 1986 diminished the tax benefits from investing in
rental housing, Related continued to develop successful
affordable-housing projects. By 1990 it had completed
85 residential projects in the Northeast and in Florida
and was managing 15,000 apartments.

Related's financial services, primarily tax syndication
of the financial benefits available to investors under various government-housing programs, also expanded during this period. Profits from these syndications allowed

COMPANY PERSPECTIVES

Our dedication to the highest possible standards in every aspect of our business is visible in everything we do. It is reflected in the distinctive architecture and interior design of our developments and in the quality of their construction, in the distinction of our partners, and in the consistently high level at which our properties operate. It is also apparent in our long-term commitment to owning and managing our properties.

Our integrated corporate structure has allowed us to develop significant synergies across our multiple areas of business activity. A good example of this is the way in which our development team draws upon company-wide expertise across a variety of markets and property types to compete effectively for large-scale development opportunities. We also benefit from the integration of our property management and residential sales teams, which provide us with direct access to real-time information about operating costs and market conditions.

the company to support its own development projects. Related became a large provider of equity capital, selling limited partnership interests in affordable housing. It also managed both public and private equity funds. In 1982, in order to reflect the organization's growth and diversity, the company name was changed from Related Housing Companies to Related Companies.

THE REAL ESTATE SLUMP: 1990–95

By 1990 the economic recession that followed the stock market crash in October 1987 was having a significant impact, particularly in the financial, insurance, and real estate industries. Related, along with other real estate organizations, was experiencing difficulties. It was burdened with unsecured debts and troubled development projects in Boston and California. The booming real estate market had collapsed, and Related had to rethink its strategies and restructure its financing.

Related's diverse business interests, however, provided Ross with the flexibility to resolve the company's problems and recover more quickly than many other firms. Related's holdings were not solely in real estate, which could be difficult to sell in a declining

market. Its tax-syndication operations had continued to be profitable, even during the economic downturn. The company withdrew from some development ventures with local partners in New England and eventually closed its regional organization there, losing nearly $40 million. In California its commercial operating company was also closed at significant financial cost.

However, in what *Crain's New York Business* characterized as "a dramatic turnaround," Related was able to restructure more than $100 million in unsecured debts, much of it transferred to Ross personally from Chemical Bank and Bankers Trust. A large portion of Related was sold to several partners, including the Moses Ginsberg family from New York and Jorge Perez in Florida, developers who had previously worked with Related. This brought in new investment capital. Additionally, Ross's uncle Max Fisher, a Detroit financier and Republican fund-raiser, purchased a partnership in the organization. Lenders in Boston and California were paid off and given some of the properties then under development. Ross retained majority interest in Related. The organization, which had begun to limit some of its nationwide expansion and restricting its financing to secured loans, was poised to focus its energies on new projects.

Meanwhile, Jeff Blau, a fellow graduate of the University of Michigan who was recruited by Ross, had joined Related in 1990 and began overseeing new development. The company had several varied projects in progress, including the Strathmore, a Manhattan building that set new standards for luxury apartments with amenities such as granite countertops, marble-tiled bathrooms, and an on-site pool and health club. Another Related building, the Monterey, demonstrated the viability of mixing low- and middle-income units. Related was also involved in the development of Ninth Square, a mixed-use residential, commercial, and retail urban-development project in New Haven, Connecticut, partially funded by Yale University. Ninth Square was completed in 1995. The company had weathered the real estate crisis.

RESTRUCTURING

In order to improve its managerial functioning, Related was organized into three separate divisions: Development, Property Management, and Financial Services. The Development Division was established to handle the acquisition, design, and construction of properties that included affordable, luxury, and government-subsidized housing, as well as commercial, retail, and mixed-use projects. The Property Management Division was created to provide operational services to residential, commercial, and retail tenants such as maintenance, administration, accounting, customer service, marketing,

KEY DATES

1972: Stephen Ross founds Related Housing Companies.
1982: Related Housing becomes Related Companies.
1993: Related restructures unsecured debts and raises new funding.
1998: Related wins bid for New York Coliseum site, which would become Time Warner Center.
2004: Time Warner Center opens.
2006: Related purchases Equinox Holdings, Inc.
2007: Investors, including a Middle East consortium, provide Related with $1.4 billion.
2009: Related wins approval for the Hudson Yards project.

and leasing. Property Management was also intended to maintain and enhance the company's real estate assets.

The Financial Services Division was set up to manage capital for several large organizations, including the State Teachers Retirement System of Ohio, GM Pension Fund, Multi-Employer Property Trust (MEPT), and California Public Employees' Retirement System (CalPERS). Financial Services also established partnerships, such as joint ventures with Credit Suisse and Zurich Financial Services, that supported financing for residential and commercial real estate development. Related's top management team was completed when Bruce Beal Jr. joined the company in 1995.

TIME WARNER CENTER: RELATED'S MAGNUM OPUS

Related was a latecomer to the competition to develop the prime New York City real estate parcel located at Columbus Circle and owned by the Metropolitan Transportation Authority (MTA). In the late 1980s the original MTA deal with Boston Properties and Salomon Brothers Inc. was jettisoned after protests headed by Jacqueline Kennedy Onassis led to three redesigns. Then Salomon pulled out of the project.

Finally, in 1998, the deal that had stymied two governors, three mayors, and a multitude of planners was finalized. Related, proposing a new headquarters for Time Warner (then AOL Time Warner), was selected for the billion dollar project, despite stiff competition that included higher offers by Donald Trump and fewer conditions by Millennium Partners.

Award-winning architect David Childs, who later designed the "Freedom Tower" to be erected at the former site of the World Trade Center, was chosen for the project. Related's partners in the enterprise included Apollo Real Estate Advisors and the Palladium Company. The groundbreaking ceremony occurred in November 2000. By the following year *Crain's New York Business* described the project with superlatives such as "the biggest construction project in New York City since the World Trade Center," "the largest construction loan for a private project in U.S. history," and "the next Rockefeller Center."

When the Time Warner Center opened on February 4, 2004, it incorporated many elements that are the hallmarks of Related developments. Its mixed-use spaces included the Time Warner corporate headquarters, CNN studios, the Mandarin Oriental luxury hotel, a jazz theater complex, an upscale retail mall, restaurants headed by noted chefs, and high-end residential apartments.

Related maintained its involvement in the center after its completion through its Property Management Division. Financing for the project included several partners and a $1.3 billion loan from GMAC Commercial Mortgage, the largest loan ever made for a private development project in the United States. Critics, including competitor Donald Trump (who hung a banner from Trump International Hotel & Tower proclaiming that it had better views), had been outplanned and outmaneuvered. Columbus Circle, the epicenter of New York City, now held the measure of Related's success.

THE NEW MILLENNIUM

Although the completion of the Time Warner Center was emblematic of Related's achievements, it did not signal any reduction in the company's activities. As with the Time Warner Center, the organization often sought to finish projects where other developers had failed, such as the $4 billion Cosmopolitan Resort and Casino venture in Las Vegas that Related was tapped by Deutsche Bank to complete.

Related also began a program of environmentally sustainable development, beginning with Tribeca Green in lower Manhattan. This building, one of the country's first LEED (Leadership in Energy and Environmental Design) Gold-certified multifamily residences, included storm-water collection for irrigating the building's garden roof, photovoltaic panels for utilizing solar power, and energy-efficient systems and appliances. The company then developed a LEED-certified retail mall in New York City, residential condominiums in the Midwest, and a subsidized-housing complex in

Colorado. The Viceroy Hotel, which opened in November 2009 in Snowmass, Colorado, featured an environmentally responsible design and construction that made it eligible for LEED Silver certification.

Related also continued its interest in large-scale, urban-redevelopment projects. Although financing delays postponed its Frank Gehry–designed Grand Avenue development in downtown Los Angeles, in December 2009 Related won final public approval for the Hudson Yards project on New York City's West Side. After a previous deal with Tishman Speyer fell through, Related was chosen to develop 26 acres above 2 rail yards near the Hudson River into a master-planned community that would include office towers, luxury and affordable apartments, retail space, and parks. At the same time, however, the New York City Council denied approval for a proposed $323 million Kingsbridge Armory retail project, objecting to Related's refusal to make a commitment that future Armory mall employees would be paid more than the minimum wage.

In late 2009 Related also resumed construction on a large mixed-use property on West 42nd Street in New York City that had been suspended due to the financial market problems in 2008. The company had renegotiated arrangements with contractors, construction unions, architects, and engineers and saved between 20 and 25 percent of the estimated project costs. The revised plan, designed for LEED Silver certification, included a hotel, condominiums, affordable housing, retail space, and several small theaters.

SIDELINES

In January 2009 Ross, independent of Related, purchased the Miami Dolphins football team from Wayne Huizenga for $1.1 billion. The deal gave Ross 95 percent ownership of the team, the stadium, and the surrounding developable land. He soon implemented his new approach to football management, adding singer/songwriter Marc Anthony, tennis stars Venus and Serena Williams, and music industry power couple Gloria and Emilio Estefan as limited partners with celebrity appeal and links in the Hispanic and African-American communities.

Related's top executive partners, Ross, Blau, and Beal, also continued to develop other innovative projects, although Related did not have a direct stake in these enterprises. As private investors without an operating bank, the partners received unprecedented approval to bid on failed lenders that had been seized by the Federal Deposit Insurance Corporation (FDIC). Their new bank, known as SJB National Bank (after the founders' first initials), invested $100 million of their own capital to help them make the transition from developing real estate to making loans.

SUSTAINING STRATEGIES

During the first decade of the 21st century, strategies that helped maintain Related through economic fluctuations continued to characterize its operations. In 2003 the company sold Related Capital, a subsidiary providing financial- and asset-management services, to CharterMac (later renamed Centerline Capital Group) but retained almost 15 percent interest in the company. Ross became chairman of the board at Centerline.

Related received further capital infusions of $1.4 billion from the 2007 equity and debt investments by the Abu Dhabi government and other backers. Goldman Sachs and MSD Capital purchased a 7.5 percent equity stake in Related. The Olayan Group, Mubadala Development Company, and the Kuwait Investment Authority made further debt investments. Blau, Related's president, was quoted in the *New York Times* (December 18, 2007) as saying, "We're now positioned to have more liquidity when the marketplace has less, setting ourselves up for the future."

In 2006 Related bought Equinox Holdings, Inc., for $505 million and added an Equinox Fitness Club to many of Related's new luxury developments. It also formed a joint venture with sportscaster and former New York Giants running back Tiki Barber to preserve and revitalize affordable-housing developments and supplement Related's strong presence in the affordable-housing market. By 2009 Related had developed or purchased more than 58,000 affordable units, and it continued to initiate affordable-housing projects around the United States.

Already aligned with investors in the Middle East, in 2009 Related planned a new international venture, based in Abu Dhabi and known as Gulf Related, to focus on luxury mixed-use destination developments. The organization also projected future projects to capitalize on the expanding real estate market in China.

Related continued its emphasis on diversity and innovation, developing massive mixed-use properties while maintaining its affordable-housing roots. It had secured the financial resources for continuing through difficult financial periods while enjoying the reputation for design and operational excellence.

Grace Murphy

PRINCIPAL SUBSIDIARIES

Related Group of Florida; Gulf Related (joint venture with Gulf Capital of Abu Dhabi); Related China (joint venture with partners in China).

PRINCIPAL DIVISIONS

Development; Financial Services; Property Management.

PRINCIPAL COMPETITORS

Icahn Enterprises L.P.; Tishman Speyer Properties, L.P.; Trump Organization.

FURTHER READING

Alldredge, Steve, "Snowmass Approves Viceroy Hotel," *Aspen Times*, September 26, 2007.

Associated Press, "Big Developer Gets $1.4 Billion in Investments," *New York Times*, December 18, 2007.

Brown, Eliot, "Related Not a Total Loser Today: Council O.K.'s Key West Side Rail Yards Rezoning," *New York Observer*, December 14, 2009.

Cuozzo, Steve, "Time's Changing in New York," *Property Week*, February 20, 2004.

Dolnick, Sam, "Voting 45-1, Council Rejects $310 Million Plan for Mall at Bronx Armory," *New York Times*, December 15, 2009.

Fung, Amanda, "Related Cos. to Re-start Project on West 42nd," *Crain's New York Business*, September 29, 2009.

Grant, Peter, "Trump Makes Last-Ditch Effort in Competition for New York Coliseum Site," *Knight Ridder/Tribune Business News*, July 14, 1998.

Hillman, Michelle, "Related Cos. Buys Former Polaroid Corp. Headquarters Site," *Boston Business Journal*, June 27, 2006, http://boston.bizjournals.com/boston/stories/2006/06/26/daily17.html.

Keehner, Jonathan, and Jason Kelly, "Related's Stephen Ross Opts for Banking over Building," *Bloomberg.com*, December 16, 2009.

Oser, Alan S., "Perspectives: Mixed-Income Housing; Finding a Way to Keep Building," *New York Times*, January 31, 1993.

———, "Perspectives: Mixed-Income Housing; In Strong Locations, Economic Diversity," *New York Times*, December 2, 1990.

Pedulla, Tom, "Glitz, Glamour of Dolphins' Owners Bring NFL to New Fans," *USA Today*, October 14, 2009.

Schwartz, Alex F., *Housing Policy in the United States: An Introduction*. New York: Routledge, 2002.

"The World's Billionaires: #191, Stephen Ross," *Forbes*, March 11, 2009, http://www.forbes.com/lists/2009/10/billionaires-2009-richest-people_Stephen-Ross_YZL6.html.

Rick's Cabaret
International, Inc.

10959 Cutten Road
Houston, Texas 77066
U.S.A.
Telephone: (281) 820-1181
Fax: (281) 820-1445
Web site: http://www.rickscabaret.com

Public Company
Incorporated: 1982 as Trumps, Inc.; 1994 as Rick's
    Cabaret International, Inc.
Employees: 1,000
Sales: $75.15 million (2009)
Stock Exchanges: NASDAQ
Ticker Symbol: RICK
NAICS: 722410 Drinking Places (Alcoholic Beverages)

■ ■ ■

A public company listed on the NASDAQ, Rick's
Cabaret International, Inc., is the Houston, Texas-based
operator of upscale adult entrainment nightclubs, so-
called gentlemen's clubs, featuring topless dancers and
catering primarily to a business clientele. The company
operates six clubs under the Rick's Cabaret name: three
in the Texas cites of Houston, San Antonio, and Fort
Worth; one in Las Vegas, Nevada; one in Minneapolis,
Minnesota; and another in New York City. A similar
club operates in Miami Gardens, Florida, as Tootsie's
Cabaret, and five Texas clubs operating as XTC Cabaret
are located in Austin, Dallas, San Antonio, and

Houston, the latter hosting two clubs. Another Rick's
Cabaret is operated in New Orleans, Louisiana, under a
licensing arrangement with the company's former
owner. Rick's holdings also include four Club Onyx
venues that cater to the African-American market,
located in Houston and Dallas, as well as in Charlotte,
North Carolina, and Philadelphia, Pennsylvania. Income
from the clubs are derived from cover charges, the sale
of food and drink, memberships to the VIP room, and
the fees the dancers pay to perform. Regarded as
independent contractors, the dancers derive their
income from patron tips. Rick's other business ventures
include adult entertainment and auction Web sites.
Rick's media division also maintains two dozen industry
Web sites, produces industry trade publications, and
hosts a pair of industry trade shows.

COMPANY ORIGINS DATE TO 1982

The seeds of Rick's Cabaret International were planted
in Houston in 1982 when, in the midst of an oil slump,
Lebanese oil man Salah Izzedin and a group of investors
formed Trumps, Inc., and opened a nightclub called
Trumps, which was essentially a supper club and disco.
When the venture failed, Izzedin brought in new investors, businessmen J. B. Gentry and Vernon Young, and,
most importantly, Dallas Fontenot, a man who had
been long involved in the topless club market. Helping
with the legal work was an attorney, tax-law specialist
Robert Watters, who would one day own Rick's and
take it public.

Rick's Cabaret International, Inc.

Watters, born in Canada, earned a law degree from the London School of Economics in 1973, followed two years later by a taxation law degree from Toronto's Osgoode Hall Law School. In 1979 he moved to Houston with his wife, who, although raised in Italy, wanted to live in Texas where her family hailed and in Houston in particular where her grandfather lived. After doing tax work at a Houston accounting firm, Watters passed the Texas bar and joined a local law firm, Hollrah, Lange and Thoma, where he met Izzedin. Quickly growing tired of practicing law, Watters welcomed the chance to become involved in the reorganized Trumps operation. Rather than open a typical, seedy strip club, all too often associated with drugs, prostitution, and organized crime, the partners wanted to create an upscale topless club, one with a respectable enough patina to attract business customers.

RICK'S CABARET OPENS: 1983

While Trumps was being converted to a gentlemen's club, Fontenot was present when someone emerged from a cab to ask if the club was open yet, mistakenly calling it Rick's. Not only was it not open, the nightclub still lacked a name, but "Rick's," with its association to the club in the film *Casablanca*, appealed to the owners. "Cabaret" was affixed to the name, again to lend an air of respectability to the topless club. Operated by Trumps, Inc., Rick's opened its doors in 1983, establishing a formula that would be followed by other gentlemen's clubs to follow: valet parking, marble floors, restaurant quality foods, and higher-caliber dancers who brought in Houston businessmen by the droves. Fontenot and Gentry had intended to eventually buy out Young and Izzedin, but the club proved so successful, quickly boasting the top liquor sales in the state, that the partners began to fight for control. The situation was complicated by the labyrinth of affiliated corporations they had established in order to pool their resources to launch Rick's. Izzedin had the edge because

he held the all-important liquor license, which he used to gain a one-third stake in Rick's. Gentry, who was accused of furnishing drugs to the dancers and other nefarious acts, was then ousted, leaving Izzedin and Fortenot half-owners and Young a passive investor.

Izzedin began spending more time at Rick's and brought in Watters essentially to serve as the front man. It was not until November 1987 that Watters received a 10 percent stake in the business. With an air of sophistication and a beguiling accent, Watters was well suited to portray Rick's as a mainstream business, although his application of sophisticated management theory to what most people would consider a strip club gilded struck some as over the top. Fontenot, in the meantime, made contributions to the business that could be quantified on the balance sheet. He was responsible for paying bonuses to cab drivers and hotel concierges for directing business to Rick's. In 1987 he created the club's VIP Room, which only membership-paying members could access by private entrance.

A series of court fights over the money Rick's generated began in 1988 when Young accused Izzedin, Fontenot, and Watters of denying him his fair share of the profits by diverting funds. According to his law suit, Izzedin admitted to taking $45,000 from Fontenot and that an audit of Rick's liquor sales funded by Gentry had revealed a $1 million shortfall. Fontenot and Watters then turned on Izzedin, accusing him of supplying narcotics to dancers and waitresses, forcing them to have sex with him, and encouraging some to act as prostitutes. Matters only grew worse when several of the club's dancers were arrested after propositioning undercover Texas Alcoholic Beverage Commission agents. Izzedin moved to Dallas where he planned to open a club under the Rick's Mansion name, prompting Fontenot and Watters to seek an injunction to prevent the use of the Rick's trademark. They also obtained a liquor license for a fictitious bar next to the proposed Dallas site as a way to block Izzedin's plan.

As alliances shifted, Izzedin joined Young in his suit, asking the courts to appoint a receiver to take control of Rick's. In answer, Watters brought a dozen of Rick's dancers into the courtroom to argue against receivership. Their appeals fell on deaf ears, and a trustee, District Judge Michael Wood, took control of Rick's in March 1989, removing Watters and Fontenot. Watters found a way to outmaneuver the court by filing for federal bankruptcy protection, which superseded the local case, and locked out Wood. When Rick's emerged from bankruptcy, a trustee more to Watters's liking was appointed, Scott C. Mitchell, a local accountant who would later be employed to do the company's books and join the board of Rick's after it went public.

KEY DATES

1982: Trumps, a supper club and disco, opens in Houston.

1983: Trumps is converted to a topless club, Rick's Cabaret.

1993: Robert Watters gains control of Rick's.

1994: Rick's Cabaret International, Inc., is formed to acquire Trumps, Inc.

1995: Rick's goes public with a listing on the NASDAQ.

1998: Eric Langan gains control of Rick's.

2004: First Club Onyx opens.

2005: New York Rick's Cabaret opens.

2008: Las Vegas Rick's Cabaret opens.

A settlement with Izzedin was reached that split ownership of Rick's between Watters and Fontenot, and Izzedin was allowed to open his Dallas club, which took the name Cabaret Royale and became a major success. Watters and Fontenot had their own aspirations, intent on opening a chain of gentlemen's clubs. They opened Colorado Bar & Grill as well as Caesar's Cabaret, and in 1990 Watters bought a Houston topless club called Caligula 21, on which he was unable to meet the payments and it was repossessed by the former owner. As it turned out, Watters and Fontenot were not well suited as partners, and they eventually fell out, leading to more litigation. In 1993 they finally parted ways. Fontenot took the Colorado venues, and Watters was now left as the sole owner of Rick's after the receivership of the company was terminated that year.

In 1994 Watters formed Rick's Cabaret International, Inc., essentially to replace Trumps, Inc. In that same year, he opened an after-hours bar in Houston, called Tantra, that he portrayed, as described in SEC filings, as a "non-sexually oriented discotheque and billiard club." He then sold it to Rick's in 1995. Earlier in the year, Watters took Rick's public, selling 48 percent of the company, netting $4.27 million in an initial public offering of stock. His goal was more than just opening a chain of gentlemen's clubs. "I want to take this industry into a wider area of accessibility," he told *Forbes* in 1996. "I want to clean it up, put in controls and have it become socially acceptable." The NASDAQ was far from convinced by Watters's platitudes and resisted his efforts to list Rick's stock. After six months and reviews by two committees, the NASDAQ concluded that because Rick's was a legitimate, licensed business, there

was no legal or regulatory basis under its rules to deny exclusion of the company's stock. Rick's was, thus, provided a listing on NASDAQ's lower-tier SmallCap Market.

RICK'S MERGES WITH TAURUS ENTERTAINMENT: 1998

In February 1996 Rick's formed a Louisiana subsidiary and later in the year opened a Rick's Cabaret club in New Orleans. The following year a club opened in Minneapolis. The company now faced stiffer competition from other gentlemen's clubs and recorded net losses of about $700,000 in fiscal 1996 and $1.29 million in fiscal 1997. In August 1998 Rick's merged with Taurus Entertainment Companies, Inc., a public company whose stock traded on an over-the-counter basis. Taurus operated topless clubs in Austin and Houston, Texas, under the XTC Cabaret name.

Taurus was controlled by 30-year-old Eric S. Langan. In March 1999 he replaced Watters as chief executive and gained majority control of Rick's. Watters, in turn, acquired the Rick's New Orleans' club and was granted a license to use the Rick's Cabaret trademarks and logos in Louisiana, Alabama, Florida, and Mississippi. By this time, Rick's stock had been trading below $1 per share for an extended period of time, resulting in a delisting notice. Langan was able to retain the NASDAQ listing by engineering a reverse stock split to reduce the number of shares and bolster the price.

Although relatively young, Langan had been involved in the adult entertainment business since 1989. Raised in Illinois, Langan moved with his family to Dallas at the age of 13. Married and divorced when he was just 19 years old, Langan was taken by some friends to a Fort Worth, Texas, topless club and began dating one of the dancers. Picking her up at work, he became aware of how much money the owner, not a good businessman, was making from a club that was not an especially impressive operation. After one semester at a junior college studying accounting, Langan quit school in 1989 and sold a baseball card collection for $40,000 to buy a shuttered topless club in Fort Worth called Sheba's Lounge. After being arrested 13 times for zoning violations, Langan decided to pursue the higher end of the market. He opened a second club in Arlington, Texas, in 1991 under the XTC Cabaret name, followed by an East Texas club and a Houston club in 1994. Langan then bought a shell corporation, which became Taurus Entertainment, to own the clubs. He began buying shares of Rick's in 1998, leading to the merger and his taking control of the combined operation.

INTERNET SITES LAUNCHED: 1999

Like Watters, Langan hoped to make gentlemen's clubs more mainstream, while also acting as a consolidator in what was a highly fragmented industry. Only a handful of the more than 3,000 gentlemen's club in the United States were not privately owned and independent. In addition, Langan sought to branch out into other parts of the adult entertainment industry, including opportunities afforded by the Internet. In October 1999 Rick's launched two sites: www.DancerDorm.com, a subscription service providing live voyeuristic views of Rick's dancers from 32 Web cams in the dormitory where they lived, and www.AmateurDan.com, a for-pay site for exclusive photos of the dancers. Other Web ventures were added in the ensuing years, including auction sites and dating sites for couples engaged in the so-called swinging lifestyle.

Although Rick's did not expand as quickly as Langan had hoped, it returned to profitability under his management. Rick's posted sales of $12.7 million in fiscal 2000, netting more than $200,000. A year later revenues improved 54 percent, to $19.7 million, and earnings increased to $1.3 million. The company began to accelerate its growth in 2003 when it acquired a controlling interest in the Wild Horse Cabaret located near Houston's Hobby Airport and then opened a sports bar next door called Hummers. Rick's then bought a north Houston club in 2004 that became the fifth XTC Cabaret. Langan also established a new format, Club Onyx, which opened in June 2004 on the site of the original Rick's Cabaret. Its target audience was affluent "urban males," essentially African Americans, which Langan believed were underserved by gentlemen's clubs. With Club Onyx, Langan hoped to find a ready market in professional athletes as well as urban businessmen.

Langan made another important move in 2004, reaching an agreement to purchase an existing club, the Paradise Club, in New York City, located on 33rd Street near Madison Square Garden, Pennsylvania Station, and the Empire State Building. Because club sites had become scarce due to stricter zoning laws, the 10,000-square-foot midtown property was an ideal location for a flagship Rick's Cabaret. The deal closed in early 2005 when Rick's paid $7.6 million for the Paradise. He then invested an additional $1.4 million to convert it to a Rick's Cabaret, which opened later in the year. Although an outsider to the market, Langan now benefited from the laws that were passed to limit the adult entertainment trade in Manhattan. Rival clubs were relegated to the less accessible West Side, and potential competitors were kept out of the market.

Rick's found a ready supply of customers from Manhattan's financial district and did particularly well when Wall Street handed out billions of dollars during bonus season each February, and throughout the year when big financial deals were celebrated.

RICK'S LICENSED IN ARGENTINA: 2006

Langan expanded in a number of directions in 2006. Dreamers Cabaret & Sports Bar was acquired in South Houston and converted to an XTC Cabaret. Club Exotica was bought in San Antonio and rechristened Club Encounters. Another San Antonio club, doing business as Centerfolds, was acquired and converted to a Rick's Cabaret. In November 2006 Playmate's Gentlemen's Club was bought and became Rick's Cabaret Austin. A Fort Worth club doing business as New Orleans Nights was purchased for conversion to the Rick's Cabaret format. Rick's also licensed its name in Argentina for a possible Rick's Cabaret in Buenos Aires and elsewhere in Latin America.

Rick's pursued further opportunities in the final years of the decade. Tootsie's Cabaret was acquired in Florida in 2007 and continued to operate under its own name. The Crazy Horse Too Cabaret in Philadelphia was acquired in 2008 and converted to the Club Onyx format. The Executive Club and Platinum Club II were acquired in Dallas, and a Rick's Cabaret opened in Las Vegas. Moreover, Rick added to its media holdings in 2008, acquiring ED Publications, Inc., publisher of trade magazine *Exotic Dancer* and the bimonthly "Club Bulletin." ED Publications was also the producer of two industry trade shows, including the Gentlemen's Club Owners Expo, the only annual national convention of its type.

The price of Rick's stock peaked in late 2007 but began to tumble as a recession took hold, despite the company's increasing revenues and strong earnings. Sales increased from $29.9 million in fiscal 2007 to more than $75 million in fiscal 2009, while net income improved from $4.4 million to $6.6 million. Nevertheless, Rick's delayed further expansion. By 2010, however, the company was making plans to open a new Rick's Cabaret near the Dallas–Fort Worth International Airport. There was every reason to expect that other club openings and acquisitions would follow.

Ed Dinger

PRINCIPAL SUBSIDIARIES

ED Publications, Inc.; RCI Holdings, Inc.; XTC Cabaret, Inc.

PRINCIPAL COMPETITORS

Galardi South Enterprises, Inc.; Million Dollar Saloon, Inc.; Scores Holding Company, Inc.

FURTHER READING

Brick, Michael, "Texas Strip Club Owner Plans a Flagship," *New York Times*, January 21, 2005, p. B1.

Dorfman, Dan, "An Adult Chain Woos Investors, Wall Streeters," *New York Sun*, August 9, 2006.

Flood, Mary, "Mr. S.O.B.," *Houston Press*, October 24, 1996.

Hudson, Kris, "Some Gentlemen's Clubs Strip Down Upscale Offerings as Business Slumps," *Wall Street Journal*, June 11, 2009, p. B1.

McVea, Denise, "Sexual Dealing," *Dallas Observer*, December 15, 1994.

Miller, Doug, "Rick's Cabaret Rocked by Feud," *Houston Business Journal*, August 28, 1989, p. 1.

Palmeri, Christopher, "Naked Claims," *Forbes*, April 8, 1996, p. 80.

Power, William, "Nasdaq Reluctantly Embraces Topless-bar Stock," *Wall Street Journal*, August 8, 1995, p. C1.

———, "Topless Bar Flirts with a Nasdaq Listing," *Wall Street Journal*, January 25, 1995, p. C1.

Pybus, Kenneth R., "Rick's Cabaret Will Go Public," *Houston Business Journal*, January 20, 1995, p. 1.

Ryckman, Pamerla, "Rick's Grows in Spite of Changing Attitudes," *New York Sun*, February 16, 2006.

Schlegel, Darrin, "Risque Business," *Houston Business Journal*, October 20–26, 1995.

Smillie, Dirk, "Wages of Sin," *Forbes*, October 27, 2008, p. 142.

Royal Shakespeare Company

——————— ■ ———————

The Courtyard Theatre
Southern Lane
Stratford-upon-Avon, Warwickshire CV37 6BB
United Kingdom
Telephone: (+44 0) 1789 403444
Fax: (+44 0) 1789 262341
Web site: http://www.rsc.org.uk

Nonprofit Company
Founded: 1961
Employees: 500
Gross Receipts: £51.2 million ($78 million) (2008)
NAICS: 711110 Repertory Companies, Theatrical

■ ■ ■

The Royal Shakespeare Company is one of the most prominent theatrical companies in the world. Based in William Shakespeare's hometown of Stratford-upon-Avon, England, the group performs a mix of plays by its namesake playwright and those of other classic and contemporary writers. The troupe is characterized by its ensemble nature, employing a resident group of artists over the course of several seasons and encouraging collaboration among the entire company. This provides a cohesiveness and depth of training almost unique in 21st-century theater. It also affords audiences the opportunity to watch an actor tackle a number of varied roles in any given season. Despite the RSC's rich history and stellar reputation, it has suffered some difficult times, most notably the internal and external controversies of the 1990s that some believed placed its

very existence in jeopardy. Michael Boyd, who was named artistic director in 2003, was instrumental in revitalizing the company. As the RSC approached its 50th anniversary in 2011, its balance sheet and reputation foretold at least as many years to come.

ORIGINS IN THE 19TH CENTURY

Although the RSC officially came into being in 1961, its roots stretch nearly a hundred years further back. In 1875 a brewer and philanthropist in Stratford-upon-Avon, Charles Edward Flower, and his wife, Sarah, donated two acres of land and the bulk of the money to build an arts center (including a theater, picture gallery, library, and music room) in Shakespeare's honor. In 1879 the 800-seat Shakespeare Memorial Theatre opened on the banks of the Avon River, with the Bard's *Much Ado About Nothing* as its first production.

The theater began modestly enough, with a short spring season and a mainly regional reach, but its stature had grown significantly by the turn of the century. It added a month-long summer season in 1910, and 1925 the theater's accomplishments were rewarded with a Royal Charter, but disaster struck just a year later when the Memorial was destroyed by fire.

In the wake of the tragedy, festival director William Bridges-Adams adhered to the theatrical tradition of "the show must go on" and continued production in a nearby cinema. The Flower family also rose to the occasion by launching an international fundraising campaign to build a new theater. A search for an architect was simultaneously begun, and the new facility, designed by Elisabeth Scott, opened on April 23 (Shakespeare's birthday) in 1932. For nearly 30 years afterward, the company's reputation grew steadily as new generations of actors, including Michael Redgrave, Ralph Richardson, John Gielgud, Peggy Ashcroft, Vivian Leigh, Laurence Olivier, and Richard Burton, graced its stage. The Memorial was one of the most prestigious artistic enterprises in England by 1960, when it came under the direction of Peter Hall.

THE HALL INFLUENCE

Peter Hall came to national recognition in 1955 as a young director at the Arts Theatre in London, where he staged the first English-language performance of Samuel Beckett's *Waiting for Godot,* which created a storm of controversy at the time and came to be considered one of the seminal works of modern theater. Thereafter Hall was to invited serve as director of the Shakespeare Memorial Theatre. Flush with success and brimming with the confidence of a 30-year-old, Hall immediately set about turning the venerable operation on its ear. Within 12 short months, he had obtained a new Royal Charter, changed the theater's name to the Royal Shakespeare Company (having found the previous name depressing), initiated the concept of a permanent company, insisted on a presence in London, and begun to add contemporary dramas to the formerly all-Shakespeare repertoire. While each of these innovations was revolutionary in its own right, creating something beyond a regional, if highly renowned, Shakespeare festival loomed especially large. So did the concept of an in-house ensemble company, which offered three-year contracts and emphasized identification with the RSC's enterprise as a whole, as opposed to starting from scratch with every production.

Hall's pioneering tactics were resoundingly effective, attracting young actors and directors who would go on to become leaders of stage and screen. Those included Peter O'Toole, Ian Holm, Vanessa Redgrave, Maggie Smith, Judi Dench, Trevor Nunn, Ian Richardson, and Jonathan Pryce. It was also a period of such landmark productions as the Shakespeare adaptation *The Wars of the Roses* (1963) and Harold Pinter's *The Homecoming* (1965). Critics raved and audiences were delighted. Hall had, in short, breathed new life into an already august institution and taken it to the next level of eminence.

UP AND DOWN AND BACK AGAIN

After Hall left the RSC in 1968, his successors made their own contributions. Trevor Nunn, who was in charge from 1968 to 1978 by himself and from 1978 to 1987 jointly with Terry Hands, broadened the RSC's reach by establishing a yearly season in Newcastle in 1977, finding it a London home at the Barbican Theatre in 1982, and opening another, smaller Stratford venue, the Swan Theatre, in 1986.

The late twentieth and early twenty-first centuries, however, were a time of upheaval and controversy. Under the direction of Adrian Noble, the RSC abandoned its permanent base at the Barbican in favor of performances at a variety of venues, which resulted in a drop in ticket revenues. At the same time, the company veered away from the ensemble concept in the hopes that it would afford actors greater freedom to accept better-paying television and film jobs, as well as allow the RSC to cast ready-made box office draws. While such ideas may have been solid in theory, their implementation proved disastrous. When Michael Boyd was named to replace Noble as artistic director in 2002, the company was running a deficit of nearly £3 million (approximately $4.8 million) and was perceived as having lost its artistic vision entirely.

Boyd, who was born in Belfast and trained in Edinburgh, Moscow, Coventry, and Sheffield, had signed on with the RSC as an associate director in 1996. His directing talents had earned him an Olivier Award for his 2000–01 productions of *Henry VI, parts I, II, III,* and *Richard III,* but it was his can-do spirit that changed the course of the company. As Mary Wakefield of the *Spectator* quoted his remarking at the time of his appointment, "We either reinvent ourselves, or we go up in flames."

Boyd proceeded to commission a substantial number of new plays and showcase a season of Shakespeare's Spanish contemporaries, in efforts designed to both place the Bard's work in context and reinforce its accessibility to all. At the same time, he also saw the wisdom in returning to the RSC's roots by insisting on reinstatement of the ensemble approach. This led to the participation of major stars in such efforts as the 2006–07 Stratford festival of all Shakespeare's plays, with Patrick Stewart appearing as Antony in *Antony and Cleopatra* and Prospero in the *Tempest.* In 2008, on the other hand, it yielded a widely acclaimed performance

KEY DATES

1879: Shakespeare Memorial Theatre opens in
Stratford-upon-Avon.
1925: First Royal Charter is awarded.
1961: Royal Shakespeare Company founded and
theater renamed by Peter Hall.
1990s: Company suffers internal and external
conflict.
2003: Michael Boyd named artistic director.

organization's gross receipts were more than £51
million. As a registered charity, the RSC received nearly
half of that figure from Arts Council England. Thirty-six
percent came from ticket sales and other commercial
revenue, while seven percent came from donations. The
RSC planned an unprecedented, six-week residency in
New York in 2011 and was scheduled to host a World
Shakespeare Festival in conjunction with the 2012
London Olympics.

Margaret L. Moser

from a company of unknowns in eight Shakespearian
histories at the same time (34 actors playing a total of
264 roles plus understudy positions), with every one of
them in seven of the eight plays. That extraordinary effort entailed two and a half years of rehearsal and
performance and emphatically underscored the value of
an ensemble company.

One of the most controversial of Boyd's campaigns
was the renovation of the Royal Shakespeare Theatre in
Stratford. While it had been belittled by many since its
dedication in 1932, there were plenty of traditionalists
who objected to any alteration of its space. Nonetheless,
in 2007 the theater was closed for a remodeling that
would retain the outside but considerably alter the
interior. The theater was due to reopen in 2010.

By 2007, the RSC was setting box office records
and had returned to profitability. In 2008 the

FURTHER READING

"All the World and Its Stage," *Economist*, March 31, 2007,
p. 92(US).
Benedict, David, "Blazing Bard Binge: RSC Dazzles with His-
tory Marathon," *Variety*, May 19, 2008, p. 50(1).
Dorn, Jennifer, "The Royal Shakespeare Company: Still Playing
the Part," *British Heritage*, November 2007.
Hastings, Chris, "Peter Hall: Everything but God in the RSC,"
Telegraph, November 23, 2008.
Healy, Patrick, "Shakespeare's New Home: Park Avenue," *New
York Times*, February 9, 2010, p. C1(L).
Jury, Louise," 'Semtex' Boyd Is Given the Chance to Shake up
the RSC," *Independent*, July 26, 2002.
———, "The Man Who Remade the RSC," *Evening Standard*,
December 4, 2007.
O'Mahoney, John, "The Fixer," *Guardian*, February 12, 2005.
Wakefield, Mary, "Liberating Shakespeare: Mary Wakefield
Talks to the RSC's Michael Boyd and Learns How He
Scared the Establishment," *Spectator*, April 5, 2008,
p. 40(2).

San Francisco Opera Association

—————————■—————————

301 Van Ness Avenue
San Francisco, California 94102
U.S.A.
Telephone: (415) 861-4008
Web site: http://sfopera.com

Nonprofit Company
Incorporated: 1923
Employees: 300 (est.)
Operating Revenues: $34 million (FY 2008–09)
NAICS: 711110 Opera Companies

■ ■ ■

The second-largest opera company in the United States after New York City's Metropolitan Opera, the San Francisco Opera Association is considered one of the best opera companies in the world. Founded in 1923, it has hosted the U.S. debuts of artists including Birgit Nilsson, Leontyne Price, and Renata Tebaldi. Committed to the presentation of contemporary opera as well as the classical repertory, the opera has commissioned important new works including *Doctor Atomic* (2005), *Appomattox* (2007), and *The Bonesetter's Daughter* (2008). The San Francisco Opera is both world-renowned and a beloved institution in its hometown. According to Jane Gross of the *New York Times,* "No other American city dotes on its opera company as San Francisco does, and opening night is the pinnacle of the social season."

TWO VISIONARIES

Much of the success of the San Francisco Opera can be traced to the vision of the company's first two general directors, Gaetano Merola and Kurt Adler. Merola was born in Naples, Italy, in 1881 and studied at the San Pietro a Maiella Conservatory of Music there before immigrating to the United States in 1899. He conducted the Metropolitan Opera, the Henry W. Savage English Opera, and the Manhattan Opera in New York, but it was on the West Coast that he came to fame.

Merola established the San Francisco Opera in 1923 with a focus on Italian works presented over a brief, two-week season. He established a fundraising operation and oversaw the building of the organization's new home, the War Memorial Opera House, which opened in 1932. Designed in the Beaux Arts style, the Opera House was the first in the United States to derive its funding from thousands of interested individuals, as opposed to a small group of wealthy patrons. Merola continued to lead his opera to increasing prominence for the next 30 years until his sudden death in 1953. Fittingly, he died in the service of music, while conducting a performance of *Madama Butterfly* at the Sigmund Stern Grove Festival in San Francisco.

Merola's successor, Kurt Herbert Adler, was born in Vienna in 1905 and made his conducting debut there at the age of 20. He went on to conduct in various European venues, including a stint as the legendary Arturo Toscanini's assistant at the 1936 Salzburg Music Festival. In 1938 he emigrated to the United States to work with the Chicago Opera, and he became a U.S. citizen in 1941. Two years later, Adler accepted an offer

COMPANY PERSPECTIVES

■

Our Mission: To present opera performances of the highest international quality available to the widest possible audiences; to perpetuate and enrich the operatic art form; to be creative and innovative in all aspects of opera; to take a leadership role in training, arts education and audience development.

from Merola to become chorus master with the San Francisco Opera.

After Merola's unexpected passing in 1953, Adler took the reins of the San Francisco Opera, first as artistic director and then as its second general director. Legendary for his formidable personality, Adler is widely acknowledged to have shaped the organization into one of the best opera companies in the world. John Rockwell of the *New York Times* described Adler as "an imperious, crusty figure who involved himself with every aspect of the company's operations" and characterized his tenure as "28 years of virtual one-man rule." Adler created the Merola Opera Program, named after his predecessor, which became one of the premier apprentice training courses in opera. He also expanded the company's repertoire (overseeing 117 different productions), introduced its touring program, and dramatically extended its season and increased its budget. Hundreds of artists, including Marilyn Horne, Jess Thomas, Boris Christoff, and Georg Solti, made their operatic or American debuts under his leadership. Together, Merola and Adler dedicated nearly six decades to the advancement of the San Francisco Opera, an unusual stretch of stability in a famously tempestuous business.

A NEW ERA

Four general directors led the San Francisco Opera from the final two decades of the 20th century into the first ten years of the next. Terence A. McEwen, who succeeded Adler in 1981, established the San Francisco Opera Center to streamline the company's various educational programs (1982) and hired the opera's first permanent musical director, Sir John Pritchard (1985), as well as presenting an extremely well received production of Wagner's *Ring Cycle* (1985). Poor health forced him to resign in 1988, coincidentally just hours before the demise of his storied predecessor.

McEwen was succeeded by Lotfi Mansouri, an experienced stage director and former head of the Canadian Opera Company. Known for his philosophy that "opera is for everyone," Mansouri brought the democratizing innovation of supertitles (subtitles projected above the stage) to the opera community. His 13 years in San Francisco saw such high points as the re-establishment of the summer season and an extensive, widely praised renovation of the Opera House. He worked to make opera more accessible as an art form, with results that Joshua Kosman of the *San Francisco Chronicle* described as a "heady, slightly uneasy blend of serious artistic achievement and frank, even garish showmanship." A "Broadway-style" production of *La Boheme* in 1996 lured young and enthusiastic audiences. However, other of his experiments were less successful, and detractors perceived an overall lowering of artistic quality during his tenure, which ended in 2001.

One of the most embattled tenures of a general director was that of Pamela Rosenberg, who served from 2001 until 2005. Fresh from a term with the Stuttgart Opera, where she won praise for her innovative programming, Rosenberg was almost instantly thrust into a financial quagmire, as the economic downturn following the dot-com boom, which hit the city particularly hard, and an alarmingly low endowment fund combined to create a $7.7 million deficit. Rosenberg cut the budget by 14 percent in 2003, one of the most brutal cutbacks in the opera's history, and discontinued an array of programming initiatives and productions. She was criticized for continuing to emphasize contemporary and innovative operas during a time of retrenchment, when some saw financial stability in staging opera's most-beloved works. However, she refused to scale back her artistic vision, telling Anthony Tommasini of the *New York Times,* "We are not going to get through this economic downturn and come out the other end by replacing quality with mediocrity. If we are going to be worthy of support, we have to make a difference in people's lives." Critics and audiences seemed to agree, and by the time she departed for the Berlin Philharmonic in 2005, the company was back in the black and many of her productions were viewed as vital infusions of fresh air. The 2005 production of John Adams's *Dr. Atomic,* for example, which was commissioned by the San Francisco Opera, was described by Tommasini as "the musical event of the year in America."

LOOKING FORWARD

David Gockley became the opera's sixth general director in 2006. He had previously spent 33 years in charge of the Houston Grand Opera, where he acquired a reputation as a bold and efficient manager. Gockley launched the company's first free outdoor simulcast (*Madama Butterfly*), the beginning of a popular series of such

---

KEY DATES

1923: San Francisco Opera is founded by Gaetano Merola.

1932: War Memorial Opera House opens.

1953: Kurt Herbert Adler takes over as general director.

2006: David Gockley assumes leadership of the opera.

---

events. Other important innovations included the installation of a permanent broadcast-standard video production facility in the Opera House and the initiation of a plan to show company operas in movie theaters. The San Francisco Opera continued to present commissioned works, including the world premieres of *Appomattox*, by composer Philip Glass and librettist Christopher Hampton (2007), and *The Bonesetter's Daughter*, by composer Stuart Wallace and librettist Amy Tan (2008).

Such artistic successes did not completely insulate the opera from the next economic downturn, which significantly reduced the opera's endowment in 2009 and took a toll on ticket sales for performing arts institutions nationwide. Nevertheless, the San Francisco Opera repeatedly performed to capacity audiences throughout the season, and this, combined with a 6.5 percent reduction in expenditures and $34 million in contributions from 9,000 donors, resulted in a balanced budget for the year. In the organization's financial statements for fiscal year 2008–09, Gockley warned of further belt-tightening to come: "We are presently forecasting a FY 2010 deficit of $2 million and are struggling mightily to balance FY 2011, the season in which we have announced three cycles of Richard Wagner's *Ring*.... Looking ahead, only significant modifica-

tions to the company's fixed cost structure will permit us to survey the future with reasonable confidence." At the same time, Opera Association President George Hume reaffirmed the company's commitment to its mission: "Although the financial realities now confronting our global economy have forced us to do some repositioning of the Company, we remain fully committed to our core values of presenting a world-class grand opera experience to our audiences both inside the Opera House and in the community."

Margaret L. Moser

FURTHER READING

Gereben, Janos, "S.F. Opera's David Gockley Maintains an Elaborate Harmony," *San Francisco Examiner*, May 24, 2009.

Gross, Jane, "San Francisco Journal; City That Loves Opera Faces a Night to Lament," *New York Times*, September 7, 1990, p. A12.

Kosman, Joshua, "Two Views of Mansouri's S.F. Era," *San Francisco Chronicle*, August 5, 2001, p. PK-48.

Ortiz, Edward, "S.F. Opera Cuts Back for 2009–10," *Sacramento Bee*, January 27, 2009.

———, "Wagner Masterpiece Will Highlight S.F. Opera Season," *Sacramento Bee*, January 20, 2010.

Rockwell, John, "Kurt Adler, Conductor Who Led San Francisco Opera, Dies at 82," *New York Times*, February 11, 1988.

Tommasini, Anthony, "Critic's Notebook; San Francisco Losing Backer of New Music," *New York Times*, July 1, 2004, p. E1.

Walsh, Michael, "Nowhere to Go but Up; the San Francisco Opera, with a New Chief, Aims to Rise Anew," *Time*, September 26, 1988, p. 95(1).

Winn, Steven, "Pamela Rosenberg's Time at the Opera was as Full of Drama as Any Production. What Are People Saying about Her Now?" *San Francisco Chronicle*, December 7, 2005, p. E-1.

SandRidge Energy, Inc.

—————————————■—————————————

123 Robert S. Kerr Avenue
Oklahoma City, Oklahoma 73102-6406
U.S.A.
Telephone: (405) 429-5500
Fax: (405) 429-5977
Web site: http://www.sandridgeenergy.com

Public Company
Incorporated: 1985
Employees: 2,095
Sales: $1.18 billion
Stock Exchanges: New York
Ticker Symbol: SD
NAICS: 211111 Crude Petroleum and Natural Gas
  Extraction; 213112 Support Activities for Oil and
  Gas Field Exploration

■ ■ ■

A product of the oil patch that stretches from San Antonio to El Paso in Texas, SandRidge Energy, Inc., was born and grew up in the entrepreneurial years following the great energy price slump of the early 1980s. It has come a long distance since then. While its oil and natural gas operations are still focused primarily on the West Texas Overthrust (WTO), an area located in Pecos and Terrell counties in West Texas, the company today is publicly traded, headquartered in Oklahoma City, and has significant operations in the Cotton Valley Trend in East Texas, the Gulf Coast area, and elsewhere. Much of its growth in recent years has been through acquisitions, including the $800 million purchase of properties in the

Permian Basin of West Texas from Forest Oil Corporation in December 2009.

ORIGINS

SandRidge's founder, N. Malone Mitchell III, was himself a product of the West Texas oil country, having grown up in Sanderson, 65 miles from Fort Stockton, where he founded the company from his bedroom and with $500 in 1985. Soon the company began acquiring other small energy producers, as well as drilling rigs through its drilling subsidiary, Lariat Services. The goal was vertical integration: to create a company that encompassed every stage of the energy exploration, production, and distribution process. By 2004 Riata Energy, as it was then known, had about $250 million in revenues from a collection of businesses that embraced most facets of the oil business, as well as construction and ranching.

By 2006 Mitchell's company could boast a fleet of 43 rigs, along with the associated heavy machinery and equipment. Through another subsidiary, PetroServices Energy Company (later called SandRidge Tertiary, LLC), it was also providing CO_2 treatment and transportation facilities and tertiary oil recovery operations. Oil and natural gas production had expanded beyond the West Texas core into Piceance Basin in northwestern Colorado. Riata was drilling one well per day and had become one of the largest privately held energy companies in the United States, as well as the nation's largest privately held land tiller.

In January of that year Mitchell and his executives decided it was time to go public. In early May, however,

COMPANY PERSPECTIVES

SandRidge Energy, Inc., is a company comprised of employees who value integrity and community. We are dedicated to harvesting and supplying this country's natural resources to the U.S. market in a safe, quick and cost-effective manner. In the process, our company protects the environment, recognizes and rewards the individual efforts of those who work for it, and enriches the communities where its employees live and work.

SandRidge Energy's name is carefully crafted to represent the company's approach to exploration. "Sand" reflects its search for high rate natural gas wells in conventional sands. "Ridge" indicates the type of geological characteristic the organization most desires when drilling wells.

an initial public offering was delayed when Tom L. Ward offered to buy a controlling share of Riata and take over as chairman and chief executive. Ward, cofounder of Chesapeake Energy Corporation, had recently stepped down as president and chief operating officer of that firm because he felt it had become too large for him to manage comfortably. Shortly thereafter he paid $500 million for a 46 percent stake in Riata and signed a three-year contract with the company. Later that year Riata moved its headquarters to Oklahoma City. In December Mitchell retired as president and COO, retaining a seat on the board. "I bought some more stock recently, and I intend to buy more stock when we go public, later this spring," he told Sharon Roosevelt of the *Fort Stockton Pioneer*.

By then Riata had launched its largest acquisition to date, the $1.52 billion purchase of NEG Oil & Gas, LLC, a Dallas-based oil and gas exploration, development, and production company, from financier Carl C. Icahn's American Real Estate Partners, L.P. The deal added to Riata's assets in the WTO, quadrupling its production in the region. It also brought new holdings in East Texas, the Gulf Coast, and the Gulf of Mexico.

Shortly thereafter, Ward announced that the combined company was changing its name to Sand-Ridge Energy, Inc., which, as he was quoted in a September 2006 press release, "encompasses the new direction and goals of the company." Early in 2007 the company made moves to bolster its capital base, easing its funding of the NEG deal. In a private transaction,

Ares Management LLC, a Los Angeles-based investment firm, bought $200 million of stock, Ward himself bought $50 million worth, and holders of SandRidge preferred shares exercised rights to buy another $70 million of common stock. At the same time, the company concluded a deal for $1 billion in term loans. The series of deals signaled Wall Street's confidence in Ward and his team, observed Bob Rader, vice president of Capital West Securities in Oklahoma City. "It's a big deal ... for SandRidge to put together this financing and bring in so much money from outside Oklahoma," he was quoted as saying by Adam Wilmoth in the *Oklahoman*. Cementing its new position in the state, SandRidge in July purchased for $22 million a parcel of property in downtown Oklahoma City, including the landmark Kerr-McGee Tower, which it planned to renovate and use as its new corporate headquarters.

SANDRIDGE GOES PUBLIC

The next step was to go ahead with the company's delayed public stock offering, which was announced in June 2007. The public market for energy shares was heating up. The oil exploration company Continental Resources Inc. had completed an initial public offering little more than a month earlier, and a like firm, Quest Resource Corp. of Oklahoma City, had just announced an IPO of a master limited partnership. Over the past two years a total of eight energy firms in the state had gone public, after a three-year period in which none had done so. SandRidge began trading on the New York Stock Exchange in November under the symbol SD, and the IPO, for 28.7 million shares at $26 each, raised $795 million shortly thereafter.

Proceeds, the company announced in an SEC filing, would be used to accelerate SandRidge's aggressive drilling program (daily production had already expanded six-fold over the past year, to 142 million cubic feet of natural gas equivalent), expand its capital expenditures, as well as pay down debt. By the end of 2007, thanks in part to a decision to link SandRidge's pipeline system to that of Equity Transfer Partners, gas production was up to 220 million cubic feet of natural gas equivalent.

The next year opened just as aggressively, with plans to expand SandRidge's CO_2 operations and new drilling in the WTO outside the core area of Pinon Field. Overall plans were to drill approximately 440 new wells. Encouragingly, the company had turned around a $3.3 million loss in the fourth quarter of 2006 to produce $14.2 million in net income for the same period in 2007. Aside from the boom in natural gas prices, Ward attributed the results to increased production (total oil and natural gas production had more than tripled to

KEY DATES

1985: Riata Energy is founded by N. Malone Mitchell III in Fort Stockton, Texas; the company quickly expands into all aspects of energy exploration, production, and distribution.

2006: Mitchell sells his controlling interest in Riata Energy to Tom L. Ward; Riata acquires NEG Oil & Gas, LLC; the company moves its headquarters to Oklahoma City and renames itself SandRidge Energy, Inc.

2007: SandRidge goes public on the New York Stock Exchange, raising $795 million in an initial public offering.

2008: SandRidge greatly expands its CO2 operations by forming a joint venture with Occidental Petroleum Corporation; a slump in natural gas prices prompts SandRidge to slash its projected capital expenditures.

2009: SandRidge acquires oil and gas properties in the Permian Basin from Forest Oil Corporation.

64.2 billion cubic feet equivalent), increased reserves, and lower per-unit production costs.

Ward continued to build his stake in the company, paying $100 million to purchase stock on the open market during the first half of 2008 even though Sand-Ridge shares were trading at 90 percent over their IPO price. Meanwhile, the company was reshaping its portfolio of properties. In May it sold its assets in Colorado's Piceance Basin to a subsidiary of Williams Companies, Inc., for $285 million. In June it augmented its CO2 operations by joining with Occidental Petroleum Corporation to build and operate a new CO2 extraction plant, as well as compression and transportation pipelines, in Pecos County, West Texas.

WEATHERING THE NATURAL GAS SLUMP

The global economic slump was by then, however, putting pressure on natural gas prices. In July SandRidge announced that its East Texas and North Louisiana assets were for sale and, in October, that it was slashing planned capital expenditures in 2009 from $2 billion to $1 billion. Two months later it halved the capital budget again, to $500 million, aiming to operate within its cash

resources while still increasing production 10 percent. In January 2009 Ward sold 23 percent of his stock in SandRidge to George Kaiser, a Tulsa businessperson, for $50 million to pay off debts, avoiding an open-market sale at a time when the company's stock price had fallen into the single digits and leaving him with a 17.5 percent stake.

SandRidge continued to repair its balance sheet in June with sales of gathering and compression rights in Pinon Field for $200 million and East Texas drilling rights for $58 million. In November it had to call off the previously announced purchase of bankrupt Crusader Energy Group Inc. The $230 million deal was expected to bolster positions that SandRidge was building in the Anadarko Basin of western Oklahoma and, with cash flow from Crusader's current production, to enhance SandRidge's balance sheet. New bidders had appeared for the company, and Ward said he did not want to participate in an auction.

SandRidge, noted Ward, would continue to pursue other opportunities and later that month announced an $800 million deal to acquire oil and gas properties in the Permian Basin from Forest Oil Corporation and one of its subsidiaries. The purchase was executed using a combination of borrowings from the company's credit facility and sales of new shares of common and preferred stock. Analysts at Standard & Poor's liked the deal. They raised SandRidge's corporate credit rating from B to B+ as a result, noting that the Permian purchase gave the company a more balanced profile between natural gas and liquids and that the company enjoyed competitive costs of development and production even though its balance sheet remained highly leveraged.

SandRidge nevertheless continued to operate in a difficult environment. Its results for the first nine months of 2009 included a net loss for common shareholders of $1.35 billion, or $7.85 per share, compared with a $137.1 million, or $0.89 per share, gain in the comparable period the year prior.

Eric Laursen

PRINCIPAL SUBSIDIARIES

Lariat Services, Inc.; SandRidge Tertiary, LLC; Sand-Ridge Midstream, Inc.

PRINCIPAL COMPETITORS

Apache Corp.; Brigham Exploration Co.; Occidental Permian Ltd.

FURTHER READING

Folsom, Geoff, "Plant Breaks Ground," *Oklahoman*, March 12, 2009.

"History," Viking Drilling, http://www.viking-drilling.com/history.

Lackmeyer, Steve, "Transformation," *Oklahoman*, January 28, 2010.

Mecoy, Don, "SandRidge Chairman Tom Ward Secures $50 Million through Stock Sale," *Oklahoman*, January 6, 2009.

Money, Jack, "SandRidge Results Soar as Chief Exec Plans to Buy More Stock," *Oklahoman*, March 4, 2008.

Roosevelt, Sharon, "Change in Management at SandRidge Energy," *Fort Stockton Pioneer*, January 25, 2007.

"SandRidge Energy Plans $100M Campus Renovation," Associated Press, January 29, 2010.

Shute, Toby, "An Oil Stock in the Short Sellers' Sights," Motley Fool, February 8, 2010, http://www.fool.com/investing/small-cap/2010/02/08/an-oil-stock-in-the-short-sellers-sights.aspx.

Wilmoth, Adam, "Oklahoma's Public Energy Market Is Heating Up Again," *Oklahoman*, June 23, 2007.

———, "SandRidge Gets $1.3B in Financing," *Oklahoman*, March 23, 2007.

Scania AB

———■———

Nyköpingsvägen 33
Södertälje, SE-151 87
Sweden
Telephone: (+46 8) 55 38 10 00
Fax: (+46 8) 55 38 10 37
Web site: http://www.scania.com

Public Company
Founded: 1891 as Vagnfabriksaktiebolaget i Södertälje
Employees: 34,777
Sales: SEK 88.98 billion ($11.46 billion) (2008)
Stock Exchanges: Stockholm
Ticker Symbol: SCVB
NAICS: 336120 Heavy Duty Truck Manufacturing

■ ■ ■

Controlled by Volkswagen AG, Sweden-based Scania AB is one of the world's leading bus and heavy-truck manufacturers. Scania supplies buses and coaches to both public transport systems and coach companies. Scania trucks include long-haul and distribution vehicles, as well as trucks geared for construction and special-purpose trucks such as fire engines, refuse collectors, road sweepers, and troop transport and other military vehicles. Scania also produces engines for industrial, marine, and power generation applications, and the company services all of its trucks, buses, and engines. Manufacturing is conducted at 11 factories located in Sweden, France, the Netherlands, Poland, Russia, Argentina, and Brazil. Sales and service is handled around the world by about 100 national distributors.

NINETEENTH-CENTURY ROOTS

Scania traces its history to 1891 when Philip Wersén and Surahammarsbruk, a venerable ironworks, formed Vagnfabriksaktiebolaget i Södertälje (Wagon Factory Ltd. in Södertälje), or Vabis in shortened form. Vabis, based in Södertälje, Sweden, initially manufactured railway carriages, but in the first years of the 20th century business fell off and out of desperation it turned its attention to engines and car and truck building. An engine and automotive plant was built, and in 1908 Vabis offered its first vehicles. Sales were poor, however. Despite building an award-winning 3-ton truck, the company fell far short of its sales target of 50 trucks a year. In 1909 the plant produced just one-tenth that number and only seven cars, and management looked to sell the business or, if necessary, dissolve the operation.

While Vabis struggled through 20 years of existence, a company called Maskinfabriksaktiebolaget Scania (Machine Factory Ltd. in Skåne; *Scania* being Latin for "Skåne") was launched in 1900 in Malmö, Sweden, to manufacture bicycles. It very quickly turned its attention to the production of cars and trucks, manufacturing its first truck in 1902. At first, Scania relied on French and German engines and other components, and only after sales picked up did it invest in the production of its own engines. Scania's prudent management stood in stark contrast to Vabis, as the younger company was able to turn a profit in the automotive field and phased out bicycles and other product lines to focus on engines

COMPANY PERSPECTIVES

Scania's mission is to supply its customers with high-quality heavy vehicles and services related to the transport of goods and passengers by road. By focusing on customer needs, high-quality products and services, as well as respect for the individual, Scania shall create value-added for the customer and grow with sustained profitability, while contributing to a sustainable society.

Scania's operations specialise in developing and manufacturing vehicles, which shall lead the market in terms of performance and life cycle cost, as well as quality and environmental characteristics. Scania's sales and service organisation shall supply customers with vehicles and services that provide maximum operating time at minimum cost, while preserving environmental characteristics, over the service life of their vehicles.

and vehicles. Scania's managing director, Per Alfred Nordeman, recognized value in the Vabis operation, and in 1910 he proposed that the two companies merge, an idea that was met with ready acceptance by the downtrodden Vabis.

1911 FORMATION OF AB SCANIA-VABIS

A merger agreement was reached in November 1910 and completed in 1911, calling for the creation of a new company, AB Scania-Vabis, and the elimination of all operations not related to engine or car and truck production. Manufacturing was consolidated at the Södertälje site. Nordeman was also tapped to serve as the company's first managing director, a position for which he had already proven himself worthy, and he further demonstrated his abilities by quickly making the combined operation a success.

Scania enjoyed excellent export sales, so that by 1915, 30 percent of sales came from Russia and other non-Nordic countries. By this time, however, war had enveloped the continent, bringing an end to exports beyond the Nordic area, but Scania more than made up for the loss in revenues through military contracts. In the meantime, Nordeman laid plans to produce standard light trucks after the war, convinced that haulers were finally ready to give up their horse-drawn wagons. Thus,

in 1919, a few months after World War I came to an end, Scania put all of its resources into standard trucks, phasing out the production of cars while immediately ending the manufacture of buses, fire engines, and other vehicles. Unfortunately, a depression gripped the world after the war, crippling truck demand. Nordeman's gamble failed, and as a result he was forced to resign his post in November 1919.

FORMATION OF NEW SCANIA: 1921

Matters did not improve following Nordeman's departure, and in 1921 the company was liquidated. With financial backing from Sweden's wealthy Wallenberg family, which had been an investor since 1916, a new company under the same name emerged, but it lacked a sales and service organization, and its prewar car and truck designs were hopelessly outdated. The new managing director, Gunnar Lindmark, had but one viable arrow in his quiver: excellent fuel-efficient engines. He was able to use that to persuade the Swedish Postal Administration and Customs Service to order 15 mail buses. Scania was able to take advantage of the postal service's shops and technicians to design a 12-passenger bus able to navigate Sweden's notoriously snow-covered roads. In addition to the new buses, Scania took advantage of its engine design capabilities to develop industrial engines and marine engines for patrol boats. With financial breathing space, Scania was able to complete new truck designs, so that by the end of the 1920s Scania had completely turned itself around, having paid off all debts to the liquidated company and erased its accumulated losses. In 1930 shareholders received their first dividend.

Scania expanded its bus business in the early 1930s following a visit of its chief designer to Ohio-based Twin Coach, which built buses with a flat front. Scania built its version of the "bulldog" bus, which was introduced in 1932. The timing proved fortuitous as the global Great Depression had sent truck sales plummeting while the need for buses and the cheap mode of transportation they provided had remained steady. The company may have lost money in 1934 but it returned to profitability in 1935, never again posting a losing year.

Also in 1935, Scania became the Swedish general agent for Germany's Volkswagen car manufacturer. The Nazi Party had already taken control of the German government and was plotting a course for war, eventually causing a disruption in the relationship. In the meantime, Scania developed its first diesel engine, followed by a unitary diesel that relied on standardized components, thus laying the foundations for a modular system, which would become a key to future success.

POSTWAR EXPANSION

Like many manufacturers, Scania became primarily a defense contractor during World War II, producing trucks for military use as well as armored personnel carriers and tanks. Nevertheless, the company began preparing for peacetime by designing new buses and truck chassis. Even before the defeat of Nazi Germany, Scania in late 1944 began selling trucks to the civilian market, setting the stage for strong growth during the postwar years. When Volkswagen reemerged, Scania became its Swedish importer in 1948. The Volkswagen vehicles proved so successful that by 1950 about half of Scania's revenues came from this import business. On other fronts, Scania introduced its highly durable direct-injection diesel engine in 1949, leading to the creation of the Regent truck model, which became the company's flagship product. In the 1950s Scania built up a dealer network that offered Scania trucks as well as Volkswagen cars and Willys-Overland jeeps and other vehicles. In addition to enjoying a large market share in Sweden, Scania enjoyed increasing success exporting its trucks, so that by the end of the 1950s more than half of the company's production was exported.

An important foreign market was Brazil, where in 1957 Scania built its first plant outside Södertälje. A year later the European Economic Community (EEC) was established, and Scania looked to take advantage of favorable customs to grow business in other EEC countries. A plant was built in the Netherlands in 1965 to spur sales. Scania also expanded through external means in the 1960s, acquiring a truck cab company as well as a coachwork company in Katrineholm, Sweden, where all bus production was moved. In 1969 Scania-Vabis merged with another Wallenberg family-owned company, the Swedish aircraft and automobile manufacturer Saab AB, creating Saab-Scania AB.

Scania grew into a pan-European company in the 1970s, expanding market share throughout the non-Communist countries of Western Europe. Scania did especially well in the long-haul segment of the truck market, primarily because of a new powerful engine it introduced in 1969 that spearheaded growth in the major European markets of France and Germany. During the 1970s Scania also expanded its business in South America, opening a factory in Argentina in 1976. The company did not, however, do business in the United States, where it remained virtually unknown.

DEVELOPMENT OF MODULAR TRUCK LINES

Scania's research and development efforts led to the introduction of important new modular truck lines in the 1980s. At the beginning of the decade the company unveiled the Program Scania line, which ranged in size from 16 tons to 36 tons. Because of the flexibility of its modular design, these trucks were available in a multitude of variations and could be tailored for specific needs. In the late 1980s Scania took the modular approach a step further with its 3-Series, which were "made-to-measure," allowing customers and dealers to essentially design a unique truck to meet their requirements. This innovation led to the 3-Series winning "Truck of the Year" honors in Europe in 1989.

Scania revamped its manufacturing operations in the 1990s to maximize economies of scale. Engine and transmission production was consolidated at Södertälje, while axle production was moved to Zwolle in the Netherlands. Cab production was moved from the Dutch town of Meppel to Oskarshamn, Sweden. A plant was also opened in Angers, France, for chassis assembly. At the same time that production was being coordinated on a large scale, at the local level Scania granted increased independence to allow factories to create and improve the way they operated.

In 1991 Saab-Scania became a wholly owned subsidiary of Investor AB, the investment arm of the Wallenberg family. Four years later Saab and Scania were split but both remained Investor subsidiaries. In 1996 Investor AB took Scania AB public, selling about 55 percent of the company in an initial public offering of stock, leading to Scania's stock being listed on both the Stockholm and New York Stock Exchanges.

OWNERSHIP MACHINATIONS

After its stock became available, and with Investor's stake reduced to 45.5 percent, Scania became vulnerable to takeover. In January 1999 such an effort was launched by a chief rival, AB Volvo, which had just sold its car business to Ford Motor Company for $6.4 billion and was eager to grow its remaining truck and bus business. Volvo began buying shares in Scania, building its stake to 21.5 percent. Investor AB initially resisted but by the summer began to see the advantages of the combination, given that the 1998 formation of Daimler-Chrysler had changed the dynamics of the vehicle industry, creating pressure to pursue greater size to achieve the economies of scale needed to effectively compete in the 21st century. Finally in August 1999, Investor AB reached a deal to sell its stake in Scania for $7.4 billion, in conjunction with an offer by Volvo to purchase the remaining outstanding shares.

The sale to Volvo never came to fruition, however. The deal was conditioned on approval by the European Union, but it was rejected in 2000 by the European Competition Commission, which maintained that the combination would create a regional monopoly. Instead, Investor AB sold a major portion of its interest in Scania to Volkswagen, so that the stake controlled by the Wallenberg family was reduced to 29 percent and Volkswagen became the largest shareholder with 34 percent. Volvo continued to own B shares, which it sold in 2004 to Deutsche Bank, which in turn sold them to the market.

In 2006 Scania faced a new hostile takeover attempt from MAN AG, a major German truck manufacturer, which assembled a 13.2 percent position. Volkswagen and Investor AB together held control and rejected MAN's bid. Moreover, Volkswagen countered by purchasing a 20 percent stake in MAN, which it then increased to 30 percent. Two years later Volkswagen bought out Investor AB and the other Wallenberg family interests, paying $4.37 billion to gain majority control of Scania, holding 68.6 percent of voting rights and 37.7 percent of the capital rights. Volkswagen had thus positioned itself to engineer a three-way merger between its truck division, MAN, and Scania to create Europe's largest truck maker. The sudden departure of MAN's chairman, Håkan Samuelsson, in November 2009 further fueled such speculation. The completion of such a merger, if pursued, was by no means certain given the regulatory hurdles. Scania, in the meantime, remained a strong competitor in its markets.

Ed Dinger

PRINCIPAL SUBSIDIARIES

Ferruform AB; Scania Credit AB; Scania Finans AB; Scania Sverige AB; Scania Argentina S.A.; Scania Leas-

ing Ges.m.b.H. (Austria); Scania Finance Belgium N.V. S.A. (99.9%); Scania Latin America Ltda. (Brazil); Scania Finance Chile S.A.; Scania Finance Czech Republic spol s.r.o.; Scania Finance France S.A.S.; Scania France S.A.S.; Scania Finance Deutschland GmbH (Germany); Scania Finance Great Britain Ltd.; Scania Finance Italy S.p.A.; Scania Finance Luxembourg S.A.; Scania Finance Nederland B.V. (Netherlands); Scania Productie Meppel B.V. (Netherlands); Scania Production Zwolle B.V. (Netherlands); Scania Finance Polska Sp.z.o.o. (Poland); Scania Production Słupsk S.A. (Poland); OOO Scania Leasing (Russia); Scania Peter OOO (Russia); Scania Finance Slovak Republic; Scania Finance Southern Africa (Pty) Ltd. (South Africa); Scania Finance Korea Ltd. (South Korea); Scania Finance Hispania EFC S.A. (Spain); Scania Finance Switzerland Ltd.; Scania Tüketici Finansmani A.S. (Turkey).

PRINCIPAL DIVISIONS

Trucks; Buses & Coaches; Engines; Services.

PRINCIPAL COMPETITORS

AB Volvo; Daimler AG; Iveco S.p.A.; MAN SE; PACCAR Inc.

FURTHER READING

Brady, Rosemary, "Sweden's Other Carmaker," *Forbes*, November 19, 1984, p. 243.

"MAN Overboard," *Economist*, November 28, 2009, p. 75EU.

Rauwald, Christoph, and Maria Akerhielm, "Scania Rejects Bid from MAN," *Wall Street Journal*, September 19, 2006, p. A10.

Reed, John, "Scania Aims for Emerging Markets," *Financial Times*, May 21, 2008, p. 20.

Sandell, Kaj, and Bo Streiffert, *Scania, 100 Years: A Century of Industrial and Automotive Progress, 1891–1991*, Södertälje, Sweden: Saab-Scania AB, Scania Division, 1990, 264 p.

Taylor, Edward, and Jenny Clevstrom, "VW Buys Scania Stake in $4.37 Billion Deal," *Wall Street Journal*, March 4, 2008, p. A4.

Walker, Jonathan, "Volvo Buys Scania: A Marriage Made in Sweden," *Diesel Progress North American Edition*, October 1999, p. 10.

Schroders plc

---

31 Gresham Street
London, EC2V 7QA
United Kingdom
Telephone: (+44 207) 658-6000
Fax: (+44 207) 658-6965
Web site: http://www.schroders.com

Public Company
Incorporated: 1818 as J. Henry Schröder & Co.
Employees: 2,307
Sales: £935.8 million ($1.35 billion) (2008)
Total Assets: £7.59 billion ($10.9 billion) (2008)
Stock Exchanges: London
Ticker Symbol: SDR
NAICS: 523920 Portfolio Management

■ ■ ■

London-based Schroders plc is one of the largest asset management banking groups in the world. The company offers a wide range of private banking services to a diverse clientele. Customers include corporations; charities; local, regional, and national governments; unit trusts; pension funds; and individual investors. Managing assets of roughly £139 billion ($222 billion), Schroders operates through 32 regional offices in 25 countries. The founding Schroder family maintains a nearly 50 percent share of the company's stock, enabling it to stick to its independent course in an era of mergers and consolidation that has resulted in a smaller field of globally operating megabanks.

MERCHANT ORIGINS IN THE 19TH CENTURY

The Schröder family had already established itself as a prominent merchant clan in Hamburg, Germany, by the beginning of the 19th century. Like many other prominent families active in trade, the Schröders had also branched out into a number of Europe's major cities. In 1804 Johann Heinrich Schröder traveled to London, joining his brother's merchant firm there.

Schröder set out on his own in 1818, founding the firm of J. Henry Schröder & Co. The new company continued the family's traditional trading activities while gradually adding a new dimension, that of merchant banking. The rise of international trade during the 19th century brought a need for more secure payment methods. Merchant banks were created in order to provide trading houses with guaranteed payments. The appearance of merchant banks was to play a central role in encouraging the growth of international trade. Johann Heinrich Schröder was succeeded by son John Henry, who took over the company at the age of 24 in 1849.

The Schröder firm (known as Schröders) profited from both the growth of international trade and the growing demand for its merchant banking services. The firm's trade financing activities were to overtake its trading operations during the 19th century; the company also moved into other financial areas, such as bond issuing and capital investments. In 1863 Schröders became the only source of foreign capital in the United States during the Civil War when it issued £3 million to the Confederates. In Europe, the company established a

COMPANY PERSPECTIVES

Long-term thinking governs our approach to investing, developing client relationships and growing our business. Our goal is to build a first class asset management business, diversified by region, product and channel, and to reward our shareholders by growing returns on a sustainable basis over the long term.

To achieve this goal we focus on: Delivering competitive and sustainable investment performance through a clear investment process; Staying close to our clients; Operational effectiveness; Being an employer of choice; and Investing in long term growth opportunities.

charitable trust, Schröder Stiftung, in 1850, which later was to earn Johann Heinrich Schröder a baronage from the king of Prussia. John Henry Schröder was similarly honored by Queen Victoria at the end of the century, in recognition for the financial assistance he had provided to the British royal family. By then the next generation of Schröders had joined the firm; John Henry's son Bruno became a partner in 1895. Bruno Schröder received a baronage from Kaiser Wilhelm II in 1904.

Schröders had by that point achieved international prominence. The company was the first to bring a foreign loan to the Japanese government, raising £1 million in order to provide funds for building the railroad between Tokyo and Yokohama. While the company continued to rise with the development of international trade through the latter half of the century, it pursued its merchant activities as well. In the 1870s, for example, Schröders acted as one of the major traders for Peruvian guano, then widely used as fertilizer.

At the dawn of the 20th century, Schröders had grown to become one of the largest merchant banks in London; by the outbreak of World War I it had claimed the number-two spot. The firm was also a leader in the issuing of foreign loans. Among the company's noteworthy transactions of the period was a controversial £15 million loan arranged for the São Paulo, Brazil, government to help stabilize coffee prices, made in 1909.

SURVIVING THE WARS: 1914–45

Schröders continued to build on its successes in the years leading up to World War I, as London became not only the focus point of a rapidly growing international trade market but also the financial capital of the world. At the same time, Schröders was quick to move into new financial markets and products being developed at the time, such as foreign exchange dealing and commodities futures trading. The company expanded rapidly during this time, with operations covering nearly all of Europe.

The outbreak of World War I inaugurated a long period of struggle for both the Schröders and their company. Despite a long history as one of England's leading merchant banking families, the Schröders had remained German citizens. The outbreak of hostilities between England and Germany opened the Schröder firm to possible seizure by the British government. Bruno Schröder himself was threatened with sequestration for the duration. Nevertheless, within days after the declaration of war, Schröder was naturalized as a British citizen.

If Schröder had avoided imprisonment, he could not avoid seeing the family firm suffer as the British and European financial markets collapsed with the war. The U.S. dollar took over from the British sterling as the world's leading currency; the international bonds market, meanwhile, shifted to New York. By the end of the war, Schröders, along with England's other merchant banks, struggled to regain their position. Schröders was able to rebuild its position as a leading acceptance house. The United States, however, had emerged from the war as the world's new financial center. In 1923 Schröders opened a new subsidiary in New York, the J. Henry Schröder Banking Corporation, which became known as Schrobanco.

In 1926 the next generation of Schröders, led by Helmut, son of Bruno Schröder, joined the bank in time to face a crisis. At that time, the company branched out into a new business, that of investment management, creating a separate department for this activity. Nevertheless, the international financial crisis and, in particular, the collapse of the German economy, nearly forced the company out of business. The ensuing buildup and then outbreak of World War II brought new difficulties for the company, which saw much of its assets frozen for the duration. As the company itself stated, "Survival was J. Henry Schröder & Co.'s foremost achievement in the depression and war years." With its European operations in disarray, the company concentrated on building up its U.S.-based Schrobanco unit. Operated as an independent company, Schrobanco remained largely protected from the misfortunes of its European parent.

When Bruno Schröder died in 1940, son Helmut took over as the firm's senior partner, as well as head of

```
┌──────────────────────────────────────────┐
│                KEY DATES                   │
│                   ■                        │
│  1818:  J. Henry Schröder & Co. is formed. │
│  1914:  Bruno Schröder is naturalized as a │
│         British citizen.                   │
│  1926:  Company launches investment        │
│         management services.               │
│  1957:  Company name drops the umlaut.     │
│  1959:  Schroders converts to private      │
│         company, then goes public.         │
│  1962:  Company merges with Helbert,       │
│         Wagg & Co.                          │
│  2000:  Schroders sells investment banking │
│         arm to Salomon Smith Barney and    │
│         acquires Liberty International      │
│         Pensions.                           │
│  2001:  Michael Dobson becomes new company │
│         CEO.                                │
│  2008:  Schroders establishes equity funds │
│         to explore new commodity investment│
│         opportunities in Korea and parts   │
│         of Europe.                          │
└──────────────────────────────────────────┘
```

Schrobanco. Following the war, the company refocused its European operations on the slowly recovering London market. The firm's London headquarters concentrated primarily on domestic business, while its U.S. subsidiary became the center of its international finance activity, as well as the largest part of the Schröder group. At home, however, Schröders focused on developing an investment funds business, which proved the motor for the company's growth in the second half of the 1940s, as London regained its prominence as one of the top financial centers in the world.

BROADENING THE COMPANY'S GLOBAL REACH: 1950–90

By the end of the 1950s, the company had largely succeeded in redeveloping its fortunes. In 1957 the company also anglicized its name, dropping the umlaut to become Schroders. Two years later, Schroders converted from a partnership to a private company, then took a listing on the London Stock Exchange, changing its name to Schroders plc. Despite going public, the Schroder family maintained firm control of the company through a majority shareholder's position. One year later, another direct descendant, also named Bruno Schroder, joined and was named to the board of directors in 1963.

In 1962 the company merged with another merchant bank, Helbert, Wagg & Co. Founded in

1823, that firm had built up a strong specialty with its brokerage operations. The newly enlarged Schroders quickly began expanding worldwide, establishing offices in the major financial markets, launching unit trusts, and broadening its asset management and lending activities. By the end of the 1970s, Schroders was present across Europe, including Switzerland, and in Hong Kong, Singapore, Japan, and Australia.

A series of bad loans to the South American market during the 1970s and 1980s brought Schrobanco into difficulty; by 1986 Schroders decided to sell this business to the Industrial Bank of Japan. At the same time, the company temporarily exited its unit trusts operations, selling that business to National Mutual Life. Under terms of that deal, Schroders agreed not to reenter that market before the end of the decade, while continuing to manage some of the unit trusts.

The so-called Big Bang deregulation of the British banking industry went into effect in 1986, opening up the country's financial markets. As a result, Schroders began concentrating more closely on its corporate finance and investment business. Boosting this was the company's acquisition of 50 percent of Wertheim & Co. Inc., based in New York. Schroders' lack of capital, however, prevented it from joining the acquisition fever of the period, as banks began acquiring brokerships and other businesses now allowed by the deregulation move. For this reason, Schroders was relatively unaffected by the stock market collapse of 1987.

ADAPTING TO A NEW ECONOMIC REALITY: THE 1990S

Schroders returned to unit trusts management at the beginning of the 1990s, focusing especially on the Japanese market. The company's funds management business was also gaining rapidly, building from just £15 billion at the end of the 1980s to more than £50 billion in 1994. In that year, the company acquired full control of Helbert, Wagg & Co., which was then renamed Schroder & Co. Inc. Schroders was also expanding its presence in the Asian markets, notably with the opening of a subsidiary in China, while building up a position in the newly opened Eastern bloc countries.

Schroders became the target of a takeover attempt by Dutch banking powerhouse ABN AMRO in 1995. The Schroder family, led by Bruno Schroder, resisted the offer, insisting on remaining independent. By then, however, the world financial community had entered into a new round of consolidation aimed at creating a very few global giants. Schroders began to find it increasingly difficult to compete with this new generation of megabanks, not only for clients but also when recruiting top personnel. Schroders itself added to its problems as its investment division struggled to keep up with the industry index. The difficult economic situation in a number of markets in the late 1990s, such as Asia and Russia, also caused the company grief.

Schroders attempted to prop up its investment side by taking on more weight. In 1999 the company entered negotiations to merge with Beacon Group, founded in 1992 by former Goldman Sachs executive Geoffrey Boisi. The deal would have enabled Schroders to capture a strong position in the international marketplace. When the deal fell through, however, the company, now led by CEO David Salisbury, reviewed its options. By the beginning of 2000, Schroders had adopted a new strategy, announcing that it was selling its investment banking arm to Salomon Smith Barney, part of Citigroup.

Meanwhile, Schroders became a dedicated assets management group. At the end of 2000, Schroders launched a new subsidiary, Schroder & Co., organized around its former Schroders Personal Investment Management Limited subsidiary and incorporating the company's acquisition of Liberty International Pensions Limited, which was renamed Schroders Pensions. Schroder & Co. was also expected to serve as the company's springboard into the wider European private banking market.

Among the moves meant to bolster this effort was the opening of a new branch in Frankfurt, Germany, in 2001. In that year also, the company launched a new institutional stakeholder pension product, designed to extend its range of services for corporate clients. At the same time, Schroders renewed its efforts to expand in the Asian markets, as the economies in that region picked up speed again. Nevertheless, the company's attempt to acquire Taiwan's Masterlink Investment Trust was thwarted when it was outbid by Prudential Insurance Company. This development seemed to highlight the company's vulnerability in an era when it found itself among the last of the remaining independent British merchant banks. Without the deep pockets of its behemoth competitors, observers wondered how long Schroders would resist any future takeover offers. At the time, however, Schroders seemed to settle in comfortably to its new identity as an assets management specialist for the 21st century.

WEATHERING ROUGH FINANCIAL SEAS: 2000–10

As Schroders continued to expand into new markets, however, it suddenly found itself struggling to retain its long-standing clients. The company saw its net earnings

drop sharply during the first half of 2001, posting profits of £41.5 million ($60.4 million) for the period, compared to figures of £129.5 million ($188.4 million) for the first six months of 2000. Over that same span, customer withdrawals totaled close to £7 billion ($10 billion), reducing the company's total asset pool to £122.6 billion ($178.3 billion), a decline of 8.3 percent in only six months. Throughout this period, Schroders was losing some of its largest clients, notably Arla Foods amba and Bass PLC, to other asset management firms.

In September 2001 Schroders CEO Salisbury was forced to resign, after only 15 months at the helm. He was replaced by Michael Dobson, former head of the hedge fund firm Beaumont Capital Management. By the beginning of 2002, it was clear that Dobson had his work cut out for him. For fiscal year 2001, Schroders posted a loss of £8.1 million ($11.7 million); it was the first time the company had finished a year in the red in its nearly 200-year history. In order to reverse this downward trend, the company embarked on an ambitious cost-reduction program. In March 2002 Schroders announced a plan to cut 20 percent of its workforce. As part of the restructuring scheme, the company planned to trim more than 600 positions over a 21-month period. By October of that year, Schroders was forced to downscale its international operations significantly, closing all its offices in South America and selling its U.S. branch to American Express. Meanwhile, in the face of a general downturn in the global investment markets, the company's financial woes continued to mount. For the third quarter of 2002, Schroders posted a loss of £9.4 million ($14.6 million).

By 2004 Dobson's aggressive management philosophy had helped steer Schroders back in the right direction. Profits for the first half of the year rose to £60.8 million ($110.8 million), more than twice the net earnings posted for the first six months of 2003, and £5 million ($9.1 million) better than the company's original projections. For the year, Schroders enjoyed net earnings of £191 million ($350.1 million), nearly tripling its profits from the year before. As its revenues continued to climb, the company once again began to shift its focus on overseas expansion, notably in the rapidly emerging Chinese market. In 2004 Schroders managed a total investment fund worth roughly £135 billion ($271.7 billion), an increase of nearly £50 billion ($100.6 billion) compared to its managed assets in 2002.

In April 2008 Schroders created an equity fund designed to explore new commodity investment opportunities in Korea. Two months later, the company established a similar fund for emerging European markets. In spite of these initiatives, Schroders soon found itself struggling to maintain brisk profit growth, as an increasingly unstable global economy began to erode the company's assets. In the face of a deteriorating investment market, the company was forced to cut 225 jobs during the second half of 2008; an additional 50 positions were terminated the following March. For the first half of 2009, profits fell 80 percent compared to the same period the previous year. As financial markets continued to reel in the wake of the global recession, it became clear that Schroders might have to place its growth strategy on hold for the immediate future.

M. L. Cohen
Updated, Stephen Meyer

PRINCIPAL SUBSIDIARIES

Burnaby Insurance (Guernsey) Limited; Gresham Founder (CIP) Limited; Gresham Manager (CIP) Limited; Leadenhall Securities Corporation Limited; New Finance Capital LLP; PT Schroder Investment Management Indonesia (99%); Schroder Administration Limited; Schroder & Co. (Asia) Limited (Singapore); Schroder & Co Bank AG (Switzerland); Schroder & Co. Limited; Schroders Australia Holdings Pty Limited; Schroder Financial Services Limited; Schroder International Finance B.V. (Netherlands); Schroder International Holdings Limited; Schroder International Holdings (Bermuda) Limited; Schroder Investment Company Limited; Schroder Investment Consulting Co. Limited (Taiwan); Schroder Investment Funds (Switzerland) AG; Schroder Investment Management Benelux N.V. (Netherlands); Schroder Investment Management Brazil DTVM S.A.; Schroder Investment Management Fondsmaeglerselskab A/S (Denmark); Schroder Investment Management GmbH (Germany); Schroder Investment Management (Guernsey) Limited; Schroder Investment Management (Hong Kong) Limited; Schroder Investment Management (Japan) Limited; Schroder Investment Management Limited; Schroder Investment Management (Luxembourg) S.A.; Schroder Investment Management North America Inc. (USA); Schroder Investment Management North America Limited; Schroder Investment Management S.A. (Argentina); Schroder Investment Management, S.A. (Mexico); Schroder Investment Management (Sin-

gapore) Ltd; Schroder Investments (Guernsey) Limited; Schroder Investments Limited; Schroder Investments (Singapore) Pte Ltd; Schroder Middle East Limited; Schroder Pension Management Limited; Schroder Property Investment (Luxembourg) s.a.r.l.; Schroder Property Investment Management GmbH (Germany); Schroder Property Investment Management Limited; Schroder Property Managers (Jersey) Limited; Schroder Property Services B.V. (Netherlands); Schroder Unit Trusts Limited; Schroder US Holdings Inc.; Schroder Venture Managers (Guernsey) Limited; Schroder Venture Managers Inc. (Bermuda); Schroders (Bermuda) Limited; Schroders Capital Investments (Singapore) Pte Ltd; Schroders (C.I.) Limited; Schroders Italy SIM S.p.A.; Schroders Korea Limited.

PRINCIPAL COMPETITORS

Aberdeen Asset Management PLC; Bank of Ireland; Barclays plc; The Charles Schwab Corporation; Close Brothers Group plc; HSBC Holdings plc; Invesco Ltd.; Jefferies Group, Inc.; Legg Mason, Inc.; Natixis S.A.; 3i Group PLC.

FURTHER READING

Brierley, David, "Schroders: The Great Survivor," *Independent on Sunday*, July 12, 1998, p. 2.

Cowell, Alan, "Schroders Ousts Chief as Funds Business Struggles," *New York Times*, September 1, 2001, p. 1.

Daley, James, "Schroders Eyes £1bn Expansion into US Retail Market," *Independent* (London), August 17, 2005, p. 56.

Flanagan, Martin, "Schroders Eyes Acquisitions after Doubling Its Profits," *Scotsman*, August 14, 2004, p. 38.

Kaban, Elif, "Schroders Courts German Rich with New Office," *Reuters*, August 1, 2001.

King, Ian, "Schroders to Cut More Jobs and Slash Pay after Funds Exodus," *Times* (London), February 13, 2009, p. 56.

Lalor, Dan, "New Schroders Starts with Cash Pile," *Reuters*, March 3, 2000.

Rossiter, James, "Schroders on Prowl as It Reaps Reward of Change in Direction," *Evening Standard* (London), August 13, 2004, p. 43.

Targett, Simon, "Determined to Steer an Independent Course," *Financial Times*, December 4, 2000.

"The Wisdom of Salomon," *Economist*, January 22, 2000.

Sealy Corporation

One Office Parkway at Sealy Drive
Trinity, North Carolina 27370
U.S.A.
Telephone: (336) 861-3500
Fax: (336) 861-3501
Web site: http://www.sealy.com

Public Company
Founded: 1882 as Sealy Inc.
Incorporated: 1912 as Ohio Mattress Company
Employees: 4,817
Sales: $1.5 billion (2008)
Stock Exchanges: New York
Ticker Symbol: ZZ
NAICS: 314129 Other Household Textile Product Mills; 337910 Mattress Manufacturing; 423210 Mattresses Merchant Wholesalers

■ ■ ■

Sealy Corporation is the world's largest mattress company, with $1.5 billion in annual sales and manufacturing facilities and branch offices on four continents. The company markets its mattresses under a variety of well-established brand names, including Sealy Posturepedic, Bassett, and Stearns & Foster. In addition to its line of mattresses, Sealy manufacturers a wide range of bedding products, including sheets, pillows, mattress pads, and bed frames. In the 21st century Sealy expanded its product line to include luxury latex mattresses, notably the Posturepedic PurEmbrace and the Posturepedic SpringFree.

EMERGENCE OF A MATTRESS GIANT, 1882–1960

Sealy was established as a licensing organization in Chicago in 1882. The company's licensees owned all the Sealy Inc. stock, and leaders of the individual affiliates comprised Sealy's board of directors. Sealy's decentralized organizational structure evolved from the nature of mattress production and distribution, with the size and weight of mattresses inhibiting both shipping and storage. Sealy licensees agreed to limit themselves to exclusive territories of 200 miles in radius, which were contractually protected from competition with other dealers. (The territories were later expanded to 300 miles as transportation methods improved.) Sealy affiliates gave the Chicago company royalties in exchange for national and cooperative brand advertising, access to research and development undertaken by the central organization, and quality-control guidelines. The decentralized organizational structure used by Sealy in the 1880s was still in use by the majority of mattress companies in the United States in the late 20th century.

In 1907 Morris Wuliger, a Hungarian immigrant, established the Ohio Mattress Company in an abandoned church. When Frank Wuliger, son of the founder, inherited the presidency of Ohio Mattress in 1924, the company bought its first Sealy license, giving it the right to use what had become the most recognized name in the industry. In 1939 Frank called his son, Ernest, home from his second year of classes at the University of Chicago to help run the family business. Ernest, who once told an interviewer that he was "born to sell mattresses," was soon recognized as an authority in the bedding industry. By the time he was 35, he was

COMPANY PERSPECTIVES

Sealy's mission is to continually help the world sleep better.

serving as chairman of Sealy's national advertising committee.

From 1951 to 1955 the annual sales of Ohio Mattress quadrupled from $1.5 million to over $6 million, and by 1956 the company was the largest of the more than 30 Sealy affiliates in the United States and Canada. In 1956 Ohio Mattress acquired the Sealy Mattress Company of Houston, Texas, signaling the start of Wuliger's push to dominate the Sealy organization and the mattress industry.

DEVELOPING A CORPORATE IDENTITY: 1963–75

Ernest succeeded his father as president of Ohio Mattress in 1963 and dedicated the seven-million-dollar company to several ambitious goals: surpassing $100 million in annual sales, expanding nationally, and receiving a listing on the New York Stock Exchange.

In defiance of the mattress industry's exclusive territory clauses, Wuliger launched intrabrand competition within other Sealy licensees' territories, undercutting their prices and squeezing their profit margins until they sold out to him. Very often, however, the threatened licensees appealed to Sealy to invoke and exercise a "right to first refusal." The clause allowed Sealy to acquire several endangered affiliates, thereby blocking Wuliger and gaining additional revenues. In 1960 the U.S. Justice Department had charged Sealy with two antitrust violations related to price fixing and the exclusive territories. Seven years of appeals brought the case before the Supreme Court in 1967, when justices ultimately found Sealy in violation of the Sherman Antitrust Act. Rather than changing its illegal business practices, Sealy simply renamed the offending clauses, retaining their content and requirements.

In 1970 Ohio Mattress became the only publicly held mattress manufacturer in the United States. Its initial public offering raised money for further expansion, and Wuliger changed the growing company's name to Ohio-Sealy Mattress Manufacturing Co. One year later, Ohio-Sealy brought its first lawsuit against the licenser, charging that it had not stopped its anticompetitive practices. The case went to court in 1974,

and within four months a jury ruled in favor of Ohio-Sealy and awarded it triple damages of $20.4 million. Appeals and a 1975 settlement with Sealy earned Ohio-Sealy $13 million, but its battle had just begun.

GROWTH THROUGH ACQUISITION: 1980–89

Wuliger tenaciously fought Sealy for more than a decade, winning a final judgment of $77 million in 1986. He forgave the damages in exchange for the right to acquire eight remaining licenses and thereby gain full control of Sealy Inc. One holdout, Sealy Mattress Co. of New Jersey, filed a suit to block Ohio-Sealy but gave in before the end of 1987. Wuliger borrowed $250 million to finance his purchases, then pared that debt down to about $75 million with the proceeds of an offering of four million new shares.

In the meantime Wuliger had also shored up Ohio-Sealy's position in the larger bedding industry with the 1983 purchases of Monterey Manufacturing Co., a leading waterbed manufacturer based in Los Angeles, and Lifetime Foam Products, a bedding manufacturer previously owned by Sears, Roebuck & Co. Ohio-Sealy also acquired TrendWest, a furniture and waterbed-frame manufacturer.

In December 1983 Wuliger purchased Stearns & Foster, a prominent mattress brand, helping him achieve two of his coveted goals. The Cincinnati-based firm cost Ohio-Sealy $52 million in cash and stock but gave Wuliger complete control of a prestigious national brand and helped catapult his company (which subsequently reassumed its Ohio Mattress Company name) over the $100 million mark. Sales more than doubled, from $98 million in 1983 to $251 million in 1984, earning Ohio Mattress a spot on the New York Stock Exchange.

Wuliger set out immediately to energize the 136-year-old Stearns & Foster brand, launching the label's first national advertising campaign since 1909. The $4 million budget was largely spent on ads in high-end shelter magazines such as *Bon Appetit, Metropolitan Home, Gourmet, Town & Country, Architectural Digest,* and *House Beautiful.* The brand's slogan, "You've earned a Stearns & Foster," was targeted toward the prosperous consumer.

In 1989, less than two years after gaining control of the world's largest mattress brand, 67-year-old Ernest suffered a heart attack and subsequently announced his intention to sell Ohio Mattress. Some observers maintained that "the vision of his own mortality caused the decision," but according to Barbara Solomon of *Management Review,* Wuliger said he was motivated by

KEY DATES

1882: Sealy Inc., a mattress licensing company, is formed.

1907: Morris Wuliger founds the Ohio Mattress Company.

1924: Ohio Mattress begins licensing Sealy products; Morris Wuliger's son, Frank, becomes president of Ohio Mattress.

1956: Ohio Mattress acquires Sealy Mattress Company of Houston, Texas.

1963: Ernest Wuliger succeeds his father, Frank, as head of Ohio Mattress.

1970: Ohio Mattress launches initial public offering.

1983: Ohio Mattress acquires Stearns & Foster mattress brand.

1989: Merchant banker Gibbons, Green van Amerongen acquires Ohio Mattress for $965 million; company once again becomes private.

1990: Company is renamed Sealy Corporation.

1993: Zell/Chilmark Fund LP acquires majority stake in Sealy Corporation.

1997: Bain Capital acquires a controlling stake in the company.

1998: Sealy relocates its corporate headquarters to Trinity, North Carolina.

2004: Kohlberg Kravis Roberts & Co. purchases Sealy for $1.5 billion.

2006: Sealy launches an initial public offering.

2008: Sealy introduces the Posturepedic PurEmbrace latex mattress.

the realization that "people would pay exorbitant amounts for companies with consumer franchises." Although Ohio Mattress was valued at $427 million late in 1988, merchant banker Gibbons, Green van Amerongen paid more than twice that amount, $965 million, to take the company private in 1989.

CONSOLIDATION

The new owners kept Wuliger on as chair and CEO and appointed Malcolm Candlish as chief operating officer and president. However, Wuliger, along with many of his top managers, resigned less than three months after the deal was completed. Wuliger's abrupt exit, as well as Ohio Mattress's 1990 assumption of the Sealy Corporation name, signaled the firm's shift from an entrepreneurial operation to a modern, consolidated corporation. Nonetheless, Candlish vowed in a 1990

interview with Solomon for *Management Review* "to retain as much as we can of what is good about being an organization of licensees, and we will complement it with all the advantages of being a national company."

Gibbons, Green van Amerongen's highly leveraged (and overpriced) buyout was also poorly timed. The firm tried to float $475 million in unsecured debentures, or junk bonds, just as that market collapsed under the weight of numerous defaults and bankruptcies. While the new owners scrambled to finance their purchase, they relied on a high-interest bridge loan from First Boston Corporation to pay for the privatization. This sticky financial situation earned Sealy the nickname "the burning bed," according to a May 1990 article in *BusinessWeek*. Without a market for its junk bonds, Gibbons, Green van Amerongen was soon compelled to exchange First Boston's debt (which was held by an affiliate, the Clipper Group) for a 40 percent equity stake in Sealy.

RESTRUCTURING: 1990–93

In spite of this overarching financial predicament, CEO Candlish was able to prune corporate expenses, keep up with interest payments, and increase revenue by 6.2 percent to $702.3 million. The new leader closed more than one-third of Sealy's 38 plants and opened 3 new, more efficient plants in strategic locations. Candlish standardized production and centralized some purchasing to take advantage of the company's newfound national buying power. He hoped to save $30 million annually through these cost-cutting measures. The divestment of surplus real estate and a subsidiary helped pay down some debt as well. In mid-1990 Sealy also invested in its largest advertising campaign ever. The national effort spent about $11 million on prime-time television spots prepared by Chicago-based ad agency Leo Burnett.

In 1991 the Clipper Group swapped its $400 million in Sealy junk bonds for an additional 53.6 percent of the mattress-maker's equity, effectively buying out Gibbons, Green van Amerongen. The deal cut Sealy's debt from $890 million to $490 million (mostly bank debt) and reduced the company's annual interest expense by half, to $56 million. This ownership transition soon led to a leadership transition. In 1992 Candlish announced that he would leave Sealy by year's end, citing conflicts with the new board, which was dominated by First Boston. In August 1992 Candlish told *Plain Dealer* that "since a change of boards following the financial restructuring, there has been a change in management philosophy that has not sat with me as well as the previous philosophy."

Sealy brought in Lyman M. (John) Beggs to succeed Candlish before the end of the month. Beggs's experience included work with global consumer products companies such as Procter & Gamble Company, Del Monte Corporation, Tambrands Inc., and Norelco Consumer Products Group. The Clipper Group's ownership of Sealy was generally viewed as a transitional investment scheme, and in 1993 the firm sold its 94 percent stake for $250 million to Zell/Chilmark Fund LP of Chicago.

EVOLUTION OF THE SEALY BRAND

The Zell/Chilmark era at Sealy Corporation proved to be short-lived. In November 1997 another venture capital firm, Bain Capital, purchased a 90 percent stake in Sealy in a deal worth $830 million. A year later Sealy relocated its corporate headquarters for the second time in 10 years, moving to a new facility in Trinity, North Carolina. In September 1999 Sealy hired Long Haymes Carr (later known as Mullen/LHC), an advertising agency based in Winston-Salem, North Carolina, to handle its marketing account. According to industry observers, the move was spurred in part because the company's previous agency, Leo Burnett, had grown dissatisfied with Sealy's decreasing marketing budget. By 1998 the company's advertising budget had shrunk to $15 million, down from $42 million in 1995.

In early 2000 Sealy Corporation unveiled a new advertising campaign stressing the importance of sleep to general health and well-being. The campaign's slogan, "We support you night and day," signified a more serious turn for the Sealy brand image. Assessing the new strategy in *Advertising Age* (February 14, 2000), Beth Snyder Bulik viewed the ads as part of the company's effort to establish a stronger "emotional connection" with its customers.

Sealy launched a more ambitious marketing push in June 2001, devoting $20 million to a series of new television and print ads. In addition, the company partnered with the National Sleep Foundation to promote sleep education among consumers, while also hiring Olympic athlete and surgeon Dot Richardson to endorse the health benefits of Sealy mattresses. Speaking to the *New York Times* on June 8, 2001, Mullen/LHC executive Pete Woods described the strategy as an attempt to "build brand conviction" in Sealy's customers. "We want people to care about their bedding, and we want them to care about the fact that Sealy is their choice," Woods explained. That same month, Sealy was named the of-ficial mattress of the 2002 Winter Olympics in Salt Lake City.

FINE-TUNING THE SEALY BRAND

Sealy continued to fine-tune its image during the early part of the decade. In May 2003 the company introduced a series of television ads featuring a new catch phrase, "It's a Sealy." The company's earnings grew steadily in 2003, with revenues of almost $1.2 billion for the year; it also saw an 8 percent jump in profits between 2002 and 2003, from $16.9 million to $18.3 million. In March 2004 Sealy changed ownership once again, when private equity firm Kohlberg Kravis Roberts & Co. (KKR) purchased the company for $1.5 billion. A year later KKR announced plans to take the mattress company public. Sealy's initial public offering was launched on April 6, 2006, raising nearly $450 million in its first day of trading.

Sealy enjoyed another strong year in 2006, with total sales of $1.58 billion. Nonetheless, even though it remained the world's leading mattress company, Sealy found itself confronting intensified competition heading into the latter part of the decade. Much of the threat to Sealy's market dominance came from Tempur-Pedic International, whose memory foam mattress had become one of the fastest-growing beds in the world. Over the course of 2007 Sealy lost half of its market value. Even as revenues rose to $1.7 billion for the year, the company's sales figures fell short of expectations. In the wake of its lackluster performance, company chairman and CEO David J. McIlquham abruptly resigned in March 2008.

In June 2008 Sealy introduced the Posturepedic PurEmbrace, a high-end mattress made entirely of latex. Touted as the "latest innovation in sleep systems" by interim CEO Larry Rogers, latex mattresses had already gained popularity outside of the United States and were considered to rival memory foam in comfort and design. Nonetheless, the growing popularity of Tempur-Pedic's memory foam mattresses continued to erode Sealy's market share, and the company's overall sales dropped to $1.5 billion for the year.

Sealy continued to struggle in 2009, as second quarter earnings fell to $298.46 million, compared to $375.38 million for the same period in 2008. The company faced another threat in September 2009, when rivals Serta and Simmons announced a $760 million merger. In the face of increasingly stiff competition, Sealy needed to remain focused on the continued innovation of its core product line if it hoped to retain its top position in the industry.

April Dougal Gasbarre
Updated, Stephen Meyer

PRINCIPAL SUBSIDIARIES

Advanced Sleep Products; Mattress Holdings International B.V. (The Netherlands); Mattress Holdings International LLC; Mattress Holding SAS (France); North American Bedding Company; Ohio-Sealy Mattress Manufacturing Co., Inc.; Sapsa Bedding SAS (France); Sealy Asia (Hong Kong) Ltd.; Sealy Canada, Ltd. (Canada); Sealy do Brasil Limitada (Brazil); Sealy, Inc.; Sealy Mattress Company; Sealy Mattress Corporation; Sealy Mattress Manufacturing Company, Inc.; Sealy Mattress Company Mexico S. de R.L. de C.V. (Mexico); Sealy Technology LLC; Western Mattress Company.

PRINCIPAL COMPETITORS

Serta International; Simmons Company; Spring Air International LLC; Tempur-Pedic International Inc.

FURTHER READING

Andresky, Jill, "Mattress Wars," *Forbes*, June 15, 1987, p. 41.

Block, Donna, "KKR Reduces Money in Mattress," *Daily Deal*, April 10, 2006.

Brunton, David, "Mattress-Making Company Is Anything but Somnolent," *Plain Dealer*, January 27, 1985, p. 4C.

Bulik, Beth Snyder, "Sealy Takes Solemn Tone in $15 Mil Mattress Push; Ads Show Woes of Lack of Sleep," *Advertising Age*, February 14, 2000, p. 12.

Gerdel, Thomas W., "Mattress Maker Is on Top," *Plain Dealer*, October 3, 1987, p. 10A.

Gleisser, Marcus, "Chicago Partners Buy Stake in Sealy," *Plain Dealer*, January 28, 1993, p. 1F.

———, "First Boston Taking Control of Sealy," *Plain Dealer*, September 20, 1991, p. 1F.

———, "New Chief Executive Named at Sealy Inc.," *Plain Dealer*, August 25, 1992, p. 1G.

———, "Sealy Chairman Trying to Liven Up Old Family Firm," *Plain Dealer*, June 12, 1990, pp. ID, 9D.

Hinton, Christopher, "Sealy Seeks Bounce from Latex Mattress; Next 'Memory Foam'," *National Post's Financial Post & FP Investing*, April 20, 2007, p. 9.

Kane, Courtney, "A Campaign to Turn a Mattress Maker into a 'Wellness Provider'," *New York Times*, June 8, 2001, p. 4.

Mallory, Maria, "Ohio Mattress Gets the Lumps Out at Last," *BusinessWeek*, May 7, 1990, pp. 127–8.

Olson, Elizabeth, Patrick McGeehan, Jane L. Levere, and Dan Fost, "Can Sealy Catch Up with the Foam Set?" *New York Times*, March 16, 2008, p. 2.

Sabath, Donald, "Mattress Company Financially Firm," *Plain Dealer*, November 9, 1980, p. 1E.

———, "No Sagging for Ohio Mattress," *Plain Dealer*, September 25, 1984, p. 1D.

"Sealy Here Acquires Operation in Texas," *Plain Dealer*, 1956.

Solomon, Barbara, "Bed Wars: A Sealy Licensee Causes Sleepless Nights," *Management Review*, December 1990, pp. 50–3.

Whitestone, Randy, "KKR to Buy Sealy in US$1.5B Deal: Buyout Specialist Takes Over No. 1 U.S. Mattress Maker," *National Post's Financial Post & FP Investing*, March 5, 2004, p. 14.

Securitas AB

---∎---

Lindhagensplan 70
Box 12307
Stockholm, SE-102 28
Sweden
Telephone: (+46 10) 470 3000
Fax: (+46 10) 470 3121
Web site: http://www.securitas.com

Public Company
Incorporated: 1934
Employees: 240,000
Sales: SEK 62.67 billion ($8.48 billion) (2009)
Stock Exchanges: Stockholm
Ticker Symbol: SECUB
NAICS: 561612 Security Guards and Patrol Services;
    561621 Security Systems Services (Except
    Lock-smiths)

■ ■ ■

Sweden's Securitas AB is locking up the world's security services market. Based in Stockholm, Securitas is the world's leading provider of security services, with a 12 percent market share in the highly fragmented industry. Through its acquisitions of Pinkerton's Inc. in 1999 and Burns International Services Corporation in 2000, Securitas has also become the leading security services firm in the United States. In 2007 Securitas restructured its operations into three business segments: Security Services North America, which includes Pinkerton Consulting & Investigations, serves the United States, Canada, and Mexico, and holds 16 percent of the market share in these regions; Security Services Europe, with a market share of 17 percent, provides aviation security to 12 countries and general security services to 23 countries; and Mobile and Monitoring, which offers call-out services, on-site security, and electronic alarm surveillance to homes and small- and medium-sized businesses. The Mobile unit operates in 11 countries, while the Monitoring unit, also known as Securitas Alert Services, serves 10 countries throughout Europe.

SECURING SCANDINAVIA IN THE 1930S

Securitas traces its roots to the dawn of the 20th century, when Kjøbenhavn Frederiksberg Nattevagt was founded by Julius Philip-Sørensen and Marius Hogrefe. The new company offered guard services in Philip-Sørensen and Hogrefe's native Denmark. Philip-Sørensen soon became the primary force behind the company's growth. In 1918 Kjøbenhavn Frederiksberg Nattevagt merged into De Forenede Vagtselskaber, the predecessor to the future ISS Group.

Julius Philip-Sørensen's son Erik Philip-Sørensen joined his father in developing the family business as it began to expand beyond Denmark. In 1934 Erik Philip-Sørensen brought the company into Sweden, buying Helsingborgs Nattvakt, based in Helsingborg. Philip-Sørensen began acquiring other Swedish security companies, building a leading position in that country's security market. The Securitas name was adopted by the company in 1938. Although Securitas remained under the ISS Group's control, the Philip-Sørensen family was

COMPANY PERSPECTIVES

Securitas is a knowledge leader in security. By focusing on providing security solutions to fit each customer's needs, Securitas has achieved sustainable growth and profitability in 40 countries in North America, Europe, Latin America, Asia, Middle East and Africa. Everywhere from small stores to airports, our 240,000 employees are making a difference.

responsible for their company's growth in Sweden and beyond.

After establishing its Swedish position, Securitas began expanding farther afield in the 1950s. For this expansion, Philip-Sørensen was aided by his sons Jørgen and Sven. During the 1950s and 1960s, Securitas' expansion helped place it among the leading European security services companies. The company's first international move came with the launch of a subsidiary in the United Kingdom in 1950. At that time, the company combined all of its operations under a single name, Securitas International. Jørgen Philip-Sørensen played an active role in the company's expansion outside of Scandinavia, which targeted especially the United Kingdom and Belgium during this period, while Sven concentrated especially on its Swedish operations, leading a series of acquisitions, including that of Svensk Nattvakt.

In 1963 Securitas formed two new subsidiaries in the United Kingdom, Store Detectives Ltd. and Securitas Alarms Ltd. While Erik Philip-Sørensen remained at the head of the company, son Jørgen was appointed to lead the company's growing U.K. operations in 1965. Three years later, the company restructured its four U.K. businesses under a new subsidiary and brand name, Group 4 (Total Security).

Jørgen and Sven Philip-Sørensen took over the company's leadership only upon Erik Philip-Sørensen's retirement in 1974. In that year, the Philip-Sørensen family bought control of Securitas from the ISS Group. The brothers maintained joint ownership of the company until 1981, when Securitas was divided equally between them. Sven Philip-Sørensen took over the company's Swedish operations, keeping the Securitas name. Jørgen Philip-Sørensen remained at the head of the company's international activities, now renamed Group 4 Securitas. Group 4 Securitas was later acquired by Falck, of Denmark, creating the world's second-largest security services group, Group 4 Falck A/S.

EXPANSION DRIVE IN THE 1980S

Sven Philip-Sørensen did not remain at the helm of Securitas for long. By 1983 he had sold his interest in the company. Although parts of Securitas were bought by Group 4, the largest part was taken over by Swedish investment firm Investment AB Latour in 1985. Latour, led by Gustaf Douglas, who also became vice chairman of Securitas, led the company on a dramatic expansion drive beginning in 1988.

In the meantime, Securitas' new management, led by Melker Schörling since 1987, had trimmed Securitas' operations, focusing the company entirely on guard and security services. Over its previous decades, Securitas had acquired a number of diversified holdings; these were now sold, leaving only a core security operation. The newly slimmed down company had sales of less than SEK 1 billion as its acquisition drive began in 1988.

In that year, the company acquired Assa, a Swedish maker of locks. By the following year, Securitas displayed an interest in the international market, acquiring security companies in Norway and Denmark, and then beyond Scandinavia to enter Portugal as well. Not all of the company's expansion came from acquisition: In 1989 the company also launched its own operations in Hungary.

By 1991 the company's sales had topped SEK 3 billion. Nevertheless, Securitas' growth had only just begun. Fueling the company's further ambitions, Securitas took a listing on the Stockholm Stock Exchange that year. The company also made its first entry into the United States in 1991, buying Arrow and thereby expanding its lock-making operations.

The following year, Securitas grew again, now with the purchase of Spain's Esabe, and then Protectas, which gave it operations in France, Austria, Switzerland, and Germany. The company moved into Finland in 1993, acquiring security operations in that country. At the same time, Securitas began focusing increasingly on security services, a fast-growing industry in the early 1990s, and merged its Swedish lock-making operations into a joint venture with Finland's Metra, creating Assa-Abloy AB. The company sold its part of the joint venture to shareholders in 1994. By then, the company's sales had topped SEK 6 billion.

NEW MARKET OPPORTUNITIES

After making no acquisitions in 1995, Securitas rejoined the acquisition trail in 1996, entering new markets, such as Estonia and Poland, and, with the acquisition of DSW Security, Germany. That last acquisition gave Se-

KEY DATES

1901: Kjøbenhavn Frederiksberg Nattevagt is founded by Julius Philip-Sørensen.

1938: Company takes Securitas name.

1950: Company expands into United Kingdom, adopts Securitas International brand name.

1991: Securitas is listed on the Stockholm Stock Exchange; company acquires U.S.-based Arrow.

1999: Securitas acquires Pinkerton's for $384 million, thus gaining a major share of the U.S. market.

2000: Securitas' second major U.S. firm, Burns International, is acquired; revenues surpass SEK 40 billion.

2001: Full control of Loomis Fargo is acquired for an estimated $100 million.

2004: Securitas acquires the Bell Group plc and Eurotelis and becomes a market leader in high security.

2007: Securitas reorganizes its operations into three decentralized business segments: Security Services North America, Security Services Europe, and Mobile and Monitoring.

2008: Loomis is listed as a separate company on the Stockholm Stock Exchange.

curitas Germany's fourth-largest security company and made the country one of its largest single markets, accounting for some 20 percent of total sales. The DSW acquisition was topped by a new acquisition in the United Kingdom, of Security Express Armaguard (SEA). The former subsidiary of Australia's Mayne Nickless, SEA had been losing money in the mid-1990s; nonetheless, the purchase boosted Securitas' cash-in-transit operations in the United Kingdom. The SEA acquisition also represented Securitas' first entry into the United Kingdom since the split-up of the company in the early 1980s.

Other acquisitions of 1996 included La Rond de Nuit and Domen Securité in France; Sonasa, in Portugal; Timetech, in Sweden; Krupp Sicherheit, in Germany; and Inkjassaator, in Estonia. In all, the company added more than SEK 2 billion in sales through acquisitions alone that year.

Securitas bundled its consumer-oriented businesses into a new subsidiary, Securitas Direct, overseeing the company's international individual home and small business alarm systems operations, in 1997. In the meantime, Securitas continued making acquisitions, particularly in France and Germany through 1997 and 1998. The company's acquisitions in these markets included Raab Karcher Sicherheit of Germany and Proteg and the Kessler Group of France. Both Proteg and Raab Karcher were leaders in their respective countries; the Raab Karcher acquisition also strengthened the company's presence in Austria and Hungary and introduced it to the Czech Republic. Also in 1998, Securitas launched its first subsidiary operations in Latvia.

By the end of 1998 Securitas' acquisition appetite had boosted its sales to nearly SEK 14 billion. One year later, the company's sales soared past SEK 25.5 billion. In that year, Securitas made its largest acquisition, one that gave it a position as the world's largest security services company, with a leading share of the U.S. market.

PINKERTON'S IS ACQUIRED: 1999

Securitas' transformation came with its acquisition of famed security services company Pinkerton's Inc. in 1999. Paying $384 million, Securitas gained control of the 150-year-old U.S. company, founded by Allan Pinkerton in Illinois in 1850. Pinkerton, originally a barrel maker, became the first private detective in the United States and, with a logo featuring an open eye, spawned the term *private eye*. Pinkerton's had been acquired by tobacco company American Brands, Inc., in 1983. In 1988 the company was merged into California Plant Protection; the larger company kept the famous Pinkerton's name. The acquisition of Pinkerton's gave Securitas a major share of the U.S. market (the company maintained the Pinkerton's name for its North and South American operations).

In 2000 Securitas swooped up another major U.S. security company, Burns International. Burns had once been part of the former Borg-Warner Corporation, when that industrial conglomerate acquired Baker Industries in 1977, giving it entry into the security services market. Baker Industries held the trademarks to two famed names, Wells Fargo and Pony Express, acquired in 1967 from American Express. Borg-Warner proceeded to go on its own acquisition binge, buying more than 70 companies to build one of the top security services in the United States by the early 1990s. Among its acquisitions was Burns International, founded in 1909 and acquired by Borg Warner in 1982. Under fire from a hostile takeover, Borg Warner escaped through a leveraged buyout at the end of the 1980s; the company's huge debt-load, however, forced it to sell off nearly all of its operations, until in 1993 all that remained of the company was its security services division, including its Wells Fargo armored car subsidiary. That company was merged with Loomis Armored in 1997, giving Borg Warner a 49 percent stake in the newly named Loomis, Fargo & Co. In 1999 Borg Warner, too, underwent a name change, to Burns International.

EMERGENCE OF THE MARKET LEADER IN THE NEW MILLENNIUM

The acquisition of Burns International by Securitas boosted the Swedish security giant's revenues past SEK 40 billion and, with a 7 percent share of the global security services market, made it the world leader in its still highly fragmented industry. Burns, folded into the Pinkerton's operation, made Securitas the out-and-out leader of the North American market as well.

Securitas had no intention of ending its drive to consolidate the worldwide security services industry. Announcing a war chest of some SEK 12 billion, the company continued to make acquisitions as the new century began. In 2000 the company acquired B&M Beveiliging & Alermering in Amsterdam, Doyle Protective Service in the United States, Baron Security of Belgium, Micro-route Ltd. of the United Kingdom, and Ausysegur of Spain. In June 2001 the company announced that it had agreed to pay more than $100 million to acquire full control of the Loomis Fargo Group.

Securitas, which had previously been organized along its geographic operations, now restructured the company into five key businesses areas. Designed to help the company achieve its future growth goals of SEK 69 billion in sales by 2005, the five segments were: Securitas Services; Securitas Systems; Securitas Direct; Cash Handling Services; and Consulting & Investigations, which also provided private security services. By the end of 2001, Securitas was ranked as the world's leading guarding company; it also held 20 percent of the U.S. security market, nearly three times that of its nearest competitor, Wackenhut Corporation.

The implementation of increased security measures across the globe was top priority after the September 11, 2001, terrorist attacks on the United States, and the demand for Securitas' services was at an all-time high. In the aftermath of the attacks, Securitas trained and deployed 10,000 new security guards over a six-week period. With an industry that was once plagued by low wages, cutbacks, and bidding wars, highly trained security guards and advanced surveillance systems were now one of corporate America's primary concerns, and Securitas' strategy of developing its services into a globally recognized quality brand was garnering attention.

In July 2002 Securitas announced that it had acquired Poland's Elberg Sp. z o.o., and Kötter Security Hungária Kft. Securitas' 2002 year-end sales were SEK 65.69 billion, an increase of more than SEK 5 billion over the previous year, and the company invested these profits in additional acquisitions. In April 2003 Securitas acquired Lincoln Security, a U.S. guard services company, for $13.7 million. This was followed with the purchase of the cash-handling business Armored Motor Services of America. In May 2004 the company announced that it would be acquiring the U.K.-based Bell Group Plc, as well as the French security systems company Eurotelis. In September 2004 Valiance Cash Handling Services of France was purchased, sealing Securitas' position as the leading service provider for banks and other high-security customers.

INCREASED SPECIALIZATION AND NEW STRATEGIES

In May 2005 Securitas made the surprising announcement that it was selling its cash-handling interests in Poland, Hungary, and the Czech Republic to Brinks Inc. Although Securitas planned to retain its guard businesses in these countries, the sale was part of its strategy to focus on its cash-handling businesses in Western Europe and the United States. Acquisitions in 2005 included Alert Services Holding S.A, strengthening the company's position in the Belgian and Dutch small alarm businesses; and Black Star, one of Spain's leading private security companies.

In April 2006 the U.S. subsidiary Securitas Systems acquired Premier System Solutions Inc., while Securitas Services Europe announced that it would be acquiring 51 percent of DAK Guvenlik, marking the company's entrance into the Turkish security services market. The following month, Securitas expanded its presence in Spain with the acquisition of Paneuropea de Seguridad Integral, a leading provider of security services to the country's larger cities. In July 2006 Securitas was awarded a five-year contract to provide security services to Sweden's Arlanda and Bromma airports. Saab Systems Security Solutions was Securitas' technical partner on the project, and the two companies would collaborate on developing a next-generation guard monitoring and dispatch system the following year. This was followed in August 2006 with the announcement that Securitas USA had signed a lucrative $800 million agreement with General Motors Corporation to provide physical guarding and security systems to its operations in North America, Europe, and Argentina over a five-year period beginning in January 2007.

In March 2007 Alf Göransson took over the reins as president and CEO and unveiled his business strategy, which included further global acquisitions, an increased range of specialized services, and expansion of the Mobile and Monitoring business segment. Göransson immediately put his plan into action with the purchase of Sweden's Larmassistans Teknik Sverige AB, 75 percent of the Italian security systems integrator CIS SpA, and the Dutch mobile guarding firm, Chubb Van den Enden Bewaking en Facilitair Beheer.

Securitas also acquired Protection Service, a French security company; Seguridad Argentina SA; and Romania's CPI Security. Securitas expanded its presence in South America further when it acquired Argentina's Cono Sur SA, a 71 percent stake in Seguridad Burns de Colombia SA, and a 90 percent share of Forza SA in Peru. Other acquisitions in 2007 included F+H Electronic of Germany; Walsons, an Indian security company; and the U.S. companies PEI Systems Inc., a security systems integrator, and Securex, a retail security business.

COMPANY RESTRUCTURES

The year-end sales for 2006 had increased to SEK 66 billion and the company began to plan another restructuring of its organization. In September 2006 Securitas Systems and Securitas Direct were distributed to shareholders and listed as separate companies on the Stockholm Stock Exchange. In January 2007 the company reverted to its geographic structure and reorganized the company into three major business segments: Security Services North America; Security Services Europe; and Mobile and Alert Services, which was later renamed Mobile and Monitoring.

Securitas Cash Handling Europe and Loomis, Fargo & Co. in the United States were combined and re-branded as Loomis Cash Handling in advance of a planned spin-off. Loomis embarked on its own spending spree before going public, acquiring France's G4S Plc, Brinks UK Ltd., and two U.S.-based firms, Guardian Armored Security Inc. and EM Armored Car Service Inc. The reorganization was completed in December 2008 when Loomis was listed as a separate company on the Stockholm Stock Exchange.

Securitas' acquisitions frenzy showed no sign of slowing down in 2008. In January Forebygget Brand-skydd AB, a Swedish provider of fire protection products and services, was acquired as part of the company's strategy to move into more specialized areas. The company also acquired three vehicle-tracking and -tracing companies from the Benelux countries: Belgium's Eureca Benelux Services, Satworld of the Netherlands, and LuxTracing SA of Luxembourg. Other global acquisitions that year included: GRB Security Ltd. (United Kingdom), G4S Sicherheitssysteme GmbH (Germany), SH Safe Home SA (Switzerland), SCP International (Siberia), Hafslund ASA (Norway), Purzeczko (Poland), El Guardian (Argentina), Grupo Guardias Blancas (Mexico), Polic Secuforce (Hong Kong), and the Agency of Security Fenix of the Czech Republic and Slovakia.

In 2009 the world was in a recession but Securitas continued its global expansion with additional acquisitions in South America, Asia, Europe, and the United States. In November 2009 Securitas acquired a 75 percent stake in Morocco's GMCE Gardiennage, mark-ing the company's first entrance into the North African market. In a February 22, 2009, interview with Manu Kaushik of India's *Business Today*, Göransson said that corporations had come to accept that security was an important investment to ensure continuity of the business, and not solely an administrative expense. Although the economy was in a downward spiral, he speculated that the security services industry was one of the few sectors which could expect annual growth. Nevertheless, when the 2009 year-end results were reported in February 2010, Göransson admitted that 2010 would be a challenging year, with customers forced to reduce costs during a period of slow recovery. With 2009 total sales of SEK 62.27 billion, Securitas shifted its focus to organic growth and profitability, continuing to explore acquisitions in both mature and emerging markets, while also being more selective during the economically challenging times.

M. L. Cohen
Updated, Marie O'Sullivan

PRINCIPAL SUBSIDIARIES

Securitas Holdings Inc. (USA); Securitas Canada Ltd; Grupo Securitas Mexico, S A de C V; Securitas Nordic Holding AB; Securitas Eesti AS (Estonia); Securitas Deutschland Finanz Holding GmbH (Germany); SL Sicherheit GmbH (Germany); Securitas Services Hold-ing U.K. Ltd; Securitas Seguridad Holding SL (Spain); Protectas S.A. (Switzerland); Securitas Sicherheitsdien-stleistungen GmbH (Austria); Securitas N V (Belgium); Securitas Services International BV (Netherlands); Secu-ritas KFT (Hungary); Securitas Polska Sp. z o. o. (Poland); Securitas CR s r o (Czech Republic); Securitas Security Services SRL (Romania; 88%); Securitas Services DOO (Serbia); Securitas Transport Aviation Security AB; Securitas Aviation Holding SL (Spain); Alert Services Holding NV (Belgium; 53%); Securitas Alert Services Polska Sp. z o.o. (Poland); Securitas

Argentina S.A.; Securitas Asia Holding AB; Securitas UAE LLC (49%); Globe Partner Services SAE (Egypt; 80%); Securitas Direct S.A. (Switzerland; 50%); Securitas Treasury Ireland Ltd; Securitas Invest AB; Securitas Group Reinsurance Ltd (Ireland); Securitas Rental AB; AB Jourmontör; Securitas Toolbox Ltd (Ireland).

PRINCIPAL DIVISIONS

Security Services North America; Security Services Europe; Mobile and Monitoring.

PRINCIPAL COMPETITORS

Allied Security Holdings LLC; Prosegur Compañía de Seguridad, S.A.; UTC Fire & Security Corporation.

FURTHER READING

George, Nicholas, "Securitas Makes Cash Bid for Burns," *Financial Times*, August 4, 2000.

Hardie, Will, "Securitas Sees Windfall from Euro Money Launch," Reuters, June 12, 2001.

Kaushik, Manu, "Security Concerns Have Changed Radically," *Business Today* (India), February 22, 2009.

Roth, Daniel, "Someone to Watch Over Us: As Corporate Fears Turn from Hacks to Attacks, Securitas Is Suddenly Finding Its Guards in Demand," *Fortune*, December 10, 2001, pp. 216+.

"Securitas AB Acquires Brinks' Cash Handling Operations in the UK," *Nordic Business Report*, August 6, 2007.

"Securitas Agrees to Acquire 49% of Long Hai Security," *Wireless News*, January 6, 2010.

"Securitas Takes Control of the American Loomis Fargo Group," *European Report*, May 30, 2001.

"Securitas to Acquire Guardforce's Operations and Assets," *Wireless News*, September 25, 2009.

"Sweden's Market Is Smiling on Securitas AB, but Some Wonder if Buying Spree Is a Bit Much," *Wall Street Journal*, August 25, 2000.

"Swedish Firm to Buy Pinkerton," *Dallas Morning News*, February 23, 1999, p. 2D.

7-Eleven, Inc.

1722 Routh Street
Dallas, Texas 75201
U.S.A.
Telephone: (972) 828-0711
Toll Free: (800) 255-0711
Fax: (972) 828-7848
Web site: http://www.7-eleven.com

Wholly Owned Subsidiary of Seven & I Holdings Co., Ltd.
Founded: 1927 as the Southland Corporation
Incorporated: 1961 as the Southland Corporation
Employees: 27,748 (est.)
Sales: $15.47 billion (est.)
NAICS: 445120 Convenience Stores; 447110 Gasoline
    Stations with Convenience Stores

■ ■ ■

With more than 37,000 locations in North America, Asia, Europe, and Australia, 7-Eleven, Inc., is the largest convenience store chain in the world. While the company owns and operates many of its locations, the majority of 7-Eleven stores are licensed or franchised. The stores sell a wide range of grocery products, including dairy items, coffee, fresh hot dogs, doughnuts, candy, prepackaged sandwiches and meals, and the company's trademark Slurpee frozen drinks. In addition to its extensive line of food and beverages, 7-Eleven also offers nonperishable goods, such as newspapers, prepaid phone cards, and personal care products. At the same time, the chain, which purchases fuel from various outside suppliers and markets it under the 7-Eleven brand, is a leading seller of gasoline. Headquartered in Dallas, Texas, the company is a wholly owned subsidiary of the Japanese conglomerate Seven & i Holdings Co., Ltd.

CREATION OF THE CONVENIENCE STORE: 1927–30

The company began as a brainstorm of John Jefferson Green. In 1927 Green approached Joe C. "Jodie" Thompson, one of five founding directors of the Dallas Southland Ice Company, with a new idea. He wanted to sell milk, eggs, and bread through his retail ice dock. "You furnish the items," he suggested, "and I'll pay the power bills." Thompson agreed, and together they established the first known convenience store.

The newly formed Southland Ice Company was composed of 4 separate ice companies and operated 8 ice plants and 21 retail ice stations. An early attempt at advertising occurred after one Southland manager visited Alaska in 1928. Upon his return to Texas, he planted a souvenir totem pole in front of his store. The pole attracted so much attention that the employees suggested placing one at every Southland-owned retail ice dock and naming the stores Tote'm Stores, because the consumers toted away their purchases.

Southland decided to go with the new name. It unified the company's diversified stores and provided a distinct identity, a key ingredient in the successful operation of numerous retail outlets. Joseph Thompson, secretary-treasurer of Southland Ice, unified the stores further by training staff with daily sales talks. He also chose a company uniform for ice station servicemen.

7-Eleven stores are part of the neighborhood and committed to serving the changing needs of our customers. Being a good neighbor and corporate citizen is part of doing business at 7-Eleven, and we are proud of our long history of supporting our neighborhoods in meaningful ways through our community relations initiatives.

Our mission is simple: to serve the needs of the communities in which 7-Eleven stores operate. We believe the most effective way to advance our mission is to support causes that are aligned with community and customer interests and enhance the overall quality of life in neighborhoods where our customers, franchisees and employees live, work and play. That's why our community relations initiatives are generally focused at the local level and on four key areas associated with strong communities and citizens: safety, education, health & wellness and community revitalization. And priority is given to youth programs to ensure we build a strong foundation for the next generation.

Thompson recognized early on that consumers should receive the same quality and service at every store. During this time Southland also began to experiment with constructing and leasing gasoline stations at 10 of its Dallas-area stores.

CHANGING FORTUNES: THE DEPRESSION AND WORLD WAR II

The Great Depression plunged Southland into bankruptcy in 1931. During a period of receivership and reorganization, Joseph Thompson was named president, a move that ensured continuity during the rocky period. The management team chosen during this time was especially strong and led Southland for a number of years. W. W. Overton, Jr., a Dallas banker, helped disentangle the young company's finances by organizing the purchase of all Southland bonds for seven cents on the dollar, which eventually put ownership of the company under the control of the board of directors. Despite the financial confusion, profits from the Tote'm Stores continued to climb, and with the repeal of Prohibition in 1933, ice and beer sales surged.

Once it was on more stable footing, Southland began vertical integration with the construction of Oak Farms Dairies in 1936, using public relations to market its new dairy products by offering a free movie to those who brought in six of its milk bottle caps. A crowd of 1,600 attended the Dallas theater sponsoring the event. By 1939 Southland operated 60 Tote'm Stores in the Dallas–Fort Worth area, triple the number operating when the company was founded 12 years earlier.

With the onset of World War II, demands for ice peaked. Southland became the chief supplier of ice for the construction and operation of Camp Hood, the U.S. Army's largest training camp. The dramatic increase in business prompted reorganization of the company. Southland bought City Ice Delivery, Ltd. The acquisition included two modern ice plants, twenty retail stations, and property on Haskell Avenue, where the new company headquarters was situated. Southland became the largest ice operator in Dallas.

RAPID POSTWAR EXPANSION: 1945–69

By 1945 Southland owned stores scattered over north-central Texas, operating from 7 in the morning to 11 at night, seven days a week. In 1946 the firm Tracey-Locke, commissioned to create a new name, chose "7-Eleven" to emphasize the firm's commitment to long operating hours to serve customers better. At this time Southland remodeled all 7-Eleven stores, doubling the amount of floor space at each retail outlet.

After the war the United States' pent-up consumer appetite surged. Refrigerators, however, were not readily available to the public. To meet demands for block ice, Southland bought Texas Public Utilities, which owned 20 ice plants, in 1947, making Southland the largest ice operator in Texas. In 1948 Joseph Thompson's oldest son, John P. Thompson, was named to the board of directors.

At a management meeting in Washington, D.C., in 1956, a blizzard blanketed the city. John Thompson noticed that in densely populated areas, people could walk to the stores even when the weather made driving impossible, and that 7-Eleven's long operating hours and unusual stock could provide exactly what customers might need, from canned soup to tissues to aspirin. Southland began to focus on the traffic patterns around potential store sites, choosing high-volume corners whenever possible.

At the end of the 1950s, John Thompson, now vice president, began to introduce 7-Eleven stores outside of Texas, in Virginia, Maryland, and eastern Pennsylvania. In reaction to mass migration to the suburbs, Southland

KEY DATES

∎

1927: John Jefferson Green and Joe C. Thompson establish Southland Ice Company and the first known convenience store.

1928: Southland stores begin operating as Tote'm Stores.

1931: The Great Depression plunges Southland into bankruptcy.

1936: Vertical integration begins with the construction of Oak Farms Dairies.

1939: The company is operating 60 Tote'm Stores in the Dallas–Fort Worth area.

1946: The stores are rebranded 7-Eleven to emphasize their long hours of operation: 7 a.m. to 11 p.m.

1947: Southland's purchase of Texas Public Utilities makes the company the largest ice operator in Texas.

1961: The Southland Corporation is incorporated; Joseph Thompson names his son John as the company's second president, and his son Jere is elected vice president of sales.

1963: The company begins franchising after being introduced to the concept through its acquisition of 100 SpeeDee Marts in California this same year.

1965: The Slurpee makes its debut in 7-Eleven stores.

1969: The company expands to the East Coast and into Canada; store count reaches 3,537.

1973: An area license for Japan is granted to Ito-Yokado Co., Ltd.

1974: The 5,000th 7-Eleven opens at the site of the company's original ice dock.

1983: Citgo Petroleum Corporation is acquired for $780 million.

1986: The company sells 50 percent interest in Citgo to the Venezuelan state-owned oil company.

1987: The Thompson brothers complete a leveraged buyout of Southland.

1988: The company completes a series of divestitures to streamline operations and reduce debt.

1990: Southland sells its remaining 50 percent stake in Citgo; after defaulting on $1.8 billion in publicly traded debt, the company files for bankruptcy.

1991: Southland emerges from bankruptcy with its debt restructured and with IYG Holding Company of Japan owning 70 percent of its common stock.

1992: To focus on its core 7-Eleven business, the company exits from the distribution and food-processing businesses.

1996: The most extensive store-remodeling program in company history is completed.

1999: The company changes its name to 7-Eleven, Inc.

2003: 7-Eleven opens its 25,000th retail location.

2005: 7-Eleven becomes a wholly owned subsidiary of the Japanese retail giant Seven & I Holdings Co., Ltd.

2006: 7-Eleven allows its 20-year fuel supply deal with Citgo to expire.

2009: 7-Eleven announces its plan to open 600 new locations in Southern California.

opened more suburban stores. Southland also refined its marketing by studying customer traffic in its stores and eliminating products that moved slowly.

In 1961 Joseph Thompson named his son John as the second president of Southland. His son Jere W. Thompson was elected vice president of sales. Upon the elder Thompson's death that year, the *Dallas Morning News* credited him with transforming "the ordinary corner ice house from an ice dispensary to a multimillion-dollar drive-in grocery enterprise." John Thompson's first goal as president was to propel South-

land from $100 million in annual sales to $1 billion within 10 years.

Southland, incorporated in 1961, moved quickly to national prominence. The unprecedented expansion began with dairy acquisitions, notably Midwest Dairy Products in 1962, with production plants and branches in Illinois, Arkansas, Louisiana, and Alabama. Purchasing continued through the 1960s and 1970s, as Southland bought existing convenience market chains in Arizona, New Jersey, Colorado, Illinois, Georgia, and Tennessee. In addition Southland experimented with its first 24-hour store, in Las Vegas, and expanded to the East Coast and into Canada in 1969.

With the acquisition of 100 SpeeDee Marts in California in 1963, Southland was introduced to the concept of franchising, a system already in operation at the very successful SpeeDee Mart stores. The company developed two-week training sessions for prospective franchisees, which allowed greater decentralization of stores. By 1965 Southland had climbed to 49th in *Fortune* magazine's top 50 merchandising firms. The Slurpee slush drink made its debut in 7-Eleven stores in 1965. By December 1969 the number of 7-Eleven stores in operation stood at 3,537.

GROWTH AND NEW PROBLEMS: 1970–74

Through a new computer inventory system, 7-Eleven was able to pinpoint its strengths and discover that single-purchase items were its best sellers. However, with such growth problems began to surface. Due in part to the operation of 24-hour stores, high employee turnover and insufficient security systems drew the attention of management. The company nonetheless committed itself to the 24-hour store, and the number of 24-hour 7-Eleven stores rose from 817 in 1972 to 3,703 by the end of 1975.

Southland reached $1 billion in sales by 1971 and became a member of the New York Stock Exchange the following year. The first regional distribution center was opened in Florida in 1971; by 1977 several such centers were fully functioning and serving more than 3,000 7-Eleven stores. Jere Thompson, named president of Southland in 1973, continued Southland's U.S. retail store expansion.

Southland began to use microwaves for fast-food sales and introduced self-service gasoline through its newly acquired Pak-a-Sak stores. In 1974 the 5,000th 7-Eleven store opened in Dallas at the site of John Jefferson Green's original ice dock.

INTERNATIONAL EXPANSION

Penetration of the European market occurred with Southland's purchase of a 50 percent interest in Cavenham Ltd., a manufacturing corporation controlling 840 retail outlets in Great Britain. By early 1974 Southland's international operations included 50 percent interest in 1,096 United Kingdom outlets, 75 7-Eleven stores in Canada, and four Super-7 stores in Mexico.

Negotiations for the introduction of 7-Eleven to Japan were completed in December 1973, when Southland granted an area license to Ito-Yokado Co., Ltd.,

one of Japan's largest retailers. Like the franchise concept in the United States, area licensing worked well in Japan because of its emphasis on the individual businessperson operating a store but able to take advantage of 7-Eleven's name and established systems of management and accounting. By late 1978 Japan had 188 7-Eleven stores open for business.

Also in 1978 Southland bought Chief Auto Parts, a California chain of 119 retail automobile parts stores. By 1986 Chief Auto Parts, operating 465 stores, was the largest convenience retailer of automobile parts in the nation. Another Southland acquisition was Tidel Systems, a manufacturer of cash-dispensing systems and underground gasoline-tank-monitoring systems.

Southland's most significant acquisition by far was the Citgo Petroleum Corporation, purchased in August 1983. Southland hoped that the $780 million acquisition would provide a smooth supply of gasoline for its convenience stores. But because of a decrease in demand and a glut in capacity throughout the oil-refining industry, the Citgo purchase resulted in a pretax loss of $50 million for Southland. Profits in 1985 exceeded the previous year's loss by $20 million, but Southland nevertheless cut Citgo's petroleum production in half, expecting Citgo's refinery in Lake Charles, Louisiana, to be unprofitable. In September 1986 Southland decided to sell a 50 percent interest in Citgo to a subsidiary of Petroleos de Venezuela, S.A., the Venezuelan state-owned oil company. Southland also signed a 20-year product purchase agreement with Citgo through which Southland agreed to purchase a certain minimum amount of gasoline from Citgo at market prices.

FROM LBO TO BANKRUPTCY: 1987–91

In mid-1987 the Thompson brothers, spurred in part by the threat of a hostile takeover bid by Canadian corporate raider Samuel Belzberg, initiated a leveraged buyout. The buyout, which involved the formation of a temporary holding company called JT Acquisitions, was completed on July 6, 1987.

By the end of 1988 Southland had completed a series of divestitures to streamline operations. Southland sold Chief Auto Parts, the snack foods division, the dairies group, Reddy Ice, Chemical/Food Labs, Tidel Systems, 1,000 convenience stores, and related real estate properties. Proceeds from the divestitures, as well as the transfer of royalties from licensees in Japan, went to repay a portion of the $4 billion debt Southland had incurred through the leveraged buyout.

Southland may well have rebounded by the early 1990s were it not for competition from convenience stores operated by the major oil companies. Although these stores emphasized gasoline retailing rather than the sale of other merchandise, they did sell the primary products of convenience stores, such as soft drinks, cigarettes, and beer. Their sheer number and financial strength changed the nature of the convenience retailing industry. Their effort was exacerbated by the decline in the U.S. economy that began in the late 1980s. Southland, along with a number of other convenience store chains, had limited capital to invest in its store base due to heavy debt loads.

Under president and CEO Clark J. Matthews II, the company began to work on a plan to restructure its balance sheet. During 1990 Southland sold its remaining 50 percent stake in Citgo to Petroleos de Venezuela. In October 1990, after defaulting on $1.8 billion in publicly traded debt, Southland filed a bankruptcy plan of reorganization after securing preliminary approval from its bondholders. The company emerged from bankruptcy less than five months later. As part of the reorganization, Southland exchanged its old leveraged buyout bonds for approximately half of the principal amount of new bonds, which had substantially lower interest rates. In addition Southland sold 70 percent of its common stock to IYG Holding Company of Japan for $430 million. Ito-Yokado Co., Ltd., the most profitable retailer in Japan, owned 51 percent of IYG, and Seven-Eleven Japan Co., Ltd., the longtime 7-Eleven licensee in Japan, owned 49 percent.

FOCUSING ON 7-ELEVEN: 1992–98

In 1992 Southland completed additional financing for a $400 million commercial paper facility backed by Ito-Yokado. Also in 1992 Southland decided to leave the distribution and food-processing businesses to focus on its core business, 7-Eleven. The company sold certain distribution centers and food-processing facilities to McLane Co., Inc., a subsidiary of Arkansas-based Wal-Mart stores. Southland also signed a service agreement with McLane, the country's largest convenience store distributor, to provide coast-to-coast distribution service to the company's 5,700 stores in the United States.

Matthews capitalized on the company's nationally recognized 7-Eleven name and enhanced the quality, appearance, and service of the famous convenience store. In late 1991 Southland remodeled and remerchandised its 50 stores in Austin, Texas, to test its new physical standards, commissary food-service program, and new merchandising process.

The new process, which deleted slow-moving items and introduced new products, was refined and introduced to 7-Eleven stores across the country by the

end of 1992. Because of the initial capital infusion by its majority owners in 1991 as well as their backing of the commercial paper facility established in 1992, Southland was able to make long-term capital investment plans for the first time in many years.

Southland's remodeling program continued throughout the mid-1990s. By 1996 the company had completed the most extensive store-remodeling program in its history. The new 7-Eleven look included improved exterior and interior lighting, a store layout with wider aisles and better organization, improved signage, and upgraded gasoline pumps that included pay-at-the-pump systems. 7-Eleven stores also changed their pricing policies, most notably doing away with what Southland itself called "insult pricing," the huge markups that customers were forced to pay for convenience. The chain thereby lowered prices on much of its inventory, adopting an "everyday fair pricing" policy. Southland closed additional underperforming stores in the mid-to-late 1990s, shuttering 202 units from 1996 through 1998.

STRATEGIES FOR GROWTH

As the next step in its slow recovery, Southland put growth back on the agenda in late 1996. Beginning in 1997 store openings started outpacing closings. The following year Southland decided to step up the pace of its U.S. expansion, aiming to open 300 to 400 units per year. During 1998 the company added 299 stores through acquisitions and new construction, the biggest jump since 1986. The acquisitions included two that closed in May 1998: the purchase of Massachusetts-based Christy's Markets, Inc., an operator of 135 convenience stores in New England; and that of 20 Red D Mart convenience stores in South Bend, Indiana, which were purchased from MDK Corporation of Goshen, Indiana.

Another key strategy that Southland adopted to revitalize the chain was to improve the quality and value of the convenience items and services offered by the stores. This included moving toward daily deliveries of fresh perishables and the introduction of new ready-to-eat fresh foods, such as sandwiches and pastries, and eventually dinner entrées.

7-Eleven stores also began an aggressive expansion of the financial services it offered. Having already gained the position as the U.S. retailer with the most ATM machines, Southland began offering prepaid phone cards in 1995 and quickly became a leading seller of money orders. In 1998 the company began selling pagers and pager services in all U.S. 7-Elevens. That year it also began testing "financial service centers," automated computer terminals that allowed customers not only to make standard ATM transactions but also to cash checks, wire money, pay bills electronically, and buy prepaid phone cards and postage stamps. After a successful trial at 36 stores in Austin, Texas, Southland began planning for the expansion of the centers into more than 200 7-Elevens in the Dallas–Fort Worth area.

Perhaps the most important element of the 7-Eleven overhaul in the United States was the implementation of a chainwide proprietary retail information system, the development of which began in 1994. Such a system had already been installed by the highly successful Seven-Eleven Japan operation, which through its nearly 8,000-unit chain was one of the most profitable retailers in Japan. Installed in phases in the United States through the end of the 1990s, the system was designed to enable each store to improve its inventory management, reduce the incidence of out-of-stock items, and tailor its product mix to better match the needs of its customers.

In April 1999 the Southland Corporation changed its name to 7-Eleven, Inc., in a move reflecting the fact that the corporation was involved in only one business. It also seemed an appropriate time for such a change as the company was well on its way to a full recovery with revenues and sales on the increase and the once-heavy debt burden significantly reduced. By mid-1999 the company had recorded eight straight quarters of U.S. same-store sales growth, the longest such stretch in the 1990s. A year later the company resumed trading on the New York Stock Exchange. This fresh influx of investment capital, coupled with the implementation of the company's retail information system, promised to help drive 7-Eleven's continued growth well into the 21st century.

NEW OPPORTUNITIES AT HOME AND ABROAD

7-Eleven received a significant financial boost in March 2000, when majority shareholder IYG Holding Company purchased an additional $540 million worth of stock in the company. With the transaction IYG Holding raised its stake in 7-Eleven from 65 percent to 72 percent. Industry observers regarded the move as a sign of significant growth potential for the convenience store giant.

About this time 7-Eleven also began to explore other ways to expand into new commercial areas. In the summer of 2001, the company announced a plan to introduce a more compact storefront model, with the aim of establishing new 7-Eleven locations within office buildings, airports, and other high-traffic spaces. The

strategy arose in response to a general decline in the availability of prime storefront real estate, a trend that compelled the company to imagine new ways to increase its market presence. The new stores, roughly half the size of traditional 7-Elevens, offered a streamlined selection of the company's typical product line. The chain officially launched the design concept in June, when it established a prototype store in the Vancouver International Airport. According to company representatives the new store was soon serving approximately 1,500 customers a day.

During the early part of the decade, 7-Eleven's sales continued to rise steadily. In 2001 the company enjoyed domestic earnings of more than $10 billion, while global revenues exceeded $31 billion. By 2003 the company had more than 5,200 stores in the United States and 25,000 locations worldwide. The chain experienced its most rapid growth in Asia, particularly in Japan, which had nearly 10,000 7-Eleven locations, an average of 77 stores for every million of the population.

The company expanded its Asian presence further in early 2004, when it received authorization from the Chinese government to open 500 new stores in and around the capital city of Beijing. At the time, China's rapid economic growth had transformed its retail sector into the second largest in Asia, with annual revenues approaching $500 billion. The company opened its first Beijing outlet in May 2004. During its first week of operation, the store averaged between 4,000 and 5,000 customers a day.

A MORE AGGRESSIVE GROWTH STRATEGY

On September 1, 2005, 7-Eleven's majority stakeholder was reorganized into a new corporation, Seven & i Holdings Co., Ltd. Two days later Seven & i Holdings launched a $1 billion bid to acquire all outstanding shares in the 7-Eleven company. With the purchase 7-Eleven became a wholly owned subsidiary of its Japanese parent company. According to a report published in the *International Herald Tribune* on September 3, 2005, the acquisition was a prelude to an aggressive new growth strategy for 7-Eleven, both in the United States and abroad. By eliminating all outside investors, Seven & i Holdings aimed to streamline the "decision-making" process considerably, enabling it to execute its expansion plans more quickly and efficiently. In the wake of the deal, 7-Eleven became a private company.

In September 2006, 7-Eleven revealed its intention not to renew its fuel supply agreement with Venezuelan oil firm Citgo. The announcement came shortly after Venezuelan president Hugo Chavez delivered an inflammatory speech at the United Nations, in which he called U.S. president George W. Bush the "devil." Although Chavez's remarks hastened the company's move to make the decision public, his rhetoric had no actual impact on the shift in the company's business plan. 7-Eleven executives had decided months earlier that it would allow the 20-year arrangement to expire, with the aim of establishing new supply deals with domestic fuel companies. As part of the new strategy, 7-Eleven would remove Citgo signs from its stores and begin marketing fuel under its own brand name.

Throughout this period 7-Eleven remained focused on continued innovation and expansion. In December 2006 the company unveiled a strategy to create 900 new North American stores over a three-year span. At the same time, 7-Eleven announced its intention to begin selling a wider range of healthy, ready-made meals, in response to increasing consumer demand for hot food.

The company identified further opportunity for growth during the economic downturn of 2008 and 2009, when the sagging real estate market enabled it to lease retail locations at bargain prices. The recession had also sparked an increase in overall convenience store sales, further fueling the chain's capacity to expand. One region with a high potential for growth was Southern California, where the company hoped to increase its total number of stores from 800 to 1,400 by the middle of the next decade. By the end of 2009, the company had more than 37,000 locations worldwide, a rise of nearly 50 percent since 2003. With its parent company devoting significant investment capital to further expansion, 7-Eleven showed every sign of continuing its rapid rate of growth for years to come.

Sina Dubovoj
Updated, David E. Salamie; Stephen Meyer

PRINCIPAL COMPETITORS

Alimentation Couche-Tard Inc.; Casey's General Stores, Inc.; Chevron Corporation; Cumberland Farms, Inc.; Exxon Mobil Corporation; Holiday Companies; Kum & Go, L.C.; The Pantry, Inc.; QuikTrip Corporation; RaceTrac Petroleum, Inc.; Royal Dutch Shell plc (The Netherlands); Sheetz, Inc.; Uni-Marts, Inc.; Wawa Inc.

FURTHER READING

"Bondholders Withdraw All Objections to Southland Plan (Bankruptcy Organization Plan)," *Los Angeles Times*, January 24, 1991.

Brennan, Terry, "7-Eleven Gets Cash Infusion," *Daily Deal*, March 1, 2000.

Copeland, Libby, "At Your Convenience: For 75 Years, 7-Eleven Has Been There for Milk Runs and Midnight Munchies," *Washington Post*, July 12, 2002, p. C01.

"Exciting Times at Southland," *Convenience Store News*, March 22, 1999, p. 25.

Fackler, Martin, "Japanese Retailer Bids for Rest of 7-Eleven," *International Herald Tribune*, September 3, 2005, p. 11.

Fairclough, Gordon, and Udorn Thani, "Shopping on the Fly: Thais Catch On to the Benefits of Convenience Stores," *Far Eastern Economic Review*, December 9, 1993, p. 70.

Francella, Barbara Grondin, "Southland and New Jersey Franchisees Face Off in a Range of Disputes," *Convenience Store News*, September 8, 1997, p. 16.

Gubernick, Lisa, "Thank Heaven for 7-Eleven," *Forbes*, March 23, 1987, p. 52.

Hackney, Holt, "Southland: The Junk Also Rises," *Financial World*, January 3, 1995, p. 24.

Hunt, Katie, and Karen Jacobs, "7-Elevens Invited in to China: The Convenience-Store Chain Won Approval to Bring up to 500 Stores to Beijing and Its Region," *Philadelphia Inquirer*, January 7, 2004, p. D02.

Klinkerman, Steve, "Why Southland Won't Unload Its Albatross," *BusinessWeek*, July 1, 1985, p. 71.

Kotabe, Masaaki, "The Return of 7-Eleven … from Japan: The Vanguard Program," *Journal of World Business*, Winter 1996, pp. 70+.

Landers, Peter, "In Japan, the Hub of E-commerce Is a 7-Eleven," *Wall Street Journal*, November 1, 1999, pp. B1, B4.

———, "Softbank, 7-Eleven Japan Go Online to Sell Books as E-commerce Expands," *Wall Street Journal*, June 4, 1999, p. A12.

Lee, Louise, "Southland Plans to Accelerate Store Openings," *Wall Street Journal*, April 6, 1998, p. A4.

Levere, Jane L., "For 7-Eleven, a Time to Open Doors," *New York Times*, July 15, 2009, p. B7.

Liles, Allen, *Oh Thank Heaven! The Story of the Southland Corporation*. Dallas: The Southland Corporation, December 1977.

McCarthy, Michael, "Shake Up at 7-Eleven," *Brandweek*, July 11, 1994, pp. 20–22, 24–27.

Miller, Karen Lowry, "A New Roll of the Dice at 7-Eleven," *BusinessWeek*, October 26, 1992.

Mufson, Steven, "Citgo Will Go, Says 7-Eleven; Chain Had Decided on Change Before Chavez's Speech," *Washington Post*, September 28, 2006, p. D03.

Nelson, Emily, "Product Development Is Always Difficult; Consider the Frito Pie," *Wall Street Journal*, October 25, 1999, pp. A1, A22.

Opdyke, Jeff D., "7-Eleven Tests Check-Cashing in Texas Stores," *Wall Street Journal*, April 29, 1998, p. T1.

Reidy, Chris, "7-Eleven Seeking a Fresh New Image—Even the Donuts," *Boston Globe*, February 5, 2003, p. C4.

Rudnitsky, Howard, "Billion-Dollar Fire Sale," *Forbes*, November 17, 1986, p. 44.

Shirouzu, Norihiko, and Jon Bigness, "7-Eleven Operators Resist System to Monitor Managers," *Wall Street Journal*, June 16, 1997, p. B1.

"Southland Chief Fires Top Aides to Cut Costs," *Wall Street Journal*, June 25, 1992.

Tannenbaum, Jeffrey A., "Franchisee Lawsuit Seeks $1 Billion from Southland," *Wall Street Journal*, April 8, 1994, p. B2.

Taylor, John H., "The Texas Chain Store Massacre," *Forbes*, February 6, 1989, p. 54.

Vincent, Roger, and Andrea Chang, "Slurping up Real Estate: 7-Eleven Plans to Add 600 Southland Stores—Just Because It's Convenient During the Recession," *Los Angeles Times*, July 24, 2009, p. B1.

Weber, Joseph, "7-Eleven Wants Out of the Glare," *BusinessWeek*, July 20, 1987, p. 78.

Weil, Jonathan, "Taking Big Gulp, Southland Moves to Revamp Stale 7-Eleven Chain," *Wall Street Journal*, September 9, 1998, p. T2.

Wilgoren, Jodi, "7-Eleven Refines the Convenience Store as Pantry," *International Herald Tribune*, July 14, 2003, p. 9.

Zellner, Wendy, and Emily Thornton, "How Classy Can 7-Eleven Get?" *BusinessWeek*, September 1, 1997, pp. 74–75.

Shubert Organization Inc.

234 West 44th Street
New York, New York 10036
U.S.A.
Telephone: (212) 944-3700
Fax: (212) 944-3755
Web site: http://www.shubertorganization.com

Wholly Owned Subsidiary of The Shubert Foundation
Founded: 1900
Incorporated: 1904 as Sam S. and Lee Shubert, Inc.
Employees: 1,600
Operating Revenues: $570 million (est.)
NAICS: 531120 Lessors of Nonresidential Buildings
(except Miniwarehouses); 711110 Theaters, Live
Theatrical Production (Except Dance).

∎∎∎

The Shubert Organization Inc. is one of the most successful business enterprises in the history of the American theater. It owns and/or operates 17 of Broadway's forty theaters, as well as one Off-Broadway and three outside of New York. It has also produced or co-produced some of Broadway's biggest hits, including the musicals *Cats* (1983) and Broadway's longest-running play ever, *The Phantom of the Opera* (1986), which was still appearing in a Shubert theater in 2010. The organization is controlled by the Shubert Foundation, a nonprofit entity established in 1945, and owns the ticketing agency Telecharge.com. In the first decade of the 21st century, the Shubert Organization had dominated Broadway for more than 100 years and displayed no signs of ceding its influence.

RISE TO THEATRICAL DOMINANCE, 1894–1924

Levi (Lee), Samuel (Sam), and Jacob (J. J.) Shubert were born in eastern Europe, probably in East Prussia or Lithuania, and grew up in poverty, with a brother and four sisters, in Syracuse, New York. Sam, the natural leader of the three, became a theatrical producer in 1894, while still in his teens. By the turn of the century the three were leasing five theaters in upstate New York and managing several stock companies. The Shuberts leased their first New York City theater in 1900, at Broadway and 35th Street. Of their first production, a *New York Times* reviewer declared, "Nothing nearly as awful has been seen in 20 years."

At this time an enterprise called the Theatrical Syndicate owned, leased, or controlled the booking of more than 700 theaters across the United States, virtually excluding competition. Sensing a growing threat from the Shuberts, the Syndicate decided in 1903 to deny them theaters and performers. Nevertheless, by the summer of 1904 they owned, leased, or booked the acts of some 50 theaters. In the fall of 1905 they presented Sarah Bernhardt in a tour that barnstormed the country. Barred from Syndicate-controlled theaters, they put on the show in rented circus tents, which held three times as many customers as the typical theater. Sam Shubert was killed in a train accident in 1905. J. J., who had been managing the firm's interests out of town, returned to Broadway. As the junior partner, he was generally responsible for musicals and for the construction and

KEY DATES

1900: Shubert brothers lease their first theatrical venue in New York City.

1945: Shubert Foundation is established.

1972: Gerald Schoenfeld and Bernard Jacobs take over the Shubert Organization.

1979: Foundation receives exemption from federal tax laws that disallow private charities from having controlling stake in profit-making enterprises.

2008: Philip J. Smith and Robert E. Wankel are named co-CEOs.

maintenance of the theaters. Lee usually handled straight plays, finances, publicity and advertising, and nontheatrical real estate.

By the fall of 1910 the Shuberts owned 73 theaters outright, held booking contracts with many more, and possessed at least 50 dramatic and musical companies. They were fully as despotic as the Syndicate and banned a number of critics from their premises for less than enthusiastic reviews. The brothers favored musical material, such as revues similar in concept to (but much less lavish than) the Ziegfeld Follies, and operettas, especially those composed by Sigmund Romberg. Sometimes as many as 20 Shubert operettas would be touring on the road. Of the straight plays, the brothers had a firm rule: "All plays have to have love interest. If you have no love interest, you have no play."

The brightest of Shubert stars was Al Jolson, who made millions for the brothers, as well as for himself. Between 1911 and 1918 six shows starring Jolson played at the Shuberts' commodious Winter Garden Theater, a converted stable at Broadway and 50th Street—far uptown at this time. The brothers also organized an unprofitable vaudeville circuit in 1921 and backed a venture that made some 350 movies between 1914 and 1919, usually under the World Film Studio name.

The Shuberts also were major owners of nontheatrical real estate, including a number of office buildings, hotels, and shops in New York, Boston, and Chicago. Between 1913 and 1917 they leased four theaters between Broadway and Eighth Avenue and 44th and 45th Streets—still the heart of New York City's theater district. Shubert Alley was constructed west of Broadway as a private street to connect the Shubert Theatre on 44th Street to the Booth Theatre on 45th Street. The Shuberts bought the four theaters and the land under

the alley in 1948 for between $3.5 million and $4 million, thereby taking full possession of the entire city block except for hotels at either end.

ZENITH AND DECLINE, 1924–72

The Shubert Theatrical Corp. was founded in 1924 as a public company taking over the business of earlier Shubert enterprises. At this time it was operating 86 theaters in 31 cities, including 30 in New York City alone, collecting 30 to 50 percent of the box office receipts as rental. The company's United Booking Office was placing shows for some 750 more theaters. In all, the Shuberts were producing one-fourth of the nation's plays and controlled three-fourths of all theatrical ticket sales. The company also claimed to hold the largest scenery, costume, and equipment inventories in the world. It even owned a shoe factory and compelled all of its dancers to buy their dancing shoes from the company.

The Shuberts were, in their heyday, heartily despised for their hammerlock on the American theater. Shrewd dealmakers, contentious litigators, and tight-fisted producers, they raised intimidation to an art form and, despite acts of charity, kept their benevolent impulses as private as possible. Their wariness even extended to each other: although Lee lived above the Shubert Theatre and J. J. in a penthouse apartment facing the theater, they rarely met and conducted necessary business through separate staffs. (Only two photos exist showing the brothers together.) They were besieged by thousands of women and girls seeking careers on stage. According to their biographer, "Although they did not invent the casting couch, it is believed that the Shuberts developed its functions."

The number of Shubert theaters reached 101 in 1928, but the corporation's net profit peaked at $3 million in 1926. Partly because of the advent of talking pictures and the growing popularity of radio programs, the American theater was beginning to pass its prime about this time. After the 1929 Wall Street crash, the value of the Shubert properties fell drastically. The brothers found it necessary to sell some of their properties—including their half-interest in five London theaters acquired in 1925—and to reduce substantially the number of shows they produced. In 1931 the Shubert Theatrical Corp. and eight other Shubert companies in one way or another affiliated with the parent—including script, music publishing, scenery, and costume companies—fell into bankruptcy.

Lee Shubert, however, was named co-receiver, and in 1933 he bought back the company's assets for $400,000—some ten cents on the dollar—renaming it Select Theatres Corp. After paying off bondholders, stockholders, and creditors of the old corporation, the Shuberts held more than 60 percent of the successor company, which included scenery, equipment, and 27 theaters. The brothers also retained many of their theaters and other real estate independent of this corporation, through their Trebuhs (Shubert spelled backwards) Realty Co.

Although the Shuberts' career as producers virtually came to an end in the 1940s, they remained active as ticket brokers, bookers, investors in shows, and operators of theatrical real estate. Tired scripts and worn sets and costumes were resurrected and recycled for touring shows and summer stock. In 1950 the Shuberts moved some 9,000 pieces of furniture, 40,000 square feet of draperies and flats, and numberless theatrical odd lots, all from the more than 1,000 shows produced, controlled, or purchased since 1900, across the Hudson River to Fort Lee, New Jersey.

In 1948 the Shuberts still owned 16 theaters in New York City and 21 elsewhere, about half of all the legitimate theaters in the United States, including all the Philadelphia theaters and all the Boston theaters but one. Through their United Booking Office, they were able to make producers book their shows exclusively in Shubert theaters around the country as a condition for renting a Shubert theater on Broadway. In a 1955 U.S. Supreme Court decision, however, the Shubert interests were found to be in violation of antitrust laws. As a result, in a 1956 consent agreement Select Theatres agreed to halt its booking activities for 25 years. It also was required to sell about a dozen theaters in six cities, including four in New York. United Booking Office was dissolved and Select Theatres ceased to exist, at least as a public company.

Lee Shubert died in 1953 and J. J. in 1963. The latter's son, John, had in 1956 taken over day-to-day operation of the business, assisted by Lawrence Shubert Lawrence, Jr., a grandnephew of the brothers who assumed management of the Shubert interests on John's death in 1962. The worth of the brothers' holdings was estimated in 1963 at $50 million and included 17 theaters in New York, two each in Chicago, Cincinnati, and Philadelphia, and one in Boston.

THE SHUBERT RESURGENCE

The Shubert Organization was a cluster of 23 corporations when its board fired Lawrence in 1972 and hired Gerald Schoenfeld and Bernard Jacobs, who were serving on the board, to run the enterprise. The two later said they found the Shubert operations in more disarray than they had suspected, and Jacobs claimed the business was losing about $2 million a year. The Broadway

houses, half of them vacant, were run-down. To fill these theaters they returned to producing plays in 1974. They met with instant success in the form of the hits *Pippin, Grease,* and *Equus.* The most successful was *A Chorus Line,* which debuted in 1975 and ran at the Shubert Theatre for 15 years. The Shubert Organization, which had been the first theatrical business to accept personal checks, telephone reservations, and credit cards, launched its own computerized system for selling theater tickets in 1979. Shubert Ticketing became the power behind Telecharge.com, the major online ticketing agency also owned by the Shubert Organization.

Lee and J. J. Shubert had established the Shubert Foundation in 1945 to lighten their income tax load and, eventually, their estate taxes. The bulk of both men's estates passed to the Foundation, which in 1972 became owner of the for-profit companies that the Shuberts had controlled. Most of the real estate continued to be held by the Shubert Organization, but certain key properties were deeded to the foundation so that rent and lease income on which the organization was paying taxes could become tax-exempt. Some of that property was sold later at substantial profit and was likewise exempt from capital gains taxes. In 1974 the state of New York charged the executors of J. J.'s estate, Lawrence, Schoenfeld, and Jacobs, with conflicts of interest depriving the foundation of millions of dollars due to "grossly excessive, unjustified and unreasonable" claims. The suit was withdrawn later when the charged parties agreed to reduce their claims on the foundation by $2 million.

In 1979 the Shubert Foundation won a ruling from the Internal Revenue Service allowing revenue from the Shubert Organization, after taxes, to flow to the foundation and be invested to produce tax-free income for the foundation. This was an exemption to federal tax laws that generally bar private charities from owning a controlling interest in a profit-making business. Otherwise, the foundation argued, it would have to sell the Broadway theaters, and as a result "the legitimate theater will be destroyed" and the new owners, most likely, would exploit the theaters for such purposes as "the showing of pornographic films" or would raze them for parking lots. (The Shubert brothers had used the same or similar arguments over the years in combating the threat of antitrust litigation.)

The rival Nederlander and Jujamcyn theater chains were most unhappy about this ruling, pointing out that the foundation gave some of the tax-exempt money to performing arts groups that used it to generate plays that then appeared in Shubert theaters. The argument that New York's theater district might cease to exist unless the Shubert Organization received favorable tax treatment seemed to lose its force when all but one of the enterprise's Broadway theaters were declared landmarks by the city in the 1980s, making them difficult to convert to any alternative use.

The Shubert Organization continued to score a number of big successes on Broadway with its own productions, including *Ain't Misbehavin'* and *Dancin'* in 1978, *Amadeus* and *Children of a Lesser God* in 1980, and *Dreamgirls* in 1981. Its biggest hit of the decade was *Cats*, which made its U.S. debut in 1982. Co-produced with Andrew Lloyd Webber's company, *Cats*, which played at the Winter Garden, broke the record previously set by *A Chorus Line* when it gave its 6,138th consecutive performance on Broadway in 1997. (*Cats* closed in 2000, and its longevity record was shattered six years later by *The Phantom of the Opera*, which was still showing in a Shubert house in 2010.) Shubert's dramas of the 1980s included Pulitzer Prize winners *Glengarry Glen Ross* and *The Heidi Chronicles*.

The Shubert Organization, in 1994, had recorded a profit in every year since 1976. That year it owned 16 Broadway theaters and the land beneath them. It also owned another one (the Music Box) jointly with the estate of Irving Berlin. In addition, it owned the Sardi Building (1501 Broadway) and the land beneath it, the land beneath the office building at 1675 Broadway, and air rights leased to the Tower 45 (120 West 45th Street) and Bertelsmann (1540 Broadway) buildings. Outside of New York City, the Shubert Organization owned Boston's Shubert Theater (which it leased to the Wang Center for the Performing Arts in 1996) and Philadelphia's Forrest Theater. It also was leasing the Shubert Theater in Los Angeles and managing the National Theatre in Washington, D.C. The Shubert Theater in Chicago was sold to the Nederlander Organization in 1991. The Shubert Organization had no remaining mortgages on their real estate holdings.

INTO THE 21ST CENTURY

Jacobs died in 1996, leaving his long-time partner Schoenfeld to continue to serve as chairman. Notable productions under Schoenfeld's direction included *Dirty Blonde* (2000), *Amour* (2002), *Passing Strange* (2008), and the Tony-Award winning revival of *Equus* (2008). *Spamalot*, which ran at the Shubert Theater from 2005 to 2009, was a particularly big hit that garnered three Tonys, including one for Best Musical. Schoenfeld, in short, never lost his touch. When he died of a heart attack in November 2008, Broadway lost one of its most influential and memorable characters.

In a move that surprised few, the close-knit Shubert Organization looked within it own ranks to find a replacement for Schoenfeld. It settled on a pair who had

long been on the company's roster and who had served as president and executive vice president since Jacob's demise in 1996. Former Shubert President Philip J. Smith was appointed chairman and former Executive Vice President Robert E. Wankel was named president in December 2008. In a nod to the successful management partnerships of the past, Smith and Wankel were also selected to serve as co-chief executive officers.

In November 2009 the new chiefs of the Shubert Organization entered into a deal with producers Robert Cole and Frederick Zollo (Tony Award winners for *Angels in America*). The three-year agreement was the first development contract the organization had entered into with producers in more than 25 years. It also marked the first time that the company had independent producers working in-house on shows in which it retained investment and development rights. How the arrangement would ultimately benefit the parties or affect the Great White Way overall remained to be seen, but it was clear that the impact and significance of the Shubert Organization would be in full force for many years to come.

Robert Halasz
Updated, Margaret L. Moser

PRINCIPAL SUBSIDIARIES

Telecharge.com; Shubert Ticketing.

PRINCIPAL COMPETITORS

Jujamcyn Theaters LLC; Live Nation Entertainment, Inc.; Nederlander Producing Company of America, Inc.

FURTHER READING

Gussow, Mel, "Bernard E. Jacobs, a Pillar of American Theater as Shubert Executive, Dies at 80," *New York Times*, August 28, 1996, p. D18.

Healy, Patrick, "Shubert Reaches a Deal with Two Stage Producers," *New York Times*, November 18, 2009, p. C2

"J. J. Shubert Dies; Last of 3 Brothers," *New York Times*, December 27, 1963, pp. 1, 23.

Kleinfield, N. R., "I.R.S. Ruling Wrote Script for the Shubert Tax Break," *New York Times*, July 11, 1994, pp. Al, B6.

Liebling, A. J., "The Boys from Syracuse," *New Yorker*, November 18, 1939, pp. 26–30; November 25, 1939, pp. 23–27; December 2, 1939, pp. 33–37.

McNamara, Brooks, *The Shuberts of Broadway*, New York: Oxford University Press, 1990.

Richards, David, "The Shuberts, Kingpins of Broadway," *Washington Post*, September 22, 1985, pp. H1, H9–H10.

Stagg, Jerry, *The Brothers Shubert*, New York: Random House, 1968.

Weber, Bruce, "He Relit Broadway: Gerald Schoenfeld Dies at 84," *New York Times*, November 26, 2008, p. A1(L).

Slaughter and May

One Bunhill Row
London, EC1Y 8YY
England
Telephone: (+44 020) 7600-1200
Fax: (+44 020) 7090-5000
Web site: http://www.slaughterandmay.com

Private Company
Founded: 1889
Employees: 1,200
NAICS: 541110 Offices of Lawyers

■ ■ ■

Slaughter and May (Slaughters) is the most profitable law firm in the United Kingdom and one of the top ten legal moneymakers in the world. Despite being the smallest member of London's Magic Circle of leading law firms, Slaughters boasts more FTSE (*Financial Times* and London Stock Exchange) 100 companies as clients than any of its competitors.

The centennial-plus firm also fosters a unique culture among its fellow corporate mavens, preferring to cultivate its internal workforce for partnership opportunities and eschewing the global expansion that began to be a widespread trend in the late 20th century. Those policies, especially the latter, paid off with stability when other businesses were reeling from the financial meltdown of the early 21st century that led to massive restructurings, layoffs, and bankruptcies. The firm even prospered during the crisis by assisting the U.K. government in rescuing faltering banks from complete ruin. By

keeping itself comparatively lean in size and remaining alert to the needs of a changing world and economy, Slaughters appeared poised to maintain its venerable status well into the years ahead.

COMPANY ORIGINS

William Capel Slaughter and William May met at the London law firm Ashurst Morris Crisp & Company, where Slaughter was an associate and May was completing his three-year term of articles (a kind of legal apprenticeship) in the 1880s. The firm had very few partners, as was customary at the time, and the addition of John Morris's son to the partnership ranks in 1887 was likely a deciding factor in Slaughter and May seeking professional fulfillment elsewhere. Slaughter was the elder and, thus, more experienced of the two, and it was he who broached the idea of the two joining forces. May passed his examinations in January of 1888 and, apparently, signed on as Slaughter's assistant directly afterward. On January 1, 1889, the partnership of Slaughter and May was officially launched.

Although the new partners became lifelong friends and colleagues, their backgrounds and personalities were starkly contrasting. Slaughter was born on May 11, 1857, the youngest of six children in a working-class family. His paternal grandfather and great-grandfather had been cheesemongers, and his father (Mihill Slaughter) had begun his career as a coal merchant. There were many independent tradesmen in his mother's (née Ann Erskine Capel) family as well, but her father, uncle, and one cousin enjoyed a comparatively higher social standing and income level

COMPANY PERSPECTIVES

At Slaughter and May, we focus on nurturing the genuinely special nature of the firm: a collegiate working style with an ambition to be the best at looking after clients; bringing a creative, quality, and business-aware approach to all of our work, however complex; fostering and developing our working relationships with leading law firms across the world—our "Best Friends" approach; (and) maintaining a sense of perspective—our clients will certainly be best served if an element of warmth and humour is in the mix.

via jobs in the financial industry. Slaughter's father became secretary of the Railway Department of the Stock Exchange after his marriage to Capel in 1846. By the time the youngest Slaughter came into the world, his family lived in a fashionable London suburb.

Slaughter was privately educated and did not attend college, a not unusual path at the time for someone who aspired to a legal career. He spent the five years in articles required of non-university graduates (graduates only needed three years) at the legal offices of Benjamin Gay Wilkinson and George Bernard Harvey Drew. In July of 1879, Slaughter qualified as a solicitor and joined Ashurst Morris Crisp & Company, one of the city's top commercial law firms. He remained affiliated with the firm for 10 years, gaining the mentorship of senior partner John Morris in the process.

May was born on May 4, 1863, into a prosperous family that had been landholders in the Thames Valley since the 16th century. His father and grandfather were both prominent surgeons, and he was reared in an immense house overlooking the Thames River. He attended boarding school at the famous Charterhouse School in Surrey before heading to Oxford University to major in classics and modern history, graduating in 1884 after staying an extra term to take a class in religious studies. May was, among other things, an avid reader, something of a poet, an accomplished musician and composer (four of his compositions were published during his lifetime), and a devoted sportsman and outdoorsman.

INSTANT SUCCESS

Thanks to an enviable relationship between Slaughter and his mentor, Morris, the firm started out with a strong client base. Recognizing Slaughter's impressive

legal acumen, Morris had allowed Slaughter to set up his own practice in 1887 while still handling clients at Ashurst Morris Crisp. After the founding of Slaughter and May in 1889, this bond was further strengthened by a special fee-sharing arrangement between the firms, as well as an informal referral setup that Morris often utilized in his role as the head of various companies in order to avoid conflicts of interest with Ashurst Morris Crisp. Slaughter and May benefited enormously from this largesse, as it leant the firm a powerful clientele and certain cachet from its inception.

Initial clients included Schroder and Company, railway contractor George Pauling, the Home & Colonial stores, and Baron Emile d'Erlanger. All were very important, but the latter two had significant impact on Slaughter and May's success. D'Erlanger was a leading French banker with business interests in many countries. In addition to keeping the partners busy with his myriad professional requirements, D'Erlanger was a major source of new clients. Pauling and Schroder and Company, for instance, had both been introductions of the baron.

The Home & Colonial stores account was also important to Slaughter and May. Cofounded in 1888 as a small retail operation by Julius Drew, the brother-in-law of Slaughter's sister, it was transformed into a vast concern under the firm's guidance (Slaughter also served as the company's chairman for nearly 30 years). It grew from just 14 shops in 1888 to 107 in 1890, 300 by 1900, and 600 by 1914. Such rapid expansion naturally necessitated a variety of legal services, thus providing Slaughters with a substantial amount of work from the time of the firm's formation.

Buttressed by such a strong starting lineup, Slaughters quickly became a force within London legal circles. Other early clients included Barings Bank, Morgan Grenfell, and Rothschild, as well as several smaller banks, and by 1932 the firm was the second largest in the city. May passed away that same year, and Slaughter had preceded him in 1917, but the legacy of the two men was lasting and indisputable as the firm reached beyond London and established itself in the global community.

UNIQUE CULTURE

As the decades passed Slaughters expanded its expertise and its frontiers. In the 1950s, for example, the firm's U.S. client base grew through its work for Bank of America and Morgan Guaranty Trust Company. In the 1960s and 1970s syndicated loans became a large part of Slaughter and May's legal efforts, while the 1970s and 1980s saw the firm play an integral part in the creation of the Eurobond market. Privatization became a

```
┌─────────────────────────────────────────────┐
│                                               │
│              KEY DATES                         │
│                    ■                           │
├─────────────────────────────────────────────┤
│                                               │
│  1889:  Firm is founded by William Capel Slaughter │
│         and William May.                       │
│  1917:  Cofounder Slaughter dies.              │
│  1932:  Slaughter and May becomes the second-  │
│         largest law firm in London; cofounder May │
│         passes away.                           │
│  1974:  Firm establishes offices in Paris and Hong │
│         Kong.                                  │
│  1989:  Slaughters celebrates its 100th anniversary. │
│  2008:  Firm is instrumental in assisting British │
│         government in the partial nationalization of │
│         distressed banks.                      │
│                                               │
└─────────────────────────────────────────────┘
```

top theme of the 1980s and 1990s, when Slaughters' legal teams were involved in restructuring a number of government-owned businesses, including British Aerospace, British Airways, Jaguar, British Telecom, and British Steel, into privately held concerns.

However, even as the world changed and Slaughters' size and status increased, the firm nourished a singular corporate culture that differed from those of its competitors. One aspect of this was a multi-specialist approach, in which the firm's lawyers were encouraged to maintain a relatively broad spectrum of expertise, thereby allowing them to shift focus when and if certain areas of work became less in demand.

Another distinctive feature of the firm was its insistence on finding its partnership material within the ranks instead of following the common lateral hiring practices of other firms. This approach resulted in a workforce with close ties to one another and exceptional loyalty to its employer. In addition, in a stance that did not become particularly relevant until the late 20th century, the firm did not engage in the global expansion that became so popular among its rivals. This too proved to be an efficient hedge against troubled economic times.

INTO THE 21ST CENTURY

Although Slaughters resisted the massive global expansion of other firms, it had, for instance, opened offices in Paris and Hong Kong as early as 1974, with presences in Brussels and Beijing to follow. Other offices, such as a New York City outpost, were opened and closed along the way. What was different was the strategy it employed. Rather than feverishly opening branch offices around the world, Slaughters initiated what it dubbed a

"Best Friends" network of leading law firms, including France's Bredin Prat, Germany's Hengeler Mueller, Italy's Bonelli Erede Pappalardo, and Spain's Uría Menéndez. The idea was to reap the benefits of international liaisons without taking the risks of unmitigated expansion.

Slaughters felt the merits of its approach as the new century's financial crisis started to take its toll on businesses and people around the world. The same was true of Slaughters' other conservative methods, such as discouraging specialization among its associates and partners. While some competitors were forced to downsize and regroup, Slaughters was prepared to address the new problems on its own terms.

In 2009 Slaughters remained the smallest of the Magic Circle firms (behind Clifford Chance, Linklaters, Allen & Overy, and Freshfields Bruckhaus Deringer). However, it was the most profitable firm in the United Kingdom and one of the ten most profitable in the world. It boasted more FTSE 100 clients than any other firm and, unlike its Magic Circle brethren, was not anticipating any employee layoffs. It had managed to prosper in the turbulent times by securing the role of legal advisor to the U.K. Treasury in 2008 and assisting in the partial nationalization of the country's many faltering banks.

The firm did have to make adjustments to stay profitable. Measures such as salary freezes and modifying its billing practices were instituted, for example. In addition, Slaughters was reportedly in talks in late 2009 with a legal-process outsourcing (LPO) provider about outsourcing some low-level work. The negotiations were reportedly at the request of a single Slaughters' client and did not imply a wider trend.

Perhaps the firm's head of corporate practice, Nigel Boardman, put it best when he said to Alex Spence of the *Times* in 2007, "We're not different because we are stupid. We're different because we think it's the right way to be. If it became clear to us that there was a better way to be, then we'd switch. It's not a religious belief. It's a business judgment, and business judgments can change. I think the demand for high-quality, individually tailored, highly committed legal services will remain the same. If we continue to do that, I don't think clients will mind whether we wear space suits or togas. Actually, clients don't care about our strategy— and rightly. I mean, why should they?"

Margaret L. Moser

PRINCIPAL COMPETITORS

Clifford Chance LLP; Linklaters LLP; Allen & Overy LLP; Freshfields Bruckhaus Deringer LLP.

FURTHER READING

Carman, Dominic, "Slaughter and May v Clifford Chance: Who Is Pursuing the Best Route?" *Times* (London), April 8, 2008.

"CC, Lovells, Slaughters All Freeze Pay," *Lawyer*, April 6, 2009, p. 5.

Chellel, Kit, "Slaughters Puts Its Faith—and Its Clients—in the Next Generation," *Lawyer*, September 1, 2008, p. 17.

Dennett, Laurie. *Slaughter and May: A Short History.* Cambridge: Granta Editions, 1989.

Hodges, Jeremy, "Magic Circle Firms Confirm Status in Global Elite," *Legal Week*, July 17, 2008.

"How Treasury Work Thrust Publicity Shy Slaughters into the Spotlight," *Lawyer*, July 13, 2009, p. 13.

"Law Firm of the Year: Slaughter and May," *Acquisitions Monthly*, December 2008, p. 34(1).

"Legal Outsourcing Trend Gains Momentum as Clients Get Tough," *Lawyer*, October 12, 2009, p. 40.

"Nigel Boardman," *Times* (London), April 21, 2008.

Novarese, Alex, "Slaughters' Best Friends—Lots of Necessity, Not So Much Virtue," *Legal Week*, May 13, 2008.

Rozenberg, Joshua, "'Magic Circle' Has Lost Its Aura as City Law Firms Feel Pain of Recession," *London Evening Standard*, February 10, 2009.

"Slaughter and May," *Lawyer*, September 16, 2008.

"Slaughter and May," *Legal Week*, August 21, 2009.

"Slaughters Bites the Bullet with New Fee Structures," *Lawyer*, February 9, 2009, p. 1.

"Slaughters Regains Top Spot on FTSE100 List," *Lawyer*, December 7, 2009, p. 5.

Spence, Alex, "Nigel Boardman: 'This Is a Correction, Not a Collapse'," *Times* (London), October 8, 2007.

———, "Slaughter and May Elects New Senior Partner," *Times* (London), January 17, 2008.

———, "Slaughter and May Sidesteps the Financial Carnage," *Times* (London), January 19, 2009.

"Survey: Slaughter & May Top UK Firm for Associate Satisfaction," *JD Journal*, July 17, 2009.

Townsend, Abigail, "The Lowdown: Why Legal Rivals Are Lambs to Slaughter," *Independent*, December 7, 2003.

Triedman, Julie, "Dealmaker of the Week: Slaughter and May's Nigel Boardman," *Am Law Daily*, October 10, 2008.

Sling Media, Inc.

1051 East Hillsdale Boulevard, Suite 500
Foster City, California 94404
U.S.A.
Telephone: (650) 293-8000
Fax: (650) 293-8800
Web site: http://www.slingmedia.com

Wholly Owned Subsidiary of EchoStar Technologies LLC
Founded: 2004
Employees: 300
Sales: $247 million (2007 est.)
NAICS: 334220 Radio and Television Broadcast and
    Wireless Communications Equipment

■ ■ ■

Sling Media, Inc., is a digital lifestyle corporation whose signature product, the Slingbox, is meant to revolutionize television viewing. The Emmy Award–winning product streams home TV content to PCs, Macs, laptops, and handheld devices anywhere in the world. Since the introduction of the basic Slingbox in 2005, Sling Media has added many software features. These include the SlingCatcher, which streams Web content to the television, and Clip+Sling, which enables TV viewers to send segments of TV programs to other viewers. Sling Media's ultimate goal is to license its technology to pay-TV providers, who would embed Slingbox software into their set-top boxes (STBs), making the Slingbox a feature rather than a product sold one at a time to consumers.

INTRODUCING THE SLINGBOX: 2004

Blake Krikorian, a technical consultant to various firms, was a resident of San Francisco and fan of the local Giants baseball team. As he told Kevin Downey in *Broadcasting & Cable*, "There was one day in the summer of 2002, working with my brother helping technology companies, and I was dying to watch my Giants play and found there was no way to watch it when I was in the office or on the road." Serendipitously, he and his brother, Jason, were then helping companies find new ways to bring media content to computers and mobile devices. They began working on a mechanism to digitalize TV content and send it to computers and mobile devices wherever they were located.

To complete their work on the mechanism, the Krikorians, along with Bhupen Shah, who had founded the digital media companies Dazzle and Emuzed, established a privately owned company called Sling Media in 2004. Blake Krikorian was the CEO, with Jason Krikorian initially as head of business development and Shah as the COO. Research centers were set up in the San Francisco Bay area and in Bangalore, India.

Sling Media introduced what would be its basic product, the Slingbox, at the International Consumer Electronics Show (CES) in January 2005. The size and trapezoidal shape of a chocolate bar and sitting right next to the TV, the first Slingboxes transferred TV streams to a single Windows XP-based PC anywhere on earth, provided there was a high-speed Internet connection. They sold for $250, and there was no periodic subscription fee.

Blake Krikorian said that the Slingbox was for "avid couch potatoes" like himself. The Slingbox technology that assured a steady video stream was named "Lebowski" by Sling Media after a laid-back, spaced-out character in the cult movie, *The Big Lebowski*. However, in the television industry, the Slingbox was taken very seriously. Some saw the Slingbox as representing a revolution in television viewing. "Timeshifting" had been made possible with the introduction of the VCR in the 1970s. That is, viewers could watch television programming *whenever* they wanted. Now the Slingbox made placeshifting possible. Viewers could watch TV *wherever* they were, with a delay of just seconds. Some television content providers expressed concern about copyright infringement, but Krikorian stated in 2005 that most of the providers understood the potential benefits of the Slingbox. He later told Matt Kapko in *RCR Wireless News*, "If anything, we're actually more of an enabler than a disruptor," Krikorian said. "What we do is actually totally additive to the Nielsen ratings system."

A WARM WELCOME: 2005

The concept of "slinging" TV content out around the globe received a warm welcome in Sling Media's early days, even before the Slingbox had even been rolled out. *Forbes* magazine included the new firm on its 2004 list of "hot" startups. That year Sling received venture funding in the amount of $10.5 million from Mobius Venture Capital, DCM-Doll Capital Management, and an undisclosed investor. This enabled the company to intensify its research. It planned, for example, to increase the size of its Bangalore staff from 25 to 100.

At the 2005 Consumer Electronics Show, the cable and satellite channel G4techTV chose the Slingbox as

"Best of CES" in the "whole house entertainment" category. CNET Networks Inc., a technology-oriented media company, declared the device as the "Next Big Thing" in the "accessories" class, and *Laptop* magazine included the product in its list of "Best of CES 2005." In 2005 it was among the 100 top-rated electronics products on Amazon.com. The following year AlwaysON, a global media company, placed Sling Media among its OnHollywood list of 100 Top Private Companies "for its significant market traction coupled with game-changing technology," according to *Wireless News*. In January 2007 the company won an Emmy Award in the Technology and Engineering category.

More important than the reception that Slingbox received was how many were sold. As a privately owned company, Sling Media did not reveal sales figures. However, in May 2006, *InternetWeek* reported that about 80,000 Slingboxes had been sold in the 14 months since it reached market. This was considered a respectable start but far short of the massive breakthrough that Sling Media sought. It was enough to attract a second round of investors. In February 2006, Sling Media obtained $46.6 million in financing from a cluster of firms headed by Goldman Sachs, Liberty Media, and EchoStar Communications.

During the second half of 2005, Hub Strategy and Communication launched a provocative advertising campaign on Sling Media's behalf. According to *ADWEEK Western Edition*, one of the ads described the Slingbox as "the best thing to happen to the business traveler since pay-per-view porn." The question, however, was whether the device would appeal beyond this base of businesspersons to the mass of consumers. In an article titled "Television's Next Big Shift," *The Economist* commented: "On the face of it, placeshifting's appeal is much narrower [than timeshifting's]: travelling executives who want to watch their home teams from their hotel rooms across the globe hardly constitute a mass market." However, CEO Blake Krikorian expressed confidence that the Slingbox had mass appeal, and the same article quoted him as saying, "This is a mainstream product already."

PURSUING WIDER MARKETS: 2006–07

To enlarge Slingbox's market, Sling Media in 2006 and 2007 introduced many innovations to make the device more versatile. Anticipating the rollout of new Slingbox software that would send TV streams to many types of mobile devices, Jason Krikorian indicated to *ExtremeTech.com* that "support for mobile devices always has been part of the company's vision but that the initial focus was on the PC because of the broadband

```
┌─────────────────────────────────────────────┐
│                                               │
│              KEY DATES                        │
│                    ■                          │
│  ┌─────────────────────────────────────────┐ │
│  │ 2004:  Sling Media is founded.            │ │
│  │ 2005:  Sling Media introduces the Sling-  │ │
│  │        box, which streams content from    │ │
│  │        a TV to a PC.                       │ │
│  │ 2007:  Sling Media introduces Sling-      │ │
│  │        Catcher, a device that sends Web   │ │
│  │        content to a TV; Sling Media is    │ │
│  │        purchased by EchoStar Communi-     │ │
│  │        cations Corp.                       │ │
│  │ 2008:  Sling Media is spun off from Echo- │ │
│  │        Star Communications Corp. and      │ │
│  │        becomes a subsidiary of EchoStar   │ │
│  │        Technologies LLC.                   │ │
│  │ 2010:  Sling Media rolls out new software │ │
│  │        for the Slingbox to facilitate its │ │
│  │        integration into set-top boxes.    │ │
│  └─────────────────────────────────────────┘ │
└─────────────────────────────────────────────┘
```

connection." Accordingly, in March 2006 Sling Media introduced software called SlingPlayer Mobile. With this new technology, Slingbox users could watch their home TVs on all network-enabled mobile phones and handheld computers (PDA) driven by Windows Mobile.

The month of March saw other innovations. SlingPlayer Mac software made it possible for the Slingbox to direct home TV content to the Macintosh line of computers by Apple. At the same time Sling Media brought out customized SlingPlayer software engineered specifically for Microsoft's new Ultra-Mobile devices that were so-called because, being the size of a paperback book, they could be used anywhere.

In September 2006 the company launched three new Slingbox models to meet varying household needs. The Slingbox Tuner, smaller than the original, was for customers without digital cable or satellite boxes. With a Slingbox AV, customers could watch content from digital cable, a satellite receiver, a DVR, and a DVD player from anywhere. The Slingbox Pro HD was the first Slingbox to stream high definition TV. Also in September, Sling Media brought out a higher level of support capability. While installing the Slingbox, customers could speak to company representatives and receive guidance. With the subscribers' permission, the representatives could even take control of the PC controls to help install the product.

In 2007 the SlingCatcher was one of Sling Media's major innovations. The new box, bringing the digital age to the TV screen, reversed the original flow from the TV to other devices. SlingCatcher sent multimedia content of any format from the Web to a TV, including a slideshow from a photo-sharing site, clips from a

video-sharing site, or films downloaded from an online movie service. Later in the year Sling Media presented the SlingLink Turbo 1 Port and SlingLink Turbo 4 Port, HomePlug power line products that enabled a higher-speed connection between the Slingbox and the router.

In 2006 Sling Media established an internal Sling Entertainment Group, headed by Jason Hirschhorn and Benjamin White, both former leaders of MTV's digital businesses. The Group's task was to create new forms of entertainment and business models. Its first initiative, marketed in June 2007, was Clip+Sling, allowing Slingbox owners to share segments of television programs online. Three months later Sling Media brought forth Slingbox Solo, which got good reviews for its very easy setup, improved streaming video quality, and its integrated HD inputs.

NEW STRUCTURES AND NEW CHALLENGES: 2007–08

In September 2007 EchoStar Communications, the third-largest pay-TV provider in the United States and a major investor in Sling Media, announced it had agreed to purchase Sling for $380 million. Acquiring Sling Media gave EchoStar a competitive advantage over its competitors. EchoStar's CEO, Charles Ergen, told Arik Hesseldahl in *BusinessWeek Online* that his corporation now could provide its customers with "innovative and convenient ways to enjoy programming on more displays and locations, including TVs, computers, and mobile phones, both inside and outside the home." Blake Krikorian said Sling Media would benefit by having available the technological resources of EchoStar, which would help expand the product range of his old firm.

During the same month EchoStar Communications announced that it would be renamed DISH Network after its satellite television operation, while parts of the company would be spun off into a new EchoStar Corporation. These parts included its technology and services operation for pay TV, in the form of the EchoStar Technologies LLC and EchoStar Satellite Services LLC, subsidiaries of the new company. Another part was Sling Media, which would be a subsidiary of EchoStar Technologies. Sling, therefore, would still have the old company's technological resources available to it. Blake Krikorian would continue as Sling Media's CEO. The split went into effect in January 2008.

In September 2007, CEO Krikorian said that the number of Slingbox customers was in the hundreds of thousands. This was significantly short of the massive sales that had been predicted. Sling Media, however, had a strategy to change the game for Slingbox. As Jason

Hirschhorn, president of the Sling Entertainment Group, told Amanda Fung in *Crain's New York Business*, "Sling's future is not in Slingbox sales." Hirschhorn went on to say that Sling wanted to license Slingbox technology to original equipment manufacturers, such as television manufacturers and cable and telecommunications companies, interested in integrating the technology into their TV sets or set-top boxes. In other words, Sling Media wanted to convert the Slingbox from a product to a built-in feature, sold wholesale rather than retail. The Slingbox, it was hoped, would become as common as DVRs.

REACHING FOR A MASS MARKET: 2008–10

Sling Media hoped to make its product more appealing to potential licensees by making "Slingbox" a household name. To help achieve this, Sling Media established a free, advertisement-supported entertainment Web site, Sling.com, in December 2008. Sling.com was based on a partnership with 90 content providers, among them CBS and HULU, and offered many television programs, video clips, and movies to consumers. More free content was added to Sling.com in January 2009 in the form of access to the Players' Network library of more than 1,500 gaming and Las Vegas lifestyle programs. Two months later Sling Media announced an agreement with HIT Entertainment, a provider of children's programs, that would add some of HIT's programming to Sling.com. In April 2009 the Tennis channel was added to the Web site's free content.

Sling Media continued to roll out product innovations to broaden its market. For instance, the company released SlingPlayer Mobile software for BlackBerry devices. The Slingbox PRO-HD was introduced in September 2008. It could stream HD content from a home television source, among them over-the-air digital signals, digital cable channels, HDTV cable boxes, HDTV satellite receivers, and HD DVRs, to a PC or laptop. In May 2009 Sling Media announced a WiFi-only version of its SlingPlayer Mobile application for iPhone and iPod touch.

In January 2009 the Krikorian brothers, Hirschhorn, and other executives left Sling Media after management differences emerged between the company and its parent. In March 2009 EchoStar and Sling Media announced a more direct effort to make the Slingbox a mass-selling product. They introduced the EchoStar T2200S, a set-top box with embedded Slingbox technology targeted specifically for the cable TV industry. Success for this product would help convert the Slingbox from a stand-alone consumer product to a built-in feature.

In conjunction with CES 2010, the company announced four new products specifically targeted for television service providers and consumer electronics manufacturers. In a press statement accompanying the announcement, John M. Paul, Sling Media's vice president of products, defined the company's strategy: "For the past 12 months, we have been fine tuning an all new product lineup. We believe manufacturers and TV service providers realize that building Sling Media products and services into their offerings is the best way to acquire new customers and delight their current ones."

Michael Levine

PRINCIPAL DIVISIONS

European Division (London); Technical Research Center (Bangalore, India).

PRINCIPAL COMPETITORS

Cisco Systems, Inc.; Sony Corporation; TiVo Inc.

FURTHER READING

Baumgartner, Jeff, "Take Your TV with You: Can 'Place-shifting' Drive the Upstream and Premium Broadband Services?" *CED*, May 2005, p. 46.

Downey, Kevin, "Blake Krikorian," *Broadcasting & Cable*, April 14, 2008, p. 40.

Fung, Amanda, "Sling Media Makes Play to Become a Household Name," *Crain's New York Business*, December 8, 2008, p. 4.

Hesseldahl, Arik, "EchoStar Raises the Bar for Mobile TV: Its Purchase of Sling Media Gives It a Competitive Edge," *BusinessWeek Online*, September 26, 2007, http://www.businessweek.com/technology/content/sep2007/tc20070925_717354.htm.

Kapko, Matt, "Sling Media Puts Customer in Control," *RCR Wireless News*, October 23, 2007, p. 6.

"Q3 2009 ECHOSTAR CORPORATION Earnings Conference Call—Final," *Fair Disclosure Wire*, November 9, 2009.

"Sling Media—CEO Interview," *Finance Wire*, December 29, 2006.

"Sling Media Unveils Suite of New OEM Products at CES 2010," Sling Media, January 6, 2010, http://www.slingmedia.com/get/io_1262761863027.html.

"Television's Next Big Shift," *The Economist*, March 11, 2006, p. 16.

Smith Micro Software, Inc.

———————————■———————————

51 Columbia
Aliso Viejo, California 92656-1456
U.S.A.
Telephone: (949) 362-5800
Fax: (949) 362-2300
Web site: http://www.smithmicro.com

Public Company
Incorporated: 1983
Employees: 359
Sales: $107.3 million (2009)
Stock Exchanges: NASDAQ
Ticker Symbol: SMSI
NAICS: 511210 Software Publishers; 541512 Computer
    Systems Design Services

■ ■ ■

Smith Micro Software, Inc., is a California-based technology company that designs, develops, and markets software products and services, primarily for the wireless communications industry. It also provides an extensive line of computer software products for business and home markets, operating on Windows, Mac, UNIX, Linux, Windows Mobile, Symbian, and Java platforms. Since its founding in 1982, the company has been noted for its cutting-edge products. Smith Micro sells directly to wireless service carriers, equipment and computer manufacturers, businesses, and consumers. It has shipped more than 100 million copies of its patented QuickLink technology worldwide for mobile connection management.

EARLY YEARS

Smith Micro's founder, William W. Smith Jr., started his career selling home finance software from the trunk of his car. In 1982, after working at Rockwell International Corporation and Xerox Data Systems in a variety of sales, technical and management positions, Smith, with his wife, Rhonda, founded Smith Micro Software.

The company initially focused on modem and fax software and sold its products to original equipment manufacturers (OEMs). By the early 1990s, Smith Micro had an established reputation for its innovative products that seamlessly integrated fax and data functions into personal computer operating systems. Building on its success with OEM data/fax software, the company began producing a wide range of retail communications software, including packages for computer telephony, remote disk access, and modem sharing, and it established international distribution channels.

In 1993 Smith Micro, looking to extend its fax software offerings to high-end and more profitable products, acquired Cross Communications Company. This allowed Smith Micro to enter the fast-growing local area network market with enhanced communications features. Smith Micro continued its growth through a strategy that included product development and product acquisition.

In September 1995 the company went public with a listing on the NASDAQ, selling 3.4 million shares of stock at a price of $12 per share via an initial public offering. That same year, Smith Micro signed a contract with International Business Machines Corporation (IBM) through which IBM began including the Quick-

COMPANY PERSPECTIVES

Through a combination of discovery, acquisitions and execution, we bring an unprecedented product portfolio to life and the breadth of our customer relationships position our business to succeed. Bringing together ingenious technologies from mobile connectivity to managing media content mobility to managing mobile devices remotely, Smith Micro products enrich the experience people have with their computers, mobile devices and wireless networks.

Link Message Center on its personal computers (PCs). This software featured integrated data, fax, and voice capabilities.

When Smith Micro, in 1996, signed an exclusive contract with Motorola, Inc., to provide communications systems for Motorola modems, William Smith, according to a press release, said it created, "a foundation to grow our relationship with Motorola through new products currently under development at Smith Micro as well as potentially providing software to other Motorola business units." At that time, Motorola was one of the world's leading providers of wireless communications devices, including cellular phones and paging and data communication equipment. That same year, Smith Micro was selected as number 30 on the *Forbes* list of the 200 best small companies in the United States.

GROWTH AND TRANSITIONS: 1996–99

Smith Micro kept expanding its capabilities through strategic acquisitions. In 1996 it purchased Performance Computing, Inc., which subsequently became Smith's video products business unit. This deal added PC-based videoconferencing software for OEM producers, as well as programs for home and small business consumers, to the Smith Micro product line. In 1997, entering into the mobile communications market, it introduced HotPage wireless messaging software, which transmitted e-mail to pagers. CommSuite, announced in 1999, allowed video and sound clips to be added to e-mail messages.

The organization also continued to develop marketing partnerships, teaming with Vivitar, Brother, Ricoh, Intel, Panasonic, and others to bundle Smith Micro software with OEM devices. In 1998 Smith Micro expanded its international operations, appointing sales managers in Europe and Australia. The company launched new international versions of its software communications products in Europe, expanded its presence in Australia, and introduced its software in New Zealand. These steps allowed Smith Micro to address growing demand from OEMs, retail vendors, and Internet service providers.

In 1999 Smith Micro introduced WebCatalog Builder, an e-commerce software program developed to create an online store for small business users. After acquiring Pacific Coast Software, Inc., a developer and marketer of e-commerce products, Smith Micro announced the formation of its Internet Solutions Division. This move, according to CEO Smith, quoted in a company press release, allowed the company "to better allocate [its] resources toward the Internet market, which [had] become Smith Micro's primary focus."

FORMATION OF NEW DIVISION: 2000

Less than a year later, in March 2000, Smith Micro responded to a dwindling market for fax technology by expanding its vision and forming a Wireless and Broadband Division. With this new division, along with a previously established Macintosh Division, the company had a structure in place to respond to what it saw as the three areas of its business with the greatest growth potential: Macintosh users, the Internet, and wireless and broadband communications.

In August 2000 the company acquired TouchStone Software Corporation's line of CheckIt products. These award-winning technologies allowed users to optimize wireless broadband and dial-up connections, check PC performance, and uncover possible problems. By December, Smith Micro had introduced QuickLink Mobile 2000, a software program enabling wireless users to connect to the Internet using their phones.

In early 2001 Smith Micro reached an agreement with Verizon Wireless to develop software for Verizon's cellular phone network. Shortly afterward, the company contracted with TELUS Mobility, a leading provider of wireless voice, data, and Internet services in Canada, to supply wireless modem kits for its customers. These kits enabled mobile phones to function as wireless modems and thus connect laptop computers to the Internet. Through these and other initiatives, Smith Micro had begun to make significant inroads into the wireless marketplace.

Meanwhile, the company was maintaining its other products and services. It developed, shortly after the terrorist attacks against the United States on September 11, 2001, a patented, computer-based, motion-responsive

KEY DATES

1982: William W. Smith Jr. founds Smith Micro Software with an initial focus on modem and fax software.

1995: Company goes public with a listing on the NASDAQ.

2000: Wireless and Broadband Division is created.

2003: Smith Micro signs deal to provide the wireless Internet connection software for Verizon Wireless customers.

2005: Company acquires Allume Systems, Inc., producer of StuffIt software.

2009: Core Mobility, Inc., producer of mobile technology products, is acquired.

video security system. It also launched FAXstfX, a fast faxing system for Mac users, and WebDNA software, which enabled businesses to create and maintain an enterprise-wide Intranet, facilitating interaction and collaboration within a company.

In early 2003 Verizon International selected QuickLink to provide Internet access for its Latin American mobile phone users in Puerto Rico, Mexico, and Venezuela. Then, in August 2003, Verizon Wireless and Smith Micro finally signed their long anticipated contract, which called for Smith to provide the wireless Internet connection software for Verizon Wireless customers. In 2004 the deal was extended. This was, for Smith Micro, its largest wireless contract and one of the most substantial agreements in the company's history.

ALLIANCES AND EXPANSION CONTINUE

At the same time, as it continued to expand in the global wireless marketplace, Smith Micro formed an alliance with ipUnplugged of Sweden for sharing technology, support, and marketing aimed at improving Wi-Fi performance for millions of mobile computer users around the world. The partnership was expected to make transferring from one Wi-Fi hotspot to another seamless and secure, without any interruption to the user's session. Smith Micro also contracted to provide data connectivity accessory kits to Thuraya Satellite Telecommunications Company, a firm based in the United Arab Emirates, for their satellite phones. Thuraya's service covered Europe, the Middle East, South and Central Asia, North and Central Africa, and adjacent bodies of water. Smith Micro then made an

agreement with QHP Systems, Inc., a technology marketing firm, to sell Smith Micro products to Chinese wireless service providers and mobile phone and camera manufacturers.

By the end of 2003, Smith Micro's QuickLink Mobile had become the leading data connectivity product in the industry. It provided support for Bluetooth and Wi-Fi technology, and users were able to instantly access e-mail, surf the Internet, and connect to business Intranets, without cables or physical connections.

Smith Micro signed a contract, in August 2004, with Dobson Communications Corporation (operating a cellular network under the brand name Cellular One) to provide its communications software. Then, in July 2005, Smith Micro acquired Allume Systems, Inc., of Watsonville, California, for $10.6 million cash and $1.9 million in Smith Micro shares. This purchase gave Smith Micro title to Allume's StuffIt software, a state-of-the-art compression technology. Smith Micro viewed this addition as providing the company with the ability to significantly improve the multimedia capacities of its wireless products. That year Smith Micro signed an agreement with Alltel Corporation to provide QuickLink Mobile to Alltel's cellular customers. With this deal, the company had contracts with carriers maintaining a significant share of the North American wireless market.

Over the next several years, Smith Micro continued to expand its products and services through strategic acquisitions. In April 2006 the company purchased PhoTags, an Israeli technology firm that held a patent for Active Images software, which allowed users to send text, music, documents, links, images, and even videos in a single JPEG file (a commonly used method for storing and transmitting photo images).

In early 2007 Smith Micro bought Ecutel Systems, Inc., a provider of secure enterprise mobility software. Incorporating Ecutel functions into Smith Micro's QuickLink Mobility Enterprise software allowed business organizations to manage their servers, users, and devices from a handset, while providing mobile workers secure and easy access to their company's network. The company also purchased Insignia Solutions, plc, a developer of mobile device software and a key provider for mobile manufacturers around the world. This acquisition enhanced Smith Micro's product line and provided access to a developed global market. That July, Smith Micro acquired an Australian firm, busineSMS Software, whose products permitted users to share multimedia content both between mobile phones and between phones and computers. In January 2008 Smith Micro spent $59.7 million for the Mobility Solutions

Group of PCTEL, Inc., gaining a large range of innovative technologies used by wireless carriers, device manufacturers, network solution providers, and business customers.

INNOVATIONS AND SOFTWARE DEVELOPMENT

While expanding its wireless products and market, Smith Micro also continued to develop its other software lines. It acquired eFrontier America, Inc., in 2007 and subsequently integrated that company's graphic and animation programs into Smith Micro's software offerings. Among other 2007 developments, Smith Micro added a powerful file recovery tool, MediaRECOVER, to its product list; introduced software for identity protection; began marketing photo animation software; released CheckIt repair and performance programs for Macintosh computers; and launched Digital TV for PC software, which brought over 1,000 television channels directly to a computer without subscription or pay-per-view fees.

In 2006 Smith Micro introduced QuickLink Music, an intuitive, PC-based multimedia manager for mobile phones that later competed with applications available for Apple Inc.'s pioneering iPhone. Verizon became the first carrier to offer the Smith Micro music software on its phones. Soon contracts with other carriers added to the wide distribution of Smith Micro's mobile software, as it signed agreements with Mexico's Iusacell, Israel-based Pelephone, U.S. Cellular, and Sprint Nextel.

The economic recession in 2008 slowed Smith Micro's momentum somewhat, but by 2009 the company was, once again, expanding its product offerings, technological expertise, and customer base. In October 2009 it acquired Core Mobility, Inc., for $10 million cash and 700,000 shares of Smith Micro Stock. Core Mobility, based in Mountain View, California, added a range of mobile technology products, including synchronization software, visual voice mail, and push-to-talk software, to Smith Micro's array of offerings.

In late 2009 Smith Micro announced that Time Warner Cable Inc. had selected the company to provide the mobile connection management software for its wireless data service, serving 3G, 4G, Wi-Fi, and WiMAX networks. Smith Micro then signed an agreement to provide its software to Bouygues Telecom, one of the largest providers of mobile products and services in France. Selected for the Deloitte Technology Fast 500 list, which ranks the fastest-growing technology companies in North America, and as a finalist for several 2009 Macworld Awards, given for innovative and successful products, Smith Micro had clearly maintained its reputation for developing pioneering technology products and creating a dynamic and responsive business organization.

Grace Murphy

PRINCIPAL SUBSIDIARIES

Allume Systems, Inc.; Core Mobility, Inc.; STF Technologies, Inc.; Smith Micro Software LLC Belgrade (Serbia); Smith Micro Software AS (Norway); Smith Micro Software UK Limited; William W. Smith Software Canada, Ltd.

PRINCIPAL COMPETITORS

Cisco Systems, Inc.; Microsoft Corporation; Polycom, Inc.; Symantec Corporation; VocalTec Communications Ltd.

FURTHER READING

Gittelsohn, John, "Smith Micro Software Buys PCTEL Unit," *Orange County Register* (Santa Ana, CA), December 11, 2007.

Loudermilk, Stephen, "Smith Micro Aims at Fax Market with Acquisition of Cross," *PC Week*, March 1, 1993, p. 119.

"Smith Micro and Silicon Metrics Expand into China with Appointments of New Sales Partners," *China Business News*, February 20, 2003.

"Smith Micro Announces Contract with Motorola," *PR Newswire*, February 1, 1996.

"Smith Micro Announces Formation of New Internet Solutions Division," *PR Newswire*, September 15, 1999.

"Smith Micro Software Announces Agreement to Acquire Core Mobility," *Business Wire*, September 14, 2009.

"Smith Micro Software Earns Spot on Deloitte Technology Fast 500," *Wireless News*, November 3, 2009.

Smurfit Kappa Group

Smurfit Kappa Group plc

Beech Hill
Clonskeagh, Dublin 4
Ireland
Telephone: (+353 1) 202-7000
Fax: (+353 1) 269-4481
Web site: http://www.smurfitkappa.com

Public Company
Incorporated: 1934 as James Magee & Sons Ltd.
Employees: 40,000
Sales: EUR 6.06 billion ($8.73 billion) (2009)
Stock Exchanges: Irish London
Ticker Symbols: SK3; SKG
NAICS: 551112 Offices of Other Holding Companies;
    322110 Pulp Mills; 322121 Paper (Except
    Newsprint) Mills; 322130 Paperboard Mills;
    322211 Corrugated and Solid Fiber Box
    Manufacturing; 322222 Coated and Laminated
    Paper Manufacturing

■ ■ ■

Dublin-based Smurfit Kappa Group plc is a world
leader in paper-based packaging, specializing in the
manufacture of containerboard, corrugated containers,
and other paper-based products. With operations in
more than 30 countries worldwide, the group is
organized into four divisions: Paper Europe, Corrugated
Europe, Specialties, and Latin America. Paper Europe,
operating in 21 countries, includes paper mills and fiber
processing. The division's headquarters are in Paris,
which is also the site for all sales and marketing efforts

related to the containerboard mills. Its research and
development (R&D) activities are based in Sweden, and
the division also has a technological center in the
Netherlands.

Through a network of national and regional offices,
Corrugated Europe handles all of the group's corrugated
packaging and fulfillment operations in Europe, and it
also runs an R&D and technical center in the
Netherlands. The Specialties Division, based in the
Netherlands, produces niche-market packaging products,
such as paper bags and solid-board containers, for a
broad range of products, including produce, dairy items,
flowers, beverages, fish, and meat. The group's Latin
American regional operation, which is based in Miami,
Florida, is involved in forestry, paper, corrugated
container, and folding carton activities in nine Latin
American countries. Smurfit Kappa Group is the
product of the 2005 merger of two major competitors
in paper-based packaging: the Irish firm Jefferson
Smurfit Group plc and the Dutch company Kappa
Packaging.

EARLY HISTORY

The history of Jefferson Smurfit Group began with a
young man from England making good in Ireland. Jefferson Smurfit, the son of a shipyard worker, was born
in Sunderland, in northeast England, in 1909. His
father died when he was 10 years old. He became an apprentice salesman in a large department store at 14; he
once said that life had made him into a little old man
by that age.

COMPANY PERSPECTIVES

The Smurfit Kappa Group strives to be a customer-oriented, market-led company where the satisfaction of customers, the personal development of employees and respect for local communities and the environment are seen as being inseparable from the aim of optimising value for the shareholders.

In 1926 he accepted his uncle's offer of work in the tailoring business in St. Helens, Lancashire. Eight years later he moved to Belfast and opened his own tailoring business, James Magee & Sons Ltd., after marrying a local woman. The priest who conducted his wedding introduced him to the box-making business in Dublin. The priest had become involved with a factory there through one of his parishioners. The priest noticed Smurfit's keen business sense and asked the young man to act as an adviser. Smurfit saw the potential of the business and turned his attention to learning more about the technology of box making. Meanwhile the tailoring business was expanding rapidly, and soon Smurfit owned four shops. He acquired full control of the Dublin box-making factory in 1938 and poured more of his energies into that business, giving up his tailor's shops and moving permanently to Dublin.

After 1939, when World War II broke out in Europe, the materials for box making became much harder to find. Smurfit was able to keep his business going because he adapted the technology and his products to meet the demands of wartime. An example of this adaptation was the production of thick paper with straw in it for use in Irish schools. Because of the scarcity of paper and packaging during the war, Smurfit was able to capitalize on the overwhelming demand. The company concentrated on corrugated box production and had two papermaking machines working at full capacity. He had good relations with the trade unions and was proud that there were no strikes. By 1950 his Dublin factory was five times its initial size and producing eight times the original revenue. By this time, the company was known as Jefferson Smurfit & Sons Limited, a name adopted in 1942.

Smurfit's sons, Michael and Jefferson Jr., were soon brought into the business. Michael, the eldest of Jefferson Smurfit's four sons, started on the factory floor (in 1952), as Jefferson Jr. did later. Their father insisted that they join the appropriate union. Both went on to specialize, Jefferson Jr. in sales, Michael in company

administration. Michael then took the opportunity to continue studying management techniques in Canada and the United States. After completing his training he ran a corrugated box factory with another brother, Alan, in his father's hometown, St. Helens, returning to his father's company in 1966 as joint managing director with Jefferson Jr.

RAPID EXPANSION THROUGH ACQUISITIONS

The 1960s were a period of considerable expansion for the company. In 1964 Jefferson Smurfit & Sons became a public company quoted on the Dublin Stock Exchange. Smurfit acquired Temple Press Ltd., a manufacturer of cartons and boxes, in 1968, and then took its first steps outside its original area of business when, in 1969, it acquired Browne & Nolan Ltd., a printing, packaging, publishing, and educational supply company. The parent company was now large enough to be quoted on the International Stock Exchange in London. Jefferson Sr. realized that his son Michael should be given more incentive to stay with the company and not become a potential rival. In 1969 he was appointed deputy chairman just as the company began to look seriously at acquisitions beyond the United Kingdom. In 1970 the company doubled its size with the purchase of the Hely Group of companies, which were involved in radio and television distribution, educational and office supplies, and packaging. Also that year, the continuing expansion of the Smurfit businesses was symbolized in a change of name, to Jefferson Smurfit Group Limited. Michael Smurfit brought the corrugated box factory in St. Helens into the new group.

The group concentrated a great deal of effort at this time on its overseas expansion plans. It acquired the British carton-making and printing company W.J. Noble and Sons in 1972. A year later its purchase of the print and packaging division of the U.K. firm Tremletts Ltd. brought plants in the United Kingdom and in Nigeria into the group. The U.S. market, however, proved to be the most lucrative of its overseas ventures. Its 40 percent investment in the paper and plastic manufacturing firm Time Industries Inc. of Chicago, in 1974, gave it a foothold in the United States. It increased this initial investment to 100 percent in 1977.

Jefferson Smurfit Sr. died in 1977, at the age of 68. Michael succeeded him as chairman, and Jefferson Jr. took over as deputy chairman. Their younger brothers moved up too, Alan to head U.K. sales and Dermot Smurfit to become managing director of the paper and board division. Their father left them a company that was beginning to diversify and internationalize itself in

KEY DATES

1934: Jefferson Smurfit opens a tailoring business, James Magee & Sons Ltd.

1942: Company name is changed to Jefferson Smurfit & Sons Limited.

1964: Company goes public with a listing on the Dublin Stock Exchange.

1970: Size of company doubles with purchase of the Hely Group of companies; company is renamed Jefferson Smurfit Group Limited.

1994: Jefferson Smurfit Corporation (JSC), the group's U.S. arm, is taken public, with the group retaining a 46.5 percent stake; company acquires Cellulose du Pin, the paper and packaging unit of France's Compagnie de Saint-Gobain.

1998: JSC and Stone Container Corporation merge to form Smurfit-Stone Container Corporation (SSCC).

2002: Jefferson Smurfit is taken private by Madison Dearborn Partners, with the deal including the spinoff of the stake in SSCC to shareholders.

2003: Company acquires SSCC's European packaging operations.

2005: Jefferson Smurfit Group and Kappa Packaging merge to form Smurfit Kappa Group (SKG).

2007: SKG raises EUR 1.3 billion in an initial public offering, marking the company's return to the stock market.

earnest yet continuing to lay stress on its base in Jefferson Sr.'s adopted homeland.

In 1968 Jefferson Sr. had seen the acquisition of Temple Press as an act of faith in the future of the Irish economy. The new chairman did not abandon this faith. The group carried on investing in Ireland, by acquiring, for example, Irish Paper Sacks Ltd.; Goulding Industries Ltd., maker of plastic film and sacks; and half the equity of the Eagle Printing Company Ltd. The more companies Jefferson Smurfit acquired, the more raw materials it needed. It decided to sell 49 percent of its corrugated box interests in Ireland and the United Kingdom to the Swedish paper company Svenska Cellulosa Aktiebolaget in return for a guaranteed supply of kraft linerboard. The sale also provided cash for further expansion abroad. Jefferson Smurfit acquired 51 percent

of the Australian company Mistral Plastics Pty Ltd. in 1978. A year later, it paid $13 million for a 27 percent share of the Alton Box Board Company, based in Alton, Illinois. At the time this was the largest investment by an Irish company in the U.S. economy. This stake was increased to 51 percent five months later.

U.S. AND OTHER INVESTMENTS IN THE EIGHTIES

Jefferson Smurfit Group established itself as a major supplier of print and packaging in the United States in the 1980s. In Ireland it bought a small stake in the Woodfab group, the largest user of native timber and a significant presence in the Irish forestry sector. Smurfit saw its greatest potential, however, in the U.S. market, where tight restrictions on foreign ownership or investment were nonexistent. Smurfit's method, a relatively cautious one, was to purchase a minority holding of a U.S. company, observe its profits rising, and then move to 100 percent ownership. Thus the 27 percent holding in the Alton Box Board Company, acquired in 1979, formed the bridgehead for complete acquisition in 1981. In a variation on the same technique, Smurfit in 1982 formed a 50-50 joint venture to take over the packaging and graphic arts divisions of Diamond International, before buying out the partner's shares in 1983 to gain full control.

Clearly, the group's long-term strategy of becoming an international competitor was coming closer to realization, and Michael Smurfit was earning his reputation as a canny businessman. In 1983 shares in the U.S. wing of the group, the Jefferson Smurfit Corporation, were floated on the market, generating $46 million for further investment. The group then decided to expand into a new area of business, setting up a joint venture with Banque Paribas, known as Smurfit Paribas Bank Ltd. Jefferson Smurfit Jr. left the group in 1984, because of ill health, and his two younger brothers were appointed joint deputy chairmen. The following year, the 50th since the company's founding, was marked by re-registration as a public limited company.

After achieving considerable success in its purchases of packaging companies, Smurfit acquired the Publishers Paper Company, based in Oregon, in 1986. This company supplied newsprint to such well-known papers as the *Los Angeles Times*. It was renamed Smurfit Newsprint Corporation and continued to supply several newspapers. The same year, in its largest deal yet, Smurfit set up a joint venture with Morgan Stanley Leveraged Equity Fund to pay Mobil $1.2 billion for its subsidiary Container Corporation of America (CCA), which produced paperboard and packaging, and in 1987 it purchased outright the manufacturing operations of

CCA on the European continent and in Venezuela. The group thus more than doubled the value of its U.S. holdings and moved into manufacturing in mainland Europe for the first time.

The second half of 1987 was a difficult time for the Smurfit family. First, Jefferson Smurfit Jr. died at the age of 50. He had contributed a great deal to the group's expansion through his expertise in sales and marketing. Then, like many other companies, Smurfit lost an enormous amount of value in the stock market crash in October. The value of its shares fell by more than half but because demand for paper products remained steady it was just a question of riding out the storm.

PHILANTHROPY IN THE LATE EIGHTIES

In 1988 Dublin marked its millennium as a city, and Jefferson Smurfit Group, with its strong ties to the Irish capital, played a part in the celebrations by donating the Anna Livia Fountain in memory of Jefferson Smurfit Sr. Anna Livia, symbolizing the River Liffey flowing through the city to the sea, is a leading character in James Joyce's novel *Finnegans Wake*. The group also contributed to the restoration of the Mansion House, the residence of the Lord Mayor of Dublin, and sponsored a Millennium Science Scholarship, to be awarded to a doctoral student specializing in high technology.

Other Smurfit activities in 1988 included the establishment of Smurfit Natural Resources to continue its own private afforestation program in Ireland and the purchase of the Spanish packaging firm Industrial Cartonera, as well as 30 percent of Papelera Navarra, also based in Spain. Adding to these a 35 percent stake in Inpacsa, acquired in 1989, gave the group interests in 4 paper mills, 8 corrugated box plants, and 20 percent of the paper and packaging market in Spain.

In 1989 the group's publishing division grew with the launch of a new weekly newspaper, the *Irish Voice*, in the United States, where it also had an interest in the magazine *Irish America*. The *Irish Post* in the United Kingdom increased its circulation, and Smurfit Print in Ireland produced more computer manuals. In the United States, an industrial dispute at Smurfit Newsprint Corporation lasted more than seven months and cost the company about $25 million in profits. The group was also affected by lengthy strikes in the packaging industry in Italy.

During this same period, Latin American operations were slowly expanding. Smurfit Carton de Colombia and Smurfit de Venezuela put much effort into researching and developing the genetic enhancement of

eucalyptus trees. Researchers believed that eucalyptus trees could be harvested in five years rather than the normal eight years. This was done by clonal reproduction, producing the fastest-growing commercial trees in the world, from which a good-quality uniform pulp could be manufactured. The Colombian company also produced writing paper, using a mix of different species of hardwood found in the tropical forests. By 1989 Smurfit Latin America had substantially more than 20 percent of the paper and board market in Venezuela and Colombia. The Latin American companies in the group provided opportunities for further education to their employees. In Colombia, for example, the company offered training in farm and forest tending as well as elementary schooling for children in the rural areas near Smurfit timberland.

REORGANIZATION AND FURTHER EXPANSION

In 1989 the group made heavy use of junk bonds to restructure its U.S. operations, which had accounted for about 65 percent of its profits in 1988. A 50-50 joint venture between Jefferson Smurfit Group and the Morgan Stanley Leveraged Equity Fund created a new private holding company, SIBV/MS Holdings, for most of the group's subsidiaries in the United States. The reorganization, which included the repurchasing of the minority stake in Jefferson Smurfit Corporation that had been publicly held, generated $1.25 billion and boosted the value of the group's shares by 50 percent.

The group next decided to continue to expand north of the U.S. border, and it purchased 30 percent of PCL Industries Ltd., a Canadian company specializing in the conversion of plastics, with its own interests in the United States. The group also formed a partnership with the Canadian firm Tembec, Inc., to build a bleached lightweight coated mill in Quebec. Meanwhile, Smurfit International, the European division of the group, added to its operations the German company C.D. Haupt, a major paper-recycling mill, placing Smurfit in a strong position to profit from new opportunities in reunited Germany and in Eastern Europe. More Italian firms such as Ondulato Imolese, an integrated corrugated manufacturer, and Euronda, producer of corrugated cases and sheets, also joined the group.

By 1990 Jefferson Smurfit Group had established itself as the largest gatherer and consumer of wastepaper in the world, and it completed the purchase of Golden State Newsprint Co. Inc., which was renamed Smurfit Newsprint Corporation of California, and Pacific Recycling Co. Inc. As environmental awareness became commercially viable, the group began to build up its recycling division by acquiring several existing units and announcing its intention to invest in a newsprint production unit, using scrap paper, in New York State.

In the United States, as in Latin America, Smurfit tried to involve itself within the community. It provided special programs for its employees, such as training at the Smurfit Technical Institute, and sponsored young children in a literacy program in Fernandina Beach, Florida. In Ireland, too, some of the universities were endowed with chairs and financial support for academic projects, of which the leading example was the Michael Smurfit School of Business at University College, Dublin.

FURTHER DIVERSIFICATION

By the beginning of the 1990s Jefferson Smurfit Group was producing a diversity of goods, from presentation boxes for Waterford crystal to takeout pizza boxes, and it continued to diversify further. It formed Nokia Smurfit Ltd. in a joint venture with Nokia Consumer Electronics, a division of the Finnish company Oy Nokia Ab that distributed televisions, video recorders, and satellite equipment in Ireland. It bought back its 49 percent interest in Smurfit Corrugated Ireland from Svenska Cellulosa and bought another 24.5 percent of U.K. Corrugated, boosting its ownership to 50 percent. One of its subsidiaries in the United Kingdom bought Texboard, a manufacturer of paper tubes. The group aimed to extend its already diversified board manufacturing and conversion business. It also purchased another U.K. firm, Townsend Hook, a leading producer of corrugated paper cases and coated papers, which gave Smurfit more than 20 percent of the corrugated case industry in Britain.

In 1991 Jefferson Smurfit added to its recycling business with the acquisition of several French companies, such as Centre de Dechets Industriels Group, the second-largest wastepaper company in France, and the Compagnie Generale de Cartons Ondules, an integrated mill and converting operation. In addition, it bought the Lestrem Group, which specialized in manufacturing solid board, accounting for about 20 percent of the market in France. It also set up a new subsidiary, Smurfit France.

Jefferson Smurfit Group carried diversification still further by deciding to invest in the leisure business in Ireland. Its activities in this area included the RiverView Racquet and Fitness Club, the Waterford Castle Golf and Country Club, and the new development of the Kildare Hotel and Country Club.

MAJOR MID-NINETIES ACQUISITIONS IN EUROPE

In the mid-1990s Jefferson Smurfit turned to continental Europe for acquisitions, beginning with France. In a deal that doubled the company's European operations, Jefferson Smurfit in late 1994 purchased Cellulose du Pin, the paper and packaging unit of France's Compagnie de Saint-Gobain, for IEP 682 million ($1.02 billion). Cellulose du Pin brought with it operations in France, Italy, Spain, and Belgium and manufactured recycled paper, corrugated boxes, coated wood-free paper, and paper bags. Following the acquisition, Jefferson Smurfit assumed the top position in the European corrugated industry.

To help fund the purchase, the company turned to its U.S. operation, taking it public once again, with Jefferson Smurfit Corporation (JSC) reemerging as a public company. About IEP 155 million ($248 million) was raised through the offering, after which Jefferson Smurfit Group retained a 46.5 percent stake in JSC.

Additional European acquisitions quickly followed that of Cellulose du Pin. In May 1995 Jefferson Smurfit paid FRF 452 million for Les Papeteries du Limousin of France, an independent corrugated packaging firm with a capacity of 220,000 metric tons of recycled containerboard. The purchase enabled Jefferson Smurfit to cancel plans to build a new mill in France. The following month saw the company make its first move into Scandinavia, with the IEP 68 million ($109 million) purchase of a 29 percent stake in Munksjö AB, a Swedish producer of bleached pulp, specialty papers, and board. Also acquired in 1995 was a 27.5 percent stake in Austria-based Nettingsdorfer Beteilgungs AG, a producer of paper and board, with interests in corrugated container operations.

These 1995 moves, coupled with the 1994 acquisition of Cellulose du Pin, meant that Jefferson Smurfit had quadrupled its continental European operations in less than two years. Further, continental Europe had become the Jefferson Smurfit Group region generating the most revenue, surpassing the Ireland/U.K. region for the first time.

Always looking for new opportunities, Jefferson Smurfit made a few inroads into Asia in 1995. In May, Jefferson Smurfit Corporation formed a joint venture in China, which soon thereafter bought a controlling interest in a linerboard mill near Shanghai. In December, Jefferson Smurfit Group formed a joint venture, called Smurfit Toyo, with the New Toyo Group of Singapore. Smurfit Toyo planned initially to manufacture folding cartons in Singapore, Hong Kong, and China. Jefferson Smurfit's approach to Asia was clearly a cautious one, although the company had a long-term goal of being an important player in the region.

Jefferson Smurfit's pace of acquisition slowed in 1996 and 1997 as the industry entered another of its cyclical downturns complete with overcapacity and the concomitant depressed prices. Revenues and profits fell significantly both years. During 1997 the company did complete some smaller deals. It purchased majority ownership of two Argentine companies—Celulosa de Coronel Suarez, S.A., maker of paperboard, and Asindus, S.A., producer of corrugated cases—and acquired outright two German producers of corrugated boxes and board: Wellit GmbH Wellpapenfabrik and Schneverdinger Wellpappenwerk GmbH & Co. KG.

LATE-NINETIES CREATION OF SMURFIT-STONE CONTAINER

During 1998 Jefferson Smurfit engineered the merger of Jefferson Smurfit Corporation and Stone Container Corporation, creating Smurfit-Stone Container Corporation (SSCC). The $1.3 billion deal was completed in November 1998, with Smurfit-Stone emerging as the largest producer of containerboard in the United States. Just prior to the transaction's completion, Jefferson Smurfit Group purchased an additional 18 percent interest in JSC for $516 million. The group's overall interest in JSC translated into a 33 percent stake in Smurfit-Stone. Two months before this merger closed, Jefferson Smurfit Group purchased from JSC 50 percent of the Canadian corrugated-container maker MacMillan-Bathurst, which was renamed Smurfit-MBI. Also in 1998, Jefferson Smurfit increased its shareholding in Nettingsdorfer to 75 percent and divested Smurfit Condat, which operated a coated paper mill in France.

Integration issues related to SSCC dominated 1999. A key rationale behind the merger had been the opportunity to reduce capacity in the containerboard sector and thereby boost prices. By late 1999 Smurfit-Stone had shut down four of its plants and laid off about 1,700 workers, reducing the company's containerboard capacity by about 20 percent. This had the desired effect of boosting prices by early 2000. Smurfit-Stone also began selling off noncore assets in order to reduce a heavy debt burden it had inherited from Stone Container. Overall, Smurfit-Stone was aiming to slash annual operating costs by $350 million. Jefferson Smurfit was also busy paring noncore assets during 1999, divesting Smurfit Finance and, with its partner Banque Paribas, selling Smurfit Paribas Bank to Anglo Irish Bank Corporation plc.

In May 2000 SSCC spent $1.4 billion to acquire St. Laurent Paperboard Inc., a Canadian producer of specialty containerboard and graphics packaging. This reduced Jefferson Smurfit's stake in Smurfit-Stone to about 29.5 percent. From 2000 to early 2002, Jefferson Smurfit completed a number of acquisitions, most of which were centered in Europe and involved the company's core containerboard and corrugated container businesses. During 2000 the company acquired U.K.-based Norcor Holdings plc; Neopac A/S, which increased its market share in Denmark to 17 percent; and Fabrica Argentina de Carton Corrugado, which doubled its market share in Argentina to 13 percent. In December 2000 the company increased its holding in Nettingsdorfer to 100 percent. In February 2001 a 25 percent interest in Leefung-Asco Printers Limited was acquired, with this investment in a Hong Kong company viewed as an initial step toward securing a meaningful position in Asia. In the early months of 2002 Jefferson Smurfit also gained full control of Munksjö AB.

In early 2002 Michael Smurfit announced plans to step down as chief executive of the group later in the year but remain chairman. Smurfit by this time was a controversial figure. He was praised in some quarters, particularly overseas, as a paper industry visionary, focusing for years on the need to prevent or eliminate industry overcapacity and thereby prop up prices. Nevertheless, in his home country (or rather, former home country, given that he officially resided in Monaco for tax reasons), his image was that of an overpaid executive unresponsive to the shareholders in his public company, who considered the firm to be perpetually underperforming. Everyone agreed, however, that it was Michael Smurfit who had created the Jefferson Smurfit of the early 21st century, be that good or bad. Moreover, because of his retention of the chairmanship, there were doubts about who would be calling the shots after Smurfit handed the chief executive office over to Gary McGann. Promoted from the post of president and chief operations officer, McGann had joined Jefferson Smurfit only in 1998, having previously been the chief executive of Aer Lingus Limited, an airline owned by the Irish state. Selected to take over McGann's previous position was Michael Smurfit's son Tony, who had headed Smurfit Europe.

TAKEOVER BY MADISON DEARBORN: 2002

One of Jefferson Smurfit's persistent problems was that the minority stake it held in SSCC made it difficult for investors to determine the actual worth of the company, which tended to depress the share price of the company's stock. By early 2002, it appeared that the company was on the verge of selling the stake. Madison

Dearborn Partners, however, a Chicago-based private-equity investment firm that had previously made several investments in the paper and packaging industry, then approached Jefferson Smurfit about a possible takeover. In June, Jefferson Smurfit accepted a EUR 3.7 billion ($3.6 billion) takeover bid from Madison Dearborn, and the deal was completed three months later. As a key part of the deal the stake in SSCC was spun off to Jefferson Smurfit shareholders, who received one Smurfit-Stone share for every 16 shares of Jefferson Smurfit that they owned. The shareholders also received EUR 2.15 per share for the Jefferson Smurfit shares themselves. The top executives of the company, including Michael Smurfit and McGann, remained with the newly privatized Jefferson Smurfit. As a group, these managers had owned about 10 percent of the company, and from the proceeds they received from the takeover, they then repurchased about a 7 percent stake in the new company.

In its first major transaction since being taken private by Madison Dearborn, Jefferson Smurfit in March 2003 acquired SSCC's European packaging operations in exchange for EUR 185 million and its 50 percent share of Smurfit-MBI. This deal severed the final ties between Jefferson Smurfit Group and Smurfit-Stone Container while reuniting the group with some of the European packaging assets it had given up in the 2002 spin-off. The packaging operations, located in Germany, Belgium, and Spain, included 11 corrugated plants, 5 recycling facilities, 2 paperboard mills, and Europa Carton, one of Europe's largest producers of corrugated containers, thereby reestablishing Jefferson Smurfit Group's presence in the region.

In the first nine months of 2004, Jefferson Smurfit's sales increased only 1 percent to EUR 3.6 billion, with pretax profits dipping to EUR 15 million as market conditions weakened in the paper and packaging industry. In an effort to raise cash, the group divested a number of noncore assets, including the Swedish specialty paper business Munksjö, which was sold in March 2005 to a Swedish venture-capital firm for EUR 450 million ($593 million). In a further effort to streamline its operations and reduce costs, Jefferson Smurfit Group in January 2005 made the surprise decision to close its Dublin paper mill after 51 years of operation.

CREATION OF THE SMURFIT KAPPA GROUP: 2005

In December 2005 Jefferson Smurfit Group and Kappa Packaging, based in Eindhoven, Netherlands, merged to create Smurfit Kappa Group Limited (SKG), which immediately ranked as the world's leading maker of cor-

rugated packaging. The merging companies had combined to generate 2004 revenues of EUR 7.6 billion ($10.3 billion). SKG was initially headed by Michael Smurfit as chairman and Kappa's CEO, Frits Beurskens, as deputy chairman, with Gary McGann serving as CEO and Tony Smurfit assuming the position of president and COO. On completion of the merger, Smurfit Kappa was jointly owned by Madison Dearborn Partners, Cinven Limited, CVC Capital Partners, and the management.

SKG, which had operations in over 20 European countries and 9 nations in Latin America, recorded a net loss during the first nine months of 2006. As it entered 2007, SKG was planning an initial public offering (IPO) to pay down debts. In what turned out to be Ireland's largest IPO in nearly eight years, the March 2007 flotation raised EUR 1.3 billion ($1.7 billion) and marked the company's return to the stock market, as Smurfit Kappa Group plc, after a five-year absence. Madison Dearborn, Cinven, and CVC Capital remained major shareholders with combined ownership of 45 percent. Shortly after the IPO, Michael Smurfit retired, and Sean Fitzpatrick, nonexecutive chairman of Allied Irish Bank Corporation plc, was named the new chairman.

In the first six months of 2007, SKG saw profits rise 40 percent to $341 million, while sales increased 3.6 percent to $2.4 billion. In addition, the group's stock had risen 14 percent since the IPO, with SKG valued at $5.8 billion. In 2008 market conditions continued to worsen throughout the industry, and SKG countered this downturn by permanently closing its less-efficient containerboard mill in Valladolid, Spain. This was followed in 2009 by the closure of the group's containerboard mill in Štúrovo, Slovakia.

The corrugated and containerboard business continued to decline through the first half of 2009 but the food and beverage packaging sectors remained strong, giving SKG extra leverage with its Specialties Division. Some within the industry were concerned about new, more-efficient containerboard machines that were slated to be introduced by the end of 2010 from such competitors as Mondi plc, Prowell Gruppe, and W. Hamburger GmbH. Undaunted, SKG viewed this potential threat as a business opportunity, announcing in January 2010 that it was in negotiations with Mondi to acquire its U.K.-based corrugated operations in exchange for SKG's European bag-converting operations.

The group turned in a better performance in 2009 than analysts had expected given the depressed market. Although earnings before interest, taxes, depreciation, and amortization had fallen from EUR 941 million in

2008 to EUR 741 million in 2009, and revenues decreased by 14 percent to EUR 6.06 billion ($8.73 billion), SKG still managed to reduce its debt by 4 percent. In a February 2010 interview with Joe Brennan of the *Irish Independent*, McGann admitted that because of a price increase of EUR 90 per ton on containerboard, a material used in the production of corrugated boxes, SKG was forced to pass on the cost to its customers for the first time since 2007. McGann acknowledged that the recession posed numerous challenges but SKG's objective was to maintain a strong cash flow and "recover our own increased costs, built up over the past few years."

Monique Lamontagne
Updated, David E. Salamie; Marie O'Sullivan

PRINCIPAL SUBSIDIARIES

Carton de Colombia, S.A. (70%); Carton de Venezuela, S.A. (88%); Grupo Smurfit Mexico, S.A. de C.V.; Smurfit Kappa Kraftliner AB (Sweden); Smurfit Kappa Nederland B.V. (Netherlands); Nettingsdorfer Papierfabrik AG & Co KG (Austria); Smurfit Kappa de Argentina, S.A.; Smurfit Kappa Treasury Funding Limited; Smurfit Kappa Deutschland GmbH (Germany); Smurfit International B.V. (Netherlands); Smurfit Kappa B.V. (Netherlands); Smurfit Kappa Participations SAS (France); Smurfit Kappa Investments UK Limited; Smurfit Kappa Ireland Limited; Smurfit Kappa Nervion, S.A. (Spain); Smurfit Kappa Holdings Italia, S.p.A. (Italy).

PRINCIPAL DIVISIONS

Paper; Corrugated; Specialties; Latin America.

PRINCIPAL COMPETITORS

DS Smith Plc; International Paper Company; Mondi plc; S.A. Industrias Celulosa Aragonesa; Svenska Cellulosa Aktiebolaget SCA.

FURTHER READING

Barrington, Kathleen, "Michael Smurfit: He Hasn't Gone Away, You Know," *Sunday Business Post* (Dublin), February 10, 2002.

Brennan, Joe, "Smurfit Kappa Earnings Fall 21pc," *Irish Independent* (Dublin), February 11, 2010.

Brown, John Murray, "Topsy-Turvy Ride Has Soft Landing," *Financial Times*, June 18, 2002, p. 27.

Jefferson Smurfit Group, 1934–1984: 50th Anniversary, Glenageary, Ireland: Irish Business Magazine, 1984, 128 p.

"JSG and Kappa Plan Merger," *Official Board Markets*, September 17, 2005, pp. 1+.

Kenny, Jim, "Jefferson Smurfit Sets Its Sights on a New Future," *Solutions—for People, Processes, and Paper*, February 2003, pp. 26+.

"SK's McGann Expresses Frustration," *Official Board Markets*, August 25, 2007, pp. 1+.

"Smurfit Jumps 8pc on Back of Demand Surge," *Irish Independent* (Dublin), March 16, 2007, p. 26.

Urry, Maggie, "A Story of Success That Turned to Excess," *Financial Times*, May 3, 2002, p. 23.

Speedway Motorsports, Inc.

5555 Concord Parkway South
Concord, North Carolina 28027
U.S.A.
Telephone: (704) 455-3239
Fax: (704) 455-2168
Web site: http://www.speedwaymotorsports.com

Public Company
Incorporated: 1994
Employees: 1,114
Sales: $611 million (2008)
Stock Exchanges: New York
Ticker Symbol: TRK
NAICS: 711212 Racetracks; 339932 Game, Toy, and
Children's Vehicle Manufacturing

∎∎∎

Speedway Motorsports, Inc. (SMI), is a leading promoter, marketer, and sponsor of motorsports entertainment in the United States, operating eight racetracks that host dozens of events sanctioned by the National Association for Stock Car Auto Racing (NASCAR). Speedway Motorsports also sponsors its own racing series called the Legends Car Racing Circuit, which features 5/8-scale vehicles that the company manufactures and sells to amateur racing enthusiasts. The company operates a joint venture in motorsports merchandising with its major competitor, International Speedway Corporation.

Speedway Motorsports is the product of founder O. Bruton Smith's aggressive attempt to develop the largest racetrack operation in the country. Smith began with Charlotte Motor Speedway and added Atlanta Motor Speedway in 1990, Bristol Motor Speedway and Sears Point Raceway in 1996, Texas Motor Speedway in 1997, and Las Vegas Motor Speedway in 1999. The firm acquired New Hampshire Motor Speedway in 2007 and Kentucky Speedway a year later. Smith owns a 67 percent share of SMI, presiding as chairman and chief executive officer of the company.

ORIGINS

Although Speedway Motorsports was not founded until 1994, the legacy of the organization stretches back to the early career of the company's founder, O. Bruton Smith. Smith trained as a professional race-car driver and began promoting races at small dirt tracks in his native North Carolina during the 1950s. In 1959 he formed Charlotte Motor Speedway (CMS) with the goal of building the region's premier racetrack facility. He broke ground on the ambitious project, but it failed due to lack of funding. By 1961 CMS had begun bankruptcy proceedings.

Smith relocated to Illinois, where he embarked on a career as a car dealer, developing his Town & Country Ford Inc. into a lucrative business that eventually ranked as the sixth-largest dealership chain in the United States. Smith used the substantial cash he accumulated with Town & Country Ford to buy back shares in CMS. By 1975 he owned nearly all of the racetrack stock and became CMS's new chief executive officer. H. A. "Humpy" Wheeler joined CMS in 1975 and in 1976 was named general manager. Together, Smith and

COMPANY PERSPECTIVES

Debuting on Wall Street in February 1995, Speedway Motorsports, Inc., became the first motorsports company to be publicly traded on the New York Stock Exchange. The Company has continuously pursued a successful five pronged business strategy. This business strategy includes enhancing and improving the speedway facilities, maximizing broadcast and sponsorship exposure, increasing the daily usage of the facilities, growing 600 Racing, Performance Racing Network, zMax, and looking for new opportunities for additional motorsports facilities through construction or acquisition.

Wheeler developed the North Carolina company into stock car racing's largest racetrack operator.

Smith's reemergence into the arena of stock car racing occurred at a pivotal point in the sport's history. Since its inception stock car racing had been a local and regional pursuit populated by drivers who generally owned their own teams and raced on privately owned tracks, attracting little national following. The dynamics of the sport changed radically in the 1970s, however, transforming stock car racing into a multibillion-dollar business.

The growth of the sport from its rural Southeastern beginnings to its modern dimensions as a national phenomenon was aided by the formation of the National Association for Stock Car Auto Racing (NASCAR) in 1947, and by several developments that coincided with Smith's return to CMS. During the mid-1970s tobacco giant R. J. Reynolds began funneling vast sums of sponsorship money into stock car racing, providing a financial foundation for the sport's future growth. Then in 1979 network television began airing NASCAR races live, introducing the sport to viewers across the country. Smith's presence in the industry was another vital key to the growth of the sport. Smith was willing to stake everything he had on grandiose projects, believing that massive, luxuriant facilities were central to stock car racing's, and his own, success.

ACQUISITIONS AND GROWTH: 1990–94

Smith's reputation as a risk taker was cemented during the 1990s, a decade of prolific growth for stock car racing. Smith first began developing a portfolio of speedway properties in 1990. He positioned himself in the vanguard of the industry's growth with the acquisition of Atlanta Motor Speedway (AMS), his second racetrack. Smith constructed additional grandstand seating at AMS, added luxury suites, improved concession facilities, and, demonstrating his far-reaching vision of stock car racing's potential, developed condominiums that overlooked the track. Smith's goal was to control a number of speedways near large metropolitan markets, each capable of seating legions of spectators and offering a breadth of conveniences and luxury services.

Smith counted on his speedways being awarded popular NASCAR-sanctioned events, and none was more coveted than the NASCAR Winston Cup Series (known since 2007 as the Sprint Cup). As the popularity of stock car racing grew during the 1990s, so too did the revenue-generating potential of hosting a Winston Cup race, which by itself could guarantee profitability for a racetrack. Smith, as he made his first advance on the acquisition front, endeavored to create racing facilities that, in consideration of their size and proximity to large markets, could not be denied the opportunity to host Winston Cup events. Toward this end, Smith aggressively pursued the expansion of his stock car racing holdings, convinced that massive investment in the sport would be substantiated by its widespread appeal.

1992 marked the debut of nighttime racing at CMS, which was the first speedway in the country to offer nighttime races. That same year the company developed the Legends Car Racing Circuit, giving aficionados of stock car racing the chance to race in scale-model versions of cars driven by early NASCAR drivers. Smith's company manufactured and sold the cars and developed a racing calendar through a subsidiary named 600 Racing. The move into amateur racing proved successful, creating a meaningful tributary of revenue ($5.7 million by 1994 and $10.9 million by 1998).

GOING PUBLIC

Smith formed Speedway Motorsports Inc. (SMI) in December 1994. In February 1995 SMI became the first company in its industry to offer shares of stock to the public, with a $68 million initial public offering (IPO). H. A. Wheeler, who served as president and chief operating officer of Speedway Motorsports, explained the decision to take the company public in a March 30, 1997, interview with the *St. Louis Post-Dispatch*: "What we saw was that NASCAR was heading into a strong power curve. We felt there would be a 10–12-year period of strong growth and we needed the capital to take advantage of it." Speedway Motorsports stock

KEY DATES

1959: O. Bruton Smith forms Charlotte Motor Speedway.
1990: Smith acquires Atlanta Motor Speedway.
1992: Smith develops the Legends Car Racing Circuit.
1994: Speedway Motorsports is incorporated.
1996: Bristol Motor Speedway and Sears Point Raceway are acquired.
1997: Texas Motor Speedway opens.
1999: Las Vegas Motor Speedway is acquired; naming rights to Charlotte Motor Speedway are sold to Lowe's Companies Inc.
2005: Speedway Motorsports and International Speedway collaborate in Motorsports Authentics, a joint motorsports merchandising venture.
2007: SMI acquires New Hampshire International Speedway.
2008: zMAX Dragway opens in Concord, North Carolina; SMI acquires Kentucky Speedway; Smith's son Marcus Smith is promoted to chief operating officer and president of the company.

debuted at $18 per share, marking the beginning of a frenetic period of growth for the company.

Speedway Motorsports' IPO touched off a trend in the industry, as Smith's competitors followed his lead into the public spotlight. Within a year, Dover Downs Entertainment, Grand Prix Association of Long Beach, and Penske Motorsports had all gone public. International Speedway Corporation (ISC) of Daytona Beach, Florida, also began as a publically traded company in 1996, and became Smith's closest competitor.

The rivalry between Speedway Motorsports and International Speedway was intriguing, a competitive battle that still necessitated a display of diplomacy by each company: the France family, who founded and controlled International Speedway, also founded and controlled NASCAR, the organization that awarded the all-important Winston Cup events to racetrack operators and upon whose beneficence Smith's fortunes rested.

The contrast between the two companies was emphasized by their corporate personalities. Speedway Motorsports was a risk-taking company, assuming an ag-

gressive and ambitious posture that it got from Smith. International Speedway, on the other hand, inherited the legacy of NASCAR, making the company far more cautious and conservative in its expansion strategy. Speedway Motorsports would build a 150,000-seat facility in a large market, banking on drawing a capacity crowd, while International Speedway erected smaller facilities in smaller markets with the goal of nurturing stock car racing's development. H. A. Wheeler, in a June 28, 1999, interview with *Knight-Ridder/Tribune Business News*, explained the differences between the two companies succinctly, remarking, "Our first priority is to build a company, and theirs is to build a sport."

CONTINUED EXPANSION

In 1996 Smith used the proceeds from the 1995 IPO to acquire two racing facilities: Bristol Motor Speedway, located in Bristol, Tennessee, and Sears Point Raceway, located near San Francisco. The following year the company built Texas Motor Speedway, a $250 million facility that seated 150,000 spectators, twice the capacity of the new racetracks International Speedway was building at the time. Some observers were shocked by Smith's audacity in building a massive complex in uncharted territory for stock car racing, but the popularity of the sport and the increasing revenue it was generating bore out his vision.

By the late 1990s stock car racing was the fastest growing sport, and the largest spectator sport, in the country. The Winston Cup races drew more than 6.1 million spectators in 1997, and an additional 123 million viewers watched the races on television. Each Winston Cup race generated between $60 million and $80 million in revenue and attracted crowds ranging between 100,000 and 150,000. Sales of NASCAR-licensed products reached $900 million, up from $80 million in 1990. During this meteoric rise Speedway Motorsports increased its total seating capacity from 176,000 in 1993 to 551,000 by 1998, and saw a threefold increase in ticket revenues.

Smith, whose racetracks hosted 9 of the 35 Winston Cup Series events in 1997, had positioned Speedway Motorsports to take advantage of the sport's enormous growth, remaining one step ahead of stock car racing's unexpected surge in popularity. Speedway Motorsports led the industry as the largest racetrack owner in the United States, eclipsing International Speedway and the industry's third-ranking contender, Penske Motorsports.

Smith furthered his reputation as an industry pioneer with the 1999 acquisition of Las Vegas Motor Speedway. He paid $215 million for the Nevada racetrack, outbidding International Speedway. In March 1999 Smith surprised the industry when he announced a first in stock car racing's history, selling naming and marketing rights at Charlotte Motor Speedway to home improvement retailer Lowe's Companies Inc. for $35 million. Marcus Smith, Bruton Smith's son, was instrumental in securing the agreement, which sent a shock wave through the industry.

In May 1999 International Speedway made an aggressive move by acquiring the industry's third-largest racetrack owner, Penske Motorsports. The $623 million deal dealt a blow to Smith's Speedway Motorsports, unseating the company from its number-one position in the industry. Smith's acquisitions had given Speedway Motorsports major facilities in three of the nation's top-ten markets, but the Penske acquisition greatly enlarged ISC's geographic coverage in markets both large and small and positioned the NASCAR owner for national growth.

LOOKING FOR AN OPENING

In 2005 Speedway Motorsports and International Speedway suspended their competition to pursue the lucrative side business of motorsports merchandising. Their joint enterprise, called Motorsports Authentics, purchased the assets of two leading companies, Team Caliber and Action Performance, which gave them majority control of the vast market for motorsports merchandise. Their products included apparel, die-cast replica cars, and a full line of novelties bearing logos of well-known drivers and teams.

Bruton Smith's next major venture was the development of a short-track drag racing strip near his Charlotte, North Carolina, flagship property. The plan drew opposition from the surrounding community because of noise concerns, which was overcome when Smith threatened to relocate his lucrative Lowe's Motor Speedway to another area. The new facility, zMAX Dragway, opened in Concord, North Carolina, in 2008.

In November 2007 Speedway Motorsports announced its first major track purchase in nearly a decade, acquiring the New Hampshire International Speedway in Loudon, New Hampshire. The track, rebranded the New Hampshire Motor Speedway, was already New England's NASCAR center, hosting annual events that included a Sprint Cup race. The acquisition gave SMI access to Boston's top-10 market and helped diversify its geographical presence.

In May 2008 the company agreed to purchase its eighth major facility, Kentucky Speedway in Sparta, Kentucky, in the heart of NASCAR's original fan base. A day before the deal was made public, H. A. Wheeler

announced his retirement from Speedway Motorsports and Lowe's Motor Speedway. To replace the legendary racing promoter, octogenarian Bruton Smith named his son Marcus president of both SMI and Lowe's.

Despite these new projects, the recession that began in 2008 cut into Speedway Motorsports' bottom line. Ticket sales, revenue, and profits were down in the first half of 2009. In August Lowe's announced it would terminate its naming agreement with Charlotte Motor Speedway, which reverted back to its original name. Speedway Motorsports cut staff and reduced ticket prices in an effort to keep the fans coming to the track. Despite NASCAR's ever-increasing popularity, the Motorsports Authentics merchandising venture failed to turn a profit in three of its first four years of operation.

Jeffrey L. Covell
Updated, Roger K. Smith

PRINCIPAL SUBSIDIARIES

Atlanta Motor Speedway Inc.; Bristol Motor Speedway Inc.; Charlotte Motor Speedway Inc.; Las Vegas Motor Speedway LLC; SPR Acquisition Corporation (d/b/a Infineon Raceway); Texas Motor Speedway Inc.; New Hampshire Motor Speedway; Kentucky Speedway; SMI Properties; Oil-Chem Research Corporation; Performance Racing Network; 600 Racing; U.S. Legend Cars International; INEX Corporation; Speedway World; Speedway Systems LLC; Speedway Funding Corporation; Sonoma Funding Corporation; Motorsports Authentics (50%).

PRINCIPAL COMPETITORS

International Speedway Corporation; Dover Motorsports Inc.

FURTHER READING

Aim, Richard, "Texas Motor Speedway Owner Sells Naming Rights to North Carolina Track," *Knight-Ridder/Tribune Business News*, February 10, 1999.

Long, Dustin, "Kentucky Could Get 2011 Cup Race," *Roanoke Times*, December 12, 2009.

Macur, Juliet, "Charlotte, N.C.-based Speedway Company Races to No. 1 in Industry," *Knight-Ridder/Tribune Business News*, June 28, 1999.

Mulhern, Mike, "Smith Buys Kentucky Speedway," *Winston-Salem Journal*, May 23, 2008.

Neelakantan, Shailaja, "Racing for Dollars," *Forbes*, December 16, 1996, p. 14.

"New NASCAR Has Fewer Track Owners," *St. Louis Post-*

Dispatch, March 30, 1997, p. 13F.

Spiegal, Peter, "Life in the Fast Lane," *Forbes*, November 1, 1999, p. 86.

Veverka, Amber, "Concord, N.C.-based Speedway Firm Sees Deals for Texas, Atlanta Tracks," *Knight-Ridder/Tribune Business News*, February 9, 1999.

Young, Lindsey, "Atlanta Date May Be Smith's Best Vegas Bet," *Chattanooga Times/Free Press*, March 15, 2009.

Teck

Teck Resources Limited

—■—

Bentall 5, 550 Burrard Street, Suite 3300
Vancouver, British Columbia V6C 0B3
Canada
Telephone: (604) 699-4000
Fax: (604) 699-4750
Web site: http://www.teck.com

Public Company
Incorporated: 1913 as Teck-Hughes Gold Mines Limited
Employees: 8,000 (est.)
Sales: CAD 7.67 billion ($7.36 billion) (2009)
Stock Exchanges: New York Toronto
Ticker Symbol: TCK (New York); TCK.A, TCK.B (Toronto)
NAICS: 211111 Crude Petroleum and Natural Gas Extraction; 212113 Anthracite Mining; 212221 Gold Ore Mining; 212222 Silver Ore Mining; 212231 Lead Ore and Zinc Ore Mining; 212234 Copper Ore and Nickel Ore Mining; 325199 All Other Basic Organic Chemical Manufacturing; 331492 Secondary Smelting, Refining, and Alloying of Nonferrous Metal (except Copper and Aluminum); 335911 Storage Battery Manufacturing

■ ■ ■

Teck Resources Limited is one of the world's leading diversified mine development and operating companies, producing gold, silver, copper, zinc, niobium, and metallurgical coal. Over the years, Teck's mining operations have extended across the globe, with the company overseeing major exploration projects in Australia,

Argentina, Bolivia, Brazil, Canada, Central Asia, Chile, Indonesia, Mexico, Panama, Peru, the United States, Venezuela, and West Africa. In addition to its mineral and coal operations, Teck Resources is also involved in oil exploration in Canada, holding a 20 percent stake in the Forest Hills Oil Sands Project. Originally founded in 1913, the present incarnation of Teck Resources was formed in 2001, when the Teck Corporation merged with Cominco Ltd.

THE RISE OF GOLD EXPLORATION IN WESTERN CANADA: 1896–1960

In 1896 gold was discovered in the Yukon Territory at Bonanza Creek by prospector George Washington Carmack. The following July two steamers carried Yukon prospectors and gold valued at over $1.2 million into the ports of Seattle and San Francisco, a groundbreaking event that opened the famous Klondike Gold Rush of the 1890s. Within two years thousands of men and women trekked north, inspired by dreams of mining their fortunes. Some were more fortunate than the majority, forming businesses that grew and prospered. Such was the case with the Yukon Consolidated Gold Corporation (YCGC). Formed in 1923, Yukon Consolidated Gold would eventually grow to become the largest operator in the area. Between 1932 and 1966, YCGC produced 1.7 million ounces of gold, all from the rich river gravels. In later years, YCGC became part of Teck Corporation through a 1978 amalgamation actuated by Norman Keevil.

Norman Keevil, father of the 1990s Teck Corporation President and CEO Norman B. Keevil, began operating as a copper miner when he started the Temagami Mining Company, Ltd., following the discovery of high-grade copper deposits in Ontario's Lake Temagami region. After purchasing several mining operations and merging with others, Keevil eventually formed Teck Corporation. Teck was derived from the Teck-Hughes Gold Mines Limited at Kirkland Lake, Ontario, an operation that had been created in 1913. At that time Teck-Hughes was a relatively small company with a few small gold mines.

GROWTH OF A MINING DEVELOPMENT COMPANY: 1960–90

Keevil's son, Norman B. Keevil, began working for Toronto-based Teck-Hughes Gold Mines Ltd. in 1962. The younger Keevil shared his father's interest in geology, according to David Berman in *Canadian Business*, but planned "to pursue a career in academia and actually accepted a job in the geology and geophysics department of a U.S. university." After half a dozen or so refusals to his father's request that he join Teck, the younger Keevil finally relented. Under his youthful and ambitious direction, the company moved its base to Vancouver, British Columbia, where it grew into a substantial mining development company and began a new phase of rapid expansion. Norman B. Keevil was appointed president and CEO in 1981.

Jewelry fabrication was the largest commercial use for gold, (one of Teck's principal products) and usually accounted for about 25 percent of the company's revenues. In 1980 Teck developed a placer gold operation around the area of the Klondike Gold Rush near Dawson City, Yukon Territory. Digging and scraping was conducted adjacent to an area that was mined by dredging between the years 1914 and 1921. Due to its location in the permafrost-zone, the harsh climate

dictated that the operation was seasonal. During the mining season, the surface operation used large tractors and scrapers to mine 800,000 cubic yards per year, resulting in 210,000 cubic yards of pay gravel that was washed through a sluice box. On average, 23 people were employed to produce approximately 7,000 ounces of gold per season, making the Klondike Placer Gold Mine one of the largest and most successful alluvial mining operations in the Yukon.

During this time, the David Bell Mine was discovered by David Bell in 1981. Teck managed the development and construction of the mine in the Hemlo Gold camp of Northern Ontario. According to company reports, the mine was developed through a 1,160-meter production shaft, and mining was done by process of longhold stoping (working a step-like part of a mine where ore is being extracted) with delayed cemented hydraulic backfill. The mill used a two-stage grinding circuit, employing semi-autogenous grinding and ball milling. Gold was recovered from solution using carbon in pulp. The gold was recovered from carbon by pressure stripping and was then electrowon (or electroextracted) from strip solution. Cathodes were smelted to produce doré bullion. Homestake Mining Company shared a 50 percent joint venture interest in the Bell Mine project.

By the end of the decade, the Williams Gold Mine was the largest gold mine in Canada, producing 450,000 ounces of gold per year. In 1989 the Supreme Court of Canada upheld a 1986 Supreme Court of Ontario judgment awarding the Williams Gold Mine to Teck and its 50 percent joint venture partner, Corona Corporation, which would later become the Homestake Mining Company. Teck's experienced management resulted in reductions in operating costs of 20 percent per ton, while increasing throughput by 1,000 tons per day. The facility operated the largest gold milling plant in Canada, using semi-autogenous grinding and a gold recovery circuit that was later expanded to produce 6,000 tons per day.

EXPANSION AND JOINT VENTURES IN THE EARLY NINETIES

As a means of balancing the volatile gold market and supply fluctuations, Teck began expanding into the major production of base metal products in the 1990s. In 1991 the Metall Mining Corporation (a Toronto-based subsidiary of Metallgesellschaft AG of Frankfurt, Germany) traded most of its holdings in Cominco Ltd. to MIM Holdings Ltd. (an Australian metals and coal producer) and Teck Corporation in a stock transfer worth about $170 million. At the same time, Metall

KEY DATES

1896: George Washington Carmack discovers gold at Bonanza Creek in the Yukon Territory.

1906: Consolidated Mining and Smelting Company (Cominco) is formed.

1913: Teck-Hughes Gold Mines Limited is founded in Kirkland Lake, Ontario.

1923: Yukon Consolidated Gold Corporation is formed.

1978: Yukon Consolidated Gold merges with Teck Corporation.

1981: Norman B. Keevil becomes president and CEO of Teck Corp.

1986: Teck Corporation purchases shares in Cominco Ltd.

2001: Teck Corporation merges with Cominco Ltd., forming Teck Cominco Ltd.

2009: Company changes name to Teck Resources Limited.

strengthened its holdings in MIM and Teck with the intention of pursuing joint-venture base metal projects that were being considered by those companies. Metall acquired 3.7 million shares of Teck's Class A and Class B stock, increasing its Teck holdings to 14.1 percent.

Metall's strategy was to streamline its investments by having one strategic investment in North America and one in the Pacific Rim area, because those areas were considered to be the main mining areas in the world. It also valued Teck and MIM as successful and reliable joint-venture partners. Cominco was the world's largest zinc concentrate producer with its Red Dog, Sullivan, and Polaris mines and would later become the third-largest refined zinc producer with its Trail zinc and lead operation and its Cajamarquilla zinc refinery in Peru. After the 1995 acquisition of the Cajamarquilla refinery, Cominco worked to steadily increase its production of zinc.

Cominco was also a significant producer of copper, a substance that was used primarily in electrical wires. Cominco's copper holdings mainly included its 50 percent interest in Highland Valley Copper and its 47.25 percent interest in the Quebrada Blanca copper mine in Chile. Norman B. Keevil explained to Edward Worden in *American Metal Market* that the Quebrada Blanca Mine's extraction and electrowinning operation would be "bypassing the smelting and refining charges which have been escalating considerably in recent years."

Worden reported that the state-owned Empresa Nacional de Minería retained a 10 percent interest in the project, while Sociedad Minera Pudahuel Ltda y Cia held a 5 percent carried interest in exchange for the use of its patented leaching technology.

Teck reported that 1991 profits declined 59 percent compared with 1990 figures, which was an occurrence attributed to lower metal prices and lower gold production. In the following year, Teck bought over 15 percent of Arauco Resources Corp., a two-year-old junior exploration company that had recently gone public. The company had numerous gold mining prospects in Chile, plus five copper prospects in Argentina. Teck also increased its share in Pacific Sentinel Gold Corp., a Vancouver exploration company.

Teck and Cominco jointly ran an extensive exploration project in Chile. The joint venture built up a very large property inventory in the high Andes and the coastal copper belts of northern Chile. During this period, Cominco was reporting substantial losses, partly attributed to the company's nickel smelting operations, which were shut down for several months. Thus, Teck also reported losses related to its 22 percent equity interest in Cominco.

In addition to diversification, a continual search for resource development locations remained critical to Teck's future profitability. The company managed an exploration team and a business development team to discover, identify, and acquire reserves that would potentially become operating mines. Teck's early explorations traditionally concentrated on Canadian sites, but the company became increasingly active internationally as it began to exhaust Canadian options. New exploration opportunities were discovered outside of North America, and offices were established in Singapore, Mexico, Peru, Panama, and Chile. The company began planning for further expansion into nearly every country in South America.

VOISEY BAY DISCOVERY: 1993

One of the most important mineral discoveries of the century in Canada was the Voisey Bay nickel deposit in Labrador. Vancouver-based Diamond Fields Resources Inc. had discovered the huge deposit almost by accident and later maintained the majority interest in the mining project. The deposit was found by two prospectors who stumbled across it in 1993. They were looking for diamonds on behalf of their company and had almost given up at the end of their three-month search. After surveying a 15,000-square-mile area, they were heading home by helicopter when they spotted a gossan (an exposed rock formation that can signal an ore deposit) and took samples that were found to be filled with copper sulfide. In addition to nickel, the site contained substantial amounts of copper and cobalt, with high-grade ore reserve estimates of approximately 25 million metric tons. Annual production was estimated to be 100 million pounds of nickel and 60 million pounds of copper. The site was especially attractive due to its high grades of ore and its proximity to the surface, which was expected to cut normal production costs in half.

More than 20 major mining companies expressed interest in participating in the Voisey Bay enterprise. Teck paid $108 million for a 10.4 percent stake in Diamond Fields. Then, due to Teck's experience with open-pit mines, Diamond Fields Resources awarded Teck the approximately $1.5 million contract to conduct a feasibility study "to address mining and concentrate production, power and water supplies, repair facilities and roads, among other things," according to Craig Schiffer in an August 31, 1995, *American Metal Market* article. It was estimated that total annual revenues of $288 million and a cash flow of $216 million could be expected from the site. Production was scheduled to begin in approximately late 1999, pending successful negotiations with both governmental entities and the Innuit and Innu Tribes, whose traditional hunting grounds and fisheries were located in the coastal waters off Voisey Bay.

FOCUSING ON THE ENVIRONMENT: THE LATE NINETIES

One of the great challenges facing the mining industry has always been to minimize environmental damage. Teck reported that it had adopted a philosophy of prevention, rather than reaction: Environmental concerns were addressed throughout the entire process in order to avoid problems instead of solving them later. The company has claimed that it tries to emphasize "local concerns and values, environmental conditions, the mining and milling methods used, and techniques for pollution prevention and reclamation technologies." Teck reported that its overall environmental performance at its operations sites continued to be excellent in 1997, with greater than 98.5 percent compliance for effluent water quality. At the company's Williams/David Bell tailings basin, a water transfer system was established to pump water from the basin into a polishing pond to eliminate the need for cyanide treatment. This also allowed the mines to control ammonia levels and to reduce the concentrations of contaminates. Environmental management teams were established to investigate opportunities for recycling at all operations, including the recycling of oil, batteries, scrap metal, paper, and hazardous waste.

Despite the company's prevention efforts, two spills occurred in 1997. One took place at Teck's Quyintette operation, due to the failure of a decant pipe on a newly constructed sediment pond. The result was the spill of approximately 800,000 cubic meters of nontoxic sediment-laden pond water into the Murray River. The other occurred at the Tarmoola operation in Australia, when a feed line to the tailings (residue) pond burst, releasing 150 tons of tailings. Cleanup was implemented and corrective steps undertaken to prevent future occurrences.

Near the end of the 1990s approximately 44 percent of Teck's total revenues came from the production of coal, which accounted for $50 million of the company's total mine operating profit in 1997. Its coal operations included the Elkview Mine (located in southeastern British Columbia), the Bullmoose Mine (located in northeastern British Columbia), and the Quintette Mine (also located in northeastern British Columbia). A Coal Task Force was established in 1997 to seek coal development opportunities in Canada and in other locations around the globe. The Task Force began by targeting government representatives, mine operators, investment bankers, and coal property owners for discussion about operating within their various countries. The Task Force also began investigating methods of working with other coal producers in Canada for the purpose of improving the structure of transportation, port, and sales operations.

Also in 1997 the discovery of a massive sulfide deposit in Zacatecas State, Mexico, indicated reserves of copper, zinc, gold, and silver that could be of potential value to Teck following further drilling and metallurgical testing. The company's net interest in the discovery was 52.5 percent. Teck was also involved in a Colorado-based chemical pilot plant for the purpose of converting titanium concentrate to commercial-grade pigment. A 1998 feasibility study was conducted to determine its viability. The site contains the largest titanium resource known to be located in North America.

Teck implemented other promising base-metal explorations in 1998 in Argentina, Chile, and Mexico, as well as in the Bathurst district of New Brunswick. The company's other investments included a 25 percent share interest in Golden Knight Resources, which holds an interest in the Tarkwa gold mine under construction in Ghana, and a 42 percent interest in Camelot Resources NL, an Australian company that shares a joint-venture with Teck in the Tarmoola gold mine in Western Australia and the Northern Territory. These and other recent investments were valued at approximately $89 million.

Prices for most metals were volatile near the end of the 1990s, with gold suffering the largest decline when its price dropped from $369 to $288 per ounce in 1997 alone. Teck reports indicated that the gold decline was influenced less by consumption than by the policies of central banks. Gold prices were expected to recover, although it was thought that the practice of forward selling (promising a product to customers and accepting payment before the product was actually available) could moderate the amount of recovery.

Facing weak metal prices, Teck reviewed its expenditure levels, including the cost of exploration and capital spending at the mines. It was decided that the development of the Lobo-Marte, Nuteck, and Petaquilla projects would be deferred. Furthermore, the Klondike placer operation was permanently shut down after the 1997 season, as was the Afton copper mine. The company remained in strong financial condition as it neared the 21st century, and Teck was optimistic about its potential to increase production at its other facilities.

THE TECK-COMINCO MERGER: 1999 AND BEYOND

In April 1999 Teck acquired more than a million additional shares in Cominco Ltd., increasing its overall stake in the company to more than 40 percent. The stock purchase came at a time when Teck was enduring a prolonged downturn in its coal business. The slump was caused primarily by decreased demand from Japanese steel companies, combined with increased competition from coal producers in Australia. In the second quarter of 1999, Teck's coal operations shipped roughly 588,000 tons of coal, compared with 1.1 million tons for the same period in 1998. Cominco, meanwhile, was enjoying rapid growth during this period, based largely on increased output from its zinc operations. For the third quarter of 1999, Cominco posted net earnings of CAD 31 million ($20.88 million).

By early 2000 Teck had increased its stake in Cominco to 44 percent, prompting some analysts to speculate that the companies might be heading toward an eventual merger. While Cominco continued its swift ascent, Teck's core businesses continued to struggle. In March 2000 Teck announced it would be forced to shut down its Quinette coal mine in August 2000, three years ahead of schedule. In the eyes of many observers, the announcement signified a dark day for the Canadian coal industry. Writing in the *National Post* on March 2, 2000, Drew Hasselback dubbed the Quinette operations "the cornerstone of the coal industry in northeastern British Columbia."

By mid-2000 Teck had increased its stake in Cominco once again, purchasing four million additional shares for roughly CAD 100 million ($67.28 million). With the transaction, Teck now controlled 50.1 percent of Cominco. The increased investment quickly proved to be a shrewd one: For the year 2000, Teck's profits rose to CAD 85 million ($57.29 million), driven largely by Cominco's continued strong performance. In April 2001 Teck launched a bid to acquire all outstanding shares in Cominco in a deal worth roughly CAD 1.46 billion ($947 million). Upon completion of the merger, the new company, Teck Cominco Ltd., became the fourth-largest mining concern on the continent.

In 2003 Teck Cominco entered a strategic alliance with two of its principal rivals. In a deal worth CAD 1.83 billion ($1.18 billion), Teck joined Fording Inc. and the Luscar Energy Partnership to create the Fording Canadian Coal Trust, a joint venture that consolidated the three companies' existing coal operations in the Elk Valley region of British Columbia. By combining their existing mines into a single entity, the companies aimed to increase efficiency and productivity while achieving cost savings in the neighborhood of CAD 50 million ($32.34 million). With the completion of the deal, the companies together became the second-largest metallurgical coal exporters in the world, accounting for 20 percent of the global supply.

In October 2008, as worldwide demand for natural resources reached its peak, Teck Cominco increased its ownership in the Fording Canadian Coal Trust to 100 percent, in a deal worth CAD 14 billion ($12 billion). Upon completing the acquisition, the new, wholly owned entity was renamed Teck Coal Limited. The takeover proved to be ill-timed, however, as the worldwide economy slipped into a deep recession later that fall, and Teck Cominco suddenly found itself CAD 11.66 ($10 billion) in debt. By January 2009 the company was compelled to cut its coal output by 20 percent in the face of declining demand, notably within the global steel industry. Faced with this decrease in operating revenues, the company was forced to sell off a number of its assets, including the majority of its gold-mining operations.

In April 2009, as it grappled with its financial struggles, Teck Cominco changed its name to Teck Resources Limited. By the middle of the year, Teck was forced to seek help from outside investors to save itself from insolvency. In July of that year, Chinese sovereign wealth fund China Investment Corporation invested CAD 1.7 billion ($1.63 billion) in Teck in exchange for 17 percent ownership in the company. By the end of the month the global demand for coal and zinc began to rebound, and the company found itself boosting production significantly. By December, Teck Resources was forecasting a 25 percent increase in coal production in 2010. Once on the brink of disaster, Teck Resources had managed to escape the global downturn relatively unscathed and was well positioned for further growth heading into the new decade.

Terri Mozzone
Updated, Stephen Meyer

PRINCIPAL SUBSIDIARIES

Compañia Minera Carmen de Andacollo (Chile); Compañia Minera Quebrada Blanca S.A. (Chile); Teck Alaska Incorporated (U.S.); Teck American Incorporated (U.S.); Teck Coal Limited; Teck Highland Valley Copper Partnership; Teck Metals Ltd.

PRINCIPAL COMPETITORS

Freeport-McMoRan Copper & Gold Inc.; Newmont Mining Corporation; Nyrstar NV; Rio Tinto Limited; Southern Copper Corporation.

FURTHER READING

Berman, David, "Mission: Excellence," *Canadian Business*, December 1996, p. 71.

Caney, Derek, J., "Comineo Resources Incurs C$5.1 M 3rd-qtr. Loss," *American Metal Market*, November 5, 1993, p. 7.

Dunn, Brian, "Voisey Bay Discovery Looms Larger by the Minute; Among Biggest Nickel, Copper, and Cobalt Finds," *American Metal Market*, May 2, 1995, p. 2.

Hasselback, Drew, "Teck Shuts B.C.'s Quintette Mine Early: $1.5B on Projects," *National Post* (Canada), March 2, 2000, p. C1.

Hoffman, Andy, "A Crushing Debt … an Astonishing Revival: Teck CEO Don Lindsay's Whirlwind Series of Deals, Asset Sales and Financings Saved Miner from Collapse," *Globe and Mail* (Toronto), January 1, 2010, p. B3.

Kennedy, Peter, and Wendy Stueck, "Cominco Merger 'Logical,' Teck CEO Says," *Globe and Mail* (Toronto), April 27, 2001, p. B7.

"Lobo-Marte Gold Project Planned," *American Metal Market*, December 9, 1996, p. 5.

"Metall Acquires Teck Corp. Shares," *American Metal Market*, July 5, 1993, p. 8.

Mumford, Christopher, "Metall Boosting MIM, Teck Stake via Stock Swap," *American Metal Market*, October 18, 1991, p. 1.

Schiffer, Craig, "Teck Chosen for Voisey Bay Study," *American Metal Market*, August 31, 1995, p. 2.

Worden, Edward, "Teck Links Up with Comineo to Develop Quebrada Blanca," *American Metal Market*, December 9, 1991, p. 2.

Tenet Healthcare Corporation

———————————■———————————

1445 Ross Avenue
Dallas, Texas 75202
U.S.A.
Telephone: (469) 893-2000
Fax: (469) 893-8600
Web site: http://www.tenethealth.com

Public Company
Incorporated: 1968 as National Medical Enterprises, Inc.
Employees: 60,297
Sales: $8.6 billion (2008)
Stock Exchanges: New York
Ticker Symbol: THC
NAICS: 622110 General Medical and Surgical Hospitals; 622210 Psychiatric and Substance Abuse Hospitals; 622310 Specialty (except Psychiatric and Substance Abuse) Hospitals; 623110 Nursing Care Facilities

■ ■ ■

Tenet Healthcare Corporation, formerly National Medical Enterprises, is one of the largest investor-owned health-care delivery systems in the United States. Through its subsidiaries the company owns or operates 49 acute-care hospitals in 12 states and 57 outpatient facilities in 11 states. These facilities offer a broad range of medical services and support regional health-care networks designed to provide communities with a full complement of care.

Over more than four decades, Tenet has continually adjusted its strategies to accommodate a rapidly chang-

ing market. Beginning as National Medical Enterprises (NME), the company spent its first decade building and acquiring medical facilities and related services. Industry changes during the mid-1980s prompted NME to shift its emphasis from acute-care to specialty hospitals. The company's Specialty Hospital Group, a division consisting of psychiatric, substance-abuse, and rehabilitation services, was NME's major strength in the late 1980s. After a damaging scandal in the early 1990s, however, NME sold off its specialty facilities, reconfiguring itself as Tenet and resuming its focus on acute-care facilities. Although the new company realized surging profits in the late 1990s, it was mired in scandal again by the end of 2002.

GROWTH AND DIVERSIFICATION: 1968–79

NME's founder and CEO, Richard K. Eamer, had degrees in accounting and law. Cofounders Leonard Cohen and John Bedrosian were also attorneys. Eamer's interest in the enterprise was piqued by his own work as a financial consultant and hospital attorney. In 1968 he joined forces with Cohen and Bedrosian, although the company is often dated to 1969, when NME acquired its first hospitals in California (four general and three convalescent) and offered public stock. That same year NME also purchased a medical office building and three potential building sites.

The building, owning, and operating of numerous hospitals allowed NME to develop cost-cutting skills. Attention to both cost management and physician input became trademarks as NME concentrated on building

COMPANY PERSPECTIVES

At Tenet, our business is health care. Our mission is to improve the quality of life for every patient who enters our doors.

Quality is at the core of everything we do and every decision we make. Quality is the reason our patients and physicians choose us, and we seek relationships with those who place a high value on quality. Our approach to quality makes us unique and defines our future.

As we seek to improve the quality of our patients' lives, we are guided by four core values. Integrity: we manage our business with integrity and the highest ethical standards. Service: We have a culture of service that values teamwork and focuses on the needs of others. Innovation: We have a culture of innovation that creates new solutions for our patients, physicians, and employees. Transparency: We operate with transparency by measuring our results and sharing them with others.

services around community hospitals. Interest in efficiency also led to NME's early diversification into hospital equipment and supplies, a hospital-consulting firm, and even a construction company that specialized in building hospitals. In the early 1970s the focus was on growth. The company launched seven construction projects in 1971, in addition to another hospital purchase, and had tripled in size within a year. In 1973 NME took its first steps outside of California by acquiring a general hospital in Seattle, Washington, and by building another in El Paso, Texas.

By this time the hospital-management and cost-cutting techniques of NME were already being hired out. NME had both domestic and international divisions to oversee management services provided to other hospitals by 1974. Management of non-NME-owned hospitals and health care–equipment rental were significant income sources during the company's growth years.

Throughout this period the central concept was to profit from cost-efficient, well-managed hospitals that satisfied both doctors and patients. NME applied standard business practices in its health-care ventures. As Eamer told *Forbes*, "In many ways, running a hospital chain is like operating a hotel or retail chain." The first

decade was devoted to building a diversified, multifacility hospital company with an eye on market needs. These efforts culminated in the 1979 purchases of Medfield Corporation and the Hillhaven Corporation. Medfield added five Florida-based hospitals, including one psychiatric institution, to NME. Hillhaven, based in Tacoma, Washington, was the nation's third-largest chain of nursing homes.

By the end of 1979, NME was the nation's fourth-largest publicly owned hospital chain, with the majority of its revenues coming from acute-care hospitals. These two major acquisitions presaged the new decade's changes. Up until this point NME, like the rest of the hospital industry, operated with an eye to the Medicare and Medicaid legislation passed in 1965, which assured reimbursement for medical care of the poor, disabled, and elderly. This assurance spawned enormous growth in the investor-owned hospital industry, a growth that in turn eventuated problems of reimbursement.

SHIFTING FOCUS FROM ACUTE-CARE HOSPITALS TO SPECIALTY FACILITIES: 1980–84

NME began to shift focus from acute-care hospitals to alternative facilities, such as nursing homes, and to develop its products-and-services segment, which included health care–equipment rental for home use and visiting-nurses agencies before the reimbursement problem became widespread. In addition, management-services contracts were booming. In 1980 NME signed a five-year, $150 million contract with Saudi Arabia to help develop health-care facilities in that country. More international contracts came in 1981, and by the end of that year NME had more than $1 billion in sales.

The health-care business was the second-largest industry in the United States during the early 1980s, second only to food and agriculture. In 1982 NME acquired National Health Enterprises, whose 66 additional long-term care facilities made NME the nation's second-largest nursing home owner. In order to better manage its own size, NME subdivided into four operating groups: international (largely consultant work), hospital, nursing homes, and medical products and services. In 1983 NME bought the Psychiatric Institutes of America (PIA), one of the nation's largest mental-health-care providers, based in Washington, D.C.

From 1981 to 1983 corporate revenues doubled. Entry into the private psychiatric industry allowed NME to profit from a sector whose size doubled every two years throughout the 1980s. In 1983 NME further streamlined its specialty interests by forming Recovery Centers of America (RCA), a subsidiary comprising

KEY DATES

1968: Richard K. Eamer, Leonard Cohen, and John Bedrosian found National Medical Enterprises (NME).

1969: NME acquires its first hospitals in California and goes public.

1983: NME forms Recovery Centers of America (RCA), a subsidiary comprising substance-abuse-recovery operations.

1990: NME spins off its long-term care facilities and related operations as the Hillhaven Corporation.

1995: Name is changed to Tenet Healthcare Corporation.

2006: The U.S. Department of Justice fines Tenet $900 million to settle charges of fraudulent Medicare billing and business practices.

2007: Tenet sells Alvarado Hospital Medical Center in San Diego, California, as part of a civil settlement resolving allegations of financial misconduct.

2008: Tenet establishes Conifer Health Solutions, a wholly owned subsidiary, to offer management services to hospitals outside the Tenet network.

substance-abuse-recovery operations.

By 1984 the hospital business had begun a decline, the result of overexpansion and of cost-containment efforts by both government and private health-care interest groups. NME continued to look to what it considered more stable and promising medical service alternatives. These included its equipment leasing and home-care services and even extended to health insurance and a Miami-based health maintenance organization (HMO) acquired in 1984.

RESTRUCTURING: 1985–90

By 1985 NME was the second-largest publicly owned health-care services company in the nation, but changes within the industry mandated adjustments and restructuring. The following year NME sold its recent HMO purchase, as well as a number of unprofitable outpatient clinics and acute-care hospitals. Emphasis was placed on the specialty facilities, especially rehabilitation and substance-abuse centers and psychiatric hospitals, in an effort to bypass nonpayment problems by shifting

away from Medicaid- or Medicare-dependent services. The Rehab Hospital Services Corporation (RHSC) of Pennsylvania had been merged with NME in 1985 for this purpose. The company also began developing academic medical center strategies.

As the industry, and NME's stock, wobbled in the late 1980s, the company concentrated on internal reorganization instead of expansion. Restructuring produced the new subdivisions of hospitals, specialty hospitals, long-term care, and retail services in 1986. NME also continued divesting the acute-care hospitals hit by the drop in occupancy rates, shorter stays, and other results of the health-care cost-containment squeeze. Within one year the company had unloaded a quarter of its businesses, including 10 acute-care hospitals. Many other hospitals were converted to specialty services. NME's specialty hospitals division (consisting of PIA, RHSC, and RCA) became the company's new core business and growth field. NME's specialty hospitals supplanted the acute-care hospitals, which had accounted for 90 percent of NME's revenues in 1969, and in 1990 NME spun off its long-term care facilities and related operations as the Hillhaven Corporation.

NME retained a 14 percent equity interest in Hillhaven, and the parent company expected this change to help it avoid the short-term challenges created by health-care legislation and the recompensation crackdown. At that time Medicaid accounted for 50 percent of Hillhaven's revenues, but less than 3 percent of the specialty hospitals division's revenues and less than 6 percent of the general hospitals division's revenues.

Because government programs had not kept pace with the rising cost of health care while private insurance rates had, NME began to focus on services that were less dependent on Medicare and Medicaid. With this safeguard and the steady growth in specialty-services industries in the late 1980s, NME seemed to have found its niche.

Still one of the nation's largest health-care providers, NME held fast to its policy of high-quality, cost-effective care. By concentrating on specialty services such as psychiatric, rehabilitative, and substance-abuse recovery and by limiting itself to profitable acute-care hospitals, NME seemed well positioned to ride out the changes in U.S. health care.

SCANDAL: 1990–94

By 1991, under Eamer's leadership, NME had more than tripled the number of psychiatric facilities it operated. Of the company's $578 million in operating profits that year, profits from psychiatric care accounted for 40 percent. As a major scandal concerning NME's psychiatric hospitals erupted, however, this specialty division brought the company to the brink of ruin.

The trouble began in 1991 when the Texas attorney general sued NME for alleged overbilling practices at its psychiatric facilities in that state. Allegations of wrongdoing were compounded that year, as individual patients began to accuse NME of having held them in psychiatric facilities against their will, only releasing them when their insurance coverage was exhausted. Eventually more than 130 patient suits would be filed.

In the summer of 1992, 19 insurance companies, including Metropolitan Life, Aetna, Prudential, and Mutual of Omaha, some of the biggest providers in the country, filed suit accusing NME of an elaborate program of insurance fraud, beginning as early as 1988, whereby NME admitted tens of thousands of patients who did not need inpatient care, paying illegal kickbacks to referring physicians, fabricating diagnoses, and charging exorbitant fees to treat them. At its peak the cost of the fraud was estimated at $750 million.

Although NME would not comment on any of its patient treatment, citing confidentiality restrictions, the company took decisive steps to mitigate the damage of the scandal. In the spring of 1993, amid rumors that the company was facing potential bankruptcy, founders and top executives Richard Eamer and Leonard Cohen were ousted, along with four other board members.

Jeffrey C. Barbakow, former chief executive and president of MGM/UA Communications Company, took over as president and CEO of NME. Barbakow was committed to lifting the company out of its legal quagmire, but his already difficult task was compounded as NME became a primary target of the Clinton administration's new initiative to crack down on health insurance fraud. In August 1993 some 600 FBI and other federal agents raided NME's headquarters and 11 of its psychiatric facilities, seizing hundreds of documents as part of an investigation into possible criminal misconduct. To his credit Barbakow insisted on full cooperation with the investigations.

The scandals significantly damaged NME's finances as well as its reputation, as operating profits from the psychiatric division fell from $234 million in 1991 to just $3 million in 1993. As for the cost of putting the past behind, by the end of 1993 settlements with only a few of the insurance companies in question had already topped $125 million. Moreover, after spending nearly $65 million in legal fees, NME pled guilty to felony federal charges in 1994 and agreed to pay $379 million to the Justice Department and the Department of Health and Human Services, the largest settlement to

that date in history between the U.S. government and a health-care provider. To offset the cost of these settlements and to excise the source of corruption from its corporate identity, NME sold off all but 10 of its 81 psychiatric facilities for about $200 million in 1994. Also that year NME sold off 73 rehabilitation hospitals and clinics for $260 million, laying the groundwork for a radical refocusing away from specialty facilities and back to the acute-care business.

RECOVERY: 1994–2001

Late in 1994, amid other dramatic consolidations in the health-care industry, NME acquired American Medical Holdings in a $3.3 billion deal, more than doubling its presence in U.S. hospitals. Together the companies would operate 84 acute-care hospitals with annual revenue in excess of $5.3 billion and become the second-largest hospital chain in the country, behind the significantly larger Columbia/HCA Healthcare Corporation. By combining operations the companies expected to realize a $60 million reduction in annual costs and other significant efficiencies. NME completed its makeover in May 1995 by reincarnating itself as Tenet Healthcare Corporation, a name that was meant to reflect the company's new, rigorously principled approach to business. Analysts were pleased with the company's cleanup efforts and projected renewed vitality for Tenet.

Tenet's performance improved significantly. Determined to remain large enough to compete with and fend off acquisition from Columbia/HCA, the company sold off its international operations, especially in Asia and Australia, to finance growth in its core U.S. market. The key to success, according to Barbakow, was to concentrate on regional markets where Tenet could create solid networks of hospitals and physicians. Tenet enjoyed a dominant presence in the southern California market and sought to establish similar positions in south Florida, Louisiana, and Texas, as well as in the Philadelphia area. Strength in regional markets enabled Tenet to exert significant pricing pressure. In addition the company increased its focus on the most lucrative fields of medicine, including cardiology, neurology, and orthopedics. By 2001 Tenet owned 111 hospitals in the United States, and profits were soaring.

NEW WAVES OF SCANDAL

Barbakow hardly had the opportunity to enjoy his success, however, before Tenet was beset by a new wave of scandals that called into question its management, billing, and diagnostic practices. In November 2002 federal agents seized documents at the Redding Medical Center in northern California, one of Tenet's. best-performing hospitals, where the director of cardiology and the chairman of cardiac surgery were suspected of performing 25 to 50 percent of their surgeries unnecessarily. While Tenet stressed that it did not participate in doctors' decisions to perform surgery, the allegations nonetheless raised serious questions about Tenet's aggressive pricing strategies and its hospital management practices.

The next month scrutiny of Tenet intensified when another of its facilities, the Alvarado Hospital Medical Center in San Diego, California, came under investigation for possible violations of anti-kickback laws. Tenet's stock value plummeted 70 percent in just two weeks. At the end of December, trading of its shares was halted altogether due to the investigations.

A third federal inquiry was launched in January 2003, when Tenet received a subpoena demanding documents from company headquarters and 19 of its hospitals, dating from January 1997 to the present. The U.S. Justice Department subsequently filed a $323 lawsuit that same month alleging that Tenet had amassed $115 million in false Medicare claims. Also in January 2003 Tenet changed the billing practices it used when charging the Medicare program for above-standard or unusually expensive patient treatment, so-called "outlier" payments. These abrupt changes to billing practices caused Tenet revenue to decline precipitously beginning in early 2003.

In May 2003 Jeffrey C. Barbakow resigned as CEO and was replaced by Tenet president Trevor Fetter. In early August 2003 Tenet reached a settlement agreement with the U.S. Department of Justice and California authorities regarding charges that two doctors at Redding Medical Center in northern California had performed unnecessary cardiac procedures and surgeries in an attempt to increase their billing revenue. Tenet admitted no wrongdoing, but the $54 million settlement ended the federal and state government criminal investigations.

Beginning in January 2004 federal subpoenas were issued for records related to business and financial practices at Tenet-owned hospitals in Texas, Florida, Louisiana, California, and Missouri.

RELOCATIONS AND SETTLEMENTS

In the first half of 2004, Tenet relocated its corporate headquarters from Santa Barbara, California, to Dallas, Texas. Described by CEO Trevor Fetter to the *New York Times* as a cost-cutting move that would streamline company operations, the relocation was financed by the sale of the company's previous headquarters in Santa Barbara, California.

During the fall of 2004, Tenet raised further capital by selling a total of ten hospitals in two states in quick succession. It began by selling three hospitals in Massachusetts to Nashville-based Vanguard Healthcare Systems, Inc., for a total of $126.7 million. In late September, Tenet went on to sell three more hospitals in Inglewood and Marina del Rey, California, to Centinela Freeman Health System. In November 2004 Tenet sold an additional four hospitals in Orange County, California, to Integrated Healthcare Holdings, Inc., of Costa Mesa, California, for a net purchase price of $70 million.

In May 2005 a short article in *Forbes* magazine reported that Tenet stock had slowly risen as it began to recover from scandals earlier in the decade. Tenet continued to predict another unprofitable year, however, in 2005.

In June 2006 the U.S. Department of Justice fined Tenet $900 million to settle charges dating from 2003 that Tenet had falsified claims for Medicare patients who required above-standard or unusually expensive care, provided illegal kickbacks to physicians to refer Medicare patients to Tenet-owned hospitals, and used illegal medical billing codes to defraud the Medicare program. The settlement amount was estimated to be one-fourth of Tenet's stock market value. The settlement did not include a finding that Tenet had broken any law. Company CEO Trevor Fetter admitted in a statement that "some of this company's past actions did not measure up to the high standards that we have imposed on ourselves." The settlement, to be paid over four years, ended investigations by federal authorities into Tenet billing practices in California, Missouri, Louisiana, Tennessee, and Texas.

SALES AGREEMENTS

Later in the summer of 2006, Tenet agreed to sell three of its New Orleans hospitals (Kenner Regional Medical Center, Meadowcrest Hospital, and Memorial Medical Center) to Ochsner Health System.

The University of Southern California (USC) filed suit against Tenet in State Superior Court in Los Angeles in August 2006 in an attempt to terminate Tenet's lease and operating agreement for USC hospitals. The suit cited "material difficulties that Tenet [had] brought upon itself" along with related cuts in financial support for the hospitals. According to an August 23 article in the *New York Times*, the university stated it had filed suit to "protect its reputation and that of its doctors." In November 2007 Tenet filed a counterclaim against USC seeking monetary damages in response to the lawsuit.

In January 2007 Tenet sold Alvarado Hospital Medical Center in San Diego, California, as part of a civil settlement with the U.S. Attorney's Office in San Diego and the U.S. Department of Health and Human Services. The settlement had resolved allegations dating from 2002 that Tenet had paid physicians illegal kickbacks to refer their Medicare patients for treatment at Alvarado.

In April 2008 Tenet reached an agreement with USC and signed a letter of intent to sell the university USC University Hospital and USC Norris Cancer Hospital, two of the best known hospitals in the Tenet network. Also in the spring of 2008, Tenet negotiated with Health Care Property Investors, Inc., (HCP) to divest itself of interest in two other California hospitals, including Irvine Regional Hospital and Medical Center. The deals left Tenet with nine hospitals in the state of California.

The End of a Decade

In November 2008 Tenet formed a new subsidiary, Conifer Health Solutions, to offer revenue-cycle management and clinical communication services to hospitals outside its network.

By the end of 2009 Tenet appeared to have survived the scandals of the early part of the decade and the national and international economic crises of the preceding two years. In 2008 Tenet facilities admitted 530,303 patients and responded to 3.8 million outpatient visits over the course of the calendar year. Tenet made available 13,149 licensed beds the following year. By the fall of 2009 strong third-quarter results allowed Tenet to raise its outlook for the year to a new range of $900 million to $950 million from a previously anticipated $810 million to $875 million. Company CEO Trevor Fetter attributed the raise to favorable trends in "payer and patient mix, bad debt expense, and volume growth."

Carol I. Keeley
Updated, Erin Brown; Joyce Helena Brusin

PRINCIPAL SUBSIDIARIES

Tenet HealthSystem Medical, Inc.; Conifer Health Solutions, Inc.

PRINCIPAL COMPETITORS

Universal Health Services, Inc.; Health Management Associates, Inc.; Community Health Systems, Inc.; LifePoint Hospitals, Inc.; Ascension Health; HCA Inc.

FURTHER READING

Abelson, Reed, "Tenet Promises to Take Steps to Reassure Investors," *New York Times*, December 20, 2002, p. C1.

Abelson, Reed, and Andrew Pollack, "More Scrutiny for Big Chain of Hospitals," *New York Times*, November 2, 2002, p. C1.

Brick, Michael, "Investing: A Hospital Chain Rises as Managed Care Suffers," *New York Times*, June 17, 2001, p. C8.

"Chief Executive Officer Resigns from Troubled Tenet Healthcare," *South Florida Sun-Sentinel*, May 28, 2003.

"Costa Mesa Hospital Management Company to Acquire Four Tenet Hospitals," *Biotech Business Week*, November 1, 2004, p. 258.

Crowe, Deborah, "Tenet Sunsets," *Los Angeles Business Journal*, July 7, 2008, p. 10(1).

Eamer, Richard K., *The History of National Medical Enterprises, Inc., and the Investor-Owned Hospital Industry.* New York: Newcomen Society in North America, 1989.

Eichenwald, Kurt, "How One Hospital Benefitted from Questionable Surgery," *New York Times*, August 12, 2003, p. A1.

———, "U.S. Awards Tenet Whistle-Blowers $8.1 Million," *New York Times*, January 8, 2004, p. C15.

Fisher, Daniel, "Critical Condition," *Forbes*, May 23, 2005, p. 230.

Galloro, Vince, "Tenet at Your Service," *Modern Healthcare*, November 10, 2008, p. 12.

Galloro, Vince, "USC, Tenet Make Peace," *Modern Healthcare*, April 21, 2008, p. 18.

Hilzenrath, David S., "Hospital Firm Plans $3 Billion Combination: National Medical Seeks to Alter Its Focus, Shed Taint of Scandal," *Washington Post*, October 12, 1994, p. F1.

"Hospital Sold," *Los Angeles Business Journal*, January 8, 2007, p. 4(1).

Kerr, Peter, "U.S. Raids Hospital Operator," *New York Times*, August 27, 1993, p. D1.

Kirchgaessner, Stephanie, "Tenet Fined $900m over Medicare Healthcare," *Financial Times*, June 30, 2006, p. 22.

Meier, Barry, "For-Profit Health Care's Human Cost: Tenet Healthcare Tries to Settle Some Old Accounts," *New York Times*, August 8, 1997, p. D1.

Myerson, Allen R., "Hospital Chain Sets Guilty Plea," *New York Times*, June 29, 1994, p. D1.

Pollack, Andrew, "California Patients Talk of Needless Heart Surgeries," *New York Times*, November 4, 2002, p. C1.

Pollack, Andrew, with Reed Abelson, "Chief Faces Problems Again After Restoring Tenet Once," *New York Times*, November 11, 2002, p. C2.

Roth, Lisa Fingeret, "Investors Punish Troubled Tenet Healthcare," *Financial Times*, June 24, 2003, p. 19.

———, "Tenet Gains After Settlement," *Financial Times*, August 8, 2003, p. 27.

Schine, Eric, "From Scandal to Second Place," *BusinessWeek*, November 27, 1995, p. 124.

Schine, Eric, with Catherine Yang, "Migraines for National Medical," *BusinessWeek*, September 13, 1993, p. 74.

"Tenet Healthcare Corporation Signs Agreement to See Three Hospitals," *Biotech Business Week*, September 27, 2004, p. 50.

"Tenet to Move Headquarters to Texas from California," *New York Times*, May 7, 2004, p. C4.

"Tenet to Sell 3 Hospitals in Massachusetts," *New York Times*, October 13, 2004, p. C5.

"Tenet in $900 Million Settlement," *New York Times*, June 30, 2006, p. C3.

"U.S.C. Files Lawsuit Against Tenet Healthcare," *New York Times*, August 23, 2006.

Yang, Catherine, and Eric Schine, " 'Put the Head in the Bed and Keep It There,' "*BusinessWeek*, October 18, 1993, p. 68.

Teva Pharmaceutical Industries Ltd.

———■———

5 Basel Street
Petah Tikva, 49131
Israel
Telephone: (+972) 3 9267267
Fax: (+972) 3 9234050
Web site: http://www.tevapharm.com

Public Company
Founded: 1935
Incorporated: 1944
Employees: 35,000 (est.)
Sales: US$13.9 billion (2009)
Stock Exchanges: Tel Aviv NASDAQ
Ticker Symbol: TEVA
NAICS: 325412 Pharmaceutical Preparation Manufacturing; 541711 Research and Development in Biotechnology

■ ■ ■

Teva Pharmaceutical Industries Ltd. is among the leading manufacturers of generic and proprietary drugs in the world. Based in Israel, Teva derives the vast majority of its business from overseas markets and is particularly dominant in the United States, where it controls more than 20 percent of the nation's generic drug sales. The company's best-selling products include generic forms of the pain medication OxyContin, the antidepressants Prozac and Zoloft, and the antibiotic Augmentin. Teva has also achieved success with several of its brand-name drugs, notably the multiple sclerosis medicine Copaxone.

In the 21st century Teva has expanded its research activities to include the development of biotechnology pharmaceuticals, one of the fastest-growing sectors in the drug industry. The company experienced steady growth in the 1990s and 2000s, largely through the acquisition of rival drug firms such as Novopharm Ltd. and Ivax Corp.

ORIGINS AND GROWTH: 1935–60

Teva (Hebrew for "nature") was founded in 1935 by Elsa Kuver and Dr. Gunter Friedlander in Jerusalem. The company's early history was influenced strongly by global politics. During the 1930s three forces converged to encourage Jewish immigration into the British-controlled area then known as Palestine. The Zionist movement strove to create a modern Jewish nation in the ancient Hebrew homeland. During the years between the two world wars, the British mandated partition of the region into separate Israeli and Arabic states and sanctioned Jewish immigration to certain areas of Palestine in order to create a Jewish majority. At the same time, Nazi persecution of German Jews drove hundreds of thousands to emigrate from that country.

Due in part to the intervention of World War II, the establishment of an Israeli state by the United Nations did not occur until 1948. In the meantime the Jewish population of Palestine increased to more than 600,000. Prior to World War II Germany was the center of the global pharmaceutical industry. Many immigrants from that country brought with them pharmaceutical expertise that provided a firm foundation upon which the Israeli drug industry, and Teva, was built.

COMPANY PERSPECTIVES

Teva differentiates itself by balancing its portfolio with generic, innovative and branded products, vertically integrating its pharmaceutical and API activities, combining local customer responsiveness with a "global edge," and by its global footprint. Teva's success lies in the leadership of its management, the skills and devotion of its people, the quality of its offerings and its focus on customers and patients.

Notwithstanding the ongoing violence in the Middle East, Teva enjoyed some advantages over its competitors around the world. For one, Israel had a high concentration of scientists, more per capita than any nation in the world. Furthermore, the Israeli government granted pharmaceutical companies tax subsidies to encourage the development and production of new drugs. It was in this environment that Teva grew, going public in 1951 on the Tel Aviv Stock Exchange.

INDUSTRY CONSOLIDATION: 1960–80

Eli Hurvitz, the man who would engineer Teva's emergence on the global drug scene, first became involved with Teva in 1968, when he was appointed to the company's board of directors. Trained as an economist, Hurvitz had started his career in 1953 at Assia Chemical Laboratories. His promotion into management at Assia in 1963 coincided with the beginning of a period of consolidation within Israel's pharmaceutical industry. This trend peaked with the 1976 union of Teva, Assia, and Zri to create the nation's largest drugmaker, Teva Pharmaceutical Industries. Hurvitz was appointed general manager, or CEO, of the merged companies.

In a bid to boost its production capacity, Teva acquired its number two competitor, Ikapharm, in 1980. The deal struck with Ikapharm's parent company Koor Industries (Israel's largest manufacturing concern) included an exchange of 20 percent of Teva's equity for the state-of-the-art drug plant. This element of the agreement would prove troublesome in the years to come. Having accumulated a 42 percent stake in Teva, Koor launched a bid for control in 1984. Teva's Founders Group, composed of the stockholding heirs to Teva's originators, thwarted the takeover attempt. Although the two groups called a truce by the end of

the year, Teva's ownership issues would not end there, for the company often used its equity to broker deals.

OVERSEAS EXPANSION: 1980–90

Having consolidated its domestic position, Teva began to expand geographically in the early 1980s. The company perceived an opportunity to penetrate the U.S. market when the federal Waxman-Hatch Act passed Congress in 1984. This legislation concerned generic drugs, which are defined as treatments that have lost their patent protection. Also known as multisource or off-patent medicines, generics are chemically identical to branded prescription drugs but are priced at 30 to 70 percent less than patented versions. Waxman-Hatch reduced the regulatory hurdles for generics, thereby cutting the time and money required to bring generic drugs to market. Thus, although generics were far less expensive to develop than new drugs, they also commanded far lower profit margins.

Teva used the generics segment as its entree into the U.S. pharmaceutical market. In 1985 the company forged an agreement with chemical conglomerate W.R. Grace to create TAG Pharmaceuticals, a 50-50 joint venture. A relative newcomer to the pharmaceutical industry, Grace contributed more than 90 percent of TAG's $23 million starting capital base, while Teva threw in $1.5 million and its decades of experience and expertise.

That same year TAG acquired Lemmon Co., a Pennsylvania-based company with a tarnished history. Infamous for marketing Quaaludes in the 1970s, Lemmon had seen four corporate owners in its scant 15 years in business. Under its newest parents, it became the sales and distribution arm for generics manufactured by Teva in Israel. Although CEO Hurvitz later reflected that "an Israeli who's coming to the States has a David and Goliath syndrome," he reminded himself that little David prevailed in the biblical battle. The potential Teva saw in Lemmon soon turned to profits; the U.S. venture's sales more than doubled from $17 million at the time of its acquisition to about $40 million in 1987, by which time it was marketing seven generic versions of branded drugs.

Teva raised $18.4 million in 1987 through the sale of American Depositary Receipts (ADRs) on the NASDAQ. Around the same time Koor Industries, which by this point was flirting with bankruptcy, sold $14.8 million worth of its Teva holding on the open market, thereby reducing its stake in Teva to about 22 percent. Teva used the proceeds of its equity offering to acquire Abic Ltd., Israel's second-ranking drug marketer, for $26.6 million in 1988. That same year Teva acquired two Israeli companies from U.S.-based Baxter

```
┌─────────────────────────────────────────────┐
│                                               │
│              KEY DATES                        │
│                  ■                            │
├───────────────────────────────────────────────┤
│ 1935: Elsa Kuver and Dr. Gunter Friedlander   │
│       establish Teva.                          │
│ 1951: Teva becomes a publicly held company.   │
│ 1976: Teva merges with Assia and Zri to create│
│       Teva Pharmaceutical Industries.          │
│ 1985: Teva joins with W.R. Grace to create TAG │
│       Pharmaceuticals and penetrate the U.S.  │
│       generics market; TAG acquires Lemmon Co. │
│ 1988: Teva purchases Abic Ltd., Travenol      │
│       Laboratories Ltd., and Travenol Trading │
│       Company Ltd.                             │
│ 1997: Teva's Copaxone drug receives FDA        │
│       approval for treatment of multiple       │
│       sclerosis.                               │
│ 1998: Teva acquires Pharmachemie Group.        │
│ 2000: Company purchases Novopharm Ltd.         │
│ 2006: Teva acquires Ivax Corp. for $7.4 billion.│
│ 2008: Company buys Barr Pharmaceuticals Inc.   │
│       for $7.46 billion.                       │
└───────────────────────────────────────────────┘
```

International Inc.: Travenol Laboratories Ltd., a manufacturer of health-care products and equipment, and Travenol Trading Company Ltd., an importer of Baxter products, for a total of $8.2 million.

Meanwhile, as part of a $1 billion debt restructuring, Koor transferred its stake in Teva to two creditors, Israeli banks Hapoalim and Leumi. The banks in turn sold about 17 percent of Teva to British publishing magnate Robert Maxwell for $30.2 million. The Maxwell connection was cut in 1993, when his estate divested the holding for $166 million, a significant appreciation. Teva severed its ties to W.R. Grace in 1991, when it purchased Grace's 50 percent share of TAG Pharmaceuticals for $35 million. Grace then divested its stake in Teva to the public for $36.4 million.

Teva's sales more than doubled from less than $100 million in 1987 to $268.5 million in 1989, and net income increased from about $7 million to more than $16 million during the same period. Although this growth rate must have been a source of pride for CEO Hurvitz and his executive team, it would pale in comparison to the increases chalked up in the 1990s.

ACQUISITIONS AND NEW DRUGS: 1990–96

In the early 1990s Teva invested aggressively in acquisitions, research and development, and increased produc-

tion capacity. From 1992 through 1996 the company spent a total of more than $420 million on a rash of acquisitions that extended its reach into France, Italy, Great Britain, and Hungary. Teva's U.S. sales surpassed its domestic revenues in 1993, and overseas employment exceeded native workers three years later. In 1996 alone Teva acquired Approved Prescription Services/Berk, the United Kingdom's second-largest generic drug marketer, and Hungary's Biogal. That same year the company catapulted to the top of the U.S. generics segment via a $290 million stock swap with America's Biocraft Laboratories, Inc. Since the merger was structured as a pooling of interests, Teva restated its financial information as if the two companies had always been one.

During this same time, Teva plowed hundreds of millions into research and development and capital improvements. The company's new drug developments concentrated on so-called "orphan" drugs in the therapeutic areas of neurological disorders and autoimmune diseases. The term is most often used to describe compounds that are discovered by major drug companies but whose patents have been allowed to lapse because the disease or condition targeted by the drug has too few patients to justify the development expenditures required to bring it to market. Smaller companies like Teva that "adopted" an orphan drug could apply for a new seven-year, exclusive patent on the compound, thereby allowing it time to make a profitable return on its investment.

Generics continued to form the core of Teva's sales. From January 1996 through July 1997 the company garnered more generic drug approvals from the U.S. Food and Drug Administration (FDA) than any other company in the world. Proprietary drugs, however, emerged as a high-profit growth vehicle in the early 1990s. The company's first major new drug, known as Copaxone, was originated more than two decades earlier in the laboratories of Israel's Weizmann Institute, where doctoral student Dvora Teitelbaum was studying the use of synthetic proteins to quell multiple sclerosis (MS) attacks in animals. Together with professors Michael Sela and Ruth Arnon, Teitelbaum spent 15 years isolating and researching the polymer COP-1 (later branded Copaxone), passing preliminary clinical trials in 1986. The treatment reduced the relapse rate for people in the early stages of relapsing-remitting MS by anywhere from 25 to 30 percent in clinical trials.

The Weizmann Institute teamed up with Teva to bring Copaxone to market. Since its patent had expired during the long development process, Teva requested and received orphan drug status from the FDA. Initially launched in Israel, Copaxone earned FDA approval in 1997. The rollout achieved several milestones, both for

Teva and for MS sufferers. Copaxone was the first drug developed in Israel to achieve FDA approval for distribution in the United States. Unlike its interferon-based competitors, it was also the first drug developed specifically to treat MS.

Since Teva had little experience marketing branded drugs on the world stage, it enlisted the help of global pharmaceutical powerhouse Hoechst Marion Roussel. This "David and Goliath" team formed a joint venture, Teva Marion Partners (TMP), to coordinate distribution. Within one month of its launch, TMP recorded 10,000 inquiries from doctors and patients about Copaxone. Within six weeks the company had 4,000 patients on the daily injection program and reported adding more than 1,000 more each month. Analysts forecasted that Copaxone alone would add at least $50 million to Teva's sales total in 1997 and increase from there.

The story of Teva's transformation from a tiny Israeli drug company into an international pharmaceutical innovator garnered a great deal of attention from investment houses around the world in the mid-1990s. Even before the Copaxone launch, Teva's sales had tripled from $295 million in 1990 to $954 million in 1996 as net income increased from $18.7 million to $73.2 million. However, while Merrill Lynch, Standard & Poor's, A.G. Edwards, and others had rated the stock a "buy," it remained a somewhat volatile equity, surging from less than $50 per share in April 1997 to $67 in June, then backsliding to $57 in September.

This roller-coaster performance could be attributed to any number of black marks on Teva's record at the time. In March 1996 CEO Hurvitz was indicted on charges of evading $18 million in corporate taxes as head of Teva's Promedico subsidiary (since divested) from 1980 to 1986. Nonetheless, Teva's board signed him to a five-year contract in January 1997. In August 1997 Teva was subjected to an FDA recall on a batch of antibiotics. The problem (which rendered the drugs "less effective but not harmful," according to Teva officials) was traced to a supplier. That same year found the company in a dispute over Copaxone royalties with its development partner, the Weizmann Institute. In addition, Teva's U.S. subsidiary GATE Pharmaceuticals was named among the nine defendants in a class-action suit over the diet drug phen-fen.

Nonetheless, most of the investment firms following Teva stood by the company. In July 1997 U.S. brokerage Gruntal & Co. asserted, "Teva should be seen as a rising star in the dynamic world medical drug market." Israeli business newspaper *Globes* called the company "this century's Israeli success story."

The development and introduction of new generics, expanding sales of Copaxone, and a variety of acquisitions and strategic alliances characterized Teva's business in the succeeding years. Whereas some manufacturers of generics, unable to differentiate their companies in the marketplace and consequently suffering declining sales and profits, changed their focus to proprietary drug development, Teva forged ahead productively. Relying partly on the momentum generated by Copaxone, it moved to create increased dominance in the generic sector. In a February 1998 interview with *Euromoney Institutional Investor*, Hurvitz said, "We are doubling our [generic] business every four years."

INCREASING THE COMPANY'S PRESENCE ABROAD: 1997–2002

In the three years following 1997, Teva purchased a number of pharmaceutical companies that furthered its access to foreign markets and enhanced its line of products. In 1998 the company bought for $87 million Dutch Pharmachemie Group, which at the time controlled 40 percent of the generic drug market in Holland. Copley Pharmaceuticals of Canton, Massachusetts, followed in 1999 for $220 million. In 2000 Teva acquired Novopharm Ltd., the second-largest producer of generics in Canada, with operations in the United States and Hungary. Through these acquisitions Teva appeared likely to obtain considerable advantage in resources and efficiency, particularly with regard to R&D and distribution.

During this period, newly formed strategic alliances also strengthened Teva's position. Such a partnership with Biovale Corp. in 1998 furnished Teva with access to an important drug delivery technology. The agreement allowed Teva to have U.S. marketing rights in connection with Biovale's line of controlled-release pharmaceuticals, an advantage for manufacturers of generics in a highly competitive market. Appraising the success of particular companies in this field in an August 2001 interview with *Chemical Market Reporter*, UBS Warburg analyst Steven Valiquette said, "We favor companies with proprietary controlled-release drug technology to develop both branded and generic drugs. These companies ultimately face less competition and thus more sustainable profit growth." A similar agreement in 1999 with Bio-Technology General Corp. brought Teva resources in the area of recombinant therapeutic products.

The company also experienced occasional setbacks. Most notably, in 1998 Teva was charged with violating the patent on U.S. pharmaceutical company Eli Lilly's drug Prozac and was ordered to pay compensation to Lilly for the losses it sustained. Sales of Copaxone continued to be strong, however. The way was prepared for even greater Copaxone sales in 1999, when, as a forerunner to general EU approval, the drug was approved in Switzerland.

The year 2000 was one of record sales. Although there was an economic slowdown in its key U.S. market, this did not injure Teva's sector. Rather, it may have proven advantageous; economic downturns tended to encourage cost-cutting measures, such as replacing expensive branded prescription drugs with generic equivalents. The period was also one in which an unprecedented number of branded pharmaceuticals were soon to relinquish their patents, an ideal situation for Teva.

A wave of new products and acquisitions followed. In 2001 Teva won a lawsuit against pharmaceutical giant GlaxoSmithKline (GSK) concerning the patent on GSK's arthritis drug Relafen, allowing Teva to begin marketing a generic equivalent. In 2002 GSK again lost out when its patent on the antibiotic Augmentin was declared invalid. In addition, Teva was able to bring to market a generic version of Roche Laboratories' Rocaltrol, used in cases of hyperthyroidism. The antidepressant Remeron, formerly under patent by Organon, also was slated to join Teva's product line.

The year 2002 also marked a change in leadership for the company. Israel Makov, who had been with Teva for eight years, was designated to succeed veteran Hurvitz as CEO. Expansion continued under Makov, as the company purchased the French generics division of Bayer Pharma AG and Honeywell's subsidiary Honeywell Pharmaceutical Fine Chemicals, with production facilities in Italy. By mid-2002 Teva's European and North American operations accounted for roughly 80 percent of its total revenues. The company enjoyed brisk profit growth during this period, posting net earnings of $91.9 million in the second quarter of 2002, an increase of 43 percent over the same period for 2001. In a generics-friendly economic climate, and with 62 drugs in the pipeline for FDA approval in the United States, Teva appeared to be well positioned to continue its dominance in the generic pharmaceuticals sector.

FURTHER CONSOLIDATION IN A CUTTHROAT GENERICS MARKET: 2003–10

In the early part of the 21st century, Teva continued to seek new opportunities overseas, particularly in Europe and North America. Europe was becoming a promising area for growth, as concerns about the precipitous rise in health-care costs prompted government officials to seek ways to expand the generic drug market. A number of

countries, notably Spain, France, and Italy, began to consider dramatic changes to their existing drug laws, which traditionally protected brand-name pharmaceutical products against the incursion of generic alternatives. According to some industry analysts, the market for generic drugs in Europe had the potential to grow by EUR 3 to EUR 4 billion ($2.98 to $3.97 billion) by the middle of the decade.

Throughout this period, Teva also remained focused on developing new product lines. In November 2003 the company agreed to acquire Sicor Inc., a California-based drug manufacturer, for $3.4 billion. A specialist in the development of injectable medicines, Sicor provided Teva with a critical pathway into the lucrative hospital sector, particularly in the areas of cancer treatment and anesthesiology. Perhaps more significant, Sicor had an extensive background in the development of biotechnology drugs, a segment that included products such as insulin and human growth hormone.

The biotech drug field was widely regarded to be one of the industry's fastest growing sectors, with global sales of $41.4 billion in 2003. At the time, U.S. law prohibited the manufacture of generic biotech pharmaceutical products, due to the high level of complexity involved with their manufacture. Because the drugs were also extremely expensive, however, many experts were predicting that a change in the law was only a matter of time. By developing the capability to manufacture bioengineered drugs, Teva clearly intended to be at the forefront of this potential generic market.

By September 2004 Teva had more than 200 generic drugs available on the U.S. market, along with an additional 110 pharmaceutical products in various stages of the FDA approval process. However, by mid-decade the generic drug market had become intensely competitive, as more companies began to enter the field. In early 2005 Teva briefly lost its position as the world's leading generic drug manufacturer, after rival Novartis absorbed German drug giant Hexal for $8.3 billion. Teva regained its top ranking in July of that year with the purchase of Miami-based pharmaceutical firm Ivax for $7.4 billion. Upon completing the merger in January 2006, Teva expanded its presence into more than 50 countries across the world, gaining a vital foothold in regions such as Latin America and Eastern Europe. The combined companies were expected to garner more than $7 billion in annual sales, while producing more than 300 different drugs.

In the years following the Ivax acquisition, Teva saw its revenues rise steadily. In 2007 the company posted sales of $9.4 billion, driven largely by its range of new generics, notably Zocor, a cholesterol drug originally developed by Merck & Company, and Pfizer's antidepressant medication Zoloft. In early 2008 Teva took another significant step toward becoming an industry leader in the biotech drug field with the acquisition of CoGenesys, a biotechnological firm, for $400 million.

In December 2008 Teva acquired rival Barr Pharmaceuticals Inc. for $7.46 billion. The merger raised the company's share of the U.S. generic drug market from 18 to 22 percent. Meanwhile, annual sales continued to rise, with Teva posting revenues of $11.1 billion in 2008 and $13.9 billion in 2009. Clearly, it had developed an effective strategy heading into the new decade.

April Dougal Gasbarre
Updated, Shawna Brynildssen; Stephen Meyer

PRINCIPAL SUBSIDIARIES

Assia Chemical Industries Ltd.; AWD Pharma GmbH & Co. KG (Germany); Galena Pharma Limited Liability Company (Russia); IVAX Pharmaceuticals Ireland (Ireland); Laboratorio Chile S.A. (Chile); Laboratorios Davur S.L. (Spain); Laboratorios Elmor, S.A. (Venezuela); Lemery S.A. de C.V. (Mexico); Novopharm Limited (Canada); Pharmachemie B.V. (The Netherlands); Plantex Chemicals B.V. (The Netherlands); Pliva Hrvatska d.o.o. (Croatia); Pliva Krakow S.A. (Poland); PLIVA RUS Ltd. (Russia); Salomon, Levin and Elstein Ltd.; Teva Animal Health, Inc. (USA); Teva Classics S.A.S. (France); Teva Deutschland GmbH (Germany); TEVA Hungary Pharmaceutical Marketing Private Limited Company (Hungary); Teva Italia S.r.l. (Italy); Teva Pharmaceuticals C.R., s.r.o. (Czech Republic); Teva Pharmaceuticals Polska s.p. z.o.o. (Poland); Teva Pharmaceuticals USA, Inc. (USA); Teva U.K. Limited (UK).

PRINCIPAL COMPETITORS

Merck & Co., Inc.; Novartis AG; Ranbaxy Laboratories Limited; Sandoz International GmbH; Watson Pharmaceuticals, Inc.

FURTHER READING

Beck, Galit Lipkis, "Teva to Raise More than $100M in US Bond Issue," *Jerusalem Post*, February 25, 1997, p. 8.

Brady, Diane, with John Carey and Amy Tsao, "Biotech: Teva's Next Triumph?" *BusinessWeek*, November 3, 2003, p. 94.

Dichek, Bernard, "Teva Pharmaceuticals Industries," *Israel Business Today*, August 27, 1993, p. 35.

Friedlin, Jennifer, "Playing with the Big Boys," *Jerusalem Post*, October 16, 1996, p. 6.

Goldgaber, Arthur, "Teva Pharmaceutical: Slammer Dunk," *Financial World*, April 15, 1997, pp. 26–27.

Hill, Miriam, "Teva Completes Acquisition of Barr," *Philadelphia Inquirer*, December 24, 2008, p. C1.

Loyd, Linda, "Top Maker of Generics in U.S. Is Not a Household Name," *Philadelphia Inquirer*, July 1, 2002.

Mann, David, and Cynthia Miller, "Israeli Company Develops Breakthrough MS Treatment," *Northern California Jewish Bulletin*, October 14, 1994.

Sherrid, Pamela, "The New Drug War," *U.S. News and World Report*, December 2, 2002, p. 41.

Sivy, Michael, "Soaring to Lofty Profits on the Wings of Peace," *Money*, November 1993, pp. 54–56.

Tiger Brands Limited

3010 William Nicol Drive
Bryanston, Gauteng
South Africa
P.O. Box 78056
Sandton, Gauteng 2146
South Africa
Telephone: (+011 2711) 840-4000
Fax: (+011 2711) 514-0084
Web site: http://www.tigerbrands.co.za

Public Company
Founded: 1921
Employees: 11,987
Sales: ZAR 20.64 billion ($2.67 billion) (2009)
Stock Exchanges: Johannesburg
Ticker Symbol: TBS
NAICS: 311211 Flour Milling; 311212 Rice Milling;
311221 Wet Corn Milling; 311230 Breakfast
Cereal Manufacturing; 311911 Roasted Nuts and
Peanut Butter Manufacturing; 325412 Pharma-
ceutical Preparation Manufacturing

■ ■ ■

Tiger Brands Limited is a South Africa-based company
with many different corporate interests. These range
from grain mills of various kinds to bakeries, fisheries,
animal feeds, pharmaceuticals, and household cleaners.
Its subsidiaries are found in several countries.

FROM SMALL BEGINNINGS

On August 21, 1921, a new venture appeared in South
Africa. Named after its creator, Jacob Frankel (Prop.)
Ltd. was created from a sum of money built on various
loans plus the sale of the family home. On this precarious financial base, Jacob Frankel confidently built a
business of pantry staples he could be sure of selling.
His list included beans of several types, rice, white and
brown sugar, high-quality peanuts, corn products such
as mealie meal, a polenta-like grain that can be cooked
to the consistency of bread, and samp, which is similar
to hominy grits in appearance if not in taste. These were
sold to several of the country's mines to feed their
workers. Frankel also sold several cattle feeds as well as
inferior peanuts used for zoo animals.

The business grew steadily, especially after Frankel's
son Rudy took over its management. From the beginning Frankel had purchased his grains from mills.
However, in 1937 the company expanded with the
acquisition of Natal Milling. This allowed the company
to produce its own grains, thus cutting its operating
costs considerably.

ENTER SIR ERNEST OPPENHEIMER

During World War II Frankel renewed an acquaintance
with Sir Ernest Oppenheimer, the head of both the Anglo American gold mining empire and De Beers, whose
main focus was diamond mining. Their talk revolved
around the possibility of supplying a line of foodstuffs
from Jacob Frankel (Prop.) Ltd. to the panoply of
diamond and gold mines in the Anglo American
portfolio. To add substance, Frankel added the fact that
he was interested in acquiring a company called Delmas
Milling, which would place his company among the
largest in the South African food industry.

In the meantime, Oppenheimer became interested in a Cape-based food company called Tiger Oats. This was a business that dated back to before 1905, when it had been bought by an entrepreneur named John Collier and known as the Cereal Manufacturing Company. Although it had previously focused on animal feeds bearing the brand name "Tiger," a name Collier seemed to have registered in 1907, Collier wanted to replace the imported oatmeal cereals with locally manufactured products for human consumption. By 1920 the company was marketing a cereal called Jungle Oats and a product called Tiger Pearl Barley. The company, however, had come down on its luck during the Great Depression. Undercapitalized and underutilized, Tiger Oats was now a company in need of firm management.

Oppenheimer decided that a merger of Tiger and Frankel would be profitable, and he added a third company named Lurie Brothers to the mix. The new company, by Oppenheimer's decree, became the Tiger Oats Company and National Milling Company, which was headed by the Frankel management. Capitalized at £1 million, an investment from Anglo American, the new company proudly displayed its new logo: a tiger drawn by British artist Charles Edward Turner, which would remain its logo into the 21st century. (The association between Tiger Oats and Anglo American was not destined to last. In 1951 Oppenheimer announced that he believed Tiger Oats had reached maturity and that he desired to make investments in developing companies. He withdrew his investment.)

OTHER VENTURES

In 1946 the Frankels decided to add more items containing vegetable protein to their animal feed products. "That meant oil cakes," Rudy Frankel wrote in his memoir, *Tiger Tapestry*. To provide oil for the feeds, the company purchased Alderton Limited, whose business focused both on expelling oil from peanuts and on producing peanut butter, both products marketed under the name Black Cat. Although Alderton was subsequently sold, the oil cakes remained with Tiger Oats. Black Cat Peanut Butter, too, would be a part of the company lineup more than 60 years later.

The year 1946 continued to be one of opportunity. In addition to purchasing the Delmas Milling Company, which helped to make Tiger Oats one of the country's largest milling concerns, Tiger Oats had a chance in October to purchase shares in a fish-canning company called Afco (African Fish Canning Company), which had been offered to Anglo American. Tiger leapt at the chance, happy to open a plant in order to produce fish meal. The product had been used as a fertilizer before the war but had become popular as an important additive to animal feeds and was now hard to obtain. This problem did not exist in America, Frankel noted in *Tiger Tapestry*, because American farmers grew soy for this purpose. However, in South Africa, the growing season for soy was too short to offer an adequate supply.

By early 1948 Afco's fishmeal plant was well on the way to profitability, so the company began to can pilchards, fish that could be prepared either in a tomato sauce or in a curry. A rock lobster processing factory was opened that year at the plant in Namibia, and Afco merged into a larger collection of companies that adopted the name United Fish Canners. Incorporated in 1948, this company was the forerunner of Oceana, long one of Tiger's most important subsidiaries.

The big news for Tiger Oats in the 1950s was the advent of radio advertising. The company was eager to promote its Jungle Oats and Black Cat Peanut Butter lines, so it began by sponsoring two programs. One was for children, featuring ads for the oats, and the other was a program for housewives featuring Black Cat. A copywriter at P. N. Barrett, the company's advertising agency, suggested using sports personalities to advertise products. The idea was adopted with great enthusiasm. Among the first sportsmen used was Vic Toweel, a boxer, who was soon joined by golfer Gary Player. Like the other sportsmen who endorsed these products, the two gave tips on training as well as advice about "champion breakfasts."

STEADY EXPANSION

These products, all of which were destined to become stalwarts of the Tiger Oats portfolio, were joined in 1964 by Tastic Rice, which, according to commercials some 40 years later, still "cooks perfectly every time." Tiger Oats CEO Rudy Frankel had been aware for some time that a parboiling process had been perfected in America that made rice less lumpy and easier to cook. This process was first introduced in South Africa by a smaller company, called S. Wainstein and Company

```
┌─────────────────────────────────────────────┐
│                                               │
│              KEY DATES                        │
│                    ■                          │
│  ───────────────────────────────────────────  │
│                                               │
│  1921:  Company is founded as Jacob Frankel   │
│         (Prop.) Ltd.                          │
│  1944:  Jacob Frankel (Prop.) Ltd. becomes a  │
│         part of the new company Tiger Oats    │
│         and National Milling Company Limited. │
│  1945:  Tiger Oats acquires Lichtenburg Mills │
│         and Malt Factory.                     │
│  1946:  Tiger Oats acquires Alderton Limited, │
│         manufacturer of the iconic Black Cat  │
│         Peanut Butter.                         │
│  1947:  Tiger Oats is listed on the London    │
│         Stock Exchange.                        │
│  2000:  Company name is changed to Tiger      │
│         Brands Limited.                        │
│                                               │
└─────────────────────────────────────────────┘
```

(Pty) Ltd., which called its product Tastic. In 1964 Tiger Oats paid ZAR 280,560 for a half-share in this business. Tastic was already familiar to South Africans because Wainstein had spent a great deal of his profits on advertising. In 1974 Wainstein disinvested from Tastic Rice, which has remained in the Tiger Oats portfolio ever since.

In the 1970s the company continued to grow, acquiring companies that would form the nuclei of future divisions. One of these was Bremer Meulens (Eindoms) Beperk, a milling company based in the Orange Free State. In line with its policy of placing its supply plants, such as mills, within easy access of its manufacturing concerns, such as bakeries, Bremer brought another flour mill and a corn mill. Bremer also had several bakeries and licenses for several new ones in the area. Frankel noted that rural bakeries were an expensive proposition for Bremer, because bread deliveries had to be made to stores in neighboring towns. The business involved drivers' wages, the purchase and maintenance of trucks, and fuel charges. This was an existing and important area of operations for Tiger, however, because it already had bakeries, developed after the acquisition of new flour mills in Gauteng and at Richard's Bay in KwaZulu. Frankel concluded that it made sense for the two companies to join forces.

One of the best-known businesses in this realm was Silverleaf Pastry and Confectionery Company (Pty) Ltd. in the Western Cape, purchased in early 1974. A new bakery was built there in August of that year to make large quantities of bread. Also joining the lineup in

1974 was Albany Bakery in Durban, linked to the mills at nearby Richard's Bay, conveniently featuring South Africa's largest harbor.

CHANGES 1980–2000

The 1980s brought great changes to Tiger Oats. By this time, having spent 50 years in the business, the original founders were ready to retire. In 1982 they sold Tiger for an undisclosed sum to become a subsidiary of C. G. Smith Foods Limited, itself a subsidiary of the Barlow-Rand Group. Barlow-Rand, now with a 65 percent interest in C. G. Smith, had a 79 percent interest in Tiger Oats.

All was not smooth sailing. Scarce rains and changes in traditional tastes brought declines in maize profits in 1987, and the crop yielded only 7.4 million tons. Nevertheless, food products overall brought 1987 sales of ZAR 3.7 billion.

In another event of the 1980s, Tiger acquired Fatti's and Moni's, a pasta company dating back to 1886 and long revered in South Africa on two fronts: as an importer of Italian olive oils, olives, and other specialties and as a manufacturer of popular pasta products.

With the beginning of the 1990s, political changes in South Africa were coming to the fore, resulting in the end of apartheid. Longtime supporters of humanitarian efforts, Tiger Oats had been hoping for this for several years. The company had been stalwart contributors to Operation Hunger, a nonprofit organization dedicated to providing necessities for underprivileged children. Looking ahead, the company began to give further assistance to disadvantaged communities by contributions of both staff expertise and money to fledgling black businesses.

In August 1999 Tiger Oats acquired a 20 percent share of Empresas Carozzi, a Chilean company, for $66 million. This business, with annual average sales of $350 million, produced tomato paste, pasta, cookies, chocolates, and flour. This cautious stake in the Chilean company had sensible roots. Empresas was a family-run business, and the Tiger Oats executives wanted to get to know their counterparts and their culture before investing too heavily.

The same year, C. G. Smith announced that Tiger Oats was to be divested in February 2000 along with two other subsidiaries, and that shareholders would receive 16.18 Tiger Oats shares for every share of C. G. Smith they held. To mark the occasion, the company changed its name to Tiger Brands Limited.

ADCOCK INGRAM: A MIXED BLESSING

In 2000 the company acquired the rest of the controlling interest in Adcock Ingram, the country's largest pharmaceutical supplier, after having bought the Tannenbaum family's controlling interest in the company in 1978. Dating back to 1890, Adcock Ingram was started by the Tannenbaum family in a small mining town called Krugersdorp. In 1950 it was listed on the Johannesburg Stock Exchange, and by the 1980s it had a long string of its own subsidiaries, Zurich Pharmaceuticals and Pharmatec among them. Under the Tiger banner, the list of expansion activities continued. These included the acquisition of Steri-Lab, a medical diagnostics business, in 2001, and the opening of a new ZAR 26 million research facility. In 2002 came the acquisition of Robertsons Homecare, the producer of household staples such as Jeyes disinfectant, Flush toilet sanitizer, and Doom insecticide.

The addition of Adcock Ingram brought Tiger several profitable product areas: over-the-counter remedies like the pain reliever Panado, Ingram's camphor cream, Allergex eye drops, baby-care products, and skin-care items, as well as antibiotics and other prescription drugs. Along with these came an array of hospital equipment products, including biopsy needles, dialysis equipment, intravenous equipment, and blood filters. Overall, Adcock Ingram was a profitable purchase, showing revenue for the year 2000 of ZAR 813.4 million for its pharmaceutical products, ZAR 490.4 million for its consumer products, and ZAR 396.7 million for its critical care (hospital) products. By 2001 Adcock Ingram's revenue had risen to ZAR 7075.4 million, a steady rise in income.

Adcock Ingram continued to perform as one of Tiger Brands' most profitable subsidiaries until 2008. At that time its Adcock Ingram Critical Care subsidiary was accused, according to Adele Shevel in the *Sunday Times*, of "collusive tendering," and a scandal erupted over the subsidiary. Tiger Brands was ordered to pay a $53 million fine for illegal tendering. The Critical Care company, dealing in hospital equipment and pharmaceuticals, was fined for participating in a price-fixing cartel along with Fresenius Kabi SA, Thusanong, and Dismed.

ANOTHER ACCUSATION OF PRICE FIXING

This was not Tiger Brands' only brush with the law. In 2007 Tiger Brands and South Africa's two other top bread producers were accused, in an anonymous letter, of price fixing by hiking bread prices by 30 to 35 cents per loaf. Because it involved a staple item, this was considered a serious charge for which the Competition Commission fined the company ZAR 98.8 million. Three company directors (CEO Nick Dennis, head of bakeries Hayden Franklin, and financial director Noel Doyle) gave up their bonuses as a result of this charge, and they later resigned as a result of the scandal.

Peter Matlare, previously the chief of strategy and business development officer for the Vodacom Company, became CEO of Tiger Brands. Matlare immediately vowed to regain public trust by ensuring company transparency and integrity in all of its dealings. Under Matlare's stewardship, the company prospered. In 2008, almost as soon as he arrived, the company acquired a 51 percent share of Haco Industries in Kenya, thus gaining a direct route to Kenya's consumer market. Haco, which imports finished products to be sold to a market of about 380 million, proved to be a good gateway for Tiger's brands of ketchup, pastas, candies, and canned beans.

Also in 2008 the company divested itself of Adcock Ingram, offering Tiger shareholders one share for each Adcock Ingram share they held. Adcock Ingram was listed on the Johannesburg Stock Exchange on August 25, 2008.

BETTER TIMES AHEAD

In 2009 Tiger Brands acquired Crosse and Blackwell from the Nestle company, gaining almost 75 percent control of its mayonnaise plant outside Cape Town. This acquisition was soon joined by Chococam, a company based in Cameroon. Manufacturing candy and other products based on cocoa since 1967, Chococam had a market stretching across West Africa. These acquisitions helped to bring Tiger Brands' sales figures for 2009 up to ZAR 20.64 billion ($2.67 billion).

Gillian Wolf

PRINCIPAL SUBSIDIARIES

Designer Group, Durban; Confectionery Works (Pty) Limited; Enterprise Foods (Pty) Limited; Langeberg Holdings Limited; Langeberg and Ashton Foods (Pty) Limited; Tiger Food Brands Intellectual Property Holding Company (Pty) Limited; Tiger Consumer Brands Limited; Haco Industries; Chocolaterie Confiserie; Pharma Investment Holdings Limited.

PRINCIPAL DIVISIONS

Domestic Food Products; Pharmaceuticals; Hospital Products; Exports; Fishing.

PRINCIPAL COMPETITORS

Associated British Foods PLC; Kraft Foods Inc.

FURTHER READING

Frankel, Rudy, *Tiger Tapestry*. Cape Town, South Africa: C. Struik, 1988.

Mawson, Nicola, "Tiger Brands Buys Crosse & Blackwell from Nestle," *Business Day*, May 25, 2009.

"New CEO for Tiger Brands," Fin24.com, February 12, 2008, http://www.fin24.com/articles/default/display_article.aspx?ArticleId=2268945.

Robbins, Tom, "Unsigned Letter Puts Tiger Boss in a Pickle," *Business Report*, November 26, 2007, http://www.busrep.co.za/index.php?fArticleId=4145282.

Shevel, Adele, "Tiger Gets New Fine for Fixing," *Sunday Times*, May 11, 2008, p. 3.

"Tiger Brands Acquisition of Haco Begins to Pay Off," *Business Daily* (Nairobi), November 25, 2009.

Tishman Construction Company

———————————— ■ ————————————

666 Fifth Avenue
New York, New York 10103-0001
U.S.A.
Telephone: (212) 399-3600
Fax: (212) 739-7065
Web site: http://www.tishmanconstruction.com

Private Company
Founded: 1898
Incorporated: 1980
Employees: 1,000
Sales: $4.69 billion (2008 est.)
NAICS: 236210 Industrial Building Construction;
236220 Commercial and Institutional Building
Construction; 237210 Land Subdivision; 531210
Offices of Real Estate Agents and Brokers

■ ■ ■

Tishman Construction Company, based in New York
City, is a leading construction management firm. Its
parent company, Tishman Realty & Construction
Company, has constructed, owned, managed, and
renovated many prominent commercial and residential
buildings in New York City and other major U.S. cities
since the late 19th century. Tishman Construction
works with five affiliates—Tishman Technologies
Corporation, Tishman Interiors Corporation, Tishman
Sustainable Construction Experience, Tishman Hotel &
Realty LP, and Tishman Advisory Services—to provide a
full range of services to construction partners. The
privately held company is led by the third and fourth

generations of Tishmans and has nine offices located
across the United States.

TENEMENT BEGINNINGS

In 1898 Julius Tishman, a Polish immigrant,
constructed the first of a series of tenement buildings on
the Lower East Side of Manhattan. During the 1910s
and 1920s, Tishman erected luxury apartment houses
on the Upper West Side and Upper East Side of the
island. Tishman's five sons joined the firm, which was
renamed Julius Tishman & Sons in 1914. Julius Tishman & Sons was one of the first of a handful of family-
owned firms that were reshaping the appearance of New
York City and which would dominate high-end urban
construction throughout the 20th century. It was also
one of the first to go public, renaming itself Tishman
Realty & Construction Co. and issuing stock on the
New York Curb Exchange in 1928. Soon, however, the
Great Depression forced the company to cease new
construction and content itself with managing its existing properties.

After World War II Tishman resumed new
construction projects with 445 Park Avenue in Manhattan, a landmark building that boasted innovations such
as central air conditioning, automatic elevators, and all-
fluorescent lighting. The booming real estate market of
Southern California attracted Norman Tishman,
company president, to expand out of New York, which
he feared was becoming overbuilt. In 1950 the company
developed a complex on Wilshire Boulevard in Los
Angeles; within a few years, Tishman became the
region's leading property manager. Tishman also erected

buildings in Buffalo, New York; Cleveland, Ohio; New Orleans, Louisiana; and Philadelphia, Pennsylvania.

Norman Tishman envisioned the Tishman firm as achieving stability through relying on rental payments. The next leader, however, Robert Tishman, who took over the family firm in 1962, steered it in a sharply different direction, emphasizing large commercial office buildings during an urban real estate boom. By the late 1960s the company sold most of its residential properties.

PIONEERS OF CONSTRUCTION MANAGEMENT

During the 1960s the Tishman company pioneered the field of construction management, in which the company acted as agent for the owner, working closely with the owner and architects at every stage but having authority over the construction site and the hiring and firing of subcontractors. Tishman Construction Company was created to handle construction manager jobs. With Tishman Realty's extensive experience as a property owner and manager, Tishman Construction could understand clients' needs and expectations more clearly than typical contractors. In addition, Tishman Construction could work on a wider range of building projects and avoid the risks of ownership.

Tishman Construction's first major project was the new Madison Square Garden in New York, constructed from 1966 to 1968. Its next set of jobs included some of the highest, and highest-profile, buildings ever built: the 100-floor John Hancock Center in Chicago, completed in 1969, and the 110-story Twin Towers at the World Trade Center complex in New York, which were the world's tallest buildings at their completion in 1973.

In the meantime, the parent company had made what turned out to be a poor bet by building a new of-

fice tower at 1166 Avenue of the Americas in Manhattan. When it opened in 1974 during a economic recession, tenants could not be found and the building went unoccupied. In 1976 the company defaulted on its construction loan, losing over $30 million. As a public company, Tishman Realty also suffered from disadvantageous accounting and tax regulations compared to its private competitors. The company seemed too large to sell intact, so the managers agreed to convert Tishman into a partnership, selling off its properties and allotting the remaining funds to its shareholders.

NEW MANAGEMENT AND REBIRTH

The construction and research division, which included Tishman Construction, was purchased by Rockefeller Center Corp. Managed by John L. Tishman, it retained the name Tishman Realty & Construction Co. Meanwhile, Robert V. Tishman and his son-in-law Jerry Speyer founded Tishman Speyer Properties in 1978, which soon grew into a leading international real estate development firm. Tishman Construction's reputation remained intact, and it attracted plenty of business. The company finished work on Detroit's Renaissance Center in 1977, and the Golden Nugget Hotel & Casino in Atlantic City, New Jersey, in 1980.

During this time, Tishman established a fruitful partnership with the Walt Disney Company, beginning by constructing additions to the Polynesian Village Resort at Walt Disney World in Florida. Its reward was to be named construction manager for EPCOT Center, a new theme park adjoining the Magic Kingdom at Walt Disney World. The project was valued at approximately $1 billion; EPCOT opened in October 1982.

REGAINING INDEPENDENCE

In 1980 a group of 16 executives, led by John Tishman, bought back Tishman Realty & Construction Co. for $6.5 million. Determined to keep firmer control over its finances and its destiny, they reestablished it as a private company. The timing was propitious, as the early and mid-1980s saw a tremendous boom for commercial construction in the United States. Initially, Tishman Realty & Construction defined itself as a construction services firm. Soon, though, it resumed developing buildings to own, but only in markets where it would not compete against its construction management clients.

Many of these build-to-own projects were hotels in leading cities and casino centers such as Atlantic City

KEY DATES

1898: Julius Tishman erects his first building in Manhattan.

1966–68: Tishman Construction manages construction of the new Madison Square Garden, its first major project.

1976: Tishman Realty & Construction is dissolved after financial reverses.

1980: Management buys back Tishman Realty & Construction and reestablishes it as a private company.

2006: Tishman Construction completes 7 World Trade Center, the first building to open on the reconstructed World Trade Center site in New York City.

and Las Vegas, Nevada. In 1982 Tishman Hotel & Realty LP was established to develop and manage these properties, usually in collaboration with Tishman Construction. Tishman Construction's relationship with Disney continued, as in 1983 it built the Hilton hotel at Walt Disney World Village, and in the late 1980s erected the Walt Disney World Swan and Dolphin resort hotels.

Tishman Construction developed other specialized services such as interior renovation and historic preservation. The company was in charge of renovating New York's Carnegie Hall, one of the world's most renowned concert halls, which was reopened in 1986 (although not without complaints that its acoustics had somehow deteriorated). A year later, the Rainbow Room nightclub and restaurants at Rockefeller Center benefited from a Tishman renovation. Tishman Construction was construction manager for Tower 49, New York's first "intelligent" building, which opened in 1984. Such buildings featured an integrated system of utilities controlled by computer through a fiber-optic network, which promised significant savings on energy costs, and incorporated devices codesigned by Tishman Research Corporation that switched lights on and off as persons entered and left rooms.

FURTHER DIVERSIFICATION IN TURBULENT TIMES

As the overheated U.S. real estate market slowed down in the late 1980s and early 1990s, Tishman Construction began pursuing jobs to build and renovate schools, prisons, and other governmental buildings, which it had

previously tended to ignore. Large-scale public jobs included the construction of the Ronald Reagan State Building in California and a comprehensive renovation of public schools in Chicago amounting to some $1 billion. Tishman Urban Development Corporation was established in 1994 to foster partnerships between public agencies and private developers.

Tishman Realty's emphasis on hotel development continued, much of it funded through a joint venture with Aoki Corporation of Japan. This relationship helped Tishman Construction become the first outside firm allowed to construct a hotel in Japan. During the 1990s the company managed hotel construction in Puerto Rico, the United Kingdom, and Poland.

In the United States, as demand for new commercial offices revived, Tishman Construction continued to reshape the Manhattan skyline with projects such as the 72-story City Spire, the Four Seasons Hotel, and the J. P. Morgan World Headquarters. The company's range of projects included airport, train, and bus terminals; convention centers; corporate data centers; and hospitals and research laboratories. Almost inevitably, not all of Tishman Construction's projects ran smoothly to completion. Most notoriously, the construction of the Condé Nast tower at 4 Times Square suffered a series of accidents, the worst of which was the collapse of an elevator tower and construction scaffolding in July 1998, which killed a resident of a nearby hotel, displaced several hundred residents and businesses, and forced the closing of streets in midtown Manhattan for almost a month.

REBUILDING THE WORLD TRADE CENTER

Into the 21st century, Tishman Construction continued to be chosen for high-profile jobs combining severe technical challenges and intense public scrutiny. One noteworthy example was the construction of the Boston Convention & Exhibition Center, completed in 2004. Nevertheless, the company had a much more sustained involvement at the most prominent (and politically charged) building project in the United States: the reconstruction of the World Trade Center site after its destruction in the September 11, 2001, terrorist attack. The first building Tishman finished was 7 World Trade Center in 2006, replacing the previous building with the same name that it had put up in the 1980s. Prolonged wrangling between officials and developers delayed construction of other buildings on the site, but by early 2010, Tishman's work on 1 World Trade Center (also known as Freedom Tower) and 4 World Trade Center was well under way.

Daniel R. Tishman succeeded his father John as the chairman and chief executive of Tishman Construction. Daniel Tishman's personal passion for environmental protection (in 2007 he was selected as chairman of the board of the Natural Resources Defense Council) merged with business opportunity as more clients appreciated the ecological benefits, as well as long-term cost savings, of energy-efficient building design. Several of Tishman Construction's projects, including 7 World Trade Center, qualified for Leadership in Energy and Environmental Design (LEED) certification, recognized as the industry standard for environmentally sensitive buildings. The massive CityCenter resort complex in Las Vegas, for which Tishman Construction was the construction manager, received LEED Gold certification as it neared completion in 2009.

Tishman Construction entered the second decade of the 2000s ranked as the number-one construction management firm in the United States according to *Building Design + Construction* magazine. Despite increasing competition from public corporations and real estate investment trusts, Tishman Construction's ability to collaborate with a wide range of public and private clients and to offer a full range of related services, seemed to ensure continued prosperity for the company even during the widespread recession that began in late 2007.

Stephen V. Beitel

PRINCIPAL SUBSIDIARIES

Tishman Construction Corporation of California; Tishman Construction Corporation of DC; Tishman Construction Corporation of Illinois; Tishman Construction Corporation of Nevada; Tishman Construction Corporation of New England; Tishman Construction Corporation of New Jersey; Tishman Construction Corporation of New York; Tishman Construction Corporation of Pennsylvania.

PRINCIPAL COMPETITORS

CB Richard Ellis Group, Inc.; Gilbane, Inc.; Trammell Crow Company; Vornado Realty Trust.

FURTHER READING

Blair, William G., "Tishman Company Back on Its Own Once More," *New York Times*, February 10, 1980, Sec. 8, pp. 1, 4.

Chen, David W., "Construction Collapse in Times Square: The Impact; Mayor Faults Offer of Aid for Victims of Collapse," *New York Times*, July 24, 1998, p. B5.

Hylton, Richard T., "At Tishman, Fewer Glamorous Jobs," *New York Times*, September 13, 1990, p. D1.

Kozinn, Allen, "Case of the Carnegie Concrete, Part II," *New York Times*, September 20, 1995, p. C13.

Madsen, Jana J., "Rising from the Ashes: Like the Mythical Phoenix Born Anew and Rising from Its Own Ashes, the New 7 World Trade Center (WTC) Embodies the Beginning of a New Downtown New York City," *Buildings*, October 2006, p. 30.

Marcus, Steven J., "The 'Intelligent' Buildings," *New York Times*, December 1, 1983.

Marino, Vivian, "Square Feet: The 30-Minute Interview: Daniel R. Tishman," *New York Times*, January 28, 2010, p. RE9.

Monroe, Linda, "Industry Innovator: Tishman Realty & Construction Co., Inc. Takes the Term Full Service beyond the Norm," *Buildings*, July 1989, p. 50.

"Stretching the Skyline," *Time*, January 12, 1968.

"Toward the Millennium," *Time*, July 21, 1958.

Tishman Speyer
Properties, L.P.

■

Rockefeller Center
45 Rockefeller Plaza
New York, New York 10111-0100
U.S.A.
Telephone: (212) 715-0300
Fax: (212) 319-1745
Web site: http://www.tishmanspeyer.com

Private Company
Founded: 1978
Employees: 300
Sales: $224 million (2008 est.)
NAICS: 531110 Lessors of Residential Buildings and
Dwellings; 531120 Lessors of Nonresidential Build-
ings (Except Miniwarehouses); 531311 Residential
Property Managers; 531312 Nonresidential
Property Managers; 237210 Land Subdivision

■ ■ ■

Tishman Speyer Properties, L.P., is a global real estate
developer with headquarters in New York City and
branch offices throughout the United States, Europe,
South America, and Asia. With stakes in the Rockefeller
Center, Chrysler Building, and MetLife Building, Tishman Speyer has become one of Manhattan's most high-
profile commercial landlords. At the same time, the
company's chief executive officer, Jerry Speyer, has
become one of the city's most prominent and celebrated
developers, both for his deal-making skill and for his
philanthropic work. In addition to establishing office
buildings in major urban locations, this private partnership creates mixed-use, retail, residential, and entertainment centers. It also provides planning services for large-
scale developments and manages the conversion of
underused tracts of land into such developments.

TISHMAN PREDECESSORS: 1898–1976

Julius Tishman was an immigrant peddler who began
building small tenements on the Lower East Side of
Manhattan in 1898. In 1910 he built a nine-story
luxury apartment building on the Upper West Side
despite warnings that no well-to-do New Yorker would
live north of 86th Street. The project was successful and
he made a small fortune erecting more apartment buildings in this neighborhood during the next 10 years. In
1923 he decided to put up an office building across
from Penn Station, even though this area around West
34th Street and Seventh Avenue was occupied mainly by
garment factories. Again, he was successful, and he followed by erecting more office buildings. Tishman Realty
& Development Co. Inc. was established as a publicly
traded firm in 1928, with Julius's son David as
president. Shortly after, the Great Depression put an
end to the firm's construction activities.

Tishman Realty & Development did not
significantly renew its growth until after World War II,
when it once again began constructing office buildings
in New York City, including Manhattan's first fully air-
conditioned office building and first metal-clad office
building, under the direction of Norman Tishman,
another of Julius Tishman's five sons. In 1950 the
company began putting up office and apartment build-

COMPANY PERSPECTIVES

Tishman Speyer is one of the leading owners, developers, operators, and managers of first-class real estate in the world, having managed a portfolio of assets since its inception of over 116 million square feet and more than 92,000 residential units in major metropolitan areas across the United States, Europe, Latin America and Asia.

In large measure, we have achieved this position by recognizing opportunities where most others see only difficulties and then transforming these opportunities into assets of even greater value.

Our ability to do so is the result of a philosophy of approaching each property or project as a stand-alone business in order to create maximum value for both tenants and partners.

This philosophy, combined with a culture that encourages creativity and unconventional thinking across a variety of disciplines, has enabled Tishman Speyer to acquire, develop and manage a property portfolio representing over US$50.2 billion in total value since 1978.

ings on Wilshire Boulevard in Los Angeles, and within a few years it was the largest landlord in Southern California. By 1958 the firm was operating 31 large office or apartment buildings and 3 shopping centers in 5 cities, with others under construction in Buffalo, New York, and Cleveland, Ohio. In 1959 the company also began leasing office and factory equipment and aircraft. The following year it began constructing buildings for other developers as well as doing so for its own account. A few years later it added a research subsidiary to help manufacturers apply new products and techniques.

Tishman Realty & Development moved into Chicago in 1962 to build the Gateway Center and soon had become the city's second-largest office landlord. It divested itself of the last of its residential properties in 1967. By this time the company was under the direction of David's son Robert. After serving as the general contractor for the 100-story John Hancock Building in Chicago and for the Renaissance Center in Detroit, the company won the contract to build the World Trade Center in New York.

The recession that began in 1970 hurt all developers, but Tishman Realty & Construction was especially hard hit because of the 44-story office building at 1166 Avenue of the Americas in midtown Manhattan that it completed in 1974. Two years later, with the building still vacant, Tishman defaulted on its construction loan from Citibank. This structure was said to have cost the company some $70 million to $80 million in cumulative losses—more money than had ever been lost before on a single building. Its management decided in 1976 to liquidate the company and use its assets for a cash distribution to the shareholders, of whom the largest group by far consisted of members of the Tishman family. Seventeen properties were purchased by the Equitable Life Assurance Society of the United States for $107.5 million. The remaining ones were sold for $78.5 million to Lazard Realty Inc., an arm of the investment house of Lazard Frères & Co. acting on behalf of a group of investors.

ESTABLISHMENT OF TISHMAN SPEYER PROPERTIES

The nine Tishmans in executive positions had no intention of putting themselves out of work, however. Tishman Realty & Construction continued as a general-contracting subsidiary of Rockefeller Center Corp. under John L. Tishman until 1980, when 16 of the senior executive officers of the subsidiary bought it back. The former company's management and leasing operations became Tishman Management and Leasing Corp., with Alan V. Tishman in charge. The finance and development arm became Tishman Speyer Properties (TSP), with Robert V. Tishman (who had been president of the old company prior to liquidation) as chairman and Speyer, his son-in-law, as president and chief executive officer.

All three successor companies took up quarters in the Tishman Building, the aluminum-clad high-rise at 666 Fifth Avenue that had served as the old company's flagship. TSP started business with assets of $17 million from the dissolution of the old firm, a staff of 13, and 2 properties worth $65 million.

TSP's first job, under contract to Lazard Realty as part of the sale, was to direct the land assemblage and construction of 520 Madison Avenue, a 38-floor slant-faced office tower clad in rose-colored granite. TSP took an equity interest in the property and moved its headquarters there after completion in 1981. The fledgling company also acquired and renovated five or six buildings at relatively low cost, tapping funds from the Lazard Realty-organized investment group.

By 1981 TSP had built enough equity from its projects to buy out this group. It then turned to brothers Lester and Henry Crown of Chicago (the largest

1978: Tishman Speyer Properties (TSP) is established with Jerry Speyer as CEO.

1981: The firm completes 520 Madison Avenue, which becomes its headquarters.

1986: TSP completes a Manhattan tower for Equitable Life Assurance.

1990: TSP completes continental Europe's tallest building in Frankfurt, Germany.

1995: The firm becomes part-owner and manager of Manhattan's Rockefeller Center.

2001: TSP sells most of its share of the rehabilitated Chrysler Building.

2005: TSP creates partnership with Indian firm ICICI Venture Funds Management Company.

2006: TSP and Black Rock Realty purchase New York's Stuyvesant Town and Peter Cooper Village apartment complexes.

2010: Ownership of Stuyvesant Town and Peter Cooper Village properties is transferred to creditors of TSP and Black Rock.

shareholders of General Dynamics Corp.) to fund joint ventures, forming both a development and an acquisition partnership with the family, and also took on Equitable Life as a limited partner. By the spring of 1983 TSP had developed 12 projects in New York, Chicago, Atlanta, Houston, and Stamford, Connecticut, worth $1.2 billion. TSP's net equity in these projects was believed to exceed $100 million.

IN THE TOP 10

In 1983 TSP completed $300 million more in construction to put it among the top 10 commercial developers in the United States. The firm developed five major projects in Chicago, including a $200 million tower for NBC, and completed a 28-story building at One Brickell Square in Miami, overlooking Biscayne Bay. The Crown brothers' connections enabled TSP to secure Chicago's Continental Illinois National Bank & Trust Co. as the anchor tenant for 520 Madison Avenue in Manhattan, which was named the Continental Illinois Center. In 1984 TSP formed a syndication company that would allow individual investors not as well-heeled as Equitable Life or the Crown brothers, but capable of putting up at least $500,000, to participate in the ownership of existing properties through private limited partnerships.

TSP was also sharing the wealth from about $550 million worth of real estate with some of its own employees. Managing partners Tishman and Speyer took 60 percent of the income and tax benefits, while three general partners and a dozen limited partners shared in the remainder, an arrangement that could double or triple their basic pay. In order to quench competition within the firm, this partnership interest applied to all of TSP's projects, not just the ones in which a given staffer was engaged.

The actual construction was in the hands of hired outside managers supervised by TSP. A company executive told Ronald Derven of *National Real Estate Investor* in 1988, "The people on our staff come from either a design or construction background. We look over the shoulders of our contractors—second-guessing them if you will—to anticipate problems before they become insurmountable."

VENTURING OUT

TSP had, in the mid-1980s, the daring to undertake Manhattan projects outside the usual locations, completing the Saatchi Building at 375 Hudson Street, north of the financial district, in 1985, and turning the ruins of the old Siegel-Cooper department store, at 620 Sixth Avenue in the Flatiron district, into a retail complex. In 1986 the firm completed a 54-story tower for Equitable Life on Seventh Avenue, the first major office building on this avenue and a trendsetter as developers began moving farther west in midtown.

Nevertheless, sensing that the market for new buildings would not last, TSP began withdrawing from further construction. "We put 7 million square feet of development on the shelf between 1985 and 1987," Speyer told Peter Hellman for *New York* in 1995. "The market was *too* hot," he explained. "It was worrisome." Instead, TSP began acquiring existing buildings, including ones in Los Angeles, Miami, and San Francisco.

By the fall of 1987 TSP's portfolio had grown to 25 properties, with 18 million square feet of space owned or managed by the firm and a cumulative market value of $4.2 billion. Only 30 percent of this portfolio was now in New York, because the managing partners considered building in Manhattan increasingly difficult and costly. TSP projects underway at this time included 3 in Florida, 2 in Chicago, 1 in Durham, North Carolina, and a joint venture with Shearson Lehman Brothers Holdings Inc. to develop, finance, and market a $150 million office and apartment complex in Beijing for foreign executives and diplomats in China. Plans for this project, however, fell apart in 1989, after Chinese security forces crushed a protest in Tiananmen Square.

EUROPEAN DESIGNS

By this time TSP had begun work on its first successful foreign project, as developer of the MesseTurm, a 62-floor pyramid-crowned office tower in Frankfurt, Germany. It was completed in 1990 as the tallest building in continental Europe. The firm followed this up with some of the largest development projects in Berlin, capital of the reunified Germany. In 1996 TSP completed Friedrichstadt-Passagen, a $500 million property with one million square feet of office, retail, and residential space fronting the city's historic Friedrichstrasse.

One Manhattan deal that proved attractive to TSP was the purchase of 1301 Avenue of the Americas, the headquarters of J.C. Penney Co., for $353 million in 1988. This 46-story, 1.8-million-square-foot tower was acquired in a joint venture with Trammell Crow Co. Once Penney moved to Plano, Texas, the prematurely aged 26-year-old building was vacant. The partners resurfaced the building's faded external panels and filled in the sunken entrance plaza, installing a Jim Dine sculpture. By late 1990, in spite of a recession, it was 80 percent rented by prestige tenants and had been renamed the Credit Lyonnais Building.

TSP essentially marked time in the early 1990s as the U.S. economy slowly recovered from recession. One of its few losers was 1515 Broadway, a 54-story midtown Manhattan office tower purchased in 1985 in partnership with Equitable Life and other investors. This venture resulted in bankruptcy and an end to TSP's relationship with Equitable Life.

MANHATTAN RESCUES

By 1995, however, TSP was ready to raise its profile again in its own backyard, by paying $306 million, in partnership with Goldman, Sachs & Co. and David Rockefeller (who also brought in Europe's superrich Gianni Agnelli and Stavros Niarchos), to purchase Rockefeller Center from Mitsubishi Estate Co., Ltd., and rescue it from imminent bankruptcy. Although the high-profile 12-building center included six million square feet of commercial and retail space, it was $900 million in debt, and Mitsubishi had incurred $2 billion in losses. Ninety percent of the space was leased but at relatively low rates, while operating costs were high. TSP wound up with only a 5 percent stake in the complex but, as manager, brought in blue-chip tenants such as Christie's International plc and Cablevision Systems Corporation, as well as fashionable retailers Banana Republic, J. Crew, Kenneth Cole, and Sephora. The

center turned profitable in 1998 and earned $45.3 million in 1999.

Another Manhattan classic was added to the TSP portfolio in 1997, when a TSP investment fund established in partnership with Travelers Group Inc. and Shearson Lehman Brothers purchased the mortgage of the Chrysler Building and adjoining 666 Third Avenue for $220 million. Speyer acknowledged that the 77-story Art Deco landmark was in need of renovation and said the firm anticipated spending about $100 million to replace elevators and the heating and air-conditioning systems. By 2000 the venerable tower was packed with tenants paying as much as $100 a square foot.

Also in 1997, TSP and Travelers Group formed a joint venture for 10 office buildings previously held by Travelers, including 125 High Street in Boston, a recently built 1.5-million-square-foot complex that included twin towers with an atrium between them, three restored 19th-century buildings, and a city fire station. The other properties consisted of buildings in Florida, California, and the Midwest, as well as one other building in Boston.

SPANNING THE WORLD

TSP was also active in Europe and South America. In addition to the previously completed German projects, the firm was, in 1998, developing a three-million-square-foot Berlin mixed-use complex, including a new train station, and, with Sony Corp., a two-million-square-foot complex near Potsdamer Platz with retail, entertainment, and office space, including Sony's new European headquarters. TSP also was developing an office building in Kraków, Poland, and had developed properties in France and Great Britain. The firm had joined with Brazil's largest construction company to erect that nation's tallest building, a 36-story office tower in São Paulo. This was followed in 2001 with the announcement that the partners would join with Deutsche Bank to put up a four-tower office complex in the city.

TSP took a trip down memory lane in 2000 when it purchased (in collaboration with a group that included the Crown family and TMW, a German investment group) the former Tishman Building at 666 Fifth Avenue. Also in 2000, TSP completed 101 West End Avenue, a 35-story, twin-tower residential rental complex between West 64th and 65th streets in Manhattan.

TSP was also active in California. In San Francisco, the firm purchased the Chevron Corp. buildings at 555 and 575 Market Street in 1998 for about $190 million after selling 525 Market Street the previous year. When

Chevron moved out of the city and new-media businesses started to fail, however, the buildings began to empty. Construction of two office towers in Mountain View and Santa Clara was scheduled to begin in 2000. In Southern California, TSP purchased Santa Monica's MGM Plaza in 2000 for $353 million, with funding from partners who included Travelers. This six-building office complex covered a whole city block.

INTO THE 21ST CENTURY

TSP had, in 2001, offices in nine U.S. cities and in Berlin, Buenos Aires, Frankfurt, Kraków, London, Madrid, Paris, São Paulo, and Warsaw. Since its formation the firm had developed or acquired a portfolio of more than 48 million square feet of constructed area, valued at over $10 billion. According to Speyer in a December 20, 1998, *New York Times Magazine* article by James Traub, TSP achieved an average annual rate of return of 47.5 percent between 1993 and 1998.

As the economy stumbled during the first decade of the 21st century, TSP briefly turned away from its historically aggressive growth strategy, selling a number of its properties in order to generate revenues for future projects. One notable deal came in March 2001, when the company and Travelers sold a 75 percent stake in the Chrysler Building to TMW for a reported $300 million. TSP continued to manage and lease the building. Even as the real estate market slowed during these years, TSP remained one of the city's most prominent and respected firms, gaining recognition for both its business acumen and its altruistic activities. By 2004 company head Speyer and his wife, Katherine Farley, had earned widespread praise for their philanthropic work. Writing in the June 2, 2004, *New York Times*, Robin Pogrebin and Charles V. Bagli described the couple as "bona fide New York royalty."

By the middle of the decade, TSP had a portfolio worth roughly $16 billion. As New York's commercial real estate market continued to grow at a rapid pace, the company remained intent on further expansion. In April 2005 TSP spent $1.72 billion to acquire the famed MetLife Building at Grand Central Station. At the time, the skyscraper's price tag was the largest paid for a single building in the history of New York. That same month, the company entered into a joint venture with Indian private-equity firm ICICI Venture Funds Management Company to explore the potential for developing a range of real estate projects in India. The move to the Indian subcontinent was part of a larger industry trend, as U.S. real estate companies intensified their search for new opportunities in emerging economies overseas. According to an industry report, by 2006 India had become one of the most desirable real estate markets in the world, second only to China.

THE PERILS OF OVERREACH

In October 2006 TSP was at the center of the largest real estate acquisition in history, when it joined Black Rock Realty to purchase the Stuyvesant Town and Peter Cooper Village apartment complexes in lower Manhattan. In a $5.4 billion deal, the companies would control 110 apartment buildings and more than 11,000 individual apartments, in an area comprising 18 city blocks. According to an October 18, 2006, *New York Times* report by Charles Bagli, the properties represented "some of the most valuable real estate in the world." The acquisition, however, quickly drew the ire of advocates for affordable housing. Originally constructed for the veterans of World War II and still largely under rent stabilization rules, the apartment complexes were widely regarded as some of the city's last bastions of affordable living space.

In order to finance this blockbuster deal, TSP quickly began to unload a number of its most valuable assets. In December of that year, the company sold its 41-story building at 666 Fifth Avenue for $1.8 billion, a new industry record, and roughly three times the price the company had paid for the building only six years earlier. In May 2007 the company sold the New York Times building to Africa Israel USA for $525 million, triple the $175 million it had paid to purchase the building in 2004. These efforts to raise capital hardly curbed TSP's appetite for new properties. In June 2007 the company spent $1.72 billion on six commercial buildings in downtown Chicago. Among the properties were the historic Civic Opera House and the Chicago Mercantile Exchange. TSP hoped to finance part of the acquisition by immediately putting three of the buildings up for sale.

As the world economy descended into a major recession, however, TSP began to feel the pinch of the credit crisis. By September 2009 TSP and Black Rock found themselves in danger of defaulting on their mortgage payment on the Stuyvesant/Peter Cooper apartment complexes. In December 2009 TSP defaulted on its loan payment for the Chicago buildings it had purchased in 2007. A month later, TSP and Black Rock officially defaulted on their payment for the Stuyvesant/Peter Cooper properties. By late January 2010 the companies were forced to turn the properties over to their creditors. Many industry observers saw the collapse of the Stuyvesant/Peter Cooper deal as a portent of worse things to come for the U.S. real estate industry. As a major player in the real estate boom of the previous

Tishman Speyer Properties, L.P.

two decades, Tishman Speyer would no doubt be facing other serious challenges as it headed into a new decade.

Robert Halasz
Updated, Stephen Meyer

PRINCIPAL COMPETITORS

Boston Properties, Inc.; Brookfield Properties Corporation; Equity Office Properties Trust; Silverstein Properties, Inc.; Vornado Realty Trust.

FURTHER READING

Bagli, Charles V., "$5.4 Billion Bid Wins Complexes in New York Deal," *New York Times*, October 18, 2006, p. A1.

———, "Huge Housing Complex in N.Y. Returned to Creditors," *New York Times*, January 25, 2010, p. 12.

Blair, William G., "Tishman Company Back on Its Own Once More," *New York Times*, February 10, 1980, Sec. 8, pp. 1, 4.

Derven, Ronald, "Tishman Speyer Celebrates 10 Years of Success," *National Real Estate Investor*, February 1988, pp. 96–98.

Ginsberg, Steve, "'Anti-Trump' Plays a New Hand," *San Francisco Business Times*, August 11, 2000, p. 1.

Gregor, Alison, "A Family Tradition Yields a $5.4 Billion Coup," *New York Times*, November 5, 2006, p. 26.

Hellman, Peter, "The Invisible Magnate," *New York*, October 16, 1995, pp. 34–39.

Pacelle, Mitchell, "Chrysler Building Gets a New Owner as Tishman Speyer Wins Bidding War," *Wall Street Journal*, November 25, 1997, p. A6.

Pogrebin, Robin, and Charles V. Bagli, "Mixing the Real Estate Business and Everyone's Pleasure," *New York Times*, June 2, 2004, p. 1E.

Scardino, Albert, "Tishman's Global Strategy," *New York Times*, October 10, 1987, pp. 43, 45.

Slatin, Peter, "Will Rock Drag Down New Owners?" *Crain's New York Business*, November 13, 1995, pp. 1, 31.

Thompson, Russell, and Matthew Williams, "How One U.S. Developer Has Found Happiness Overseas," *Barron's*, July 6, 1998, pp. 36–37.

Traub, James, "The Anti-Trump," *New York Times Magazine*, December 20, 1998, pp. 62–68.

TPI Composites, Inc.

---■---

8501 North Scottsdale Road
Gainey Center II, Suite 280
Scottsdale, Arizona 85253-2759
U.S.A.
Telephone: (480) 305-8910
Fax: (480) 305-8315
Web site: http://www.tpicomposites.com

Private Company
Incorporated: 1968 as Tillotson-Pearson, Inc.
Employees: 2,000
Sales: $8.8 million (2008 est.)
NAICS: 326130 Laminated Plastics Plate, Sheet (Except Packaging), and Shape Manufacturing

■ ■ ■

TPI Composites, Inc., is a manufacturer of composite structures serving three markets: energy, transportation, and military. The company offers wind turbine blades for the wind energy market, while its transportation products include decks for shipping cars by rail and other railcar floors, as well as lightweight vehicle bodies for buses and "people movers." For the military market, TPI uses composite materials to produce lighter and corrosive-resistant vehicle bodies that also offer greater personnel protection. At the heart of TPI is its patented SCRIMP (Seemann Composites Resin Infusion Molding Process) technology, which produces materials that are not only lighter and stronger than traditional fiber-reinforced polymer (FRP) composites but also more versatile. Headquartered in Scottsdale, Arizona, TPI

maintains development and manufacturing operations in Warren, Rhode Island, its former home base. Other manufacturing facilities are located in Springfield, Ohio; Newton, Iowa; Ciudad Juárez, Mexico; and Taicang, China.

COMPANY FOUNDER PEARSON

Behind the TPI initials were the two men who founded TPI in 1968: Neil Tillotson, the financier, and Everett Pearson, the innovator and acclaimed fiberglass ship builder. Born in 1933, Pearson grew up in a tenant house in New York City but was fortunate that his family was able to build a cottage that became a summer home on a piece of land on the Rhode Island coast. As a youth, Pearson fixed up an old 8-foot punt provided by a family friend and taught himself to sail. In 1955 Pearson and his cousin, Clinton Pearson, tried their hand at building dinghies using polyester resin and fiberglass, which had been the subject of a *Popular Mechanics* article read by a friend of theirs. They bought the necessary materials and began producing dinghies in a barn in Seekonk, Rhode Island, and then sold the vessels on the lawn with a hand-painted "For Sale" sign. The seeds for Pearson Yachts were thus planted, and they began to take root after the cousins, both Brown University graduates, completed military service in the U.S. Navy. In 1958 they were asked to build a fiberglass sailboat that could be sold for less than $10,000. They accepted the challenge and in January 1959 displayed their creation at the New York Boat Show. They arrived in town with not enough cash to pay for their hotel room but left with $170,000 in orders.

Pearson Yachts was taken public in April 1959 and later in the year acquired the famous Herreshoff Yard in Bristol, Rhode Island. The company enjoyed rapid growth but lacked the funds it needed, leading Grumman Allied Industries to acquire a controlling interest in Pearson Yachts in 1961. The Pearson cousins were able to expand their boat lines as the company became a major player in its field. While the financial backing that Grumman provided was crucial to the growth of Pearson Yachts, the cousins chafed under corporate control. Not only did they have to build fiberglass rooftops and fronts for the United Parcel Service trucks Grumman produced, they had to spend time writing quarterly reports and attending board meetings, time they felt could be better devoted to building yachts. Clinton Pearson left in 1964, and two years later Everett Pearson sold his stake to Grumman.

THE TILLOTSON-PEARSON PARTNERSHIP

Because of an agreement he signed with Grumman, Everett Pearson was not permitted to compete against Grumman in midsize sailboats for three years. Instead of boats, he decided to use FRP technology to build industrial fiberglass products, in particular chemical storage tanks. It was not long, however, before he was asked to build a boat. The Boston firm of John Alden Co. asked him to oversee the construction of a boat it designed for the company's owner, 70-year-old Neil Tillotson. Grumman granted Pearson permission to take on the job.

Although little remembered today, Tillotson was a minor celebrity of a peculiar sort. Growing up in Vermont, he quit high school to go to work for a rubber company in Massachusetts. He then started his own rubber company in the 1930s to make children's balloons and later grew it into an international concern manufacturing industrial products. In 1954 he bought a resort in the White Mountains of New Hampshire and established a home in Dixville Notch. Because the closest polling place was 50 miles away at the county seat, Tillotson incorporated Dixville Notch to establish a

polling place. By tradition New Hampshire was the first state to hold a presidential primary every four years, and Tillotson decided to bring attention to Dixville Notch by opening its polling place a moment after the stroke of midnight on primary day, the results then to be reported across the country by the newswire services. As town moderator, Tillotson had the honor of being the first to vote, thus becoming known as the first presidential primary voter every four years. Tillotson continued the tradition for nearly a half-century through the 2000 election, finally passing away at the age of 102 in 2001.

Pearson spent a winter with Tillotson building his boat. At some point Tillotson suggested they go into business together: He would supply the funding, Pearson the work, and the profits would be split equally. There was no contract, just a handshake deal between two sailors. In 1968 Tillotson-Pearson, Inc., was formed, and with Tillotson's money an FRP molding company in Warren, Rhode Island, was purchased and became the home for the new venture. "Our business philosophy," Pearson once explained, "was to employ good people, take care of our employees, and create new things."

VENTURES OUTSIDE BOAT BUILDING

Because Pearson was still not allowed to build boats and compete against Grumman-owned Pearson Yachts, TPI focused on such industrial products as ductwork, cooling towers, lighting poles, burial vaults, and windmill blades. The company even developed torpedoes for the U.S. Navy. Of these initial products, the streetlight poles and blades provided the most revenues. Although composite light poles eventually lost out to aluminum, the blade business proved especially resilient by finding a new use in the wind energy market. Other projects included people movers for United Technologies and Disney World rides and a prototype design for fiberglass harbor pilings developed in conjunction with the San Diego Port Authority. In 1986 TPI acquired SwimEx, Inc., a developer of small-space pools for exercise and rehabilitation, primarily geared toward athletic training.

Soon after the noncompete clause expired, of course, Pearson returned to his lifelong passion and resumed building boats. TPI acquired the Alden Yacht line and in 1976 introduced J Boat racing sailboats, which, despite a high price tag, proved to be extremely popular. TPI's boats and industrial products combined to generate $42 million in revenues by the end of the 1980s. Facing increased competition from other boat builders, TPI elected to sell the power boat and sailboat division and invest the proceeds in product research to achieve more diversity. As a result, sales fell to $24 million, but only 35 percent of that amount came from boat building as opposed to 65 percent the prior year. Being less dependent on boat building soon proved to have been an extremely wise decision. Because of a recession, the U.S. Congress in 1990 imposed a luxury tax on yachts and other items costing more than $100,000. Rather than generate more revenues, the tax prompted wealthy consumers to put off buying new boats, and the boat industry in the United States was all but destroyed.

ACQUIRING SCRIMP TECHNOLOGY

Because of the manufacturing process it used, TPI was one of Rhode Island's largest emitters of volatile organic compounds (VOCs). To lower its emissions, as mandated by the Environmental Protection Agency, the company had for many years pursued vacuum technology. The Pearson cousins had initially attempted to produce fiberglass dinghies using molds and vacuum suction but ended up building up layers by hand. The process worked but VOC emissions were the price. It was a du Pont salesman who told TPI that a man named Bill Seemann was having success with a closed vacuum system. Pearson immediately recognized that Seemann had solved the decades-long puzzle of working with resin in a closed vacuum system, and in 1992 TPI secured a license to refine and promote the so-called SCRIMP technology, which was consistent and repeatable, an ideal process for both boat making and producing other fiberglass products. Later in the year, TPI, Seemann, and Hardcore Composites formed SCRIMP Systems, LLC, to promote and license the technology to others.

In 1993 Tillotson sold his share of Tillotson-Pearson to John Walton, son of Wal-Mart Stores, Inc., founder Sam Walton. The company was renamed TPI, Inc., and subsequently became TPI Composites, Inc. TPI used the SCRIMP technology for both boat building and the manufacture of its other products. In the

late 1990s the company developed a lightweight fiberglass bus body that was more fuel efficient and environmentally friendly than aluminum bus bodies. It was also during this period, in 1999, that Pearson was able to buy back the Pearson Yachts trademark. In 1986 Grumman had sold the company to a private investor group. A dozen years later, Pearson tracked down the current owners and acquired the trademark while discarding the molds and other equipment that had become outdated.

REFOCUSING UNDER NEW OWNERSHIP

The new century brought manifold changes to TPI. In 2002 the company formed VienTek Mexico, a joint venture with Mitsubishi Power Systems Americas, Inc., a supplier of wind turbines, to manufacture wind turbine blades. A year later Pearson struck out on his own. He bought the SwimEx division and also used some of TPI's research to form Pearson Pilings within SwimEx. Greater changes were to follow in the fall of 2004 when TPI Composites was bought by Landmark Growth Capital Partners, LP and members of TPI's senior management team. In addition, the marine business composed of J Boats, Pearson Yachts, and Alerion sailboats was spun off as a separate company under the Pearson Composites name. The split allowed Pearson Composites to focus on the boat sector, while TPI was better positioned to take advantage of opportunities in the wind energy, transportation, and military markets.

In its more focused form, TPI in 2005 won a development contract from the U.S. Army to build next-generation composite Humvees that were lighter, and therefore more mobile, while providing occupants with greater armor protection. The transportation business also expanded. In 2006 a new plant opened in Springfield, Ohio, to produce a lightweight platform deck for vehicle-transport railcars. In addition, wind energy was gaining momentum as oil prices rose and greater emphasis was placed on renewable forms of energy. TPI opened a plant in Taicang, China, in 2008 to supply China and the western United States with large fiberglass turbine blades, up to 150 feet in length. Wind towers were also emerging across the Midwest, and later in the year TPI opened a new plant in Newton, Iowa, in 2008 to produce turbine blades. At the same time, the production of blades was tripled at the TPI-Mitsubishi joint venture plant in Mexico.

Because of its growing global footprint, TPI moved its headquarters to a more centralized location in 2007, opening new offices in Scottsdale. The potential of its business also attracted investors. Shortly before moving to Arizona, the company raised $22 million from new and existing investors. In early 2009 another $20 million was received from such prominent investors as the investment arm of General Electric Company, and at the end of the year another $26 million was raised from new and existing investors. Moreover, in 2010 TPI received $9 million in manufacturing tax incentives from the U.S. Department of Energy for its wind-blade business. Demand for both lightweight blades and lightweight bodies for commercial and military vehicles was likely to accelerate, placing TPI in a strong position for years to come.

Ed Dinger

PRINCIPAL SUBSIDIARIES

TPI Iowa LLC; TPI Ohio; TPI Taicang Composites (China).

PRINCIPAL COMPETITORS

Blade Dynamics Ltd.; LM Glasfiber Holding A/S; Polymarin Composites USA Limited.

FURTHER READING

Goldstein, Richard, "Neil Tillotson, 102, First Presidential Voter," *New York Times*, November 5, 2001.

Pillsbury, Fred, "Boatbuilder Is Taking a Spin with a New Line," *Boston Globe*, November 7, 1982, p. 1.

Rusnak, Andrew, "Tough as Glass," pts. 1 and 2, *Composites Fabrication*, March 1999, pp. 3–7; April 1999, pp. 3–5.

Sneyd, Ross, "Flexibility Serves Boat Builder," *Boston Globe*, August 25, 1991, p. 46.

Stein, Mara Lemos, "Incentives Add Players to Wind," *Wall Street Journal*, January 13, 2010, p. B4A.

Taylor, Ed, "Scottsdale Company Finds an Edge with High-Tech Wind Blades," *Mesa (AZ) Tribune*, September 26, 2008.

Tumi, Inc.

1001 Durham Avenue
South Plainfield, New Jersey 07080
U.S.A.
Telephone: (908) 756-4400
Toll Free: (800) 322-8864
Fax: (908) 756-5878
Web site: http://www.tumi.com

Wholly Owned Subsidiary of Doughty Hanson & Co.
Founded: 1975
Employees: 1,000 (est.)
NAICS: 448320 Luggage and Leather Goods Stores;
316991 Luggage Manufacturing; 316992 Women's
Handbag and Purse Manufacturing; 316993
Personal Leather Good (except Women's Handbag
and Purse) Manufacturing

■ ■ ■

Tumi, Inc., a subsidiary of Doughty Hanson & Co., is
known for its high-end luggage, business and travel
bags, and luxury accessories. It is an international brand
that distributes its products through its own stores
and Web site, as well as through department and
specialty stores around the globe. Tumi has a reputation for indestructible materials, innovative and
functional designs, cutting-edge technology, and
celebrity customers. It holds more than 25 patents for
engineering and design advances.

BEGINNINGS

In 1969 Charlie Clifford returned to New Jersey after
two years in the Peace Corps in Peru. He got a dog

called Tumi (named after a Peruvian god) and a job
with a small importing company that dealt in everything
from rugs to hand-carved gourds. In 1975 Clifford left
to form his own company, specializing in leather goods,
and he selected what he described as a "sentimental
choice" for the organization's name: Tumi. Clifford's
company was started with $10,000 in capital, and in the
first year it grossed over $625,000. Its early customers
were small stores that specialized in hand-made leather
goods, and most of Tumi's products were imported from
Colombia.

By the early 1980s, economic recession had affected
Tumi's early success. The company was faced with
declining sales and high interest rates on business loans,
and it was compelled to reassess both its products and
its business plans. Tumi lost money for several years and
then came up with a design innovation that catapulted
the company in a whole new direction. Its soft, ballistic
nylon travel bags with U-shaped and expandable pockets
became, within a few years, an industry standard. Clifford now felt that his original partner envisioned a less
aggressive business model, so with the help of an investment by his father-in-law, Clifford bought his partner
out. Tumi began expanding both its products and its
markets.

DESIGN ADVANCES AND
DEVELOPING MARKETS: THE
NINETIES

During the 1990s Tumi continued to be a design innovator for travel and business bags. In addition to soft
luggage made from the fabric used in bullet-proof vests,

Tumi produced carry-on luggage that used the same wheels as high-quality in-line skates. In 1994 the company introduced custom-molded zinc snap hooks with a swivel platform and riveted construction. Three years later Tumi invented the Safecase protection system whose shock absorption guarded the bag's contents if the bag was dropped.

Emphasizing the virtual indestructibility of its bags, Tumi originally offered a lifetime guarantee (later modified to a limited warranty). It introduced bags with secure lock systems and the Tumi Tracer, which featured an individual 20-digit code affixed to each bag and a toll-free number to help reunite Tumi customers with their lost or stolen bags. The company began putting its bags through testing to insure their quality. The tests included dropping a bag, loaded with 40 kilos of weight, more than 5,000 times, rubbing abrasive material on the luggage fabric for more than 24 hours, and putting the wheels on a bumpy treadmill. Tumi also began marketing leather cases for laptop computers before other luggage manufacturers, and the company included pockets for cell phones, business cards, and other small items in its product designs.

Tumi entered the international market in the 1990s and found new ways to distribute its products. For most of its early history, Tumi had sold its bags through department and specialty stores. In 1997 a Tumi retailer was opening a mall in Santa Monica, California, and suggested that Tumi launch its own shop in an available space. After opening this first store, Tumi continued with its regular distribution channels but now also sold directly to it customers. By November 2000, when Tumi opened its New York City store in Rockefeller Center, it already had 15 Tumi shops worldwide.

TRANSITIONS

As the new millennium began, Tumi was exploring various options for product and business development. After the terrorist attacks on the World Trade Center and the Pentagon in 2001, however, the travel industry and related businesses declined precipitously. Tumi deferred several planned store openings and laid off 25 percent of its employees, including Clifford's daughter. As it had in the early 1980s, Tumi used this difficult time as a catalyst to change.

In 2002 Oaktree Capital Management, a Los Angeles-based private investment bank, made what was described in *Women's Wear Daily* as a "substantial" investment in Tumi. Clifford, although retaining considerable interest in the company, stepped down as CEO. The capital infusion was intended to improve the financial functioning of the company, expand the retail-store business, aggressively pursue the international market, and increase brand awareness.

The new strategy included establishing new fiscal policies, creating new partnerships, designing new product lines to appeal to women and younger customers, and developing new direct-retail outlets using catalogs and online sales. Tumi moved its production facilities from the United States to Asia. In 2004 Doughty Hanson, a London investment fund, bought Tumi for $276 million and planned even more expansion.

A NEW DIRECTION

Tumi's signature black ballistic nylon bag did not appeal to all travelers, and some considered its standard black bag too conservative. Tumi wanted to increase its customer pool with more fashion-conscious designs. In addition, Tumi stores attracted customers that Tumi could serve with products beyond its luggage line. Consequently, in 2002 Tumi launched its T-Tech line, a collection of bags not intended for travel and targeted for the young, urban consumer. In 2005 Tumi entered into collaboration with Ducati, the Italian motorcycle manufacturer, for a co-branded red-and-black line of luggage, including an expandable knapsack that could hold a motorcycle helmet. At the same time, Tumi signed a licensing agreement with Umbro, a European soccer brand, to market sportswear designed to travel well.

By 2006, 15 percent of Tumi's sales came from fashion items such as watches, umbrellas, and key rings. That same year, Tumi began a partnership with the artist Anish Kapoor. Tumi sponsored the installation of Kapoor's Sky Mirror sculpture at Rockefeller Center, and Kapoor collaborated on the design of a backpack with a solar charger for cell phones. The joint project was for the benefit of Doctors without Borders, an organization providing international medical care.

In 2007 David Chu, founder and designer of Nautica, a company noted for its popular activewear, joined Tumi as an equity partner and executive creative director. Chu had already proven successful with his

KEY DATES

1975: Charlie Clifford founds Tumi.
1983: Tumi introduces its ballistic bag.
1997: The company opens its first Tumi store.
2002: Tumi is bought by Oaktree Capital Management.
2004: Tumi is bought by Doughty Hanson & Co.

fashionable and appealing designs and business savvy. According to Tumi CEO Laurence Franklin, quoted by Helen Walters in *BusinessWeek*, Chu was now expected to "supercharge the creative side of the business."

Before Chu's partnership with Tumi, about 70 percent of the brand's users were men aged 35 to 60. Chu's initial design targets were women, and four new handbag collections were launched in 2007. He also created the luxury Townhouse collection. Chu's brother, architect Peter Chu, redesigned the Tumi stores to be more attractive to women, including red Murano glass chandeliers that matched the Tumi logo, textured walls, and ebony and chrome fixtures, evoking the experience of luxury travel. The first new concept store, which opened on Madison Avenue in New York City, featured women's products and did not carry Tumi's functional luggage lines. When Chu left Tumi at the end of 2008, its global sales of luxury products had increased from 5 percent to 15 percent of Tumi's business.

NEW MARKETING STRATEGIES

With each management shift, Tumi introduced more aggressive marketing strategies as well as new designs and products. Tumi's initial online presence had been limited to advertising and information. In 2002 Tumi developed a partnership with eBags Technology Services to create a Web site that would sell Tumi products directly to the consumer. For the first time, customers could view, select, and order Tumi bags online.

In 2009 Tumi decided to redesign its Web presence, and the company chose GSI Commerce to provide a comprehensive package that would incorporate e-commerce, customer care, marketing, e-mail, and social media services. The redesigned Web stores were planned to launch in late 2010 and initially serve the United States, the United Kingdom, and Germany.

Tumi also changed its retail strategies in the new millennium. In 2003 it began leaving department stores and specialty shops that did not perform well or did not

fit the new fashionable image Tumi wanted to project. By 2005 Tumi's own stores generated 25 percent of its sales, and international sales accounted for 30 percent of its business.

Among the marketing alliances the company developed, in 2003 Tumi partnered with Starwood Preferred Guest, a hotel customer loyalty program that included Westin, Sheraton, St. Regis, and W hotels. Members received incentive rewards that provided access to Tumi private sales, special Tumi rewards for frequent stays, and the option to redeem program points for Tumi products. Tumi also announced an "Alliance of Style" with Seabourn Cruises, and Tumi document portfolios and luggage tags were added to the amenities provided on Seabourn's opulent voyages.

After many years of partially relying on word-of-mouth advertising, in 2005 Tumi hired Publicis and Publicis Dialog for a $10 million global campaign to include event sponsorship, print advertising, and direct and point-of-sale marketing. Although Tumi did not pay for product endorsements, the celebrities who owned Tumi bags, including Madonna, Tom Cruise, Shaquille O'Neal, and Cameron Diaz, continued to provide publicity for the company. Even U.S. President Barack Obama's briefcase of choice, known as the Obama bag, was a Tumi.

FASHION AND FUNCTION GOING FORWARD

As the first decade of the 21st century was ending, Tumi continued to grow, maintaining its design standards of functionality, endurance, and ease and incorporating marketing responsiveness and flexibility. In 2009 Jerome Griffith took over as CEO following the retirement of Laurence Franklin, who had held the post since 2002. Griffith had over 20 years of industry experience working with brands like Coach, Tommy Hilfiger, Lord and Taylor, and Esprit.

Tumi then introduced the Alpha Bravo line, a new collection of casual travel and business bags, designed to infuse a modern fashion sense into the iconic Tumi ballistic nylon bags and costing about 20 percent less. Tumi products continued to be available at leading department stores such as Bloomingdale's, Harrods, and Neiman Marcus, but Tumi now had more than 80 of its own stores around the globe, including stores in New York, Los Angeles, London, Paris, and Tokyo.

Grace Murphy

PRINCIPAL COMPETITORS

Coach, Inc.; LVMH Möet Hennessy Louis Vuitton SA; Samsonite.

FURTHER READING

Bailey, Ellen Askin, "Tumi Expands with Two Licensing Pacts: Luxury Travel Brand Ventures into Apparel and Co-branded Luggage While Continuing Retail Drive," *Daily News Record*, September 19, 2005, p. 4.

Braude, Jonathan, "Doughty Hanson Pockets Tumi," *Daily Deal/The Deal*, October 6, 2004.

Butler, Elisabeth, "Putting a New Face on an Old Bag," *Crain's New York Business*, March 7, 2005, p. 8.

Harris, Jessica, "Charlie Clifford: Founder, Tumi," *From Scratch*, National Public Radio, http://www.fromscratchradio.com/show/?p=127.

Scheidnes, Jean, "David Chu and Tumi Go Separate Ways," *WWD*, December 29, 2008, p. 3.

Tanaka, Hiroshi, "A Study of Brands: Tumi Trades on Trust, Tradition," *The Daily Yomiuri* (Tokyo, Japan), October 24, 2009, p. 5.

"Tumi Launches New E-commerce Web Site," PR Newswire, October 4, 2002.

"Tumi Selects GSI Commerce as Global Strategic E-Commerce Partner: Tumi to Re-platform Its Web Stores as Part of Multiyear Agreement That Includes Technology, Customer Care and Marketing Services," Business Wire, December 15, 2009.

Walters, Helen, "Tumi's New Itinerary: With Nautica Founder David Chu at the Creative Helm, the Luggage Maker Eyes Growth through a Complementary Market: Women's Accessories," *BusinessWeek*, January 24, 2007.

Zammit, Deanna, "Publicis to Lift Tumi's Global Image," *Adweek*, October 11, 2005.

Unisys Corporation

Unisys Way
Blue Bell, Pennsylvania 19424
U.S.A.
Telephone: (215) 986-4011
Fax: (215) 986-2312
Web site: http://www.unisys.com

Public Company
Incorporated: 1886 as American Arithmometer Company
Employees: 26,000
Sales: $5.23 billion (2008)
Stock Exchanges: New York
Ticker Symbol: UIS
NAICS: 334111 Electronic Computer Manufacturing; 334112 Computer Storage Device Manufacturing; 334113 Computer Terminal Manufacturing; 511210 Software Publishers; 541512 Computer Systems Design Services; 541611 Administrative Management and General Management Consulting Services

∎∎∎

Unisys Corporation is a major provider of computer and information technology products to customers in the financial services, communications, transportation, and government sectors. Over the years the company has forged contracts with a number of prominent public and private clients, notably the U.S. Department of Defense and the U.S. Department of Homeland Security. In addition to manufacturing high-end, mission-critical servers, Unisys offers a range of consult-

ing, systems integration, and outsourcing services. At the same time, it designs, implements, and maintains computer networks and multivendor information systems for various business applications. Headquartered in Pennsylvania, the company employs more than 26,000 people worldwide, with offices throughout North America, Europe, Asia, and Australia.

ADDING MACHINE ORIGINS

Unisys, formed from the 1986 merger of the Burroughs Corporation with the Sperry Corporation, traces its beginnings to 1885, when William Seward Burroughs invented the first recording adding machine. Burroughs called his device an arithmometer, and the next year he and three partners founded the American Arithmometer Company in St. Louis. Creating a commercially viable version proved difficult. Burroughs was unable to patent a salable model until 1892, although once on the market the adding machine became a success. In 1897 Burroughs was awarded the Franklin Institute's John Scott Medal in honor of his invention. He died of tuberculosis the next year, however, sadly before realizing much profit from his invention. The company, which moved to Detroit in 1905, was renamed the Burroughs Adding Machine Company in his memory.

During the early years of the 20th century, Burroughs consolidated a position in the adding machine business by acquiring both Universal Adding Machine and Pike Adding Machine in 1908 and Moon-Hopkins Billing Machine in 1921. By 1914 the company offered 90 different types of data-processing machines, which, with the help of interchangeable parts, could be modified into 600 different configurations. Accountants formed the core customer base, and in 1917 Burroughs increased courtship of those clients with the debut of *Burroughs Clearing House*, a magazine devoted to accounting. By the 1920s Burroughs was an established mainstay of the office-machine industry and remained so for the next three decades, with adding machines still at the heart of the product line.

EXPANDING INTO COMPUTERS

All of that changed, however, as a result of J. Presper Eckert and John W. Mauchly's invention of ENIAC, the first electronic computer, in 1946. At first the market for computers appeared to be limited to a handful of government agencies that used them for large-scale number crunching. The only companies to commit themselves to computer research and development were large electronics and office-machine firms for which the computer was a natural extension. When the U.S. Defense Department awarded the design contract for the new SAGE early-warning computer system in 1952, Burroughs, IBM, RCA, Remington Rand, and Sylvania were all prime choices. IBM won, giving that company an advantage competitors would struggle to overcome.

Burroughs did not immediately plunge wholeheartedly into computer technology, preferring, along with Sperry Rand's UNIVAC unit, NCR, Control Data, and Honeywell, to just keep up with IBM during the 1950s. At the end of the decade, Burroughs's reputation was

still, in the words of a *Time* magazine correspondent, that of "a stodgy old-line adding machine maker." Even so, in 1952 the company developed an add-on memory for Eckert and Mauchly's ENIAC. The following year the company name was shortened to Burroughs Corporation, in recognition of its diversification. In 1956 Burroughs introduced its first commercial electronic computer and acquired ElectroData Corporation, a leading maker of high-speed computers. Burroughs also entered the field of automated office machines, introducing the Sensitronic electronic bank bookkeeping machine in 1958.

Burroughs entered the computer field during the tenure of John Coleman, whose last major act as president was to negotiate a partnership between his company's computer operations and those of RCA, which was also looking for a way to catch up to IBM through a pooling of financial resources. RCA approved the agreement in 1959, but the plan was never realized because Coleman died before he could sway Burroughs's board of directors. Business historian Robert Sobel wrote that the Burroughs-RCA partnership might have produced "the best possible challenger for IBM."

STRUGGLING TO COMPETE WITH IBM: 1960–69

Coleman was succeeded by executive vice president Ray Eppert. Under Eppert, Burroughs expanded its place in the rapidly growing bank-automation market in 1960, as the company began selling magnetic inks and automatic check-sorting equipment. In 1961 the company introduced the B5000 computer, which was less expensive and simpler to operate than other commercial mainframes. Expansion and diversification during the early years of the computer age led to a fourfold increase in sales between 1948 and 1960, from $94 million to $389 million. At the same time, however, increased research and development costs cut profit margins, a problem the company struggled with until the late 1960s.

Despite this surge in earnings, Burroughs remained among the smallest of IBM's main competitors in the early 1960s. Although the B5000's distinctive design had earned a solid following, Burroughs's computer product line remained narrow, and the company was still too dependent on accounting machines. Research and development costs continued hacking away at profit margins, leaving the company's future clouded.

In 1964 Ray Macdonald became executive vice president and began overseeing the company's day-to-day operations. With the help of several like-minded executives, he took control of Burroughs from Eppert and committed the company to a course of steady profit growth through cost cutting. Macdonald succeeded Eppert as CEO in 1967. Burroughs's financial performance continued improving, and the company became a Wall Street favorite before the decade was out.

The U.S. Defense Department awarded Burroughs a contract in 1967 to build the Illiac IV supercomputer, which had been designed by a team at the University of Illinois and was a major coup for the company. The Illiac IV was 10 to 20 times faster than any existing supercomputer in 1972 and was delivered to NASA's Ames Research Center in California.

Despite the success of the Illiac IV, the sudden lag in research and development created by Macdonald's policy of cutting costs contributed to two significant technical failures around this time. The B8500 mainframe, which had been scheduled for delivery in 1967, had to be scrapped altogether in 1968, after Burroughs engineers realized they could not produce reliable components at a reasonable price. The B6500 was riddled with breakdowns caused by the development team's strategy for bringing the project in on time and under budget (namely, cutting corners in the high-speed circuitry design and neglecting to properly test the completed machines before delivery).

MULTIPLE LEADERS, LOW MORALE: 1974–81

An interesting aspect of Macdonald's stewardship was his reemphasis on accounting machines as an integral part of Burroughs's product line. Foremost among his talents was a genius for salesmanship; the company won a considerable chunk of the high-speed accounting machines market from rival NCR. In 1974 Burroughs entered the facsimile equipment business, acquiring Graphic Services for $30 million. The next year the company paid $8.8 million for Redactron, a maker of automatic typewriters and computer-related equipment.

Macdonald retired in 1977 and was replaced by Paul Mirabito, his handpicked successor. During Mirabito's brief tenure, the consequences of Macdonald's fiscal policies began manifesting themselves in earnest. In 1979 IBM announced a powerful new generation of computer systems. Burroughs countered by introducing its own new series of systems. Unfortunately, although Burroughs's design ideas were good, the company did not have the development or manufacturing resources to translate them into actual computers.

Burroughs's inability to deliver finished products resulted in an embarrassing stream of canceled orders. Years of salary cuts and other forms of budget tightening had engendered low morale among field engineers and a reputation for poor service among clients. Customer complaints came to a head in 1981 when 129 Burroughs users sued the company over product unreliability and difficulty in getting their machines fixed.

Mirabito had retired in 1979 and, in a move that surprised many industry observers, was replaced by W.

Michael Blumenthal, the former chairman of U.S. manufacturing and engineering company Bendix and secretary of the Treasury during the Carter administration. Blumenthal took over a company that was deceptively profitable, chalking up record sales of $2.8 billion in 1979. He immediately set about shaking up Burroughs's corporate culture, firing veteran executives and replacing them with his own appointees, phasing out the adding machine and calculator businesses, implementing a plan to improve repair service, and discontinuing accounting practices that tended to inflate earnings. Blumenthal's reforms did not come without cost, however; in July 1980, the company reported its first drop in quarterly profits in 17 years.

Blumenthal concentrated on Burroughs's computer business in an effort to secure the position of the largest of IBM's U.S. competitors. In 1981 the company covered one weak spot by acquiring System Development Corporation, a software development firm, for $9.6 million. That year Burroughs also procured Memorex, maker of disc drives and other data-storage equipment, for $85.2 million, despite Memorex's shaky financial condition. These moves added $1 billion to the company's annual sales.

BURROUGHS AND SPERRY MERGER

Blumenthal eventually decided that economies of scale were necessary to compete with IBM. In 1985 Burroughs launched a $65-per-share takeover bid, worth $3.7 billion, for Sperry Corporation. Sperry had been a takeover candidate since holding unsuccessful merger talks with ITT Corporation in March 1984. The Sperry board of directors and investors, from whom Burroughs hoped to obtain shares, balked at the offer and the deal fell through.

In May 1986 Burroughs came back with a $70-per-share bid, worth $4.1 billion, and a four-week battle ensued. Sperry executives, anxious to preserve the company's independence, argued against selling out. The board put up a defense that included an $80-per-share stock buyback offer while casting about for a white knight. Sperry eventually agreed to a $76.50-per-share deal, worth $4.8 billion at the time, which was by far the largest merger in the history of the computer industry and one of the largest in U.S. corporate history. The resulting company was the second-largest computer firm in the nation, leapfrogging over Digital Equipment Corporation.

Sperry, which was founded in 1933 but traced its roots back to the 1910-formed Sperry Gyroscope Co., originally made aircraft instruments. In 1955 the manufacturer jumped into the computer business, merging with Remington Rand, whose history dated back farther than Burroughs or Sperry. In 1873 E. Remington & Sons, forerunner of Remington Typewriter Co., introduced the earliest commercially successful typewriter. After producing the first "noiseless" typewriter in 1909, Remington debuted the original electric typewriter in the United States in 1925.

Two years later Remington Typewriter merged with Rand Kardex to form Remington Rand. The latter introduced the world's first business computer, the 409, in 1949. The following year Remington Rand acquired Eckert-Mauchly Corporation, the company founded by the developers of the ENIAC and UNIVAC computers. The 1955 merger of Sperry and Remington Rand resulted in Sperry Rand, which quickly became one of the industry's leading companies due to its technical prowess. By the 1960s the company had gained a reputation for wonderful products, however, Sperry had also inherited a legacy of poor management and marketing from Remington Rand. By the time Burroughs showed interest, the renamed Sperry Corporation had profitable defense-electronics operations but a struggling computer business.

Six months after the acquisition, the combined company adopted the name Unisys Corporation. The name was selected from suggestions submitted by Burroughs and Sperry employees and was conceived as a synthesis of the words "United Information Systems." However, the real work of fusing the two companies still remained. Over the next two years the Unisys workforce was reduced by 20 percent (24,000 of the 121,000 positions were eliminated) while unwanted and redundant businesses were placed on the market in order to generate cash. In December 1986 Unisys sold Sperry Aerospace to Honeywell and later sold Memorex's marketing arm.

SINKING FORTUNES: 1987–91

Meanwhile Unisys stepped up diversification of its product line. In 1987 it obtained Timeplex, a high-tech communications equipment company, for $300 million, and Convergent Technologies, a maker of office workstations, for $351 million. By 1989 the company had begun to move into the small and midsize computer market, adopting AT&T's popular Unix operating system as the standard configuration for Unisys machines. In 1989 Unisys also began manufacturing its own personal computers for the first time.

Unisys was not entirely successful in the late 1980s, however. Despite strong earnings growth from the time of the Sperry deal through 1988, the company posted a loss of nearly $100 million in the first quarter of 1989. Management shakeups in 1987 had resulted in the departure of two key executives: vice chairman Joseph Kroger, the former president of Sperry who commanded intense loyalty from former Sperry employees, and Paul G. Stern, a physicist whom Blumenthal had brought into the company from IBM and made president and chief operating officer in 1982. Sluggish sales, manufacturing cost overruns, and fierce price competition among the many companies using the Unix system all cut into revenues.

Unisys also found itself caught up in the Pentagon procurement scandal of 1988. Federal prosecutors brought charges of fraud against some Unisys executives, including former vice president Charles Gaines, who headed the Washington, D.C., office of one of the company's defense units. Prosecutors claimed that, prior to the Sperry and Burroughs merger, executives at Sperry bribed U.S. Defense Department officials into yielding classified procurement documents and made illegal campaign contributions to members of Congress.

Unisys had already begun an internal investigation when the government made the accusations public. According to Paul Mann of *Aviation Week & Space Technology*, the company settled its part in the Operation 111 Wind court case in September 1991, pleading guilty to fraud and bribery and agreeing to pay a record of up to $190 million in damages, penalties, and fines. In the same article, James A. Unruh, who succeeded Blumenthal in 1990, said, "We as a company must accept responsibility for the past actions of a few people, even though today we have a completely different management team and different shareholders."

RESTRUCTURING AND TURNAROUND

Unisys's difficulties deepened in the early 1990s, with much of the troubles easily traced back to the merger of Burroughs and Sperry. The operations of the two companies had never been properly integrated, leaving duplicate R&D, marketing, and accounting departments. Already saddled with a huge debt load from the 1986 merger, Unisys was forced to take on an additional $1.4 billion in debt to cover negative cash flow, as the company's mainframe computers were quickly losing market share to IBM and Amdahl. The company's stock, which sold for about $50 in 1987, collapsed to a low of $1.75 during 1990. Unisys posted successive net losses of $639 million in 1989, $436 million in 1990, and $1.39 billion in 1991. Bankruptcy neared.

Amid a depressed global economy, Unruh managed to turn Unisys's fortunes around by 1992 through a dra-

conian restructuring, the success of which surprised many observers. Unisys exacted additional drastic employee reductions, eliminating some 23,000 people from 1989 through 1991. At the end of 1991, the remaining Unisys workforce was roughly half the size of that at the time of the merger. An additional 6,000 jobs were cut in 1992, leaving a workforce of 54,300. Other major restructuring costs led Unisys to take massive charges of $1.2 billion in 1991, directly contributing to overall unprofitability for the year. These measures, however, were expected to reduce costs on an annual basis by approximately $800 million.

In its aggressive drive to cut costs, Unisys reduced its 50,000-product line by 15,000 items, having determined that 10 percent of its products were bringing in 90 percent of the revenue. Its mainframe computer lines were reduced from four to two (Sperry's 2200 series and Burroughs's A series). The Timeplex subsidiary, responsible for only a small fraction of overall revenues, was divested. The company shuttered 7 of its 15 manufacturing facilities, and Unisys began concentrating on those market sectors where it was traditionally the strongest: banking, airlines, government, and communications. Debt was brought down to a more manageable $1.4 billion from its peak of $3.5 billion.

This massive reengineering effort not only pulled Unisys from the brink of disaster but also resulted in two solid years of financial performance: for 1992 net income of $361.2 million on sales of $8.7 billion and for 1992 net income of $565.4 million on $7.74 billion in revenues. Unisys was much smaller (revenues had totaled $10.11 billion in 1990) but much more profitable.

SHIFT TO SERVICES: 1992–97

As the turnaround was taking shape, Unruh pushed the company in a new direction. With a clear shift taking place from mainframes to networked computing, Unruh moved to deemphasize the former through an expansion into computer services. Beginning in 1992 with the formation of a unit dedicated to providing information technology services, Unisys became active in the areas of systems consulting and design and systems integration services. One rationale behind the shift to services was that as computer systems grew ever more complex, in-house personnel were less and less able to cope, leading to a growing market for outside information technology expertise. Building on its existing mainframe maintenance activities, Unisys was able to generate $1.3 billion from services in 1992, then $2 billion the following year. By 1994 the company's support services unit was generating more revenue than the mainstay mainframe hardware operations.

Unfortunately, Unisys's comeback proved short-lived. Services revenues were growing about 30 percent per year, but the company had failed to make a profit from its new activities, losing about $54 million during 1995 alone. Part of a 1994 profit decline was attributed to a delay in getting the company's latest servers, the 550 and 580, to market. Another factor was a $186 million charge for a further restructuring of the mainframe operations, including a workforce reduction of 4,000 and the long overdue merging of the 2200 series and the A series into a single mainframe line. After the depressed profit figure of $100.5 million for 1994, Unisys posted a net loss of $624.6 million in 1995 thanks to a $717.6 million charge for another restructuring (the fifth in seven years).

This time the company reorganized itself into three units: hardware and software, which included mainframes, servers, and a recent foray into PCs; maintenance and networking, which concentrated on servicing and connecting computers; and services, which involved consulting and outsourcing in integrated systems design. This restructuring also involved the paring of a few thousand more workers from the payroll and the consolidating of facilities and manufacturing, as well as the 1995 sale of its defense contracting unit to Loral Space & Communications for $862 million.

The following year Unisys introduced to positive market reaction the ClearPath line of computers, which combined proprietary mainframes with open systems capable of running standard Unix and Windows NT software and applications in a single system. In April 1996 Unruh managed to defeat Greenway Partners' proposal to shareholders for a breakup of Unisys into three parts. (Greenway held nearly a 5 percent stake in Unisys.) A similar breakup proposal one year later failed as well. In September 1997 Unruh stepped aside from his leadership position at Unisys, having kept the company alive but having never fully turned it around. The financial ups and downs and the frequent restructurings had left the remaining workforce demoralized. Nevertheless, most observers praised Unruh's shift into services, and during 1997 that unit finally turned its first profit.

CONTINUED RESTRUCTURING: 1997–99

Unruh helped select his successor, Lawrence A. Weinbach, former head of accounting and consulting giant Andersen Worldwide. The new chairman, CEO, and president immediately began working to improve

employee morale, meeting with more than one-third of the workforce and revoking unpopular policies from recent austerity programs, such as the elimination of the company match on 401(k) contributions. Weinbach also initiated $1.04 billion in fourth-quarter 1997 charges, which resulted in a net loss for the year of $853.6 million. Some $900 million of the charges were to write down the value of goodwill left from the acquisition of Sperry, with the remainder going toward reducing debt. At year-end 1997 debt stood at $1.4 billion but was reduced to less than $1 billion by the end of 1999.

In addition to focusing on debt reduction, Weinbach moved Unisys out of the manufacturing of PCs and smaller servers. The company began outsourcing the manufacture of such hardware to Hewlett-Packard in 1998. He also jettisoned the company's three-unit structure in favor of a simpler division between hardware, which would now focus on high-end servers and mainframes, and services, which included maintenance as well as consulting and systems design.

On the hardware side, Unisys worked to upgrade its existing mainframe line while also introducing in 1999 a mainframe-class server called the Unisys e-@ction ClearPath Enterprise Server, which used an Intel microprocessor and ran Windows NT (later Windows 2000) software. This server was part of a comprehensive and integrated portfolio of hardware and services (known as Unisys e-@ction Solutions) that the company unveiled in 1999 to support the burgeoning e-business market. On the services side, Unisys became more selective in the type of projects it took on, concentrating on key markets where it had the most expertise, including financial services, government, communications, transportation, and publishing.

By 1999 70 percent of the company's revenues were being generated by the services operations. For the year, Unisys posted net income of $510.7 million on sales of $7.54 billion, its best year since 1993. It was difficult to predict whether this turnaround would last longer than that of the early 1990s. As Unisys's services side grew, profit increases were likely to be harder won, as its services business was markedly less profitable than its hardware side. Nevertheless, one possible avenue for early-21st-century growth was in international markets, and Unisys was seeking acquisitions to fuel an overseas push in services. In 1999 the company made several acquisitions, including Datamec, a Brazilian application outsourcing company, and City Lifeline Systems Limited, a U.K.-based provider of services and solutions for firms trading in fixed-income securities.

INNOVATION AND DIVERSIFICATION AFTER DOT-COM CRASH

At the beginning of the new century, as the technology sector fell into a prolonged slump, Unisys found itself struggling to maintain steady earnings growth. While the company had reduced its overall debt from $2.3 billion to $600 million by April 2000, it was still faced with declining sales, with revenues falling 8 percent in the year's first quarter. During this time Unisys also witnessed a dramatic drop in its stock value, from $49 a share in 1999 to $23 per share less than a year later.

Some analysts attributed the company's slide to the relatively narrow scope of its core business. While many of Unisys's competitors were able to maintain strong revenues through sales of personal computers and other general consumer products, Unisys's reliance on corporate clients left it particularly vulnerable to the latest downturn in the economy. As more and more businesses cut their operating budgets during the early part of the decade, demand for the company's high-end business servers dropped dramatically.

In order to weather this financial storm, Unisys embarked on the first of what would become a series of cost-cutting measures. In October 2000, as third quarter earnings fell nearly 70 percent compared with the same period a year earlier, the company announced the implementation of a new early retirement program, with the aim of reducing its U.S. workforce by 1,500 employees. At the same time it began to explore a range of new business opportunities.

In January 2001, following the controversy surrounding the 2000 presidential election, Unisys entered into a joint venture with Dell and Microsoft to create a new electronic voting system aimed at state governments. Unisys had already achieved success developing electronic voting machines for Brazil and Italy and estimated that the U.S. market for its technology could be worth more than $3 billion. A year later the company was awarded a $1 billion contract to build and maintain a computer network for the newly formed U.S. Department of Homeland Security.

Nonetheless, Unisys continued to contend with sluggish sales, and in 2001 it absorbed a $67 million loss. Facing this decline in revenues, it announced another round of staff reductions, cutting 2,600 jobs between fall 2001 and spring 2002. Even as the company returned to profitability in 2002, its stock value remained stagnant, falling to as low as $6 a share at one point in the year. By 2003 the company was still underperforming in its sector, lagging well behind rivals such as IBM.

Speaking to the *Philadelphia Inquirer* on September 23, 2003, Unisys CEO Lawrence Weinbach pointed to the company's lack of name recognition in the mainstream computing market as a source of its struggles. "We don't have anything that you'd call a consumer product," Weinbach said. "It's easy to advertise if you have a consumer product. The best way for us to get to consumers is delivering what we say we're going to deliver."

In order to fulfill this goal, the company continued to increase its presence in the growing homeland security industry. In April 2004 Unisys landed an important new contract with the U.S. Department of Defense, in a deal potentially worth $345 million. As part of the agreement, Unisys was assigned to create an integrated counterintelligence network for the U.S. military, enabling diverse agencies and departments to share information more efficiently. That same month Unisys opened an office in Bangalore, India, with the aim of building a staff of 3,000 Indian employees over a five-year span. At the time computer programmers in India earned roughly one-eighth of the salaries of their U.S. counterparts, making the outsourcing measure a potential source of significant operating-cost reductions over the long term.

FURTHER CUTS AND A NEW PLAN

Unisys continued to shed jobs throughout the middle of the decade, as it struggled to maintain consistent profitability. Total profits for 2004 came to $38.6 million, down from $258.7 million for the previous year. In January 2005 Weinbach stepped down as CEO; he was succeeded by Joseph W. McGrath. In October 2005, following a quarterly loss of $54.3 million, Unisys announced its intention to cut another 3,500 employees, or roughly 10 percent of its total workforce. A month later it unveiled a marketing campaign aimed at increasing consumer recognition of the company's brand identity. As part of the new strategy, Unisys intended to focus on five strategic areas, including network security and outsourcing services. In the midst of these efforts, the company's financial woes continued to mount. For fiscal year 2005, Unisys suffered losses of $1.73 billion.

By mid-2006, the company was forced to implement more staff reductions, while shifting a number of positions to lower cost labor markets in Asia and Eastern Europe. The company was dealt another blow in January 2007 when Congress launched an investigation into security breaches involving the company's Homeland Security project. In the wake of these allegations, Homeland Security began to seek new bidders to build its network. Since Unisys received roughly one-sixth of its total earnings from federal projects, the loss of the Homeland Security contract represented a potentially devastating blow to the company.

In October 2008 as its earnings and stock value continued to slide, the company appointed a new CEO, J. Edward Coleman. Under Coleman's leadership, Unisys was soon able to regain profitability, due largely to a continued emphasis on cutting costs. While company earnings remained relatively flat in 2009, its operating expenses dropped by $200 million for the year. By December its workforce had fallen to approximately 26,000 employees, compared with 39,000 at the beginning of the decade. While Unisys's streamlining efforts had helped it achieve fiscal stability, it remained to be seen when the company's new strategy would finally drive up earnings figures.

PRINCIPAL SUBSIDIARIES

Intelligent Processing Solutions Limited (UK); Unisys Funding Corporation I; Unisys Limited (UK).

PRINCIPAL COMPETITORS

Accenture Limited; Computer Sciences Corporation; DecisionOne Corporation; Dell Inc.; Electronic Data Systems Limited; Fujitsu Limited; Getronics NV; Hewlett-Packard Company; Hitachi, Ltd.; International Business Machines Corporation; Microsoft Corporation; NCR Corporation; Perot Systems Corporation; Sun Microsystems, Inc.

FURTHER READING

Benoit, Ellen, "All Dressed Up," *Forbes*, March 24, 1986, pp. 106+.

Bock, Gordon, and Russell Mitchell, "How Burroughs Finally Won Sperry," *BusinessWeek*, June 9, 1986, pp. 28+.

Bulkeley, William M., "Unisys, Back from the Edge, Stresses Service, Comfort," *Wall Street Journal*, April 22, 1999, p. B4.

———, "Unisys Expects Profit to Trail Forecasts," *Wall Street Journal*, June 30, 2000, p. B6.

Byrne, John A., "Univacuum," *Forbes*, June 6, 1983, pp. 156+.

DiStefano, Joseph N., "Successful Turnaround at Unisys," *Philadelphia Inquirer*, December 6, 2009, p. D03.

England, Robert Stowe, "A Bet Against: Whither Mainframes? At Unisys, James Unruh Is Betting the Company That

Their Future Is Bleak," *Financial World*, August 1, 1995, pp. 46–48.

———, "Ugly Duckling," *Financial World*, October 12, 1993, pp. 36–7.

Hooper, Laurence, "Unruh Saves Unisys, Now Aims to Put It on Cutting Edge," *Wall Street Journal*, September 25, 1992, p. B4.

"The Long Road Back for Burroughs," *BusinessWeek*, May 18, 1981, pp. 119+.

Macdonald, Ray W. *Strategy for Growth: The Story of Burroughs Corporation*. New York: Newcomen Society in North America, 1978.

Mann, Paul, "Unisys Admits Bribery and Fraud, Will Pay Record $190 Million Fine," *Aviation Week & Space Technology*, September 16, 1991.

Narisetti, Raju, "Campaign at Unisys Emphasizes Firm's Vigor in Bid for New Image," *Wall Street Journal*, September 24, 1998, p. B12.

———, "Unisys's New Chairman Is Bullish Despite Slow Sales: Weinbach's Plan Calls for Paring Debt and Relying on New Technologies," *Wall Street Journal*, January 7, 1998, p. B12.

Petre, Peter, "The Struggle over Sperry's Future," *Fortune*, December 9, 1985, pp. 78+.

Reingold, Jennifer, "Unisys: Nobody Said Diversifying Was Easy," *BusinessWeek*, July 15, 1996, p. 32.

Reingold, Jennifer, and Phillip L. Zweig, "Can He Stop the Unisys Slide?" *BusinessWeek*, June 3, 1996, pp. 64–67.

"Sperry: Pouring Its Resources into High-Growth Products," *BusinessWeek*, February 15, 1982, pp. 80+.

Tanaka, Wendy, "Unisys Getting No Respect," *Philadelphia Inquirer*, September 23, 2003, p. D01.

Uttal, Bro, "A Surprisingly Sexy Computer Marriage," *Fortune*, November 24, 1986, pp. 46+.

———, "The Blumenthal Revival at Burroughs," *Fortune*, October 5, 1981, pp. 128+.

———, "How Ray Macdonald's Growth Theory Created IBM's Toughest Competitor," *Fortune*, January 1977.

Verity, John W., and Joseph Weber, "So Far, Married Life Seems to Agree with Unisys," *BusinessWeek*, October 3, 1988, p. 123.

Weber, Joseph, "This Is Hardly the Turning Point Unisys Had in Mind," *BusinessWeek*, August 28, 1989, pp. 82+.

———, "Unisys: Out of the Bleak and into the Black," *BusinessWeek*, June 8, 1992.

Ziegler, Bart, and Joann S. Lublin, "Task at Unisys Isn't for 'Faint of Heart' As Unruh Confirms Plans to Step Down," *Wall Street Journal*, June 20, 1997, p. B6.

United Way Worldwide

701 North Fairfax Street
Alexandria, Virginia 22314-2045
U.S.A.
Telephone: (703) 836-7112
Toll Free: (800) 892-2757
Fax: (703) 519-0097
Web site: http://www.liveunited.org

Nonprofit Organization
Founded: 1887 as Charity Organizations Society
Incorporated: 1932
Employees: 304
Sales: $66.43 million (gross revenues) (2008)
NAICS: 813212 Voluntary Health Organizations;
    813211 Charitable Trusts, Awarding Grants

∎ ∎ ∎

United Way Worldwide (UWW) is the largest nonprofit in the world. With an international network in 45 countries and territories, including nearly 1,300 local organizations in the United States, UWW raises more than $5 billion annually. Mobilizing local volunteers, the organization works at the community level to design, fund, and measure the success of projects to foster education, improve health, and increase income throughout the world.

BEGINNINGS: 1887–1949

Charity provided by well-intentioned people and groups led to the origin in the United States of what became United Way Worldwide. The body can be traced back to several disparate societies, the earliest of which was the Charity Organizations Society, founded in Denver, Colorado, in 1887. Several related groups began distributing financial and other aid both nearby and in other cities and states, operating under various names but with the same goals. By 1888 the Denver outfit had organized its first campaign and raised $21,700 for its causes, an impressive amount of money at the time.

In 1894, when a federal law decreed that for-profit companies must pay taxes, charitable groups or nonprofit agencies received a major coup: tax exemption. With relief from any tax burden, nonprofit groups flourished. However, the tax-free status attracted a number of unsavory characters, who had no intention of dispersing their funds for altruistic purposes. These imitators led to the creation of the Committee on Benevolent Associations, formed by the Chamber of Commerce in Cleveland, Ohio, in 1900. This committee was the earliest attempt to regulate charitable and philanthropic endeavors, to set clear guidelines, and to safeguard the interests of both those contributing and those receiving funds.

Over the next several years, after the reelection and assassination of President William McKinley and into the Teddy Roosevelt administration, charitable organizations grew rapidly around the country. In Chicago alone, there were over 3,000 registered charities by 1905. In 1913 the first Community Chest was formed, a name brought to fame by the wildly popular Parker Brothers *Monopoly* game, in which players were given a yellow card for landing on the "Community Chest" space. The cards either rewarded players with cash gifts

---

COMPANY PERSPECTIVES

United Way Worldwide Mission: To improve lives by mobilizing the caring power of communities around the world to advance the common good. To do this we will ignite a worldwide social movement, and thereby mobilize millions to action—to give, advocate and volunteer to improve the conditions in which they live; galvanize and connect all sectors of society—individuals, businesses, non-profit organizations and governments—to create long-term social change that produces healthy, well-educated and financially-stable individuals and families.; raise, invest and leverage billions of dollars annually in philanthropic contributions to create and support innovative programs and approaches to generate sustained impact in local communities; hold ourselves accountable to this cause through our steadfast commitment to continually measure—in real terms—improvement in education, income and health.

---

or sought "a donation" for various community-related projects.

As nonprofit agencies blossomed, so did efforts at self-regulation. Through a number of committees and associations, including the Associated Charities (founded in 1908), the National Association of Societies for Organizing Charity (1911), the National Information Bureau (1918), and the American Association for Community Organizations (1918), standards and policies continued to evolve. The American Association for Community Organizations (AACO), created by the leaders of 12 charitable groups in Chicago to gain a clearer focus on community planning and the role of social work, was considered the breeding ground of what led to the formation of the United Way. Those involved with the AACO formulated the critical tenets of what a charitable organization should be and how its goals should be met.

If World War I and its aftermath gave humanitarian groups a sobering glimpse into the depths of human suffering, the onset of the Great Depression revealed a true panorama of despair. Charity was in high demand, and those who had freely contributed in the past found themselves hard put to donate much of anything. Even after the United States recovered and a majority of Americans were back on their feet, sharper, deeper lines had been drawn between the haves and the have-nots.

United Way chapters struggled to provide for their constituents, and relief came ironically with another declaration of war. World War II production fueled the nation's economy in the 1940s; in the postwar years, with the baby boom and widespread financial security, the urgent need for charity itself declined while donations from both corporations and individuals increased.

A LARGER FOCUS: 1950–79

Into the late 1950s, charitable agencies continued to evolve on local, state, and national levels. More service organizations were created, including the National Council on Community Foundations (renamed the Council on Foundations in 1964), the Institute of Community Studies (which evolved into the Management and Community Studies Institute), the Commerce and Industry Combined Health Appeal, and the National Budget and Consultation Committee (NBCC), created by the merging of the American Way Community Services and the Joint Budget Committee of the Community Chests and Councils. From the NBCC came the 1963 publication *Standards for National Voluntary Health, Welfare, and Recreations Agencies*, a much-needed procedural for the ever-growing nonprofit societies popping up across the country. In the same year that the procedural came out, more than two dozen Community Chests and United Fund chapters in Los Angeles, California, joined forces and officially began using the name United Way, Inc.

Two presidential executive orders (the first in 1957 from President Dwight D. Eisenhower and the second in 1963 from President John F. Kennedy) allowed charitable groups to receive contributions from federal employees. The 1957 order created the Uniform Federal Fund-Raising Program, permitting federal employee gift-giving to local accredited groups. The second presidential order broadened the network of health and welfare agencies eligible to receive gifts from federal employees. In 1964 United Way chapters, echoing President Lyndon B. Johnson, declared their own "War on Poverty" and instituted various programs to combat hunger in the United States. Help for the crusade came from the newly initiated federal employee payroll deduction plan, while the charitable groups eligible for these deductions (those originally instituted under presidents Eisenhower and Kennedy) merged to form the Combined Federal Campaign (CFC).

By the mid-1960s United Way had become a well-known organization with more than 30,000 affiliated agencies nationwide, and it sought consolidation and cooperation from the federal government and national groups. To promote these goals, the organization issued the *Statement of Consensus on Government and the*

Voluntary Sector in Health and Welfare in 1966. By 1967 the population of the United States totaled more than 195.8 million people, and a generation was in turmoil over the Vietnam War. War supporters marched down Fifth Avenue in New York City, antiwar demonstrators gathered at the Lincoln Memorial, and United Way agencies managed to collect more than $700 million through 31,300 individual agencies across the country. Funds were distributed to more than 27 million families in need.

United Way's national governing body, the United Community Funds and Council of America (UCFCA), reorganized itself into the streamlined and more simply named United Way of America (UWA) in 1970. William Aramony was appointed to head the group, and he brought forth what he called the Thirteen Point Program for Rebirth and Renewal of United Way. The new program's purpose included attracting more volunteers on local, regional, and national levels, as well as raising public awareness of just what the United Way chapters did and for whom. Additionally, in an effort to bring uniformity to its many chapters, UWA leaders passed a resolution to discontinue the use of names other than "United Way," and in 1973 the national headquarters moved from New York City to Alexandria, Virginia.

In 1973 UWA scored a major coup in the public promotion of its goals by partnering with the National Football League (NFL). Players and coaches made public service announcements about their involvement with United Way chapters, and these associations brought widespread attention to UWA's programs. The NFL exposure helped UWA garner support and initiate its Program for the Future, in which national goals were applied at local levels, in 1976. A year later the Program for the Future's success led to annual contributions of more than $1 billion for the first time. Leaders of the UWA agencies continued to plan for the future and identified five areas in which to concentrate their efforts: inclusiveness, area-wide services, volunteers and public policies, agency relations, and personalization of services.

ALWAYS READY TO HELP: 1980–93

With the emergence of another decade came diversified goals within the charity sector. Programs were instituted to address newer issues affecting the country, including environmental concerns and societal pressures on women and minorities. As UWA's focus became more all-encompassing, its member agencies' money-raising abilities increased as well. Nationally more than $1.68 billion was raised in 1981, amounting to the greatest single-year increase in funds (more than 10 percent over 1980). In 1982 the organization opened its new National Service and Training Center in Alexandria, with all costs covered by a $4 million fundraiser sponsored by John V. James, chairman of Dresser Industries, and John R. Opel, chairman and CEO of IBM. At the same time, a Volunteer Leadership Development Program was established to educate and train group leaders to maximize their skills.

Both new programs came in handy when the government established the Federal Emergency Management Agency (FEMA) in 1983 with an initial $50 million grant, which was followed by a grant of $40 million a few months later. Charged with the responsibility of managing FEMA funds, UWA created a national board with its own representatives as well as those from five other nonprofit groups, so funds could be administered on an as-needed basis to local agencies throughout the United States.

By the middle of the 1980s UWA had come a long way from its humble origins in Colorado. What began as a handful of like-minded charitable agencies had become a multifaceted alliance of thousands, united in purpose and achievement. In 1985 contributors anted up an amazing $2.33 billion, up some 9 percent from the previous year. As the organization approached its 100-year anniversary in 1987, it published *Rethinking the Future and Beyond*, which discussed UWA's current focus as well as ideas for its second hundred years and beyond. During the centennial year, the U.S. Postal Service honored UWA with a commemorative stamp as more than 3,000 gathered in the nation's capital for the Centennial Volunteer Leaders Conference. In addition, UWA established a program for young people called the Young Leaders Conference.

Continuing its focus on America's youth, UWA gave gifts totaling more than $100,000 to youth volunteer programs in four cities across the United States in 1987. Two years later northern and central California were devastated by an earthquake, and UWA led the emergency services. Local chapters not only coordinated operations with FEMA teams but brought in major contributions from the NFL ($1.25 million), Sony Corporation ($1 million), and scores of concerned Americans.

With the debut of the 1990s, UWA again put its ideals and beliefs on paper in a 1990 publication called *Mobilizing a Caring America: Principles for the 1990s*. The 103-year-old organization was definitely doing something right: Americans donated more than $3 billion to UWA chapters in 1990, just in time for the next imbroglio, the outbreak of the Gulf War in 1991. UWA set up an Operations Center and coordinated services with the U.S. military and other groups such as the American Red Cross and USO.

The early 1990s, however, also brought controversy to the UWA. In 1992 Aramony resigned as president, and the post was temporarily filled by Kenneth W. Dam. Aramony was under investigation for fraud and mismanagement of funds, and the organization underwent intense scrutiny for its policies and dealings, including specific transactions with seven agencies that had been spun off in recent years. After soliciting suggestions from some 6,000 UWA volunteers throughout the country and seeking outside counsel, UWA's board of governors voted for sweeping changes and reformed much of the organization's financial operation. The board itself was expanded to 45 members, 15 of whom were United Way representatives, and a new president and CEO was installed: Elaine L. Chao, a former director of the Peace Corps. Chao was UWA's first woman president and its first Asian-American director. (Chao later served as secretary of labor under President George W. Bush.)

Next came the trial of Aramony and two codefendants. All were found guilty in 1995, with Aramony convicted on 25 counts of fraud, filing false tax returns, conspiracy, and money laundering. Sentenced to seven years in prison, three years of probation, and a fine of over $550,000, Aramony appealed his sentence, although unsuccessfully. He also failed in an attempt to win $2 million in extra pension benefits. UWA suffered a black eye from the extensive publicity, but the organization was soon back to doing what it did best when much of the Midwest was ravaged by floods, although it received noticeably less in donations. After the Aramony scandal, contributions fell to their lowest point since World War II, and many United Way chapters withdrew from the national organization, Most, however, would later return. To boost its public image, UWA initiated several new programs, including Sky-Wish with Delta Airlines, wherein travelers donated frequent flyer mileage to critically ill patients in need of life-saving transportation.

RECOVERY AFTER THE ARAMONY CRISIS

In the middle and late years of the 1990s, UWA invested in technological advances and promoted the organization through its first major advertising campaign. Temerlin McCain of Irving, Texas, donated the time and effort necessary to create UWA's latest "helping hands" logo, as well as the catchphrase "Reaching those who need help. Touching us all." Fortunately for UWA, Aramony's trial and sentencing had quickly faded from the memory of most Americans, and in 1994 *Financial World* named the organization its leading charity. The following year UWA was involved in the torch relays for the Atlanta Olympics and published *Strategic Direction for United Way: Charting the Path for Building Better Communities*, outlining plans for the future. Then, another catastrophic event occurred requiring the expertise of UWA's many dedicated volunteers: the bombing of the Alfred P. Murrah Federal Building in Oklahoma City on April 19, 1995. UWA agencies not only helped survivors and the families of victims but sent a technology team to the site as well.

The national UWA organization received a jolt in 1996 when Aramony filed a $5 million lawsuit for earnings and retirement benefits he claimed were due to him. Moreover, Chao resigned as president and CEO. Chao was replaced by Betty Stanley Beene, formerly the chief executive of Tri-State (New York) United Ways chapters. As Beene took the reins in 1997, there were 4,400 UWA chapters across the United States, and the organization had gone global with a UWA Web site (www.unitedway.org) and United Way Online for use by its local agencies. The next year, 1998, UWA and the NFL celebrated 25 years of collaboration, an alliance that had brought recognition to both parties. The cost of the commercial air time donated by the NFL before, during, and after televised games was worth upwards of $1 billion, but the exposure had been priceless. Additionally, another humanitarian-themed postage stamp was unveiled by the U.S. Postal Service, with the words "Giving & Sharing: An American Tradition" printed on the stamp.

By the late 1990s UWA was stronger than ever, with leadership programs for all ages and agencies working to conquer need at all levels of society. For its efforts on behalf of children, UWA was given two remarkable gifts from the Bank of America Foundation: a grant for $10 million followed by one for $40 million. The latter was one of the largest corporate grants ever. Annual contributions also hit another all-time high, with donations totaling more than $3.5 billion for 1998 and $3.77 billion for 1999, due in large part to support from individuals (including Bill Gates, Infoseek's Steve Kirsch, and Alexis de Tocqueville Society members) and such corporations as Bank of America, Boeing Company, General Motors Corporation, IBM, J.C. Penney Company, Pfizer, United Parcel Service, and Wal-Mart Stores.

FIRST DECADE OF THE NEW MILLENNIUM

The coming of the new millennium found United Way in a strong position. It also brought internal conflict over policies, changes in leadership, and the evolution of a new approach to United Way's role. Gift-giving had fully recovered from the post-Aramony era, providing a record $3.91 billion in resources in 2001. In January 2001 Beene resigned as president after losing a bid to set and enforce national standards on local United Ways. This effort drew such intense opposition that some local affiliates withheld part of their dues to United Way of America.

After a yearlong search, the board of directors appointed Brian Gallagher to replace Beene. A 20-year veteran of United Way, Gallagher was president of the United Way of Central Ohio. He had been in the forefront of urging United Ways to shift from acting as a club of member charities to focusing on how to use donations to improve social conditions. Shortly before hiring him, the Board had initiated an extensive review of the organization's structure and governance system and had started to look into ways to evolve from community fundraiser to catalyst for change in the quality of life. The result was the adoption in December 2001 of a new mission statement: "to improve lives by mobilizing the caring power of communities."

As a new president with new priorities, Gallagher was faced early on with issues involving the local affiliates. In January 2002 board members of the United Way of the National Capital Area (UWNCA), the second-largest affiliate, were beginning to question the propriety of the affiliate's spending and administration. After a suppressed audit report uncovered serious fiscal mismanagement, the problem got the attention of Senator Charles E. Grassley, a Republican from Iowa, who made inquiries into UWNCA's management practices. In September 2002 director Norman O. Taylor stepped down, bowing to pressure from both local critics and United Way of America.

In response to this crisis, in January 2003 the nation's local United Ways decided to overhaul the board of directors and added actor George Clooney in an attempt to improve the damaged image of United Way. More substantively, they voted overwhelmingly to approve standards to enhance financial disclosure and expand the role of the national organization. For the first time, affiliates were required to submit detailed annual reports to the national office for review by financial and management experts. The standards thereby allowed the national organization to more closely monitor the 1,400 affiliates, compare their practices, and spot any early signs of impropriety or ineffectiveness.

NEW PROGRAMS AND CRISES RESPONSE

With the UWNCA corruption issue slowly receding, United Way of America immediately refocused in 2003 on implementing its new community-impact effort. However, the public continued to view UWA as a fundraising mission, so there was a need to change perceptions. UWA therefore undertook a massive rebranding campaign, built around the slogan "What Matters," which was intended to articulate the new commitment to having a direct impact on communities across America. It followed this up in 2005 by updating its guiding "Standards of Excellence" to provide benchmark standards and best practices in implementing its new mission of addressing the long-term needs of communities.

Over the next few years, UWA introduced some new programs. In 2005 it unveiled Born Learning, an innovative public engagement campaign designed to provide parents and caregivers with resources for creating better early-learning opportunities for young children. In 2007 it introduced the United Way Financial Stability Partnership, designed to help lower-income people to achieve financial independence. Effectively codifying these two efforts under a larger policy umbrella, in 2008 UWA announced, in its report *Goals for the Common Good*, a three-pronged focus on education, income, and health as a way to help advance the common good. United Way set three goals for the country to reach by 2018: cut by half the number of young people who drop out of high school, cut by half the number of working families that lack financial stability, and increase by one-third the percentage of healthy young people and adults.

While redefining and redirecting its mission during the 2000s, United Way responded in many ways to the major natural and man-made catastrophes of the decade. In response to the September 11, 2001, terrorist attacks on the World Trade Center in New York City and the Pentagon in Washington, D.C., local affiliates joined to establish the September 11th Fund, which sought to meet the pressing needs of the victims. In response to devastating hurricanes in Florida and to Hurricane Katrina in the New Orleans area, United Way chapters throughout Florida and the Gulf of Mexico area led response and recovery efforts by identifying the most serious needs in devastated communities. A special telephone 2-1-1 network to assist victims was later adopted in many other states. The tragic tsunami of 2004 that struck South Asia prompted United Way of America to develop a Coordinated Crisis Response Team that worked collaboratively with staff from United Way International and United Way affiliates in India, Indonesia, Kenya, Malaysia, and Thailand to collectively respond to the Indian Ocean communities impacted by the disasters. In 2006 United Way and MTV created Storm Corps, a spring break program that mobilized young people to help rebuild the hurricane-decimated Gulf Coast. After the catastrophic earthquake in Haiti early in 2010, United Way immediately began working through its members and other partners in Haiti to raise money and assist in the recovery of the devastated Haitian communities.

At the end of the first decade of the 21st century, with its domestic agenda expanded to provide aid to communities while raising money, United Way now focused on its international structure. In 1974 United Way International had been founded to coordinate with and assist affiliates around the world. In 2009 United Way of American and United Way International merged to become United Way Worldwide. At this auspicious time in its history, United Way received what must have been, after the woes and crises of the previous two decades, a heartening vote of confidence in its prestige: A major public relations firm determined that United Way ranked third among nonprofit brands in the United States. This boded well for further support from major corporations, which valued donating to and basking in the glow of prestigious charities.

Nelson Rhodes
Updated, Judson MacLaury

PRINCIPAL COMPETITORS

American Red Cross; Goodwill Industries International, Inc.; The Salvation Army USA.

FURTHER READING

Clifford, Sarah, "Charity: When Big Is Better," *Inc.*, February 1987, p. 11.

Gabor, Andrea, "Fundraising in Trying Times; James Robinson of American Express on Marketing United Way," *U.S. News & World Report*, May 4, 1987, p. 53.

Galper, Joseph, "Generosity by the Numbers," *American Demographics*, August 1998, p. 24.

Gattuso, Greg, "How Much Is Too Much?" *Fund Raising Management*, October 1996, p. 3.

Johnston, David Cay, "Ohio Chapter Head Named United Way President," *New York Times*, November 6, 2001, p. A14

McLaughlin, Thomas, "Lessons from United Way," *Association Management*, August 1995, p. 24.

"Planning the United Way," *American Demographics*, November 1986, p. 24.

Santoro, Elaine, "Salvation Army Breaks United Way Ties," *Fund Raising Management*, September 1996, p. 6.

Sanz, Cynthia, "A Little Help for His Friends: William Aramony Faces Prison for Diverting the United Way His Way," *People Weekly*, April 17, 1995, p. 89.

"United Way Outlines Ambitious 10 Year Goals around High School Graduation Rates, Financial Stability and Health," United Way of America, May 15, 2008, http://www.liveunited.org/news/upload/Goals_Press_Release_2008.pdf.

Vedanta Resources plc

16 Berkeley Street
London, W1J 8DZ
England
Telephone: (+44 20) 7499-5900
Fax: (+44 20) 7491-8440
Web site: http://www.vedantaresources.com

Public Company
Founded: 1976
Employees: 30,000 (est.)
Sales: $6.6 billion (2009 est.)
Stock Exchanges: London
Ticker Symbol: VED
NAICS: 551112 Offices of Other Holding Companies; 212231 Lead Ore and Zinc Ore Mining; 212234 Copper Ore and Nickel Ore Mining; 212299 All Other Metal Ore Mining; 331419 Primary Smelting and Refining of Nonferrous Metal (except Copper and Aluminum); 331492 Secondary Smelting, Refining, and Alloying of Nonferrous Metal (except Copper and Aluminum)

∎ ∎ ∎

Vedanta Resources plc is a leading diversified metals and mining group and the first Indian manufacturing company to be listed on the London Stock Exchange. Vedanta holds a substantial share of India's copper, zinc, and aluminum markets and is the country's largest iron ore producer-exporter. With corporate offices in London, Vedanta operates in India, Zambia, and Australia through five main business segments. The subsidiaries in the copper segment include Sterlite Industries (India) Limited based in Mumbai, Konkola Copper Mines (KCM) in Zambia, and Copper Mines of Tasmania Pvt. Ltd. (CMT) in Australia. Located in Udaipur, the zinc segment operates through Hindustan Zinc Limited (HZL), India's only integrated zinc producer. India's Bharat Aluminium Company Limited (BALCO) in Korba, Madras Aluminium Company Limited (MALCO) in Mettur, and Vedanta Aluminium Limited in Lanjigarh make up the aluminum segment. Sesa Goa Limited in Panaji, India, controls the iron ore segment. The company's newest business segment, the commercial power generation business, operates through Sterlite Energy Limited, a wholly owned subsidiary of Sterlite Industries. Sterlite Industries is India's leading copper producer, while BALCO and MALCO are the country's second-largest primary producers of aluminum. Vedanta fosters an entrepreneurial spirit, with a view to becoming a world-class metals and mining company through further acquisitions and organic growth.

VEDANTA'S EARLY YEARS

Anil Agarwal, founder, chairman, and majority stakeholder of Vedanta Resources plc, grew up in Patna, a small city in the state of Bihar in northeastern India. He left school at the age of 15 without knowing a word of English and having no formal education. His father was a fabricator of grills, grates, and aluminum conductors. Agarwal began his career as a scrap metal trader, collecting materials from aluminum cable and copper wire companies to sell in Bombay (Mumbai).

Agarwal's humble beginnings and lack of education were no deterrent to the young, focused, and aggressive go-getter. A shrewd entrepreneur, Agarwal had identified a niche for the copper market within India's burgeoning telecommunications business. A small business opportunity brought Agarwal to Mumbai in 1975. Agarwal said in a Rediff.com interview in February 2005 that it was in Mumbai that he learned English, "how to dress well, and the other tricks of the trade." Using a phone rented from an upstairs office, Agarwal set up operations in an 80-square-foot room in an old neighborhood of Mumbai called Kalbadevi. In 1976 Agarwal founded Vedanta Resources and established India's first copper smelting plant. Agarwal's first big break came when he began to help the Indian government privatize its mining assets.

In 1979 Agarwal entered into the enameled copper wire and aluminum overhead power transmission cable markets with the acquisition of Shamsher Sterling Corporation at auction. In 1983, with a $1.5 million bank loan, Agarwal headed to Decatur, Illinois, to purchase a copper cable manufacturing plant that he shipped back to India, thus making Vedanta the first multinational to have a significant portion of its physical assets in the country. In 1986 Agarwal entered into the jelly field cable business by setting up a factory at INR 7 million against the normal INR 30–40 million. That same year Sterling Industries (India) Limited was born when Sterlite Cables Limited, a Vedanta subsidiary, acquired Shamsher Sterling. By 1988 Sterling Industries was India's largest private producer of cast copper rod plants, and the company made an initial public offering (IPO) of its shares and convertible debentures.

EXPANSION AND DIVERSIFICATION

Agarwal's empire was beginning to take shape, and, in keeping with his practice of going abroad to buy cheap and shipping back to India, he traveled to Australia, where he used his persuasive charms to buy a copper smelting plant for INR 9 billion, although the asking price was INR 25 billion. With his copper business well established, Agarwal next moved into aluminum and, in 1993, established a plant for the manufacture of aluminum sheets and foils. This same year he established Sterlite Communications in Aurangabad, Maharashtra, for the manufacture of optical fiber. Agarwal failed at his attempt to buy Indian Aluminium (Indal), but in 1995 he acquired an 80 percent interest in Madras Aluminium Company Limited (MALCO).

In 1997 Sterlite Industries commissioned the first privately developed copper smelter in Tuticorin, India. In its first year of operation, the new plant was steeped in controversy when an explosion killed two workers and emitted sulfur dioxide into the surrounding residential community. Ten years later the plant would be rated as one of the world's top 10 custom copper smelters and the largest producer in India. The acquisition of Copper Mines of Tasmania Pvt. Ltd. and Thalanga Copper Mines Pvt. Ltd., both in Queensland, Australia, followed in 1999.

In 2000 Agarwal demerged the telecommunications cables and optical fiber business into a new company, Sterlite Optical Technologies Limited. Agarwal once again faced controversy when the Indian government put the Bharat Aluminium Company (BALCO) up for sale, and Sterlite bid $121 million, nearly twice that of the next highest bidder. Although Sterlite succeeded in acquiring 51 percent of BALCO in 2001, lawsuits were filed, and the labor union went on strike. With the plant sitting idle for more than two months, its molten aluminum solidified. It took several months before the plant was fully operational, and Agarwal moved swiftly to make the newly privatized company competitive. Within the year, Agarwal had implemented measures that reduced the staff by 30 percent, while increasing production by 35 percent at a cost savings of $400 per ton.

As the Indian government continued to privatize, Sterlite entered into the zinc business with the acquisition of 26 percent of Hindustan Zinc Limited in 2002. An additional 20 percent of the company was acquired through an open market offer and, in 2003, another 18.9 percent through a government call option. Immediately getting to work on maximizing the operation's efficiency, Agarwal built a 30-megawatt power plant that reduced electricity costs by 35 percent.

KEY DATES

1976: Anil Agarwal founds Vedanta Resources.
1979: Vedanta acquires Shamsher Sterling Corporation.
1986: Sterlite Industries (India) Limited is founded.
1993: Sterlite Communications is established.
1995: Vedanta acquires an 80 percent interest in Madras Aluminium Company Limited (MALCO).
1999: Vedanta acquires Copper Mines of Tasmania Pvt. Ltd. and Thalanga Copper Mines Pvt. Ltd.
2000: Agarwal demerges the telecommunications cables and optical fiber business to form Sterlite Optical Technologies Limited, renamed Sterlite Technologies Limited in 2007.
2001: Sterlite acquires a 51 percent interest in Bharat Aluminium Company Limited (BALCO).
2002: Sterlite acquires a 26 percent interest in Hindustan Zinc Limited.
2003: Vedanta Resources plc is fully listed on the London Stock Exchange.
2004: Vedanta acquires a 51 percent interest in Konkola Copper Mines plc.
2007: Sterlite Industries (India) Limited is listed on the New York Stock Exchange.

He also cut the number of workers from 8,100 to 6,000 and stretched out the tread wear hours on company vehicle tires before replacing them. These measures helped bring down the cost of zinc from $870 per ton to $570.

VEDANTA RESOURCES LISTS ON THE LONDON STOCK EXCHANGE

By the end of 2003 Vedanta Resources had achieved a full listing on the London Stock Exchange, the first Indian manufacturing company to do so. Its subsidiary Sterlite Industries would be listed on the New York Stock Exchange four years later, the largest IPO by an Indian company in U.S. history. "This marks the climax of my ambition to have my company listed on the London Stock Exchange. I am delighted with the success of this Initial Public Offer of 3 billion dollars," Agarwal said to the Press Trust of India.

In 2004 Vedanta expanded into Zambia with the purchase of a 51 percent stake in Konkola Copper

Mines plc for $50 million. Agarwal estimated that Konkola, which was Zambia's largest private sector company with sales in excess of $600 million annually, would contribute about $150 million per year to the group's profits. The stake would later be increased to 79.4 percent, with Vedanta having full management control over the company.

With the added profits from the international expansion efforts, Vedanta was well positioned to increase its investment in India. In 2005 Vedanta expanded the copper smelter at Tuticorin to 300,000 tons per annum (tpa) and commissioned a new 154-megawatt power plant and zinc smelter at Chanderiya, which had a production capability of 170,000 tpa. The company also completed expansion of the Rampura Agucha lead and zinc mine.

In January 2006 Agarwal's global metal business was estimated to be worth more than $1.9 billion. With shares at an all-time high, Vedanta announced that it was raising $725 million through a convertible bond arranged by Barclays Bank, which also included the option to increase the bond by an additional $125 million. The funds would be used to refinance existing debts, including the ambitious $2.1 billion Jharasaguda aluminum smelter in Orissa, India.

This was followed in 2006 with the commissioning of an additional 50,000 tpa lead smelter at Chanderiya and the completion of BALCO expansion projects that increased aluminum output by 250,000 tpa. In October 2006 Vedanta announced that it had acquired Canadian-listed Sterlite Gold, marking the company's first entrance into the precious metals market. One year later Vedanta sold its 84.2 percent stake to GEoProm-Mining Ltd. for $86 million.

RECORD GROWTH

In 2007, after successfully completing a $2 billion American Depository Share (ADS) issue, Sterlite Industries was listed on the New York Stock Exchange (NYSE). Also in 2007 Vedanta acquired 51 percent of Sesa Goa Limited in Panaji, India. With a majority stake in the company, Vedanta had management control of India's largest producer-exporter of iron ore. In 2008 the group marked its fourth consecutive year of record growth, with the Chanderiya zinc smelter and Sesa Goa cited as two of the main contributors to the company's success. Vedanta also reported increased efficiencies and reduced operating costs across all businesses, with the exception of its operation in Konkola, Zambia. To remedy the situation Vedanta announced in May 2008 that it was investing $1 billion to double the production output of the copper mine.

In June 2008 Vedanta announced that its subsidiary Sterlite Industries was acquiring Asarco LLC, the third-largest copper mine in the United States, which had filed for Chapter 11 bankruptcy protection. Grupo-Mexico, Asarco's parent company, challenged the deal. Agarwal was keen on closing the sale, which would substantially increase the group's presence, adding a fourth continent 'feather' to his cap. Agarwal was quick to point out, however, that Sterlite would only be acquiring Asarco's assets and not its environmental liabilities, such as outstanding asbestos litigation. "All the money we pay will go to the creditors and to settle environmental claims," Agarwal is reported to have said on Indian television on May 1. By November 2009 the right of ownership was still unresolved, although Asarco's management, creditors, and the mining union were all in favor of Sterlite. The fate of Asarco was now in the hands of a Texas bankruptcy court judge.

HIT BY THE ECONOMIC DOWNTURN

The global economy was in decline, and Vedanta reported a 25 percent drop in profits after its half-year review ending on September 30, 2008. Earlier that month Vedanta had announced that it would be investing $9.8 million toward its aluminum smelting operation, but with the current economic conditions, the company was forced to reduce this expenditure to $5.1 billion.

Vedanta had also planned to undertake a corporate restructuring, but the plan was temporarily put on hold on the recommendation of its investors. "When the whole world is collapsing, the best decision we have taken is not to pursue it at this point of time, but we are committed to simplify our structure," said Agarwal to *Financial Express*. With the collapse of the U.S. housing market, the demand for copper, used in plumbing and electrical wiring, plummeted. Vedanta, now the largest copper producer in India, reported a staggering 98 percent decline in earnings by the end of its fiscal third quarter. From a high of $671.5 million a year earlier, earnings before interest, tax, depreciation, and amortization had fallen to $10.1 million by the end of 2008.

While metal prices continued to drop, Agarwal remained true to his strategy of reducing costs and optimizing efficiencies, resulting in a $621 million improvement in working capital. At the end of the March 2009 fiscal year, the company had a healthy bottom line even though the fall in metal prices meant a $1.4 billion decline in earnings. In June 2009, one day after Sesa Goa announced that it would be acquiring VS Dempo Mining Corporation Pvt. Ltd., Vedanta launched a $1.25 billion convertible bond issue to finance acquisitions and support organic growth.

Although Vedanta's earnings for the first quarter of the 2009 fiscal year were half of what they had been the year before, Agarwal remained focused on his mission of making Vedanta one of the world's top five metal producers and the global leader of zinc by 2010. Entering the third quarter of the 2009 fiscal year, Vedanta's iron ore and aluminum production were up, and the company was considering moving into the nickel and gold businesses.

About the future, the self-made, self-taught billionaire said, "India is a fast-emerging and attractive resource destination, and we believe our strategy and business objectives will harness India's high-quality wealth of mineral resources at low costs of development, positioning it as a leader on the global metals and mining market."

Marie O'Sullivan

PRINCIPAL SUBSIDIARIES

Bharat Aluminium Company Limited (India, 51%); Copper Mines of Tasmania (Australia); Hindustan Zinc Limited (India, 64.9%); Konkola Copper Mines plc (Zambia, 79.4%); Madras Aluminium Company Limited (India, 93.2%); Sesa Goa Limited (India, 52.7%); Sterlite Energy Limited (India); Sterlite Industries (India) Limited (57.9%); Vedanta Aluminium Limited (India, 70.5%).

PRINCIPAL OPERATING UNITS

Copper; Zinc; Aluminum; Iron Ore; Commercial Power Generation.

PRINCIPAL COMPETITORS

BHP Billiton Limited; Outokumpu; Rio Tinto Limited.

FURTHER READING

Advani, Sangitaa, "Anil Agarwal: Wheel of Fortune," Livemint. com/ *Wall Street Journal*, http://www.livemint.com/2008/02/01002118/Anil-Agarwal--Wheels-of-fortu.html.

"Anil Agarwal," The Equity Desk, http://www.theequitydesk.com/anil_agarwal.asp.

"Anil Agarwal, Vedanta Resources," Survival: The Movement for Tribal Peoples, http://www.survivalinternational.org/about/anilagarwal.

"Anil Agarwal Bags Mining Journal Award," *Business Standard* (India), December 11, 2009.

Bajaj, Kapil, "A Self-Made Billionaire," *Business Today* (India), August 27, 2006.

Bolger, Joe, "Vedanta Ends Its Record-Breaking Run on News of Convertible Bond," Stock Markets, *Times* (London), January 24, 2006, p. 53.

"E&Y Gives Away Entrepreneur of the Year Awards," *Financial Express*, November 27, 2008.

Freedman, Michael, "Billionaires: All Mine," *Forbes*, March 15, 2004.

"Governance Update: Vedanta Vindicated in Director Selection," *Pensions Week*, August 1, 2005.

Hopkins, Kathryn, "Vedanta Resources Dismisses Human Rights Abuse Claims," *Guardian* (London), November 5, 2009.

Kripalani, Manjeet, David Rocks, Alex Halperin, and Nandini Lakshman, "India Plays Catch-Up in Africa," *BusinessWeek*, May 26, 2008, p. 55.

Li, Martin, "Vedanta Outperforms Again," *Investors Chronicle*, May 19, 2008.

MacNamara, William, "Battle for Asarco Enters Final Phase," *Financial Times*, November 16, 2006, p. 23.

Mathiason, Nick, "Profile: Anil Agarwal," *Guardian* (London), July 28, 2009.

————, "Vedanta Resources—India's Largest Copper Mining Firm," *Guardian* (London), October 12, 2009.

"Metal Companies' Cup of Woes Full in 2008," *Financial Express*, December 31, 2008.

Nair, Suresh, "Proving Its Mettle: Vedanta Has Its Ear to the Ground," *Asia Africa Intelligence Wire*, October 22, 2005.

"'Not Right Time for Vedanta to Restructure'," *Financial Express*, March 4, 2009.

O'Sullivan, Daniel, "Vedanta Pushing Ahead," *Investors Chronicle*, May 8, 2009.

————, "Vedanta's Resources Continue to Bloom," *Investors Chronicle*, November 5, 2009.

"The Rediff Interview: Anil Agarwal, CEO, Vedanta Resources Plc," Rediff.com, February 16, 2005, http://www.rediff.com/money/2005/feb/16inter.htm.

"Sterlite Raises $1.5 bn via ADS Issue," *Financial Express*, July 17, 2009.

"Sterlite's Anil Agarwal Set to Join Britain's Elite," Rediff.com. November 16, 2003, http://www.rediff.com/money/2003/nov/16sterlite.htm.

"Sterlite to Match Rival Bid for Asarco," *Financial Express*, April 30, 2009.

"Vedanta Earnings Fall 98%, Nalco Net Dips," *Financial Express*, January 29, 2009.

"Vedanta Ebidta Halves on Steep Metal Price Fall," *Financial Express*, August 1, 2009.

"Vedanta Eyes Gold, Nickel Biz," *Financial Express*, August 13, 2009.

"Vedanta Resources plc Announces Successful Acquisition of Sterlite Gold Ltd. and Extension of Offer," *CNW Group*, October 2, 2006.

"Vedanta Sells Sterlite Gold for $86m," *Metals Place*, August 16, 2007.

"Vedanta's Q2 Aluminium, Iron Ore Production Up," *Financial Express*, October 9, 2009.

"Vedanta Subsidiary Acquires Bankrupt Asarco," *Corporate Financing Week*, June 9, 2008, p. 5(1).

"Vedanta to Cut Capex by $5.1 bn as Profits Dip," *Financial Express*, November 7, 2008.

"Vedanta to Raise $1bn Via Bonds," *Financial Express*, June 13, 2009.

Verma, Virendra Kumar, "Anil Agarwal," *Business Today* (India), July 13, 2008.

Vivendi

42 Avenue de Friedland
Paris, 75380 Cedex 08
France
Telephone: (+33 1) 71-71-10-00
Fax: (+33 1) 71-71-10-01
Web site: http://www.vivendi.com

Public Company
Incorporated: 1853 as Compagnie Générale des Eaux
Employees: 43,208
Sales: €25.39 billion ($35.79 billion) (2008)
Stock Exchanges: Euronext Paris
Ticker Symbol: VIV
NAICS: 334611 Software Reproducing; 512220 Integrated Record Production/Distribution; 515210 Cable and Other Subscription Programming; 517110 Wired Telecommunications Carriers; 517210 Wireless Telecommunications Carriers (except Satellite)

■ ■ ■

Formerly known as the Compagnie Générale des Eaux, Vivendi is one of the world's leading entertainment conglomerates with interests in music, television, telecommunications, video games, and Internet-related businesses. Based in Paris, France, Vivendi controls the Universal Music Group (the largest record company in the world), the Canal+ Groupe (the leading pay-television firm in Europe), SNR (the largest private telecommunications operator in France), and Activision Blizzard (one of the world's largest video game developers). During the 1990s and early 2000s, Vivendi embarked on a major expansion program, purchasing stakes in film, television, and publishing interests throughout Europe and the Americas. The company's ambitious acquisition strategy soon saddled it with crushing debt, however, and by the end of the decade it had scaled back its holdings considerably.

BIRTH OF A NEW BUSINESS: 1850–59

Compagnie Générale des Eaux was founded in 1852 during the reign of Napoleon III and is often described as France's first capitalist venture. The company was authorized by imperial decree on December 14, 1853, and from the start benefited enormously from the emperor's personal interest, as well as from support and investment from the international business communities in Paris, London, and Lyons, which had studied the water supply companies of the United States and the United Kingdom and realized rich pickings could be had. The list of founders included the Rothschild family, a Fould, a Lafitte, the Duc de Morny (the emperor's half brother), and a large proportion of the imperial nobility. Shareholders included James de Rothschild (who had the largest single subscription of 5,000 shares) and a cross-section of members of the nobility, stockbrokers, and bankers. The initial capital was FRF 20 million, which was raised from an 80,000 share subscription.

The political and financial influence of its founders and shareholders gave the new company a high profile from the start, but the company also caught the mood

COMPANY PERSPECTIVES

The Vivendi group's business lines have numerous common points: they each belong to the digital and new technologies sector and they are aimed specifically at end-consumers through the leveraging of strong brands (i.e., Activision Blizzard, UMG, SFR, Maroc Telecom and Canal+) which provide customers with subscription-based access to digital quality and creative content. These common points give Vivendi competitive advantages through fruitful know-how and advanced technology sharing, which in turn generate considerable expertise in the management of subscribers, brands, distribution platforms, creation and copyrights.

of the day with its declared objective of providing "assistance for municipal authorities in implementing schemes of fundamental importance to public health." Not only was the notion of water-for-all part of a new municipal socialism that had already taken root in the United Kingdom and Germany, but also France's growing industries were becoming insatiable in their need for water and power. Without an industrial base France could not compete with its neighbors, the United Kingdom and Germany.

If the foundation of Compagnie Générale des Eaux was a calculated political move, it was also an astute financial one. "We shall be opening up a mine, the wealth of which has not been explored," reported the first board of management to the shareholders, which claimed that "as the first occupants of this mine, it will be our privilege to select and exploit the best seams." The shareholders were not disappointed.

Projected returns of 4 percent were realized at 25 percent from the first year of business. Lyons and Nantes headed the list of municipal authorities anxious to receive Générale des Eaux water. Within months a 99-year agreement had been concluded with Lyons to provide water for domestic and industrial consumption. For an initial investment of FRF 6 million and operating costs of FRF 80,000 per year, Générale des Eaux guaranteed a gross annual income of FRF 381,500 before a drop of water had even flowed through the pipes. A contract with Nantes followed in 1854, with Générale des Eaux undercutting the haphazard services of current suppliers but still managing to make a healthy 20 percent profit.

EXPANDING INTO NEW TERRITORIES: 1860–90

Securing the contract for the Paris water supply took a little longer. Initially turned down for the bid to supply the capital's water, Générale des Eaux began buying into small local water companies in the suburbs. When in 1860 the suburbs were annexed to the city, the company was in a strong position to negotiate with the prefecture of the Seine and the city of Paris authorities. Slow penetration into and around the desired market was a clever strategy and became something of a hallmark of Générale des Eaux's acquisition policies thereafter.

The seven-year wait was worth it. Générale des Eaux won a 50-year contract to supply Paris and the suburbs. The city of Paris, for its part, took possession of all water machinery and installations that had previously belonged to the company. Générale des Eaux guaranteed a supply of water that they charged back to the authorities. As the population of Paris grew and the demand for both domestic and industrial water increased, the water supplier saw its profits grow.

The character of Générale des Eaux was beginning to emerge. The company preferred to deal with large municipal authorities that would contract agreements for long periods of time and sought out projects that would bring high profits to enable greater investment. It also displayed a strong speculative and entrepreneurial streak, the latter of which is particularly remarkable. Anticipating the growth of the Côte d'Azur and the so-called Emerald Coast of Brittany some 20 to 30 years before the resorts became fashionable, Générale des Eaux installed water supplies and drainage systems in Nice and the surrounding areas from the 1860s and subsequently supplied Antibes, Menton, Hyères, and Monaco in the 1870s and 1880s. Toward the end of the century, the coastal towns and large cities of Brittany and Normandy were supplied by Générale des Eaux.

NEW CHALLENGES: 1890–1940

Despite heady successes in the company's first 50 years, the end of the century brought an unforeseen problem. In 1892 there was a major typhoid epidemic in Paris. The authorities acted by ordering a systematic sampling of water for laboratory analysis, and in 1902 the Public Hygiene Act laid down standards for public health in relation to the water supply. The connection between water supply and cholera and typhoid was finally understood. From then on municipal authorities demanded not just efficiency but guarantees that the water being delivered for domestic consumption was clean and disease free. For Générale des Eaux, the Public Hygiene Act meant hefty investment in research and new machinery. Treating wastewater before it ran back

```
┌─────────────────────────────────────────────┐
│                                               │
│               KEY DATES                       │
│                    ■                          │
│  ─────────────────────────────────────        │
│                                               │
│  1852:  Compagnie Générale des Eaux is founded.│
│  1860:  The company secures a 50-year contract│
│         to supply water to Paris and its suburbs.│
│  1981:  Profits reach FRF 331 million; Compagnie│
│         Générale d'Electricité purchases a 15 │
│         percent stake in Générale des Eaux.   │
│  1983:  Saint-Gobain is forced by the French govern-│
│         ment to cut its stake in the firm.    │
│  1996:  Jean-Marie Messier is named chairman and│
│         begins a reorganization program.      │
│  1998:  The company changes its name to Vivendi.│
│  2000:  Company merged with Canal+ and Seagram│
│         Company Ltd. and is renamed Vivendi   │
│         Universal S.A.                         │
│  2001:  MP3.com Inc. and Houghton Mifflin     │
│         Company are acquired; plans are set in mo-│
│         tion to purchase USA Networks Inc.    │
│  2004:  Vivendi sells 80 percent of its Vivendi│
│         Universal Entertainment subsidiary to NBC,│
│         creating NBC Universal.               │
│  2007:  Vivendi purchases a controlling stake in the│
│         video game developer Activision, creating Ac-│
│         tivision Blizzard.                    │
│                                               │
└─────────────────────────────────────────────┘
```

into the clean water supplies also became a priority.

There was, too, a new competitor in the field. Société Lyonnaise des Eaux et de L'Eclairage was founded in 1880 and by the start of the 20th century had established itself as a force to be reckoned with. From then on something of a race developed between the two companies to acquire market shares in the supplying of water to unserviced municipalities. Between 1900 and 1940 the rate at which water supply networks spread through France accelerated with each decade. Both companies expanded their areas of influence by buying up local water companies and overhauling their operations, so that by the outbreak of World War II Compagnie Générale des Eaux and Société Lyonnaise des Eaux et de L'Eclairage supplied 50 percent of all town dwellers.

THE GUY DEJOUANY ERA

Dominating the fortunes of Compagnie Générale des Eaux in the postwar years was the personality of Guy Dejouany. An engineer by profession, he was educated at the Ecole Polytechnique and, after appointments in Metz and Paris, joined Générale des Eaux in 1950. His rise through the company was swift. A director in 1960, he became deputy director general in 1965, director general in 1972, and president and director general in 1976.

In the 1960s Dejouany was instrumental in the development of a thermal energy program, showing himself to be a strong advocate of diversification beyond the traditional water concerns. Moreover, he turned the company from a fairly institutional concern into a dynamic, highly diversified group that, in 1991, was one of the most successful companies on the Paris Stock Exchange. Dejouany remained a decidedly nonpublic figure, declining to give interviews and running an unusually small headquarters with only 15 managers. Dejouany was involved in the first tentative moves, in the 1970s, into urban cleaning and maintenance, waste, electrical contracting, house building, and construction.

By 1981 Compagnie Générale des Eaux was beginning to make the headlines with its profits of FRF 331 million. Ironically its attractiveness nearly brought about its downfall. At the start of the 1980s, 75 percent of shares were held by small investors, headed by Dejouany. In March 1981 Compagnie Générale d'Electricité announced a 15 percent stake, a significant interest held by a large company. Two years later glass and pipe manufacturer Saint-Gobain, which had already bought enthusiastically into Olivetti and Bull CH Honeywell only to have the government insist that it pull out, announced a 33 percent holding in Compagnie Générale des Eaux. Months of complicated maneuvers on the Paris Stock Exchange had been necessary, but Générale des Eaux had exposed itself to the risk of being acquired by a large company when it issued new shares at the start of 1983 to raise capital for investment.

The announcement brought crises within the water company and within the government. Dejouany and a number of government critics complained that Saint-Gobain, one of France's six major companies nationalized in 1982, was attempting a creeping nationalization of the water company. Saint-Gobain replied that it was merely seeking to expand its business by ordinary means but was soon requested by the government to cut its stake to 20.7 percent. Dejouany further redressed the balance by asking Schlumberger, a Franco-American service and electronics group, to buy a 10 percent share at a cost of FRF 550 million to offset Saint-Gobain's interest.

INTERNATIONAL EXPANSION: 1980–91

This share purchase ended the crisis and signaled the end, too, of the growing pains of Générale des Eaux.

The company multiplied its interests abroad and bought into some of France's leading companies at home. The results were dramatic. The 1980s, as a whole, saw sales at home increase six and a half times, from FRF 11.5 billion to FRF 76.5 billion, and sales abroad multiply 35 times, from FRF 630 million to FRF 22 billion. Net profits rose from FRF 331 million in 1981 to FRF 766 million in 1986 and then took off sharply to finish at FRF 1.8 billion in 1989.

The weighty program of investment and activity abroad produced both admiration and controversy in countries targeted for Générale des Eaux treatment. By 1991 Générale des Eaux was the second-largest water distributor in Spain and the third-largest distributor of bottled water in the United States. The company also supplied water in Portugal, Malta, and Italy. It collected waste in Bogota and Prague, cleaned the streets and underground system of Madrid, supplied cable television in Montreal, and managed industrial waste and thermal power from California to Benelux.

Générale des Eaux also moved across the English Channel. Britain in the late 1980s, with a water industry heading for privatization and local authorities beginning to put many of their service contracts out for tender, was ripe for investment. Lyonnaise des Eaux and Société d'Aménagement Urbain et Rural (SAUR) made large tenders for the 10 regional water companies, Lyonnaise paying £47.6 million for Essex Water in June 1988 and SAUR paying £58.6 million for Mid Southern Water in January 1989.

Générale des Eaux, in contrast, focused on buying shares in a number of smaller companies, including Three Valleys, Folkestone & District, Mid-Kent, Severn and Trent, and Bristol, and looked to the wider areas of energy, waste, health care, construction, and cable television to establish a foothold in Britain. The foothold was designed to be flexible. When British electricity companies were privatized in 1990, Générale des Eaux dropped some of its water interests and bought into Associated Electricity. Similarly, when television franchises were put up for bids in 1991, Générale des Eaux bought shares in a number of cable television operations.

Less expected was the purchase of American Medical International's chain of private hospitals in Britain in March 1990 and an 83 percent stake in Norwest Hoist. In June 1991 Générale des Eaux's U.K. waste company Onyx announced a seven-year rubbish collection contract with the city of Liverpool, the latest of 20 such contracts with municipalities all over Britain.

CONTINUED GROWTH AND DIVERSIFICATION

The progress of Générale des Eaux in Britain mirrored the development of the company in France during its early days in the 19th century. The profits were just as rich. In 1990 the company made £900 million in Britain, representing almost 10 percent of total group sales revenue worldwide.

In the general spread of its international and home operations there were similarities, too, to company behavior in the previous century and during the early 1990s. Générale des Eaux was responsive to current environmental issues. In May 1990 it paid $100 million for a 16 percent stake in Air and Water Technologies, a major U.S. pollution-control company based in New Jersey. Air, water, and soil pollution prevention was high on the list of priorities for Générale des Eaux in the 1990s. Its activities by that time had already earned it attention from Europe's press for its environmental concerns.

By 1991 Générale des Eaux's interests in cable television and cellular car phones included a 21.6 percent share in Canal+, 90 percent of Générale d'Images, and 80 percent of Compagnie Générale de Vidéo-communications, making Générale des Eaux the leading operator of cable networks in France. Although the 1991 Gulf War boosted viewing figures, cable television had yet to take off in a big way. It was thought, however, that the mid-1990s would see a large increase in the subscription base. The launch of cellular phones showed quicker returns. Between the inception of the service in March 1989 and the end of the year, there were 10,000 subscribers. At a European level the earphone subsidiary, Compagnie Financière pour le Radio Téléphone, worked with BMW and Veba in Germany to install telephones directly.

In addition to entering the communications sector, since 1986 Générale des Eaux had bought into a number of French blue chip companies, including Saint-Gobain. Saint-Gobain's major subsidiary, Société Générale d'Entreprise (which had in turn been acquired from Compagnie Générale d'Electricité) was bought out by Générale des Eaux in 1988, thereby giving it a major position in France's construction industry. Phénix, Seeri, and Sari added to Générale des Eaux's command in this area, with projects such as the La Defense building in Paris. In Paris the company cleaned the Louvre, the Métro, the Ministry of Finance, and the Musée d'Orsay art gallery. It also collected waste for Peugeot, Air France, the SNCF (Société Nationale des Chemins de Fer Français), and Nestlé.

A NEW FOCUS AND A NEW NAME: 1995–98

Continuing with its expansion efforts, Générale des Eaux underwent a series of strategic changes during the mid-to-late 1990s that turned the company into a major entertainment and environmental concern. In 1996 Dejouany retired, leaving Jean-Marie Messier to take over the helm. The 39-year-old executive quickly initiated a hard-core restructuring effort with a focus on its environmental and communications-related businesses and began selling off more than $25 billion in holdings.

At the time, Générale des Eaux was referred to as a "corporate octopus," having more than 2,200 subsidiaries involved in the property, construction, health, energy, mobile phone, amusement park, cable television, and railway industries. A 1996 article in the *European* claimed that the company had "begun to spin out of control following reckless investment, mainly in property, the disappointing performance of the private healthcare division, and problems in maximizing investments in mobile phones and cable TV, which have lagged behind in France."

As part of Messier's grand scheme, he implemented a strategy on which the company was focused on gaining world leadership in the environmental services industry, as well as in both the media and communications industries. During 1996 plans were set in motion to create the Groupe Cegetel, a subsidiary that would cover fixed and mobile phone businesses in France. (The telecommunications market in France was deregulated in 1998.) As part of its push into publishing, the company acquired a 30 percent interest in Havas in 1997 and then merged with Havas the following year. It afterward purchased Cendant Software Corp., an electronic publishing firm. In 1998 the company adopted a new name, Vivendi, chosen to suggest life and vitality.

ENTERING THE NEW MILLENNIUM

Vivendi marked its entrance into the new millennium with a $34 billion stock purchase of Seagram Company Ltd. The deal added Universal Music Group and Universal Studios to Vivendi's holdings, giving it control of the world's largest music company. It also purchased the remaining shares of Canal+ and then changed its name once again, to Vivendi Universal. During this time period companies that had traditionally focused on either content or distribution began seeking out strategic purchases that would align both content and distribution holdings. The merger of America Online Inc. and Time Warner was one such purchase that signaled the

industry's changing landscape. Messier commented on the AOL deal in a 2001 Time International article, stating that "nothing in the world of communications would ever be the same again. Being strong in content is not enough. You also need to own part of your own distribution network."

As such Vivendi began to seek out a distribution partner that would give it a stronger foothold in the U.S. market. Along with its purchases of U.S.-based publisher Houghton Mifflin Company and Internet music service provider MP3.com Inc., the company announced its intent to purchase the entertainment assets of USA Networks Inc. for more than $10 billion in December 2001, along with a 10 percent stake in Echo-Star Communications Corp., the second-largest satellite-television operator in the United States. The USA Network deal would give Vivendi access to more than 84 million U.S. television viewers and bring it closer to competing with the likes of rival AOL Time Warner.

In just seven years Messier had transformed the Générale des Eaux Group of the 1800s into a leading entertainment conglomerate with a net income of $2.1 billion in 2000 and sales of nearly $50 billion in 2001. While the company's recent acquisition spree left it with debt equaling $18 billion (a 50 percent debt-to-equity ratio, which was higher than most of its competitors), management was confident that the firm was on the right track to securing future growth. Messier held strong to his belief that Vivendi Universal would become the world's preferred creator and provider of entertainment.

FINANCIAL STRUGGLES

As the decade progressed Vivendi Universal soon found itself buckling beneath the weight of its massive financial liabilities. The company absorbed losses of EUR 13.6 billion ($11.86 billion) in 2001, driven largely by a drop in the value of several new assets, notably Canal+ and Seagram. At the same time, the company's stock plummeted in the first two years of the new century, falling 75 percent between early 2000 and April 2002. Vivendi executives worked hard to allay investor concerns, arguing that many of the company's losses were write-offs relating to recent acquisitions.

By May 2002 Vivendi's debt had ballooned to EUR 31.3 billion ($28.6 billion). For the first half of the year, the company posted losses of EUR 13.38 billion ($12 billion). In July embattled CEO Jean-Marie Messier resigned. According to some industry analysts, Messier's troubles stemmed primarily from his inability to elucidate a clear rationale behind the company's recent acquisition strategy, coupled with his failure to identify an effective way to pay down its debt. Messier was replaced by Jean-René Fourtou, who immediately set out to streamline the company's holdings. As part of Fourtou's vision, the company planned to sell off a number of its assets, with the ultimate goal of raising EUR 10.02 billion ($9.8 billion).

REVISING EXPECTATIONS: 2002 ON

In November 2002 Vivendi sold the American publishing house Houghton Mifflin, which had been acquired only a year earlier under Messier's stewardship, for $1.7 billion (EUR 1.7 billion). That same month the company announced its intention to sell half of its 40.4 percent stake in Vivendi Environnement, its core water and waste management business. The shares were valued at roughly EUR 1.85 billion ($1.85 billion). During this period Vivendi also sold all of its remaining publishing concerns, both in Europe and abroad, and divested portions of its Canal+ holdings. Between July and November 2002, the company sold more than EUR 5 billion ($4.93 billion) worth of its holdings.

Meanwhile the company's new strategy began to take shape. In December 2002 it spent EUR 4 billion ($4.08 billion) to acquire an additional 26 percent stake in Cegetel, a French telecommunications firm. Although Vivendi suffered total losses of EUR 23.3 billion ($25 billion) for the year 2002, a record for a French corporation, the company's six principal businesses, among them Vivendi Universal Entertainment and Cegetel, saw net profits increase 18 percent. By the end of the year, the company had reduced its overall debt to EUR 12.3 billion ($12.57 billion).

By mid-2003 the company was still struggling to regain its financial footing. In June of that year, as a way of paying off its debt more aggressively, Vivendi announced that it was putting the movie, theme park, and television divisions of Vivendi Universal Entertainment up for sale. In November of that year, the company entered into a preliminary agreement with broadcast giant NBC to create a new joint venture, NBC Universal, with an estimated value of $43 billion (EUR 36.7 billion). Under the terms of the deal, Vivendi would retain a 20 percent stake in the company. The merger was completed in May 2004.

Vivendi's corporate image continued to evolve during the second half of the decade, as the rapidly shifting nature of new technologies presented new opportunities for growth. One surprising success from this period came from the company's relatively small video game subsidiary, Blizzard Entertainment. The unit's swift growth came from its interactive online role-playing game *World of Warcraft*, which by 2007 had amassed more than 9 million players across the world. In December of that year, Vivendi acquired a controlling share in American video game maker Activision to create a new subsidiary, Activision Blizzard. That same month Vivendi acquired an additional 29 percent stake in Neuf Cegetel, with the aim of eventually owning the entire company.

As the decade drew to a close, Vivendi's former chief, Jean-Marie Messier, was forced to stand trial on accounting fraud charges, the culmination of an investigation dating back to the year 2001. The company itself soon came under scrutiny and in late January 2010 was found guilty of fraud by the U.S. District Court in Manhattan. In the midst of these legal issues, Vivendi entered into negotiations to sell its 20 percent stake in NBC Universal, as a prelude to the proposed merger of NBC and cable giant Comcast. With the prospect of another major debt looming, Vivendi's decision to sell another lucrative asset seemed particularly well timed.

Catriona Luke
Updated, Christina M. Stansell; Stephen Meyer

PRINCIPAL SUBSIDIARIES

Activision Blizzard, Inc. (U.S., 57%); Canal+ Groupe; GVT (Brazil); Maroc Télécom Group (Morocco, 53%); SFR (56%); Universal Music Group (U.S.); Vivendi Mobile Entertainment.

PRINCIPAL COMPETITORS

Electronic Arts Inc.; France Télécom; Orange; Sony Corporation; Viacom Inc.

FURTHER READING

"All Vivendi Wants for Christmas," *BusinessWeek*, December 24, 2001.

Carter, Bill, "G.E. Finishes Vivendi Deal, Expanding Its Media Assets," *New York Times*, October 9, 2003, p. C1.

Guyon, Janet, "Can Messier Make Cash Flow Like Water?" *Fortune*, September 3, 2001, p. 148.

Kapner, Suzanne, "Vivendi's Latest Spin Campaign: No Sale Option Is Left Unspun," *New York Times*, September 14, 2002, p. C1.

"Master of the Universe," *Time International*, August 6, 2001, p. 32.

Mathieson, Clive, "Vivendi Chief Still Has a Lot to Prove," *Times* (London), April 13, 2002.

McClellan, Steve, "Vivendi Deal Makes It Truly Universal," *Broadcasting & Cable*, December 31, 2001, p. 8.

Nicholson, Chris V., "With Sale of NBC, Analysts Say Vivendi Can Pursue Other Acquisitions," *New York Times*, December 2, 2009, p. B4.

Tillier, Alan, "Golden Boy Dips His Toe in the Water," *European*, May 23, 1996, p. 32.

———, "Vivendi Makes Its Multimedia Play," *European*, November 30, 1998, p. 19.

"Veni Vidi Vivendi," *Economist*, December 22, 2001.

"Why Vivendi's Shuffling Has Only Just Begun," *Fortune*, July 10, 2000, p. 38.

Vornado Realty Trust

888 Seventh Avenue
New York, New York 10019
U.S.A.
Telephone: (212) 894-7000
Fax: (201) 587-0600
Web site: http://www.vno.com

Public Company
Founded: 1947 as Two Guys from Harrison
Incorporated: 1957 as Two Guys from Harrison, Inc.
Employees: 3,529
Sales: $1.96 billion (2008)
Stock Exchanges: New York
Ticker Symbol: VNO
NAICS: 531120 Lessors of Nonresidential Buildings (except Miniwarehouses); 531210 Offices of Real Estate Agents and Brokers; 531311 Residential Property Managers; 531312 Nonresidential Property Managers

■ ■ ■

Vornado Realty Trust is a real estate investment trust (REIT) that owns, leases, develops, and manages real estate properties. The company operates primarily in the Northeast and Mid-Atlantic states, while also controlling major properties in Chicago and San Francisco. Vornado was a retailer until 1980, when Steven Roth wrested control of the firm and converted it into a developer of the properties occupied by its Two Guys from Harrison store chain. In the 1990s Roth positioned Vornado to become a major developer of commercial real estate in

Midtown Manhattan, acquiring numerous properties in the area surrounding Madison Square Garden. By the 21st century Vornado controlled more than 100 million square feet of commercial real estate, with major office and retail holdings in New York City, Chicago, the Washington, D.C., metropolitan area, and Puerto Rico.

DISCOUNT STORE ORIGINS

Vornado's corporate history dates back to 1947, when Herbert Hubschman and his brother Sidney opened a household-appliance store in a converted diner in Harrison, New Jersey. This was the first in a discount chain named Two Guys from Harrison, which originally sold major appliances and later added other appliances and housewares. The Hubschmans were pioneers in the development of one-stop shopping centers in New Jersey, consisting chiefly of leased departments. Vital to the brothers' success was their policy of locating the stores in outlying areas, where they could obtain less expensive land and offer customers larger parking lots than other retailers. Sales grew from $6.8 million in fiscal 1952 to $38 million in fiscal 1957. Net income rose from $162,723 to $816,675 over this period.

Two Guys from Harrison was operating, through subsidiaries, 16 discount stores (14 of them in northern New Jersey) when it went public as Two Guys from Harrison, Inc., in 1957, offering one-fourth of its common stock at $9 a share. In 1959 Two Guys entered a new field by acquiring O. A. Sutton Corp., Inc., for stock. Since 1954 Sutton had been manufacturing Vornado electric fans and room air conditioners; fuel tanks for the air force; and air conditioners under the West-

COMPANY PERSPECTIVES

Our business objective is to maximize shareholder value. We intend to achieve this objective by continuing to pursue our investment philosophy and executing our operating strategies through maintaining a superior team of operating and investment professionals and an entrepreneurial spirit; investing in select markets, such as New York City and Washington, D.C., where we believe there is a high likelihood of capital appreciation; acquiring quality properties at a discount to replacement cost and where there is significant potential for higher rents; investing in retail properties in select under-stored locations such as the New York City metropolitan area; investing in fully integrated operating companies that have a significant real estate component; and developing and redeveloping existing properties to increase returns and maximize value.

inghouse, Hotpoint, and Kelvinator trade names in Wichita, Kansas. Auto air conditioners and dehumidifiers were later added to its product line.

Sutton's net sales rose from $3.1 million in fiscal 1949 to $38 million in fiscal 1954, while net income grew from $282,859 to nearly $1.5 million over this period. In fiscal 1957, however, Sutton lost $1.7 million on sales of $37.9 million. The next year it suspended manufacturing and began liquidating its inventories to pay off bank notes.

The acquisition of Sutton provided Two Guys with additional working capital, the Vornado line of appliances, and an income-tax shelter later challenged by the Internal Revenue Service. Renamed Vornado, Inc., in less than 3 years the consolidated company expanded the Vornado line of appliances to more than 50. Although manufacturing operations were now contracted out, the Two Guys chain and other dealers sold Vornado ranges, freezers, hair dryers, electronic can openers, and other items. By the end of 1965 the company was the nation's fifth-largest discount chain, with 25 stores in 5 states, stretching from Connecticut to Maryland. Sales in fiscal 1966 reached $247.2 million, with net income of $8 million.

Two Guys's units, which included seven company-owned properties, were among the largest in the discount industry, with average store size close to 146,000 square feet. All but seven included company-operated supermarkets. Food, appliances, and clothing and apparel contributed the most to sales volume, with other items including housewares, home furnishings, shoes, auto accessories, jewelry, cosmetics, toys, and seasonal merchandise. Leased departments now accounted for only 5 percent of sales. Vornado maintained a fleet of almost 200 trailers and trucks and had in-house advertising, service, and construction departments. Herbert Hubschman died in 1964; since his brother had previously left the company, an associate, Frederick Zissu, succeeded as chairman.

LATE SIXTIES TO 1980: MORE STORES, DECLINING SALES

In 1967 Vornado acquired Food Giant Markets, Inc., a West Coast supermarket chain that also held a discount-store division and other retail enterprises, for an estimated $50 million of company stock. The purchase seemed to be a bargain: for its stock Vornado acquired a company doing $350 million worth of business a year, with 70 supermarkets, 241 Fosters Freeze franchised fast-food drive-ins, 14 Unimart general-merchandise discount stores, 5 package liquor stores, and a chain of more than 20 Builders Emporium stores selling do-it-yourself supplies. Vornado's sales immediately more than doubled, and its profits rose, although by a lesser amount.

Before long, however, security analysts were characterizing the acquisition as a serious drag on profits. Food Giant, still under its old management, instituted discounting but alienated shoppers by shortening hours and eliminating trading stamps. When managers from the East Coast took over, they did away with established California brands in favor of Vornado's own private labels, which were unknown out West. Unimart ended up with a huge inventory of unsalable merchandise. Company debt had reached $97.2 million by 1971.

In fiscal 1972 the Vornado empire enjoyed record sales of $827.1 million and record net income of $12.1 million. There were 53 Two Guys stores (including 4 in California), 65 Food Giant stores, 240 Fosters Freezes, and 31 Builders Emporium units. Most of the Unimarts had been phased out or were being converted into Two Guys outlets. In addition the company had purchased 12 Disco Fair stores in California from Beck Industries Inc. and owned a bakery and a dairy-products company. The Food Giant chain was disposed of piecemeal in 1971 and 1972, but this failed to stem a steady decline in profits. In fiscal 1977 Vornado earned only $145,000 on sales of $946.5 million.

In 1978 Vornado sold 22 Two Guys stores in California and a Builders Emporium to Fed-Mart Corp.

Guys, which was doing $600 million a year in business but had an operating loss of more than $20 million in the first half of 1981, disposing of $196 million of inventory. Montgomery Ward & Co., Inc., had leased 12 Philadelphia-area locations from Vornado in 1980; in March 1982 Stop & Shop Cos., Inc., agreed to lease 11 more Vornado shopping centers for its Bradlees discount department stores.

While seeking tenants for its 34 other shopping centers and its 8 warehouses, the company retained 3 Sutton Place catalog stores, which were subsequently phased out, and the Steinwurtzel finished-apparel wholesaling operation. Company revenues, $36.2 million in 1982, had reached $66.3 million in 1985, when real estate outstripped merchandising from Steinwurtzel (which was discontinued in 1991) as the chief source of sales. In 1989 Vornado had net income of $10.4 million on sales of $81.6 million.

Roth, through Interstate Properties, had entered the Manhattan real estate market in 1985 by buying a small stake in Alexander's, a failing retailer whose land holdings included a flagship store that occupied the entire block between East 58th and 59th streets and Lexington and Third avenues. Interstate and developer Donald Trump raised their respective shares of Alexander's to 22 percent each in 1987 and agreed to jointly expand or sell their interests in the firm. In 1988 they each raised their stakes to 27 percent. The agreement lapsed in 1991, when Trump turned over his holdings in Alexander's to Citicorp, which had been holding them as collateral for a personal loan. The following year Roth and Alexander's creditors forced the firm into bankruptcy. They closed the remaining stores in operation and raised $120 million by leasing a half dozen of its properties to Caldor, a chain of discount stores.

Alexander's emerged from bankruptcy in 1993 but as a REIT. Two years later Vornado, which already held a small portion of the retailer, bought Citicorp's share for $54.8 million (about 25 percent under market value). Roth, who now held majority control through Vornado and Interstate, became chief executive officer of the company. Vornado's plans for Alexander's East Side property (perhaps the most conspicuously unoccupied tract of prime Manhattan real estate in the 1990s) remained uncertain.

Vornado Inc. was converted to Vornado Realty Trust, a REIT, in 1993. By this time the company held $115 million in cash and $421 million in total assets. Its shares had increased in value by about 17 times since 1981, and Roth had realized $29.2 million the previous year by exercising options on 1.5 million shares of Vornado stock. The new equity offering raised $172 million and left Roth, through Interstate Properties and his

---

KEY DATES

1947: Brothers Herbert and Sidney Hubschman found the appliance chain Two Guys from Harrison.

1957: Two Guys from Harrison, Inc., goes public.

1959: Two Guys from Harrison acquires O. A. Sutton Corp., Inc.; company is renamed Vornado, Inc.

1967: Vornado acquires Food Giant Markets, Inc.

1979: Interstate Properties Inc. acquires 17 percent stake in Vornado.

1980: Interstate Properties assumes control over Vornado's business activities.

1993: Vornado, Inc., becomes Vornado Realty Trust.

1996: Michael Fascitelli becomes president of Vornado.

2001: Vornado signs Bloomberg LP as anchor tenant at former Alexander's department store site.

2002: Company acquires Charles E. Smith Commercial Realty for $1.58 billion.

2005: Vornado partners with KKR and Bain Capital to purchase Toys "R" Us retail chain.

2008: Company forms joint venture with Reliance Industries Limited to develop retail properties in India.

---

for $38.3 million and the assumption by the buyer of $27.3 million in mortgage debt. It sold the other 59 Builders Emporium stores to Wickes Corp. for $56.3 million in cash and the assumption of $10.7 million in mortgage debt. This left the company with 60 Two Guys stores and some $100 million in cash but also about $103 million in debt.

By the fall of 1979, Interstate Properties Inc., a private partnership engaged in shopping-center development, had taken a 17 percent stake in Vornado. In fiscal 1980 the company reported a loss of $750,000 on sales of $733.4 million, and later that year Interstate Properties took control of the firm after winning a proxy struggle.

1980–95: FROM RETAIL TO REAL ESTATE

Steven Roth, the active Interstate Properties partner, regarded Vornado's real estate holdings as more valuable than its declining retail operations. He liquidated Two personal holdings, with 38 percent of the outstanding shares. A special dividend of $54 million was distributed to shareholders.

1995–98: GROWTH THROUGH ACQUISITION

At the end of fiscal 1995, Vornado had posted an average 3-, 5-, and 10-year annual total returns of 27.4, 33.7, and 28.9 percent, respectively. The company suffered a blow when Bradlees, now the anchor store in 21 of Vornado's 56 shopping centers, filed for bankruptcy protection in 1995. Standard & Poor's concluded, however, that most of the leases would survive the bankruptcy because of the above-average sales of the stores involved, the superior locations, and Bradlees' lease guarantees from its former owner, Stop & Shop. Bradlees held 17 leases from Vornado at the end of 1996. They were mostly in New Jersey but also included the location of its store near Manhattan's Union Square.

Michael Fascitelli, a Goldman, Sachs & Co. real estate investment banker, was recruited to become president of Vornado in December 1996 with a compensation package valued between $50 million and $100 million or more. The lucrative deal was seen as evidence that Vornado was ready to buy downtown office buildings and regional malls. Rumors about the company's intentions sent the price of its stock to $61 a share in March 1997, compared to $37 a share a year earlier. Shortly thereafter Vornado confirmed one source of speculation by purchasing Mendik Co. for $437 million in cash and securities from developer Bernard Mendik, who became cochairman of Vornado. Vornado also assumed $217 million in debt. Mendik Co. held control of seven Midtown Manhattan office buildings totaling four million square feet of space.

One of Mendik's buildings was adjacent to Madison Square Garden, and another was across the street. A few months later Vornado agreed to buy another nearby building, the Hotel Pennsylvania, in a $160 million joint venture with Ong Beng Seng, a Singaporean hotel developer and financier. In June 1997 Vornado purchased three small buildings a block north of the hotel, plus leases of retail spaces in two buildings previously acquired by Vornado, for about $75 million. These transactions aroused speculation that Vornado was contemplating a multilevel shopping and entertainment complex in the area, which included not only Madison Square Garden but also the Manhattan passenger terminals for Amtrak and the Long Island Rail Road.

At the end of 1996 Vornado owned 57 shopping centers in New Jersey, New York, Pennsylvania, Maryland, Connecticut, Massachusetts, and Texas, containing 10 million square feet of space. They were generally located on major regional highways in densely populated areas. Shopping centers accounted for 92 percent of Vornado's rental revenues in 1996, and the occupancy rate was 90 percent. The company also owned eight warehouse/industrial properties in New Jersey and two office buildings. In addition, Vornado was leasing its executive headquarters in Saddle Brook, New Jersey.

In 1996 Vornado enjoyed record income from continuing operations of $61.4 million, on record revenues of $116.9 million. Interstate Properties, a general partnership in which Roth was managing general partner, held 24.4 percent of its shares. Vornado held 29.3 percent of Alexander's common stock at this time and was managing, developing, and leasing Alexander's properties under a three-year agreement.

The company's growth during this period was driven primarily by its acquisitions. In a two-year span between early 1996 and spring 1998, Vornado devoted more than $3 billion to new real estate deals. In April 1998 the company purchased the Merchandise Mart, a massive wholesale trade complex in Chicago, for $630 million. Among its numerous functions, the building is perhaps best-known for hosting trade shows for the furniture industry. According to company estimates, roughly 65 percent of the nation's office furniture sales were contracted at the Merchandise Mart.

SCALING BACK ACQUISITIONS

As the decade drew to a close, however, Vornado began to scale back its real estate purchases. In the eyes of some industry observers, this slowdown was the result of a steep drop in Vornado's stock value, which ultimately diminished the company's buying power. Roth dismissed these speculations, insisting that the company had more than $1 billion earmarked for strategic acquisitions. The problem, as Roth argued at an industry conference in fall 1998, was that real estate prices had become artificially inflated, as more and more sellers began to overvalue their properties. While Vornado had remained active in property auctions over the course of the year, its bids had typically fallen far short of the final sale price.

While the company's acquisition rate had slowed considerably, it continued to remain active heading into the new century. In early 1999 Vornado demolished the old Alexander's retail store on Manhattan's Upper East Side. By September the company had begun construction of a new building on the site, even though it had not finalized plans for the new structure and had secured only one tenant. According to a report published in the *Daily News* on September 20, 1999, the company's rush to commence excavation activities was driven by upcoming changes to the city's zoning laws, which were expected to impose new restrictions on the height of buildings in the neighborhood. By launching construction ahead of the rezoning, Vornado would be "grandfathered" into the previous requirements.

2001–09: EXPANDING INTO NEW GEOGRAPHICAL TERRITORIES

Entering the new century, Vornado embarked on an aggressive growth strategy, with its eye focused squarely on some of the most prominent real estate properties in New York City. In March 2001 the company's $3.5 billion offer was the highest bid on a 99-year lease for the World Trade Center. The deal ultimately fell apart, however, after Vornado altered its bid in a way that was unacceptable to the Port Authority of New York and New Jersey, which owned the twin towers. In light of the terrorist attacks that occurred six months later, Vornado's inability to close the deal represented one of the most fortunate business failures of Roth's career.

In the ensuing months Vornado scored a string of major successes. In April 2001, with the recent completion of a new 55-story building at the former Alexander's site, the company secured financial media firm Bloomberg LP as the tower's anchor tenant. In October of that year, Vornado bid $1.58 billion to acquire Charles E. Smith Commercial Realty, the largest commercial real estate developer in the Washington, D.C., area. The purchase was completed in 2002. With the acquisition, Vornado assumed control of more than 18 million square feet of retail and office property in and around the nation's capital. At the same time the deal made Vornado the fourth-largest real estate investment trust in the United States.

By 2005 Vornado had a market value of roughly $16 billion. In New York and Chicago alone, it owned nearly 50 million square feet of office and retail space, in addition to a wide range of other real estate investments. Heading into the second half of the decade, Vornado remained focused on further diversifying its portfolio. In July 2005 it partnered with equity capital firms KKR and Bain Capital to acquire the struggling Toys "R" Us retail chain, in a deal worth $6.1 billion. A year later the company joined developer John B. Hynes III to revitalize the Filene's department store in downtown Boston. In November 2006 Vornado purchased the Manhattan Mall, a Midtown complex with close to one million square feet of retail and office space, for $689 million.

These acquisitions paled in comparison to Vornado's bid to acquire industry leader Equity Office Proper-

ties Trust in early 2007, in a proposed deal worth $41 billion in cash and stock. At the time, Equity office controlled more than 100 million square feet of commercial real estate across the country, nearly double Vornado's holdings. More significantly for Vornado, the proposed deal would give the company major properties in Los Angeles and San Francisco, providing it with the opportunity to develop a national presence. The deal ultimately fell through, however, after Equity Office shareholders rejected Vornado's overture in favor of an all-cash offer from Blackstone Group LP. In the wake of its failed bid, Vornado entered into a partnership with Donald Trump in May 2007 to acquire two commercial properties, one of which was the prestigious Bank of America building in San Francisco.

At the same time, Vornado began to eye real estate opportunities overseas. In August 2008 the company formed a $250 million alliance with Reliance Industries Limited to purchase and develop retail properties in India. As the world slipped into an economic crisis in late 2008, Vornado launched an aggressive push to raise investment capital, with the aim of capitalizing on the steep decline in real estate values. Over the course of 2009, the company raised $1.2 billion, primarily through share sales. With commercial real estate selling at bargain prices, the strategy seemed a way for Vornado to ensure further growth heading into the new decade.

Robert Halasz
Updated, Stephen Meyer

PRINCIPAL COMPETITORS

Boston Properties, Inc.; Brookfield Properties Corporation; Equity Office Properties Trust; Mack-Cali Realty Corporation; The Trump Organization.

FURTHER READING

Allimadi, Milton G., "Vornado Nears Vote to Convert Firm to a REIT," *Wall Street Journal*, April 23, 1993, p. A7E.

Bagli, Charles V., "Big Realty Trust to Take Over 7 Manhattan Office Towers, Long a Family's Domain," *New York Times*, March 13, 1997, p. B7.

Barmash, Isadore, "Marriage at Vornado Is Mended," *New York Times*, September 22, 1968, p. F15.

"Cash at a Discount?" *Forbes*, May 15, 1978, p. 192.

Daly, Brenon, "Bain, KKR, Vornado Buy Toys 'R' Us," *Daily Deal*, March 18, 2005.

Elman, David, "Vornado Buys Manhattan Mall," *Daily Deal*, November 29, 2006.

Feldman, Amy, "Roth Flashes Alexander's Trump Card," *Crain's New York Business*, August 20, 1990, pp. 3, 25.

Freeman, William, "Trading Stamps? Chain Takes All," *New York Times*, August 26, 1962, p. F9.

Griffith, L. Timothy, "Vornado, Inc.," *Wall Street Transcript*, January 6, 1969.

Gross, Daniel, "Building Expectations," *New York*, July 7, 1997, pp.22–23, 87.

Halbfinger, David M., "A Developer Buys a Swath of Midtown with a Garden View," *New York Times*, June 28, 1997, p. 23.

"Herbert Hubschman Dies at 52; Chairman of Discount Chain," *New York Times*, September 22, 1964, p. 39.

Herman, Eric, "Top of World: Vornado WTC Winner," *Daily News*, February 23, 2001, p. 46.

Kirkpatrick, David A., "Vornado Realty Trust, Long a Bottom-Fisher, Is Buying at Top Dollar," *Wall Street Journal*, February 24, 1998, p. A1.

Lewis, Christina S. N., "Vornado Targets Ailing Retailers but May Face Hurdles of Its Own," *Wall Street Journal*, October 21, 2009, p. B1.

Louis, Brian, and Bob Ivry, "Blackstone Wins Real Estate Battle; Shareholders Approve $22.9-billion Sale of Equity Office after Vornado Pulls Out," *Globe and Mail* (Toronto), February 8, 2007, p. B15.

"O.A. Sutton Says It's Liquidating Stocks to Pay Off Bank Debt," *Wall Street Journal*, September 17, 1958, p. 11.

Pacelle, Mitchell, "Control of Alexander's to Be Acquired by Real-Estate Developer Steven Roth," *Wall Street Journal*, February 7, 1995, p. A8.

"The Price of a White Elephant," *Forbes*, December 15, 1968, p. 19.

Pristin, Terry, "Vornado Chief Keeps Competitors on Their Toes," *New York Times*, February 16, 2005, p. 7.

"Profits of Vornado Sweep Toward New Record High," *Barron's*, March 7, 1966, p. 26.

Rudnitsky, Howard, "No More Mr. Nice Guy," *Forbes*, September 13, 1993, pp. 100–1.

Spinner, Jackie, "Vornado to Buy Commercial Arm of Smith Realty Giant," *Washington Post*, October 20, 2001, p. E01.

Vinocur, Barry, "Deal Maker Leaves Goldman Sachs for Big-Buck Job at REIT," *Barron's*, December 9, 1996, pp. 46–47.

———, "Steve Roth's Property Company Takes Big Stake in Alexander's, the Old Store Chain," *Barron's*, February 13, 1995, p. 46.

Winans, R. Foster, "Vornado Becomes Attractive to Institutions, but Buyers Advised Not to Expect Quick Payoff," *Wall Street Journal*, February 4, 1983, p. 43.

Yu, Hui-yong, "New Salvo in Battle for U.S. Office Space; Vornado Raises Bid for Equity Office," *International Herald Tribune*, February 2, 2007, p. 15.

Vorwerk & Co. KG

Mühlenweg 17-37
Wuppertal, North Rhine-Westphalia D-42270
Germany
Telephone: (+49 202) 564 0
Fax: (+49 202) 564 1301
Web site: http://www.vorwerk.com

Private Company
Incorporated: 1883 as Barmer Teppichfabrik Vorwerk & Co. KG
Employees: 23,000, in addition to a contractual sales force of about 555,000
Sales: €2.44 billion (2008)
NAICS: 443111 Household Appliance Stores; 442210 Floor Covering Stores; 442299 All Other Home Furnishing Stores; 335212 Household Vacuum Cleaner Manufacturing; 335221 Household Cooking Appliance Manufacturing; 314110 Carpet and Rug Mills

■ ■ ■

For more than a century, Vorwerk & Co. KG has been a fixture in German and international households. What began as a family-owned carpet business has become a diversified international corporate group. Vorwerk & Co. KG designs and manufactures carpets, household appliances, and fitted kitchens, selling them mainly through a direct sales network. The company also designs, produces, and sells carpeting to commercial and industrial customers, as well as under contract to third-party carpet suppliers.

Vorwerk's U.S.-based subsidiary Jafra sells cosmetics and skin and body care products. The direct sales approach remains the company's worldwide signature. In addition to its high-quality product line, Vorwerk offers infrastructural facility services, such as cleaning and security services through its HECTAS subsidiary, as well as financial services in its banking subsidiary akf. Vorwerk remains a privately owned, family-controlled company, with the Scheid family at the helm since 1904. Vorwerk is an "unknown giant." Worldwide approximately 560,000 people work with Vorwerk, some 30,000 of whom are advisers selling household appliances and more than 500,000 of whom work for Jafra Cosmetics. Vorwerk generates a business volume of more than €2.3 billion a year and operates in more than 60 countries.

CARPETING SPECIALIST

Vorwerk & Co. KG was founded by the brothers Carl and Adolf Vorwerk in 1883 as the Barmer Teppichfabrik Vorwerk & Co. The company's focus, as its name implied, was the production of carpeting for the domestic German market. While Vorwerk & Co. would soon expand its product line, carpeting remains a key company product.

Vorwerk's 20th-century growth began with the Scheid family's participation in the company, which was structured as a limited partnership. In 1904 August Mittelsten Scheid, Carl Vorwerk's son-in-law, took over management at Vorwerk, representing the first Scheid family generation at the helm of the company. Under Scheid, Vorwerk began to expand its operations. In

1908 the company-run machine shop used for supplying its carpet production activities was converted to a full-fledged production facility for the manufacturing of machinery, mainly looms. The company's focus nevertheless remained on carpets, and by 1909 Vorwerk was a registered carpet trademark, offering an alternative and strong competition to Oriental carpets.

Vorwerk's expertise in carpeting, coupled with its increasing production capacity, presented new opportunities that came to define the company for much of its domestic clientele. In 1929 the Kobold, the first handheld vacuum cleaner developed by the chief engineer Engelbert Gorissen, left the Wuppertal production line and revolutionized cleaning in German households. (In German folklore, a kobold is a mischievous yet sometimes helpful elf said to inhabit people's homes.) The Kobold quickly found acceptance in German homes, as Vorwerk now provided not only carpets but a means to clean them as well.

In 1930 Vorwerk adopted the then popular direct sales approach for its vacuum cleaners. Sending its sales force door-to-door allowed customers to witness the qualities of Vorwerk products in their own homes. Seeing the results on their own floors and carpets gave customers confidence in the products. Indeed Vorwerk's sales approach inspired its domestic customers to make Vorwerk the country's top supplier of vacuum cleaners.

In the 1930s Vorwerk began to expand its domestic appliance line, first adding to the Kobold diverse and innovative attachments, such as a hair dryer and a grooming attachment for horses. In 1937 Vorwerk began producing refrigerators. The following year marked Vorwerk's first international expansion, with the founding of Vorwerk Folletto in Italy, the first international Kobold company.

POSTWAR GROWTH

As was the case with many other German companies, the onset of World War II in 1938 forced Vorwerk to convert its production facilities to supply the war effort. By 1943 the Allies had turned the tide of the war, and raw materials and manpower became increasingly rare in a Germany heading toward defeat. As a result, Vorwerk had to cut its own operations, shut down its direct sales force, and end production of its vacuum cleaners. In the same year, Scheid retired, making room for the second generation of Scheids, his sons Erich and Werner Mittelsten Scheid.

In 1945 Vorwerk resumed production of its Kobold vacuum cleaners. With the younger Scheid generation at the helm, Vorwerk's direct sales force once again took to the country's doorsteps and in 1949 celebrated the sale of the millionth Kobold. The postwar reconstruction and the German "economic miracle" provided Vorwerk with a receptive market for its vacuum cleaners and other household appliances. Systematically the company expanded its home appliances line to include refrigerators, washing machines and spinners, and, of course, new vacuum cleaners and attachments. In 1959 the company launched a new line of electric-powered carpet brushes, dubbed the Europas.

Thus far Vorwerk's sales had remained mainly domestic. As the European market began to open up in the late 1950s and throughout the 1960s, the company expanded into neighboring countries. In 1961 Vorwerk & Co. set up a new subsidiary for its foreign operations, the Auslandsholding Vorwerk & Co., which was renamed Vorwerk International in 1971. Thus began Vorwerk's march into international homes.

DIVERSIFICATION

The sustained economic boom of the 1960s throughout Europe and the United States encouraged the trend toward corporate conglomerates. Vorwerk too was inspired by this trend and began to seek market op-

KEY DATES

1883: Carl and Adolf Vorwerk found Barmer Teppichfabrik Vorwerk und Co.

1907: August Mittelsten Scheid becomes sole managing partner.

1929: The Kobold vacuum system is patented and introduced in Germany.

1930: Werner Mittelsten Scheid introduces the direct sales and marketing system.

1937: The product line expands to include refrigerators.

1938: Vorwerk Folletto, the first international Kobold company, is founded in Italy.

1943: Direct sales halt during World War II.

1949: The millionth Kobold vacuum cleaner is sold.

1968: Vorwerk expands its product line to include kitchen appliances; Vorwerk launches the akf bank, a financial services unit in Wuppertal.

1974: Vorwerk launches the Hygienic Service Gebäudereiniging und Umweltplfege GmbH subsidiary, later called HECTAS.

2000: Vorwerk sells its Brugman fitted kitchen subsidiary.

2001: Vorwerk takes over Lux Asia Pacific; Vorwerk launches its first advertising campaign.

2004: Vorwerk takes over the U.S.-based Jafra Cosmetics.

portunities beyond its traditional base of manufacturing and direct sales, adding services to its product line. In 1968, under the leadership of Jörg Mittelsten Scheid, Vorwerk launched a financial services unit, the akf bank in Wuppertal. Over the years akf developed into a leading specialist for financing mobile assets.

Scheid, who led the company through the end of the 20th century, represented the third generation of Scheids at the helm. His leadership was marked by vigorous diversification. In addition to financial services, Vorwerk added a data processing arm, the subsidiary ZEDA Informationsverarbeitung. Vorwerk's next expansion seemed more organic. In 1974 the company created its Hygienic Service Gebäudereiniging und Umweltplfege GmbH subsidiary, renamed HECTAS in 1997. The new subsidiary complemented the company's industrial carpeting installations with building cleaning, maintenance, and security services.

The 1970s were also marked by product diversification. Vorwerk launched a fitted kitchen concept (sold door-to-door), which provided a complete, modular kitchen unit that could be adapted to customers' homes. The direct sales "adviser" helped the customer plan the kitchen, which was then manufactured in a new Vorwerk production facility established exclusively for this product line. A more or less independent structure, with its own back wall, the fitted kitchen could be refitted according to clients' changing needs and could even follow a customer who moved to a new home.

In 1971 Vorwerk launched the Thermomix, a new kitchen appliance that would become as much a staple as the Kobold first in German and then in international households. A multipurpose, all-in-one home cooking appliance, the Thermomix was designed to replace many of the common tools and appliances used in the modern kitchen. For manufacturing and distributing the new product, the company founded its Vorwerk & Co. Thermomix GmbH. Vorwerk also introduced a new sales method. Thermomix was marketed through the "party sales" approach that had proven effective for Mary Kay Cosmetics, Tupperware, and others. Soon Vorwerk was able to claim a sales-per-demonstration success rate of 85 percent.

RESTRUCTURING AND INTERNATIONAL EXPANSION

Vorwerk's fitted kitchen concept caught on quickly in the domestic German market. Rather than export the fitted kitchen, however, in 1991 Vorwerk purchased Brugman Keukens, a Netherlands-based kitchens manufacturer with a chain of retail kitchen specialist stores. In this way Vorwerk entered the foreign kitchen market.

In the 1990s, as a response to the long economic crisis in Europe and especially the recessionary period provoked by the difficulties of German reunification, Vorwerk stepped up its international expansion. Following the proven direct sales approach, the company's sales advisers took to doors in eastern and western Europe. Vorwerk also targeted the Far East, bringing the company's door-to-door sales approach to the countries of that region, particularly China. In 2001 Vorwerk consolidated its position in the Asian market by purchasing the Lux Asia Pacific direct sales organization from the Swedish Electrolux group. Lux Asia Pacific, based in Singapore, sells primarily the Vorwerk home appliance line throughout Asia, providing a strong foothold in a market with a high growth potential.

Also in 2001 Vorwerk began a restructuring process by selling its Dutch kitchen subsidiary Brugman to Plana Kuechenland. Two years later, in 2003, Vorwerk's data processing arm, ZEDA, was sold to T-Systems, essentially outsourcing Vorwerk's IT systems to T-Mobile for 11 years. In 2002 Vorwerk launched a new product line, introducing the Feelina ironing system. Because of the limited growth potential of this division, Vorwerk ceased distribution in January 2009.

The acquisition in May 2004 of the American cosmetics manufacturer Jafra Cosmetics proved more successful. Jafra, one of the world's fastest-growing direct sales companies, offers skin and body care products, cosmetics, and fragrances. With its firm foothold in the United States and Mexico, Jafra would become Vorwerk's third-largest division by the end of 2008, behind only the company's signature Kobold sales division and the akf financial group.

NEW MARKETING STRATEGIES

The new century brought not only international expansion and product diversification but also new marketing strategies. Like many other direct sales companies, Vorwerk had never engaged in classic advertising. In 2001, however, Vorwerk launched a broad-based image campaign focusing on the "Family Concept," creating the slogan "Vorwerk—Our Best for Your Family," which became part of the company's logo. The campaign included television and radio commercials, print ads, and competitions for "Family Manager of the Year," raising awareness for the value, difficulties, and rewards of managing a household.

This campaign increased the awareness and popularity of the company throughout Germany, particularly among the relevant target group of stay-at-home wives and husbands. The campaign helped create a more contemporary company image, which, in part because of its seemingly outdated sales approach of the traveling salesman, seemed more traditional than its product. It also included the Vorwerk Family Fund, established in 2002, which supports SOS Children's Villages.

In 2005 Jörg Mittelsten Scheid, who had presided over the company since 1969 and made it a successful international corporate group, left his position as chairman of the executive board, moving to the advisory board.

In 2008 Vorwerk celebrated its 125th anniversary. What had begun as a local carpet company had grown into an international corporation with a diverse product and service line. As a result of the sustained strategy of international expansion, foreign sales were generating 59 percent of the company's business volume by 2008. Despite its international operations, two-thirds of the company's electric products still bore the coveted stamp "Made in Germany."

M. L. Cohen
Updated, Helga Schier

PRINCIPAL SUBSIDIARIES

Vorwerk & Co. Interholding GmbH; Vorwerk & Co. KG; Vorwerk & Co. Beteiligungsgesellschaft mbH; Vorwerk Mittelsten Scheid & Co.; Vorwerk & Co. KG Büro Brüssel (Belgium); Vorwerk Direct Selling Ventures GmbH; Vorwerk Folletto SRL (Italy); Vorwerk Contempera S.r.l. (Italy); Vorwerk Deutschland Stiftung & Co. KG; Vorwerk España (Spain); Vorwerk France S.C.S.; Vorwerk Household appliances Co., LTD (UK); Vorwerk Portugal Electrodomésticos Lda. (Portugal); Vorwerk Austria GmbH & Co. KG (Austria); Vorwerk Polska sp.z.o.o. (Poland); Vorwerk CS K.S. (Czech Republic); Vorwerk Lux (Far East) Ltd. (Taiwan); Vorwerk CIS, LLC (Russia); Vorwerk Mexico S. De R.L. de C.V. (Mexico); Vorwerk Elektrowerke GmbH & Co. KG; Vorwerk Semco S.A.S. (France); Vorwerk Household Appliances Manufacturing Co. Ltd. (Shanghai); Jafra Cosmetics International (USA); Lux Asia Pacific Pte. Ltd. (Singapore); akf bank GmbH & Co. KG; akf leasing Gmbh & Co. KG; akf Servicelease GmbH; Hectas Gebudedienste Stiftung & Co. KG; Hectas Gebäudereinigung Stiftung & Co. KG; Hectas Gebäudemanagement GmbH & Co. KG; Hectas Sicherheitsdienste GmbH; Vorwerk & Co. Teppichwerke GmbH & Co. KG.

PRINCIPAL DIVISIONS

Direct Sales, Kobold; Direct Sales, Thermomix; Direct Sales, Jafra Cosmetics; Direct Sales, Lux Asia Pacific; Vorwerk Carpets; HECTAS Facility Services; akf group.

PRINCIPAL COMPETITORS

Amway; Avon Products, Inc; BSH Bosch und Siemens Hausgeräte GmbH; Mary Kay Inc.; Miele & Cie. KG.

FURTHER READING

"Im Porträt: Vorwerk-Chef Peter Oberegger," *Frankfurter Allgemeine Zeitung*, August 12, 2008, http://www.faz.net/f30/common/Suchergebnis.aspx?term=Vorwerk+Und+Co.&x=0&y=0&allchk=1.

Kazim, Hasnaim, "Hilfe mein Teppich funkt," *Spiegel Online*, March 13, 2006, http://www.spiegel.de/wirtschaft/0,1518,405652,00.html.

"Propeller am Penis," *Spiegel Online*, January 17, 1986, http://www.spiegel.de/spiegel/print/d-13517743.html.

Scheele, Martin, "Familie Mittelsten Scheid: Klinkenputzer und Staubfänger," *Manager Magazin*, January 5, 2005, http://www.manager-magazin.de/koepfe/unternehmerarchiv/0,2828,335493-2,00.html.

Vorwerk & Co.—Datum zur Unternehmensgeschichte. Wuppertal, Germany: Vorwerk & Co.: 1991.

Wacker-Chemie AG

Hanns-Seidel-Platz 4
München, Bavaria D-81737
Germany
Telephone: (+49 89) 6279-01
Fax: (+49 89) 6279-1770
Web site: http://www.wacker.com

Public Company
Founded: 1903
Incorporated: 1914
Employees: 16,000
Sales: €4.3 billion ($5.9 billion) (2008)
Stock Exchanges: Frankfurt
Ticker Symbol: WCH (Frankfurt) CHM/WCK.GR
(Bloomberg) CHE/WCHG.DE (Reuters)
NAICS: 325211 Plastics Material and Resin Manufacturing; 325212 Synthetic Rubber Manufacturing; 334413 Semiconductor and Related Device Manufacturing; 325199 All Other Basic Organic Chemical Manufacturing; 325188 All Other Basic Inorganic Chemical Manufacturing

∎ ∎ ∎

Wacker-Chemie AG is a worldwide leader in the production and sales of chemicals. Headquartered in Munich, Germany, the company focuses on semiconductors, polysilicon, polymers and specialty chemicals, and silicones. Wacker strongly supports innovative chemistry and new technologies. The company supplies solutions that are market oriented, energy saving, and environmentally compatible.

Wacker-Chemie has more than 60 subsidiaries in 27 countries around the world. Manufacturing plants are located throughout Europe, the United States, and Asia. Wacker-Chemie AG is traded on the Frankfurt Stock Exchange. Descendants of the Wacker family hold more than 50 percent of the company's shares.

THE LATE 19TH CENTURY: WACKER AND SCHUCKERT START A BUSINESS

The origins of the Wacker-Chemie AG can be traced to Alexander Wacker, who was born in 1846 in Heidelberg, Germany. As an apprentice clerk in the textile industry, Wacker acquired the business skills that would prove an asset when he met Sigmund Schuckert in 1877. Schuckert, a gifted mechanic, had invented a flatring dynamo machine that transformed waterpower into electricity. Together Wacker and Schuckert started a partnership at Schuckert's Nuremberg workshop. While Schuckert ran the workshop, Wacker oversaw the business, which employed 12 assistants and 3 apprentices.

As a result of Wacker's successful marketing efforts, S. Schuckert & Co. grew rapidly. By 1885 the company employed 46 clerks and 228 workers. The company's dynamos powered Munich's first electric tram line, which started service in 1886.

Along with such dynamic growth came financial pressures, and Wacker decided to take the company to the next level. In 1892 he reorganized the company as the Elektrizitäts AG, vormals Schuckert & Co. That same year Schuckert retired, and Wacker became managing director. By 1902 the "Schuckertwerke" employed

COMPANY PERSPECTIVES

Vision: We believe that, long term, the chemical industry makes a vital contribution to global progress and sustainable development. In the future, social and economic success will rest more than ever on worldwide collaboration and interconnected skills. Flexible and specialist units will therefore profit the most from the opportunities available today and tomorrow.

Mission: WACKER is a technology leader in the chemical sector, pushing ahead with technical innovations and the development of new products for the world's key industries. In this way, WACKER helps improve people's lives. WACKER is organized as a group of independently operating units with considerable responsibility under a strong roof. This gives us the necessary flexibility and resolve. Everything we do is conducive to global networking and cultural integration.

7,413 workers and 1,082 clerks in 36 branches and technical offices in Germany. In addition, the Elektrizitäts AG set up a worldwide sales network.

In 1902 Wacker started a venture of his own. Backed by financial support from a friend, he bought out the electrochemical side of the Schuckert business, specifically its carbide factories. Together with three business partners (the Bosnian Bosnische Elektrizitäts AG, the Swiss Lonza AG, and the Norwegian Aktieselkabet Hafslund), Wacker formed a new company for the production of carbide. One year later Wacker transformed the electrochemical laboratory he had founded before the turn of the century into the Consortium für elektrochemische Industrie, an independent limited liability company.

The Consortium became the central research lab for the new group of chemical companies All were shareholders in the facility. The company's goal was to develop technologies for the industrial use of acetylene, which would become one of the most important basic chemicals for the next five decades until petrochemistry took its place in the 1960s. The Consortium was a breeding ground for numerous patents.

Around 1907 Wacker took further innovative steps. He tested Bavarian rivers for their potential as a source of sustainable energy for the energy-intensive production of basic chemicals. He also researched the best location for a new carbide plant and purchased a property in the Burghausen forest on the banks of the Bavarian river Salzach. Two months after Germany declared war on Russia in 1914, Wacker registered the first enterprise of his own under the name Dr. Alexander Wacker, Gesellschaft für elektrochemische Industrie KG, eventually shortened to Wacker-Chemie.

At age 70, Wacker had finally achieved his dream. In December 1916 in the Burghausen plant, Wacker-Chemie started mass production of the basic chemicals acetaldehyde, acetic acid, and acetone. The company's headquarters moved to Munich. At that time Wacker-Chemie employed 403 workers and 51 clerks.

Acetone was one of the chemicals urgently needed by Germany's war economy. The plant had to begin production immediately, even before it could finish its own power supply. Power came from nearby Reichenhall by means of Bavaria's first high-voltage power line. The first tank of acetone was shipped from the Burghausen plant in January 1917.

In 1918 the Burghausen plant started producing tetrachloroethane and trichloroethylene. Wacker's research lab was also moved to Munich. That same year Bosnische Elektrizitäts and Aktieselkabet Hafslund withdrew from the partnership. After World War I (in 1919) Wacker-Chemie began the production of acetic ester, oxybutyric aldehyde, crotonaldehyde, butanol, and butyl acetate.

EARLY SUCCESSES THROUGH 1939

The 1920s brought economic turmoil to Germany and the world: hyperinflation early in the decade and the stock market crash in 1929 followed by the Great Depression. Despite this turmoil, the 1920s were a decade of dynamic growth for Wacker-Chemie. In 1920 the production of ethyl acetate began in the Burghausen plant. A year later a new technology for acetylene purification was implemented, and chlorine-alkali electrolysis with diaphragm cells made the production of chlorinated hydrocarbons possible.

In 1922 Wacker-Chemie produced its first synthetic, shellac. The company started developing pesticides as well. Wacker's dream had surpassed even his own expectations. At age 75 he died at the height of his success.

Over the following years Wacker-Chemie continued to expand its product range, introducing low-carbon ferroalloys, polyvinyl alcohol, acetic anhydride from acetic acid, Wacker acetate silk from acetyl cellulose, and vinyl acetate. Wacker's copper oxychloride-based "Kupferkalk" turned out to be a powerful fungicide for infested hop crops and vineyards. Wacker-Chemie also played a role in the development of stainless steels as Germany's only producer of calcium-silicon alloys and low-carbon ferrochromium. Another important product for Wacker-Chemie during this time was carbide as an end product, for example welding carbide.

The 1920s were also successful years for the Consortium. In 1922 it registered a patent for a technology to produce anhydride from cellulose acetate, or ketene. Another field for research was in the usefulness of chlorine products as pesticides. In 1924 researchers at the Consortium discovered polyvinyl alcohol, which led to the production of the first solely synthetic fiber, called Polyviol. In 1928 the Consortium first published the results of their work on the polymerization of vinyl chloride and started intense testing the year after.

During this time Wacker-Chemie significantly improved its infrastructure. The necessary financial boost came from a new business partner, Farbwerke Hoechst AG, which acquired 50 percent of Wacker's share capital in 1921. In 1922 Wacker's own waterpower sta-

tion (the "Alzwerke") began to deliver electricity to the Burghausen plant. In the same year the company opened its own railway station. Wacker-Chemie also invested in its Bavarian distribution partner Christian Dederer GmbH. In 1924 Wacker obtained a 30-year lease on a salt mine to secure the supply of rock salt for chlorine electrolysis.

By 1930 Wacker's Burghausen plant had grown into a significant chemical production complex. However, the effects of the Depression required that Wacker reduce its workforce by 10 percent. In 1933 Wacker-Chemie acquired Elektroschmelzwerk Kempten, a silicon carbide producer. New production lines were opened almost every year.

The highlight for Wacker-Chemie's research was the development of a suspension technology for the production of polyvinyl chloride (PVC), which opened a new chapter in the history of plastics. In 1938 Wacker-Chemie started PVC production in Burghausen. Other Wacker products of that time included synthetic belt drives, medical sutures, shatter-proof glass, and Drawinella, the first acetate staple fiber similar to wool.

THE RECONSTRUCTION YEARS THROUGH 1959

By 1939, the year in which Adolf Hitler attacked Poland and World War II began, Wacker-Chemie had 4,125 employees and was generating DEM 75 million in sales. Basic chemicals were a necessary commodity during the war, and Wacker-Chemie expanded its production capacities. However, toward the end of World War II, Wacker-Chemie suffered significant setbacks. In 1943 and 1944 the Consortium and laboratories at its headquarters were completely destroyed. Three anti-Nazi activists had been killed at the Burghausen plant just before the German surrender, and when Wacker-Chemie came under American administration in 1945, two managing directors were arrested.

Nearly all production facilities closed down between May and October 1945. Two of the production plants, the salt mine and the Alzwerke power plant, were split from the company in order to prevent too great a concentration of economic power. Most significantly, the Soviets dismantled the Burghausen facilities, and Wacker's two eastern German production plants in Mückenberg and Tschechnitz, which accounted for two-thirds of Wacker's total output, were expropriated and nationalized. The survival of Wacker-Chemie was at stake.

In 1947 research resumed in Burghausen, and Wacker-Chemie opened the silicon chapter of its history. Three years later an experimental production facility was established. That facility produced silanes (the first preliminary ingredient for silicones) as well as the first silicon products, such as a silicone-insulated high-voltage motor. In 1951 the range of Wacker-Chemie silicon products was expanded to include impregnating agents for textiles, release and antifoam agents, pastes, and emulsions.

In 1953 Wacker-Chemie produced the first hyperpure silicon for semiconductors as well as the first silicon rubber. In 1955, the year in which the Federal Republic of Germany regained sovereignty and the last prisoners were returning from Russia, Wacker-Chemie started building its first facility for silane and silicone mass production. On April 8, 1953, the company became a limited liability private company, and its name changed to Wacker-Chemie GmbH. The shares were held in equal parts by Hoechst and the Wacker family. By the end of the 1950s, Wacker had grown to employ more people than before the war.

RAPID GROWTH THROUGH 1979

The German economy boomed in the 1960s, as did the German plastics industry. It was during the same time period that polyvinyl plastics based on carbide were succeeded by more economical petrochemical-based materials. In 1960 a new Wacker plant, the first production line that used ethylene instead of carbide acetylene to make acetaldehyde, started operation in Cologne. Three years later the acetylene-based production of acetaldehyde at the Burghausen plant was closed down.

In 1965 Wacker-Chemie, Farbwerke Hoechst, and Marathon Oil agreed to build a petrochemical refinery in Burghausen. The refinery began deliveries of ethylene and petrochemical acetylene three years later. Finally, on May 9, 1969, the carbide production in Burghausen, which had significantly contributed to the early success of Wacker-Chemie, was closed down. Other production lines that were shut down during the 1960s included chemical purification equipment, the cellulose acetate fiber Drawinella, and hexachlorethane.

At the same time, demand for silicon products was on the rise. Beginning in 1961 hyperpure silicon was produced regularly, and semiconductor production was expanded in Burghausen. In 1960 Wacker's hyperpure silicon was sold to the United States for the first time. In 1965 Wacker-Chemie acquired Monosilicon, a manufacturer of hyperpure silicon based in Los Angeles, California, and established its American subsidiary, Wacker Chemicals Corp., based in New York.

Three years later Wacker's German silicon activities were organized under the new Wacker-Chemitronic Gesellschaft für Elektronik Grundstoffe GmbH in

Burghausen. Another important step for Wacker-Chemie in the 1960s was the acquisition of the Stetten salt mine. This acquisition secured the supplies of rock salt needed for the chemical processes at the Wacker plants.

The 1970s marked the beginning of massive international expansion for Wacker-Chemie. Initiated by two of Wacker's top executives, Chief Executive Officer (CEO) Ekkehard Maurer and Marketing Director Hans Denis, the company started establishing numerous foreign subsidiaries around the world. Wacker-Mexicana S.A. was set up in 1971. It was followed by the Wormerveer-based Wacker-Chemie Nederland B.V. in the Netherlands and the Vienna-based Wacker-Chemie Ges. m.b.H. Salzburg in Austria in 1972.

In 1973 the marketing subsidiaries Wacker-Chemie (Schweiz) AG in Liestal, Switzerland, and Wacker-Chemie S.A. in Brussels, Belgium, were set up. Subsidiaries in Denmark, Great Britain, Brazil, and Spain were founded between 1975 and 1978. Moreover, in 1978 Wacker-Chemie founded two more companies in the United States: Wacker Siltronic Corporation based in Portland, Oregon, and the silicon carbide producer ESK Corporation based in Hennepin, Illinois. In 1979 Wacker bought a share in the Canadian firm Henley Chemicals Ltd., located in Ontario, which had represented Wacker in Canada.

THE LATE 20TH CENTURY

With the rise of personal computers and other electronics products based on microchips, silicon was Wacker's flagship product in the 1980s. In 1980 a new silicon factory was opened at Wacker Siltronic in Portland. Another began production in São Paulo, Brazil, the following year. In 1985 the first Wacker plant started making silicone in Japan, and by 1987 Wacker-Chemie was the third-largest producer of silicone in the world.

In 1988 the silicone division contributed DEM 713 million, or 26.5 percent, to Wacker's total sales. Besides the well-known silicon wafers used in the microelectronics industry, Wacker-Chemie made more than 1,500 silicon products used in construction, transportation, pharmaceuticals, cosmetics, paper, textiles, and many other industries in the form of fluids, resins, or elastomers. These products were made in the most sophisticated production facility of its kind in Europe, in Burghausen, as well as in the United States, Mexico, Brazil, Australia, and Japan.

During the 1980s Wacker's network of worldwide subsidiaries expanded significantly into Italy, Portugal, Greece, Sweden, Finland, Singapore, and South Africa. In 1988 the company was reorganized into five business divisions: vinyl acetate, polymers and organic chemicals, materials, PVC and chlorine derivatives, semiconductors, and silicones, silanes, and silicas. Each division was under separate management and was responsible for its own profits and losses. Wacker's sales surpassed DEM 3 billion for the first time in 1988, with 14,000 employees on the company's payroll worldwide. In 1995 Peter-Alexander Wacker, the great grandson of the company's founder, joined the company's management board as the first Wacker family member since the 1960s.

In the late 1990s, Wacker-Chemie's semiconductor division suffered during the Asian economic crisis. In 1998 Wacker's profits decreased by two-thirds. Despite this setback, Wacker continued to pursue a vivid globalization strategy. In 1998 Wacker-Chemie entered a joint venture with India's largest silicone manufacturer, Metroark. In the same year the company launched two joint ventures with air products and chemicals: the emulsions producer Air Products Polymers L.P. and the redispersible powders producer Wacker Polymer Systems L.P. A new production facility for silicone wafers in Singapore began production in 1999, and technical service centers were opened in São Paulo and Shanghai, China.

In 2000 Wacker-Chemie withdrew from the PVC business and sold its two PVC joint ventures with Celanese, Vinnolit Kunststoff GmbH, and Vintron GmbH, concluding the company's divestment strategy in the field of inorganic chemicals. In one of the most significant company developments at the turn of the century, Wacker's longtime partner Hoechst AG, which had merged with Rhone-Poulenc to form Aventis SA, sold its 50 percent ownership of Wacker-Chemie GmbH back to the Wacker family. In January 2001 the Alexander Wacker Familien GmbH, a holding company that already owned the other 50 percent of Wacker-Chemie GmbH, acquired the majority of voting rights via capital increase and thus gained management control over the company. Peter-Alexander Wacker became president and CEO of the executive board.

NEW MARKETS IN THE 21ST CENTURY

To secure future growth and sustainability in the 21st century, Wacker-Chemie continued aggressively to pursue the emerging Asian marketplace. Rising living standards in Asia promised continued growth of business sectors relevant to Wacker-Chemie. Construction activity, as well as the digitization and infrastructural expansion typical of the growing industrialization and westernization of an emerging market, created an increased need for Wacker products and services. A joint venture between Wacker-Chemie and Dow Corning Corp. to manufacture siloxane and pyrogenic silica (raw

materials for silicone production) in Zhangjiagang, China, began in 2003. In 2004 Wacker-Chemie commissioned a production plant for silicone emulsions in Shanghai. One year later, in 2005, Wacker took over the polymers business of Wuxi Xinda Fine Chemical Co. Ltd. in China. In addition, Wacker and China's Dymatic Chemicals Inc. established joint ventures for the production and marketing of silicone products.

Construction being one of the main markets for Wacker-Chemie, the company took over its former partners Air Products Polymers L.P. and the redispersible powders producer Wacker Polymer Systems L.P. in 2007. This move made Wacker-Chemie the only company in the market that could cover the entire dispersion and powder production supply chain for the construction industry in Asia, Europe, and the United States.

Wacker-Chemie also aggressively pursued the environmental sector. In 2005 Wacker purchased the biotech company ProThera GmbH, based in Jena, Germany, and changed its name to Wacker Biotech GmbH. In an effort to remain competitive in this sector and true to its long history of continued innovation, Wacker-Chemie invested approximately 5 percent of all profits in research and development, making Wacker one of the most research-intensive chemical companies in the world. In early 2010 research included such fields as photovoltaics, catalysis and processes, functional materials, polymers, organic synthesis, and biotechnology.

As a result of separating from its former long-term partner Hoechst in 2001, Wacker-Chemie GmbH became a public stock company and was renamed Wacker-Chemie AG in 2005. Wacker-Chemie AG was first introduced at the Frankfurt Stock Exchange on April 10, 2006, at €80 per share with extraordinary success. According to the company's 2006 financial report, the initial public offering grossed approximately €430 million in treasury shares. In early 2010 the Alexander Wacker Familien GmbH still held more than 50 percent of the company's stock. Peter-Alexander Wacker remained at the new company's helm as president and CEO.

In the first two years of public trading, Wacker-Chemie AG reported a sales increase of 13 percent in 2007 and 14 percent in 2008, benefiting mostly from the solar sector's demand for polysilicone. Despite this positive trend, the new president and CEO Rudolf Staudigl, who took office in 2008 when Peter-Alexander Wacker moved to the supervisory board, took measures to counteract the growing global economic crisis: short-time work, temporary plant shutdowns, budget cuts, and efforts to create leaner production and administrative structures. The most far-reaching restructuring took place in the company's polysilicone division. Wacker Polysilicone decided to withdraw from the business of producing solar wafers and to terminate its 2007 joint venture with Schott Solar. Instead Wacker Polysilicone would focus on the production of hyperpure polycrystalline silicon.

In its 2009 third-quarter report, company management predicted that the emerging Asian economies would provide the main impulse for the recovery of the world economy and the future growth of Wacker-Chemie AG. Growing affluence in emerging markets would continue to increase the demand for Wacker products, particularly in electronics, consumer goods, cosmetics, pharmaceuticals, textiles, and medical technology promise future profits.

Evelyn Hauser
Updated, Helga Schier

PRINCIPAL SUBSIDIARIES

Wacker-Chemie has more than 50 subsidiaries worldwide.

PRINCIPAL DIVISIONS

Wacker Silicones; Wacker Polymers; Wacker Fine Chemicals; Wacker Polysilicone; Siltronic.

PRINCIPAL COMPETITORS

Dow Corning Corp.; General Electric Company; Compagnie de Saint-Gobain S.A.

FURTHER READING

"Air Products, Wacker-Chemie Launch Venture," *Adhesives Age*, December 1998, p. 38.

Alperowicz, Natasha, "Wacker-Chemie Confirms Huls Deal," *Chemical Week*, December 9, 1998, p. 17.

Hume, Claudia, "Wacker Family Negotiates Purchase of Hoechst's 50% Stake," *Chemical Week*, November 10, 1999, p. 24.

Kuehnen, Eva, "Wacker Chemie to Take Over Polymer Joint Ventures," Reuters, December 11, 2007, http://www.reuters.com/article/idUSL116809520071211.

Milmo, Sean, "Wacker Targets Biochemistry for Rapid Growth," *Chemical Market Reporter*, November 8, 1999.

"Wacker Chemie-Tochter und Samsung bauen Wafer-Fabrik in Singapur für 1 Mrd USD," Sueddeutsche.de, June 14, 2006, http://www.sueddeutsche.de/finanzen/283/410056/text/.

"Wacker; Chemische Spaltung," *Focus*, May 31, 1999, p. 254.

"Wacker Negotiates Silicon Carbide Divestment," *Chemical Week*, April 19, 2000, p. 8.

"Wacker to Consolidate Pyrogenic Silica Production," Azom.com, January 18, 2010, http://www.azom.com/news.asp?newsID=20390.

Washington H. Soul
Pattinson and Company
Limited

—————— ∎ ——————

First Floor, 160 Pitt Street Mall
Sydney, New South Wales 2000
Australia
Telephone: (+61 2) 9232-7166
Fax: (+61 (2)) 9235-1747
Web site: http://www.whsp.com.au

Public Company
Founded: 1872
Incorporated: 1903
Employees: 2,130
Sales: AUD 764.5 million (2009)
Stock Exchanges: Australian Securities Exchange
Ticker Symbol: SOL
NAICS: 551112 Offices of Other Holding Companies;
    523920 Portfolio Management; 212111 Bituminous
    Coal and Lignite Surface Mining; 424210 Drugs
    and Druggists' Sundries Merchant Wholesalers.

∎ ∎ ∎

Washington H. Soul Pattinson and Company Limited is
a diversified public Australian company whose major
activities include ownership of properties and shares,
coal mining, retailing of pharmaceutical products,
operation of a licensed commercial television station,
and retailing of telecommunications products and
services. The company owns controlling investments in
New Hope Corporation and Pitt Capital Partners and
major investments in Australian Pharmaceutical
Industries Limited, Brickworks Limited, Clover
Corporation Limited, Ruralco Holdings Limited, and

SP Telemedia Limited. In 2000 the company sold the
wholesaling and manufacturing operations of its original
pharmacy business, including the Soul Pattinson brand
name, to Australian Pharmaceutical Industries (API) in
return for a 25 percent stake in API.

FOUNDATIONAL YEARS

Washington H. Soul Pattinson and Company Limited
traces its legacy to two British entrepreneurs, Caleb Soul
and Lewy Pattinson, who separately came to Australia,
established pharmacy businesses, and became friends
before their namesake pharmacies were later combined.
Soul was a druggist and chemist who worked for 18
years for a drug manufacturing firm known for supplying the British armed forces during the Crimean War.
After moving to Australia in 1863 and working in various fields, Soul began importing patented drugs from
the United States and Britain. In 1872 Caleb Soul and
his son, Washington Handley, established a drugstore
and dispensary in Sydney named Washington H. Soul
and Co. Caleb Soul named the business after his son
because, according to popular legend, he thought his
son's name sounded more honest than his own.
Washington H. Soul and Co. advertised that "all [its]
goods [were] sold at New York and London prices"
because all pharmaceuticals at that time were imported
and prices for products in Australia were extremely high.
The business quickly became profitable and soon
became popular locally for other reasons: its décor and
soda fountain modeled on those in American drugstores.

The drugstore's "milk bar" sold a variety of drinks,
the favorite of which was Soul's Spartan Tonic, compris-

COMPANY PERSPECTIVES

■

Washington H. Soul Pattinson is a significant investment house with a portfolio encompassing many industries—its traditional field of pharmacy as well as building materials, natural resources, food technology and beverages, equity investments, media and telecommunications, merchant banking and funds management.

ing alcohol, minerals, and salts. Teetotalers were known to frequent the milk bar, coming in for a mid-morning or pre-lunch Spartan Tonic. Soul's became well known also for a variety of products manufactured in-house, several of which, because of their popularity, were marketed nationally. These products included Soyer's baking powder, which Soul made by following a published recipe. Newspapers during the period frequently published prescriptions attributed to well-known doctors, and manufacturers in turn borrowed those recipes and often named their products after the inventing physicians. Such was the case with numerous products Soul's manufactured: Dr. Richardson's Hair Restorer, Dr. Thompson's Coltsfoot Linctus, Sir Benjamin Brodie's Gout and Rheumatic Cure, Dr. Erasmus Wilson's Heart Tonic, Dr. Jones's Corn and Wart Cure, and Clayton's Kidney and Bladder Pills.

Lewy Pattinson worked in his brother's pharmacy in England, where he read about and became inspired by the success of Soul's business in Australia. After a sojourn to Sydney to meet Soul himself, Pattinson moved to Australia in 1886 to open his own pharmacy in Balmain, a suburb of Sydney. Pattinson followed Soul's business strategy, and, like Soul, Pattinson imported all of his raw drugs and medicines. Pattinson soon purchased several other local drugstores, set up his own warehouse, and established his own laboratories. Among his most successful patents was Scott's Compound of Glycerine and Linseed, a cough medicine that became a popular national product and, as of the 2000s, remained available for purchase. Other popular products produced by Pattinson included Howard's Zono English Aspirin, Nadys Complexion Cream, Ziris Perfumes and Cosmetics, and Bay Rum and Cantharades for dandruff, as well as the highly successful product Dr. McKenzie's Influenza Mixture. McKenzie was well known as Queen Victoria's physician who, in an ironic twist of fate, died of influenza.

By 1888 Caleb and Washington Soul had 30 employees and a one-of-a-kind store in Australia that was the source of numerous relaxing drinks that made Soul's a social gathering place. After Pattinson's business was quarantined in the 1890s due to the bubonic plague, Caleb Soul allowed Pattinson to share office space, which informally began a business partnership and solidified a friendship. About this same time John Spence, another pharmacist, joined Pattinson's operation.

1903 A NEW CORPORATION IN A NEW CENTURY

Caleb Soul died in 1894, and his son, Washington, assumed the role of general manager of Soul's. During the early years of the next century, Washington, who had no sons, was preparing for retirement and asked Pattinson if he would buy out Washington H. Soul and Co., which included16 shops, a warehouse, and a factory, as well as a glass company Washington H. Soul and Co. used to produce its own bottles. Pattinson agreed. The acquisition became effective in April 1902, and stock was privately placed in December. In January 1903 Lewy Pattinson incorporated the new company: Washington H. Soul Pattinson and Company Limited. Washington Soul retired after the new corporation was created, and Lewy's brother William Pattinson and John Spence were named managing directors.

In 1903 the newly incorporated firm acquired a pharmacy in Annandale, and John Spence Jr. was named its manager. The following year Lewy Pattinson's brother William retired to the Isle of Man. In 1904 Soul Pattinson opened a new pharmacy in Maitland (roughly between Sydney and Newcastle). Because the area was prone to flooding, the pharmacy was built on one of the highest places in town.

Soul Pattinson built a new factory and warehouse in Sydney in 1916. In 1920 Lewy's son Dr. William Lewy Pattinson, fresh from a tour of duty in World War I, joined the company as manager of all company shops. John Spence Jr. was named supervisor of the factory and warehouse. In 1921 Ken Mulholland was named supervisor of all the shops in Newcastle, a major city about 100 miles northeast of Sydney. Those shops performed so well that a separate subsidiary, Soul Pattinson (Newcastle) Pty. Ltd., was established with Mulholland named managing director.

EXPANSION AND THE SPREAD OF SHOPS

Meanwhile the rest of Soul Pattinson's retail business expanded rapidly under the direction of Dr. Pattinson.

KEY DATES

1872: Caleb Soul and his son, Washington Handley, establish the drugstore and dispensary Washington H. Soul and Co.

1903: Lewy Pattinson incorporates a company combining Washington H. Soul and Co. with his company Pattinson and Co.; the new firm is named Washington H. Soul Pattinson and Company Limited.

1969: Soul Pattinson and Brickworks Ltd., both concerned about a possible takeover, exchange one million shares of stock to facilitate cross-ownership of the two firms.

1982: The company acquires a 50 percent interest in the coal-mining firm Surrey Properties (renamed New Hope Corporation).

2000: The company sells 260 stores in Australia and the wholesaling and manufacturing operations of its pharmacy business, including the Soul Pattinson brand name, to Australian Pharmaceutical Industries (API) in return for a 25 percent stake in API.

The company continued to import all its raw pharmaceuticals, as well as new gift lines, including popular items like ladies' compacts, known then as flapjacks. In 1928 Dr. Pattinson and John Spence Jr. were named joint managing directors after John Spence Sr. died. During the 1920s and 1930s, the company added more than 15 New South Wales retail outlets in Sydney and nearby suburbs. Many of these new shops involved a share ownership, whereby the manager of the shop put in a share investment and in return received that percentage of profits. By 1937 Soul Pattinson boasted more than three dozen stores in Sydney, its suburbs, and Newcastle.

By 1940 the pharmacy market was controlled by Soul Pattinson, with 42 shops, and Hallams Ltd., with 13 shops. Soul Pattinson's growth was stymied, though, in 1940 after the Australian Parliament approved legislation limiting pharmacies to the number in existence at the time. As a result of the Pharmacy Act, the growth of Soul Pattinson came to a virtual standstill for the next 15 years.

Lewy Pattinson died in 1944 at the age of 96, and John Spence was named to replace Pattinson as chairman. In 1950 a new generation assumed a major role in the company when the grandson of Lewy Pattinson, James Sinclair (Jim) Millner, was named general manager of the company. John Spence retired in 1957, and Dr. Pattinson was named chairman and Jim Millner a new director.

PRICING PROBLEMS AND TAKEOVER PREVENTION

Through the early 1960s manufacturers established the retail price of products and refused to sell their wares to any retailer who deviated from selling at those prices. As a result prices for patented medicines and toiletries were consistent throughout Australian drugstores. Additionally some manufacturers restricted products to only pharmacy businesses. In the early 1960s, however, Bristol Myers broke with the policy of price maintenance, and several toiletries moved into supermarkets and variety chain stores at reduced prices. This trend spread to other manufacturers.

Faced with a major business dilemma, the Soul Pattinson board, persuaded by Jim Millner, agreed to undercut prices offered by supermarkets and variety stores. Specials were offered at lower discount prices, with products placed in wire baskets at the front of stores. The move was successful, and by 1963 Soul Pattinson was again highly profitable. By the mid-1960s all former "chemist-only" products were available to all retailers, and such retail price maintenance was later made illegal.

In the late 1960s Soul Pattinson began diversifying. To generate acquisition funds, the company in 1968 publicly issued one million shares of stock through the Australian Stock Exchange at $12 a share. This was the company's first and only share issue not made to existing preferred shareholders. Previously the company had only distributed bonus share issues to existing holders. After the share sale Soul Pattinson acquired the Australian finance company Deposit & Investment Co. Ltd., a firm in which it already had a sizable stake.

Recognizing that it could be a potential takeover target, Millner contacted a number of large Australian companies with sizable assets, which could likewise be attractive to other firms, in order to discuss mutually beneficial agreements. Millner met with W. F. Dawes, chief executive of Brickworks Ltd., who also was concerned about a possible takeover. In an unusual stock swap to facilitate cross-ownership, the two firms agreed to exchange one million shares at $10 a share. As a result Soul Pattinson owned 25 percent of Brickworks, which in turn owned 22 percent of Soul Pattinson.

LABOR ISSUES, A NEW EXPORT BUSINESS, AND DIVERSIFICATION

After Gough Whitlam became Australia's prime minister in 1972, the first member of the Labor Party to hold the position in more than 20 years, he succeeded in instituting a number of legislative reforms, and wages rose dramatically. As a result Soul Pattinson turned to self-service checkouts at its shops to keep overhead down. It also was during this period of the early 1970s when the major retailers in New South Wales came under pressure to enforce a trend toward compulsory unionism, with all existing staff of Soul Pattinson strongly urged to join a union. According to the company all of its staff objected to being compelled to join, and, despite union picketing of the firm and attempted black bans (whereby union members were not allowed to work for a particular employer) against Soul Pattinson, the company remained union free.

Looking for ways to expand its business, Soul Pattinson began an export trade in the early 1970s, shipping its manufactured products to Fiji, Hong Kong, Malaysia, Malta, New Guinea, Nigeria, and Singapore. In 1975 Soul Pattinson established a pharmaceutical manufacturing plant in Malaysia as part of a joint venture with Apex Pharmacy. With Soul Pattinson's export business growing rapidly, in 1976 the company acquired McGloin Pty Ltd., a well-respected producer and distributor of chemist product lines that sold to every pharmacy in Australia. Requiring larger warehouse facilities and a new factory, Soul Pattinson initiated a major construction program. Between the late 1970s and early 1980s, J. McGloin relocated its business into part of Soul Pattinson's former warehouse, and the company opened new warehouses in Kingsgrove, in Brisbane to serve Queensland, and in Perth to supply Western Australia.

In 1982 Soul Pattinson acquired a 50 percent stake in Surrey Properties (renamed New Hope Corporation). New Hope was an independent energy company focusing on mining and marketing of open-cut-mine derived coal, with a majority of production shipped to Asian-Pacific markets. Soul Pattinson continued diversifying in 1989 through the acquisition of NBN Ltd., a regional Newcastle-based television station. In 1991 NBN became an affiliate of the Nine Network, then the most watched television network in Australia. With this new affiliation NBN expanded its coverage to include all of northern New South Wales while extending programming to 24 hours a day.

A NEW GENERATION OF MANAGEMENT, A NEW CORPORATE DIRECTION

After experiencing some dramatic peaks and valleys, Soul Pattinson's share price began a significant upswing in 1999, buoyed by NBN, boasting Australia's highest television audience share, and improvement in global coal markets. At a time when the company's diversified assets were increasingly playing a larger role in Soul Pattinson's revenues than was pharmaceutical retailing, Jim Millner retired (in 1999), and his nephew Robert Millner, the great-grandson of Lewy Pattinson, became chairman. The younger nephew, while honoring the conservative style of the company, soon began guiding the firm into an expanded position of an investment holding company. Increasingly Soul Pattinson began selling, floating, or spinning off its holdings, while maintaining sizable stock in the firms sold, as investments.

While Soul Pattinson was best known for its drugstore and pharmacy chain, in 2000 it sold 260 stores in Australia and the wholesaling and manufacturing operations of its pharmacy business, including the Soul Pattinson brand name, to Australian Pharmaceutical Industries (API). In return Soul Pattinson received a 25 percent stake in API, which became the country's second-largest pharmaceutical wholesaler as a result of the transaction.

While pharmaceuticals were reduced to a more minor role in the company's ledger, brick manufacturing was playing a greater role in Soul Pattinson's earnings. This fact was not lost on those like Sir Ron Brierley, who, in 2000, acquired a 10 percent stake in Brickworks in an initial move to undo the Soul Pattinson–Brickworks cross-ownership pact that had stood since the late 1960s. Since then Soul Pattinson's stake in Brickworks had grown from 25 percent to 49.8 percent, and Brickworks' interest in Soul Pattinson had increased from 22 percent to 42.9 percent. Brierley apparently recognized that the smaller Brickworks was the foundation for the value of the larger Soul Pattinson. However, shareholders of the latter remained loyal to the century-old firm, declined Brierley's offer to acquire a larger share of Brickworks, and Brierley sold his interest in the brick operation within two years of acquiring it.

INVESTING IN TELECOMMUNICATIONS, COAL, AND BRICKS

In 2001 the company established Soul Pattinson Telecommunications Ltd. (SPT) to provide a more economical television-based Internet alternative to the provider Telstra for customers living between Sydney and Brisbane. SPT, initially designed to provide Internet, voice, and data services through its broadcast television infrastructure, went public its first year. Its services were later expanded to include fiber, fixed line, and wireless phone services.

Soul Pattinson in April 2002 announced a 10-1 stock split designed to increase share liquidity. The announcement followed a report of a six-month earnings increase of more than 60 percent over the previous year. Six months later, after the firm logged a 28 percent increase in yearly earnings that rose to $72.74 million, Chairman Robert Millner defended his company's "conservative" business strategy and boasted that the 100-year-old Soul Pattinson had paid a shareholder dividend every year since 1903.

In 2003 Soul Pattinson acquired the boutique funds management firm Veritas Investment Management, which it renamed Souls Funds Management. That same year Soul Pattinson spun off New Hope Corporation to its own shareholders but retained nearly a 64 percent stake in NHC. Prior to the spin-off the company sold NHC's most promising mine, Adaro, for $406 million. Brickworks, in 2003, acquired the building materials firm Metro Brick Bristile Limited, making Brickworks (with operations in all six Australian states as well in some offshore areas) the largest brick manufacturer in Australia and a major force in the roofing and floor tile production business.

On its route to becoming a burgeoning telecom firm, SPT acquired a handful of troubled companies during the early 2000s. In 2004 it also purchased NBN Television, the affiliate of the Nine Network Newcastle affiliate formerly owned by Soul Pattinson. About the same time, SPT changed its name to SP Telemedia after Soul Pattinson transferred control of NBN to the telecommunications firm.

A GROWING INVESTMENT FIRM

By 2005 Soul Pattinson owned nearly 64 percent of New Hope Corporation, which had three major coal mines that were responsible for generating a majority of Soul Pattinson's annual revenues. By mid-decade Soul Pattinson also was associated with three listed investment companies, including Milton Corporation with a capitalization of more than $1 billion and Choiseul Investments capitalized at about $400 million. The third listed investment company was Brickworks Investment Company, a firm that Brickworks had spun off a year prior while retaining a 25 percent interest. In addition Soul Pattinson owned a 50.4 interest in the biscuit and cakes manufacturer KH Foods Limited, a nearly 20 percent interest in the rural services and merchandise

provider Ruralco Holdings Limited, and a stake in the fish oil producer Clover Corporation. Soul Pattinson also held a sizable portfolio of investments in other listed and unlisted businesses. These included a 64 percent interest in Souls Funds Management (which in 2004 produced extremely impressive investment results), Calliden Group (an insurance underwriter), ARB Corporation (an automotive parts manufacturer and distributor), Reece Holdings (later Reece Australia Limited; a bathroom and plumbing parts supplier), Noni B (a women's apparel and accessories retailer), and Souls Private Equity (a namesake investment capital provider in companies with high-growth potential).

In 2007 Soul Pattinson boosted its stake in the ailing bakery business KH Foods from 52 percent to nearly 87 percent. KH, which had traded in its well-known spice business to enter the bakery field, continued to lose money and was sold in 2008. Soul Pattinson agreed to underwrite KH's losses.

Soul Pattinson's telecommunications investments proved more fruitful. In February 2008 SP Telemedia paid AUD 150 million to merge with the TPG Group, an Internet service provider. The combined firm boasted one of the largest DSLAM (Digital Subscriber Line Access Multiplexer) networks in the country, allowing it to provide Internet service at a variety of customer-chosen speeds. Annual revenues in 2009 for the merged company was projected to be $607 million. Prior to the merger Soul Pattinson owned about 46 percent of SP Telemedia. Afterward it owned about 28 percent of the merged business because of diluted shareholdings.

In 2008 BHP Billiton Mitsubishi Alliance purchased from New Hope its New Saraji coal project. For the 2008–09 fiscal year Soul Pattinson posted an underlying net profit of AUD 225 million, but the sale of New Hope assets pushed total net profit in excess of AUD 1 billion. New Hope reportedly contributed a majority of revenue for Soul Pattinson. Brickworks for the same year posted a net profit of AUD 305 million on revenue of AUD 594 million. Soul Pattinson, before consideration of the sale of assets, nearly doubled its annual earnings.

SOUL PATTINSON'S CONSERVATIVE FUTURE

Soul Pattinson sold its Souls Funds Management Limited to Treasury Group Ltd. in November 2009. In February 2010 Soul Pattinson boosted its stake in CBD Energy Limited, a diversified renewable energy storage company and provider of fossil-fuel alternatives for renewable energy, from about 10 percent to17 percent.

Soul Pattinson closed one decade and entered another by acquiring investments in growing and proven fields that held solid growth prospects, such as renewable energy and telecommunications. The company was also, under Robert Millner, becoming much more of an investment holding company, with its one-time namesake drugstore business having become one of its investments while coal and bricks seemed to constitute the foundation for the company's long-term profitability. As the *Intelligent Investor* observed in 2005, "The Millners are archetypal value investors. They buy high quality assets cheaply, hold plenty of cash for opportunistic investment, and don't worry too much about diversifying simply for the sake of it. And they keep those investments for the long term."

That formula had seemed to work for more than a century. It took more than a century before Soul Pattinson shed most of the pharmaceutical interests upon which the company was built. As it entered a new decade, Soul Pattinson appeared positioned to remain conservative in terms of being "value investors" albeit a bit more liberal, perhaps, at least under Robert Millner, in terms of what investments it might select or abandon.

Roger Rouland

PRINCIPAL SUBSIDIARIES

New Hope Corporation Limited; Pitt Capital Partners Limited.

PRINCIPAL COMPETITORS

Australian United Investment Company Limited; Diversified United Investment Limited; Southern Cross Airports Corporation Holdings Limited.

FURTHER READING

"Australia's Soul Pattinson Telecom, New Skies, Form Alliance," *AsiaPulse News*, May 9, 2001.

Durie, John, "Soul Pattinson Pushes Asset for Sale," the *Australian* with the *Wall Street Journal*, November 26, 2009, http://www.theaustralian.com.au/business/opinion/shell-takes-coal-stake-as-soul-pattinson-pushes-asset-for-sale/story-e6frg9io-1225804163238?from=public_rss.

"Hats off to the Millners," *Intelligent Investor*, July 6, 2005, http://www.intelligentinvestor.com.au/articles/179/Hats-off-to-the-Millners.cfm?articleID=10001047.

Hughes, Anthony, Geoff Wilson, and Matthew Kidman, *Masters of the Market: Secrets of Australia's Leading Sharemarket Investors*. Melbourne: John Wiley & Sons, 2005.

"Millner Looking but in No Hurry to Spend Cash Pile," *Australasian Business Intelligence*, February 15, 2010.

Nicklin, Lenore, "The Heart of Soul," the *Bulletin* with *Newsweek*, December 1, 1998, p. 44.

"Programs Build Confidence," *Australasian Business Intelligence*, January 26, 2010.

Rochfort, Scott, "Soul Patts Sticks to Its Guns—and the Old Ways," *TheAge.com*, October 10, 2002, http://www.theage.com.au/articles/2002/10/09/1034061256166.html.

———, "WH Soul Pattinson Plods to $72m Profit," *Sydney Morning Herald*, October 10, 2002, http://www.theage.com.au/articles/2002/10/09/1034061256166.html.

"Souls Doses Out the Good Investment Medicine," *Money Management* (Australia), January 20, 2005.

Western Union Company

12500 East Belford Avenue
Englewood, Colorado 80112
U.S.A.
Telephone: (720) 332-1000
Toll Free: (866) 405-5012
Web site: http://www.westernunion.com

Public Company
Incorporated: 1851 as The New York and Mississippi
   Valley Printing Telegraph Company
Employees: 5,900
Sales: $5.3 billion (2008)
Stock Exchanges: New York
Ticker Symbol: WU
NAICS: 522390 Money Transmission Services

■ ■ ■

The Western Union Company operates the world's largest money-transfer company, with approximately 400,000 locations in 200 countries worldwide. Through its vast global network, Western Union enables consumers and businesses to transfer money or make payments with money orders and other electronic systems. Since the early 21st century, Western Union's business has been driven largely by the steady rise in the global population of migrant workers, who use the company's remittance services to wire money to relatives in their native countries. From 1994 to 2006 the company was a subsidiary of First Data Corporation, operating under the name Western Union Financial Services. First Data decided to spin off the subsidiary in 2006, forming the Western Union Company.

ORIGINS AND GROWTH IN THE 19TH CENTURY

Western Union started operations in 1851 as the New York and Mississippi Valley Printing Telegraph Company. The company, its name defining the boundaries of its operating territory, was formed by a group of Rochester, New York, businessmen, whose geographic ambitions soon escalated. In 1856 the company changed its name to the Western Union Telegraph Company, reflecting the union of telegraph lines in the western United States with telegraph lines in the eastern United States. An integrated system was formed by cobbling together a number of rival telegraph lines. The Western Union name soon became a household word.

Throughout its history, Western Union was an innovator. The company's 10th anniversary in 1861 saw the completion of the first transcontinental telegraph line and coincided with the outbreak of the Civil War. The new service enabled fast coast-to-coast communications during the war. Many of the company's pioneering developments during its formative years could be credited to one of its employees, an icon of U.S. ingenuity. Thomas Edison was a Morse operator for Western Union, tapping out the code that conveyed the company's telegrams. Many of Edison's early inventions were completed under the auspices of Western Union. The glass-domed stock ticker that provided brokerage firms with New York Stock Exchange quotations was his invention, first introduced by Western Union in 1866.

The stock ticker lent unprecedented sophistication and geographic expansion to the stock distribution side of the company's business. Five years after its introduction Western Union entered what became its single most important business during the modern era. In 1871 Western Union introduced the concept of wiring money, a business that would eventually replace message sending as the company's primary business.

The importance of the foray into wiring money was not to be underestimated, but its importance grew gradually. During the late 19th century and for much of the 20th century, Western Union made its money and earned its reputation as a conveyor of communications, with the company's uniformed messengers serving as the living symbol of telegrams to a fast-growing population sometimes separated by thousands of miles. Western Union's role in enabling individuals, companies, and institutions to communicate with each other became an indispensable component of U.S. life.

Western Union developed new ways to communicate, and increasingly, the company's efforts tilted toward the financial sector, as first highlighted by its involvement in the stock distribution business. Before entering the 20th century, Western Union celebrated one last distinction that confirmed the company's significance. In 1884 Western Union was selected as one of the original 11 companies whose stock values became the benchmarks of the Dow Jones Industrial Average.

EMERGING AS AN INDUSTRY INNOVATOR: 1900–80

Western Union's development during the first half of the 20th century was punctuated by an impressive list of innovations. In 1914 the company introduced the first consumer charge card. In 1923 Western Union introduced teletypewriters, which enabled companies to communicate with their branch offices. During the 1920s the company also pioneered the first practical use of a device that could send pictures over telegraph wires for press services, a precursor to the modern-day facsimile machine.

A little more than a decade later, in 1935, Western Union introduced the first public facsimile service, connecting Buffalo, New York, and New York City. The company's knack for delivering revolutionary technology exhibited itself one more time before the end of the first half of the century. Midway through World War II, in 1943, Western Union introduced the first commercial microwave system to connect one city with another city.

Despite the remarkable achievements recorded by Western Union during its first century of existence, the company's centennial anniversary was dampened considerably by its financial condition. From the end of World War II into the 1950s, Western Union struggled with its balance sheet. To correct the ills, the company diversified into the telex, developing a desk-model machine that provided direct-dial, consumer-to-consumer teleprinter service. The advent of the machine sounded the death knell for the uniformed Western Union messenger. The singing telegram, introduced in 1933 by Western Union's publicity director George P. Oslin, soon disappeared.

During the 1960s Western Union intensified its attempts at diversification. The broadening of the company's operational scope engendered growth, prompting Western Union's management to embark on a diversification program that progressed throughout the 1970s and into the 1980s. Against the backdrop of growth and diversification, the Western Union legacy of innovation continued.

In 1964 the company unveiled its transcontinental microwave radio beam system. The use of the system rendered obsolete the myriad poles and wires stretching across the country. A decade later Western Union could claim it had expanded into space. In 1974 the company launched the first domestic communications satellite for the United States, the Westar 1. In 1982, less than a decade after launching Westar 1, Western Union became the first company with five satellites in orbit.

BANKRUPTCY AND RESTRUCTURING: 1982-94

Not long after launching its fifth satellite, Western Union began to experience the backlash from decades of diversification. Although the company's sprawling domestic and international operations had experienced robust growth, increases in sales had not always led to increased profits. As the company entered the mid-1980s, signs of financial trouble began to emerge. When the extent of the damage was revealed fully, the company found itself floundering in financial straits far worse than its postwar financial crisis.

Western Union's pursuit of new business and new markets created problems on the company's balance sheet. Over time its operations had become too far-flung and incurred too much debt for it to survive without making wholesale changes. In 1984 the problems related to overextending itself became manifest, as Western Union found itself suffering from a severe liquidity crisis. The problem hobbled the company's progress for a decade. Ultimately Western Union's sour financial condition required the most severe of corporate responses. The venerable company, one of the leading pioneering enterprises of the world, was forced to declare bankruptcy, filing for protection from creditors under Chapter 11 of the U.S. Bankruptcy Code in 1994.

The reorganization required by Western Union's Chapter 11 status engendered the company's final transformation into a financial-services business. The company's telecommunications businesses were divested

during the reorganization. Once stripped of these businesses, Western Union was left to concentrate exclusively on financial services, primarily the money wiring business it had invented more than a century earlier. The final stage of the company's attempt to resurrect itself came on September 19, 1994, when the auction of Western Union was scheduled to occur. Thoroughly revamped, Western Union waited during the summer of 1994 to find out who its new owner would be.

NEW LIFE AS A SUBSIDIARY COMPANY: 1994-2002

The two companies who expressed the greatest interest in acquiring Western Union were Forstmann, Little & Co. and First Data Corporation. By August 1994 First Data, a payment services company based in Hackensack, New Jersey, had emerged as the leading contender. First Data submitted a $660 million bid in August. At roughly the same time the Federal Trade Commission (FTC) launched its first antitrust challenge to the merger.

Because of the similarity of the two entities, the FTC alleged the merger would create a monopoly, combining Western Union's own massive money-transfer business with First Data's payment system, known as MoneyGram. To ease the FTC's concerns First Data signed a consent decree in August. By the following month, First Data had prevailed. Western Union, an independent concern for nearly 125 years, became a private subsidiary of First Data, marking the beginning of a new era for the company.

Under the governance of First Data, Western Union emerged from its decade-long malaise with renewed vitality. Since Western Union's invention of the money-transfer business in 1871, the way in which the system operated, not surprisingly, had changed substantially. The Morse keys and sounders operated by Thomas Edison had been replaced with a network of agents connected through the Western Union computer system. The agents were located in supermarkets, check-cashing outlets, mailbox stores, and sundry other retail establishments.

Money transfer, aside from the technological changes, had become an incredibly large business, enjoying exponential growth during Western Union's final transformation into a financial-services company. In 1986, there were eight million money-transfer transactions. A decade later, as Western Union embarked on its new era of existence under the control of First Data, there were more than 30 million money-transfer transactions.

As Western Union focused on dominating the business it had first developed, the company increasingly bolstered its global presence. In 1992 the company began the first consumer instant money-transfer service between the United States and Russia. In 1993, while still in the throes of its financial crisis, the company launched its Dinero en Minutos (Money in Minutes) service in Mexico, a new currency-transfer service that enabled travelers in Mexico to pick up cash in pesos at any of the nearly 300 locations operated by Elektra, a leading furniture and electronics retail company based in Mexico.

At roughly the same time, the company introduced electronic fund transfers in Africa, entering Ghana in 1993 and expanding into South Africa, Ethiopia, Zambia, Senegal, Kenya, Nigeria, Uganda, and Eritrea during the subsequent two years. International expansion fueled much of the company's growth during the mid-1990s, particularly its advances in Mexico, which accounted for a fifth of its international financial growth in 1995. The company strengthened its ties with Elektra at the beginning of 1996, signing a 10-year agreement with the retailer. Later in the year Western Union opened its North American headquarters in Englewood, Colorado, and opened new regional sales offices in Paris, Vienna, and Hong Kong.

Western Union's aggressive expansion during the 1990s could be charted by the growth of its agent network. The company had fewer than 20,000 agent locations during the early 1990s. By 1998 Western Union's money-transfer service had expanded to 50,000 agent locations worldwide, representing the world's largest money-transfer network. By the end of the decade there were more than 80,000 Western Union agent locations scattered throughout more than 140 countries.

As Western Union entered the 21st century it promised to figure as a dominant player in the money-transfer business. The company launched westernunion.com in 2000, inaugurating the extension of money transfer to the Internet. The following year the company celebrated its 150th anniversary with 100,000 agent locations, a more than fivefold increase in less than a decade. In 2002, as part of its consistent efforts to expand payment options on the Internet, Western Union launched its Consumer Web Payment Service, enabling customers' funds to be debited or credited electronically through their checking accounts.

A NEW ERA OF GROWTH: 2003 ON

As the decade progressed, Western Union Financial Services found itself facing increased competition as the global market for financial remittances continued to expand. Much of the industry's growth during this period was driven by the steady rise in the number of migrant workers worldwide, who depended on money-transfer services to send money to family members in their home countries. By 2003 analysts estimated that roughly 80 million workers would transfer up to $150 billion over the course of the year. Western Union controlled approximately 12 percent of the remittance sector.

This lucrative business was quickly attracting new rivals, however, as financial companies such as Wells Fargo and Bank of America began to carve out their own niches within the industry, particularly in the Central and South American markets. In late 2003 Western Union devoted $300 million to a new marketing campaign aimed at building and solidifying consumer awareness of the Western Union brand. At the same time the company set out to explore growth possibilities in rapidly emerging markets, notably China and India, where the wire-transfer business remained virtually undeveloped.

As part of its growth strategy, Western Union also worked to expand its physical presence across the globe. In September 2004 the company celebrated the opening of its 200,000th location, in Athens, Greece, shortly after the city hosted the Summer Olympics. Two months later the company opened new branch offices in India, Singapore, and China. The Chinese market was especially enticing to Western Union, with annual remittances estimated to top $11 billion.

As the company expanded into new territories, revenues continued to rise. In 2005 Western Union earned $3.8 billion from money transfers, an increase of 14 percent over the previous year. Total revenues topped $4 billion for the year, of which $1.2 billion was profit. As the money-transfer business became one of the fastest growth industries in the world, however, the company's telegram division was rapidly becoming extinct. Western Union terminated its telegram and message business on January 27, 2006.

At around the same time Western Union was closing its historic telegram business, parent company First Data announced its intention to divest Western Union. An initial public offering took place on September 20, 2006, and Western Union was once again a public company. By November of that year the newly christened Western Union Company had roughly 285,000 locations worldwide. A year later this number had grown to 320,000, with nearly a third of the company's offices in the swiftly expanding Asian market.

In 2007 the company's revenues rose to $4.9 billion, an increase of 10 percent over 2006. Sales continued to climb in 2008, when the company posted total revenues of $5.3 billion. During this period

Western Union also expanded through acquisition. In February 2009 the company acquired the money-transfer division of Fexco, a financial-services company based in Ireland, for $159.5 million. Three months later Western Union purchased Canadian foreign-exchange firm Custom House Ltd. for $370 million. By early 2010 the company had more than 400,000 locations worldwide.

Jeffrey L. Covell
Updated, Stephen Meyer

PRINCIPAL SUBSIDIARIES

Western Union has approximately 100 major subsidiaries worldwide, all of which are involved in various aspects of the company's core money-transfer business.

PRINCIPAL COMPETITORS

American Express Company; MoneyGram International, Inc.; PayPal, Inc.

FURTHER READING

Ankomah, Baffour, "The Money Transfer Revolution," *African Business*, October 1995, p. 28.

Barthel, Matt, "1st Data Agrees to Sell a Money-Transfer Business If It Wins Western Union," *American Banker*, August 22, 1994, p. 14.

"Bumiputra-Commerce Western Union Tie Up," *New Straits Times*, March 13, 2001.

Fairlamb, David, with Geri Smith and Frederik Balfour, "Can Western Union Keep On Delivering?" *Business Week*, December 22, 2003, p. 52.

Fickenscher, Lisa, "Western Union Beefs Up in Mexico, Signing 10-Year Deal with Retailer," *American Banker*, January 30, 1996, p. 17.

Levin, Gary, "Western Union Not Fading into Sunset; New Services Are Added as Telegrams Drop," *Advertising Age*, April 27, 1992, p. 54.

Malhotra, Priya, "More E-Billing at Western Union," *American Banker*, July 29, 2002, p. 23.

Sileo, Olia, "Marking 125 Years of Wiring Money," *Record*, January 31, 1997, p. B1.

"Western Union Buys Commerce Group," *Cardline*, June 17, 2002, p. 1.

Zadvydas, Thomas, "Western Union Adds Custom House for $370M," *Daily Deal*, May 7, 2009.

Wizards of the Coast LLC

———————————■———————————

1600 Lind Avenue SW, Suite 400
Renton, Washington 98057
U.S.A.
Telephone: (425) 226-6500
Toll Free: (800) 324-6496
Web site: http://www.wizards.com

Wholly Owned Subsidiary of Hasbro, Inc.
Founded: 1990
Incorporated: 1990
Employees: 1500
NAICS: 339932 Game, Toy, and Children's Vehicle
      Manufacturing; 511130 Book Publishers

■ ■ ■

Wizards of the Coast LLC (WotC) is an international
leader in the adventure game industry and is perhaps
best known as the publisher of the world's best-selling
trading card game, *Magic: The Gathering*. Through its
purchase of fellow gaming company TSR Inc., Wizards
acquired the rights to *Dungeons & Dragons*, another
hobby game that has long held cult status as the original
role-playing game. The company had another big hit
with the *Pokemon* trading card game.

The multinational toy company Hasbro purchased
Wizards of the Coast in 1999, but the subsidiary has
maintained its identity and lively market niche. WotC
has also profited handsomely from publishing adventure
books based on the characters and worlds of its games.

WIZARDS OF THE WHAT?: BEGINNINGS, 1991

Wizards of the Coast was founded in 1990 by Peter Adkison, a systems analyst at Boeing. With a dream of
establishing a career in the adventure gaming business,
Adkison and six other young visionaries began creating
and developing role-playing games in their spare time.
Adkison asked game aficionado Richard Garfield to
design a card game that was fun and portable and could
be played in under an hour. Garfield, who had been
designing his own games since age 15, and George Skaff
Elias, a fellow graduate student in mathematics, started
working on it.

Two years later, in August 1993, the trading card
game *Magic: The Gathering* was released by the newly
formed WotC (rhymes with Yahtzee). The company's
staff of eight operated out of the basement of Adkison's
home. The game, set in the imaginary realm of Do-
minia, features wizards challenging one another for
control of the land. Players use cards representing
fantastic creatures and spells to reduce their opponents'
score from 20 to 0 and win the game.

GATHERING THE MAGIC

Both a game and a collectible item, *Magic: The Gathering* was the first product of its kind to be released. It
surprised the gaming industry by becoming one of the
most popular games in history, outselling *Monopoly* and
Trivial Pursuit and spawning an entire new subindustry
within the gaming industry: trading cards. Each deck of
40 or so cards is different from every other deck, giving
players/collectors no lack of items to buy. The extremely

COMPANY PERSPECTIVES

The story of Wizards is one of independence, inspiration, and opportunity. It's the epic story of a humble game company starting in its owner's basement and climbing to its current perch atop the global hobby gaming business. It entails a journey of discovery, in which entirely new worlds were conceived and brought to life through the vibrant shards of countless pieces of fantastic art. It's the story of the pioneering days of our industry, when icons like Gary Gygax and Richard Garfield created unprecedented types of games and introduced the world to entirely new play experiences. It's the story of our firsts and the foundation of gaming that's still being shaped by our efforts to this day. It's also the personal story of any gamer and the paths we open up to their individual creativity. It's a celebration of face-to-face connectivity and spontaneous imagination. It's the story of individual gaming groups coming together to celebrate their shared passion. It's the story of those who live to game.

rare *Black Lotus* card, for example, has sold for more than $1,000 in a flourishing black market for cards.

More than 10 million trading cards were sold in 6 weeks. More than 5 million players throughout the world would go on to play *Magic*, and it would be published in 9 languages and in more than 65 countries. A bimonthly magazine called the *Duelist*, which offers rules, strategy tips, and tournament news, was also created.

Due to the success of *Magic*, Garfield was able to quit his teaching job at Whitman College in Walla Walla, Washington, and pursue his true passion of game design, coming on board with WotC full time in June 1994. In October of that year, WotC released *RoboRally*, the company's first major board game, designed by Garfield while he was still a graduate student at the University of Pennsylvania. In the fast-paced, futuristic game, players attempt to be the first to maneuver their robots across a wild and treacherous factory floor.

NEW ACQUISITIONS AND PARTNERSHIPS, 1994–96

Trading card collecting in general surged in popularity from 1992 to 1995, losing a bit of momentum in the wake of 1994's Major League Baseball strike. The company's skyrocket to the top allowed it to relocate to an office in Renton, Washington, in 1994 and open international offices in Milan, Paris, and Antwerp. In 1995 Garfield created a card game called *The Great Dalmuti*, which was WotC's first game to be distributed through retail channels. The game is based on a medieval theme, and players are either kings, peons, or merchants. That year the company also purchased Ohio-based Andon Unlimited, a company that ran trade shows. However, suffering from growing pains, WotC eliminated its *Everway*, *Ars Magica*, and *Slay Industries* games.

In 1996 telecommunications giant MCI entered into a partnership with WotC, with an estimated $750,000 three-year sponsorship of the *Magic: The Gathering* U.S. Tournament and releasing prepaid phone cards featuring *Magic* artwork. A perfect premium for a collectible-friendly market, the phone cards provided a hotline for fans wanting up-to-the-minute tournament information, including tour dates, individual player rankings, and game strategy.

In November 1996 WotC released a *BattleTech* trading card game based on FASA Corporation's popular board game of the same name. The WotC strategic card game transports players into the 31st century, where they assume the role of commanders and control armies of 30-foot-tall walking tanks known as "BattleMechs." The game would become the second-best-selling trading card game in the United States, behind *Magic*.

DAVID BUYS GOLIATH

By February 1997, in order to not dilute *Magic*'s pure gamer image, WotC had teamed with only eight licensees, including software developers Acclaim Entertainment Inc. and Microprose Inc., book publishers Workman and Carlton Books Limited, and apparel manufacturer Nice Man, to generate approximately $1 million in licensed *Magic* business. The company had also already received movie and television offers but was holding off for the time being. Acclaim's comics division began publishing a *Magic* comic book series, and publisher HarperCollins released 12 paperback science fiction and fantasy novels based on the game under the HarperPrism imprint.

In April 1997 WotC announced its intent to acquire struggling veteran gaming company TSR Inc. for an undisclosed amount. The move stunned the gaming world, as Wizards was still considered an upstart by many analysts despite the staggering success of *Magic*.

During its 25 years in business, TSR had created hundreds of games, including children's board games,

1990: Wizards of the Coast (WotC) is founded by Peter Adkinson.

1993: Company launches collectible card game *Magic: The Gathering.*

1997: WotC acquires TSR and its *Dungeons & Dragons* franchise; company obtains patent on trading card games.

1999: Wizards publishes *Pokemon* trading card game, an immediate hit; Hasbro acquires WotC.

2000: Third edition of *Dungeons & Dragons* and company's first *Star Wars* role-playing game are launched.

2004: Wizards introduces children's book imprint, Mirrorstone.

adult strategy games, dice games, card games, war games, and numerous role-playing games, translated into more than a dozen languages and sold in over 50 countries. TSR was best known for its publication of former insurance underwriter E. Gary Gygax's highly successful fantasy/adventure role-playing games *Dungeons & Dragons*, which debuted in 1974. This was followed by *Advanced Dungeons & Dragons*, which was ultimately played by millions of gamers throughout the world, singlehandedly creating the billion-dollar role-playing game industry.

The *D&D* concept ultimately expanded into supporting settings such as *Greyhawk Adventures*, the *Forgotten Realms* campaign set in a medieval world; the *Planescape* campaign set in alternate realities; and the *Ravenloft* classic gothic horror campaign. Another setting for *Advanced D&D* was the successful *DragonLance* saga.

A second gaming system by TSR, *Saga*, concentrates more on roles than rules in an easy-to-use role-playing system that revolves around drama and storytelling. Notable titles within this format include the *Marvel Super Heroes Adventure Game*, which features Spider-Man, the X-Men, the Avengers, the Fantastic Four, and other popular licensed characters.

TSR also ranked as one of the world's top fantasy and science fiction book publishers. Since first publishing in the early 1980s, the company had sold millions of copies of its novels, most derived from its gaming series. Some of these titles would reach *New York Times* best-selling status. In addition, TSR published two successful gaming periodicals, *Dragon Magazine* and

Dungeon Adventures Magazine, both of which focused on the role-playing game industry, specifically TSR's games. The company also licensed its properties to other media, including television (Total Entertainment Network) and electronic games (Interplay Inc. and Sierra On-Line).

TSR headquarters and most of the staff were moved from their longtime home of Lake Geneva, Wisconsin, to WotC's facility in Washington state. One of the major issues to be resolved in the purchase was the payment of royalties owed to a number of TSR authors. At the time of its purchase, the company was publishing nearly 60 books per year, all of which were distributed by Random House Inc. The Science Fiction and Fantasy Writers of America Inc. (SFWA) led a vocal group of writers into negotiations, which finally resulted in WotC agreeing to cover TSR's debts.

MORE ACQUISITIONS AND RELEASES

In addition to its TSR acquisition in 1997, WotC purchased Five Rings Publishing Group Inc., best known for its *Legends of the Five Rings* trading card game, the *Star Trek: The Next Generation* collectible dice game, and the *Dune: Eye of the Storm* trading card game. WotC also released two new games designed by Garfield. *Corporate Shuffle*, a card game based on the United Features Syndicate *Dilbert* comic strip by Scott Adams, was released in May 1997. The game, featuring full-color cartoons of Dilbert; his ignorant superiors; his clueless coworkers (including the delightful Ratbert and evil Human Resources Director Catbert); and his cynical dog, Dogbert, appealed to gamers of all ages. It satirizes the chaos and quirks of 1990s corporate life as players compete in a mad dash to climb the corporate ladder and assume the title of "Big Boss," with all its perks.

By this time the fervor for *Magic* cards had sparked criminal acts, with dealers reporting theft of the cards from their stores. *BRANDWEEK*'s article "The 'Gathering' Storm" highlighted a report that "four street toughs mugged a trio of gamers at knifepoint for their collection of *Magic* cards valued at nearly $2,400." Other stories surfaced about riots in Japan, precipitated by dwindling supply.

WotC insisted such stories were exaggerated, but the company took tighter rein of its image in June 1997 by launching its first national ad campaign. The campaign, which accounted for 62 percent of WotC's entire advertising budget, was supplemented by ads appearing in *Rolling Stone*, *Spin*, and *Swing*, among others, and demos appearing at state fairs, music tours, in-line skating and mountain biking events, and military bases.

Hoping to extend the popularity of its highly successful *Magic* game beyond a young, male demographic, WotC released in 1997 an introductory version of the game called *Portal*, which introduced new players to the same sophisticated game mechanics, portability, and professional artwork that made *Magic* an international success. *Portal Second Age* was released in 1998, followed by the advanced-level *Fifth Edition* game of *Magic* and expert-level products like the *Tempest* and *Stronghold* expansion decks.

WOTC GAME CENTER OPENS

Also in 1997, WotC opened the Wizards of the Coast Game Center in Seattle, the first gaming environment and entertainment center for adventure gaming enthusiasts in the world. The facility featured more than 250 games, including the *BattleTech* virtual reality center, with a dozen interactive simulator pods, 3,800 square feet of state-of-the-art video game and pinball machines, a retail store, and a tournament center for organized game playing. The center became a testing site for other top gaming manufacturers such as Atari and Williams/Bally and also the headquarters for the official *Magic: The Gathering* World Tournament, featuring more than $1 million in prize money. WotC soon opened a chain of retail gaming stores in shopping malls across the United States. The company also received a U.S. patent on the trading card game method of play.

WotC started 1998 with a bang, releasing four card games (*Twitch, Pivot, AlphaBlitz,* and *Go Wild!*) in February. Several months later came *C-23,* a science fiction trading card game with comic-style art by famed comic artist Jim Lee and story by comics writer Brandon Choi. The release was accompanied by a *C-23* comic book series. In May WotC announced an agreement with Viacom Consumer Products, the licensing division of Paramount Pictures, for the premiere issue of the relaunch of *Amazing Stories,* the world's oldest science fiction magazine. The publication was founded in 1926 by Hugo Gernsback, the father of modern science fiction.

FURTHER SUCCESS AND A BUYER

In early 1999 Wizards unveiled another trading card game that became a gigantic hit: *Pokemon,* an adaptation of a Japanese video game created by Nintendo. WotC caught the wave of *Pokemon*'s popularity, which included a successful television series, comic books, toys, and *anime* home videos based on the characters, and brought it to another level. Children bought pack after pack of cards to build their collection of battling monsters, hoping to collect all 150. For a brief period,

sales levels rivaled *Magic*'s peak popularity; shops could hardly keep supplies on their shelves. Nintendo USA later reclaimed the rights to distribute the Pokemon card game and released an updated version in 2003.

The addition of *Pokemon* to the Wizards catalog raised the company's profile and stature to the point that it attracted the interest of larger corporate players. In September 1999 the multinational toy maker Hasbro announced that it had acquired Wizards with an initial payment of $325 million. Later payments raised the total transaction cost to roughly $500 million. Despite becoming a Hasbro subsidiary (and absorbing Avalon Hill, another Hasbro acquisition), little changed in the company's operations and growth plan.

In 2000 WotC commanded an 85 percent share of the hobby game market, according to *Forbes* magazine. That year the company released the third edition of *Dungeons & Dragons,* still the world's most popular role-playing game. The new edition included a revised set of game mechanics known as the "d20 system" (named for the 20-sided die well known to *D&D* fanatics) as well as the concept of the "open game license" to allow third-party creative use of licensed intellectual property such as the basic game rules. The d20 system also supported other role-playing games, including the *Star Wars Role-playing Game,* which made its debut in 2000.

FANTASY IMPRINTS

Wizards has also achieved remarkable success as a book publisher. The company inherited its literary wing in the acquisition of TSR and continued producing book series and titles emanating from the fantasy worlds of *D&D* and other role-playing games in its catalog. The *Dragon-Lance* and *Forgotten Realms* series have proven the most potent: many published novels take place in these campaign settings and have achieved mainstream success. The genre's leading author, R. A. Salvatore, has written more than 20 *New York Times* best sellers and sold more than 15 million books under Wizards of the Coast imprints. The company's book publishing division earned in excess of $12 million in 2002, according to *Publishers Weekly,* as the *Harry Potter* phenomenon and the *Lord of the Rings* films invigorated sales of fantasy literature. The company launched a children's and young adult imprint, Mirrorstone, in 2004. In 2005 Random House signed on to distribute WotC's literary output.

In 2008 the company built upon two of its most successful product lines. In April it added to its expansive set of *Star Wars* role-playing games and miniatures (action figures used in the game play). The characters included in the set went beyond the familiar figures from the original movies to include those represented in the new *Clone Wars* film series, comic books, novels, and TV show. Two months later came *Dungeons & Dragons* fourth edition, complete with interactive features allowing dungeon masters to automate the creation of environments. An online "tabletop" interface allows remote players to participate. In January 2010 the company announced that it would be discontinuing its *Star Wars* licensing agreement, citing the economic downturn.

Daryl F. Mallett
Updated, Roger K. Smith

PRINCIPAL SUBSIDIARIES

Five Rings Publishing Group Inc.; TSR Inc.; Avalon Hill.

PRINCIPAL COMPETITORS

Steve Jackson Games; Bio Ware Corporation; Chaosium Inc.; White Wolf, Inc.; Iron Crown Enterprises.

FURTHER READING

Adler, Jerry, "Magic's Kingdom," *Newsweek*, May 26, 1997, p. 68.

Baker, M. Sharon, "Wizards' Magic Is Powerful, but Other Games Falter," *Puget Sound Business Journal*, December 15, 1995, p. 3.

Engle, Tim, "Try to Understand…the Magic Man," *Starmagazine*, March 15, 1998.

Miller, Brian, "Playing the Corporate Game," *South County Journal*, February 14, 1997, p. Bl.

Milliot, Jim, "Wizards of the Coast Whips Up Sales," *Publishers Weekly*, February 24, 2003, p. 10.

Rodkin, Dennis, "Card Sharks," *Entrepreneur*, October 1996, p. 164.

Rose, Cynthia, "It's Magic," *Seattle Times*, August 14, 1997, p. El.

Schoenberger, Chana R., "House of Cards," *Forbes*, March 20, 2000, p. 130.

"TSR to Be Sold," *Publishers Weekly*, April 14, 1997, p. 12.

Warner, Bernhard, "The 'Gathering' Storm," *BRANDWEEK*, February 17, 1997, p. 20.

World Fuel Services Corporation

9800 N.W. 41st Street, Suite 400
Miami, Florida 33178
U.S.A.
Telephone: (305) 428-8000
Fax: (305) 392-5600
Web site: http://www.wfscorp.com

Public Company
Incorporated: 1984 as International Recovery Corp.
Employees: 1,164
Sales: $18.51 billion (2008)
Stock Exchanges: New York
Ticker Symbol: INT
NAICS: 424720 Fuel Oil Merchant Wholesalers (Except Bulk Stations, Terminals)

■ ■ ■

World Fuel Services Corporation is the world's leading downstream marketer of fuel for the aviation, marine, and ground transportation sectors. World Fuel markets fuel products at more than 2,500 airports and seaports across the globe, while serving clients in 163 countries. In addition, World Fuel provides a range of financing and other services to its customers, including brokering, reselling, credit services, risk management, and logistical support. The company's aviation division specializes in servicing small and mid-sized carriers, while its marine division helps shipping companies obtain the vital fuel they need every day from the highly fragmented world oil market. At the same time, World Fuel's ground transportation segment offers fuel supply and management services in cities throughout the United States.

ORIGINS OF A FUEL PROVIDER: 1984–94

World Fuel began as a regional used oil recycling company with sales of $6 million a year. It was incorporated in Florida on July 20, 1984, as International Recovery Corporation. Ralph Weiser and Jerrold Blair were cofounders of the company, which was based in Miami Springs. Blair became president and chief operating officer in January 1985. After trading over-the-counter under the symbol IRPC, International Recovery began listing on the American Stock Exchange in June 1987 under the symbol INT.

In 1986 International Recovery acquired a three-year-old aviation fuel company, Advance Petroleum, Inc. (later doing business as World Fuel Services of Florida). Thus the company entered a promising new line of business, which was expanded into an international sales operation covering airports throughout the world. One of Advance Petroleum's founders, Philip S. Bradley, was made CEO of World Fuel's Aviation Fuel Services division.

International Recovery acquired another aviation fueling business, JCo Energy Partners, Ltd., in October 1989 and renamed it World Fuel Services, Inc. A new subsidiary, International Petroleum Corporation of Delaware, was formed in April 1993 upon the completion of an oil and water recycling plant in Wilmington. The business involved collecting waste oil, wastewater, and other petroleum-contaminated liquids from auto

World Fuel Services offers its customers an unprecedented level of service for the supply, quality control, logistical support and price risk management of fuel products and related services, under one roof. We pride ourselves in providing you with the highest quality of service, reliability, flexibility and stability. Our highly diverse team with years of experience in all areas of fuel management is ready to serve you around the world, 24 hours a day, 365 days a year.

shops, utilities, and other generators. The recycled products were sold to industrial and commercial customers.

MAKING WAVES IN THE MID- TO LATE 1990S

World Fuel entered the marine fuel business via the January 1995 acquisition of the Trans-Tec Services group of companies, based in New York, Costa Rica, the United Kingdom, and Singapore. Trans-Tec had been founded in 1985 by Paul H. Stebbins and Michael J. Kasbar; both became executives at World Fuel. The company changed its name from International Recovery Corp. to World Fuel Services Corporation in August 1995. World Fuel's revenues were about $500 million in fiscal 1996. The company had a presence at more than 1,100 airports and 1,000 seaports in more than 150 countries.

World Fuel acquired Baseops, a Houston-based corporate aviation services company, in January 1998 for $3.5 million in cash and stock. Baseops had been formed seven years earlier by former employees of Air Routing International, which itself had been formed by former employees of Universal Weather and Aviation. According to Jenalia Moreno in the *Houston Chronicle*, these companies were the industry's top three players, although Baseop's annual sales ($15.3 million in 1997) were dwarfed by those of the other two (estimated at more than $150 million for Universal and $100 million for Air Routing). These companies provided weather information and flight plans for pilots and performed a variety of services for private jet owners.

The operations of the Bunkerfuels companies, a substantial marine fuel brokerage, were acquired in April 1999 in a deal worth $8.5 million. Bunkerfuels had 1998 earnings of $1.7 million on revenues of $84

million. Based in Cranbury, New Jersey, it had been founded in 1978 by Robert Fitzgerald, chairman, who was retiring. Bunkerfuels was credited as the first to establish a worldwide presence to serve international fleets. It was to operate independently from Trans-Tec Services. Combined with the other holdings, the acquisition made World Fuel the world's largest marine fuels brokerage.

GROWING PAINS

Plans to form a subsidiary in Indonesia, PT World Fuel Services, were announced in April 1999. Trans-Tec, which had a 10 percent share of the world bunker market, was opening an office in Tokyo, its 11th.

In August 1999 company officials reported an unusual act of piracy. A shipment of fuel to the Nigerian offshore oil industry did not reach its intended customers. World Fuel recorded a $3.3 million charge as a result and filed a claim with its insurance company. This was settled for $1 million in 2001. Earlier in 1999, the company had taken a $2.2 million charge related to bad debts, particularly in Ecuador.

In spite of the growth, World Fuel executives perceived the company's stock to be undervalued. After hitting $22 per share earlier in the year, in April the stock was trading at slightly more than $11. One of the main difficulties was a lack of similar companies available for comparison by analysts. World Fuel weathered a stockholders' class-action lawsuit that was dismissed in December 2000.

EXITING OIL RECYCLING IN 2000

In February 2000 World Fuel exited the used-oil recycling business by divesting its International Petroleum Corporation subsidiaries to the EarthCare Company of Dallas. Net income fell by a third to $9.6 million in fiscal 2000 on sales of $1.2 billion, up from 1999's $720 million.

In December 2000 World Fuel entered an aviation fuel marketing joint venture called PAFCO (formerly Page Avjet Fuel Corporation) with Signature Flight Support Services Corporation. Signature, described as the world's largest flight support operator and distribution network for business and commercial aviation services, was a subsidiary of the BBA Group.

Company president Jerrold Blair was named chairman and CEO in August 2000 upon the retirement of fellow cofounder Ralph R. Weiser. In the following few months, the company cut its staff by nearly 40 percent as part of a bid to make its financial performance less unpredictable.

KEY DATES

1984: International Recovery Corporation is founded.
1986: The company enters the aviation fuel business with purchase of Advance Petroleum.
1989: JCo Energy Partners is acquired; company is renamed World Fuel Services, Inc.
1995: World Fuel enters the marine fuel business with acquisition of Trans-Tec Services.
1998: World Fuel acquires Baseops International, provider of ancillary aviation services.
2001: PAFCO joint venture increases World Fuel's involvement in corporate aviation; World Fuel acquires Dutch fuel firm Oil Shipping Group.
2004: World Fuel Services acquires British fuel supplier Tramp Holdings.
2007: World Fuel acquires business jet fuel supplier AVCARD for $55 million.

President and COO Paul Stebbins, a cofounder of Trans-Tec (along with Michael J. Kasbar, CEO of the Marine Fuel Services division since 1995), explained the business to John T. Fakler in the *South Florida Business Journal*. The world fuel market, they contended, was highly fragmented and unpredictable. World Fuel provided volume buying power, and its specialized staff tracked the many variables of market dynamics.

GREAT RESULTS IN 2001

Total revenues increased 27 percent to $1.5 billion for the fiscal year ending March 31, 2001. Net income rose 10 percent to $10.6 million. A rise in world fuel prices in the winter of 2000–01 helped send belt-tightening customers to the firm. World Fuel also was emphasizing the logistics side of the business, rather than the credit side, as it had in the past.

In March 2001 World Fuel acquired the software company TransportEdge as it worked to move its business online. Two marine fuel brokerage companies, Norway-based Norse Bunker A.S. and Marine Energy of Dubai, also were acquired during the fiscal year. Both were located in vitally important seafaring areas.

World Fuel launched a new fuel management division in spring 2001 aimed at helping airlines manage their exposure to variations in jet fuel prices. This move promised to broaden the company's customer base to include larger commercial and corporate accounts.

A decline in passenger airline traffic followed the terrorist attacks on the United States on September 11, 2001, yet cargo traffic, charters, and military support flights all posted an increase. One of World Fuel's largest customers was the U.S. government. Analysts expected the increasing trend toward fractional ownership of business jets to continue, to the benefit of World Fuel.

RAPID GROWTH IN THE NEW CENTURY

Over the course of the next several years, World Fuel embarked on an ambitious acquisition strategy, aimed at both increasing the company's marketing capacity and broadening its global reach. In December 2001 the company purchased the Oil Shipping Group, a major fuel supplier based in Rotterdam, Netherlands. In addition to giving World Fuel a strategic position in the European marine fuel market, the acquisition expanded the company's presence in Asia, where Oil Shipping had branches in Hong Kong and Singapore. This expansion of its business volume, coupled with a rise in marine fuel prices, helped drive up the company's revenues during the first half of 2002. For the first two quarters of the year, World Fuel enjoyed sales of $969.5 million, compared with $687.8 million for the same period in 2001.

World Fuel continued to achieve brisk sales in 2003, primarily due to steep rises in global fuel prices. The company's marine fuel segment saw revenues of $397 million in the year's first quarter, an increase of 55 percent over the first quarter of 2002. However, the volume of the company's sales of marine fuel actually fell 8 percent during this period. World Fuel's aviation fuel sales, on the other hand, more than doubled between 2002 and 2003, with first quarter revenues rising from $94 million to $261 million. By late 2003 the company provided fuel marketing services at more than 1,100 locations worldwide.

World Fuel concluded another key acquisition in April 2004, when it purchased Tramp Holdings, owner of British bunker firm Tramp Oil. The move increased the company's sales capacity by 6 million tons per year, while giving it offices in 10 new countries across the globe. With the merger, World Fuel became the leading independent fuel provider in the world. Carly Fields and Martyn Wingrove reported in the April 6, 2004, edition of *Lloyd's List* that the acquisition signaled World Fuel's aim to achieve "total domination of the independent bunkers market." For the first three quarters of 2004, the company's revenues were $3.87 billion, compared with $1.96 billion for the same period the previous year.

In 2007 World Fuel acquired AVCARD, a major provider of fuel for business jets. That same year, the company hired Ira Birns, longtime treasurer of Arrow Electronics, as its new chief financial officer. From the beginning, Birns set out to emphasize a new focus on fiscal discipline at the company. Birns's experience proved particularly important in late 2008 as the world sank into a recession. To maintain its own financial health, World Fuel Services began to impose a stricter payment policy on its clients. Under Birns's guidance, the company began to renegotiate its credit terms in an effort to eliminate long delays in repayment. In some instances, World Fuels cut the amount of allowable time between service and payment by 40 percent. The company also began to pay closer attention to the credit ratings of its customers, with the aim of eliminating clients at risk of becoming insolvent.

At first, some company insiders feared that the tighter credit restrictions would cause some longstanding customers to sever their ties with World Fuel. As the financial crisis worsened, however, and fewer corporations were able to extend any sort of credit to their customers, World Fuel's new regulations seemed like a relatively minor inconvenience. In the end, the company lost only one regular customer as a result of the revised credit terms. Meanwhile, World Fuel's revenues soared during the later part of the decade, with total sales exceeding $18.5 billion in 2008. With its market dominance growing every year, World Fuel had even more reason to feel confident about its financial future.

Frederick C. Ingram
Updated, Stephen Meyer

PRINCIPAL SUBSIDIARIES

Advance Petroleum, Inc.; Baseops International, Inc.; Casa Petro S.R.L. (Costa Rica); Kropp Holdings, Inc.; World Fuel Services Canada, Inc.; World Fuel Services Company, Inc.; World Fuel Services Corporate Aviation Support Services, Inc.; World Fuel Services, Inc.

PRINCIPAL DIVISIONS

Aviation; Ground; Marine.

PRINCIPAL COMPETITORS

BBA Aviation plc (UK); Mercury Air Group, Inc.; SMF Energy Corporation; Sun Coast Resources Inc.

FURTHER READING

Alderstein, David, "World Fuel Services Names CEO," *South Florida Business Journal*, August 1, 2000.

Cordle, Ina Paiva, "Miami-based Fuel Reseller Blames Fraud, Theft for $3.3 Million Charge," *Miami Herald*, August 27, 1999.

Fakler, John T., "World Fuel Stoked by Energy Pinch," *South Florida Business Journal*, February 23, 2001.

Fields, Carly, and Martyn Wingrove, "World Fuel Shares Leap on Tramp Purchase: Tramp Oil Buy Will Supply Vital Foothold in Europe and Asia," *Lloyd's List*, April 6, 2004, p. 3.

Flynn, Matthew, "Bunker Giant Bucks the Trend by Putting Down Tokyo Roots," *Lloyd's List*, July 17, 1999, p. 6.

Johnson, Sarah, "Leadership in Finance: World Fuel's Ira Birns," CFO.com, May 26, 2009, http://www.cfo.com/article.cfm/13724762.

Martinez, Matthew, "World Spans Globe for Options," *Mergers & Acquisitions Report*, May 10, 1999, p. 4.

McLaughlin, John, "World Fuel Looks to Realise Value," *Lloyd's List*, April 30, 1999, p. 1.

———, "World Fuel Snaps Up Oil Shipping," *Lloyd's List*, December 20, 2001, p. 1.

Moreno, Jenalia, "Success in the Air; Corporate Aviation Takes Flight; Industry Booms with Competition, Expanded Services," *Houston Chronicle*, March 7, 1998, p. 1.

Osier, David, "World Fuel in Major Bunker Buy," *Lloyd's List*, March 24, 1999, p. 1.

Pachymuthu, Luke, "US' World Fuel Services Buys Bunker Player Tramp Oil for $83-Mil," *Platts Oilgram Price Report*, April 6, 2004, p. 11.

Smith, Neville, "World Fuel Services Profits Rise," *Lloyd's List*, August 11, 2005, p. 3.

Wingrove, Martin, "World Fuel Scoops Global Market with Tramp Holdings," *Lloyd's List*, April 5, 2004, p. 1.

"World Fuel Acquires Norse Bunker," *South Florida Business Journal*, February 15, 2001.

"World Fuel Hails Dismissal of Lawsuit," *South Florida Business Journal*, December 15, 2000.

"World Fuel Services to Form Joint Venture with Signature Flight Support," *South Florida Business Journal*, December 26, 2000.

"World Fuel Settles Suit over Loss of Oil Shipments," *Broward Daily Business Review*, July 11, 2001, p. A3.

WPP

WPP Group plc

---

6 Ely Street
Dublin, 2
Ireland
Telephone: (+353) 1669 0333
Fax: (+353) 1669 0334
Web site: http://www.wpp.com

Public Company
Incorporated: 1971 as Wire & Plastic Products Ltd.
Employees: 112,000
Sales: £7.48 billion ($13.88 billion) (2008)
Gross Billings: £36.93 billion ($68.51 billion) (2008)
Stock Exchanges: London NASDAQ
Ticker Symbol: WPP (London) WPPGY (NASDAQ)
NAICS: 541613 Marketing Consulting Services; 541810
  Advertising Agencies; 541820 Public Relations
  Agencies

■ ■ ■

WPP Group plc operates as one of the largest communications services companies in the world. The company is the creation of Sir Martin Sorrell, a brash, charismatic entrepreneur who transformed a small manufacturing firm into a global advertising and marketing giant. A diversified, multinational corporation, WPP offers communications services to some of the world's leading corporations. Among WPP's major clients are the Ford Motor Company, IBM, Dell Inc., and HSBC Holdings plc. The company's subsidiaries include the international media advertising giants JWT Group Inc., Ogilvy & Mather, Young & Rubicam, and

the Grey Group. Also included are the public relations firm Hill and Knowlton Inc. and information and consultancy firm the Kantar Group. The group's companies provide services in advertising, media investment management, information and consultancy, public relations and public affairs, branding and identity, and specialist communications.

THE BIRTH OF AN ADVERTISING EMPIRE: 1980–89

WPP is largely the creation of English businessman Martin Sorrell. Armed with an economics degree from Cambridge and an M.B.A. from Harvard, he made his name as financial director of the advertising giant Saatchi & Saatchi plc, joining the firm in 1977 and playing a key role in its growth through acquisitions. In 1986 Sorrell set out to build his own advertising empire. In need of a quoted company as a nucleus for acquisitions, he and a stockbroker friend had already bought a 27 percent stake in Wire and Plastics Products plc in 1985. Having gone public in 1971, the U.K. firm was the holding company for a group of wire and plastic manufacturing businesses whose main products were shopping baskets and other domestic wire products. Sorrell became chief executive, changed the name of the company to WPP Group plc, and with the support of the other directors began adding marketing services to its activities.

In 1986 WPP made 11 acquisitions in this field, including design houses, incentive specialists, sales promotion consultants, and an audio-visual company. Sorrell's experience with Saatchi & Saatchi plc had

COMPANY PERSPECTIVES

Our mission: To develop and manage talent; to apply that talent, throughout the world, for the benefit of clients; to do so in partnership; to do so with profit.

taught him to be adept at publicizing his firm in the business press. He also followed his former company's acquisition technique, buying companies on a five-year "earn-out" basis. In this way, the cost of the buyout is spread over a period of years, and the price finally paid for the company depends on how well the management increases its pre-takeover profits.

The Saatchi brothers, with whom Sorrell was in close association, had taken a 10 percent stake in WPP. The price of WPP's shares was boosted, increasing its attractiveness as takeover currency. Investment bankers subsequently began suggesting takeover candidates to Sorrell.

In the first half of 1987, WPP turned its attention to the United States and acquired several companies there. Still purchasing marketing services companies, Sorrell professed to be uninterested in buying conventional advertising agencies at that time. In June 1987, however, WPP launched a bid for the JWT Group Inc., a media advertising agency in financial trouble in the mid-1980s. Although it had posted a loss in the first quarter of 1987 and takeover rumors were rife, some analysts were surprised to find the JWT Group bought out by a British company that had never owned a mainstream advertising agency. The two companies agreed to terms within two weeks, and the whole JWT Group, including the public relations giant Hill & Knowlton Inc. and several satellite companies, became part of WPP.

WPP had to borrow part of the $566 million cost of this purchase. JWT's profit margin had dropped to 4 percent. However, with a few management changes and tough new profit targets, and with overstaffing and extravagant spending curbed, within three years both the JWT Group Inc. and Hill & Knowlton Inc. had raised their profit margins to 10 percent. In addition to increasing revenue, a large property windfall helped to cover the purchase cost. A sale and lease-back arrangement was organized with JWT's Tokyo office, which, when found to be worth over £100 million, was promptly sold along with other valuable properties.

A SERIES OF KEY ACQUISITIONS: 1989–96

Despite its borrowings, WPP's profits rose steeply, from £1.7 million pre-tax in 1986 to £40.3 million in 1988. Sorrell's reputation as a financial wizard grew as well, and he continued to make other acquisitions. His biggest coup came in 1989, when he added the Ogilvy Group to his empire. Like the JWT Group, it was at the time an international network of agencies and satellite companies about equal in size to the WPP Group. Interpublic Group Inc. also put in a bid for Ogilvy, but after a brief tussle it fell to WPP for $864 million. David Ogilvy, the Ogilvy Group's founder, was persuaded to become chairman of WPP to help reassure Ogilvy clients.

WPP was now larger than Saatchi & Saatchi, the largest advertising group of the time. However, the financing of its new purchases involved the company in preference shares and further large borrowings. Sorrell was convinced that he could pay these debts from increasing profits, but the task proved harder than it had with JWT because the Ogilvy group's margins were already averaging 8 percent.

WPP eventually overtook Saatchi & Saatchi in worldwide billings, however, and its pre-tax profits hit new peaks in 1989 (£75 million) and 1990 (£90 million). Its earnings per share also rose in both years. It was only in the recession of the last quarter of 1990 that the company was forced to issue a warning of lower profits in 1991. Investors suddenly scrambled to get out, and within a week WPP's shares lost two-thirds of their value.

In 1991 the company suspended all dividend payments and was forced to renegotiate its debts. Not helped by the effects of the Persian Gulf War and the continuing economic recession, the group's billings fell for the first time, and by the end of the year its profits had fallen by 38 percent before taxes. In 1992 WPP refinanced again, and in return the banks took more of the equity but had limited voting rights. While Martin Sorrell remained chief executive of the firm, a new chairman was appointed.

After spending a few years restructuring, WPP gradually began to expand its operations. In 1992 the firm launched CommonHealth, a virtual health care marketing communications network. Three years later the Kantar Group was created to act as a holding company for the company's research businesses. Then, in 1996, WPP purchased a stake in Media Technology Ventures, a venture capital partnership designed to invest in emerging technology firms.

```
┌─────────────────────────────────────────────┐
│                                               │
│               KEY DATES                       │
│                  ■                            │
│ ───────────────────────────────────────────  │
│                                               │
│  1971:  Wire & Plastics Products is incorpo-  │
│         rated and goes public.                │
│  1985:  Martin Sorrell and a stockbroker      │
│         friend purchase a 27 percent stake    │
│         in Wire and Plastics.                 │
│  1986:  Sorrell is named chief executive and  │
│         changes the name of the company to    │
│         WPP Group plc.                        │
│  1987:  WPP acquires the JWT Group.           │
│  1989:  The company purchases the Ogilvy      │
│         Group and becomes the largest         │
│         advertising group in the world.       │
│  1992:  CommonHealth, a virtual healthcare    │
│         marketing network, is launched.       │
│  1995:  The Kantar Group is created to act    │
│         as a holding company for the firm's   │
│         research businesses.                  │
│  1997:  The group begins a major expansion    │
│         effort.                               │
│  2007:  WPP forges advertising and marketing  │
│         agreement with Dell Computers.        │
│  2008:  WPP acquires Taylor Nelson Sofres.    │
│                                               │
└─────────────────────────────────────────────┘
```

RAPID GROWTH: FROM THE LATE NINETIES INTO THE 21ST CENTURY

Because of its financial troubles of the early 1990s, WPP had put its growth strategy on the back burner. The group's financial position improved, however, and beginning in the late 1990s the group made a series of key purchases, launched new start-ups, and invested in media ventures. In 1997 WPP purchased a stake in Peapod (an online shopping service based in the United States), Syzygy (a digital media firm based in London), and HyperParallel (a San Francisco-based data mining firm). The company also invested in media firms in Latin America, Singapore, and Germany. In 1998 the firm acquired three high-technology marketing consulting concerns along with U.S.-based Management Ventures Inc., the Canada-based marketing research firm Goldfarb Consultants, Conway/Milliken, a research company based in Chicago, the U.S.-based Alexander Communications, a technology public relations concern, and Asatsu-DK Inc., the third-largest advertising agency in Japan.

By this time WPP had also launched MindShare, a new company involved in media planning, buying, and research in Europe and Asia. The firm also created Sava-

tar, a start-up focused on new technology marketing in the United States. During 1998 profits rose by nearly 20 percent, and non-media advertising, including Internet and Internet-related billings, accounted for 50 percent of the group's revenue for the first time in its history. WPP's frantic expansion pace continued in 1999 as the group made further investments in advertising communications-related firms and also acquired several companies, including Steve Perry Consultants, Shire Hall Group, Perspectives, the Brand Union, Blanc and Otus, Dazai Advertising, and P. Four.

WPP entered the new millennium focused on growth. While the group made a slew of acquisitions during 2000, its most publicized purchase of the year was that of Young & Rubicam Inc., a U.S. marketing concern. Sorrell made the firm's initial offer in January, which was followed by several months of hostile negotiations. The $4.7 billion transaction was finally completed in September. It was the largest such deal in the advertising industry at the time and created the world's leading marketing services group. That year, operating profits grew by 43 percent over the previous year to $631 million.

Sir Martin Sorrell, who had been knighted in 2000, found himself involved in another attention-grabbing deal in 2001 when he made a bid for the Tempus Group plc, a media buying concern. By this time, WPP had amassed a 22 percent stake in the firm. Tempus, however, was not keen on a WPP takeover. Its chairman, Chris Ingram, had made public the fact that he would never work for Sorrell, and Tempus looked to advertising conglomerate Havas to make a white knight bid. When Havas made its offer, WPP responded with a higher bid of $630 million.

The advertising industry as a whole suffered as the terrorist attacks against the United States on September 11, 2001, sent the U.S. economy into a deeper decline. As a result of the weakening market conditions, Havas allowed its bid to expire, leaving WPP the sole bidder. Sorrell tried to back out of the deal, but his efforts were denied by the U.K. Takeover Panel. The deal was completed in late 2001.

WPP characterized 2001 as a brutal year in its annual report. The year 2001 was challenging for the industry in general, as advertising revenues fell 5 percent for the year. Nevertheless, the company continued to report significant profits despite the downturn in the industry. Sales increased by nearly 50 percent over 2000 figures, and pre-tax profits climbed by 12 percent. By this time, marketing services accounted for just over half of the group's revenues, while countries outside of the United States secured 56 percent of sales.

WPP's long-term goal was to become the world's most successful and preferred provider of communications services to multinational and local companies. With Sorrell at the helm, the group was focused on overcoming hardships related to economic challenges, integrating both its Young & Rubicam and Tempus purchases, and increasing its marketing services business to 65 percent of total revenues.

EXPANDING INTO EMERGING MARKETS: 2002 AND BEYOND

WPP's earnings took a hit during the early part of 2002, as the general economic downturn continued to erode advertising budgets throughout the business world. Revenues for the first half of the year dipped to £1.96 billion ($2.83 billion), a 2 percent decline from the same period in 2001. The company's net earnings fell even more precipitously over this span, with pre-tax profits dropping to £210.38 million ($303.8 million), a decrease of 17 percent.

At the time, WPP CEO Martin Sorrell saw the industry's struggles as part of a general shift in the nature of advertising and marketing in the digital age. In Sorrel's view, the rise of the Internet was providing consumers with an unprecedented level of knowledge about a wide range of products and services. In response to this development, Sorrel argued, companies like WPP needed to devote more attention to understanding the specific needs and desires of their target audiences. The WPP chief told Bernice Harrison in the *Irish Times* on March 22, 2002, "Sellers of products and services need the clearest possible understanding of consumer behaviour and the ability to differentiate broadly similar products from each other by means of their communications."

In spite of this general downturn, WPP remained an industry leader during the early part of the decade. In April 2003 the company's U.S. subsidiary Young & Rubicam landed a coveted advertising account with the Burger King fast food chain, in a deal worth £230 million ($360 million). Two months later WPP reached an agreement to purchase the smaller advertising firm Cordiant Communications, formerly known as Saatchi & Saatchi, the advertising giant where Sorrel had gotten his start. The total value of the transaction was estimated to be £260 million ($409.5 million), of which £250 million ($393.75 million) represented Cordiant's outstanding debt. According to industry analysts, the deal gave WPP an important foothold in the Asian market, where Cordiant had achieved some recent success. Perhaps more significantly, the purchase helped WPP surpass rival Interpublic to become the second-largest advertising and marketing firm in the world.

Entering the middle of the decade, WPP began to seek new ways to expand its presence in geographical areas with a high potential for growth. In early 2004 WPP derived roughly 45 percent of its total revenues from the United States. Europe accounted for another 35 percent of sales, while Asia and the Pacific Rim accounted for 20 percent. With earnings potential in the U.S. and European markets beginning to stagnate, however, WPP was determined to create more of a balance between these three core regions. To pursue this goal, the company began to devote more resources to generating higher business volume in emerging markets, particularly in China and India.

Throughout this period, WPP continued to forge important strategic partnerships with new clients. The company landed one of its largest accounts in May 2004, when banking giant HSBC hired WPP to manage its global marketing campaign. The deal was particularly noteworthy for its scope. While companies typically hired advertising and marketing firms to handle specific areas of their business, HSBC was entrusting WPP with all of its marketing needs. While some analysts remained skeptical about WPP's ability to coordinate its various global divisions to produce a consistent, integrated message for HSBC, others wondered if the company's "network" approach might signal a shift in the industry as a whole. Martin Sorrell remained unwilling to speculate on the deal's broader implications. Speaking to Emiko Terazono for the *Financial Times* on May 18, 2004, Sorrell was quoted as saying, "Whether this is a trend or not, we will have to see over time."

In September 2004 WPP announced another major acquisition, purchasing Grey Global Group, the world's seventh-leading advertising firm, for £848.2 million ($1.52 billion). The deal put WPP in a position to rival Omnicom as the largest advertising and marketing company in the world. In 2003 WPP and Grey Global had combined revenues of £4.96 billion ($8.1 billion), barely trailing Omnicom's sales of £5.26 billion ($8.6 billion) for the same year. By March 2005 WPP had achieved a market value of £7.7 billion ($14.71 billion).

WPP continued to enjoy strong earnings throughout 2005. The company's brisk sales were fueled in large part by rapid growth in Asia, the Middle East, and Latin America, where revenues rose 27 percent during the first half of the year. India and China were particularly strong areas for WPP, especially toward the end of the year, when the Chinese relaxed a number of trade restrictions, enabling foreign companies to launch business operations in the country without first partnering with a domestic corporation. By April 2006 China accounted for 4 percent of the company's total revenues, while India accounted for 3 percent.

Toward the end of the decade WPP also began to seek ways to expand its presence in the online advertising and marketing segment. In May 2007 the company acquired U.S. Internet advertising firm 24/7 Media, in a deal worth £328 million ($649 million). In December of that year WPP added computer firm Dell Inc. to its list of prominent clients, in what was widely considered to be one of the industry's biggest contracts of the year. The company's revenues remained strong throughout the first half of 2008, driven largely by the strength of its business in China, where sales grew 17 percent for the period.

In October 2008, as the world sank into a recession, WPP moved its corporate headquarters from London to Dublin, Ireland. The change was part of a larger trend among English corporations, which were drawn to Ireland by the nation's generous tax breaks. While WPP's decision to relocate promised to help it streamline costs during the economic downturn, many analysts worried that it would ultimately have a negative impact on the company's public image. Even with its acquisition of market research firm Taylor Nelson Sofres in late 2008, which drove the company's revenues past those of rival Omnicom for the year, WPP still faced formidable challenges. With the firm's profits falling sharply in the first half of 2009, maintaining the strength of the WPP brand became more crucial than ever.

John Swan
Updated, Christina M. Stansell; Stephen Meyer

PRINCIPAL SUBSIDIARIES

24/7 Real Media (USA); A. Eicoff & Company (USA); Alliance Agency (USA); Bates 141 (Hong Kong); BDG McColl (UK); Blanc & Otus (USA); BLUE Interactive Marketing Pte. Ltd. (Singapore); Bridge Worldwide (USA); Brouillard Communications, Inc. (USA); Buchanan Communications (UK); Catalyst Online (USA); Clarion Communications (UK); Coley Porter Bell (UK); CommonHealth (USA); DELIVER (USA); The Dewey Square Group (USA); Dialogue 141 (UK); Everystone (UK); EWA Bespoke Communications (UK); Feinstein Kean Healthcare (USA); Finsbury Limited (UK); The Forward Group (UK); The Geppetto Group (USA); Grey Group (USA); GroupM (USA); GT London Ltd. (UK); Headcount Worldwide Field Marketing Ltd (UK); Hill & Knowlton, Inc. (USA); JWT (USA); the Kantar Group (USA); Mando Corporation Limited (UK); Ogilvy & Mather Worldwide, Inc. (USA); Ohal (UK); Pace Advertising (USA); PRISM (UK); Public Strategies, Inc. (USA); Quasar Media Private Limited (India); Santo (Argentina); Soho Square (USA); Spafax (UK); Tapsa (Spain); Timmons & Company (USA); The United Network (UK); Warwicks UK Ltd.; Young & Rubicam Inc. (USA).

PRINCIPAL COMPETITORS

Havas S.A.; The Interpublic Group of Companies Inc.; Omincom Group Inc.; Publicis Groupe S.A.

FURTHER READING

Andrews, Amanda, "WPP's Chief Predicts a Bumpy Ride," *Times* (London), October 20, 2007, p. 59.

Benady, Alex, "Cordiant Captured by an Aggressive Dealmaker with an Eye for a Bargain," *Financial Times*, June 21, 2003, p. 3.

Boyle, Catherine, "Emerging Markets Help WPP to Take Shelter from the Storm," *Times* (London), August 23, 2008, p. 61.

Brady, Diane, "Now, WPP and Y&R Have to Kiss, Make Up—and Get to Work," *Business Week*, May 12, 2000.

Clark, Nick, "Sorrell Bemoans WPP's 47% Fall in Profit; We Got Our Sums Wrong, Admits Boss of World's No 3 Advertising Agency," *Independent* (London), August 27, 2009, p. 38.

Davey, Jenny, "WPP Saw Promise of the East and Is Reaping the Rewards," *Times* (London), April 22, 2006, p. 75.

Fass, Allison, "Profit Down at WPP Group, and Chief Is Not Optimistic," *New York Times*, August 21, 2002, p. 1.

Fildes, Nick, "WPP Lands $4.5bn Deal to Revitalise Dell's Image," *Independent* (London), December 4, 2007, p. 38.

Grande, Carlos, "Buying 24/7 Real Media Is Significant Step Change for WPP," *Financial Times*, May 19, 2007, p. 17.

Harrison, Bernice, "Tribal Leader Shuns Ad Man Tag in Favour of Businessman," *Irish Times*, March 22, 2002, p. 54.

Hasell, Nick, "Account Win Fuels Advance for WPP," *Times* (London), April 16, 2003, p. 26.

Houlder, Vanessa, "Tax Factor Beats Patriotism in WPP Relocation; Companies with 'Brass Plate' Headquarters Risk PR Damage," *Financial Times*, October 6, 2008, p. 16.

Kapner, Suzanne, "A Master Deal Maker Got More Than He Bargained For," *New York Times*, November 20, 2001, p. C8.

Katz, Richard, "WPP Group Merges for Clout," *MediaWeek*, April 7, 1997, p. 6.

McCarthy, Michael, "WPP Is in a Deal-Making Mood," *AdWeek*, September 15, 1997, p. 3.

McGregor, Richard, "Sorrell Sees a Market Ripe for Expansion: Head of WPP Advertising Group Says Any Slowdown in Chinese Market Could Lead to Further Acquisitions," *Financial Times*, June 23, 2004, p. 10.

McMains, Andrew, "WPP Takes Reins of Y&R," *AdWeek*, October 9, 2000, p. 5.

O'Leary, Noreen, "WPP's Martin Sorrell," *AdWeek*, May 22, 2000, p. 26.

Piggott, Stanley, *OBM, A Celebration: 125 Years in Advertising.* London: Ogilvy Benson & Mather, 1975.

Snoddy, Raymond, "WPP Brings Local Touch to Global Operations," *Times* (London), January 12, 2004, p. 22.

Terazono, Emiko, "A Slippery Slope, or Nirvana? HSBC's Decision to Hand Its Entire Global Business to WPP Has Left the World—and Sir Martin Sorrell—Watching," *Financial Times*, May 18, 2004, p. 2.

Timmons, Heather, and Eric Pfanner, "WPP Is on Track to Becoming the World's Second-largest Agency in a Deal to Take Over Grey Global," *New York Times*, September 14, 2004, p. C10.

"Uneasy Lies the Head," *The Economist*, February 24, 2001, p. 9.

Wentz, Laurel, and Richard Linnett, "Tempus Tempest," *Advertising Age*, November 5, 2001, p. 3.

"WPP Group's Pre-Tax Profit Jump 20 Percent," *Campaign*, February 19 1999, p. 2.

Cumulative Index to Companies

After Hours Formalwear Inc., 60 3–5

Aftermarket Technology Corp., 83 16–19

AG Barr plc, 64 9–12

Ag-Chem Equipment Company, Inc., 17 9–11 *see also* AGCO Corp.

Ag Services of America, Inc., 59 11–13

Aga Foodservice Group PLC, 73 18–20

AGCO Corp., 13 16–18; 67 6–10 (upd.)

Agence France-Presse, 34 11–14

Agere Systems Inc., 61 17–19

Agfa Gevaert Group N.V., 59 14–16

Aggregate Industries plc, 36 20–22

Aggreko Plc, 45 10–13

Agilent Technologies Inc., 38 20–23; 93 28–32 (upd.)

Agilysys Inc., 76 7–11 (upd.)

Agland, Inc., 110 6–9

Agnico-Eagle Mines Limited, 71 11–14

Agora S.A. Group, 77 5–8

AGRANA *see* Südzucker AG.

Agri Beef Company, 81 5–9

Agria Corporation, 101 9–13

Agrigenetics, Inc. *see* Mycogen Corp.

Agrium Inc., 73 21–23

AgustaWestland N.V., 75 18–20

Agway, Inc., 7 17–18; 21 17–19 (upd.) *see also* Cargill Inc.

AHL Services, Inc., 27 20–23

Ahlstrom Corporation, 53 22–25

Ahmanson *see* H.F. Ahmanson & Co.

AHMSA *see* Altos Hornos de México, S.A. de C.V.

Ahold *see* Koninklijke Ahold NV.

AHP *see* American Home Products Corp.

AICPA *see* The American Institute of Certified Public Accountants.

AIG *see* American International Group, Inc.

AIMCO *see* Apartment Investment and Management Co.

Ainsworth Lumber Co. Ltd., 99 18–22

Air & Water Technologies Corporation, 6 441–42 *see also* Aqua Alliance Inc.

Air Berlin GmbH & Co. Luftverkehrs KG, 71 15–17

Air Canada, 6 60–62; 23 9–12 (upd.); 59 17–22 (upd.)

Air China Limited, 46 9–11; 108 15–19 (upd.)

Air Express International Corporation, 13 19–20

Air France–KLM, 108 20–29 (upd.)

Air-India Limited, 6 63–64; 27 24–26 (upd.)

Air Jamaica Limited, 54 3–6

Air Liquide *see* L'Air Liquide SA.

Air Mauritius Ltd., 63 17–19

Air Methods Corporation, 53 26–29

Air Midwest, Inc. *see* Mesa Air Group, Inc.

Air New Zealand Limited, 14 10–12; 38 24–27 (upd.)

Air Pacific Ltd., 70 7–9

Air Partner PLC, 93 33–36

Air Products and Chemicals, Inc., I 297–99; 10 31–33 (upd.); 74 6–9 (upd.)

Air Sahara Limited, 65 14–16

Air T, Inc., 86 6–9

Air Wisconsin Airlines Corporation, 55 10–12

Air Zimbabwe (Private) Limited, 91 5–8

AirAsia Berhad, 93 37–40

Airborne Freight Corporation, 6 345–47; 34 15–18 (upd.) *see also* DHL Worldwide Network S.A./N.V.

Airborne Systems Group, 89 39–42

AirBoss of America Corporation, 108 30–34

Airbus Industrie *see* G.I.E. Airbus Industrie.

Airgas, Inc., 54 7–10

Airguard Industries, Inc. *see* CLARCOR Inc.

Airlink Pty Ltd *see* Qantas Airways Ltd.

Airstream *see* Thor Industries, Inc.

AirTouch Communications, 11 10–12 *see also* Vodafone Group PLC.

Airtours Plc, 27 27–29, 90, 92

AirTran Holdings, Inc., 22 21–23

Aisin Seiki Co., Ltd., III 415–16; 48 3–5 (upd.)

Aitchison & Colegrave *see* Bradford & Bingley PLC.

Aiwa Co., Ltd., 30 18–20

Ajegroup S.A, 92 1–4

Ajinomoto Co., Inc., II 463–64; 28 9–11 (upd.); 108 35–39 (upd.)

AK Steel Holding Corporation, 19 8–9; 41 3–6 (upd.)

Akamai Technologies, Inc., 71 18–21

Akbank TAS, 79 18–21

Akeena Solar, Inc., 103 6–10

Akerys S.A., 90 17–20

AKG Acoustics GmbH, 62 3–6

Akin, Gump, Strauss, Hauer & Feld, L.L.P., 33 23–25

Akorn, Inc., 32 22–24

Akro-Mills Inc. *see* Myers Industries, Inc.

Aktiebolaget SKF, III 622–25; 38 28–33 (upd.); 89 401–09 (upd.)

Akzo Nobel N.V., 13 21–23; 41 7–10 (upd.); 112 1–6 (upd.)

Al Habtoor Group L.L.C., 87 9–12

Al-Tawfeek Co. For Investment Funds Ltd. *see* Dallah Albaraka Group.

Alabama Farmers Cooperative, Inc., 63 20–22

Alabama National BanCorporation, 75 21–23

Aladdin Knowledge Systems Ltd., 101 14–17

Alain Afflelou SA, 53 30–32

Alain Manoukian *see* Groupe Alain Manoukian.

Alamo Group Inc., 32 25–28

Alamo Rent A Car, 6 348–50; 24 9–12 (upd.); 84 5–11 (upd.)

ALARIS Medical Systems, Inc., 65 17–20

Alascom, Inc. *see* AT&T Corp.

Alaska Air Group, Inc., 6 65–67; 29 11–14 (upd.)

Alaska Communications Systems Group, Inc., 89 43–46

Alaska Railroad Corporation, 60 6–9

Alba-Waldensian, Inc., 30 21–23 *see also* E.I. du Pont de Nemours and Co.

Albany International Corporation, 8 12–14; 51 11–14 (upd.)

Albany Molecular Research, Inc., 77 9–12

Albaugh, Inc., 105 9–12

Albemarle Corporation, 59 23–25

Alberici Corporation, 76 12–14

The Albert Fisher Group plc, 41 11–13

Albert Heijn NV *see* Koninklijke Ahold N.V. (Royal Ahold).

Albert's Organics, Inc., 110 10–13

Alberta Energy Company Ltd., 16 10–12; 43 3–6 (upd.)

Alberto-Culver Company, 8 15–17; 36 23–27 (upd.); 91 9–15 (upd.)

Albertson's, Inc., II 601–03; 7 19–22 (upd.); 30 24–28 (upd.); 65 21–26 (upd.)

Albtelecom Sh. a, 111 1–5

Alcan Aluminium Limited, IV 9–13; 31 7–12 (upd.)

Alcatel-Lucent, 9 9–11; 36 28–31 (upd.); 109 12–17 (upd.)

Alco Health Services Corporation, III 9–10 *see also* AmeriSource Health Corp.

Alco Standard Corporation, I 412–13

Alcoa Inc., 56 7–11 (upd.)

Alderwoods Group, Inc., 68 11–15 (upd.)

Aldi Einkauf GmbH & Co. OHG, 13 24–26; 86 10–14 (upd.)

Aldila Inc., 46 12–14

Aldus Corporation, 10 34–36 *see also* Adobe Systems Inc.

Aleris International, Inc., 110 14–17

Alès Groupe, 81 10–13

Alex Lee Inc., 18 6–9; 44 10–14 (upd.)

Alexander & Alexander Services Inc., 10 37–39 *see also* Aon Corp.

Alexander & Baldwin, Inc., 10 40–42; 40 14–19 (upd.)

Alexander's, Inc., 45 14–16

Alexandra plc, 88 5–8

Alexandra Real Estate Equities, Inc., 101 18–22

Alexon Group PLC, 107 6–10

Alfa Corporation, 60 10–12

Alfa Group, 99 23–26

Alfa-Laval AB, III 417–21; 64 13–18 (upd.)

Alfa Romeo, 13 27–29; 36 32–35 (upd.)

Alfa, S.A. de C.V., 19 10–12

Alfesca hf, 82 1–4

Alfred A. Knopf, Inc. *see* Random House, Inc.

Alfred Dunhill Limited *see* Vendôme Luxury Group plc.

Alfred Kärcher GmbH & Co KG, 94 9–14

Alfred Ritter GmbH & Co. KG, 58 3–7

Basin Electric Power Cooperative, 103 43–46

The Basketball Club of Seattle, LLC, 50 93–97

Bass PLC, I 222–24; 15 44–47 (upd.); 38 74–78 (upd.)

Bass Pro Shops, Inc., 42 27–30

Bassett Furniture Industries, Inc., 18 52–55; 95 44–50 (upd.)

BAT Industries plc, I 425–27 *see also* British American Tobacco PLC.

Bata Ltd., 62 27–30

Bates Worldwide, Inc., 14 48–51; 33 65–69 (upd.)

Bath Iron Works Corporation, 12 27–29; 36 76–79 (upd.)

Battelle Memorial Institute, Inc., 10 138–40

Batten Barton Durstine & Osborn *see* Omnicom Group Inc.

Battle Mountain Gold Company, 23 40–42 *see also* Newmont Mining Corp.

Bauer Hockey, Inc., 104 31–34

Bauer Publishing Group, 7 42–43

Bauerly Companies, 61 31–33

Baugur Group hf, 81 45–49

Baumax AG, 75 56–58

Bausch & Lomb Inc., 7 44–47; 25 53–57 (upd.); 96 20–26 (upd.)

Bavaria S.A., 90 44–47

Baxi Group Ltd., 96 27–30

Baxter International Inc., I 627–29; 10 141–43 (upd.)

Baxters Food Group Ltd., 99 47–50

The Bay *see* The Hudson's Bay Co.

Bay State Gas Company, 38 79–82

Bayard SA, 49 46–49

BayBanks, Inc., 12 30–32

Bayer A.G., I 309–11; 13 75–77 (upd.); 41 44–48 (upd.)

Bayerische Hypotheken- und Wechsel-Bank AG, II 238–40 *see also* HVB Group.

Bayerische Motoren Werke AG, I 138–40; 11 31–33 (upd.); 38 83–87 (upd.); 108 95–101 (upd.)

Bayerische Vereinsbank A.G., II 241–43 *see also* HVB Group.

Bayernwerk AG, V 555–58; 23 43–47 (upd.) *see also* E.On AG.

Bayou Steel Corporation, 31 47–49

BayWa AG, 112 45–49

BB&T Corporation, 79 57–61

BB Holdings Limited, 77 50–53

BBA *see* Bush Boake Allen Inc.

BBA Aviation plc, 90 48–52

BBAG Osterreichische Brau-Beteiligungs-AG, 38 88–90

BBC *see* British Broadcasting Corp.

BBDO Worldwide *see* Omnicom Group Inc.

BBGI *see* Beasley Broadcast Group, Inc.

BBN Corp., 19 39–42

BBVA *see* Banco Bilbao Vizcaya Argentaria S.A.

BCE, Inc., V 269–71; 44 46–50 (upd.)

Bci, 99 51–54

BDO Seidman LLP, 96 31–34

BE&K, Inc., 73 57–59

BEA *see* Bank of East Asia Ltd.

BEA Systems, Inc., 36 80–83

Beacon Roofing Supply, Inc., 75 59–61

Bear Creek Corporation, 38 91–94

Bear Stearns Companies, Inc., II 400–01; 10 144–45 (upd.); 52 41–44 (upd.)

Bearings, Inc., 13 78–80

Beasley Broadcast Group, Inc., 51 44–46

Beate Uhse AG, 96 35–39

Beatrice Company, II 467–69 *see also* TLC Beatrice International Holdings, Inc.

BeautiControl Cosmetics, Inc., 21 49–52

Beazer Homes USA, Inc., 17 38–41

bebe stores, inc., 31 50–52; 103 47–51 (upd.)

Bechtel Corporation, I 558–59; 24 64–67 (upd.); 99 55–60 (upd.)

Beckett Papers, 23 48–50

Beckman Coulter, Inc., 22 74–77

Beckman Instruments, Inc., 14 52–54

Becton, Dickinson and Company, I 630–31; 11 34–36 (upd.); 36 84–89 (upd.); 101 69–77 (upd.)

Bed Bath & Beyond Inc., 13 81–83; 41 49–52 (upd.); 109 63–70 (upd.)

Beech Aircraft Corporation, 8 49–52 *see also* Raytheon Aircraft Holdings Inc.

Beech-Nut Nutrition Corporation, 21 53–56; 51 47–51 (upd.)

Beef O'Brady's *see* Family Sports Concepts, Inc.

Beer Nuts, Inc., 86 30–33

Beggars Group Ltd., 99 61–65

Behr GmbH & Co. KG, 72 22–25

Behring Diagnostics *see* Dade Behring Holdings Inc.

BEI Technologies, Inc., 65 74–76

Beiersdorf AG, 29 49–53

Bekaert S.A./N.V., 90 53–57

Bekins Company, 15 48–50

Bel *see* Fromageries Bel.

Bel Fuse, Inc., 53 59–62

Bel/Kaukauna USA, 76 46–48

Belco Oil & Gas Corp., 40 63–65

Belden CDT Inc., 19 43–45; 76 49–52 (upd.)

Belgacom, 6 302–04

Belk, Inc., V 12–13; 19 46–48 (upd.); 72 26–29 (upd.)

Bell and Howell Company, 9 61–64; 29 54–58 (upd.)

Bell Atlantic Corporation, V 272–74; 25 58–62 (upd.) *see also* Verizon Communications.

Bell Canada Enterprises Inc. *see* BCE, Inc.

Bell Canada International, Inc., 6 305–08

Bell Helicopter Textron Inc., 46 64–67

Bell Industries, Inc., 47 40–43

Bell Resources *see* TPG NV.

Bell Sports Corporation, 16 51–53; 44 51–54 (upd.)

Bellcore *see* Telcordia Technologies, Inc.

Belleek Pottery Ltd., 71 50–53

Belleville Shoe Manufacturing Company, 92 17–20

Bellisio Foods, Inc., 95 51–54

BellSouth Corporation, V 276–78; 29 59–62 (upd.) *see also* AT&T Corp.

Bellway Plc, 45 37–39

Belo Corporation, 98 19–25 (upd.)

Beloit Corporation, 14 55–57 *see also* Metso Corp.

Belron International Ltd., 76 53–56

Belvedere S.A., 93 77–81

Bemis Company, Inc., 8 53–55; 91 53–60 (upd.)

Ben & Jerry's Homemade, Inc., 10 146–48; 35 58–62 (upd.); 80 22–28 (upd.)

Ben Bridge Jeweler, Inc., 60 52–54

Ben E. Keith Company, 76 57–59

Ben Hill Griffin, Inc., 110 43–47

Benchmark Capital, 49 50–52

Benchmark Electronics, Inc., 40 66–69

Benckiser N.V. *see* Reckitt Benckiser plc.

Bendix Corporation, I 141–43

Beneficial Corporation, 8 56–58

Benesse Corporation, 76 60–62

Bénéteau SA, 55 54–56

Benetton Group S.p.A., 10 149–52; 67 47–51 (upd.)

Benfield Greig Group plc, 53 63–65

Benguet Corporation, 58 21–24

Benihana, Inc., 18 56–59; 76 63–66 (upd.)

Benjamin Moore and Co., 13 84–87; 38 95–99 (upd.)

Benninger AG, 107 40–44

BenQ Corporation, 67 52–54

Benton Oil and Gas Company, 47 44–46

Berean Christian Stores, 96 40–43

Beretta *see* Fabbrica D' Armi Pietro Beretta S.p.A.

Bergdorf Goodman Inc., 52 45–48

Bergen Brunswig Corporation, V 14–16; 13 88–90 (upd.) *see also* AmerisourceBergen Corp.

Berger Bros Company, 62 31–33

Beringer Blass Wine Estates Ltd., 22 78–81; 66 34–37 (upd.)

Berjaya Group Bhd., 67 55–57

Berkeley Farms, Inc., 46 68–70

Berkshire Hathaway Inc., III 213–15; 18 60–63 (upd.); 42 31–36 (upd.); 89 92–99 (upd.)

Berkshire Realty Holdings, L.P., 49 53–55

Berlex Laboratories, Inc., 66 38–40

Berliner Stadtreinigungsbetriebe, 58 25–28

Berliner Verkehrsbetriebe (BVG), 58 29–31

Berlinwasser Holding AG, 90 58–62

Berlitz International, Inc., 13 91–93; 39 47–50 (upd.)

Bernard C. Harris Publishing Company, Inc., 39 51–53

Bernard Chaus, Inc., 27 59–61

Bernard Hodes Group Inc., 86 34–37

Bruno's Supermarkets, Inc., 7 60–62; 26 46–48 (upd.); 68 70–73 (upd.)

Brunschwig & Fils Inc., 96 62–65

Brunswick Corporation, III 442–44; 22 113–17 (upd.); 77 68–75 (upd.)

Brush Engineered Materials Inc., 67 77–79

Brush Wellman Inc., 14 80–82

Bruster's Real Ice Cream, Inc., 80 51–54

Bryce Corporation, 100 80–83

BSA *see* The Boy Scouts of America.

BSC *see* Birmingham Steel Corporation

BSH Bosch und Siemens Hausgeräte GmbH, 67 80–84

BSN Groupe S.A., II 474–75 *see also* Groupe Danone

BT Group plc, 49 69–74 (upd.)

BTG, Inc., 45 68–70

BTG Plc, 87 80–83

BTR plc, I 428–30

BTR Siebe plc, 27 79–81 *see also* Invensys PLC.

Bubba Gump Shrimp Co. Restaurants, Inc., 108 128–31

Buca, Inc., 38 115–17

Buck Consultants, Inc., 55 71–73

Buck Knives Inc., 48 71–74

Buckeye Partners, L.P., 70 33–36

Buckeye Technologies, Inc., 42 51–54

Buckhead Life Restaurant Group, Inc., 100 84–87

The Buckle, Inc., 18 84–86

Bucyrus International, Inc., 17 58–61; 103 80–87 (upd.)

The Budd Company, 8 74–76 *see also* ThyssenKrupp AG.

Buderus AG, 37 46–49

Budgens Ltd., 59 93–96

Budget Group, Inc., 25 92–94 *see also* Cendant Corp.

Budget Rent a Car Corporation, 9 94–95

Budweiser Budvar, National Corporation, 59 97–100

Buena Vista Home Video *see* The Walt Disney Co.

Bufete Industrial, S.A. de C.V., 34 80–82

Buffalo Grill S.A., 94 87–90

Buffalo Wild Wings, Inc., 56 41–43

Buffets Holdings, Inc., 10 186–87; 32 102–04 (upd.); 93 105–09 (upd.)

Bugatti Automobiles S.A.S., 94 91–94

Bugle Boy Industries, Inc., 18 87–88

Buhrmann NV, 41 67–69

Buick Motor Co. *see* General Motors Corp.

Build-A-Bear Workshop Inc., 62 45–48

Building Materials Holding Corporation, 52 53–55

Bulgari S.p.A., 20 94–97; 106 82–87 (upd.)

Bull *see* Compagnie des Machines Bull S.A.

Bull S.A., 43 89–91 (upd.)

Bulley & Andrews, LLC, 55 74–76

Bulova Corporation, 13 120–22; 41 70–73 (upd.)

Bumble Bee Seafoods L.L.C., 64 59–61

Bundy Corporation, 17 62–65

Bunge Ltd., 62 49–51

Bunzl plc, IV 260–62; 31 77–80 (upd.)

Burberry Group plc, 17 66–68; 41 74–76 (upd.); 92 33–37 (upd.)

Burda Holding GmbH. & Co., 23 85–89

Burdines, Inc., 60 70–73

The Bureau of National Affairs, Inc., 23 90–93

Bureau Veritas SA, 55 77–79

Burelle S.A., 23 94–96

Burger King Corporation, II 613–15; 17 69–72 (upd.); 56 44–48 (upd.)

Burgett, Inc., 97 88–91

Burke, Inc., 88 39–42

Burke Mills, Inc., 66 41–43

Burlington Coat Factory Warehouse Corporation, 10 188–89; 60 74–76 (upd.)

Burlington Industries, Inc., V 354–55; 17 73–76 (upd.)

Burlington Northern Santa Fe Corporation, V 425–28; 27 82–89 (upd.); 111 55–65 (upd.)

Burlington Resources Inc., 10 190–92 *see also* ConocoPhillips.

Burmah Castrol PLC, IV 381–84; 30 86–91 (upd.) *see also* BP p.l.c.

Burns International Security Services, 13 123–25 *see also* Securitas AB.

Burns International Services Corporation, 41 77–80 (upd.)

Burns, Philp & Company Ltd., 63 83–86

Burpee & Co. *see* W. Atlee Burpee & Co.

Burr-Brown Corporation, 19 66–68

Burroughs & Chapin Company, Inc., 86 52–55

The Burton Corporation, V 20–22; 94 95–100 (upd.)

The Burton Group plc, *see also* Arcadia Group plc.

Burton Snowboards Inc., 22 118–20, 460

Burt's Bees, Inc., 58 47–50

Busch Entertainment Corporation, 73 73–75

Bush Boake Allen Inc., 30 92–94 *see also* International Flavors & Fragrances Inc.

Bush Brothers & Company, 45 71–73

Bush Industries, Inc., 20 98–100

Business Men's Assurance Company of America, 14 83–85

Business Objects S.A., 25 95–97

Business Post Group plc, 46 71–73

Butler Manufacturing Company, 12 51–53; 62 52–56 (upd.)

Butterick Co., Inc., 23 97–99

Buttrey Food & Drug Stores Co., 18 89–91

buy.com, Inc., 46 74–77

Buzztime Entertainment, Inc. *see* NTN Buzztime, Inc.

BVR Systems (1998) Ltd., 93 110–13

BW Group Ltd., 107 28–32

BWAY Corporation, 24 91–93

C

C&A, 40 74–77 (upd.)

C&A Brenninkmeyer KG, V 23–24

C&G *see* Cheltenham & Gloucester PLC.

C&J Clark International Ltd., 52 56–59

C&K Market, Inc., 81 59–61

C & S Wholesale Grocers, Inc., 55 80–83

C-COR.net Corp., 38 118–21

C-Cube Microsystems, Inc., 37 50–54

C-Tech Industries Inc., 90 90–93

C. Bechstein Pianofortefabrik AG, 96 66–71

C.F. Martin & Co., Inc., 42 55–58

The C.F. Sauer Company, 90 86–89

C.H. Boehringer Sohn, 39 70–73

C.H. Guenther & Son, Inc., 84 39–42

C.H. Heist Corporation, 24 111–13

C.H. Robinson Worldwide, Inc., 11 43–44; 40 78–81 (upd.)

C. Hoare & Co., 77 76–79

C.I. Traders Limited, 61 44–46

C. Itoh & Co., I 431–33 *see also* ITOCHU Corp.

C.R. Bard, Inc., 9 96–98; 65 81–85 (upd.)

C.R. Meyer and Sons Company, 74 58–60

CAA *see* Creative Artists Agency LLC.

Cabela's Inc., 26 49–51; 68 74–77 (upd.)

Cable & Wireless HKT, 30 95–98 (upd.)

Cable and Wireless plc, V 283–86; 25 98–102 (upd.)

Cabletron Systems, Inc., 10 193–94

Cablevision Electronic Instruments, Inc., 32 105–07

Cablevision Systems Corporation, 7 63–65; 30 99–103 (upd.); 109 87–94 (upd.)

Cabot Corporation, 8 77–79; 29 79–82 (upd.); 91 74–80 (upd.)

Cabot Creamery Cooperative, Inc., 102 65–68

Cache Incorporated, 30 104–06

CACI International Inc., 21 85–87; 72 49–53 (upd.)

Cactus Feeders, Inc., 91 81–84

Cactus S.A., 90 94–97

Cadbury plc, 105 60–66 (upd.)

Cadbury Schweppes PLC, II 476–78; 49 75–79 (upd.)

Cadence Design Systems, Inc., 11 45–48; 48 75–79 (upd.)

Cadence Financial Corporation, 106 88–92

Cadmus Communications Corporation, 23 100–03 *see also* Cenveo Inc.

CAE USA Inc., 48 80–82

Caere Corporation, 20 101–03

Caesars World, Inc., 6 199–202

Caffè Nero Group PLC, 63 87–89

Caffyns PLC, 105 67–71

Cagle's, Inc., 20 104–07

Curtice-Burns Foods, Inc., 7 104–06; 21 154–57 (upd.) *see also* Birds Eye Foods, Inc.

Curtiss-Wright Corporation, 10 260–63; 35 132–37 (upd.)

Curves International, Inc., 54 80–82

Cushman & Wakefield, Inc., 86 96–100

Custom Chrome, Inc., 16 147–49; 74 92–95 (upd.)

Cutera, Inc., 84 78–81

Cutter & Buck Inc., 27 112–14

CVPS *see* Central Vermont Public Service Corp.

CVRD *see* Companhia Vale do Rio Doce Ltd.

CVS Caremark Corporation, 45 133–38 (upd.); 108 186–93 (upd.)

CWM *see* Chemical Waste Management, Inc.

Cyan Worlds Inc., 101 148–51

Cybermedia, Inc., 25 117–19

Cyberonics, Inc., 79 128–31

Cybex International, Inc., 49 106–09

Cydsa *see* Grupo Cydsa, S.A. de C.V.

Cygne Designs, Inc., 25 120–23

Cygnus Business Media, Inc., 56 73–77

Cymer, Inc., 77 125–28

Cypress Semiconductor Corporation, 20 174–76; 48 125–29 (upd.)

Cyprus Airways Public Limited, 81 103–06

Cyprus Amax Minerals Company, 21 158–61

Cyprus Minerals Company, 7 107–09

Cyrela Brazil Realty S.A. Empreendimentos e Participações, 110 115–18

Cyrk Inc., 19 112–14

Cystic Fibrosis Foundation, 93 177–80

Cytec Industries Inc., 27 115–17

Cytyc Corporation, 69 112–14

Czarnikow-Rionda Company, Inc., 32 128–30

D

D&B *see* Dun & Bradstreet Corp.

D&H Distributing Co., 95 118–21

D&K Wholesale Drug, Inc., 14 146–48

D-Link Corporation, 83 103–106

D.A. Davidson & Company, 106 133–37

D. Carnegie & Co. AB, 98 79–83

D.F. Stauffer Biscuit Company, 82 82–85

D.G. Yuengling & Son, Inc., 38 171–73

D.R. Horton, Inc., 58 82–84

D. Swarovski & Co., 112 133–37 (upd.)

Dachser GmbH & Co. KG, 88 57–61

D'Addario & Company, Inc. *see* J. D'Addario & Company, Inc.

Dade Behring Holdings Inc., 71 120–22

Daesang Corporation, 84 82–85

Daewoo Group, III 457–59; 18 123–27 (upd.); 57 90–94 (upd.)

Daffy's Inc., 26 110–12

D'Agostino Supermarkets Inc., 19 115–17

DAH *see* DeCrane Aircraft Holdings Inc.

Dai-Ichi Kangyo Bank Ltd., II 273–75

Dai Nippon *see also* listings under Dainippon.

Dai Nippon Printing Co., Ltd., IV 598–600; 57 95–99 (upd.)

Daido Steel Co., Ltd., IV 62–63

The Daiei, Inc., V 39–40; 17 123–25 (upd.); 41 113–16 (upd.)

Daihatsu Motor Company, Ltd., 7 110–12; 21 162–64 (upd.)

Daiichikosho Company Ltd., 86 101–04

Daikin Industries, Ltd., III 460–61

Daiko Advertising Inc., 79 132–35

Daily Journal Corporation, 101 152–55

Daily Mail and General Trust plc, 19 118–20

The Daimaru, Inc., V 41–42; 42 98–100 (upd.)

Daimler-Benz Aerospace AG, 16 150–52

Daimler-Benz AG, I 149–51; 15 140–44 (upd.)

DaimlerChrysler AG, 34 128–37 (upd.); 64 100–07 (upd.)

Dain Rauscher Corporation, 35 138–41 (upd.)

Daio Paper Corporation, IV 266–67; 84 86–89 (upd.)

Dairy Crest Group plc, 32 131–33

Dairy Farm International Holdings Ltd., 97 125–28

Dairy Farmers of America, Inc., 94 143–46

Dairy Mart Convenience Stores, Inc., 7 113–15; 25 124–27 (upd.) *see also* Alimentation Couche-Tard Inc.

Dairy Queen *see* International Dairy Queen, Inc.

Dairyland Healthcare Solutions, 73 99–101

Dairylea Cooperative Inc., 111 82–85

Daishowa Paper Manufacturing Co., Ltd., IV 268–70; 57 100–03 (upd.)

Daisy Outdoor Products Inc., 58 85–88

Daisytek International Corporation, 18 128–30

Daiwa Bank, Ltd., II 276–77; 39 109–11 (upd.)

Daiwa Securities Company, Limited, II 405–06

Daiwa Securities Group Inc., 55 115–18 (upd.)

Daktronics, Inc., 32 134–37; 107 91–95 (upd.)

Dal-Tile International Inc., 22 169–71

Dale and Thomas Popcorn LLC, 100 131–34

Dale Carnegie & Associates Inc., 28 85–87; 78 78–82 (upd.)

Dalgety PLC, II 499–500 *see also* PIC International Group PLC

Dalhoff Larsen & Horneman A/S, 96 95–99

Dalian Shide Group, 91 136–39

Dalkia Holding, 66 68–70

Dallah Albaraka Group, 72 83–86

Dallas Cowboys Football Club, Ltd., 33 122–25

Dallas Semiconductor Corporation, 13 191–93; 31 143–46 (upd.)

Dalli-Werke GmbH & Co. KG, 86 105–10

Dallis Coffee, Inc., 86 111–14

Damark International, Inc., 18 131–34 *see also* Provell Inc.

Damartex S.A., 98 84–87

Dames & Moore, Inc., 25 128–31 *see also* URS Corp.

Dan River Inc., 35 142–46; 86 115–20 (upd.)

Dana Holding Corporation, I 152–53; 10 264–66 (upd.); 99 127–134 (upd.)

Danaher Corporation, 7 116–17; 77 129–33 (upd.)

Danaos Corporation, 91 140–43

Daniel Measurement and Control, Inc., 16 153–55; 74 96–99 (upd.)

Daniel Thwaites Plc, 95 122–25

Danisco A/S, 44 134–37

Dannon Company, Inc., 14 149–51; 106 138–42 (upd.)

Danone Group *see* Groupe Danone.

Danske Bank Aktieselskab, 50 148–51

Danskin, Inc., 12 93–95; 62 88–92 (upd.)

Danzas Group, V 441–43; 40 136–39 (upd.)

D'Arcy Masius Benton & Bowles, Inc., 6 20–22; 32 138–43 (upd.)

Darden Restaurants, Inc., 16 156–58; 44 138–42 (upd.)

Dare Foods Limited, 103 135–38

Darigold, Inc., 9 159–61

Darling International Inc., 85 81–84

Dart Group PLC, 16 159–62; 77 134–37 (upd.)

Darty S.A., 27 118–20

DASA *see* Daimler-Benz Aerospace AG.

Dassault-Breguet *see* Avions Marcel Dassault-Breguet Aviation.

Dassault Systèmes S.A., 25 132–34 *see also* Groupe Dassault Aviation SA.

Data Broadcasting Corporation, 31 147–50

Data General Corporation, 8 137–40 *see also* EMC Corp.

Datapoint Corporation, 11 67–70

Datascope Corporation, 39 112–14

Datek Online Holdings Corp., 32 144–46

Dauphin Deposit Corporation, 14 152–54

Dave & Buster's, Inc., 33 126–29; 104 98–103 (upd.)

The Davey Tree Expert Company, 11 71–73

The David and Lucile Packard Foundation, 41 117–19

The David J. Joseph Company, 14 155–56; 76 128–30 (upd.)

David Jones Ltd., 60 100–02

Davide Campari-Milano S.p.A., 57 104–06

David's Bridal, Inc., 33 130–32

Davis Polk & Wardwell, 36 151–54

Davis Service Group PLC, 45 139–41

FormFactor, Inc., 85 128–31

Formica Corporation, 13 230–32

Formosa Plastics Corporation, 14 197–99; 58 128–31 (upd.)

Forrester Research, Inc., 54 113–15

Forstmann Little & Co., 38 190–92

Fort Howard Corporation, 8 197–99 *see also* Fort James Corp.

Fort James Corporation, 22 209–12 (upd.) *see also* Georgia-Pacific Corp.

Fortis, Inc., 15 179–82; 47 134–37 (upd.); 50 4–6

Fortum Corporation, 30 202–07 (upd.) *see also* Neste Oil Corp.

Fortune Brands, Inc., 29 193–97 (upd.); 68 163–67 (upd.)

Fortunoff Fine Jewelry and Silverware Inc., 26 144–46

Forward Air Corporation, 75 147–49

Forward Industries, Inc., 86 152–55

The Forzani Group Ltd., 79 172–76

The Foschini Group, 110 160–64

Fossil, Inc., 17 189–91; 112 188–93 (upd.)

Foster Poultry Farms, 32 201–04

Foster Wheeler Corporation, 6 145–47; 23 205–08 (upd.); 76 152–56 (upd.)

FosterGrant, Inc., 60 131–34

Foster's Group Limited, 7 182–84; 21 227–30 (upd.); 50 199–203 (upd.); 111 141–47 (upd.)

The Foundation for National Progress, 107 141–45

Foundation Health Corporation, 12 175–77

Fountain Powerboats Industries, Inc., 28 146–48

Four Seasons Hotels Limited, 9 237–38; 29 198–200 (upd.); 106 191–95 (upd.)

Four Winns Boats LLC, 96 124–27

4imprint Group PLC, 105 187–91

4Kids Entertainment Inc., 59 187–89

Fourth Financial Corporation, 11 144–46

Fox Entertainment Group, Inc., 43 173–76

Fox Family Worldwide, Inc., 24 170–72 *see also* ABC Family Worldwide, Inc.

Fox, Inc. *see* Twentieth Century Fox Film Corp.

Foxboro Company, 13 233–35

FoxHollow Technologies, Inc., 85 132–35

FoxMeyer Health Corporation, 16 212–14 *see also* McKesson Corp.

Fox's Pizza Den, Inc., 98 121–24

Foxworth-Galbraith Lumber Company, 91 188–91

FPL Group, Inc., V 623–25; 49 143–46 (upd.); 111 148–53 (upd.)

Framatome SA, 19 164–67 *aee also* Alcatel S.A.; AREVA.

France Telecom S.A., V 291–93; 21 231–34 (upd.); 99 173–179 (upd.)

Francotyp-Postalia Holding AG, 92 123–27

Frank J. Zamboni & Co., Inc., 34 173–76

Frank Russell Company, 46 198–200

Franke Holding AG, 76 157–59

Frankel & Co., 39 166–69

Frankfurter Allgemeine Zeitung GmbH, 66 121–24

Franklin Covey Company, 11 147–49; 37 149–52 (upd.)

Franklin Electric Company, Inc., 43 177–80

Franklin Electronic Publishers, Inc., 23 209–13

The Franklin Mint, 69 181–84

Franklin Resources, Inc., 9 239–40

Frank's Nursery & Crafts, Inc., 12 178–79

Franz Haniel & Cie. GmbH, 109 250–55

Franz Inc., 80 122–25

Fraport AG Frankfurt Airport Services Worldwide, 90 197–202

Fraser & Neave Ltd., 54 116–18

Fred Alger Management, Inc., 97 168–72

Fred Meyer Stores, Inc., V 54–56; 20 222–25 (upd.); 64 135–39 (upd.)

Fred Perry Limited, 105 192–95

Fred Usinger Inc., 54 119–21

The Fred W. Albrecht Grocery Co., 13 236–38

Fred Weber, Inc., 61 100–02

Freddie Mac, 54 122–25

Frederick Atkins Inc., 16 215–17

Frederick's of Hollywood Inc., 16 218–20; 59 190–93 (upd.)

Fred's, Inc., 23 214–16; 62 144–47 (upd.)

Freedom Communications, Inc., 36 222–25

Freeport-McMoRan Copper & Gold, Inc., IV 81–84; 7 185–89 (upd.); 57 145–50 (upd.)

Freescale Semiconductor, Inc., 83 151–154

Freese and Nichols, Inc., 107 146–49

Freeze.com LLC, 77 156–59

FreightCar America, Inc., 101 192–95

Freixenet S.A., 71 162–64

French Connection Group plc, 41 167–69

French Fragrances, Inc., 22 213–15 *see also* Elizabeth Arden, Inc.

Frequency Electronics, Inc., 61 103–05

Fresenius AG, 56 138–42

Fresh America Corporation, 20 226–28

Fresh Choice, Inc., 20 229–32

Fresh Enterprises, Inc., 66 125–27

Fresh Express Inc., 88 97–100

Fresh Foods, Inc., 29 201–03

Fresh Mark, Inc., 110 165–68

FreshDirect, LLC, 84 130–133

Fretter, Inc., 10 304–06

Freudenberg & Co., 41 170–73

Fried, Frank, Harris, Shriver & Jacobson, 35 183–86

Fried. Krupp GmbH, IV 85–89 *see also* ThyssenKrupp AG.

Friedman, Billings, Ramsey Group, Inc., 53 134–37

Friedman's Inc., 29 204–06

Friedrich Grohe AG & Co. KG, 53 138–41

Friendly Ice Cream Corporation, 30 208–10; 72 141–44 (upd.)

Friesland Coberco Dairy Foods Holding N.V., 59 194–96

Frigidaire Home Products, 22 216–18

Frisch's Restaurants, Inc., 35 187–89; 92 128–32 (upd.)

Frito-Lay North America, 32 205–10; 73 151–58 (upd.)

Fritz Companies, Inc., 12 180–82

Fromageries Bel, 23 217–19; 25 83–84

Frontera Foods, Inc., 100 170–73

Frontier Airlines Holdings Inc., 22 219–21; 84 134–138 (upd.)

Frontier Corp., 16 221–23

Frontier Natural Products Co-Op, 82 121–24

Frontline Ltd., 45 163–65

Frost & Sullivan, Inc., 53 142–44

Frozen Food Express Industries, Inc., 20 233–35; 98 125–30 (upd.)

Frucor Beverages Group Ltd., 96 128–31

Fruehauf Corp., I 169–70

Fruit of the Loom, Inc., 8 200–02; 25 164–67 (upd.)

Fruth Pharmacy, Inc., 66 128–30

Frymaster Corporation, 27 159–62

Fry's Electronics, Inc., 68 168–70

FSI International, Inc., 17 192–94 *see also* FlightSafety International, Inc.

FTD Group, Inc., 99 180–185 (upd.)

FTI Consulting, Inc., 77 160–63

FTP Software, Inc., 20 236–38

Fubu, 29 207–09

Fuchs Petrolub AG, 102 132–37

Fuddruckers Inc., 110 169–72

Fuel Systems Solutions, Inc., 97 173–77

Fuel Tech, Inc., 85 136–40

FuelCell Energy, Inc., 75 150–53

Fugro N.V., 98 131–34

Fuji Bank, Ltd., II 291–93

Fuji Electric Co., Ltd., II 22–23; 48 180–82 (upd.)

Fuji Photo Film Co., Ltd., III 486–89; 18 183–87 (upd.); 79 177–84 (upd.)

Fuji Television Network Inc., 91 192–95

Fujisawa Pharmaceutical Company, Ltd., I 635–36; 58 132–34 (upd.) *see also* Astellas Pharma Inc.

Fujitsu-ICL Systems Inc., 11 150–51

Fujitsu Limited, III 139–41; 16 224–27 (upd.); 42 145–50 (upd.); 103 171–78 (upd.)

Fulbright & Jaworski L.L.P., 47 138–41

Fuller Smith & Turner P.L.C., 38 193–95

Funai Electric Company Ltd., 62 148–50

Funco, Inc., 20 239–41 *see also* GameStop Corp.

Fuqua Enterprises, Inc., 17 195–98

Fuqua Industries Inc., I 445–47

Furmanite Corporation, 92 133–36
Furniture Brands International, Inc., 39 170–75 (upd.)
Furon Company, 28 149–51 *see also* Compagnie de Saint-Gobain.
Furr's Restaurant Group, Inc., 53 145–48
Furr's Supermarkets, Inc., 28 152–54
Furukawa Electric Co., Ltd., III 490–92
Future Now, Inc., 12 183–85
Future Shop Ltd., 62 151–53
Fyffes PLC, 38 196–99; 106 196–201 (upd.)

G

G&K Holding S.A., 95 159–62
G&K Services, Inc., 16 228–30
G-III Apparel Group, Ltd., 22 222–24
G A Pindar & Son Ltd., 88 101–04
G.D. Searle & Co., I 686–89; 12 186–89 (upd.); 34 177–82 (upd.)
G. Heileman Brewing Co., I 253–55 *see also* Stroh Brewery Co.
G.I.E. Airbus Industrie, I 41–43; 12 190–92 (upd.)
G.I. Joe's, Inc., 30 221–23 *see also* Joe's Sports & Outdoor.
G. Leblanc Corporation, 55 149–52
G.S. Blodgett Corporation, 15 183–85 *see also* Blodgett Holdings, Inc.
Gabelli Asset Management Inc., 30 211–14 *see also* Lynch Corp.
Gables Residential Trust, 49 147–49
Gadzooks, Inc., 18 188–90
GAF, I 337–40; 22 225–29 (upd.)
Gage Marketing Group, 26 147–49
Gaiam, Inc., 41 174–77
Gainsco, Inc., 22 230–32
Galardi Group, Inc., 72 145–47
Galaxy Investors, Inc., 97 178–81
Galaxy Nutritional Foods, Inc., 58 135–37
Gale International LLC, 93 221–24
Galenica AG, 84 139–142
Galeries Lafayette S.A., V 57–59; 23 220–23 (upd.)
Galey & Lord, Inc., 20 242–45; 66 131–34 (upd.)
Galiform PLC, 103 179–83
Gallaher Group Plc, 49 150–54 (upd.)
Gallaher Limited, V 398–400; 19 168–71 (upd.)
Gallo Winery *see* E. & J. Gallo Winery.
Gallup, Inc., 37 153–56; 104 156–61 (upd.)
Galoob Toys *see* Lewis Galoob Toys Inc.
Galp Energia SGPS S.A., 98 135–40
Galtronics Ltd., 100 174–77
Galyan's Trading Company, Inc., 47 142–44
The Gambrinus Company, 40 188–90
Gambro AB, 49 155–57
The GAME Group plc, 80 126–29
GameStop Corp., 69 185–89 (upd.)
GAMI *see* Great American Management and Investment, Inc.
Gaming Partners InternationalCorporation, 92225–28

Gander Mountain Company, 20 246–48; 90 203–08 (upd.)
Gannett Company, Inc., IV 612–13; 7 190–92 (upd.); 30 215–17 (upd.); 66 135–38 (upd.)
Gano Excel Enterprise Sdn. Bhd., 89 228–31
Gantos, Inc., 17 199–201
Ganz, 98 141–44
GAP *see* Grupo Aeroportuario del Pacífico, S.A. de C.V.
The Gap, Inc., V 60–62; 18 191–94 (upd.); 55 153–57 (upd.)
Garan, Inc., 16 231–33; 64 140–43 (upd.)
The Garden Company Ltd., 82 125–28
Garden Fresh Restaurant Corporation, 31 213–15
Garden Ridge Corporation, 27 163–65
Gardenburger, Inc., 33 169–71; 76 160–63 (upd.)
Gardner Denver, Inc., 49 158–60
Garmin Ltd., 60 135–37
Garst Seed Company, Inc., 86 156–59
Gart Sports Company, 24 173–75 *see also* Sports Authority, Inc.
Gartner, Inc., 21 235–37; 94 209–13 (upd.)
Garuda Indonesia, 6 90–91; 58 138–41 (upd.)
Gas Natural SDG S.A., 69 190–93
GASS *see* Grupo Ángeles Servicios de Salud, S.A. de C.V.
Gasunie *see* N.V. Nederlandse Gasunie.
Gate Gourmet International AG, 70 97–100
GateHouse Media, Inc., 91 196–99
The Gates Corporation, 9 241–43
Gateway Corporation Ltd., II 628–30 *see also* Somerfield plc.
Gateway, Inc., 10 307–09; 27 166–69 (upd.); 63 153–58 (upd.)
The Gatorade Company, 82 129–32
Gatti's Pizza, Inc. *see* Mr. Gatti's, LP.
GATX, 6 394–96; 25 168–71 (upd.)
Gaumont S.A., 25 172–75; 91 200–05 (upd.)
Gaylord Bros., Inc., 100 178–81
Gaylord Container Corporation, 8 203–05
Gaylord Entertainment Company, 11 152–54; 36 226–29 (upd.)
Gaz de France, V 626–28; 40 191–95 (upd.) *see also* GDF SUEZ.
Gazprom *see* OAO Gazprom.
GBC *see* General Binding Corp.
GC Companies, Inc., 25 176–78 *see also* AMC Entertainment Inc.
GDF SUEZ, 109 256–63 (upd.)
GE *see* General Electric Co.
GE Aircraft Engines, 9 244–46
GE Capital Aviation Services, 36 230–33
GEA AG, 27 170–74
GEAC Computer Corporation Ltd., 43 181–85
Geberit AG, 49 161–64
Gecina SA, 42 151–53

Gedney *see* M.A. Gedney Co.
Geek Squad Inc., 102 138–41
Geerlings & Wade, Inc., 45 166–68
Geest Plc, 38 200–02 *see also* Bakkavör Group hf.
Gefco SA, 54 126–28
Geffen Records Inc., 26 150–52
GEHE AG, 27 175–78
Gehl Company, 19 172–74
GEICO Corporation, 10 310–12; 40 196–99 (upd.)
Geiger Bros., 60 138–41
Gelita AG, 74 114–18
GEMA (Gesellschaft für musikalische Aufführungs- und mechanische Vervielfältigungsrechte), 70 101–05
Gemini Sound Products Corporation, 58 142–44
Gemplus International S.A., 64 144–47
Gen-Probe Incorporated, 79 185–88
Gencor Ltd., IV 90–93; 22 233–37 (upd.) *see also* Gold Fields Ltd.
GenCorp Inc., 9 247–49
Genentech, Inc., I 637–38; 8 209–11 (upd.); 32 211–15 (upd.); 75 154–58 (upd.)
General Accident plc, III 256–57 *see also* Aviva PLC.
General Atomics, 57 151–54; 112 194–98 (upd.)
General Bearing Corporation, 45 169–71
General Binding Corporation, 10 313–14; 73 159–62 (upd.)
General Cable Corporation, 40 200–03; 111 154–59 (upd.)
The General Chemical Group Inc., 37 157–60
General Cigar Holdings, Inc., 66 139–42 (upd.)
General Cinema Corporation, I 245–46 *see also* GC Companies, Inc.
General DataComm Industries, Inc., 14 200–02
General Dynamics Corporation, I 57–60; 10 315–18 (upd.); 40 204–10 (upd.); 88 105–13 (upd.)
General Electric Company, II 27–31; 12 193–97 (upd.); 34 183–90 (upd.); 63 159–68 (upd.)
General Electric Company, PLC, II 24–26 *see also* Marconi plc.
General Employment Enterprises, Inc., 87 172–175
General Growth Properties, Inc., 57 155–57
General Host Corporation, 12 198–200
General Housewares Corporation, 16 234–36
General Instrument Corporation, 10 319–21 *see also* Motorola, Inc.
General Maritime Corporation, 59 197–99
General Mills, Inc., II 501–03; 10 322–24 (upd.); 36 234–39 (upd.); 85 141–49 (upd.)

General Motors Corporation, I 171–73; 10 325–27 (upd.); 36 240–44 (upd.); 64 148–53 (upd.)

General Nutrition Companies, Inc., 11 155–57; 29 210–14 (upd.) *see also* GNC Corp.

General Public Utilities Corporation, V 629–31 *see also* GPU, Inc.

General Re Corporation, III 258–59; 24 176–78 (upd.)

General Sekiyu K.K., IV 431–33 *see also* TonenGeneral Sekiyu K.K.

General Signal Corporation, 9 250–52 *see also* SPX Corp.

General Tire, Inc., 8 212–14

Generale Bank, II 294–95 *see also* Fortis, Inc.

Générale des Eaux Group, V 632–34 *see also* Vivendi.

Generali *see* Assicurazioni Generali.

Genesco Inc., 17 202–06; 84 143–149 (upd.)

Genesee & Wyoming Inc., 27 179–81

Genesis Health Ventures, Inc., 18 195–97 *see also* NeighborCare,Inc.

Genesis Microchip Inc., 82 133–37

Genesys Telecommunications Laboratories Inc., 103 184–87

Genetics Institute, Inc., 8 215–18

Geneva Steel, 7 193–95

Genmar Holdings, Inc., 45 172–75

Genovese Drug Stores, Inc., 18 198–200

Genoyer *see* Groupe Genoyer.

GenRad, Inc., 24 179–83

Gentex Corporation, 26 153–57

Genting Bhd., 65 152–55

Gentiva Health Services, Inc., 79 189–92

Genuardi's Family Markets, Inc., 35 190–92

Genuine Parts Company, 9 253–55; 45 176–79 (upd.)

Genzyme Corporation, 13 239–42; 38 203–07 (upd.); 77 164–70 (upd.)

geobra Brandstätter GmbH & Co. KG, 48 183–86

Geodis S.A., 67 187–90

The Geon Company, 11 158–61

GeoResources, Inc., 101 196–99

Georg Fischer AG Schaffhausen, 61 106–09

Georg Jensen A/S, 110 173–77

George A. Hormel and Company, II 504–06 *see also* Hormel Foods Corp.

The George F. Cram Company, Inc., 55 158–60

George P. Johnson Company, 60 142–44

George S. May International Company, 55 161–63

George W. Park Seed Company, Inc., 98 145–48

George Weston Ltd., II 631–32; 36 245–48 (upd.); 88 114–19 (upd.)

George Wimpey plc, 12 201–03; 51 135–38 (upd.)

Georgia Gulf Corporation, 9 256–58; 61 110–13 (upd.)

Georgia-Pacific LLC, IV 281–83; 9 259–62 (upd.); 47 145–51 (upd.); 101 200–09 (upd.)

Geotek Communications Inc., 21 238–40

Gerald Stevens, Inc., 37 161–63

Gerber Products Company, 7 196–98; 21 241–44 (upd)

Gerber Scientific, Inc., 12 204–06; 84 150–154 (upd.)

Gerdau S.A., 59 200–03

Gerhard D. Wempe KG, 88 120–25

Gericom AG, 47 152–54

Gerling-Konzern Versicherungs-Beteiligungs-Aktiengesellschaft, 51 139–43

German American Bancorp, 41 178–80

Gerresheimer Glas AG, 43 186–89

Gerry Weber International AG, 63 169–72

Gertrude Hawk Chocolates Inc., 104 162–65

Gesellschaft für musikalische Aufführungs-und mechanische Vervielfältigungsrechte *see* GEMA.

Getrag Corporate Group, 92 137–42

Getronics NV, 39 176–78

Getty Images, Inc., 31 216–18

Gevaert *see* Agfa Gevaert Group N.V.

Gévelot S.A., 96 132–35

Gevity HR, Inc., 63 173–77

GF Health Products, Inc., 82 138–41

GFI Informatique SA, 49 165–68

GfK Aktiengesellschaft, 49 169–72

GFS *see* Gordon Food Service Inc.

Ghirardelli Chocolate Company, 30 218–20

Gianni Versace S.p.A., 22 238–40; 106 202–07 (upd.)

Giant Cement Holding, Inc., 23 224–26

Giant Eagle, Inc., 86 160–64

Giant Food LLC, II 633–35; 22 241–44 (upd.); 83 155–161 (upd.)

Giant Industries, Inc., 19 175–77; 61 114–18 (upd.)

Giant Manufacturing Company, Ltd., 85 150–54

GIB Group, V 63–66; 26 158–62 (upd.)

Gibbs and Dandy plc, 74 119–21

Gibraltar Steel Corporation, 37 164–67

Gibson Greetings, Inc., 12 207–10 *see also* American Greetings Corp.

Gibson Guitar Corporation, 16 237–40; 100 182–87 (upd.)

Gibson, Dunn & Crutcher LLP, 36 249–52

Giddings & Lewis, Inc., 10 328–30

Giesecke & Devrient GmbH, 83 162–166

GiFi S.A., 74 122–24

Gifts In Kind International, 101 210–13

GigaMedia Limited, 109 264–68

Gilbane, Inc., 34 191–93

Gildan Activewear, Inc., 81 165–68

Gildemeister AG, 79 193–97

Gilead Sciences, Inc., 54 129–31

Gillett Holdings, Inc., 7 199–201

The Gillette Company, III 27–30; 20 249–53 (upd.); 68 171–76 (upd.)

Gilman & Ciocia, Inc., 72 148–50

Gilmore Entertainment Group L.L.C., 100 188–91

Ginnie Mae *see* Government National Mortgage Association.

Giorgio Armani S.p.A., 45 180–83

Girl Scouts of the USA, 35 193–96

The Gitano Group, Inc., 8 219–21

GIV *see* Granite Industries of Vermont, Inc.; Gruppo Italiano Vini

Givaudan SA, 43 190–93

Given Imaging Ltd., 83 167–170

Givenchy *see* Parfums Givenchy S.A.

GKN plc, III 493–96; 38 208–13 (upd.); 89 232–41 (upd.)

GL Events S.A., 107 150–53

Glaces Thiriet S.A., 76 164–66

Glacier Bancorp, Inc., 35 197–200

Glacier Water Services, Inc., 47 155–58

Glamis Gold, Ltd., 54 132–35

Glanbia plc, 59 204–07, 364

Glatfelter Wood Pulp Company *see* P.H. Glatfelter Company

Glaverbel Group, 80 130–33

Glaxo Holdings plc, I 639–41; 9 263–65 (upd.)

GlaxoSmithKline plc, 46 201–08 (upd.)

Glazer's Wholesale Drug Company, Inc., 82 142–45

Gleason Corporation, 24 184–87

Glen Dimplex, 78 123–27

Glico *see* Ezaki Glico Company Ltd.

The Glidden Company, 8 222–24

Global Berry Farms LLC, 62 154–56

Global Cash Access Holdings, Inc., 111 160–63

Global Crossing Ltd., 32 216–19

Global Hyatt Corporation, 75 159–63 (upd.)

Global Imaging Systems, Inc., 73 163–65

Global Industries, Ltd., 37 168–72

Global Marine Inc., 9 266–67

Global Outdoors, Inc., 49 173–76

Global Payments Inc., 91 206–10

Global Power Equipment Group Inc., 52 137–39

GlobalSantaFe Corporation, 48 187–92 (upd.)

Globe Newspaper Company Inc., 106 208–12

Globex Utilidades S.A., 103 188–91

Globo Comunicação e Participações S.A., 80 134–38

Glock Ges.m.b.H., 42 154–56

Glon *see* Groupe Glon.

Glotel plc, 53 149–51

Glu Mobile Inc., 95 163–66

Gluek Brewing Company, 75 164–66

GM *see* General Motors Corp.

GM Hughes Electronics Corporation, II 32–36 *see also* Hughes Electronics Corp.

GMAC, LLC, 109 269–73

GMH Communities Trust, 87 176–178

GN ReSound A/S, 103 192–96

N.V. Holdingmaatschappij De Telegraaf, 23 271–73 *see also* Telegraaf Media Groep N.V.

Holiday Inns, Inc., III 94–95 *see also* Promus Companies, Inc.

Holiday Retirement Corp., 87 221–223

Holiday RV Superstores, Incorporated, 26 192–95

Holidaybreak plc, 96 182–86

Holland & Knight LLP, 60 171–74

Holland America Line Inc., 108 262–65

Holland Burgerville USA, 44 224–26

Holland Casino, 107 191–94

The Holland Group, Inc., 82 174–77

Hollander Home Fashions Corp., 67 207–09

Holley Performance Products Inc., 52 157–60

Hollinger International Inc., 24 222–25; 62 184–88 (upd.)

Holly Corporation, 12 240–42; 111 205–10 (upd.)

Hollywood Casino Corporation, 21 275–77

Hollywood Entertainment Corporation, 25 208–10

Hollywood Media Corporation, 58 164–68

Hollywood Park, Inc., 20 297–300

Holme Roberts & Owen LLP, 28 196–99

Holmen AB, 52 161–65 (upd.); 111 211–17 (upd.)

Holnam Inc., 8 258–60; 39 217–20 (upd.)

Hologic, Inc., 106 233–36

Holophane Corporation, 19 209–12

Holson Burnes Group, Inc., 14 244–45

Holt and Bugbee Company, 66 189–91

Holt's Cigar Holdings, Inc., 42 176–78

Holtzbrinck *see* Verlagsgruppe Georg von Holtzbrinck.

Homasote Company, 72 178–81

Home Box Office Inc., 7 222–24; 23 274–77 (upd.); 76 178–82 (upd.)

Home City Ice Company, Inc., 111 218–22

The Home Depot, Inc., V 75–76; 18 238–40 (upd.); 97 208–13 (upd.)

Home Hardware Stores Ltd., 62 189–91

Home Inns & Hotels Management Inc., 95 195–95

Home Insurance Company, III 262–64

Home Interiors & Gifts, Inc., 55 202–04

Home Market Foods, Inc., 110 213–16

Home Product Center plc, 104 205–08

Home Products International, Inc., 55 205–07

Home Properties of New York, Inc., 42 179–81

Home Retail Group plc, 91 242–46

Home Shopping Network, Inc., V 77–78; 25 211–15 (upd.) *see also* HSN.

HomeBase, Inc., 33 198–201 (upd.)

Homestake Mining Company, 12 243–45; 38 229–32 (upd.)

Hometown Auto Retailers, Inc., 44 227–29

HomeVestors of America, Inc., 77 195–98

Homex *see* Desarrolladora Homex, S.A. de C.V.

Hon Hai Precision Industry Co., Ltd., 59 234–36

HON Industries Inc., 13 266–69 *see* HNI Corp.

Honda Motor Company Ltd., I 174–76; 10 352–54 (upd.); 29 239–42 (upd.); 96 187–93 (upd.)

Honeywell International Inc., II 40–43; 12 246–49 (upd.); 50 231–35 (upd.)109 300–07 (upd.)

Hong Kong and China Gas Company Ltd., 73 177–79

Hong Kong Dragon Airlines Ltd., 66 192–94

Hong Kong Telecommunications Ltd., 6 319–21 *see also* Cable & Wireless HKT.

Hongkong and Shanghai Banking Corporation Limited, II 296–99 *see also* HSBC Holdings plc.

Hongkong Electric Holdings Ltd., 6 498–500; 23 278–81 (upd.); 107 195–200 (upd.)

Hongkong Land Holdings Ltd., IV 699–701; 47 175–78 (upd.)

Honshu Paper Co., Ltd., IV 284–85 *see also* Oji Paper Co., Ltd.

Hoogovens *see* Koninklijke Nederlandsche Hoogovens en Staalfabricken NV.

Hooker Furniture Corporation, 80 143–46

Hooper Holmes, Inc., 22 264–67

Hooters of America, Inc., 18 241–43; 69 211–14 (upd.)

The Hoover Company, 12 250–52; 40 258–62 (upd.)

Hoover's, Inc., 108 266–69

HOP, LLC, 80 147–50

Hops Restaurant Bar and Brewery, 46 233–36

Hopson Development Holdings Ltd., 87 224–227

Horace Mann Educators Corporation, 22 268–70; 90 237–40 (upd.)

Horizon Food Group, Inc., 100 225–28

Horizon Lines, Inc., 98 197–200

Horizon Organic Holding Corporation, 37 195–99

Hormel Foods Corporation, 18 244–47 (upd.); 54 164–69 (upd.)

Hornbach Holding AG, 98 201–07

Hornbeck Offshore Services, Inc., 101 246–49

Hornby PLC, 105 221–25

Horsehead Industries, Inc., 51 165–67

Horserace Totalisator Board (The Tote), 107 201–05

Horseshoe Gaming Holding Corporation, 62 192–95

Horton Homes, Inc., 25 216–18

Horween Leather Company, 83 183–186

Hoshino Gakki Co. Ltd., 55 208–11

Hospira, Inc., 71 172–74

Hospital Central Services, Inc., 56 166–68

Hospital Corporation of America, III 78–80 *see also* HCA, Inc.

Hospitality Franchise Systems, Inc., 11 177–79 *see also* Cendant Corp.

Hospitality Worldwide Services, Inc., 26 196–98

Hoss's Steak and Sea House Inc., 68 196–98

Host America Corporation, 79 202–06

Host Hotels & Resorts, Inc., 112 211–13

Hot Dog on a Stick *see* HDOS Enterprises.

Hot Stuff Foods, 85 171–74

Hot Topic Inc., 33 202–04; 86 190–94 (upd.)

Hotel Properties Ltd., 71 175–77

Hotel Shilla Company Ltd., 110 217–20

Houchens Industries Inc., 51 168–70

Houghton Mifflin Company, 10 355–57; 36 270–74 (upd.)

House of Fabrics, Inc., 21 278–80 *see also* Jo-Ann Stores, Inc.

House of Fraser PLC, 45 188–91 *see also* Harrods Holdings.

House of Prince A/S, 80 151–54

Household International, Inc., II 417–20; 21 281–86 (upd.) *see also* HSBC Holdings plc.

Houston Industries Incorporated, V 641–44 *see also* Reliant Energy Inc.

Houston Wire & Cable Company, 97 214–17

Hovnanian Enterprises, Inc., 29 243–45; 89 254–59 (upd.)

Howard Hughes Medical Institute, 39 221–24

Howard Johnson International, Inc., 17 236–39; 72 182–86 (upd.)

Howden Group Limited, 111 223–26

Howmet Corporation, 12 253–55 *see also* Alcoa Inc.

HP *see* Hewlett-Packard Co.

HSBC Holdings plc, 12 256–58; 26 199–204 (upd.); 80 155–63 (upd.)

HSN, 64 181–85 (upd.)

Huawei Technologies Company Ltd., 87 228–231

Hub Group, Inc., 38 233–35

Hub International Limited, 89 260–64

Hubbard Broadcasting Inc., 24 226–28; 79 207–12 (upd.)

Hubbell Inc., 9 286–87; 31 257–59 (upd.); 76 183–86 (upd.)

Huddle House, Inc., 105 226–29

The Hudson Bay Mining and Smelting Company, Limited, 12 259–61

Hudson Foods Inc., 13 270–72 *see also* Tyson Foods, Inc.

Hudson River Bancorp, Inc., 41 210–13

Hudson's Bay Company, V 79–81; 25 219–22 (upd.); 83 187–194 (upd.)

HuffingtonPost.com, Inc., 111 227–30

Imetal S.A., IV 107–09
IMG, 78 177–80
IMI plc, 9 288–89; 29 364
Immucor, Inc., 81 192–96
Immunex Corporation, 14 254–56; 50 248–53 (upd.)
Imo Industries Inc., 7 235–37; 27 229–32 (upd.)
IMPATH Inc., 45 192–94
Imperial Chemical Industries plc, I 351–53; 50 254–58 (upd.)
Imperial Holly Corporation, 12 268–70 *see also* Imperial Sugar Co.
Imperial Industries, Inc., 81 197–200
Imperial Oil Limited, IV 437–39; 25 229–33 (upd.); 95 196–203 (upd.)
Imperial Parking Corporation, 58 182–84
Imperial Sugar Company, 32 274–78 (upd.)
Imperial Tobacco Group PLC, 50 259–63
IMS Health, Inc., 57 174–78
In Focus Systems, Inc., 22 287–90
In-N-Out Burgers Inc., 19 213–15; 74 153–56 (upd.)
In-Sink-Erator, 66 195–98
InaCom Corporation, 13 276–78
Inamed Corporation, 79 213–16
Inchcape PLC, III 521–24; 16 276–80 (upd.); 50 264–68 (upd.)
Inco Limited, IV 110–12; 45 195–99 (upd.)
Incyte Genomics, Inc., 52 174–77
Indel, Inc., 78 181–84
Independent News & Media PLC, 61 129–31
Indian Airlines Ltd., 46 240–42
Indian Oil Corporation Ltd., IV 440–41; 48 210–13 (upd.)
Indiana Bell Telephone Company, Incorporated, 14 257–61
Indiana Energy, Inc., 27 233–36
Indianapolis Motor Speedway Corporation, 46 243–46
Indigo Books & Music Inc., 58 185–87
Indigo NV, 26 212–14 *see also* Hewlett-Packard Co.
Indosat *see* PT Indosat Tbk.
Indus International Inc., 70 127–30
Industria de Diseño Textil S.A. (Inditex), 64 193–95
Industrial and Commercial Bank of China Ltd., 109 308–12
Industrial Bank of Japan, Ltd., II 300–01
Industrial Light & Magic *see* Lucasfilm Ltd.
Industrial Services of America, Inc., 46 247–49
Industrias Bachoco, S.A. de C.V., 39 228–31
Industrias Peñoles, S.A. de C.V., 22 284–86; 107 215–19 (upd.)
Industrie Natuzzi S.p.A., 18 256–58
Industrie Zignago Santa Margherita S.p.A., 67 210–12
Inergy L.P., 110 234–37

Infineon Technologies AG, 50 269–73
Infinity Broadcasting Corporation, 11 190–92; 48 214–17 (upd.)
InFocus Corporation, 92 172–75
Infogrames Entertainment S.A., 35 227–30
Informa Group plc, 58 188–91
Information Access Company, 17 252–55
Information Builders, Inc., 22 291–93
Information Holdings Inc., 47 183–86
Information Resources, Inc., 10 358–60
Informix Corporation, 10 361–64; 30 243–46 (upd.) *see also* International Business Machines Corp.
InfoSonics Corporation, 81 201–04
InfoSpace, Inc., 91 259–62
Infosys Technologies Ltd., 38 240–43
Ing. C. Olivetti & C., S.p.A., III 144–46 *see also* Olivetti S.p.A
ING Groep N.V., 108 270–75
Ingalls Shipbuilding, Inc., 12 271–73
Ingenico—Compagnie Industrielle et Financière d'Ingénierie, 46 250–52
Ingersoll-Rand Company, III 525–27; 15 223–26 (upd.); 55 218–22 (upd.)
Ingles Markets, Inc., 20 305–08
Ingram Industries, Inc., 11 193–95; 49 217–20 (upd.)
Ingram Micro Inc., 52 178–81
INI *see* Instituto Nacional de Industria.
Initial Security, 64 196–98
Inktomi Corporation, 45 200–04
Inland Container Corporation, 8 267–69 *see also* Temple-Inland Inc.
Inland Steel Industries, Inc., IV 113–16; 19 216–20 (upd.)
Innovative Solutions & Support, Inc., 85 175–78
Innovo Group Inc., 83 195–199
INPEX Holdings Inc., 97 230–33
Input/Output, Inc., 73 184–87
Inserra Supermarkets, 25 234–36
Insight Enterprises, Inc., 18 259–61
Insilco Corporation, 16 281–83
Insituform Technologies, Inc., 83 200–203
Inso Corporation, 26 215–19
Instinet Corporation, 34 225–27
Instituto Nacional de Industria, I 459–61
Insurance Auto Auctions, Inc., 23 285–87
Integra LifeSciences Holdings Corporation, 87 244–247
Integrated BioPharma, Inc., 83 204–207
Integrated Defense Technologies, Inc., 54 178–80
Integrity Inc., 44 241–43
Integrity Media, Inc., 102 180–83
Integrys Energy Group, Inc., 109 313–17
Intel Corporation, II 44–46; 10 365–67 (upd.); 36 284–88 (upd.); 75 196–201 (upd.)
IntelliCorp, Inc., 45 205–07
Intelligent Electronics, Inc., 6 243–45
Inter Link Foods PLC, 61 132–34

Inter Parfums Inc., 35 235–38; 86 201–06 (upd.)
Inter-Regional Financial Group, Inc., 15 231–33 *see also* Dain Rauscher Corp.
Interactive Intelligence Inc., 106 243–47
Interbond Corporation of America, 101 257–60
Interbrand Corporation, 70 131–33
Interbrew S.A., 17 256–58; 50 274–79 (upd.)
Interceramic *see* Internacional de Ceramica, S.A. de C.V.
Interco Incorporated, III 528–31 *see also* Furniture Brands International, Inc.
InterContinental Hotels Group, PLC, 109 318–25 (upd.)
IntercontinentalExchange, Inc., 95 204–07
Intercorp Excelle Foods Inc., 64 199–201
InterDigital Communications Corporation, 61 135–37
Interep National Radio Sales Inc., 35 231–34
Interface, Inc., 8 270–72; 29 246–49 (upd.); 76 195–99 (upd.)
Interfax News Agency, 86 207–10
Intergraph Corporation, 6 246–49; 24 233–36 (upd.)
The Interlake Corporation, 8 273–75
Intermec Technologies Corporation, 72 187–91
INTERMET Corporation, 32 279–82; 77 207–12 (upd.)
Intermix Media, Inc., 83 208–211
Intermountain Health Care, Inc., 27 237–40
Internacional de Ceramica, S.A. de C.V., 53 174–76
International Airline Support Group, Inc., 55 223–25
International Assets Holding Corporation, 111 244–47
International Brotherhood of Teamsters, 37 211–14
International Business Machines Corporation, III 147–49; 6 250–53 (upd.); 30 247–51 (upd.); 63 195–201 (upd.)
International Controls Corporation, 10 368–70
International Creative Management, Inc., 43 235–37
International Dairy Queen, Inc., 10 371–74; 39 232–36 (upd.); 105 248–54 (upd.)
International Data Group, Inc., 7 238–40; 25 237–40 (upd.)
International Family Entertainment Inc., 13 279–81 *see also* Disney/ABC Television Group
International Flavors & Fragrances Inc., 9 290–92; 38 244–48 (upd.)
International Game Technology, 10 375–76; 41 214–16 (upd.)
International House of Pancakes *see* IHOP Corp.

Jack B. Kelley, Inc., 102 184–87

Jack Henry and Associates, Inc., 17 262–65; 94 258–63 (upd.)

Jack in the Box Inc., 89 265–71 (upd.)

Jack Morton Worldwide, 88 215–18

Jack Schwartz Shoes, Inc., 18 266–68

Jackpot Enterprises Inc., 21 298–300

Jackson Hewitt, Inc., 48 234–36

Jackson National Life Insurance Company, 8 276–77

Jacmar Companies, 87 266–269

Jaco Electronics, Inc., 30 255–57

Jacob Leinenkugel Brewing Company, 28 209–11

Jacobs Engineering Group Inc., 6 148–50; 26 220–23 (upd.); 106 248–54 (upd.)

Jacobs Suchard (AG), II 520–22 *see also* Kraft Jacobs Suchard AG.

Jacobson Stores Inc., 21 301–03

Jacor Communications, Inc., 23 292–95

Jacques Torres Chocolate *see* Mrchocolate.com LLC.

Jacques Whitford, 92 184–87

Jacquot *see* Établissements Jacquot and Cie S.A.S.

Jacuzzi Brands Inc., 23 296–98; 76 204–07 (upd.)

JAFCO Co. Ltd., 79 221–24

Jaguar Cars, Ltd., 13 285–87

Jaiprakash Associates Limited, 101 269–72

JAKKS Pacific, Inc., 52 191–94

JAL *see* Japan Airlines Company, Ltd.

Jalate Inc., 25 245–47

Jamba Juice Company, 47 199–202

James Avery Craftsman, Inc., 76 208–10

James Beattie plc, 43 242–44

James Hardie Industries N.V., 56 174–76

James Original Coney Island Inc., 84 197–200

James Purdey & Sons Limited, 87 270–275

James River Corporation of Virginia, IV 289–91 *see also* Fort James Corp.

Jani-King International, Inc., 85 191–94

JanSport, Inc., 70 134–36

Janssen Pharmaceutica N.V., 80 164–67

Janus Capital Group Inc., 57 192–94

Japan Airlines Corporation, I 104–06; 32 288–92 (upd.); 110 242–49 (upd.)

Japan Broadcasting Corporation, 7 248–50

Japan Leasing Corporation, 8 278–80

Japan Post Holdings Company Ltd., 108 281–85

Japan Pulp and Paper Company Limited, IV 292–93

Japan Tobacco Inc., V 403–04; 46 257–60 (upd.)

Jarden Corporation, 93 255–61 (upd.)

Jardine Cycle & Carriage Ltd., 73 193–95

Jardine Matheson Holdings Limited, I 468–71; 20 309–14 (upd.); 93 262–71 (upd.)

Jarvis plc, 39 237–39

Jason Incorporated, 23 299–301

Jay Jacobs, Inc., 15 243–45

Jayco Inc., 13 288–90

Jaypee Group *see* Jaiprakash Associates Ltd.

Jays Foods, Inc., 90 258–61

Jazz Basketball Investors, Inc., 55 237–39

Jazzercise, Inc., 45 212–14

JB Oxford Holdings, Inc., 32 293–96

JBS S.A., 100 233–36

JCDecaux S.A., 76 211–13

JD Group Ltd., 110 250–54

JD Wetherspoon plc, 30 258–60

JDA Software Group, Inc., 101 273–76

JDS Uniphase Corporation, 34 235–37

JE Dunn Construction Group, Inc., 85 195–98

The Jean Coutu Group (PJC) Inc., 46 261–65

Jean-Georges Enterprises L.L.C., 75 209–11

Jeanneau *see* Chantiers Jeanneau S.A.

Jefferies Group, Inc., 25 248–51

Jefferson-Pilot Corporation, 11 213–15; 29 253–56 (upd.)

Jefferson Properties, Inc. *see* JPI.

Jefferson Smurfit Group plc, IV 294–96; 19 224–27 (upd.); 49 224–29 (upd.) *see also* Smurfit Kappa Group plc

Jel Sert Company, 90 262–65

Jeld-Wen, Inc., 45 215–17

Jelly Belly Candy Company, 76 214–16

Jenkens & Gilchrist, P.C., 65 180–82

Jennie-O Turkey Store, Inc., 76 217–19

Jennifer Convertibles, Inc., 31 274–76

Jenny Craig, Inc., 10 382–84; 29 257–60 (upd.); 92 188–93 (upd.)

Jenoptik AG, 33 218–21

Jeppesen Sanderson, Inc., 92 194–97

Jerónimo Martins SGPS S.A., 96 213–16

Jerry's Famous Deli Inc., 24 243–45

Jersey European Airways (UK) Ltd., 61 144–46

Jersey Mike's Franchise Systems, Inc., 83 223–226

Jervis B. Webb Company, 24 246–49

Jet Airways (India) Private Limited, 65 183–85

JetBlue Airways Corporation, 44 248–50

Jetro Cash & Carry Enterprises Inc., 38 266–68

Jewett-Cameron Trading Company, Ltd., 89 272–76

JFE Shoji Holdings Inc., 88 219–22

JG Industries, Inc., 15 240–42

Jillian's Entertainment Holdings, Inc., 40 273–75

Jim Beam Brands Worldwide, Inc., 14 271–73; 58 194–96 (upd.)

The Jim Henson Company, 23 302–04; 106 255–59 (upd.)

The Jim Pattison Group, 37 219–22

Jimmy Carter Work Project *see* Habitat for Humanity International.

Jimmy John's Enterprises, Inc., 103 227–30

Jitney-Jungle Stores of America, Inc., 27 245–48

JJB Sports plc, 32 302–04

JKH Holding Co. LLC, 105 260–63

JLA Credit *see* Japan Leasing Corp.

JLG Industries, Inc., 52 195–97

JLL *see* Jones Lang LaSalle Inc.

JLM Couture, Inc., 64 206–08

JM Smith Corporation, 100 237–40

JMB Realty Corporation, IV 702–03 *see also* Amfac/JMB Hawaii L.L.C.

Jo-Ann Stores, Inc., 72 200–03 (upd.)

Jockey International, Inc., 12 283–85; 34 238–42 (upd.); 77 217–23 (upd.)

Joe's Sports & Outdoor, 98 218–22 (upd.)

The Joffrey Ballet of Chicago, 52 198–202

Johanna Foods, Inc., 104 221–24

John B. Sanfilippo & Son, Inc., 14 274–76; 101 277–81 (upd.)

John Brown plc, I 572–74

The John D. and Catherine T. MacArthur Foundation, 34 243–46

John D. Brush Company Inc., 94 264–67

The John David Group plc, 90 266–69

John Deere *see* Deere & Co.

John Dewar & Sons, Ltd., 82 182–86

John F. Kennedy Center for the Performing Arts, 106 260–63

John Fairfax Holdings Limited, 7 251–54 *see also* Fairfax Media Ltd.

John Frieda Professional Hair Care Inc., 70 137–39

John H. Harland Company, 17 266–69

John Hancock Financial Services, Inc., III 265–68; 42 193–98 (upd.)

John Laing plc, I 575–76; 51 171–73 (upd.) *see also* Laing O'Rourke PLC.

John Lewis Partnership plc, V 93–95; 42 199–203 (upd.); 99 233–240 (upd.)

John Menzies plc, 39 240–43

The John Nuveen Company, 21 304–065

John Paul Mitchell Systems, 24 250–52; 112 224–28 (upd.)

John Q. Hammons Hotels, Inc., 24 253–55

John W. Danforth Company, 48 237–39

John Wiley & Sons, Inc., 17 270–72; 65 186–90 (upd.)

Johnny Rockets Group, Inc., 31 277–81; 76 220–24 (upd.)

Johns Manville Corporation, 64 209–14 (upd.)

Johnson *see* Axel Johnson Group.

Johnson & Higgins, 14 277–80 *see also* Marsh & McLennan Companies, Inc.

Johnson & Johnson, III 35–37; 8 281–83 (upd.); 36 302–07 (upd.); 75 212–18 (upd.)

CUMULATIVE INDEX TO COMPANIES

Marks Brothers Jewelers, Inc., 24 318–20 *see also* Whitehall Jewellers, Inc.

Marlin Business Services Corp., 89 317–19

The Marmon Group, Inc., IV 135–38; 16 354–57 (upd.); 70 167–72 (upd.)

Marquette Electronics, Inc., 13 326–28

Marriott International, Inc., III 102–03; 21 364–67 (upd.); 83 264–270 (upd.)

Mars, Incorporated, 7 299–301; 40 302–05 (upd.)

Mars Petcare US Inc., 96 269–72

Marsh & McLennan Companies, Inc., III 282–84; 45 263–67 (upd.)

Marsh Supermarkets, Inc., 17 300–02; 76 255–58 (upd.)

Marshall & Ilsley Corporation, 56 217–20

Marshall Amplification plc, 62 239–42

Marshall Field's, 63 254–63 *see also* Target Corp.

Marshalls Incorporated, 13 329–31

Martek Biosciences Corporation, 65 218–20

Martell and Company S.A., 82 213–16

Marten Transport, Ltd., 84 243–246

Martha Stewart Living Omnimedia, Inc., 24 321–23; 73 219–22 (upd.)

Martha White Foods Inc., 104 284–87

Martignetti Companies, 84 247–250

Martin-Baker Aircraft Company Limited, 61 195–97

Martin Franchises, Inc., 80 236–39

Martin Guitar Company *see* C.F. Martin & Co., Inc.

Martin Industries, Inc., 44 274–77

Martin Marietta Corporation, I 67–69 *see also* Lockheed Martin Corp.

Martini & Rossi SpA, 63 264–66

MartinLogan, Ltd., 85 248–51

Martins *see* Grupo Martins.

Martin's Super Markets, Inc., 101 330–33

Martz Group, 56 221–23

Marubeni Corporation, I 492–95; 24 324–27 (upd.); 104 288–93 (upd.)

Maruha Group Inc., 75 250–53 (upd.)

Marui Company Ltd., V 127; 62 243–45 (upd.)

Maruzen Company Ltd., 18 322–24; 104 294–97 (upd.)

Marvel Entertainment, Inc., 10 400–02; 78 212–19 (upd.)

Marvell Technology Group Ltd., 112 268–71

Marvelous Market Inc., 104 298–301

Marvin Lumber & Cedar Company, 22 345–47

Mary Kay Inc., 9 330–32; 30 306–09 (upd.); 84 251–256 (upd.)

Maryland & Virginia Milk Producers Cooperative Association, Inc., 80 240–43

Maryville Data Systems Inc., 96 273–76

Marzotto S.p.A., 20 356–58; 67 246–49 (upd.)

The Maschhoffs, Inc., 82 217–20

Masco Corporation, III 568–71; 20 359–63 (upd.); 39 263–68 (upd.); 111 295–303 (upd.)

Maserati *see* Officine Alfieri Maserati S.p.A.

Mashantucket Pequot Gaming Enterprise Inc., 35 282–85

Masland Corporation, 17 303–05 *see also* Lear Corp.

Mason & Hanger Group Inc., 110 310–14

Masonite International Corporation, 63 267–69

Massachusetts Mutual Life Insurance Company, III 285–87; 53 210–13 (upd.)

Massey Energy Company, 57 236–38

MasTec, Inc., 55 259–63 (upd.)

Mastellone Hermanos S.A., 101 334–37

Master Lock Company, 45 268–71

Master Spas Inc., 105 292–95

MasterBrand Cabinets, Inc., 71 216–18

MasterCard Worldwide, 9 333–35; 96 277–81 (upd.)

MasterCraft Boat Company, Inc., 90 290–93

Matalan PLC, 49 258–60

Match.com, LP, 87 308–311

Material Sciences Corporation, 63 270–73

The MathWorks, Inc., 80 244–47

Matra-Hachette S.A., 15 293–97 (upd.) *see also* European Aeronautic Defence and Space Company EADS N.V.

Matria Healthcare, Inc., 17 306–09

Matrix Essentials Inc., 90 294–97

Matrix Service Company, 65 221–23

Matrixx Initiatives, Inc., 74 177–79

Matsushita Electric Industrial Co., Ltd., II 55–56; 64 255–58 (upd.)

Matsushita Electric Works, Ltd., III 710–11; 7 302–03 (upd.)

Matsuzakaya Company Ltd., V 129–31; 64 259–62 (upd.)

Matt Prentice Restaurant Group, 70 173–76

Mattel, Inc., 7 304–07; 25 311–15 (upd.); 61 198–203 (upd.)

Matth. Hohner AG, 53 214–17

Matthews International Corporation, 29 304–06; 77 248–52 (upd.)

Mattress Giant Corporation, 103 254–57

Matussière et Forest SA, 58 220–22

Maui Land & Pineapple Company, Inc., 29 307–09; 100 273–77 (upd.)

Maui Wowi, Inc., 85 252–55

Mauna Loa Macadamia Nut Corporation, 64 263–65

Maurices Inc., 95 255–58

Maus Frères SA, 48 277–79

Maverick Ranch Association, Inc., 88 253–56

Maverick Tube Corporation, 59 280–83

Maverik, Inc., 103 258–61

Max & Erma's Restaurants Inc., 19 258–60; 100 278–82 (upd.)

Maxco Inc., 17 310–11

Maxicare Health Plans, Inc., III 84–86; 25 316–19 (upd.)

The Maxim Group, 25 320–22

Maxim Integrated Products, Inc., 16 358–60

MAXIMUS, Inc., 43 277–80

Maxtor Corporation, 10 403–05 *see also* Seagate Technology, Inc.

Maxus Energy Corporation, 7 308–10

Maxwell Communication Corporation plc, IV 641–43; 7 311–13 (upd.)

Maxwell Shoe Company, Inc., 30 310–12 *see also* Jones Apparel Group, Inc.

MAXXAM Inc., 8 348–50

Maxxim Medical Inc., 12 325–27

The May Department Stores Company, V 132–35; 19 261–64 (upd.); 46 284–88 (upd.)

May Gurney Integrated Services PLC, 95 259–62

May International *see* George S. May International Co.

Mayer, Brown, Rowe & Maw, 47 230–32

Mayfield Dairy Farms, Inc., 74 180–82

Mayflower Group Inc., 6 409–11

Mayo Foundation, 9 336–39; 34 265–69 (upd.)

Mayor's Jewelers, Inc., 41 254–57

Maytag Corporation, III 572–73; 22 348–51 (upd.); 82 221–25 (upd.)

Mazda Motor Corporation, 9 340–42; 23 338–41 (upd.); 63 274–79 (upd.)

Mazeikiu Nafta *see* Orlen Lietuva

Mazel Stores, Inc., 29 310–12

Mazzio's Corporation, 76 259–61

MBB *see* Messerschmitt-Bölkow-Blohm.

MBC Holding Company, 40 306–09

MBE *see* Mail Boxes Etc.

MBIA Inc., 73 223–26

MBK Industrie S.A., 94 303–06

MBNA Corporation, 12 328–30; 33 291–94 (upd.)

MC Sporting Goods *see* Michigan Sporting Goods Distributors Inc.

MCA Inc., II 143–45 *see also* Universal Studios.

McAfee Inc., 94 307–10

McAlister's Corporation, 66 217–19

McBride plc, 82 226–30

MCC *see* Morris Communications Corp.

McCain Foods Limited, 77 253–56

McCarthy Building Companies, Inc., 48 280–82

McCaw Cellular Communications, Inc., 6 322–24 *see also* AT&T Wireless Services, Inc.

McClain Industries, Inc., 51 236–38

The McClatchy Company, 23 342–44; 92 231–35 (upd.)

McCormick & Company, Incorporated, 7 314–16; 27 297–300 (upd.)

McCormick & Schmick's Seafood Restaurants, Inc., 71 219–21

McCoy Corporation, 58 223–25

McDATA Corporation, 75 254–56

McDermott International, Inc., III 558–60; 37 242–46 (upd.)

McDonald's Corporation, II 646–48; 7 317–19 (upd.); 26 281–85 (upd.); 63 280–86 (upd.)

McDonnell Douglas Corporation, I 70–72; 11 277–80 (upd.) *see also* Boeing Co.

McGrath RentCorp, 91 326–29

The McGraw-Hill Companies, Inc., IV 634–37; 18 325–30 (upd.); 51 239–44 (upd.)

MCI *see* Melamine Chemicals, Inc.

MCI WorldCom, Inc., V 302–04; 27 301–08 (upd.) *see also* Verizon Communications Inc.

McIlhenny Company, 20 364–67

McJunkin Corporation, 63 287–89

McKechnie plc, 34 270–72

McKee Foods Corporation, 7 320–21; 27 309–11 (upd.)

McKesson Corporation, I 496–98; 12 331–33 (upd.); 47 233–37 (upd.); 108 334–41 (upd.)

McKinsey & Company, Inc., 9 343–45

McLanahan Corporation, 104 302–05

McLane Company, Inc., 13 332–34

McLeodUSA Incorporated, 32 327–30

McMenamins Pubs and Breweries, 65 224–26

McMoRan *see* Freeport-McMoRan Copper & Gold, Inc.

McMurry, Inc., 105 296–99

MCN Corporation, 6 519–22

McNaughton Apparel Group, Inc., 92 236–41 (upd.)

McPherson's Ltd., 66 220–22

McQuay International *see* AAF-McQuay Inc.

MCSi, Inc., 41 258–60

McWane Corporation, 55 264–66

MDC Partners Inc., 63 290–92

MDU Resources Group, Inc., 7 322–25; 42 249–53 (upd.)

The Mead Corporation, IV 310–13; 19 265–69 (upd.) *see also* MeadWestvaco Corp.

Mead Data Central, Inc., 10 406–08 *see also* LEXIS-NEXIS Group.

Mead Johnson & Company, 84 257–262

Meade Instruments Corporation, 41 261–64

Meadowcraft, Inc., 29 313–15; 100 283–87 (upd.)

MeadWestvaco Corporation, 76 262–71 (upd.)

Measurement Specialties, Inc., 71 222–25

MEC *see* Mitsubishi Estate Company, Ltd.

Mecalux S.A., 74 183–85

Mechel OAO, 99 278–281

Mecklermedia Corporation, 24 328–30 *see also* Jupitermedia Corp.

Medarex, Inc., 85 256–59

Medco Containment Services Inc., 9 346–48 *see also* Merck & Co., Inc.

Médecins sans Frontières, 85 260–63

MEDecision, Inc., 95 263–67

Media Arts Group, Inc., 42 254–57

Media General, Inc., 7 326–28; 38 306–09 (upd.)

Media Sciences International, Inc., 104 306–09

Mediacom Communications Corporation, 69 250–52

MediaNews Group, Inc., 70 177–80

Mediaset SpA, 50 332–34

Medical Action Industries Inc., 101 338–41

Medical Information Technology Inc., 64 266–69

Medical Management International, Inc., 65 227–29

Medical Staffing Network Holdings, Inc., 89 320–23

Medicine Shoppe International, Inc., 102 253–57

Medicis Pharmaceutical Corporation, 59 284–86

Medifast, Inc., 97 281–85

MedImmune, Inc., 35 286–89

Mediolanum S.p.A., 65 230–32

Medis Technologies Ltd., 77 257–60

Meditrust, 11 281–83

Medline Industries, Inc., 61 204–06

Medtronic, Inc., 8 351–54; 30 313–17 (upd.); 67 250–55 (upd.)

Medusa Corporation, 24 331–33

Mega Bloks, Inc., 61 207–09

Megafoods Stores Inc., 13 335–37

Meggitt PLC, 34 273–76

Meguiar's, Inc., 99 282–285

Meidensha Corporation, 92 242–46

Meier & Frank Co., 23 345–47 *see also* Macy's, Inc.

Meijer, Inc., 7 329–31; 27 312–15 (upd.); 101 342–46 (upd.)

Meiji Dairies Corporation, II 538–39; 82 231–34 (upd.)

Meiji Mutual Life Insurance Company, III 288–89

Meiji Seika Kaisha Ltd., II 540–41; 64 270–72 (upd.)

Mel Farr Automotive Group, 20 368–70

Melaleuca Inc., 31 326–28

Melamine Chemicals, Inc., 27 316–18 *see also* Mississippi Chemical Corp.

Melco Crown Entertainment Limited, 103 262–65

Melitta Unternehmensgruppe Bentz KG, 53 218–21

Mello Smello *see* The Miner Group International.

Mellon Financial Corporation, II 315–17; 44 278–82 (upd.)

Mellon-Stuart Co., I 584–85 *see also* Michael Baker Corp.

The Melting Pot Restaurants, Inc., 74 186–88

Melville Corporation, V 136–38 *see also* CVS Corp.

Melvin Simon and Associates, Inc., 8 355–57 *see also* Simon Property Group, Inc.

MEMC Electronic Materials, Inc., 81 249–52

Memorial Sloan-Kettering Cancer Center, 57 239–41

Memry Corporation, 72 225–27

The Men's Wearhouse, Inc., 17 312–15; 48 283–87 (upd.)

Menard, Inc., 104 310–14 (upd.)

Menasha Corporation, 8 358–61; 59 287–92 (upd.)

Mendocino Brewing Company, Inc., 60 205–07

The Mentholatum Company Inc., 32 331–33

Mentor Corporation, 26 286–88

Mentor Graphics Corporation, 11 284–86

MEPC plc, IV 710–12

Mercantile Bankshares Corp., 11 287–88

Mercantile Stores Company, Inc., V 139; 19 270–73 (upd.) *see also* Dillard's Inc.

Mercer International Inc., 64 273–75

The Merchants Company, 102 258–61

Mercian Corporation, 77 261–64

Merck & Co., Inc., I 650–52; 11 289–91 (upd.); 34 280–85 (upd.); 95 268–78 (upd.)

Merck KGaA, 111 304–10

Mercury Air Group, Inc., 20 371–73

Mercury Communications, Ltd., 7 332–34 *see also* Cable and Wireless plc.

Mercury Drug Corporation, 70 181–83

Mercury General Corporation, 25 323–25

Mercury Interactive Corporation, 59 293–95

Mercury Marine Group, 68 247–51

Meredith Corporation, 11 292–94; 29 316–19 (upd.); 74 189–93 (upd.)

Merge Healthcare, 85 264–68

Merial Ltd., 102 262–66

Meridian Bancorp, Inc., 11 295–97

Meridian Gold, Incorporated, 47 238–40

Meridian Industries Inc., 107 265–68

Merillat Industries, LLC, 13 338–39; 69 253–55 (upd.)

Merisant Worldwide, Inc., 70 184–86

Merisel, Inc., 12 334–36

Merit Medical Systems, Inc., 29 320–22

Meritage Corporation, 26 289–92

MeritCare Health System, 88 257–61

Merix Corporation, 36 329–31; 75 257–60 (upd.)

Merlin Entertainments Group Ltd., 105 300–03

Merriam-Webster Inc., 70 187–91

Merrill Corporation, 18 331–34; 47 241–44 (upd.)

Merrill Lynch & Co., Inc., II 424–26; 13 340–43 (upd.); 40 310–15 (upd.)

Merry-Go-Round Enterprises, Inc., 8 362–64

The Mersey Docks and Harbour Company, 30 318–20

NOW *see* National Organization for Women, Inc.

NPC International, Inc., 40 340–42

The NPD Group, Inc., 68 275–77

NPM (Nationale Portefeuille Maatschappij) *see* Compagnie Nationale à Portefeuille.

NPR *see* National Public Radio, Inc.

NRG Energy, Inc., 79 290–93

NRJ Group S.A., 107 300–04

NRT Incorporated, 61 267–69

NS *see* Norfolk Southern Corp.

NSF International, 72 252–55

NSK *see* Nippon Seiko K.K.

NSP *see* Northern States Power Co.

NSS Enterprises, Inc., 78 262–65

NSTAR, 106 324–31 **(upd.)**

NTCL *see* Northern Telecom Ltd.

NTD Architecture, 101 373–76

NTK Holdings Inc., 107 305–11 **(upd.)**

NTL Inc., 65 269–72

NTN Buzztime, Inc., 86 308–11

NTN Corporation, III 595–96; **47** 278–81 **(upd.)**

NTTPC *see* Nippon Telegraph and Telephone Public Corp.

NU *see* Northeast Utilities.

Nu-kote Holding, Inc., 18 386–89

Nu Skin Enterprises, Inc., 27 350–53; **31** 386–89; **76** 286–90 **(upd.)**

Nucor Corporation, 7 400–02; **21** 392–95 **(upd.)**; **79** 294–300 **(upd.)**

Nufarm Ltd., 87 345–348

Nuplex Industries Ltd., 92 280–83

Nuqul Group of Companies, 102 311–14

NuStar Energy L.P., 111 354–57

Nutraceutical International Corporation, 37 284–86

The NutraSweet Company, 8 398–400; **107** 312–16 **(upd.)**

Nutreco Holding N.V., 56 256–59

Nutrexpa S.A., 92 284–87

NutriSystem, Inc., 71 250–53

Nutrition 21 Inc., 97 307–11

Nutrition for Life International Inc., 22 385–88

Nuveen *see* John Nuveen Co.

NV Umicore SA, 47 411–13

NVIDIA Corporation, 54 269–73

NVR Inc., 8 401–03; **70** 206–09 **(upd.)**

NWA, Inc. *see* Northwest Airlines Corp.

NYK *see* Nippon Yusen Kabushiki Kaisha (NYK).

NYMAGIC, Inc., 41 284–86

NYNEX Corporation, V 311–13 *see also* Verizon Communications.

Nypro, Inc., 101 377–82

NYRG *see* New York Restaurant Group, Inc.

NYSE *see* New York Stock Exchange.

NYSEG *see* New York State Electric and Gas Corp.

O

O&Y *see* Olympia & York Developments Ltd.

O.C. Tanner Co., 69 279–81

Oak Harbor Freight Lines, Inc., 53 248–51

Oak Industries Inc., 21 396–98 *see also* Corning Inc.

Oak Technology, Inc., 22 389–93 *see also* Zoran Corp.

Oakhurst Dairy, 60 225–28

Oakleaf Waste Management, LLC, 97 312–15

Oakley, Inc., 18 390–93; **49** 297–302 **(upd.)**; **111** 358–65 **(upd.)**

Oaktree Capital Management, LLC, 71 254–56

Oakwood Homes Corporation, 13 155; **15** 326–28

OAO AVTOVAZ *see* AVTOVAZ Joint Stock Co.

OAO Gazprom, 42 261–65; **107** 317–23 **(upd.)**

OAO LUKOIL, 40 343–46; **109** 428–36 **(upd.)**

OAO NK YUKOS, 47 282–85

OAO Severstal *see* Severstal Joint Stock Co.

OAO Siberian Oil Company (Sibneft), 49 303–06

OAO Surgutneftegaz, 48 375–78

OAO Tatneft, 45 322–26

Obagi Medical Products, Inc., 95 310–13

Obayashi Corporation, 78 266–69 **(upd.)**

Oberoi Group *see* EIH Ltd.

Oberto Sausage Company, Inc., 92 288–91

Obie Media Corporation, 56 260–62

Obrascon Huarte Lain S.A., 76 291–94

Observer AB, 55 286–89

Occidental Petroleum Corporation, IV 480–82; **25** 360–63 **(upd.)**; **71** 257–61 **(upd.)**

Océ N.V., 24 360–63; **91** 359–65 **(upd.)**

Ocean Beauty Seafoods, Inc., 74 209–11

Ocean Bio-Chem, Inc., 103 308–11

Ocean Group plc, 6 415–17 *see also* Exel plc.

Ocean Spray Cranberries, Inc., 7 403–05; **25** 364–67 **(upd.)**; **83** 284–290

Oceaneering International, Inc., 63 317–19

Ocesa *see* Corporación Interamericana de Entretenimiento, S.A. de C.V.

O'Charley's Inc., 19 286–88; **60** 229–32 **(upd.)**

OCI *see* Orascom Construction Industries S.A.E.

OCLC Online Computer Library Center, Inc., 96 324–28

The O'Connell Companies Inc., 100 306–09

Octel Messaging, 14 354–56; **41** 287–90 **(upd.)**

Ocular Sciences, Inc., 65 273–75

Odakyu Electric Railway Co., Ltd., V 487–89; **68** 278–81 **(upd.)**

Odebrecht S.A., 73 242–44

Odetics Inc., 14 357–59

Odfjell SE, 101 383–87

ODL, Inc., 55 290–92

Odwalla Inc., 31 349–51; **104** 349–53 **(upd.)**

Odyssey Marine Exploration, Inc., 91 366–70

OEC Medical Systems, Inc., 27 354–56

OENEO S.A., 74 212–15 **(upd.)**

Office Depot, Inc., 8 404–05; **23** 363–65 **(upd.)**; **65** 276–80 **(upd.)**

OfficeMax Incorporated, 15 329–31; **43** 291–95 **(upd.)**; **101** 388–94 **(upd.)**

OfficeTiger, LLC, 75 294–96

Officine Alfieri Maserati S.p.A., 13 376–78

Offshore Logistics, Inc., 37 287–89

Ogden Corporation, I 512–14; **6** 151–53 *see also* Covanta Energy Corp.

Ogilvy Group Inc., I 25–27 *see also* WPP Group.

Oglebay Norton Company, 17 355–58

Oglethorpe Power Corporation, 6 537–38

Ohbayashi Corporation, I 586–87

The Ohio Art Company, 14 360–62; **59** 317–20 **(upd.)**

Ohio Bell Telephone Company, 14 363–65; *see also* Ameritech Corp.

Ohio Casualty Corp., 11 369–70

Ohio Edison Company, V 676–78

Oil and Natural Gas Commission, IV 483–84; **90** 313–17 **(upd.)**

Oil-Dri Corporation of America, 20 396–99; **89** 331–36 **(upd.)**

Oil States International, Inc., 77 314–17

Oil Transporting Joint Stock Company Transneft, 92 450–54

The Oilgear Company, 74 216–18

Oji Paper Co., Ltd., IV 320–22; **57** 272–75 **(upd.)**

OJSC Novolipetsk Steel, 99 311–315

OJSC Wimm-Bill-Dann Foods, 48 436–39

Oki Electric Industry Company, Limited, II 72–74; **15** 125; **21** 390

Oklahoma Gas and Electric Company, 6 539–40

Okuma Holdings Inc., 74 219–21

Okura & Co., Ltd., IV 167–68

Olan Mills, Inc., 62 254–56

Old America Stores, Inc., 17 359–61

Old Dominion Freight Line, Inc., 57 276–79

Old Kent Financial Corp., 11 371–72 *see also* Fifth Third Bancorp.

Old Mutual PLC, IV 535; **61** 270–72

Old National Bancorp, 15 332–34; **98** 266–70 **(upd.)**

Old Navy, Inc., 70 210–12

Old Orchard Brands, LLC, 73 245–47

Old Republic International Corporation, 11 373–75; **58** 258–61 **(upd.)**

Old Spaghetti Factory International Inc., 24 364–66

Old Town Canoe Company, 74 222–24

Old Vic Productions plc, 108 371–74

Petrobras Energia Participaciones S.A., 72 278–81

Petroecuador *see* Petróleos del Ecuador.

Petrof spol. S.R.O., 107 352–56

Petrofac Ltd., 95 332–35

PetroFina S.A., IV 497–500; 26 365–69 (upd.)

Petrogal *see* Petróleos de Portugal.

Petrohawk Energy Corporation, 79 317–20

Petróleo Brasileiro S.A., IV 501–03

Petróleos de Portugal S.A., IV 504–06

Petróleos de Venezuela S.A., IV 507–09; 74 235–39 (upd.)

Petróleos del Ecuador, IV 510–11

Petróleos Mexicanos (PEMEX), IV 512–14; 19 295–98 (upd.); 104 373–78 (upd.)

Petroleum Development Oman LLC, IV 515–16; 98 305–09 (upd.)

Petroleum Helicopters, Inc., 35 334–36

Petroliam Nasional Bhd (Petronas), 56 275–79 (upd.)

Petrolite Corporation, 15 350–52 *see also* Baker Hughes Inc.

Petromex *see* Petróleos de Mexico S.A.

Petron Corporation, 58 270–72

Petronas, IV 517–20 *see also* Petroliam Nasional Bhd.

Petroplus Holdings AG, 108 381–84

Petrossian Inc., 54 287–89

Petry Media Corporation, 102 326–29

PETsMART, Inc., 14 384–86; 41 295–98 (upd.)

Peugeot S.A., I 187–88 *see also* PSA Peugeot Citroen S.A.

The Pew Charitable Trusts, 35 337–40

Pez Candy, Inc., 38 355–57

The Pfaltzgraff Co. *see* Susquehanna Pfaltzgraff Co.

Pfizer Inc., I 661–63; 9 402–05 (upd.); 38 358–67 (upd.); 79 321–33 (upd.)

PFSweb, Inc., 73 254–56

PG&E Corporation, 26 370–73 (upd.)

PGA *see* The Professional Golfers' Association.

Phaidon Press Ltd., 98 310–14

Phantom Fireworks *see* B.J. Alan Co., Inc.

Phar-Mor Inc., 12 390–92

Pharmacia & Upjohn Inc., I 664–65; 25 374–78 (upd.) *see also* Pfizer Inc.

Pharmion Corporation, 91 379–82

Phat Fashions LLC, 49 322–24

Phelps Dodge Corporation, IV 176–79; 28 352–57 (upd.); 75 319–25 (upd.)

PHH Arval, V 496–97; 53 274–76 (upd.)

PHI, Inc., 80 282–86 (upd.)

Philadelphia Eagles, 37 305–08

Philadelphia Electric Company, V 695–97 *see also* Exelon Corp.

Philadelphia Gas Works Company, 92 301–05

Philadelphia Media Holdings LLC, 92 306–10

Philadelphia Suburban Corporation, 39 326–29

Philharmonic-Symphony Society of New York, Inc. (New York Philharmonic), 69 293–97

Philip Environmental Inc., 16 414–16

Philip Morris Companies Inc., V 405–07; 18 416–19 (upd.); 44 338–43 (upd.) *see also* Altria Group Inc.

Philip Services Corp., 73 257–60

Philipp Holzmann AG, 17 374–77

Philippine Airlines, Inc., 6 106–08; 23 379–82 (upd.)

Philips Electronics N.V., 13 400–03 (upd.) *see also* Koninklijke Philips Electronics N.V.

Philips Electronics North America Corp., 13 396–99

N.V. Philips Gloeilampenfabriken, II 78–80 *see also* Philips Electronics N.V.

The Phillies, 106 364–68

Phillips Foods, Inc., 63 320–22; 90 330–33 (upd.)

Phillips International, Inc., 78 311–14

Phillips Lytle LLP, 102 330–34

Phillips Petroleum Company, IV 521–23; 40 354–59 (upd.) *see also* ConocoPhillips.

Phillips-Van Heusen Corporation, 24 382–85

Phillips, de Pury & Luxembourg, 49 325–27

Philly Pretzel Factory *see* Soft Pretzel Franchise Systems, Inc.

Phoenix AG, 68 286–89

Phoenix Footwear Group, Inc., 70 220–22

Phoenix Mecano AG, 61 286–88

The Phoenix Media/Communications Group, 91 383–87

Phones 4u Ltd., 85 328–31

Photo-Me International Plc, 83 302–306

PHP Healthcare Corporation, 22 423–25

PhyCor, Inc., 36 365–69

Physician Sales & Service, Inc., 14 387–89

Physio-Control International Corp., 18 420–23

Piaggio & C. S.p.A., 20 426–29; 100 348–52 (upd.)

PianoDisc *see* Burgett, Inc.

PIC International Group PLC, 24 386–88 (upd.)

Picanol N.V., 96 335–38

Picard Surgeles, 76 305–07

Piccadilly Cafeterias, Inc., 19 299–302

Pick 'n Pay Stores Ltd., 82 280–83

PictureTel Corp., 10 455–57; 27 363–66 (upd.)

Piedmont Investment Advisors, LLC, 106 369–72

Piedmont Natural Gas Company, Inc., 27 367–69

Pier 1 Imports, Inc., 12 393–95; 34 337–41 (upd.); 95 336–43 (upd.)

Pierce Leahy Corporation, 24 389–92 *see also* Iron Mountain Inc.

Piercing Pagoda, Inc., 29 382–84

Pierre & Vacances SA, 48 314–16

Pierre Fabre *see* Laboratoires Pierre Fabre S.A.

Piggly Wiggly Southern, Inc., 13 404–06

Pilgrim's Pride Corporation, 7 432–33; 23 383–85 (upd.); 90 334–38 (upd.)

Pilkington Group Limited, II 724–27; 34 342–47 (upd.); 87 375–383 (upd.)

Pillowtex Corporation, 19 303–05; 41 299–302 (upd.)

Pillsbury Company, II 555–57; 13 407–09 (upd.); 62 269–73 (upd.)

Pillsbury Madison & Sutro LLP, 29 385–88

Pilot Air Freight Corp., 67 301–03

Pilot Corporation, 49 328–30

Pilot Pen Corporation of America, 82 284–87

Pinault-Printemps-Redoute S.A., 19 306–09 (upd.) *see also* PPR S.A.

Pindar *see* G A Pindar & Son Ltd.

Pinguely-Haulotte SA, 51 293–95

Pinkerton's Inc., 9 406–09 *see also* Securitas AB.

Pinnacle Airlines Corp., 73 261–63

Pinnacle West Capital Corporation, 6 545–47; 54 290–94 (upd.)

Pinskdrev Industrial Woodworking Company, 110 367–71

Pioneer Electronic Corporation, III 604–06; 28 358–61 (upd.) *see also* Agilysys Inc.

Pioneer Hi-Bred International, Inc., 9 410–12; 41 303–06 (upd.)

Pioneer International Limited, III 728–30

Pioneer Natural Resources Company, 59 335–39

Pioneer-Standard Electronics Inc., 19 310–14 *see also* Agilysys Inc.

Piper Jaffray Companies, , 22 426–30 ; 107 357–63 (upd.)

Pirelli & C. S.p.A., V 249–51; 15 353–56 (upd.); 75 326–31 (upd.)

Piscines Desjoyaux S.A., 84 310–313

Pitman Company, 58 273–75

Pitney Bowes Inc., III 156–58, 159; 19 315–18 (upd.); 47 295–99 (upd.); 111 389–96 (upd.)

Pittsburgh Brewing Company, 76 308–11

Pittsburgh Plate Glass Co. *see* PPG Industries, Inc.

Pittsburgh Steelers Sports, Inc., 66 255–57

The Pittston Company, IV 180–82; 19 319–22 (upd.) *see also* The Brink's Co.

Pittway Corporation, 9 413–15; 33 334–37 (upd.)

Pixar Animation Studios, 34 348–51

Pixelworks, Inc., 69 298–300

Pizza Hut Inc., 7 434–35; 21 405–07 (upd.)

Pizza Inn, Inc., 46 346–49

PKF International, 78 315–18

Ritter Sport *see* Alfred Ritter GmbH & Co. KG.

Ritter's Frozen Custard *see* RFC Franchising LLC.

Ritz Camera Centers, 34 375–77

The Ritz-Carlton Hotel Company, L.L.C., 9 455–57; 29 403–06 (upd.); 71 311–16 (upd.)

Ritz-Craft Corporation of Pennsylvania Inc., 94 365–68

Riunione Adriatica di Sicurtà SpA, III 345–48

Riva Fire *see* Gruppo Riva Fire SpA.

The Rival Company, 19 358–60

River Oaks Furniture, Inc., 43 314–16

River Ranch Fresh Foods LLC, 88 322–25

Riverbed Technology, Inc., 101 428–31

Riverwood International Corporation, 11 420–23; 48 340–44 (upd.) *see also* Graphic Packaging Holding Co.

Riviana Foods, 27 388–91; 107 373–78 (upd.)

Riviera Holdings Corporation, 75 340–43

Riviera Tool Company, 89 373–76

RJR Nabisco Holdings Corp., V 408–10 *see also* R.J Reynolds Tobacco Holdings Inc., Nabisco Brands, Inc.; R.J. Reynolds Industries, Inc.

RM Auctions, Inc., 88 326–29

RMC Group p.l.c., III 737–40; 34 378–83 (upd.)

RMH Teleservices, Inc., 42 322–24

Roadhouse Grill, Inc., 22 464–66

Roadmaster Industries, Inc., 16 430–33

Roadway Express, Inc., V 502–03; 25 395–98 (upd.)

Roanoke Electric Steel Corporation, 45 368–70

Robbins & Myers Inc., 15 388–90

Roberds Inc., 19 361–63

Robert Bosch GmbH, I 392–93; 16 434–37 (upd.); 43 317–21 (upd.); 108 418–25 (upd.)

Robert Half International Inc., 18 461–63; 70 281–84 (upd.)

Robert Mondavi Corporation, 15 391–94; 50 386–90 (upd.)

Robert Talbott Inc., 88 330–33

Robert W. Baird & Co. Incorporated, 67 328–30

Robert Wood Johnson Foundation, 35 375–78

Robertet SA, 39 347–49

Roberts Dairy Company, 103 364–67

Roberts Pharmaceutical Corporation, 16 438–40

Robertson-Ceco Corporation, 19 364–66

Robins, Kaplan, Miller & Ciresi L.L.P., 89 377–81

Robinson Helicopter Company, 51 315–17

ROC *see* Royal Olympic Cruise Lines Inc.

Rocawear Apparel LLC, 77 355–58

Roche Biomedical Laboratories, Inc., 11 424–26 *see also* Laboratory Corporation of America Holdings.

Roche Bioscience, 14 403–06 (upd.)

Roche Holding AG, 109 469–76

Rochester Gas And Electric Corporation, 6 571–73

Rochester Telephone Corporation, 6 332–34

Röchling Gruppe, 94 369–74

Rock Bottom Restaurants, Inc., 25 399–401; 68 320–23 (upd.)

Rock-It Cargo USA, Inc., 86 339–42

Rock of Ages Corporation, 37 329–32

Rock-Tenn Company, 13 441–43; 59 347–51 (upd.)

The Rockefeller Foundation, 34 384–87

Rockefeller Group International Inc., 58 303–06

Rocket Software, Inc., 110 403–06

Rockford Corporation, 43 322–25

Rockford Products Corporation, 55 323–25

RockShox, Inc., 26 412–14

Rockwell Automation, Inc., 43 326–31 (upd.); 103 368–76 (upd.)

Rockwell Collins, 106 423–27

Rockwell International Corporation, I 78–80; 11 427–30 (upd.)

Rockwell Medical Technologies, Inc., 88 334–37

Rocky Brands, Inc., 26 415–18; 102 357–62 (upd.)

Rocky Mountain Chocolate Factory, Inc., 73 280–82

Rodale, Inc., 23 415–17; 47 336–39 (upd.)

Rodamco N.V., 26 419–21

Rodda Paint Company, 98 329–32

Rodriguez Group S.A., 90 357–60

ROFIN-SINAR Technologies Inc, 81 345–48

Rogers Communications Inc., 30 388–92 (upd.) *see also* Maclean Hunter Publishing Ltd.

Rogers Corporation, 61 310–13; 80 313–17 (upd.)

Rohde & Schwarz GmbH & Co. KG, 39 350–53

Röhm and Haas Company, I 391–93; 26 422–26 (upd.); 77 359–66 (upd.)

ROHN Industries, Inc., 22 467–69

Rohr Incorporated, 9 458–60 *see also* Goodrich Corp.

Roland Berger & Partner GmbH, 37 333–36

Roland Corporation, 38 389–91

Roland Murten A.G., 7 452–53

Rolex *see* Montres Rolex S.A.

Roll International Corporation, 37 337–39

Rollerblade, Inc., 15 395–98; 34 388–92 (upd.)

Rollins, Inc., 11 431–34; 104 397–403 (upd.)

Rolls-Royce Allison, 29 407–09 (upd.)

Rolls-Royce Group PLC, 67 331–36 (upd.)

Rolls-Royce Motors Ltd., I 194–96

Rolls-Royce plc, I 81–83; 7 454–57 (upd.); 21 433–37 (upd.)

Rolta India Ltd., 90 361–64

Roly Poly Franchise Systems LLC, 83 326–328

Romacorp, Inc., 58 307–11

Roman Meal Company, 84 331–334

Ron Tonkin Chevrolet Company, 55 326–28

RONA, Inc., 73 283–86

Ronco Corporation, 15 399–401; 80 318–23 (upd.)

Ronson PLC, 49 337–39

Room and Board, Inc., 111 427–31

Rooms To Go Inc., 28 389–92

Rooney Brothers Co., 25 402–04

Roosevelt Hospital *see* Continuum Health Partners, Inc.

Roots Canada Ltd., 42 325–27

Roper Industries, Inc., 15 402–04; 50 391–95 (upd.)

Ropes & Gray, 40 377–80

Rorer Group, I 666–68

Rosauers Supermarkets, Inc., 90 365–68

Rose Acre Farms, Inc., 60 255–57

Rose Art Industries, 58 312–14

Roseburg Forest Products Company, 58 315–17

Rosemount Inc., 15 405–08 *see also* Emerson.

Rosenbluth International Inc., 14 407–09 *see also* American Express Co.

Rose's Stores, Inc., 13 444–46

Rosetta Stone Inc., 93 375–79

Rosneft, 106 428–31

Ross-Simons Jewelers Inc., 109 477–81

Ross Stores, Inc., 17 408–10; 43 332–35 (upd.); 101 432–37 (upd.)

Rossignol Ski Company, Inc. *see* Skis Rossignol S.A.

Rossmann *see* Dirk Rossmann GmbH.

Rostelecom Joint Stock Co., 99 374–377

Rostvertol plc, 62 308–10

Rosy Blue N.V., 84 335–338

Rotary International, 31 395–97

Rothmans UK Holdings Limited, V 411–13; 19 367–70 (upd.)

Roto-Rooter, Inc., 15 409–11; 61 314–19 (upd.)

Rotork plc, 46 361–64

The Rottlund Company, Inc., 28 393–95

Rouge Steel Company, 8 448–50

Rougier *see* Groupe Rougier, SA.

Roularta Media Group NV, 48 345–47

Rounder Records Corporation, 79 357–61

Roundy's Inc., 14 410–12; 58 318–21 (upd.)

The Rouse Company, 15 412–15; 63 338–41 (upd.)

Roussel Uclaf, I 669–70; 8 451–53 (upd.)

Rover Group Ltd., 7 458–60; 21 441–44 (upd.)

Rowan Companies, Inc., 43 336–39

Skandia Insurance Company, Ltd., 50 431–34

Skandinaviska Enskilda Banken AB, II 351–53; 56 326–29 (upd.)

Skanska AB, 38 435–38; 110 422–26 (upd.)

Skechers U.S.A. Inc., 31 413–15; 88 368–72 (upd.)

Skeeter Products Inc., 96 391–94

SKF *see* Aktiebolaget SKF.

Skidmore, Owings & Merrill LLP, 13 475–76; 69 332–35 (upd.)

SkillSoft Public Limited Company, 81 371–74

skinnyCorp, LLC, 97 374–77

Skipton Building Society, 80 344–47

Skis Rossignol S.A., 15 460–62; 43 373–76 (upd.)

Skoda Auto a.s., 39 373–75

Skyline Chili, Inc., 62 325–28

Skyline Corporation, 30 421–23

SkyMall, Inc., 26 439–41

Skype Technologies S.A., 108 452–55

SkyWest, Inc., 25 420–24

Skyy Spirits LLC, 78 348–51

SL Green Realty Corporation, 44 383–85

SL Industries, Inc., 77 383–86

Slaughter and May, 112 376–79

SLC Participaçoes S.A., 111 442–45

Sleeman Breweries Ltd., 74 305–08

Sleepy's Inc., 32 426–28

SLI, Inc., 48 358–61

Slim-Fast Foods Company, 18 489–91; 66 296–98 (upd.)

Sling Media, Inc., 112 380–83

Slinky, Inc. *see* Poof-Slinky, Inc.

SLM Holding Corp., 25 425–28 (upd.)

Slough Estates PLC, IV 722–25; 50 435–40 (upd.)

Small Planet Foods, Inc., 89 410–14

Smart & Final LLC, 16 451–53; 94 392–96 (upd.)

Smart Balance, Inc., 100 398–401

SMART Modular Technologies, Inc., 86 361–64

SmartForce PLC, 43 377–80

Smarties *see* Ce De Candy Inc.

SMBC *see* Sumitomo Mitsui Banking Corp.

Smead Manufacturing Co., 17 445–48

SMG *see* Scottish Media Group.

SMH *see* Sanders Morris Harris Group Inc.; The Swatch Group SA.

Smith & Hawken, Ltd., 68 343–45

Smith & Nephew plc, 17 449–52; 41 374–78 (upd.)

Smith & Wesson Corp., 30 424–27; 73 306–11 (upd.)

The Smith & Wollensky Restaurant Group, Inc., 105 418–22

Smith Barney Inc., 15 463–65 *see also* Citigroup Inc.

Smith Corona Corp., 13 477–80

Smith International, Inc., 15 466–68; 59 376–80 (upd.)

Smith Micro Software, Inc., 112 384–87

Smith-Midland Corporation, 56 330–32

Smithfield Foods, Inc., 7 477–78; 43 381–84 (upd.)

SmithKline Beckman Corporation, I 692–94 *see also* GlaxoSmithKline plc.

SmithKline Beecham plc, III 65–67; 32 429–34 (upd.) *see also* GlaxoSmithKline plc.

Smith's Food & Drug Centers, Inc., 8 472–74; 57 324–27 (upd.)

Smiths Group plc, 25 429–31; 107 406–10 (upd.)

Smithsonian Institution, 27 410–13

Smithway Motor Xpress Corporation, 39 376–79

Smoby International SA, 56 333–35

Smorgon Steel Group Ltd., 62 329–32

Smucker's *see* The J.M. Smucker Co.

Smurfit Kappa Group plc, 26 442–46 (upd.) ; 83 360–368 (upd.)112 388–95 (upd.)

Snap-On, Incorporated, 7 479–80; 27 414–16 (upd.); 105 423–28 (upd.)

Snapfish, 83 369–372

Snapple Beverage Corporation, 11 449–51

SNC-Lavalin Group Inc., 72 330–33

SNCF *see* Société Nationale des Chemins de Fer Français.

SNEA *see* Société Nationale Elf Aquitaine.

Snecma Group, 46 369–72 *see also* SAFRAN.

Snell & Wilmer L.L.P., 28 425–28

SNET *see* Southern New England Telecommunications Corp.

Snow Brand Milk Products Company, Ltd., II 574–75; 48 362–65 (upd.)

Soap Opera Magazine see American Media, Inc.

Sobeys Inc., 80 348–51

Socata *see* EADS SOCATA.

Sociedad Química y Minera de Chile S.A.,103 382–85

Sociedade de Jogos de Macau, S.A.*see* SJM Holdings Ltd.

Società Finanziaria Telefonica per Azioni, V 325–27

Società Sportiva Lazio SpA, 44 386–88

Société Air France, 27 417–20 (upd.) *see also* Air France–KLM.

Société BIC S.A., 73 312–15

Societe des Produits Marnier-Lapostolle S.A., 88 373–76

Société d'Exploitation AOM Air Liberté SA (AirLib), 53 305–07

Société du Figaro S.A., 60 281–84

Société du Louvre, 27 421–23

Société Générale, II 354–56; 42 347–51 (upd.)

Société Industrielle Lesaffre, 84 356–359

Société Luxembourgeoise de Navigation Aérienne S.A., 64 357–59

Société Nationale des Chemins de Fer Français, V 512–15; 57 328–32 (upd.)

Société Nationale Elf Aquitaine, IV 544–47; 7 481–85 (upd.)

Société Norbert Dentressangle S.A., 67 352–54

Société Tunisienne de l'Air-Tunisair, 49 371–73

Society Corporation, 9 474–77

Sodexho SA, 29 442–44; 91 433–36 (upd.)

Sodiaal S.A., 19 50; 36 437–39 (upd.)

SODIMA, II 576–77 *see also* Sodiaal S.A.

Soft Pretzel Franchise Systems, Inc., 108 456–59

Soft Sheen Products, Inc., 31 416–18

Softbank Corporation, 13 481–83; 38 439–44 (upd.); 77 387–95 (upd.)

Sojitz Corporation, 96 395–403 (upd.)

Sol Meliá S.A., 71 337–39

Sola International Inc., 71 340–42

Solar Turbines Inc., 100 402–06

Solarfun Power Holdings Co., Ltd., 105 429–33

Sole Technology Inc., 93 405–09

Solectron Corporation, 12 450–52; 48 366–70 (upd.)

Solo Cup Company, 104 424–27

Solo Serve Corporation, 28 429–31

Solutia Inc., 52 312–15

Solvay & Cie S.A., I 394–96; 21 464–67 (upd.)

Solvay S.A., 61 329–34 (upd.)

Somerfield plc, 47 365–69 (upd.)

Sommer-Allibert S.A., 19 406–09 *see also* Tarkett Sommer AG.

Sompo Japan Insurance, Inc., 98 359–63 (upd.)

Sonae SGPS, S.A., 97 378–81

Sonat, Inc., 6 577–78 *see also* El Paso Corp.

Sonatrach, 65 313–17 (upd.)

Sonera Corporation, 50 441–44 *see also* TeliaSonera AB.

Sonesta International Hotels Corporation, 44 389–91

Sonic Automotive, Inc., 77 396–99

Sonic Corp., 14 451–53; 37 360–63 (upd.); 103 386–91 (upd.)

Sonic Innovations Inc., 56 336–38

Sonic Solutions, Inc., 81 375–79

SonicWALL, Inc., 87 421–424

Sonnenschein Nath and Rosenthal LLP, 102 384–87

Sonoco Products Company, 8 475–77; 89 415–22 (upd.)

SonoSite, Inc., 56 339–41

Sony Corporation, II 101–03; 12 453–56 (upd.); 40 404–10 (upd.); 108 460–69 (upd.)

Sophus Berendsen A/S, 49 374–77

Sorbee International Ltd., 74 309–11

Soriana *see* Organización Soriana, S.A. de C.V.

Soros Fund Management LLC, 28 432–34

Sorrento, Inc., 19 51; 24 444–46

SOS Staffing Services, 25 432–35

Sotheby's Holdings, Inc., 11 452–54; 29 445–48 (upd.); 84 360–365 (upd.)

Soufflet SA *see* Groupe Soufflet SA.

Sound Advice, Inc., 41 379–82

SWH Corporation, 70 307–09

Swift & Company, 55 364–67

Swift Energy Company, 63 364–66

Swift Transportation Co., Inc., 42 363–66

Swinerton Inc., 43 397–400

Swire Pacific Ltd., I 521–22; 16 479–81 (upd.); 57 348–53 (upd.)

Swisher International Group Inc., 23 463–65

Swiss Air Transport Company Ltd., I 121–22

Swiss Army Brands, Inc. *see* Victorinox AG.

Swiss Bank Corporation, II 368–70 *see also* UBS AG.

The Swiss Colony, Inc., 97 395–98

Swiss Federal Railways (Schweizerische Bundesbahnen), V 519–22

Swiss International Air Lines Ltd., 48 379–81

Swiss Reinsurance Company (Schweizerische Rückversicherungs-Gesellschaft), III 375–78; 46 380–84 (upd.)

Swiss Valley Farms Company, 90 400–03

Swisscom AG, 58 336–39

Swissport International Ltd., 70 310–12

Sybase, Inc., 10 504–06; 27 447–50 (upd.)

Sybron International Corp., 14 479–81

Sycamore Networks, Inc., 45 388–91

Sykes Enterprises, Inc., 45 392–95

Sylvan, Inc., 22 496–99

Sylvan Learning Systems, Inc., 35 408–11 *see also* Educate Inc.

Symantec Corporation, 10 507–09; 82 372–77 (upd.)

Symbol Technologies, Inc., 15 482–84 *see also* Motorola, Inc.

Symrise GmbH and Company KG, 89 436–40

Syms Corporation, 29 456–58; 74 327–30 (upd.)

Symyx Technologies, Inc., 77 420–23

Synaptics Incorporated, 95 394–98

Synchronoss Technologies, Inc., 95 399–402

Syneron Medical Ltd., 91 471–74

Syngenta International AG, 83 391–394

Syniverse Holdings Inc., 97 399–402

SYNNEX Corporation, 73 328–30

Synopsys, Inc., 11 489–92; 69 339–43 (upd.)

SynOptics Communications, Inc., 10 510–12

Synovus Financial Corp., 12 465–67; 52 336–40 (upd.)

Syntax-Brillian Corporation, 102 405–09

Syntel, Inc., 92 356–60

Syntex Corporation, I 701–03

Synthes, Inc., 93 434–37

Sypris Solutions, Inc., 85 421–25

SyQuest Technology, Inc., 18 509–12

Syratech Corp., 14 482–84

SYSCO Corporation, II 675–76; 24 470–72 (upd.); 75 357–60 (upd.)

System Software Associates, Inc., 10 513–14

Systemax, Inc., 52 341–44

Systems & Computer Technology Corp., 19 437–39

Sytner Group plc, 45 396–98

T

T-Netix, Inc., 46 385–88

T-Online International AG, 61 349–51

T.J. Maxx *see* The TJX Companies, Inc.

T. Marzetti Company, 57 354–56

T. Rowe Price Associates, Inc., 11 493–96; 34 423–27 (upd.)

TA Triumph-Adler AG, 48 382–85

TAB Products Co., 17 467–69

Tabacalera, S.A., V 414–16; 17 470–73 (upd.) *see also* Altadis S.A.

TABCORP Holdings Limited, 44 407–10

TACA *see* Grupo TACA.

Taco Bell Corporation, 7 505–07; 21 485–88 (upd.); 74 331–34 (upd.)

Taco Cabana, Inc., 23 466–68; 72 344–47 (upd.)

Taco John's International Inc., 15 485–87; 63 367–70 (upd.)

Tacony Corporation, 70 313–15

TAG Heuer S.A., 25 459–61; 77 424–28 (upd.)

Tag-It Pacific, Inc., 85 426–29

Taiheiyo Cement Corporation, 60 298–301 (upd.)

Taittinger S.A., 43 401–05

Taiwan Semiconductor Manufacturing Company Ltd., 47 383–87

Taiwan Tobacco & Liquor Corporation, 75 361–63

Taiyo Fishery Company, Limited, II 578–79 *see also* Maruha Group Inc.

Taiyo Kobe Bank, Ltd., II 371–72

Takara Holdings Inc., 62 345–47

Takashimaya Company, Limited, V 193–96; 47 388–92 (upd.)

Take-Two Interactive Software, Inc., 46 389–91

Takeda Chemical Industries, Ltd., I 704–06; 46 392–95 (upd.)

The Talbots, Inc., 11 497–99; 31 429–32 (upd.); 88 393–98 (upd.)

Talisman Energy Inc., 9 490–93; 47 393–98 (upd.); 103 425–34 (upd.)

Talk America Holdings, Inc., 70 316–19

Talley Industries, Inc., 16 482–85

TALX Corporation, 92 361–64

TAM Linhas Aéreas S.A., 68 363–65

Tambrands Inc., 8 511–13 *see also* Procter & Gamble Co.

TAME (Transportes Aéreos Militares Ecuatorianos), 100 407–10

Tamedia AG, 53 323–26

Tamfelt Oyj Abp, 62 348–50

Tamron Company Ltd., 82 378–81

TAMSA *see* Tubos de Acero de Mexico, S.A.

Tandem Computers, Inc., 6 278–80 *see also* Hewlett-Packard Co.

Tandy Corporation, II 106–08; 12 468–70 (upd.) *see also* RadioShack Corp.

Tandycrafts, Inc., 31 433–37

Tanger Factory Outlet Centers, Inc., 49 386–89

Tanimura & Antle Fresh Foods, Inc., 98 379–83

Tanox, Inc., 77 429–32

TAP—Air Portugal Transportes Aéreos Portugueses S.A., 46 396–99 (upd.)

Tapemark Company Inc., 64 373–75

TAQA North Ltd., 95 403–06

Target Corporation, 10 515–17; 27 451–54 (upd.); 61 352–56 (upd.)

Targetti Sankey SpA, 86 385–88

Tarkett Sommer AG, 25 462–64

Tarmac Limited, III 751–54; 28 447–51 (upd.); 95 407–14 (upd.)

Taro Pharmaceutical Industries Ltd., 65 335–37

TAROM S.A., 64 376–78

Tarragon Realty Investors, Inc., 45 399–402

Tarrant Apparel Group, 62 351–53

Taschen GmbH, 101 465–68

Taser International, Inc., 62 354–57

Tastefully Simple Inc., 100 411–14

Tasty Baking Company, 14 485–87; 35 412–16 (upd.)

Tata Motors, Ltd., 109 526–30

Tata Steel Ltd., IV 217–19; 44 411–15 (upd.); 109 531–38 (upd.)

Tata Tea Ltd., 76 339–41

Tate & Lyle PLC, II 580–83; 42 367–72 (upd.); 101 469–77 (upd.)

Tati SA, 25 465–67

Tatneft *see* OAO Tatneft.

Tattered Cover Book Store, 43 406–09

Tatung Co., 23 469–71

Taubman Centers, Inc., 75 364–66

TaurusHolding GmbH & Co. KG, 46 400–03

Taylor & Francis Group plc, 44 416–19

Taylor Corporation, 36 465–67

Taylor Devices, Inc., 97 403–06

Taylor Guitars, 48 386–89

Taylor Made Group Inc., 98 384–87

Taylor Nelson Sofres plc, 34 428–30

Taylor Publishing Company, 12 471–73; 36 468–71 (upd.)

Taylor Woodrow plc, I 590–91; 38 450–53 (upd.)

TaylorMade-adidas Golf, 23 472–74; 96 423–28 (upd.)

TB Wood's Corporation, 56 355–58

TBA Global, LLC, 99 435–438

TBS *see* Turner Broadcasting System, Inc.

TBWA/Chiat/Day, 6 47–49; 43 410–14 (upd.) *see also* Omnicom Group Inc.

TC Advertising *see* Treasure Chest Advertising, Inc.

TCBY Systems LLC, 17 474–76; 98 388–92 (upd.)

TCF Financial Corporation, 47 399–402; 103 435–41 (upd.)

Thomas & Betts Corporation, 11 515–17; 54 370–74 (upd.)

Thomas & Howard Company, Inc., 90 409–12

Thomas Cook Travel Inc., 9 503–05; 33 394–96 (upd.)

Thomas Crosbie Holdings Limited, 81 384–87

Thomas H. Lee Co., 24 480–83

Thomas Industries Inc., 29 466–69

Thomas J. Lipton Company, 14 495–97

Thomas Nelson Inc., 14 498–99; 38 454–57 (upd.)

Thomas Publishing Company, 26 482–85

Thomaston Mills, Inc., 27 467–70

Thomasville Furniture Industries, Inc., 12 474–76; 74 339–42 (upd.)

Thomsen Greenhouses and Garden Center, Incorporated, 65 338–40

The Thomson Corporation, 8 525–28; 34 435–40 (upd.); 77 433–39 (upd.)

THOMSON multimedia S.A., II 116–17; 42 377–80 (upd.)

Thor Equities, LLC, 108 487–90

Thor Industries Inc., 39 391–94; 92 365–370 (upd.)

Thorn Apple Valley, Inc., 7 523–25; 22 508–11 (upd.)

Thorn EMI plc, I 531–32 *see also* EMI plc; Thorn plc.

Thorn plc, 24 484–87

Thorntons plc, 46 424–26

ThoughtWorks Inc., 90 413–16

Thousand Trails, Inc., 33 397–99

THQ, Inc., 39 395–97; 92 371–375 (upd.)

Threadless.com *see* skinnyCorp, LLC.

365 Media Group plc, 89 441–44

3Com Corporation, 11 518–21; 34 441–45 (upd.); 106 465–72 (upd.)

The 3DO Company, 43 426–30

3i Group PLC, 73 338–40

3M Company, 61 365–70 (upd.)

Thrifty PayLess, Inc., 12 477–79 *see also* Rite Aid Corp.

Thrivent Financial for Lutherans, 111 452–59 (upd.)

Thumann Inc., 104 442–45

ThyssenKrupp AG, IV 221–23; 28 452–60 (upd.); 87 425–438 (upd.)

TI Group plc, 17 480–83

TIAA-CREF *see* Teachers Insurance and Annuity Association-College Retirement Equities Fund.

Tianjin Flying Pigeon Bicycle Co., Ltd., 95 421–24

Tibbett & Britten Group plc, 32 449–52

TIBCO Software Inc., 79 411–14

TIC Holdings Inc., 92 376–379

Ticketmaster, 13 508–10; 37 381–84 (upd.); 76 349–53 (upd.)

Tidewater Inc., 11 522–24; 37 385–88 (upd.)

Tiffany & Co., 14 500–03; 78 396–401 (upd.)

TIG Holdings, Inc., 26 486–88

Tiger Aspect Productions Ltd., 72 348–50

Tiger Brands Limited, 112 420–24

Tigre S.A. Tubos e Conexões, 104 446–49

Tilcon-Connecticut Inc., 80 373–76

Tilia Inc., 62 363–65

Tillamook County Creamery Association, 111 460–63

Tilley Endurables, Inc., 67 364–66

Tillotson Corp., 15 488–90

TIM *see* Telecom Italia Mobile S.p.A.

Tim-Bar Corporation, 110 459–62

Tim Hortons Inc., 109 543–47 (upd.)

Timber Lodge Steakhouse, Inc., 73 341–43

The Timberland Company, 13 511–14; 54 375–79 (upd.); 111 464–70 (upd.)

Timberline Software Corporation, 15 491–93

Time Out Group Ltd., 68 371–73

Time Warner Inc., IV 673–76; 7 526–30 (upd.) ; 109 548–58 (upd.)

The Times Mirror Company, IV 677–78; 17 484–86 (upd.) *see also* Tribune Co.

TIMET *see* Titanium Metals Corp.

Timex Group B.V., 7 531–33; 25 479–82 (upd.); 111 471–77 (upd.)

The Timken Company, 8 529–31; 42 381–85 (upd.)

Tiscali SpA, 48 396–99

TISCO *see* Tata Iron & Steel Company Ltd.

Tishman Construction Company, 112 425–28 (upd.)

Tishman Speyer Properties, L.P., 47 403–06; 112 429–34

Tissue Technologies, Inc. *see* Palomar Medical Technologies, Inc.

Titan Cement Company S.A., 64 379–81

The Titan Corporation, 36 475–78

Titan International, Inc., 89 445–49

Titan Machinery Inc., 103 446–49

Titanium Metals Corporation, 21 489–92

TiVo Inc., 75 373–75

TJ International, Inc., 19 444–47

The TJX Companies, Inc., V 197–98; 19 448–50 (upd.); 57 366–69 (upd.)

TLC Beatrice International Holdings, Inc., 22 512–15

TMP Worldwide Inc., 30 458–60 *see also* Monster Worldwide Inc.

TNT Freightways Corporation, 14 504–06

TNT Limited, V 523–25

TNT Post Group N.V., 27 471–76 (upd.); 30 461–63 (upd.) *see also* TPG N.V.

Tnuva Food Industries Ltd., 111 478–81

Tobu Railway Company Ltd., 6 430–32; 98 404–08 (upd.)

Today's Man, Inc., 20 484–87

TODCO, 87 439–442

The Todd-AO Corporation, 33 400–04 *see also* Liberty Livewire Corp.

Todd Shipyards Corporation, 14 507–09

Todhunter International, Inc., 27 477–79

Tofutti Brands, Inc., 64 382–84

Tohan Corporation, 84 402–405

Toho Co., Ltd., 28 461–63

Tohuku Electric Power Company, Inc., V 726–28

The Tokai Bank, Limited, II 373–74; 15 494–96 (upd.)

Tokheim Corporation, 21 493–95

Tokio Marine and Fire Insurance Co., Ltd., III 383–86 *see also* Millea Holdings Inc.

Tokyo Electric Power Company, V 729–33; 74 343–48 (upd.)

Tokyo Gas Co., Ltd., V 734–36; 55 372–75 (upd.)

TOKYOPOP Inc., 79 415–18

Tokyu Corporation, V 526–28; 47 407–10 (upd.)

Tokyu Department Store Co., Ltd., V 199–202; 32 453–57 (upd.); 107 434–40 (upd.)

Tokyu Land Corporation, IV 728–29

Toll Brothers Inc., 15 497–99; 70 323–26 (upd.)

Tollgrade Communications, Inc., 44 424–27

Tom Brown, Inc., 37 389–91

Tom Doherty Associates Inc., 25 483–86

Tombstone Pizza Corporation, 13 515–17 *see also* Kraft Foods Inc.

Tomen Corporation, IV 224–25; 24 488–91 (upd.)

Tomkins plc, 11 525–27; 44 428–31 (upd.)

Tommy Bahama Group, Inc., 108 491–95

Tommy Hilfiger Corporation, 20 488–90; 53 330–33 (upd.)

Tomra Systems ASA, 103 450–54

Tom's Foods Inc., 66 325–27

Tom's of Maine, Inc., 45 414–16

TomTom N.V., 81 388–91

Tomy Company Ltd., 65 341–44

Tone Brothers, Inc., 21 496–98; 74 349–52 (upd.)

Tonen Corporation, IV 554–56; 16 489–92 (upd.)

TonenGeneral Sekiyu K.K., 54 380–86 (upd.)

Tong Yang Cement Corporation, 62 366–68

Tonka Corporation, 25 487–89

Too, Inc., 61 371–73

Toolex International N.V., 26 489–91

Tootsie Roll Industries, Inc., 12 480–82; 82 392–96 (upd.)

The Topaz Group, Inc., 62 369–71

Topco Associates LLC, 60 302–04

Topcon Corporation, 84 406–409

Toppan Printing Co., Ltd., IV 679–81; 58 340–44 (upd.)

University of Phoenix *see* Apollo Group, Inc.

Univision Communications Inc., 24 515–18; 83 434–439 **(upd.)**

UNM *see* United News & Media plc.

Uno Restaurant Holdings Corporation, 18 538–40; 70 334–37 **(upd.)**

Unocal Corporation, IV 569–71; 24 519–23 **(upd.); 71 378–84 (upd.)**

UNUM Corp., 13 538–40

UnumProvident Corporation, 52 376–83 **(upd.)**

Uny Co., Ltd., V 209–10; 49 425–28 **(upd.)**

UOB *see* United Overseas Bank Ltd.

UPC *see* United Pan-Europe Communications NV.

UPI *see* United Press International.

Upjohn Company, I 707–09; 8 547–49 **(upd.)** *see also* Pharmacia & Upjohn Inc.; Pfizer Inc.

UPM-Kymmene Corporation, 19 461–65; 50 505–11 **(upd.)**

The Upper Deck Company, LLC, 105 462–66

UPS *see* United Parcel Service, Inc.

Uralita S.A., 96 438–41

Uranium One Inc., 111 515–18

Urban Engineers, Inc., 102 435–38

Urban Outfitters, Inc., 14 524–26; 74 367–70 **(upd.)**

Urbi Desarrollos Urbanos, S.A. de C.V., 81 400–03

Urbium PLC, 75 389–91

URS Corporation, 45 420–23; 80 397–400 **(upd.)**

URSI *see* United Road Services, Inc.

US *see also* U.S.

US Airways Group, Inc., I 131–32; 6 131–32 **(upd.); 28 506–09 (upd.); 52** 384–88 **(upd.); 110 472–78 (upd.)**

US 1 Industries, Inc., 89 475–78

USA Interactive, Inc., 47 418–22 (upd.)

USA Mobility Inc., 97 437–40 (upd.)

USA Truck, Inc., 42 410–13

USAA, 10 541–43; 62 385–88 (upd.) *see also* United Services Automobile Association.

USANA, Inc., 29 491–93

USCC *see* United States Cellular Corp.

USF&G Corporation, III 395–98 *see also* The St. Paul Companies.

USG Corporation, III 762–64; 26 507–10 **(upd.); 81 404–10 (upd.)**

Ushio Inc., 91 496–99

Usinas Siderúrgicas de Minas Gerais **S.A., 77 454–57**

Usinger's Famous Sausage *see* Fred Usinger Inc.

Usinor SA, IV 226–28; 42 414–17 **(upd.)**

USO *see* United Service Organizations.

USPS *see* United States Postal Service.

USSC *see* United States Surgical Corp.

UST Inc., 9 533–35; 50 512–17 (upd.)

USTA *see* United States Tennis Association

USX Corporation, IV 572–74; 7 549–52 **(upd.)** *see also* United States Steel Corp.

Utah Medical Products, Inc., 36 496–99

Utah Power and Light Company, 27 483–86 *see also* PacifiCorp.

UTG Inc., 100 430–33

Utilicorp United Inc., 6 592–94 *see also* Aquila, Inc.

UTStarcom, Inc., 77 458–61

UTV *see* Ulster Television PLC.

Utz Quality Foods, Inc., 72 358–60

UUNET, 38 468–72

Uwajimaya, Inc., 60 312–14

Uzbekistan Airways National Air **Company, 99 470–473**

V

V&S Vin & Sprit AB, 91 504–11 (upd.)

VA TECH ELIN EBG GmbH, 49 429–31

Vail Resorts, Inc., 11 543–46; 43 435–39 **(upd.)**

Vaillant GmbH, 44 436–39

Vaisala Oyj, 104 459–63

Valassis Communications, Inc., 8 550–51; 37 407–10 **(upd.); 76** 364–67 **(upd.)**

Valeo, 23 492–94; 66 350–53 (upd.)

Valero Energy Corporation, 7 553–55; 71 385–90 **(upd.)**

Valhi, Inc., 19 466–68; 94 431–35 **(upd.)**

Vallen Corporation, 45 424–26

Valley Media Inc., 35 430–33

Valley National Gases, Inc., 85 434–37

Valley Proteins, Inc., 91 500–03

ValleyCrest Companies, 81 411–14 **(upd.)**

Vallourec SA, 54 391–94

Valmet Oy, III 647–49 *see also* Metso Corp.

Valmont Industries, Inc., 19 469–72

Valora Holding AG, 98 425–28

Valorem S.A., 88 427–30

Valores Industriales S.A., 19 473–75

The Valspar Corporation, 8 552–54; 32 483–86 **(upd.); 77 462–68 (upd.)**

Value City Department Stores, Inc., 38 473–75 *see also* Retail Ventures, Inc.

Value Line, 16 506–08; 73 358–61 **(upd.)**

Value Merchants Inc., 13 541–43

ValueClick, Inc., 49 432–34

ValueVision International, Inc., 22 534–36

Valve Corporation, 101 483–86

Van Camp Seafood Company, Inc., 7 556–57 *see also* Chicken of the Sea International.

Van de Velde S.A./NV, 102 439–43

Van Hool S.A./NV, 96 442–45

Van Houtte Inc., 39 409–11

Van Lanschot NV, 79 456–59

Van Leer N.V. *see* Royal Packaging Industries Van Leer N.V.; Greif Inc.

Vance Publishing Corporation, 64 398–401

Vanderbilt University Medical Center, 99 474–477

The Vanguard Group, Inc., 14 530–32; 34 486–89 **(upd.)**

Vanguard Health Systems Inc., 70 338–40

Vann's Inc., 105 467–70

Van's Aircraft, Inc., 65 349–51

Vans, Inc., 16 509–11; 47 423–26 **(upd.)**

Vapores *see* Compañía Sud Americana de Vapores S.A.

Varco International, Inc., 42 418–20

Vari-Lite International, Inc., 35 434–36

Varian Associates Inc., 12 504–06

Varian, Inc., 48 407–11 (upd.)

Variety Wholesalers, Inc., 73 362–64

Variflex, Inc., 51 391–93

VARIG S.A. (Viação Aérea **Rio-Grandense), 6 133–35; 29** 494–97 **(upd.)**

Varity Corporation, III 650–52 *see also* AGCO Corp.

Varlen Corporation, 16 512–14

Varsity Brands, Inc., 15 516–18; 94 436–40 **(upd.)**

Varta AG, 23 495–99

VASCO Data Security International, **Inc., 79 460–63**

Vastar Resources, Inc., 24 524–26

Vattenfall AB, 57 395–98

Vaughan Foods, Inc., 105 471–74

Vauxhall Motors Limited, 73 365–69

VBA - Bloemenveiling Aalsmeer, 88 431–34

VCA Antech, Inc., 58 353–55

Veba A.G., I 542–43; 15 519–21 (upd.) *see also* E.On AG.

Vebego International BV, 49 435–37

VECO International, Inc., 7 558–59 *see also* CH2M Hill Ltd.

Vector Aerospace Corporation, 97 441–44

Vector Group Ltd., 35 437–40 (upd.)

Vectren Corporation, 98 429–36 (upd.)

Vedanta Resources plc, 112 457–61

Vedior NV, 35 441–43

Veeco Instruments Inc., 32 487–90

Veidekke ASA, 98 437–40

Veit Companies, 43 440–42; 92 398–402 **(upd.)**

Velcro Industries N.V., 19 476–78; 72 361–64 **(upd.)**

Velocity Express Corporation, 49 438–41; 94 441–46 **(upd.)**

Velux A/S, 86 412–15

Venator Group Inc., 35 444–49 (upd.) *see also* Foot Locker Inc.

Vencor, Inc., 16 515–17

Vendex International N.V., 13 544–46 *see also* Koninklijke Vendex KBB N.V. (Royal Vendex KBB N.V.).

Vendôme Luxury Group plc, 27 487–89

Venetian Casino Resort, LLC, 47 427–29

Ventana Medical Systems, Inc., 75 392–94

Ventura Foods LLC, 90 420–23

Venture Stores Inc., 12 507–09

Veolia Environnement, SA, 109 566–71

Wella AG, III 68–70; 48 420–23 (upd.)

WellCare Health Plans, Inc., 101 487–90

WellChoice, Inc., 67 388–91 (upd.)

Wellco Enterprises, Inc., 84 427–430

Wellcome Foundation Ltd., I 713–15 *see also* GlaxoSmithKline plc.

Wellman, Inc., 8 561–62; 52 408–11 (upd.)

WellPoint, Inc., 25 525–29; 103 505–14 (upd.)

Wells' Dairy, Inc., 36 511–13

Wells Fargo & Company, II 380–84; 12 533–37 (upd.); 38 483–92 (upd.); 97 453–67

Wells-Gardner Electronics Corporation, 43 458–61

Wells Rich Greene BDDP, 6 50–52

Wendell *see* Mark T. Wendell Tea Co.

Wendy's International, Inc., 8 563–65; 23 504–07 (upd.); 47 439–44 (upd.)

Wenner Bread Products Inc., 80 411–15

Wenner Media, Inc., 32 506–09

Werhahn *see* Wilh. Werhahn KG.

Werner Enterprises, Inc., 26 531–33

Weru Aktiengesellschaft, 18 558–61

Wesfarmers Limited, 109 591–95

Wessanen *see* Koninklijke Wessanen nv.

West Bend Co., 14 546–48

West Coast Entertainment Corporation, 29 502–04

West Corporation, 42 435–37

West Fraser Timber Co. Ltd., 17 538–40; 91 512–18 (upd.)

West Group, 34 502–06 (upd.)

West Linn Paper Company, 91 519–22

West Marine, Inc., 17 541–43; 90 438–42 (upd.)

West One Bancorp, 11 552–55 *see also* U.S. Bancorp.

West Pharmaceutical Services, Inc., 42 438–41

West Point-Pepperell, Inc., 8 566–69 *see also* WestPoint Stevens Inc.; JPS Textile Group, Inc.

West Publishing Co., 7 579–81

Westaff Inc., 33 454–57

Westamerica Bancorporation, 17 544–47

Westar Energy, Inc., 57 404–07 (upd.)

WestCoast Hospitality Corporation, 59 410–13

Westcon Group, Inc., 67 392–94

Westdeutsche Landesbank Girozentrale, II 385–87; 46 458–61 (upd.)

Westell Technologies, Inc., 57 408–10

Western Atlas Inc., 12 538–40

Western Beef, Inc., 22 548–50

Western Company of North America, 15 534–36

Western Digital Corporation, 25 530–32; 92 411–15 (upd.)

Western Gas Resources, Inc., 45 435–37

Western Oil Sands Inc., 85 454–57

Western Publishing Group, Inc., 13 559–61 *see also* Thomson Corp.

Western Refining Inc., 109 596–99

Western Resources, Inc., 12 541–43

The WesterN SizzliN Corporation, 60 335–37

Western Union Company, 54 413–16; 112 492–96 (upd.)

Western Wireless Corporation, 36 514–16

Westfield Group, 69 366–69

Westin Hotels and Resorts Worldwide, 9 547–49; 29 505–08 (upd.)

Westinghouse Electric Corporation, II 120–22; 12 544–47 (upd.) *see also* CBS Radio Group.

WestJet Airlines Ltd., 38 493–95

Westmoreland Coal Company, 7 582–85

Weston Foods Inc. *see* George Weston Ltd.

Westpac Banking Corporation, II 388–90; 48 424–27 (upd.)

WestPoint Stevens Inc., 16 533–36 *see also* JPS Textile Group, Inc.

Westport Resources Corporation, 63 439–41

Westvaco Corporation, IV 351–54; 19 495–99 (upd.) *see also* MeadWestvaco Corp.

Westwood One Inc., 23 508–11; 106 490–96 (upd.)

The Wet Seal, Inc., 18 562–64; 70 353–57 (upd.)

Wetterau Incorporated, II 681–82 *see also* Supervalu Inc.

Weyco Group, Incorporated, 32 510–13

Weyerhaeuser Company, IV 355–56; 9 550–52 (upd.); 28 514–17 (upd.); 83 454–461 (upd.)

WFS Financial Inc., 70 358–60

WFSC *see* World Fuel Services Corp.

WGBH Educational Foundation, 66 366–68

WH Smith PLC, 42 442–47 (upd.)

Wham-O, Inc., 61 390–93

Whataburger Restaurants LP, 105 493–97

Whatman plc, 46 462–65

Wheaton Industries, 8 570–73

Wheaton Science Products, 60 338–42 (upd.)

Wheelabrator Technologies, Inc., 6 599–600; 60 343–45 (upd.)

Wheeling-Pittsburgh Corporation, 7 586–88; 58 360–64 (upd.)

Wheels Inc., 96 458–61

Wherehouse Entertainment Incorporated, 11 556–58

Whirlpool Corporation, III 653–55; 12 548–50 (upd.); 59 414–19 (upd.)

Whitbread PLC, I 293–94; 20 519–22 (upd.); 52 412–17 (upd.); 97 468–76 (upd.)

White & Case LLP, 35 466–69

White Castle Management Company, 12 551–53; 36 517–20 (upd.); 85 458–64 (upd.)

White Consolidated Industries Inc., 13 562–64 *see also* Electrolux.

The White House, Inc., 60 346–48

White Lily Foods Company, 88 435–38

White Martins Gases Industriais Ltda., 111 526–29

White Mountains Insurance Group, Ltd., 48 428–31

White Rose, Inc., 24 527–29

White Wave, 43 462–64

Whitehall Jewellers, Inc., 82 429–34 (upd.)

Whiting Petroleum Corporation, 81 424–27

Whiting-Turner Contracting Company, 95 446–49

Whitman Corporation, 10 553–55 (upd.) *see also* PepsiAmericas, Inc.

Whitman Education Group, Inc., 41 419–21

Whitney Holding Corporation, 21 522–24

Whittaker Corporation, I 544–46; 48 432–35 (upd.)

Whittard of Chelsea Plc, 61 394–97

Whole Foods Market, Inc., 20 523–27; 50 530–34 (upd.); 110 479–86 (upd.)

WHX Corporation, 98 464–67

Wickes Inc., V 221–23; 25 533–36 (upd.)

Widmer Brothers Brewing Company, 76 379–82

Wieden + Kennedy, 75 403–05

Wienerberger AG, 70 361–63

Wikimedia Foundation, Inc., 91 523–26

Wilbert, Inc., 56 377–80

Wilbur Chocolate Company, 66 369–71

Wilco Farm Stores, 93 490–93

Wild Oats Markets, Inc., 19 500–02; 41 422–25 (upd.)

Wildlife Conservation Society, 31 462–64

Wilh. Werhahn KG, 101 491–94

Wilh. Wilhelmsen ASA, 94 459–62

Wilhelm Karmann GmbH, 94 463–68

Wilkinson Hardware Stores Ltd., 80 416–18

Wilkinson Sword Ltd., 60 349–52

Willamette Industries, Inc., IV 357–59; 31 465–68 (upd.) *see also* Weyerhaeuser Co.

Willamette Valley Vineyards, Inc., 85 465–69

Willbros Group, Inc., 56 381–83

William Grant & Sons Ltd., 60 353–55

William Hill Organization Limited, 49 449–52

William Jackson & Son Ltd., 101 495–99

William L. Bonnell Company, Inc., 66 372–74

William Lyon Homes, 59 420–22

William Morris Agency, Inc., 23 512–14; 102 448–52 (upd.)

William Reed Publishing Ltd., 78 467–70

William Zinsser & Company, Inc., 58 365–67

Williams & Connolly LLP, 47 445–48

Williams Communications Group, Inc., 34 507–10

Index to Industries

Accounting

American Institute of Certified Public Accountants (AICPA), 44
Andersen, 29 (upd.); 68 (upd.)
Automatic Data Processing, Inc., III; 9 (upd.); 47 (upd.)
BDO Seidman LLP, 96
BKD LLP, 96
CPP International, LLC, 103
CROSSMARK, 79
Deloitte Touche Tohmatsu International, 9; 29 (upd.)
Ernst & Young Global Limited, 9; 29 (upd.); 108 (upd.)
FTI Consulting, Inc., 77
Grant Thornton International, 57
Huron Consulting Group Inc., 87
JKH Holding Co. LLC, 105
KPMG International, 33 (upd.); 108 (upd.)
L.S. Starrett Co., 13
McLane Company, Inc., 13
NCO Group, Inc., 42
Paychex, Inc., 15; 46 (upd.)
PKF International 78
Plante & Moran, LLP, 71
PRG-Schultz International, Inc., 73
PricewaterhouseCoopers International Limited, 9; 29 (upd.); 111 (upd.)
Resources Connection, Inc., 81
Robert Wood Johnson Foundation, 35
RSM McGladrey Business Services Inc., 98
Saffery Champness, 80
Sanders\Wingo, 99
Schenck Business Solutions, 88
StarTek, Inc., 79
Travelzoo Inc., 79

Univision Communications Inc., 24; 83 (upd.)

Advertising & Business Services

ABM Industries Incorporated, 25 (upd.)
Abt Associates Inc., 95
Accenture Ltd., 108 (upd.)
AchieveGlobal Inc., 90
Ackerley Communications, Inc., 9
ACNielsen Corporation, 13; 38 (upd.)
Acosta Sales and Marketing Company, Inc., 77
Acsys, Inc., 44
Adecco S.A., 36 (upd.)
Adelman Travel Group, 105
Adia S.A., 6
Administaff, Inc., 52
Advertising Council, Inc., The, 76
Advisory Board Company, The, 80
Advo, Inc., 6; 53 (upd.)
Aegis Group plc, 6
Affiliated Computer Services, Inc., 61
AHL Services, Inc., 27
Allegis Group, Inc., 95
Alloy, Inc., 55
Amdocs Ltd., 47
American Building Maintenance Industries, Inc., 6
Amey Plc, 47
Analysts International Corporation, 36
aQuantive, Inc., 81
Arbitron Company, The, 38
Ariba, Inc., 57
Armor Holdings, Inc., 27
Asatsu-DK Inc., 82
Ashtead Group plc, 34
Associated Press, The, 13

Avalon Correctional Services, Inc., 75
Bain & Company, 55
Barrett Business Services, Inc., 16
Barton Protective Services Inc., 53
Bates Worldwide, Inc., 14; 33 (upd.)
Bearings, Inc., 13
Berlitz International, Inc., 13; 39 (upd.)
Bernard Hodes Group Inc., 86
Bernstein-Rein, 92
Big Flower Press Holdings, Inc., 21
Billing Concepts, Inc., 26; 72 (upd.)
Billing Services Group Ltd., 102
BISYS Group, Inc., The, 73
Booz Allen Hamilton Inc., 10; 101 (upd.)
Boron, LePore & Associates, Inc., 45
Boston Consulting Group, The, 58
Bozell Worldwide Inc., 25
BrandPartners Group, Inc., 58
Bright Horizons Family Solutions, Inc., 31
Brink's Company, The, 58 (upd.)
Broadcast Music Inc., 23; 90 (upd.)
Bronner Display & Sign Advertising, Inc., 82
Buck Consultants, Inc., 55
Bureau Veritas SA, 55
Burke, Inc., 88
Burns International Services Corporation, 13; 41 (upd.)
Cambridge Technology Partners, Inc., 36
Campbell-Ewald Advertising, 86
Campbell-Mithun-Esty, Inc., 16
Cannon Design, 63
Capario, 104
Capita Group PLC, 69
Cardtronics, Inc., 93
Carmichael Lynch Inc., 28
Cash Systems, Inc., 93
Cazenove Group plc, 72
CCC Information Services Group Inc., 74

Aerospace

Agribusiness & Farming

Airlines

Bio-Technology

Peter Kiewit Sons' Inc., 8
Philipp Holzmann AG, 17
Pinguely-Haulotte SA, 51
Post Properties, Inc., 26
Pulte Homes, Inc., 8; 42 (upd.)
Pyramid Companies, 54
Redrow Group plc, 31
Rinker Group Ltd., 65
RMC Group p.l.c., III; 34 (upd.)
Robertson-Ceco Corporation, 19
Rooney Brothers Co., 25
Rottlund Company, Inc., The, 28
Roy Anderson Corporation, 75
Ryan Companies US, Inc., 99
Ryland Group, Inc., The, 8; 37 (upd.);
   107 (upd.)
Sandvik AB, IV; 32 (upd.); 77 (upd.)
Schuff Steel Company, 26
Seddon Group Ltd., 67
Servidyne Inc., 100 (upd.)
Shimizu Corporation, 109
Shorewood Packaging Corporation, 28
Simon Property Group Inc., 27; 84 (upd.)
Skanska AB, 38; 110 (upd.)
Skidmore, Owings & Merrill LLP, 69
   (upd.)
SNC-Lavalin Group Inc., 72
Speedy Hire plc, 84
Stabler Companies Inc. 78
Standard Pacific Corporation, 52
Structure Tone Organization, The, 99
Stone & Webster, Inc., 64 (upd.)
Sundt Corp., 24
Swinerton Inc., 43
Tarmac Limited, III; 28 (upd.); 95 (upd.)
Taylor Woodrow plc, I; 38 (upd.)
Technical Olympic USA, Inc., 75
Terex Corporation, 7; 40 (upd.); 91
   (upd.)
ThyssenKrupp AG, IV; 28 (upd.); 87
   (upd.)
TIC Holdings Inc., 92
Tishman Construction Company, 112
Toll Brothers Inc., 15; 70 (upd.)
Trammell Crow Company, 8
Tridel Enterprises Inc., 9
Turner Construction Company, 66
Turner Corporation, The, 8; 23 (upd.)
Urban Engineers, Inc., 102
Urbi Desarrollos Urbanos, S.A. de C.V.,
   81
U.S. Aggregates, Inc., 42
U.S. Home Corporation, 8; 78 (upd.)
VA TECH ELIN EBG GmbH, 49
Veidekke ASA, 98
Veit Companies, 43; 92 (upd.)
Wacker Construction Equipment AG, 95
Walbridge Aldinger Co., 38
Walter Industries, Inc., III; 22 (upd.); 72
   (upd.)
Weitz Company, Inc., The, 42
Whiting-Turner Contracting Company, 95
Willbros Group, Inc., 56
William Lyon Homes, 59
Wilson Bowden Plc, 45
Wood Hall Trust PLC, I
Yates Companies, Inc., The, 62
Zachry Group, Inc., 95

Containers

Ball Corporation, I; 10 (upd.); 78 (upd.)
BWAY Corporation, 24
Chesapeake Corporation, 8; 30 (upd.); 93
   (upd.)
CLARCOR Inc., 17; 61 (upd.)
Constar International Inc., 64
Continental Can Co., Inc., 15
Continental Group Company, I
Crown Cork & Seal Company, Inc., I; 13
   (upd.); 32 (upd.)
Crown Holdings, Inc., 83 (upd.)
Gaylord Container Corporation, 8
Golden Belt Manufacturing Co., 16
Graham Packaging Holdings Company,
   87
Greif Inc., 15; 66 (upd.)
Grupo Industrial Durango, S.A. de C.V.,
   37
Hanjin Shipping Co., Ltd., 50
Heekin Can Inc., 13
Inland Container Corporation, 8
Interpool, Inc., 92
Kerr Group Inc., 24
Keyes Fibre Company, 9
Libbey Inc., 49
Liqui-Box Corporation, 16
Longaberger Company, The, 12
Longview Fibre Company, 8
Mead Corporation, The, 19 (upd.)
Metal Box PLC, I
Mobile Mini, Inc., 58
Molins plc, 51
National Can Corporation, I
Owens-Illinois, Inc., I; 26 (upd.); 85
   (upd.)
Packaging Corporation of America, 51
   (upd.)
Pochet SA, 55
Primerica Corporation, I
Printpack, Inc., 68
PVC Container Corporation, 67
Rexam PLC, 32 (upd.); 85 (upd.)
Reynolds Metals Company, 19 (upd.)
Royal Packaging Industries Van Leer N.V.,
   30
RPC Group PLC, 81
Sealright Co., Inc., 17
Shurgard Storage Centers, Inc., 52
Smurfit Kappa Group plc, 112 (upd.)
Smurfit-Stone Container Corporation, 26
   (upd.); 83 (upd.)
Sonoco Products Company, 8; 89 (upd.)
Thermos Company, 16
Tim-Bar Corporation, 110
Toyo Seikan Kaisha, Ltd., I
U.S. Can Corporation, 30
Ultra Pac, Inc., 24
Viatech Continental Can Company, Inc.,
   25 (upd.)
Vidrala S.A., 67
Vitro Corporativo S.A. de C.V., 34

Drugs & Pharmaceuticals

A. Nelson & Co. Ltd., 75
A.L. Pharma Inc., 12
Abbott Laboratories, I; 11 (upd.); 40
   (upd.); 93 (upd.)

Aché Laboratórios Farmacéuticas S.A., 105
Actavis Group hf., 103
Actelion Ltd., 83
Adolor Corporation, 101
Akorn, Inc., 32
Albany Molecular Research, Inc., 77
Alfresa Holdings Corporation, 108
Allergan, Inc., 77 (upd.)
Alpharma Inc., 35 (upd.)
ALZA Corporation, 10; 36 (upd.)
American Home Products, I; 10 (upd.)
American Oriental Bioengineering Inc., 93
American Pharmaceutical Partners, Inc.,
   69
AmerisourceBergen Corporation, 64
   (upd.)
Amersham PLC, 50
Amgen, Inc., 10; 89 (upd.)
Amylin Pharmaceuticals, Inc., 67
Andrx Corporation, 55
Angelini SpA, 100
Aspen Pharmacare Holdings Limited, 112
Astellas Pharma Inc., 97 (upd.)
AstraZeneca PLC, I; 20 (upd.); 50 (upd.)
AtheroGenics Inc., 101
Axcan Pharma Inc., 85
Barr Pharmaceuticals, Inc., 26; 68 (upd.)
Bayer A.G., I; 13 (upd.)
Berlex Laboratories, Inc., 66
Biovail Corporation, 47
Block Drug Company, Inc., 8
Boiron S.A., 73
Bristol-Myers Squibb Company, III; 9
   (upd.); 37 (upd.); 111 (upd.)
BTG Plc, 87
C.H. Boehringer Sohn, 39
Cahill May Roberts Group Ltd., 112
Caremark Rx, Inc., 10; 54 (upd.)
Carter-Wallace, Inc., 8; 38 (upd.)
Celgene Corporation, 67
Cephalon, Inc., 45
Chiron Corporation, 10
Chugai Pharmaceutical Co., Ltd., 50
Ciba-Geigy Ltd., I; 8 (upd.)
CSL Limited, 112
D&K Wholesale Drug, Inc., 14
Discovery Partners International, Inc., 58
Dr. Reddy's Laboratories Ltd., 59
Egis Gyogyszergyar Nyrt, 104
Eisai Co., Ltd., 101
Elan Corporation PLC, 63
Eli Lilly and Company, I; 11 (upd.); 47
   (upd.); 109 (upd.)
Endo Pharmaceuticals Holdings Inc., 71
Eon Labs, Inc., 67
Express Scripts Inc., 44 (upd.)
F. Hoffmann-La Roche Ltd., I; 50 (upd.)
Fisons plc, 9; 23 (upd.)
Forest Laboratories, Inc., 52 (upd.)
FoxMeyer Health Corporation, 16
Fujisawa Pharmaceutical Company, Ltd.,
   I; 58 (upd.)
G.D. Searle & Co., I; 12 (upd.); 34
   (upd.)
Galenica AG, 84
GEHE AG, 27
Genentech, Inc., I; 8 (upd.); 75 (upd.)
Genetics Institute, Inc., 8

Education & Training

Electrical & Electronics

Engineering & Management Services

Entertainment & Leisure

Financial Services: Banks

Financial Services: Excluding Banks

Food Products

Whittard of Chelsea Plc, 61
Whole Foods Market, Inc., 20; 50 (upd.);
110 (upd.)
Wild Oats Markets, Inc., 19; 41 (upd.)
Willow Run Foods, Inc., 100
Winchell's Donut Houses Operating
Company, L.P., 60
WinCo Foods Inc., 60
Winn-Dixie Stores, Inc., II; 21 (upd.); 59
(upd.)
Wm. Morrison Supermarkets plc, 38; 110
(upd.)
Wolfgang Puck Worldwide, Inc., 26, 70
(upd.)
Worldwide Restaurant Concepts, Inc., 47
Yoshinoya D & C Company Ltd., 88
Young & Co.'s Brewery, P.L.C., 38
Yucaipa Cos., 17
Yum! Brands Inc., 58
Zingerman's Community of Businesses,
68
Zpizza International Inc., 105

Health, Personal & Medical Care Products

A-dec, Inc., 53
Abaxis, Inc., 83
Abbott Laboratories, I; 11 (upd.); 40
(upd.); 93 (upd.)
Abiomed, Inc., 47
Accuray Incorporated, 95
Acuson Corporation, 10; 36 (upd.)
Advanced Medical Optics, Inc., 79
Advanced Neuromodulation Systems, Inc.,
73
Akorn, Inc., 32
ALARIS Medical Systems, Inc., 65
Alberto-Culver Company, 8; 36 (upd.); 91
(upd.)
Alco Health Services Corporation, III
Alès Groupe, 81
Allergan, Inc., 10; 30 (upd.); 77 (upd.)
American Medical Alert Corporation, 103
American Oriental Bioengineering Inc., 93
American Safety Razor Company, 20
American Stores Company, II; 22 (upd.)
Amway Corporation, III; 13 (upd.)
Andis Company, Inc., 85
AngioDynamics, Inc., 81
Ansell Ltd., 60 (upd.)
ArthroCare Corporation, 73
Artsana SpA, 92
Ascendia Brands, Inc., 97
Atkins Nutritionals, Inc., 58
Aveda Corporation, 24
Avon Products, Inc., III; 19 (upd.); 46
(upd.); 109 (upd.)
Ballard Medical Products, 21
Bally Total Fitness Holding Corp., 25
Bare Escentuals, Inc., 91
Bausch & Lomb Inc., 7; 25 (upd.); 96
(upd.)
Baxter International Inc., I; 10 (upd.)
BeautiControl Cosmetics, Inc., 21
Becton, Dickinson and Company, I; 11
(upd.); 36 (upd.); 101 (upd.)
Beiersdorf AG, 29
Big B, Inc., 17

Bindley Western Industries, Inc., 9
Biolase Technology, Inc., 87
Biomet, Inc., 10; 93 (upd.)
BioScrip Inc., 98
Biosite Incorporated, 73
Block Drug Company, Inc., 8; 27 (upd.)
Body Shop International plc, The, 11; 53
(upd.)
Boiron S.A., 73
Bolton Group B.V., 86
Borghese Inc., 107
Bristol-Myers Squibb Company, III; 9
(upd.)
Bronner Brothers Inc., 92
Burt's Bees, Inc., 58
C.R. Bard Inc., 9; 65 (upd.)
Candela Corporation, 48
Cantel Medical Corporation, 80
Cardinal Health, Inc., 18; 50 (upd.)
Carl Zeiss AG, III; 34 (upd.); 91 (upd.)
Carma Laboratories, Inc., 60
Carson, Inc., 31
Carter-Wallace, Inc., 8
Caswell-Massey Co. Ltd., 51
CCA Industries, Inc., 53
Chanel SA, 12; 49 (upd.)
Chattem, Inc., 17; 88 (upd.)
Chesebrough-Pond's USA, Inc., 8
Chindex International, Inc., 101
Chronimed Inc., 26
Church & Dwight Co., Inc., 68 (upd.)
Cintas Corporation, 51 (upd.)
Clorox Company, The, III; 22 (upd.); 81
(upd.)
CNS, Inc., 20
COBE Cardiovascular, Inc., 61
Cochlear Ltd., 77
Colgate-Palmolive Company, III; 14
(upd.); 35 (upd.)
Combe Inc., 72
Conair Corporation, 17; 69 (upd.)
CONMED Corporation, 87
Connetics Corporation, 70
Cook Group Inc., 102
Cooper Companies, Inc., The, 39
Cordis Corporation, 19; 46 (upd.); 112
(upd.)
Cosmair, Inc., 8
Cosmolab Inc., 96
Coty, Inc., 36
Covidien Ltd., 91
Cyberonics, Inc., 79
Cybex International, Inc., 49
Cytyc Corporation, 69
Dade Behring Holdings Inc., 71
Dalli-Werke GmbH & Co. KG, 86
Datascope Corporation, 39
Del Laboratories, Inc., 28
Deltec, Inc., 56
Dentsply International Inc., 10; 109
(upd.)
DEP Corporation, 20
DePuy Inc., 30; 37 (upd.)
DHB Industries Inc., 85
Diagnostic Products Corporation, 73
Dial Corp., The, 23 (upd.)
Direct Focus, Inc., 47
Drackett Professional Products, 12

Drägerwerk AG, 83
drugstore.com, inc., 109
Drypers Corporation, 18
Duane Reade Holdings Inc., 109 (upd.)
Dynatronics Corporation, 99
E-Z-EM Inc., 89
Edwards Lifesciences LLC, 112
Elizabeth Arden, Inc., 8; 40 (upd.)
Elscint Ltd., 20
Empi, Inc., 26
Enrich International, Inc., 33
Essie Cosmetics, Ltd., 102
Essilor International, 21
Estée Lauder Companies Inc., The, 9; 30
(upd.); 93 (upd.)
Ethicon, Inc., 23
Exactech, Inc., 101
Farnam Companies, Inc., 107
Farouk Systems Inc. 78
Forest Laboratories, Inc., 11
Forever Living Products International Inc.,
17
FoxHollow Technologies, Inc., 85
Franz Haniel & Cie. GmbH, 109
French Fragrances, Inc., 22
G&K Holding S.A., 95
Gambro AB, 49
General Nutrition Companies, Inc., 11;
29 (upd.)
Genzyme Corporation, 13; 77 (upd.)
GF Health Products, Inc., 82
Gillette Company, The, III; 20 (upd.); 68
(upd.)
Given Imaging Ltd., 83
GN ReSound A/S, 103
GNC Corporation, 98 (upd.)
Golden Neo-Life Diamite International,
Inc., 100
Goody Products, Inc., 12
Groupe Yves Saint Laurent, 23
Grupo Omnilife S.A. de C.V., 88
Guerlain, 23
Guest Supply, Inc., 18
Guidant Corporation, 58
Guinot Paris S.A., 82
Hanger Orthopedic Group, Inc., 41
Health O Meter Products Inc., 14
Helen of Troy Corporation, 18
Helene Curtis Industries, Inc., 8; 28
(upd.)
Henkel KGaA, III; 34 (upd.); 95 (upd.)
Henry Schein, Inc., 31; 70 (upd.)
Herbalife Ltd., 17; 41 (upd.); 92 (upd.)
Huntleigh Technology PLC, 77
ICON Health & Fitness, Inc., 38; 102
(upd.)
Immucor, Inc., 81
Inamed Corporation, 79
Integra LifeSciences Holdings
Corporation, 87
Integrated BioPharma, Inc., 83
Inter Parfums Inc., 35; 86 (upd.)
Intuitive Surgical, Inc., 79
Invacare Corporation, 11; 47 (upd.)
Invivo Corporation, 52
IRIS International, Inc., 101
IVAX Corporation, 11
IVC Industries, Inc., 45

Health Care Services

Hotels

Information Technology

Insurance

Legal Services

Materials

Mining & Metals

Nonprofit & Philanthropic Organizations

Paper & Forestry

Personal Services

Petroleum

Publishing & Printing

Real Estate

Retail & Wholesale

World Duty Free Americas, Inc., 29
(upd.)
Yamada Denki Co., Ltd., 85
Yankee Candle Company, Inc., The, 37
Yingli Green Energy Holding Company
Limited, 103
Young's Market Company, LLC, 32
Younkers, 76 (upd.)
Younkers, Inc., 19
Zale Corporation, 16; 40 (upd.); 91
(upd.)
Zany Brainy, Inc., 31
Zappos.com, Inc., 73
Zara International, Inc., 83
Ziebart International Corporation, 30
Zion's Cooperative Mercantile Institution,
33
Zipcar, Inc., 92
Zones, Inc., 67
Zumiez, Inc., 77

Rubber & Tires

AirBoss of America Corporation, 108
Aeroquip Corporation, 16
Avon Rubber p.l.c., 108
Bandag, Inc., 19
BFGoodrich Company, The, V
Bridgestone Corporation, V; 21 (upd.); 59
(upd.)
Canadian Tire Corporation, Limited, 71
(upd.)
Carlisle Companies Incorporated, 8
Compagnie Générale des Établissements
Michelin, V; 42 (upd.)
Continental AG, V; 56 (upd.)
Continental General Tire Corp., 23
Cooper Tire & Rubber Company, 8; 23
(upd.)
Day International, Inc., 84
Elementis plc, 40 (upd.)
General Tire, Inc., 8
Goodyear Tire & Rubber Company, The,
V; 20 (upd.); 75 (upd.)
Hankook Tire Company Ltd., 105
Kelly-Springfield Tire Company, The, 8
Kumho Tire Company Ltd., 105
Les Schwab Tire Centers, 50
Myers Industries, Inc., 19; 96 (upd.)
Pirelli S.p.A., V; 15 (upd.)
Safeskin Corporation, 18
Sumitomo Rubber Industries, Ltd., V; 107
(upd.)
Trelleborg AB, 93
Tillotson Corp., 15
Treadco, Inc., 19
Ube Industries, Ltd., III; 38 (upd.)
Yokohama Rubber Company, Limited,
The, V; 19 (upd.); 91 (upd.)

Telecommunications

A.H. Belo Corporation, 30 (upd.)
Abertis Infraestructuras, S.A., 65
Abril S.A., 95
Acme-Cleveland Corp., 13
ADC Telecommunications, Inc., 10; 89
(upd.)
Adelphia Communications Corporation,
17; 52 (upd.)

Adtran Inc., 22
Advanced Fibre Communications, Inc., 63
AEI Music Network Inc., 35
AirTouch Communications, 11
Alaska Communications Systems Group,
Inc., 89
Albtelecom Sh. a, 111
Alcatel S.A., 36 (upd.)
Alcatel-Lucent, 109 (upd.)
Allbritton Communications Company,
105
Alliance Atlantis Communications Inc., 39
ALLTEL Corporation, 6; 46 (upd.)
América Móvil, S.A. de C.V., 80
American Tower Corporation, 33
Ameritech Corporation, V; 18 (upd.)
Amstrad plc, 48 (upd.)
AO VimpelCom, 48
AOL Time Warner Inc., 57 (upd.)
Arch Wireless, Inc., 39
ARD, 41
ARINC Inc., 98
ARRIS Group, Inc., 89
Ascent Media Corporation, 107
Ascom AG, 9
Aspect Telecommunications Corporation,
22
Asurion Corporation, 83
AT&T Bell Laboratories, Inc., 13
AT&T Corporation, V; 29 (upd.); 68
(upd.)
AT&T Wireless Services, Inc., 54 (upd.)
Avaya Inc., 104
Basin Electric Power Cooperative, 103
BCE Inc., V; 44 (upd.)
Beasley Broadcast Group, Inc., 51
Belgacom, 6
Bell Atlantic Corporation, V; 25 (upd.)
Bell Canada, 6
BellSouth Corporation, V; 29 (upd.)
Belo Corporation, 98 (upd.)
Bertelsmann A.G., IV; 15 (upd.); 43
(upd.); 91 (upd.)
BET Holdings, Inc., 18
Bharti Tele-Ventures Limited, 75
BHC Communications, Inc., 26
Blackfoot Telecommunications Group, 60
Bonneville International Corporation, 29
Bouygues S.A., I; 24 (upd.); 97 (upd.)
Brasil Telecom Participaçoes S.A., 57
Brightpoint Inc., 18; 106 (upd.)
Brite Voice Systems, Inc., 20
British Broadcasting Corporation Ltd., 7;
21 (upd.); 89 (upd.)
British Columbia Telephone Company, 6
British Telecommunications plc, V; 15
(upd.)
Broadwing Corporation, 70
BT Group plc, 49 (upd.)
C-COR.net Corp., 38
Cable & Wireless HKT, 30 (upd.)
Cable and Wireless plc, V; 25 (upd.)
Cablevision Systems Corporation, 7; 30
(upd.); 109 (upd.)
CalAmp Corp., 87
Canadian Broadcasting Corporation
(CBC), The, 37
Canal Plus, 10; 34 (upd.)

CanWest Global Communications
Corporation, 35
Capital Radio plc, 35
Carlton Communications PLC, 15; 50
(upd.)
Carolina Telephone and Telegraph
Company, 10
Carphone Warehouse Group PLC, The,
83
Carrier Access Corporation, 44
CBS Corporation, 28 (upd.)
CBS Television Network, 66 (upd.)
Centel Corporation, 6
Centennial Communications Corporation,
39
Central European Media Enterprises Ltd.,
61
Century Communications Corp., 10
Century Telephone Enterprises, Inc., 9; 54
(upd.)
Cesky Telecom, a.s., 64
Chancellor Media Corporation, 24
Channel Four Television Corporation, 93
Charter Communications, Inc., 33
Chello Zone Ltd., 93
China Mobile Ltd., 108
China Netcom Group Corporation (Hong
Kong) Limited, 73
China Telecom, 50
Chris-Craft Corporation, 9, 31 (upd.); 80
(upd.)
Christian Broadcasting Network, Inc.,
The, 52
Chrysalis Group plc, 40
Chugach Alaska Corporation, 60
Chunghwa Telecom Co., Ltd., 101 (upd.)
CIENA Corporation, 54
Cincinnati Bell, Inc., 6; 105 (upd.)
Citadel Communications Corporation, 35
Citizens Communications Company, 79
(upd.)
Clear Channel Communications, Inc., 23
Clearwire, Inc., 69
Cogent Communications Group, Inc., 55
COLT Telecom Group plc, 41
Comcast Corporation, 24 (upd.); 112
(upd.)
Comdial Corporation, 21
Commonwealth Telephone Enterprises,
Inc., 25
CommScope, Inc., 77
Comsat Corporation, 23
Comtech Telecommunications Corp., 75
Comverse Technology, Inc., 15; 43 (upd.)
Corning Inc., III; 44 (upd.); 90 (upd.)
Corporation for Public Broadcasting, 14;
89 (upd.)
Cox Radio, Inc., 89
Craftmade International, Inc., 44
Cumulus Media Inc., 37
DDI Corporation, 7
Deutsche Telekom AG, V; 48 (upd.); 108
(upd.)
Dialogic Corporation, 18
Digital Angel Corporation, 106
Directorate General of
Telecommunications, 7
DIRECTV, Inc., 38; 75 (upd.)

Textiles & Apparel

Tobacco

Transport Services

OMI Corporation, 59
Oppenheimer Group, The, 76
Oshkosh Corporation, 7; 98 (upd.)
Österreichische Bundesbahnen GmbH, 6
OTR Express, Inc., 25
Overnite Corporation, 14; 58 (upd.)
Overseas Shipholding Group, Inc., 11
Pacer International, Inc., 54
Pacific Basin Shipping Ltd., 86
Patriot Transportation Holding, Inc., 91
Peninsular and Oriental Steam Navigation Company, The, V; 38 (upd.)
Penske Corporation, V; 19 (upd.); 84 (upd.)
Peter Pan Bus Lines Inc., 106
PHH Arval, V; 53 (upd.)
Pilot Air Freight Corp., 67
Plantation Pipe Line Company, 68
PODS Enterprises Inc., 103
Polar Air Cargo Inc., 60
Port Authority of New York and New Jersey, The, 48
Port Imperial Ferry Corporation, 70
Post Office Group, V
Poste Italiane S.p.A., 108
Preston Corporation, 6
RailTex, Inc., 20
Railtrack Group PLC, 50
REpower Systems AG, 101
Réseau Ferré de France, 66
Roadway Express, Inc., V; 25 (upd.)
Rodriguez Group S.A., 90
Rock-It Cargo USA, Inc., 86
Royal Olympic Cruise Lines Inc., 52
Royal Vopak NV, 41
Russian Railways Joint Stock Co., 93
Ryder System, Inc., V; 24 (upd.)
Saia, Inc., 98
Santa Fe Pacific Corporation, V
Schenker-Rhenus AG, 6
Schneider National, Inc., 36; 77 (upd.)
Sea Ray Boats Inc., 96
Seaboard Corporation, 36; 85 (upd.)
SEACOR Holdings Inc., 83
Securicor Plc, 45
Seibu Railway Company Ltd., V; 74 (upd.)
Seino Transportation Company, Ltd., 6
Simon Transportation Services Inc., 27
Skeeter Products Inc., 96
Smithway Motor Xpress Corporation, 39
Société Nationale des Chemins de Fer Français, V; 57 (upd.)
Société Norbert Dentressangle S.A., 67
Southern Pacific Transportation Company, V
Spee-Dee Delivery Service, Inc., 93
Stagecoach Group plc, 30; 104 (upd.)
Stelmar Shipping Ltd., 52
Stevedoring Services of America Inc., 28
Stinnes AG, 8; 59 (upd.)
Stolt-Nielsen S.A., 42
Sunoco, Inc., 28 (upd.); 83 (upd.)
Swift Transportation Co., Inc., 42
Swiss Federal Railways (Schweizerische Bundesbahnen), The, V
Swissport International Ltd., 70

Teekay Shipping Corporation, 25; 82 (upd.)
Tibbett & Britten Group plc, 32
Tidewater Inc., 11; 37 (upd.)
TNT Freightways Corporation, 14
TNT Post Group N.V., V; 27 (upd.); 30 (upd.)
Tobu Railway Company Ltd., 6; 98 (upd.)
Todd Shipyards Corporation, 14
Tokyu Corporation, V
Totem Resources Corporation, 9
TPG N.V., 64 (upd.)
Trailer Bridge, Inc., 41
Transnet Ltd., 6
Transport Corporation of America, Inc., 49
Trico Marine Services, Inc., 89
Tsakos Energy Navigation Ltd., 91
TTX Company, 6; 66 (upd.)
U.S. Delivery Systems, Inc., 22
Union Pacific Corporation, V; 28 (upd.); 79 (upd.)
United Parcel Service of America Inc., V; 17 (upd.)
United Parcel Service, Inc., 63
United Road Services, Inc., 69
United States Postal Service, 14; 34 (upd.); 108 (upd.)
Universal Truckload Services, Inc., 111
US 1 Industries, Inc., 89
USA Truck, Inc., 42
Velocity Express Corporation, 49
Werner Enterprises, Inc., 26
Wheels Inc., 96
Wincanton plc, 52
Wisconsin Central Transportation Corporation, 24
Wright Express Corporation, 80
Yamato Transport Co. Ltd., V; 49 (upd.)
Yellow Corporation, 14; 45 (upd.)
Yellow Freight System, Inc. of Delaware, V
YRC Worldwide Inc., 90 (upd.)

Utilities

AES Corporation, 10; 13 (upd.); 53 (upd.)
Aggreko Plc, 45
Air & Water Technologies Corporation, 6
Akeena Solar, Inc., 103
Alberta Energy Company Ltd., 16; 43 (upd.)
Allegheny Energy, Inc., V; 38 (upd.)
Alliant Energy Corporation, 106
Ameren Corporation, 60 (upd.)
American Electric Power Company, Inc., V; 45 (upd.)
American States Water Company, 46
American Water Works Company, Inc., 6; 38 (upd.)
Aquarion Company, 84
Aquila, Inc., 50 (upd.)
Arkla, Inc., V
Associated Natural Gas Corporation, 11
Atlanta Gas Light Company, 6; 23 (upd.)
Atlantic Energy, Inc., 6
Atmos Energy Corporation, 43

Avista Corporation, 69 (upd.)
Baltimore Gas and Electric Company, V; 25 (upd.)
Basin Electric Power Cooperative, 103
Bay State Gas Company, 38
Bayernwerk AG, V; 23 (upd.)
Berlinwasser Holding AG, 90
Bewag AG, 39
Big Rivers Electric Corporation, 11
Black Hills Corporation, 20
Bonneville Power Administration, 50
Boston Edison Company, 12
Bouygues S.A., I; 24 (upd.); 97 (upd.)
British Energy Plc, 49
British Gas plc, V
British Nuclear Fuels plc, 6
Brooklyn Union Gas, 6
BW Group Ltd., 107
California Water Service Group, 79
Calpine Corporation, 36
Canadian Utilities Limited, 13; 56 (upd.)
Cap Rock Energy Corporation, 46
Carolina Power & Light Company, V; 23 (upd.)
Cascade Natural Gas Corporation, 9
Cascal N.V., 103
Centerior Energy Corporation, V
Central and South West Corporation, V
Central Hudson Gas and Electricity Corporation, 6
Central Maine Power, 6
Central Vermont Public Service Corporation, 54
Centrica plc, 29 (upd.); 107 (upd.)
ČEZ a. s., 97
Chesapeake Utilities Corporation, 56
China Shenhua Energy Company Limited, 83
Chubu Electric Power Company, Inc., V; 46 (upd.)
Chugoku Electric Power Company Inc., V; 53 (upd.)
Cincinnati Gas & Electric Company, 6
CIPSCO Inc., 6
Citizens Utilities Company, 7
City Public Service, 6
Cleco Corporation, 37
CMS Energy Corporation, V, 14 (upd.); 100 (upd.)
Coastal Corporation, The, 31 (upd.)
Cogentrix Energy, Inc., 10
Columbia Gas System, Inc., The, V; 16 (upd.)
Comisión Federal de Electricidad, 108
Commonwealth Edison Company, V
Commonwealth Energy System, 14
Companhia Energética de Minas Gerais S.A. CEMIG, 65
Compañia de Minas Buenaventura S.A.A., 93
Connecticut Light and Power Co., 13
Consolidated Edison, Inc., V; 45 (upd.); 112 (upd.)
Consolidated Natural Gas Company, V; 19 (upd.)
Consumers Power Co., 14
Consumers Water Company, 14
Consumers' Gas Company Ltd., 6

Sonat, Inc., 6
South Jersey Industries, Inc., 42
Southern Company, The, V; 38 (upd.)
Southern Connecticut Gas Company, 84
Southern Electric PLC, 13
Southern Indiana Gas and Electric
    Company, 13
Southern Union Company, 27
Southwest Gas Corporation, 19
Southwest Water Company, 47
Southwestern Electric Power Co., 21
Southwestern Public Service Company, 6
State Grid Corporation of China, 108
Statnett SF, 110
Suez Lyonnaise des Eaux, 36 (upd.)
SUEZ-TRACTEBEL S.A., 97 (upd.)
TECO Energy, Inc., 6
Tennessee Valley Authority, 50
Tennet BV 78
Texas Utilities Company, V; 25 (upd.)
Thames Water plc, 11; 90 (upd.)
Tohoku Electric Power Company, Inc., V
Tokyo Electric Power Company, The, V;
    74 (upd.)
Tokyo Gas Co., Ltd., V; 55 (upd.)
TransAlta Utilities Corporation, 6
TransCanada PipeLines Limited, V
Transco Energy Company, V
Tri-State Generation and Transmission
    Association, Inc., 103
Trigen Energy Corporation, 42
Tucson Electric Power Company, 6
UGI Corporation, 12
Unicom Corporation, 29 (upd.)
Union Electric Company, V
United Illuminating Company, The, 21
United Utilities PLC, 52 (upd.)
United Water Resources, Inc., 40
Unitil Corporation, 37
Utah Power and Light Company, 27
UtiliCorp United Inc., 6
Vattenfall AB, 57
Vectren Corporation, 98 (upd.)

Vereinigte Elektrizitätswerke Westfalen
    AG, V
VEW AG, 39
Viridian Group plc, 64
Warwick Valley Telephone Company, 55
Washington Gas Light Company, 19
Washington Natural Gas Company, 9
Washington Water Power Company, 6
Westar Energy, Inc., 57 (upd.)
Western Resources, Inc., 12
Wheelabrator Technologies, Inc., 6
Wisconsin Energy Corporation, 6; 54
    (upd.)
Wisconsin Public Service Corporation, 9
WPL Holdings, Inc., 6
WPS Resources Corporation, 53 (upd.)
Xcel Energy Inc., 73 (upd.)

Waste Services

Allied Waste Industries, Inc., 50
Allwaste, Inc., 18
American Ecology Corporation, 77
Appliance Recycling Centers of America,
    Inc., 42
Azcon Corporation, 23
Berliner Stadtreinigungsbetriebe, 58
Biffa plc, 92
Brambles Industries Limited, 42
Browning-Ferris Industries, Inc., V; 20
    (upd.)
Casella Waste Systems Inc., 102
Chemical Waste Management, Inc., 9
CHHJ Franchising LLC, 105
Clean Harbors, Inc., 73
Clean Venture, Inc., 104
Copart Inc., 23
Darling International Inc., 85
E.On AG, 50 (upd.)
Ecolab Inc., I; 13 (upd.); 34 (upd.); 85
    (upd.)
Ecology and Environment, Inc., 39
Empresas Públicas de Medellín S.A.E.S.P.,
    91

Fuel Tech, Inc., 85
Industrial Services of America, Inc., 46
Ionics, Incorporated, 52
ISS A/S, 49
Jani-King International, Inc., 85
Kelda Group plc, 45
McClain Industries, Inc., 51
MPW Industrial Services Group, Inc., 53
Newpark Resources, Inc., 63
Norcal Waste Systems, Inc., 60
Oakleaf Waste Management, LLC, 97
1-800-GOT-JUNK? LLC, 74
Onet S.A., 92
Pennon Group Plc, 45
Perma-Fix Environmental Services, Inc.,
    99
Philip Environmental Inc., 16
Philip Services Corp., 73
Republic Services, Inc., 92
Roto-Rooter, Inc., 15; 61 (upd.)
Safety-Kleen Systems Inc., 8; 82 (upd.)
Saur S.A.S., 92
Sevenson Environmental Services, Inc., 42
Severn Trent PLC, 38 (upd.)
Servpro Industries, Inc., 85
Sims Metal Management, Ltd., 109
Shanks Group plc, 45
Shred-It Canada Corporation, 56
Stericycle, Inc., 33; 74 (upd.)
TRC Companies, Inc., 32
Valley Proteins, Inc., 91
Veit Companies, 43; 92 (upd.)
Veolia Environnement, SA, 109
Waste Connections, Inc., 46
Waste Holdings, Inc., 41
Waste Management Inc., V; 109 (upd.)
Wheelabrator Technologies, Inc., 60
    (upd.)
Windswept Environmental Group, Inc.,
    62
WMX Technologies Inc., 17

Geographic Index

Albania
Albtelecom Sh. a, 111

Algeria
Sonatrach, IV; 65 (upd.)

Argentina
Acindar Industria Argentina de Aceros S.A., 87
Adecoagro LLC, 101
Aerolíneas Argentinas S.A., 33; 69 (upd.)
Alpargatas S.A.I.C., 87
Aluar Aluminio Argentino S.A.I.C., 74
Arcor S.A.I.C., 66
Atanor S.A., 62
Coto Centro Integral de Comercializacion S.A., 66
Cresud S.A.C.I.F. y A., 63
Grupo Clarín S.A., 67
Grupo Financiero Galicia S.A., 63
IRSA Inversiones y Representaciones S.A., 63
Ledesma Sociedad Anónima Agrícola Industrial, 62
Loma Negra C.I.A.S.A., 95
Mastellone Hermanos S.A., 101
Molinos Río de la Plata S.A., 61
Nobleza Piccardo SAICF, 64
Penaflor S.A., 66
Petrobras Energia Participaciones S.A., 72
Quilmes Industrial (QUINSA) S.A., 67
Renault Argentina S.A., 67
SanCor Cooperativas Unidas Ltda., 101
Sideco Americana S.A., 67
Siderar S.A.I.C., 66
Telecom Argentina S.A., 63
Telefónica de Argentina S.A., 61
YPF Sociedad Anonima, IV

Australia
ABC Learning Centres Ltd., 93
Amcor Limited, IV; 19 (upd.), 78 (upd.)
Ansell Ltd., 60 (upd.)
Aquarius Platinum Ltd., 63
Aristocrat Leisure Limited, 54
Arnott's Ltd., 66
Austal Limited, 75
Australia and New Zealand Banking Group Limited, II; 52 (upd.)
AWB Ltd., 56
BHP Billiton, 67 (upd.)
Billabong International Limited, 44; 112 (upd.)
Blundstone Pty Ltd., 76
Bond Corporation Holdings Limited, 10
Boral Limited, III; 43 (upd.); 103 (upd.)
Brambles Industries Limited, 42
Broken Hill Proprietary Company Ltd., IV; 22 (upd.)
Burns, Philp & Company Ltd., 63
Carlton and United Breweries Ltd., I
Cochlear Ltd., 77
Coles Group Limited, V; 20 (upd.); 85 (upd.)
Colorado Group Ltd., 107
Commonwealth Bank of Australia Ltd., 109
CRA Limited, IV; 85 (upd.)
CSL Limited, 112
CSR Limited, III; 28 (upd.)
David Jones Ltd., 60
Elders IXL Ltd., I
Fairfax Media Ltd., 94 (upd.)
Foster's Group Limited, 7; 21 (upd.); 50 (upd.); 111 (upd.)
Goodman Fielder Ltd., 52
Harvey Norman Holdings Ltd., 56

Hills Industries Ltd., 104
Holden Ltd., 62
James Hardie Industries N.V., 56
John Fairfax Holdings Limited, 7
Lend Lease Corporation Limited, IV; 17 (upd.); 52 (upd.)
Lion Nathan Limited, 54
Lonely Planet Publications Pty Ltd., 55
Macquarie Bank Ltd., 69
McPherson's Ltd., 66
Metcash Trading Ltd., 58
MYOB Ltd., 86
National Australia Bank Ltd., 111
News Corporation Limited, IV; 7 (upd.); 46 (upd.)
Nufarm Ltd., 87
Orica Ltd., 112
Pacific Dunlop Limited, 10
Pioneer International Limited, III
PMP Ltd., 72
Publishing and Broadcasting Limited, 54
Qantas Airways Ltd., 6; 24 (upd.); 68 (upd.)
Repco Corporation Ltd., 74
Ridley Corporation Ltd., 62
Rinker Group Ltd., 65
Rural Press Ltd., 74
Santos Ltd., 81
Sims Metal Management, Ltd., 109
Smorgon Steel Group Ltd., 62
Southcorp Limited, 54
Suncorp-Metway Ltd., 91
TABCORP Holdings Limited, 44
Telecom Australia, 6
Telstra Corporation Limited, 50
Village Roadshow Ltd., 58
Washington H. Soul Pattinson and Company Limited, 112
Wesfarmers Limited, 109

Germany

GEOGRAPHIC INDEX

Merrill Lynch & Co., Inc., II; 13 (upd.);
40 (upd.)
Merry-Go-Round Enterprises, Inc., 8
Mervyn's California, 10; 39 (upd.)
Mesa Air Group, Inc., 11; 32 (upd.); 77
(upd.)
Mesaba Holdings, Inc., 28
Mestek Inc., 10
Metal Management, Inc., 92
Metalico Inc., 97
Metatec International, Inc., 47
Metavante Corporation, 100
Meteor Industries Inc., 33
Methode Electronics, Inc., 13
Metris Companies Inc., 56
Metro Information Services, Inc., 36
Metro-Goldwyn-Mayer Inc., 25 (upd.); 84
(upd.)
Metrocall, Inc., 41
Metromedia Company, 7; 14; 61 (upd.)
Metropolitan Baseball Club Inc., 39
Metropolitan Financial Corporation, 13
Metropolitan Life Insurance Company,
III; 52 (upd.)
Metropolitan Museum of Art, The, 55
Metropolitan Opera Association, Inc., 40
Metropolitan Transportation Authority, 35
Mexican Restaurants, Inc., 41
Meyer Natural Angus L.L.C., 112
MFS Communications Company, Inc., 11
MGA Entertainment, Inc., 95
MGIC Investment Corp., 52
MGM MIRAGE, 17; 98 (upd.)
MGM/UA Communications Company, II
Miami Herald Media Company, 92
Miami Subs Corporation, 108
Michael Anthony Jewelers, Inc., 24
Michael Baker Corporation, 14; 51 (upd.)
Michael C. Fina Co., Inc., 52
Michael Foods, Inc., 25
Michaels Stores, Inc., 17; 71 (upd.)
Michigan Bell Telephone Co., 14
Michigan National Corporation, 11
Michigan Sporting Goods Distributors,
Inc., 72
Micrel, Incorporated, 77
Micro Warehouse, Inc., 16
MicroAge, Inc., 16
Microdot Inc., 8
Micron Technology, Inc., 11; 29 (upd.)
Micros Systems, Inc., 18
Microsemi Corporation, 94
Microsoft Corporation, 6; 27 (upd.); 63
(upd.)
MicroStrategy Incorporated, 87
Mid-America Apartment Communities,
Inc., 85
Mid-America Dairymen, Inc., 7
Midas Inc., 10; 56 (upd.)
Middleby Corporation, The, 22; 104
(upd.)
Middlesex Water Company, 45
Middleton Doll Company, The, 53
Midland Company, The, 65
Midway Airlines Corporation, 33
Midway Games, Inc., 25; 102 (upd.)
Midwest Air Group, Inc., 35; 85 (upd.)
Midwest Grain Products, Inc., 49

Midwest Resources Inc., 6
Mikasa, Inc., 28
Mike-Sell's Inc., 15
Mikohn Gaming Corporation, 39
Milacron, Inc., 53 (upd.)
Milbank, Tweed, Hadley & McCloy, 27
Miles Laboratories, I
Millennium Pharmaceuticals, Inc., 47
Miller Brewing Company, I; 12 (upd.)
Miller Industries, Inc., 26
Miller Publishing Group, LLC, 57
Milliken & Co., V; 17 (upd.); 82 (upd.)
Milliman USA, 66
Millipore Corporation, 25; 84 (upd.)
Mills Corporation, The, 77
Milnot Company, 46
Milton Bradley Company, 21
Milton CAT, Inc., 86
Milwaukee Brewers Baseball Club, 37
Mine Safety Appliances Company, 31
Miner Group International, The, 22
Minerals Technologies Inc., 11; 52 (upd.)
Minnesota Mining & Manufacturing
Company (3M), I; 8 (upd.); 26 (upd.)
Minnesota Power, Inc., 11; 34 (upd.)
Minnesota Twins, 112
Minntech Corporation, 22
Minute Maid Company, The, 28
Minuteman International Inc., 46
Minyard Food Stores, Inc., 33; 86 (upd.)
Mirage Resorts, Incorporated, 6; 28 (upd.)
Miramax Film Corporation, 64
Mirant Corporation, 98
Misonix, Inc., 80
Mississippi Chemical Corporation, 39
Mississippi Power Company, 110
Mitchell Energy and Development
Corporation, 7
MITRE Corporation, 26; 107 (upd.)
Mity Enterprises, Inc., 38
MIVA, Inc., 83
MN Airlines LLC, 104
MNS, Ltd., 65
Mobil Corporation, IV; 7 (upd.); 21
(upd.)
Mobile Mini, Inc., 58
Mobile Telecommunications Technologies
Corp., 18
Mocon, Inc., 76
Modern Woodmen of America, 66
Modine Manufacturing Company, 8; 56
(upd.)
Modtech Holdings, Inc., 77
Moen Inc., 12; 106 (upd.)
Mohawk Fine Papers, Inc., 108
Mohawk Industries, Inc., 19; 63 (upd.)
Mohegan Tribal Gaming Authority, 37
Moldflow Corporation, 73
Molex Incorporated, 11; 54 (upd.)
Molson Coors Brewing Company, 77
(upd.)
Monaco Coach Corporation, 31
Monadnock Paper Mills, Inc., 21
Monarch Casino & Resort, Inc., 65
Monarch Cement Company, The, 72
MoneyGram International, Inc., 94
Monfort, Inc., 13
Monro Muffler Brake, Inc., 24

Monrovia Nursery Company, 70
Monsanto Company, I; 9 (upd.); 29
(upd.); 77 (upd.)
Monster Cable Products, Inc., 69
Monster Worldwide Inc., 74 (upd.)
Montana Coffee Traders, Inc., 60
Montana Power Company, The, 11; 44
(upd.)
Monterey Pasta Company, 58
Montgomery Ward & Co., Incorporated,
V; 20 (upd.)
Moody's Corporation, 65
Moog Inc., 13
Moog Music, Inc., 75
Mooney Aerospace Group Ltd., 52
Moore Medical Corp., 17
Moore-Handley, Inc., 39
Moran Towing Corporation, Inc., 15
Morgan Group, Inc., The, 46
Morgan, Lewis & Bockius LLP, 29
Morgan Stanley Dean Witter &
Company, II; 16 (upd.); 33 (upd.)
Morgan's Foods, Inc., 101
Morgans Hotel Group Company, 80
Morinda Holdings, Inc., 82
Morningstar Inc., 68
Morris Communications Corporation, 36
Morris Travel Services L.L.C., 26
Morrison & Foerster LLP, 78
Morrison Knudsen Corporation, 7; 28
(upd.)
Morrison Restaurants Inc., 11
Morrow Equipment Co. L.L.C., 87
Morse Shoe Inc., 13
Morton International Inc., I; 9 (upd.); 80
(upd.)
Morton Thiokol, Inc., I
Morton's Restaurant Group, Inc., 30; 88
(upd.)
Mosaic Company, The, 91
Mosinee Paper Corporation, 15
Mossimo, 27; 96 (upd.)
Motel 6, 13; 56 (upd.)
Mothers Against Drunk Driving
(MADD), 51
Mothers Work, Inc., 18
Motiva Enterprises LLC, 111
Motley Fool, Inc., The, 40
Moto Photo, Inc., 45
Motor Cargo Industries, Inc., 35
Motorcar Parts & Accessories, Inc., 47
Motorola, Inc., II; 11 (upd.); 34 (upd.);
93 (upd.)
Motown Records Company L.P., 26
Mott's Inc., 57
Mount Sinai Medical Center, 112
Mountain States Mortgage Centers, Inc.,
29
Movado Group, Inc., 28; 107 (upd.)
Movie Gallery, Inc., 31
Movie Star Inc., 17
Mozilla Foundation, 106
MPS Group, Inc., 49
MPW Industrial Services Group, Inc., 53
Mr. Coffee, Inc., 15
Mr. Gasket Inc., 15
Mr. Gatti's, LP, 87
Mrchocolate.com LLC, 105

Puritan-Bennett Corporation, 13
Purolator Products Company, 21; 74 (upd.)
Putt-Putt Golf Courses of America, Inc., 23
PVC Container Corporation, 67
PW Eagle, Inc., 48
Pyramid Breweries Inc., 33; 102 (upd.)
Pyramid Companies, 54
Q.E.P. Co., Inc., 65
Qdoba Restaurant Corporation, 93
QRS Music Technologies, Inc., 95
QSC Audio Products, Inc., 56
QSS Group, Inc., 100
Quad/Graphics, Inc., 19
Quaker Chemical Corp., 91
Quaker Fabric Corp., 19
Quaker Foods North America, 73 (upd.)
Quaker Oats Company, The, II; 12 (upd.); 34 (upd.)
Quaker State Corporation, 7; 21 (upd.)
QUALCOMM Incorporated, 20; 47 (upd.)
Quality Chekd Dairies, Inc., 48
Quality Dining, Inc., 18
Quality Food Centers, Inc., 17
Quality Systems, Inc., 81
Quanex Corporation, 13; 62 (upd.)
Quanta Services, Inc. 79
Quantum Chemical Corporation, 8
Quantum Corporation, 10; 62 (upd.)
Quark, Inc., 36
Quest Diagnostics Inc., 26; 106 (upd.)
Questar Corporation, 6; 26 (upd.)
Quick & Reilly Group, Inc., The, 20
Quicken Loans, Inc., 93
Quidel Corporation, 80
Quigley Corporation, The, 62
Quiksilver, Inc., 18; 79 (upd.)
QuikTrip Corporation, 36
Quill Corporation, 28
Quinn Emanuel Urquhart Oliver & Hedges, LLP, 99
Quintiles Transnational Corporation, 21; 68 (upd.)
Quixote Corporation, 15
Quizno's Corporation, The, 42
Quovadx Inc., 70
QVC Inc., 9; 58 (upd.)
Qwest Communications International, Inc., 37
R&B, Inc., 51
R&R Partners Inc., 108
R.B. Pamplin Corp., 45
R.C. Bigelow, Inc., 49
R.C. Willey Home Furnishings, 72
R.G. Barry Corporation, 17; 44 (upd.)
R.H. Macy & Co., Inc., V; 8 (upd.); 30 (upd.)
R.J. Reynolds Tobacco Holdings, Inc., 30 (upd.)
R.L. Polk & Co., 10
R. M. Palmer Co., 89
R.P. Scherer, I
R.R. Bowker LLC, 100
R.R. Donnelley & Sons Company, IV; 9 (upd.); 38 (upd.)
Racal-Datacom Inc., 11

RaceTrac Petroleum, Inc., 111
Racing Champions Corporation, 37
Rack Room Shoes, Inc., 84
Radian Group Inc., 42
Radiant Systems Inc., 104
Radiation Therapy Services, Inc., 85
@radical.media, 103
Radio Flyer Inc., 34
Radio One, Inc., 67
RadioShack Corporation, 36 (upd.); 101 (upd.)
Radius Inc., 16
RAE Systems Inc., 83
Rag Shops, Inc., 30
RailTex, Inc., 20
Rain Bird Corporation, 84
Rainbow Media Holdings LLC, 109
Rainforest Café, Inc., 25; 88 (upd.)
Rainier Brewing Company, 23
Raley's Inc., 14; 58 (upd.)
Rally's, 25; 68 (upd.)
Ralphs Grocery Company, 35
Ralston Purina Company, II; 13 (upd.)
Ramsay Youth Services, Inc., 41
Ramtron International Corporation, 89
RAND Corporation, 112
Rand McNally & Company, 28
Randall's Food Markets, Inc., 40
Random House Inc., 13; 31 (upd.); 106 (upd.)
Range Resources Corporation, 45
Rapala-Normark Group, Ltd., 30
Rare Hospitality International Inc., 19
RathGibson Inc., 90
Ratner Companies, 72
Raven Industries, Inc., 33
Raving Brands, Inc., 64
Rawlings Sporting Goods Company, 24; 107 (upd.)
Raychem Corporation, 8
Raycom Media, Inc., 106
Raymond James Financial Inc., 69
Rayonier Inc., 24
Rayovac Corporation, 13; 39 (upd.)
Raytech Corporation, 61
Raytheon Aircraft Holdings Inc., 46
Raytheon Company, II; 11 (upd.); 38 (upd.); 105 (upd.)
Razorfish, Inc., 37
RCA Corporation, II
RCM Technologies, Inc., 34
RCN Corporation, 70
RDO Equipment Company, 33
RE/MAX International, Inc., 59
Read-Rite Corp., 10
Reader's Digest Association, Inc., The, IV; 17 (upd.); 71 (upd.)
Reading International Inc., 70
Real Times, Inc., 66
RealNetworks, Inc., 53; 109 (upd.)
Realogy Corporation, 112
Reckson Associates Realty Corp., 47
Recording for the Blind & Dyslexic, 51
Recoton Corp., 15
Recovery Engineering, Inc., 25
Recreational Equipment, Inc., 18; 71 (upd.)
Recycled Paper Greetings, Inc., 21

Red Apple Group, Inc., 23
Red Hat, Inc., 45
Red McCombs Automotive Group, 91
Red Robin Gourmet Burgers, Inc., 56
Red Roof Inns, Inc., 18
Red Spot Paint & Varnish Company, Inc., 55; 112 (upd.)
Red Wing Pottery Sales, Inc., 52
Red Wing Shoe Company, Inc., 9; 30 (upd.); 83 (upd.)
Redback Networks, Inc., 92
Reddy Ice Holdings, Inc., 80
Redhook Ale Brewery, Inc., 31; 88 (upd.)
Redken Laboratories Inc., 84
Redlon & Johnson, Inc., 97
Redner's Markets Inc., 111
RedPeg Marketing, 73
Reebok International Ltd., V; 9 (upd.); 26 (upd.)
Reed & Barton Corporation, 67
Reed's, Inc., 103
Reeds Jewelers, Inc., 22
Regal Entertainment Group, 59
Regal-Beloit Corporation, 18; 97 (upd.)
Regence Group, The, 74
Regency Centers Corporation, 71
Regent Communications, Inc., 87
Regions Financial Corporation, 106
Regis Corporation, 18; 70 (upd.)
Reichhold, Inc., 10; 112 (upd.)
Reiter Dairy, LLC, 94
Rejuvenation, Inc., 91
Related Companies, L.P., 112
Reliance Electric Company, 9
Reliance Group Holdings, Inc., III
Reliance Steel & Aluminum Company, 19; 70 (upd.)
Reliant Energy Inc., 44 (upd.)
Reliv International, Inc., 58
Remedy Corporation, 58
RemedyTemp, Inc., 20
Remington Arms Company, Inc., 12; 40 (upd.)
Remington Products Company, L.L.C., 42
Renaissance Learning, Inc., 39; 100 (upd.)
Renal Care Group, Inc., 72
Renfro Corporation, 99
Reno Air Inc., 23
Rent-A-Center, Inc., 45
Rent-Way, Inc., 33; 75 (upd.)
Rental Service Corporation, 28
Rentech, Inc., 110
Rentrak Corporation, 35
Replacements, Ltd., 110
Republic Engineered Products Inc., 7; 26 (upd.); 106 (upd.)
Republic Industries, Inc., 26
Republic New York Corporation, 11
Republic of Tea, Inc., The, 105
Republic Services, Inc., 92
Res-Care, Inc., 29
Research Triangle Institute, 83
Reser's Fine Foods, Inc., 81
Resorts International, Inc., 12
Resource America, Inc., 42
Resources Connection, Inc., 81
Response Oncology, Inc., 27
Restaurant Associates Corporation, 66

Wallace Computer Services, Inc., 36
Walsworth Publishing Co., 78
Walt Disney Company, The, II; 6 (upd.); 30 (upd.); 63 (upd.)
Walter E. Smithe Furniture, Inc., 105
Walter Industries, Inc., II; 22 (upd.); 72 (upd.)
Walton Monroe Mills, Inc., 8
Wang Laboratories, Inc., III; 6 (upd.)
Warnaco Group Inc., The, 12; 46 (upd.)
Warner Communications Inc., II
Warner Music Group Corporation, 90 (upd.)
Warner-Lambert Co., I; 10 (upd.)
Warners' Stellian Inc., 67
Warrantech Corporation, 53
Warrell Corporation, 68
Warwick Valley Telephone Company, 55
Washington Companies, The, 33
Washington Federal, Inc., 17
Washington Football, Inc., 35
Washington Gas Light Company, 19
Washington Mutual, Inc., 17; 93 (upd.)
Washington National Corporation, 12
Washington Natural Gas Company, 9
Washington Post Company, The, IV; 20 (upd.); 109 (upd.)
Washington Scientific Industries, Inc., 17
Washington Water Power Company, 6
Waste Connections, Inc., 46
Waste Holdings, Inc., 41
Waste Management, Inc., V; 109 (upd.)
Water Pik Technologies, Inc., 34; 83 (upd.)
Waterhouse Investor Services, Inc., 18
Waters Corporation, 43
Watkins-Johnson Company, 15
Watsco Inc., 52
Watson Pharmaceuticals Inc., 16; 56 (upd.)
Watson Wyatt Worldwide, 42
Watts Industries, Inc., 19
Wausau-Mosinee Paper Corporation, 60 (upd.)
Waverly, Inc., 16
Wawa Inc., 17; 78 (upd.)
WAXIE Sanitary Supply, 100
Waxman Industries, Inc., 9
WD-40 Company, 18; 87 (upd.)
We-No-Nah Canoe, Inc., 98
Weather Central Inc., 100
Weather Channel Companies, The, 52
Weather Shield Manufacturing, Inc., 102
Weatherford International, Inc., 39
Weaver Popcorn Company, Inc., 89
Webasto Roof Systems Inc., 97
Webber Oil Company, 61
Weber-Stephen Products Co., 40
WebEx Communications, Inc., 81
WebMD Corporation, 65
Webster Financial Corporation, 106
Weeres Industries Corporation, 52
Wegmans Food Markets, Inc., 9; 41 (upd.); 105 (upd.)
Weider Nutrition International, Inc., 29
Weight Watchers International Inc., 12; 33 (upd.); 73 (upd.)
Weil, Gotshal & Manges LLP, 55

Weiner's Stores, Inc., 33
Weingarten Realty Investors, 95
Weirton Steel Corporation, IV; 26 (upd.)
Weis Markets, Inc., 15; 84 (upd.)
Weitz Company, Inc., The, 42
Welbilt Corp., 19
Welch Foods Inc., 104
Welcome Wagon International Inc., 82
Welk Group Inc., The, 78
WellCare Health Plans, Inc., 101
WellChoice, Inc., 67 (upd.)
Wellco Enterprises, Inc., 84
Wellman, Inc., 8; 52 (upd.)
WellPoint, Inc., 25; 103 (upd.)
Wells Fargo & Company, II; 12 (upd.); 38 (upd.); 97 (upd.)
Wells Rich Greene BDDP, 6
Wells' Dairy, Inc., 36
Wells-Gardner Electronics Corporation, 43
Wendy's International, Inc., 8; 23 (upd.); 47 (upd.)
Wenner Bread Products Inc., 80
Wenner Media, Inc., 32
Werner Enterprises, Inc., 26
West Bend Co., 14
West Coast Entertainment Corporation, 29
West Corporation, 42
West Group, 34 (upd.)
West Linn Paper Company, 91
West Marine, Inc., 17; 90 (upd.)
West One Bancorp, 11
West Pharmaceutical Services, Inc., 42
West Point-Pepperell, Inc., 8
West Publishing Co., 7
Westaff Inc., 33
Westamerica Bancorporation, 17
Westar Energy, Inc., 57 (upd.)
WestCoast Hospitality Corporation, 59
Westcon Group, Inc., 67
Westell Technologies, Inc., 57
Westerbeke Corporation, 60
Western Atlas Inc., 12
Western Beef, Inc., 22
Western Company of North America, 15
Western Digital Corporation, 25; 92 (upd.)
Western Gas Resources, Inc., 45
Western Publishing Group, Inc., 13
Western Refining Inc., 109
Western Resources, Inc., 12
WesterN SizzliN Corporation, The, 60
Western Union Company, 54; 112 (upd.)
Western Wireless Corporation, 36
Westfield Group, 69
Westin Hotels and Resorts Worldwide, 9; 29 (upd.)
Westinghouse Electric Corporation, II; 12 (upd.)
Westmoreland Coal Company, 7
WestPoint Stevens Inc., 16
Westport Resources Corporation, 63
Westvaco Corporation, IV; 19 (upd.)
Westwood One Inc., 23; 106 (upd.)
Wet Seal, Inc., The, 18; 70 (upd.)
Wetterau Incorporated, II
Weyco Group, Incorporated, 32

Weyerhaeuser Company, IV; 9 (upd.); 28 (upd.); 83 (upd.)
WFS Financial Inc., 70
WGBH Educational Foundation, 66
Wham-O, Inc., 61
Whataburger Restaurants LP, 105
Wheaton Industries, 8
Wheaton Science Products, 60 (upd.)
Wheelabrator Technologies, Inc., 6; 60 (upd.)
Wheeling-Pittsburgh Corporation, 7; 58 (upd.)
Wheels Inc., 96
Wherehouse Entertainment Incorporated, 11
Whirlpool Corporation, III; 12 (upd.); 59 (upd.)
White & Case LLP, 35
White Castle Management Company, 12; 36 (upd.); 85 (upd.)
White Consolidated Industries Inc., 13
White House, Inc., The, 60
White Lily Foods Company, 88
White Rose, Inc., 24
Whitehall Jewellers, Inc., 82 (upd.)
Whiting Petroleum Corporation, 81
Whiting-Turner Contracting Company, 95
Whitman Corporation, 10 (upd.)
Whitman Education Group, Inc., 41
Whitney Holding Corporation, 21
Whittaker Corporation, I; 48 (upd.)
Whole Foods Market, Inc., 20; 50 (upd.); 110 (upd.)
WHX Corporation, 98
Wickes Inc., V; 25 (upd.)
Widmer Brothers Brewing Company, 76
Wieden + Kennedy, 75
Wilbert, Inc., 56
Wilbur Chocolate Company, 66
Wilco Farm Stores, 93
Wild Oats Markets, Inc., 19; 41 (upd.)
Wildlife Conservation Society, 31
Wikimedia Foundation, Inc., 91
Willamette Industries, Inc., IV; 31 (upd.)
Willamette Valley Vineyards, Inc., 85
William L. Bonnell Company, Inc., 66
William Lyon Homes, 59
William Morris Agency, Inc., 23; 102 (upd.)
William Zinsser & Company, Inc., 58
Williams & Connolly LLP, 47
Williams Communications Group, Inc., 34
Williams Companies, Inc., The, IV; 31 (upd.)
Williams Scotsman, Inc., 65
Williams-Sonoma, Inc., 17; 44 (upd.)
Williamson-Dickie Manufacturing Company, 14; 45 (upd.)
Willkie Farr & Gallagher LLP, 95
Willow Run Foods, Inc., 100
Wilmer Cutler Pickering Hale and Dorr L.L.P., 109
Wilmington Trust Corporation, 25
Wilson Sonsini Goodrich & Rosati, 34
Wilson Sporting Goods Company, 24; 84 (upd.)

Uruguay

Uzbekistan

Vatican City

Venezuela

Vietnam